The Advanced Pilot's Flight Manual

Based on the original text by
William K. Kershner
8th Edition | Edited by William C. Kershner

Aviation Supplies & Academics, Inc.
Newcastle, Washington

After doing his first spin at the age of 16 in an Aeronca TAC, **William K. Kershner** flew and taught aerobatics for 60 years. Bill put his degree in technical journalism and aerodynamics, along with his ability to make complex ideas seem simple, to work in writing *The Student Pilot's Flight Manual, The Instrument Flight Manual, The Advanced Pilot's Flight Manual, The Flight Instructor's Manual* and *The Basic Aerobatic Manual.* He also wrote *Logging Flight Time,* a collection of aviation anecdotes and experiences collected over a lifetime in aviation. The Kershner Flight Manual Series has influenced hundreds of thousands of pilots, with over 1.3 million copies printed in at least 3 languages.

Bill received the General Aviation Flight Instructor of the Year and the Ninety-Nines Award of Merit, among many other honors. To date he is the only person to have been inducted into both the International Aerobatic Club Hall of Fame and the Flight Instructor's Hall of Fame. He was among the first to be inducted into the Tennessee Aviation Hall of Fame.

Kershner operated an aerobatic school for many years at the Sewanee-Franklin County airport in Tennessee using a Cessna 152 Aerobat. His airplane, N7557L, is on display at the National Air and Space Museum's Udvar-Hazy Center at Dulles International Airport. Bill Kershner died January 8th, 2007.

Editor **William C. Kershner** received his early flight training from his father, William K. Kershner. He holds Commercial, Flight Instructor and Airline Transport Pilot certificates and has flown 22 types of airplanes, ranging in size from Cessna 150s to Boeing 777s, in his 12,000+ flight hours. He works as an airline pilot and lives in Sewanee, Tennessee.

The Advanced Pilot's Flight Manual
Eighth Edition
William K. Kershner
Illustrated by the Author

First Edition published 1970, Iowa State University Press. Eighth Edition published 2014 by Aviation Supplies & Academics, Inc.

Aviation Supplies & Academics, Inc.
7005 132nd Place SE, Newcastle, WA 98059
Email: asa@asa2fly.com Internet: www.asa2fly.com

Printed in the United States of America

2018 2017 2016 2015 9 8 7 6 5 4 3 2 1

ASA-FM-ADV-8
ISBN 978-1-61954-213-6

Library of Congress Cataloging-in Publication Data:
Kershner, William K.
The advanced pilot's flight manual / William K. Kershner—7th ed.
p. cm.
Includes bibliographical references and index.
1. Airplanes—Piloting. I. Title.
TL710.K42 2003
629.132'dc21 2002152289

Contents

To Mac and Sarah Lisenbee

Introduction

W.K. Kershner's Notes on the Seventh Edition

It has long been the writer's opinion that the average pilot could learn the basics of airplane performance very easily if the involved mathematics were bypassed. One of the purposes of *The Advanced Pilot's Flight Manual* is to bridge the gap between theory and practical application. If pilots know the principles of performance they can readily understand the effects of altitude, temperature, and other variables of airplane operation.

GAMA (General Aviation Manufacturer's Association) and the FAA together have established a *Pilot's Operating Handbook*, which will include information now scattered among several different sources. It has a standardized format so that the pilot can quickly find information (for instance, emergency procedures), whether flying a Piper, Cessna, or other makes. The older planes will still have several sources for finding operating information. *Pilot's Operating Handbook* will be used as a general term to cover all sources of information available to the pilot.

When it is said here for instance, "You can find the center of gravity limits in the *Pilot's Operating Handbook*," the term is meant to cover all sources of information currently available to the operator. You may be able to open the *Owner's Handbook* and get this information or you may have to go out to the airplane and look at something called "Operations Limitations" or "Airplane Flight Manual."

So, rather than repeat each time, "You can find this information in either the *Owner's Handbook* (or *Owner's Manual*) or *Pilot's Handbook*, or *Flight Handbook*, or *Airplane Flight Manual*, or "Operations Limitations," or in the form of placards or markings, the writer has used one term: *Pilot's Operating Handbook* (POH).

Thumb rules are used throughout as a means of presenting a clearer picture of the recommended speeds for various performance requirements such as maximum range, maximum endurance, or maximum angle of climb. Such rules of thumb are not intended in any way to replace the figures as given by the POH or comparable information sources, if available. However, the knowledge of even the approximate speed ranges for various maximum performance requirements will enable pilots to obtain better performance than if they had no idea at all of the required airspeeds. Naturally, this practice must be tempered with judgment. If a pilot flies a rich mixture and high power settings until only a couple of gallons of fuel are left, setting up either the rule of thumb or the manufacturer's recommended airspeed for maximum range still won't allow making an airport 75 miles farther on. The same applies to maximum endurance. Waiting to the last minutes of fuel to set up the maximum endurance speed will have no perceptible effect on increasing endurance.

Many of the rules of thumb are based on the use of calibrated stall airspeeds, which are in turn based on the max certificated weight of the airplane (unless otherwise noted). Airplane weight variation effects on recommended airspeeds are to be ignored unless specifically mentioned.

The material in this book includes what the writer believes is of the most interest to the pilot who wants to go into more detail about airplane performance. For instance, the chapters on checking out in advanced models and types are intended to cover the questions most often asked by pilots checking out in those airplanes.

It is hoped that the material whets the reader's desire for more information. If so, then the mission of this book will have been accomplished. The books listed in the Bibliography are recommended for further study.

Introduction to the Eighth Edition

When you get your Commercial certificate you open up a lot of possibilities: from flying local charters to getting that CFI and instructing; from flying a high-performance airplane for a corporation or fractional to flying for the airlines, whether domestic or long-haul international. Performing a wider variety of flying gives opportunities to see and experience things few others can. As inspiring as it is to fly over the mountains of Alaska, it can be just as fulfilling to show someone their hometown on their first airplane ride.

A pilot's everyday flying is filled with habits that seem as normal as walking, but abnormal situations can require actions that seem unnatural in comparison. Spin recovery, pitching down to extend the glide when you are below best glide speed, or chopping power on the good engine of a twin in order to maintain control are examples of what might be called counter-intuitive flying—all covered in *The Advanced Pilot's Flight Manual*. These are situations that require both solid use of the POH procedures and an in-depth knowledge of how the airplane flies.

As is said many times in this book, the Pilot's Operating Handbook has precedence on procedures for a particular airplane. Of course, the charts in the book are not to be used for navigation or flight planning. Thoroughly reviewing the latest Practical Test Standards will have you much more comfortable on your check ride.

For this Eighth Edition, my thanks go to the ASA Editing and Production department for their patience, skill and professionalism, especially editor Jennie Trerise and graphic artist Sarah Hager.

William C. Kershner
Sewanee, Tennessee

Photo by Dan Akins
Shreveport, Louisiana (KSHV)
February 1990
Boeing 727-223

Part One **Airplane Performance and Stability for Pilots** 1

1

Airplane Performance and Stability for Pilots

A Review of Mathematics for Pilots

A pilot doesn't have to know calculus to fly an airplane well, and there have been a lot of outstanding pilots who could add, subtract, multiply, and divide—and that's about it. *But* since you are going to be an "advanced pilot," this book goes a little more deeply into the whys and hows of airplane performance, including a little math review.

Trigonometry

Trigonometry can turn into a complex subject if you let it, but the trigonometry discussed here is the simple kind you've been using all along in your flying and maybe never thinking of it as such.

Take a crosswind takeoff or landing: you've been using Tennessee windage in calculating how much correction will be needed for a wind of a certain strength at a certain angle from the runway centerline. You correct for the crosswind component and know that the headwind component will help (and a tailwind component will hurt).

You have been successfully using a practical approach to solving trigonometric functions. (If an instructor had mentioned this factor earlier, some of us might have considered quitting flying.)

What it boils down to is this—whenever you fly you're unconsciously (or maybe consciously) dealing with problems that involve working with the two sides and hypotenuse of a right triangle. Flight factors involved include (1) takeoffs and landings in a crosswind, (2) max angle climbs, (3) making good that ground track on a VFR *or* IFR cross-country, (4) working a max range curve (if you are an engineer, too), and (5) calculating max distance glides. The following chapters will cover all these areas of performance in more detail.

Looking at a takeoff in a crosswind, you're dealing with the sines and cosines of a *right triangle*, a triangle with a 90° angle in it (Figure 1-1).

Sine

The sine (normally written as "sin," which perks it up a little) for an angle (α here) is the ratio of the nonadjacent side A to the hypotenuse (side C) (Figure 1-1). The Greek letters α (alpha) and β (beta) are used for the angles here because, well, it gives the book more class, and the Greek letters *are* used in aerodynamics equations. More Greek letters will be along shortly. The sides of a triangle are normally denoted by our alphabet (A, B, C).

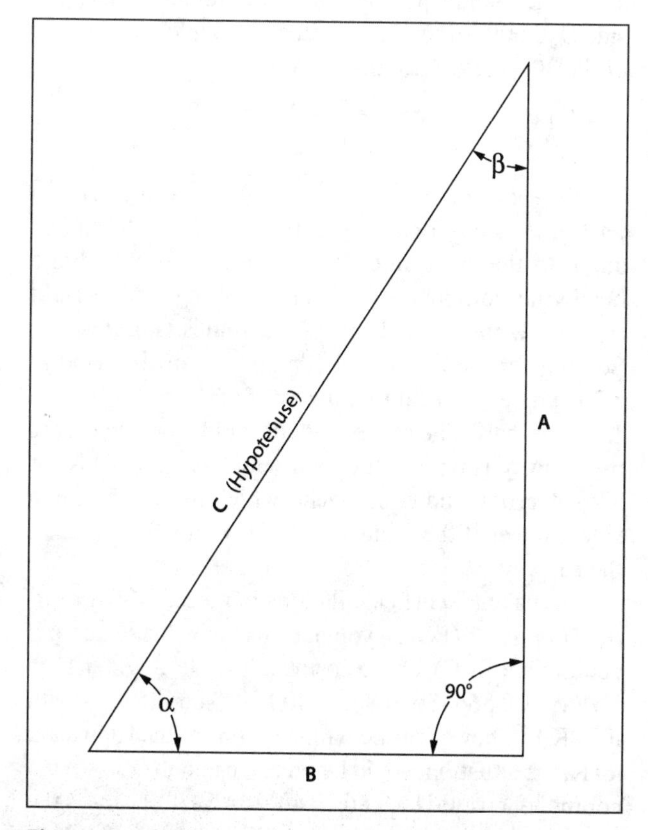

Figure 1-1. Right triangle components.

Look at a 30°-60°-90° triangle (Figure 1-2). The internal angles always add up to 180°; thus the other two angles of the right triangle (which has a 90° angle) always add up to 90° (10° and 80°, 45° and 45°, etc.). Another interesting point about right triangles is that the sum of the squares of the two sides is equal to the square of the hypotenuse, or $A^2 + B^2 = C^2$ (Figure 1-3). (This is what the Scarecrow recited after the Wizard of Oz gave him a diploma—and a brain.)

Cosine

For a 30° angle (β in Figure 1-2), the relationship of sides A and C (the hypotenuse), side A is *always* 0.866 of the length of side C (the cosine of 30° is 0.866; A/C = 0.866). Engineers add a zero before the decimal point for a value less than 1 so that it is clear that there isn't a missing number.

Looking at the angle α in Figure 1-2, note that the relationship of length of the adjacent side B at the 60° angle to the hypotenuse (side C) is the *cosine* of *that* angle, *always* 0.50 (B/C = 0.50).

Looking from the same angle of 60° (α), it is a fact that the *sine* (the nonadjacent side A divided by the hypotenuse, or A/C), is 0.866; that is, the length or value of side A is 0.866 the length of the hypotenuse. The sine of the 60° angle is the same as the cosine of a 30° angle—and why not? That's the same side (A). For side B, 0.500 is the cosine of the 60° angle and the sine of the 30° angle. (Got that?)

(Figure 1-2)—cosine $\alpha = B/C = 0.500$
sine $\beta = B/C = 0.500$

Take a practical situation: You are taking off in a jet fighter from a runway with a 40-K wind at a 30° angle to the centerline. What are the crosswind and headwind components? You're working with a right triangle with 30° and 60° acute angles (Figure 1-4). Solving for the crosswind component for the wind at a 30° angle you find that the ratio of A to C is 0.50 to 1, or one-half. The component of wind working across the runway is 0.50 of the total wind speed of 40 K, or a 20-K crosswind component, which means the same side force as if the wind were at 20 K at a 90° angle to the runway.

To make takeoff calculations in the *Pilot's Operating Handbook* (POH), you need to know the headwind component (B/C), or the cosine of the 30° angle, which is *always* 0.866. So, 0.866 × 40 K is 34.64 K. (Just call it 35 K.) If, however, the wind was 60° to the runway at 40 K, the situation would be reversed and the *crosswind* component would be 0.866 × 40 = 34.64 (35) K (and the *headwind* component would be 0.50 × 40 = 20 K), as

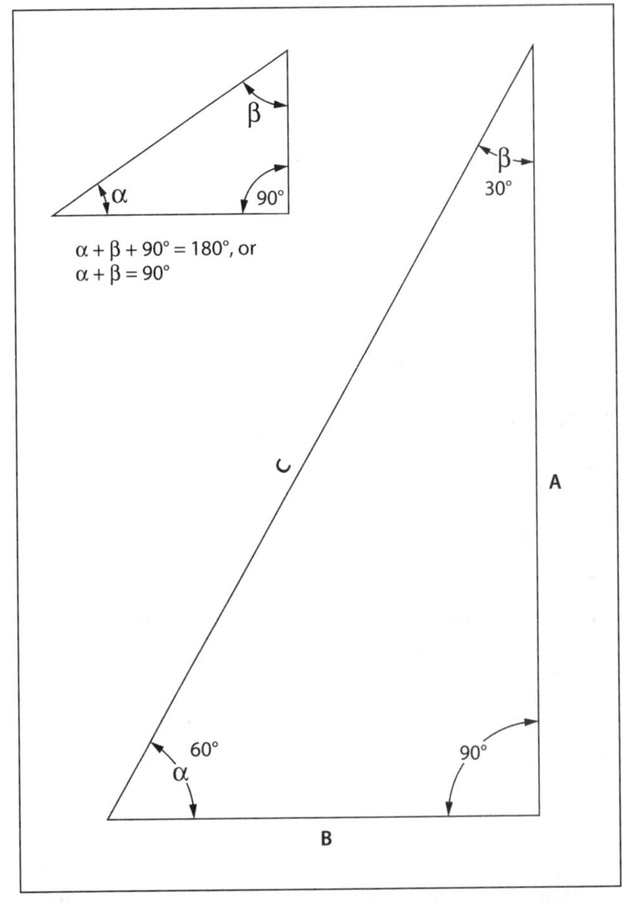

Figure 1-2. A right triangle with 30° and 60° acute (less than 90°) angles.

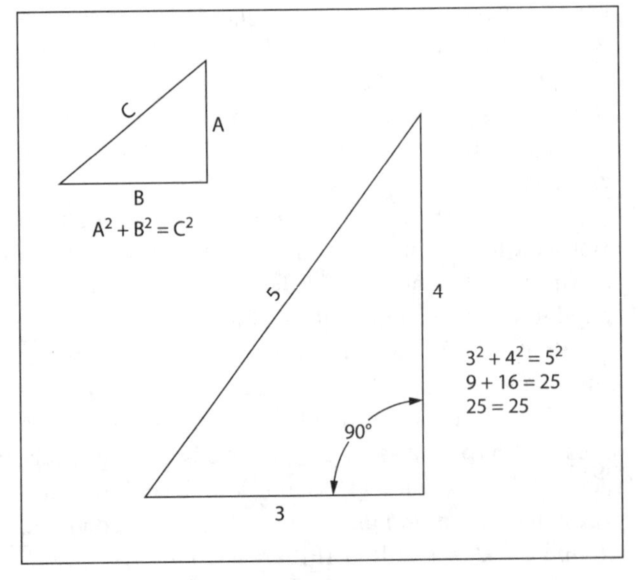

Figure 1-3. Classic example of the relationship of the hypotenuse of a right triangle. (Another is a triangle with 7 and 24 sides and a 25 hypotenuse: $7^2 + 24^2 = 49 + 576 = 625$; $25^2 = 625$).

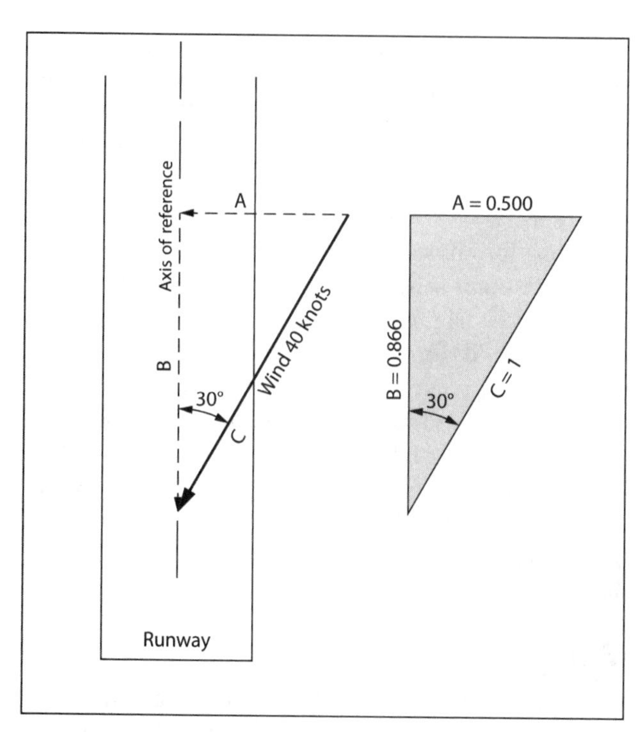

Figure 1-4. Finding the headwind and crosswind components.

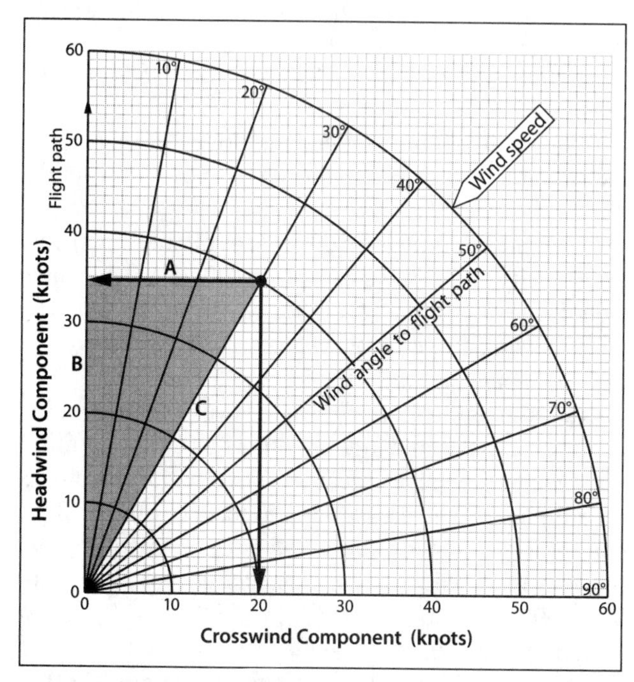

Figure 1-5. The wind component chart is a prepared set of right triangles, with sines and cosines precalculated and drawn. Horace Endsdorfer, private pilot, assumes that Figure 1-5 can only be used for crosswinds from the right, since that's the way it's drawn, but Horace has other problems as well (see Chapter 7—Endurance).

can be seen by checking the graph (Figure 1-5). What we've started here is a wind component chart like that found in a POH; here the engineers work out the sines and cosines for various angles the wind may make with the runway and all you have to do is read the values off the graph. Note that the triangle in Figure 1-4 and the shaded area of Figure 1-5 are the same. The wind speed in the graph is always the hypotenuse (side C) of the triangle.

Tangents

The tangent is the relationship between the *far side* (the nonadjacent side) and the *near side* (the side adjacent to the angle in question). Look back at Figure 1-2. The relationship A/B is the tangent of the angle α (60° shown there), and looking ahead at Figure 1-8 you can see that the tangent of 60° is 1.732. In a 60° angle, side A is 1.732 times as long as side B. The tangent is useful in such factors as finding the angle of climb, where the relationship of feet upward versus feet forward is essential.

To digress a little, Figure 1-6 shows the procedure probably first used in measuring the height of an object too high to be scaled easily. Although the example is better as a problem in geometry, it shows that for a given angle (the sun's rays forming the shadow), the sides of a right triangle have the same ratio.

If you were assigned the job of finding the height of the flagpole on a sunny day you could set up a vertical pole 4 feet tall and measure the shadow (3 feet here). You would then quickly measure the flagpole shadow to establish the ratio of the two poles (Figure 1-6). Your numbers would not likely work out as evenly as these, however, and there would be a problem on a cloudy day or at night.

If you had a device set on the ground for measuring the angle α (53° here) and knew the distance of that device from the flagpole (B), you would come up with $\tan \alpha = A/30$; $A = 30 \tan \alpha$; $\alpha = 53°$, $\tan \alpha = 1.33$, $A = 30 \times 1.33 = 40$ feet.

Okay, to review:

The sine of an angle is the ratio between, or relative value of, the "far" (nonadjacent) side of the right triangle and its hypotenuse and, like the cosine and tangent, is always the same for any given angle.

The cosine is the ratio between, or relative value of, the "near" (adjacent) side of the right triangle and its hypotenuse.

The tangent is the ratio of the "far" side to the "near" side of an angle of the right triangle.

The tangent shows the relationship in a climb between vertical and horizontal distances covered.

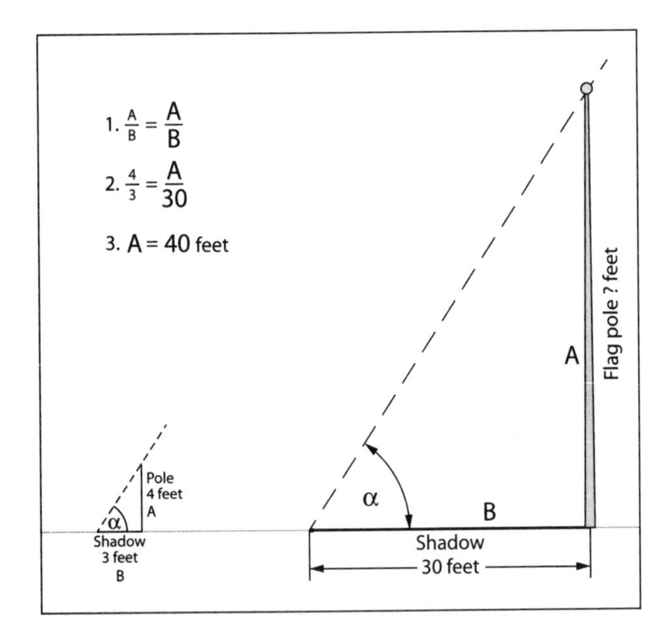

Figure 1-6. Using the relationship between similar triangles to find the height of a flagpole by measuring sides A and B of the small triangle and side B of the large triangle to find side A (the height of the flagpole). It is assumed that the flagpole is greased so that it cannot be climbed and measured with a tape. (There's the old story of two physics students who were each given a very expensive barometer and told to find the height of a certain tall building. One dropped the barometer off the top and measured its fall with a stopwatch. The other went to the janitor and said, "If you tell me exactly how high this building is, I'll give you this fine barometer." Scientific research methods vary, it seems.)

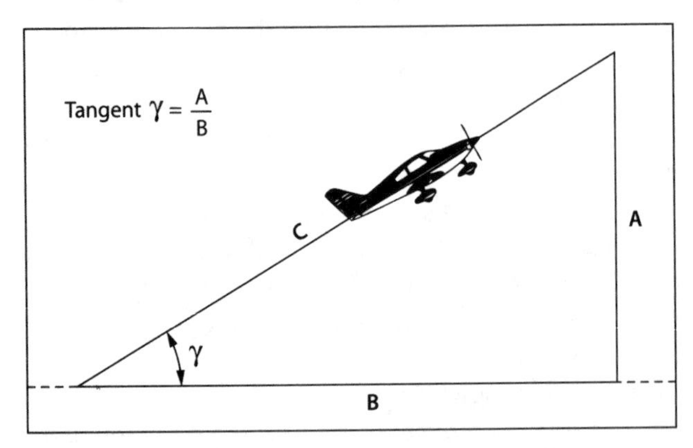

Figure 1-7. Max angle of climb (γ) is a tangent function and depends on the highest ratio of A (vertical height) to B (horizontal distance). Gamma (γ) is normally used to depict climb or descent angles.

The sine (0.500) of a 30° angle is the same as the cosine of a 60° angle. The sine of 55° equals the cosine of 35°, sine 20° equals cosine 70°, etc. (The "etc." is to cover the fact that the first time you encounter it this can be as confusing as an FAA directive.)

Figure 1-8 is a table of sine, cosine, and tangent functions for angles from 0° to 90° in 5° increments, plus three other selected angles that will be discussed later. Using a trig table (or the right kind of calculator app) you could, for instance, find the sine of an angle of 6°36' (6 degrees 36 minutes) or 6.6°, which turns out to be 0.1149372. (That's *all* you need—to be fumbling around with a trig table or calculator while you're flying.) But again, what it says is that the ratio of the value of the *far side* of the triangle to its hypotenuse is 0.115 (rounded off in Figure 1-8); it's about 11.5% as long as the hypotenuse.

Max Angle Climb

A good example of finding the max angle of climb of an airplane at a particular density-altitude is shown in Figure 1-9, which is a variation of Figure 6-7. (You might take a look ahead at Figure 6-7 now.)

As noted in Chapter 6, the max angle climb speed is found by running a line from the origin of the graph (zero climb and zero knots) tangent to or touching (and passing) the curve.

The angle of climb (γ, or gamma) is the tangent, or the ratio of A to B (A/B); tan γ = rate of climb/velocity—or is it?

The rate of climb is 1,200 feet per minute (fpm) and the velocity is 75 K, so tan γ = 1,200/75 = 16, which would give a climb angle (after referring to your trig table or using a calculator) of 86.4°, *Now that's a climbing airplane!* (Figure 1-10).

Of course, 86.4° is *not* the answer because we're dealing in apples and oranges, knots and feet per minute. One of the values must be converted to the other; for simplicity, convert the 75 K to feet per minute. The conversion factor for knots to feet per second is 1.69; multiply that by 60 to get the distance covered in a minute: 1.69 × 75 × 60 = 7,605 (call it 7,600).

So the tangent of the angle is 1,200/7,600 = 0.158, or, looking at Figure 1-8, the angle of climb is 8.98° (call it 9°). Wait a minute. It's easy to fall into a trap using the graph shown in Figure 1-9, although at shallow angles of climb the error is not too great. At first glance, it seems a simple matter of solving the tangent: you just plot climb distance versus airspeed and look up the tangent. The kicker is that the airplane is traveling up along its *climb path flight angle* at the airspeed given for max climb.

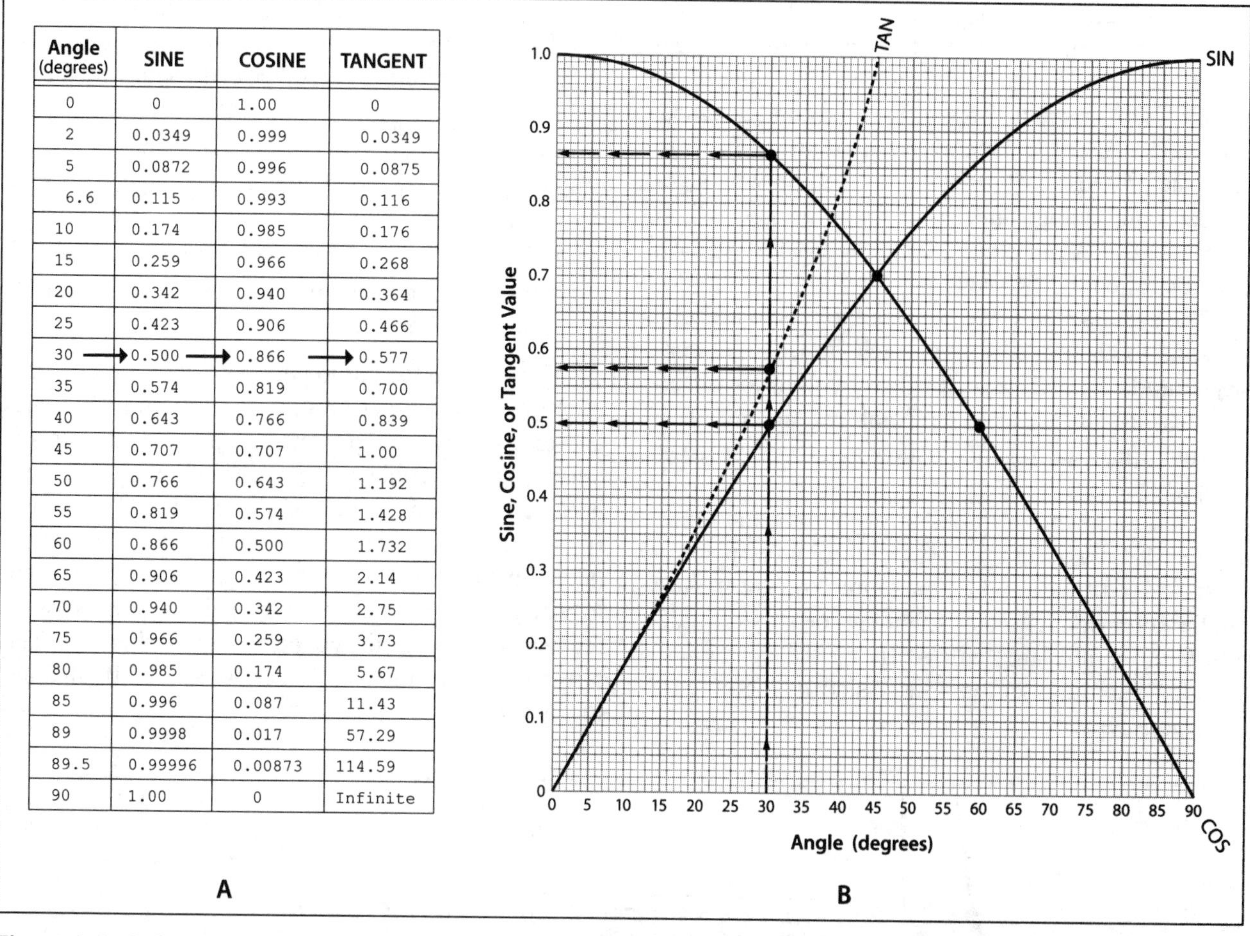

Angle (degrees)	SINE	COSINE	TANGENT
0	0	1.00	0
2	0.0349	0.999	0.0349
5	0.0872	0.996	0.0875
6.6	0.115	0.993	0.116
10	0.174	0.985	0.176
15	0.259	0.966	0.268
20	0.342	0.940	0.364
25	0.423	0.906	0.466
30 ⟶	0.500 ⟶	0.866 ⟶	0.577
35	0.574	0.819	0.700
40	0.643	0.766	0.839
45	0.707	0.707	1.00
50	0.766	0.643	1.192
55	0.819	0.574	1.428
60	0.866	0.500	1.732
65	0.906	0.423	2.14
70	0.940	0.342	2.75
75	0.966	0.259	3.73
80	0.985	0.174	5.67
85	0.996	0.087	11.43
89	0.9998	0.017	57.29
89.5	0.99996	0.00873	114.59
90	1.00	0	Infinite

Figure 1-8. A. Sine, cosine, and tangent values. Notice how the tangent value increases rapidly as the angle approaches 90°; for instance, from 85° to 89.5° (4.5°) the value increases over 10 times and goes to infinity at 90°. **B.** A graphical representation of the sine, cosine, and tangent values. Note that the tangent goes off the scale at a value of 1.0 at 45°. The examples are for the sine, cosine, and tangent at 30°.

Look at the problem again after setting up equal values: sin γ = 1,200/7,600 = 0.158; γ = 9.09° (call it 9.1°). The point is that at *shallow* angles (usually considered as less than 15°) the sine and tangent are quite close together and in this case would create an error of 0.11°, or a little over 0.1° (9.09°–8.98° = 0.110).

A problem might be set up as follows: Through earlier flight testing it was found that the max angle of climb for our new Rocket Six is 10.0° at sea level density. Find the horizontal distance required from *lift-off* to clear a 50-foot obstacle under the condition given. Assume that the airplane has the max angle climb speed at lift-off.

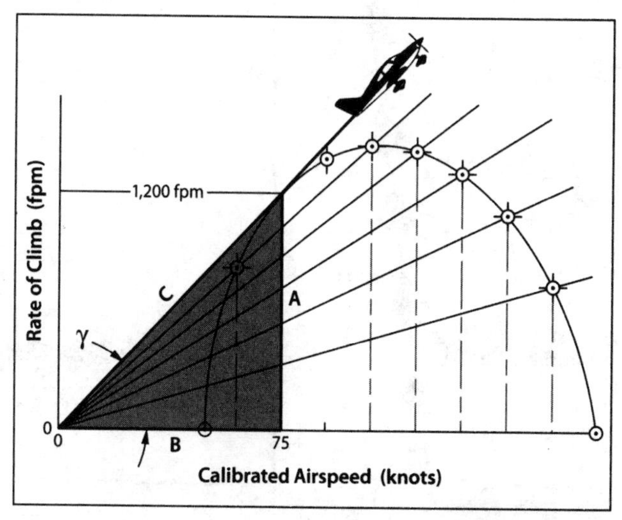

Figure 1-9. Rate of climb versus airspeed, finding the angle of climb at sea level (no wind).

The *tangent* of the angle of climb is important here because you're finding the distance to clear a 50-foot obstacle as part of the takeoff and climb distance for insertion in the POH. The vertical part of the triangle is known (A = 50 feet), as is the angle of climb (10.0°), so you would need to find B, or the horizontal distance required (Figure 1-11). Tan γ = tangent of 10.0°

(checking Figure 1-8, you'll find the answer is 0.176). Note again in Figure 1-8 that the tangent of the angle is very close to the sine value. So A (the height of 50 feet) is 0.176, or about 17.6% of B, the ground distance. You can see that the distance required after lift-off to clear the obstacle is 50/0.176 = 284 feet. Solving algebraically and doing some reshuffling, tan γ = A/B; B tan γ= A; B = A/tan γ, or 50/0.176, or 284 feet. (That's why it's called the "Rocket.")

The ground run would be added to this to get total distance to clear a 50-foot obstacle at sea level density-altitude. The same idea would be used for different pressure altitudes and temperatures (and different weights) until the takeoff distance chart or graph is complete.

Look at a general problem of finding the climb angle at the maximum *rate* of climb for an airplane at a particular altitude and temperature. You are the test pilot and set up a climb at 5,000 feet density-altitude. You (and the airplane) will be flying the hypotenuse (side C); the rate of climb will be side A. (See Figure 1-11 again.) So...

1. If two sides of a right triangle are known, or
2. If one side and one of the acute angles of a right triangle are known, all other factors may be found.

Two items are known:

1. The IAS is read off the airspeed indicator, converted to CAS (or EAS, as needed) and then to TAS (knots).
2. The rate of climb is either timed or read off the extra-accurate vertical speed indicator especially built for this problem.

The TAS up the climb path is in knots and the rate of climb is in feet per minute (fpm). Again it's apples and oranges, so you convert one of the values to the other. For this problem, the TAS along the climb path is to be 89 K and the rate of climb is found to be 900 fpm. One solution is to convert both to *feet per second* (although you could convert the TAS to feet per minute to match the rate of climb usage). To convert 89 K to feet per second, use the conversion multiplier 1.69. The airplane is traveling at 150 feet per second (fps) along the hypotenuse.

Figure 1-10. Using the dimensions cited in the example gives the airplane extraordinary climb performance.

The rate of climb is 900 fpm, or 60 seconds × 15 (fps).

The sine of the angle of climb, then, is side A/hypotenuse or rate of climb (fps)/TAS (fps) = 15/150 = 0.10. See Figure 1-8B to get the angle.

$$\sin \gamma = 0.10$$
$$\gamma = 5.8° = 5°48'$$

You could use "fathoms per fortnight" for both TAS and rate of climb, just as long as both factors are given in the same terms.

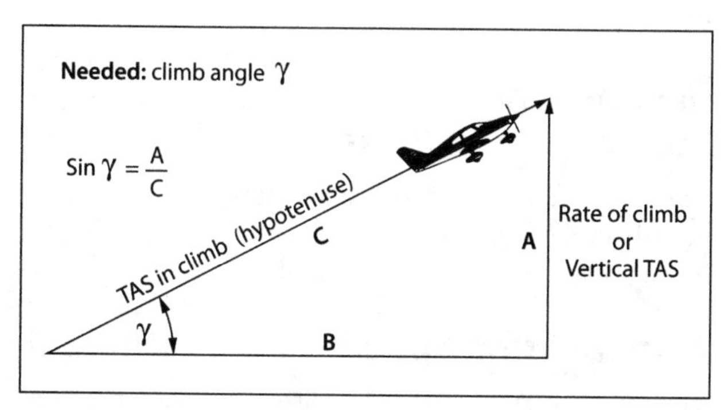

Figure 1-11. Finding the climb angle of an airplane at a particular climb speed (TAS) and rate of climb.

Fixed Angle of Attack Performance Factors

There are several factors in calculating airplane performance based on a fixed angle of attack; in order to fly at that angle of attack (without an angle of attack indicator), the airspeed must be varied as the square root of the weight change. The following performance parameters for reciprocating engine airplanes depend aerodynamically on a constant coefficient of lift (or constant angle of attack).

Stall Speed

The stall occurs at the maximum coefficient of lift (C_{Lmax}) for the configuration chosen (clean or a chosen flap setting). The C_{Lmax} with flaps extended will be higher than unflapped, naturally, which means that the stall speed (V_{stall}) will be *lower.* (See Figure 2-11, right side.)

Look at the equation for lift (see Chapter 2 for a more thorough discussion): lift = $C_L S(\rho/2)V^2$, where ρ = air density (slugs per ft³), C_{Lmax} = maximum coefficient of lift, S = wing area (ft²), and V^2 = true velocity (fps²). Assuming that lift = weight (W), and solving for V_{stall}, you'd find $V_{stall} = \sqrt{2W/S\rho C_{Lmax}}$

Following are the steps used in finding the stall speed:

$$L = W = C_{Lmax}S(\rho/2)V^2_{stall}$$

$$V^2_{stall} = \frac{W}{C_{Lmax}S(\rho/2)} = \frac{2W}{C_{Lmax}S\rho}$$

(The "2" is moved to the top of the equation to simplify things a little.)

To solve for V_{stall}, square roots are taken of each side of the equation:

$$V_{stall} = \sqrt{2W/C_{Lmax}S\rho}$$

You can see that the greater the C_{Lmax}, the lower the stall speed. (V_{stall} is TAS here.)

Double the weight and the stall speed is increased by a factor of the square root of 2 ($\sqrt{2}$), or 1.414. Two numbers to remember if you plan to follow up on this are $\sqrt{2}$ = 1.414 and $\sqrt{3}$ = 1.732. Spend your time memorizing them instead of watching TV news; it's less depressing.

Max Range Airspeed

Max range distance depends on maintaining the maximum ratio of C_L to C_D (C_L/C_D) or maintaining a constant *angle of attack* throughout the trip. As fuel is burned off, the weight decreases and the dynamic pressure must be reduced to reduce lift so as to maintain straight and level flight at this constant angle of attack. If you don't reduce power as weight decreases, the airplane will climb. (This is one technique of long-range cruise control, that is, letting the airplane gain altitude as weight decreases; but the usual procedure for max range is to maintain a constant altitude and reduce airspeed as fuel is burned.)

Looking at the lift equation again, assuming straight and level flight:

$$L = W = C_{LR}S(\rho/2)V^2 = C_{LR} \times S \times \rho/2 \times V^2$$

where C_{LR} = coefficient of lift at the max *range* angle of attack and $(\rho/2)V^2$ = dynamic pressure (pounds per square foot, or psf).

Taking a fictitious airplane weighing 3,600 pounds at the start of a max range exercise at a constant 5,000-ft density-altitude and a wing area of 180 ft², find the speeds for max range at weights of 3,600 pounds and 2,700 pounds near the end of the trip. The C_L for max range (C_{LR}, or max C_L/C_D), is 0.500 for this airplane. The density at 5,000 feet is 0.002049 slugs per ft³ (see Figure 4-4). Of course, you aren't going to carry a standard atmosphere chart around in the airplane, but do the problem anyway.

The true airspeed (V_T) to be carried at 5,000 feet at a weight 3,600 pounds is

$$V_T^2 = \frac{2W}{C_{LR}S\rho} = \frac{2 \times 3{,}600}{0.002049 \times 180 \times 0.500} = \frac{7{,}200}{0.1844}$$

$$= 39{,}096$$

$$V_T = \sqrt{\frac{2W}{C_{LR}S\rho}} = \sqrt{39{,}096} = 198 \text{ fps}$$

To convert from feet per second to knots, the factor is 1.69; 198/1.69 = *117 K* (rounded off). The true airspeed to be carried for max range at 5,000 feet density-altitude at 3,600 pounds is 117 K. Using an E-6B computer or calculator app, the *calibrated* airspeed is found to be *109 K* at 5,000 feet.

At a weight of 2,700 pounds near the end of the trip, the *only* variable is weight. Going through the process again to find TAS:

$$V_T^2 = \frac{2W}{C_{LR}S\rho}$$

$$V_T = \sqrt{\frac{2W}{C_{LR}S\rho}} = \sqrt{\frac{5{,}400}{0.18441}} = \sqrt{29{,}283}$$

You would again use a calculator to find the CAS at 5,000 feet (94 K) at 2,700 pounds at destination.

The question comes up as to the variation of max range indicated (or calibrated) airspeed with respect to different *density-altitudes*. Take still another look at the lift equation (lift = weight): $L = W = C_{LR}S(\rho/2)V^2$.

Assume that the weight is the same at the different density-altitudes so that L (or W) is constant but ρ varies. Since $(\rho/2)V^2$ is dynamic pressure (CAS), if the other factors (L, C_{LR}, and S) are constant, then dynamic pressure must remain so.

The *combination* of one-half the density of the air molecules moving past the airplane times the velocity (TAS) squared gives the dynamic pressure required to support it.

Suppose that an airplane at a certain weight and C_L requires a minimum calibrated airspeed of 100 K, or a dynamic pressure of 33.9 psf, to maintain level flight. The 33.9 psf may be obtained by flying at sea level at a calibrated and true airspeed of 100 K (169 fps), or at 10,000 feet with a true airspeed of 116 K. In both cases the calibrated airspeed is 100 K. The point is this: Once the C_{LR} is found, you would fly the airplane at the same calibrated (or indicated) airspeed at any of the lower operating altitudes to get max range.

Max Endurance

Maximum endurance for propeller airplanes is also a function of a constant coefficient of lift (C_{LE}, or max endurance coefficient of lift) as far as aerodynamics is concerned. Max endurance is found at a higher angle of attack than max range and, in aerodynamic theory at least, is the lowest point on the power-required curve.

As in the cases of maximum range and the stall speed, the airspeed required to maintain the C_{LE} is decreased with the *decrease of the square root of the weight* (and for the same reasons). More about this in Chapter 7.

Max Distance and Minimum Sink Glides

These are fixed angle of attack performance factors that also vary with the square root of the weight change. More about this in Chapter 8.

Maneuvering Speed

The maneuvering speed (V_A) also depends on a constant C_L (C_{Lmax}, or the stall angle of attack); therefore V_A must be reduced with the decrease of the square root of the weight:

$$V_{A2} = V_{A1}\sqrt{W_2/W_1}\ ;\ V_A = \sqrt{n} \times V_S$$

where n = limit load factor (discussed in Chapter 11).

A thumb rule for finding the effects of weight change on airspeed for *any parameter requiring a constant* C_L *is to reduce the airspeed* (V_A here) *by one-half of the percentage of the weight reduction.*

Suppose at 3,000 pounds an airplane has a maneuvering speed of 100 K (chosen for simplifying the arithmetic). At 2,400 pounds, or at 20% weight reduction, this rule says to reduce the 3,000-lb maneuvering speed by 10% to 90 K. At 1,800 pounds, a weight reduction of 40%, the original 3,000-lb (100-K) maneuvering speed should drop by 20%, to 80 K.

To check it out, actually solve for the square roots (the technical way of doing it) and compare. Instead of the thumb rule of 90 K at the lower weight of 2,400 pounds, the computer gives an answer of 89.44 K. At the weight drop of 40%, the "real" answer is 77.45 K, as compared with the estimate of 80 K.

Figure 1-12 is a graph used to see the relationship between weight change and required airspeeds for the performance parameters that result from, or require, a fixed angle of attack, or more accurately, a constant C_L. The graph is a quick and easy way to get the numbers; you can still work it out yourself if you like.

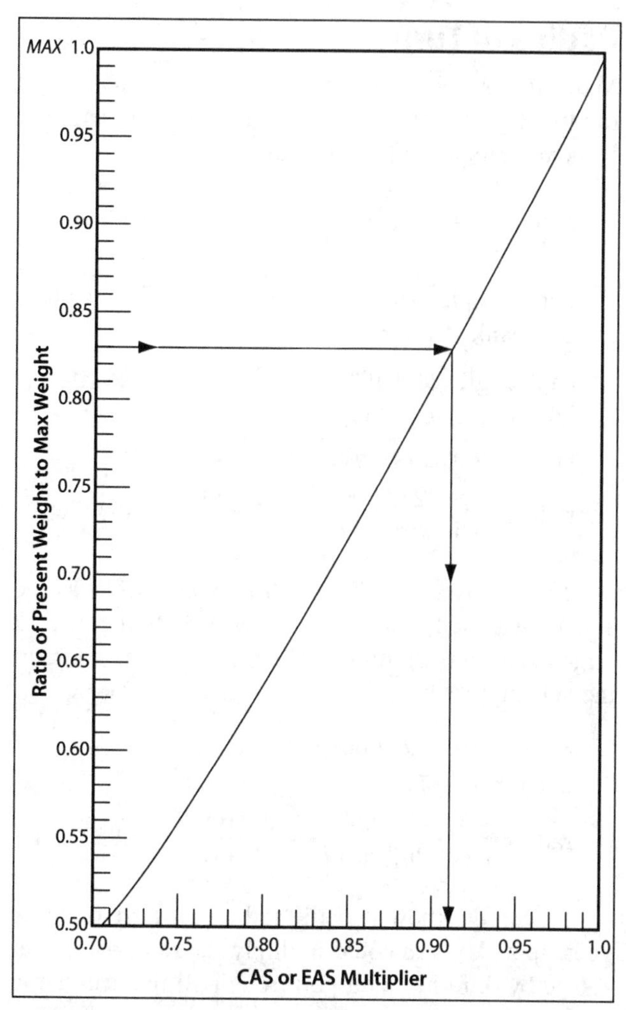

Figure 1-12. CAS or EAS multipliers to correct for weight change with the fixed angle of attack performance factors (stall speeds, maneuvering, max range, and max endurance speeds). It's assumed for the graph that the lowest weight will not be less than 50% (0.50) of that of the maximum weight. You could use the graph to find weights much lower than the 2,990 pounds used as an example by having it as the "new" max weight. For instance, to find the maneuvering speed at 1,555 pounds for that same (originally 3,600-lb) airplane you could set up the ratio 1,555/2,990 = 0.52. Looking at 0.52 on the ratio of weights scale in this figure and moving over to the line and down—as was done eariler—you'd get an answer of about 0.72. The V, at 1,555 pounds, is 0.72 that of 2,990 pounds. V, at 2,990 pounds, was 109 K, as was found earlier. V, at 1,555 pounds, would be 0.72 x 109 = 78 K (rounded off).

Following are operating speeds (CAS):

Stalls = V_{S0}, V_{S1} (landing configuration and clean, respectively).

Maneuvering speed = V_A

Maximum range speed = V_{MR}

Maximum endurance speed = V_{ME}

Each of these operating speeds decreases as a function of the square root of the decrease in weight. V_{S1}, as noted in Chapter 4, is the stall speed for a particular configuration; in this book it will be the clean stall speed at a particular weight.

To use Figure 1-12, assume a fictitious airplane with a maximum certificated weight of 3,600 pounds. The airspeeds (CAS or EAS) at that weight for this problem are V_{S1} = 62 K, V_A = 120 K, V_{MR} = 106 K, V_{ME} = 80 K. To find the required airspeeds at a weight of 2,990 pounds, divide: 2,990/3,600 = 0.83. The new weight is 0.83 of the max certificated weight (rounded off).

Selecting 0.83 on the ratio of weights scale, move across to intercept the reference line and then down to find the CAS (or EAS) multiplier of 0.91 for this problem. Solving for the *new* airspeeds (rounded off) at the lower weight of 2,990 pounds: $V_{S1} = 0.91 \times 62 =$ 56 K; $V_A = 0.91 \times 120 = 109$ K; $V_{MR} = 0.91 \times 106 = 96$ K; $V_{ME} = 0.91 \times 80 = 73$ K. Figure 1-12 works for any weight ratio you may use; 3,600 and 2,990 pounds were just examples.

Turns

Looking at a 2,000-lb airplane in a steady state, coordinated, constant-altitude turn in a bank of 60° (Figure 1-13): The "up" and "down" forces must be in balance if the airplane is to maintain a constant altitude. The items known are the airplane's weight, which is acting directly downward, and the 60° angle of bank. It is also known that lift acts perpendicular to the wingspan (the hypotenuse, or side C), and for now it can be given a value of 1.

Side B (the vertical component of lift) must be 2,000 pounds in order to balance the weight of 2,000 pounds, and here it is 0.500 of the value of the total lift (the hypotenuse, or side C) required to maintain a constant altitude. The lift (C) acting perpendicular (as always) to the wingspan must be 4,000 pounds. Lift required = $1/\cos \phi = 1/0.500 = 2$, or C = 2B's (B = 2,000 pounds).

The g's being pulled here are lift/weight = 4,000/2,000 = 2 g's. In any constant-altitude balanced turn, the load factor being exerted is the lift-to-weight ratio, or load factor (LF) = $1/\cos \phi$.

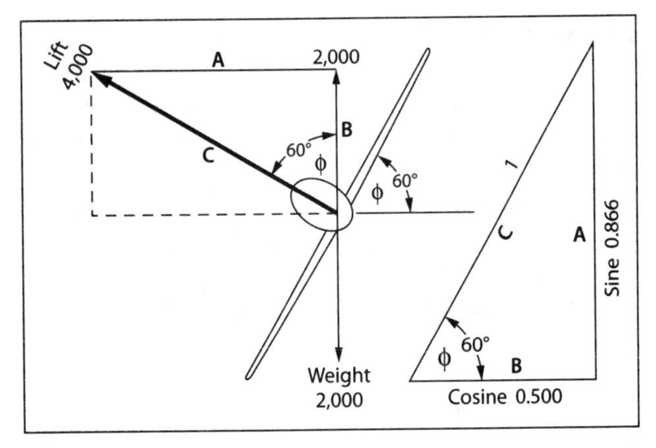

Figure 1-13. The cosine of 60° is 0.500; the weight is 2,000 pounds. Cosine ϕ (phi or phee, the Greek letter used to denote bank) = cosine 60° = 0.500. The lift required = $1/\cos\phi = 1/0.500 = 2$. Lift required = 2 x 2,000 = 4,000 pounds.

Look back at Figure 1-8, or use your calculator, and find the load factor for a 25° banked turn; $\cos\phi = 8/C$, or $\cos\phi = 0.906$, or LF = 1/0.906 = 1.104 g's. You could make up your own curve as shown in various textbooks or POHs by picking bank angles from 0 to 90°, plotting the points, and joining them. You can use Figure 1-8 to find the cosine of a particular bank and divide "1" by that.

This brings up the point about the *stall speed increase* with increased bank angle in the balanced, constant-altitude turn; the stall is affected by the load factor, which is an indication of how much the airplane "weighs." The stall speed increases as the *square root* of the load factor increases (or weight increases, as was discussed earlier and is shown in Figure 1-12).

Suppose that the airplane is in a bank of 35° (ϕ = 35°). What is the load factor and increase in stall speed? Referring to Figure 1-8 you'd see that the cosine of 35° is 0.819 (call it 0.82). The load factor in the 35°-banked constant-altitude turn is $1/\cos\phi = 1/0.82 = 1.22$. The pilot (and airplane) is feeling 1.22 g's flying the 35°-banked turn. The stall speed increase is the *square root* of the load factor (or apparent weight increase), or $\sqrt{1.22}$, or 1.10. The stall speed has increased by 10% in the turn (more about this in Chapter 2).

Radius of Turn

Many times you'd like to have a good idea of what radius of turn would be expected at a given angle of bank and airspeed (TAS, knots).

$$\text{radius (ft)} = \frac{V^2}{11.26 \tan\phi}$$

For example, what is the turn radius of an airplane at a 30° bank at 150 K?

$$\text{bank angle } (\phi) = 30°$$
$$V^2 = (150)^2 = 22{,}500$$
$$\tan 30° = 0.577 \text{ (look back at Figure 1-8)}$$
$$\text{radius} = \frac{22{,}500}{(11.26)(0.577)} = \frac{22{,}500}{6.497} = 3{,}463 \text{ feet}$$

The radius at 300 K (which is twice as fast as the 150 K just used) and 30° bank will be four times as large because the radius is a function of the square of the velocity.

$$V^2 = (300)^2 = 90{,}000$$
$$\tan 30° = 0.577$$
$$\text{radius} = \frac{90{,}000}{(11.26)(0.577)} = \frac{90{,}000}{6.497} = 13{,}852 \text{ feet}$$

Since you know that the radius for a given bank goes up as V^2, you could multiply the radius found at 150 K by 4, rather than go through all the arithmetic again.

The "new" radius, if you know the "old" one, is proportional to $(V_2/V_1)^2$ times the "old" radius. For example, the radius at 150 K was 3,463 feet. What would be the "new" radius of turn at 190 K?

$$(190/150)^2 = (1.267)^2 = 1.604, \text{ or}$$
$$1.604 \times 3{,}463 = 5{,}554 \text{ feet}$$

Don't forget that you'll need ***twice*** the radius to do the 180° turn needed to escape the box canyon. This might be the time to pitch up and turn (even if you can't climb out of the canyon). The airspeed loss in the climbing turn will reduce the radius of turn (cutting the airspeed by a quarter, which reduces the turn radius by 44%), at the same bank angle.

Turn Rate

For those interested in instrument flying, the rate of turn is an important factor; the rule of thumb of dividing the TAS (K) by 10 and adding one-half of that answer works very well for the standard rate of turn of 3° per second. As an example, the rule of thumb indicates that at an airspeed of 130 K, a standard rate of turn would require a bank of 19.5° (call it 20°).

$$\text{turn rate (degrees per second)} = \frac{1{,}091 \tan \phi}{V}$$

where ϕ is the bank angle and V is TAS in knots (130 K here). The turn rate is 3° per second, so turning the equation around a little:

$$3 = 1{,}091 \tan \phi / V$$
$$3V = 1{,}091 \tan \phi;\ 3V/1{,}091 = \tan \phi$$
$$\tan \phi = (3 \times 130)/1{,}091 = 390/1{,}091 = 0.3575.$$

Using a calculator or trig table (or Figure 1-8), you'd find that the angle of bank (ϕ) is 19.67°, a value "easily" flown on the attitude indicator (sure it is). You could look at Figure 1-8 and see that the tangent of 20° is 0.3640 and that the tangent of the angle sought here would be slightly less than that. Or you could interpolate between 0.3640 (for 20°) and 0.2680 (for 15°).

There is a certain amount of error involved in interpolating between tangent values because as the angle increases the tangent value increases at a *much* higher rate. For instance, the tangent of 60° is *not* just 3 times the value of the tangent of 20°. Looking back at Figure 1-8 you'd note that the tangent of 60° is 1.732; the tangent of 20° is 0.364, for a ratio of 4.76 to 1 (1.732 divided by 0.364), not 3 to 1. It gets even more out of hand as the angle approaches 90°.

Summary

This chapter is an introduction or review of trigonometry, as well as briefly covering certain aspects of airplane performance. The following chapters will cover climbs, turns, glides, and cruise performance in much greater detail. After you've read each chapter on performance, you might want to check back to this one for a quick review of the basic factors involved.

2

The Four Forces

Background

Lift, Drag, Thrust, and Weight are the Four Forces acting on an airplane in flight (Figure 2-1). The actions of the airplane are affected by the balance (or imbalance) of these forces, and while each will be discussed separately in this chapter, don't get the idea that each works completely separately.

Sure, you can fly an airplane without knowing how Lift or the other of the Four Forces work, but a good understanding of the factors affecting each of them can lead to analyzing and predicting the performance of your airplane under different conditions of Weight, altitude, etc. This chapter takes a look at how each Force is developed, and Chapter 3 shows how it *acts* in flight.

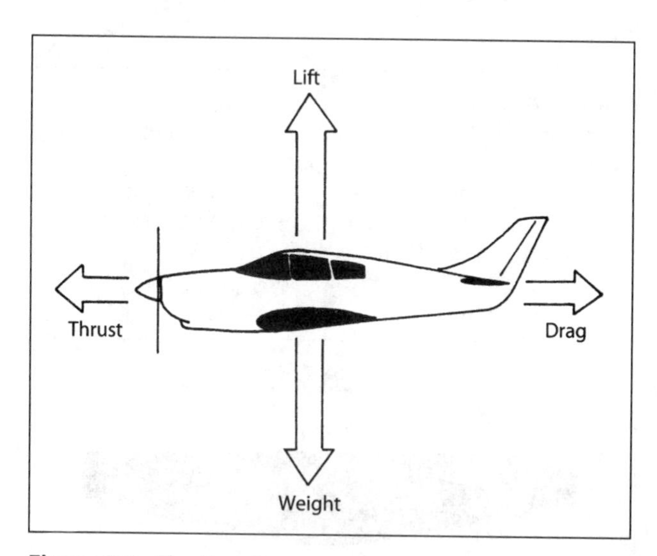

Figure 2-1. The Four Forces.

Lift

Lift is the force exerted primarily by the wings (although the fuselage contributes, and even the tail helps under certain special conditions) and is created by the action of the air moving past the airfoil (cross-section of the wing). *Lift is considered to act perpendicularly to the relative wind and to the wingspan* (Figure 2-2).

The airfoil produces effective lift because of its shape, which is such that the pressure, velocity, and downwash distribution results in *effective* lift, meaning that the lift required for the airplane's various performance actions does not result in excessive drag and high power requirements. In other words, the airfoil gives a high lift-to-drag ratio (more about that later).

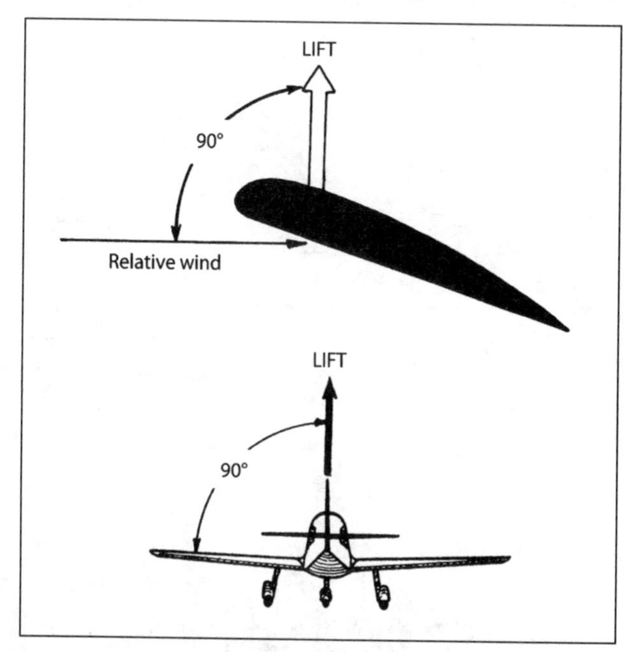

Figure 2-2. Lift acts perpendicular to the relative wind and to the wingspan.

You might use a flat plate of sufficient size to "lift" a 2,000-lb (or 200,000-lb) airplane, but the power required to fly it would be prohibitive.

As the airfoil moves through the air, either in powered or gliding flight—or as the air moves past it as in a wind tunnel—pressure distributions around it result in a downwash action (Figure 2-3). This action creates the reaction of the airplane being supported in flight. (Figure 3-5 shows some pressure distribution patterns around an airfoil at two different low angles of attack.) The air, moving past the airfoil, has different velocities at different positions.

Figure 2-4 gives some airfoil nomenclature. Note that the mean camber (average curve) line is equidistant from each surface. Figure 2-5 shows a symmetrical airfoil (no camber) at zero angle of attack. The pressure distributions on each side of the airfoil are lower but equal, there is no downwash, and lift doesn't exist. In Figure 2-6 downwash is present and the pressure distribution is such that lift is being produced.

If you are interested in the mathematics of lift, take another look at the following equation, which was introduced in Chapter 1.

$$L = C_L S(\rho/2)V^2, \text{ or Lift} = C_L \times S \times \frac{\rho}{2} \times V^2$$

where L = lift, in pounds.

C_L = coefficient of lift (It varies with the type of airfoil used and angle of attack.)

S = wing area, in square feet (Figure 2-7 shows how it is usually measured.)

$\rho/2$ = air density (ρ divided by 2). (Rho, or ρ, is air density, which for standard sea level conditions is 0.002378 slugs per cubic foot. If you want to know the mass of an object in slugs, divide the weight, in pounds, by the acceleration of gravity, or 32.16. The acceleration caused by gravity is 32.16 feet per second per second at the earth's average surface.)

V^2 = true velocity (true airspeed) of the air particles in feet per second (fps) squared.

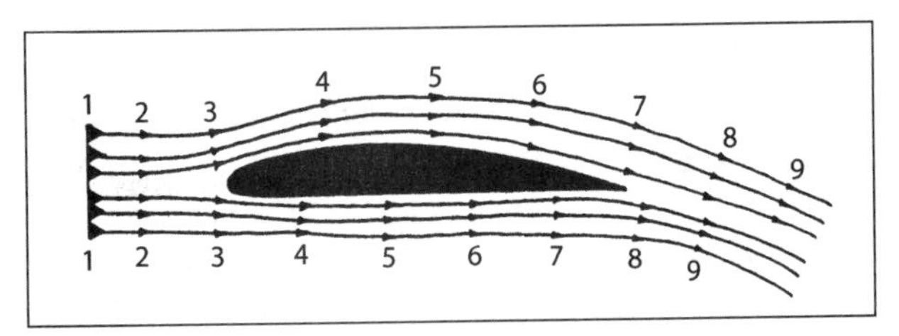

Figure 2-3. Relative velocities and down wash around a nonsymmetrical airfoil.

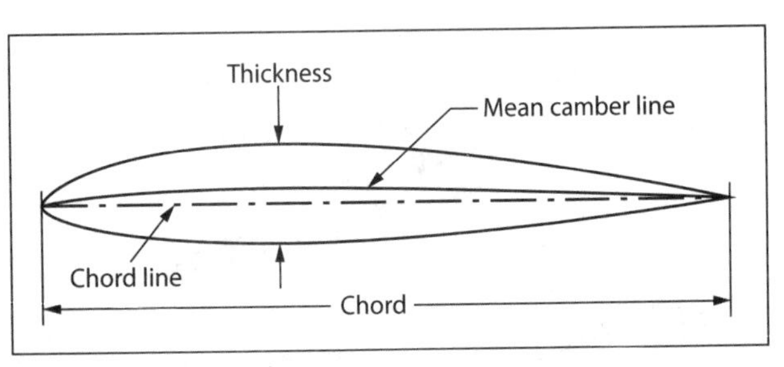

Figure 2-4. Airfoil nomenclature. The chord line is the shortest distance between the leading edge to the trailing edge of the airfoil.

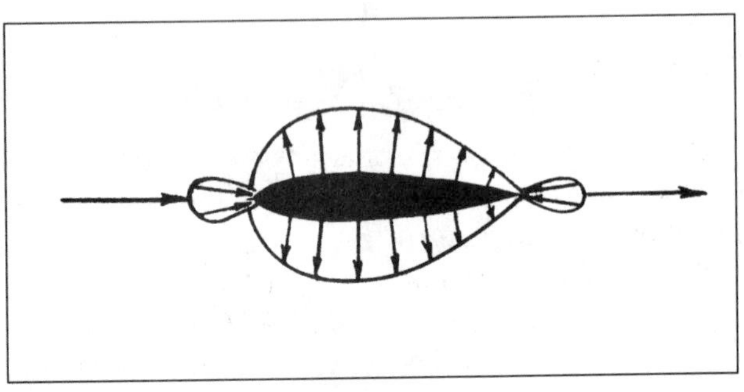

Figure 2-5. Pressure patterns around a symmetrical airfoil moving at a zero angle of attack.

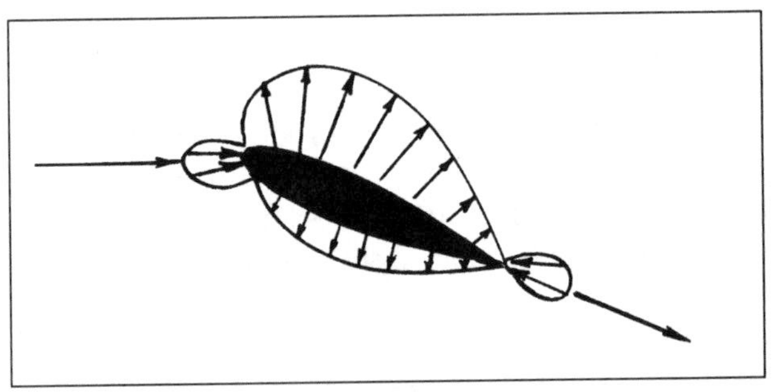

Figure 2-6. Pressure patterns around a symmetrical airfoil at a positive angle of attack. By comparing Figures 2-5 and 2-6 you can see that lift isn't produced by a symmetrical airfoil until an angle of attack occurs. Most aeroabatic airplanes have symmetrical or near-symmetrical airfoils for better inverted flight characteristics. (The airfoil in Figure 2-3 would be inefficient in inverted flight.)

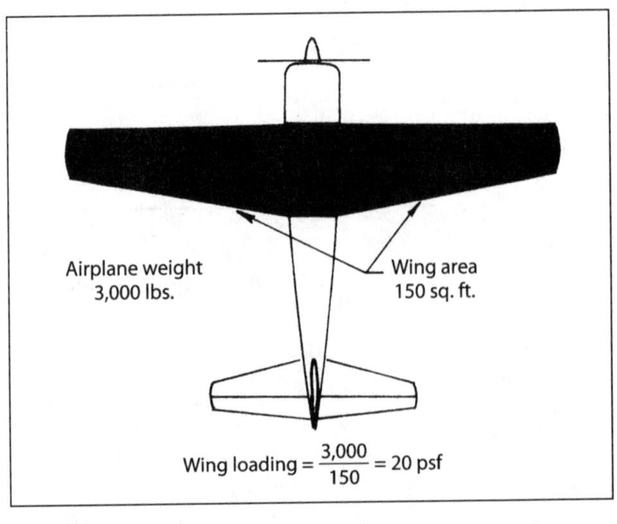

Figure 2-7.

Coefficient of lift is a relative measure of an airfoil's lifting capabilities. Comparatively high-lift airfoils, such as the Clark Y type with its curved or cambered upper surface and flat lower surface, may have a maximum C_L of 1.8. A thin airfoil, such as might be used on a jet, may have a maximum C_L of only 0.9. The airplane having the higher maximum coefficient of lift, or C_{Lmax}, will use less runway on landing (assuming two airplanes of equal wing loading operating in the same air density). Having available the C_L versus angle of attack curves of various airfoils, the engineer can decide which airfoil would be better to use for a particular airplane. Your contact with the term is only through control of the angle of attack while flying.

A plot of C_L versus angle of attack for a typical general aviation airplane type of airfoil shows that the C_L increases in a straight line with an increase in angle of attack until the stalling angle is reached, at which point the C_L drops off rapidly (Figure 2-8).

Figure 2-9 shows the C_L versus angle of attack for a high-speed symmetrical airfoil such as may be used on jets. Its maximum C_L is only 0.9, which means that the airplane would have a high landing speed.

These airfoil designations describe the airfoil properties and shape. The 23012 is an unsymmetrical airfoil. The "12" indicates that the airfoil maximum thickness is 12% of its chord. The 0006 airfoil is a symmetrical airfoil (the first two zeros tell this) with a thickness ratio of 0.06 or 6%.

Take the 3,000-lb plane with the 150-ft² wing area in the earlier example. Assume that there are two airplanes exactly alike with this weight and wing area; one has a 23012 airfoil, and the other a 0006. The plane with the 0006 high-speed airfoil will cruise faster because of less drag but will also land faster. In fact, it may land so fast as to be useless for many smaller airports.

It has been found that a "birdlike" airfoil (Figure 2-10) has a comparatively high C_{Lmax}. Earlier planes used this type and had low landing speeds—but also had low cruise speeds because of the higher drag at all angles of attack. A good setup would be to have a 0006 airfoil for cruising and a birdlike airfoil for landing. Flaps accomplish just that; when you lower the flaps you raise the C_{Lmax} and have a lower landing speed.

Figure 2-11 shows plots of the C_L versus angle of attack for two airfoils. Notice the similarity of the curves of the 0006 with flaps and the 23012. It can be readily seen that although the flaps installation adds weight, flaps make it possible for fast airplanes to land at low speeds. The two airplanes of the same weight and configuration in the example would probably use the same amount of runway for landing, assuming the plane with the 0006 airfoil used 60° of flaps and the one with the 23012 airfoil did not have flaps and, of course, the air density (density-altitude) was the same for both airplanes.

By using the lift equation $L = C_L S(\rho/2)V^2$, and solving for velocity, an actual comparison of the landing speeds of the two airplanes can be found. For convenience, assume that the two airplanes are landing at sea level, that lift just equals weight at the touchdown, and

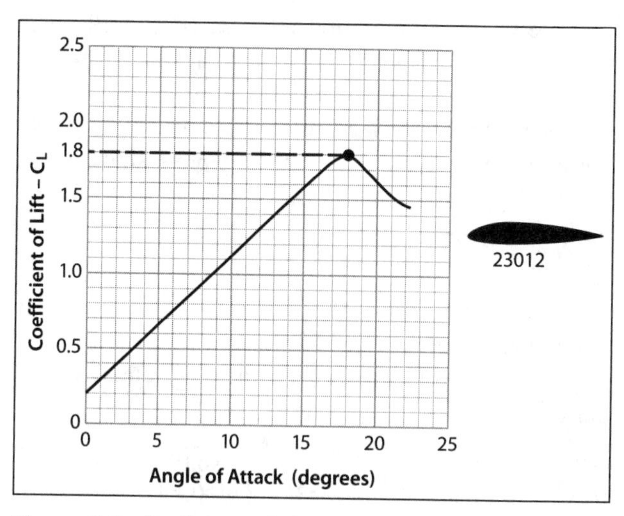

Figure 2-8. Coefficient of lift versus angle of attack, NACA 23012 airfoil.

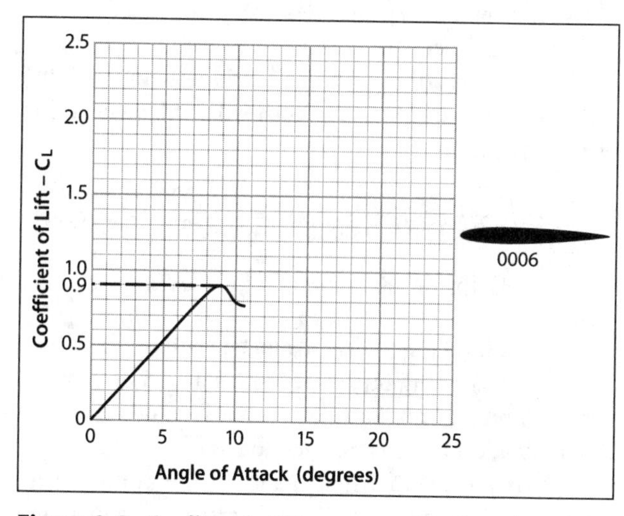

Figure 2-9. Coefficient of lift versus angle of attack, NACA 0006 airfoil.

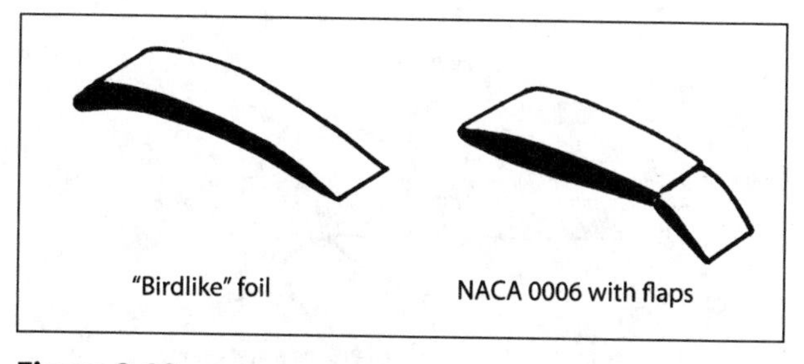

Figure 2-10.

that the C_L in the equation is C_{Lmax} (both will touch down at the maximum angle of attack or minimum speed).

First solve for the landing speed of the airplane with the 23012 airfoil and do a little algebraic shuffling of the lift equation:

$$V = \sqrt{2L/C_{Lmax}S\rho}$$

Everything inside the square root enclosure is known: L (weight) = 3,000 pounds, C_{Lmax} (for this airfoil) = 1.8, S = 150 square feet, and ρ = 0.002378 slugs per cubic foot.

$$V = \sqrt{\frac{6{,}000}{1.8 \times 150 \times 0.002378}} = \sqrt{\frac{6{,}000}{0.64}} = \sqrt{9{,}380}$$

$$= 97 \text{ fps}$$

Thinking in terms of miles per hour, V = 66 mph or 57 K (true airspeed, or TAS).

Do the same thing for the airplane with the 0006 airfoil (no flaps); C_{Lmax} is 0.9 instead of 1.8 (everything else is the same):

$$V = \sqrt{\frac{6{,}000}{0.9 \times 150 \times 0.002378}} = \sqrt{\frac{6{,}000}{0.32}} = \sqrt{18{,}750}$$

= 137 fps or *93.5 mph* or *81 K* (TAS)

(At sea level the indicated and true airspeeds will be the same, assuming no airspeed instrument or position error.) A pretty "hot" airplane—but it could be cooled down by adding the flaps mentioned earlier.

Getting back to lift in general, the funny thing about it is that you really don't worry about how much lift you have in normal flying—you fly by the airplane and lift takes care of itself. Sure, you can be flying along at cruise and increase lift by pulling back on the wheel, but you can *feel* that lift is greater than it should be by the way you are being pressed down in the seat. As drag is increased by the increase of lift, you'll find that the airplane slows—and lift will tend to regain its old value again.

One time when you *are* interested in watching lift increase is on takeoff. If your 3,000-lb airplane with the 23012 airfoil (or any airfoil) is taking off at a high elevation (where the density is low), it must have a higher V^2 (TAS, squared) in order to make up for the lower density to get the required lift for lift-off. This is *one* of the reasons why a longer takeoff run is required at airports at higher elevations. (The big reason is that the engine is producing less power in the less dense air, but this will be covered in later chapters.)

High-Lift Devices

The effects of flaps, as noted, can increase the maximum C_L compared with the wing without flaps. While the term *high-lift device* is commonly used, actually *the purpose of flaps, slots, or slats is to provide the same lift as before (say 3,000 pounds) at a lower airspeed, not to increase the lift over that required.* If you are flying at a high speed and suddenly put the flaps down, it is true that lift will be increased suddenly and the airplane will *accelerate* upward—and you will again be pressed down sharply in the seat. You could find that "increasing the lift" in such a fashion could cause certain problems (such as leaving a trail of flaps and other parts of the airplane fluttering behind). *So the high-lift devices are used at low speeds.* More about this in Chapter 11.

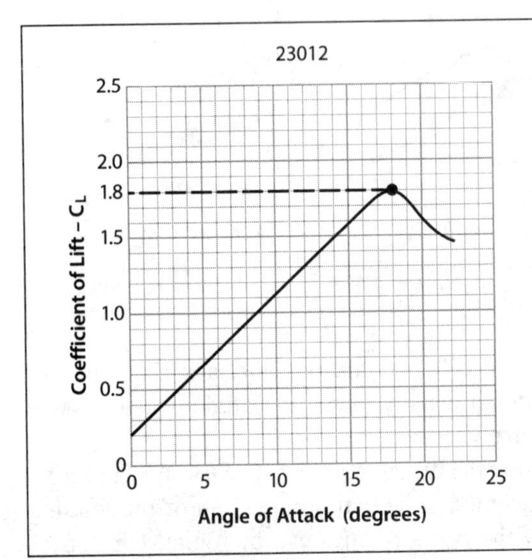

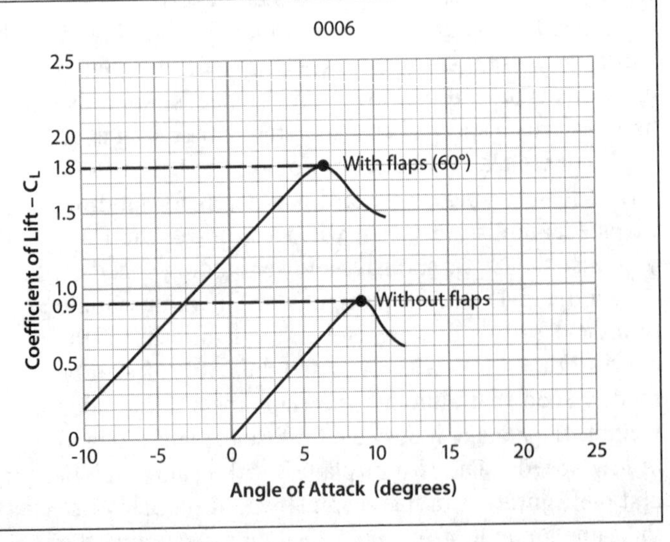

Figure 2-11. Comparison of plain NACA 23012 airfoil and NACA 0006 airfoil with and without flaps.

Flaps

Flaps are the most widely used high-lift device. Many types are in use, a few of which will be covered here.

1. *Plain flap*—A simple means of changing the camber of the airfoil for use at low speeds (Figure 2-12).
2. *Split flap*—You can see in Figure 2-13 that there is a low-pressure region between the flap and the wing so that for equal flap areas and settings, the split flap tends to cause greater drag than the plain flap, particularly at lesser angles of deflection.
3. *Fowler flap*—This flap combines a camber change with an increase in wing area—a good combination to lower the stall speed for landing, but the system may be too complex and heavy for some lighter planes (Figure 2-14).
4. *Zap flap*—This split-type flap increases wing area in the same way as the Fowler type (Figure 2-15).
5. *Double-slotted flap*—By putting slots in the flaps, a combination of camber change and smoother flow is obtained (Figure 2-16).

Slots

The leading-edge slot is a means of keeping a smooth flow at higher angles of attack than would be possible with an unslotted wing. Slots usually are placed near the wingtip to aid in lateral (aileron) control at the stall and to ensure that the tips don't stall first, but they may be used along the entire span.

You are familiar by now with the idea of a wing dropping during the stall and, like most pilots, probably prefer an airplane that has a good, straight-ahead stall break (Figure 2-17).

Slats

Slats are movable leading-edge vanes that form slots. The slot causes drag at higher speeds and, as the slat can be retracted more or less flush with the leading edge, it is a boon to higher-speed airplanes. Some jets use a "droop snoot" in combination with flaps to obtain a birdlike airfoil for lower landing speeds (Figure 2-18).

The high-lift devices complement each other—that is, by adding flaps to a plain airfoil, the maximum C_L is raised; adding slots or slats to this flap-equipped wing results in a further increase in C_{Lmax}.

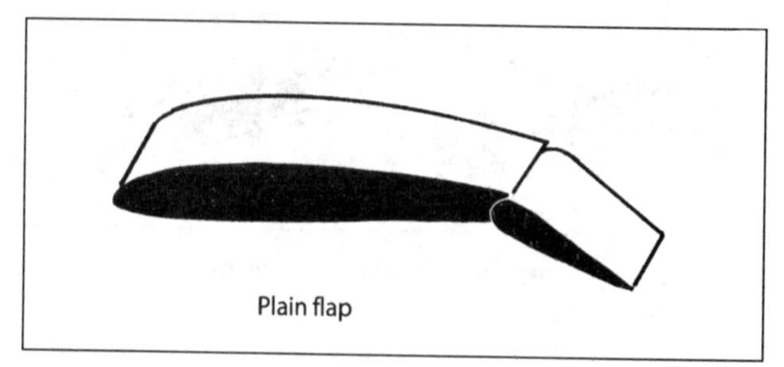

Figure 2-12.

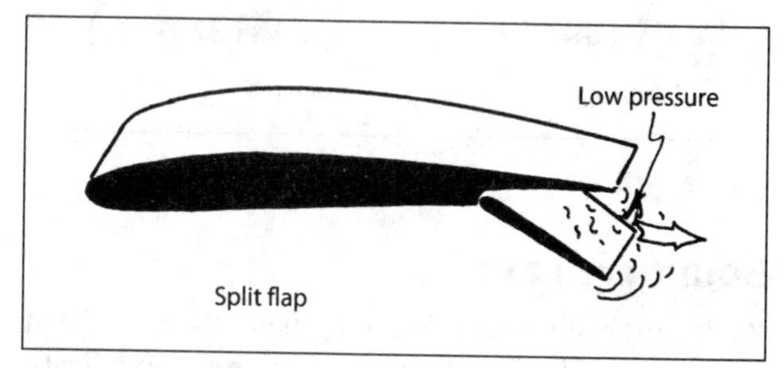

Figure 2-13.

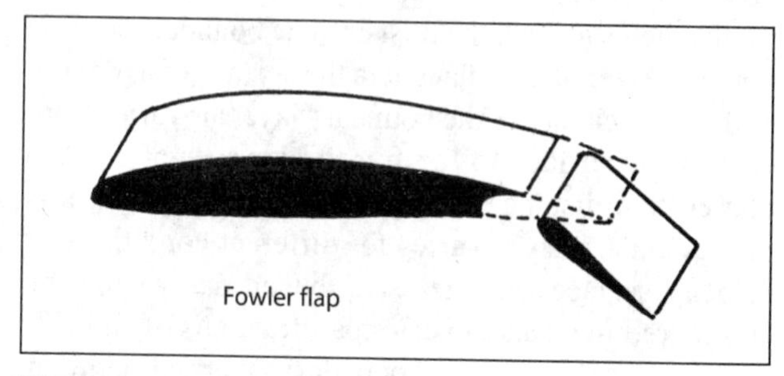

Figure 2-14.

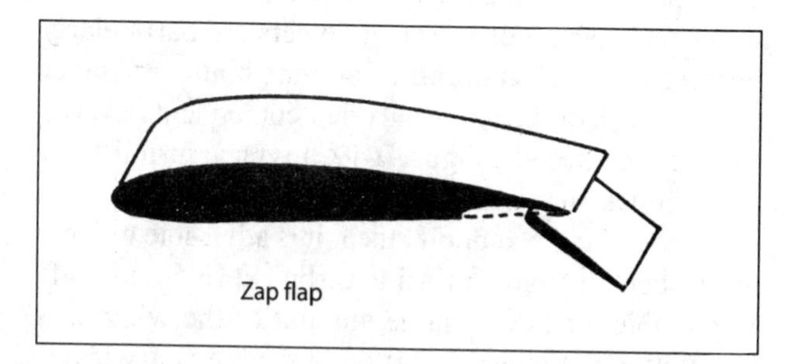

Figure 2-15.

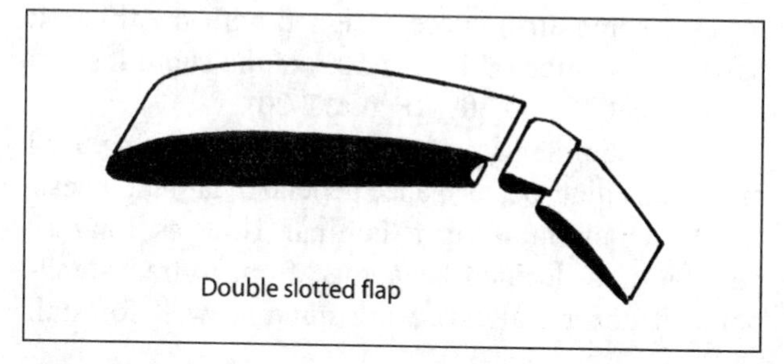

Figure 2-16.

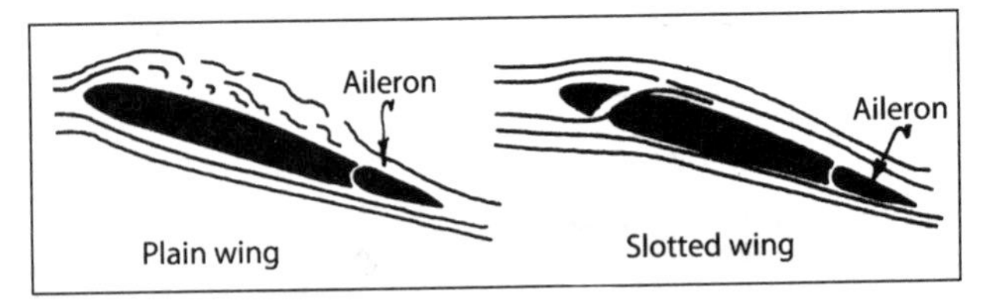

Figure 2-17. Comparison of plain and slotted wings at higher angles of attack.

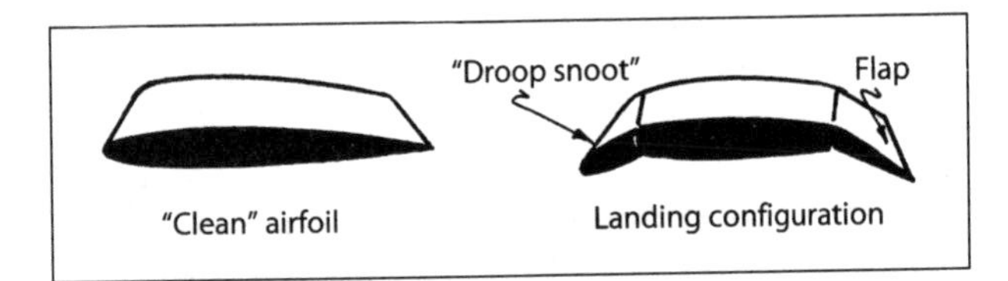

Figure 2-18.

Boundary Layer

You've probably heard this term many times. A good illustration of boundary layer can be seen on a dusty wing; you fly the airplane at speeds up to 200 K, but the dust isn't affected. The boundary layer effect is one factor that helps to keep the dust on. The boundary layer is that thin layer of air adjacent to the surface of a moving body. The velocity of the boundary layer air varies from zero at the surface to the free-stream velocity (TAS) at a certain distance from the surface. The thickness of a boundary layer varies for different conditions of velocity, surface roughness, etc., but normally it may be considered in terms of very small fractions of an inch.

There are two types of boundary layers: (1) laminar or layered smooth flow and (2) turbulent. The laminar type creates much less skin friction drag than the turbulent type; aeronautical engineers are particularly interested in maintaining a laminar boundary layer over as much of the wing and other components as possible at high speeds. Figure 2-19, a typical airfoil for a light trainer, shows that both types are present.

From a drag standpoint then, it is advisable to have this transition from laminar to turbulent flow as far aft as possible, or have a large amount of the wing surface within the *laminar* portion of the boundary layer. Because the transition usually occurs at approximately the thickest part of the airfoil (where the pressure is lowest), some airfoils are designed with the thickest parts at a position of 40% to 50% of the chord instead of the usual 25% to 30% (Figure 2-20).

These laminar types of airfoils are now being used on various high-performance general aviation planes.

While maintaining a laminar flow as long as possible is a decided advantage from a drag standpoint, it doesn't always work quite so well for stall characteristics. One of the first steps in a stall is the separation of the boundary layer, and the longer it remains intact the more delayed the stall (higher angle of attack and a greater C_{Lmax} at stall). The laminar layer tends to break down more suddenly than the turbulent layer so that the laminar flow airfoil usually does not have quite as good stall characteristics as found in older airfoil types (all other things being equal). The designer must compromise between low drag and good stall characteristics on the airplane using the laminar flow airfoil.

Some general aviation trainers use NACA 64 and 65 series airfoils, which are considered to be in the laminar flow family. The Piper Cherokee 140 has a 65_2-415 airfoil, which has the maximum thickness of 40% aft of the leading edge (the "4" in its designation) and a thickness-to-chord ratio of 0.15, or 15%.

One problem encountered in actual operations is that mud or other protrusions on the wing surface may cause the laminar flow to become turbulent at a point well forward of the desired or designed point. Figure 2-20 shows the "perfect" situation. But insects smashed against the leading edge may cause the flow behind the point to become turbulent, with a resulting loss of cruise efficiency. It would seem that any kind of roughness (scratches or protrusions) could cause problems, but aerodynamicists note that a scratch or depression has little effect on transition, compared with a protruberance of the same dimension.

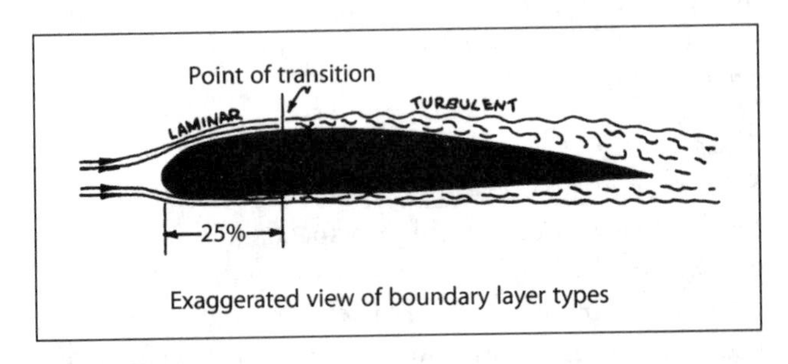

Figure 2-19.

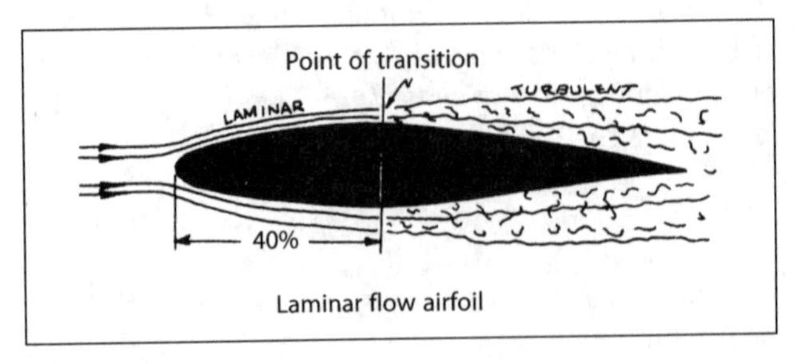

Figure 2-20.

Boundary Layer Control

For many years engineers have worked to find artificial means of delaying boundary layer separation at higher angles of attack. Two methods have been tried: (1) suction, which removes the boundary layer at various points of the airfoil, drawing it inward, and (2) blowing, which adds energy to the boundary layer and in essence works as if the entire airfoil has a turbulent layer (with its resulting better stall characteristics because of later separation). Boundary layer control requires a great deal of energy, which only can be furnished by adding weight in the forms of pumps, piping, etc. Jets use bleed-air from the compressor sections.

Angle of Attack Indicators

The U.S. Navy has for some years used angle of attack (α) indicators both for operational carrier airplanes and for those in the Training Command preparing pilots for flying with the fleet.

The airplane will always stall, clean, at a certain α and, with a given amount of flap deflection, at another constant α—weight, airspeed, or g force has no effect on it. The max range and max endurance will each have a requirement for a certain fixed C_L as will the max distance or minimum sink glide. By knowing the different angles of attack (sometimes given in degrees, but more often in *units*) required for the various performance phases just cited, the pilot may hold them constant during the period of that particular phase. The same value of angle of attack would be maintained on the AOA indicator throughout, say, a 5-hour max range flight where, because of fuel burn, the weight may decrease by 30% to 40%. To maintain the max range conditions without an AOA indicator, the airspeed must be reduced as the square root of the weight change, as was noted in Chapter 1. (See Figure 1-12 for a graph to correct the airspeed for constant phases, depending on a constant C_L value.)

Since angle of attack is the criterion for performance in these earlier mentioned areas, variable weight or density (atmospheric pressure and temperature) has no effect on the AOA readings for the various maneuvers. If, for example, the airplane stalls at an indicated 15 units with full flaps in bitterly cold Antarctica at a very light weight, it will also stall at 15 units with full flaps at max weight in Central Africa on a hot summer day. The calibrated airspeeds at stall will be different, but in this case only because of the weight. The approach units would be the same value in both cases; the approach *airspeeds* would be different, however.

The AOA indicator uses a probe (well calibrated and usually on the fuselage) to check the airflow. Taken into account are the angle of incidence and other factors that would result in different angles between fuselage and wing flow.

Many airliners have AOA gauges installed as part of the glass cockpit. The display may be in the corner of the PFD (primary flight display). The display can show a needle on a long arc that has a red line for the critical α and a green band for ideal α. The green and red mark indications are based on current flap setting; i.e., keep it in the green band and you are safe, even as you configure for landing.

Design of the Wing

Every airplane is made up of compromises, and this is particularly noticeable in wing design. For speed, a tapered wing is better than a rectangular wing. But the tapered wing with no twist has poor stall characteristics, as the tips tend to stall first. Common sense tells you that the tapered wing has less drag because of less area near the tip—which results in less induced (vortex) drag than a rectangular wing of equal area (assuming the two planes have the same span loading). The elliptical wing (like that of the WW II *Spitfire*) is more efficient but does not have as good stall characteristics as the rectangular wing (other factors being equal).

Wing Design and the Stall

There are several solutions to this problem of the stall. In every case the tips should stall *last*. You want lateral (aileron) control throughout the stall. An airplane with bad rolling tendencies at the stall break is viewed with a jaundiced eye by pilots. The best stall pattern is to have the wing stall at the root area first, with the stall progressing outward toward the tips. This may be accomplished by several means: washout (twist), slots, stall strips, or spanwise airfoil variation.

Washout

The wing may have a built-in twist so that the tip, having a lower angle of incidence (resulting in a lower angle of attack during the approach to a stall), will be flying after the root section has stalled. Generally this difference in incidence is no more than 2° to 3° from root to tip. The tips are said to have washout in this case (Figure 2-21). Washed-in tips would have a higher angle of incidence—hardly conducive to pilot ease during the stall because the tips naturally tend to stall first.

Slots

Slots are not only a high-lift device but also a lateral control aid. Planes with slots usually have them only in the section near the wingtip so that lateral control can be maintained throughout the stall, or at least so that a wing won't drop suddenly with little warning, as may sometimes happen in a landing or practice stall (unmodified tapered wings have this tendency). Slots give the tapered-wing airplane the benefit of added lateral control in the stall and tend to dampen any rolling tendency. If the tips stalled first (remember, some airplanes have a different twist in each wing to counteract torque), a sizable rolling moment could be produced.

Some STOL (short takeoff and landing) airplanes have full-length slots or slats, which make for good slow-speed characteristics (Figure 2-22).

Stall Strips

Stall strips, or spin strips as they are sometimes called, are strips attached to the leading edge of the wing, usually near the root. As the angle of attack increases, these strips break up the flow, which gives the desired effect of the root area stalling first (Figure 2-23).

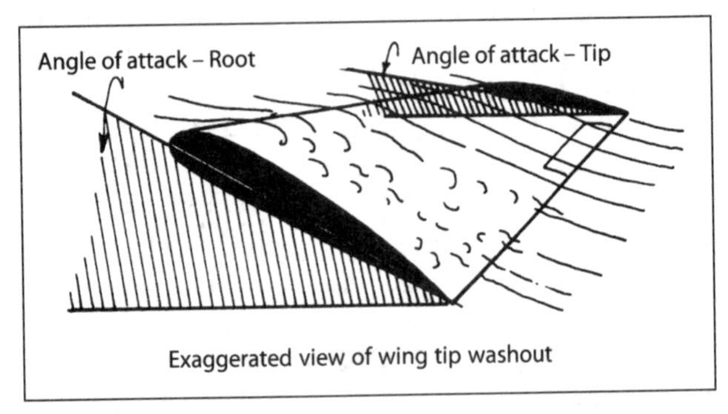

Figure 2-21. Wingtip washout as a means of maintaining lateral control during the stall.

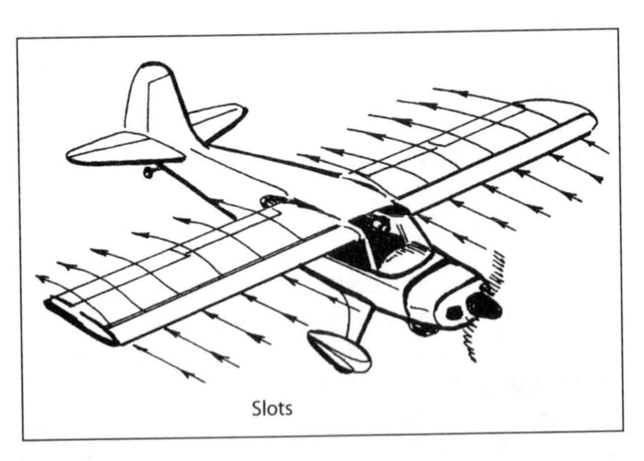

Figure 2-22.

Spanwise Airfoil Variation

This high-sounding title simply means that some wings may have a high-speed-type airfoil at the root and a low-speed-type at the tip. An extreme example would be a laminar flow airfoil at the root and a birdlike airfoil at the tip. The birdlike tip will be flying after the high-speed section at the wing root has stalled (Figure 2-24). In some cases several of these wing design techniques may be combined. The fact that the root section stalls first tends to cause a flow disturbance that usually results in tail buffeting and a warning of the impending stall.

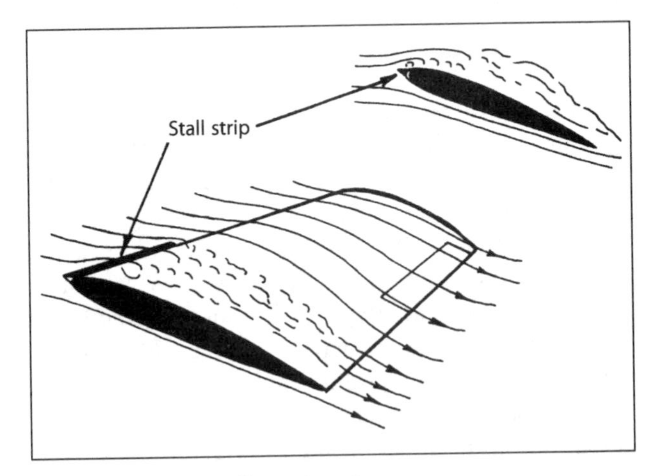

Figure 2-23. The stall or spin strip.

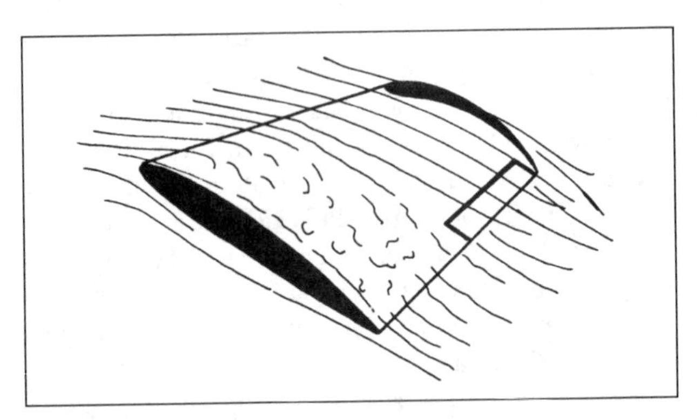

Figure 2-24. Different airfoils at root and tip.

Wingtip Tanks and Winglets

Many jets and several of the high-performance general aviation airplanes use tip tanks. The aerodynamic effect of tip tanks or end plates is an increase in effective aspect ratio (ratio of span to average chord), and you'll see in the next section that a larger aspect ratio results in lower induced drag. In most cases, the tip tanks more than offset any additional penalty such as increased frontal area or skin friction area.

A large percentage of transport category airplanes are now equipped with winglets. The reduction in drag increases the effective range of the airplane without the need for increased fuel capacity (same Mach at a lower power setting). Winglets have been installed on planes already in service, allowing markets to be flown that the winglet-less model of the same aircraft couldn't reach with adequate reserves. There is some weight penalty involved, plus the need for structural analysis of the stresses the winglet might add to the airframe; it's not a free lunch but often a cost effective one.

Drag

Anytime a body is moved through a fluid such as air, drag is produced. Airplane aerodynamic drag is composed of two main parts: induced drag (the drag caused by lift being created) and parasite drag (form drag, skin friction, and interference drag). Drag acts rearward and parallel to the flight path.

Parasite Drag

The following factors affecting parasite drag are similar to those affecting lift (assume as each factor is discussed that the others remain constant).

Coefficient of parasite drag—A relative measure of the parasite drag of an object. The more streamlined an object the lower its coefficient of parasite drag (Figure 2-25).

Air density—The greater the density of the fluid moving past an object, the greater the parasite drag, assuming the velocities are the same. Note the difference in effort required to move your hand through water and air at the same speeds.

Velocity—Double the airspeed and parasite drag is quadrupled.

Area—Parasite drag increases directly with the size of the object in the airstream. The engineers normally base the total drag of an airplane on its wing area, so as to establish some basis for comparison between airplanes.

The total coefficient of drag is the sum of C_{Di} (coefficient of induced drag) and the C_{Dp} (coefficient of parasite drag), or $C_{Dtotal} = C_{Di} + C_{Dp}$ (more about C_{Di} later). Total drag = $(C_{Di} + C_{Dp})S(\rho/2)V^2$.

Form Drag

This is the drag caused by the frontal area of the airplane components. When you were a kid you no doubt stuck your hand out the car window when you went riding. When your hand was held palm forward, the drag you felt was nearly all form drag. When your hand was held palm down the drag was caused mostly by skin friction. This can probably be best described by looking at a very thin flat plate (Figure 2-26).

Note that in Figure 2-26A the drag existing is principally caused by the form of the plate whereas in Figure 2-26B the largest part of the drag is skin friction. This form drag is the reason why streamlining is necessary to reach higher cruise speeds (Figure 2-27).

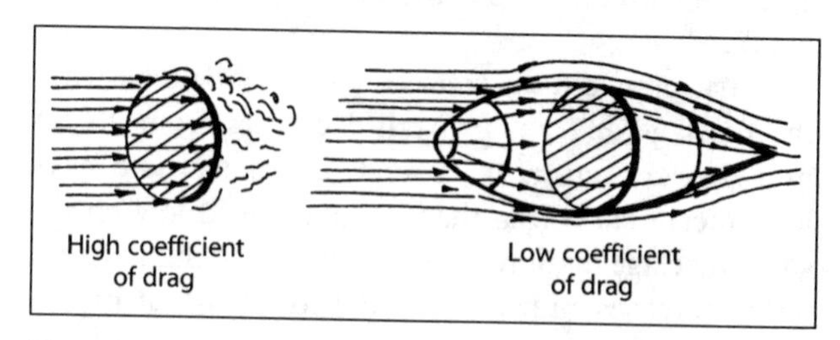

Figure 2-25. A comparison of the drag of a flat plate and a streamlined shape with the same cross-section area at the same air density and velocity.

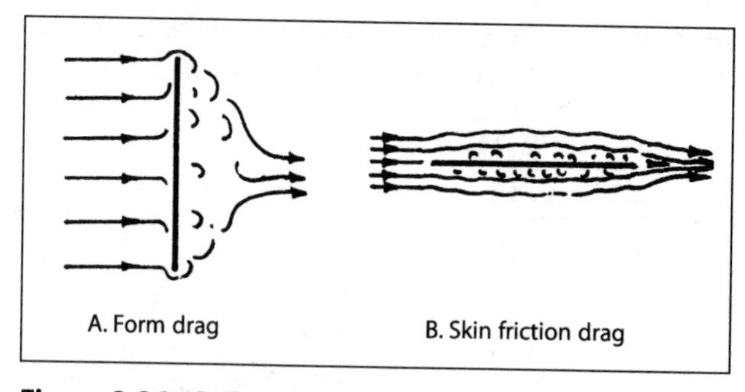

Figure 2-26. A. Form drag and **B.** skin friction drag.

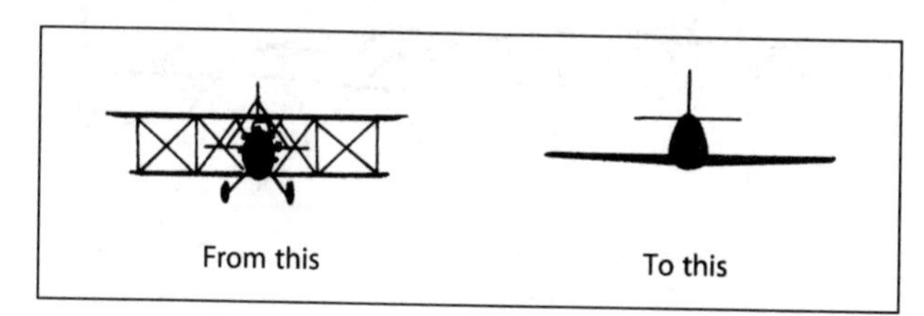

Figure 2-27.

Skin Friction Drag

This is the drag caused by the air passing over the airplane's surfaces. Flush riveting and smooth paint are good ways of decreasing skin friction drag. A clean, polished airplane may be several miles per hour faster than another of the same model that is dirty and unpolished. Waxing and buffing will help an aerodynamically clean airplane because a large proportion of its parasite drag is due to skin friction. Waxing the Wright Brothers' Flyer would have been a waste of elbow grease as far as getting a noticeable added amount of airspeed because the largest percentage of its drag was form drag.

Interference Drag

Interference drag is caused by the interference of the airflow between parts of the airplane such as are found at the intersection of the wings or empennage with the fuselage. This drag is lessened by filleting these areas so that the mixing of the airflow is more gradual (Figure 2-28).

Interference drag *increases* as the angle between the fuselage and wing or tail decreases from 90°. A midwing configuration (round fuselage) would have less interference drag than a wing placed low on the same fuselage (assuming no fairing). Without fairings, drag increases radically for the low wing at higher angles of attack.

A good example of increased interference drag is during gear retraction or extension. The acute angles between the landing gear and wing or fuselage can raise the drag considerably, and this can be a problem during a lift-off in close-to-stall conditions.

Induced Drag

Induced drag is a byproduct of lift. As discussed in the section on lift, there is a difference in the pressure on the top and bottom of the wing, and as nature abhors a vacuum (or at least tries to equalize pressures in a system such as unconfined air), the higher-pressure air moves over the wingtip toward the lower pressure on top. Wingtip vortices result because as a particular mass of air gets over the tip the wing and has moved on out from under it (Figure 2-29).

Because of action of these vortices, the relative wind passing the wing is deflected downward in producing lift. The downward deflection of the air means that the wing is actually operating at a lower angle of attack than would be seen by checking the airplane's flight path, because it's flying in an "average" relative wind partly of its own making (Figure 2-30).

Figure 2-30 shows that the "true" lift of the wing is operating perpendicularly to its own relative wind rather than perpendicularly to the air moving relative to the whole airplane (or the relative wind you, as a pilot, think about). Of course, you know that the angle of attack is the angle between the chord line of the wing and its relative wind.

As the C_L (angle of attack) increases, the strengths of the wingtip vortices get greater with a resulting increase in downwash (and differences in angles of attack). This makes the difference between effective lift and the wing's "true" lift even greater, which would make the retarding force, induced drag, increase (Figure 2-30).

Keep in mind that wingtip vortices can be very powerful for large airplanes (which are producing many pounds of lift) and are particularly vicious when they

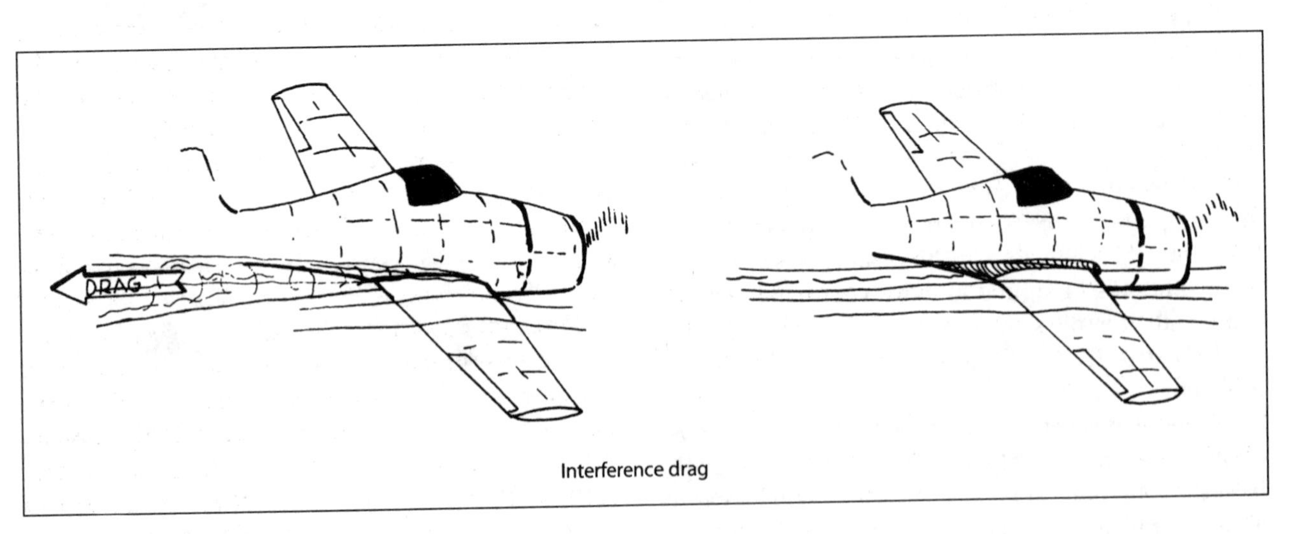

Figure 2-28.

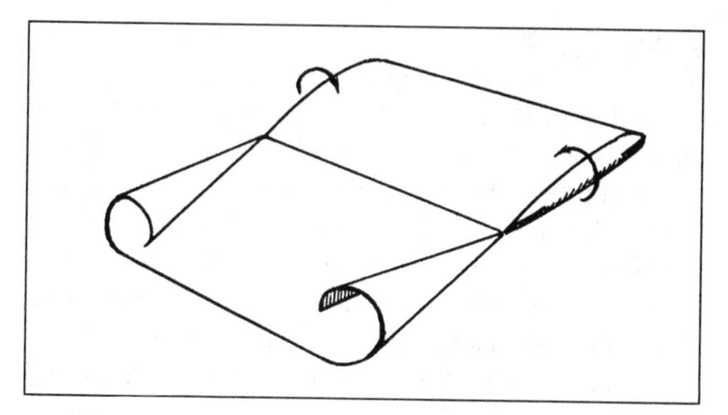

Figure 2-29. Wingtip vortices.

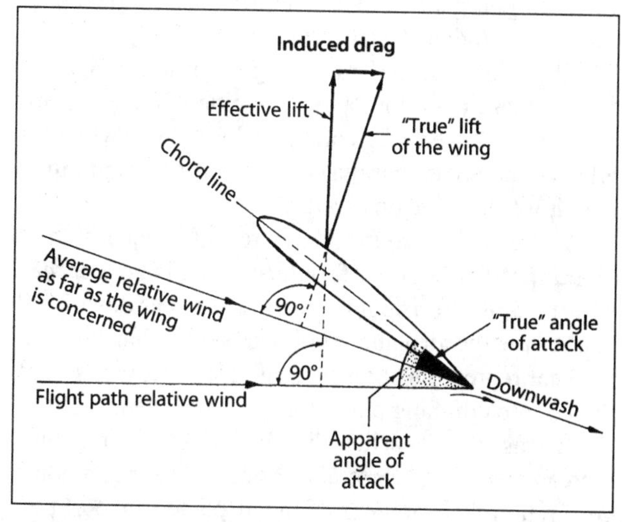

Figure 2-30. Induced drag.

are flying at low speeds (high C_L). Following closely behind an airliner on approach or takeoff can be an extremely exciting activity for a smaller, general aviation airplane.

Figure 2-31 plots parasite and induced drag versus airspeed for a fictitious airplane at a specific weight in the clean condition. As you can see, the total drag at various speeds is made up of the sum of the two types. Induced drag rises sharply as the airplane slows and approaches the stall speed (or more correctly as it approaches the maximum C_L), and at a point just above the stall speed, it may be 80% to 85% of the total drag. It gets lower as the speed increases (as the angle of attack, or C_L, decreases). It will never disappear because as long as any lift is being produced, it's a resulting evil.

Induced drag is inversely proportional to the aspect ratio of the wing; that is, longer thinner wings mean less induced drag if indicated airspeed, airplane weight, and wing area are equal. (Aspect ratio is the wingspan-to-average-chord ratio or, more correctly, the ratio of the span squared, divided by the wing area.) If the wing had an infinite span the wingtip vortices would naturally not exist and induced drag would be zero. The

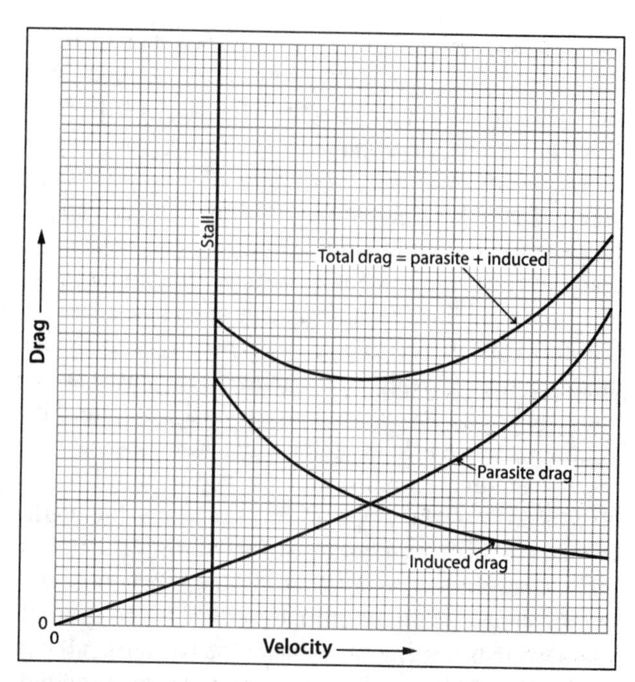

Figure 2-31. Total drag is a combination of parasite and induced drag.

power of the wingtip vortices is tied in directly with "span loading" (the amount of lift produced per foot of wingspan), which is another way of talking about aspect ratio. Aircraft that require good aerodynamic efficiency rather than high speed and that operate the majority of the time at comparatively high coefficients of lift need high-aspect-ratio wings (sailplanes and the U-2). For airplanes such as jet fighters that operate at high speeds, where induced drag is small compared with parasite drag, the aspect ratio must be low, both from an aerodynamic and a structural standpoint.

Ground Effect

When the airplane wing operates close to the ground, the downwash characteristics are altered, with a resulting decrease in induced drag. This happens because the strength of the vortices is decreased and the downwash angle is also decreased for a particular amount of lift being produced. This means that the wing's true lift and effective lift are working closer to each other (the angle between the two forces is less) and the retarding force (induced drag) is less. (Check Figure 2-30 again.)

When the airplane approaches the ground as for a landing, ground effect really enters the picture at about a wingspan distance above the surface. Its effects are then increased radically as the plane nears the ground, until at about touchdown, induced drag *can* possibly drop by about 48%. Figure 2-32 shows the decrease in percent of induced drag in terms of span height for airplanes of general configuration. (Remember the effects vary with aspect ratio.)

Basically, ground effect means that you are getting the same lift for less induced drag. As induced drag can make up 80% to 85% of the total drag at lift-off or touchdown, a 48% decrease in induced drag could mean a *decrease in total drag of around 40%* for a specific angle of attack. This amount of drag decrease could fool a pilot into thinking on takeoff that the airplane is ready to fly and climb out like a tiger, only to discover after getting a few feet above the ground that it's more like an anemic house cat. The power required to fly the airplane rises sharply as the induced drag increases, and a deficit in power would result in a sink rate. The pilot meanwhile is holding the same nose attitude, trying to get some climb out of the suddenly inherited "lead sled." As the airplane starts settling, the angle of attack is increased because of the downward movement; since the angle was at the raw edge to begin with, the airplane stalls and abruptly contacts the ground again (sounds of bending metal in the background).

Ground effect also has a bearing on the longitudinal (pitch) stability of the airplane. An airplane is more stable in ground effect; that is, the nose is "heavier" for any trim setting. In fact, ground effect is a major factor in deciding the forward center of gravity (CG) limits of the airplane. More up-elevator is needed near the ground because the wing downwash angle is decreased. The down force exerted on the stabilizer-elevator is a mixture of free-stream velocity, slipstream (which is weak in the power-off condition), and downwash from the wing. It may take anywhere from 4° to 15° more up-elevator to obtain the max angle of attack at landing as compared with that in free flight at altitude, depending on the make and model of the airplane.

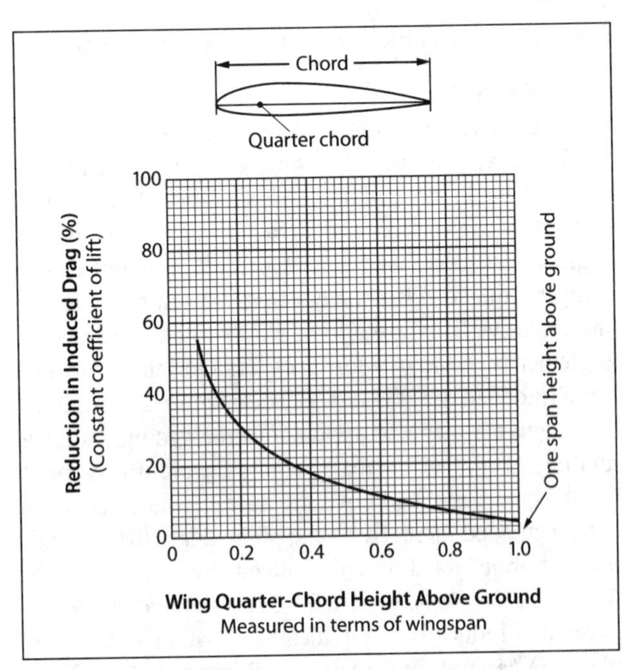

Figure 2-32. Reduction of induced drag with decrease in height above the ground.

As the airplane is more nose heavy in ground effect, an airplane loaded at (or past) the rearward CG limits might appear to be acceptably stable immediately following the takeoff, but as it gained a few feet, it could tend to nose up, catching the pilot sleeping. The influence of ground effect on stability will be covered more thoroughly in Chapter 10.

You can see by looking at Figure 2-32 that the wing quarter chord would have to be about 3½ to 4 feet above the surface (this is about one-tenth the span of most current light, general aviation airplanes) to get a 48% decrease in induced drag.

The pilot's misunderstanding of ground effect has caused more than one landing accident when the airplane has "floated" the length of the runway while the pilot sat there with paralysis of the throttle hand thinking "it would settle on any day now."

You can use ground effect to aid acceleration to climb speed after takeoff. Induced drag is greater than parasite drag at this point, so leave the gear down until you're sure the airplane is going to stay airborne (landing gear represents parasite drag). Don't let yourself be fooled into climbing out before the airplane is ready.

It was noted earlier that interference drag may increase during gear retractions as the gear and doors go through their process. If the airplane's takeoff performance is depending on ground effect, the retraction of the landing gear while moving up and out of ground effect could be the factor that puts the airplane back on the ground—with the gear partially retracted. Chapter 5 will cover this idea again.

Another reason for not getting the gear up too soon is that an engine failure could result in a gear-up landing with plenty of landing area ahead. Under normal conditions leave the gear down until you can no longer land on the runway ahead.

Ground effect has also enabled pilots to get out of ticklish situations on takeoff and landing and has been used by pilots of multiengine airplanes on overwater flights when an engine (or engines) failed. Taking advantage of this phenomenon allowed them to keep flying under conditions that would have otherwise resulted in a ditching. Glassy water, which is best for ground effect, can be hazardous as far as judging heights are concerned. This writer used it during a power problem after a deck run (takeoff) on a carrier in an F4U-5N Corsair. You can see in Figure 2-32 that a few feet can make a lot of difference as far as ground effect is concerned.

The wing's lifting function is more efficient in ground effect (it's as if the wing has a higher aspect ratio) and needs a *lower angle of attack* to get the required lift. The C_L versus angle of attack curve (straight line portion) is steeper. Looking back at Figure 2-8, you can see that at an angle of attack of 10°, a C_L of about 1.10 is obtained; in ground effect the slope of the line might be steeper so that at 10° the C_L could be 1.3 or so. Of course, as an airplane climbs *out* of the ground effect it loses this advantage; the C_L versus angle of attack curve reverts to the situation shown in Figure 2-8, and a *higher* angle of attack is needed to get the required lift. This could cause problems in increased drag and result in a stall if the pilot pulls the nose up sharply to keep from settling back in.

Lift-to-Drag Ratio

One measure of an airplane's aerodynamic efficiency is its maximum lift-to-drag ratio. The usual engineering procedure is to use the term C_L/C_D since the other factors of lift and drag (density, wing area, and velocity) are equally affected. (The C_D is the coefficient of *total* drag.) This means that at a certain angle of attack the airplane is giving more for your money. The angle of attack and ratio of this special point varies with airplanes as well as with a particular airplane's configuration (clean or dirty). Pilots hear the term C_L/C_D maximum and automatically assume that this point is found at C_{Lmax}, or close to the stall. This is not true because, while the C_L is large at large angles of attack, the total C_D is *much* larger in proportion because of induced drag. Following are figures showing how the lift-to-drag (or C_L/C_D) ratio varies for a sample airplane in the clean condition.

C_L	C_D	C_L/C_D Ratio
0.935	0.080	11.7 (low speed)
0.898	0.075	12.0
0.860	0.070	12.1
0.820	0.065	12.6
0.772	0.060	12.9
0.725	0.055	13.2
0.671	0.050	13.4
0.620	0.045	13.7
0.562	0.040	14.1
0.500	***0.035***	***14.3***
0.418	0.030	13.9
0.332	0.025	13.3
0.200	0.020	10.0 (high speed)

The figures in bold italics show the values for C_L/C_D maximum.

The maximum lift-to-drag ratio is the condition at which maximum range and maximum glide distance will be found for propeller (recip) airplanes (this will be covered in more detail later).

Thrust

Thrust, the force exerted by a propeller, jet, or rocket, is used to overcome aerodynamic drag and other forces acting to retard the airplane's motion in the air and on the ground. It can be explained by one of Newton's laws of motion: For every action there is an equal and opposite reaction.

The propeller is a rotating airfoil that accelerates a comparatively large mass of air rearward, resulting in an equal and opposite reaction—the airplane moves forward. The thrust exerted is proportional to the mass and the velocity of the accelerated air.

The jet engine accelerates a mass of air and fuel at a faster velocity than does the propeller. The rocket takes a mass (of its fuel and oxidizer) and accelerates it to a very high speed.

Thrust Available and Drag

The greatest thrust for the *propeller-driven* airplane is found in the static condition; that is, when you are sitting on the end of the runway with the engine running at full power, the propeller is producing the greatest thrust. As the plane moves, the thrust force available decreases with speed increase.

For straight and level flight, the thrust available (pounds) and drag (pounds) are considered equal if a constant airspeed is maintained. For speeds in the area of cruise where the airplane's thrust line is acting along the flight path (the nose is not "cocked up" as is the case for slower speeds), this assumption is a valid one (Figure 2-33). The variations of the Four Forces in different maneuvers will be shown in Chapter 3, and this particular point will be covered.

Propeller

The propeller, a rotating airfoil, is subject to stalls, induced drag, and other troubles that affect airfoils. As you have noticed, the blade angle of the propeller changes from hub to tip with the greatest angle of incidence (highest pitch) at the hub and the smallest at the tip (Figure 2-34).

This twist is necessary because of the difference in the actual speed through the air of the various portions of the blade. If the blade had the same geometric pitch all along its length (say 20°), at cruise the inner portion near the hub would have a negative angle of attack and the extreme outer portion would be stalled.

This is hardly conducive to get up and go—so the twist is necessary.

Fixed-pitch propellers come in two main categories, climbing and cruising. Regardless of which prop is on the plane, you always wish you had the other one. The climbing prop with its lower pitch results in higher RPM and more horsepower developed, which gives efficient takeoff and climb performance—but poor cruise characteristics. The cruise propeller with its higher pitch results in lower RPM and less horsepower developed, which is efficient for cruise but gives comparatively poor performance in takeoff and climb. Two terms are used in describing the angles of incidence and propeller effectiveness: (1) *geometric pitch*, or the built-in angle of incidence, the path a chosen portion of the blade would take in a nearly solid medium such as gelatin and (2) *effective pitch*, or the actual path the propeller is taking in air at any particular time. Looking at geometric pitch you might see a number on the fixed-pitch prop of an airplane such as M58 D74 or D7458. The "74" tells you the diameter of the propeller (74 inches), and the "58" tells the advance of a particular station of the blade, per revolution (58 inches). A "D7452" propeller would be more of a "climb" prop (the selected station only advances 52 inches per revolution, hence a lower pitch); the engine would be revving up more, and it would be more efficient at lower airspeeds. Different prop manufacturers may have different codes, but you should ask some of the local mechanics about the code for a particular prop if you aren't sure.

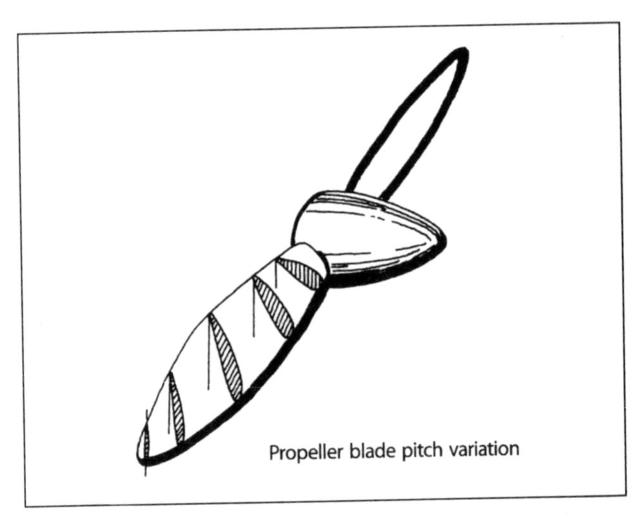

Figure 2-34.

The difference between the geometric pitch and the effective pitch is the angle of attack (Figure 2-35). The climbing propeller has a lower *average* geometric pitch than the cruising prop and revs up more, developing more horsepower (Figure 2-36).

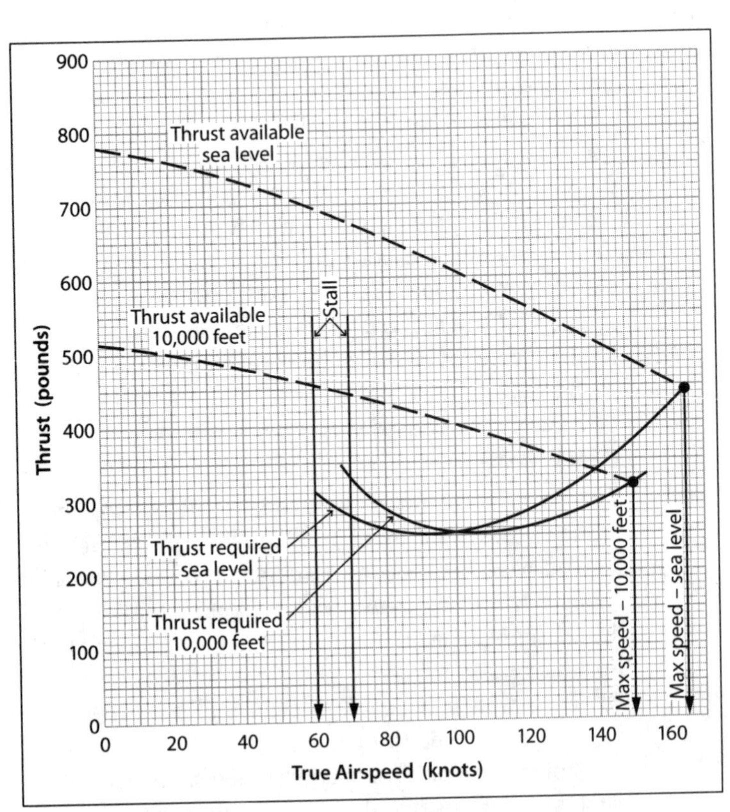

Figure 2-33. Thrust required and maximum thrust available versus true airspeed at sea level and 10,000 feet for a fictitious high-performance four-place airplane (gross weight).

Take an airplane sitting at the end of a runway with a cruise-type propeller revolving at 2,400 RPM. Figure 2-37 shows that because the plane is not moving, the geometric pitch and angle of attack are the same, and a large portion of the blade is stalled. A vector diagram would show the difference in the efficiency of a propeller at 0 mph and 100 mph (at 2,400 RPM).

The velocity of a *particular station* of the blade can be readily found. Pick a station at a point slightly more than 1½ feet from the hub center so that the point chosen travels 10 feet each revolution. At 2,400 RPM the velocity at this point is 400 fps. Assuming a geometric pitch of 30° at this point, the prop stalls at an angle of attack of 20°, so this portion of the blade is stalled.

Therefore the only part of the blade developing thrust under this condition would be the portion having a geometric pitch of less than 20°—or the outboard portion of the blades. The thrust pattern would look like that shown in Figure 2-38.

For the same airplane moving at 89 K, or 150 fps (again chosen for convenience), the result can be seen by vectors (Figure 2-39).

You will notice that the blade is operating at a more efficient angle of attack. As the propeller is an airfoil, it is most efficient at the angle of attack giving the greatest lift-to-drag ratio. A climb prop would be more efficient at low airspeeds because a greater portion of the blade is operating in this range. At high airspeeds it is operating at a lower angle of attack and is not producing efficient thrust.

At a higher pitch the drag of the blades is higher and the engine is unable to get as high an RPM and develop as much horsepower as would be obtained with a lower-pitch propeller. *The fixed-pitch propeller is efficient only at one particular speed range.*

The solution to this is the variable-pitch propeller, which can be set to suit the pilot:

1. For takeoff and climb—LOW PITCH, which results in HIGH RPM and high power. (The British call this "fine pitch.")
2. For cruise—HIGH PITCH, which results in LOW RPM and efficient cruise. (The British call this "coarse pitch.")

With a variable-pitch prop, the RPM still varies with airspeed, as with the fixed-pitch prop. In other words, if you set a cruise RPM of 2,400, a climb or dive will cause it to vary. The constant-speed prop, which is an "automatic" variable-pitch propeller, will maintain a constant RPM after being set. Once the desired setting is made, changes in airspeed do not affect it.

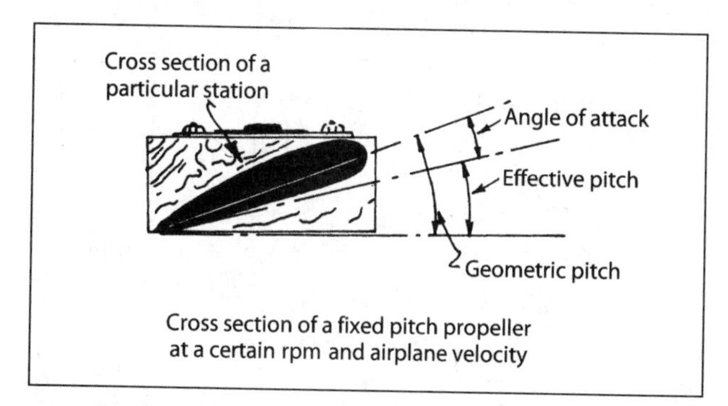

Figure 2-35.

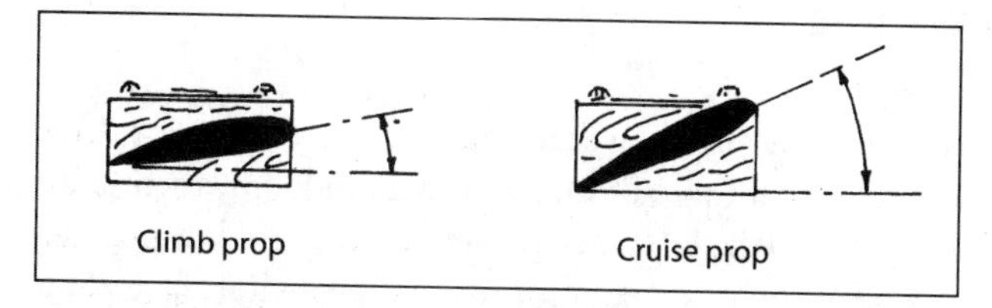

Figure 2-36. Climbing and cruising propellers—a comparison of geometric pitch at the same station (same distance from the hub).

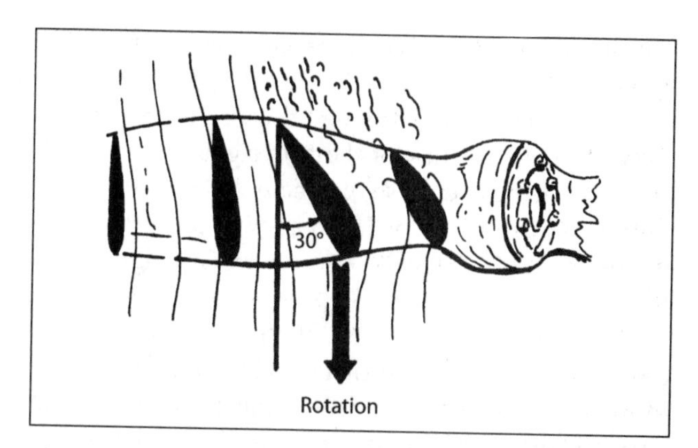

Figure 2-37. Airplane stationary—portion of the blade stalled.

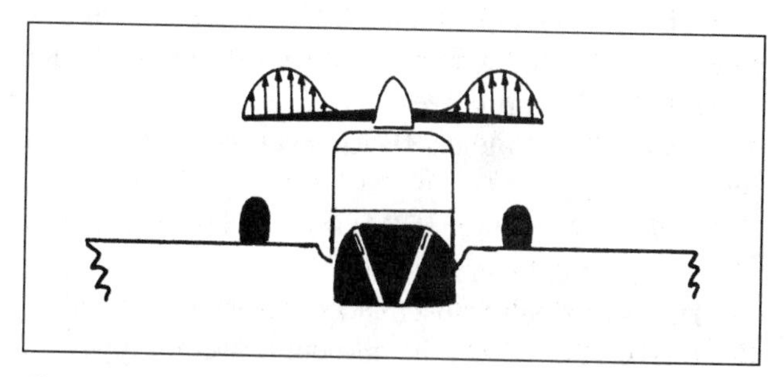

Figure 2-38. Thrust pattern of the propeller of a stationary airplane.

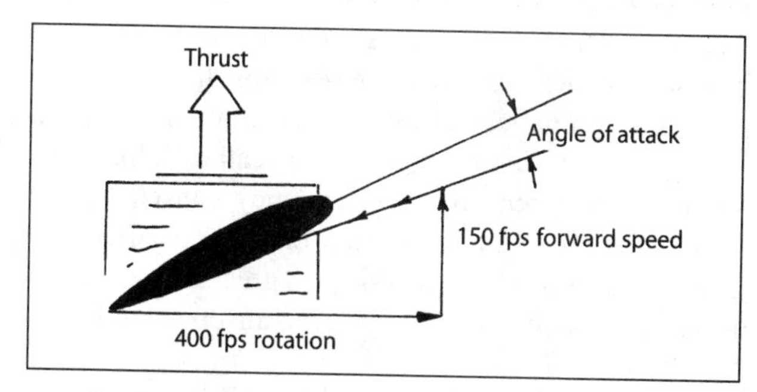

Figure 2-39. Angle of attack of the same portion of the blade at a forward speed of 150 fps (89 K).

The Constant Speed Propeller (Oil-Counterweight Type)

The constant-speed propeller setting is the result of a balance between oil pressure (using engine oil) and the centrifugal force exerted by the propeller counterweights. This balance is maintained by the governor, which is driven by the crankshaft through a series of gears. The governor has two main parts, the flyweight assembly and the oil pump. The governor is set by the prop control(s) in the cockpit. Assume you have set the RPM at 2,400 for cruise. The oil pressure and counterweight forces are equal because the flyweights in the governor are turning at a constant speed and the oil valve to the prop pistons is closed, with oil pressure locked in the propeller hub. Now assume that you pull the nose up. The airspeed drops, causing the prop RPM and engine RPM to drop. The centrifugal force on the governor flyweights decreases because of the drop in RPM. The contraction of the flyweight causes a two-way valve to be opened so that increased pressure to the pistons moves the propeller to a lower pitch, allowing it to maintain 2,400 RPM. (Look ahead to Figure 12-4 for an example.)

If the plane were dived, the prop would tend to overspeed; the resulting increase in centrifugal force of the governor flyweight would cause the oil valve to open so that the oil pressure in the propeller hub dome would decrease. Centrifugal force on the propeller counterweights would then cause the prop to be pulled into a higher pitch; the increased blade angle of attack would result in more drag and the propeller would not overspeed. To summarize:

Lower pitch (higher RPM) is caused by added oil pressure.

Higher pitch (lower RPM) is caused by centrifugal force on prop counterweights.

The operation of most noncounterweight propellers is the reverse of that of the oil-counterweight types. In creating thrust, the blade creates a moment that tends to decrease its pitch (the same thing happens to a wing, as will be covered in Chapter 3). A spring may be added to help this natural force. This is opposed by governor oil pressure, which tends to increase its pitch.

Some propellers use compressed air or nitrogen in the dome to increase pitch and feather. This force opposes the pitch-lowering tendency caused by the blade moment and the governor oil pressure. Because counterweights are not necessary, a great deal of weight is saved. In effect, the compressed air does the job of the counterweights.

To get an idea of how a variable-pitch or constant-speed propeller can increase the efficiency of a propeller, let's set up a hypothetical situation. To simplify matters, assume that a certain engine can only be run at a certain RPM for cruise—no other can be used; 2,400 is a good round figure, so that's the number for this problem. (The propeller is direct-drive and turns at this same RPM.) Figure 2-40 shows the efficiencies of a particular propeller at different pitch settings of the propeller blade (at a station three-quarters, or 75%, of the radius from the hub) at various airspeeds.

The constant-speed propeller will change its angle to maintain a constant RPM so as the airspeed increases, the pitch setting will also increase automatically. The dashed line (envelope) shows that as the airspeed increases, the efficiency remains fairly constant over the entire range. The propeller pitch changes as needed to keep a constant angle of attack.

Notice that the solid-line curves for different pitch settings have a comparatively narrow range of airspeed for peak efficiency. For this airplane a pitch (at the station at 75% of the radius of the prop) of 15° is 80% (or higher) efficient only between the speeds of 85 and 104 K, or has its peak efficiency at about 95 K. At a pitch setting of 20° the range of 80% or higher efficiencies is from about 104 to 140 K, with the peak at about 128 K, etc. Shown are the ranges of efficiencies for fixed-pitch versions of that propeller at 15°, 20°, and 25° pitch respectively. Notice in Figure 2-40 that the efficiencies for these pitches drop rapidly at the upper ends of their speed ranges. The constant-speed prop has practically an infinite number of pitch settings available within the airplane's operating speed ranges; this is shown by the envelope of peak efficiencies.

Use of the variable-pitch and constant-speed propeller also will be covered in later chapters.

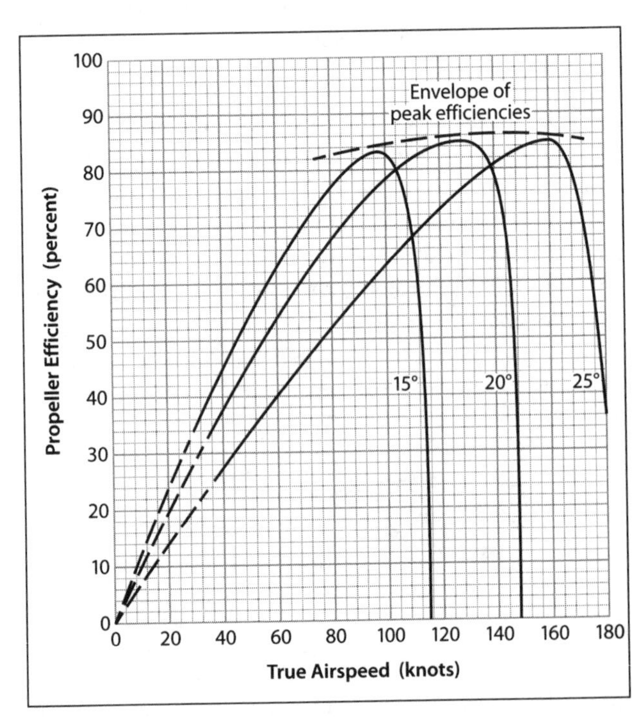

Figure 2-40. Efficiency of a particular propeller at various blade settings and airspeeds (contant 2,400 rpm).

Torque

You have long been familiar with torque, the pilot's term for that force or moment that tends to yaw or turn the plane to the left when power is applied at low speeds. It is also the price paid for using a propeller. Knowing that the propeller is a rotating airfoil, you realize that it exerts some drag as well as lift. This drag creates a moment that tends to rotate the airplane around its longitudinal (fuselage) axis opposite to prop rotation.

Although torque is normally thought of as one force, it is, in fact, several combined forces.

1. *Slipstream effects*—As the propeller turns clockwise, a rotating flow of air is moved rearward, striking the left side of the fin and rudder, which results in a left yawing moment. The fin may be offset to counteract this reaction, with the fin setting built in for maximum effectiveness at the rated cruising speed of the airplane, because the plane will be flying at this speed most of the time (Figures 2-41 and 2-42).

If it were not for the offset fin, right rudder would have to be held at all speeds. As it is, the balance of forces results in no yawing force at all, and the plane flies straight at cruise with no right rudder being held (Figure 2-41).

Sometimes the fin may not be offset correctly, due to manufacturing tolerances, and a slight left yaw is present at cruise, making it necessary to use right rudder to keep the airplane straight. To take care of this, a small metal tab is attached to the trailing edge of the rudder and bent to the left. The pressure of the relative air against the tab forces the rudder to the right (Figure 2-42).

On lighter planes this adjustment can be done only on the ground, and it may require several flights before a satisfactory setting is found. For heavier planes a controllable rudder tab is used, allowing the pilot to correct for torque at all speed ranges. If the tab has been bent correctly (or has been set in the cockpit) for cruise, the torque and impact forces are balanced.

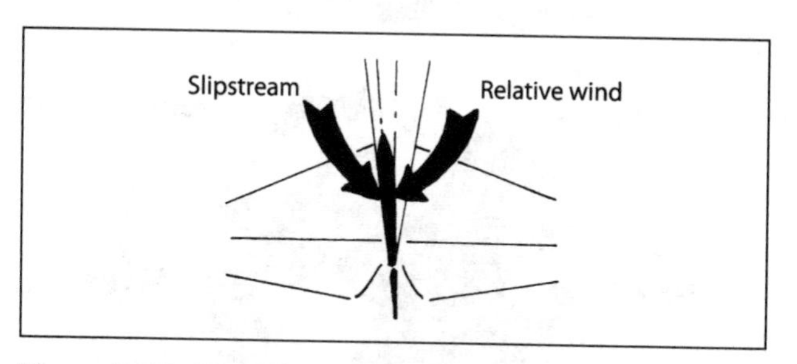

Figure 2-41. The offset fin is designed so that the angle of attack of the fin is zero (the forces balance) at cruise.

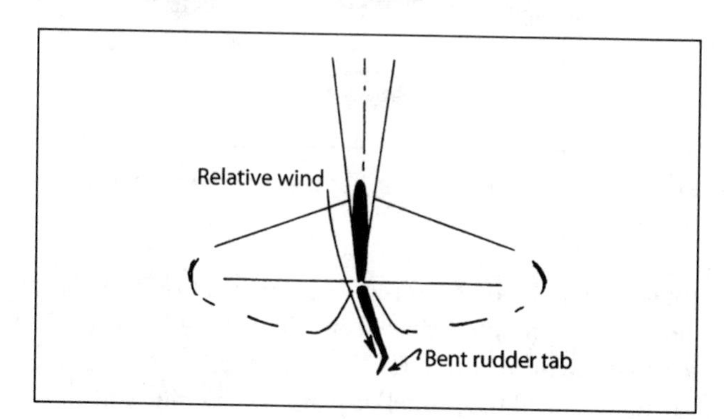

Figure 2-42. The rudder trim tab.

Some manufacturers use an offset thrust line, or "cant" the engine, to counteract torque at cruise; the airplane's reactions are the same as for the offset fin.

In a climb, right rudder must be held to keep the plane straight. In a dive, left rudder is necessary to keep it straight. In larger planes the rudder tab may be adjusted during flight for these variations from cruise.

In a glide there is no yawing effect. Although the engine is at idle and torque is less, the impact pressure on the fin is also less. *The slipstream effect is the most important torque force working on the single-engine airplane.*

2. *Equal and opposite reactions*—Newton's Law of equal and opposite reactions is only a minor factor in torque effects. The airplane tends to rotate in a direction opposite that of the propeller's rotation. In some cases the left wing or wingtip area may have *wash-in* to compensate for this. Wash-in means that the angle of incidence is increased and the wing is bent up into the airstream for more lift. *Washout* can be thought of as the wing turning down out of the relative wind for less lift, as noted earlier in the chapter. Wash-in may also contribute very slightly to a left-turning effect.

3. *Asymmetric loading*, or propeller disk asymmetric loading (also called P-factor)—This condition, caused by the air not striking the prop disk at exactly a 90° angle, is usually encountered in a constant positive angle of attack such as in a climb or in slow flight. The down-moving propeller blade, which is on the right side as seen from the cockpit, has a higher angle of attack and consequently a greater thrust, which results in a left-turning effect. This can be visualized by checking Figure 2-43.

To find the exact difference in the thrust of the two sides of the propeller disk, a vector diagram must be drawn that includes the propeller blade angles, rotational velocity, and the airplane's forward speed and angle of attack. If the airplane is yawed, the P-factor effect is encountered. A left yaw would mean a slight nose-down tendency and a right yaw a slight nose-up tendency (you can reason this out). As climbs and slow flights are more usual maneuvers than are yaws, these will be the most likely spots to encounter P-factor effects.

P-factor has been given a great deal of credit for contributing to left-turning tendencies in situations where it has little, if any, effect on the airplane's yawing tendencies. For instance, the attitude of the tricycle gear on the takeoff roll pretty well assures that the prop disk is perpendicular to the line of "flight"—yet the airplane still turns radically to the left. Let's see, there's

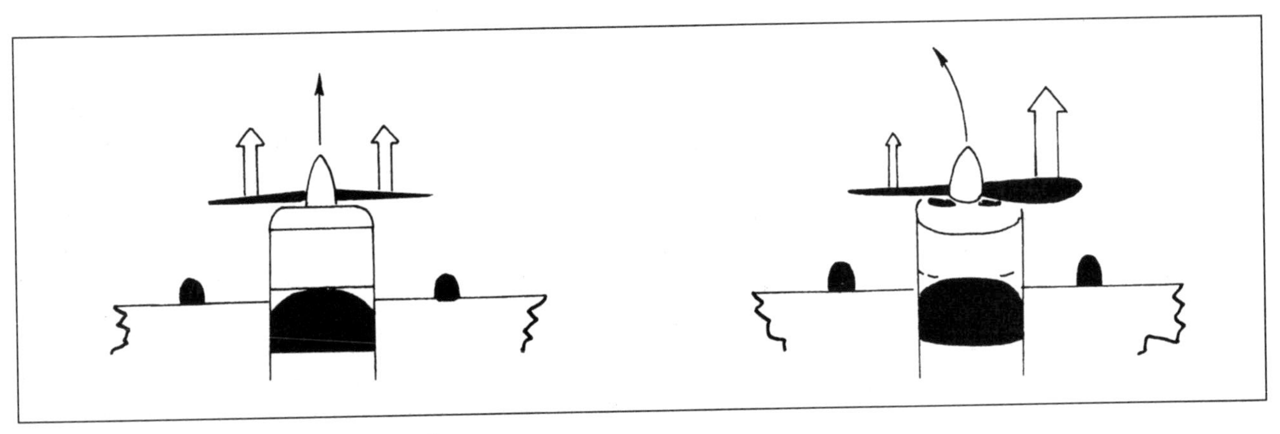

Figure 2-43. Asymmetric disk loading effects.

no problem with torque (sure, the left wheel may be pressing a few pounds harder on the runway because of "equal and opposite reaction," but the turning effect is negligible). There is little or no difference in the angle at which the prop encounters the relative wind, so the rotating slipstream is the culprit here.

Prop manufacturers are advised to take the P-factor effect into account when running a vibration evaluation of their propellers (FAA AC 20-66).

Some older twins used to have engines toed-in or -out and this gave a "permanent" P-factor effect. You can get an idea of P-factor roughness in an airplane parked in a strong crosswind with the engine idling.

4. *Precession*—You encounter precession when, in a tailwheel-type airplane, you try to force the tail up quickly on a takeoff run. The airplane wants to get away from you as it suddenly yaws to the left (U.S. engines). Precession affects the airplane only *during* attitude changes.

Precession is a gyroscopic property (the gyro will be covered more thoroughly in Chapter 4). If a force is exerted against the side of the gyro, it reacts as if the force had actually been exerted in the same direction at a point 90° around the wheel (Figure 2-44).

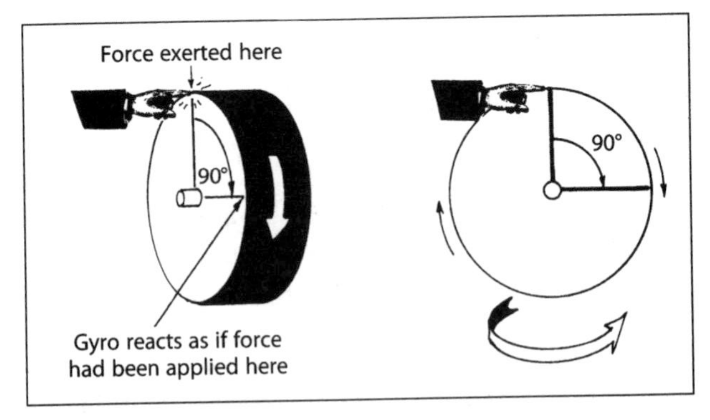

Figure 2-44. Precession.

The propeller disk makes a good gyro wheel, as it has mass and a good rotational velocity. Another property of a gyro is "rigidity in space." This property is used in ships' gyros and aircraft attitude indicators and heading indicators. The rotating gyro wheel tends to stay in the same plane of rotation in space and resists any change in that plane (Figure 2-45). If a force is insistent enough in trying to change this plane of rotation, precession results.

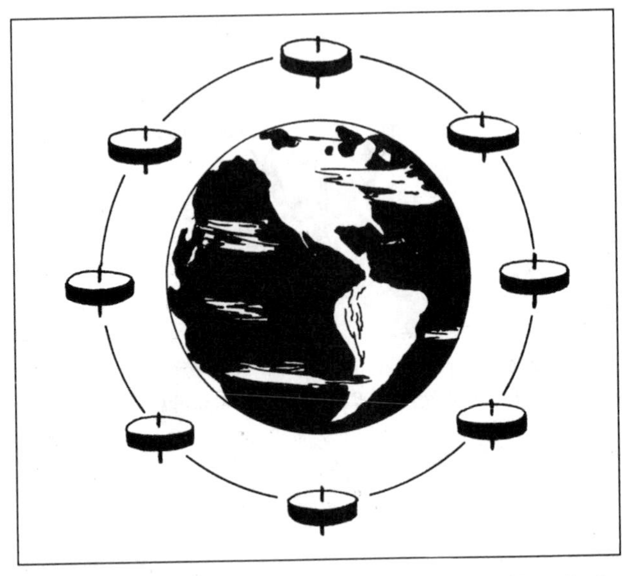

Figure 2-45. The gyro wheel has the property of "rigidity in space."

When you're rolling down the runway in the three-point position (in a tailwheel-type plane), the propeller is in a certain rotational plane. You are using full power and are fighting the other torque effects (rotating slipstream, asymmetric loading, etc.). When you shove the wheel or stick forward and the tail rises, the plane reacts as if the force were exerted on the right side of the propeller disk from the rear. The result is a brisk swing to the left. You can further figure out the reactions of the propeller plane to yawing, pull-ups, or push-overs. You're most likely, however, to notice precession effects when getting the tail up for takeoff because the rudder is comparatively ineffective at this low speed and the sudden yaw is harder to control.

Summary of Torque

These forces or combinations of them make up what pilots call "torque," the force that tends to yaw the plane to the left at low speeds and high power settings. This discussion is presented so that you may understand your airplane better; the objective is to compensate for torque and to fly the airplane in the proper manner. There are a lot of good pilots flying around who wouldn't know what "asymmetric disk loading" was if they were hit in the face with it. The nose yaws to the left and they correct for it—and so should you.

The Power Curve

Force, Work, and Power

In order to understand power and horsepower it is necessary to discuss *force* and *work*.

A *force* may be considered a pressure, tension, or weight. Thrust, lift, weight, and drag are forces; our present system uses the term *pounds* to express the value or strength of a force.

You can exert a *force* against a heavy object and nothing moves; that still doesn't alter the fact that force has been exerted. If the object doesn't move, no *work* has been done as far as the engineering term is concerned (tell this to your aching back). So *work*, from an engineering standpoint, is a measure of a *force* times *distance* (in the direction in which the force is being exerted). If a constant force of 100 pounds is exerted to move an object 10 feet, the deed has accomplished 1,000 ft-lb of *work*.

For instance, your Zephyr Six airplane weighs 2,200 pounds and you must push (or pull) it by hand 100 feet to the gas pit. It does not require 220,000 ft-lb of work to accomplish this as you could see by attaching a scale to the tow bar and checking the force required to move the airplane at a steady rate; for our purposes, we'll say that it requires a constant force of 55 pounds to keep the airplane rolling across the ramp. This job would require 5,500 ft-lb of work on your part (55 pounds times 100 feet).

If you lifted the airplane to a *height* of 100 feet at a constant rate, the work done would be 2,200 pounds × 100 feet or 220,000 ft-lb. The force you would need to exert would be the weight of the airplane, once you got it moving at a steady rate upward. And, obviously you would do less work pulling the airplane 100 feet than lifting it the same distance because less force is required to pull it than to lift it.

The amount of work done has nothing to do with time; you can take a second or all week to do the 5,500 ft-lb of work in pulling the airplane. This brings up another term—*power. Power* is defined as a time rate of work. If you pulled the airplane the 100 feet over to the gas pit in 1 second, you would have been exerting a power of 5,500 ft-lb per second. (And if you are strong enough to accomplish such a feat you don't need an airplane; just flap your arms when you want to fly.) Suppose that it takes 10 seconds to do the job. The power used would be work/time = 5,500 ft-lb/10 seconds = 550 ft-lb per second. You would have to exert 1 HP for 10 seconds to do the job. The most common measurement for power is the term *horsepower*, which happens to be a power of 550 ft-lb per second.

Thrust horsepower (THP) is the horsepower developed by a force (thrust) exerted to move an object (the airplane) at a certain rate. Remembering that a *force* times the distance it moves an object is *work*, and when divided by time, *power* is found, the equation is THP = TV/550, where T = propeller thrust (pounds) and V = the airplane's velocity (fps). As velocity can be considered to be distance divided by time, TV (or T × V) is *power* in foot-pounds per second. The power (TV) is divided by 550 to obtain the HP being developed. If you wanted to think in terms of *miles per hour* for V, the equation would be THP = TV/375 (375 is the constant number used for miles per hour). For V in knots, THP = TV/325.

As far as the airplane is concerned, there are several types of horsepower of interest.

Indicated horsepower is the actual power developed in the cylinders and might be considered to be a calculated horsepower based on pressure, cubic-inch displacement, and RPM.

Brake horsepower (BHP) is so named because in earlier times it was measured for smaller engines by using a braking system or absorption dynamometer such as the "prony brake." The horsepower thus exerted by the crankshaft was known as *brake horsepower* or *shaft horsepower*. The fact that there is internal friction existing in all engines means that all the horsepower in the cylinders doesn't get to the crankshaft, so a loss of horsepower from indicated horsepower, called *friction horsepower loss*, results. The reciprocating engine is always rated in BHP. If your airplane has an unturbocharged (or normally aspirating) engine, for example, the specification will note that the engine is rated as a certain horsepower at full throttle at a certain RPM at sea level (meaning standard sea level conditions of air density). For turbocharged engines, the specification cites a specific manifold pressure and RPM at sea level and also at the critical altitude (above which even full throttle can't hold the required manifold pressure to get the rated horsepower). This idea will be covered in more detail in later chapters.

The term 75% power means *75% of the normal rated horsepower; or max continuous power available at sea level on a standard day* (59°F and a pressure of 29.92 inches of mercury). For instance, a particular engine may have a takeoff power rating of 340 HP and a *normal rating* of 320 HP. The takeoff rating label means that the engine can be run at this power only for a *limited time*, as given in the engine specifications. If you use the engine power chart and set up manifold pressure and RPM to get 75% power for that engine, your horsepower will be 75% of 320 (the normal rated power), or 240 HP.

For other engines, the takeoff rating and normal rating are the same. That is, they develop a certain maximum amount of horsepower and can be run continuously at this power if necessary. In effect, there is no takeoff rating, or no special, higher-than-normal, limited-time power setting.

BHP also increases slightly with intake ram effect but is normally considered to remain constant, hence its use as a standard for setting power by the power chart.

Thrust horsepower, as discussed earlier, is considered to be a percentage of BHP if propeller efficiency is taken into account: THP = η BHP. The term η (eta) is the propeller efficiency that runs at best up to 0.85 (85%) for most engine-propeller combinations and varies with airspeed. (This was covered back in the section on the propeller.)

As an example of the various steps of getting from the ignition of the fuel-air mixture to the THP being developed, take a look at the following:

Indicated HP (work done in cylinders)	325 HP
Drive loss (friction and accessories)	–25 HP
Resulting *Shaft* or *Brake HP*	300 HP
Loss from propeller (80% efficient at particular speed)	–60 HP
Horsepower available as *THP*	240 HP

Figure 2-46 shows the maximum HP available for the two types of power at various speeds. The point at which the maximum HP available equals the HP required establishes the maximum level flight speed of the airplane, whether in terms of HP or THP (points 1 and 2):

Notice how the available THP varies with airspeed. As THP = TV (knots)/325, you can see that although at zero velocity the thrust might be high, no HP is being developed because V = 0, and a number times zero is still zero. As the airplane picks up speed, THP starts being developed, increasing fairly rapidly at first. This is because thrust is high at the lower speeds (check back to Figure 2-33). THP increases at a lower rate as the speed picks up (and thrust decreases.)

You will also note that more BHP than THP is required by the airplane at any speed; this is because, as was mentioned, the propeller is not 100% efficient and there's some loss. In other words, the engine has to produce more than enough effort to get the required amount of HP actually working to fly the airplane.

For the same airplane of Figure 2-46 the amount of BHP necessary to get the THP required rises sharply at lower speeds because the propeller efficiency drops rapidly in that area. The THP required does not rise as sharply in this area as either the drag or BHP-required curves because, while the drag is rising rapidly, the required THP is also a function of velocity—THP = TV/325 or DV/325 and the decrease in speed *tends* to offset the effects of the increase in drag (the velocity used here is in knots).

To give an idea of the comparison between BHP and THP, suppose that instead of the prop an iron bar of equal weight and drag is attached on the hub. The engine would still be putting out a certain amount of BHP as measured by a dynamometer, but the iron bar would be producing no thrust and therefore no THP

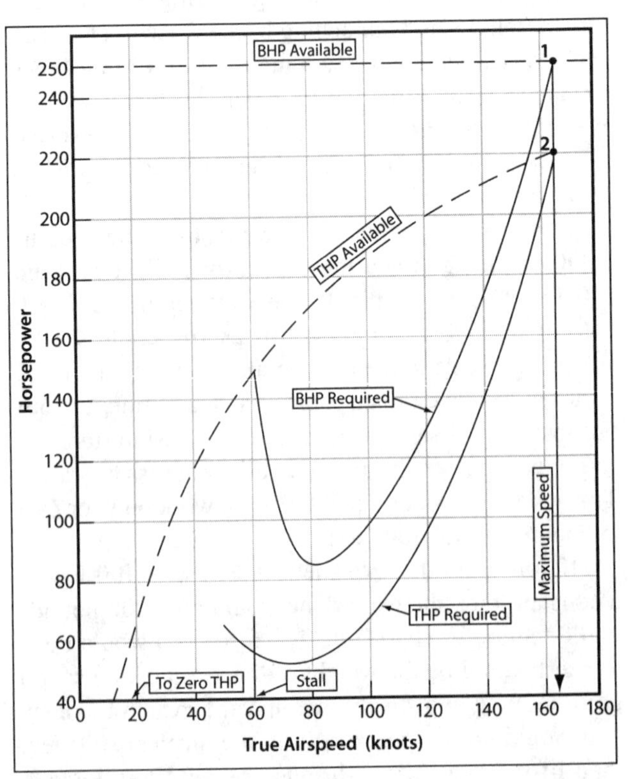

Figure 2-46. Brake and thrust horsepower available and required versus true airspeed for a four-place airplane with the engine rated 250 BHP at sea level (gross weight). (In order to save space the HP was started at 40 rather than 0.)

could ever be developed by the engine in that configuration—the efficiency (η) would be zero.

When thinking in terms of setting power, a curve for BHP is more effective; for performance items such as climbs or glides, THP gives a clearer picture.

Figure 2-47 shows some pertinent points on a power-available and power-required versus velocity curve as expressed in BHP for a fictitious airplane at the maximum certificated weight of 3,000 pounds at sea level in the clean condition.

The shaded area shows the areas of normal cruise power settings and airspeeds for this particular airplane. As you know, power settings most commonly used are from 60% to 75% of the normal rated power. The majority of reciprocating engine airplanes avoid cruise (or continuous) power settings above 75% because of increased fuel consumption and engine wear.

By now you've also noticed that the power-required curve (for both THP and BHP) has a characteristic U shape similar to the drag curve. This is because the power required to fly the airplane at a constant altitude varies with the drag existing at different airspeeds—the values, of course, are different because one is expressed in pounds and the other in horsepower. If you had a drag versus airspeed curve for your airplane, you could draw your own THP-required curve by selecting particular airspeeds and using the drags in the equation for THP.

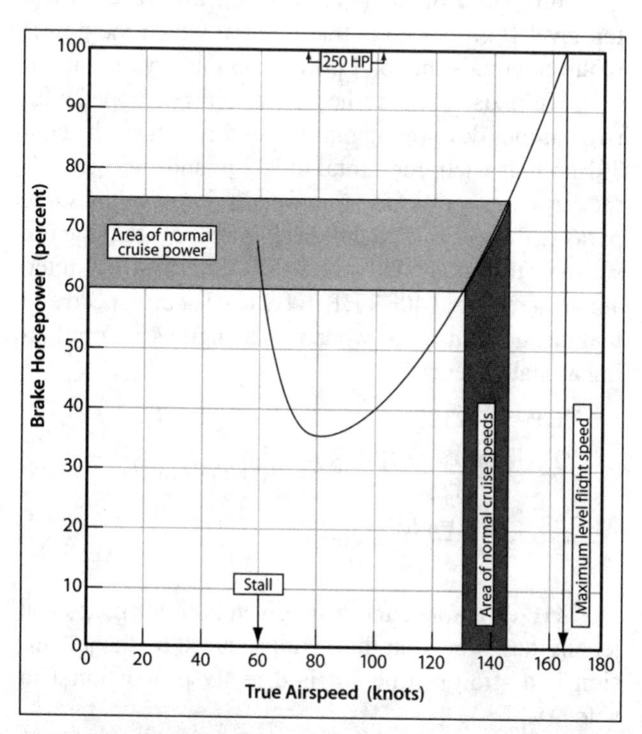

Figure 2-47. Brake horsepower required and available versus airspeed for a particular airplane at sea level (gear and flaps retracted). Assume TAS = CAS.

Because of the varying power needed to maintain a constant altitude, the airplane can fly at two speeds for the lower power settings (Figure 2-47). It is unlikely that in actuality it could fly at a slow enough speed to require close to 100% power (250 BHP for this airplane) to maintain a constant altitude because the stall characteristics of the airplane wouldn't allow it—the break would occur at an airspeed higher than that. If the stall could be delayed appreciably through use of, say, boundary layer control, it might well work out that it could fly at a slow speed where 100% power is required to maintain a constant altitude.

The power required varies with weight, altitude, and airplane configuration. Figure 2-48 shows the effects of various weights on the power required for the airplane in Figure 2-47. The solid line represents the curve of Figure 2-47.

Added or subtracted weight affects the existing induced drag and power required at various airspeeds. (The engineers speak of this as induced power required.) You can also see that the stall speed is lower with less weight and vice versa. *Notice that a variation in weight has comparatively little effect on the max speed.* The effects of weight are felt mostly where induced drag is predominant.

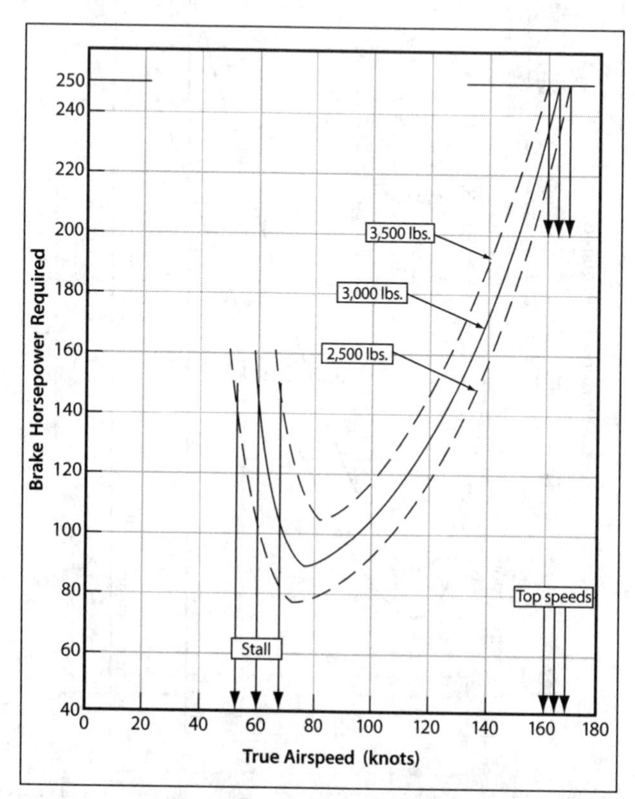

Figure 2-48. The effects of weight on the airplane in Figure 2-47 (TAS = CAS). The stall speed effects are slightly exaggerated here for clarity. For calculating the exact stall speeds for weight change use Figure 1-12.

Figure 2-49 shows the effects of parasite drag on the power-required curve. The new curve represents the power required (at the original weight of 3,000 pounds) with the gear extended. In this case, the maximum speed would be greatly affected because parasite drag (or parasite power required) is the largest factor in that area. The cruise speed would be affected because it is also in an area of high parasite drag. In this example, *the stall speed would not vary and comparatively small effects would be felt at the lower flight speeds where parasite drag is low.*

The total power required equals induced power required *plus* parasite power required.

Figure 2-50 shows THP required and available versus airspeed for a light twin at gross weight at sea level. This curve is important in that the rate of climb of the airplane depends on the excess THP available. The maximum rate of climb, then, is found at the airspeed where the maximum excess THP is available because that is the HP working to raise the airplane. Notice that as you slow down past the point of minimum power required (point 1), the THP required starts increasing

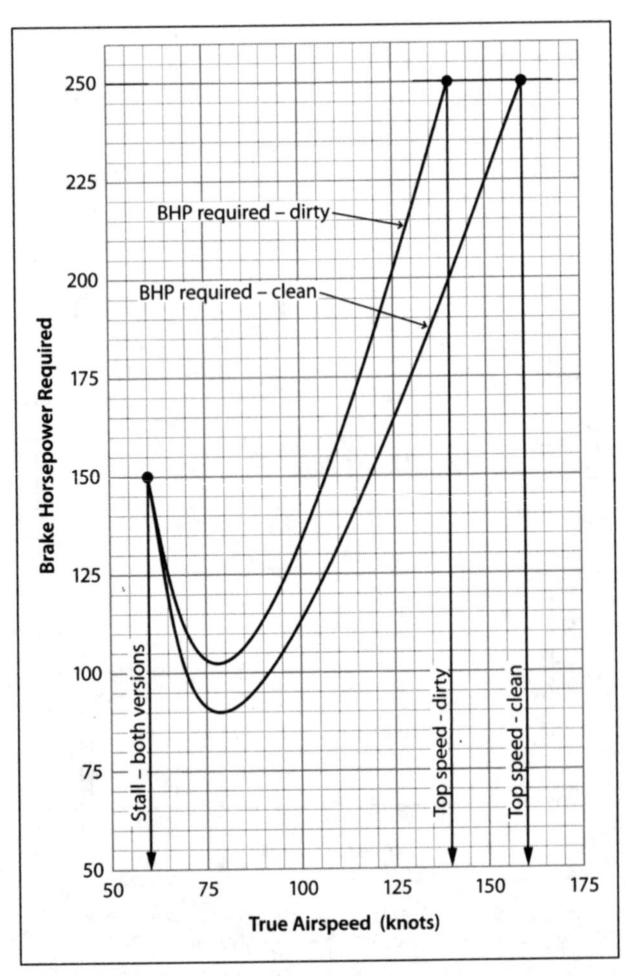

Figure 2-49. The effects of parasite drag (extended gear) on the airplane in Figure 2-47.

again. The excess HP available depends on the characteristics of *both* the THP-available and THP-required curves. The airspeed at which the maximum excess horsepower exists (Point 2) is therefore the speed for a max rate of climb for this airplane at the particular weight and altitude. Point 3 shows the maximum level flight speed at sea level.

Chapters 3 and 6 will go into more detail on climb requirements and how excess THP works in making the airplane climb.

Jets and Props

The jet engine is considered to exert a constant thrust at all airspeeds, compared with that shown for the propeller in Figure 2-33. Therefore, the THP developed by the jet increases in a straight line with velocity: THP = TV (mph)/375 or TV(K)/325.

Figure 2-51 is a power-required and power-available versus velocity curve for the light twin of Figure 2-50 when it is equipped with either jets or reciprocating engines. To simplify, assume that the airplane could be equipped with either jet engines or reciprocating engines with no difference in parasite drag or gross weight. This means that the *power-required* curve in Figure 2-51 would be exactly the same for either version.

Suppose that the top speed of the reciprocating version of our fictitious airplane is 180 K at sea level and it requires 400 (thrust) HP to fly at this speed. (The top level flight speed is that point at which the power required equals the total power available, you remember.) We'll also say that the jet version is equipped with two engines developing maximum thrust at sea level of 361 pounds each, for a total of 722 pounds of thrust. If the airplanes are at the same weight and have the same parasite drag, it can be shown (Figure 2-51) that the top speed of the jet version is also 180 K because, as noted above, it required 400 THP to fly level at this speed and that just happens to be what our jet engines are producing at that speed:

$$\text{THP} = \text{TV}/325$$

$$\frac{722\,(\text{lb thrust}) \times 180\,(\text{K})}{325} = 400 \text{ THP or}$$

$$\frac{722 \times 208\,(\text{mph})}{375} = 400 \text{ THP}$$

THP-available curves are given both for props and jet engines. Note that the THP produced by the jet version is a straight line—it is directly proportional to velocity.

As was mentioned before, the rate of climb for any airplane is proportional to the excess THP available. Note in Figure 2-51 that the maximum rate of climb is

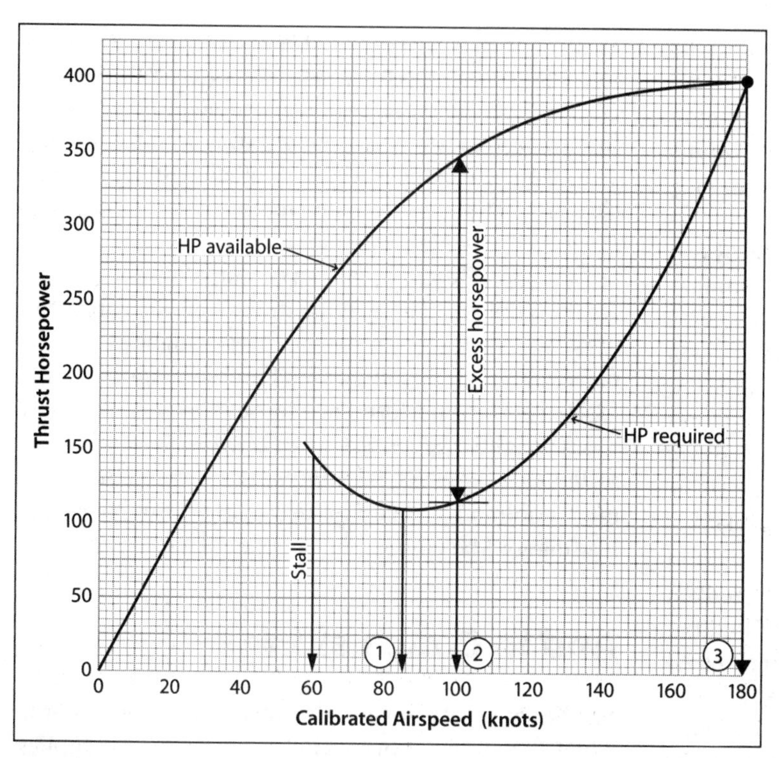

Figure 2-50. Thrust horsepower available and required versus airspeed for a light twin at gross weight at sea level. Assume CAS = TAS at sea level.

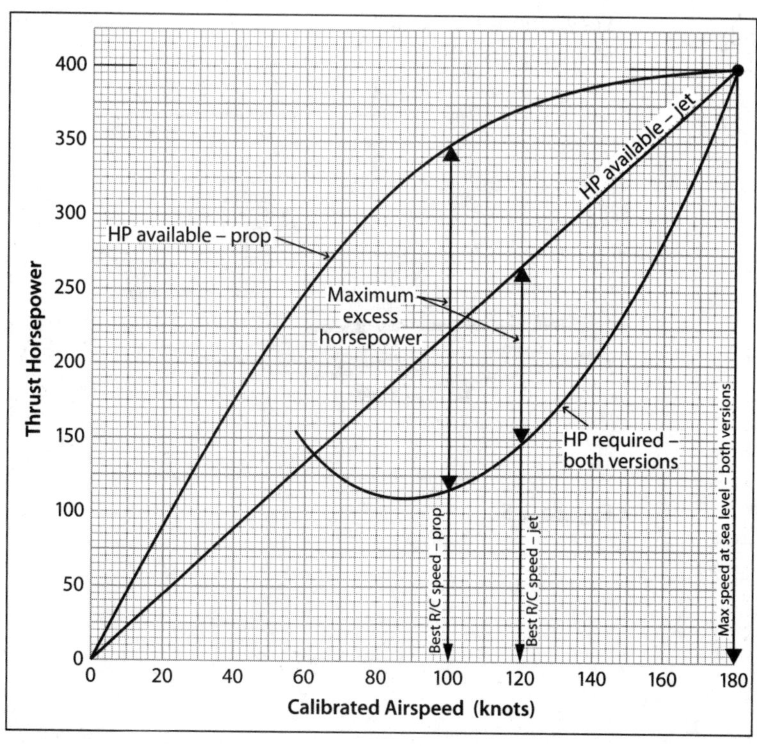

Figure 2-51. A comparison of prop and jet versions of the light twin in Figure 2-50.

found for the airplane at a speed of 100 K when it uses reciprocating engines, and at the higher speed of 120 K when the jet engines are installed.

The higher speed used for climb in a jet airplane is one of the hardest things for the ex-prop pilot to get used to. Notice in Figure 2-51 that the performance of the jet-equipped version would be poor in the climb and low-speed regime because of the smaller amount of excess THP available, compared with one with props. In fact, at speeds close to the stall, a power deficit could exist in that airplane. If you tried to hurry the airplane off the ground at takeoff, you might get it too cocked up and find that you can't get, or stay, airborne. (This sometimes happens even in airplanes with a reasonable amount of power or thrust available.)

Obviously this jet version is underpowered—even though it has the same top speed as the propeller version of the airplane. The low-thrust engines in this example certainly would not be used for this particular airplane; the jet engines would actually be more streamlined, and the manufacturer would put higher-thrust engines in so that the jet version would be much faster. The big point here is that jet engines just aren't very practical in an airplane designed for a top speed of 180 K.

Because of its relatively poor acceleration at low speeds and because of the time required for the engine to develop full thrust when the throttle is opened all the way from idle (it may take several seconds), a comparatively high amount of power is usually carried by some jet airplanes on approach until the landing is assured.

Modern jets have an "approach idle," a higher idle that is triggered by extension of the gear or flaps. This higher idle speed, perhaps 5–10% increased rpm, shortens the "spool-up" time to go-around power. The higher idle may also engage anytime the anti-ice systems are turned on, ensuring enough bleed air to heat the engine inlets and wing leading edges.

The power curve will be covered in more detail as it applies to flight requirements throughout the book.

Weight

The weight of the airplane, as the weight of any other object, always acts downward toward the center of the earth. Weight and drag, the detrimental forces, are the main problems facing aeronautical engineers.

Weight acts toward the center of the earth, so you can see by Figure 2-52 that the Australians and other people in that area fly upside down as far as we're concerned. However, they seem quite happy about it, have been doing it for years, and it's too late to mention it to them.

There are several weight terms with which you should be familiar:

1. *Empty Weight as weighed* is the actual weight that is obtained from the scale readings (after the weight of extra items such as braces or chocks is subtracted). It may be empty of oil, any fuel, or hydraulic fluid, but these are considered later in weight and balance problems worked for the airplane.

2. *Licensed Empty Weight* as set earlier by some manufacturers is the empty weight of the airplane including *undrainable oil, unusable fuel,* and *hydraulic fluid.* This term applies to airplanes *manufactured before* 1976 and indicates that the airplane is painted and ready to go except for oil and usable fuel (and pilot).

3. *Basic Empty Weight* is the term used for general aviation airplanes in models produced in 1976 and after and includes *full oil, unusable fuel,* and *hydraulic fluid.* In other words, oil is considered in this empty weight. The airplane may be actually weighed without oil or be bare of paint; these are added mathematically to get the *Basic Empty Weight and moment.*

4. *Gross Weight* is the maximum allowable weight for the airplane. The manufacturer's performance figures are usually given for the gross weight of the airplane, although in some cases graphs or figures in the POH also show performance for several weights below gross weight. *The term as used in this book refers only to the maximum FAA-certificated weight.* This is the most commonly accepted use of the term. Airplane loading will be covered in Chapter 10.

And In Conclusion

Maybe some of the material in this chapter needs a little thought, and much of it will be repeated as it applies in following chapters. It's possible after reading this that you may subscribe to Dr. Horatio Zilch's belief that airplanes, etc., are really held up by a very strong and very fine wire, which simplifies the subject considerably (Figure 2-53).

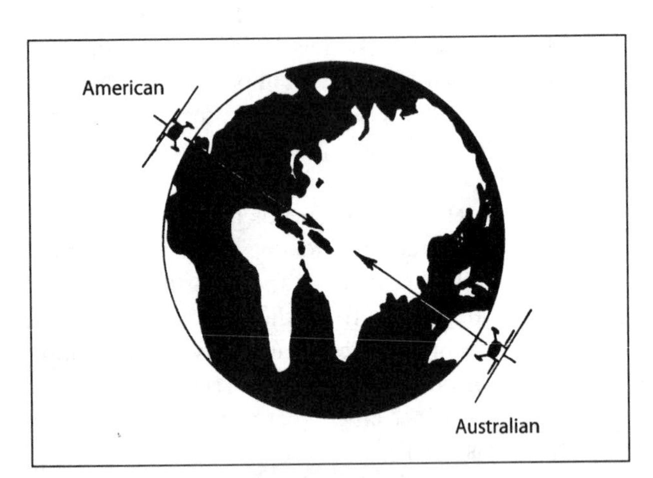

Figure 2-52. As far as Americans are concerned, the Australians fly inverted all the time (and vice versa).

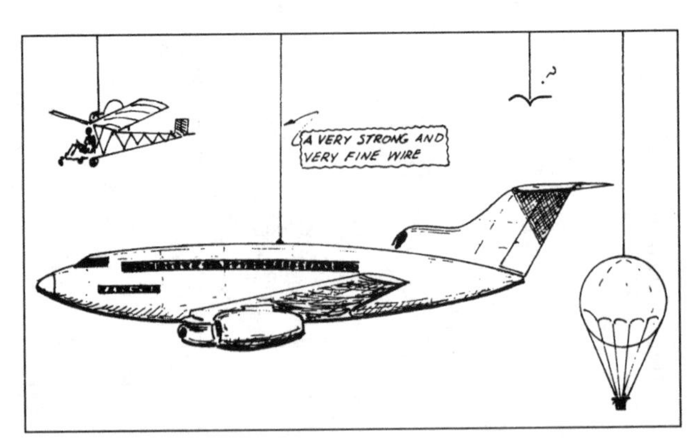

Figure 2-53.

3

Flight Mechanics

This chapter has nothing to do with the people who work on aircraft; *flight mechanics* are the forces and moments acting on the airplane in flight. While the Four Forces are fresh in your mind from the last chapter, it would be well to see how they act on the airplane.

The term *force* was covered in the last chapter, and you've used moments in computing weight and balance problems. A moment normally results from a force (or weight) acting at the end of an arm (at a 90° angle to it) and is usually expressed as pound-inches or pound-feet (Figure 3-1).

The airplane in steady-state flight—that is, in a steady climb, a glide, or in level unaccelerated flight—must be in *equilibrium*; that is, the forces acting in opposite directions on the airplane must cancel each other out. (The same thing goes for the moments.)

A *vector* is an arrow used to represent the direction and strength of a force. You've had experience with vectors in working out wind triangles in navigation and also unconsciously discuss vector systems when you talk about headwind and crosswind components for takeoffs and landings (Figure 3-2). As a pilot you use the runway centerline as a reference and consciously (or unconsciously) divide the wind into components acting along and perpendicular to this reference axis.

You are interested in the component of wind acting across the runway (for example, 15 K) and, if you were interested in computing the takeoff run, you would use the headwind component, or the component of the wind acting down the runway (say, 26 K). You usually don't go so far as to figure out the exact crosswind component but note the wind velocity and its angle to the runway and make a subconscious estimate of how much trouble it might give you on takeoff or landing. You set up your own axis and work with what would seem like a most complicated system if people started talking about axes, vectors, and components. What you do is break down the wind's vector into the two components of most interest to you, as was done in Chapter 1. The same general idea will be used here for the forces acting on the airplane.

The reference axis for operating the airplane is the flight path or line of flight, and the forces are measured as operating parallel and perpendicular to it (Figure 3-3). For an airplane in a *steady-state condition* of flight such as straight and level unaccelerated flight, a constant-airspeed climb or glide, or a constant-altitude balanced turn of a constant rate, the forces acting parallel to the flight path must be balanced. The same thing applies to those forces acting perpendicular, or at 90° ("up" or "down"), to the flight path—they must cancel

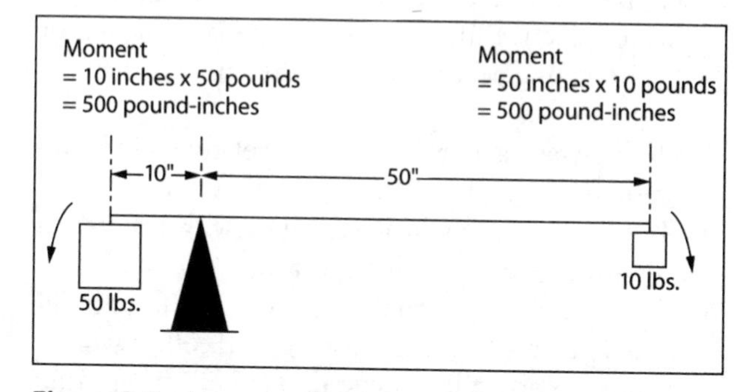

Figure 3-1. A system of moments in equilibrium.

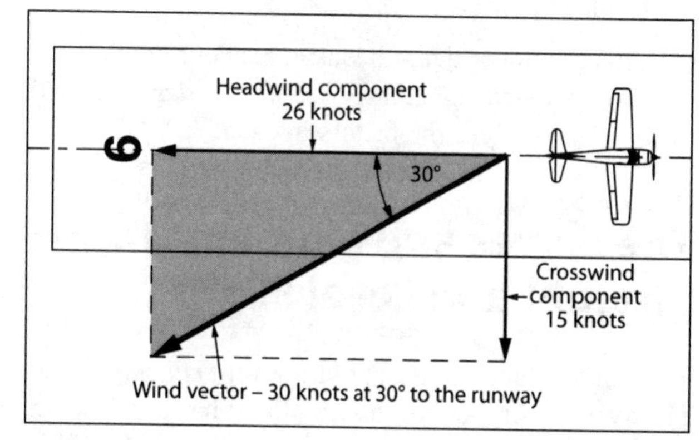

Figure 3-2. A vector system as faced by the pilot during a takeoff or landing in a crosswind that is 30° to the runway at 30 K (Chapter 1).

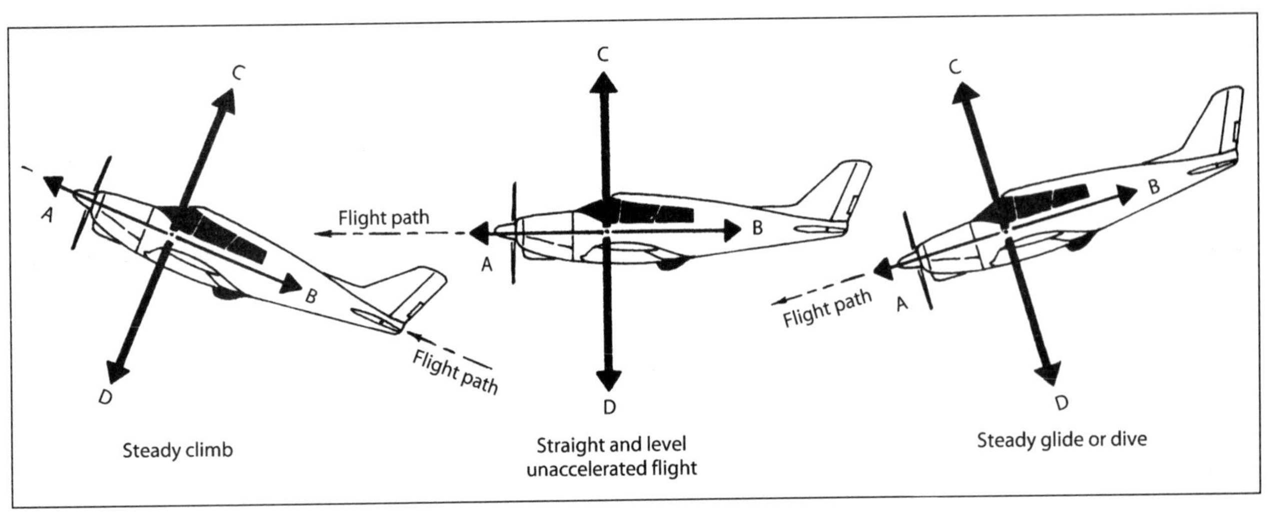

Figure 3-3. In a steady-state flight, the sum of the forces acting parallel to the flight path (A–B) must equal zero; the same applies to those acting perpendicular. Minus signs may be given to forces acting in a "downward" or "rearward" direction.

each other. Each of the vectors shown in Figure 3-3 may represent the total of several forces acting in the direction shown.

The following must be realized in order to see the mechanics of flight:

1. *Lift* always acts perpendicular to the relative wind (and, hence, perpendicular to the flight path). This is the effective lift discussed in the last chapter, or the lift acting perpendicular to the actual path of the airplane.
2. *Drag* always acts parallel to the relative wind (and flight path) and in a "rearward" direction.
3. *Weight* always acts in a vertical (downward) direction toward the center of the earth.
4. *Thrust*, for these problems, always acts parallel to the centerline of the fuselage. (In other words, at this point we'll assume no "offset" thrust line and that thrust is acting parallel to the axis of the fuselage.)

This chapter will take a look at the Four Fundamentals of flight—*straight and level, climbs, descents,* and *turns*—and analyze the factors in each.

The Forces and Moments in Straight and Level Flight

Take an airplane in straight and level *cruising* flight: The average airplane in this condition has a tail-down force because it is designed that way (the need for this will be covered in Chapter 10). Let's examine the forces and moments acting on a typical four-place airplane in straight and level flight at a constant speed at *cruise*.

For simplicity, rather than establishing the vertical acting forces with respect to the center of gravity (CG), which is the usual case, these forces will be measured fore and aft from the center of lift. Assume at this point that lift is a string holding the airplane up; its value will be found later (this is legal). The airplane in Figure 3-4 weighs 3,000 pounds, is flying at 154 K CAS, and at this particular loading the CG is 5 inches ahead of the "lift line."

Summing up the major moments acting on the airplane (check Figure 3-4 for each):

1. *Lift-weight moment*—The weight (3,000 pounds) is acting 5 inches ahead of the center of lift, which results in a 15,000-lb-in. *nose-down* moment (5 inches × 3,000 pounds = 15,000 lb-in.).
2. *Thrust moment*—Thrust is acting 15 inches above the CG and has a value of 400 pounds. The *nose-down* moment resulting is 15 × 400 = *6,000 lb-in.* (The moment created by thrust will be measured with respect to the CG.) For simplicity it will be assumed that the drag is operating back through the CG. Although this is not usually the case, it saves working with another moment.
3. *Wing moment*—The wing, in producing lift, creates a nose-down moment, which is the result of the forces working on the wing itself. Figure 3-5 shows force patterns acting on a wing at two airspeeds (angles of attack). These moments are acting with respect to the aerodynamic center, a point considered to be located about 25% of the distance from the leading edge to the trailing edge for all airfoils.

Notice that as the speed increases (the angle of attack decreases) the moment becomes greater as the force pattern varies. If the airfoil is not a symmetrical type, the nose-down moment created by

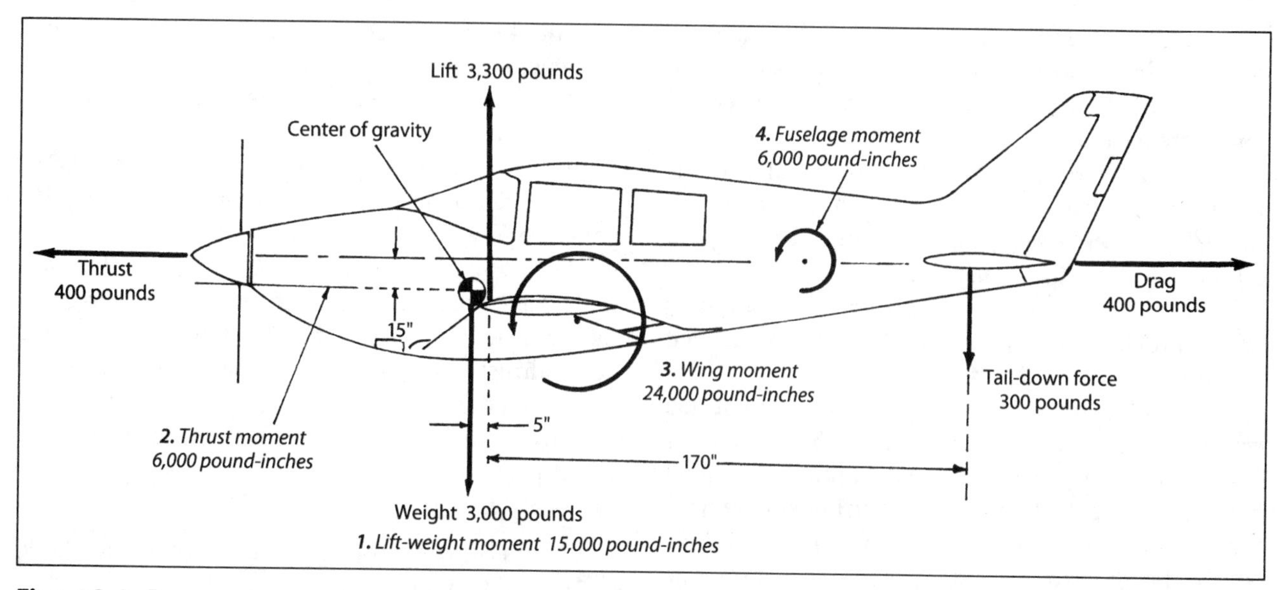

Figure 3-4. Forces and moments acting on an airplane in steady straight and level flight.

the wing increases as the *square* of the airspeed. (There is no wing moment if the airfoil is symmetrical because all of the forces are acting through the aerodynamic center of the airfoil.)

For an airplane of the type, airspeed, and weight used here, a nose-down moment created by the wing of 24,000 lb-in. would be a good round figure. Remember that this would vary with indicated airspeed. *Nose-down moment created by wing = 24,000 lb-in.*

4. *Fuselage moment*—The fuselage may also be expected to have a moment about its CG because it, too, has a flow pattern, which, for the airplane type and airspeed in this example, would be about *6,000 lb-in. nose-down.* (This is not always the case.)

Summing up the nose-down moments:

Lift-weight moment	= 15,000 lb-in.
Thrust moment	= 6,000 lb-in.
Wing moment (at 154 K)	= 24,000 lb-in.
Fuselage moment (at 154 K)	= 6,000 lb-in.
Total nose-down moment	= 51,000 lb-in.

For equilibrium to exist, there must be a *tail-down* moment of 51,000 lb-in., and this is furnished by the tail-down force. Figure 3-4 shows that the *arm* (the distance from the lift line to the center of the tail-down force) is 170 inches. So, the moment (51,000 lb-in.) and the arm (170 inches) are known; the force acting at the end of that arm (the tail-down force) can be found: 51,000 lb-in./170 inches = 300 pounds. The airplane nose does not tend to pitch either way.

The *forces* must also be balanced for equilibrium to exist. Summing up the forces acting perpendicular to the flight path: in this case because the flight path is level, it can be said also that the *vertical* forces must be equal—in a climb or glide the forces acting perpendicular to the flight path will not be vertical (Figure 3-3). The "down" forces are the weight (3,000 pounds) and the tail-down force (300 pounds). The "up" force (lift) must equal the down forces for equilibrium to exist, thus its value must be 3,300 pounds. Now the moments and forces acting perpendicular to the flight path are in equilibrium. As can be seen, lift is not normally the same as weight in straight and level unaccelerated flight. Of course, the CG can be moved back to a point where no nose-down moment exists and no tail-down force is required. This, however, could cause stability problems, which will be covered in Chapter 10.

In the situation just discussed, it was stated that the airplane was at a *constant cruise* speed so that the force (pounds) acting rearward (drag) and the force (pounds) acting forward (thrust) are equal. (It is assumed that at higher speeds the thrust line is acting parallel to the flight path so it can be considered to be equal to drag.)

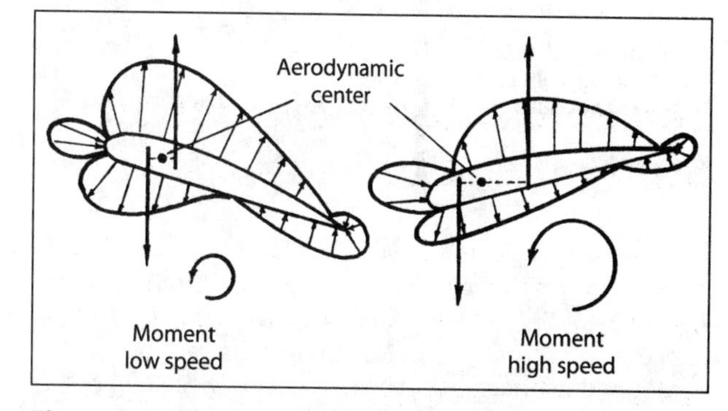

Figure 3-5. The moments created by the unsymmetrical airfoil at two different airspeeds. The angles of attack and pressure patterns around the airfoil have been exaggerated.

Thus it can be said without too much loss of accuracy that, in the cruise regime, thrust equals drag and normally lift is slightly greater than weight when the forces are balanced.

But what about a situation where the airplane is flying straight and level at a constant airspeed in *slow flight?* Again the forces must be summed as shown in Figure 3-6. Now the thrust line is *not* acting parallel to the flight path (and opposite to drag); for purposes of this problem, it will be assumed that it is inclined upward from the horizontal by 15°.

As a pilot, for straight and level slow flight you set up the desired airspeed and use whatever power is necessary to maintain a constant altitude; you don't know the value of drag, thrust, or lift (and may have only a vague idea as to what the weight is at that time, but for this problem it's 3,000 pounds, as before). The tail-down force will be assumed to be 200 pounds. (At this high angle of attack it likely will be less than for cruise.) In the problem of straight and level *cruising* flight it was just assumed that thrust equaled drag and we weren't particularly interested in the values. Look at Figure 3-7 for a typical drag versus airspeed curve for the type of airplane being discussed.

In summing up the forces parallel to the flight path in slow flight with this airplane, drag is 350 pounds; the component of thrust acting opposite drag must be 350 pounds also. No doubt you are already ahead of this in your thinking and realize that because it is inclined at an angle, the actual thrust must be greater than drag if its "forward" component along the flight path is equal to drag. You could look in a trigonometry table and find that at a 15° angle, the *actual* thrust must be about 3½% higher, or about 362 pounds compared with 350 pounds of drag.

Thrust also has a component acting at a 90° angle to the flight path parallel to lift. A check of a trigonometric table would show that this force is 26% of the actual thrust and has a value of about 94 pounds (which is a fair amount).

Now, summing up the forces perpendicular to the flight path (the "up" forces must equal the "down" forces):

Forces "down" = weight + tail-down force = 3,000 + 200 = 3,200 pounds

Forces "up" = lift + vertical component of thrust = lift + 94 pounds = 3,200 pounds

Lift, of course, is found as 3,200 – 94 = 3,106 pounds, using our arbitrary values. So lift is less at low-speed level flight (3,106 pounds) than at cruise (3,300 pounds), if you are talking strictly about each of the Four Forces. You don't worry about this in practical application but fly the airplane and set the power and airspeed to get the desired result.

As the vertical component of thrust helps support the airplane, the wings only have to support 3,106 pounds rather than the full 3,200 pounds (weight plus tail-down force) in slow flight and therefore the wing

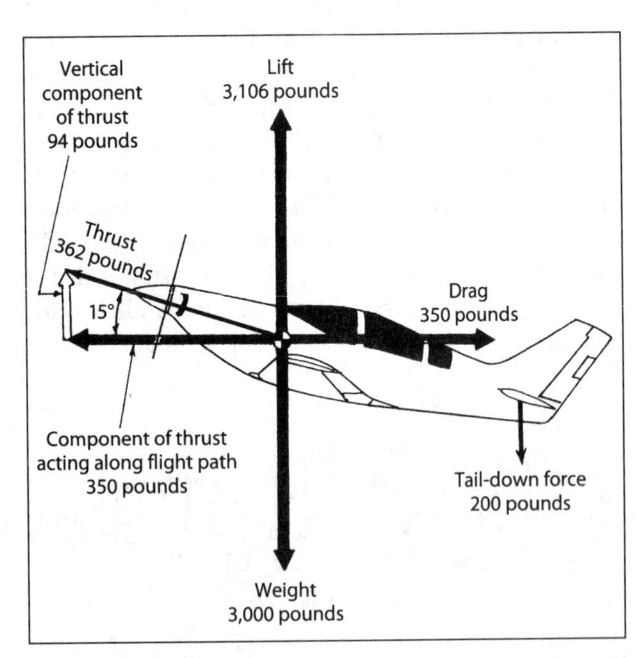

Figure 3-6. The forces at work on an airplane in straight and level slow flight just above the stall. The vertical component of thrust has been moved out ahead of the airplane for clarity. Because of the placement of the various forces, it would appear that the moments are not in equilibrium. They will be assumed to be so for this problem.

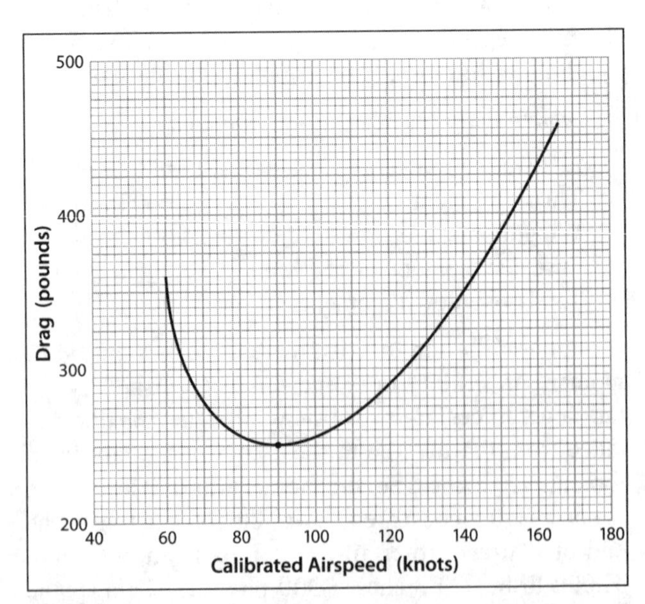

Figure 3-7. A drag versus airspeed curve for a fictitious, four-place, high-performance, single-engine airplane at gross weight. The values are in the area currently expected of that type of airplane.

loading is less than would be expected. The airplane always stalls at a lower airspeed with power on (for the same flap setting and weight) than in the power-off condition. The effect of the slipstream across the wing helps lower the stall speed, too.

The greater that thrust is in proportion to weight, the greater this effect. For instance, if the airplane had an engine-propeller combination capable of producing 3,000 pounds of thrust, the airplane would be capable of "hanging on its prop" and in theory the power-on stall speed would be zero.

So, in summary, in straight and level flight in the *slow flight regime*, it may be expected that (1) the actual thrust exerted by the propeller (pounds) is greater than the drag of the airplane and (2) lift is less than at higher speeds. The location of the CG, the angle the thrust line makes with the flight path, and other factors can have an effect on these figures, of course.

Forces in the Climb

To keep from complicating matters, the tail-down force will be ignored for the first part of each section of flight mechanics. It exists, of course, and varies with CG and angle of attack (airspeed) but is comparatively small in most cases, so lift will be considered equal to weight, at least at the beginning. We'll also assume that all moments are balanced and won't have to consider them further, and the Four Forces will be drawn as acting through a single point (the CG) of the airplane to avoid complicating the drawings.

One of the biggest fallacies in pilots' thinking is believing that the airplane climbs because of "excess lift." For purposes of this problem, the drag (pounds) of the example airplane will be 250 pounds at the recommended climb speed of 90 K (Figure 3-7). The figures for the values for drag have been rounded off.

Again, remembering that all forces (and moments) must be in balance for such equilibrium to exist, the following is noted. Because the flight path is no longer level, weight, for the first time, is no longer operating in a direction 90° to the flight path. As the forces must be in equilibrium, both parallel and perpendicular to the flight path, weight must be broken down into the components acting in these directions (as you do with the wind when it is neither right down the runway nor straight across it) (Figure 3-8).

Figure 3-9 shows the forces acting on the airplane in a steady-state climb of 90 K (CAS). The airplane has an angle of climb of 8° to the horizontal and requires an angle of attack of 6° to fly at the climb airspeed of 90 K. We are assuming that the angle of incidence is zero (the wing chord line is exactly parallel to the fuselage centerline) and that the thrust line is offset "upward" from the flight path by 6° in this climb. In the following drawings the angles will be exaggerated and a simplified airplane silhouette used for clarity.

To sum up the forces *parallel* to the flight path:

The forces acting rearward along the flight path are aerodynamic drag (250 pounds) (see Figure 3-7 again) *plus* the rearward component of weight, which by checking a trigonometric table for the 8° angle of climb (in round numbers) is found to be 417 pounds. The total rearward acting force is aerodynamic drag (250 pounds) plus the rearward acting component of weight (417 pounds), or *667 pounds*.

For the required equilibrium (steady-state climb condition) to exist, there must be a balancing force acting forward along the flight path; this is furnished by thrust. The fact that the thrust line is offset upward from the flight path by 6° further complicates the problem. Because of its inclination the actual thrust produced by the propeller must be greater than 667 pounds in order to have that force acting along the flight path. The actual thrust, you will note, is the hypotenuse of a

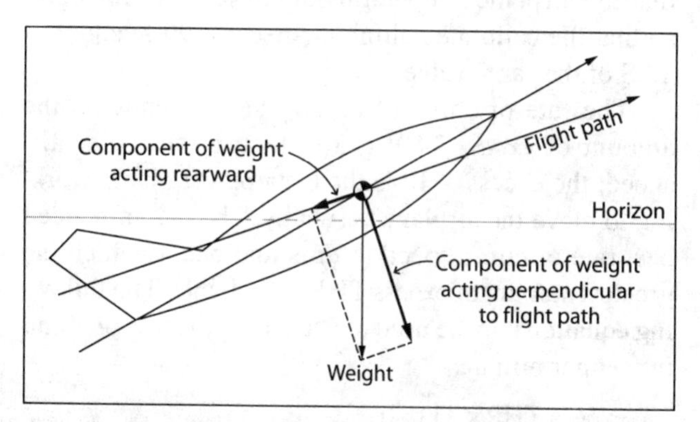

Figure 3-8. Weight is no longer acting perpendicular to the flight path, therefore it must be broken down into components as shown.

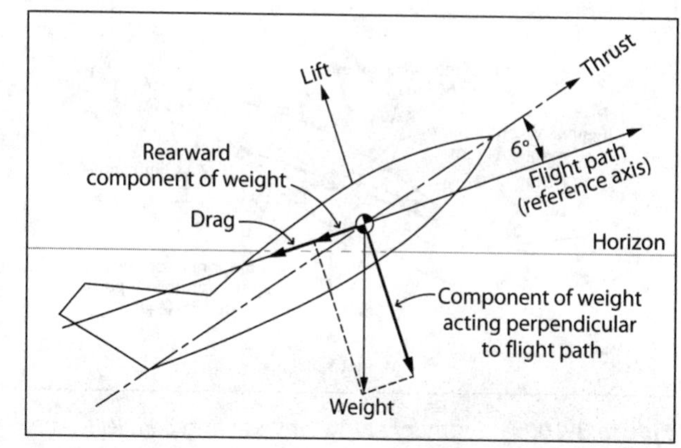

Figure 3-9. The rearward forces acting on an airplane in a steady-state climb.

right triangle, and you remember from your geometry (and Chapter 1) that the hypotenuse of a right triangle is always longer than either one of its sides; the longer of the two other sides is the component of thrust acting along the flight path, which must be equal to the rearward acting force(s). The sum of the forces equals zero.

Again, a check of a trigonometric table shows that to have 667 pounds along the flight path the *actual* thrust must be about 0.55% greater (a little more than one-half of 1%) so that its value is 3 pounds greater, or about 670 pounds (a nit-picking addition, to be sure). The forces acting *parallel* to the flight path at the climb speed of 90 K and weight of 3,000 pounds are balanced (Figure 3-10).

To summarize the forces acting *perpendicular* to the flight path: The component of weight acting perpendicular (more or less "downward") to the flight path at the climb angle of 8° turns out to be 2,971 pounds according to the trigonometric table (the cosine of 8° is 0.9902). Because this is considered to be the only force acting in that direction (now that the tail-down force is being neglected), it must be balanced by an equal force (or forces) in the opposite direction. The two forces acting in that direction are (1) lift and (2) the component of thrust acting at 90°, or perpendicular, to the flight path (Figure 3-11).

As thrust is now a known quantity, we can solve for that component acting in the same direction as lift. For a 6° angle of inclination, the component for 670 pounds of thrust is 70 pounds (rounded off). This means that lift must have a value of 2,901 pounds in this case (2,971 – 70 = 2,901 pounds), or lift (2,901 pounds) + thrust component (70 pounds) = weight component (2,971 pounds). The forces acting perpendicular to the flight path are balanced.

Lift (2,901 pounds) is found here to be *less* than the airplane's weight (3,000 pounds) in the steady-state

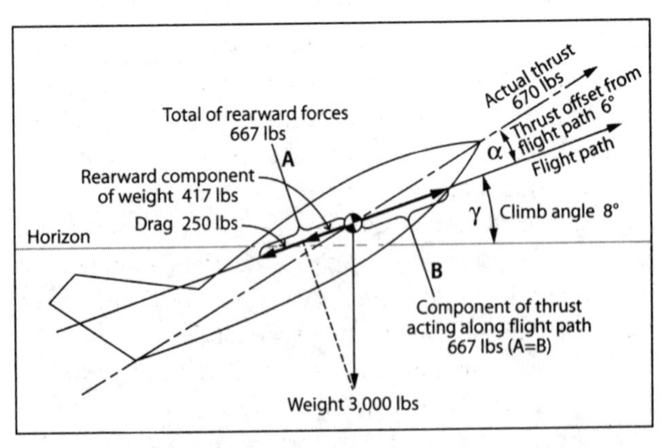

Figure 3-10. A summary of the forces acting *parallel* to the flight path in the steady-state climb.

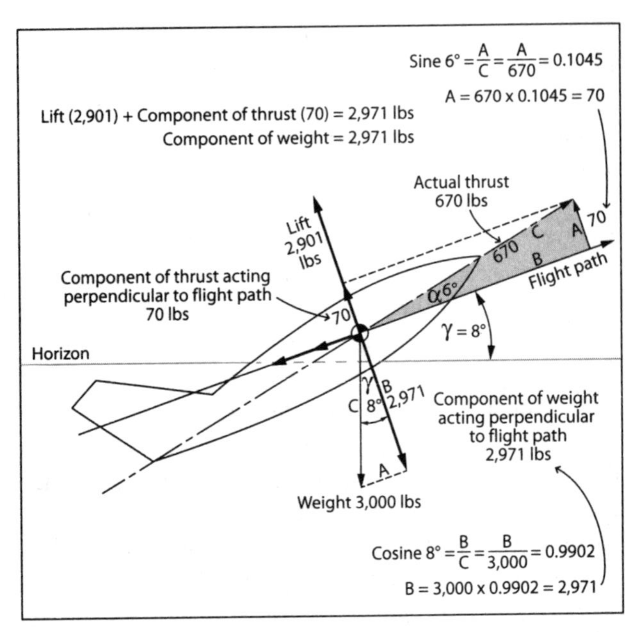

Figure 3-11. A summary of the forces acting *perpendicular* to the flight path in the climb.

climb. Thrust (670 pounds) is *greater* than aerodynamic drag (250 pounds).

What happened to the idea that an airplane makes a steady climb because of "excess" lift? Even considering the tail-down force, which for this airplane's airspeed, weight, and CG location could be expected to be about 250 pounds, lift is hardly greater than weight. In any event, there is no "excess lift" available—it's all being used to balance the tail-down force and the component of weight acting perpendicular to the flight path. (lift would have to be 2,901 pounds + 250 pounds, or 3,151 pounds.)

Remember from the last chapter that the thrust horsepower equation is THP = TV/325 (the 325 is for the airspeed in knots), so that the THP being developed along the flight path is (667 × 90)/325 = 185 THP. The "V" in the equation is *true* airspeed; it will be assumed that the airplane is operating at sea level at this point so that the calibrated climb airspeed of 90 K equals a TAS of the same value.

The rate of climb of an airplane depends on the amount of *excess* THP available at a particular airspeed; the excess THP is the horsepower that is working to move the airplane vertically. The recommended best rate of climb speed (V_Y) is that one at which the greatest amount of excess THP is available. The following equation may be used to determine the rate of climb in feet per minute:

$$\frac{\text{excess THP} \times 33{,}000}{\text{airplane weight}}$$

Power is *force* times *distance per unit of time* and 1 HP is equal to 550 ft-lb per second or 33,000 ft-lb per minute. That's where the 33,000 in the equation comes in; it's set up for a rate of climb (RC), or vertical displacement, in feet per minute. Going back to the original idea for horsepower (in this case THP), the equation for the THP (excess THP) used to climb would be as follows:

$$\frac{\text{airplane weight} \times \text{RC (fpm)}}{33{,}000}$$

The THP required to climb is that raising a certain weight (the airplane) a certain vertical distance in a certain period of time.

But to find the rate of climb for the example airplane, it would be best to first find out how much THP is required to fly the airplane *straight and level* at a constant altitude at sea level at 90 K. As weight in *level flight* will not have a component acting rearward to the flight path, the only retarding force is aerodynamic drag, which was found to be 250 pounds. The thrust component acting along the flight path must be equal to this, or 250 pounds. Assuming that the angle of attack and the angle thrust makes with the flight path is 6°, to get this value the actual thrust would be about 251 pounds (rounded off to the 250) (Figure 3-12).

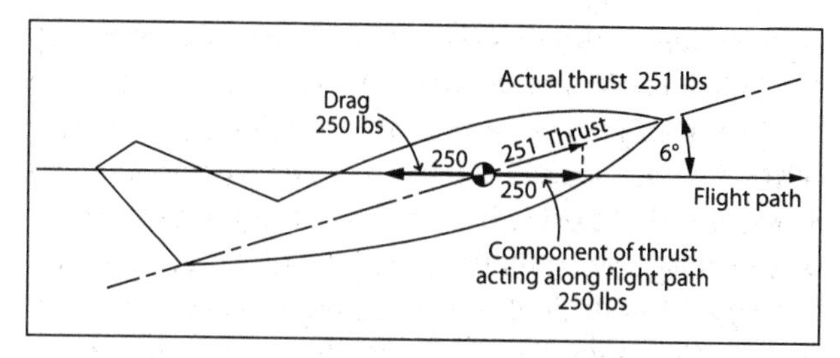

Figure 3-12. The forces acting parallel to the flight path for the airplane flying *straight and level* at the recommended climb speed of 90 K.

In the earlier look at the climb at 90 K, 667 pounds of thrust was being exerted along the flight path. This is 417 pounds more than required for level flight and is, in effect, the "excess thrust" needed for a climb angle of 8° at 90 K. (The rearward component of weight was 417 pounds.)

Solving for excess thrust horsepower (ETHP):

$$\text{ETHP} = \frac{\text{excess thrust} \times \text{velocity (K)}}{325}$$

$$\text{ETHP} = \frac{417 \times 90}{325} = 115 \text{ THP}$$

Solving for rate of climb:

$$\text{RC} = \frac{\text{ETHP} \times 33{,}000}{\text{weight}}$$

$$\text{RC} = \frac{115 \times 33{,}000}{3{,}000} = 1{,}265 \text{ fpm}$$

The brake horsepower (BHP) required to get such performance for a 3,000-lb airplane with the described characteristics could be estimated. It can be assumed here that at the climb speed the propeller is 74% efficient (efficiency varies with airspeed, you remember from Chapter 2) and that the THP being developed is 74% of the BHP being developed at the crankshaft. The *total* THP being used in the climb is THP = (T × V)/325 = (670 × 90)/325 = 185 THP (rounded off). The thrust acting along the flight path was 667 pounds, but the *total* thrust exerted was 670 pounds; this is what must be used to work back to the BHP requirement.

This, then, is approximately 74% of the horsepower developed at the crankshaft, so the BHP required to get this performance for the fictitious airplane would be 185/0.74, or approximately 250 BHP (0.74 × 250 = 185).

The rate of climb found is in the ball park for current four-place retractable-gear airplanes ("our" airplane may be cleaner or dirtier aerodynamically than others). All of this resulted from our arbitrarily selecting an aerodynamic drag (250 pounds), an angle of attack (and offset thrust from the path) in the climb (6°), and a climb angle of 8° at a climb speed of 90 K. The figures were picked to give a reasonable idea of how such airplane types get their climb performance. The 74% used for propeller efficiency is also arbitrary, although the figure is close to that expected for the airplane type and speed discussed.

The more practical aspects of the climb will be covered in Chapter 6.

Forces in the Glide

As you have probably already reasoned, anytime the flight path of the airplane is not horizontal, weight has to be broken down into two components. The glide or descent at an angle of 8° to the horizontal would have the same percentages of weight acting perpendicular and parallel to the flight path as for the 8° of climb mentioned—except that in the glide, the component of weight parallel to the glide path is not a retarding force but is acting in the direction of the flight.

For this situation it is assumed that the power is at idle and *no thrust exists*. The tail-down force will be neglected at first. The forces acting parallel to the flight path are (1) the component of weight, which must be balanced by (2) aerodynamic drag in order to keep the airspeed constant in the descent. For an 8° angle of descent the component of weight acting along the flight path would be 417 pounds, as for the climb—except that it's now working in the direction of motion. The aerodynamic drag must equal the component of weight acting along the flight path for a steady-state condition to exist. Looking back to Figure 3-7, you see that for an 8° angle of descent, this value of drag (417 pounds) exists at about 157 K.

The more usual situation would be to use the power-off glide speed recommended by the manufacturer. For this example, 90 K will be used as the recommended (clean) glide speed. We'll also ignore the effects of power decrease or windmilling prop on the drag curve and say that aerodynamic drag at 90 K is 250 pounds, as it was for the power-on climb. The speed of 90 K may or may not be the best one for maximum glide efficiency (it depends on the airplane), but the niceties of that will be covered later on.

Illustrating the same reasoning as in the other steady-state flight conditions, Figure 3-13 shows the forces acting parallel to the flight path in a power-off glide. (Again, the tail-down force is neglected for simplicity.)

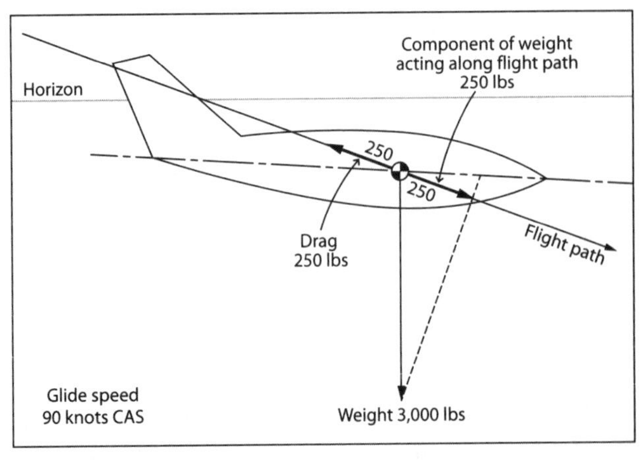

Figure 3-13. The forces acting parallel to the flight path in the power-off glide at 90 K.

Realizing that the component of weight acting along the flight path must have a value equal to the 250 pounds of aerodynamic drag, the glide path will be of a certain angle for this condition to occur; a check of a trig table shows this to be 4°47' (4 degrees and 47 minutes), or nearly a 5° angle downward in relation to the horizon. Knowing the glide angle, the forces acting 90° to the flight path (lift and the component of weight acting perpendicular to the flight path) can be found (Figure 3-14).

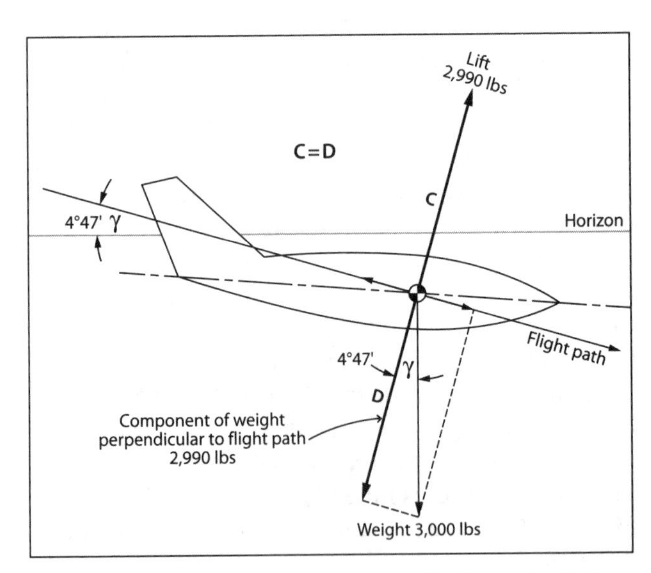

Figure 3-14. The forces acting perpendicular to the flight path in the glide.

That weight component, which can be found by reference to a trig table, is 2,990 pounds, so lift must also equal this value for a steady-state (or constant) glide under the conditions of ignoring the tail-down force.

For shallow angles of glide, the variation of lift from weight is usually ignored. In this case, lift is 2,990 pounds to a weight of 3,000 pounds, a variation of about one-third of 1%.

In the climb, a final figure for lift required at 90 K (considering the tail-down force) was 3,151 pounds. For the glide, the tail-down force for this airplane would be in the vicinity of 225 pounds because of the lack of a moment created by thrust. The component of weight acting perpendicular to the flight path at the 90 K glide was 2,990 pounds, and lift required to take care of this would be 2,990 + 225 or *3,215 pounds. There are 64 more pounds of lift in the glide than in the climb, or lift would be greater in the glide than in the climb under the conditions established!*

The angle that weight varies from being perpendicular to the flight path is also the angle of glide or descent. If *aerodynamic drag is cut to a minimum, the components of weight acting parallel to the flight path can also be a minimum for a steady-state glide.* In other words, if the aerodynamic drag could somehow be halved for this airplane, the angle of glide would be halved; the airplane would descend at an angle of about 2.5° to the horizontal *and would glide twice as far for the same altitude loss.*

Because the airplane's weight is considered to be constant for a particular instant of time, the solution is that the farthest distance may be covered with the airplane flying at the angle of attack (or airspeed) with the minimum aerodynamic drag. For instance, assuming that at small angles of descent lift equals weight (3,000 pounds), the angle of glide of the example airplane is 3,000 pounds (lift or weight)/250 pounds (aerodynamic drag) = 12. The glide ratio for our example airplane at 90 K is 12 to 1, or 12 feet forward for every 1 foot down. And as the point of minimum aerodynamic drag (250 pounds at 90 K CAS) was determined from Figure 3-7, this would be the minimum glide angle (or *maximum distance* glide) for the example airplane. Any time drag is increased, the efficiency of the glide is *decreased.* With a faster or slower glide speed than the 90 K chosen, a check of Figure 3-7 shows that drag will increase—and the glide ratio will suffer.

One method of increasing drag would be to glide with the landing gear extended (an increase in parasite drag, which would result in an increase in total drag). With the gear down a typical figure for drag for an airplane of this type at 90 K would be 300 pounds. The glide angle would be greater and the glide ratio would suffer.

Assume that the pilot starts gliding "clean" and the glide ratio is 12 to 1. The nose is at a certain attitude to get the 90 K (and the 4°47' angle of descent); for most airplanes of that type the nose will be approximately level.

The gear is extended and suddenly the forces acting parallel to the flight path are no longer in balance; drag is greater than the component of weight, and the airplane would start slowing if the nose were kept at the same position. Deciding to glide at 90 K as before, the pilot must drop the nose and change the flight path so that the component of weight acting along the flight path would equal the 300 pounds of aerodynamic drag. The new glide ratio at 90 K with the gear down would be lift (3,000 pounds)/drag (300 pounds), or about 10 to 1; the glide angle would be about 6° relative to the horizon.

The method of finding the rate of sink of the airplane can be compared to that of solving for the rate of climb. The rate of sink, however, is a function of the *deficit* THP existing at the chosen airspeed:

$$\frac{\text{defecit THP} \times 33{,}000}{\text{airplane weight}}$$

The aerodynamic drag for the airplane is a force of 250 pounds acting rearward along the flight path at the airspeed of 90 K (the airplane is clean and weighs 3,000 pounds). The equivalent THP required to be acting in the direction of flight to equal the effects of drag at 90 K would be THP = DV/325 = (250 × 90)/325 = 69. The combination of thrust and velocity would have to equal 69 THP for level flight at 90 K, or TV/325 = 69 THP. However, in this case thrust is zero and, as you know, zero times any number (90 K in this case) is still zero. So, there's no THP being developed by the engine; the airplane is 69 THP in the hole, or there is a deficit of 69 THP. The rate of sink can be calculated: (69 × 33,000)/3,000 = 760 fpm (rounded off).

This could be checked by looking at the situation in Figure 3-13 again. The airplane is descending down a path inclined at an angle of 4°47' at 90 K forward speed. Converting the 90 K to feet per minute it can be said that the airplane is moving down the path at a rate of 9,130 fpm. It was already found that the glide ratio was 12 to 1, so the feet down per minute would be one-twelfth that traveled along the glide path, or about 760 fpm.

Forces in the Turn

Analysis of the turn can be quite complicated but we'll take a simple look at it.

For normal flying (the Four Fundamentals), the turn is the only maneuver in which lift is deliberately and maliciously made greater than weight and is the only one of the Four Fundamentals in which g forces exist in a steady-state condition.

For a balanced turn at a constant altitude, the up forces must equal the down forces as in straight and level flight. For ease of discussion we'll ignore the tail-down force in this section on the turn.

As noted in Chapter 2, lift acts perpendicular to the relative wind and *to the wingspan.* The latter consideration is of particular importance in discussing the turn.

As you know from turning a car, your body is forced toward the "outside of the circle," and that force increases as an inverse function of the turning radius. (The smaller the radius or tighter the turn for a given speed, the greater the apparent "side force" working on you.) If you drive faster and try to turn in the same radius as that at a slower speed, the force is greater. So, your discomfort is a function of either the radius or the velocity during the turn, or both. If, in a turn, the car would suddenly hit a spot of oil or ice, it would move toward the outside of the circle (or more correctly, its path would be tangent to the circle). The tendency for the car to travel in a straight line is normally offset by the *centripetal* force, or the holding (friction) force of the tires against the road surface. When the oil spot or ice is encountered, the friction providing the centripetal force decreases suddenly and the car departs the beaten path for new adventures through somebody's hedge.

You'll hear, and probably use, the term "centrifugal force," which is not a true force (and not even a proper term in physics) but is the result of a body (the airplane, for example) tending to continue in a straight line.

To repeat: the acceleration, or g forces in a balanced turn, depends on the bank; a Cessna 152 and an F-15 in a 30° bank at cruise will have the same force acting on each of the pilots. The turn radius of the F-15 will be much greater as will be reviewed later.

You can set up a balanced turn and play airspeed versus bank angle to vary the effects of rate and radius of turn. You also know that in doing steep turns you could control altitude by changing bank angle and back pressure (angle of attack). Generally you don't increase airspeed in a constant-altitude turn (you don't have all that much capacity in the average general aviation airplane), but if you did you'd have to relax back pressure (*decrease* the angle of attack) or *increase* the bank angle if a constant altitude is to be held.

In balanced, constant-altitude and constant-radius turns, the tendency of the airplane to continue in a straight line is overcome by the component of lift (centripetal force) acting toward the center of the turn (after the turn is established).

Centripetal force (C.F.) = WV^2/gR = horizontal component of lift (L).

where W = weight of the airplane (pounds)
V^2 = tangential velocity (fps), squared.
(You can call it TAS in feet per second, squared.)
g = acceleration of gravity (32.16 feet per second per second)
R = radius of turn (feet)

$WV^2/gR = L \sin \phi$ (ϕ = bank angle)

If the velocity is *doubled* at the same bank, the g forces will remain the same but the turn radius will be *quadrupled.* (More about this later.)

Figure 3-15 shows that the airplane would like to go straight (A), but you are in command and want to turn (left in this particular case) (B).

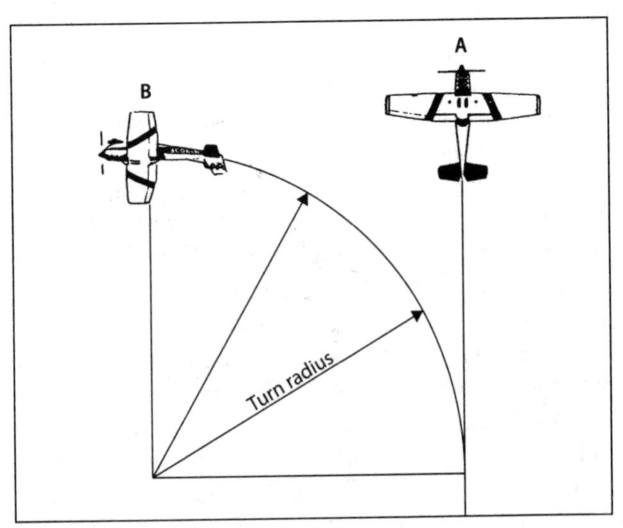

Figure 3-15. The airplane wants to proceed straight ahead (A), but your skillful control of the lift force direction and value, you are able to follow path (B).

Figure 3-16 shows the forces acting to keep the airplane in a constant-altitude balanced turn. The vertical component of lift (A) is balancing the weight of the airplane, while the horizontal component (B) of lift is acting to turn it.

For instance, take two airplanes of the same weight; one has a great deal more power and can maintain a level turn at twice the cruising speed of the other. Both will be banked at 30° in a balanced level turn (Figure 3-17). Both airplanes are pulling the same load factor or number of g's, but there is quite a difference in their turn radii. (The load factor is a function of the lift-to-weight ratio if the tail-down force is ignored; lift in each case is 3,460 pounds; the airplanes are pulling 3,460/3,000, or 1.15 g's.) In the balanced turn, as was mentioned earlier, centripetal force is furnished by the horizontal component of lift, which for the bank of 30° is found to be 1,730 pounds (Figure 3-17).

Everything is known except the radius of turn (R) for each airplane under the conditions given (W = 3,000 pounds, g = 32.16 feet per second per second, CF [horizontal component of lift] = 1,730 pounds, V = 150 and 300 fps). Solving for R of Airplane A requires a little algebraic shuffling and rounding off:

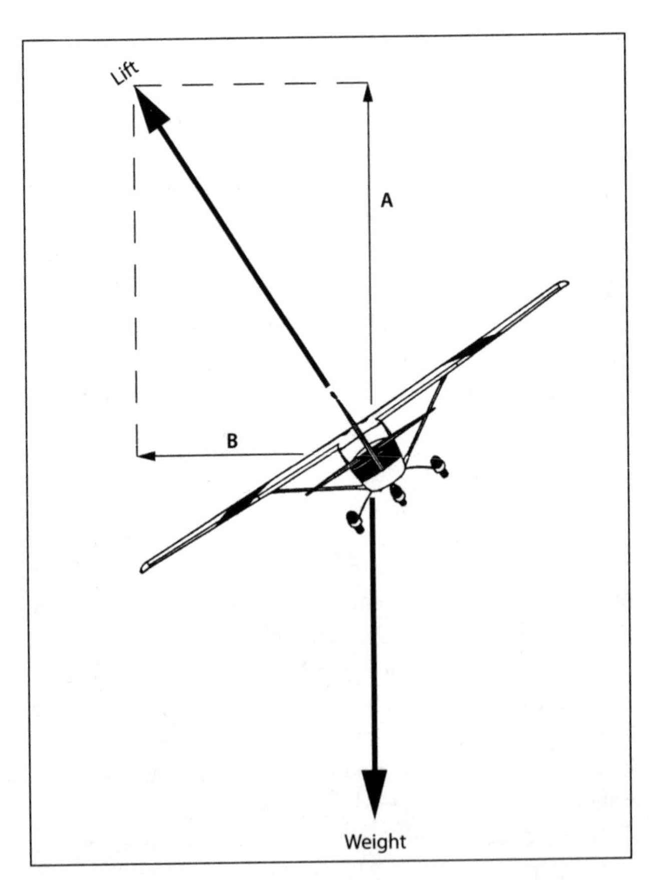

Figure 3-16. In a balanced constant-altitude turn, lift may be considered to be broken down into a vertical component (A) and a horizontal component (B).

$$R = \frac{WV^2}{g(CF)} = \frac{3{,}000 \times (150)^2}{32.16 \times 1{,}730} = 1{,}210 \text{ feet}$$

The turning radius of airplane A in a 30°-banked turn at 150 fps, or about 90 K, is about 1,210 feet, or slightly less than ¼ mile. If it made a 360° turn, the diameter of the turn would be a little less than ½ mile.

For airplane B, turning at a velocity of 300 fps, the radius of turn would be (rounded off):

$$\frac{3{,}000 \times (300)^2}{32.16 \times 1{,}730} = 4{,}850 \text{ feet, or } r = \frac{V^2(K)}{11.26 \tan \phi}$$

The radius of its turn would be 4,850 feet, or *four times* that of the airplane of the same weight and angle of bank traveling at one-half the speed. (The numbers in this exercise have all been rounded off to 10 feet.)

Suppose the pilot of airplane B wanted to make the *same radius of turn* as A but still at the higher speed of 300 fps (about 178 K). You've no doubt already figured out that the airplane must be banked more steeply; this can be found by reshuffling the equation and working back to the bank required to get a radius of turn of 1,210 feet, like airplane A.

This time the centripetal force required at the speed of 300 fps for a radius of turn of 1,210 feet is (rounded off):

$$CF = \frac{WV^2}{g(R)} = \frac{3{,}000 \times (300)^2}{32.16 \times 1{,}210} = 6{,}940 \text{ pounds}$$

So, the horizontal component of lift must equal this value of 6,940 pounds. It's also a fact that the vertical component of lift *must* be 3,000 pounds (to equal weight) so the lift value and angle could be readily found by checking a trig table (Figure 3-18). It's found that the angle of bank must be about 66.6°. The lift value must be 7,560 pounds, or the airplane's lift-to-weight ratio is 7,560/3,000 = 2.52 g's. The pilot's face is sagging downward trying to stay in the turning circle of the slower airplane (the pilot of which probably feels quite comfortable at a 1.15-g loading in the 30° bank). Figure 3-19 shows the two airplanes in the turn.

In instrument flying, the *time* to make a turn (rate of turn) is important, and you'll find that the faster the airplane the steeper the bank must be in order to make a balanced standard-rate turn of 3° per second (Chapter 1). Chapter 4 will also go into this requirement in more detail.

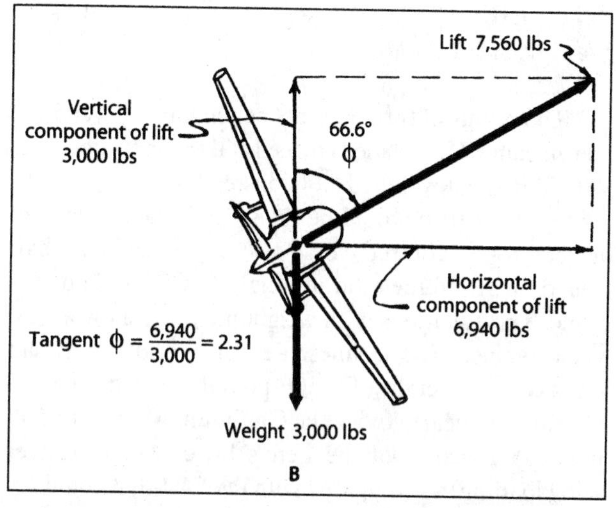

Figure 3-18. Forces existing and bank required for Airplane B to make a turn with a radius of 1,210 feet at its speed of 300 fps.

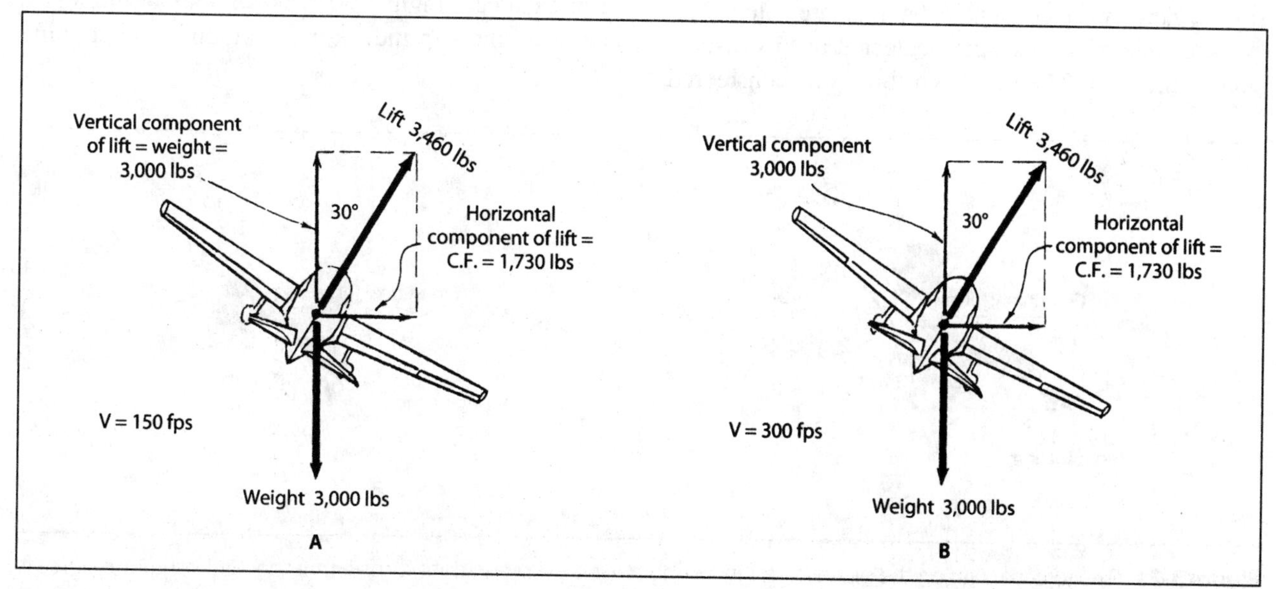

Figure 3-17. Forces in the balanced level turn for two airplanes flying at *different speeds* at a 30° bank. Note that the forces are the same.

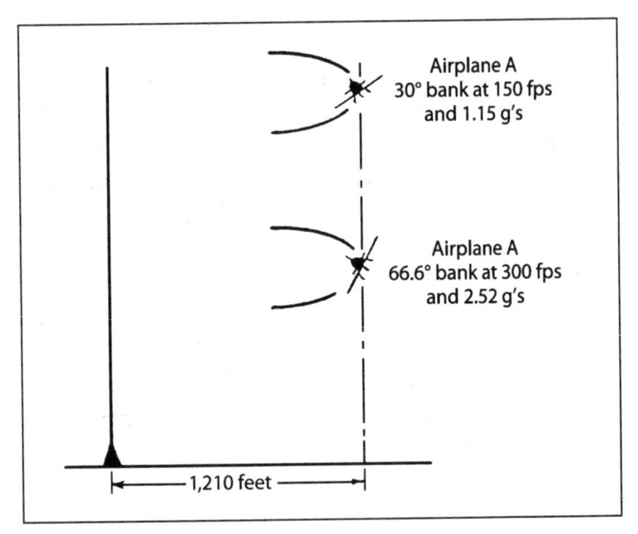

Figure 3-19. A comparison of the two airplanes making the same radius of turn.

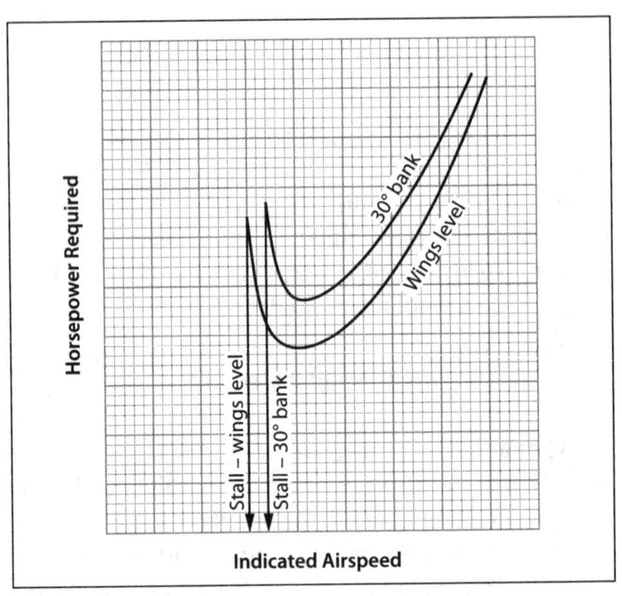

Figure 3-20. A comparison of the horsepower required to maintain a constant altitude (and stall speeds), wings level and in a 30° bank.

The radius of turn does not depend on the weight of the airplane. If airplane B turned at the same velocity as A (150 fps) but weighed 6,000 instead of 3,000 pounds, its radius of turn would be the same because the centripetal force required would also be doubled (in a balanced turn) and the ratio of weight to CF would be the same. The equations with weight included show actual vector values. The Japanese Zero in World War II had a maximum weight of 6,500 pounds, and the F4U-4 Corsair had nearly twice the maximum weight (12,500 pounds). Because of the Zero's lower weight (lower wing loading) as compared with the F4U-4, it could fly (and turn) at a *much slower speed.* U.S. pilots knew better than to try to out turn the Zero. (This writer had the honor of flying the F4U-5N Corsair during an 8-month carrier deployment in the Far East in 1954. Needless to say, no Zeros were encountered at that late date.)

A couple of things were neglected in this discussion of the turn. The tail-down force was considered to be zero, which it certainly would not be in a turn (you could expect it to increase appreciably in steeper turns). And because of the increased angle of attack in the turn, thrust has components acting inward (helping centripetal force) and upward. However, putting all this into an illustration might result in a pretty confusing situation.

Figure 3-20 shows the power-required curves for an airplane in straight and level flight and in a 30°-banked constant-altitude turn. Note that it is quite similar to Figures 2-48, 7-3, and 7-5, since the airplane does "weigh" more in the turn.

As was mentioned, the turns in this chapter have been balanced; Figure 3-21 takes a look at the forces acting on the slip indicator in skidding and slipping turns.

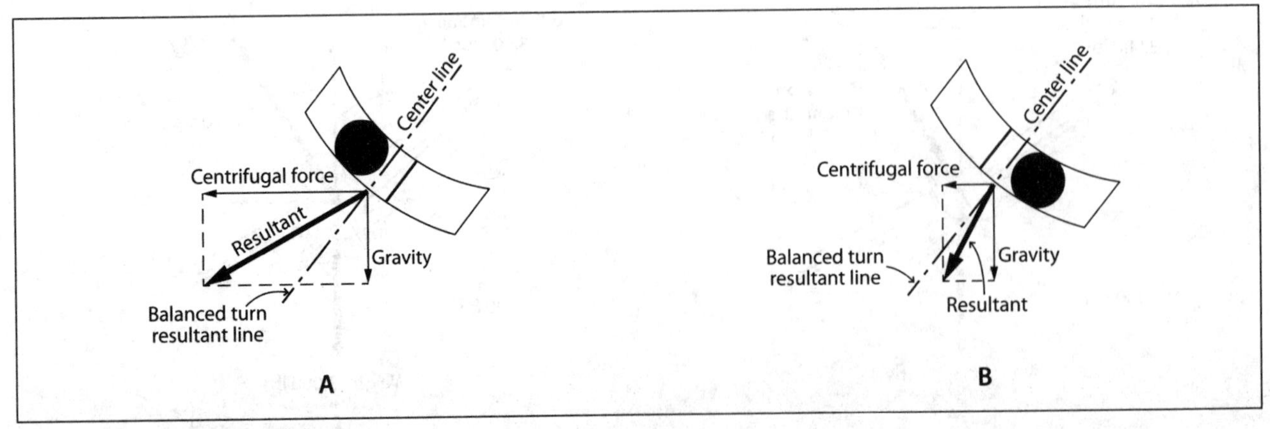

Figure 3-21. The forces acting on the slip indicator in a skidding and a slipping right turn. Remember that centrifugal force is only an apparent force and is a popular, *not* a physics, term.

Another Look at the Turn

Interestingly enough, the usual idea is to think of the balanced, constant-rate, level turn as a "static" condition even though the nose is moving around the horizon and g's are being pulled. In a wings-level turn (assuming a bank of, say, 0.001° and also that the longitudinal axis is level with the horizon), a steeper bank would require pulling the nose up and spoiling this initial concept.

During a banked, level turn, the airplane is actually rotating about the vertical (Z) axis *and* the lateral (Y) axis. Take two exaggerated examples. In a "flat" (no-bank), constant-altitude turn, the airplane is rotating only around the vertical axis (yaw). In a 90°-banked, nose-level turn, the airplane would be rotating (pitching) only about the lateral (Y) axis (Figure 3-22).

In the foregoing discussion the notation was made that those were nose-level turns. (Nothing was mentioned about maintaining altitude—which would be a chore in the 90°-banked turn.)

Take a look at a chandelle: It's a maximum performance climbing turn with 180° change in direction. The maneuver requires that the last 90° of turn has a constant (fairly high) nose position and the maneuver ends with the airplane just above stall. One fallacy in describing a chandelle is that it is "a loop on an inclined plane." Not so—the nose does not rise perpendicularly to the wingspan as would be the case of a loop. (A loop, straight up or inclined, is movement *only* around the lateral axis, or pitch only; the nose movement and path of the airplane are as shown in Figure 3-23.)

Assume that a bank of 30° is set at the beginning of the chandelle and the stick or control wheel is brought straight back; the bank will increase to about 45°—as 90° of turn is reached because the airplane's pitch is not changing as much as the turn change (Figure 3-23C).

You can take a model airplane and see how under some circumstances and attitudes movement around one axis can affect the attitude of the airplane about one or both of the others.

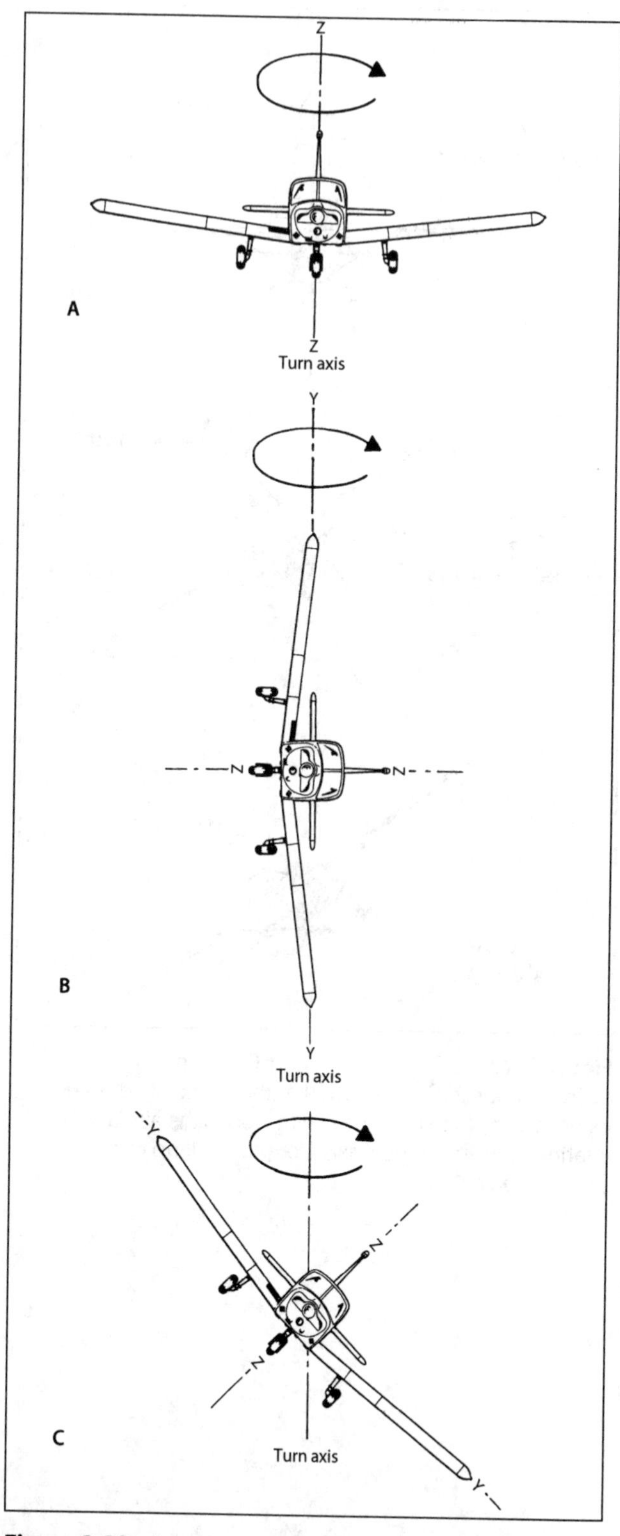

Figure 3-22. An exaggerated look at constant-altitude turns. **A.** The skidding, wings-level turn; the airplane is rotating only about the vertical (Z) axis; yaw. **B.** The 90°-banked, nose-level turn; the airplane is rotating only about the lateral (Y) axis; pitch. **C.** A 45°-banked, nose-level turn; the airplane is rotating equally about the Y and Z axes, but neither of the two is the turn axis. The ratio of rotation about the Y and Z axes depends on the bank angle. (Don't bank 90° in a normal category airplane.)

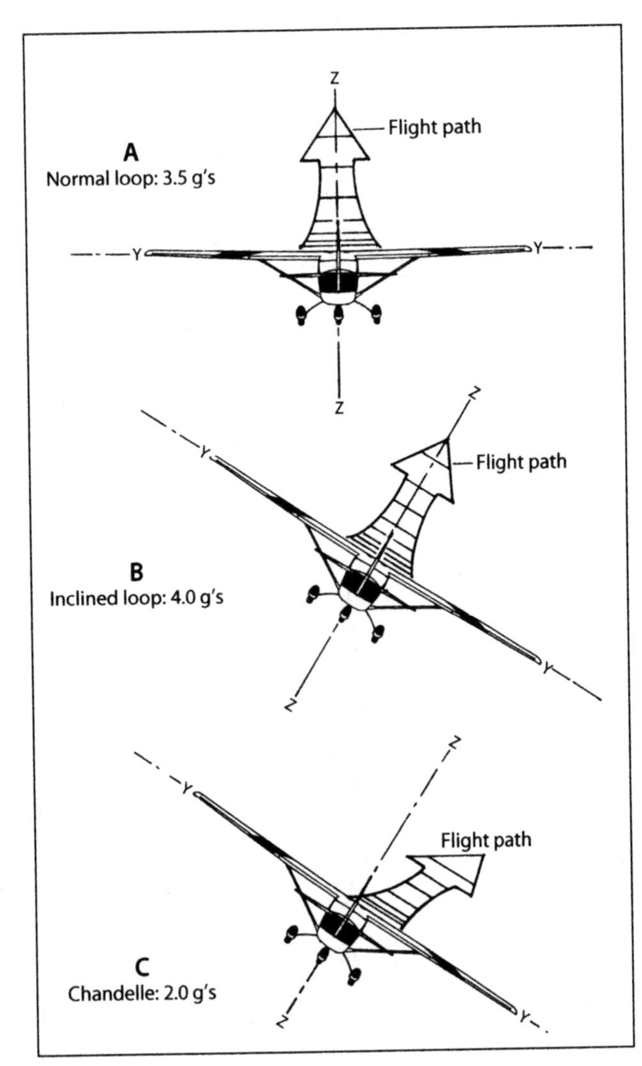

Figure 3-23. A. The "normal" loop. **B.** The inclined loop. **C.** The chandelle. You can see that the chandelle does not follow the inclined loop idea. In the loops the airplane is rotating only about the Y axis. Note the pull-up forces in each maneuver.

Summary

There is a lot of misunderstanding concerning the actions of the Four Forces in various maneuvers, and the most common one is that "excess lift" is what makes the airplane climb. This is not to deny that it will climb when an excess lift exists, but in that case acceleration forces, or g's, will be exerted. Suppose you are flying along at cruise and suddenly exert back pressure on the wheel or stick. Assuming that you didn't overdo it and the wings are still with you, the airplane will *accelerate* upward (and then assume a normal steady-state climb if that's what you wanted). When you exerted back pressure the up force (lift) was greater than the down forces (weight, etc.) at that time—you increased the angle of attack almost instantly and the airplane was still at the cruise speed so the dynamic pressure q, which is $(\rho/2)V^2$, was still of the same high value.

The measurement of positive g's is the lift-to-weight ratio, and at the instant of rotation lift may be increased radically. Of course, as you know, an increase in angle of attack (coefficient of lift) means an increase in drag (induced), and lift will tend to reassume its old value, depending on the new flight path. If you had wanted to climb at a certain airspeed (with a certain angle and rate of climb resulting) lift would soon settle down to the required value. In flying the airplane, you, as a pilot, decide what the airplane must do and keep this requirement by using power, the airspeed, and/or altimeter. When you have established a steady-state condition such as a steady climb or glide or straight and level flight, the forces settle down of their own accord. *You* balance the forces automatically by setting up a steady-state condition. If the up forces (working toward the ceiling of the airplane cabin) are greater than the down forces (working toward the floor) you feel positive g's and feel heavier in the seat; this is the effect in a normal level turn, the steeper the turn the greater the effect.

Probably a large number of stall-type accidents have occurred because the pilot unconsciously thought in terms of "increasing the lift" to climb over an obstacle.

Another idea not often considered is that a tail-down force exists for the majority of airplanes throughout most of the range of flight speeds and loadings. Most laymen think that the "little wing back there is always helping to hold the airplane up." In one sense perhaps it is, in that it is required for good stability, which is important to flight.

You can prove that a tail-down force exists by a very simple experiment. In Chapter 2 the drawings showed that the wing tip vortices curled over the tip toward the low pressure or "lifting" (top) side of the wing. Knowing this to be the case, you can "see" this wing tip vortex action by taping a ribbon or string (with a light plastic funnel on the free end) to each wing tip and to the tip of each stabilizer. The rotation of the string will be as shown in Figure 3-24.

Note in Figure 3-24 that the string-funnel combination is rotating in the opposite direction at the stabilizer tips than it is at the wings—the low pressure or "lifting" side is on the bottom—so a tail-down force exists.

You need only to do one wing and stabilizer tip to see the action. Check the actions of the strings at cruise and watch the wing tip as the airplane is slowed (the angle of attack or C_L is increased). You can readily see that vortex strength increases with a decrease in speed (increase in C_L).

By now you have likely figured that the airplane is actually flown by the thrust-to-drag relationship and that little is done in the way of controlling lift in normal 1-g flight. By setting up a steady-state condition, lift takes care of itself and actually varies very little in wings-level climbs and glides and straight and level flight. *Keep it in mind.*

From the turn theory in this chapter, you can note some information that could be of practical value. The radius of the turn is a function of the velocity squared, $R = (f)V^2$, for a given bank angle. If you get into marginal VFR weather with poor visibilities in strange territory, slow the airplane up so that you can make small-radius turns if necessary to avoid an obstruction such as a mountain or TV tower that suddenly looms up out of the mist. (Don't stall.) *Don't go* boring along at low altitudes in low visibilities at full cruise speed. (Better yet, preplan so that you avoid such a possibility.)

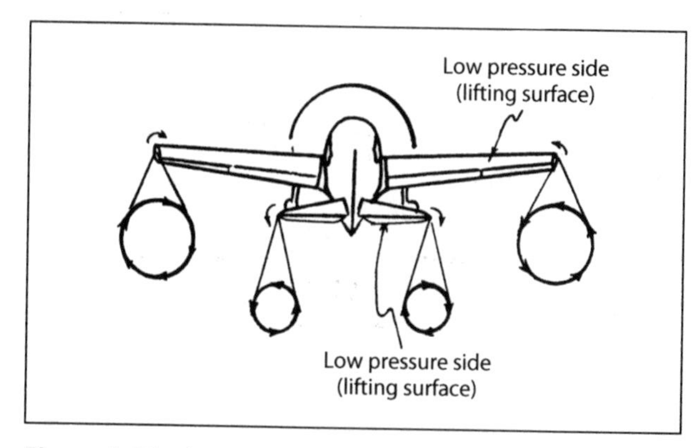

Figure 3-24. An experiment for checking if a tail-down force exists.

4

The Airplane Instruments

Flight Instruments and Airplane Performance

The earlier chapters were somewhat theoretical in their approach to airplane performance and were necessary for background in preparation for this and the following chapters in Part 1.

In order to get the most from your airplane you must have a good understanding of its instruments and know what affects their operation. Whether you plan to go on to the commercial certificate or to continue to fly for personal business or pleasure, pride in your flying ability will cause you to want to learn more about your airplane.

There are certain relationships between the density, temperature, and pressure of the atmosphere. An airplane's performance depends on the density-altitude, and density-altitude has an interlocking relationship with temperature and pressure. For instance, cold air is denser than warm air—so a *decrease* in temperature (if the pressure is not changed) means an *increase* in density. If the pressure is *increased* (assuming no change in temperature), the density is *increased* (more particles of air compressed into the same volume). This chapter on instruments is a review, but it may introduce information that you didn't run into during your study and training for the private certificate.

Equation of State

For those interested in the mathematics, the equation of state explains the exact relationships between the three variables: temperature, pressure, and density.

$$\rho = \frac{P}{1{,}716 T_R}$$

This form of the equation of state says that the air density (ρ, or "rho"), in slugs per cubic foot, equals the pressure (P), in pounds per square foot (psf), divided by 1,716 times the temperature (T), in degrees Rankine.

The figure 1,716 is a constant number derived from the product of the constant for air (53.3) and the acceleration of gravity (32.2).

A slug is a unit of mass, as was mentioned in Chapter 2. The mass of an object in slugs may be found by dividing the weight by the acceleration of gravity, 32.16 feet per second (fps) per second; hence a 161-lb man has a mass of 5 slugs (rounded off) (161/32.16 = 5).

The temperature in degrees Rankine may be found by adding 460° to the Fahrenheit reading; for a standard sea level day the temperature is 59°F or 519° Rankine.

The density at sea level on a standard day may be found as follows: ρ (rho, air density) = 2,116 (sea level pressure, psf)/(1,716 × 519), or ρ = 0.002378 slugs per cubic foot. Or, checking for pressure, pressure= density × temperature × 1,716.

The equation of state and the symbols for density, pressure, and temperature will be used throughout the book.

The three factors directly affect each other. If you know your pressure altitude and the temperature, the density-altitude can be found with a graph or computer.

A Review of Pressure Flight Instruments

As the name implies, these instruments operate because of air pressure or air pressure changes.

Airspeed Indicator

The airspeed indicator is nothing more than a specialized air pressure gage. The airspeed system comprises the pitot and static tubes and the airspeed indicator instrument. An airplane moving through the air creates its own relative wind. This relative wind exerts a ram pressure in the pitot tube where its effects are passed on into a diaphragm linked to an indicating hand (Figure 4-1).

This relative wind force is calibrated in miles per hour, or knots, rather than pounds per square foot of pressure. The static tube acts as a neutralizer of the static pressure around the airplane and within the instrument, so that *only* the dynamic pressure is measured. For some planes the pitot and static tube inlets are together, but for greater accuracy, the static tube opening is placed at some point on the airplane where the most accurate measurement of the actual outside air static pressure is found. A usual spot is on the side of the fuselage somewhere between the wing and stabilizer. No doubt you've noticed these static pressure sources, accompanied by a sign, "Keep this hole free of dirt." These points are selected as being the places where the static pressure is least affected by the airflow about the airplane. It is difficult to find a spot on the airplane entirely free of static pressure error—and so the term *position error.* The proper placing of the static tube opening to minimize this error is responsible for more than a few ulcers in aircraft manufacturing. In

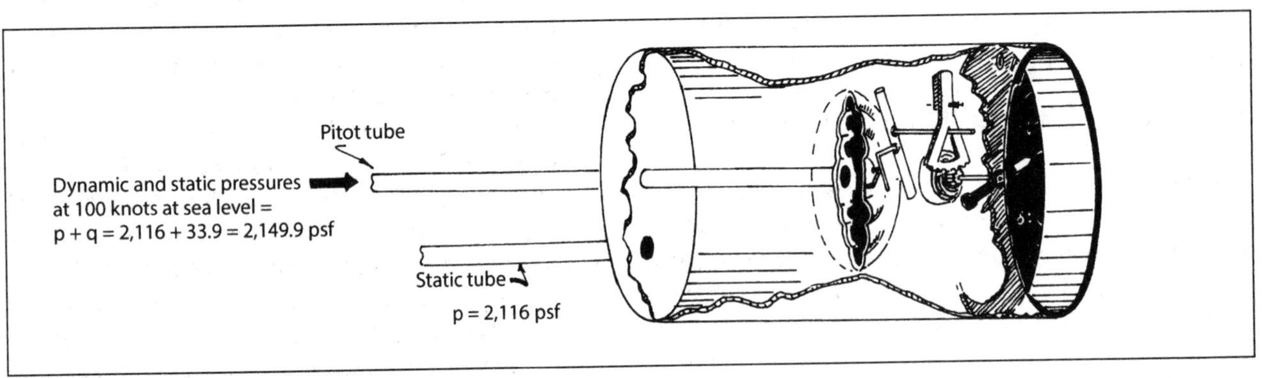

Figure 4-1. Airspeed indicator. The combination of the static and dynamic pressures in the pitot tube is labeled *total pressure,* or $P_T = p + q$.

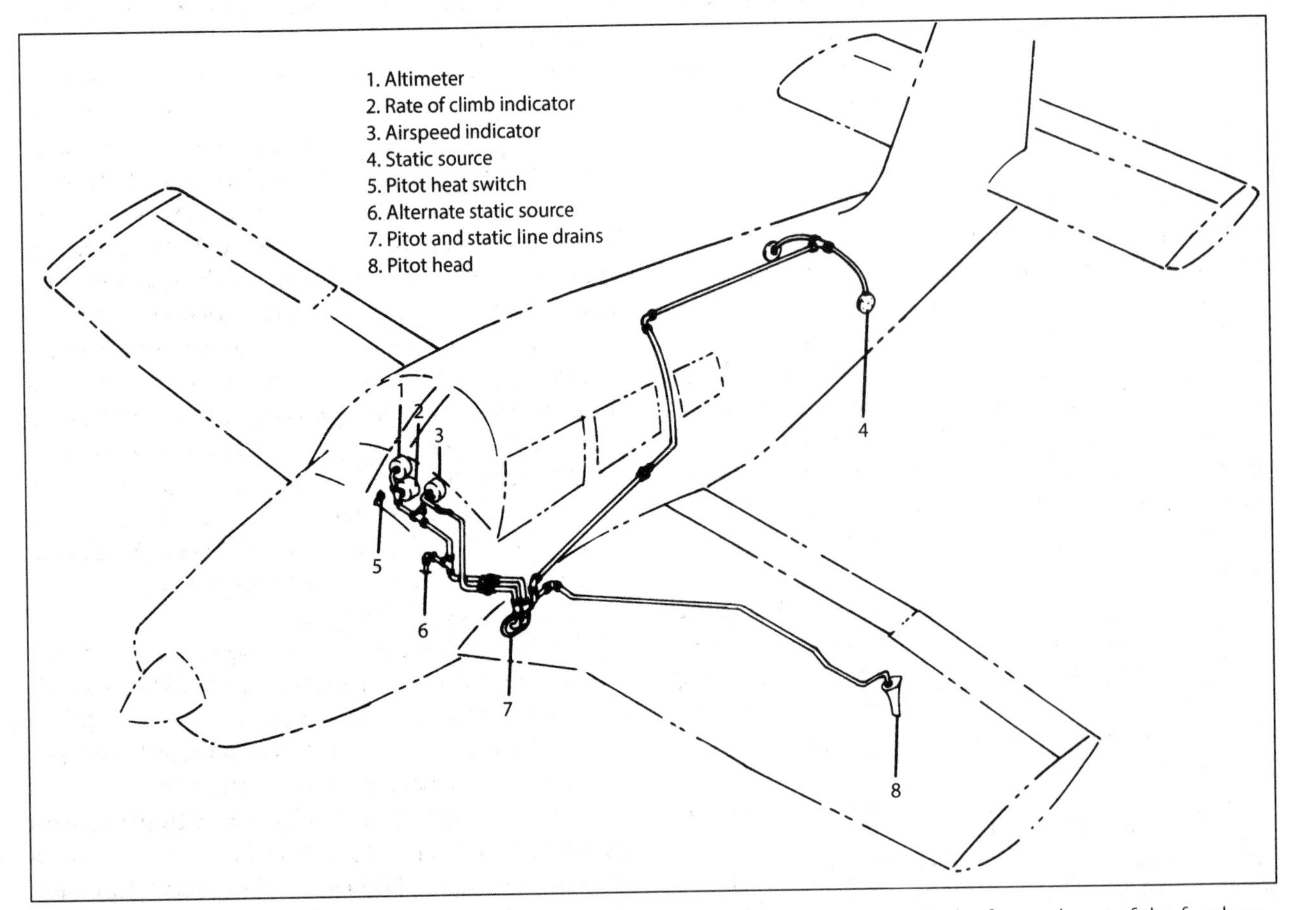

Figure 4-2. A pitot/static system for a four-place airplane. Others may have static sources in the forward part of the fuselage just aft of the engine compartment.

addition to the position error in the system, there is usually some error in the airspeed indicator instrument itself. This *instrument error* is another factor to contend with in airspeed calibration (Figure 4-2).

The pitot tube position is also important. It must be placed at a point where the actual relative wind is measured, free from any interfering aerodynamic effects. A particularly bad place would be just above the wing where the air velocity is greater than the free stream velocity.

Error is introduced into the airspeed indicator at high angles of attack or in a skid. You've seen this when practicing stalls. The airplane had a stall speed of 50 K according to the POH, yet there you were, still flying (though nearly stalled) with the airspeed indicator showing 40 K (or even zero). It wasn't because of your skill that you were able to fly the airplane at this lower speed—the angle of the airplane to the airstream introduced an error. While at first the pitot tube, being at a fairly high angle of attack, seems to be the culprit, this is not the case. For the airplane that stalls at the usual 15° to 20° angle of attack, this effect is small, although for STOL-type airplanes it could be a real factor in airspeed error. Flight test airplanes use an elaborate extended boom with a swivel pitot head, which results in much greater accuracy at high angles of attack. This is obviously not practical in cost or weight for normal lightplane installation. The *major* source of error, however, is the static system; the pitot tube contributes a minor amount.

So, static pressure error can also be introduced at angles of attack or angles of yaw, the amount of error depending on the location of the static opening; this will be covered again a little later.

The dynamic pressure measured by the airspeed indicator is called "q" (the letter q) and has the designation $(\rho/2)V^2$, as indicated earlier. You will notice that dynamic pressure is a part of the lift and drag equations. This *dynamic pressure*, which is one-half the *air density* (slugs per cubic foot) *times* the *true air velocity* (feet per second squared), is pressure in *pounds per square foot.*

At sea level on a standard day, at a speed of 100 K (169 fps), q would be $0.002378 \times (169)^2/2 = 33.9$ psf. The lightplane airplane airspeed indicator is calibrated for standard sea level conditions with a temperature of 15°C or 59°F and a pressure of 29.92 inches of mercury, or 2,116 psf.

The perfect airspeed indicator would work as follows:

Pitot tube measures dynamic and static pressure.

Static tube equalizes static pressure or "subtracts" it from the pitot tube reading.

Airspeed indicator indicates dynamic pressure only. So the airspeed indicator only measures the dynamic pressure, which is a combination of density and airstream velocity (squared). As altitude increases, the air density decreases so that an airplane indicating 100 K (or 33.9 psf dynamic pressure) at 10,000 ft actually has a higher TAS than the airplane at sea level *indicating* the same dynamic pressure (airspeed).

This airspeed correction for density change can be worked on your computer, but a good rule of thumb is to add 2% per 1,000 feet to the indicated airspeed. A plane with a calibrated airspeed of 100 K at 10,000 feet density-altitude will have a TAS close to 120 K. (By computer it's found to be 116 K.)

There are airspeed indicators today that correct for TAS; the TAS can be read directly off the dial. One type has a setup where the pilot adjusts the dial to compensate for altitude and the temperature effects (density-altitude) and the needle indicates the TAS in the cruising range. Another more expensive instrument does this automatically for certain speeds well above stall or approach speeds. The reason for not having corrections at lower speeds is that the pilot might fly by *true airspeed* and get into trouble landing at airports of high elevation and/or high temperatures. Perhaps an explanation is in order.

An airplane will stall at the same indicated (or calibrated) airspeed regardless of its altitude or the temperature (all other things such as weight, angle of bank, etc., being equal). An airplane that stalls at an indicated 50 K at sea level will stall at an indicated 50 K at a density-altitude of 10,000 feet because the airspeed indicator measures q and it still takes the same amount of q to support the airplane. However, the *true airspeed* at 10,000 feet would be approximately 60 K. If you were flying by a TAS instrument, you might get a shock when the plane dropped out from under you at an airspeed 10 K higher than you expected (it always stalls at 50 K down at sea level—what gives?). Of course, the airspeed indicator isn't likely to be accurate at the speeds close to the stall anyway, but you might not give yourself enough leeway in the approach in this case. (These are unaccelerated stalls.)

Several terms are used in talking about airspeed:

Indicated airspeed (IAS)—the airspeed as read off the standard airspeed indicator.

Calibrated airspeed (CAS)—indicated airspeed corrected for instrument and position error.

Equivalent airspeed (EAS)—calibrated airspeed corrected for compressibility effects.

True airspeed (TAS)—equivalent airspeed corrected for density effects.

Some Airspeed Theory

Notes on Equivalent Airspeed

Equivalent airspeed (EAS) is the "correct" calibrated airspeed, and you can't go wrong by using the term in all of your hangar flying discussions for *corrected* indicated airspeed. Calibrated is fine for lower airspeeds and lower altitudes.

EAS, the actual dynamic pressure acting on the airframe, is used to get a correct picture of stresses on the airplane or to work out TAS problems if compressibility error is a factor. Figure 4-3 is an exaggerated example of CAS versus EAS for sea level, 5,000-ft and 10,000-ft pressure altitudes.

The point is that CAS is equal to, *or greater than*, EAS; the difference becomes greater with an increase in altitude and airspeed. The speed of sound decreases with altitude (and the temperature decrease), and as the airplane's airspeed increases, the compressibility "edge" is reached. One way it has been explained is that as the airplane gets into compressibility effects, the *static pressure in the pitot tube* (and within the diaphragm as shown in Figure 4-1) increases, causing the indicated- and calibrated-airspeeds to read erroneously high. A detailed correction table for a number of altitudes and airspeeds is available to pilots of higher-performance airplanes. (One table works for *all* airplanes for various airspeeds and pressure altitudes.)

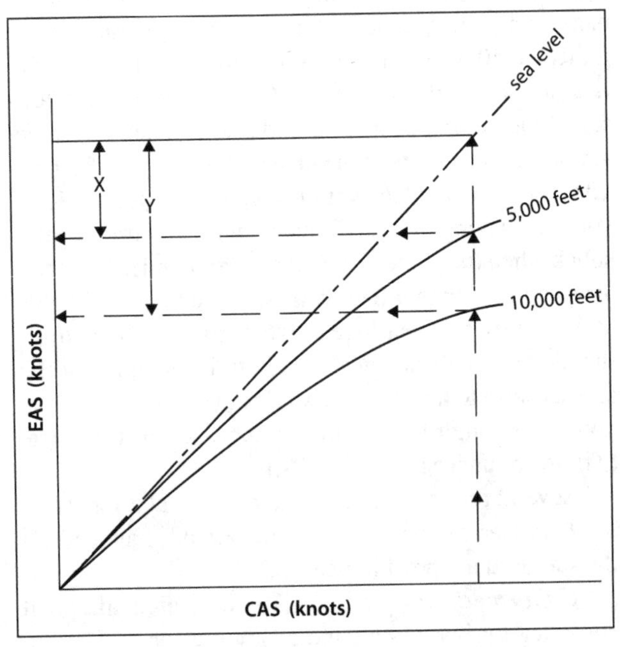

Figure 4-3. CAS versus EAS. At sea level and less than 250 K, EAS and CAS are equal. At higher speeds and altitudes, EAS is less. The differences at 5,000 feet and 10,000 feet are noted by X and Y respectively.

EAS, then, is the indicated airspeed corrected for instrument and position error (which gives CAS), and CAS is then corrected for compressibility effects.

One point about compressibility effects—it's assumed by a lot of people that the airplane itself has to be flying right at the speed of sound for the phenomenon to occur. However, curved parts of the airplane (canopy, wing, etc.) have the relative wind moving past them at near sonic velocities because of Bernoulli's theorem, even though the airplane's TAS is significantly lower than the transonic range. Some WW II fighters began to nibble at the edges of compressibility because of this factor, but stories of propeller fighters diving to supersonic speeds were exaggerated. Some late and post-WW II prop fighters had speed brakes to use if compressibility problems were encountered.

True Airspeed

To find TAS or to establish a performance relationship between altitudes, engineers use the density ratio σ (sigma), which is the ratio between the air density at some altitude (ρ_a) and at sea level (ρ_o):

$$\sigma = \frac{\rho_a}{\rho_o}$$

The *true airspeed* (V) portion of the dynamic pressure, or $(\rho/2)V^2$, is a function of the *square root* of the ratio of densities, or $V = f\sqrt{\rho_a/\rho_o}$, or $V = f\sqrt{\sigma}$, the relationship of dynamic pressure for a given CAS is

$$\left(\frac{\rho_a}{2}\right)V_a^2 = \left(\frac{\rho_o}{2}\right)V_o^2$$

To repeat, a CAS of 100 K at sea level is the same dynamic pressure as a CAS of 100 K at 10,000 feet; the airspeed indicator can't determine which factors (density or velocity) are making the diaphragm expand to register the same CAS (V_{cal}) in both instances. To solve for TAS (V_a) at, say, 10,000 feet you could use the square root of the density ratio. (The 2's can be eliminated since there's one on each side of the equation.)

$$V_a^2 = \frac{V_o^2}{\left(\frac{\rho_a}{\rho_o}\right)} = \frac{V_o^2}{\sigma}; \quad V_a = \frac{V_o}{\sqrt{\sigma}}$$

$$\text{TAS} = \frac{\text{CAS (or EAS)}}{\sqrt{\text{density ratio}}} = \frac{\text{CAS}}{\sqrt{\sigma}}$$

$$V_{T10} = \frac{V_{cal}}{\sqrt{\sigma}}$$

See Figure 4-4 for a standard atmosphere chart. At 10,000 feet ρ is 0.001756; at sea level it's 0.002378, so using your calculator, or working it out in longhand and giving V_{cal} a universal value of 1:

$$V_{T10} = \frac{V_{cal}}{\sqrt{\frac{0.001756}{0.002378}}} = \frac{V_{cal}}{0.85933} = \frac{1}{0.85933} = 1.16369$$

The TAS at 10,000 feet is about 16% more than, or 1.164 times, that at sea level for the same calibrated (or better yet, equivalent) airspeed. A CAS of 100 K would give a TAS of about 116 K, as noted earlier.

For another problem, find the TAS for an airplane with a calibrated (equivalent) airspeed of *186 K* at a standard altitude of 17,000 feet. The value of ρ at sea level is (still) 0.002378, and at 17,000 feet it's 0.001401 (Figure 4-4). So the CAS (EAS) is divided by the square root of the ratio of the two densities. Under normal circumstances you'll have no problem figuring out that the square root of the ratio would be *less* than 1 because the TAS will *normally* be higher than the CAS or EAS (more about the word *normally* a little later). So

$V_T = \frac{V_{cal}}{\sqrt{\sigma}}$, the divisor of the CAS is

$$\sqrt{\frac{0.001401}{0.002378}}, \text{ or } \sqrt{\frac{1401}{2378}} = \sqrt{0.589} = 0.7675$$

(rounded off)

The TAS = 186/0.7675 = 242 K. Your computer does this for you.

The earlier comment about TAS *normally* being greater than CAS or EAS is correct, but in an unusual situation where the airplane is flying in an air density greater than sea level, the TAS may be less than CAS or EAS. Suppose you are flying just off the surface of the Dead Sea in standard conditions. Because the Dead Sea is below mean sea level, the airspeed indicator could have a density error "the wrong way." In extremely cold conditions at lower altitudes (but still above sea level), the density could be well above standard so that things would be the reverse of normal. The airspeed indicators used for lower speeds and altitudes (say, below 250 K and below 10,000 feet) are set up on the base using sea level density, and you must correct for variations of the density *either way* from sea level. In usual (above sea level) flying, the density at the altitude being flown is always less than the density at sea level, so the usual correction is made (TAS greater than CAS or EAS).

STANDARD ATMOSPHERE CHART

Altitude (ft)	Pressure (in. Hg)	Pressure (psi)	Temp (°C)	Temp (°F)	Density-slugs per cubic foot
0	29.92	2116.22	15.0	59.0	.002378
1,000	28.86	2040.85	13.0	55.4	.002309
2,000	27.82	1967.68	11.0	51.9	.002242
3,000	26.82	1896.64	9.1	48.3	.002176
4,000	25.84	1827.69	7.1	44.7	.002112
5,000	24.89	1760.79	5.1	41.2	.002049
6,000	23.98	1695.89	3.1	37.6	.001988
7,000	23.09	1632.93	1.1	34.0	.001928
8,000	22.22	1571.88	–0.9	30.5	.001869
9,000	21.38	1512.70	–2.8	26.9	.001812
10,000	20.57	1455.33	–4.8	23.3	.001756
11,000	19.79	1399.73	–6.8	19.8	.001701
12,000	19.02	1345.87	–8.8	16.2	.001648
13,000	18.29	1293.70	–10.8	12.6	.001596
14,000	17.57	1243.18	–12.7	9.1	.001545
15,000	16.88	1194.27	–14.7	5:5	.001496
16,000	16.21	1146.92	–16.7	1.9	.001448
17,000	15.56	1101.11	–18.7	–1.6	.001401
18,000	14.94	1056.80	–20.7	–5.2	.001355
19,000	14.33	1013.93	–22.6	–8.8	.001310
20,000	13.74	972.49	–24.6	–12.3	.001267

Figure 4-4. Standard atmosphere chart.

Mach and Mach Number

Ernst Mach (1838-1916), an Austrian physicist, published works on ballistics and fast-moving bodies in gases in the late 1870s and the 1880s. His major work preceded even the advent of aviation, much less transonic and supersonic flight, but it could be that he was getting ready for the airplane. (Many people also believe that the Federal Aviation Administration was established in 1803, a hundred years early, just in case somebody should ever invent a flying machine." It's not true about the FAA, but Mach's studies were ready when higher-speed flight was attained.)

The term *Mach number* is the ratio of the velocity of a body in a gas to the speed of sound in that gas. As a pilot, you are interested in the speed of sound in air; it would be different in other gases and other mediums.

The speed of sound in air, 661 K at standard sea level, decreases with altitude (temperature), becoming 584 K at 36,000 feet where the temperature stabilizes for another 30,000 feet—at roughly -69°F.

An equation for finding the speed of sound (fps) is $49.1\sqrt{T_R}$ (49.1 times the square root of the temperature in degrees Rankine, which was discussed at the beginning of this chapter). You'd add 460° to the temperature (Fahrenheit) and take the square root of the sum. For instance, standard temperature at sea level is 59°F; 460 + 59 = 519°F. The speed of sound at sea level is $49.1\sqrt{519}$ = 1,118 fps, or 661 K.

Mach Meter

The Mach meter is designed to give the pilot the ratio of the airplane's airspeed to that of the speed of sound for both subsonic and supersonic flight (with corrections for the usual airspeed indicator problems of position and instrument errors). It has bellows to correct for static pressure and total and static pressure differences and reads this ratio at all altitudes and speeds.

More About Airspeed Errors

Starting out with IAS, which, as you've heard since you started flying, is what the instrument indicates, you may manipulate the system to get some far-off readings. One less than scrupulous used-airplane seller some years ago had a plastic ring set up around the pitot/static head of an airplane so that it would indicate higher airspeeds than could be explained by natural law. The lightplane, which at cruise normally would indicate about 90 mph, was suddenly converted into a 120-mph bombshell. The new owner was proud to have the hottest Buzzwind Two in the area, since it cruised 30 mph faster than the others and required much more pilot skill because it also landed at about 75 mph, compared with 45 mph for run-of-the-mill models. The seller got the money and the new owner the prestige (temporarily at least).

A *particular* airspeed indicator may indicate wrong because somebody dropped it on the way to installing it in the airplane, but this is an unusual situation.

14 CFR Part 23 *(Airworthiness Standards: Normal, Utility and Acrobatic Category Airplanes)* sets up the following maximum allowable system error for the manufacturer:

> **§23.1323 Airspeed indicating system.**
>
> (a) Each airspeed indicating instrument must be calibrated to indicate true airspeed (at sea level with a standard atmosphere) with a minimum practicable instrument calibration error when the corresponding pitot and static pressures are applied.
>
> (b) Each airspeed system must be calibrated in flight to determine the system error. The system error, including position error, but excluding the airspeed indicator instrument calibration error, may not exceed three percent of the calibrated airspeed or five knots, whichever is greater, throughout the following speed ranges:
>
> (1) $1.3V_{S1}$ to V_{MO}/M_{MO} or V_{NE}, whichever is appropriate with flaps retracted.
>
> (2) $1.3V_{S1}$ to V_{FE} with flaps extended.

(V_{MO}/M_{MO}, the Maximum Operating limit or Mach speed, is associated with higher-speed aircraft.)

The airspeed correction tables in the POH (Figure 4.5) assume that all the instruments in the various airplanes have the same problems and that no individual needles were bent, etc. Figure 4-5 is for the normal static system and doesn't include the changes associated with use of alternate air sources (to be covered later). (Airplanes manufactured as 1975 models or earlier have the airspeed indicator markings as calibrated airspeed and usually in *mph.*)

To get CAS, corrections must be made for instrument and position error; if, for instance, you aren't sure of the accuracy of your airspeed indicator, you can fly the airplane between two points a known distance apart and work out your own correction table for instrument and system error. For example, to calibrate the airplane's airspeed system, it would be nice to have a convenient straight railroad track with white-painted ties at each end of the run (Figure 4-6).

In books, the distances are always easy to make even. "Your" track, however, could be 1.79 (or 2.87, etc.) miles long so you have to set up a correction factor. Picking a calm, early morning period and taking along an observer with a stopwatch, you would fly the route both ways at a low altitude at each airspeed desired. You might end up with a table like that in Figure 4-7.

The point is that in calm conditions, groundspeed (GS) equals TAS, and since you have set your airplane's well-calibrated altimeter to 29.92, you're flying a known pressure altitude. With this, combined with the outside air temperature at that altitude read from

AIRSPEED INDICATOR MARKINGS

MARKING	KIAS VALUE OR RANGE	SIGNIFICANCE
White Arc	42 - 85	Full Flap Operating Range. Lower limit is maximum weight V_{S_O} in landing configuration. Upper limit is maximum speed permissible with flaps fully extended.
Green Arc	47 - 107	Normal Operating Range. Lower limit is maximum weight V_S at most forward C.G. with flaps retracted. Upper limit is maximum structural cruising speed.
Yellow Arc	107 - 141	Operations must be conducted with caution and only in smooth air.
Red Line	141	Maximum speed for all operations.

AIRSPEED CORRECTION TABLE

(Flaps Up)

IAS	40	50	60	70	80	90	100	110	120	130	140
CAS	51	57	65	73	82	91	100	109	118	127	136

(Flaps Down)

IAS	40	50	60	70	80	90	100				
CAS	49	55	63	72	81	89	98				

Figure 4-5. Airspeed indicator markings and correction table (normal source).

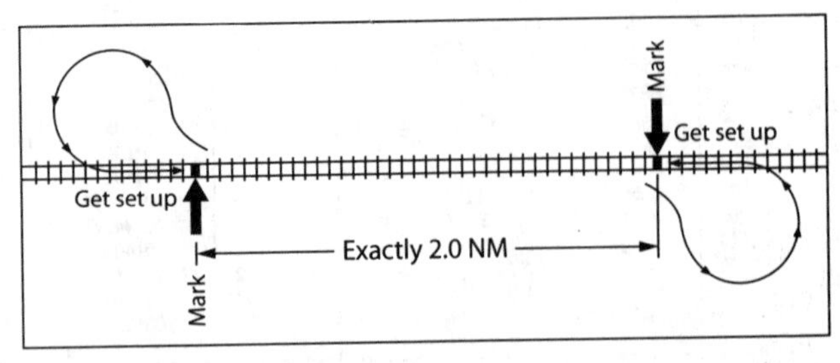

Figure 4-6. Using a conveniently located railroad track or other straight reference, get set up and then start and stop the timing at the tick marks.

the well-calibrated outside air temperature (OAT) gage on board, you can find density-altitude and work back from TAS (GS) to CAS. So for each IAS picked, you come up with a number of indicated and calibrated airspeeds to set up a table like that found in a POH (Figure 4-8).

GPS is a useful aid for calibrating airspeeds (rather than a railroad track).

In flying the airspeed calibration, if there is a crosswind you don't correct for drift but maintain a heading parallel to the railroad track (Figure 4-9). The time start would be made when the reference point(s) is directly off the wingtip. The error is negligible for the distance flown because the airplane is flying within the air mass and doesn't "know" it's drifting.

There is some argument as to whether headwind and tailwind components cause error to creep in. By picking the calmest conditions possible, any error introduced is minimized, but look at an exaggerated example. If flying the 2-mile route in *no-wind* conditions requires 60 seconds for each leg, the GS and TAS would be 120 K; the average for the two legs would be (120 + 120)/2 = 120 K.

Suppose there is a 30-K steady direct headwind on one leg and a 30-K direct tailwind on the other. The time required to fly the 2-mile leg in the headwind condition would be at 90 K, or 80 seconds. With a 30-K tailwind the stopwatch time for that distance would be at 150 K and would take 48 seconds. Comparing:

Total time to go 4 miles (no wind) = 120 seconds, or GS = 120K

Total time to go 4 miles (30-K wind) = 128 seconds; 128/4 = 32 seconds per NM, or 112.5 K.

Airspeed calibration shouldn't be done in such conditions and any error would be much smaller as conditions approach calm, but the principle should be considered.

As noted earlier, flight test airplanes use an extended boom to get more accurate pitot (total pressure) and static pressure readings. This is fine for accuracy but would be too expensive for use on all airplanes.

Another one of the several methods for calibrating airspeeds is the *pacer method*, in which the airplane to be tested is "paced" at various indicated airspeeds by an airplane with a corrected airspeed system.

Sometimes pilots ask if each airplane manufactured is flown to the design dive speed (V_D—see Chapter 11), or has the airspeed indicator calibrated as just discussed, or has stability and control testing done. The answer is *no*. The prototype and test bed airplanes come up with the numbers and manufacturing tolerances that apply to all the airplanes that are manufactured later. Figure 4-10 is actual airspeed calibration for a normal static source given in a POH.

Ground effect, or rather an airplane's proximity to the ground, can affect an airspeed system so that some POHs may have an additional correction graph or table for the takeoff run ("rotation at 90 K IAS = 94 K CAS"). The airplane in Figure 4-10 has an alternate air source that supplies static pressure from inside the cabin if it's suspected that the normal static source (a

FLAPS UP

PA 1500′ OAT 10°C CAS = TAS x $\sqrt{\sigma}$

RUN	IAS-Knots	TIME-Sec	GS = TAS	AVER. TAS	CAS	
EAST	60	110	65	—	—	
WEST	60	108	67	66	65	
2 E	70	96	75	—	—	
W	70	98	74	74	73	
3 E	80	87	83	—	—	
W	80	88	82	82	81	
4 E	90	79	91	—	—	
W	90	79	91	91	90	
5 E	100	72	100	—	—	
W	100	73	99	99	97	RERUN
6 E	110	66	110	—	—	
W	110	66	110	110	108	
7 E	120	60	120	—	—	
W	120	60	120	120	118	
8 E	130	55	130	—	—	
W	130	55	130	130	128	
9 E	140	52	137	—	—	
W	140	52	137	137	135	
10 E	150	49	147	—	—	
W	150	49	147	147	145	

Figure 4-7. A table made up from the runs in Figure 4-6 (flaps up).

FLAPS UP

KIAS	60	70	80	90	100	110	120	130	140	150
KCAS	65	73	81	90	97	108	118	128	135	145

Figure 4-8. A correction card made for the airplane in Figures 4-6 and 4-7.

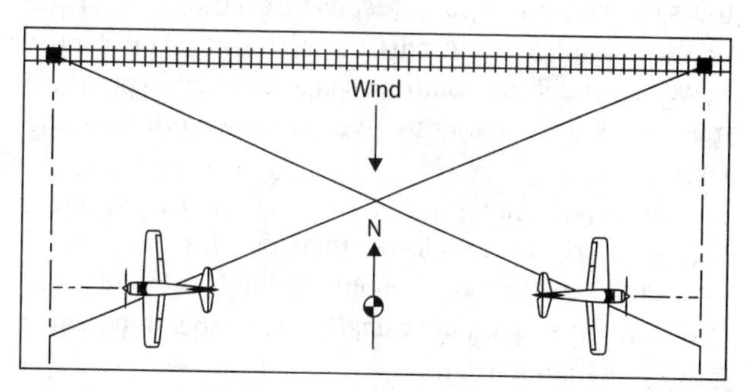

Figure 4-9. Flight path in a crosswind.

AIRSPEED CALIBRATION
NORMAL STATIC SOURCE

CONDITIONS:
Power required for level flight or maximum power during descent.

FLAPS UP												
KIAS	50	60	70	80	90	100	110	120	130	140	150	160
KCAS	55	63	71	80	89	99	108	118	128	138	147	157
FLAPS 10°												
KIAS	40	50	60	70	80	90	100	110	120	130	---	---
KCAS	50	54	62	71	81	91	100	110	120	130	---	---
FLAPS 30°												
KIAS	40	50	60	70	80	90	100	---	---	---	---	---
KCAS	47	54	62	71	81	90	101	---	---	---	---	---

Figure 4-10. Airspeed calibration, normal static source, for a four-place retractable-gear airplane.

AIRSPEED CALIBRATION
ALTERNATE STATIC SOURCE

Heater and defroster full on and windows closed.

FLAPS UP										
NORMAL KIAS	50	60	70	80	90	100	110	120	140	160
ALTERNATE KIAS	46	58	69	79	88	98	108	117	136	155
FLAPS 10°										
NORMAL KIAS	50	60	70	80	90	100	110	120	130	---
ALTERNATE KIAS	45	58	69	80	90	100	109	119	128	---
FLAPS 30°										
NORMAL KIAS	50	60	70	80	90	100	---	---	---	---
ALTERNATE KIAS	46	58	68	78	87	96	---	---	---	---

Figure 4-11. Airspeed calibration (alternate static source) for the airplane in Figure 4-10.

port on each side of the forward fuselage in this airplane) is being affected by ice or water. Figure 4-11 is an airspeed calibration for the alternate static source.

Note that the calibration is with the heater and defroster full ON and the windows closed, a likely setup when flying in icing or cold rain conditions (where problems with the normal system are most apt to occur).

Figure 4-11 brings up an interesting point. It's usually considered that the pressure in the cabin (unpressurized airplane) will be slightly less than the ambient (outside) static pressure because of the effects of the relative wind moving past the airframe. Apparently, however, under the conditions cited, the cabin pressure must be slightly higher to give the shown effect on the IAS.

Notice, too, in Figure 4-11 that the alternate system IAS is nearly always lower than that for the normal system. There are some equal readings at 80, 90, and 100 K at 10° flaps, but basically the airspeed indicator reads less than normal.

Look at Figure 4-11 and assume for purposes here that the KIAS with the *normal* source is "correct," that is, KIAS = KCAS. Also assume that the airplane is flying at sea level (pressure = 2,116 psf, density = 0.002378 slugs per cubic foot) at a normal KIAS (KCAS) of 120 K, flaps up. There is a 3-K difference caused by the higher cabin pressure here. You can find the difference between cabin pressure and outside pressure by the following equation: KIAS (KCAS also, for this example) = $(\rho_0/2)V^2$. (It's assumed for now that the static pressure in the diaphragm and in the case are equal at 2,116 psf. In other words, it's easier at first to assume that the imbalance is caused by a *low* dynamic pressure, find the value, and then correctly give that value to a higher cabin, or instrument case, pressure.)

Check the dynamic pressures (rounded off), as if the airplane were *actually* going through the air at 120 K and 117 K respectively and converting to feet per second (1.69 factor):

At 120 K,

$$\left(\frac{\rho_0}{2}\right)V^2 = \frac{0.002378}{2} \times (120 \times 1.69)^2$$

$$= \frac{0.002378}{2} \times (202.8)^2 = 48.9 \text{ psf}$$

At 117 K,

$$\left(\frac{\rho_0}{2}\right)V^2 = \frac{0.002378}{2} \times (117 \times 1.69)^2$$

$$= \frac{0.002378}{2} \times (197.7)^2 = 46.5 \text{ psf}$$

The 3-K drop was actually caused by a 2.4-psf *increase in cabin pressure* rather than a change (drop) in dynamic pressure (a change of pressure of 2.4/2,116 = 0.001134, or a little over 0.11%).

The *total* pressure *P*, which equals the static and dynamic pressures p + q, at an indicated 120 K is 2,116 + 48.9 = 2,164.9. The actual total pressure (in the pitot tube and in the diaphragm) at an indicated 117 K should be the same (2,164.9) because the airplane is actually moving at 120 K, but an error in indication has been introduced by a change in static pressure in the cabin and in the instrument case. (It has increased and is causing the diaphragm to be "compressed," resulting in a lower airspeed indication.) Figure 4-12 gives an idea of what's happening.

The POH in this example does not have an altimeter correction for the alternate static source, but based on the just-learned facts, you know the altimeter would read *lower* on the alternate static source than on the normal source. (The reason, of course, is that the substitute *static* pressure being furnished to the altimeter

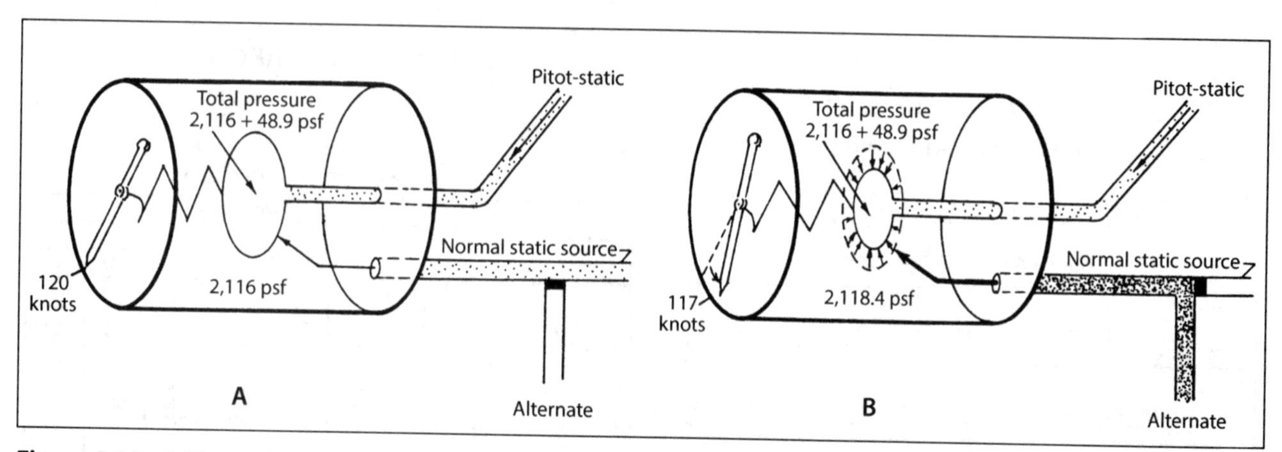

Figure 4-12. A. The static pressure within the diaphragm and within the case are equal, so only the dynamic pressure is read, as it should be. **B.** Even though the total pressure (within the diaphragm) is correct, the *extra* pressure in the case induced by the alternate source allows the diaphragm to expand only about 117 K worth.

is higher *so the altimeter "thinks" the airplane has descended.*)

Checking Figure 4-4 again and doing a little arithmetic, you will find that the altimeter, if zeroed at sea level on the normal source, would read about 32 feet lower when on the alternate source. The reason is that sea level pressure is 2,116 psf while at 1,000 feet it's 2,041 psf (rounded off), or a drop of 75 psf in that 1,000 feet. The static pressure is 2.4 psf higher than standard for that altitude so it will change the altimeter indication downward by the following factor:

$$\frac{\text{static error (psf)} \times 1{,}000}{\text{pressure change per 1,000 feet (psf)}} = \frac{2.4}{75} \times 1{,}000 = 32 \text{ feet}$$

The error would have to be 75 psf to get a 1,000-ft change, but it was only 2.4 psf; 2.4/75 × 1,000, or about 32 feet. So the altimeter will read about 32 feet low under the conditions cited.

Not too much error would be introduced if this was also the assumption for altitudes 1,000 feet either side of sea level. Again, checking Figure 4-4 and subtracting, you'll find the pressure drop is 75 psf from sea level to 1,000 feet, 73 psf from 1,000 to 2,000 feet, and 71 psf from 2,000 to 3,000 feet.

Figure 4-13 has correction tables for a twin for airspeed and altimeter when on the alternate system. The alternate system is vented within the nose section. Note that altitude is not a factor when correcting for CAS because calibrated airspeed (again) is a function of the combination of $(\rho/2)V^2$. You can have a large ρ and a comparatively small V, or at altitude ρ may be small and V large. But at a particular airspeed (CAS or EAS, as applicable), q will always be the same, so a graph like Figure 4-14 could be made.

You'll note, however, that altitude does have an effect on the altimeter correction because of the difference in rate of pressure change at various altitudes (Figure 4-4). If the airspeed reads higher when on the alternate static source, so should the altimeter. In other words, if the static system pressure lowers when on the alternate system, it means that *the pressure in the ASI and altimeter instrument cases will be low.* And conversely, if the airspeed on alternate indicates lower than the actual value, the altimeter will read lower than actual, as was worked out earlier.

The real point, of course, is to use the available POH corrections for airspeed and altimeter.

14 CFR Part 23 cites the following standards for a static pressure system:

§23.1325 Static pressure system.

(a) Each instrument provided with static pressure case connections must be so vented that the influence of airplane speed, the opening and closing of windows, airflow variations, moisture, or other foreign matter will least affect the accuracy of the instruments except as noted in paragraph (b)(3) of this section.

(b) If a static pressure system is necessary for the functioning of instruments, systems, or devices, it must comply with the provisions of paragraphs (b)(1) through (3) of this section.

(1) The design and installation of a static pressure system must be such that—

(i) Positive drainage of moisture is provided;

(ii) Chafing of the tubing, and excessive distortion or restriction at bends in the tubing, is avoided; and

(iii) The materials used are durable, suitable for the purpose intended, and protected against corrosion.

(2) A proof test must be conducted to demonstrate the integrity of the static pressure system in the following manner:

(i) *Unpressurized airplanes.* Evacuate the static pressure system to a pressure differential of approximately 1 inch of mercury or to a reading on the altimeter 1,000 feet above the aircraft elevation at the time of the test. Without additional pumping for a period of 1

AIRSPEED CALIBRATION

ALTERNATE STATIC SOURCE

NOTES:

1. Indicated airspeed assumes zero instrument error.
2. The following calibrations are not valid in the pre-stall buffet.

VENTS AND HEATER CLOSED

FLAPS UP								
NORMAL KIAS	80	100	120	140	160	180	200	210
ALTERNATE KIAS	87	112	133	154	175	195	215	225
FLAPS 10°								
NORMAL KIAS	70	80	90	100	120	140	160	175
ALTERNATE KIAS	74	85	97	108	130	151	172	186
FLAPS 30°								
NORMAL KIAS	60	70	80	90	100	110	125	---
ALTERNATE KIAS	66	75	85	96	106	117	133	---

VENTS AND/OR HEATER OPEN

FLAPS UP								
NORMAL KIAS	80	100	120	140	160	180	200	210
ALTERNATE KIAS	85	108	130	151	171	192	211	221
FLAPS 10°								
NORMAL KIAS	70	80	90	100	120	140	160	175
ALTERNATE KIAS	73	84	95	106	127	147	167	182
FLAPS 30°								
NORMAL KIAS	60	70	80	90	100	110	125	---
ALTERNATE KIAS	62	72	81	93	102	113	129	---

ALTIMETER CORRECTION

ALTERNATE STATIC SOURCE

NOTE:
Add correction to desired altitude to obtain indicated altitude to fly.

VENTS AND HEATER CLOSED

CONDITION	CORRECTION TO BE ADDED - FEET							
	KIAS							
	80	90	100	120	140	160	180	200
FLAPS UP								
Sea Level	40	60	90	150	200	240	290	330
10,000 Ft.	50	80	120	180	250	310	370	430
20,000 Ft.	60	110	160	250	340	430	510	590
FLAPS 10°								
Sea Level	30	40	60	110	150	200	250	---
10,000 Ft.	40	60	90	140	200	260	330	---
20,000 Ft.	60	90	130	210	290	375	460	---
FLAPS 30°								
Sea Level	30	50	70	100	---	---	---	---
10,000 Ft.	40	60	80	130	---	---	---	---
20,000 Ft.	---	---	---	---	---	---	---	---

VENTS AND/OR HEATER OPEN

CONDITION	CORRECTION TO BE ADDED - FEET							
	KIAS							
	80	90	100	120	140	160	180	200
FLAPS UP								
Sea Level	20	30	50	90	130	190	240	300
10,000 Ft.	30	50	70	120	180	250	310	380
20,000 Ft.	50	80	110	180	260	350	440	530
FLAPS 10°								
Sea Level	10	30	40	80	110	150	190	---
10,000 Ft.	20	40	60	100	140	190	240	---
20,000 Ft.	30	60	90	150	210	270	340	---
FLAPS 30°								
Sea Level	10	20	30	50	---	---	---	---
10,000 Ft.	10	30	50	70	---	---	---	---
20,000 Ft.	---	---	---	---	---	---	---	---

Figure 4-13. Alternate source corrections for the airspeed and altimeter of a particular airplane.

minute, the loss of indicated altitude must not exceed 100 feet on the altimeter.

(ii) *Pressurized airplanes.* Evacuate the static pressure system until a pressure differential equivalent to the maximum cabin pressure differential for which the airplane is type certificated is achieved. Without additional pumping for a period of 1 minute, the loss of indicated altitude must not exceed 2 percent of the equivalent altitude of the maximum cabin differential pressure or 100 feet, whichever is greater.

(3) If a static pressure system is provided for any instrument, device, or system required by the operating rules of this chapter, each static pressure port must be designed or located in such a manner that the correlation between air pressure in the static pressure system and true ambient atmospheric static pressure is not altered when the airplane encounters icing conditions. An anti-icing means or an alternate source of static pressure may be used in showing compliance with this requirement. If the reading of the altimeter, when on the alternate static pressure system differs from the reading of the altimeter when on the primary static system by more than 50 feet, a correction card must be provided for the alternate static system.

(c) Except as provided in paragraph (d) of this section, if the static pressure system incorporates both a primary and an alternate static pressure source, the means for selecting one or the other source must be designed so that—

(1) When either source is selected, the other is blocked off; and

(2) Both sources cannot be blocked off simultaneously.

(d) For unpressurized airplanes, paragraph (c)(1) of this section does not apply if it can be demonstrated that the static pressure system calibration, when either static pressure source is selected, is not changed by the other static pressure source being open or blocked.

(e) Each static pressure system must be calibrated in flight to determine the system error. The system error, in indicated pressure altitude, at sea level, with a standard atmosphere, excluding instrument calibration error, may not exceed ±30 feet per 100 knot speed for the appropriate configuration in the speed range between 1.3 V_{S0} with flaps extended, and 1.8 V_{S1} with flaps retracted. However, the error need not be less than 30 feet.

(f) [Reserved]

(g) For airplanes prohibited from flight in instrument meteorological or icing conditions, in accordance with §23.1559(b) of this part, paragraph (b)(3) of this section does not apply.

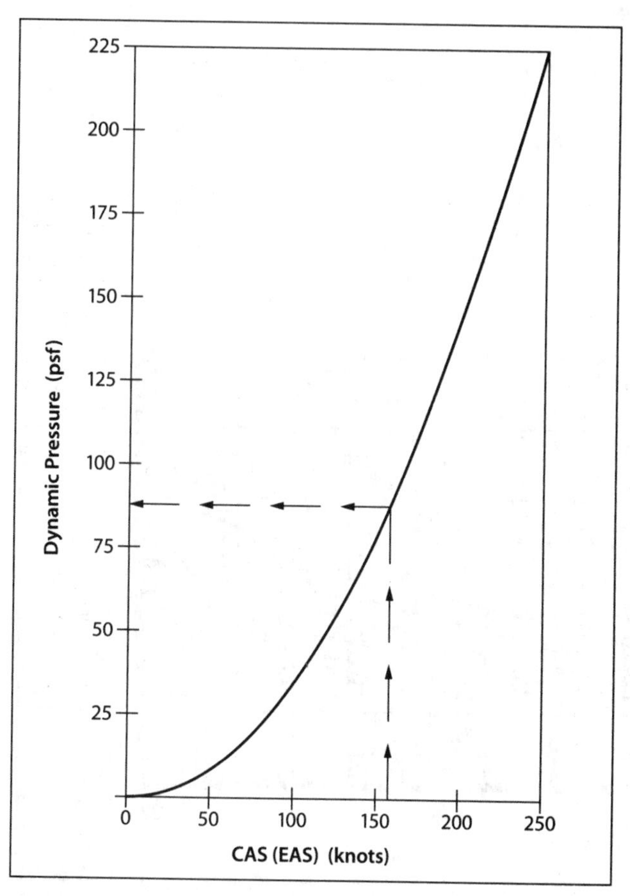

Figure 4-14. Approximate pressure (psf) for various calibrated (or more accurately, equivalent) airspeeds. For example, at 160 K the dynamic pressure is approximately 87 psf.

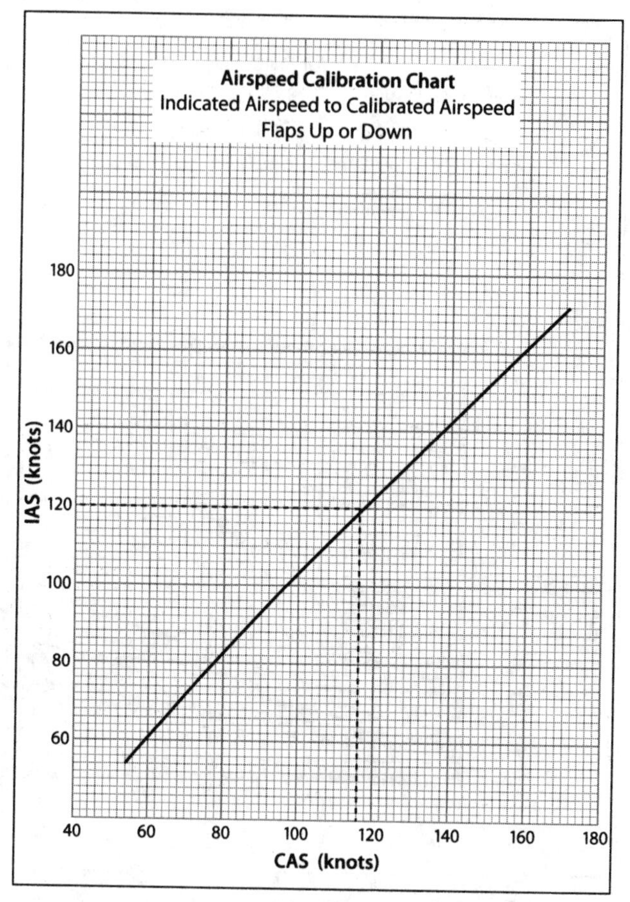

Figure 4-15. Graphical presentation of an airspeed calibration chart.

Figure 4-15 is a graphical presentation of an airspeed calibration chart (normal source). As an example, an IAS of 120 K results in a CAS of approximately 118 K.

Other Airspeed Factors

Figure 4-16 is a correction graph for the outside air temperature gage. At 160 K IAS at 10,000 feet you should *subtract* approximately 4°C (7°F) from what the OAT gage indicates.

While it might not directly apply to the previous discussion about airspeed, you should be aware that most airplanes of normal configuration, with a stabilizer or stabilator and a tail-down force, stall at a higher indicated (or calibrated or equivalent) airspeed with a forward CG because, as was noted earlier, as the CG moves forward the tail-down force must be increased to maintain equilibrium. Figure 4-17 is an actual stall speed chart for most rearward and forward CGs for a particular weight.

The altimeter problems associated with using the alternate static system were discussed briefly earlier. However, any problems caused by use of the alternate are minor compared with having a totally plugged static system. In many nonpressurized airplanes the alternate static system gets static pressure from the cabin area; this wouldn't work for pressurized airplanes, because the cabin may be at 8,000 feet and the airplane (and outside pressure) at 20,000 feet. Figure 4-18 shows the normal pitot/static system and the alternate static system for a popular pressurized twin.

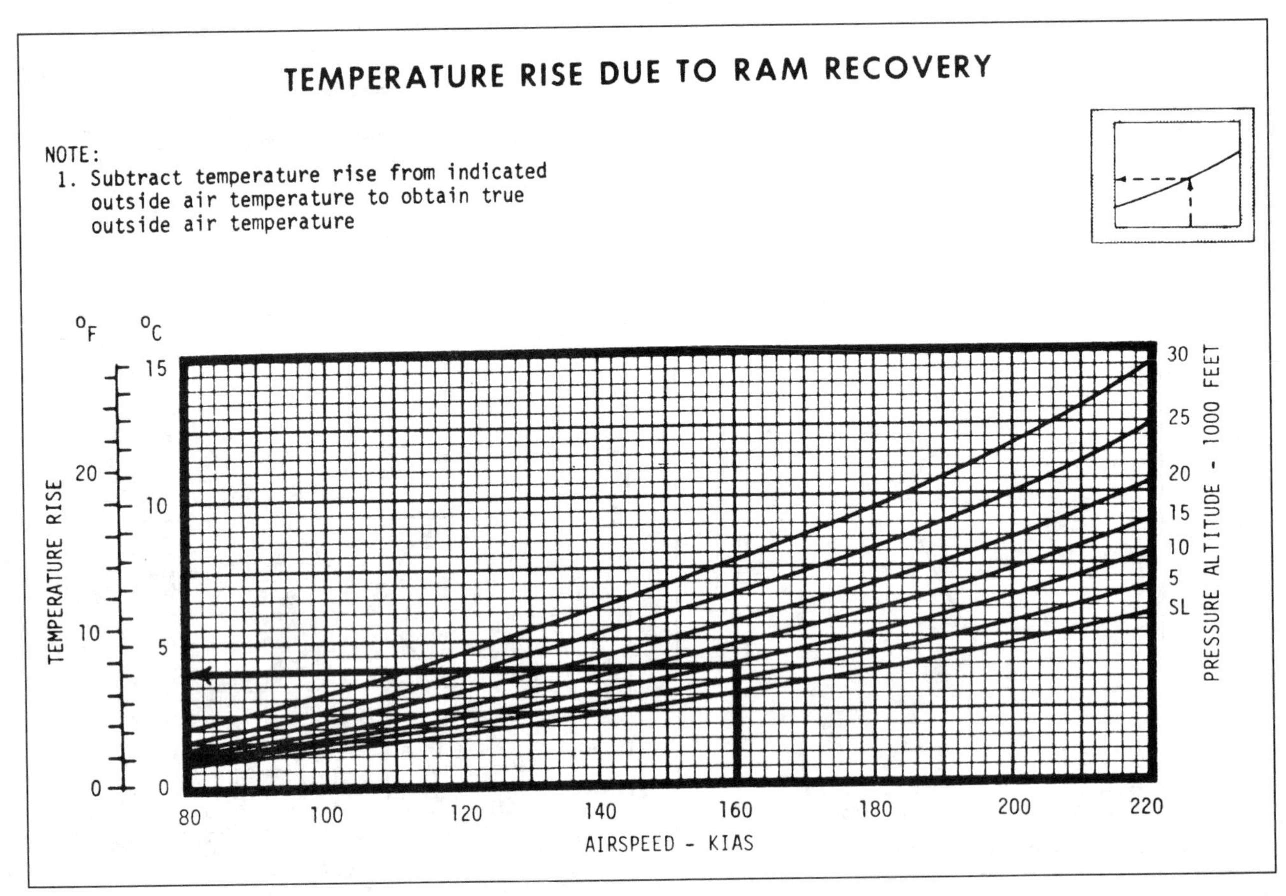

Figure 4-16. Outside air temperature correction graph.

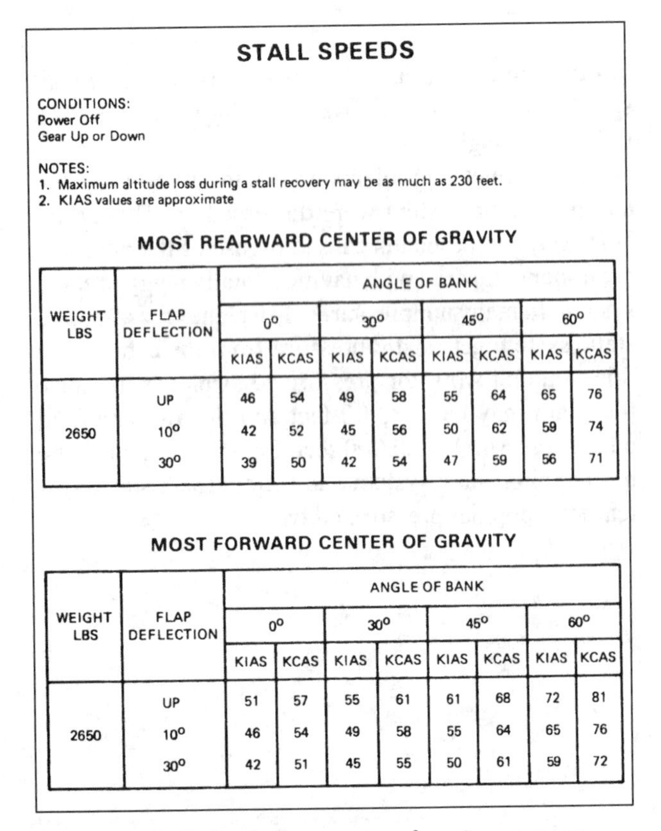

STALL SPEEDS

CONDITIONS:
Power Off
Gear Up or Down

NOTES:
1. Maximum altitude loss during a stall recovery may be as much as 230 feet.
2. KIAS values are approximate

MOST REARWARD CENTER OF GRAVITY

WEIGHT LBS	FLAP DEFLECTION	ANGLE OF BANK							
		0°		30°		45°		60°	
		KIAS	KCAS	KIAS	KCAS	KIAS	KCAS	KIAS	KCAS
2650	UP	46	54	49	58	55	64	65	76
	10°	42	52	45	56	50	62	59	74
	30°	39	50	42	54	47	59	56	71

MOST FORWARD CENTER OF GRAVITY

WEIGHT LBS	FLAP DEFLECTION	ANGLE OF BANK							
		0°		30°		45°		60°	
		KIAS	KCAS	KIAS	KCAS	KIAS	KCAS	KIAS	KCAS
2650	UP	51	57	55	61	61	68	72	81
	10°	46	54	49	58	55	64	65	76
	30°	42	51	45	55	50	61	59	72

Figure 4-17. Stall speeds at center of gravity extremes.

Airspeed Indicator Markings

The FAA requires that the airspeed indicator be marked for various important speeds and speed ranges.

Red line—never-exceed speed (V_{NE}). This speed should not be exceeded at any time.

Yellow arc—caution range. Strong vertical gusts could damage the airplane in this speed range; therefore it is best to refrain from flying in this speed range when encountering turbulence of any intensity. The caution range starts at the maximum structural cruising speed and ends at the never-exceed speed (V_{NE}).

Green arc—normal operating range. The airspeed at the lower end of this arc is the flaps-up, gear-up, power-off stall speed at gross weight (V_{S1}) (for most airplanes, the landing gear position has no effect on stall speed). The upper end of the green arc is the maximum structural cruising speed (V_{NO}), the maximum IAS where no structural damage would occur in moderate vertical gust conditions.

White arc—flap operating range. The lower limit is the stall speed at gross weight with the flaps in the *landing position*, and the upper limit is the maximum flap operating speed.

Airplanes manufactured as 1976 models or later have the airspeed indicator markings as *indicated*

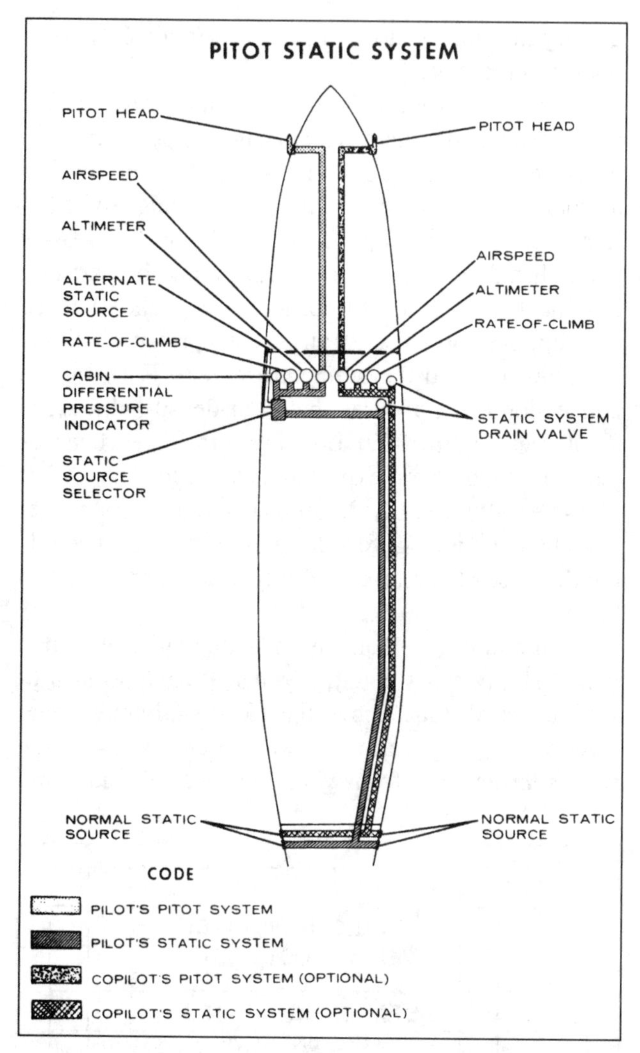

Figure 4-18. Pitot/static system for a pressurized twin. Note that the alternate static air source is in the unpressurized nose compartment.

airspeed and knots. (Instrument markings before that were CAS and usually mph.)

14 CFR Part 1 gives the following definitions of various airspeeds (the maneuvering speed V_A and max landing gear speeds V_{LE} and V_{LO} are not marked on the airspeed indicator):

V_A means design maneuvering speed.

V_B means design speed for maximum gust intensity.

V_C means design cruising speed.

V_D means design diving speed.

V_{DF}/M_{DF} means demonstrated flight diving speed.

V_F means design flap speed.

V_{FC}/M_{FC} means maximum speed for stability characteristics.

V_{FE} means maximum flap extended speed.

V_H means maximum speed in level flight with maximum continuous power.

V_{LE} means maximum landing gear extended speed.

V_{LO} means maximum landing gear operating speed.

V_{LOF} means lift-off speed.

V_{MC} means minimum control speed with the critical engine inoperative.

V_{MO}/M_{MO} means maximum operating limit speed.

V_{MU} means minimum unstick speed.

V_{NE} means never-exceed speed.

V_{NO} means maximum structural cruising speed.

V_R means rotation speed.

V_S means the stalling speed or the minimum steady flight speed at which the airplane is controllable.

V_{S0} means the stalling speed or the minimum steady flight speed in the landing configuration.

V_{S1} means the stalling speed or the minimum steady flight speed obtained in a specific configuration.

V_X means speed for best angle of climb.

V_Y means speed for best rate of climb.

V_1 means takeoff decision speed (formerly denoted as critical engine failure speed).

V_2 means takeoff safety speed.

V_{2min} means minimum takeoff safety speed.

Altimeter Review

The altimeter is an aneroid barometer calibrated in feet instead of inches of mercury. Its job is to measure the static pressure (or ambient pressure as it is sometimes called) and register this fact in terms of feet or thousands of feet.

The altimeter has an opening that allows static (outside) pressure to enter the otherwise sealed case. A series of sealed diaphragms or "aneroid wafers" within the case are mechanically linked to the three indicating hands. Because the wafers are sealed, they retain a constant internal "pressure" and expand or contract in response to the changing atmospheric pressure surrounding them in the case. As the aircraft climbs, the atmospheric pressure decreases and the sealed wafers expand; this is duly noted by the indicating hands as an increase in altitude (or vice versa).

Standard sea level pressure is 29.92 inches of mercury and the operations of the altimeter are based on this fact. Any change in local pressure must be corrected for by the pilot. This is done by using the setting knob to set the proper barometric pressure (corrected to sea level) in the setting window.

True altitude is the height above sea level.

Absolute altitude is the height above terrain.

Pressure altitude is the altitude read when the altimeter is set to 29.92. This indication shows what your altitude would be if the altimeter setting were 29.92—that is, if it were a standard pressure day.

Indicated altitude is the altitude read when the altimeter is set at the local barometric pressure corrected to sea level.

Density-altitude is the pressure altitude computed with temperature. The density-altitude is used in performance. If you know your density-altitude, air density can be found by tables and airplane performance calculated. You go through this step every time you use a computer to find the TAS. You use the pressure altitude and the outside air temperature and get the TAS. Usually there's not enough difference in pressure altitude and indicated altitude to make it worthwhile to set up 29.92 in the altimeter setting window, so the usual procedure is to use the *indicated* altitude.

The fact that the computer used pressure altitude and temperature to obtain density-altitude in finding TAS didn't mean much as you were only interested in the final result. You may not even have been aware that you were working with the density-altitude during the process. Some computers also allow you to read the density-altitude directly by setting up pressure altitude and temperature. This is handy in figuring the performance of your airplane for a high-altitude and/or high-temperature takeoff or landing. The POH gives graphs or figures for takeoff and landing performance at the various density-altitudes. After finding your density-altitude, you can find your predicted performance in the POH.

The newest routine is for the manufacturer to furnish performance data for various temperatures and pressure altitudes (a combination resulting in density-altitudes); you can then use the graph or table information to get answers for particular situations. Figure 4-19 is an altitude conversion chart that might be part of a graphical presentation of, for instance, a takeoff chart.

Suppose you are at an airport at a pressure altitude of 6,000 feet and the temperature is 80°F. Using the conversion chart you see that your density-altitude is 8,500 feet (Figure 4-19). Looking at the takeoff curves you can see that your expected distance to clear a 50-ft obstacle will be nearly 2,300 feet at your gross weight of 4,800 pounds (Figure 4-20). This is more than double the distance at sea level and might be a handy fact to know.

You and other pilots fly indicated altitude. When you're flying cross-country, you will have no idea of your exact altitude above the terrain (although over level country you can check airport elevations on the way, subtract this from your indicated altitude, and

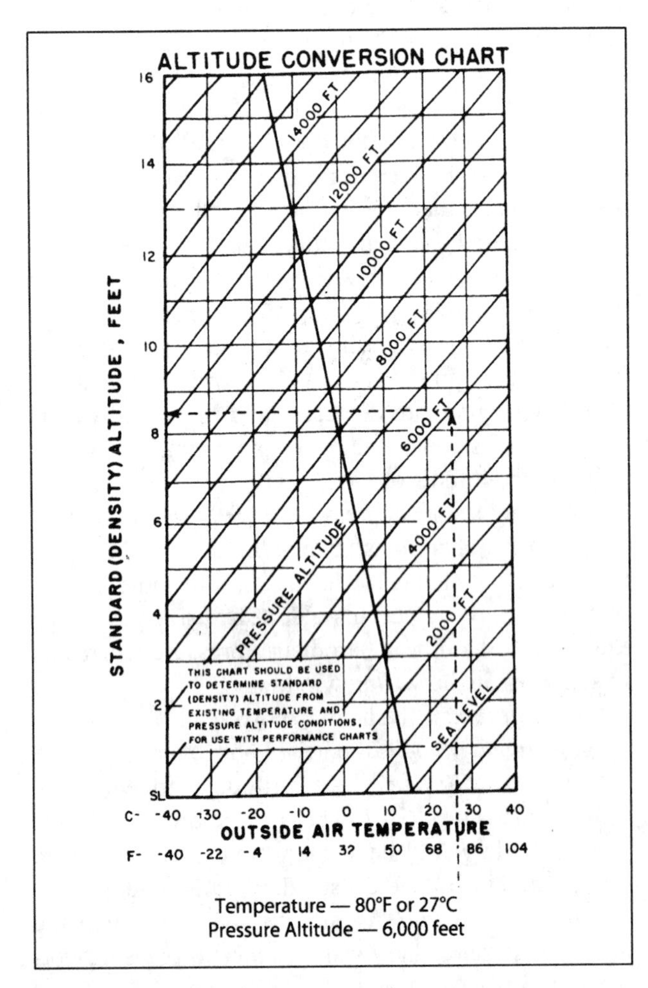

Figure 4-19. Altitude conversion chart.

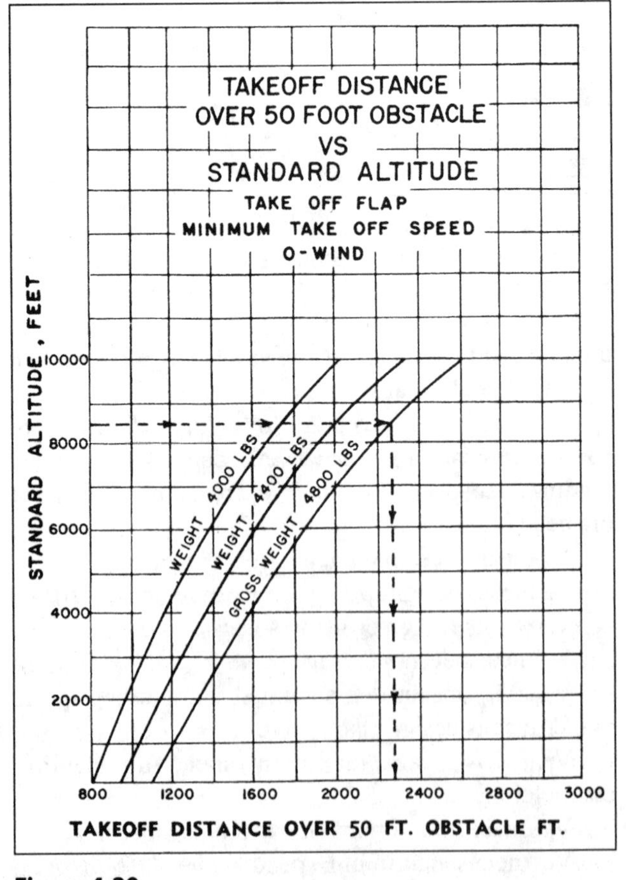

Figure 4-20.

have a ballpark figure). Over mountainous terrain this won't work, because the contours change too abruptly for you to hope to keep up with them. As you fly you'll get altimeter settings from various ground stations and keep up to date on pressure changes.

The use of indicated altitude for all planes makes good sense in that all pilots are using sea level as a base point. If each pilot set the altimeter at zero before taking off, you can imagine what pandemonium would reign.

Altimeter Errors

Instrument error—Being a mechanical contrivance, the altimeter is subject to various quirks. If you set the current barometric pressure—corrected to sea level—for your airport (if you have a tower or ASOS/AWOS), the altimeter should indicate the field elevation when you're on the ground.

14 CFR Part 91 specifies that airplanes operating in controlled airspace (IFR) must have had each static pressure system and each altimeter instrument tested by the manufacturer or an FAA-approved repair station within the past 24 calendar months.

Pressure changes—When you fly from a high-pressure area into a low-pressure area, the altimeter "thinks" you have climbed and will register accordingly—even if you haven't changed altitude. You'll see this and fly the plane down to the "correct altitude," and actually will be low. When you fly from a low- to a high-pressure area, the altimeter thinks you've let down to a lower altitude and registers too low. A good way to remember (although you can certainly reason it out each time) is HLH—High to Low, (altimeter reads) High; LHL—Low to High, (altimeter reads) Low.

You can see that it is worse to fly from a high- to a low-pressure area as far as terrain clearance is concerned. You might find that the clouds have rocks in them. So get frequent altimeter settings as you fly cross-country. "High to low, look out below."

Temperature errors—Going back to the equation of state for air where pressure = density × temperature × 1,716, you see the relationship between temperature and pressure. For our purposes we can say that pressure is *proportional* (P) to density (ρ) × temperature (T) and get rid of the constant number 1,716. Assuming the density remains constant, for simplicity you can then say that pressure is proportional to temperature. Therefore, if you are flying at a certain altitude and the temperature is higher than normal, the pressure at your altitude is higher than normal. *The altimeter registers this as a lower altitude.* If the temperature is lower, the pressure is lower and the altimeter will register accordingly—*lower temperature, altimeter reads higher.*

You might remember it this way, using the letters H and L as in pressure changes: temperature High, (altimeter reads) Low—HL; temperature Low, (altimeter reads) High—LH. Or perhaps you'd prefer to remember HALT (High Altimeter because of Low Temperature). The best thing, however, is to know that higher temperature means higher pressure (and vice versa) at altitude and reason it out from there.

The temperature error is zero at the surface point at which the setting is obtained and increases with altitude, so the error could easily be 500 to 600 feet at the 10,000-ft level. In other words, you can have this error at altitude even if the altimeter reads correctly at the surface point at which the setting originated. Temperature error can be found with a computer (Figure 4-21). For indicated altitude, this error is neglected, but it makes a good question for an FAA knowledge exam or practical test—and it has been used!

These errors (particularly temperature errors, which are normally ignored) affect everybody in that area (though slightly differently for different altitudes) so that the altitude separation is still no problem. Temperature errors *could* cause problems as far as terrain clearance is concerned, however.

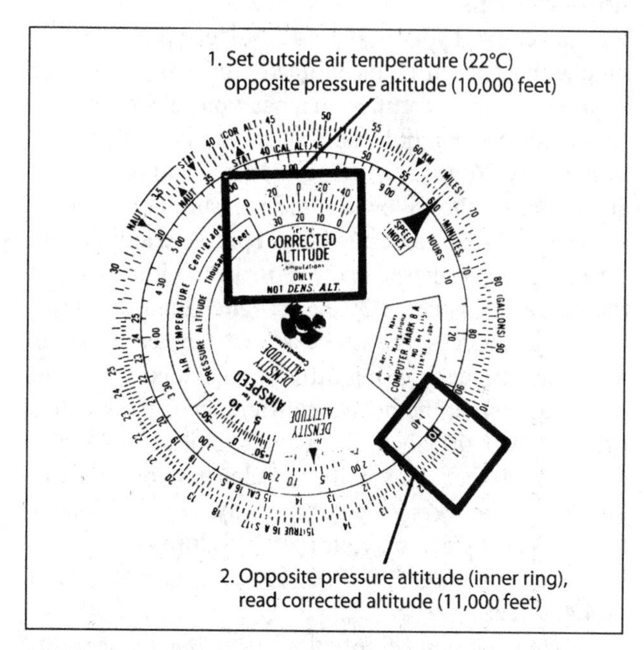

Figure 4-21. Using the computer to find corrected pressure altitude.

Hugh R. Skinner (see the Acknowledgments, Page B-4) has suggested some pilot considerations to observe before and during flight; here are a couple of particularly important ones:

1. Check the static ports. If the static ports are clogged or if there are large dents or protrusions *in the vicinity* of the ports, a considerable static pressure error can be created, especially at high airspeeds. (For instance, mud blobs may have been splashed up on the airframe *near* the ports and cause an erroneous static pressure.) You generally check the static ports themselves but may not notice that dried mud or new large dent near them.
2. Check for barometric correlation as often as possible, preferably before departure. Unless a large error exists don't jump on the instrument too quickly. Temperature, pressure, aircraft elevation, mechanical recovery (has it settled down?). and other problems cause short-term discrepancies in the indication of a good altimeter. Note the error and apply it to subsequent altimeter setting reports until further checks can be made. If the error persists, corrective service should be done.

Altimeter Tips

You can convert your indicated altitude to pressure altitude without resetting the altimeter to 29.92 by looking at your altimeter setting. Suppose your altimeter registers 4,000 feet and the current setting is 30.32 inches of mercury. Your pressure altitude is 3,600 feet and is arrived at by the following: the pressure corrected to sea level is 30.32 inches, but to get pressure altitude the setting should be based on 29.92 inches This shows that the actual pressure of 30.32 is *higher* than standard; therefore the pressure altitude is *less*. (Higher pressures at lower altitudes.) Using a figure of 1 inch per 1,000 feet you see that the pressure difference is 0.40 inches of mercury or 400 feet. The pressure altitude is 4,000 – 400 = 3,600 feet. This will be as close as you can read an altitude conversion chart anyway. If the altimeter setting had been 29.52 your pressure altitude would be 400 feet higher (29.92 – 29.52 = 0.40 inches = 400 feet) or 4,400 feet.

For estimation of pressure altitude without resetting: If your altimeter setting is *lower* than 29.92, *add* 100 feet to your indicated altitude for each 0.10 inch difference. If your altimeter setting is *higher* than 29.92, *subtract* 100 feet from your indicated altitude for each 0.10 inch difference to get the pressure altitude. The reason for this little mental exercise is to get you familiar with working between pressure and indicated altitude. You may prefer to note your altimeter setting (so you can return the altimeter to the indicated altitude after getting the pressure altitude), and then set the altimeter to 29.92 to get the pressure altitude. After this is done you can return to the original indicated altitude setting.

For computer work you are told to use the *pressure altitude* to find the TAS. For practical work use *indicated altitude* (current sea level setting) for TAS computations. Remember that the TAS increases about 2% per 1,000 feet so the most you will be off will be 2%. That is, your sea level altimeter setting could possibly be 28.92 or 30.92, but this is extremely unlikely. So...

Assume that a total error of no more than 1% will be introduced by using indicated altitude. For a 200-K airplane this means you could be 2 K off for TAS. But the instrument error or your error in reading the instrument could be this much.

One thing to remember concerning the altimeter that is useful for knowledge tests and hangar flying sessions: *If you increase the numbers in the setting window* (by using the setting knob, naturally), *the altitude reading is also increased*—and vice versa. If you have the altimeter originally set at 29.82 as the sea level pressure while flying and get an altimeter setting of 30.02 from a station in your area, you'll find that in rolling in that *additional* 0.20 inch you've also given the altimeter an *additional* 200 feet of *indicated* altitude.

This also follows the earlier LHL idea; when flying from a Low (29.82) to a High (30.02) the altimeter reads Low (until you put it right by rolling in the added 0.20 inch in the setting window and adding another 200 feet to your indicated altitude).

Encoding Altimeter

As you progress in aviation (you are likely to have your instrument rating before you read this), you'll use more sophisticated electronics equipment, including encoding altimeters (Figure 4-22).

The encoding altimeter, which is part of the transponder system (Mode C), provides automatic altitude reporting to equipped ATC facilities. A 4096 code transponder with Mode C equipment is required for operating within Class B areas.

The two basic types of installations are (1) an altimeter with an internal altitude encoder and (2) a "blind" encoder for use with an existing altimeter. (Or matched sets are available as shown in Figure 4-22.)

Altimeter Summary

On the commercial knowledge test (airplane), be ready to answer questions on the relationship of temperature and pressure effects on indicated and density-altitude. There are also questions on the test about the altimeter

Figure 4-22. Two types of encoders. (*King Radio Corporation*)

and alternate air sources, and the usual assumption is that, if the emergency alternate static source of an airplane is used, the altimeter will always read *high*. In some airplanes, particularly with vents or windows open, the "correct" altitude may be noticeably lower than on the altimeter, and the amount will vary with airspeed. The answer is, of course, to check the POH for *your* airplane.

Rate of Climb or Vertical Speed Indicator

Like the altimeter, the vertical speed indicator has a diaphragm. But unlike the altimeter, it measures the *rate of change* of pressure rather than the pressure itself.

The diaphragm has a tube connecting it to the static tube of the airspeed indicator and altimeter (or the tube may just have access to the cabin air pressure in the case of cheaper or lighter installations). This means that the inside of the diaphragm has the same pressure as the air surrounding the airplane. Opening into the otherwise sealed instrument case is a capillary tube.

As an example, suppose the airplane is flying at a constant altitude. The pressure within the diaphragm is the same as that of the air surrounding it in the instrument case. The rate of climb is indicated as zero.

When the plane is put into a glide or dive, air pressure inside the diaphragm increases at the same rate as that of the surrounding air. However, because of the small size of the capillary tube, the pressure in the instrument case does not change at the same rate. In a glide or dive, the diaphragm expands, the amount of expansion depending on the difference of pressures. Because the diaphragm is mechanically linked to a hand, the appropriate rate of descent in hundreds (or thousands) of feet per minute is read on the instrument face. In a climb, the pressure in the diaphragm decreases faster than that within the instrument case, so the needle will indicate an appropriate rate of climb.

Because the pressure in the case during a climb or dive is always "behind" the diaphragm pressure in the above described instrument, a lag of 6 to 9 seconds results. The instrument will still indicate a vertical speed for a short time after the plane is leveled off. For this reason, the rate of climb indicator is not used to maintain altitude. On days when the air is bumpy, this lag is particularly noticeable. The rate of climb indicator is used as a check of the plane's climb, dive, or glide rate. The altimeter is used to maintain a constant altitude.

There is a more expensive rate of climb indicator (instantaneous vertical speed indicator) on the market that does not have lag and is very accurate even in bumpy air. It contains a piston-cylinder arrangement whereby the airplane's vertical acceleration is immediately noted. The pistons are balanced by their own weights and springs. When a change in vertical speed occurs, the pistons are displaced and an immediate change of pressures in the cylinders is created. This

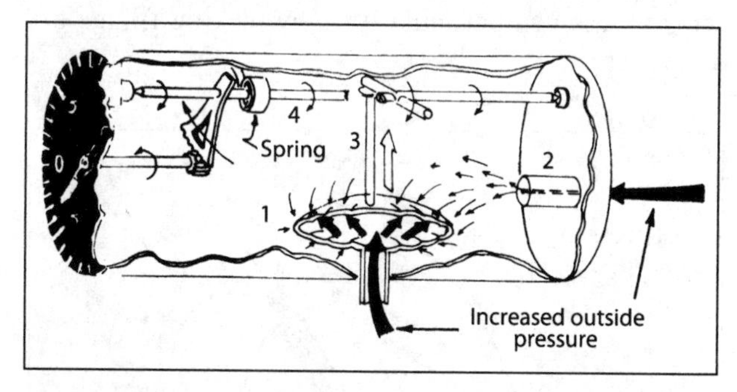

Figure 4-23. Vertical speed indicator. As the airplane descends, the outside pressure increases. The diaphragm expands immediately (1). Because of the small size of the capillary tube (2), the pressure within the case is not increased at the same rate. The link (3) pushes upward rotating the shaft (4), which causes the needle to indicate the proper rate of descent. The spring helps return the needle to zero when pressures are equal and also acts as a dampener.

pressure is transmitted to the diaphragm, producing an almost instantaneous change in indication. After the acceleration-induced pressures fade, the pistons are no longer displaced, and the diaphragm and capillary tube act as in the old type of indicator (as long as there is no acceleration). The actions of the acceleration elements and the diaphragm-capillary system overlap for smooth action.

It's possible to fly with this type of instrument as accurately as with an altimeter, but the price may be out of the range of the owner of a lighter plane.

Magnetic Compass

The Earth's Magnetic Field

As noted in hundreds of aviation books, the magnetic poles are not located at the geographic poles; this may be a large or small factor in navigation, depending on where you are.

The earth may be considered as a bar magnet in a sphere (Figure 4-24). It would seem by looking at Figure 4-24 that the solution is a straightforward, straight line correction for the "angle" between the poles and that the flux lines would be symmetrical, as illustrated in a simple experiment with a magnet and iron filings. It's not that simple for the earth. As shown on navigation charts and in Figure 4-25, the isogonic lines (lines of equal variation) seem to have a random pattern. The line system gets rather cluttered close to the poles and there are some prodigious variation values there. (Incidentally, if you do the experiment with the magnet and iron filings, keep a sheet of paper between the two systems unless you particularly enjoy picking filings off a magnet.)

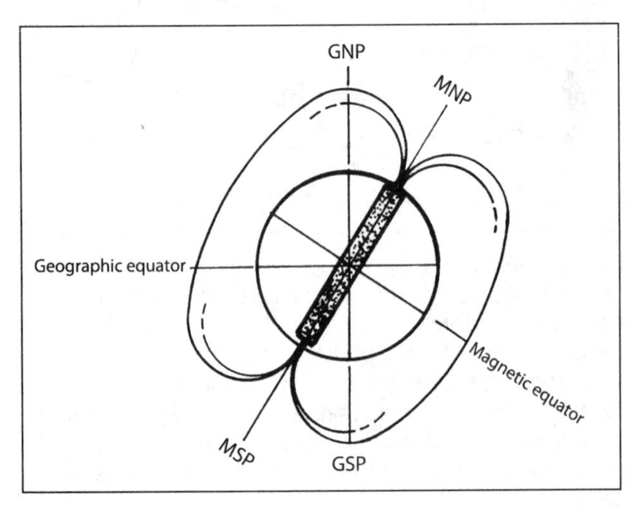

Figure 4-24. The earth as a bar magnet.

Note that the western hemisphere and the United States have relatively small variation values, which is an aid to navigation in those major aviation areas; it's doubtful if nature planned it that way.

Figure 4-26 shows the isogonic lines for the United States in 1980 (the date these example charts are from). The agonic line (0° variation) runs down the eastern edge of Lake Michigan, through the western edge of Franklin County, Tennessee (point A), and along the west coast of the Florida peninsula.

A brief review to jog your memory: The magnetic compass naturally points to the Magnetic North Pole, and this leads to the necessity of correcting for the angle between the Magnetic and Geographic North Poles. Normally a course will be measured on the chart from a meridian at a midpoint distance; this is the "true course" (the course referred to the True or Geographic North Pole). To get the magnetic course, remember that *going from true to magnetic* (whether a course or heading):

East is least—subtract East variation as shown on the sectional or WAC chart.

West is best—add West variation as shown on the sectional or WAC chart.

The variation (15° E or 10° W) given by the isogonic lines means that the Magnetic North Pole is 15 degrees east or 10 degrees west of the True North Pole. from your position as far as the compass is concerned. Naturally, if you happen to be at a point where the two poles are magnetically in line, the variation will be zero.

Figure 4-27 shows that the variation is a magnetic angle rather than a geometric one. In this exaggerated example, at Perry County airport the geometric angle between the poles is 30° but the variation (magnetic angle) is 0° because the agonic and isogonic lines wander and set up their own "magnetic meridians."

In addition to the overall effects of the earth's magnetic field, there are also local and regional anomalies. These are considered to be the result of clockwise and counterclockwise vortices of electric currents located at the earth's core beneath these points. Large deposits of iron ore may affect the magnetic compass indications in certain locations (Figure 4-28).

Magnetic pole reversals have been indicated over the past 6,000,000 years (don't ask who did the studies), and during that period the average lifetime of a geomagnetic field polarity, either normal or reverse, was 230,000 years but individual lifetimes varied considerably. This means that you'd better quit dragging your feet and get that commercial certificate before these data on magnetism are obsolete.

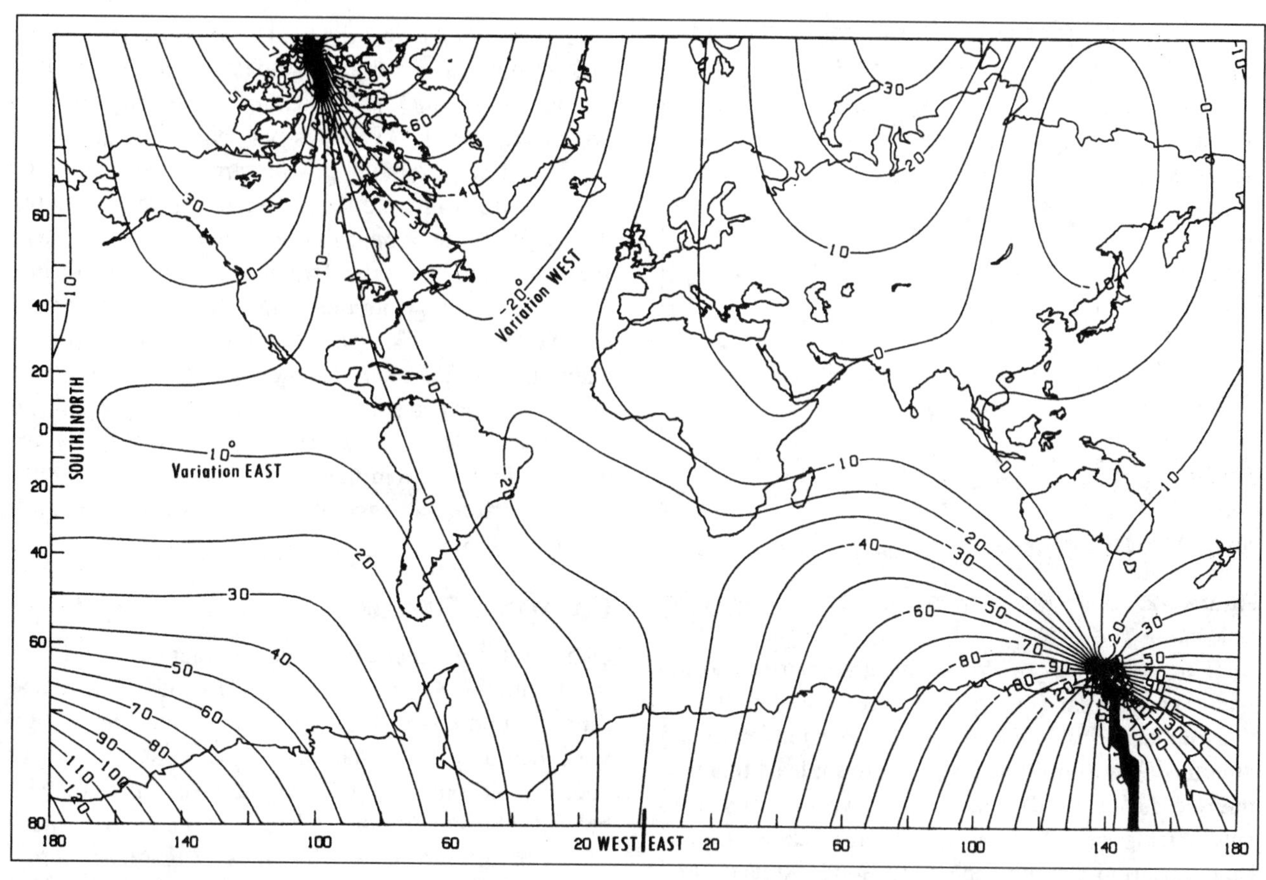

Figure 4-25. Worldwide variation values (example charts from 1980). A minus sign indicates westerly variation. (*NASA*)

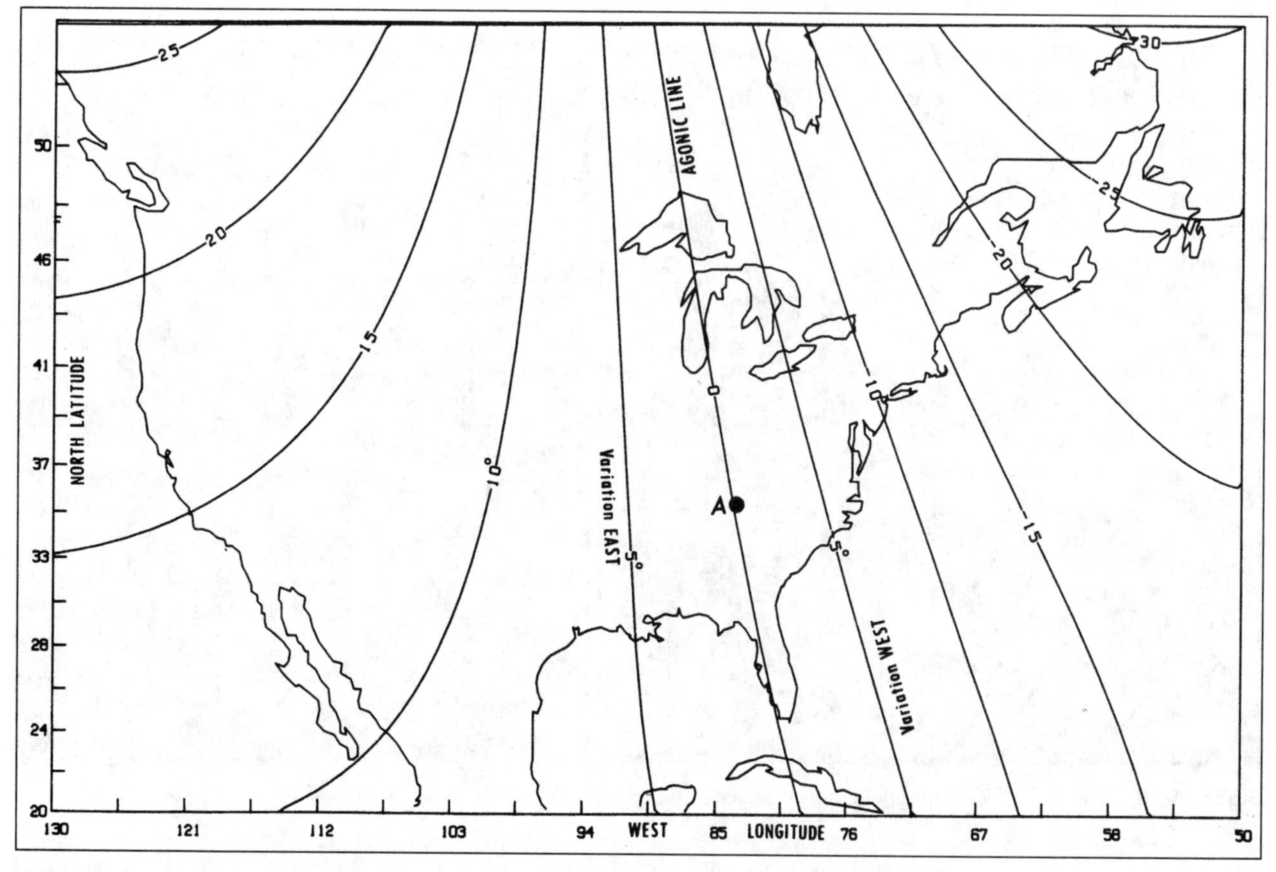

Figure 4-26. Example of variation for the United States. (Point A shown here will come up again in Figure 4-30.) (*NASA*)

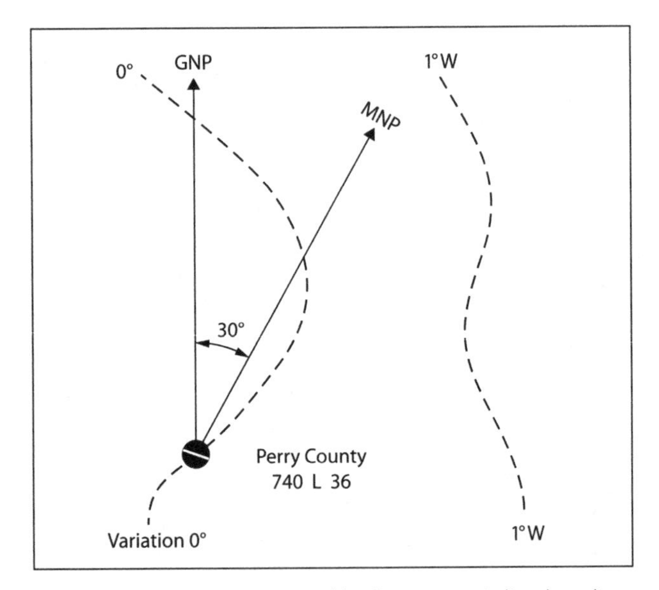

Figure 4-27. An exaggerated look at isogonic line bending.

Variation of variation—Variation varies (sorry) from year to year (Figure 4-29). You'll notice that in the southeastern United States the variation is moving "westerly" by 10 minutes per year (or at least that was the rate during 1980). The rate may vary from year to year. As Figure 4-29 shows, there are pockets of fairly high variation change such as in South America and southern Africa.

Figure 4-30 shows the change in variation for the United States and part of Canada. The area at point A (on the agonic line) has westward movement of variation at the rate of 10 minutes per year; in other words, variation lines are moving westward at that rate.

To better illustrate this, look at Figure 4-31. Note that in 1960 the agonic line was at Knoxville, but in 1982 that line had moved geographically *west* to just east of Nashville, from there meandering southward to near Sewanee. Looking at a point just east of Nashville where the 1982 agonic line and the 1960 3° E isogonic line cross, you can see that variation at that geographic point has changed 3° (180 minutes) in 22 years, an average of a little over 8 minutes per year. This was slightly below the actual change of 10 minutes given for 1980 in Figure 4-30.

Compass Factors

Okay, so the magnetic compass is a magnet that aligns itself with the Magnetic North Pole while the airplane turns around it (Figure 4-32). You are familiar enough with the compass so that an involved description isn't needed, but some review on using the compass may be helpful. The magnets in the compass tend to align themselves parallel to the earth's lines of magnetic force. This tendency is more noticeable as the Magnetic North Pole is approached. The compass would theoretically

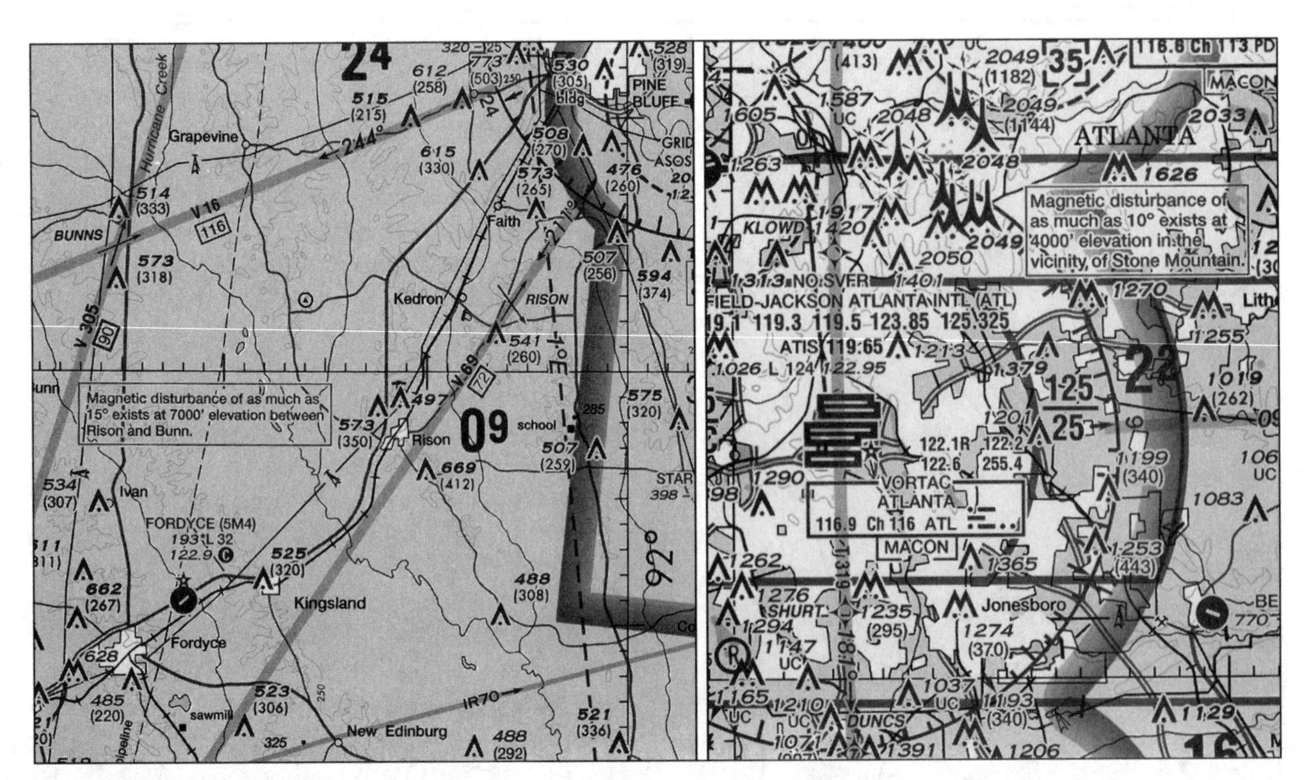

Figure 4-28. Examples of local magnetic disturbance warnings, near Pine Bluff, Arkansas and Atlanta, Georgia.

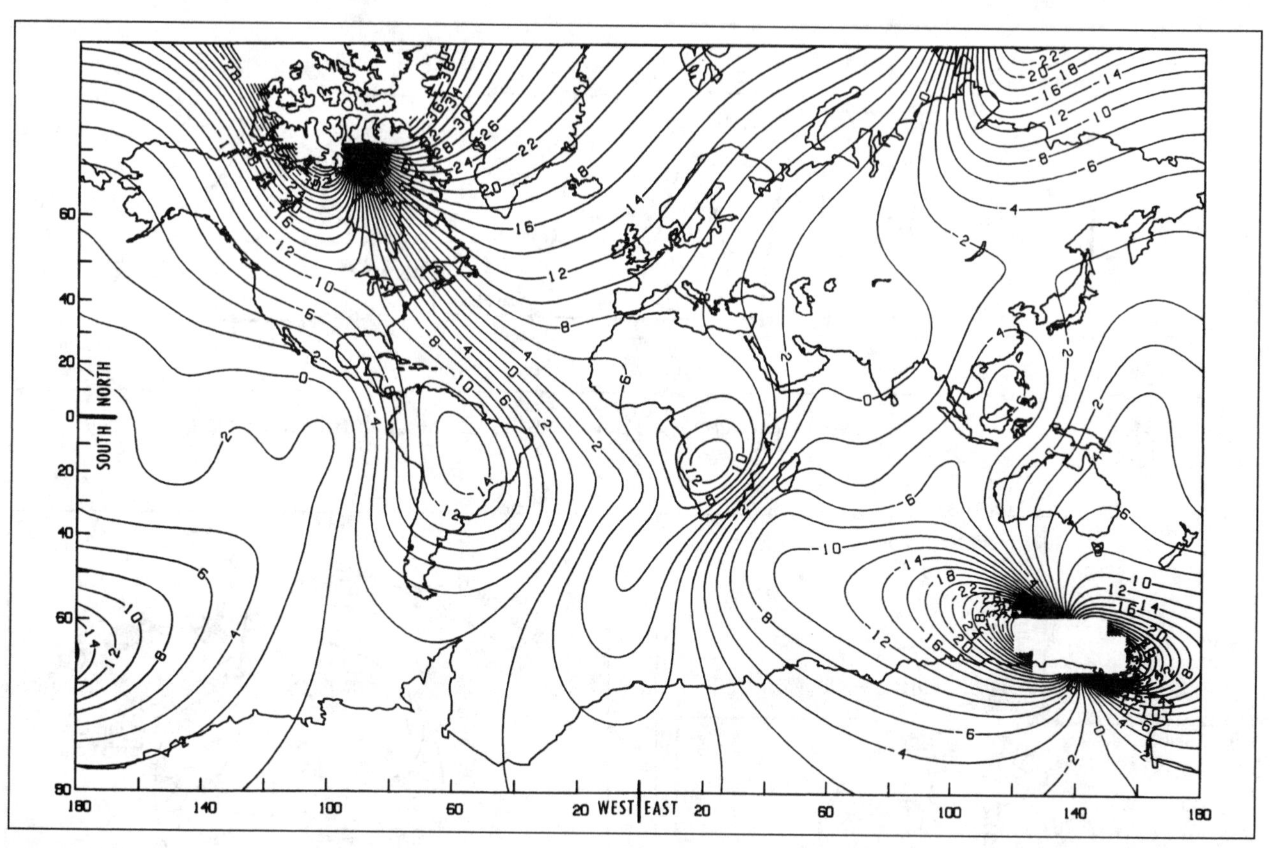

Figure 4-29. Example of worldwide variation change, minutes of longitude per year (for this example period). A minus sign indicates the variation is becoming more westerly. *(NASA)*

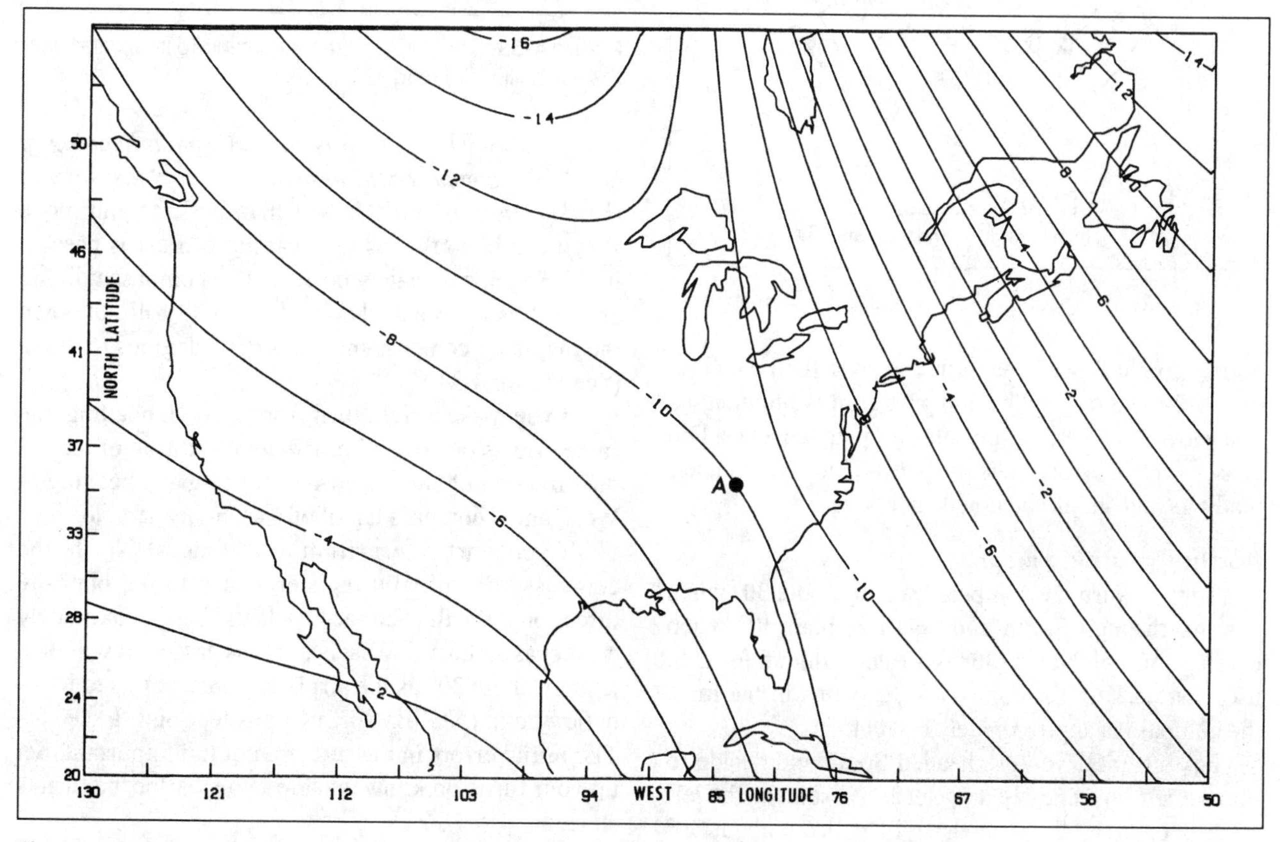

Figure 4-30. Example variation change, United States and part of Canada (same period,1980). Point A is Sewanee, Tennessee. *(NASA)*

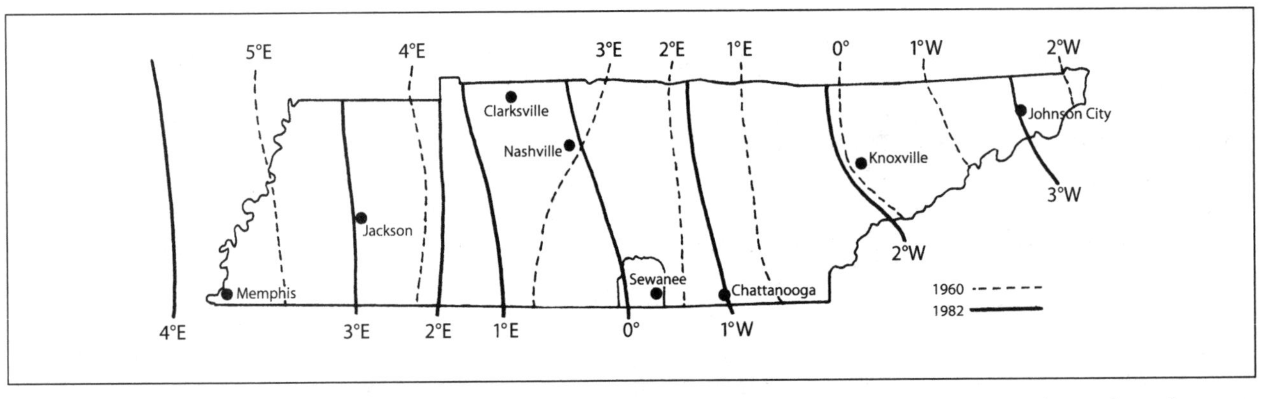

Figure 4-31. Changes in isogonic lines over time in Tennessee (solid lines are 22 years later). Check your latest charts for current values.

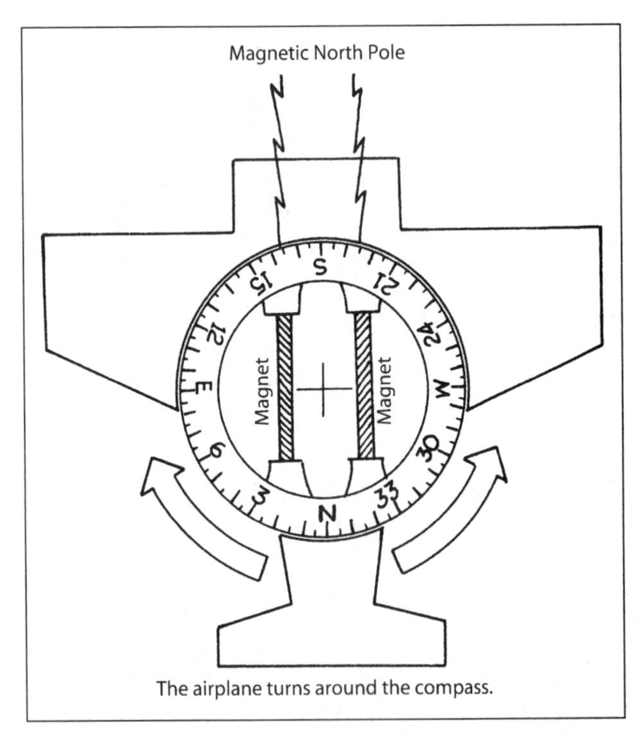

Figure 4-32. The magnetic compass (as seen from above).

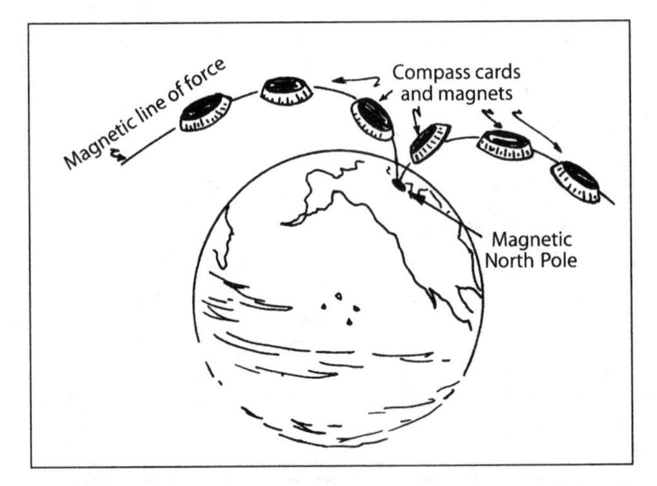

Figure 4-33. The compass magnets tend to lie parallel with the earth's lines of magnetic force.

point straight down when directly over the pole (Figures 4-24 and 4-33). The compass card is mounted so that a low CG location fights this dipping tendency. Dip causes certain errors to be introduced into the compass readings and should be noted as follows.

Northerly Turning Error

In a shallow turn the compass leads by about 30° when passing through South and lags by about 30° when passing through North (30° is a rule of thumb for U.S. use). On passing East and West headings in the turn, the compass is approximately correct.

For instance, you are headed South and decide to make a *left* turn and fly due North. As soon as the left bank is entered, the compass will indicate about 30° of left turn, when actually the nose has hardly started to move. *So, when a turn is started from a heading of South, the compass will indicate an extra fast turn in the direction of bank.* It will then hesitate and move slowly again so that as the heading of East is passed, it will be approximately correct. The compass will lag as North is approached so that you will roll out when the magnetic compass indicates 030° degrees (or "3"). (See Figure 4-34.)

If you make a right turn from a South heading, the same effects occur: an immediate indication of turn in the direction of bank, a correct reading at a heading of West, and a compass lag of 30° when headed North.

If you start a turn from a heading of North, the compass will initially register a turn in the opposite direction but will soon race back and be approximately correct as an East or West heading is passed. It will then lead by about 30° as the airplane's nose points to Magnetic South. (NOSE: North Opposite, South Exceeds.) The initial errors in the turn are not too important. Set up your turn and know what to expect after the turn is started.

Here is a simple rule to cover the effects of bank (assuming a shallow bank of 20° or less—if the bank is too steep the rule won't work).

Northerly Turning Errors—Northern Hemisphere

North heading—compass *lags* 30° at start of turn, or in the turn.

South heading—compass *leads* 30° at start of turn, or in the turn.

East or West heading—compass correct at start of turn, or in the turn.

Just remember that North *lags* 30° and South *leads* 30°, and this covers the problem. Actually, 30° is a round figure; the lead or lag depends on the latitude, but 30° is close enough for the work you'll be doing with the magnetic compass and is easy to remember.

Acceleration Errors

Because of its correction for dip, the compass will react to acceleration and deceleration of the airplane. This is most apparent on East or West headings, where *acceleration results in a more northerly indication. Deceleration gives a more southerly indication.* You might check this the next time you're out just boring holes in the sky. (Remember ANDS? Acceleration = North, Deceleration = South.)

The magnetic compass reads correctly *only* when the airplane is in straight and level unaccelerated flight (and sometimes not even then). In bumpy air the compass oscillates so that readings are difficult to take and more difficult to hold. The fluid in the case (acid-free white kerosene) is designed to keep the oscillations at a minimum, but the problem is still there.

Deviation

The compass also has an instrument error due to electrical equipment and metal parts of the plane. This error varies between headings and a correction card is placed near the compass, showing these errors for each 30°. The compass is "swung," or corrected, on a *compass rose*—a large calibrated circle painted on the concrete ramp or taxiway away from metal interference such as hangars. The airplane is taxied onto the rose and corrections are made in the compass with a nonmagnetic screwdriver (the engine should be running and normal radio and electrical equipment on). Attempts are made to balance out the errors—better to have all headings off a small amount than some correct and others badly in error.

In order to use the compass, you must allow for corrections, and for navigation purposes the following steps apply:

1. True course (or heading) plus or minus Variation gives Magnetic course (or heading).
2. Magnetic course (or heading) plus or minus Deviation gives Compass course (or heading).

You can remember TVMDC (TV Makes Dull Children, or The Very Mean Department of Commerce—left over from the days when aviation was under the jurisdiction of the Department of Commerce).

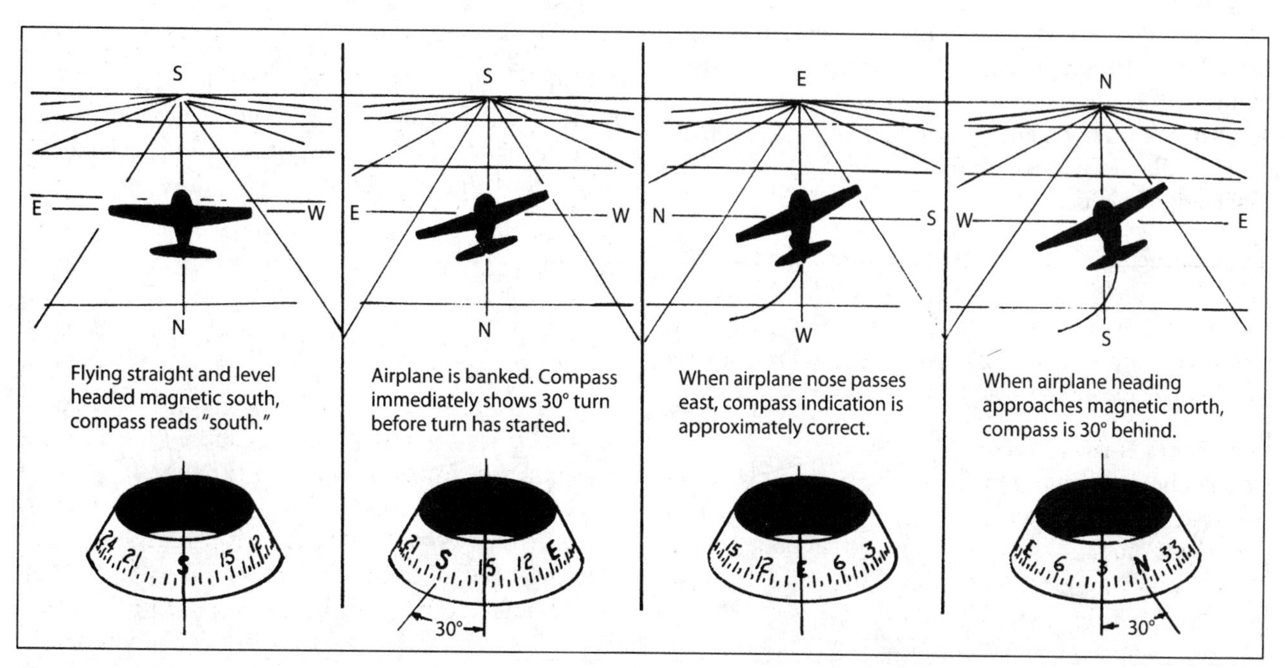

Figure 4-34. Compass reactions to a turn.

Swinging the Compass

You may never be called upon to swing a compass, but as a professional pilot, you should have some idea of the procedure so as to understand whether the magnetic compass in your airplane indicates within a few degrees of what it should. If you work as a flight instructor, as your career progresses you may be disappointed at the conditions of some of the magnetic compasses in the trainers on the line. It may have been so long since some of the compass correction cards have been corrected that they're in Gothic script, or even have Magellan's signature on them. Also, you'll note that some of the cards have *no* deviation indicated and apparently are accurate indeed. Later when you become chief instructor or chief pilot of an organization, it may be your responsibility to see that the trainers' compasses are accurate enough to ensure that the student pilots flying on solo cross-countries don't end up at unplanned destinations.

The Compass Rose

The compass is "swung" on the compass rose with the engine running at a speed at which the alternator is working, and with radios on. For the most accuracy, the airplane should be in the level flight position. Tricycle-gear airplanes give little problem in this regard. Again, the compass rose should be painted on a ramp in an area well away from outside ferrous (iron or steel) or electrical influences. It is oriented with respect to Magnetic North and has lines painted every 30° around the circle (Figure 4-35).

The magnetic compass has two compensating magnets: the North-South magnet has its own screw adjustment as does the East-West magnet. A nonmagnetic screwdriver (easily made by grinding a short section of 3⁄16-inch-diameter copper wire if necessary) is used to make adjustments.

Aircraft Alterations (AC 43.13-l and 2), which gave acceptable methods, techniques, and practices for aircraft inspection and repair and some techniques for swinging aircraft magnetic indicators on the ground:

a. Move the aircraft to a location free from the influence of steel structures, underground pipes and cables, reinforced concrete, or other aircraft.
b. Place the aircraft in level flight position.
c. Check the indicator for fluid level and cleanliness. If fluid is required, the compass is defective.
d. Remove the compensating magnets from the chambers or reset the fixed compensating magnets to neutral positions, whichever is applicable, before swinging.
e. Check the pivot friction of the indicator by deflecting the card with a small magnet. The card should rotate freely in a horizontal plane.
f. Align the aircraft with North magnetic heading and compensate with the compensating magnets. Repeat for the East magnetic heading. Then place on South and West magnetic headings and remove half of the indicated error by adjusting the compensators. The engine(s) should be running.
g. Turn the aircraft to successive 30° headings through 360°. Prepare a placard to show the correction to be applied at each of these headings. When significant errors are introduced by operation of electrical/electronic equipment or systems, the placard should also be marked at each 30° heading showing the correction to be applied when such equipment or systems are turned on or energized.

Adjustment of remote indicating gyro compasses and other systems of this type may be accomplished by the "ground swinging" technique. Reference should be made to the manufacturer's manual for special tools, instructions, and procedures.

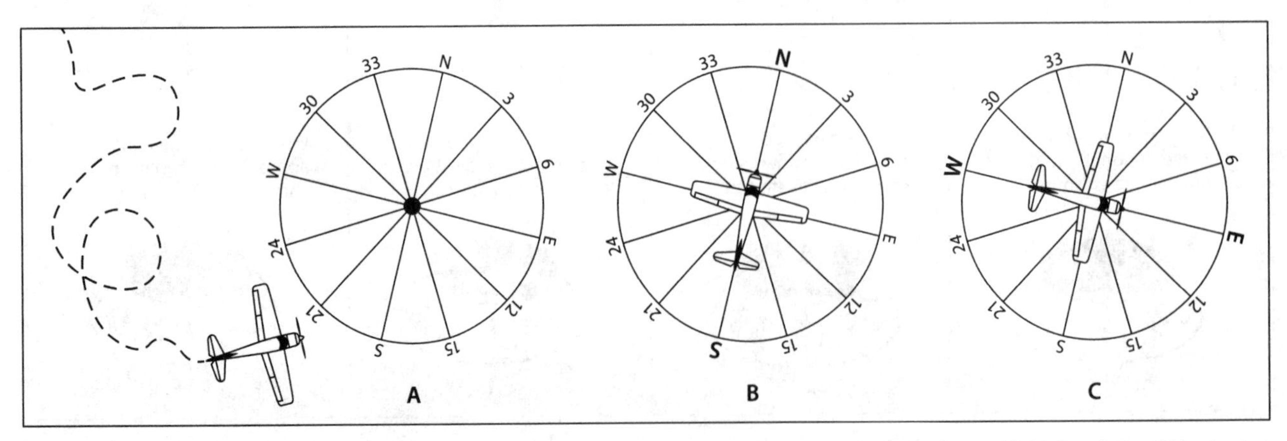

Figure 4-35. The compass rose. **A.** The pilot taxis skillfully onto the rose. **B.** and **C.** North and East (then South and West) headings are corrected. The correction placard is filled for every 30° heading.

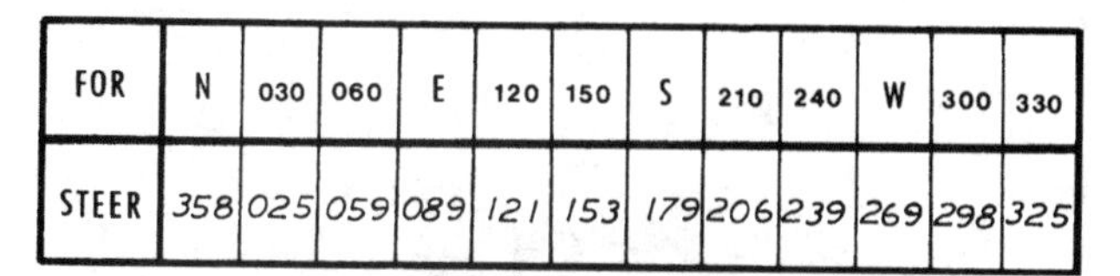

FOR	N	030	060	E	120	150	S	210	240	W	300	330
STEER	358	025	059	089	121	153	179	206	239	269	298	325

Figure 4-36. A deviation card for an aircraft compass.

Figure 4-36 is a correction card for an aircraft compass that this writer "swung" on a small compass rose on his (wooden) desk (no electrical or ferrous metal inputs). Naturally, turning that compass was much easier than turning a full-sized airplane.

One point you may not have considered is that the magnetic compass may be used as a direction *and* bank indicator if you've lost all the gyro instruments. Back in the section "Northerly Turning Error," you'll note that when the compass turned from a heading of South it turned the correct way but exaggerated the amount of turn. You can use this fact to make a straight descent on a South heading through an overcast because bank (and turn) will be indicated more quickly and in the proper direction so that early deviations may be corrected. (Because when on a North heading the compass initially turns to the opposite direction, great confusion might result. On East or West, deviations are not so exaggerated.)

The magnetic compass has many quirks, but once you understand them, it can be a valuable aid. One thing to remember—the mag compass "runs" on its own power and doesn't need electricity or suction to operate. This feature may be important to you some day when your other more expensive direction indicators have failed.

Gyro Flight Instruments

Vacuum-Driven Instruments

For the less expensive airplanes, the gyro instruments are usually vacuum driven, either by an engine drive pump or (rarely) venturi system. A disadvantage of the venturi system is that its efficiency depends on airspeed, and the venturi tube itself causes slight aerodynamic drag. Although a venturi system can be installed on nearly any airplane in a short while, the engine-driven vacuum pump is best for actual instrument operations, because it starts operating as soon as the engine(s) start. Multiengine airplanes usually have a vacuum pump on each engine so that the vacuum-driven instruments will still operate in the event of an engine failure. Each pump has the capacity to carry the system.

Errors in the instruments may arise as they get older and bearings get worn, or the air filters get clogged with dirt. Low suction means low rpm and a loss in efficiency of operation.

Some airplanes use a pneumatic (pressure) pump rather than a vacuum pump to move air through the gyro instruments. The instruments work effectively, and, in addition, the positive pressure system may be set up to operate de-icer boots or work with the turbochargers to pressurize the cabin. (More about that in Chapter 19.)

Electric-Driven Instruments

The electric-driven gyro instruments got their start when high-performance aircraft such as jets began to operate at very high altitudes. The suction-driven instruments lost much of their efficiency in the thin air, and a different source of power was needed.

Below 30,000 feet either type of gyro performs equally well. It is common practice to use a combination of electric- and vacuum-driven instruments for safety's sake, should one type of power source fail. A typical gyro flight instrument group for a single-pilot plane would probably include a vacuum-driven attitude gyro and heading indicator, and an electric turn and slip or turn coordinator. Large airplanes have two complete sets of flight instruments, one set vacuum-driven and one set electric-driven, or two independently-supplied electric instrument sets.

More About Rigidity in Space

You know that, once a gyro is rotating at its operating speed, it resists any force trying to change its plane of rotation or its axis alignment (that is, it has rigidity in space). The resistance to change is a function of the angular velocity, weight (mass), and radius at which the weight is located. To confirm this, take two objects of the same weight and diameter and drill a hole in the center of each to insert an axis and establish equal rotation rates (Figure 4-37). The dumbbell-shaped object (lower) has more "gyroscopic inertia" because its mass is distributed farther out from the axis and the moment of inertia depends on the *square* of the radius of the center of the mass. (Inertia is the property of matter by which it either wants to stay put or, when moving, to continue in a straight line, according to Newton's First Law.) The moment of inertia—and you've run enough weight and balance problems by now to know what a moment is—the distance (radius) squared, times the mass. In other words, the farther out the center of the mass of *each half* of the shapes shown in Figure 4-37 is from the axis, the much greater the inertia.

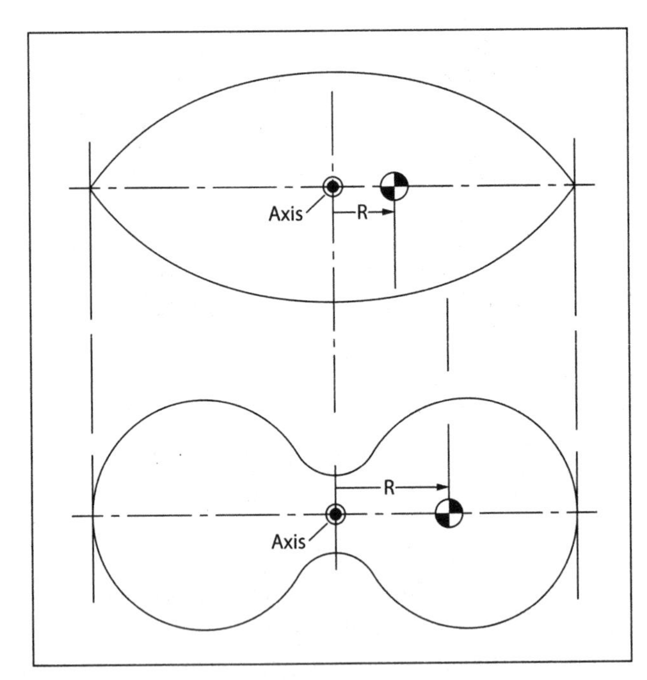

Figure 4-37. Cross sections of two differently shaped objects of equal weight (mass), diameters, and rpm. Note the radii of the CGs of the rotating shapes.

In order to take advantage of this property, the older gyro wheel (rotor) was made so that as much of the mass (weight) as possible is located near the rim (Figure 4-38). From a physics standpoint, it would be good to have section A in Figure 4-38 very thin so as to move the CG of a rotor segment as far out toward the rim as possible, but structural considerations limit this, since the rotation rate in newer gyros may in some cases be up to 30,000 rpm and precession forces could cause destruction of the rotor-axis system. (Precession will be covered shortly.)

Or looking at it another way—Newton's Law stating that a body in motion tends to remain in motion and move in a straight line unless disturbed by an outside force doesn't, at first glance, seem to apply to rotating bodies. However, it does if you look at the gyro as a "bunch of chunks" (Figure 4-39). As the wheel rotates at a high speed, each particle tends to continue in a straight line and leave the system, but it can't because it's attached to the rest. The particle wants to continue in a line in the plane of rotation since there are no forces from the side acting on it for this example.

Looking at two of the equal-weight particles at different radii on the wheel (Figure 4-39), you can note the following. The wheel in Figure 4-39 has a radius of just over 2 inches and is rotating at 10,000 rpm. The circumference of a circle is $2\pi r$. Particle 1 is centered 1 inch from the center; particle 2 is 2 inches from the center and close to the edge of the wheel. The velocity for particle 1 is $2\pi r = 2 \times 3.1416$ in.= 6.2832 inches per

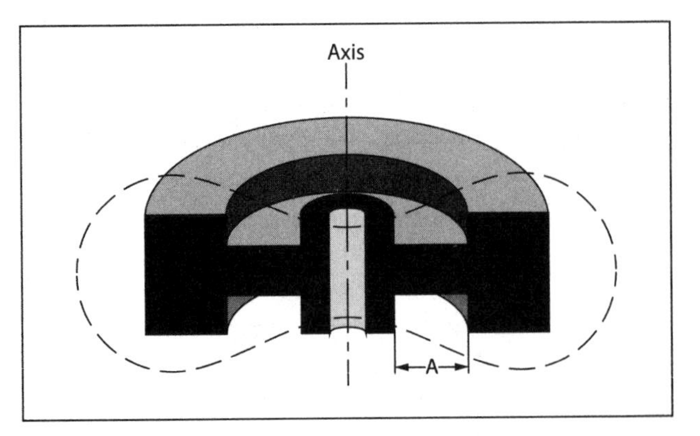

Figure 4-38. Gyro rotor mass distribution.

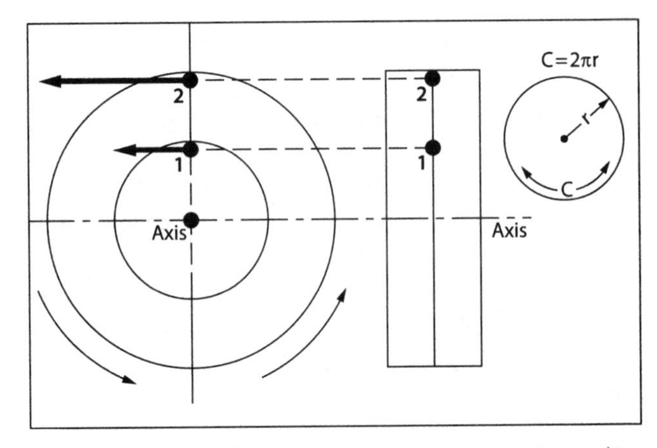

Figure 4-39. Particles with the same mass at varying radii on a rotating wheel.

revolution, or 62,832 inches per minute at 10,000 rpm. Converting to feet per second, you'd divide the inches by 12 to get feet per minute, and then divide that answer by 60: 62,832/12 = 5,236; 5,236/60 = 87.3 fps (linear velocity at any point in that radius).

Doing the same thing for particle 2 the linear velocity is found to be 174.6 fps.

Since kinetic energy (KE) is a function of one-half the mass times the velocity squared, particle 2 contributes 4 times as much to the gyro inertia; $KE = \frac{1}{2}MV^2$. Both have the same weight or mass so that's not a factor. The point is that the "outside" particle (2) is contributing 4 times as much as the inside particle (1), and it's a gaining proposition to move as many "particles" outboard as is structurally possible.

A 12-inch-diameter heavy gyro rotor turning at a very high speed would provide an effective gyro system. The only problem is that size and weight have to be considered for installation in an airplane instrument panel. The older attitude indicators and heading indicators (directional gyros) were both larger and heavier with lower rpm used (Figure 4-40).

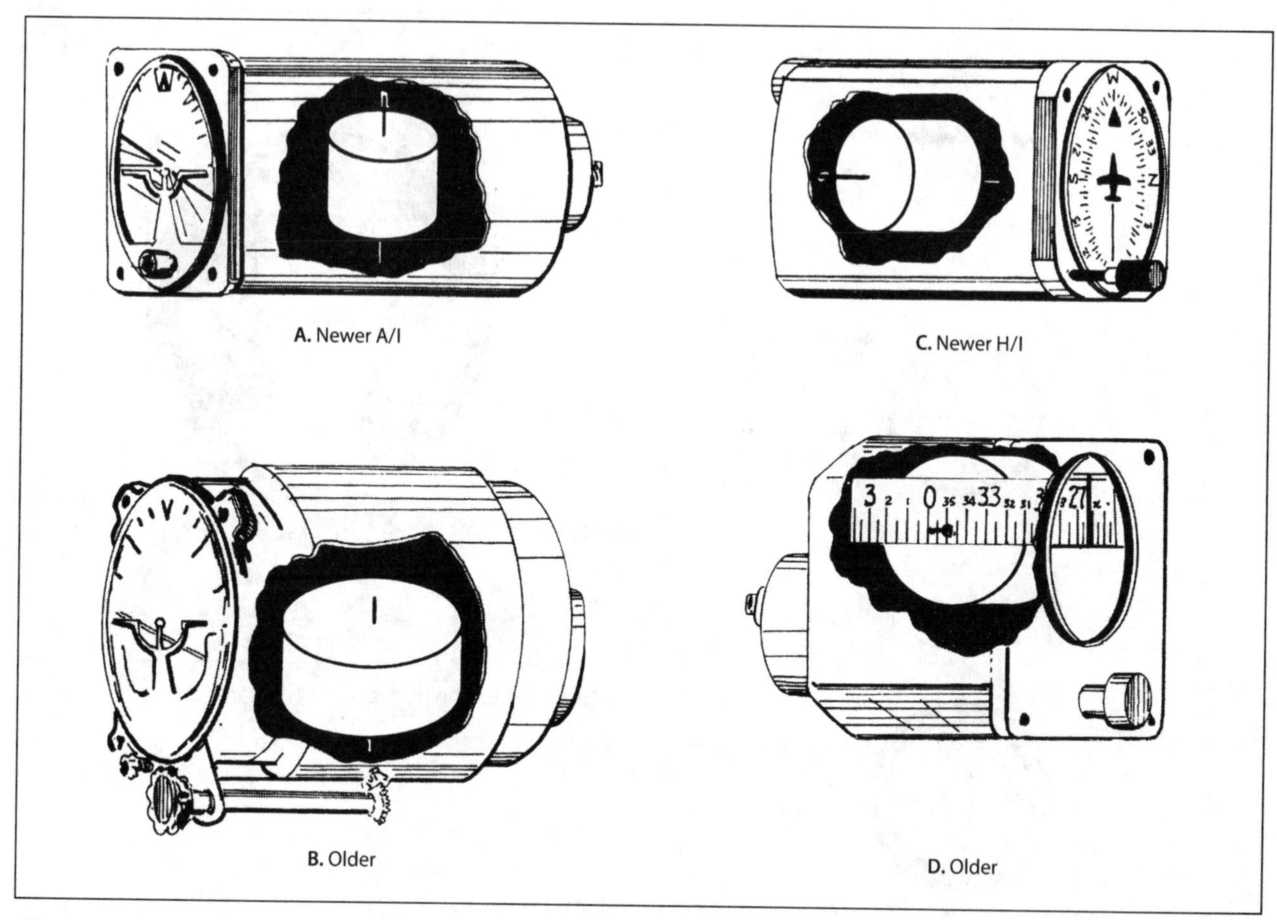

Figure 4-40. A comparisonof old and new gyro instruments. The rotor diameters were decreased so the instruments could be smaller, requiring a higher rpm to get the same gyroscopic inertia.

Gyros and Gimbals

It's all well and good to see the theory of how gyros work, but they have to be mounted into the instruments and here's where the gimbals (supporting rings) come in (Figure 4-41).

When the gyro wheel is mounted (Figure 4-41D), it has freedom around two axes. Following the logic, the gyro system is now complete. The gyro gimbals (support rings) stand (sit?) on the earth, which in turn (or at least legend has it) sits on the back of a great turtle (Figure 4-42).

Attitude Indicator

The plane of rotation of the attitude indicator (A/I) is horizontal (the axis is vertical), and the airplane rolls, pitches, and yaws around it (Figure 4-40 A,B). A/I's may be powered electrically or by vacuum pressure sources.

The electrically driven type may be further divided into those that use 14- and 28-volt DC (direct current) sources and those that have 115-volt AC (alternate current) sources. The latter must be equipped with an inverter to provide the required AC power. These electric A/I's are usually 360° rotation in pitch and roll and may be more expensive than the vacuum-/pressure-driven types (some of which also are considered non-tumbling, self-erecting) (Figure 4-43).

When you're checking out in that more complex twin your corporation is buying, you'll need to know which gyro instruments depend on electrical and which on vacuum/pressure sources. Most lighter airplanes use a vacuum-/pressure-driven attitude indicator and heading indicator ("directional gyro") with an electrically driven turn and slip or turn coordinator as a backup. You may find an installation with an electric-powered A/I and H/I with a vacuum-/pressure-driven turn and slip, particularly on the copilot's side in heavier twins.

The electric instruments have a warning flag or indicator that pops into view when power to the instrument is lost, which should also be showing when the airplane is shut down and sitting at the ramp. (A quick look and an "I see that the A/I on the pilot's side is electric" will establish your expertise at once.)

A/I power requirements—Newer, vacuum-/pressure-driven A/Is normally require a suction of from 4.5 to 5.2 inches of mercury differential at a maximum

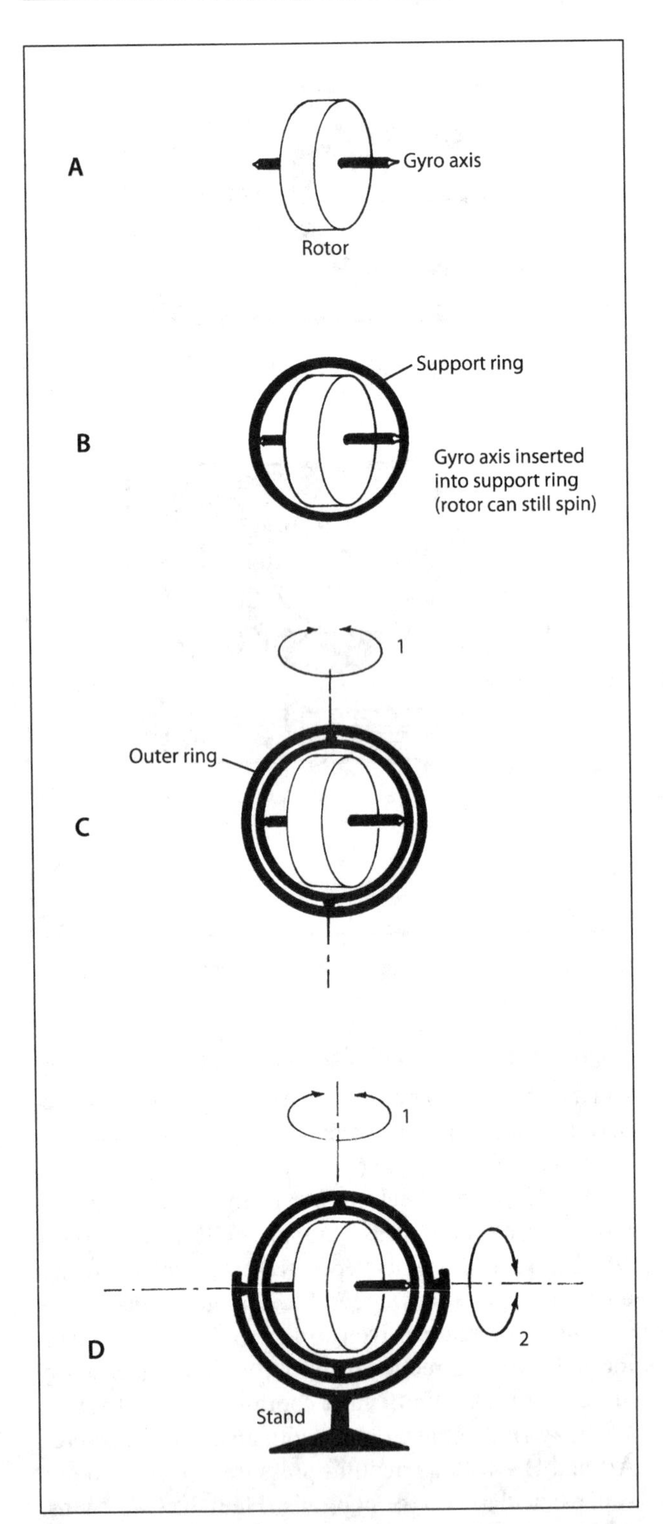

Figure 4-41. Building up a gyro system (assume for now the gyro isn't rotating). **A.** A gyro rotor and axis (axle). **B.** Since a gyro can't just hang around without support, it's inserted into a support ring (or gimbal) that allows it to rotate. **C.** An outer ring is added and attached so that the gyro rotor and support ring can turn within it (1). The rotor and supporting ring are restricted to turning in only one plane at this point. **D.** By adding a stand with axis attachments as shown, the *gyro system* can also turn 360° around that axis (2). By rotating the system (1 and 2) an infinite number of positions relative to the stand can be attained. If the gyro rotor is rotating and rigidity in space is maintained, the outer ring and stand may be moved around the wheel, as would be the case when an airplane does rolls or loops around the horizontal rotor in the attitude indicator.

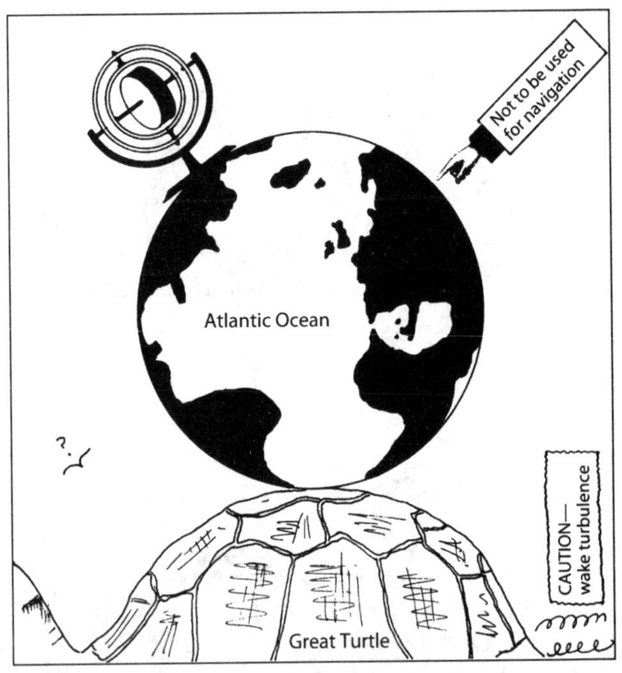

Figure 4-42. The gyro system and earth on the back of a great turtle.

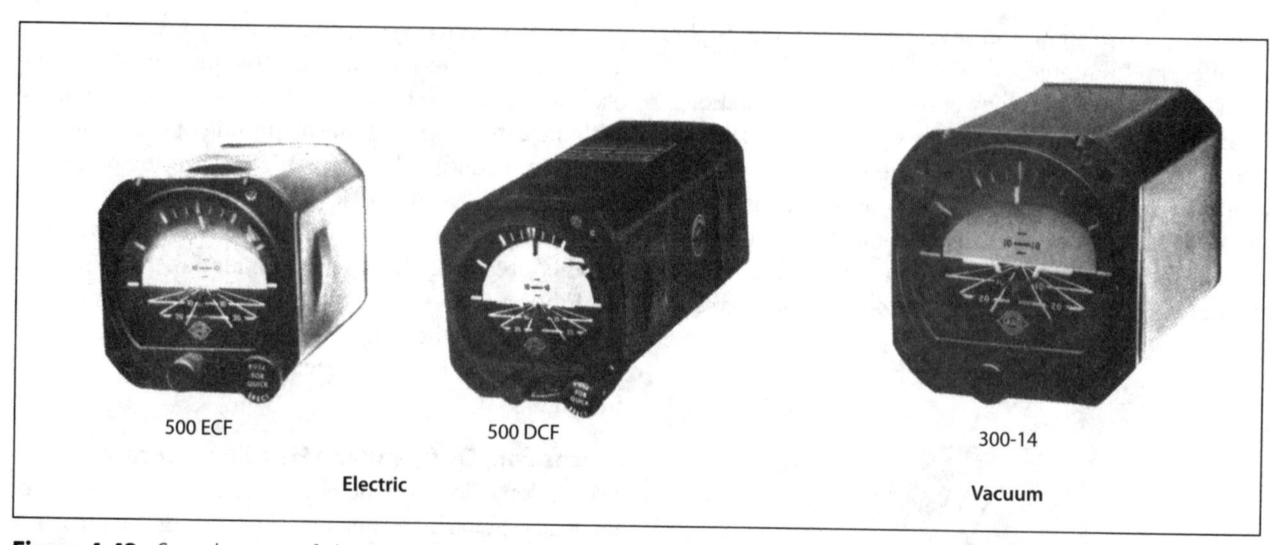

Figure 4-43. Sample types of electric and vacuum attitude indicators. *(Aviation Instrument Manufacturing Corporation)*

flow of 2.1 ft^3 of air per minute (measured at the instrument) as compared with 3.8 or 4.2 inches for earlier models (which makes sense because of the higher rpm required for the smaller-sized gyro rotors). Some of the electric types require the following power:

28-volt DC systems—0.8 amperes

14-volt DC system—1.5 amperes

115-volt AC system—16 volt-amperes for starting and 13 volt-amperes while running.

The newer A/I gyro rotors are 1.375 inches in diameter and 1.300 inches "long," and usually rotate at 20,000 to 25,000 rpm. The *heading indicator* (H/I) rotors have a diameter of 1.375 inches and are 1.500 inches "long."

Incidentally, older A/I instruments have an operating rotor speed of approximately 12,000 rpm and weigh about 4.5 pounds as compared with 2.7 pounds for a current, lighter model. Most of these older models also have pitch and bank limits (before tumbling) of 70° and 100° respectively.

Attitude indicator problems—If the A/I is slow to erect or shows deviation from level flight when you, with your great skills, are really flying level, the problem could be caused by worn bearings or maybe the gyro rotor isn't getting the power (electric or vacuum) that it should. After the flight and you've shut down the engine and the gyros are winding down, listen for noise indicating bearing wear or damage. You should also check the vacuum gage or electric power indicators and power source connections for problems. Smoking in the cabin is bad for vacuum-driven instruments because the filters eventually clog up, and air flow is cut resulting in a decrease in rotor rpm (and gyro inertia).

A/I's precess and react to *acceleration* by falsely indicating a *nose-high* attitude. This can be bad on an actual instrument takeoff when the airplane is accelerating for climb; the pilot thinks the airplane's nose is too high and may ease it over, settling back into the surface (trees, etc.). These A/I's falsely indicate a *nose-low* attitude during *deceleration*. Also, precession error is at a maximum after a 180° turn, when all of the forces have been acting in the same direction. A 180° turn in the opposite direction or continuing the turn for 360° cancels the error.

Note in Figure 4-43 that those electric A/I's have a manual quick erection system in addition to the normal adjustment knob for the small airplane.

The Heading Indicator (or Directional Gyro)

The heading indicator (H/I) functions because of rigidity in space, as does the A/I; but note, looking back at Figure 4-40, that the plane of the rotor is "vertical" (or the axis is "horizontal," if you prefer to look at it that way). The gyro is fixed relative to the card, and the airplane turns around it. Most heading indicators, both old and new types, have the gyro axis lined up with North and South indications.

The newer H/I's with vertical faces, although mechanically attached (through gears), also indicate North or South when the gyro axis is aligned with the long axis of the instrument.

The older H/I's weighed as much as 3.75 pounds and operated at 10,000 rpm, compared with 2.9 pounds and 24,000 rpm for some more-recent models. Both types use the same gyro position (vertical plane) for their principle of operation (Figure 4-44).

The nonslaved heading indicator must be reset to the magnetic compass when it is reading correctly; this is usually in straight and level, unaccelerated flight about every 15 minutes.

The older and some newer models have limitations of 55° pitch or bank, although if you are, for instance, doing a roll with the H/I indicating North or South, or a loop on an indication of East or West, this limitation does not apply because the airplane is moving *around* the rotor in these cases and is not forcing the rotor against the stops. *(Don't do loops or rolls except in an aerobatic airplane.)*

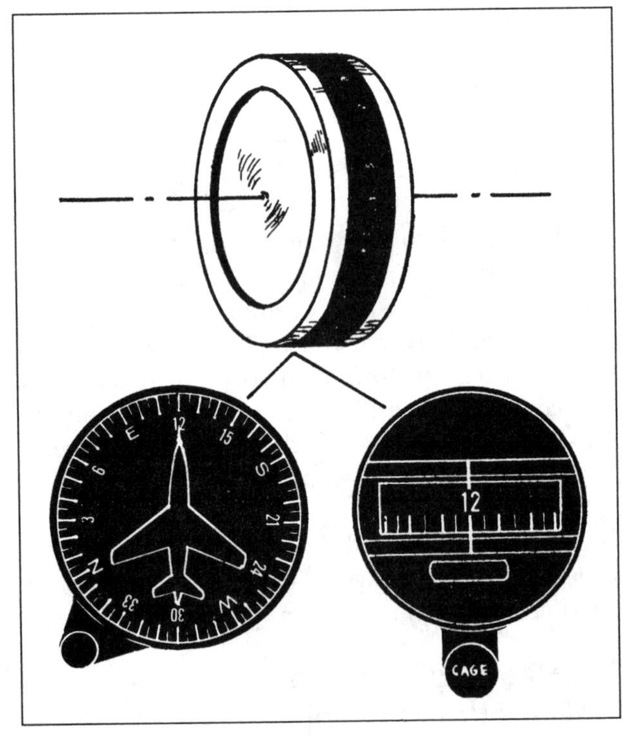

Figure 4-44. The heading indicator. The airplane turns around the vertical gyro wheel.

A slaved gyro system continually corrects for gyro drift and compensates for magnetic dip, deviation, and oscillation. You set the H/I to the magnetic compass with the card set knob at the beginning of the flight and the system continually corrects itself while operating. The remotely mounted flux detector (the magnet portion of the system) is normally mounted in the wingtip or other area away from ferrous material.

Figure 4-45 shows different types of vacuum-/pressure-driven heading indicators. Figure 4-46 shows some different types of electrically powered heading indicators.

Precession, Drift, and the Heading Indicator

Precession effects on the H/I are caused by three main factors: (1) bearing problems, (2) effect of the airplane being turned and hence trying to "turn" or move the gyro wheel from its plane of rotation, and (3) apparent precession ("drift" caused by the earth's rotation). Of these, only gyro drift can be predicted because the condition of the bearings depends on (1) the age and history of the particular instrument and (2) the number (and degree) of turns done within a given time during a flight.

Computing the effect of the earth's rotation (gyro drift) can be complicated, but a look at the idea will give you a chance to use some of that trigonometry you did so well with in Chapter 1. The value of the error caused by the earth's rotation (apparent precession) *per hour* is 15.04 × sin latitude. The earth turns 15.04° per hour. We've always rounded it off to 15° in basic navigation and Coordinated Universal Time (UTC) problems. The sine of an angle, if you recall, is zero at 0° and 1 at 90° (Figure 4-47).

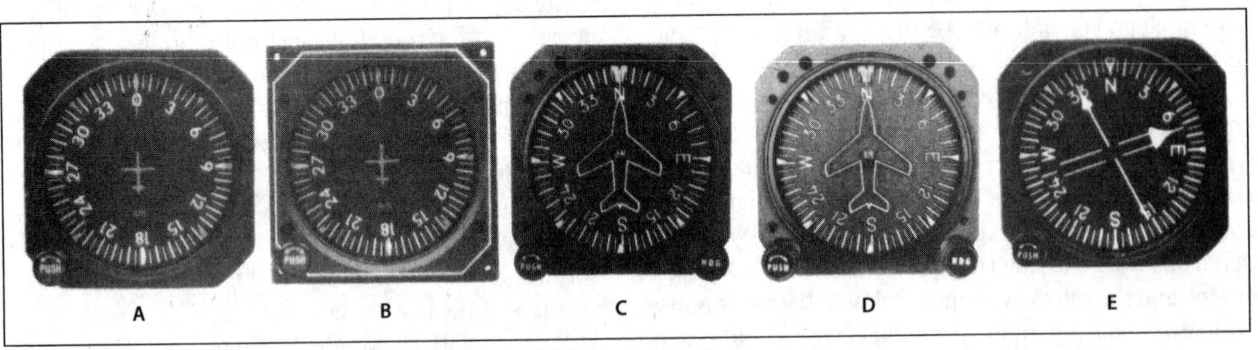

Figure 4-45. Vacuum/pressure heading indicators (directional gyros) using 4.5–5.2 inches of mercury. **A.** A "standard" type of instrument used on many trainers. **B.** H/I with an ARINC or international standards bezel (pronounced "bezzle") or panel cutout shape. The standard bezel for an instrument is round with a diameter of 3.125 inches. Notice that this instrument has a modified octagonal cutout (white outline). **C.** H/I with a different indicator and a movable "bug" and 45° references to aid the pilot in setting a heading reference. **D.** This model provides autopilot heading select outputs. **E.** Slaved instrument. It has optional RMI (radio magnetic indicator) pointers for simultaneous VOR/ADF displays. Included with the installation is a slaving indicator and a magnetic flux detector (usually in the wing tip or in a part of the airplane well away from ferrous or electrical influence). *(Aviation Instrument Manufacturing Corporation)*

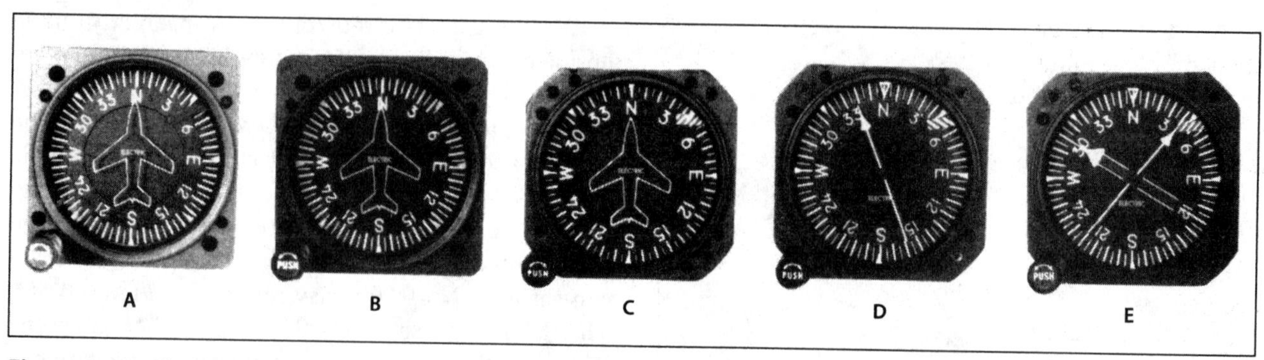

Figure 4-46. Electric heading indicators. **A.** 28- or 14-volt DC free (nonslave) gyro. **B.** 115-volt, 400-Hz (cycles) free directional gyro. **C.** 115-volt, 400-Hz slaved heading indicator. **D.** Slaved H/I with RMI (115-volt, 400-Hz). **E.** Slaved H/I and RMI with dual pointers (115-volt, 400-Hz). *(Aviation Instrument Manufacturing Corporation)*

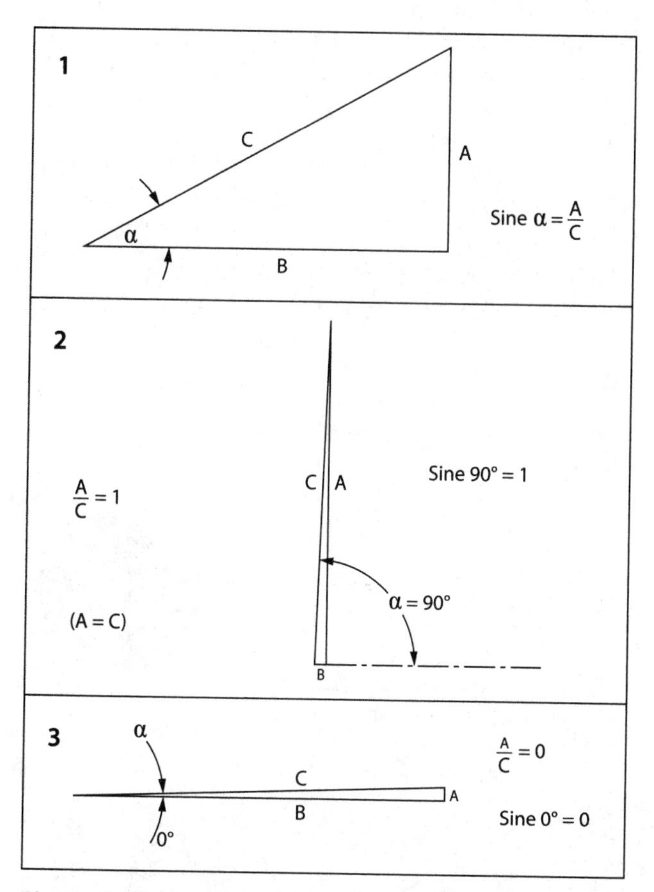

Figure 4-47. A review of sine values for 0° and 90°.

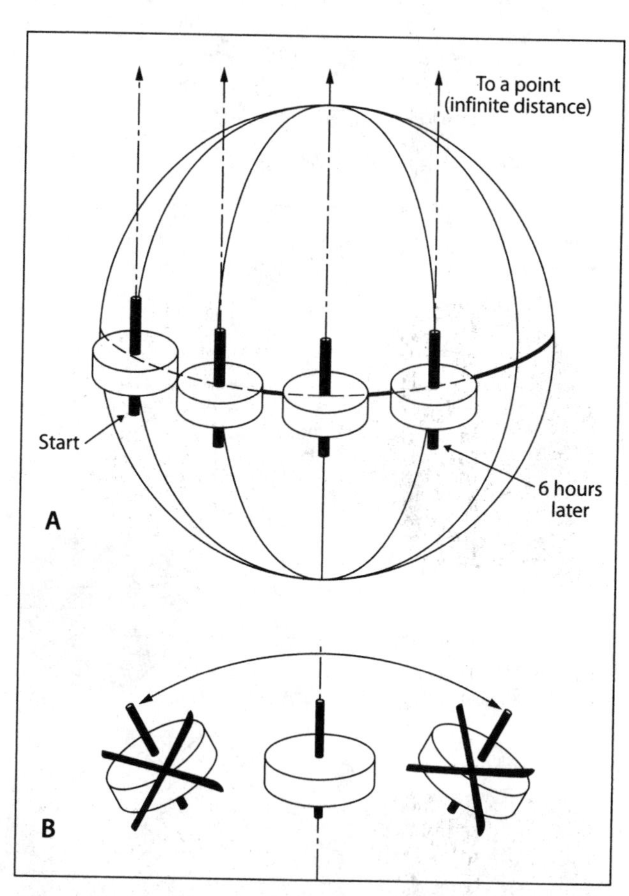

Figure 4-48. A. A gyro rotating at the equator with the axis parallel to the surface and aligned True North and South. **B.** The gyro axis will remain constant as the earth rotates.

Suppose the airplane is sitting tied down on the ramp at the equator (latitude = 0) facing North with the heading indicator in operation. The gyro axis is lined up with a point in space, say, an infinite distance away. The earth turns 15.04° per hour, so in 6 hours it will have turned a little over 90°. The gyro axis is still lined up with that point, with no measurable error because of the angle involved (Figure 4-48).

The gyro principle of rigidity in space keeps the gyro axis pointed at that point an infinite distance away. You are rotating *around* that line but have not changed the angle of the gyro axis in reference to that line. The point is that the gyro hasn't turned with respect to the original setting.

Figure 4-49 shows the top view of an operating gyro system at the equator that has the plane of the gyro pointing toward North (or the axis pointing toward the ground, rather than parallel to it as in Figure 4-48). Note that as the earth rotates, the gyro rotor, while maintaining a constant rigidity in space, is radically changing its relationship to the earth. The "face" of the wheel is pointing at the ground at position 1. At position

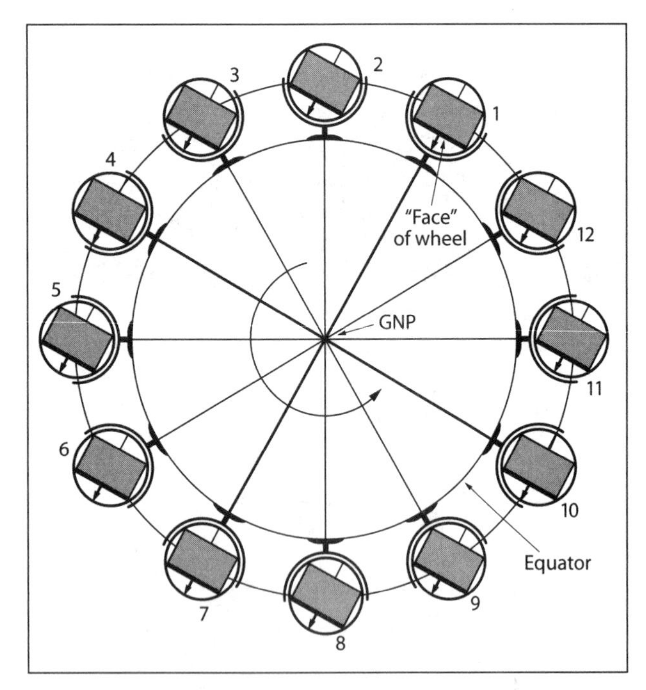

Figure 4-49. A gyro system (rotor at speed) at the equator with the "face" of the wheel pointing at the ground. As the earth rotates for 24 hours, the gyro rotor apparently turns 360° in its gimbal system.

7, 12 hours later (180° rotation), it has apparently turned upside down and is pointing straight up. After another 12 hours it will be back to "normal."

Take an airplane sitting *tied down* with the engine running and the H/I in operation right at the Geographic (or True) North Pole. You've set the H/I on a heading of North for this example. (Actually all headings from the True North Pole are South but for this example you can set it on North for easy reference) (Figure 4-50). The H/I that was set on North 6 hours earlier now reads West even though the H/I was not reset and the airplane is still tied down, pointing directly at the same igloo, or the original "North." The equation to determine precession error (per hour) is 15.04 × sin latitude. At the equator (latitude 0°), $15.04 \times \sin 0° = 15.04 \times 0 = 0$, or *no error*. At the True North or South Pole (latitude = 90°, $15.04 \times \sin 90° = 15.04 \times 1 = 15.04°$ precession error per hour, or the *maximum possible*.

The question now is, How does that affect the H/I, or *in which direction* is the correction to be made for the stationary H/I used in the example in Figure 4-50? The airplane is still pointed at the igloo, our original "North" (360°), but the H/I shows 270, or West. To

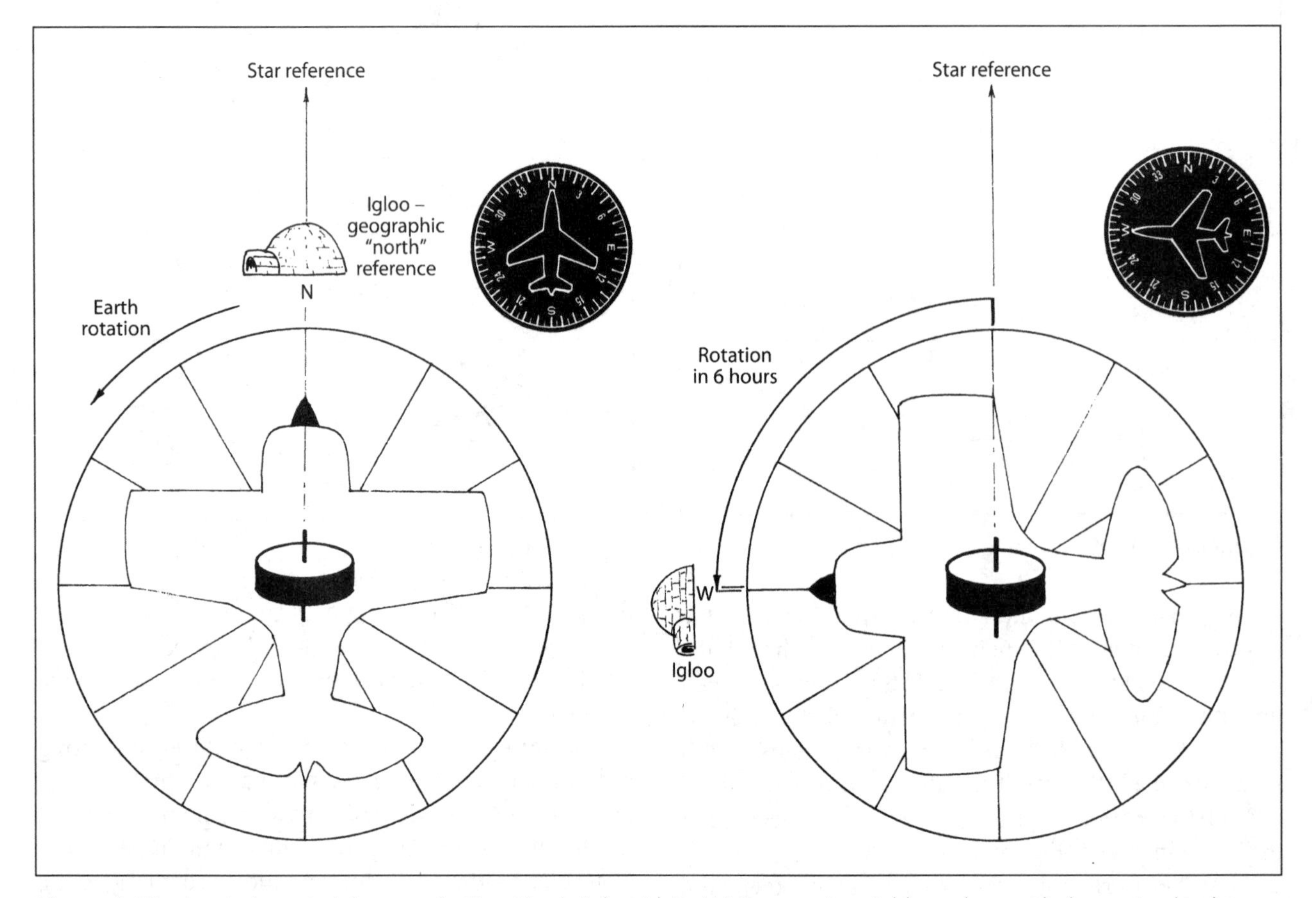

Figure 4-50. An airplane tied down at the True North Pole with its H/I in operation. Add numbers with the setting knob to correct for the apparent drift.

use the same geographic reference and starting over (the pilot slept for 6 hours and woke up to discover the problem), the H/I must be mechanically rotated clockwise 90° (*add* numbers) from a reading of West to a reading of North. This effect lessens as the airplane (or fixed H/I) is closer to the equator. In the northern hemisphere, *add* numbers to correct the error caused by the earth's rotation.

At a latitude of 30° N you would expect an error per hour of 15:04 × sin 30° = 15.04 × 0.5 = 7.52° per hour (fixed position). You must *add* this amount to the H/I indication each hour to correct the error.

What if an airplane were tied down with the H/I at the *True South Pole?* Look at Figure 4-51. From a point directly "below" the True South Pole, the earth's rotation appears to be in reverse, but you're looking at it from the opposite direction from that in Figure 4-50. The earth is rotating to the "East." The airplane is tied down at the True South Pole on a heading of North, pointing at the mountain peak (geographic reference) with the H/I in operation.

After 6 hours the H/I is indicating East (090°) while the airplane is still facing *its* North reference (the peak). The reading would have to be *decreased* by 090° to correct for the gyro drift caused by the earth's rotation. Figures 4-50 and 4-51 show the extreme of the contrasts between north and south latitudes; each hemisphere's *error would decrease* as the positions chosen *approach the equator.*

In review, *to correct for gyro drift or apparent precession:*

North *latitudes—increase* numbers on the H/I
South *latitudes—decrease* numbers on the H/I

This is the error for a stationary gyro.

You're not going to go into the problem so deeply in every flight; the old "set your H/I with the magnetic compass every 15 minutes" works fine, but later you may use the Inertial Navigation Systems or other advanced equipment and should have a look at the principle involved.

Looking at some other factors: Suppose that an airplane at 30° N latitude is flying on a heading of True East (the airspeed to be decided later).

You know that on the equator every degree of longitude is 60 NM and when a stationary point there has turned 90° (earth's rotation) it will have "moved" 5,400

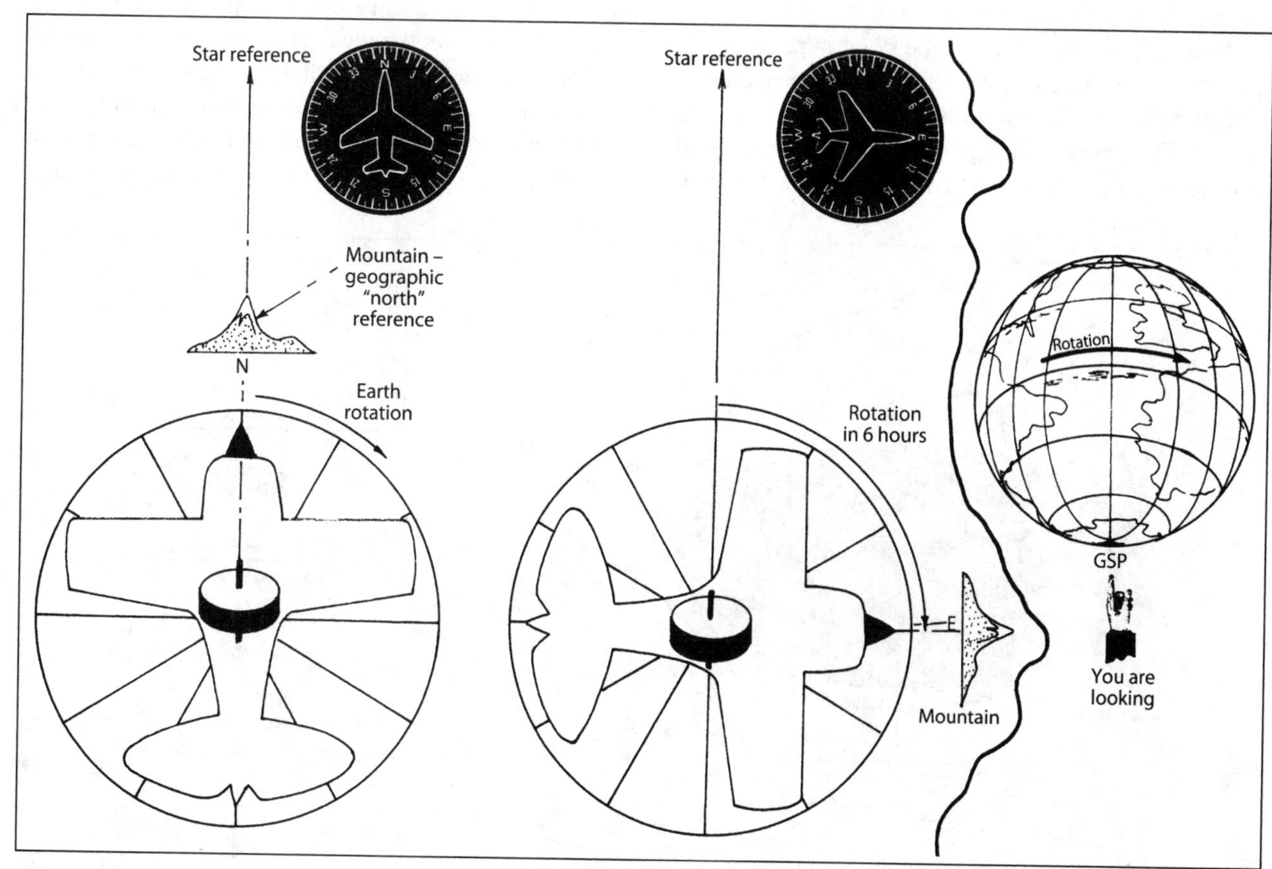

Figure 4-51. An airplane tied down at the True South Pole with its H/I in operation. Subtract numbers with the setting knob to correct for the apparent drift.

NM. (For example purposes here, round off the earth's rotation to 15° per hour and 900 NM per hour at the equator.) You also know that the meridians converge at the True North and South Poles and every degree of longitude on those points is 0 NM.

Figure 4-52 shows an idea of "mileage covered" for a stationary point on the equator and one at 30° N latitude when the earth has rotated 90°. The cosine of 30° is 0.866 (Figure 1-8); a point at 30° N would move a distance of 0.866 as far as the point (moving 900 K) at the equator. That point at 30° N will move "East" 0.866 × 900 = 780 NM per hour (rounded off). The numbers show the comparative distance covered in 6 hours.

An example: You are flying a jet on a true course of 270° (True West) at 30° N latitude at 780 K groundspeed and pass over a city (Figure 4-53, point A) at 1100Z. The situation is that the airplane is staying at that *point in space* and no gyro drift is occurring. The airplane is certainly traveling hell-bent-for-election west over the earth itself but is holding its own with respect to that point in space when time zero (1100Z) occurs. The jet is canceling out the movement of that point on the earth's surface, which is moving east at 780 K with respect to the original reference an infinite distance away.

You are staying over the same point in reference to space while geographically flying 780 miles due west, cancelling out the apparent drift. An analogy would be that of a person walking down an "up" escalator at its exact speed, moving with reference to the escalator (that is, stepping on different steps) but not moving as far as the store "space" is concerned. (Astronomers: Don't write to mention that the earth is moving around the sun and the universe is expanding and ask for some extra velocity components to be thrown in here—we're having enough trouble as it is.)

If the airplane is traveling due *east* at 780 K at 30° N, the *apparent drift error* is *compounded*; the airplane is aiding and abetting the problem by adding its speed to that of the earth's rotation.

Earlier it was noted that the drift (precession) error at 30° N latitude would be 7.52° per hour and also that a point on the earth at that latitude would be traveling "eastward" at 780 K because of the rotation. If that airplane is traveling due east at 780 K, its apparent drift would be another 7.52° for a total error of 15.04°, or the same error that would be present at the geographic poles (and obviously this is a canned problem).

So, in the northern hemisphere, *if the airplane is flying westerly, the component of its flight path parallel to the equator, or parallel to the earth's rotation, decreases the drift error. Flying easterly, the error is compounded.*

The component of its flight path parallel to the equator is the one causing (or helping) the problem. Figure 4-54 shows the idea. The airplane's component of flight parallel to the equator is 780 K and equal to the travel of a fixed point on the earth, so here, too, the error is apparently doubled. Actually the fact that the airplane is traveling in a northerly direction at that

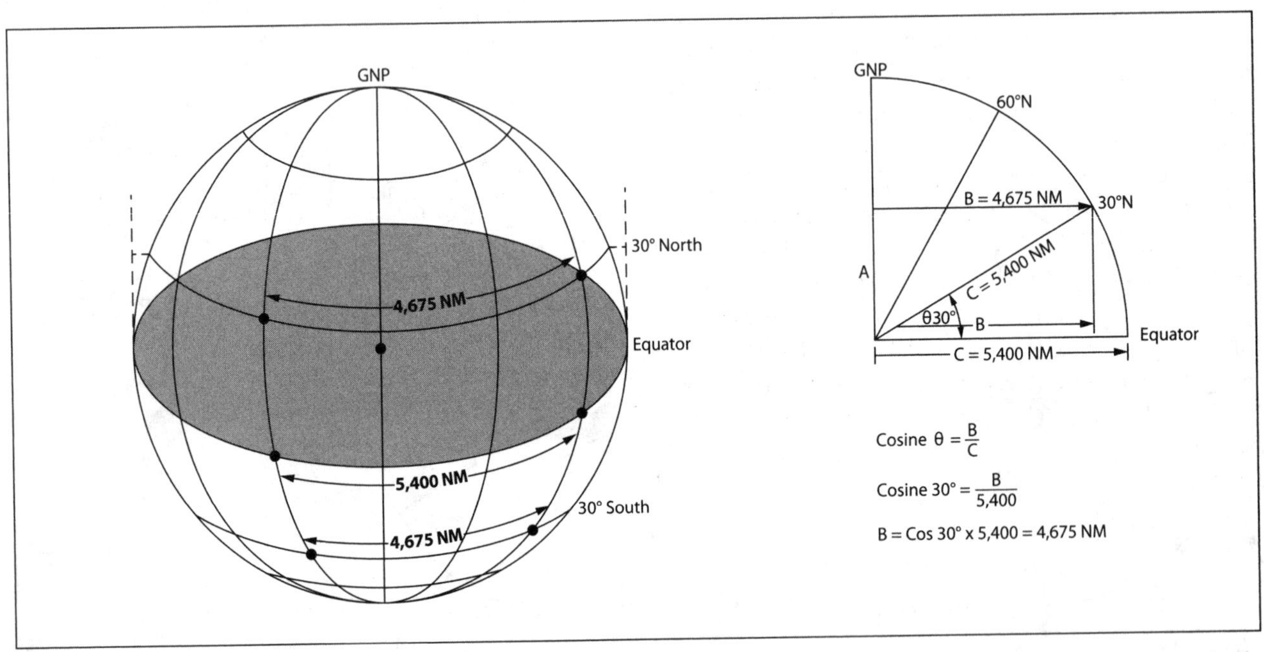

Figure 4-52. Distances between meridians at the equator (5,400 miles) and at 30° N or 30° S (4,675 miles). The numbers have been rounded off for neatness and clarity of thought.

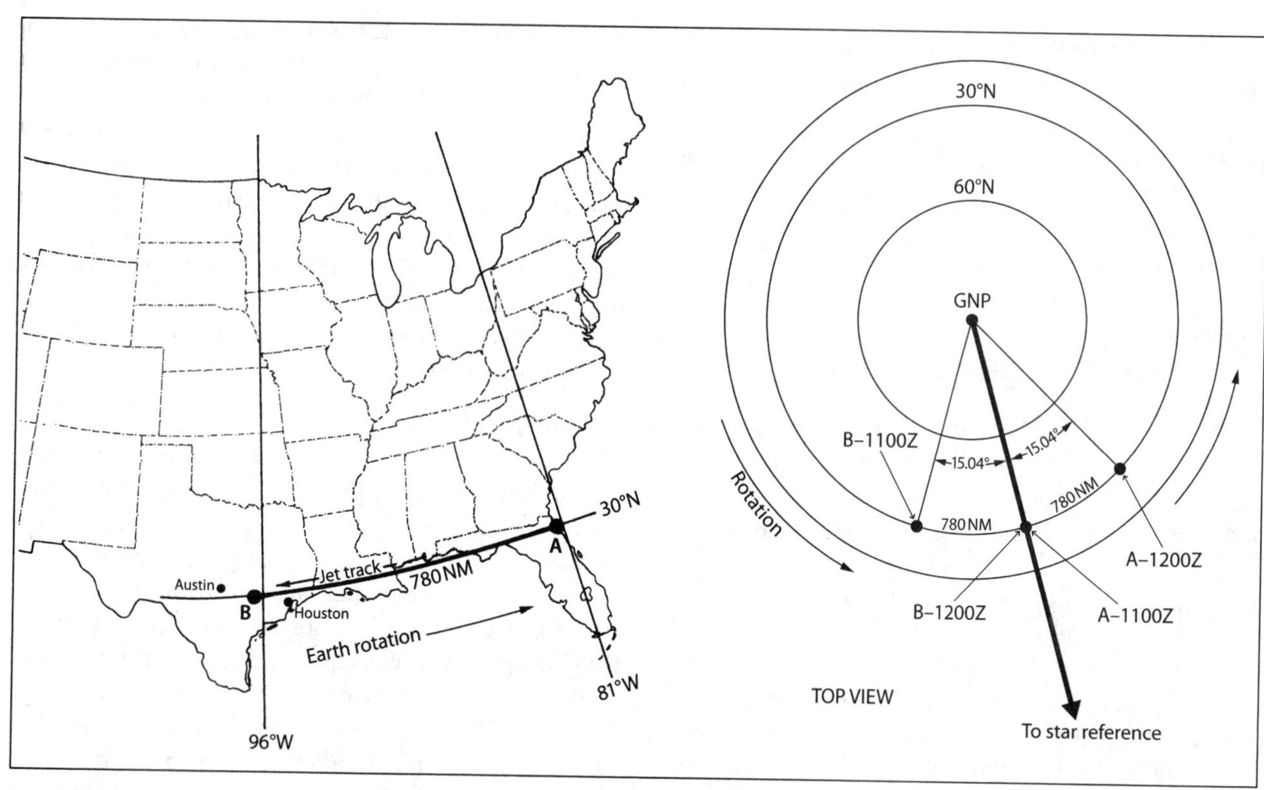

Figure 4-53. A jet flying True West at 30° N at 780 K would cancel out the gyro drift effects. It departed point A at 1100Z and arrived at point B at the same point in space at 1200Z.

speed causes the error to be more than doubled. As the latitude is increased (which would be the case of a course of 060°) *the drift error is increased* because the error is a function of 15.04 × sin latitude. Flying *east* or *north* (northern hemisphere), the apparent drift error is increased over that of the stationary gyro. Flying *west* or *south* (again northern hemisphere) would decrease the apparent drift error from that of a stationary gyro.

You can calculate the error caused by the increase in latitude for the airplane in Figure 4-54 by simple trigonometry: The flight angle from True East is 30°; at the end of an hour, the airplane will have traveled north by the factor $\sin \alpha = A/C$; $A = C \times \sin \alpha = 900 \times 0.5 = 450$ NM. Realizing that each 60 NM north adds another degree of latitude to the 30° N at the start, the airplane would be at 37.5° N at the end of 1 hour (450/60 = 7.5). The error would be greater at the end of the hour. If the airplane is flying a heading of 120° true, the error at the end of the hour would be that for 22.5° N, using the reasoning above.

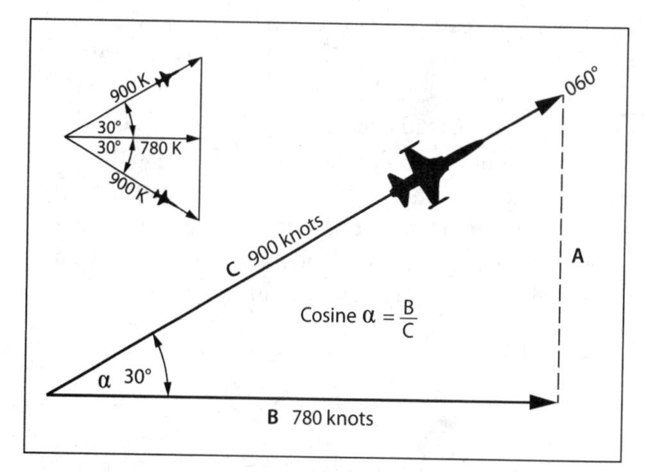

Figure 4-54. The airplane traveling at 900 K on a true course of 060° is moving True East at 780 K.

The Precession Instruments

The turn and slip (T/S) and turn coordinator (T/C) use the principle of precession for operation, as you've been aware of since you first read about it as a student pilot. The point is that the gyro rotor tends to stay in the same plane of rotation (or keeps the axis pointed in the same direction relative to space, whichever you prefer), and any outside force acting perpendicular to the plane of rotation causes the gyro wheel to move as if the force had been applied 90° around the rim in the direction of rotation.

Precession depends on the gyro rotor rpm and the force acting to tilt the rotor. The higher the gyro inertia (which again depends on the mass, radius of the center of the mass, and rpm), the more resistant it is to precession. The greater the value and/or rate of application of the acting side force, the greater the precession effects if all other considerations are equal.

A toy gyroscope may be used to illustrate precession. If the end of the axis of the nonspinning rotor is placed on the pedestal, it will obviously fall off as gravity cannot be denied (Figure 4-55). The CG of the system is well outside the point of support. Strange things happen if the gyro rotor is rotating within a certain rpm value range. The rotor wants to fall but, if the rpm is right, will instead precess or rotate around the stand, the axis remaining level. Gravity causes the rotor to want to tilt forward and down, but its rotation sets up a coupling that instead causes the gyro rotor and axis to rotate horizontally on the stand. In Figure 4-56 the rotor itself is shown rotating counterclockwise around the axis as seen from "head-on," and you can see in the top view that the system (rotor and axis) is rotating around the stand in a counterclockwise direction.

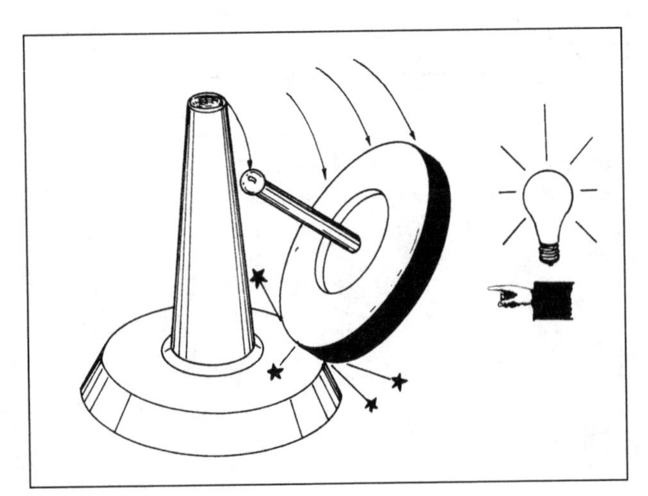

Figure 4-55. The nonrotating gyro will fall off the stand. A degree in physics is not necessary to predict this.

In trying to fall, the weight of the rotor sets up a force-couple system that reacts with the counterclockwise rotation so that the system turns to the left (as seen from above) rather than falling. As the rotation slows, the forces and couples will no longer be in balance and the rotor will oscillate and move downward and eventually fall.

The T/S and T/C are limited to movement of one degree of freedom. The gyro wheel "tilts" in two directions with respect to the instrument, "leftward" and "rightward" (Figure 4-57).

The Turn and Slip

The turn and slip (or needle and ball, or turn and bank as it used to be known) was *the* instrument for "blind flying" in earlier days. It was powered by a venturi on the side of the fuselage, usually most effective at around 85 K, which meant that the airplane was airborne and committed before the pilot knew whether the instrument was working or not. Also, structural ice could be a "minor nuisance" as it plugged the venturi.

The tilting movement of the rotor is limited by stops; the instruments have springs to dampen the movement and to lower chances of shock damage as the

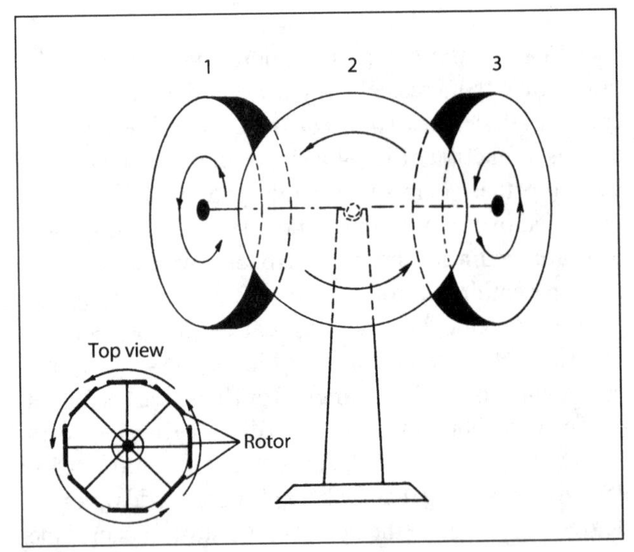

Figure 4-56. Rotating gyro wheel reactions at a certain rpm.

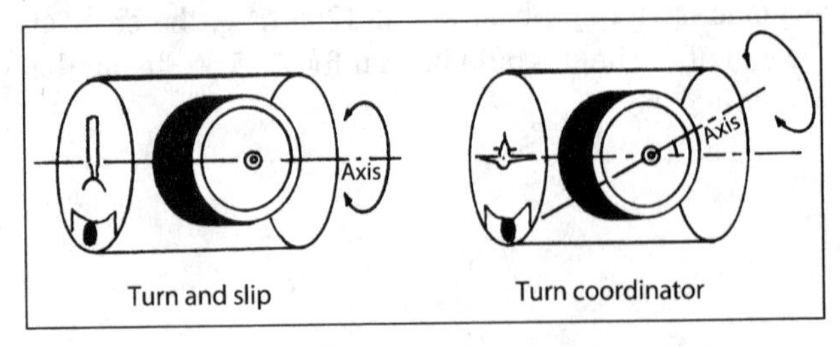

Figure 4-57. Turn and slip and turn coordinator axis alignment.

system reaches its stops. The needle of the T/S reacts to the yaw component only, so that a "flat" turn (skid) would give the most accurate value of the rate of nose movement around the horizon (Figures 4-58 and 4-59).

It's best to have the flight instruments on different power sources so that all won't fail at once, thus the usual installation is to have the A/I and H/I vacuum pressure-driven and the T/S electric. Other setups have electric A/I and H/I with a vacuum-pressure T/S. For larger airplanes, the instruments may be the two combinations just discussed, one for the pilot and the opposite arrangement for the copilot's panel.

A note with the literature for a particular T/S indicates that the instrument can be installed and used with instrument panels that are tilted as much as 8° from vertical.

There is some confusion about the markings on various models of the T/S because some have "4 minutes" on the face, others "2 minutes," and others have no indication of any kind. The "2 minutes" indicates the time required to complete a standard rate turn of 360° at 3° per second *if the needle is deflected one needle width from center.* The 4-minute-turn instrument is used for higher-speed airplanes where 1½° per second is a standard rate to avoid too-steep banks.

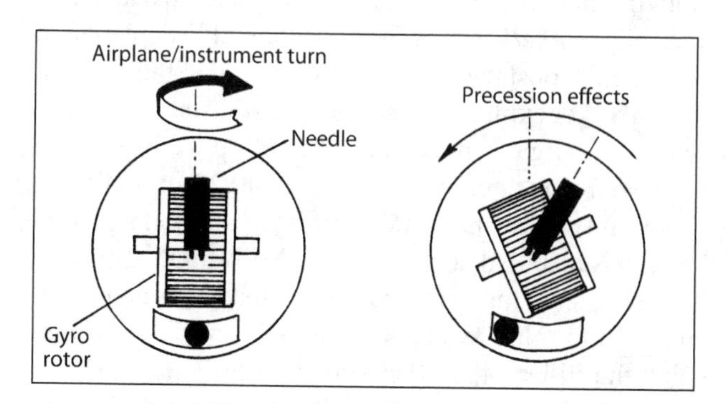

Figure 4-58. Needle and ball reactions to a "flat turn."

In Chapter 1 it was explained that the turn rate was a function of the tangent of the angle of bank, or working further and using 3° per second as a fixed rate, it's possible to set up this equation: $\tan \phi = 3V/1{,}091$. You would set in the airspeed (knots here) to solve for the tangent of the angle of bank and use Figure 1-8 to find the bank.

Turn Coordinator

At this writing, turn coordinators are electrically driven. The axis of lateral movement of the T/C rotor is at a 30° angle to the long axis of the instrument. The T/S reacted only to yaw because of its installation and the fact (again) that precession acts 90° around the rotor.

The T/C is designed so that the pilot gets a roll input, as well as a response to yaw. The primary role of the instrument, however, is to measure the yawing of the nose (rate of turn) so the long axis is angled up only 30°, leaving yaw as the primary mover of the indicator (Figure 4-57).

Figure 4-60 shows an electric T/C and vacuum/pressure and electric T/S's.

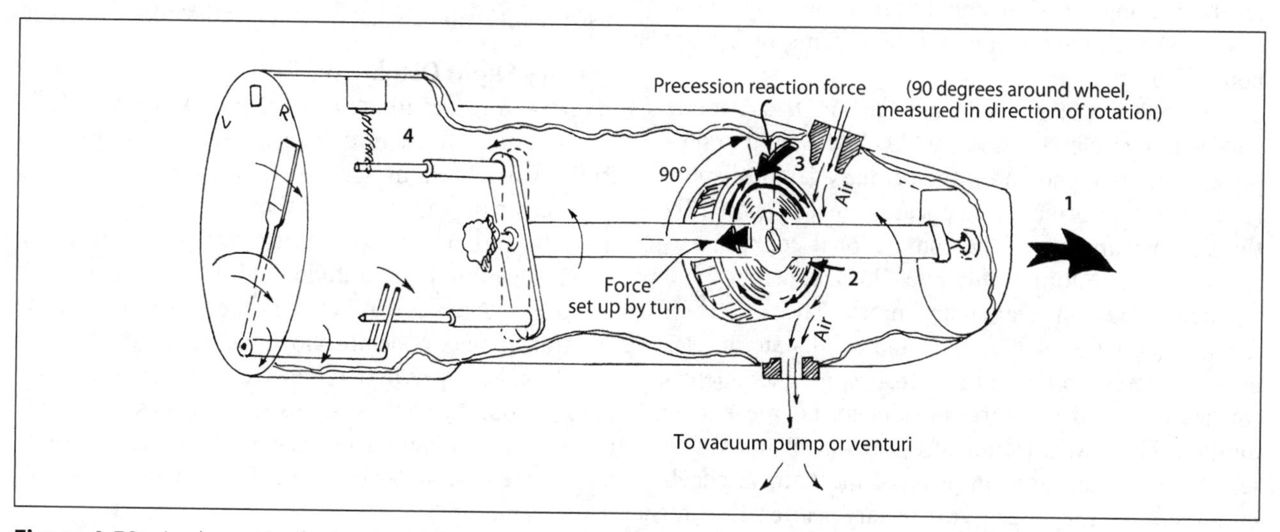

Figure 4-59. A schematic of a vacuum-driven turn and slip reacting to a right turn.

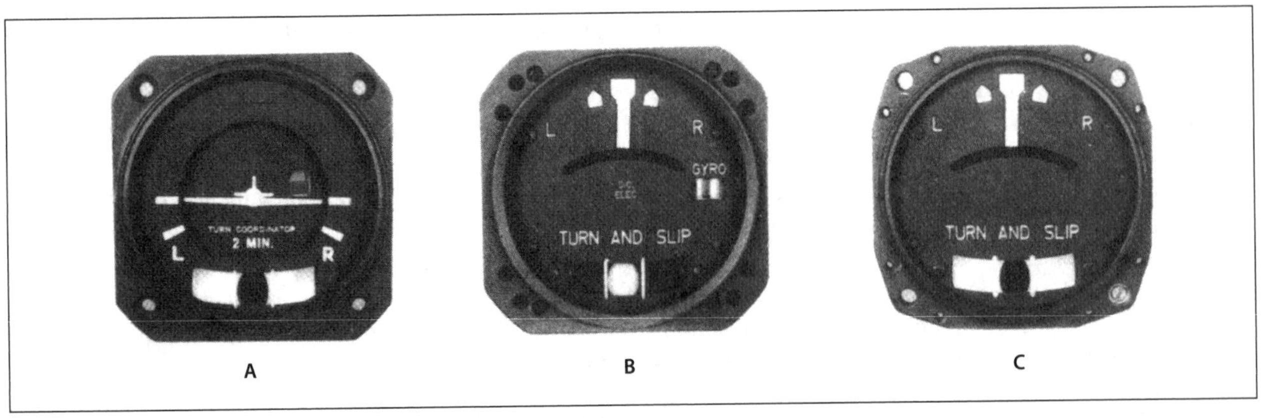

Figure 4-60. A. Turn coordinator (electric 14 or 28 volts DC). Note the warning flag that indicates electrical power is not getting to the instrument. **B.** Electric turn and slip indicator (28 volts DC) with warning flag. **C.** A vacuum/pressure turn and slip indicator. This instrument can use differentials of 1.8 to 2.2 inches or 4.6 to 5.2 inches of mercury as desired. Lighting is optional for these instruments. *(Aviation Instrument Manufacturing Corporation)*

Glass Cockpits

Glass cockpits (flight information displayed on screens instead of round mechanical dials) are a fairly recent development in instrument flight and have vastly increased the pilot's awareness of what the airplane is doing now and in the near future. The biggest benefit of current glass cockpits is the overall situational awareness, especially when "synthetic vision" is incorporated (this is explained below). Since most newly manufactured airplanes come with glass, you'll soon have the chance to try it (if you haven't already). It's a big step forward.

One example of a complete glass cockpit system is the Dynon Avionics "Skyview" system. Although meant for airplanes with experimental type certificates and light sport aircraft, this system is representative of all the leading glass cockpit systems and is far more advanced than most of the airliners flying over your home airport.

Dynon's Skyview system uses an Air Data Attitude and Heading Reference System (ADAHRS) unit to supply information shown on the primary flight display (PFD). This information duplicates what is shown by the six instruments of the conventional cockpit: airspeed, attitude, altitude, turn rate/slip/skid, heading and vertical speed (plus a great deal more). The ADAHRS is small (about 5" × 3" × 1.2") and solid state. It uses accelerometers, rotation rate sensors, magnetometers for heading, and pressure transducers for measuring air data. These MEMS (micro-electro-mechanical systems) sensors are used in place of mechanical accelerometers or ring laser gyros in larger aircraft. Pitot and static air pressure are piped into the unit, along with optional angle of attack (AOA) data. A second ADAHRS can be installed to automatically take over if the primary one fails.

The flight information from the ADAHRS, when supplemented with GPS and a GPS database, allows a moving map display. Adding terrain and obstacle data permits *synthetic vision*—an accurate PFD depiction of the terrain, obstacles and runways ahead of the aircraft.

Glass cockpit systems are user adjustable, in most cases. A single screen might be set up to display the PFD and map equally, or have a 40/40/20 split of PFD, map, and engine instruments (if integrated). If a second screen is installed, it can act as an MFD (multi-function display), showing combinations of map, engine instruments and other systems, while still available to display the PFD if the other screen fails. The MFD can be changed to show what's most important for that phase of flight; at night, over the mountains, the engine instruments can be what most holds the pilot's interest.

Primary Flight Display (PFD)

Figure 4-61 is an illustration of the Skyview PFD in use. The aircraft has initiated a go-around from an ILS Runway 31L at Palm Springs, California (PSP).

The top bar of the display shows two autopilot functions (the numbers in parentheses refer to Figure 4-61):

(1) Heading hold/altitude hold, which are inactive due to no "AP" shown between them. The UTC time and transponder code are shown here also, in (2).

(3) is the slip/skid ball (need a little right rudder on the go-around). Some systems show this as a movable base on the triangular pointer on the attitude indicator—if the base slides out to the left, you need left rudder to center it.

(4) is the airspeed indicator. From the top: the "---KTS" means no airspeed bug is set. Current airspeed

is 93 knots and slowing. The magenta trend line shows that you will be at 82 knots in 6 seconds (if nothing changes). TAS is 95 knots and ground speed is 90 knots. All of the normal ASI arcs are present, but only the green and white arcs are in view at this airspeed.

Item (5) is a graphic display of the wind direction at your altitude with a digital speed and calculated crosswind component.

(6) The word "TRAFFIC" at the top of the ASI shows that traffic may be a factor, and it tells you to search the PFD for a solid yellow ball that indicates the nearby traffic's position (in this case, off to the right). The "2" inside the ball indicates distance from you (2 NM, SM, or km, depending on how you've programmed the system). The traffic is below your altitude because it's below the horizon line, but might not be for long since it is climbing (shown by the up arrow). This display makes it much easier to find traffic visually. The system must have a traffic sensing device connected and the other traffic must have equipment that allows it to be displayed.

(7) is a stall warning/angle of attack (AOA) display showing proximity to the stall. The green tape disappears into the bottom of the box as critical AOA is approached. Slow flight would leave little or no green band visible. As you approach the red, the direction of the red chevrons encourage you to push the nose over. AOA is sensed by a special pitot tube that has an additional orifice angled forward and down toward the bottom of the pitot tube. The system compares the air pressure of each orifice and calculates AOA.

(8) is the altimeter display which shows that the altitude bug is set at 1,700 feet and is off scale (only half of the bug is showing—see the complete bug on the VSI). Current altitude is about 515 feet with the estimated altitude in 6 seconds of 565 feet shown as by the magenta trend line. The altimeter setting is 30.00 inches and the density altitude (DA) is 484 feet MSL. This is calculated using the outside air temperature (OAT), #18.

(9) is the vertical speed indicator. The VSI bug was set at -500 fpm (as shown by the bug's location and the digits at the top of the VSI) for the approach, but the airplane is now climbing at 550 feet per minute.

The navigation status display in (10) indicates that the internal GPS is being used for navigation (GPS 0)

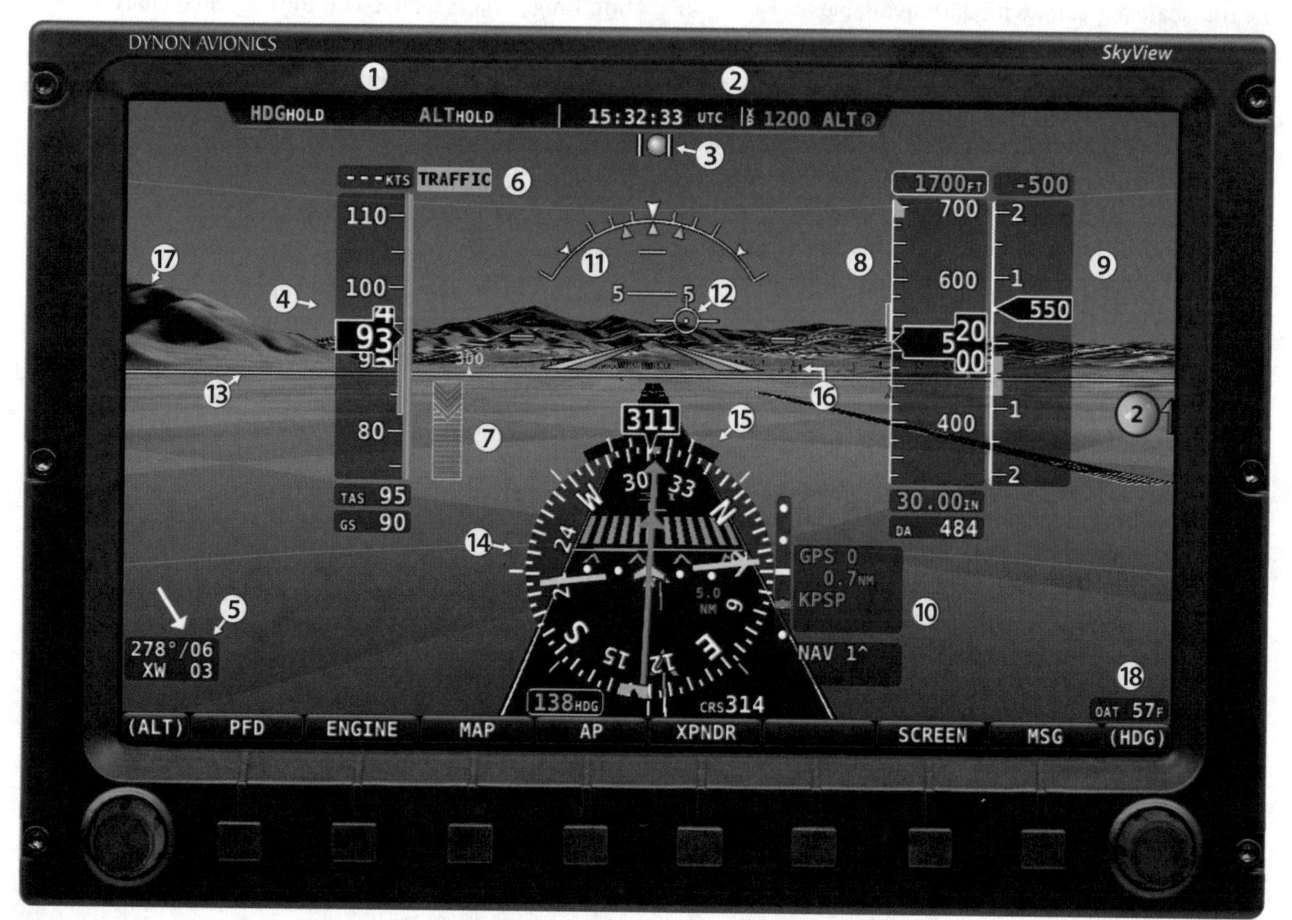

Figure 4-61. The Skyview PFD (primary flight display) with synthetic vision showing runways, obstacles, and terrain. *(Courtesy Dynon Avionics)*

and the aircraft is 0.7 nautical miles from the Palm Springs (KPSP) airport reference point. The NAV1 shows that the yellow pointer on the HSI is tied to navigation radio 1 and indicates bearing only.

The attitude indicator in (11) has the airplane's pitch reference (adjustable as on a gyro attitude indicator) passing through the 2 yellow sidebars and the point of the inverted V. There are pitch marks (5°, etc.) as on round gauges. There are also curved 10° pitch lines stretching across the screen both above and below the horizon line. The horizon line has marks every 30° of the compass.

Extreme pitch (±45°) will expose large red arrows pointing to the horizon. This type of display will always show the shortest way to the horizon by displaying some small amount of blue (if you are pointing down) or brown (if you have to pitched up drastically).

The bank angle arc shows the bank angle on the outside (large pointer is 0°, small ones are 45°). The amber pointer aligns with the bank angle as read on the outside scale and the blue triangles are the calculated bank angle needed for a standard-rate (2 minute) turn at the current airspeed. As bank is increased, more of the roll scale appears, with 360° available.

Item (12) is the flight path marker (FPM), a two-dimensional track. It currently shows the aircraft traveling upward at about 3° and drifting to the right, due to the 3-knot crosswind component shown in (5). A stalled airplane could have the nose above the horizon (attitude indicator), but be traveling downward (flight path marker). Some systems call this the flight path vector (FPV). With synthetic vision, putting the flight path marker on the runway threshold as you approach (and keeping it there) will take you right to the runway.

(13) is the extended zero-pitch line with magnetic heading markers every 30°. Relative altitude of other traffic is indicated by being above or below this line (on the line is at *your* altitude).

The heading indicator/HSI in (14) is similar to the older versions with the very useful addition of a GPS track indicator, the small magenta triangle just below the 311° magnetic heading. This shows your current track. If you are on course and this indicator eases off the proper course number (say 128° outbound from the NDB, on the approach to Boondox International), you will soon be OFF course. The lower display shows the heading bug setting ("138HDG") along with the course that has been set for the magenta CDI needle ("CRS314"). The amber needle shows the bearing to the station set on navigation radio 1 (NAV 1). Lateral and vertical (GS) deviation scales are also shown (on course, but 1 dot high).

(15) Rate of turn would be shown in the black arc at the top of the HSI, just below the 311° indicated heading. A magenta band will appear in the direction of turn as the aircraft turns, with the band length being proportional to the turn rate. To do a standard-rate turn to the right, bank to the right until the magenta band stretches out to the taller of the two white hash marks (the smaller one is ½-standard-rate). This is also a 6-second trend line: the standard-rate turn mark is 18° from the lubber-line (3°/second, standard-rate × 6 seconds = 18°). The large white triangle on the attitude indicator bank scale would now point at the appropriate blue triangle.

(16) Obstacles are shown as towers. They will only be displayed if within 1,000 feet of your altitude. From 1,000 feet below to 100 feet below the aircraft altitude they appear yellow. If they reach within 100 feet below your altitude or taller, they will be shown as red. Make sure your database is updated.

(17) Terrain on the PFD is shown in the same elevation-range colors as used on the sectional chart.

(18) is the outside air temperature (OAT), used for density altitude calculations, the pilot's performance calculations and icing awareness. (Temperature can be displayed as Celsius.)

The bottom row of controls consist of "joysticks" at each end to change settings and to control the functions of the keys between them.

This PFD shows the airplane climbing straight ahead on the missed approach, airspeed decaying, but it appears that a pitch (down) correction is being made since the flight path marker is showing above the pitch of the attitude indicator (not usual for steady-state flight). There is a slight right drift due to the wind from left front, so the ground speed is less than TAS. A little more right rudder is needed, and the pilot needs to keep the traffic off to the right in mind—but also not forget the mountains, especially from 12 o'clock and left. Most of those towers ahead are red, meaning they top out at least 415 feet MSL and possibly much taller. The reader must bear in mind that this is not the view out the window, it's synthetic vision—the airplane may be IMC at this point.

Moving Map Display

The map display in Figure 4-62 is an overhead view of the airplane and its surroundings. With GPS and terrain/obstacle databases, it displays the (non-weather) hazards to flight much like the PFD.

The map display is oriented magnetic "track up" with the thin white line (1) showing the airplane's current track across the map and magenta box displaying it digitally (1). The airplane symbol (2) shows the current location and is pointed to the aircraft's magnetic heading (i.e., a fierce crosswind would show the airplane crabbed off course, but tracking up). The magenta line is the active leg of the current flight plan (with subsequent legs being white). With no crosswind, there is not much difference between track, heading and course in Figure 4-62.

The range of the display can be selected from a scale of 0.3 nautical miles to 1,200 nautical miles (or in units of statute miles or kilometers). The range scale selected is shown by the number (4) which describes the distance from the airplane symbol to the inner ring circle (4). The outer ring (5) has compass markings (magnetic) and is twice the range of (4).

The cyan (light blue) heading bug (6) has been moved out of the way in this example.

Traffic is displayed on the map somewhat similarly to the PFD. No traffic is present, but the system is operating normally (7, lower right). Since there is no horizon line, traffic will be displayed with a +/- altitude (see Figure 4-63) and an arrowhead indicating its climb or descent (no arrowhead means level). The map displays a long arrow indicating the traffic's ground track (Figure 4-63).

The bearing-to-waypoint (BTW) is shown lower right (8) and the distance-to-waypoint (DTW) is shown lower left (9). Unlike the PFD, this map has no pitot/static information. The GPS ground speed (10) is in the upper left and the GPS altitude (11) is in the upper right.

Terrain (12) and obstacles are shown with the same colors and symbology as a sectional chart. The alert colors of yellow (-1,000 feet to -100 feet of airplane altitude) and red (-100 feet to above the aircraft) are used for terrain and obstacle awareness. Towers are shown in the upper right of Figure 4-63.

Airports (13) are shown with runway orientation, if that information is available. S43 is Harvey Field and 96WA is Jim and Julie's airport (private as indicated

Figure 4-62. Dynon Avionics' map display shows the airplane's situation from an overhead perspective. *(Courtesy Dynon Avionics)*

by the "R"). Airspace (14) is shown with floors and ceilings (if applicable), color-coded by type (solid blue line is class B; red is restricted/prohibited, etc.). TFRs are not displayed on this unit. They can be implemented quickly, so check for new ones before each flight.

Navigation aids (15) are depicted as on the sectional charts. The pointer (16) always points to true North.

A map display like Skyview can give a very clear picture of where the airplane is and where it is going:

Assuming an altitude of 2,500 feet MSL (versus the 2,726 feet GPS altitude shown), we can get a good idea of what the airplane is doing in Figure 4-62—southbound through the KPAE Class D airspace and underflying the KSEA Class B airspace. On the current track, we'll pass to the west of KSEA under the 3,000-ft floor. The altimeter is squawking 1200 and reporting altitude (as required within 30 NM of KSEA). There is little or no crosswind, as shown by the airplane symbol alignment with the track. ETA to the next waypoint is 20:42 UTC (59.4 DTW divided by 76 knots ground speed equals 47 + the 19:55 current time equals 20:42).

There are MOAs and restricted areas 12 miles to our right (yellow/red outlines, using the range circle for reference). There is high terrain both left and right up ahead. If airliners, especially "heavies," are landing south at KSEA, wake turbulence may be a factor as we pass under the final approach to KSEA. There are some airports around for emergency purposes, but note that some are seaplane bases. The large amount of water needs to be taken into consideration if the engine acts up—do you want to cross miles of open water to WA61 with a rough running engine when a return along your course will keep you over dry land? The NRST button will give the nearest airports, but the closest may not be the best due to terrain, crossing water or weather.

Modern glass cockpits provide an incredible amount of information and situational awareness. A good pilot will be able to use what's important for the current situation, but not become overloaded or spend too much time "heads-down" in the air (or on the ground). Most importantly, the pilot should never forget the duty that ranks above all else—*fly the airplane.*

Figure 4-63. A Skyview screen used as a multi-function display (MFD)—engine instruments (left), map display (right). *(Courtesy Dynon Avionics)*

Engine Instruments

Tachometer

For airplanes with fixed-pitch propellers, the tachometer is the engine instrument to check for an indication of power being used. The centrifugal tachometer operates on the same principle as an older car speedometer. One end of a flexible shaft is connected to the engine crankshaft and the other connected to a shaft with counterweights within the instrument. The rate of turning of the crankshaft (and cable) causes expansion of the counterweight system. The instrument hand is mechanically linked to the counterweight assembly so that the engine speed is indicated in revolutions per minute (rpm).

For direct-drive engines, the engine and propeller rpm are the same (Lycoming O-320, O-540, O-360). The geared engine (Lycoming GO-480, etc.) has different engine and propeller speeds; this is noted in the POH (the propeller rpm is less than the engine rpm). The tachometer measures engine rpm and this is the basis for your power setting. (There are a few exceptions to this "rule.")

A simple type of tachometer is magnetic, which utilizes a flexible shaft that turns a magnet within a special collar in the instrument. The balance between the magnetic force and a hairspring is indicated as rpm by a hand on the instrument face. This type of tachometer does not oscillate as sometimes happens with the less expensive centrifugal type.

A third type of tachometer is electric, which depends on a generator unit driven by a tachometer drive shaft. The generator is wired to an electric motor unit of the indicator, which rotates at the same rpm and transmits this through a magnetic tachometer unit that registers the speed in rpm. This type of tachometer is also smoother than the centrifugal type.

Most airplanes have a recording tachometer from which various maintenance requirements may be made, such as 100-hour checks, oil changes, or airworthiness directives. As an example, one recording tach is based on 2,310 rpm, and if the engine is at lower power settings, "tach time" is not built up as fast as "real time." Check how your tach is powered.

When trailing behind another airplane, you can "check" its rpm by looking through your prop at its prop. You would move the throttle (or propeller control with a constant-speed prop) until the other propeller "stops." Assuming that *your* tachometer is accurate, you can then read the other airplane's rpm on it. This is particularly useful when you're flying cross-country behind a friend who has the same make and model airplane but is running away from you (who swears to be carrying only 2,100 rpm but you find that 2,400 is indicated through your prop). Stroboscopic effect and science triumph!

Manifold Pressure Gage

For airplanes with controllable (which includes constant-speed) propellers, this instrument is used in combination with the tachometer to set up desired power from the engine. The manifold absolute pressure (map) gage measures the air or fuel-air mixture pressure going to the cylinders and indicates it in inches of mercury.

The map gage is an aneroid barometer like the altimeter, but instead of measuring the outside air pressure, it measures the *actual* pressure of the mixture or air in the intake manifold. When the engine is not running, the outside air pressure and the pressure in the intake manifold are the same so that the map gage will indicate the outside air pressure as would a barometer. At sea level on a standard day, this would be 29.92 inches of mercury, but you can't read the map this closely—it would appear as approximately 29 or 30 inches.

You start the engine with the throttle cracked or closed. This means that the throttle valve or butterfly valve is nearly shut. The engine is a strong air pump, taking in fuel and air and discharging residual gases and air. At a closed- or cracked-throttle setting the engine is pulling air (and fuel) at such a rate past the throttle valve that a decided drop in pressure is found in the intake manifold and is duly registered by the map gage. As the engine starts, the indication of 30 inches drops rapidly to 10 inches or less at idle. It will never reach zero for this would mean a complete vacuum in the manifold (most map gages don't even have indications of less than 10 inches). Besides, if you tried to shut off all air (and fuel) completely, the engine would quit running.

As you open the throttle, you are allowing more and more fuel and air to enter the engine and the manifold pressure increases accordingly (Figure 4-64).

As you can see in Figure 4-64, the unturbocharged engine will never indicate the full outside pressure on the map gage. The usual difference is 1 to 2 inches of mercury. The maximum indication on the map gage you can expect to get is 28 to 29 inches on takeoff.

The turbocharged engine has compressors that bring the fuel-air mixture to a higher pressure than the outside air before it goes into the manifold. This makes it possible to register more than the outside pressure and results in more HP being developed for a given rpm, because HP is dependent on rpm and the amount of fuel and air (map) going into the engine.

When the engine is shut down, the map gage indication moves to the outside air pressure. The techniques in using a map gage will be discussed later in Part 2, Checking Out in Advanced Models and Types. Figure 4-65 shows some examples of various map gages available. (Mp *or* Map is used in flying.)

Oil Pressure Gage

The older oil pressure gage consists of a curved Bourdon tube with a mechanical linkage to the indicating hand that registers the pressure in pounds per square inch (Figure 4-66). As is shown, oil pressure tends to straighten the tube and the appropriate oil pressure indication is registered. This is the direct-pressure-type gage.

Another type of oil pressure gage uses a unit containing a flexible diaphragm that separates the engine oil from a nonflammable fluid that fills the line from the unit into the Bourdon tube. The oil pressure is transmitted through the diaphragm and to the Bourdon tube by this liquid because liquids are incompressible (Figure 4-67). Others may use an electrical-resistance type, using the airplane's electrical system.

Oil Temperature Gage

The vapor type of gage is the most common type of oil temperature gage for older airplanes. This instrument, like the oil pressure gage, contains a Bourdon tube connected by a fine tube to a metal bulb containing a volatile liquid. Vapor expansion due to increased

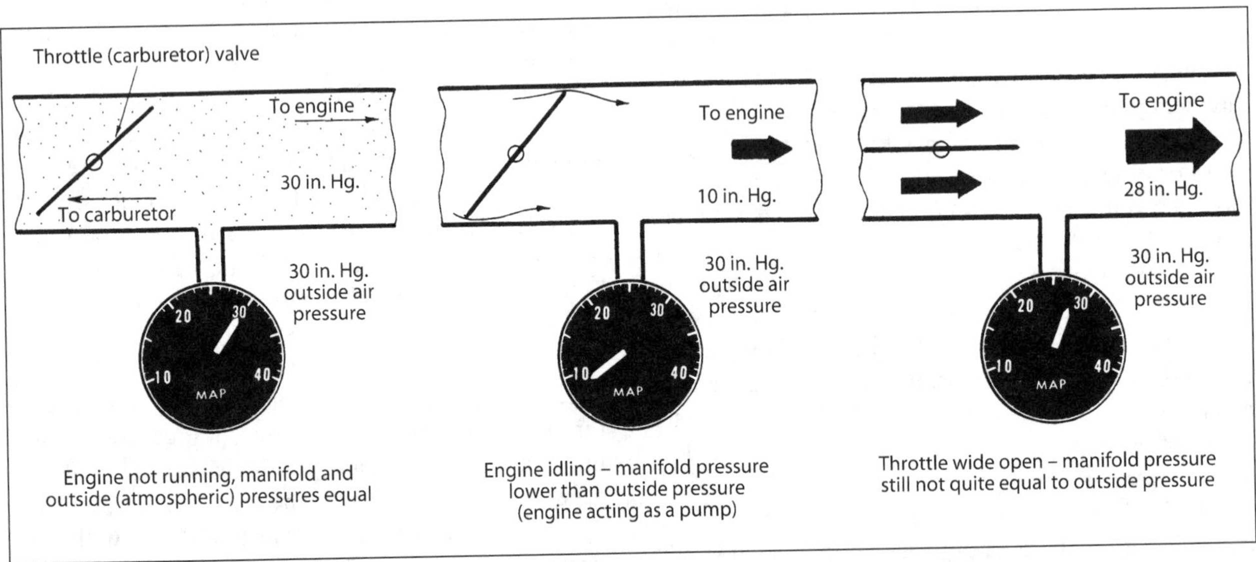

Figure 4-64. The manifold pressure gage principle (unturbocharged engine). A value of 30 inches is used as an example, but you might see 29 inches (or lower) before start, depending on the pressure altitude at the airport.

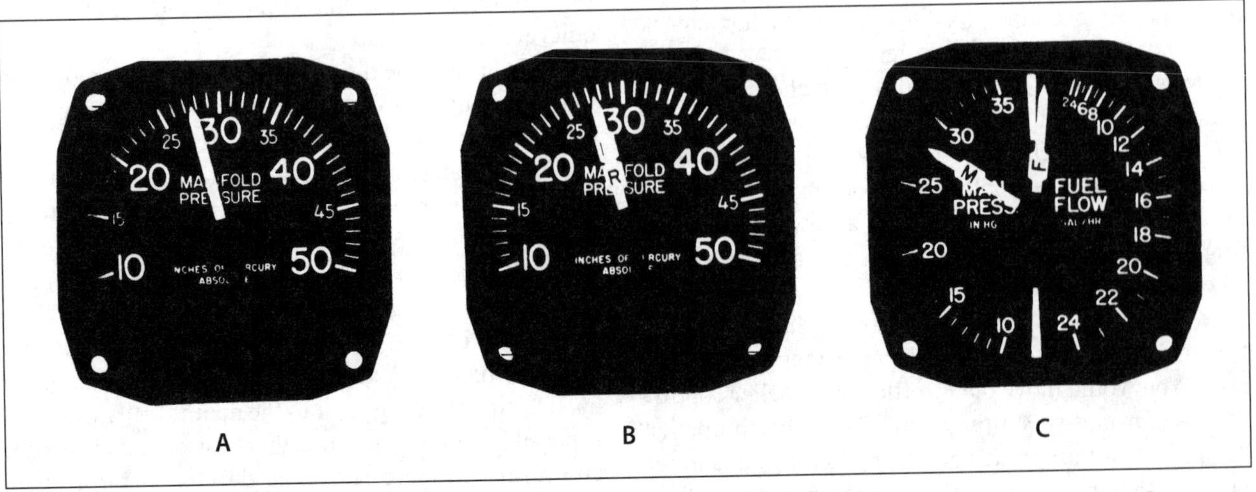

Figure 4-65. Manifold pressure gages. **A.** Simple gage for single-engine airplane. **B.** Dual needles used for a twin. **C.** Combination fuel-flow and manifold pressure gage. (*Sigma Tek*)

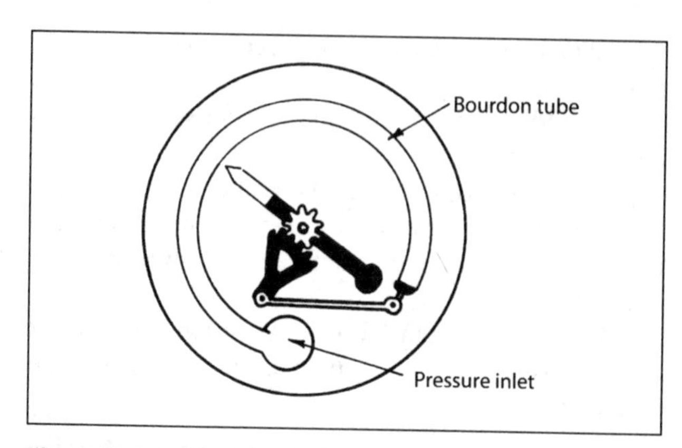

Figure 4-66. Oil pressure gage.

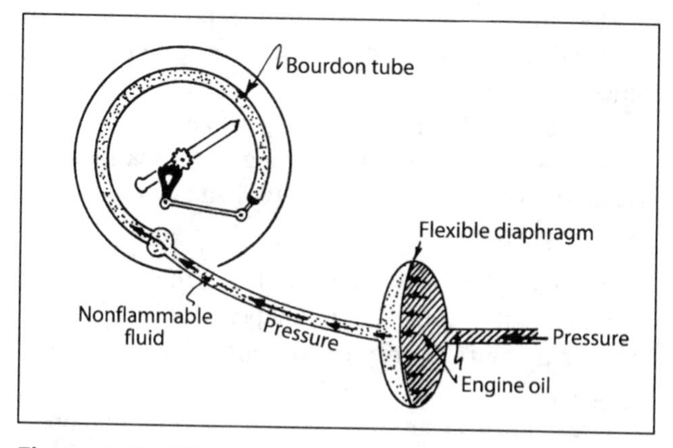

Figure 4-67. Oil pressure gage utilizing a flexible diaphragm and nonflammable fluid.

temperature exerts pressure, which is indicated as temperature on the instrument face.

Other types of oil temperature gages may use a thermocouple rather than a Bourdon tube. The Cessna 172 RG oil temperature gage is operated by an electrical resistance-type temperature sensor, which receives power from the airplane's electrical system.

Cylinder Head Temperature Gage

The cylinder head temperature gage is an important instrument for engines of higher compression and/or higher power. Engine cooling is a major problem in the design of a new airplane. Much flight testing and cowl modification may be required before satisfactory cooling is found for all airspeeds and power settings. The engineers are faced with the problem of keeping the engine within efficient operating limits for all air temperatures. An engine that has good cooling for summer flying may run too cool in the winter. Cowl flaps, which are controlled by the pilot, aid in compensating for variations in airspeed and power setting. Many of the older high-performance airplanes use "augmenter cooling" instead of cowl flaps. Air is drawn over the cylinders by venturi action of a tube around the exhaust stacks (Figure 4-68).

The cylinder head temperature gage usually warns of any possible damage to the engine before the oil temperature gage gives any such indication.

The "hottest" cylinder, which is usually one of the rear ones in the horizontally opposed engine, is chosen during the flight testing of the airplane. A thermocouple lead replaces one of the spark plug washers on this cylinder.

The cylinder head temperature gages are likely to be operated by the electrical-resistance-type temperature sensor on each engine powered by the airplane's electrical system.

Some pilots use cylinder head temperature as an aid in proper leaning of the mixture. Generally, richer mixtures mean lower head temperatures; leaner mixtures mean higher head temperatures, all other things (airspeed, power settings, etc.) being equal. But the engine may not be developing best power at the extremes. Too rich a mixture means power loss plus excessive fuel consumption, and too lean a mixture means power loss plus the possibility of engine damage. Leaning procedures will be discussed in more detail in Part 2.

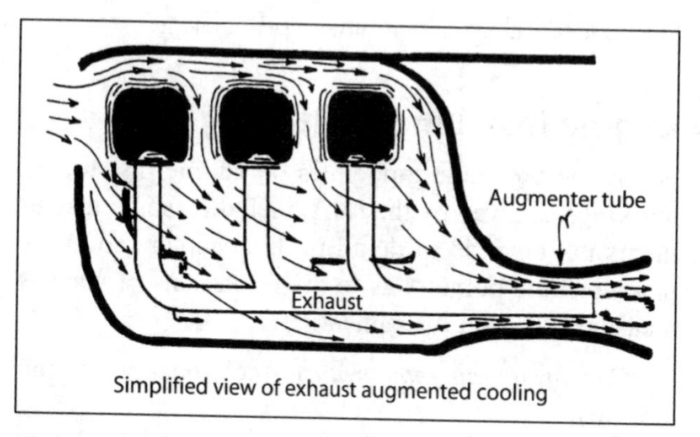

Figure 4-68.

Fuel Gage

The cork float-and-wire fuel gages of earlier days have gone by the board. The corks sometimes got "fuel logged" and registered empty all the time. Worse, the wire sometimes got bent and the pilot had an unrealistic picture of fuel available. These indicators were followed by metal floats and indicators, and finally by the electric transmitter type now in popular use. (Always check your fuel visually before the flight.)

The electric transmitter type may be broken down into the following components: (1) float and arm, (2) rheostat-type control, and (3) the indicator, a voltmeter indicating fuel either in fractions or in gallons. The float and arm are attached to the rheostat, which is connected by wires to the fuel gage. As the float level in the tank (or tanks) changes, the rheostat is rotated, changing the electrical resistance in the circuit—which changes the fuel gage indication accordingly. This is the most popular type of fuel measuring system for airplanes with electrical systems (Figure 4-69).

Frequent checks of the fuel gage are a good idea; sudden dropping of the fuel level indication may be caused by a serious fuel leak and you should know about it. For many airplanes, both the fuel quantity and oil temperature indicators may be turned OFF if "somebody" inadvertently turns the master switch OFF in flight.

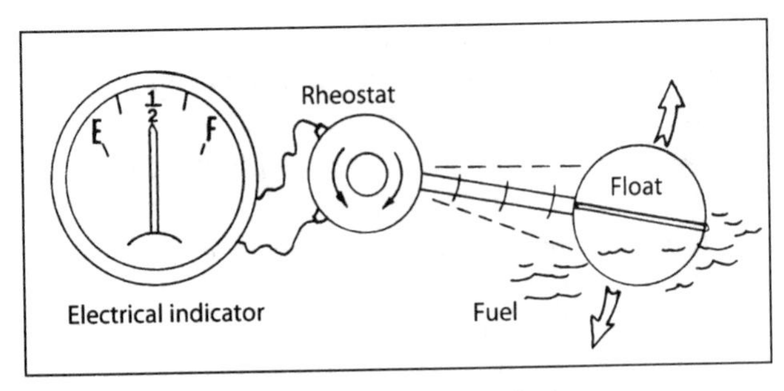

Figure 4-69. Electric transmitter-type fuel gage.

Engine Instrument Marking

Following are some guidelines on engine instrument markings as given by the FAA, including some instruments not covered in detail in this chapter. You may pick up some pointers as to the limitations of what is measured by each instrument.

Carburetor air temperature (reciprocating engine aircraft)

Red radial—At the maximum permissible carburetor inlet air temperature recommended by the engine manufacturer.

Green arc—Normal operating range for trouble-free operation with the upper limit at the maximum permissible carburetor inlet air temperature and the lower limit at the point where icing may be anticipated. Additional green arc may be required in the temperature range below the icing range.

Yellow arc—Range indicating where icing is most likely to be encountered.

Cylinder head temperature (reciprocating engine aircraft)

Red radial—At the maximum permissible cylinder head temperature.

Green arc—From the maximum permissible temperature for continuous operation to the minimum recommended by the engine manufacturer for continuous operation.

Yellow arc—From the maximum temperature for continuous operation to the maximum permissible temperature.

Fuel pressure (reciprocating and turbine engine aircraft)

Red radial—At the maximum and/or minimum permissible pressures established as engine operating limitations.

Green arc—Normal operating range.

Yellow arc—Cautionary ranges indicating any potential hazard in the fuel system such as malfunction, icing, etc.

Manifold pressure (reciprocating engine aircraft)

Red radial—At the maximum permissible manifold absolute pressure for dry or wet operation, whichever is greater.

Green arc—From the maximum permissible pressure for continuous operation to the minimum pressure selected by the aircraft manufacturer for cruise power.

Yellow arc (if present)—From the maximum pressure for continuous operation to the maximum permissible pressure.

Oil pressure (reciprocating and turbine engine aircraft)

Red radial—At the maximum and/or minimum permissible pressures established as engine operating limitations

Green arc—Normal operating range.

Yellow arc—Cautionary ranges indicating any potential hazard due to overpressure during cold start, low pressure during idle, etc.

Oil temperatures (reciprocating and turbine engine aircraft)

Red radial—At the maximum and/or minimum permissible temperatures established as engine operating limitations.

Green arc—Normal operating range.

Yellow arc—Cautionary ranges indicating any potential hazard due to overheating, high viscosity at low temperature, etc.

Tachometer (reciprocating engine aircraft)

Red radial—At the maximum permissible rotational speed (rpm).

Green arc—From the maximum rotational speed for continuous operation to the minimum recommended for continuous operation (except in the restricted ranges, if any).

Yellow arc—From the maximum rotational speed for continuous operation to the maximum permissible rotational speed.

Red arc—Range(s) in which operation is restricted, except to pass through, for all operating conditions because of excessive stresses, etc.

Electrical System

Figure 4-70 is a diagram of an electrical system for a four-place airplane. This is a 28-volt DC system with a belt-driven 60-amp alternator to maintain the battery's state of charge. (Alternators have replaced generators because alternators provide more electrical power at lower engine rpm.)

The *ammeter* indicates the amount of current, in amperes, from the alternator to the battery or from the battery to the electrical system. When the engine is operating and the master switch is on, the ammeter indicates the charging rate applied to the battery. If the alternator isn't working, or the electrical load is too high, the ammeter shows the battery discharge rate. A low-voltage light is included in the system to warn of an alternator problem. The master switch can be turned off and then back on to reset the alternator control unit.

Learn which circuit breakers protect which units of the electrical system for *your* airplane.

Vacuum System

Figure 4-71 is a schematic of the vacuum system for a four-place single-engine airplane. Note that the low-vacuum warning light circuit breaker is the 8th breaker from the top in Figure 4-70.

Figure 4-72 is the vacuum system for a twin with a vacuum pump on each engine. The system is set up so that one pump can carry the load if the other fails. Chapter 19 will discuss a pressure or pneumatic pump system for the instruments.

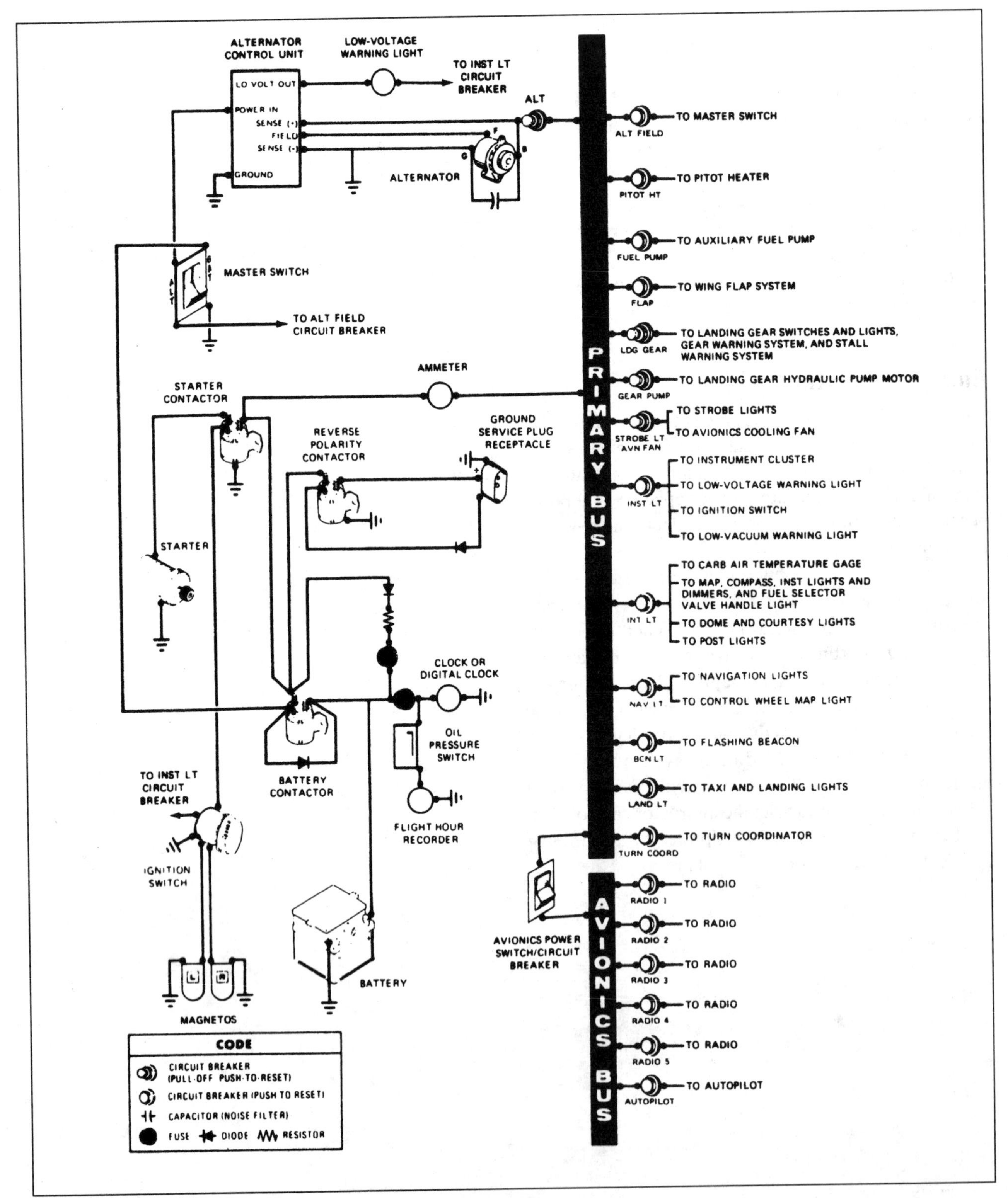

Figure 4-70. Electrical system. Note that most of the circuit breakers are push-to-reset but the strobe lights, landing gear hydraulic pump motor, and landing gear switches and lights are protected by pull-off-type CBs. The clock and flight-hour recorder have fuses. You no doubt have long known that the magnetos have self-contained magnets and aren't part of the airplane's electrical system.

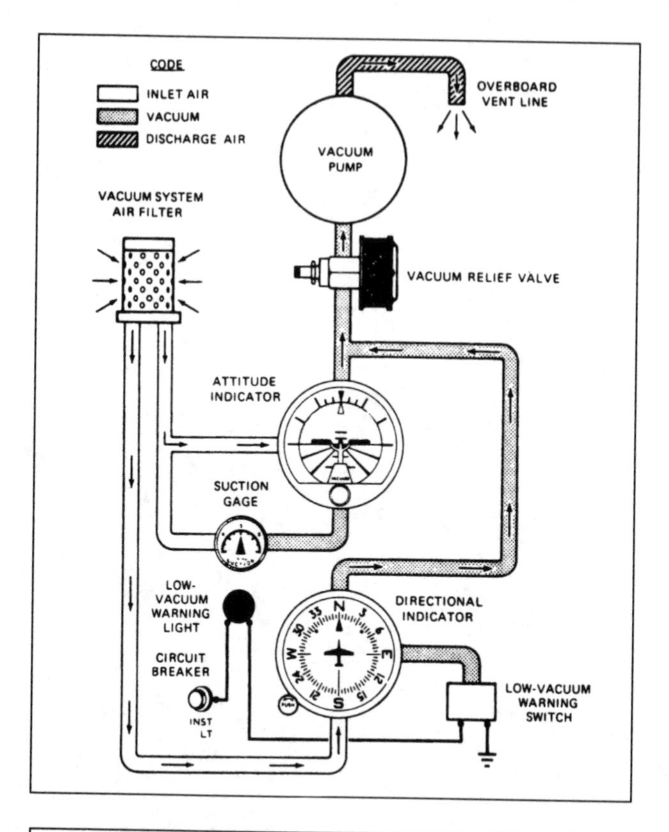

Figure 4-71. Vacuum system for a single-engine airplane.

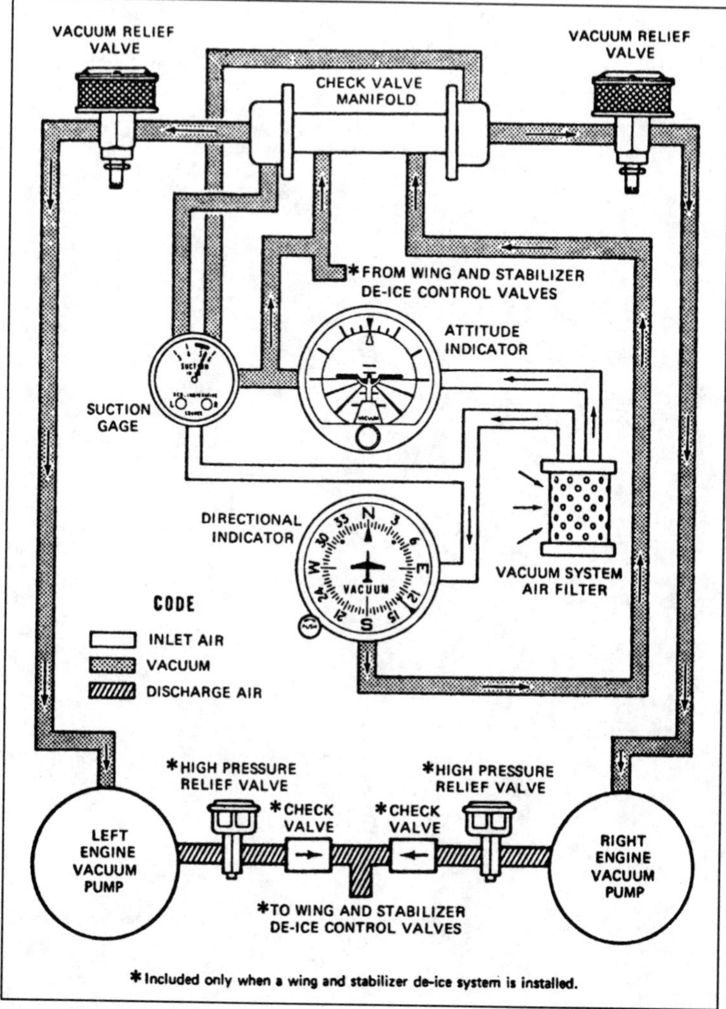

Figure 4-72. Vacuum system for a light twin.

5

Takeoff Performance

The first measurement of a good pilot is headwork—thinking well in an airplane. Running a close second for the experienced pilot is the ability to get the most out of the plane when it is needed. If you don't know what your airplane can do, you may either set such a high safety margin that performance suffers, or such a low margin as to damage your airplane and yourself. Sometimes it takes a great deal of intestinal fortitude to do what's right—for instance, during a short-field takeoff with high trees at the far end. Logic and knowledge tell you that forcing the plane off too soon will cost takeoff performance, while instinct pushes for you to get it off now. It requires an understanding of airplane performance and sometimes a lot of argument with yourself to do what's right in a particular situation.

The following chapters on performance will be based on your understanding of the following:

1. The air density in slugs per cubic foot is 0.002378 at sea level (standard day) and decreases with altitude.
2. The sea level standard pressure is 29.92 inches of mercury, or 2,116 pounds per square foot, and decreases at the rate of approximately 1 inch of mercury, or 75 pounds per square foot, per 1,000 feet. This is only an approximation. We will be considering only the lower part of the atmosphere (up to 10,000 feet) in this chapter.
3. The standard sea level temperature is 59°F, or 15°C, and decreases 3½°F, or 2°C, per 1,000 feet (the temperature normal lapse rate is 3½°F or 2°C per 1,000 feet). Performance thumb rules and data are based on normally aspirated engines (no turbochargers) unless specifically stated.

Takeoffs in General

The takeoff is usually the most critical part of the flight because (1) the plane is most heavily loaded at this point, and (2) if the field is somewhat soft or has high grass or snow, the takeoff suffers (but the landing roll is helped if it's not so soft as to cause a nose-over). Because of these two factors in particular, it's possible for you to get into a field from which you can't fly out.

Takeoff Variables

Altitude and Temperature Effects

The air density decreases with altitude and, as you remember, air density (ρ) is a factor of lift.

Let's say that at the point of takeoff, lift just equals weight (this is for a takeoff at any altitude). It also simplifies our discussion to say that the plane lifts off at the maximum angle of attack. In most cases this doesn't happen—that is, you don't "stall it off"—but it makes for easier figuring here, so we'll do it. So, the maximum angle of attack (without stalling) and wing area are the same for the takeoff at any altitude, and the density is less at higher altitudes. Assuming the weight of the airplane is the same as you had at a sea level airport, at higher altitudes you'll have to make up for the decrease in density by an increased true airspeed before the airplane can lift off. The *indicated* airspeed will be the same for a high-altitude takeoff as it is at sea level, but it will take longer to get this indicated airspeed, the big reason being that the engine can't develop sea level HP. The result is that more runway is required with an increase in density-altitude. This increase in takeoff run can be predicted. As one pilot said after trying to take off from a short field at a high altitude and going off the end of the runway, through two fences, a hedge, across a busy highway, and through a yard, "About this time I began to wonder if I was going to get off."

The atmospheric density does not decrease in a straight line, like temperature. At 20,000 feet the density is about half that of sea level. At 40,000 feet the density is approximately half that of 20,000 feet, and so on, with the density halving about every 18,000 to 20,000 feet. Density is a function of pressure altitude and temperature.

The FAA earlier produced two density-altitude computers, one for fixed-pitch-propeller airplanes and the other for variable-pitch-propeller airplanes. The computers were used to check the takeoff and climb performance of these two airplane types at higher density-altitudes.

How do you find the density-altitude without a computer? Here are the temperatures for standard altitudes (density-altitudes) from sea level to 8,000 feet (rounded off to the nearest degree):

Sea level	59°F	15°C
1,000 feet	55°F	13°C
2,000 feet	52°F	11°C
3,000 feet	48°F	9°C
4,000 feet	45°F	7°C
5,000 feet	41°F	5°C
6,000 feet	38°F	3°C
7,000 feet	34°F	1°C
8,000 feet	31°F	–1°C

Keep this in mind: For every ±15°F or ±8½°C variation from standard temperature at your pressure altitude, the density-altitude is increased or decreased 1,000 feet.

For instance, you are ready to take off and set the altimeter to 29.92. The pressure altitude given is 3,000 feet and the outside air temperature is +22°C. The *standard* temperature at 3,000 feet is +9°C, or the temperature is 13°C *higher than normal.* This higher temperature means that the air is less dense and the airplane is operating at a *higher* density-altitude. This 13°C higher-than-standard temperature means adding another 1,500 feet, for a *density-altitude* of 4,500 feet.

You should always use the POH figures if they are available rather than using the FAA computers or the following thumb rules.

A high temperature, even at sea level or a low altitude airport, can hurt the airplane's takeoff performance. You can check by looking at the equation of state: $\rho = P/1{,}716T$. If the temperature increases, the density decreases and vice versa (constant pressure). The relative humidity also affects performance. *Moist air at the same temperature, is less dense than dry air.* Common sense would seem to tell you that water is heavier than air and the more water vapor present, the denser the air should be. *This is not the case.*

If you had high school or college chemistry you might be interested in the following analogy: As you know, the air is made up of approximately 78% nitrogen and 20% oxygen, with other gases making up the very small remainder. For this example, forget the other gases and say that air is composed of a ratio of 4 molecules of nitrogen to 1 molecule of oxygen. The atomic weights of the basic elements are hydrogen—1, oxygen—16, nitrogen—14. The molecular weights of the basic elements (2 atoms to a molecule) are H_2—2, N_2—28, O_2—32. (H_2O [water] is 18.) Assuming then that a particle of air has 4 nitrogen and 1 oxygen molecules, the total weight would be $N_2 = 4 \times 28 = 112$ and $O_2 = 1 \times 32 = 32$; $112 + 32 = 144$. So, a particle of "dry" air composed of 5 molecules "weighs" (has a relative density of) 144.

If all 5 of those molecules were replaced by water molecules, the results would be $5 \times 18 = 90$.

The moist air, based on this highly exaggerated example, would have a density of $90/144 = 0.62$, or 62% of the completely dry air. Well, it's not quite that simple, for several reasons, but the fact is that moist air is "lighter" than dry air and won't allow as much lift—and particularly HP and thrust—to be produced. If you calculated the effects of changing air from a very low relative humidity to 100% relative humidity at 100°F (which is a highly moist condition since every 20°F increase in temperature allows a parcel of air to double its ability to hold moisture), you'd find that a given air density would decrease approximately 2 to 3%. The effects on *lift* would be negligible in reasonable situations, but the reciprocating engine may lose up to 12% power depending on the amount of existing moisture. So, the aerodynamics of the takeoff are not so affected as is the power. Turbojet engines are not affected so much by increased moisture.

Back in Chapter 4, in discussing altimeter errors, it was mentioned that wide variations from standard temperature at your altitude can cause errors in the altimeter indications. In the case of a takeoff or landing at the airport giving the altimeter setting, any errors due to variations from standard temperature will have been compensated for in the setting. (On takeoff you will set your altimeter to field elevation, anyway.) Remember that the altimeter-temperature error is zero at the surface of the airport at which the setting is obtained (sea level is often used as an example but it's true for any airport elevation).

Aircraft Loading Effects

Aircraft loading and its effect on stability and control will be covered in a later chapter, but the effects of weight itself on takeoff runs should be noted here. Weight has a decided influence on the distance required for lift-off; the factor is (present weight/max certificated weight)^2. If the airplane is 10% over the weight given for a particular ground run value, the new distance would be $(1.1)^2 = 1.21$, or at least 21% longer. (The worst situation for takeoff would be an overloaded airplane on a short, soft field at high altitude on a hot, moist day in tailwind or no-wind conditions—but more about the other factors later.)

Getting back to weight effects alone, the same equation applies for lower weights as well. For instance, an airplane requiring a ground run (roll) of 1,000 feet at its max certificated weight of 3,000 pounds would require a run of approximately 640 feet at a weight of 2,400 pounds at that same density-altitude and wind and runway conditions, or $(2{,}400/3{,}000)^2 = (0.8)^2 = 0.64$. The airplane would require about 640 feet to lift off at the lower weight. The POHs give takeoff distances at several weights (as well as at different pressure altitudes and temperatures).

Runway Surface Effects

A soft or rough field, high grass, or deep snow can affect your takeoff distance—but common sense has been telling you this for some time. The ground drag of your airplane caused by the runway surface is called *rolling resistance*. The equation for this resistance is $R = \mu\,(\text{weight} - \text{lift})$, where μ is the coefficient of friction for that particular runway surface. The following table shows rolling resistance coefficients and thumb rules for added takeoff roll for some surfaces at *sea level*.

Takeoff Surface	μ	Required Takeoff Roll
Concrete or asphalt	0.02	POH figure
Firm turf	0.04	POH figure + 7%
Short grass	0.05	POH figure + 10%
Tall grass	0.10	POH figure + 25%
Soft field, deep snow	0.10–0.30	POH figure + 25%–infinity

These figures are approximate only and are based on airplanes with a power loading of 10 to 16 pounds per HP, or max weight per takeoff HP = 10 to 16 pounds per HP. These figures vary with power loading. Airplanes with a lower power loading, that is, *less weight per HP, are affected proportionately less* by increased rolling resistance than are heavy airplanes with little power. At a higher density-altitude, the required takeoff distance increases for a given airplane because the engine is unable to develop full sea level HP, yet the airplane has the same max certificated weight. Its power loading is increased and so are the rolling resistance effects. That's why it should be noted that the thumb rules for runway surface here are for *sea level*.

The percentage of additional runway required rises sharply at a μ higher than 0.15. In fact, none of the airplanes used as samples could even move at a μ of 0.30.

For example, a certain four-place airplane has a max certificated weight of 3,000 pounds and a static thrust of 865 pounds at sea level. At a μ of 0.30 (soft field, deep snow, etc.), the rolling resistance at gross weight is $\mu\,(\text{weight} - \text{lift})$ or $0.30\,(3{,}000 - 0)$. There is no lift at the beginning of the roll and the result is μ times weight $= 0.30 \times 3{,}000 = 900$ pounds, *or 35 pounds more than the thrust available at full power.* It won't move. That's where the term infinity comes in, although in this extreme case, infinity would be a better term for the *time* required to get airborne, since the distance traveled would be 0 feet.

One point—pilots' definitions of short or tall grass vary. One of your flying buddies may consider grass as being short if it's less than waist high, while you may think that grass on a putting green is tall.

Figure 5-1. Overloading means extra-long takeoff runs.

Because of this rolling resistance, for a soft-field takeoff you need to get the weight off the wheels as soon as possible. (Okay, so you knew that already.)

Figure 5-2 is a general look at the two retarding forces (drag and rolling resistance) versus calibrated airspeed from zero motion to lift-off speed on a *level concrete surface*. The total retarding force is the sum of the two, and you can note that rolling resistance is the big factor for the first part of the run, becoming zero at the lift-off (where there's no weight on the wheels). Aerodynamic drag is the big factor in the later part of the ground run (after the airspeed at point A).

Figure 5-3 shows some exaggerated effects of short and tall grass compared with the concrete surface of Figure 5-2. All surfaces are level.

Points A, B, and C (airspeeds) indicate that (as you probably know by now) the higher the rolling resistance, the sooner the weight should be taken off the wheels. If when taking off in tall grass you keep the nose down, maintaining a level-flight altitude, the total retarding force (mainly rolling resistance) will considerably extend the required lift-off distance.

Figure 5-4 is a look at some approximate numbers for that 3,000-lb airplane with 865 pounds of static thrust that was mentioned earlier. Some actual numbers are used, though rounding off was done and some assumptions made (for instance, that the pilot held a certain constant coefficient of lift, or C_L, in the run until 55 K, then rotated to the lift-off altitude or lift-off C_L, and accomplished lift-off at 65 K). Note that the thrust decreases from 865 pounds at 0 K to 640 pounds at 65 K (lift-off).

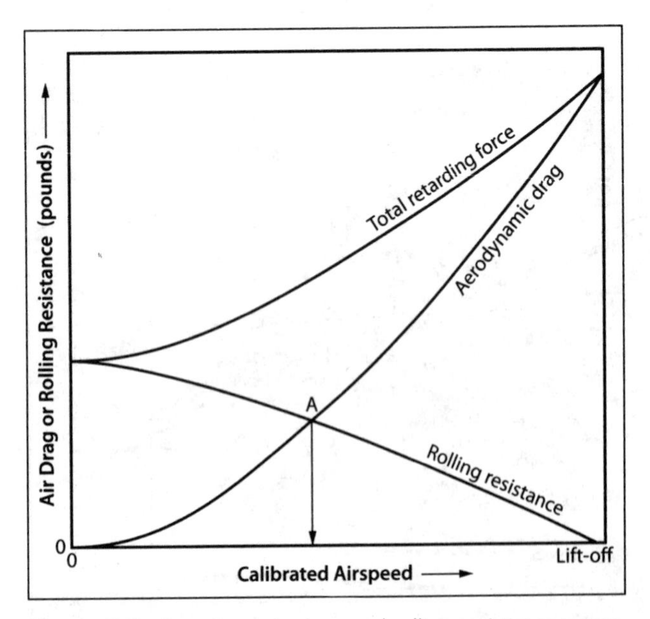

Figure 5-2. Aerodynamic drag and rolling resistance versus calibrated airspeed.

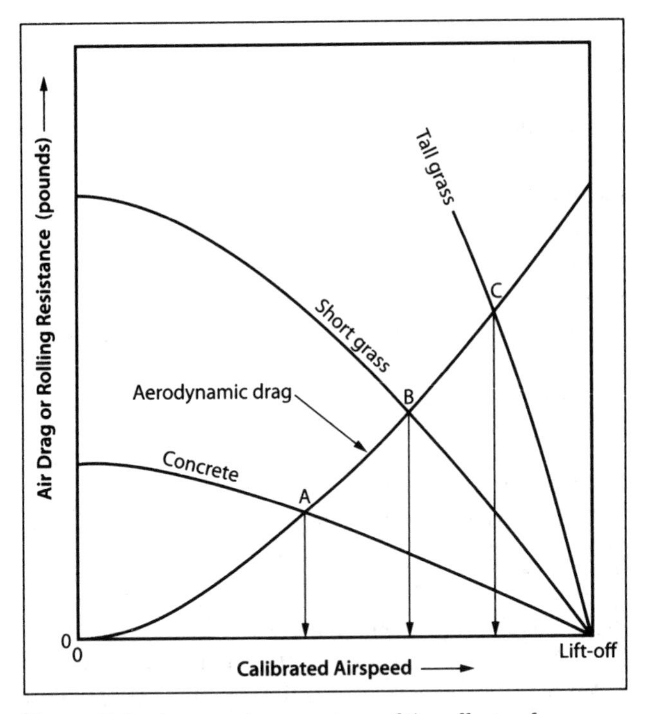

Figure 5-3. A general comparison of the effects of concrete, short grass, and tall grass surfaces for the ground run portion of the takeoff.

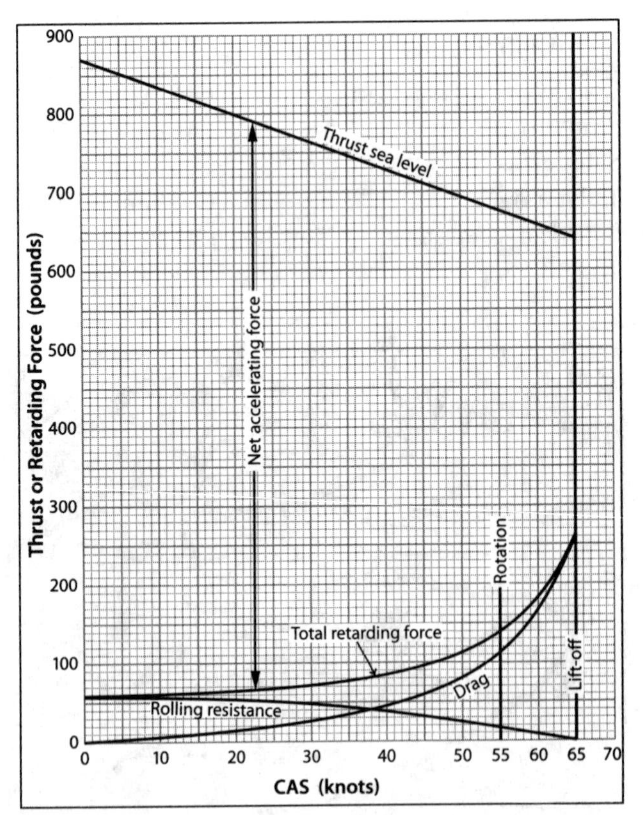

Figure 5-4. Thrust and retarding forces for a 3,000-lb, four-place airplane developing 865 pounds of static thrust at sea level on a dry concrete runway surface.

The *net accelerating force* (NAF) is the difference between the thrust available and the total retarding force, and as you can see *in this case, the NAF decreases as the airspeed increases.* Note also that total aerodynamic drag increases at a fairly predictable rate until at 55 K when the pitch attitude is increased. The aerodynamic drag increases rapidly there (because of the increased induced drag) until 65 K is obtained, and then it is the total retarding force after lift-off.

Wait a minute—there seems to be a problem here. Earlier you read that in straight and level unaccelerated flight, thrust and drag are equal, or the maximum level-flight speed of an airplane is when the maximum thrust is equal to the total drag. Looking at Figure 5-4 and extending the thrust and drag curves, you'll see that they would intersect at (roughly) 80 K. Based on that, it would seem that this airplane is close to the mythical one you've heard about that takes off, cruises, and lands at the same airspeed.

Figure 5-5 shows that the physics of takeoffs (ground portion) and flight have two different requirements. The airplane in Figure 5-4 has different drag characteristics in the two types of operation; "use power to go faster" doesn't always work when airborne. When you lift off you are transitioning from a ground vehicle to one of flight. If your technique is smooth, the transition is not abrupt as implied by Figure 5-5. (Note in Figure 5-5 that the maximum level-flight speed is 145 K, not the approximately 80 K that might be derived from extending the curves in Figure 5-4.)

Figure 5-6 shows the same 3,000-lb airplane taking off at sea level, again rotating at 55 K and lifting off at 65 K. This time, the plane is in tall grass with a μ of 0.10, so that the initial rolling resistance is $3{,}000 \times 0.10 = 300$ pounds. Comparing the NAF with that of dry concrete in Figure 5-4, you can see that NAF (the tall graph) is lower at the beginning of the run but is the same value at lift-off (since aerodynamic drag is the same). The point is that it is better to rotate earlier than 55 K to do the job. Again note that the total retarding force is the sum of the two forces (drag and rolling resistance).

Runway Slope Effects

This one is hard to handle. If you have figures on the slope of the particular runway you're using and are handy with mathematics (as well as having plenty of time), you can figure it out. Obviously if you are taking off uphill, more runway will be required; downhill, less. It's factors like runway slope that shoot some beautiful takeoff calculations right out the window. For safety, add 10% for an uphill run at sea level. At higher

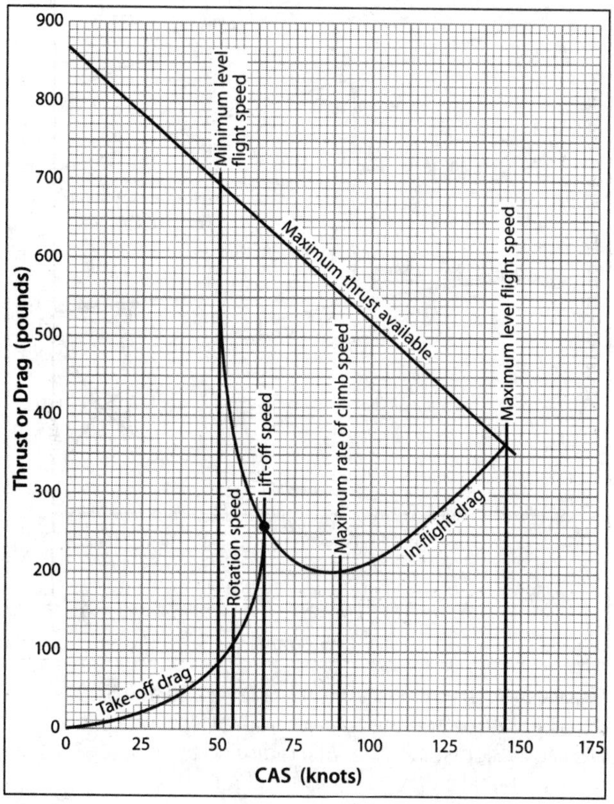

Figure 5-5. Thrust and aerodynamic drag during the takeoff run (dry concrete) and in flight at sea level for the airplane in Figure 5-4.

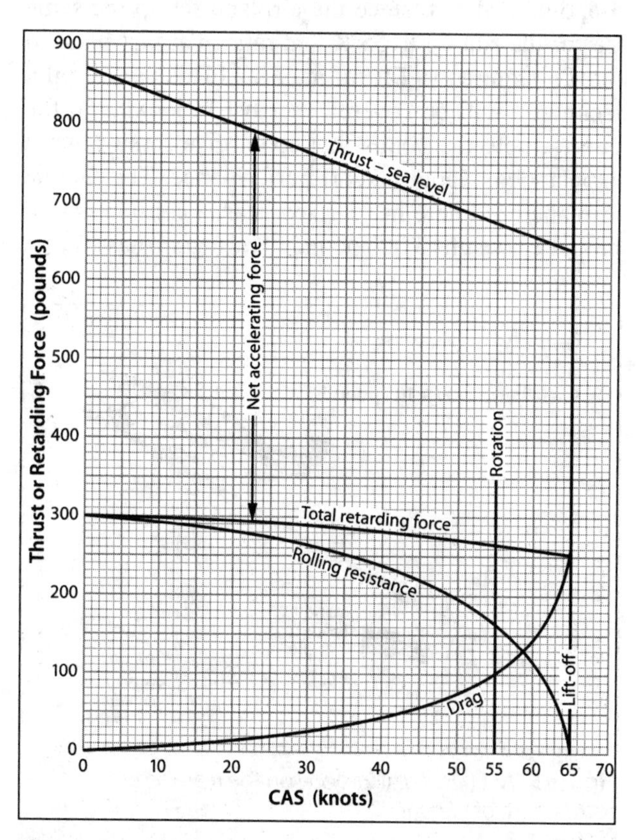

Figure 5-6. Thrust and retarding forces, at a weight of 3,000 pounds, at sea level, in tall grass ($\mu = 0.10$).

density-altitudes, the slope effects will be a bigger factor because available thrust for acceleration will be less.

There is always the question of whether to take off uphill and upwind or downhill and downwind. This depends on the wind and runway slope, of course. If you are operating from the average hard-surface airport where slopes are within certain maximum allowable values, it is better to take off into the wind and uphill *if the headwind component is 10% or more of your take-off speed.* On off-airport landings or at small airports where slopes may be comparatively steep, you'll have to make your own decision according to the conditions.

FAA airport design standards (utility airports) limit the maximum slope on portions of the runway to 2%, or a little over 1.2°. Figure 5-7 shows the effects of a 2° slope on a 3,000-lb airplane. (The angle is exaggerated a *little.*) As you can see, the rearward component of weight has a value of 105 pounds, which has a significant effect even at sea level, since the static thrust available is only 865 pounds.

Figure 5-8 shows the effects of a 2° slope, aerodynamic drag, the rolling resistance of tall grass, and a density-altitude of 5,000 feet on the net accelerating force. (Compare Figures 5-4 and 5-8 to see how the added factors can increase the takeoff run.)

The aerodynamic drag is equal for Figures 5-4, 5-5, 5-6, and 5-8, since the airplane set up the same C_L for the run up to 55 K and rotated at that point to the C_L required to lift off at 65 K. (This part of pilot technique will be covered shortly.) In looking at the curves, note the points that could give some general expectations about takeoff performance. The sample airplane used here has a fixed gear, a constant-speed propeller, weighs 3,000 pounds, and (again) has a *static* thrust of 865 pounds that decreases to 640 pounds at 65 K at sea level.

The rate of acceleration will generally decrease as the takeoff run continues. The net acceleration force (NAF) will be less as the calibrated airspeed picks up, as noted earlier. The point is that if the acceleration is bad at the beginning, it's not apt to *increase* as the airspeed picks up. Comparing Figures 5-4 and 5-6 (remember that both are for sea level), you can see that the total retarding force is greatly affected by the rolling resistance existing, but the *drop* of thrust available with increasing airspeed is the big factor in the decrease in the NAF. On soft-field takeoffs your subjective feeling may be that the airplane, in the initial part of the run, is not accelerating as on dry concrete (naturally) but seems to be doing as expected for this condition. There seems to be a point about halfway to the expected lift-off spot that the airspeed stops increasing and sort of hovers around a particular (too-low) value. *This is the decision time:* (1) close the throttle and taxi back for another shot at it (this can be a useful technique in some cases, to pack the snow or press the grass down with a

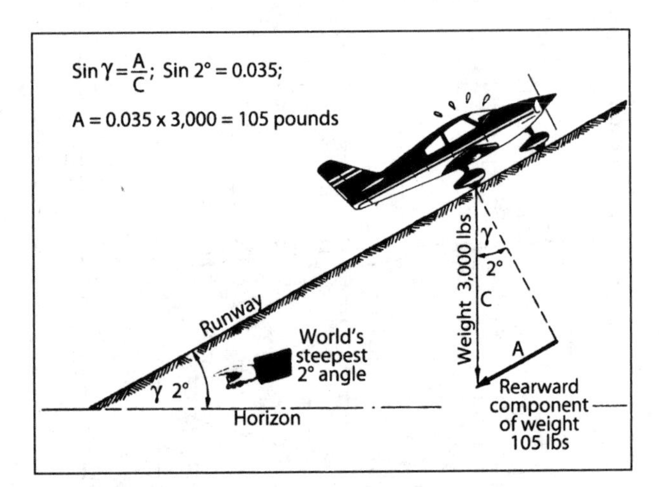

Figure 5-7. Effects of a 2° slope on the rearward component of weight.

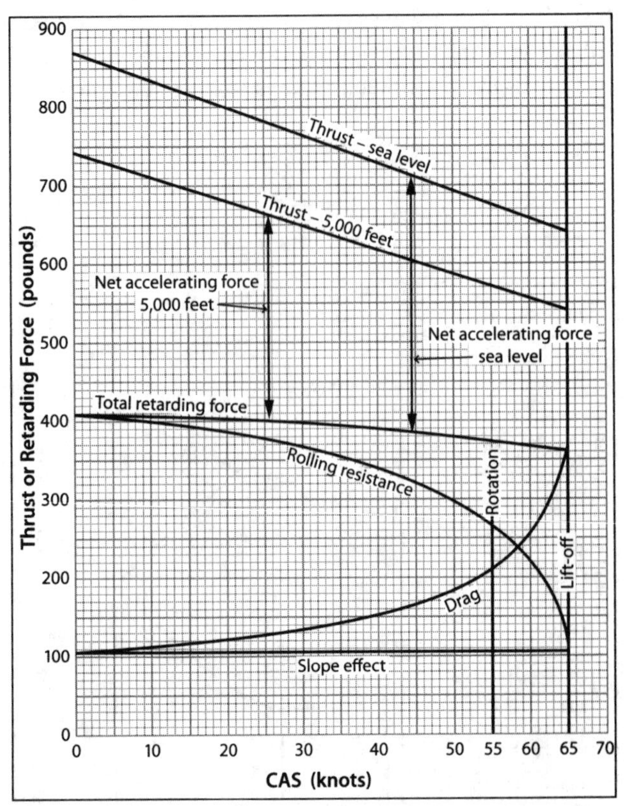

Figure 5-8. Thrust available at sea level and at a 5,000-ft density-altitude and the total retarding force in tall grass with an upslope of 2°. The total retarding force at any point in the takeoff run is the sum of rolling resistance, aerodynamic drag, and slope effect.

few dummy runs) or (2) keep at it and hope that it will pick up airspeed again, break loose, and let you clear the trees? You might prepare for the decision by stepping off the limit of the distance available to get off and safely clear obstacles. Use 2.5 feet as your measure for each "normal" step and if you are slogging through snow or tall grass better cut this down to 2 feet. If you assume a 3-foot pace, you might find out the hard way that a 400-pace (what you think is 1,200-ft) distance could be much closer to 800 feet. One possibility is to correctly pace off the *safe distance for lift-off* and put a marker at the halfway point. If you don't have an indicated (calibrated) airspeed of 0.7 (or 70%) of the lift-off speed at that halfway marker, you will not likely have lift-off speed at the end point. (This naturally assumes a constant coefficient of rolling resistance—if the "second half" of the surface is softer, the airplane may slow down and never get off.)

For example, you are taking off from a small grass airport and you've estimated that, to clear the trees, 1,800 feet is the maximum that can be used for the takeoff run. The airplane has to break ground at the usual rotation speed to get the max angle climb speed, V_X, and get over the obstacle(s). You put a rag or marker that can be readily seen on the side of the takeoff area at the 900-ft point. With a lift-off speed (CAS) of 65 K, you'll need $(0.7 \times 65) = 45.5$ K. Call it 45 K, an easily seen value on the airspeed indicator.

Look at Figures 5-4 and 5-8 to compare the net accelerating forces if you had been accustomed to dry, level, concrete runways at sea level and now find yourself with a gross weight at a 5,000-ft density-altitude on a runway with tall grass. At 40 K (for instance) the sea level NAF (dry, level concrete) is about 640 pounds; in the example at 5,000 feet, the NAF is about 230 pounds. You won't have to worry about passengers' whiplash injuries during the run in the latter case.

Wind Condition Effects

The wind affects the takeoff both in time and distance; of the two, distance is the most important. The headwind component is the important factor, and you need to know its value. For instance, a 30-K wind at a 30° angle to the runway would have a headwind component of 26 K—you might take a look back at Figures 1-5, 1-8, and 3-2. (The cosine of 30° is 0.866; $0.866 \times 30 = 26$ K, rounded off.)

The graph in Figure 5-9 shows that the wind effects are not as straightforward as they might at first seem. For instance, if the wind down the runway is 25% of the takeoff speed, Figure 5-9 shows that the length required for lift-off would be only 58% of that required under no-wind conditions. Common sense would seem to tell you that 75% is the answer.

Figure 5-10 is a quick way to find the multipliers for headwind and crosswind components. For instance, if the wind is at a 20° angle to the runway at 20 K you would see by referring to Figure 5-10 that the headwind and crosswind components would be 18 K and 7 K respectively. You gain more by having a headwind than you might at first think.

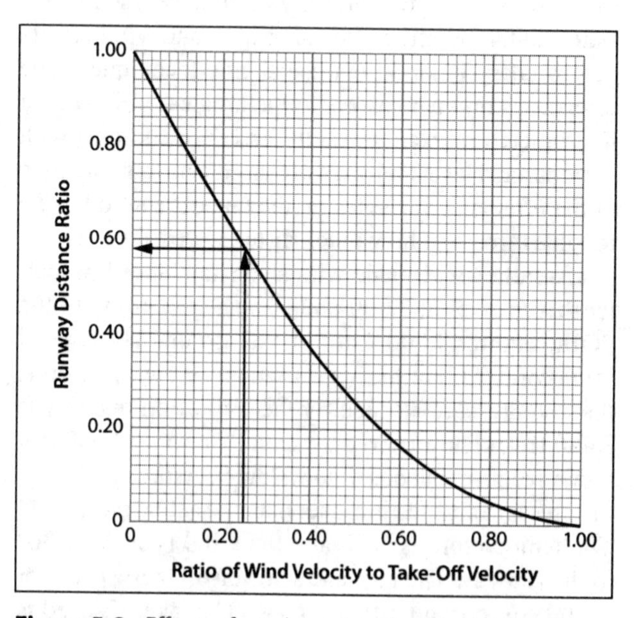

Figure 5-9. Effects of wind on takeoff run (or roll). Use the headwind component.

The angle that the wind makes with the runway	Cos α multiplier for headwind component	Sin α multiplier for crosswind component
0° (straight down the runway)	1.0	0
10°	1.0	0.15
15°	0.95	0.25
20°	0.90	0.35
30°	0.85	0.50
40°	0.75	0.65
45°	0.70	0.70
60°	0.50	0.85
75°	0.25	0.95
90° (direct crosswind)	0	1.0

Figure 5-10. Headwind and crosswind components for the wind at various angles to the runway (rounded off).

Pilot Technique Effects

The figures for takeoff distance in the POH are obtained by experienced test pilots and show better performance than a 100-hour private pilot might get, but these published figures at least give some basis for comparison. The disheartening thing is that takeoff techniques vary even among equally experienced pilots. In fact, it's very doubtful whether anyone could make two consecutive takeoffs just alike even though runway and wind conditions were exactly the same.

Assume that you carefully calculate pressure altitude and temperature effects, weight, and wind effects before takeoff—and then use sloppy techniques. The effect is as if you measured something carefully with a micrometer, marked it exactly, and then cut it off with a blunt ax. Nevertheless, you should have some idea of the effects of variables on the takeoff run to have a rough estimate of how much distance you'll need.

Assume an airplane with a constant-speed propeller that grosses at 3,000 pounds and, according to the POH, requires 1,000 feet to break ground at sea level on a standard day (no wind). Suppose the pilot finds that the pressure altitude for the airport on that day is 3,400 feet. (The airport may actually be only 3,000 feet above sea level but due to local low-pressure conditions the pressure altitude is higher than the actual elevation.) The temperature is 76°F and the wind is 10 K at 30° to the runway. The airplane's power-off stall speed for the takeoff configuration is 60 K. The takeoff speed is generally considered to be 1.2 times the power-off stall speed, so 72 K will be the takeoff speed used for these calculations. Assume that the runway is hard surfaced and level. The plane weighs 3,300 pounds because, although it's illegal to be over gross, the pilot wants to take an extra passenger wedged in the back seat (plus some extra baggage).

The following steps apply:

1. *Pressure altitude and temperature effects*—Note that the pressure altitude is 3,400 feet (standard temperature for this altitude is 47°F or 8°C) and the temperature is 76°F (24°C) or 29°F higher than normal. Remember that each added 15°F or 8½°C above standard equals another 1,000 feet of density-altitude. The density-altitude is 2,000 feet higher (rounded off) than the pressure altitude. *The airplane will perform at a density-altitude of 5,400 feet, no matter what the altimeter says.* Add 12% per 1,000 feet ($5.4 \times 12 = 65\%$). *The takeoff roll at this point will be 1,650 feet.*
2. *Weight effects*—The airplane's weight is (present weight/gross weight)^2 = $(3{,}300/3{,}000)^2 = (1.1)^2 = 1.21$; $1.21 \times 1{,}650 = 1{,}995$ feet now needed to break ground (call it 2,000 feet).
3. *Wind effects*—Assuming that the takeoff is into the wind (although anyone who overloads an airplane so much might decide to take off downwind just for the heck of it), the multiplier for the headwind component for a wind at an angle of 30° to the runway is 0.85 (Figure 5-10); $0.85 \times 10 = 8.5$ K. If your airspeed indicator is in mph, you can convert this wind speed to mph by multiplying by 1.15; $1.15 \times 8.5 = 9.8$ mph (call it 10 mph).

In order to use Figure 5-9, the ratio of wind velocity to takeoff velocity is needed; $V_{wind}/V_{takeoff} = 8.5$ K/72 K = 0.118 or 0.12. Referring to Figure 5-9 you find that the ratio takeoff distance (wind)/takeoff distance (no wind) = 0.80. So finally: $0.80 \times 2{,}000$ = *about 1,600 feet runway required at a pressure-altitude of 3,400 feet, temperature of 76°F; weight of 3,300 pounds and a wind of 10 K at an angle of 30° to the runway. This doesn't take into account runway slope or bad pilot technique.* Another thing to remember (again) is that tall grass, snow, or mud could possibly double this distance.

What about the climb? It's affected also. At sea level you can expect the distance (after lift-off) to clear a 50-foot obstacle to be about 90% of the takeoff roll. The sample airplane with a takeoff roll of 1,000 feet would likely require another 900 feet to clear a 50-foot obstacle. The distance to clear a 50-foot obstacle increases with increase in density-altitude and weight, but the airplane with the fixed-pitch propeller suffers more. For instance, a popular trainer at sea level density-altitude and gross weight has a climb ratio of 1 to 12; at 5,000-feet density-altitude, the climb ratio is 1 to 20.

Rule of Thumb Takeoff Variables for Non-Turbocharged Engines

1. *Add 12% to the takeoff run, as given in the POH for sea level, for every 1,000 feet of pressure altitude at the takeoff point.*
2. *Add 12% to the above figure for every 15°F or 8.5°C above standard for the field pressure altitude.*
3. *Weight effects*—The POH takeoff figures are for the gross weight of the airplane unless otherwise stated. The takeoff run is affected approximately by the square of the weight change. For example, a 10% weight change causes at least a 21% change in length of takeoff run.
4. *Wind effects*—The ratio of wind velocity (down the runway) to your takeoff speed (in percentage) subtracted from 90% gives the expected ratio of

runway length needed to break ground. If wind = 20% of takeoff velocity, 90 – 20 = 70%. You'll use *70%* of the runway distance as given by the POH for no-wind conditions. This rule of thumb can be used if you don't have Figure 5-9 handy. Consider any headwind component less than 5 K to be calm and to have no effect on takeoff run if you use the just-mentioned rule of thumb.

The Normal Takeoff

Tricycle-Gear

For computing takeoff distance, engineers sometimes use a speed at lift-off of 1.1 times the power-off stall speed. You know, as a pilot, that you can lift a plane off at stall speed, but this is usually reserved for special occasions such as soft-field takeoffs. The 1.1 figure is recommended to preclude your getting too deeply in the backside of the power-required curve.

If you pull the plane off in a cocked-up attitude and try to climb too steeply, you will use a great deal of your power just keeping the plane flying, much less getting on with your trip.

This nose-too-high attitude was particularly critical for the earlier jet takeoffs. Jet pilots pulling the nose too high during the takeoff run found themselves running out of runway with the plane having no inclination to get airborne. In fact, a 100-mile-long runway wouldn't be any better—you'd still be sitting there waiting for something to happen when there was no more runway left (Figure 5-11).

The prop plane has more HP to spare at low speeds and will accelerate or climb out of the bad situation more quickly. But accelerating takes time and distance, and if there are obstacles off the end of the runway, you may wish you had shown a little more discretion in your method of lift-off. This problem is (again) more evident in propeller planes of high power loadings (power loading = weight/HP).

The "back side of the power curve" is also important on approaches. You can get your airplane so low and slow on final that by the time you accelerate or climb out of this condition, you may have gone through a fence and killed somebody's prize Hereford bull a good quarter mile short of the runway. You can get out of this region, but it may take more distance than you can spare at the moment.

If you feel that the nose is too high on the takeoff roll and the plane isn't accelerating as it should, then the nose must be lowered and the plane given a chance to accelerate—even though you don't particularly want to do this when there's not much runway left.

In an airplane that has an effective elevator and a not-so-effective rudder, it doesn't make for ease of mind if you yank the nosewheel off at the first opportunity, particularly in a strong left crosswind. On the other hand, nothing seems quite so amateurish as the pilot who runs down the runway hell-for-leather on all three wheels until the tires are screaming and then yanks it off. Just because it's a tricycle-gear doesn't

Figure 5-11. Sometimes you don't have time for computing.

mean that it should be ridden like a tricycle. The best normal takeoff in a tricycle-gear plane is one in which, after a proper interval of roll, the nosewheel is gently raised and shortly afterward the airplane flies itself off. No book can tell you just when to raise the nosewheel for all the different airplanes. *In fact, no book can tell you just how to fly, as you are well aware of by now.*

Although retractable-gear airplanes will be covered in detail later, there are a couple of points to be mentioned here. Too many pilots have the idea that it makes them look "hot" to pull up the gear as soon as the plane breaks ground. Airplanes have been known to settle back on the runway after a takeoff. The plane doesn't roll too well with the gear partially retracted. Don't retract the gear too soon, even if you are *definitely* airborne. That is, don't pull up the gear until you have reached the point where in case of engine failure the airplane can no longer be landed on the runway wheels down. It would be very embarrassing to use 500 feet of a 10,000-foot runway and then have to belly it in when the engine quit because you didn't have time to get the gear back down (Figure 5-12).

Delaying the gear raising has its aerodynamic and performance advantages, too. For some airplanes, the transitioning of the gear (up or down) can increase parasite drag as the gear doors open and shut. An airplane that has been forced off in a marginal condition and is barely holding its own, staggering along just above the runway, may have enough added interference drag and form drag during the gear raising that aerodynamic laws would require it to settle back down on partially retracted gear, no matter how good your pilot technique might be (Figure 5-13).

Common Errors (Tricycle-Gear)

1. Holding the nosewheel on and jerking the airplane off the ground (a less violent technique similar to this is good for takeoffs in strong crosswinds but some people do it under all wind and weather conditions).
2. The other extreme, pulling the nose up too high and too early, which increases chances of poor directional control in a crosswind and extends the takeoff run. A typical case is one in which the pilot pulls the nosewheel off by brute force before it's ready, and has to apply lots of right rudder. The nose, not ready to stay up, falls back down with nosewheel cocked. This makes for a funny feeling.

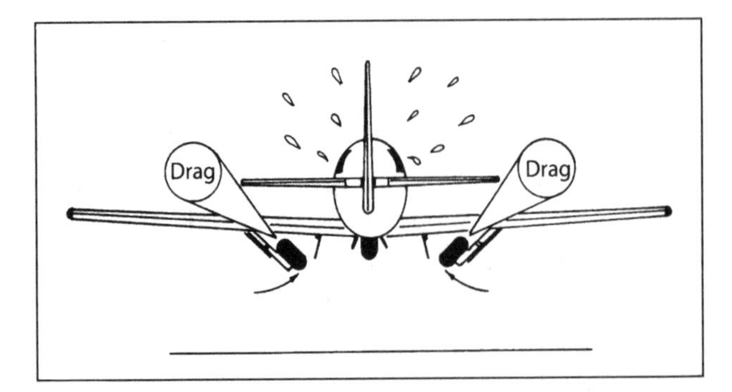

Figure 5-13. The transition of the landing gear may cause unacceptable drag.

Takeoffs for Tailwheel Types

Things being as they are today, it may be that you haven't checked out in a tailwheel airplane yet. For a long time there were few if any tricycle-gear trainers, and everybody learned to fly in airplanes with tailwheels. Now the trend is reversed and nearly all the planes are tricycle gear. This section is presented to give you a little background if you get a chance to check out in the tailwheel type.

The takeoff roll may be broken down into three phases.

Phase 1

This phase usually gives the most trouble to the pilot checking out in the tailwheel type. It's slightly harder to go from the tricycle-gear to the tailwheel type than vice versa, but you'll have no trouble after the first few takeoffs and landings.

The big problem in this phase seems to be the inability to see over the nose at the beginning of the takeoff roll. You've been used to looking directly over the nose all through the tricycle-gear takeoff, and this habit may be hard to break. You'll have to get used

Figure 5-12. Haste can make waste.

to looking down the side of the nose in most cases, although some tailwheel airplanes have low nose positions comparable to tricycle-gear types.

Ease the throttle open. This is important for the tailwheel airplane because (1) the rudder-tailwheel combination has less positive control at low speeds, and the sudden application of power causes torque effects that could make directional control a problem at first and (2) the high nose makes it harder to detect this torque-induced movement and may delay your corrective action.

The tailwheel will be doing most of the steering with the rudder becoming more effective as the airspeed picks up. In a high-powered, propeller airplane it may take a great deal of rudder to do the job at the beginning of the takeoff run.

The elevators should be left at neutral or only slightly ahead of neutral because you don't want to force the tail up too quickly and lose directional control.

You may for the first takeoff or two have a tendency to "walk the rudder." You've had enough experience by now to recognize this mistake and correct it yourself.

Phase 2

As the plane picks up speed, allow (or assist slightly) the tail to come up until the airplane is in the attitude of a shallow climb. When the tail comes up, tailwheel steering is lost and the rudder itself is responsible for keeping the airplane straight. This means that added rudder deflection must make up for the loss of steering of the tailwheel. Your biggest steering problems will be at the beginning of the takeoff and at the point at which the tail comes up.

If the tail is abruptly raised, our old friend "precession" has a chance to act. The rotating propeller makes an efficient gyro, and when the tail is raised, it is as if a force were exerted at the top of the propeller arc, from the rear. The airplane reacts as if the force had been exerted at a point 90° around the propeller arc, or at the right side (Figure 5-14). The precession force is added to the torque forces and could cause a *left* swerve if you are unprepared. The opposite occurs if the nose is abruptly raised in flight.

Phase 3

The airplane is now in a shallow climb attitude and will fly itself off. However, you can help a little with slight back pressure. The rest of the takeoff and climb are just like the procedures you've been using with the tricycle-gear plane.

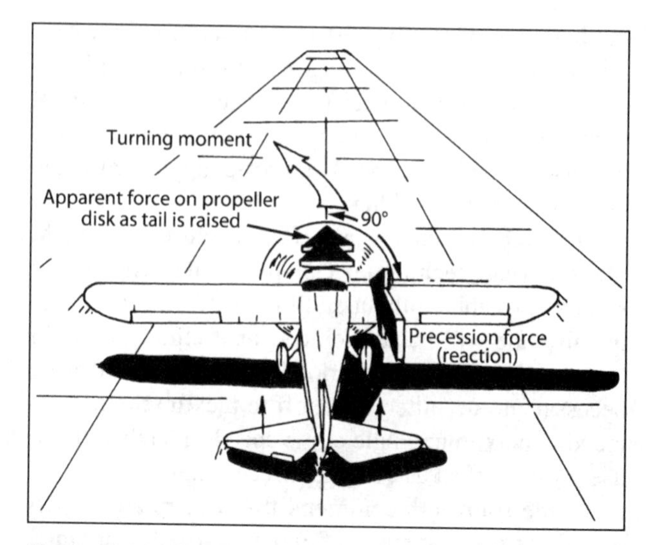

Figure 5-14. Precession effects due to abrupt raising of the tail.

Common Errors (Tailwheel-Type)

1. Poor directional control.
2. Raising the tail abruptly and too high.
3. Trying to pull the plane off too early.

The Short-Field Takeoff

The short-field takeoff is used in conjunction with the climb to clear an obstacle. Only the ground roll will be covered in this section; the maximum angle or obstacle climb will be covered in Chapter 6.

The airplane accelerates best when in the air if it is not "stalled off." The comparative amount of acceleration between the airplane at a given speed on the ground and airborne naturally depends on the surface. The airplane is ready to fly before the average pilot wants to; the pilot generally uses more runway than is necessary in becoming airborne. This is good under normal takeoff conditions as well as in gusty air, because it gives a margin of safety at lift-off. *But* in the case of the short-field takeoff, you don't have the runway to spare.

Some pilots are firm believers in the idea of holding the plane on until the last instant and then hauling back abruptly and screaming up over the obstacle. This makes the takeoff look a great deal more flashy and difficult than if the pilot had gotten the plane off sooner and set up a maximum angle or obstacle clearance climb. The rate of climb is a function of the excess HP available, as will be discussed in Chapter 6. In the maximum angle climb, you are interested in getting *more altitude per foot of ground covered*, rather than the best rate of climb. This is a compromise between a lower airspeed and lower rate of climb in order to clear an obstacle at a specific distance. True, you're not climbing at quite as great a rate, but on the other hand, because of the lower speed you're not approaching the obstacle as quickly either.

The recommended takeoff procedure is close to the soft-field technique. Get the plane airborne as soon as possible without stalling it off. In most cases the airplane will be accelerating as it climbs. Only in underpowered and/or overloaded airplanes will it be necessary to definitely level off to pick up the recommended maximum angle climb speed, though you can use ground effect as an aid to acceleration.

Some sources recommend that you rotate to lift-off just as the best angle of climb airspeed is attained and maintain that speed until the assumed obstructions have been cleared. This is a standardized procedure. The main drawback is that the average pilot tends to let the airspeed pick up after lift-off and get well over the best angle of climb speed, thus losing performance. You can talk with pilots experienced in your airplane and work out the best technique for takeoff and climb. It may very well be that rotating at V_X is best, and you can hold this exact speed after lift-off.

Use of Flaps

Manufacturers recommend a certain flap setting for the short-field takeoff because they have found that this flap setting results in a shorter takeoff run and better angle of climb. For some airplanes, the manufacturers recommend that no flaps be used on the short-field takeoff, and for best performance, it is wise to follow the recommendations given in the POH.

There are two schools of thought on the technique of using flaps for a short-field takeoff. One is to use no flaps at all for the first part of the run and then apply flaps (generally full flaps) when the time seems ripe. This technique generally disregards the fact that there is rolling resistance present. The first part of the roll usually is made with the airplane in a level-flight attitude, the pilot counting on the sudden application of flaps to obtain lift for the takeoff. There is no doubt that aerodynamic drag is less in the level-flight attitude than in a tail-low attitude, but rolling resistance is the greatest factor in the earlier part of the run and this is often overlooked. If the field is soft, an inefficient and perhaps dangerous (particularly in the tailwheel type) condition may be set up because weight is not being taken from the main wheels and a nosing-over tendency is present.

The ideal point at which to lower flaps differs widely between pilots.

The effect of full flaps on the obstacle climb (unless the plane design calls specifically for the use of full flaps) results in a low lift-to-drag ratio—that is, an increase of proportionally more drag for the amount of lift required, so the climb angle suffers.

There is usually a loss in pilot technique (particularly in the tailwheel type) during the flap lowering. The pilot has to divide attention between the takeoff and flap manipulation. This can be overcome as the pilot becomes more familiar with the airplane, but in most cases the flap handle is located in an awkward position or requires attention to operate. The flaps generally are designed to be operated at a point where the pilot can direct attention to them if necessary—that is, *before* takeoff, on the base leg or on final. The takeoff itself requires more attention than these other procedures. The pilot attempting to deflect the flaps the correct amount during the takeoff run may get two notches instead of three, or over- or undershoot the desired setting if the flaps are hydraulically or electrically actuated. It's just not worth the danger and distraction during a critical phase of flight.

The other, and better, technique is to set the flaps at the recommended angle *before* starting the takeoff run and then forget about them until the obstacle is well cleared. Fly the airplane off and attain, *and maintain*, the recommended climb speed. *After* the obstacle is cleared, ease the nose over slightly and pick up airspeed until you have a safe margin to ease the flaps up. Some pilots clear the obstacle, breathe a sigh of relief, jerk the flaps up, and grandly sink back into the trees. On some airplanes the *POH-recommended* maximum angle of climb speed is fairly close to the power-on stall speed. Although you had a good safety margin with the flaps down, when you jerk them up at this speed at a low altitude, you could have problems in gusty air. (A common error, however, is to be overly cautious.)

Short-Field Takeoff Procedure (Tailwheel or Tricycle-Gear)

1. Before takeoff, use a careful pretakeoff check and a full-power run up to make sure the engine is developing full power. Don't waste runway; start at the extreme end. Set flaps as recommended by the POH. (Lean the mixture per POH at high density altitudes.)
2. Open the throttle wide (smoothly) as you release the brakes. (Don't wait until the throttle is completely open before releasing the brakes.)
3. Keep the airplane straight and avoid "rudder walking," because this slows the takeoff.
4. Get the airplane airborne as soon as is safely possible without "stalling it off." This means that the

nosewheel of the tricycle-gear type is raised as soon as practicable (not *too* high) and on the tailwheel-type the attitude is tail low, similar to that of the soft-field takeoff. In both cases, the airplane is flown off at a slightly lower-than-usual airspeed.

5. Attain and *maintain* the recommended maximum angle climb or obstacle clearance speed as given in the POH. Continue to use full power until the obstacle is cleared or as recommended. (It may be a couple of hundred feet.)
6. Retract the landing gear (if so equipped).
7. Assume a normal climb. (The climb will be discussed later.)
8. Retract flaps when clear of the obstacles and at the recommended IAS.

Some pilots argue for a 90° rolling takeoff, but this is hard on tires and landing gear assemblies for very little, if any, gain. It's agreed that the fixed-pitch prop is inefficient at low speeds (Chapter 2) but you might ground loop using the 90°-run technique.

It's possible that a too-sharp turn onto the runway could "unport the fuel" on one side. Suppose you're making an extra-sharp high-speed left turn onto the runway and have selected the right wing tank for takeoff. (That was the fullest and the one selected before the run-up.) As you make that turn, centrifugal force moves the fuel away from the port opening of the fuel line. You could have a loss of power during the takeoff run or right after lift-off (Figure 5-15).

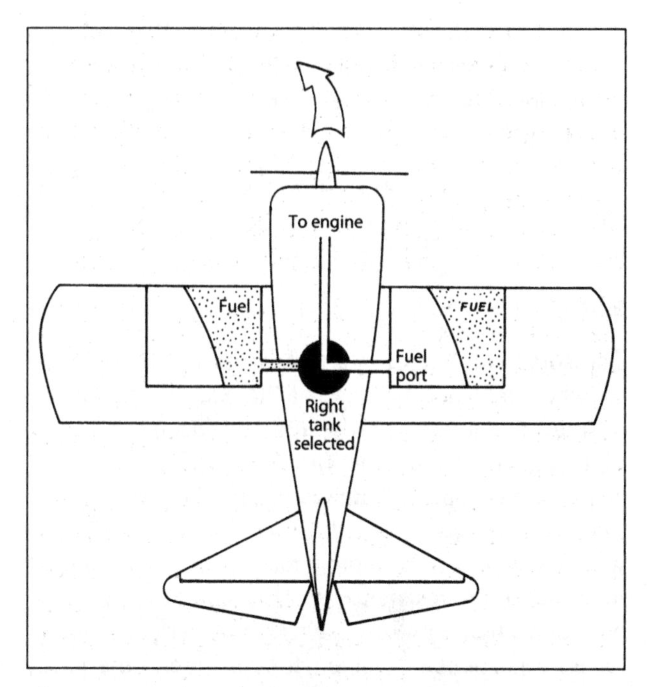

Figure 5-15. The centrifugal force of the sharp left turn moved the fuel from the tank port and the engine is being starved at a bad time. (There is usually just enough fuel left in the line to let the airplane get too far to land on the runway.) One solution used over the years is that of baffles in the fuel tank to slow, or stop, fuel "sloshing."

Common Errors

1. Poor directional control when the brakes are released.
2. Trying to hurry the plane off the ground, resulting in high drag and actually slowing the takeoff.
3. Holding the plane down after breaking ground, letting the airspeed pick up past the maximum angle of climb speed and losing climb efficiency.

The Soft-Field Takeoff

(Use flaps as recommended by the POH.)

Maybe the only soft-field takeoff procedures you've used so far were the simulated ones practiced for the private flight test. But sooner or later you'll find yourself in a spot where the field may be too soft for a normal takeoff.

Generally speaking, mud, snow, and high grass can be considered to fall into the category where a special takeoff technique is required. This same technique is useful on a rough field where it's better to get the plane off as soon as possible to minimize chances of damaging the landing gear.

Tricycle-Gear

Keep the airplane rolling. If you stop to think things over in the middle of the takeoff area, you may find yourself watching the wheels slowly sinking in the muck. It may take full power to even move once you've stopped. The propeller will pick up mud and gravel and throw it into the stabilizer or stabilator. This doesn't help either the prop or the tail surfaces.

Rolling resistance is high, so you will want a tail-low attitude on the takeoff run to help overcome this resistance.

1. The airplane is kept rolling, full throttle is applied, and the wheel (or stick) is held back for two reasons: (1) to get the weight off the nosewheel, which will decrease rolling resistance as well as lessen chances of the nosewheel hitting an extra-soft spot and being damaged and (2) to increase the angle of attack as soon as possible so that the weight on the main wheels is minimized.
2. As soon as the plane is definitely airborne, lower the nose and establish a normal climb.

Common Errors (Tricycle-Gear)

1. Not keeping the airplane moving as it is lined up with the takeoff area, thus requiring a great deal of power to get rolling again and increasing the possibility of prop damage.

2. Not enough back pressure. Most pilots tend to underestimate the amount of back pressure required to break the nosewheel from the ground at lower airspeeds.

Of course, you may be able to get the nose too high and suffer the same results as in the normal takeoff under these conditions—that is, no takeoff at all.

Tailwheel Type

The soft-field takeoff is a little more touchy with the tailwheel airplane because of the greater chances of nosing up if a particularly soft spot, deeper snow, or higher grass is suddenly encountered. The tailwheel airplane has some advantage in that there is no large third wheel to cause added rolling resistance. The tailwheel is small and has comparatively little weight on it to cause rolling resistance. *But* this could cause a nose over in a situation where the tricycle-gear plane would have no particular trouble. (It could break the nosewheel, however.)

You had soft-field takeoffs on the private flight test and, if you used a tailwheel-type plane, you have a pretty good idea of the technique.

As with the tricycle-gear plane, the plane should be kept rolling onto the runway (invariably someone else is coming in for a landing and you'll have to wait anyway, but if you do, try to pick a firmer spot so you won't get mired down). This means that the pretakeoff check should be run at a good spot so that after ascertaining that there is no traffic coming in, you can get on the takeoff area and get about your business (Figure 5-16).

Review Figure 5-3 to get a nonquantitative comparison of the effects of tall grass or soft ground. By comparing Figures 5-4 and 5-6, you can see that the initial (V = 0) rolling resistance for concrete and tall grass is 60 pounds and 300 pounds respectively.

Procedure

1. Keep the airplane rolling onto the runway and apply full power in the same manner as for a normal takeoff. Don't ram it open!
2. Keep the wheel (or stick) back to stop any early tendencies to nose over. Then—
3. Ease the tail up to a definitely tail-low position so that (1) the plane doesn't have a tendency to flip over and (2) the angle of attack is such as to get the plane airborne (and the weight off the main wheels) as soon as possible.
4. As soon as the airplane is definitely airborne, lower the nose slightly and establish a normal climb.

Common Errors (Tailwheel Type)

1. Holding the stick back too firmly and too long, causing added tailwheel rolling resistance as well as aerodynamic drag.
2. Getting the tail too high, with the danger of nosing over.

A Review of Crosswind Takeoffs

Tricycle-Gear

The wind's effect on both the tricycle-gear and tailwheel airplane on the ground generally is the same. That is, the airplane tends to weathercock into the wind and lean over as well (Figure 5-17). The tricycle-gear plane does not have as strong a tendency to weathercock because the nosewheel is large and there is more weight on it, so there is a greater ground resistance, compared with the tailwheel type.

In order to make a smooth crosswind takeoff you'll have to overcome these wind effects. Some lightplanes are hard to control when taking off in a strong left crosswind. The weathercocking tendency plus torque effects make it extremely difficult to have a straight takeoff run.

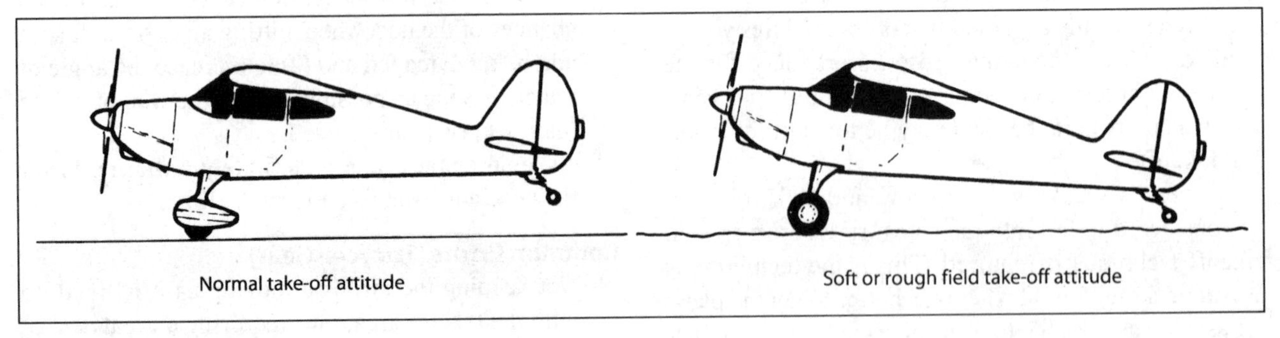

Figure 5-16. Takeoff attitudes.

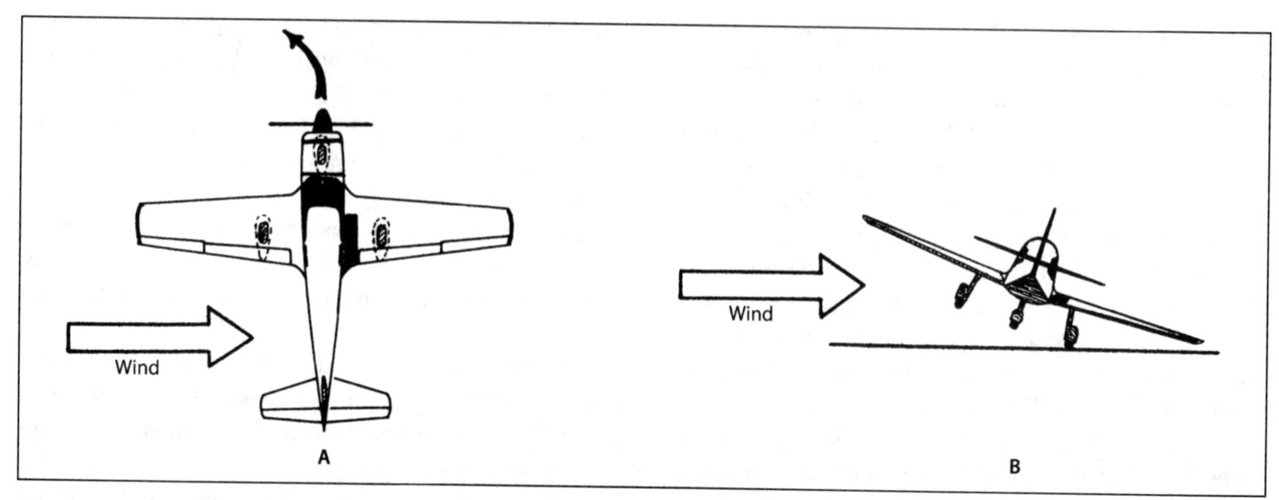

Figure 5-17. Airplane tends to weathercock **(A)** as well as lean **(B)**.

Procedure

Line up with the centerline of the runway, or on the downwind side if you think weathercocking will be so great as to make it impossible to keep the plane straight. If the wind is this strong, however, you might be better off to stay on the ground.

Assume, for instance, there is a fairly strong left crosswind component (10 K). It will require conscious effort on your part to apply and hold aileron into the wind. This is probably the most common fault of the relatively inexperienced pilot. It doesn't feel right to have the wheel or stick in such an awkward position. It is natural that the correction be eased off unconsciously shortly after the run begins. This may allow the wind to lift that upwind wing.

Another common error is the other extreme. The pilot uses full aileron at the beginning of the run and gets so engrossed in keeping the airplane straight that, when the plane does break ground, the full aileron may cause the airplane to start a very steep bank into the wind. This does little for the passengers' peace of mind and is actually useful only if the pilot is interested in picking up a handkerchief with his wing tip.

Notice in Figures 5-18 and 5-19 that the aileron into the wind actually has two effects: (1) it offsets the "leaning over" tendency (the ailerons have no effect in a 90° crosswind until the plane gets moving, though) and (2) the drag (both form and induced) of the down aileron (and its long arm) help fight the weathercocking tendency. Even with the differential aileron movement of modern light planes (they move farther up than down), ailerons into the wind fight both leaning and weathercocking in a crosswind.

This is a takeoff where you definitely should not rush the airplane into flying. The crosswind takeoff feels uncomfortable. It's perfectly natural to want to get the plane airborne and stop all this monkey business. Keep the plane on the ground until you are certain it is ready to fly, then lift it off with definite, but not abrupt, back pressure. If the plane should skip into the air, try to keep it flying, if possible. It will start drifting as soon as you are off the ground, and it won't help the tires and landing gear assembly to hit again when you're moving sideways.

In other words, don't try to ease the nosewheel off as in a normal takeoff. The weathercocking effect in a large crosswind component may be more than you can handle with rudder alone (no nosewheel help). Again, this is particularly true in a left crosswind. In a right crosswind, torque and weathercocking tend to work against each other. The airplane should be kept on all three wheels until at the lift-off point.

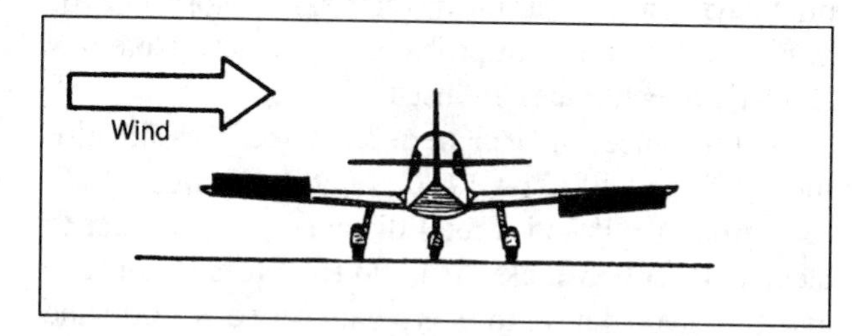

Figure 5-18. Tricycle-gear attitude and use of ailerons to compensate for a crosswind.

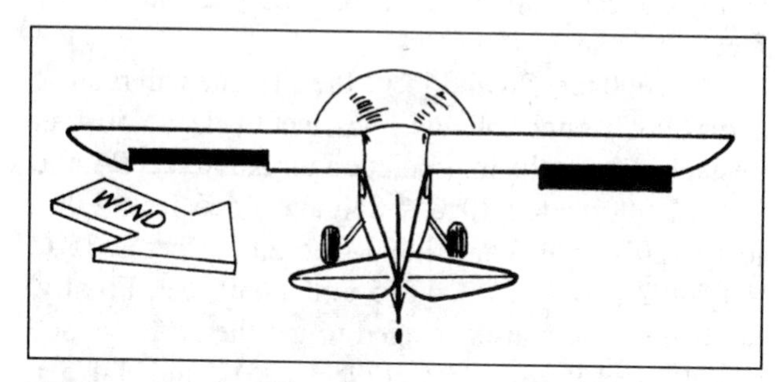

Figure 5-19. Aileron deflection at the beginning of the crosswind takeoff (tailwheel-type).

The idea of keeping the plane on the ground longer applies to the tailwheel type for the same reasons as for the tricycle-gear airplane. The attitude of the plane during the run will be slightly more tail high than for the normal takeoff (which for the tailwheel type, you remember, was the attitude of a shallow climb).

A common failing of pilots in both types of airplanes is that a poor drift correction is set up on the climbout. There are the hardy but misguided souls who still believe that holding rudder into the wind or holding the upwind wing down is the best way to correct for a crosswind *on the climbout.*

You know by now that the average plane, if trimmed properly, will make its own takeoff, but this may not be the most efficient procedure, particularly under abnormal conditions. Many pilots have never flown their airplanes at gross weight until one day they attempt it under adverse conditions—and leave an indelible impression on some object off the end of the runway.

Some Practical Considerations

It's good to know the theory and factors that affect takeoff performance, but you'll have to know how to use the charts for *your* airplane. The following charts are examples for review, starting with the simple and moving on to the more complex. Some people prefer a graphical presentation and others a tabular listing, but you should be prepared to use either one.

Figure 5-20 is for a noncomplex trainer; you may have used this chart in your student and earlier private pilot days. The tabular form is self-explanatory, but you might work a couple of problems for review. Note that short-field techniques are used.

For instance, an airplane at 3,000 feet pressure altitude (PA) and 10°C (at 1,670 pounds) requires a 925-foot ground roll and a total distance of 1,730 feet to clear a 50-foot obstacle. At 1,500 feet pressure altitude and 15°C, you'd have to interpolate between 1,000 and 2,000 feet at 10°C and at 20°C. For example, 1,000 feet at 10°C = 765 and 1,420 feet; 1,000 feet at 20°C = 825 and 1,530 feet; 1,000 feet at 15°C = 1,590/2 and 2,950/2 feet = 795 and 1,475 feet.

At 1,000 feet PA and 15°C, the airplane will require a 795-foot ground roll and 1,475 feet to clear a 50-foot obstacle. Doing the interpolation for 2,000 feet PA and 15°C, 2,000 feet at 10°C = 840 and 1,565 feet; 2,000 feet at 20°C = 910 and 1,690 feet; 2,000 feet at 15°C = 1,750/2 and 3,255/2 = 875 and 1,630 feet. Finally, the two answers are averaged to get the performance at 1,500 feet PA and 15°C: (795 + 875)/2 and (1,475 + 1,630)/2 = 835 and 1,555 feet (rounded off).

Assuming no wind and taking off on a dry, grass runway at 1,500 feet PA and 15°C, you would add 15% of the ground roll (run?) figure to both distances: 0.15 × 835 = 125 feet; 835 + 125 = 960 feet ground roll; 1,555 + 125 = *1,680 feet total distance over a 50-foot obstacle* (note 4).

Assuming that a 9 K headwind has suddenly sprung up just as you start the roll on that dry grass runway you would use approximately 10% less of the distance (note 3).

Figure 5-21 is a takeoff distance chart for a more complex airplane with performance for two weights given. You can interpolate altitudes, temperatures, and weights with this.

Figure 5-22 is the takeoff ground distance chart for a four-place airplane (0° flaps). The example is self-explanatory.

Figure 5-23 is a chart for the *total distance* over a 50-foot barrier for the airplane in Figure 5-22. (Note the headwind difference for the two examples.) Figure 5-24 is the same type of graphical presentation but for a heavier twin.

Check the notes on the charts so that you aren't computing the performance for the wrong weight or flap configuration. These charts, like all performance or navigation charts in this book, are not to be used in actual situations.

Study and know the POH. If in doubt, read it again, and, above all, *always give yourself a safety factor, particularly in takeoffs.*

TAKEOFF DISTANCE

SHORT FIELD

CONDITIONS:
Flaps 10°
Full Throttle Prior to Brake Release
Paved, Level, Dry Runway
Zero Wind

NOTES:
1. Short field technique as specified in Section 4.
2. Prior to takeoff from fields above 3000 feet elevation, the mixture should be leaned to give maximum RPM in a full throttle, static runup.
3. Decrease distances 10% for each 9 knots headwind. For operation with tailwinds up to 10 knots, increase distances by 10% for each 2 knots.
4. For operation on a dry, grass runway, increase distances by 15% of the "ground roll" figure.

WEIGHT LBS	TAKEOFF SPEED KIAS		PRESS ALT FT	0°C		10°C		20°C		30°C		40°C	
	LIFT OFF	AT 50 FT		GRND ROLL	TOTAL TO CLEAR 50 FT OBS	GRND ROLL	TOTAL TO CLEAR 50 FT OBS	GRND ROLL	TOTAL TO CLEAR 50 FT OBS	GRND ROLL	TOTAL TO CLEAR 50 FT OBS	GRND ROLL	TOTAL TO CLEAR 50 FT OBS
1670	50	54	S.L.	640	1190	695	1290	755	1390	810	1495	875	1605
			1000	705	1310	765	1420	825	1530	890	1645	960	1770
			2000	775	1445	840	1565	910	1690	980	1820	1055	1960
			3000	855	1600	925	1730	1000	1870	1080	2020	1165	2185
			4000	940	1775	1020	1920	1100	2080	1190	2250	1285	2440
			5000	1040	1970	1125	2140	1215	2320	1315	2525	1420	2750
			6000	1145	2200	1245	2395	1345	2610	1455	2855	1570	3125
			7000	1270	2470	1375	2705	1490	2960	1615	3255	1745	3590
			8000	1405	2800	1525	3080	1655	3395	1795	3765	1940	4195

Figure 5-20. Takeoff chart for a light trainer.

TAKEOFF DISTANCE

2500 LBS AND 2300 LBS

SHORT FIELD

CONDITIONS:
Flaps Up
2700 RPM and Full Throttle Prior to Brake Release
Cowl Flaps Open
Paved, Level Dry Runway
Zero Wind

NOTES:
1. Short field technique as specified in Section 4.
2. Prior to takeoff from fields above 3000 feet elevation, the mixture should be leaned to give maximum power in a full throttle, static runup.
3. Decrease distances 10% for each 9 knots headwind. For operation with tailwinds up to 10 knots, increase distances by 10% for each 2 knots.
4. For operation on a dry, grass runway, increase distances by 15% of the "ground roll" figure.

WEIGHT LBS	TAKEOFF SPEED KIAS		PRESS ALT FT	0°C		10°C		20°C		30°C		40°C	
	LIFT OFF	AT 50 FT		GRND ROLL	TOTAL TO CLEAR 50 FT OBS	GRND ROLL	TOTAL TO CLEAR 50 FT OBS	GRND ROLL	TOTAL TO CLEAR 50 FT OBS	GRND ROLL	TOTAL TO CLEAR 50 FT OBS	GRND ROLL	TOTAL TO CLEAR 50 FT OBS
2500	56	61	S.L.	835	1400	895	1495	960	1595	1025	1705	1100	1820
			1000	910	1525	975	1635	1045	1745	1120	1865	1200	1995
			2000	995	1670	1070	1790	1145	1915	1225	2050	1315	2195
			3000	1090	1835	1170	1965	1255	2105	1345	2260	1440	2420
			4000	1195	2015	1280	2165	1375	2325	1475	2500	1580	2685
			5000	1310	2230	1410	2400	1515	2580	1625	2780	1740	2990
			6000	1440	2470	1550	2665	1665	2875	1790	3105	1920	3355
			7000	1585	2760	1710	2980	1840	3230	1975	3500	2120	3800
			8000	1755	3095	1890	3360	2035	3655	2185	3980	2350	4350
2300	54	59	S.L.	690	1160	740	1240	790	1320	845	1405	905	1500
			1000	750	1265	805	1350	860	1440	920	1535	985	1635
			2000	820	1380	880	1475	940	1575	1010	1680	1080	1795
			3000	895	1505	960	1610	1030	1725	1105	1845	1180	1970
			4000	980	1650	1050	1770	1130	1895	1210	2025	1295	2170
			5000	1075	1815	1155	1950	1240	2090	1325	2240	1420	2400
			6000	1180	2005	1265	2150	1360	2310	1460	2485	1565	2670
			7000	1295	2220	1395	2385	1500	2570	1610	2765	1725	2980
			8000	1430	2465	1540	2660	1655	2875	1775	3105	1905	3355

Figure 5-21. Takeoff chart for a four-place airplane at two weights.

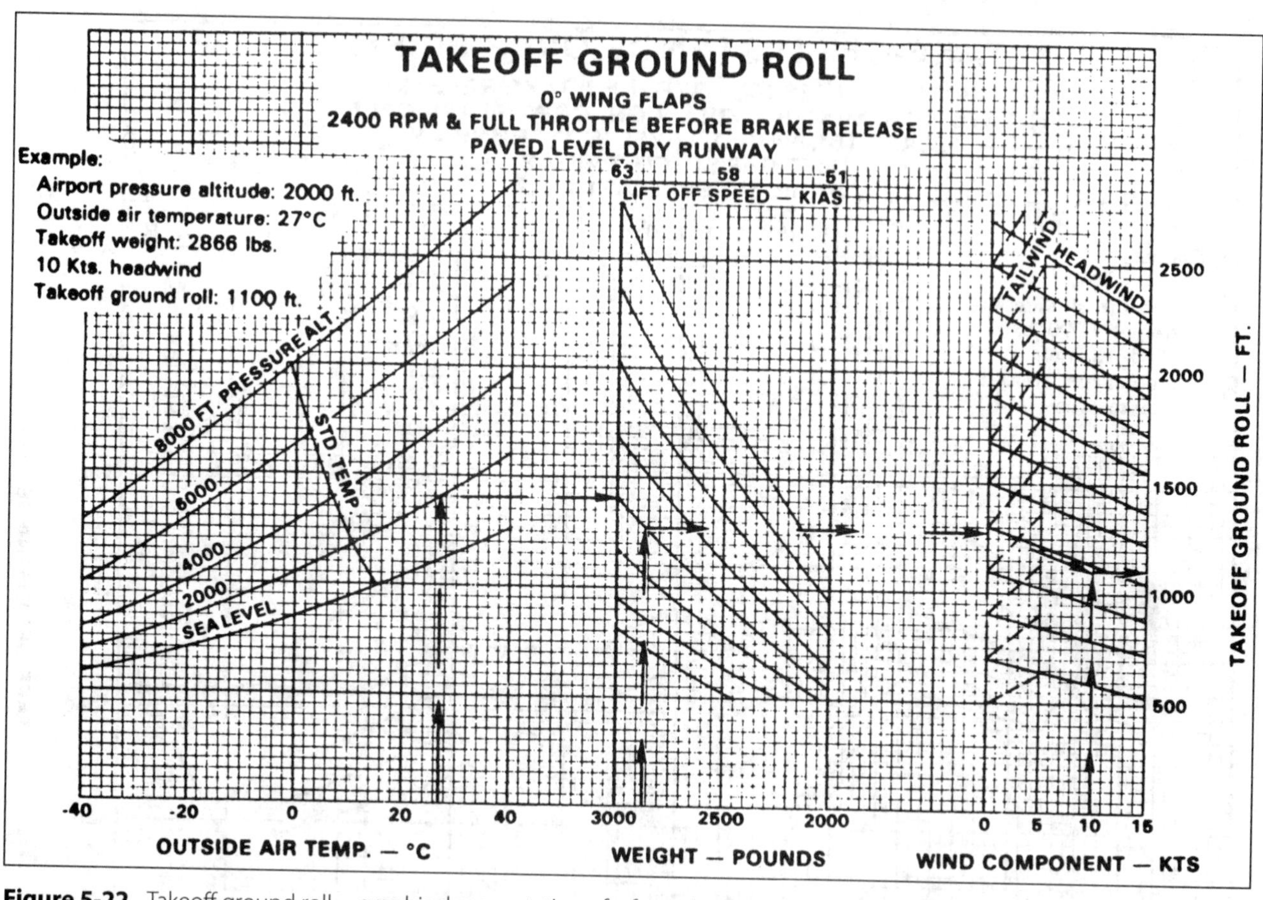

Figure 5-22. Takeoff ground roll—graphical presentation of a four-place airplane.

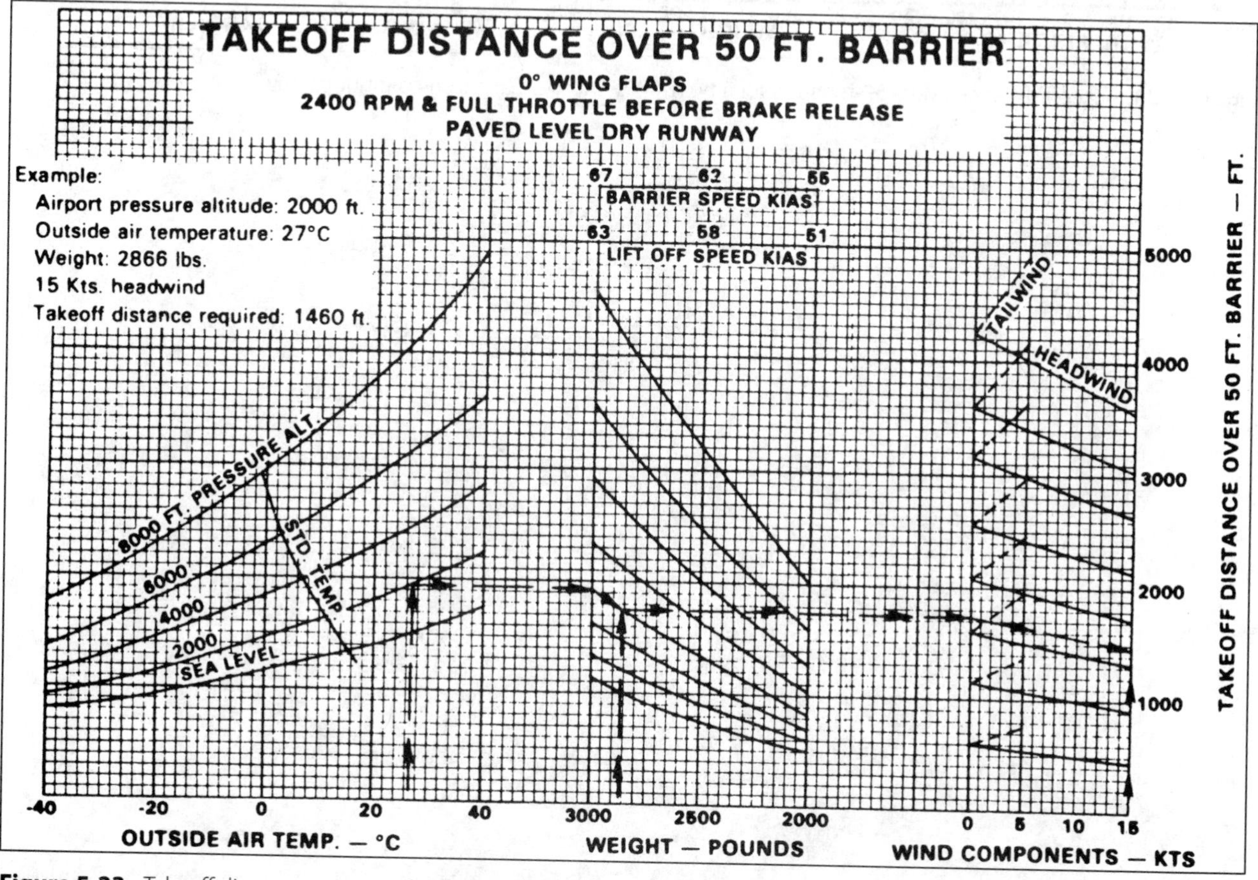

Figure 5-23. Takeoff distance over a 50-ft barrier for the airplane in Figure 5-22.

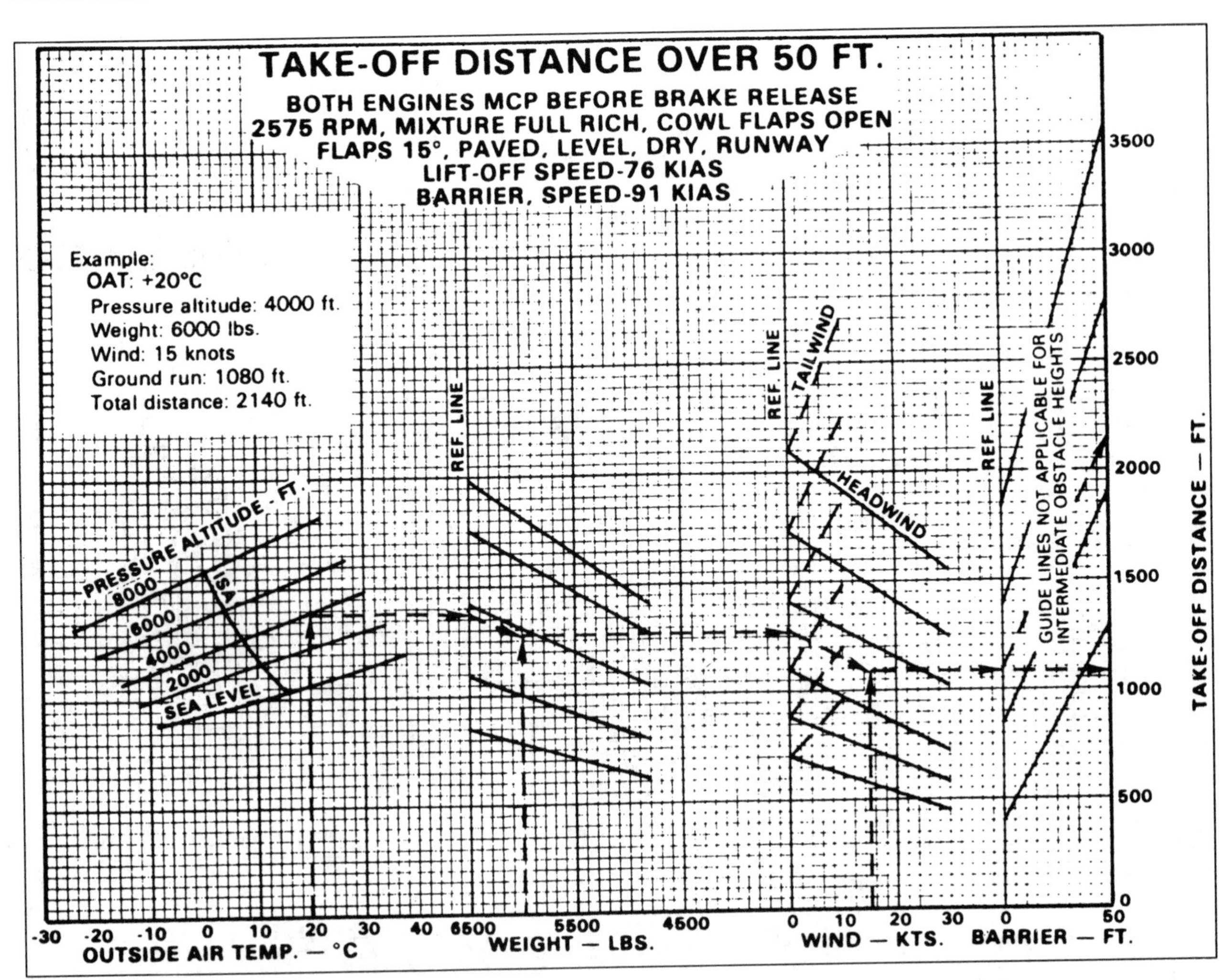

Figure 5-24. Takeoff distance over a 50-ft barrier for a twin. (MCP means maximum continuous power.)

6
The Climb

An airplane's rate of climb is a function of excess HP available. This can be approximated by this equation: rate of climb (fpm) = (excess thrust horsepower × 33,000)/airplane weight, or R/C (fpm) = (ETHP × 33,000)/W, or

$$R/C = ETHP \times \frac{33{,}000}{W}$$

Looking again at a HP-required and HP-available (THP) versus velocity curve for a particular altitude (we'll choose sea level for simplicity), note the following (Figure 6-1). At a particular velocity, the difference between the THP available at recommended climb power and the HP required is the maximum. By looking at this graph for a particular airplane, you immediately know the best rate of climb speed at sea level. With a series of these curves up to the airplane's ceiling, you can find the speed for best rate of climb for any altitude (Figure 6-2). Looking at Figure 6-2, you can see that, at 90 K at sea level, a power of about 59 THP is required to fly the airplane straight and level and 178 THP is the available power, or an excess of 119 THP exists. Using the equation for rate of climb: R/C = (ETHP × 33,000)/weight (the weight for this airplane is 3,000 pounds), R/C = (119 × 33,000)/3,000 = 1,309 fpm at sea level. The climb angle is found to be 8°15' relative to the horizon. If you remember back in Chapter 3, the rate of climb for this fictitious airplane was found to be 1,265 fpm (a climb angle of an *even* 8° was set up for the climb speed of 90 K and the problem was worked "backward"). The higher rate of climb here shows that the airplane was slightly underrated by that method (and numbers were rounded off).

Checking the rate of climb at 10,000 feet at the best climb speed (given as TAS here), the pilot would use IAS or CAS, which computed for the TAS of 97 K at 10,000 feet would work out to be a CAS of about 84 K. The THP required is about 62 and the THP available is 120 (Figure 6-2), an excess of 58 THP: R/C = (58 × 33,000)/3,000 = 638 fpm—a reasonable figure at that altitude for an airplane of that weight and THP required. (Assume IAS = CAS for this discussion.)

Some POHs include graphs of the best rate of climb speeds for various altitudes (IAS or CAS) (Figure 6-3).

In cases where a graph like Figure 6-3 is unavailable for lighter (older) planes such as trainers, which have a simplified type of POH, a rule of thumb may be applied: the standard sea level recommended best rate of climb speed is available in these abbreviated

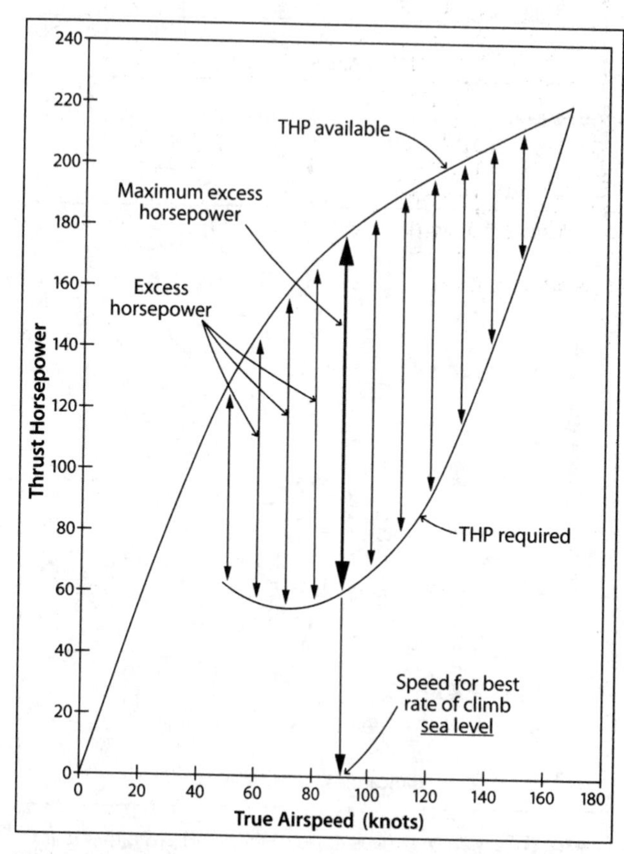

Figure 6-1. THP-available and THP-required curve for a high-performance general aviation airplane at sea level. (Calibrated airspeed equals true airspeed at sea level.) The best rate of climb is found at the speed where there is the greatest amount of excess THP available. (Airplane weight = 3,000 pounds)

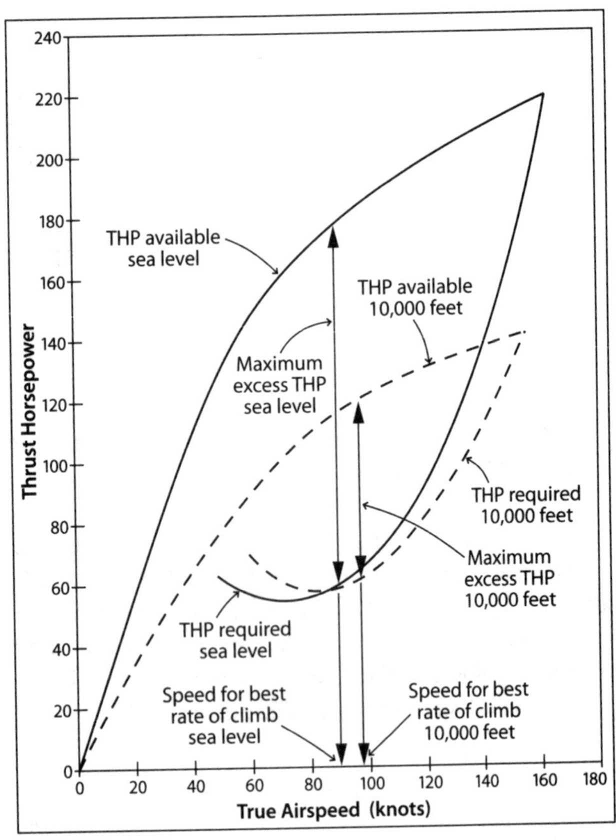

Figure 6-2. Best rate of climb speed (TAS) at sea level and 10,000 feet (density-altitude), unturbocharged engine.

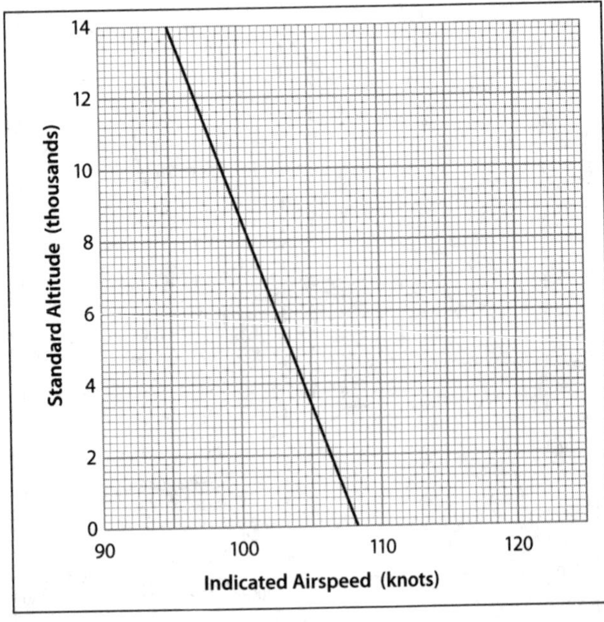

Figure 6-3. The max (best) rate of climb versus altitude for a light trainer.

Owner's Manuals, and the idea of maintaining a nearly constant TAS may be used; that is, the TAS and the CAS are the same under sea level standard conditions. You can find the (rough) indicated airspeed by *subtracting* 1% per 1,000 feet from the published figure. Note that in order to maintain the same TAS at various altitudes, the rule of thumb would be to subtract 2% per 1,000 feet from the sea level indicated climb speed, but the best rate of climb *true* airspeed increases about 1% per 1,000 feet (assuming no instrument error).

The 1% per 1,000 feet decrease in *indicated* airspeed takes care of this. It must be repeated that this rule of thumb is for light trainers, but it also works pretty well for heavier airplanes. You can't go too far wrong by maintaining the same IAS throughout the climb in the trainer, although a slight loss in efficiency will result. This type of plane normally does not operate much over 5,000 feet anyway.

There are two *ceilings* commonly mentioned: (1) *service ceiling* (that altitude at which the rate of climb is 100 fpm) and (2) *absolute ceiling* (the absolute altitude the plane can reach, where the rate of climb is zero). These ceilings are normally based on gross weight but can be computed for any weight. If you want to come right down to it, the absolute ceiling as a part of a climb schedule at gross weight could never really be reached. In the first place, the airplane would be burning fuel and getting lighter as it climbed so it wouldn't reach the absolute ceiling at the correct weight; secondly, even if the weight could be kept constant, the situation would be somewhat like that of the old problem of the frog 2 feet from a wall who jumps 1 foot the first time, 6 inches the second, etc., halving the length each hop. In theory, he would never reach the wall. For the airplane, that last *inch* up to the absolute ceiling would take a very long time. The rate of climb for single-engine airplanes and light twins with both engines operating is 100 fpm at the normal service ceiling but the light twin service ceiling with *one engine inoperative* is listed at the altitude at which the rate of climb is 50 fpm.

The service and absolute ceilings can be approximated by extrapolation. Measure the rate of climb at sea level and at several other altitudes and join these points (Figure 6-4).

For instance, set your altimeter to 29.92, noting the outside air temperature and the rate of climb for several altitudes. Then convert your pressure-altitude to density-altitude and, using a piece of graph paper, determine your absolute and service ceilings, correcting for the difference in weight from the gross weight. You're not likely to do this, but it will give you some idea of the rate of climb of your plane for various standard altitudes if you are interested. The POH lists the rate

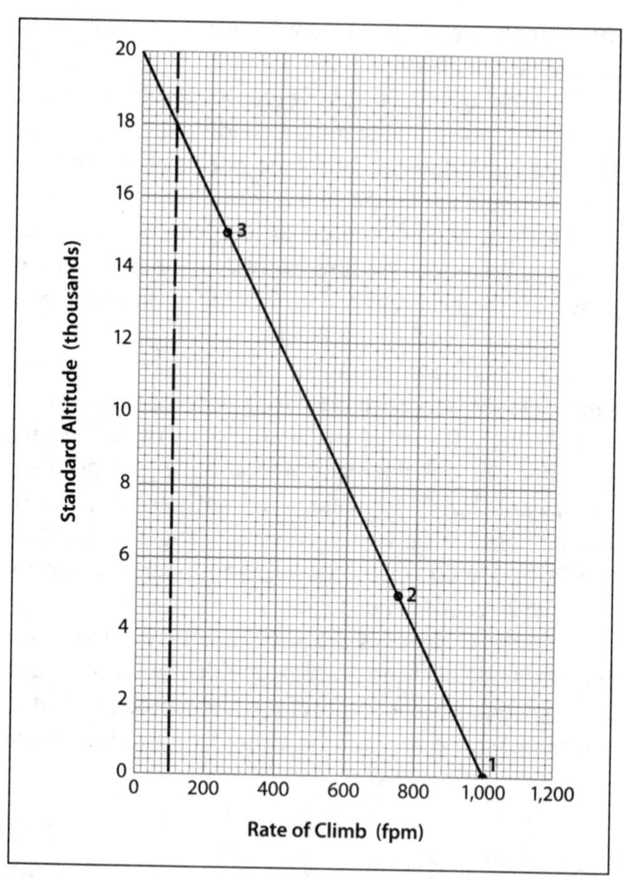

Figure 6-4. Establishing a rate of climb graph.

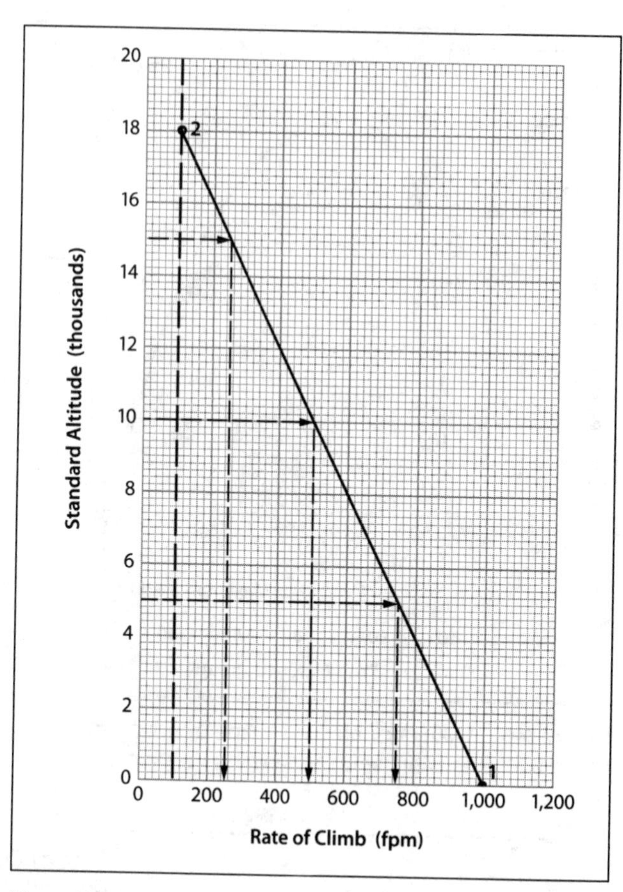

Figure 6-5. Making an approximate rate of climb graph (gross weight) by using the rate of climb at sea level and the published service ceiling.

of climb at sea level and also the service and, in some cases, operational ceilings. You can use this information to check your rates of climb at various altitudes by making a graph such as in Figure 6-5. Suppose your POH gives a rate of climb at sea level of 1,000 fpm and a service ceiling of 18,000 feet. Knowing that the service ceiling rate of climb is always 100 fpm, you can set it up as in Figure 6-5. Set up points 1 and 2; by connecting them with a straight line you can pick off the rate of climb for any standard altitude. (Your expected rate of climb in Figure 6-5 is about 500 fpm at 10,000 feet.)

You can also work out a rule of thumb for your airplane. If your rate of climb drops from 1,000 fpm at zero altitude to 100 fpm at 18,000 feet, it means a drop of 900 fpm in 18,000 feet. A little division shows a rate of climb drop of 50 fpm for every 1,000 feet, so a good approximation of your expected rate of climb at various altitudes is 1,000 fpm at sea level, 950 fpm at 1,000 feet, 900 fpm at 2,000 feet, etc. You can work out the figures for the plane you are flying (but it's doubtful if they would work out as evenly as this "fixed" problem).

Rate of climb varies inversely with weight, and at first thought it would seem that variations in rate of climb could be simply calculated for variations in weight. However, induced drag is also affected by weight change, and the excess THP (and rate of climb) suffers more with added poundage than would be considered by a straight weight ratio.

The rate of climb depends on excess THP available, and this depends on the *density-altitude*. Your rate of climb is affected by pressure-altitude and temperature (which combine to give you density-altitude).

Two important speeds concern the climb: (1) the speed for the best rate of climb and (2) the speed for the maximum angle of climb. These speeds are obtained by flight tests. Generally the manufacturer will measure the rates of climb at various airspeeds, starting from just above the stall to the maximum level-flight speed. This is done for several altitudes and the rate of climb is plotted against the TAS and a curve drawn for each (Figure 6-6). Corrections are made for weight changes during the testing process.

You can see that the rate of climb would be zero at speeds near the stall and at the maximum level-flight speed because no excess HP is available. Looking back at Figure 6-1, note that the excess THP drops off to nothing at the maximum level-flight speed as all the HP is being used to maintain altitude at that speed. At the lower end of the speed range, the same thing occurs, but

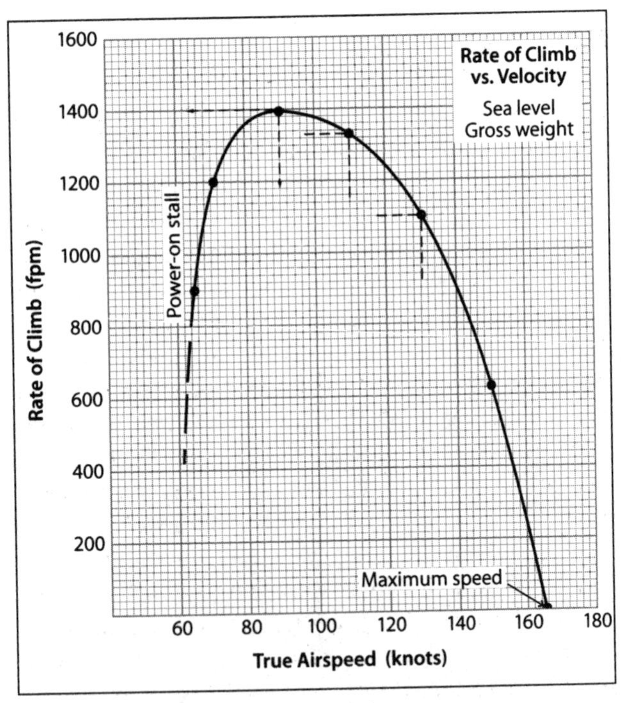

Figure 6-6. A rate of climb curve made by noting the rate of climb at various airspeeds and joining the points.

the stall characteristics of the airplane may not allow such clear-cut answers.

By looking at the resulting graph after these figures have been reduced to standard conditions and plotted, you can learn the speed for best rate of climb and for the maximum angle of climb (Figure 6-7).

The best rate of climb is at the peak of the curve. Reading the velocity below point A, you can find the speed for the best rate of climb. This is the published figure for sea level in the POH.

A line is drawn from the origin (0) on the graph tangent to the curve. Mathematically speaking this will give the highest ratio of climb to velocity (which means the same thing as the maximum altitude gain per foot of forward flight). The velocity directly below point B is the published figure for maximum angle of climb at sea level. Each airplane make and model is tested to find these recommended speeds. The tangent lines for the other two altitudes are shown in Figure 6-7; note that the angle of climb decreases with altitude as might be expected. This is important to remember, in that a 50-foot obstacle that can be cleared easily at the max

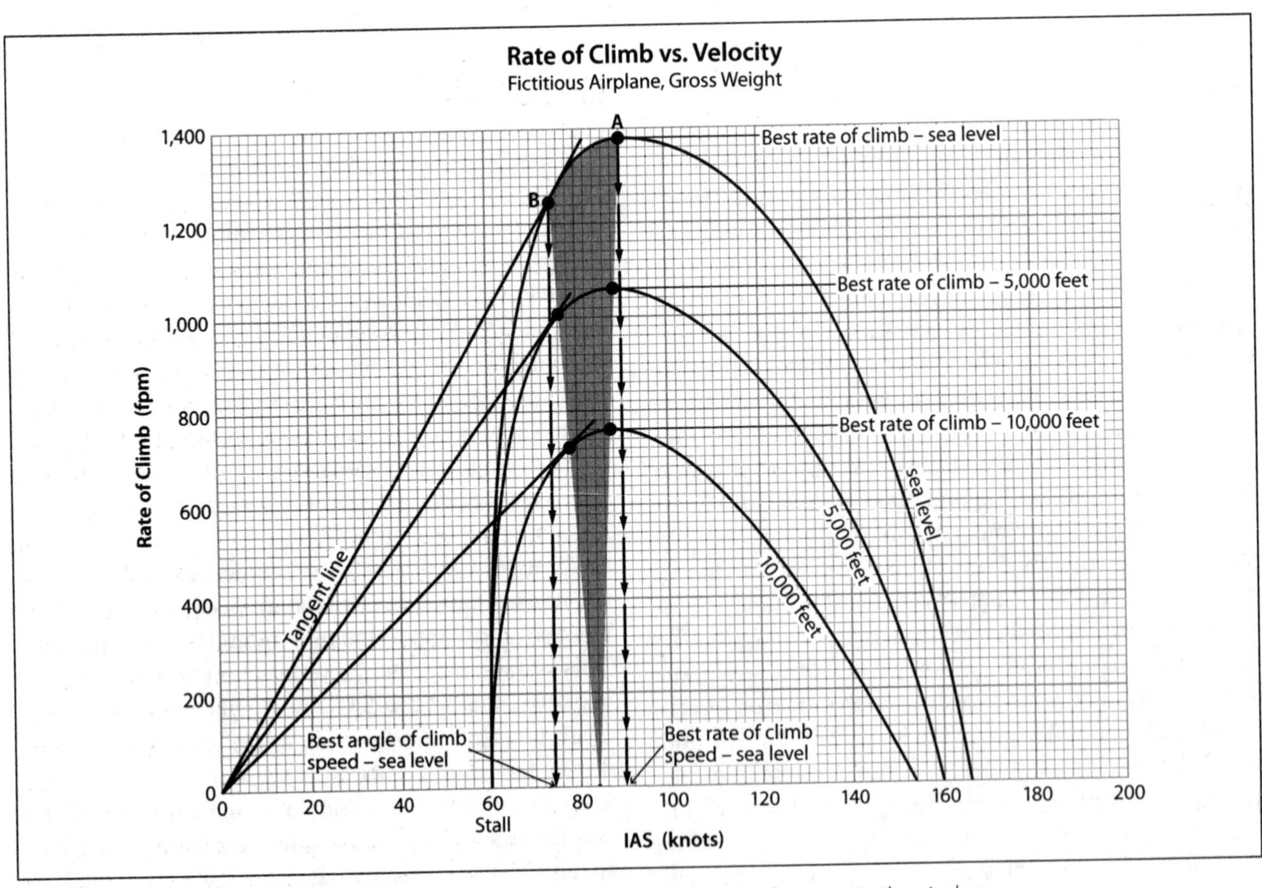

Figure 6-7. Rate of climb versus velocity curve for several density-altitudes for a particular airplane.

angle climb at sea level could be a problem at airports of higher elevation (and/or higher density-altitude).

Figure 6-7 is shown in terms of IAS to give a clearer picture of altitude effects. As shown, if the points of maximum angle are connected by a straight line and the same thing done for the points for the best rate of climb, the lines (in theory) converge at the same airspeed at the *absolute* ceiling of the airplane (zero rate of climb). In other words, the curves would get smaller and smaller until the "curve" for the absolute ceiling would be a point at some airspeed (and the rate of climb would be zero—all of the power available would be needed to keep from losing altitude at that one and only airspeed). The airspeeds for max angle and best rate get closer to each other as the altitude increases. The required IAS for best rate *decreases* with altitude, and the required IAS for max angle *increases* with altitude; they will (in theory) be the same as the airplane reaches its absolute ceiling. The best rate of climb is always found at a higher airspeed than that for the max angle of climb up to that imaginary point, the absolute ceiling (Figure 6-8).

For the particular airplane in Figure 6-8, the service and absolute ceilings are given as 12,000 and 14,000 feet respectively. Note how the indicated airspeeds for best (or max) angle and best rate of climb speeds converge at the absolute ceiling. (The same condition would apply if the climb speeds were drawn in terms of TAS.)

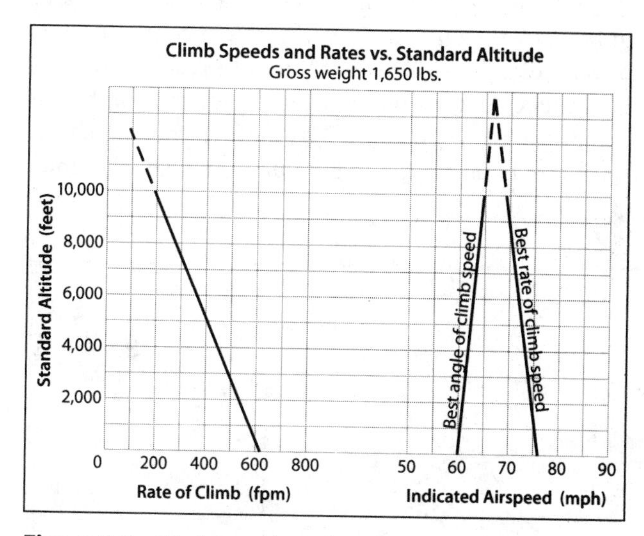

Figure 6-8. Climb speeds and rates versus standard altitude for a two-place trainer.

Normal Climb

The normal climb is the best rate of climb possible without overworking the engine. The manufacturer recommends a certain airspeed and power setting for the normal climb. Pilots sometimes get impatient during a prolonged climb and start to cheat a little by easing the nose up. This does nothing more than decrease the rate of climb and strain the engine by decreasing the relative wind's cooling effects. Review Figure 6-7 to see that when the speed is varied in either direction from the peak at A, the rate of climb is not at a maximum. You could lower the nose an equivalent amount and the rate of climb would not suffer any more than if you raised it—and the engine would be a lot better off!

After takeoff, the landing gear is raised, and as the speed approaches the best rate of climb speed, the flaps are raised and the power retarded to the recommended climb setting. As a rule of thumb for airplanes with unturbocharged engines, knock off 1% per 1,000 feet from your climb *indicated* airspeed. For airplanes up through the light twins, this can be considered to be up to 1 K per 1,000 feet.

Cruise Climb

This climb, which results in a good rate of climb as well as a high forward speed, is from 10 to 30 K faster than the recommended best rate, or normal climb speed. The cruise climb is ideal for a long cross-country where you want to fly at a certain altitude but don't want to lose much of your cruise speed getting there. Of course, if it's bumpy at lower altitudes, you may want to use the best rate of climb up to smooth air and a cruise climb from that point up to your chosen altitude. An advantage to the cruise climb is that because of the higher airspeed (and higher air flow) the engine will generally be cooler during the climb.

Looking back at Figure 6-7 (the sea level curve), note that by climbing at 110 K the rate of climb is *decreased* by about 75 fpm or about 5½%, while the forward speed (110 K, compared with the best rate of climb speed of 90 K) is *increased* by 22%—an advantage if you are interested in going places as you climb. Notice that as the climb speed increases past this value the rate of climb begins to drop off at a faster and faster rate. One method of setting up a cruise climb condition for your airplane (particularly for the cleaner, higher performance type) is to add the difference between the recommended max angle and max rate speeds to the max rate speed. In other words, if the recommended max rate speed at sea level and gross weight is 90 K and the max angle speed (same conditions) is 75 K, you add the difference (15 K) to the speed for max rate and come up with a cruise climb speed of 105 K. Speaking simply, you're operating on the opposite side of the climb curve from the max angle speed but not at such a speed that the rate of climb has dropped radically. (Notice on the curves in Figures 6-6 and 6-7 that, as the airspeed increases above that for best rate, the rate of climb decreases at a greater and greater rate per knot.) The speed for cruise climb found this way is at best an approximation and you should, as always, use the manufacturer's figure if available. Lower the cruise climb speed about 1% per 1,000 feet, as was done for the max rate climb.

Maximum Angle Climb

This climb usually is not an extended one and seldom continues for more than a couple of hundred feet altitude. As soon as the plane is firmly airborne, retract the landing gear (per POH) and attain and maintain the recommended max angle climb speed. Keep the engine at full power. You'll need all the HP you can get, and the short length of time that full power will be used won't hurt the engine. Leave the flaps alone until the obstacle has been well cleared. After you have sufficient altitude and the adrenalin has stopped racing around, raise the flaps (if used), throttle back, and assume a normal climb. For the *best angle of climb add ½% per 1,000* feet (about ½ K) to the *indicated* airspeed.

The max angle of climb is found at the speed at which the maximum excess thrust is found. It will be found at the speed at which the greatest amount of thrust component is available to move the airplane upward, compared with its forward motion. The max *rate* of climb is a function of *time* (the max angle is not) and so is dependent on the excess thrust *horsepower* working to move the airplane upward at a certain rate (Figure 6-9). Figure 6-10 shows how the max angle climb speed is found.

The recommended *obstacle clearance* airspeed may be slightly less than the extended max angle climb because the airplane is dirty (has more parasite drag) with the gear and flaps down.

Climb Charts

Figure 6-11 shows the maximum rates of climb and the time, fuel, and distance needed to climb at max rate for a high-performance, four-place airplane. A is pretty much self-explanatory, but you might look at B briefly.

Suppose that you are taking off from an airport at 1,500 feet elevation and will level off at 7,500 mean sea level (MSL). You would interpolate between 1,000 and 2,000 to get (1) a time of 2 minutes, (2) 0.6 gal. fuel used (in the climb itself), and (3) a distance (no-wind) of 3 miles. To go from *sea level* to 7,500 feet (interpolated), it would take 12 minutes, 3.1 gallons, and 18 miles. The difference, or 10 minutes, 2.5 gallons, and 15 miles, is required to climb from 1,500 feet MSL to 7,500 feet MSL. To get total fuel used until level-off, you'd add 1.4 gallons for engine start, taxi, and takeoff (Figure 6-11, Notes) for a requirement of 3.9 gallons.

Note that wind will not affect time or gallons used, unless strong winds result in turbulence and performance loss. The mileage required to reach a particular altitude depends on the wind during the climb; you could use an "average" winds aloft if you wanted to work it out that closely with your computer. The time,

Figure 6-9. Exaggerated comparison of max angle and best rate of climb.

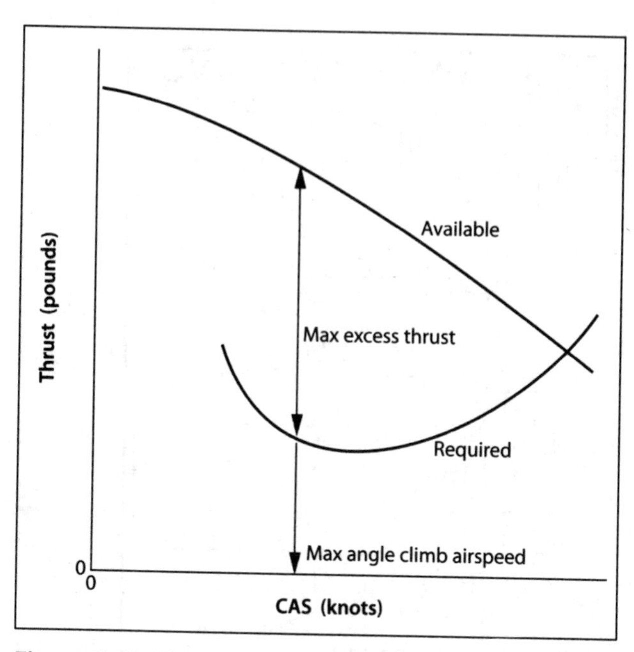

Figure 6-10. The max angle of climb speed is found at the point of greatest excess thrust.

fuel, and distance are increased by 10% for each 10°C above standard temperature, as noted.

Figure 6-12 is a graphical presentation of climb performance and fuel, time, and distance to climb. This example shows that, as in Figure 6-11, the numbers (fuel, time, and distance) for the pressure-altitude and temperature of takeoff must be subtracted from the cruise pressure-altitude and outside air temperature. Check the example.

A MAXIMUM RATE OF CLIMB

CONDITIONS:
Flaps Up
Gear Up
2700 RPM
Full Throttle
Mixture Leaned above 3000 Feet
Cowl Flaps Open

WEIGHT LBS	PRESS ALT FT	CLIMB SPEED KIAS	RATE OF CLIMB - FPM			
			-20°C	0°C	20°C	40°C
2650	S.L.	84	925	855	780	710
	2000	83	825	755	685	620
	4000	81	720	655	590	525
	6000	80	620	560	495	435
	8000	78	525	465	405	340
	10,000	77	430	370	310	---
	12,000	75	330	275	220	---

B TIME, FUEL, AND DISTANCE TO CLIMB

MAXIMUM RATE OF CLIMB

CONDITIONS:
Flaps Up
Gear Up
2700 RPM
Full Throttle
Mixture Leaned above 3000 Feet
Cowl Flaps Open
Standard Temperature

NOTES:
1. Add 1.4 gallons of fuel for engine start, taxi, and takeoff allowance.
2. Increase time, fuel and distance by 10% for each 10°C above standard temperature.
3. Distances shown are based on zero wind.

WEIGHT LBS	PRESSURE ALTITUDE FT	TEMP °C	CLIMB SPEED KIAS	RATE OF CLIMB FPM	FROM SEA LEVEL		
					TIME MIN	FUEL USED GALLONS	DISTANCE NM
2650	S.L.	15	84	800	0	0.0	0
	1000	13	83	760	1	0.4	2
	2000	11	83	715	3	0.8	4
	3000	9	82	675	4	1.1	6
	4000	7	81	635	6	1.6	8
	5000	5	81	590	7	2.0	10
	6000	3	80	550	9	2.4	13
	7000	1	79	510	11	2.9	16
	8000	-1	78	465	13	3.3	19
	9000	-3	78	425	15	3.8	22
	10,000	-5	77	385	18	4.3	26
	11,000	-7	76	340	21	4.9	30
	12,000	-9	75	300	24	5.5	35

Figure 6-11. A. Maximum climb rates. **B.** Time, fuel, and distance to climb.

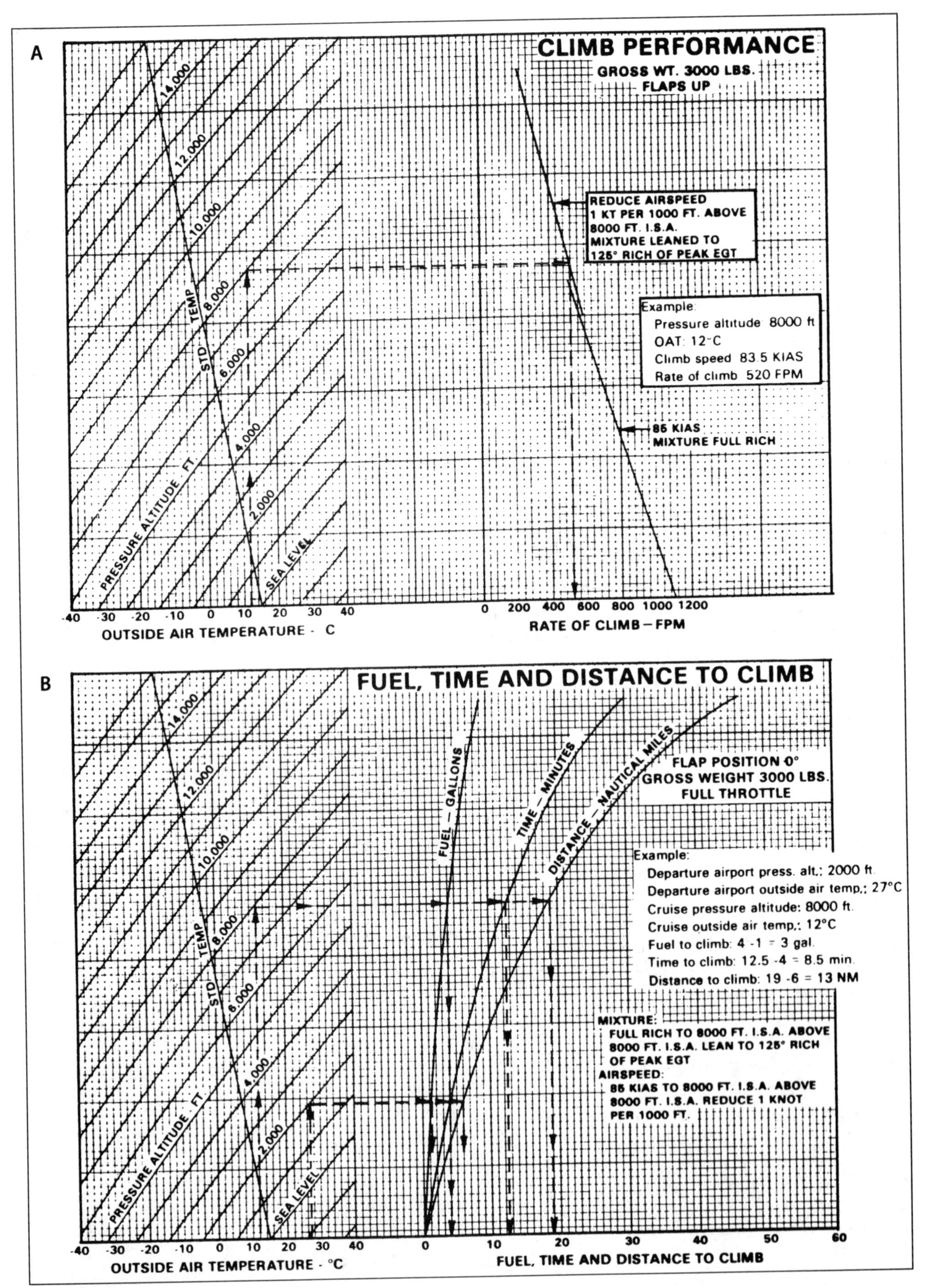

Figure 6-12. A. Climb performance. **B.** Fuel, time, and distance to climb.

7

Cruise Control—Range and Endurance

Cruise Control in General

Cruise control is an area too often ignored by pilots, and unfortunately the performance charts that come with the airplane are often classed with the writing on the walls of a Pharaoh's tomb. This chapter is a general coverage of cruise control. *Specific methods* of setting up power will be covered later.

Figure 7-1 is a typical TAS versus standard altitude (density-altitude) curve for a high-performance retractable-gear, four-place airplane. This presentation is also known as a speed-power chart. Point 1 is the maximum level-flight speed and, like all airplanes with unturbocharged engines, it is found at sea level where the maximum amount of power is available to allow the airplane to maintain altitude at such a high speed.

The normal cruise settings usually vary between 55 and 75%, with 65 and 75% being the most popular. Most engine manufacturers recommend that no continuous power settings over 75% be used because of increased fuel consumption and added engine wear. You remember from Chapter 2 that these percentages of power are based on normal rated power, or the maximum *continuous* power allowed for the engine (brake horsepower).

Looking at Figure 7-1, note that for the higher cruise power settings, true airspeed (TAS) is gained with altitude, so if a power setting of 75% is desired, it would be best to fly at an altitude of 7,000 feet (point 2) to get the most knots per HP—assuming outside factors such as ceiling, IFR-assigned altitude requirements, and winds aloft are not considered. Above 7,000 feet, even full throttle will no longer furnish this airplane the required manifold pressure to maintain 75% power. If 65% power is used, this setting can be maintained to about 10,000 feet (point 3); this would be the best altitude for that setting. As the desired cruise setting decreases, the best altitude increases, but the loss of time in climbing to the optimum altitude could offset TAS gains, particularly on shorter trips. Note that as the cruise power setting decreases from 75%, the TAS gain *per 1,000 feet* also decreases until at 40% (point 4), there is no gain shown with altitude increase.

At the higher power settings, it can also be expected that, because the TAS increases with altitude for a specific power (and fuel consumption), the range is also increased with altitude for a fixed percentage of power being used—except for one condition, that of maximum range, which will be discussed later.

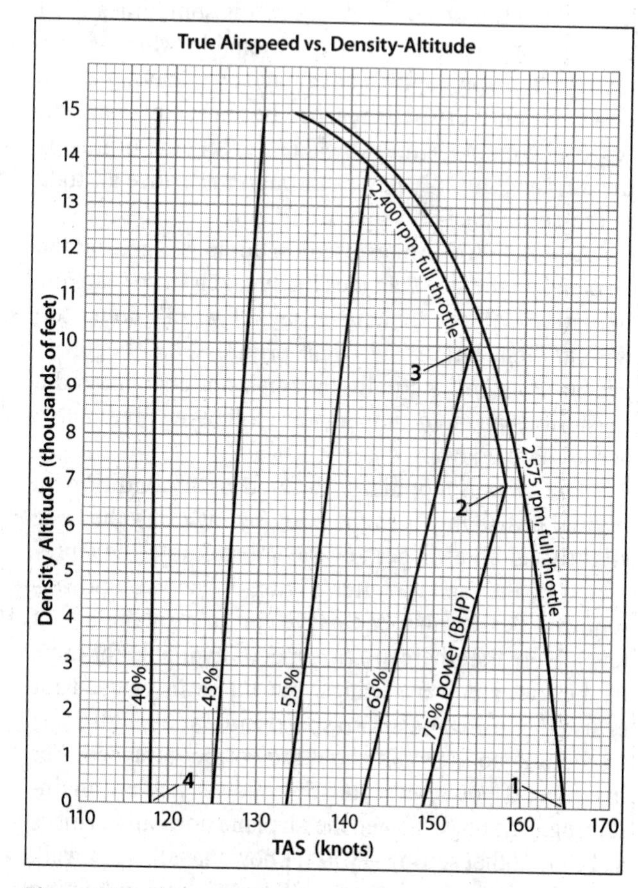

Figure 7-1. A true airspeed versus standard altitude chart for a four-place high-performance airplane.

Establishing the Cruise Condition

As the desired altitude is reached, there are three main techniques used by pilots in establishing the cruise: (1) as soon as the altitude is reached, immediately retarding power from climb to cruise setting, (2) maintaining climb power after level-off until cruise speed is attained, and (3) climbing about 200 feet past the altitude and diving to attain cruise speed and then setting power.

The first technique is the least effective method of attaining cruise (as far as time is concerned) and also means the resetting of power after the area of cruise speed is reached. Because the airplane is slow (at climb speed) when power is set, the increased airspeed as cruise is approached means that, for the fixed-pitch propeller, the rpm will have increased past that desired and, for the constant-speed type, ram effect may have increased the manifold pressure above the original setting. Acceleration to cruise speed is necessarily slow compared with maintaining climb power (the second technique), assuming a constant altitude.

Climbing past the altitude and diving down to aid in establishing cruise (technique 3) is sometimes used for cleaner airplanes. It is questionable whether this method has a perceptible advantage over leaving climb power on until cruise is reached because any comparison of the methods must include starting the timing as the airplane initially passes through the cruise altitude in the climb-past-and-dive technique.

A phrase sometimes used by pilots is, "getting the airplane on the step," an idea likely taken from seaplane operations. Pilots sometimes say, "I wasn't doing too well at first, but as the flight progressed, I began to get on the step." Actually they had not encountered a mysterious phenomenon but were following predictable aerodynamic laws.

The *step* is popularly defined as a condition in normal cruise in which the pilot, by lowering the nose slightly, is able to get several more knots than predicted by the manufacturer. Figure 7-2 shows a power-required versus airspeed curve for an airplane at sea level. Note that there are *two* speeds available for most of the lower power settings, but for settings used for cruise (55 to 75%), the two speeds are far enough apart so there is no question about the correct airspeed. For instance, if you're carrying 55% power and are maintaining, say, 65 K—when the airplane normally cruises at 140 K at that setting—you'll know that all is not well. However, if you are carrying 35 to 40% and indicating 80 K when you *could* be indicating 90 K the problem is not so obvious.

Getting back to the idea of getting on the step as the flight progresses, Figure 7-3 shows the power required

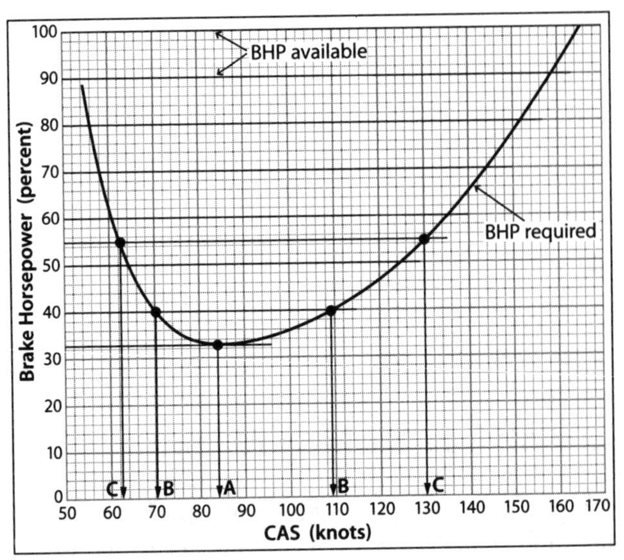

Figure 7-2. Brake horsepower versus calibrated airspeed at a *constant* altitude for a fictitious high-performance airplane. This would be what the pilot would obtain by maintaining a constant altitude at various airspeeds, taking note of the manifold pressure and rpm necessary for each airspeed and later checking the percentage of power used after landing and referring to a power-setting chart. For instance, point C represents the two speeds available for this airplane, using 55% of normal rated power.

for a particular airplane at gross weight and when it is nearly empty of fuel. The airplane *will* indicate a higher airspeed at the lighter weight, and this is expected and predictable. The difference in airspeeds depends on the ratio of fuel weight to airplane weight. Chapter 2 also discusses this idea.

Down in the area of max range and max endurance, at 35 to 45% power, the speeds are not so far apart and the pilot might be flying at the low speed when it's possible to cruise several knots faster (Figure 7-2). The principle is still the same: the pilot can fly at the higher speed rather than the low but *cannot* fly at an even higher speed than the highest airspeed allowed at one of the intersections of the power-required/power-available curve. The pilot cannot, for example, go faster than the greater of the two speeds (shown by B using 40% power) and still maintain a constant altitude. The pilot's problem is not being aware of the higher speed available, since both speeds are likely to be close together; the airplane would be quite happy to maintain that airspeed and altitude until weight changes begin to have their effect.

Pilots unaware of the two available speeds may experiment by lowering the nose and, lo and behold, seem to have gotten "on the step." It might be hard to convince them they haven't beaten the game, but they have obtained only what is obtainable from the laws of aircraft performance.

Another fallacy of cruising flight, one often put forth by those of the "step" school of thought, is that the airplane should be loaded for a forward center of gravity (CG). One reason for this theory of loading might be the belief that with the CG forward the airplane wants to run "downhill." The pilot doesn't let it lose any altitude, goes the theory, but still benefits in added speed from this downhill-running tendency.

Actually, the airplane with the CG as far back as safely possible is usually faster. When two airplanes of the same model and weight carry the same power, the one with the more aft CG will cruise slightly faster. The airplane with the aft CG will also not be as longitudinally stable as the other and will be more easily disturbed from its trim. This doesn't mean that the airplane becomes unsafe; flight characteristics could be quite reasonable once the airplane is in smooth air and trimmed. If you went too far with this idea, however, serious problems of instability could arise.

Just how can aft loading add to performance? Take a look at an average high-performance airplane (Figure 7-4). You'll find it has a tail-down force at cruise, the result of the CG location for any particular airplane-weight combination. The center of lift is considered to be fixed, as shown by both planes in Figure 7-4. This produces a nose-down moment, which must be balanced by a tail-down moment furnished by the horizontal tail surfaces.

A moment is usually measured in pound-inches (lb-in.) and is the result of distance times a force or weight. For this problem, we will measure the moments around the center of lift rather than around the CG, as was done back in Chapter 3.

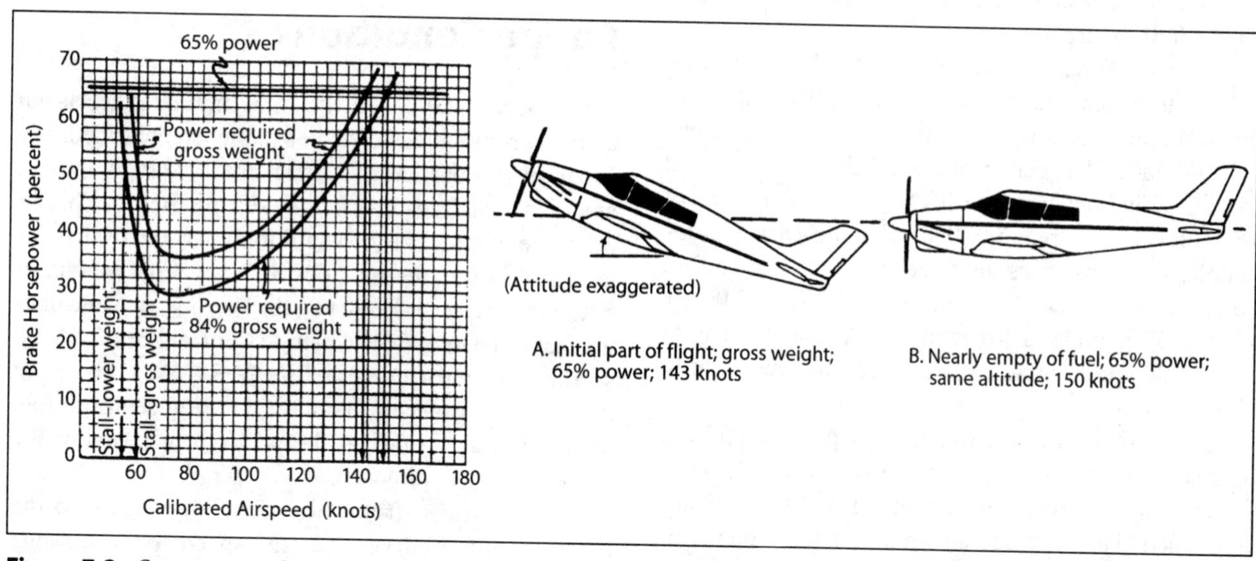

Figure 7-3. Comparison of BHP required and airplane flight speeds at gross weight and nearly empty of fuel at the same power setting of 65%.

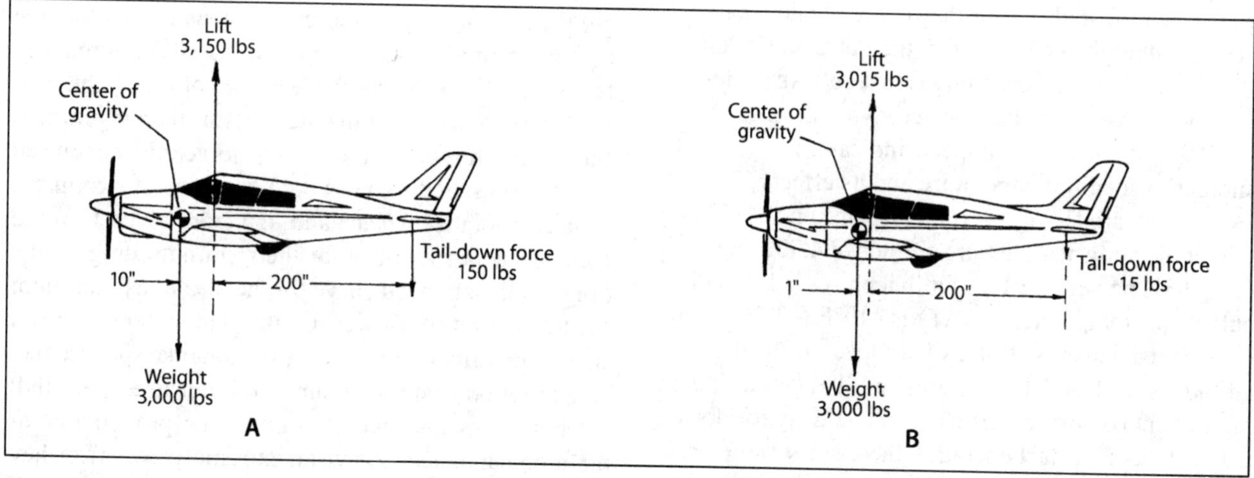

Figure 7-4. The effects of CG position and resulting lift (and power) required for an airplane in cruising flight.

Airplane A is loaded so that the CG is 10 inches ahead of the center of lift. The airplane weighs 3,000 pounds, so the nose-down moment is 10 inches × 3,000 pounds or 30,000 lb-in. The tail-down moment must equal this (or the airplane will want to do an outside loop), and the center of the tail-down force in this case is 200 inches behind the center of lift. This calls for a force of 150 pounds (the 30,000 lb-in. must equal 200 inches times the force, which is 150 pounds). When the moments are equal, the airplane's nose does not tend to pitch either way. (The other moments covered in Chapter 3 will be ignored for this problem.)

If equilibrium exists and Airplane A is to maintain level flight, the *vertical* forces must also be equal; up must equal *down* in other words. Down forces are weight (3,000 pounds) and the tail-down force (150 pounds)—a total of 3,150 pounds down. Lift must equal this same value, so 3,150 pounds of lift are required to fly a 3,000-lb airplane.

Airplane B has a more aft CG. It is loaded so that the CG is 1 inch ahead of the center of lift. The nose-down moment here is 1 inch times the 3,000 pounds, or 3,000 lb-in. The center of the tail-down force is 200 inches behind the center of lift so that a down force of 15 pounds is required (3,000 lb-in. in this case, a product of 200 inches times the force, which must therefore be 15 pounds). To sum up the vertical forces: 3,000 + 15 = 3,015 pounds of lift required. Airplane B has to fly at an angle of attack and airspeed to support only 3,015 pounds.

Both airplanes would weigh 3,000 pounds if placed on a scale, of course, but airplane A weighs 5% more as far as the combined angle of attack and airspeed are concerned. That airplane also requires more power to fly at a constant altitude, and because both airplanes are carrying the same power setting, the heavier airplane A would cruise more slowly. To believers riding on airplane B and noting that it flies faster than airplane A, it might well seem that their airplane is "on the step," yet all that is happening is that both airplanes are merely following predictable aerodynamic laws.

Relying solely on airspeed indicators can lead to another oversight: temperature and its effects.

Say you are flying a certain airplane on a Canadian winter morning at a pressure altitude of 4,000 feet, carrying 65% power; the TAS for that power is 161 K. The outside air temperature (OAT) is –10°F (–23°C). This gives you a density-altitude of sea level. If the density-altitude is sea level, the IAS will be 161 K (assuming no instrument or position error). You could fly to Florida the next day and start operating there at the same pressure-altitude of 4,000 feet and the same weight at 65%, but at an OAT of 75°F (+24°C). The density-altitude is 6,000 feet, giving a TAS of 170 K. In getting this *TAS of 170*, however, you are indicating only *155 K*. By just comparing indicated airspeeds, you come up with the fact that yesterday—at the same pressure-altitude, power setting, and weight—you were indicating *6 K more*. Yesterday, it might seem, you were "on the step"; today, you just can't seem to make it. Even once, perhaps, you try to ease the nose down today to get on the step but just lose altitude, so you're more convinced than ever that the "step" is a mysterious thing only found once in a while. Quite possibly, you might have noted the variation from standard temperature in setting up your manifold pressure, but fell nevertheless into that oft-repeated trap of comparing indicated airspeeds only. *So forget the "step."*

A Look at Maximum Range Conditions

It has been established that maximum range, as far as the aerodynamics of the airplane is concerned, is a function of a particular coefficient of lift (C_L), the one at which the lift-to-drag ratio is at a maximum. This C_L (or angle of attack) is constant for a particular airplane (and configuration) and does not vary with weight, as noted in Chapter 1. However, the average airplane does not have means of measuring C_L or angle of attack, so the pilot must decrease the IAS (CAS) as weight decreases in order to maintain the required optimum angle of attack. Look at the problem in terms of the power curve (Figure 7-5).

A line drawn from the origin (0) tangent to the power-required curve gives the speed for best range at this altitude for each weight. Assuming that the altitude remains constant, the TAS (and IAS) must be constantly decreased with decreasing weight in order to get the absolute maximum range. This means that the power setting (brake horsepower, or BHP) is reduced from, say, 40 to 35% over the period of the flight.

From an aerodynamic standpoint, the tangent line should be drawn on the *thrust* horsepower-required curve. The speed found would be point of maximum efficiency of the airplane and, in theory at least, would coincide with the speed for the minimum drag on the drag-versus-airspeed curve for the airplane (maximum lift-to-drag ratio). However, other factors are involved such as propulsive efficiency (η) and brake specific fuel consumption (bsfc, or pounds of fuel used per BHP per hour). For instance, if your engine-propeller combination happened to have an extremely low efficiency at the speed found by using the THP-required curve, a compromise must be found. As an exaggeration, suppose at the aerodynamically ideal speed for best range that the efficiency of the engine propeller combination is only 33%, or *three* BHP is required to get *one* THP, but at a slightly higher speed the efficiency jumps up to 85%. A compromise would be in order. The same thing applies to bsfc. Figure 7-6 illustrates that the bsfc changes with power and this might also be a factor.

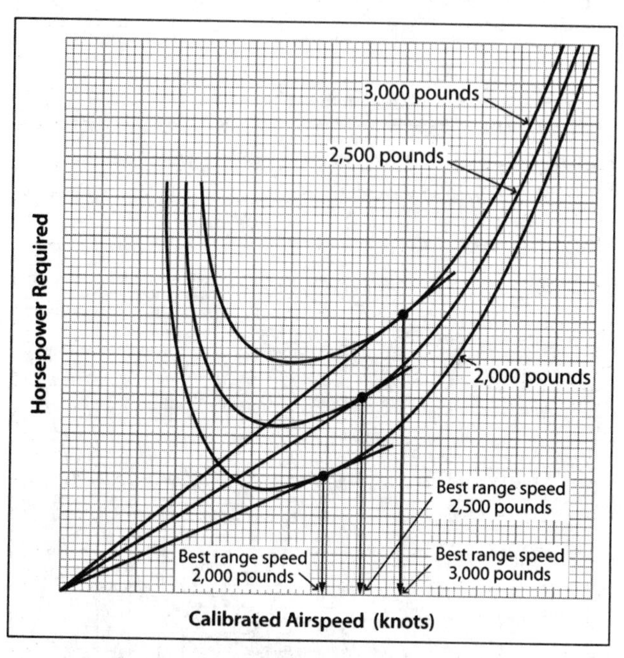

Figure 7-5. Power-required curves for a particular airplane at various weights. Notice that, for maximum range, the airspeed must be decreased as weight decreases.

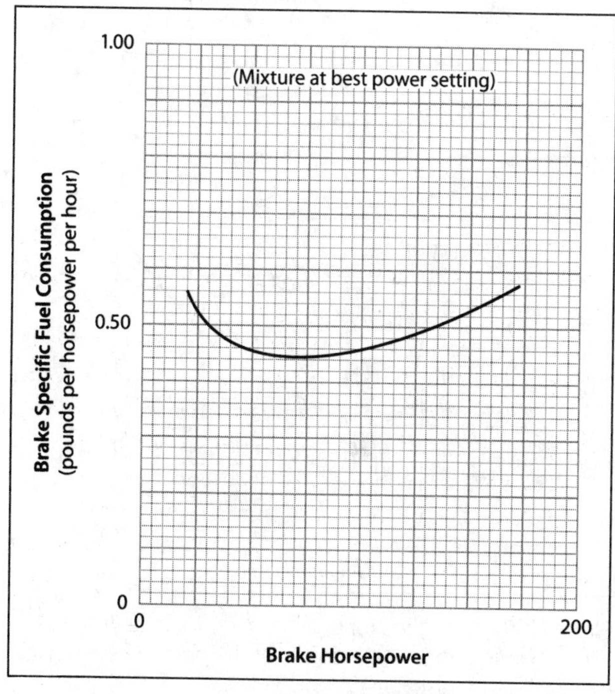

Figure 7-6. Specific fuel consumption curve for a typical reciprocating engine as is used in light planes.

Basically, max range would be found at a condition at which the combination L/D × efficiency/bsfc is a maximum. You may have to fly at a *lower* lift-to-drag ratio in order to *increase* efficiency or *decrease* bsfc and get an overall greater range than would result from sticking to the max L/D speed and ignoring low efficiency or high bsfc at that speed. Manufacturers take this into consideration when they publish max range figures. In order to show the expected power settings for various airspeeds for max range and endurance, Figures 7-5, 7-7, 7-8, and 7-9 are actually based on BHP as you can see by the shape of the curves.

You can see that the normal cruise speed, which is well above that of the maximum range speed, is a compromise between speed and economy. Naturally everybody would like to get from A to B as rapidly as possible, but this is neither aerodynamically nor economically feasible.

One thing you'll find is that, after careful planning for winds and other factors, you may save some time en route—only to lose it at the other end by a delayed landing or ground transportation troubles. On a 200-NM trip, a plane that cruises at 150 K takes 16 minutes less than one that cruises at 125 K, and these savings can easily be lost at the destination. Of course, the longer the trip the greater the time savings, but more time is lost at airports than is generally considered.

A study of current general aviation airplanes shows that a rule of thumb may be used to approximate the maximum range airspeeds for gross weight. The following ratios, based on three major airplane types, are the ratio of the maximum range speed to the flaps-up, power-off stall speeds (wings level and calibrated airspeeds). After using the ratio, *you may convert to IAS* by checking the airspeed calibration chart for your airplane.

Single-engine, fixed-gear	1.5 × power-off stall speed
Single-engine, retractable-gear	1.8 × power-off stall speed
Twin-engine, retractable-gear	1.7 × power-off stall speed

Suppose you find in the POH or by rule of thumb that the IAS is 120 K for max range of gross weight; how do you take care of the weight change as fuel is burned? Looking at the lift equation and working to solving for V: $V = \sqrt{2W/C_L S\rho}$. (Assume here for simplicity that lift equals weight.) The coefficient of lift (C_L) is to be held constant because it is the one found for max L/D, or max range, and the wing area (S) does not change, nor does the density (r) for a constant altitude, so the only variable in the square root symbol is W, or weight. (The "2" is also a constant, as always.) This means that as weight changes, V must also change as the square root of the weight change. Put in simple terms, V must change one-half the percentage of that of the weight. If weight decreases 20%, the V (or airspeed) must be decreased by 10% to keep the required constant C_L. If the gross weight of the airplane is 3,000 pounds and the required airspeed for max range is 120 K, the airspeed at 2,400 pounds (a decrease in weight of 20%) should be 108 K (a decrease in airspeed of 10%). This works for the maximum expected decrease from gross to minimum flyable weight for most airplanes. Figure 1-12 can be used for determining airspeed change required with weight change, as was discussed in Chapter 1.

A higher percentage of normal rated power is required to maintain a required CAS (IAS) at higher altitudes, but the TAS will be increased so that the ratio of miles per gallon remains essentially the same (Figure 7-7). Why do you try to use the same IAS for all altitudes (assuming equal weights)? Basically, it goes back to the lift equation of earlier chapters, $L = C_L S(\rho/2) V^2$. The C_L is the fixed one found for max range (or max lift-to-drag ratio). The weight, or lift required, is the same for a particular time, the wing area (S) is the same, and hence the final $(\rho/2)V^2$ must be the same under all conditions if the C_L is to remain constant. The dynamic pressure q, or $(\rho/2)V^2$, is that as measured by the airspeed instrument as IAS.

The ratios given are the approximate CAS (IAS) for maximum range for a chosen altitude. For most airplanes with unturbocharged engines, the altitude for best *normal* cruise is roughly 8,000 feet standard altitude (call it 7,000 to 10,000). In this altitude range, wide open throttle is necessary to get the 65 to 75% recommended power setting for normal flying. But getting back to the idea of obtaining max range, once you have the ratio for your type of airplane and have found the maximum range speed for sea level, you can *use this figure as an approximate IAS* for your chosen flight level. This would give you the best range under no-wind conditions for that particular altitude at gross weight. This holds true up to the altitude where you are no longer able to get the necessary power to maintain altitude at the recommended CAS (IAS). The drawback is that you may burn some fuel getting up to this altitude, but if the trip is a long one, it might be worthwhile timewise because of the increased TAS (taking winds aloft into account).

For maximum range, you would climb to the chosen altitude and set up an IAS at the correct max range-to-stall speed ratio (1.5, 1.7, or 1.8, depending on your airplane type). You would then set up the power necessary to maintain altitude at this IAS and would lean the mixture (leaning will be discussed later). Remember,

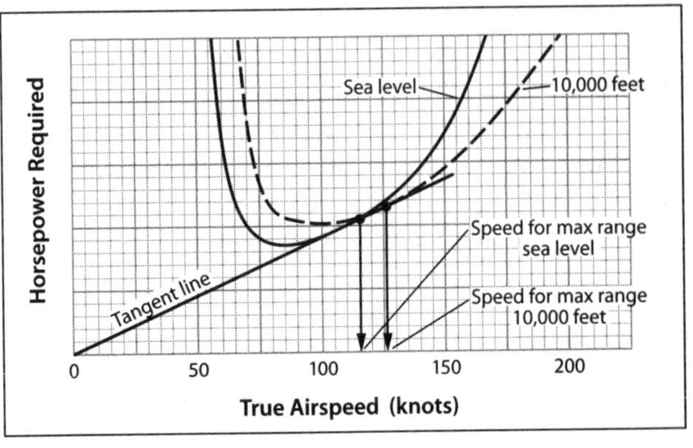

Figure 7-7. Best-range speeds (TAS) for a particular airplane at sea level and at 10,000 ft.

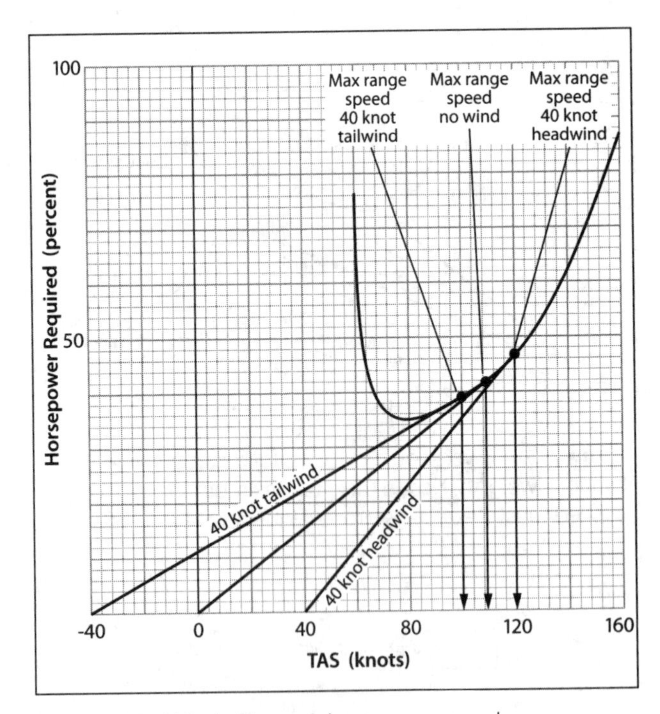

Figure 7-8. Wind effects on best-range speed.

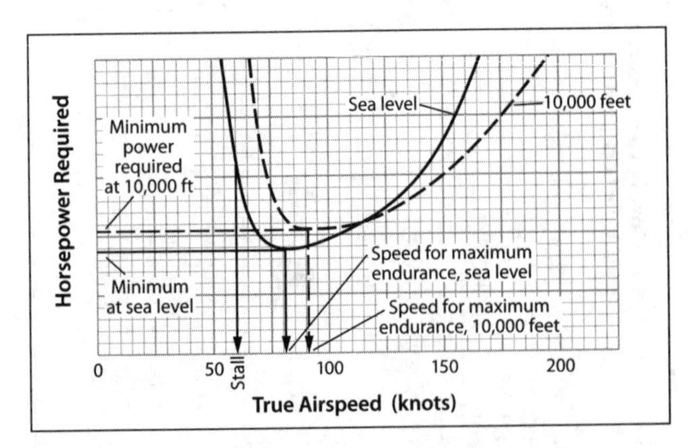

Figure 7-9. The speed for maximum endurance (from an aerodynamic standpoint) is found at the point where power required is the least.

the stall speed must be CAS for the multipliers, *then* the final number is converted to IAS.

Figure 7-7 shows the relationship between the sea level maximum range speed and that at some altitude expressed in terms of TAS. Your project is to maintain the same IAS at higher altitudes. You are unable to maintain the *normal* cruise IAS to very high altitudes with an unturbocharged engine because you start with a high percentage of power to begin with (65 to 75%) and cannot obtain this above a certain altitude. If you start at 40 to 55%, as is required to maintain the lower maximum range speed, you will be able to use the required power at a higher altitude (Figure 7-10).

The average pilot is more interested in saving time than extending range. There is no question that the max range speed may be only 60 to 70% of the normal cruise speed. If you are interested in getting somewhere in a reasonable length of time, you are willing to operate at a higher, though costlier, speed.

These ratios are presented for you to remember in case they are needed. Suppose you are at a point where you have overestimated your range under normal cruise conditions. It's night and there is some bad country to cross before getting to a lighted airport. You can extend the remaining range by pulling the power back and judiciously leaning the mixture until you are able to maintain altitude at a CAS of 1.5, 1.7, or 1.8 times your power-off, flaps-up stall (calibrated) airspeed. You can then convert to IAS as—or if—necessary.

These ratios are not completely accurate, but they do give you an approximate speed to extend your range if you have to. Propeller and engine efficiency at lower speeds, specific fuel consumption at various power settings, and other variables may result in slightly different airspeeds than given here. Figure 7-6 shows a specific fuel consumption graph for a typical lightplane engine.

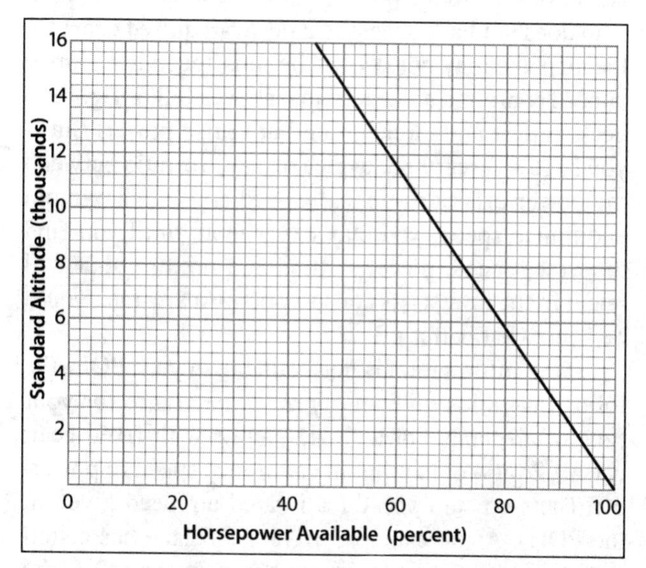

Figure 7-10. Percentage of brake horsepower available at various altitudes, typical unturbocharged engine.

The max range speed at gross weight will be found at power settings of approximately 40 to 45%, as given on the power chart in your airplane (unturbocharged engines). A variation of 5 K from these figures will make very little difference in max range.

To review: Maximum range conditions depend on the lift-to-drag ratio, propulsive efficiency, and brake specific fuel consumption. The speed at which the max L/D is found as far as the aerodynamics of the airplane is concerned might be one at which the propeller efficiency is low and/or bsfc is proportionally higher. So, actually max range is found at the airspeed at which the value $C_L/C_D \times$ prop efficiency/bsfc is greatest. The max range speed for various aircraft is found by flight testing; the rules of thumb were taken from data of current airplanes, which take the above-mentioned variables into consideration.

Wind Effects on Range

There's no doubt that wind affects the range of your airplane as well as your groundspeed. Obviously, with a tailwind the range is greater than under no-wind conditions and much greater than under headwind conditions—the difference depends on the wind. So what's new?

What's new is that you can compensate for wind effects by varying airspeed for a particular altitude. Suppose you are in the situation cited previously—the night is dark and it looks like it'll be touch-and-go making the next available airport. After pulling the power back, you remember that there is a 10- to 15-K headwind. This hurts, but there's something you can do about it. You can increase the indicated airspeed about 5% for heavy headwinds. *You will never get as much range with a headwind as under no-wind conditions, but you will be doing the best possible in this situation.* What you have done is decreased the time spent in this predicament.

Conversely, if you have a moderate tailwind, you can stretch your range even farther by subtracting about 5% from the speed given for maximum range under no-wind conditions (Figure 7-8).

Summary of Range

These ideas are presented to give you a greater safety factor, not to get you to push the range of the airplane to the limit. You may never use these points, but they could come in handy if you get into a bind and *have* to stretch it. It will require a great deal of willpower to throttle back when you feel like increasing power so as to "get there before you run outa gas."

The added time required to get to the airport may make you a nervous wreck, but you'll make it under conditions that wouldn't allow you to otherwise.

Incidentally, remember that you probably won't need to use max range techniques if in your preflight planning you adhere to FAR 91 (VFR fuel requirements), which basically states that no person may begin a flight under VFR unless (considering wind and forecast weather conditions) there is enough fuel to fly to the first point of intended landing and, assuming normal cruising speed (1) during the day, to fly after that for at least 30 minutes, or (2) at night, to fly after that for at least 45 minutes.

But of course, there may be unforecast wind and weather conditions that may require that you have to fly much farther than originally planned.

Endurance

The maximum endurance of an airplane is seldom needed but when it is, it's really needed! You should be familiar with the idea of maximum endurance, particularly with an instrument rating, because under extreme conditions you may have to hold over a certain fix and then discover the destination field has gone below Instrument Flight Rules minimums and you have to go to an alternate airport. Things could get tense, particularly if you haven't tried to conserve fuel but have been boring holes in the soup all this time on full-rich mixture and cruise power settings.

Or take a VFR situation: You're coming into a large airport after a long trip, it's below VFR minimums, but the weather is good enough for you to get a special VFR clearance into the field; however, there's a lot of instrument traffic (and maybe other controlled-VFR pilots like yourself). The tower orders you to hold outside the controlled airspace. The local weather is 1,000 overcast and 1½ mi—good enough for you to fly underneath "elsewhere" but not good enough to enter controlled airspace without clearance, so you hold just outside and "await further clearance." Here, too, would be a good place to use maximum endurance unless you have plenty of fuel.

For reciprocating engines, maximum endurance is found at sea level. Refer to the power-required-versus-velocity curve of Figure 7-9.

You are interested in minimum gas consumption while still maintaining altitude. The low point of the power curve is where the least power is required and the point where gas consumption is a minimum if you properly lean the mixture. For most retractable-gear airplanes (including unturbocharged light twins), this will require a power setting of 30 to 35% of max continuous power at sea level. Few power charts go this low. The minimum BHP required (in percentages) depends on the aerodynamic cleanness and power loading of the airplane. An aerodynamically dirty, heavy airplane with comparatively little power might need a *minimum* of 50 to 55% or more of its available power to maintain a constant altitude.

After examining Figure 7-9 you can readily see that contrary to what might be expected, the maximum endurance speed is not the lowest speed possible for the airplane to fly without stalling. Many pilots, when confronted with the need for maximum endurance for the first time, automatically assume that the lower the speed, the less power required.

Horace Endsdorfer, private pilot, flew around just above a stall for 2 hours one day when he needed maximum endurance and was worn out keeping the airplane under control. Needless to say, he was one disgusted pilot when he learned that he was burning only slightly less gas than at cruise—and working like heck all the time (Figure 7-11). It should have struck him as being odd that he had to use so much power to maintain altitude in the holding pattern.

Manufacturers' recommended figures on speeds for maximum endurance are not always available. In many cases this is true because of the airplane's low-speed handling, and the constant-speed propeller-governing characteristics at low rpm. A compromise may be desired, such as a slight loss of endurance by increasing airspeed to have smoother operation.

A few manufacturers publish the figure and the others leave it up to the pilot. The only trouble is, the pilot who does not have access to a power-required chart for the airplane may not know what this speed is and may either fly around at a speed just above stall or figure to heck with it and circle around at cruise power. But if you have an approximate idea of, say, the ratio between the power-off, flaps-up stall speed and the maximum endurance speed, you may experiment until you find the exact speed, power setting, and mixture that will result in the lowest gas consumption. At any rate, you'll be somewhat better off.

If the information is not available in your POH, the following ratios give an *approximate* figure for your type of airplane. For a single-engine with fixed gear, use a 1.2 ratio of maximum endurance speed to power-off, flaps-up stall speed (calibrated airspeed given in the POH). As an example, if your airplane has a stall speed of 60 KCAS (flaps up) given in the POH, the maximum endurance speed would be $1.2 \times 60 = 72$

K. For a single-engine or a twin with retractable gear, use a ratio of 1.3. (These are formulas for max gross weight.)

The speeds found by this method are calibrated airspeeds and will apply at all altitudes—although the lower the better for reciprocating engines. This doesn't mean get down to 20 feet above the ground when you could be at 500 or 1,000 feet. It does mean that if you have a choice, an altitude of 1,000 feet is better for maximum endurance than 10,000 feet.

To set up maximum endurance, take the following steps:

1. Throttle back and slow the plane to the recommended airspeed.
2. Retard the prop control (if so equipped) until you get the lowest rpm possible and still have a reasonably smooth prop operation. In the case of a constant-speed prop, this means no "hunting" by the propeller as it reaches the lower limits of governor control. Low rpm means low friction losses.
3. Set the throttle so that the recommended speed and a constant altitude are maintained. Trim the airplane.
4. Lean the mixture as much as possible without the possibility of damaging the engine. You may then have to experiment again with the throttle to obtain the optimum setting for your particular condition (hot day, cold day, etc.).

Some of the above steps may not apply; for example, if you are flying an older light trainer that has neither a mixture control nor a constant-speed prop.

You are trying to maintain altitude with the minimum fuel consumption. This means minimum power (*not* minimum speed) and judicious leaning of the mixture. You'll be using about 30 to 35% power.

If you have to hold or "endure," it's usually over a particular spot, and this means *turns*. Keep your turns as shallow as possible, without wandering over into the next county, because steeper turns mean increased back pressure to maintain altitude—and this is a speed killer. Making steep turns usually results in constant variation of throttle as altitude or speed is lost and regained at a cost of increased power and fuel consumption. Of course, if you start out high enough, you may just be lucky enough to get cleared into the airport before you run out of altitude. However, if you are on Instrument Flight Rules, it's not considered cricket to go blindly barging down into the next fellow's holding pattern.

Wind has no effect on endurance, but turbulence decreases it.

You may find the approximate max endurance speed for your airplane by flying at various airspeeds, maintaining a constant altitude. Figure 7-12 shows an *actual* test of an airplane with a fixed-pitch propeller and fixed gear (flaps-up, power-off stall speed—56 K), using IAS. (In other words, the airspeeds required for various power settings were read directly off the instrument.)

Notice that 65 K is the indicated airspeed at which minimum power is required. The ratio of max endurance speed to flaps-up, power-off stall speed is 65/56 = 1.16, reasonably close to the predicted ratio of 1.20 for

Figure 7-11.

Indicated Airspeed (knots)	RPM
101	2,700
96	2,600
90	2,500
86	2,400
78	2,300
74	2,200
70	2,150
65	2,075
61	2,250
57	2,300

Figure 7-12.

this type of airplane. (The 1.20 figure assumes a maximum endurance speed of 1.20 × 56, or 67 K.)

You could find the max endurance speed for an airplane with a constant-speed propeller by leaving the rpm at the lowest smooth value and making a table like Figure 7-12, noting manifold pressure required rather than rpm. Don't use too high a manifold pressure with low rpm, because the engine could be damaged. Actually, since the max endurance speed normally falls within 50% of the stall speed, this is the only area that needs to be investigated. Make a note of the lowest manifold pressure, rpm, and airspeed at this value for future use. You may find that the airplane doesn't handle well at that speed and may want to add a few knots. At any rate you'll have an approximation if needed. If the test is run at less than gross weight, remember that the required speed should be slightly higher at gross.

Note: In using the thumb rule multipliers in this and following chapters, if the airspeed indicator is marked as KIAS (1976 models and after), convert the bottom of the green arc to CAS, use the multiplier; and then reconvert to IAS.

More about Ratios—Why Use CAS?

Back in Chapter 4, it was noted that airplanes manufactured as 1976 models and later have the airspeed indicator marked as *indicated airspeeds* and *in knots* (KIAS). Some airplanes have a significant error between IAS and CAS near the stall, and if you used the value of the bottom of the green arc (which is now IAS), your ratios would be different. For instance, one fixed-gear airplane POH shows that, at 4,000 feet standard altitude (density-altitude), the *calibrated* airspeed should be 72 K for approximate max range conditions at gross weight. The thumb rule multiplier for this type of airplane for max range is 1.5, as given earlier in the chapter. The stall speed is 40 KIAS and 46 KCAS. By using KIAS (the bottom of the green arc) for the later airplanes, the result would be 1.5 × 40 (IAS) = 60 K, which is too low. The proper procedure would be 1.5 × 46 (CAS) = 69 KCAS, which would be within reason of the book figure of 72 KCAS.

A procedure that would work for all airplanes would be as follows:

Ratio (1.3, 1.5, etc.), × *calibrated* stall speed = thumb rule CAS. You could then convert this to IAS for your reference to remember if you should later leave the POH back in the airport office. The airplane just used has an airspeed calibration table showing a CAS 1 K lower than the IAS in the 70-K area, so you would add 1 K and *indicate* 70 K instead of the 69 KCAS obtained with the thumb rule.

Again, the POH figures, if available, are to be used for performance areas in this book. The thumb rules are basically given to show the airspeed ratios that different performance areas require.

Cruise Performance Charts

Figure 7-13 is the cruise performance chart for a two-place trainer. You may have used this one when working on your private certificate, but a couple of points should be brought out:

1. For a fixed-pitch-propeller airplane, a rule of thumb for maintaining a constant power (65%, 75%, etc.) is to add 25 rpm per 1,000 feet of altitude gain. As an example, suppose you are at 2,000 feet pressure-altitude (standard temperature) and are carrying 75% power (BHP). The chart shows that, at 2,000 feet, 2,400 rpm is required for 75%, and at 4,000 feet 2,450 rpm, a required 50 rpm added for the added 2,000 feet. A check of 6,000 and 8,000 feet at 75% shows an added 25 rpm per 1,000 feet is required to maintain that percentage of power.
2. Another thumb rule, used for an airplane engine in cruise and properly leaned, is to multiply the actual BHP being used by 0.08. For most normally aspirating general aviation engines, a bsfc (leaned) is in the vicinity of 0.48 pounds per HP per hour. Talking in terms of 6 pounds per gallon, the 0.48 is divided by 6 and the number 0.08 gallons per HP per hour is derived.

The engine of Figure 7-13 is rated at 110 BHP, so at 75% power, a total of 0.75 × 110 = 82.5 BHP is being developed. To find the gallons per hour (gph) consumed, multiply 82.5 by the thumb rule figure of 0.08 to get 6.6 being on the safe side, when compared with gph. This is higher than the book figure of 6.1 gph, but it is close enough for a general estimate if the POH isn't handy at the time. Note also in Figure 7-13 that

CRUISE PERFORMANCE

CONDITIONS:
1670 Pounds
Recommended Lean Mixture (See Section 4, Cruise)

NOTE:
Cruise speeds are shown for an airplane equipped with speed fairings which increase the speeds by approximately two knots.

PRESSURE ALTITUDE FT	RPM	20°C BELOW STANDARD TEMP			STANDARD TEMPERATURE			20°C ABOVE STANDARD TEMP		
		% BHP	KTAS	GPH	% BHP	KTAS	GPH	% BHP	KTAS	GPH
2000	2400	---	---	---	75	101	6.1	70	101	5.7
	2300	71	97	5.7	66	96	5.4	63	95	5.1
	2200	62	92	5.1	59	91	4.8	56	90	4.6
	2100	55	87	4.5	53	86	4.3	51	85	4.2
	2000	49	81	4.1	47	80	3.9	46	79	3.8
4000	2450	---	---	---	75	103	6.1	70	102	5.7
	2400	76	102	6.1	71	101	5.7	67	100	5.4
	2300	67	96	5.4	63	95	5.1	60	95	4.9
	2200	60	91	4.8	56	90	4.6	54	89	4.4
	2100	53	86	4.4	51	85	4.2	49	84	4.0
	2000	48	81	3.9	46	80	3.8	45	78	3.7
6000	2500	---	---	---	75	105	6.1	71	104	5.7
	2400	72	101	5.8	67	100	5.4	64	99	5.2
	2300	64	96	5.2	60	95	4.9	57	94	4.7
	2200	57	90	4.6	54	89	4.4	52	88	4.3
	2100	51	85	4.2	49	84	4.0	48	83	3.9
	2000	46	80	3.8	45	79	3.7	44	77	3.6
8000	2550	---	---	---	75	107	6.1	71	106	5.7
	2500	76	105	6.2	71	104	5.8	67	103	5.4
	2400	68	100	5.5	64	99	5.2	61	98	4.9
	2300	61	95	5.0	58	94	4.7	55	93	4.5
	2200	55	90	4.5	52	89	4.3	51	87	4.2
	2100	49	84	4.1	48	83	3.9	46	82	3.8
10,000	2500	72	105	5.8	68	103	5.5	64	103	5.2
	2400	65	99	5.3	61	98	5.0	58	97	4.8
	2300	58	94	4.7	56	93	4.5	53	92	4.4
	2200	53	89	4.3	51	88	4.2	49	86	4.0
	2100	48	83	4.0	46	82	3.9	45	81	3.8
12,000	2450	65	101	5.3	62	100	5.0	59	99	4.8
	2400	62	99	5.0	59	97	4.8	56	96	4.6
	2300	56	93	4.6	54	92	4.4	52	91	4.3
	2200	51	88	4.2	49	87	4.1	48	85	4.0
	2100	47	82	3.9	45	81	3.8	44	79	3.7

Figure 7-13. Cruise performance chart for a trainer.

75% power has a fuel consumption of 6.1 gph at 2,000, 4,000, 6,000, and 8,000 feet (even though the required rpm increases with altitude), since it's assumed that judicial leaning will be used in each case.

The cruise performance charts for a higher-performance airplane at pressure-altitudes of 6,000 and 10,000 feet are shown in Figure 7-14. This airplane has a 180-HP engine, and looking at the 6,000-ft table you can see that, for instance, 65% power is available at several rpm-manifold pressure combinations at the different temperatures given. At 65% and 2,300 rpm (standard temperature), a manifold pressure of 22 inches of mercury is required and the fuel consumption is 8.8 gph. Using the rule of thumb for finding fuel consumption at cruise: at 65%, 117 BHP is being used ($0.65 \times 180 = 117$); $117 \times 0.08 = 9.4$ gph. Things won't always work out exactly, but you'll have a fair idea of the fuel being used at various power settings for your engine if the POH isn't handy right then.

Look over Figure 7-14 and make sure you can use this type of presentation. You might have to interpolate for both temperature and BHP in some cases, for example, at 6,000 feet at 2,400 rpm and 10°C above standard temperature if you needed the manifold pressure for 70% power.

CRUISE PERFORMANCE

PRESSURE ALTITUDE 6000 FEET

CONDITIONS:
2650 Pounds
Recommended Lean Mixture
Cowl Flaps Closed

NOTE
For best fuel economy, operate at the leanest mixture that results in smooth engine operation or at peak EGT if an EGT indicator is installed.

RPM	MP	20°C BELOW STANDARD TEMP -17°C			STANDARD TEMPERATURE 3°C			20°C ABOVE STANDARD TEMP 23°C		
		% BHP	KTAS	GPH	% BHP	KTAS	GPH	% BHP	KTAS	GPH
2500	23	---	---	---	75	136	10.0	72	136	9.6
	22	73	132	9.7	70	132	9.4	68	132	9.1
	21	68	128	9.1	66	128	8.8	63	128	8.6
	20	63	123	8.6	61	123	8.3	59	123	8.1
2400	24	---	---	---	77	137	10.2	74	138	9.9
	23	75	133	10.0	72	134	9.6	70	134	9.3
	22	70	130	9.4	68	130	9.1	66	130	8.8
	21	66	126	8.8	63	126	8.6	61	125	8.3
2300	24	77	134	10.2	74	135	9.8	71	136	9.5
	23	72	131	9.6	70	132	9.3	67	132	9.0
	22	68	127	9.1	65	128	8.8	63	127	8.5
	21	63	123	8.5	61	123	8.3	59	123	8.0
2200	24	74	132	9.9	71	133	9.5	69	133	9.2
	23	70	129	9.3	67	129	9.0	65	129	8.7
	22	65	125	8.8	63	125	8.5	61	125	8.2
	21	61	121	8.3	59	120	8.0	57	120	7.8
2100	23	67	126	8.9	64	126	8.7	62	126	8.4
	22	62	122	8.5	60	122	8.2	58	122	7.9
	21	58	118	8.0	56	117	7.7	54	117	7.5
	20	54	113	7.5	52	112	7.3	50	110	7.0
	19	50	108	7.0	48	106	6.8	46	103	6.6

PRESSURE ALTITUDE 10,000 FEET

CONDITIONS:
2650 Pounds
Recommended Lean Mixture
Cowl Flaps Closed

NOTE
For best fuel economy, operate at the leanest mixture that results in smooth engine operation or at peak EGT if an EGT indicator is installed.

RPM	MP	20°C BELOW STANDARD TEMP -25°C			STANDARD TEMPERATURE -5°C			20°C ABOVE STANDARD TEMP 15°C		
		% BHP	KTAS	GPH	% BHP	KTAS	GPH	% BHP	KTAS	GPH
2700	20	72	136	9.7	70	136	9.3	67	136	9.0
	19	67	131	9.0	65	131	8.7	62	130	8.4
2600	20	70	134	9.4	68	134	9.0	65	133	8.8
	19	65	129	8.8	63	128	8.5	61	128	8.2
	18	60	123	8.2	58	123	7.9	56	121	7.7
2500	20	68	132	9.1	66	132	8.8	63	131	8.5
	19	63	127	8.5	61	126	8.3	59	125	8.0
	18	58	121	8.0	56	120	7.7	54	119	7.5
	17	54	115	7.4	52	113	7.2	50	110	7.0
2400	20	66	130	8.9	63	129	8.6	61	129	8.3
	19	61	124	8.3	59	124	8.0	57	123	7.8
	18	56	119	7.7	54	118	7.5	52	115	7.3
	17	52	112	7.2	50	110	7.0	48	107	6.8
2300	20	64	127	8.6	61	127	8.3	59	126	8.0
	19	59	122	8.0	57	121	7.8	55	119	7.5
	18	54	116	7.5	52	114	7.3	51	112	7.1
	17	50	109	7.0	48	106	6.8	46	103	6.6
2200	20	61	125	8.3	59	124	8.0	57	123	7.8
	19	57	119	7.8	55	118	7.5	53	116	7.3
	18	52	113	7.3	50	111	7.0	49	108	6.9
2100	20	59	122	8.0	57	121	7.8	55	119	7.5
	19	55	116	7.5	52	115	7.3	51	112	7.1
	18	50	110	7.0	48	107	6.8	47	104	6.6

Figure 7-14. Cruise performance chart for 6,000 and 10,000 feet for a high-performance general aviation airplane.

POWER SETTING TABLE — AVCO LYCOMING O-540-J3A5D, 235 HP @ 2400 RPM

Press. Alt. Feet	Std. Alt. Temp. °F	129 HP - 55% Rated RPM & MAN. PRESS.				153 HP - 65% Rated RPM & MAN. PRESS.				175 HP - 75% Rated RPM & MAN. PRESS.			200 HP - 85% Rated RPM & MAN. PRESS.		
		2100	2200	2300	2400	2100	2200	2300	2400	2200	2300	2400	2200	2300	2400
SL	59	20.8	20.0	19.4	18.7	23.2	22.4	21.7	21.0	24.6	23.9	23.1	27.2	26.4	25.5
1000	55	20.5	19.8	19.2	18.5	22.9	22.2	21.5	20.8	24.3	23.6	22.9	26.9	26.1	25.3
2000	52	20.3	19.5	19.0	18.3	22.7	21.9	21.2	20.6	24.1	23.4	22.6	F.T.	25.8	25.0
3000	48	20.0	19.3	18.8	18.1	22.4	21.7	21.0	20.4	23.8	23.1	22.4		F.T.	24.7
4000	45	19.8	19.1	18.5	17.9	22.1	21.4	20.8	20.2	23.5	22.8	22.1			F.T.
5000	41	19.5	18.9	18.3	17.7	21.9	21.2	20.5	20.0	23.2	22.6	21.9			
6000	38	19.3	18.6	18.1	17.5	21.6	21.0	20.3	19.7	F.T.	22.3	21.7			
7000	34	19.1	18.4	17.9	17.3	21.3	20.7	20.1	19.5	—	F.T.	21.5			
8000	31	18.8	18.2	17.7	17.2	21.1	20.5	19.9	19.3	—	—	F.T.			
9000	27	18.6	18.0	17.5	17.0	F.T.	20.2	19.7	19.1						
10,000	23	18.3	17.7	17.2	16.8	—	F.T.	19.4	18.9						
11,000	20	18.1	17.5	17.0	16.6	–		F.T.	F.T.						
12,000	16	17.8	17.3	16.8	16.4										
13,000	13	F.T.	17.0	16.6	16.2										
14,000	9	—	F.T.	16.4	16.0										
15,000	6	–	—	F.T.	15.8										
16,000	1				F.T.										

A

NOTE: To maintain constant power, correct manifold pressure approximately 0.17" Hg. for each 10° F. variation in carburetor air temperature from standard altitude temperature. Add manifold pressure for air temperatures above standard; subtract for temperatures below standard.

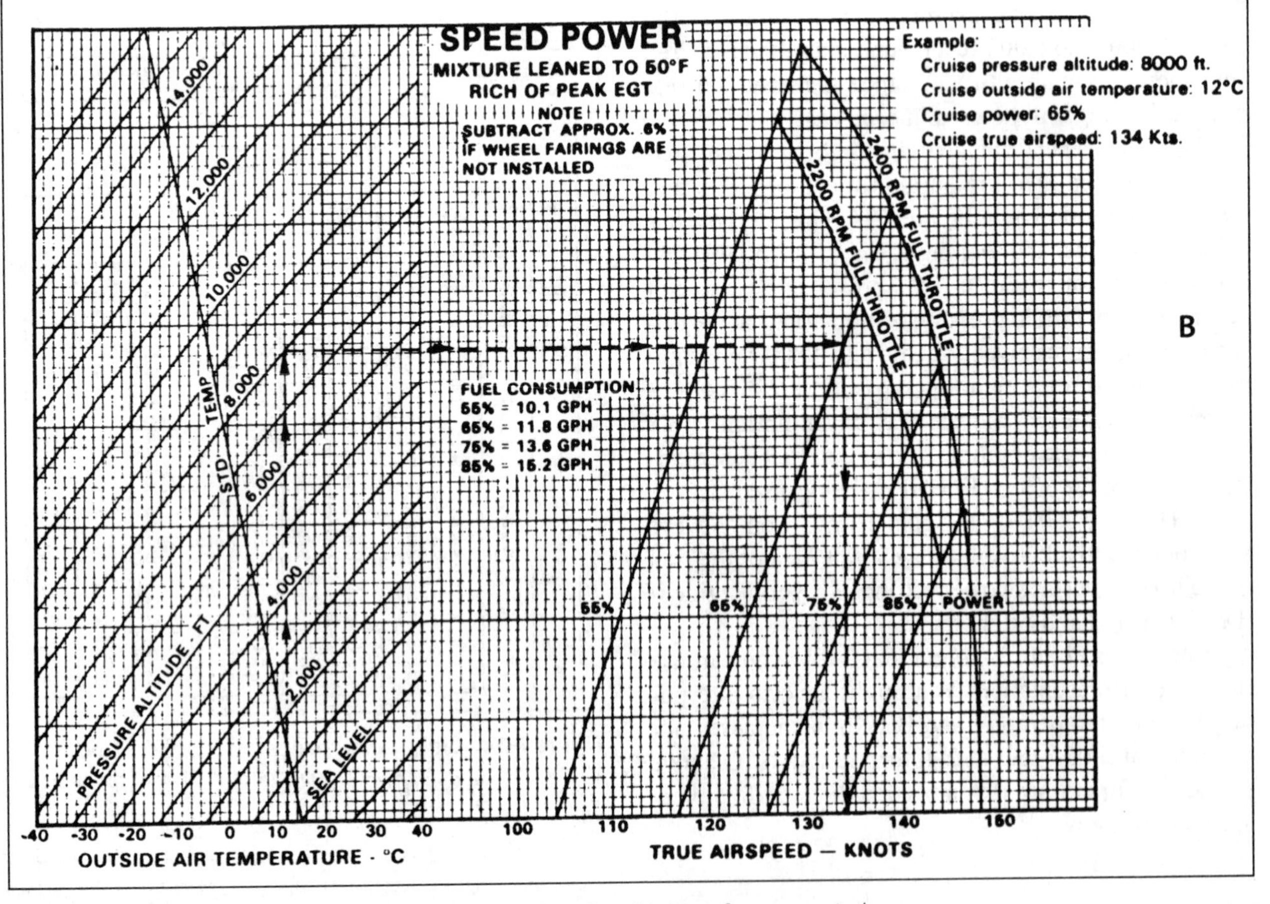

Figure 7-15. Power-setting table and speed-power chart for a high-performance airplane.

Figure 7-15 contains a power-setting table and a speed-power graph (see Figure 7-1 again) for a particular airplane. You decide what power setting you want to use, set it up using Figure 7-15A, and check your expected performance at various altitudes using Figure 7-15B. This airplane also has a speed-power graph for the mixture leaned to peak EGT (exhaust gas temperature) (not included here).

Figure 7-16 shows the range and endurance profiles of the airplane in Figure 7-14. Note that at 45% power the airplane has approximately 18 minutes more endurance at sea level than at 11,000 feet. The range profile chart has a note that the chart "allows for the fuel used for engine start, taxi, takeoff, and climb (etc.)." See Figure 6-11 for that information.

Remember that POH performance numbers have precedence over any thumb rules in this book.

RANGE PROFILE
45 MINUTES RESERVE
44 GALLONS USABLE FUEL

CONDITIONS:
2650 Pounds
Recommended Lean Mixture for Cruise
Standard Temperature
Zero Wind

NOTE:
This chart allows for the fuel used for engine start, taxi, takeoff and climb, and the distance during a normal climb up to 8000 feet and maximum climb above 8000 feet.

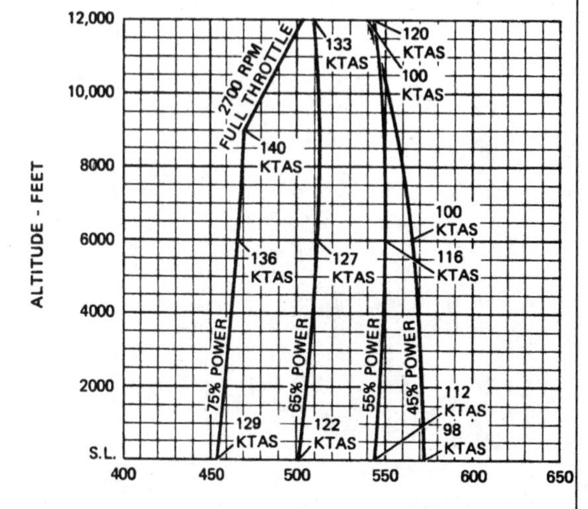

ENDURANCE PROFILE
45 MINUTES RESERVE
44 GALLONS USABLE FUEL

CONDITIONS:
2650 Pounds
Recommended Lean Mixture for Cruise
Standard Temperature

NOTE:
This chart allows for the fuel used for engine start, taxi, takeoff and climb, and the time during a normal climb up to 8000 feet and maximum climb above 8000 feet.

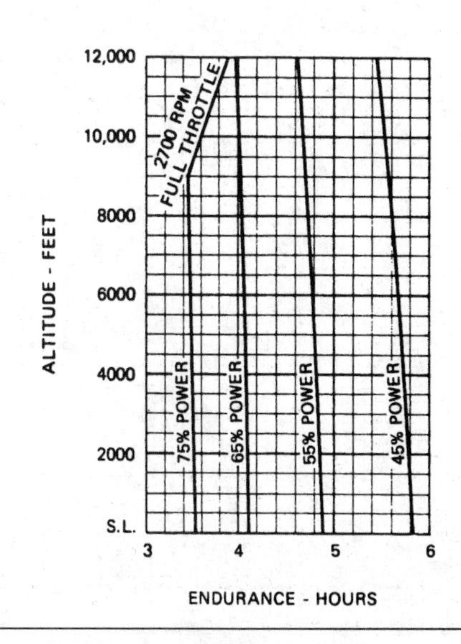

Figure 7-16. Range and endurance profiles for a high-performance airplane.

8

Glides

Pilots pay comparatively little attention to the airplane's glide characteristics these days. The trend has been toward power approaches for all airplanes no matter how light, and pilots sometimes have been caught short by an engine failure.

For airplanes with higher wing loadings, power approaches are usually necessary in order to avoid steep angles of approach to landing. If the approach angle is steep and the airspeed low, you may find that the airplane will "rotate" for landing but will continue downward at an undiminished (or even greater) rate of descent, making a large airplane-shaped hole in the runway (Figure 8-1). The stall characteristics of the swept wing make it particularly susceptible to this type of trouble.

Because of this and the fact that some jet engines give poor acceleration from idle settings, pilots must plan farther ahead on landing approaches, if a go-around is required.

This chapter discusses airplane clean glide characteristics. Back in the old days when engines were not as reliable as they are now, the pilot's knowledge of the airplane's power-off glide characteristics was of supreme importance. Nearly all approaches were at engine idle and made so that should the engine quit at some point during the process the field could still be reached. Even now, applicants for the commercial certificate are required to land beyond and within a certain distance from a point on the runway. They are allowed to use flaps or slip to hit the spot—in earlier times even these aids were taboo. Every pilot should make occasional power-off (idle) approaches to keep in practice in case of engine failure at altitude.

Two glide speeds will be of interest to you: (1) airspeed for minimum rate of sink and (2) airspeed for farthest glide distance. The two conditions are not the same, although they might appear to be at first glance. These figures are arrived at by flight tests. Glide the airplane at various airspeeds and plot the rates of sink for each airspeed and altitude. The graph for one altitude and weight looks like Figure 8-2.

Figure 8-1.

The Minimum Sink Glide

Point A on Figure 8-2 represents the velocity at which rate of sink is a minimum. Point B is that at which the max distance glide is found. Remember that the rate of climb is a function of excess thrust horsepower (THP). The less HP you "require," the less the rate of sink in the power-off condition. The best velocity for this is at point A for a particular airplane. (Check Figure 8-3 also.)

Remember from Chapter 2 that the power-required curve would be moved by the effects of weight or altitude. It can also be affected by a change in parasite drag. So while in theory the speeds for the minimum sink and maximum distance glides should be the same as that for maximum endurance and maximum range respectively, for propeller airplanes certain practical factors are involved. When you are flying at the maximum endurance (or max range) speed, you naturally have power on. Power, even the comparatively small amount used for endurance, normally increases the efficiency of the airplane by furnishing a slipstream across the wing center section. The airspeed ratios arrived at in Chapter 7 are based on power-on configurations. With the power off, thrust and slipstream effects are missing. If the propeller is windmilling, parasite drag increases sharply (a windmilling prop is like a barn door out front—remember how much force it takes to manually move the prop). To maintain the new, *lower* lift-to-drag ratio, the airplane must fly at a slower airspeed in order to get the best performance in this less-efficient condition. For the light twin, the props should be feathered if the engines are out of action.

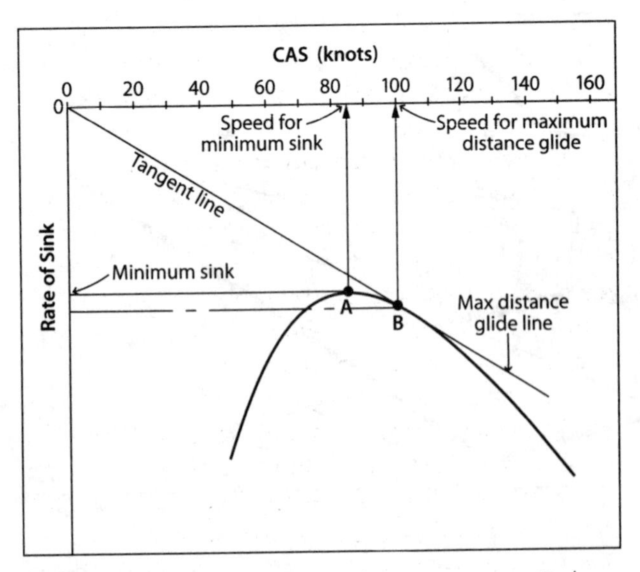

Figure 8-2. Rate of sink versus velocity curve; a particular altitude and weight for a fictitious airplane in the clean condition.

Figure 8-4 is a comparison of the rate of sink curves for an airplane in the clean condition (prop feathered or removed) and one with the prop windmilling in low pitch. By looking at the curves, you can see the effects of increased parasite drag from the windmilling prop on the rate of sink curves. Points A and B represent respectively the speeds of minimum sink and max distance glides for the clean airplane; A' and B' represent the same speeds for the dirty airplane. Notice that for the dirty condition the airspeed for max distance glide must be decreased. Parasite drag varies (increases) with airspeed squared so that a lower speed is necessary to help keep it to a minimum in the dirty configuration.

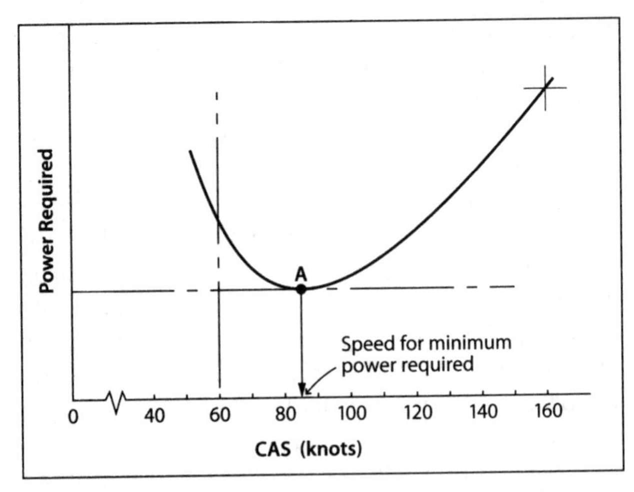

Figure 8-3. Power-required versus velocity curve (thrust horsepower).

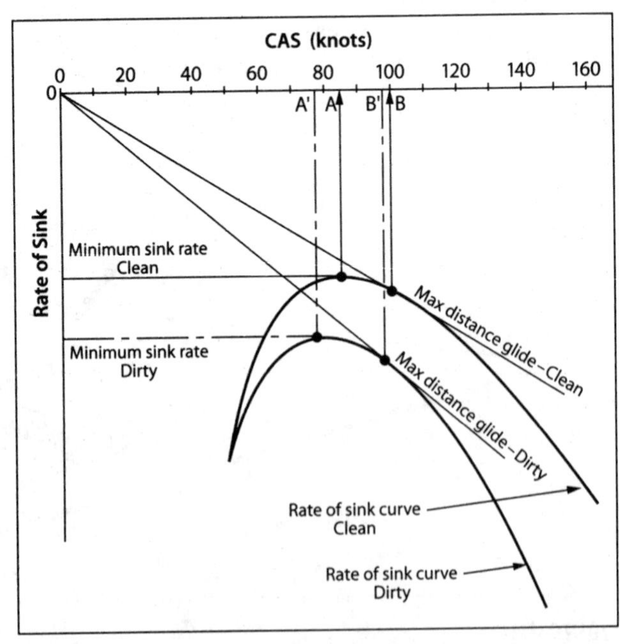

Figure 8-4. Rate of sink curves for an airplane in the clean and dirty conditions (prop windmilling in low pitch). Both curves are for the same altitude and weight.

Incidentally, all the rate of sink curves in this chapter are exaggerated, particularly at the lower end of the speed ranges, in order to show the theory more clearly.

There's another tie-in between minimum sink and max endurance—you'll do better at low altitudes for both; the minimum sink rate will be less at lower altitudes.

The glide is one of the most difficult factors of airplane performance to pin down for rule of thumb purposes. Minimum sink speed will be in the vicinity of the speed for maximum endurance but somewhat lower because of the effects discussed earlier. The glide properties not only vary between airplanes of the same general classification (single-engine, fixed-gear, etc.) but also vary for the same airplane, depending on propeller blade setting if a variable-pitch prop is used. Here are some propeller settings and their effects on the glide:

Very bad—prop windmilling, low pitch
Better—prop windmilling, high pitch
Even better—prop stopped
Best—prop feathered (applicable to multiengine only)
Fixed-pitch prop—stopped, but read on...

Of course, you can usually stop the propeller by slowing up to about a flaps-down stall speed (after pulling the mixture to idle cutoff), but you may not feel like doing stalls with a dead engine at low altitudes.

For most airplanes it's difficult to slow up enough to stop the propeller, and in some cases, full flaps and a near-stall condition is required to accomplish it. Pilots who've deliberately stopped the prop of a single-engine airplane (at a high altitude above a very large airport) have noted that (1) the glide ratio is improved, (2) it is extremely quiet, and (3) there is some worry about getting the engine started again. Also, some pilots have been known to forget to move the mixture out of the idle cutoff before trying to start the engine, using up a considerable amount of perspiration and altitude before getting things straightened out. It is particularly interesting if, after putting your total concentration on (not) getting the engine started, you found that the large airport is now well out of gliding range.

Here are some approximations of the airspeed for minimum sink as a ratio to the flap-up, power-off stall speed (CAS) at gross weight.

Single-engine, fixed-gear
(flaps up, prop windmilling).................................. 1.1

Single-engine, retractable-gear
(gear and flaps up, prop windmilling in high pitch).. 1.2

Twin-engine, retractable-gear
(gear and flaps up, props feathered) 1.3

The minimum rate of sink condition will probably be used only in an emergency situation (you have engine failure at night and don't know the terrain below). This rate of sink will be low enough so that you will have a good chance in flat territory where there isn't something like a solid stone wall to hit. This would be the best approach for an engine failure at night over water, marsh grass, or snow, where altitude is hard to judge. Notice that you won't have much safety margin in gusty air.

Maximum Distance Glide

Point B on Figure 8-2 gives the speed for the maximum glide distance (or maximum forward distance per foot down). This happens to be the airspeed for the max lift-to-drag ratio, which you remember was also the speed for maximum range. The speed for maximum range was with power; for the maximum glide distance, power effects are not present. Because of this, the recommended airspeed is somewhat lower.

This type of glide is used more often, particularly in a single-engine airplane where engine failure can give some small concern. *The more drag your airplane has, the less its glide ratio,* so naturally the gear should be up (if possible) and the flaps retracted.

This maximum distance glide speed, in the case of a forced landing, is used to make sure that you get to the field and the "key point" or "key position box," after which you set up the familiar approach speed for the final part of the problem. A possible forced-landing situation might be like this: You are on a cross-country in a single-engine plane at 3,000 feet AGL when the engine quits. Carburetor heat, switching tanks, turning on the electric boost pump, or other corrective measures cannot remedy the situation and you are faced with landing whether you want to or not. There's a decent-looking field over to one side that will allow an into-the-wind landing.

The first time this happens (or the tenth, or the hundredth) you are "shook." The best procedure would be to set up the maximum distance glide speed as you turn toward the field. This means that you will be slowing the airplane to this speed from cruise, which will be almost automatic as you unconsciously try to maintain altitude—the trouble is that many pilots tend to overdo it. In too many cases, though, the pilot keeps the airspeed too high, losing valuable altitude too soon.

The new POH gives you the airspeed for maximum distance glide (some older *Owner's Manuals* do not). Use the *POH-recommended* speed if it is available. Here are some multipliers you can use to get an approximate max distance glide speed (CAS) if your older POH doesn't list one (as multipliers of the clean, power-off stall speed in CAS):

Single-engine, fixed-gear
(flaps up, prop windmilling).................................... 1.3

Single-engine, retractable-gear
(gear and flaps up, prop windmilling in high pitch).. 1.4

Twin-engine, retractable-gear
(gear and flaps up, *props feathered*)........................ 1.5

Notice that the single-engine, retractable-gear airplane is the most affected by the windmilling propeller. The max range speed is about 1.8 times the flaps-up, power-off stall speed, but the max glide distance speed is only 1.4 times the reference stall speed. The difference is greater for this type as it is normally cleaner than the other two groups, and the windmilling propeller (parasite drag) affects it more (Figure 8-4).

The feathered propellers on the light twin cause its max glide distance speed to be comparatively closer to the max range speed than the other two groups because the parasite drag is not increased so radically due to windmilling.

So while the maximum lift-to-drag ratio for the airplane in its cleanest condition may be 10:1 or 12:1, with a windmilling propeller the maximum ratio may be cut down to 8:1 or less. You are trying to maintain the best airspeed for this new ratio. You have to do the best with what you have. Remember that cowl flaps cause drag, also. Figure 8-5 shows an exaggerated comparison between a minimum sink and a maximum distance glide.

About "stretching the glide"—there is *one indicated airspeed* for maximum distance for your airplane at a given weight and configuration. Any deviation from this means less distance per foot of altitude. The airspeed for maximum glide distance decreases with weight decrease. *The maximum glide ratio is the maximum lift-to-drag ratio for the airplane in the glide condition and is independent of weight.* This means you can glide the same distance at gross weight as at a near empty weight—but you'll use different airspeeds for the different weights (Figure 8-6). (Also see Figure 1-12.)

As the glide ratio is that of the lift-to-drag ratio, cleaner airplanes will get more feet forward per foot of altitude. When a jet trainer or light jet transport weighing 12,000 pounds and a J-3 Cub weighing 1,200 pounds each passes through 10,000 feet at its *particular max distance glide speed* (throttle at idle), which will glide farther from 10,000 feet? The jet would likely glide about 50% farther than the Cub under the conditions cited—the weights were just put in to cloud the issue. The jet would likely have a max lift-to-drag ratio of 15:1 whereas the Cub would likely fall in the area of a max ratio of about 10:1. A max distance glide speed of 180 K would be reasonable for some of the earlier light jets while the Cub's best glide speed would likely be in the neighborhood of 45 K at gross weight.

The jet's glide angle would be only about two-thirds as steep as that of the Cub, but it would be moving down the shallower slope 4 times as fast. The sum total is that the jet would reach the ground long before the Cub—but it would end up much farther away. (Figure 8-5 is an example of these two airplanes, the Cub naturally being the airplane on the right.)

Take a look at Figure 8-7, which is the rate of sink versus velocity (IAS) for a particular airplane. While it might appear that gliding too slowly is better than

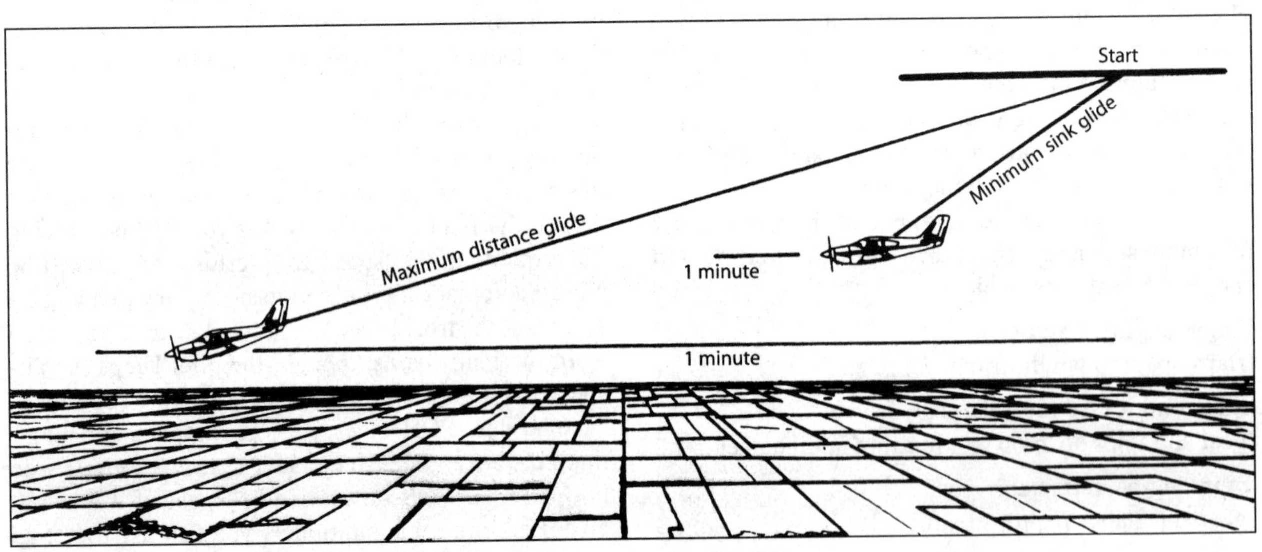

Figure 8-5. Exaggerated view of minimum sink and maximum distance glides.

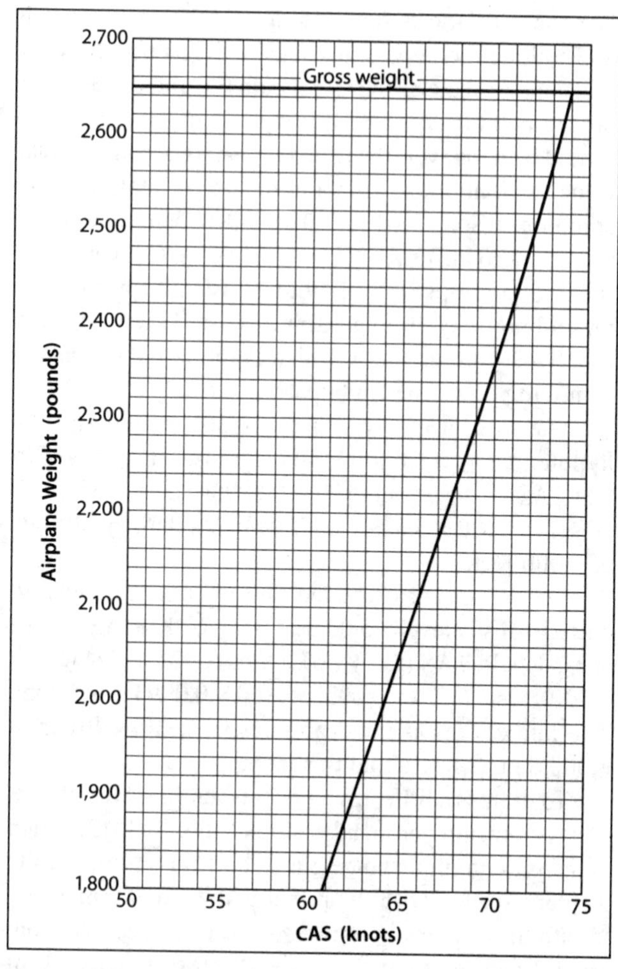

Figure 8-6. Airspeed for maximum distance glide versus weight for a particular airplane.

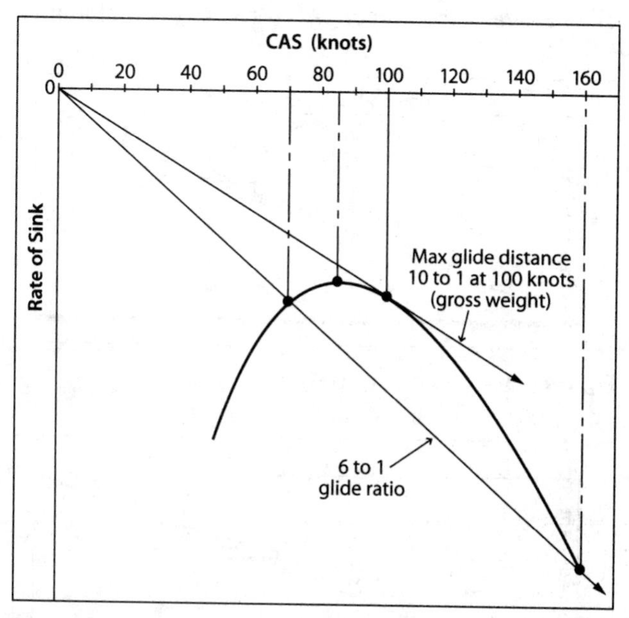

Figure 8-7. Assume IAS = CAS at all speed ranges for all the graphs shown.

gliding too fast, the glide angle for 70 K is the same as that for 160 K. Figure 8-7 shows that for the two airspeeds, although the glide angle is the same at 70 and 160 K, there is a great deal of difference in the rates of sink. The lower airspeed gives a smaller rate of sink, but *as far as the distance covered is concerned, both speeds would be bad.*

Back to stretching the glide—suppose you have an engine failure and are trying to make a field. You don't know the maximum distance glide speed for your airplane (which is 100 K—the one used for the graphs) so you use a speed of 70 K. Figure 8-7 shows that you are definitely *not* getting the maximum distance and you soon see that it will be very close—if you're going to make the field at all.

So, like a lot of pilots, you try to stretch the glide by pulling the nose up until you're indicating 60 K. Figure 8-8 shows that the 10-K slowdown has resulted in a much steeper glide angle and higher rate of sink—now you surely won't make it! You'd have been much better off to have *added* 10 K and held 80 K.

As the graphs show, the closer to the stall you get, the more the glide ratio and the sink rate are affected by a change in airspeed. Know the max distance glide speed(s) for your airplane and stick with it—don't try to stretch the glide.

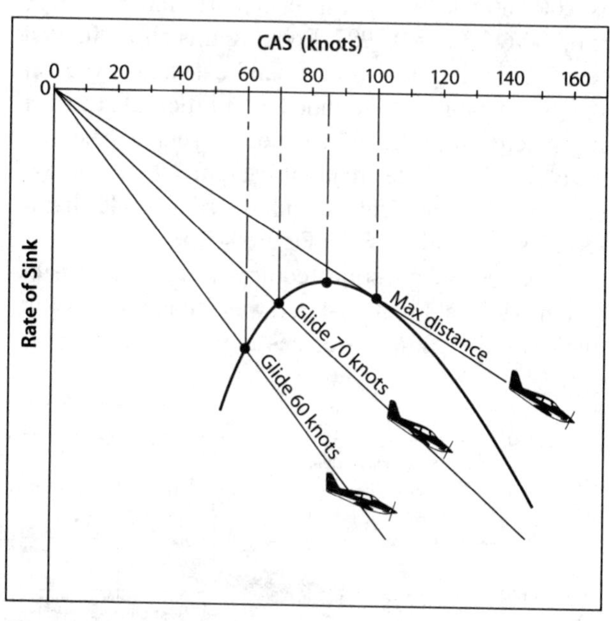

Figure 8-8. What happens to the glide angle if you slow down.

Altitude Effects on the Glide

It was mentioned earlier that weight has no effect on the maximum distance glide if the condition of maintaining the max L/D angle of attack is followed. (And with no angle of attack indicator, your only course is to vary the airspeed with weight change to maintain the constant angle of attack.)

Figure 8-9 is the maximum distance glide ratio for a retractable-gear airplane in the configuration and wind condition indicated. The following is presented for those interested in the mathematics of the glide. Assume that (1) the height above terrain is also height above mean sea level on a standard day (that is, the heights given are also density-altitude), (2) the airplane is at a weight of 2,250 pounds at the time of the start of the descent, and (3) KIAS = KCAS at 67 K.

1. What is the *glide angle* of the airplane as shown on the graph in Figure 8-9?
2. What is the *rate of descent* at 67 KCAS at 6,000-ft density-altitude *at that glide angle?*

The *first* answer can be found by simply reading the graph. At 6,000-ft density-altitude, the glide distance is 10 NM. Apples and oranges again—convert 10 NM to feet ($10 \times 6{,}080 = 60{,}800$ feet). This problem requires a tangent function because you are working with the sides of a triangle and the tangent of the angle of glide is $6{,}000/60{,}800 = 0.0987$ (rounded off): $\tan \gamma = A/B'$, or $= 6{,}000/60{,}800 = 0.0987$. Looking this all up in a trig table, using Figure 1-8 or a hand calculator, you find that the angle is 5.7° (rounded off a little). That's working strictly from the information presented. The glide ratio is a little better than 10:1. Figures 8-10 and 8-11 show a low-wing airplane with the same glide characteristics as the airplane in Figure 8-9.

The *second* question requires a little more background (look at Figure 8-11). It was found that the glide angle was 5.7°; now it becomes a matter of finding how fast the airplane is descending (side A) as it travels down along the hypotenuse (side C). You use the same units of speed along the flight path (C) and descent (A). Since rate of descent (RD) is usually in fpm, the move should be to convert the true *airspeed* (which is the true velocity along the flight path) to fpm. (Break out your computer.) So, 67 KCAS at 6,000-ft density-altitude works out to be 73 KTAS (rounded off). Converting to fpm, you multiply it by 1.69 to convert to fps and then multiply *that* by 60 to get fpm: $1.69 \times 73 \times 60 = 7{,}400$ fpm TAS (rounded off), which is the rate the airplane is moving down the flight path.

The sine is involved here (opposite side and the hypotenuse—see Figure 8-11 again); $\sin \gamma = A/C = RD/TAS$; $\gamma = 5.7°$; $\sin 5.7° = 0.0993$; $RD = TAS \times \sin \gamma$; $RD = 7{,}400 \times 0.0993 = 735$ *fpm* at a density-altitude of 6,000 feet.

Just out of curiosity, the rate of sink at a density-altitude of sea level would be TAS = 67 K (CAS = TAS at sea level); TAS (fpm) $= 67 \times 1.69 \times 60 = 6{,}794$ (call it 6,800); $\sin \gamma\ (5.7°) = 0.0993$; $6{,}800 \times 0.0993 = 675$ fpm. The rate of sink is noticeably less at sea level than at 6,000 feet. (More about this later.)

To digress a little, if you're curious about the effects of a windmilling prop, take a look at Figure 8-12, which is the maximum distance glide chart for a twin-engine airplane (clean, with the props feathered). Comparing it with the airplane in Figure 8-9, you can see that from 10,000 feet the twin can glide 20 NM or nearly 3 mi farther than the single with its windmilling prop.

Altitude does not change the maximum distance glide *angle* if the proper IAS (or CAS) is maintained

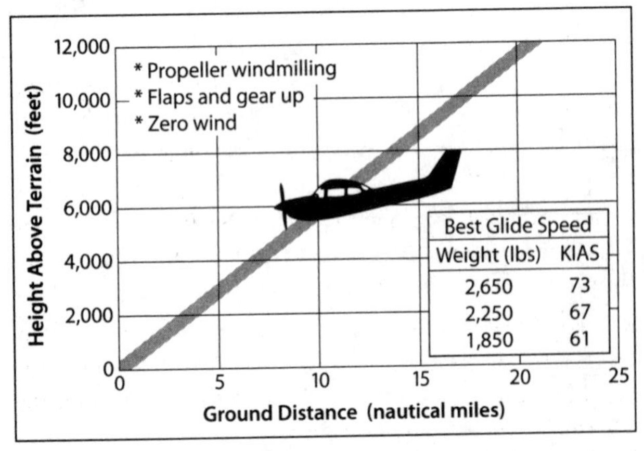

Best Glide Speed	
Weight (lbs)	KIAS
2,650	73
2,250	67
1,850	61

Figure 8-9. Altitude versus maximum distance glide. Note the required decrease in IAS (CAS) with weight decrease.

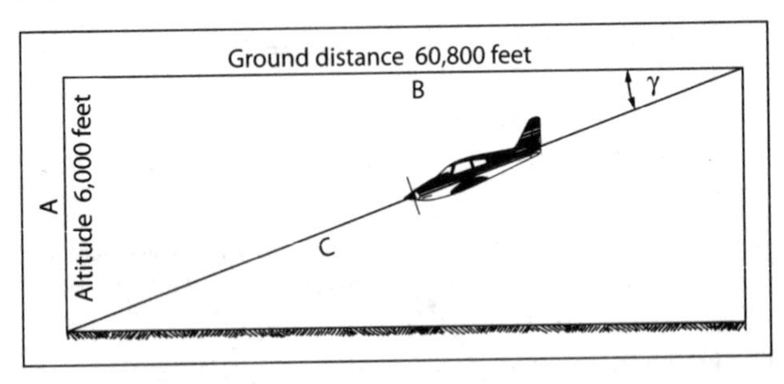

Figure 8-10. Solving for glide angle.

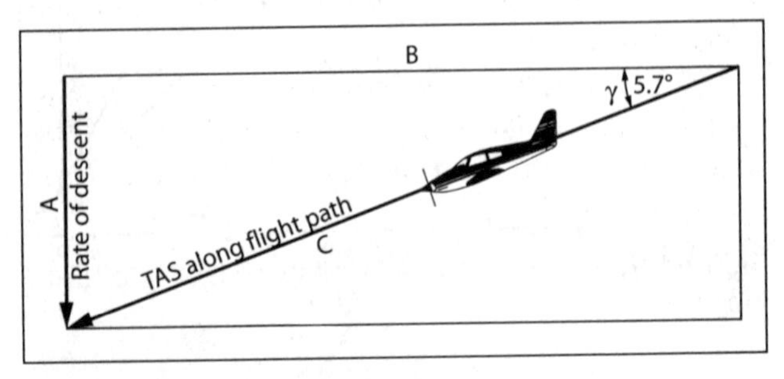

Figure 8-11. Solving for rate of descent.

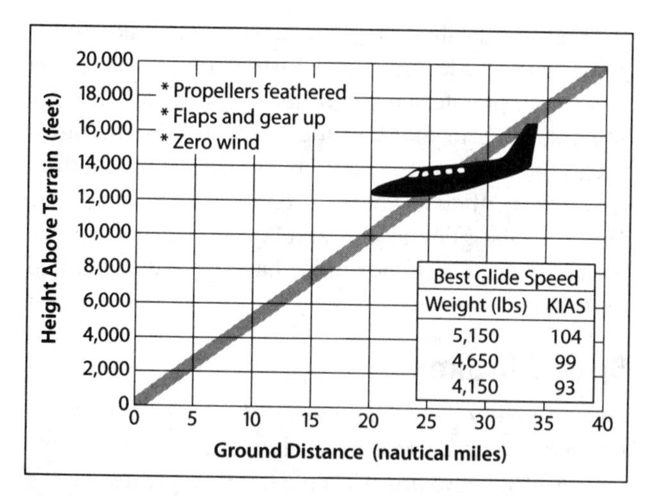

Figure 8-12. Altitude versus maximum distance glide for a twin (propellers feathered).

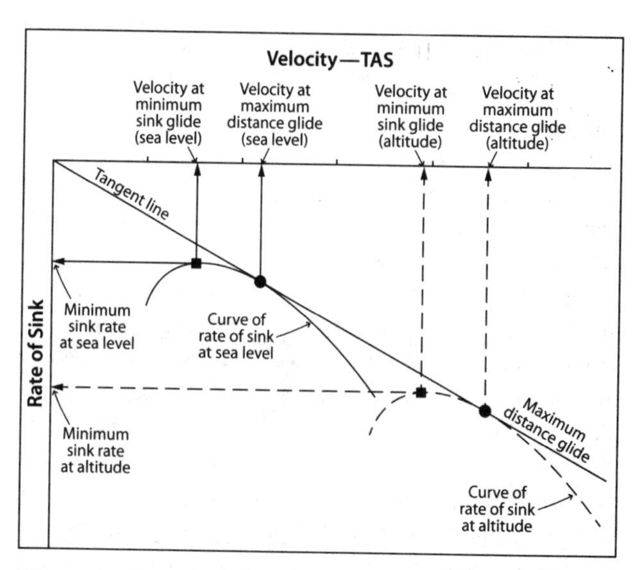

Figure 8-13. Rate of sink versus velocity curves for a particular airplane at two altitudes (same weight).

for the current weight. Figure 8-13 shows a rate of sink versus *true* airspeed curve for an airplane at sea level and some altitude at the same weight. The curves have been "stretched" apart for clarity. Notice that the line that represents the maximum distance glide is tangent to both curves. The difference is that the TAS is greater at altitude—the airplane, although indicating the same airspeed, is moving down the slope at a greater rate and hence has a greater rate of descent.

There have been arguments about whether a higher approach speed should be used for landings at airports of higher elevations. Assuming that the airplane weighs the same in both instances, it will stall at the same *indicated* airspeed (and calibrated airspeed) at altitude as at sea level, but its *true* airspeed will be much higher at touchdown; hence it will use more runway at the airport of higher elevation (but the landing roll is a subject for another chapter).

Now, it's agreed that the airplane will stall at the same indicated (calibrated) airspeed at higher altitude so there should be no problem—except that the rate of descent is greater for that same approach speed (IAS) (Figure 8-13).

If you are in the habit of crossing the fence at an IAS just above a stall, you might find that at higher elevations you'd require just a touch more power than usual to sweeten the landing because of this greater rate of descent.

The chances are good that you wouldn't even notice the difference on landing except at very high altitudes and, as it's a matter of judgment or "eyeballing," you would handle it with no problem. Adding airspeed would increase the landing roll (which will be covered in Chapter 9).

A problem could be encountered on a short-field approach at a higher elevation (and higher density-altitude). If you chop power and start sinking, the increased sink rate compared with sea level (for the same IAS) might fool you. Added to this is the fact that there is less HP available (for unturbocharged engines) to stop the sink rate at the higher altitude. The best thing would be to exercise care to avoid getting into such a condition at higher altitudes.

Wind Effects on the Glide

Wind affects the glide distance (and angle) for a particular airspeed—as you've noticed, particularly on power-off approaches. From a practical standpoint it is unlikely that in an engine-out emergency you would want to take the time to worry about working out a new max distance glide speed for a headwind or tailwind. The theoretical side of the problem is that you would add a few knots of IAS to the best glide speed for a moderate headwind and subtract airspeed for a moderate tailwind, basically the same idea as was discussed in Chapter 7. It has been shown, for instance, that increasing the airspeed to take care of a headwind (or decreasing for a tailwind) makes only a slight difference in glide distance in these conditions for normal winds. So you would most likely be better off in an actual emergency using the no-wind glide speed for headwind or tailwind conditions rather than further complicating an already complicated situation. You have other things to do such as picking a landing spot, trying to locate the trouble in the cockpit, and deciding whether to land gear-up or down.

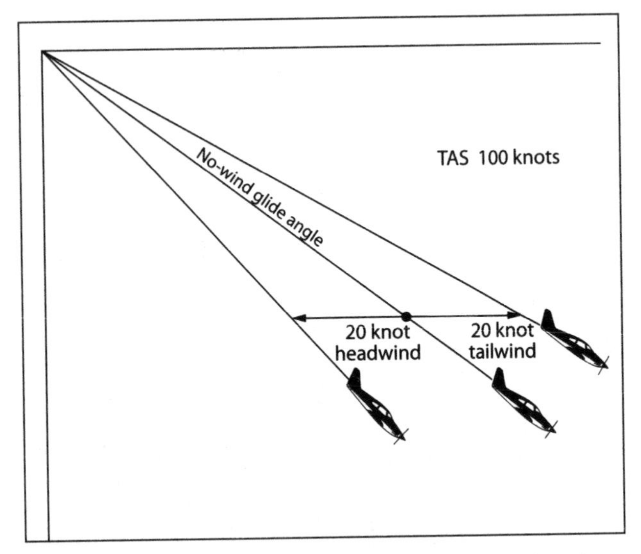

Figure 8-14. The effects of a headwind or tailwind on the glide angle of an airplane at a particular true airspeed.

Figure 8-14 shows the effects of a headwind or tailwind on the glide angle for a particular airspeed.

You may note the similarity to the wind triangles you did earlier in your training; here the only difference is that the vectors are in a vertical plane. The length of the no-wind glide vector represents the TAS, and others represent the glide angles and "groundspeed" for the winds given. The glide angles have been exaggerated for clarity.

Speed Brakes

One company produced a speed brake kit for installation on some current general aviation airplanes, the principle being to provide a means for a greater rate of descent (and steeper angle) without picking up airspeed. The speed brakes are usually located fairly well aft on the chord and are retractable. There may be one or two pairs of brakes, depending on the airplane, and each pair has an area of 55 inches. The nearly 0.4 feet (per pair) additional area can make a significant difference.

The glide is a function of the C_L/C_D ratio, and if C_D (or drag) is increased, the glide will be steeper and the added drag will keep the airspeed low for that new angle of descent. (See Figure 8-4 again.)

9

Landings

Approach

The Normal Approach

The rule that a good landing is generally preceded by a good approach is a true one. If you approach at too high an airspeed (adding 5 K for the wife, 2 K for each of the kids, and maybe a little because it's Sunday), you'll use more runway than necessary, and you won't be flying the airplane efficiently. Murgatroyd Sump, private pilot, has a beautiful wife and eleven fine children at home. It is usually necessary to shoot him down to keep him from using the whole 5,000 feet of runway (Murgatroyd doesn't fly into a field any shorter). He hasn't read his POH for a recommended approach speed nor does he know that a rule of thumb for normal approaches is a calibrated airspeed of approximately 1.3 times stall (CAS) at the flap setting (no flaps) he uses. If he used full flaps, then it would be 1.3 times the figure given for the stall speed (calibrated) as given in the POH. With no flaps he would use the POH figure (CAS) for the flaps-up stall in setting up his approach speed. Also, although his plane has flaps, Murgatroyd originally trained in an airplane that didn't have flaps and old habits die hard. Besides, he tried using flaps once and it felt "funny."

The Use of Flaps During the Approach

For a normal approach and landing, use as much flaps as is consistent with the wind conditions. For strong, gusty winds you may use less or, perhaps, no flaps. Some airplanes have steep glide angles with no power and full flaps, and it may be preferable to use some setting of less than full flaps when planning a power-off approach.

Using flaps will help you maintain the recommended approach speed, whereas with no flaps you will nearly always be too fast on final and at the start of the landing. With flaps, you will land at a lower airspeed, using less runway and making it easier on the tires. This makes an even bigger difference if they are *your* tires.

Have the final flap setting completed on base and do it in one move so that you can put your attention to using the wheel, rudder, and throttle—not the flap handle. Set your flaps, set up power (if necessary), trim, and fly the airplane. This means that no matter what flap setting you plan to use on the landing, from one-fourth to full, this should be completed before you reach a mid-base-leg position (Figure 9-1).

Another reason for having the final flap setting completed on base is that airspeed is easier to control. If you are too fast on final, the sudden application of flaps may result in altitude gain and the possibility of being too high. Unless you have a very long final (and this is bad at an uncontrolled airport), you won't have time to get set up in attitude and airspeed. Generally, the base leg is slightly faster (about 5 to 10 K) than the final. (This is no absolute law—student pilots in training airplanes should use final approach speed all the way around.)

A major area of disagreement among pilots is *when* to put the flaps down on approach. For light trainers (and low-time pilots), it's usually better under normal conditions to have the final flap setting on base so that you can direct attention to using ailerons, rudder, and

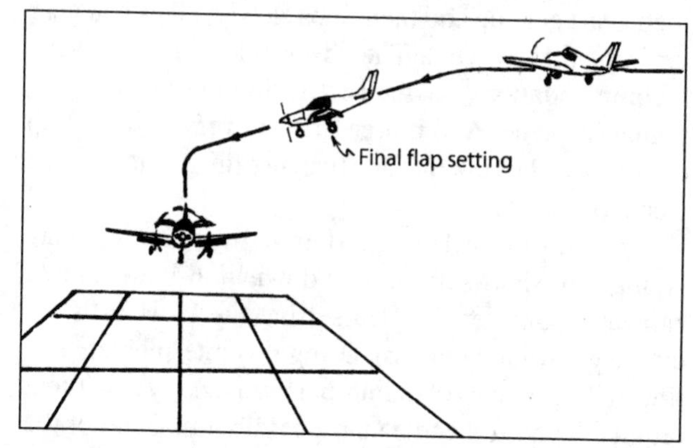

Figure 9-1. Recommended flap-setting procedure for a light trainer under normal wind and traffic conditions.

throttle—and to watching the runway— rather than putting the flaps down in small increments, requiring retrimming and possible distraction from flying the airplane. In this case, to repeat, no matter what flap setting you plan to use, one-fourth to full, this should be completed by the mid-base position (Figure 9-1).

As you fly heavier and more-complex airplanes (particularly twins), you may not want to commit yourself to full flaps on base but would likely prefer making the last setting on final when you're sure the runway is made. You could put the flaps down in increments with perhaps half-flaps on base (or even less depending on the wind or whether you have one propeller feathered), but Chapter 15 goes into detail on engine-out approaches in the twin.

If you are making a power-off accuracy approach and landing, for fun or profit, it would behoove you not to be too hasty in putting down full flaps too soon in the approach. But in the case above, you *would* put them down in increments and, if undershooting the spot, might stay at zero or stop at one-fourth flap deflection, as necessary.

If you have to make a go-around, after adding full power you'll want to clean the airplane as expeditiously as possible. Gear and flaps create drag (and require HP). There is an argument against raising the flaps too fast in a critical situation right at the stall, but the average pilot, new to the use of flaps, tends to be too timid in bringing them up in such a case. For many airplanes the addition of full power will just about offset the difference in stall speeds between flaps up and full flaps down. Some POHs recommend raising flaps before raising the gear in a go-around. At any rate, don't be so particular about seeing how slowly and smoothly you can raise the flaps that you fly into some object off the far end of the runway. When you check out in a different airplane, do some simulated go-arounds at altitude in the full-dirty condition; pick a "base" altitude for the ground and try different techniques (flaps up slowly, then gear; gear up and then flaps slowly; flaps and gear up immediately, etc.). The check pilot will also have recommendations for the best technique for that particular airplane. Add power first in every case to stop or decrease the sink rate and then use the recommended cleanup procedure.

In choosing a landing flap setting for everyday flying (not short/soft field or downwind with limited runway), consider the flap setting the POH calls for on the go-around (or less). Using this intermediate setting will give good landing performance, yet without requiring you to handle (and possibly mis-handle) the flap handle close to the ground when you're very busy controlling the airplane (low airspeed/high power). Of course, conditions requiring full-flaps will demand more concentration on both the approach and go-around, so thoroughly review the procedures in your mind before starting.

Traffic Pattern

Nothing looks worse or delays traffic more than a drawn-out final approach. You'll be operating into some pretty busy airports, and traffic controllers don't appreciate some pilot in a lightplane with an approach speed of 60 K who happens to be making a 3-mile final. The results are cumulative. The pilot in a faster airplane will have to make an even longer final to keep from running over you, and the cycle begins; each plane following must go farther before turning final and you are the instigator of all this.

Figure 9-2 shows a typical landing procedure for a heavier retractable-gear plane using flaps.

There'll be times at a busy airport when you'll be rushed (there's a jet back there that looks as if it'll run into your tail feathers any minute). It's best to have the gear down before reaching a point opposite the spot of intended landing. *But always have the gear down before you turn onto the base leg.* This must become an ingrained habit. In some cases, in order to expedite the approach, you may not use flaps and will come in "hot." The runways will be long enough at these big airports to handle you without flaps but not without landing gear. If you persist in cluttering up busy runways with airplanes resting on their bellies, you won't be welcome after a while. Make a last landing gear check after turning final.

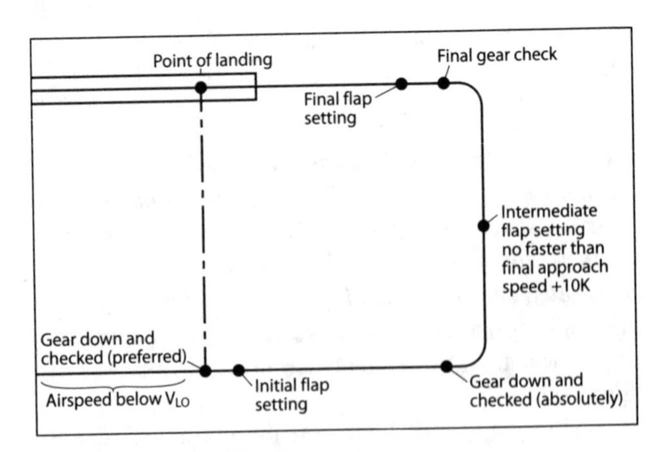

Figure 9-2. Typical landing pattern.

The Landing

Landings in General

The goal of any normal landing is to have the airplane touch down as slowly as possible, consistent with conditions. This is sometimes forgotten by pilots who fly by themselves for many hours. When they start practicing for the commercial flight test they find that old habits are hard to break.

The most prevalent misconception about landings among private pilots, even among those who learned to fly on tailwheel airplanes, is that the tricycle-gear requires a special technique in landing. Maybe it should be put another way—they think that no technique is required. They may listen to the instructor during the checkout, but sooner or later they get in the habit of landing the tricycle-gear in a too-nose-low attitude. Some even go so far as to land on all three wheels at the same time on all occasions and in all wind conditions. This means that the airplane is not stalled and lands at a much higher speed than is necessary.

You can think of the landing distance in terms of kinetic energy that must be dissipated before the airplane is stopped: Kinetic energy = $(M/2)V^2$, where M = mass of the particular airplane (weight in pounds divided by 32.2) and V^2 = the touchdown velocity (fps), squared.

Although your landing distance is directly affected by weight (double the weight and you *double* the energy to be dissipated), the effect of velocity is even more pronounced (double the velocity at landing and the energy to be dissipated is *quadrupled*).

An approximation for landing roll distance can be obtained: landing roll = (landing velocity)^2/–2a, where –a is equal to a deceleration of 7 fps per second. This is for airplanes on a concrete runway with normal braking. Converting this to miles per hour, or knots: ground roll (no wind) = $0.225V_L^2$ (mph) or $0.3V_L^2$ (K). Figure 9-3 shows some comparative ground roll figures for various airplanes.

You will notice that the POH figures are usually lower than those arrived at using the equation. The POH figures come from flight tests by test pilots who are old pros with new brakes and tires they didn't have to buy. Pilot technique can make a lot of difference on takeoff and landing. Maximum range and endurance airspeeds are precomputed figures, but even there a pilot who is more skillful in leaning the engine will get more out of the airplane. Pilot technique shows up the most on takeoffs or landings. The test pilots can get these published figures for landing, but can you? Their braking may be greater than you normally use.

Airplane	Flaps-down stall speed (knots)	Landing Roll	
		POH figures (feet)	Equation figures (feet)
1	43	360	565
2	49	350	705
3	53	600	835
4	48	560	680
5	42	500	540
6	47	500	655
7	37	350	415
8	54	900	870
9	49	750	710
10	64	620	1,230
11	51	535	780
12	61	700	1,130
13	72	1,000	1,530

Figure 9-3. Landing rolls, sea level, no wind (gross weight).

Airplane manufacturers are in a highly competitive business, and they will get the best performance possible. The given equation is an approximation—but don't cut your planning too closely.

Variables Affecting the Landing Roll

Altitude Effects

The landing is not affected as greatly by altitude as is the takeoff. Engine performance is not a critical factor on the landing, because it is usually at idle at touchdown, so the altitude effect generally can be more easily predicted.

In the ground roll equation, $0.225V_L^2$ (mph) or $0.3V_L^2$ (K), the V_L (landing velocity) is the true airspeed. At sea level, *true airspeed* and *calibrated airspeed* are the same. Remember that the airplane will stall at the same wings-level indicated and calibrated airspeed at *all altitudes* (assuming the same weights), but the true airspeed will increase 2% per 1,000 feet. This means that, if you stall the airplane at sea level and then at 10,000 feet, the IAS at the "break" will be the same at both altitudes, but your actual speed with reference to the air at 10,000 feet is 20% (10 × 2%) faster than at sea level (using the rule of thumb in an earlier chapter). In calm air this means that you'll also contact the ground at landing 20% faster—which results in a longer ground roll. V_L goes up 2% per 1,000 feet, but this figure is squared in the landing equation so that *the effect on the landing roll is to add 4% per 1,000 feet for density-altitude effects.* For every 1,000 feet of density-altitude above sea level add 4% to the landing roll given for sea level standard conditions in the POH.

Temperature

Computing density-altitude and using it directly for landing computations involves the use of a conversion table. It may be easier to compute for altitude and temperature effects separately. A rule of thumb may be of some help.

If you know the pressure altitude, you know the standard temperature for this altitude (from 59°F subtract 3½°F for every 1,000 feet of pressure altitude). For a pressure-altitude of 6,000 feet the standard temperature should be 59 – 21 = 38°F. *For every 15°F above the standard temperature for this altitude, add 4% to the landing run computed for pressure altitude effects* (subtract 4% for every 15°F below this figure). If you are working with Celsius, the rule is that for every 8.5°C above or below standard, add or subtract 4% respectively.

Remember that a nonstandard temperature affects the pressure altitude indication of the altimeter. However, for the thumb rule used here, it is normally ignored.

For example, suppose your airplane uses 800 feet for a landing roll at sea level in no-wind conditions. You are landing at an airport at a 6,000-ft pressure altitude and the last sequence report gives the surface temperature as 48°F.

The temperature (48°F) is 10° above normal for the field altitude standard (38°F). The pressure altitude is 6,000 feet, which means an increased landing run of 6 × 4 = 24% for altitude effects: 1.24 × 800 = 992 feet. Added to this figure is 2⅔% (call it 3) for the extra 10° of temperature; 0.03 × 800 = 24 feet. Your landing roll will be 216 feet longer at this airport. The 2⅔% figure was arrived at by the ratio 10°F/15°F = x%/4%; x = 2⅔% (total roll = 1,016 feet).

Using an altitude conversion chart, you would find that at a pressure altitude of 6,000 feet and a temperature of 48°F (9°C), the density-altitude would be 6,800 feet. You would then use straight altitude effects: 6.8 × 4% = 27.2%; 1.272 × 800 = 1,018 feet. In either case you are close enough to be in the ball park (or the airport).

In step 1 above you converted to the correct density-altitude the hard way by working with pressure altitude and temperature separately. You assumed the density-altitude to be 6,000 feet and then corrected this assumption for temperature effects.

If you know the field elevation of the destination airport and are able to get the altimeter setting and temperature from a METAR, you could work out your probable landing run on the way in if you think it's going to be a close squeeze on landing.

Take the same airport discussed earlier, where the pressure altitude was 6,000 feet. Here's one way we could have arrived at that figure. The field elevation is 5,700 feet and the latest altimeter setting for the area is 29.62. If the pressure altitude had been the same, the altimeter setting would have been 29.92 (remember that setting an altimeter to 29.92 gives the pressure altitude). But this altimeter setting is 0.30 inch low for the pressure altitude setting of 29.92. This means that the pressure altitude at the destination is approximately 300 feet higher than the field elevation. The pressure altitude is 5,700 plus 300, or 6,000 feet (another canned problem). If you had ignored the 0.30 inch, or 300 feet of pressure altitude, what would have happened? Suppose you call the field elevation the pressure altitude. The altitude effects would have been 5.7 × 4 = 22.8%; 1.228 × 800 = 982 feet. Correcting for temperature as before (plus 3%): 24 + 982 = 1,006 feet, a difference of 12 feet from the first calculation. If the destination altimeter setting is within 0.50 inch of 29.92 inches (29.42 to 30.42), use the field elevation for your pressure altitude correction and then correct for temperature. The altimeter setting is nearly always within the above stated limits. Even if the corrected altimeter setting was *1 inch* off, it would only mean a difference of 4% (about 40 feet) in the landing run in the above problem. You can use up 40 feet or considerably more by poor pilot technique; *so for an approximation of pressure altitude, the field elevation works fine for landing.* For simplicity, the effect of temperature on the landing roll can be ignored unless the temperature is extremely high or low for the landing altitude. An approximation to correct for altitude and higher temperature effects calls for *adding 5% per 1,000 feet of field elevation. This saves a lot of computing.* Actually it's pretty ridiculous to work it out to the nearest 6 feet (1,006 feet), and it was done only to show the arithmetic involved.

High humidity is much less of a problem for landings than for takeoffs because engine power is normally not a factor when landing, as noted earlier. (Power may be increased on a soft-field landing, just before touchdown, but any humidity effects there would not be measurable.) The *aerodynamic* effects at sea level of 100°F and *100%* humidity might increase the roll slightly less than 2%. On *takeoff* some reciprocating engines could lose up to 12% at full power under the temperature and moisture conditions just cited, and *that* would be a factor (see Chapter 5).

Airplane Weight

The effect of weight on landing roll is generally considered to be straightforward—increase the airplane weight 20% and the landing roll increase is close to this figure. POH figures show that there is a difference of about 5% between the two figures. That is, if the weight is decreased 20%, the landing roll is decreased only about 15%. Or, if the weight is increased 20%, the landing roll is increased about 15%. *But for estimation purposes, the percentage of weight change equals the percentage of approach and/or rolling distance change.* Landing roll is directly proportional to weight at landing.

Assume that braking is being used—added weight would increase the touchdown (stall) speed but would result in better braking (more weight on the braking wheels); therefore it would approximately balance out. However, the brakes would be hotter at the end of the roll because of the greater energy that had to be dissipated. Braking effectiveness on dry concrete is usually considered to be from 0.4 to 0.6; that is, the coefficient of friction, m, is that value. A 3,000-lb airplane could have a braking retarding force of $0.4 \times 3{,}000 = 1{,}200$ pounds if lift is not present. Comparing that to Figure 5-4's "Net Accelerating Force" of about 730 pounds at 40 K, you get the idea of why you can land in a field that's too short for takeoff.

Runway Condition

Added rolling resistance in the form of high grass, soft ground, or snow naturally shortens the landing roll. The effect of increased rolling resistance on the landing is to help in all cases—unless it becomes so great as to cause a nose-over. Because you will probably be using brakes in the later part of the roll, no set figures can be given here.

Wind

The wind affects the landing roll exactly as it does the takeoff run, and a rule of thumb, 90% – wind velocity/landing speed = percentage of no-wind runway, can be used. If the wind velocity is 20% of your landing speed, you'll use 70% of the published figure for no-wind conditions (90% – 20% = 70%).

Braking

For normal landings, use aerodynamic braking by holding the nosewheel off (in the tricycle-gear type) and leaving the flaps down. Aerodynamic drag $(D) = C_D S (\rho V^2/2)$, a function of the square of the velocity. As you slow down on the roll to one-half your landing speed, the aerodynamic drag is approximately one-fourth that at touchdown. Aerodynamic drag is not as important as wheel braking. Use aerodynamic drag for what you think is about one-fourth of the expected landing roll, then lower the nose and use brakes as needed (on dry concrete). In lowering the nose you increase the rolling resistance by decreasing lift, remembering that rolling resistance = μ(weight – lift). The less the lift, the greater the rolling resistance.

Some pilots start applying brakes as soon as they touch down. The brake effectiveness is not at its best because the airplane still has some lift (though not enough to support the airplane), and this usually results in skidding and less braking effect.

Once you've lowered the nose, flaps can still give aerodynamic drag, so for normal landings leave them down, particularly if you're using full flaps. For cleaner airplanes, *full* flaps help more in aerodynamic drag than they hinder the braking action by furnishing lift by being down. Leave 'em down throughout the roll and save your brakes. For short fields, get the flaps up shortly after landing, as soon as you feel you've gotten the most drag out of them. In this case you are not interested in taking care of the brakes but want to stop in as short a distance as possible. *Hold the wheel full back as you brake. Do not retract the landing gear.*

To get the most out of your brakes, you want to apply them as much as possible *without skidding*. Not only will skidding result in the possibility of blown tires, but it will give much less braking action than found with proper brake usage (the coefficient of friction drops dramatically as soon as the tire starts sliding).

Some of the larger airplanes have antiskid devices (as do cars), so if the wheels start to skid, the brakes are automatically relaxed, even though the pilot continues to hold full force against the pedals. If the device is working properly, this may mean up to twice the braking effectiveness of braking by "feel."

In the situation where braking action is poor, such as on frost-covered, wet, or icy runways, it's best not to count on the brakes. Although skidding sideways is not as critical for an airplane as it is for a car (it says here), improper brake action could result in the airplane skidding sideways on an icy runway; if a clear spot of runway is hit, landing gear failure could result. Also, if you apply full brakes on ice, even headed straight, and suddenly hit a bare spot of runway, a tire may blow or, in the tailwheel-type airplane, a nose-over could occur.

The brake effectiveness on ice is a great deal less than that for dry concrete, so aerodynamic drag will be the big factor for an icy or wet runway. Plan on it!

Figure 9-4 shows some comparison of rolling resistance caused by braking and aerodynamic drag for concrete and ice-covered runways for a particular airplane. Note that the aerodynamic drag is the same, as it is assumed that the airplane touches down at the minimum speed and at the same weight both times.

Some landing distance charts note that the figures are based on zero wind and a paved, level, dry runway with factors added for wind and a dry, grass runway. Figure 9-13 at the end of this chapter indicates that distances (ground roll and totals over 50 feet) should be increased by 40% of the ground roll figure if operating on a dry, grass runway. The initial thought is that since a dry, grass runway would be expected to have a higher coefficient of friction (see Chapter 5 again), the landing roll would be less than on pavement. You'll note, however, that the distances are based on *short-field techniques with maximum braking.* Dry grass is "slicker" than pavement as far as braking is concerned, and the airplane will use up more ground roll on dry grass.

Runway Slope Effects

Little can be said here except that if the slope is great, it is better to land uphill and downwind (unless the wind is very strong). As you saw back in Figure 5-7, a 2° slope can mean a retarding component about 3½% of the weight, which is approximately 105 pounds for a 3,000-lb airplane. This factor would be of significance in an off-airport landing on an upslope of 5°. (The retarding component of weight would give a respectable 261-lb retarding force on the rollout.)

Pilot Technique

As in takeoffs, here is the item that can shoot all your careful computations. Landing too fast, poor brake usage, and other goof-ups can cause you to lose all you have gained. The only answer is to get an occasional check ride in your airplane with an instructor and know the variables that can affect your landings.

Short-Field Landing

When landing area is critical, you want to land as short as possible without damaging the airplane. You want a safety margin of speed, but not enough to cause floating, because every foot of runway counts.

Power is used to control your approach path at the recommended speed. Fly a wider pattern so you won't be rushed or have to make steep turns at this near-critical airspeed. The power approach angle will be 1° or 2° shallower than the normal power-off approach for your airplane and you'll need more room.

A rule of thumb for short fields uses an approach speed of no more than 1.3 times the *power-off, full flaps-down stall speed* (calibrated airspeed); you'll be using full flaps for a short-field landing, and this ratio will give a safety factor if you think you'll be too high and suddenly chop the throttle.

For gusty air, this speed should be increased by 5 to 10 K, because sudden changes in wind velocity can affect your airplane, and you are interested in not suddenly finding yourself with a critically low airspeed at a bad time. One rule used is to add one-half the gust velocity to the approach speed. For instance, if the wind is 15 K gusting to 25 K, add one-half the difference of the 10-K gust (5 K) to the approach airspeed. Note that gusty winds could make a normally acceptable landing area too short due to the extra airspeed needed for the winds.

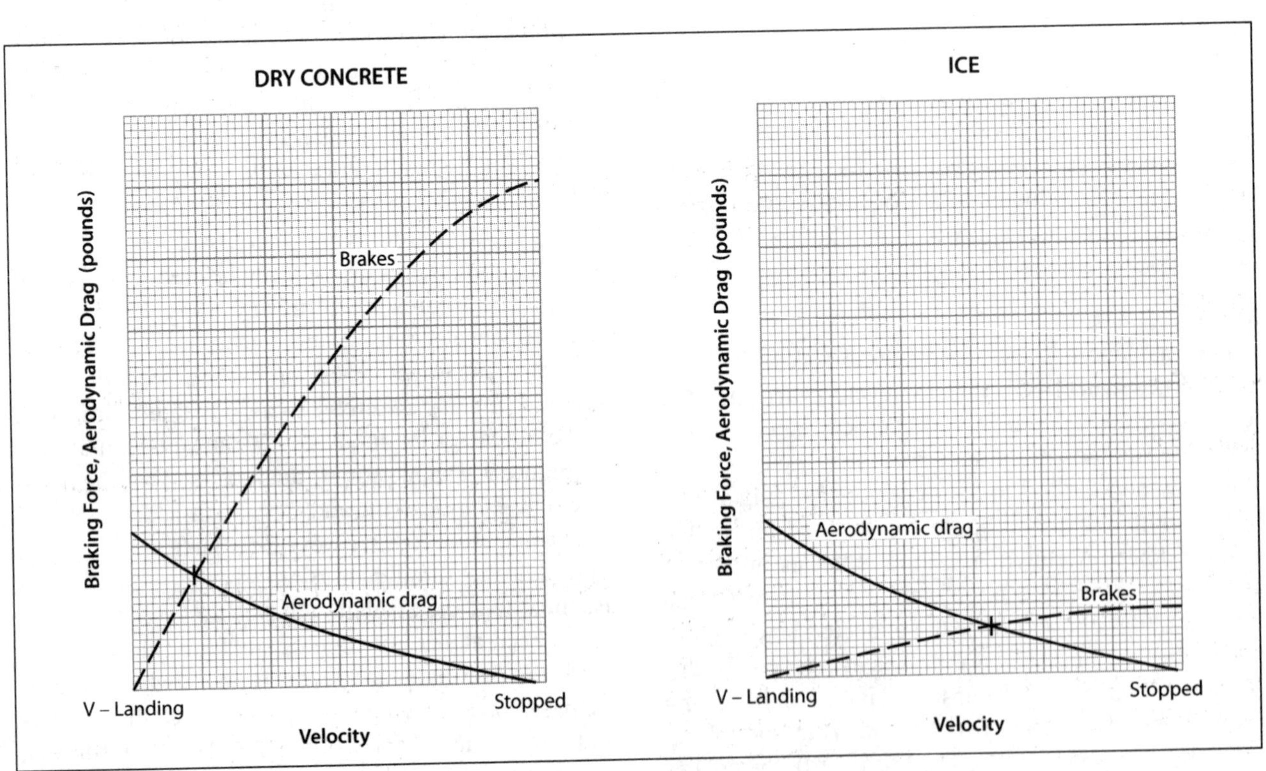

Figure 9-4. An exaggerated comparison of brake effectiveness on dry concrete and ice.

Obstacle approaches require a steeper angle of descent in that you must clear the obstacle and still land as short as possible (Figure 9-5). The danger here is that you approach at a low airspeed, and after the obstacle is passed, a steep angle of descent is continued toward the ground. You may possibly find that there is not enough airspeed to allow you to flare. The airplane is rotated quickly but stalls. A sudden short burst of power just before touching can be used to cushion the landing if you get too slow. Don't leave the power on too long or you'll use too much runway.

1. Start the approach from a slightly wider downwind leg.
2. Have full flaps set and attain recommended short-field approach speed on base. If you plan a long final, wait until after the final turn to set up your recommended airspeed.
3. Control the approach angle with throttle after turning on final. Don't be a throttle jockey; use minor adjustments.
4. Use power as necessary to make the spot. You'll have to use power all the way to the ground if you get low and slow.

Figure 9-5. The obstacle approach.

Soft-Field Landing

Approach

The approach for the soft-field landing is usually a normal one—only the actual touchdown is different from other landings. Of course, in an emergency situation, you may be running low on fuel and have to land in a pasture—which may be both short and soft. This would require a short-field approach and a soft-field landing. Never make an approach to a soft field at a higher-than-normal approach speed because the airplane will float and usually is "put on" at a higher-than-minimum speed (pilots get impatient, it seems).

If you make a short-field type of approach to a soft field, you can pick the firmest possible landing spot. There may be parts of a muddy field where the grass cover is better or the snow is not drifted as deeply on a snow-covered field.

Landing

The same principle applies on a soft-field landing for both tricycle-gear and tailwheel-type airplanes. Touch down as slowly as possible and with a higher nose attitude than for the normal landing. This means the use of power during touchdown (Figure 9-6).

If you know beforehand that you'll have to land in snow or on a soft field, it would be a good idea to have the speed fairings removed before the trip. Speed fairings look good and help out on speed a little, but they get clogged up in short order on a muddy field or in snow. (If conditions are such that they are liable to get clogged up on the landing run itself, things can get pretty hairy.) The reason speed fairings weren't mentioned in more detail on the soft-field takeoff is that, if the field is really soft, you won't get to the takeoff area anyway.

After touching down, keep the wheel or stick *full back*. The point is to keep the tail on the ground with the tailwheel-type, and to keep as much weight as possible *off* the nosewheel for as long as possible with the tricycle-gear airplane.

Check into the idea of retracting the flaps after touchdown to keep down damage from mud, slush, snow, etc. (This is more of a problem with low-wing airplanes.) For pete's sake, don't pull the gear up by mistake.

If conditions require that you land on a plowed field, land parallel to the rows if possible.

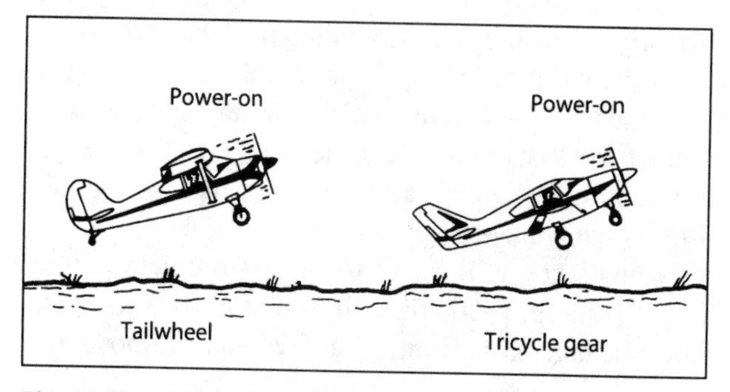

Figure 9-6. The soft-field landing, tailwheel and tricycle-gear airplanes (attitudes exaggerated).

Gusty and Crosswind Landings

Approaches in Gusty Wind Conditions

In gusty wind conditions, the approach must be flown 5 to 10 K faster than for a normal approach, as indicated earlier. Less flaps than normal may be used so that when the airplane is landed it won't be as apt to be lifted off again by a sudden sharp gust. If the wind is strong your landing run will be short anyway, so the higher approach speed and lower setting of flaps won't particularly hurt the landing roll. The approach is naturally the same for tricycle-gear or tailwheel-type airplanes.

Wheel Landings

The wheel landing is a good method of landing the tailwheel airplane in strong and/or gusty wind conditions, because the plane contacts the ground at a low angle of attack. You are literally flying the plane onto the ground.

Two-place trainers and other lightplanes of low wing loading generally do not require power to make the landing; in fact, the use of power makes the problem more knotty. A "power juggler" will use up more runway than is necessary.

Procedure

Make an approach about 5 K faster than for a normal glide. The landing transition is made at a lower height for two reasons: (1) the airplane must touch down at a higher speed and (2) the attitude will be only slightly tail-low—not three-point. For the lighter planes, power is only used to control the approach—not to make the landing. Make your path a curved one, tangent to the runway at the touchdown point (Figure 9-7).

The correct procedure is to land in a slightly tail-low attitude by properly "rounding off" the glide. After the plane has touched, apply slight forward pressure to keep the tail up—and maintain a low angle of attack. If you are too hasty in bringing the tail down, the chances are good of becoming airborne once more—and you will probably have to go around.

Impatience will be your biggest problem on the wheel landing, particularly if you're gliding too fast. The airplane is skimming a few inches above the runway and you may try to "put it on." This results in some fancy "crow hopping" and usually means you'll have to open it up and take it around. Then there are pilots who hold the plane off too long and wind up making a half-three-point, half-wheel, and all-bouncing type of landing when the plane settles fast on the front two wheels.

As the plane slows, continue to hold more forward pressure until you run out of elevator and the tail moves down; then hold the wheel (or stick) back to keep it on the ground.

Some airplanes have comparatively poor directional control at lower speeds with the tailwheel off the ground. There just may not be enough rudder effectiveness to do the job. In these airplanes, it's best to maintain the forward pressure held at touchdown—don't push forward. As the speed decreases, the tail will come down before you lose rudder control; then you may move the wheel smoothly back to the full aft position. This is a good technique in a strong crosswind for all types of tailwheel airplanes.

The crosswind correction for a wheel landing is the same as for the three-point landing. Lower the wing and hold opposite rudder as needed. Land on one wheel; the other will come down immediately. Hold aileron into the wind and apply rudder as needed to keep it straight.

Common Errors

1. Too fast an approach—the plane floats.
2. Too slow an approach or leveling off too high—the plane settles fast on the main gear and bounces.
3. Getting impatient—trying to put it on.

A bounce usually means taking it around, but you can lower the nose, apply power, and reland if there is enough runway left.

Keep in mind that wheel landings and soft-field conditions don't mix very well.

Gusty Wind Landing for the Tricycle-Gear

The approach in gusty air is the same for both types of airplanes and the landing technique is very similar (Figure 9-8).

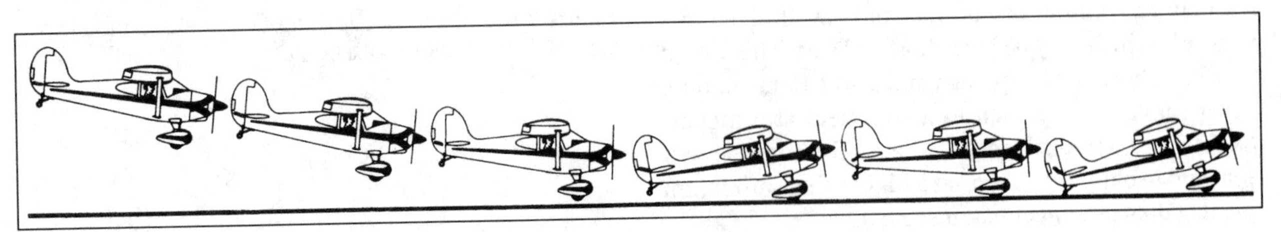

Figure 9-7. The wheel landing.

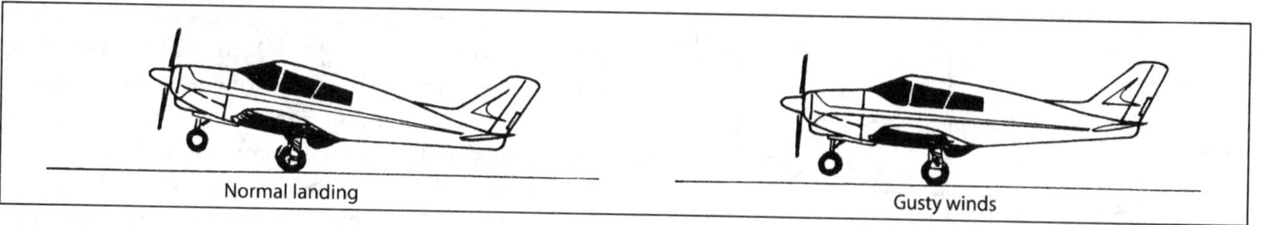

Figure 9-8. Landing attitudes.

You remember that the recommended procedure for normal landings for the tricycle-gear is to land on the main wheels and hold the nosewheel off during the initial portion of the landing roll. For strong, gusty wind conditions, however, holding the nose up may result in a sudden gust lifting the airplane off again. The best technique for this wind condition is to touch down in a nearly level-flight attitude. If you used flaps, get them up immediately after touchdown to lessen any chance of a gust picking you up. Again, the objection to pulling up the flaps during the landing roll is that, in a retractable-gear airplane, you could inadvertently pull up the *landing gear.* This would preclude a sudden gust picking you up as you would slow down very quickly, but it's more expensive than pulling up the flaps.

After you touch down, lower the nose immediately to decrease the angle of attack, and raise the flaps. If the wind is very strong, you may not want to use flaps for landings. Check the POH.

Common Errors

1. Flying the airplane on and "slamming" it on the ground with the possibility of damaging the nosewheel.
2. Failure to take into consideration the gusty conditions and holding the nosewheel off after landing.

Crosswind Landings

As in the gusty wind landings, the approach is the same for the two types of landing gear. You have four choices in making the approach and landing for either type of landing gear.

1. *The wing-down method*—This was probably the method taught to you because it is the simplest for light-to-moderate crosswinds. It's easy because you do not need to raise the wing or kick rudder to straighten the airplane at the last second. Hold the wing down with aileron and use opposite rudder all through the final approach and landing as necessary to keep the nose lined up with the runway (Figure 9-9). With strong crosswind components, the wing may be down to such a degree that the slipping approach is uncomfortable to the passengers. In extreme cases, the lowered wing may be in danger of striking the ground, particularly in a low-wing airplane. Chances are in such conditions you wouldn't land at that airport but would find one having a runway more into the wind. If you are low on fuel and must land, this method may limit your correction for strong crosswind.

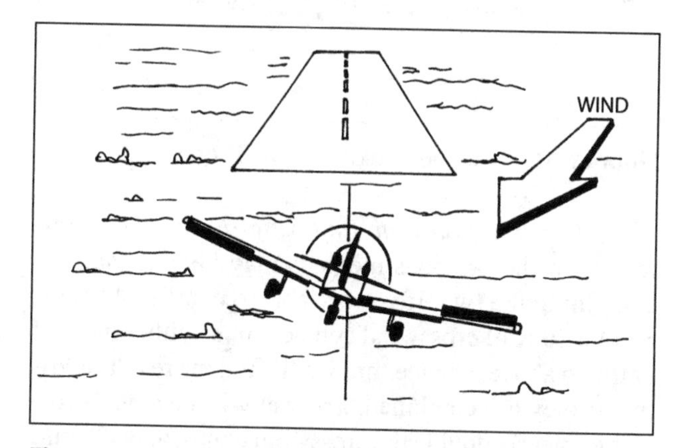

Figure 9-9. Wing-down method of crosswind correction.

Common errors: Probably the most common error committed by private pilots in this type of correction is using too much top rudder, thus yawing the nose away from the runway. The nose should be lined up with the runway during the approach and landing. Also, some pilots try to raise the down wing at the last instant. This isn't necessary.

2. *Crab method*—This makes for a comfortable approach because the plane is not slipping, but it has the disadvantage of requiring fine judgment in knowing when to "kick" the airplane straight. Also, if the crosswind is strong, the crab angle will have to be so great as to make it doubtful that you would have enough rudder effectiveness left to completely straighten the airplane before it touched—and this makes for a possible ground loop. If the airplane hits in a crab, you'll have a weathercocking tendency. In the tailwheel-type airplane, forces will be set up to aggravate the ground loop once it has started. So, the crab method also is limited to moderate crosswind components (Figure 9-10).

Common errors: Not straightening the airplane at the right time. Gusts may cause the airplane to float and start drifting after you've kicked it straight, or you may touch down before you're ready, still in a crab.

Figure 9-10. Crab method of crosswind correction.

3. *Combination crab and wing-down*—The limitations of the previous methods may be overcome by combining the two. If you are able to comfortably correct for 10 K of crosswind component by either method outlined above, chances are you'll find the results additive if they are combined, and you will be able to correct for nearly double the crosswind component (Figure 9-11).

You'll be crabbed *and* have the wing down, which means that the wing is not uncomfortably low and the crab is not such that the plane cannot be yawed straight as it touches. The idea is to yaw the plane straight, not to bother trying to raise the wing. Land on the upwind wheel as was done in the wing-down method.

Common errors: Getting so engrossed in one of the corrections that the other is neglected. Usually you forget you're in a crab as well as having the wing down.

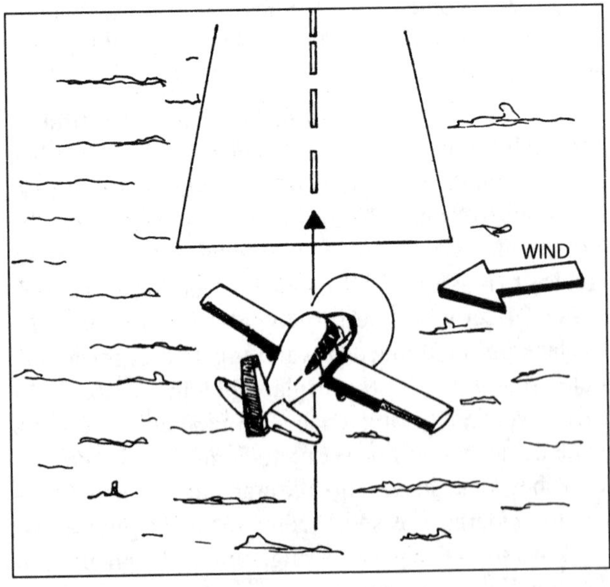

Figure 9-11. Combination wing-down and crab methods.

4. *Crab approach and wing-down landing*—This makes a comfortable approach for light-to-moderate crosswinds. The crab is used during the final approach, and before the landing flare is begun, the nose is straightened and the wing lowered. From this point on, it is the wing-down method. This avoids the long slipping approach, but it may require a couple of practice periods to make a smooth transition from the crab to the wing-down attitude.

Common errors: Poor transition from crab to wing-down attitude, with some frantic scrambling around and poor use of controls.

Note that the crab method (2) has the disadvantage of "timing is everything": if you don't kick it straight soon enough, you'll land in a crab traveling along the centerline. If you kick it straight too soon, you drift downwind and land in a crab traveling towards the downwind side of the runway. In either case, the side load on the gear is high.

On the other hand, remember that any method requiring a transition from a crab to a slip will result in a sink. You must increase pitch (using some airspeed), add a little power to offset the increased descent rate (especially in transports) or both. So getting into the side-slip by about 100 feet AGL gives you time to get stabilized, but isn't too long a time with everyone bunched up on the low side of the cabin.

The Ground Roll

Here's where the tricycle-gear pays for itself. The CG is ahead of the main wheels, which tends to straighten the airplane out. The tailwheel-type reacts just the opposite. The ground roll is the toughest part of the problem in strong crosswinds. Keep that aileron into the wind to help fight wing-lifting tendencies and to also utilize the down-aileron drag to help keep you straight. The aileron is more important for the tailwheel airplane during the ground roll because of the airplane's attitude, but use it for both types.

Tailwheel-type—Keep that wheel back (if you made a three-point landing) because this will allow the tailwheel to get a good grip and help fight the weathercocking tendency.

Tricycle-gear—Ease the nosewheel on but don't hold forward pressure; you may wheelbarrow.

Hydroplaning

As you progress to faster airplanes with their higher-speed ground rolls and fly in more adverse weather conditions, hydroplaning will be more of a problem.

There are three types of hydroplaning:

1. *Dynamic.* In total dynamic hydroplaning, water standing on the runway exerts pressure between the tires and the runway. The tires are lifted and are not in contact with the runway surface. The rolling coefficient of friction (and also brake effectiveness) is reduced to nearly nothing. This means also that steering is not effective. A strong crosswind can cause added problems of control. Dynamic hydroplaning starts at high speeds and in standing water on the runway.

A thumb rule for predicting the minimum dynamic hydroplaning speed (knots) is $8.6\sqrt{\text{tire pressure, psi}}$. At a tire pressure of 25 pounds, the expected minimum dynamic hydroplaning speed is 43 K ($8.6 \times \sqrt{25} = 8.6 \times 5 = 43$). Expect problems above this speed. See Figure 9-12.

2. *Viscous hydroplaning.* When the runway has painted areas or rubber deposits that make it smooth, the tire can't fully displace the moisture film. You can feel this effect in driving a car when your car slips momentarily as you cross an extra thick painted highway centerline covered with rain or dew. When a large area of the runway or taxiway is involved, you could lose steering and braking ability. *This can occur at a much lower speed than dynamic hydroplaning.*

If you are landing on a wet runway with rubber deposits and lots of painted markings, get the airplane slowed to taxi speed early. The middle portion of the runway will have better braking than either end and you can't count on that same braking action as you roll out onto the rubber and paint at the far end. This will be more important when you're flying transports into far-off, exotic locales that have runways that may not be crowned or grooved.

3. *Reverted rubber hydroplaning.* Suppose you are touching down on a wet runway and (wrongly) apply brakes immediately after touchdown. The airplane starts dynamic hydroplaning because the brakes are locked. The airplane slows, the dynamic hydroplaning decreases, and the locked tires heat up because of added friction. A layer of steam occurs between the tires and the runway and the rubber melts. This prevents water dispersal because the tire is riding on a layer of steam and molten rubber.

This is the worst of the hydroplaning variations because it can happen down to zero speed. *Locking the brakes for prolonged periods causes reverted (melted) rubber hydroplaning.*

Some runways are grooved to cut down on hydroplaning effects, but you should be ready for it anytime you are taking off or landing on a wet runway. Think of braking or directional control problems and avoid excessive use of the rudder pedals or brakes. Assume that the liquid water will have the friction properties of ice (which it will, under the conditions just mentioned).

References for further reading: (1) ATP. K.T. Boyd, Iowa State University Press; (2) You vs. Hydroplaning (article), *Aerospace Safety*, Norton AFB, Calif.

As was indicated earlier in this chapter, a dry grass runway doesn't allow as good braking as pavement (wet grass is even worse), so the ground roll and total distances for a given pressure-altitude and temperature are to be increased by 40% of the ground roll figure. Looking at 2,000 feet and 10°C in Figure 9-13, you'll see that the ground roll is 660 feet with a *total* distance of 1,395 feet required to clear a 50-foot obstacle. When landing on dry grass the added distance required will be $0.40 \times 660 = 264$ feet. Add 264 feet to both values: 924-ft ground roll and 1,659-ft total over the 50-foot obstacle.

Figure 9-14 is a graphical presentation of two landing performance charts. The examples show the procedure for using the charts.

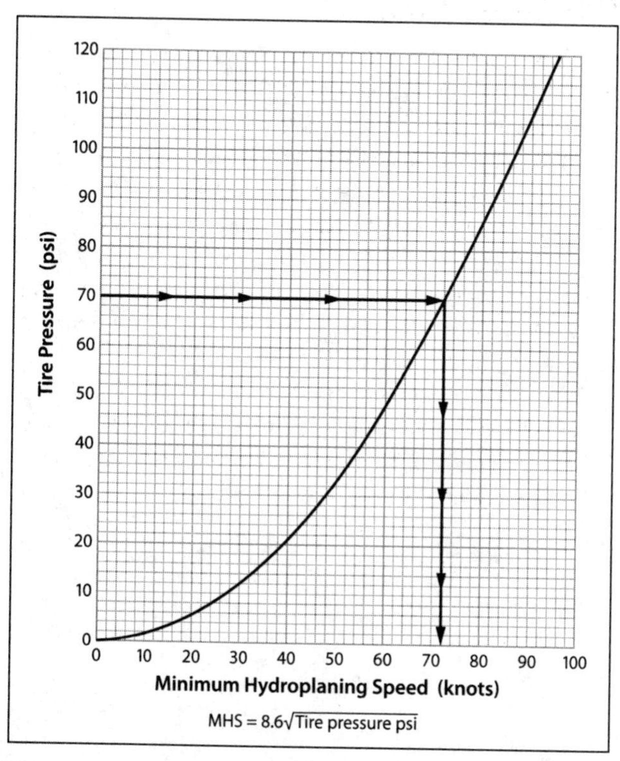

Figure 9-12. Tire pressure versus minimum hydroplaning speed (72 K at 70 psi).

CONDITIONS:
Flaps 30°
Power Off
Maximum Braking
Paved, Level, Dry Runway
Zero Wind

LANDING DISTANCE

SHORT FIELD

NOTES:
1. Short field technique as specified in Section 4.
2. Decrease distances 10% for each 9 knots headwind. For operation with tailwinds up to 10 knots, increase distances by 10% for each 2 knots.
3. For operation on a dry, grass runway, increase distances by 40% of the "ground roll" figure.
4. If a landing with flaps up is necessary, increase the approach speed by 9 KIAS and allow for 35% longer distances.

WEIGHT LBS	SPEED AT 50 FT KIAS	PRESS ALT FT	0°C		10°C		20°C		30°C		40°C	
			GRND ROLL	TOTAL TO CLEAR 50 FT OBS	GRND ROLL	TOTAL TO CLEAR 50 FT OBS	GRND ROLL	TOTAL TO CLEAR 50 FT OBS	GRND ROLL	TOTAL TO CLEAR 50 FT OBS	GRND ROLL	TOTAL TO CLEAR 50 FT OBS
2650	63	S.L.	590	1290	615	1325	635	1355	660	1390	680	1425
		1000	615	1325	635	1355	660	1395	680	1425	705	1460
		2000	635	1355	660	1395	685	1430	705	1465	730	1500
		3000	660	1395	685	1430	710	1470	735	1505	760	1545
		4000	685	1430	710	1470	735	1510	760	1545	785	1585
		5000	710	1470	740	1515	765	1550	790	1590	815	1630
		6000	740	1515	765	1555	795	1595	820	1635	850	1680
		7000	770	1560	795	1600	825	1645	850	1685	880	1725
		8000	800	1605	825	1645	855	1690	885	1735	915	1780

Figure 9-13. Landing distance chart (short-field techniques).

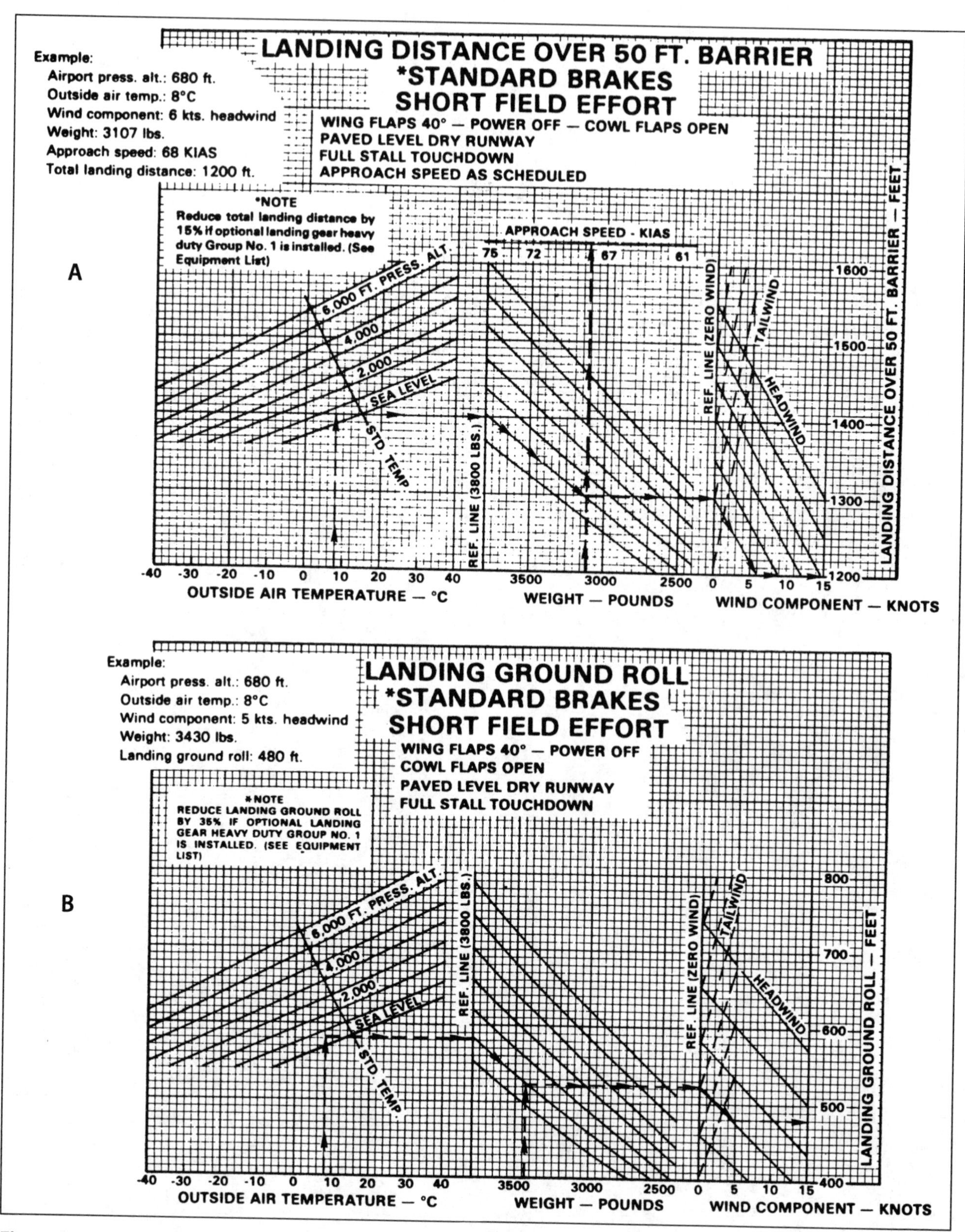

Figure 9-14. Landing distance charts. **A.** Distance over 50-ft barrier. **B.** Landing ground roll.

10

Airplane Stability and Control

The Three Axes

There are three axes around which the airplane moves. These axes pass through the airplane's center of gravity, or the point where the airplane weight is considered to be concentrated (Figure 10-1).

An airplane that is stable requires little pilot attention after it is trimmed for a certain airspeed and power setting. Airplanes certificated by the FAA for use in private and commercial flying must meet certain stability requirements around all three axes—otherwise the pilot could get into a dangerous situation because of a momentary lapse of attention. All the airplanes you have flown to date, certificated as "normal" or "utility" category, can be trimmed to maintain prescribed limits within certain airspeed ranges.

Stability in General

Stability, as defined by the dictionary, means "fixedness, steadiness, or equilibrium." An object that is *positively stable* resists any displacement. One that is *negatively stable* does not resist displacement; indeed, it tends to displace itself more and more if acted upon by an outside force. An object that is *neutrally stable* doesn't particularly care what happens to it. If acted on by a force it will move, but it does not tend to return to its position or to move farther after the force is removed.

Static Stability

Static (at rest) stability is the initial tendency of a body to return to its original position after being disturbed. An example of positive static stability is a steel ball sitting inside a perfectly smooth bowl (Figure 10-2). You can see that the ball has an initial tendency to return to its original position if displaced.

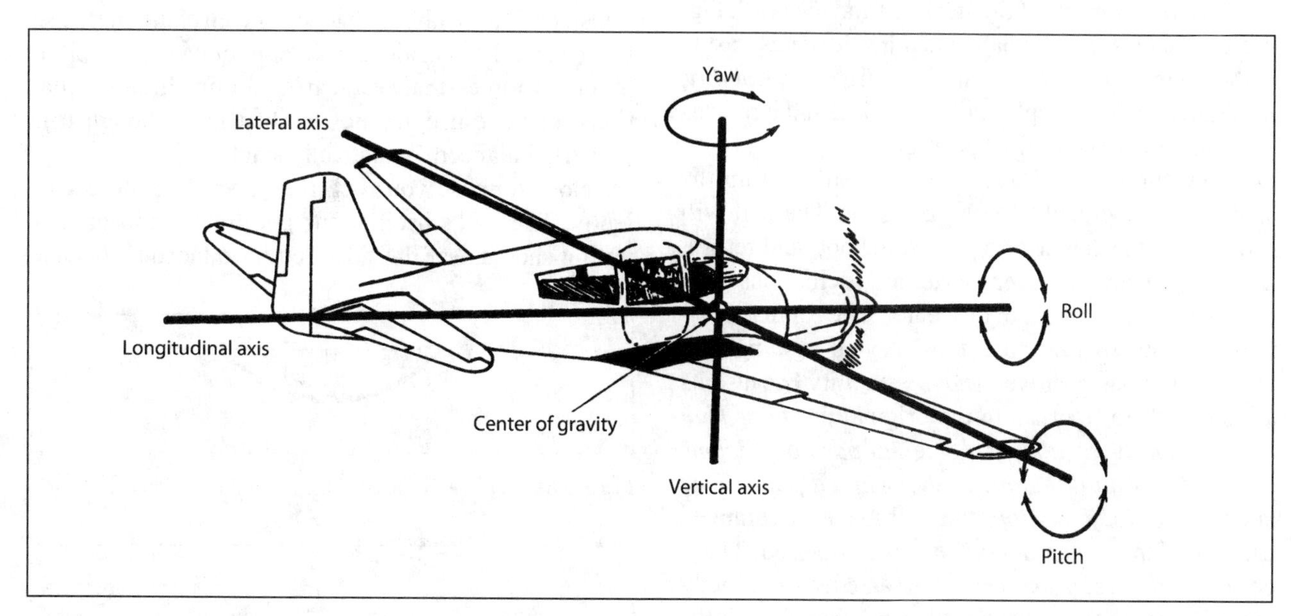

Figure 10-1. The three axes.

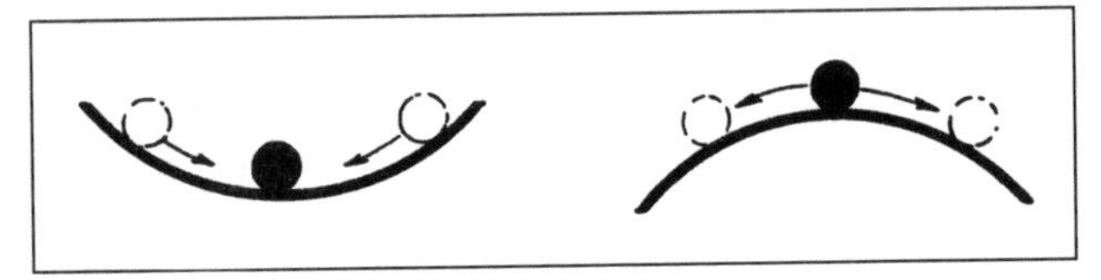

Figure 10-2. (Left) Positive static stability.
Figure 10-3. (Right) Negative static stability.

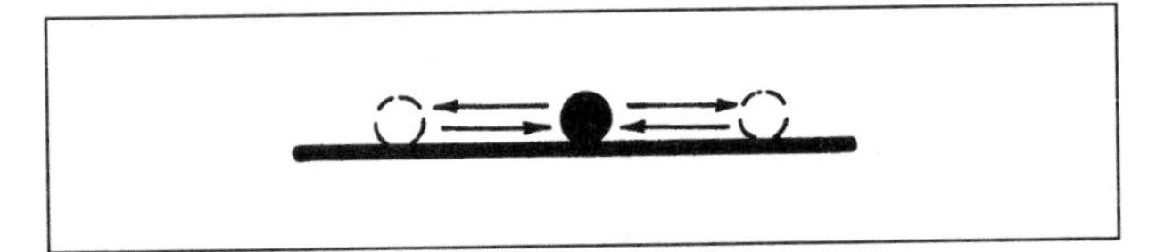

Figure 10-4. Neutral static stability.

Figure 10-3 is an example of negative static stability. The ball is carefully balanced on the peak of the bowl, and the application of outside force results in its falling. It does not tend to return to its original position; on the contrary, it gets farther and farther from the original position as it falls.

Neutral static stability can be likened to a steel ball on a perfectly flat smooth surface. If a force is exerted on it, the ball will move and stop at some new point after the force is removed (Figure 10-4).

Dynamic Stability

The actions a body takes in response to its static stability properties show its dynamic (active) stability. This dynamic stability usually is considered to be the time history of a body's response to its inherent static stability.

Take the example of the steel ball and the bowl. Figure 10-2 shows that the ball, when inside, tends to stay in the center of the bowl—it has *positive static stability.* It requires force to displace it up the side, and it returns immediately to its original position.

Now suppose you push the steel ball well up the side of the bowl and quickly release it. The ball will roll toward the center position, overshoot, and return, keeping this up with ever shortening oscillations until finally it returns to rest in the center. The ball has positive *static* stability because it resists your pushing it up the side and has positive *dynamic* stability because its actions tend to return it to the original position. *That is, the oscillations about its original position become less and less until it stops at the original point.* This is called *periodic motion;* the ball makes a complete oscillation in a given interval of time or period. These periods remain approximately the same length (exactly the same under theoretical conditions) even though the *amplitude* (movement) is less and less.

You can also see periodic motion by suspending a heavy weight on a string, making a homemade pendulum. The pendulum at rest has positive *static* stability—it resists any attempt to displace it. It has positive *dynamic* stability in that it finally returns to its original position through a series of periodic oscillations of decreasing amplitude.

The ball in the bowl could be given the property of *aperiodic* (nontimed) positive dynamic stability by filling the bowl with a heavy liquid such as oil (Figure 10-5). The liquid would damp the oscillations to such an extent that the ball would probably return directly, though more slowly, to the original position with no overshooting and hence no periodic motion. Through manipulation of the system (adding oil), you have caused its motions to be aperiodic.

Unlike the steel ball *inside* the bowl, which is statically stable, resists any displacement, and has positive dynamic stability, a properly designed airplane does not necessarily have positive dynamic stability under all conditions (see the section, Longitudinal Dynamic Stability of the Airplane, later in this chapter). And the fact that an airplane sometimes has positive static stability does not mean that its dynamic stability is also positive. Outside forces may act on the airplane so that the oscillations stay the same or even become greater.

Back to the ball inside the bowl. Suppose you start the ball rolling and then rock the bowl with your hand so that the oscillations do *not* decrease. Because of the outside force you set up, the ball's oscillations retain the same amplitude. The system has positive static stability but neutral dynamic stability—the ball's oscillations continue without change. The airplane may also be affected by outside (aerodynamic) or inside (pilot-induced) forces that result in undiminishing oscillations, or neutral dynamic stability, even though it is properly balanced, or statically stable.

Now suppose you rock the bowl even more violently. The ball's oscillations get greater and greater until it shoots over the side. You introduced an outside

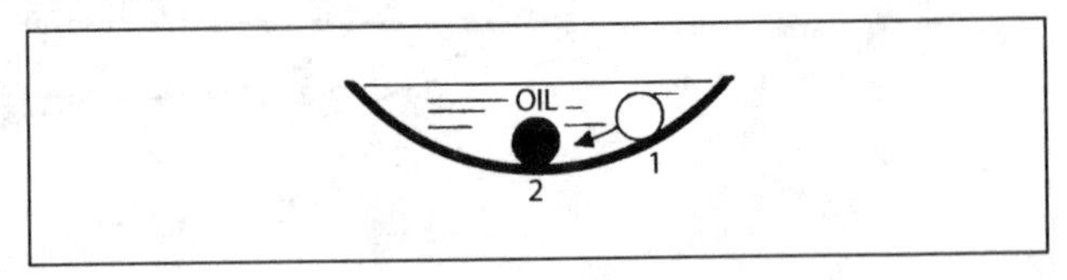

Figure 10-5. A periodic positive dynamic stability.

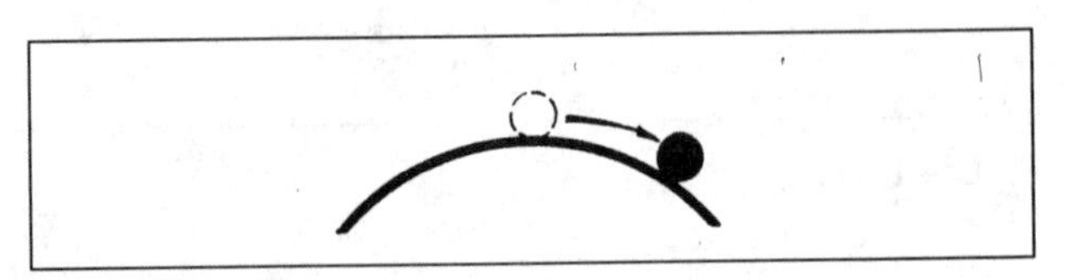

Figure 10-6. A statically unstable system.

factor that resulted in negative dynamic stability—the oscillations increasing in size until *structural damage* occurred (the ball went over the side).

Thus, the system (or airplane) with positive *static* stability may have positive, neutral, or negative *dynamic* stability. *A system that is statically stable will have some form of oscillatory behavior.* This tendency may be so heavily damped (the oil in the bowl) that it is not readily evident. The oscillations show that the system is statically stable; the ball (or airplane) is trying to return to the original position. Outside forces may continually cause it to equally overshoot this position or may be strong enough to cause the oscillations to increase until structural damage occurs.

For a system that has *neutral* static stability such as a ball on a smooth flat plate, there are no oscillations because the ball isn't trying to return to any particular position. It's displaced and stays displaced.

A system that has *negative* static stability or is statically *unstable* (the terms mean the same thing) will have no oscillations; there will be a steady divergence. Let's use the ball and bowl again. This time turn the bowl over and balance the ball carefully on the peak (sure you can) and take another look at the statically unstable system (Figure 10-6).

If even a small force is applied, the ball rolls down the side of the bowl. The ball does not resist any force to offset it from its position—on the contrary, it wants to leave in the first place and when displaced leaves its original position at a faster and faster rate. There are no oscillations because there is no tendency to return at all. *The statically unstable system has no dynamic (oscillatory) characteristics but continually diverges.* The action this system takes in diverging is not always that simple, but *that* we'll leave for the programmers.

A statically stable system (or airplane) may have either positive, neutral, or negative dynamic stability characteristics.

How this applies to you as a pilot will be shown shortly.

Longitudinal or Pitch Stability

The elevators control the *pitch* (the movement around the lateral axis) (Figure 10-7). The pilot's ability to control the airplane about this axis is very important. In designing an airplane, a great deal of effort is spent in making it stable around all three axes. But *longitudinal stability* (stability about the pitch axis) is considered to be the most affected by variables introduced by the pilot, such as airplane loading.

Take a look at an airplane in balanced, straight and level flight (Figure 10-8). Making calculations from the center of gravity (CG), you find the *moment* (force × distance) about the CG caused by the wing's lift is 5 × 3,100 or 15,500 lb-in. In Chapter 7, such measurements were made from the center of lift, but that's okay. This is a nose-down moment. To maintain straight and level flight there must be an equal moment in the opposite direction or the airplane would be attempting to do an outside loop. This opposite moment is furnished by a down force on the tail. Its moment must be 15,500 lb-in. in a tail-down direction. The distance shown from the CG to the center of tail lift is 155 inches; therefore the down force at the tail must be 100 pounds (force × distance = 100 pounds × 155 inches). The tail-down moment is also 15,500 lb-in., which balances the nose-down moment. The airplane is statically balanced.

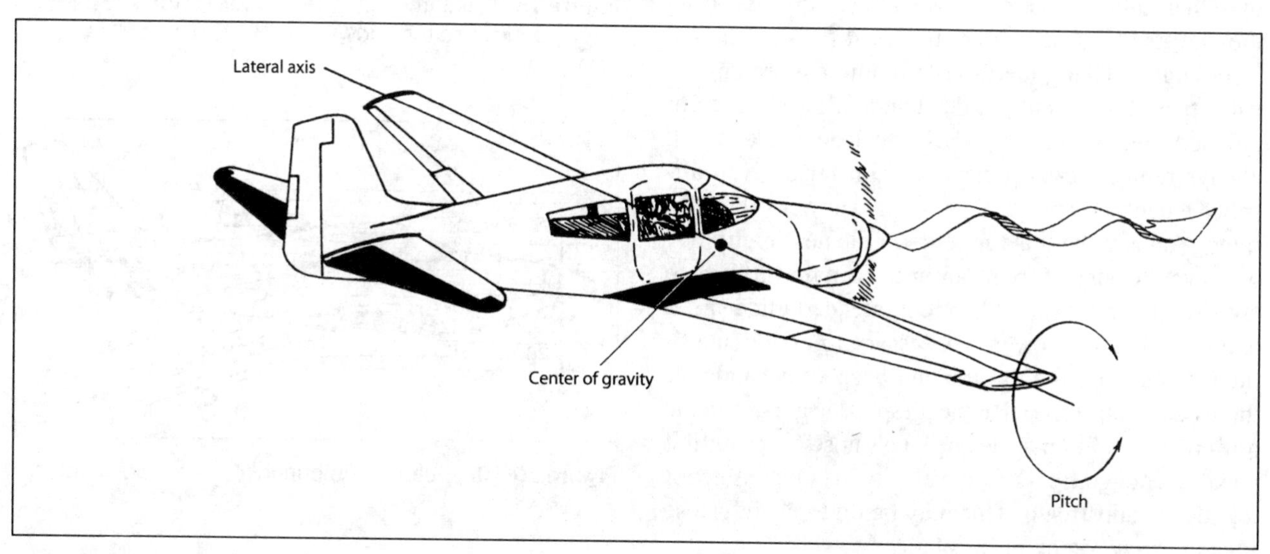

Figure 10-7. The elevators control movement about the lateral axis (pitch).

In order for the airplane to maintain level flight, the upward forces must balance the downward forces, as was covered in Chapter 3 (Figure 10-9).

The down forces are the airplane's weight (3,000 pounds) and the tail-down force (100 pounds), which total 3,100 pounds. In order to balance this, the up force (lift) must be 3,100 pounds. The wing itself contributes some pitching effects, as was mentioned in Chapter 3.

For airplanes with fixed, or nonadjustable, stabilizers, the stabilizer is set by the manufacturer at an angle that furnishes the correct down force at the expected cruising speed and CG position.

The tail-down force is the result of propeller slipstream, downwash from the wing, and the free-stream velocity (airspeed) (Figure 10-10).

Suppose you're flying straight and level (hands-off) at the design cruise speed and power setting and suddenly close the throttle. The slipstream force suddenly drops to practically nothing; the airplane starts slowing as thrust is no longer equal to drag, and the free-stream velocity also drops. You've suddenly lost some of the tail-down force. The result is that the nose drops. This is a healthy situation; the airplane is trying to pick up speed and reestablish the balance (Figure 10-11).

Of course, as the airplane slows, lift decreases and the airplane starts to accelerate downward for a very short time, but this is not so noticeable to you as the nosing-down action.

We'll disregard the airplane settling and think only in terms of the rotational movement caused by closing the throttle. One way of looking at it is to return to the seesaw of your earlier days. When the kid on the other end suddenly jumped off you set up your own "nose down" (the moments were no longer balanced).

You set the desired tail force for various airspeeds by either holding fore or aft wheel pressure or setting the elevator trim. If you are trimmed for straight and level flight, closing the throttle requires more up-elevator trim if you want to glide hands-off at the recommended glide speed. A propeller-driven airplane will always require less up-elevator trim for a given airspeed when using power than when in power-off conditions. You can see this for yourself the next pretty day when you're out just flying around. Trim the airplane to fly straight and level at the recommended glide speed and use whatever power is necessary to maintain altitude. Then close the throttle and keep your hands off the wheel. You'll find that the airspeed is greater in the power-off condition—the airplane's nose drops until it picks up enough free-stream velocity to compensate for the loss of slipstream. This may be up to about cruise speed, depending on the airplane.

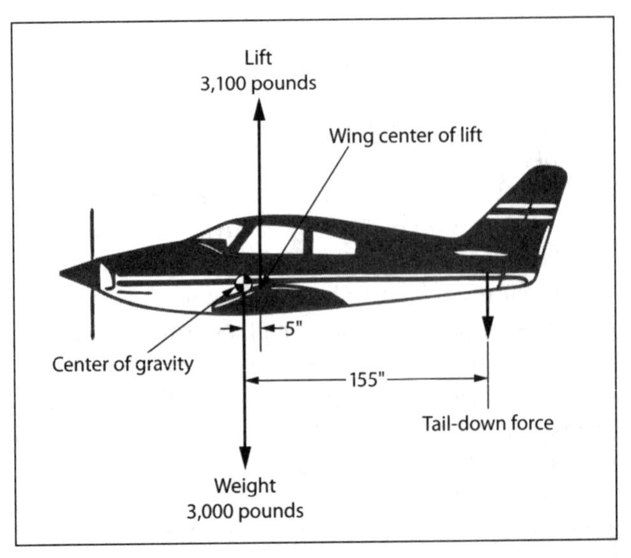

Figure 10-8. Airplane in balanced in straight and level flight.

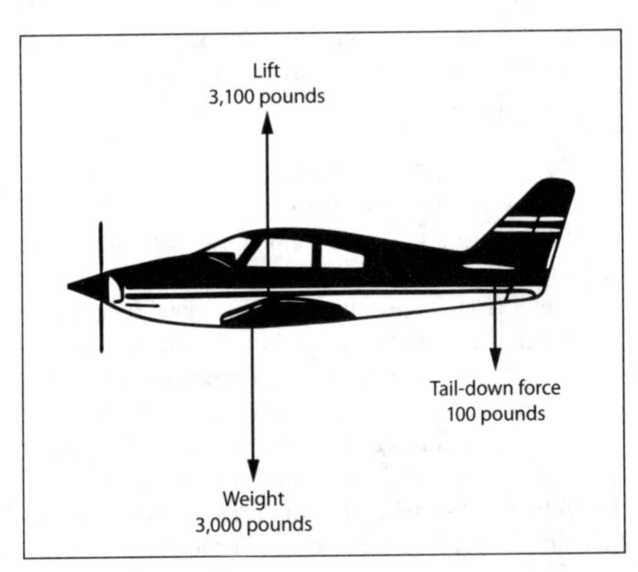

Figure 10-9. Summation of vertical forces: total up force 3,100 pounds and total down force 3,100 pounds—forces balanced.

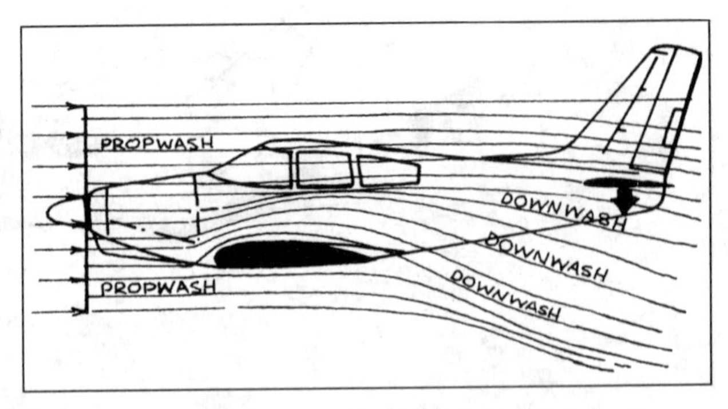

Figure 10-10. Factors contributing to the tail-down force.

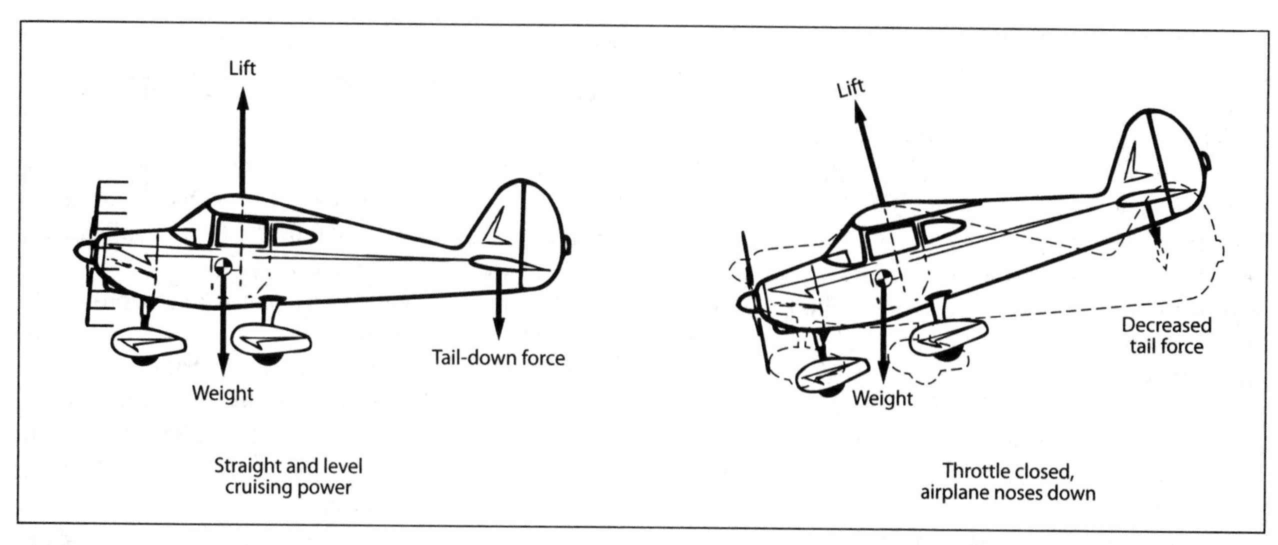

Figure 10-11.

The arrangement of having the CG ahead of the center of lift, and an aerodynamic tail-down force, results in the airplane always trying to return to a safe condition. Pull the nose up and the airplane slows and the tail-down force decreases. The nose will soon drop unless you retrim it or hold it up with increased back pressure. Push the nose down and it wants to come back up as the airspeed increases the tail-down force. The stable airplane wants to remain in its trimmed conditions, and this *inherent* (built-in) *stability* has gotten a lot of pilots out of trouble.

A hypothetical arrangement is shown in Figure 10-12. A lifting tail is necessary on this airplane in order to maintain balance. From a purely aerodynamic standpoint, the two lifting surfaces (wing and tail) are a good idea; from a stability standpoint, this type of configuration is not so good.

When you throttle back, the tail lift decreases and the nose tends to go up! This is not conducive to easy pilot control. The engineers would rather have a little less aerodynamic efficiency and more stability. So this arrangement is avoided—although it is not nearly as critical in a jet airplane. Actually, in some conditions

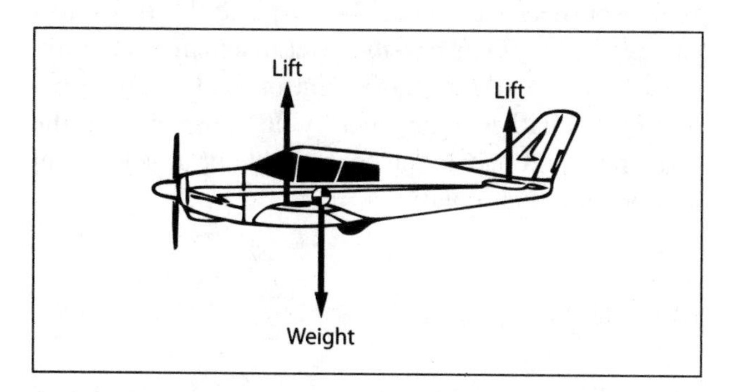

Figure 10-12. A different loading and tail force.

(high C_L, a tail upload may be present, even for the "standard" airplane that has a tail-down force at cruise.

The *canard* (horizontal-tail-first) designs have appeared again in the past few years. Some of these airplanes are quite efficient because both the wings and horizontal tail are lifting, versus the more conventional arrangement in Figure 10-9. One advantage of the canard-type is that it is stall and spin resistant if the forward surface is designed to lose its lift (and pitch the nose down to decrease the angle of attack of the main wing before it reaches the critical angle). The canard arrangement is not new (see photos of the Wright brothers' first powered flight), but the state of the art has improved so much that the newer designs are making a strong impact on the industry.

Power Effects on Stability

Power is considered to be destabilizing; that is, the addition of power tends to make the nose rise. The designer may offset this somewhat by having a high thrust line. The line through the center of the propeller disk passes above the CG so that, as thrust is increased, a moment is produced to counteract slipstream effects on the tail (Figure 10-13). Or the designer may offset the thrust line so that it passes above the CG (Figure 10-14).

A very low thrust line would be bad because it would tend to add to the nose-up effect of the slipstream on the horizontal tail surfaces (Figure 10-15).

You can get an idea of how an airplane will respond to power increase or decrease by its configuration. An older airliner like the MD-80, with aft-mounted engines near the longitudinal axis, won't have dramatic pitch changes with power changes, while a Boeing 737 will pitch up with added power due to its low-mounted engines. A Lake amphibian, with its very high-mounted pusher engine, pitches down with added

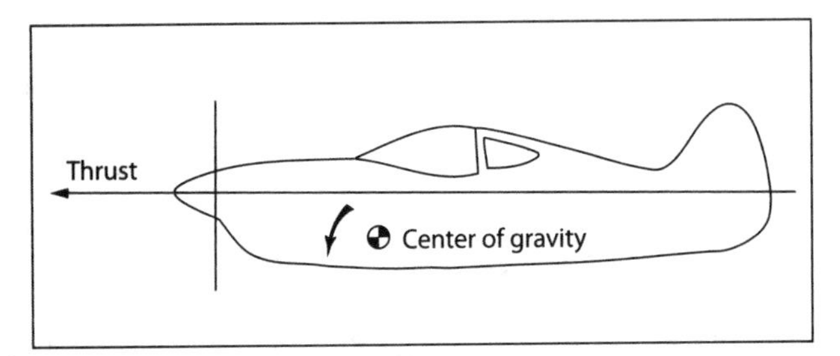

Figure 10-13. Exaggerated view of a high thrust line as an aid to stability.

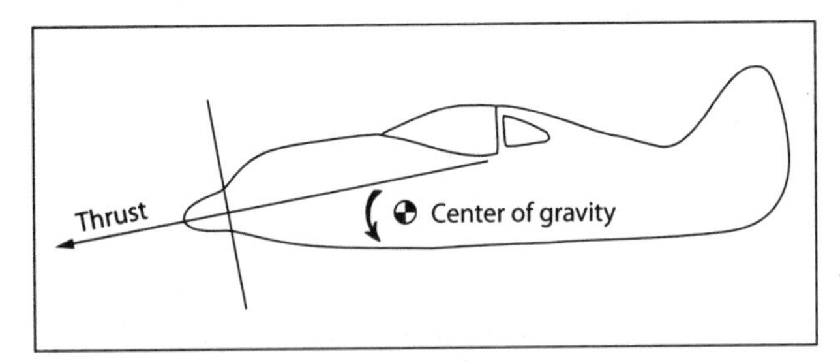

Figure 10-14. Offset thrust line.

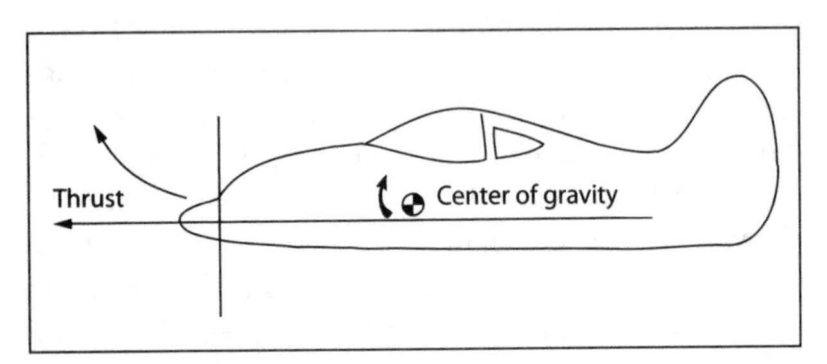

Figure 10-15. Low thrust line effects with application of power.

power. The fly-by-wire system of the Boeing 777 automatically compensates for the "pitch up with power" tendency from its underslung engines. The pitch change is there—that's basic physics—but the flight controls compensate for both power and configuration changes. Only speed changes cause the hand-flying 777 pilot to need pitch trim.

The thrust line of your airplane is fixed and there's nothing you can do about it; this has been presented only for your interest. All these factors have been taken into consideration in the certification. No airplane will be certificated in the normal or utility categories if it has dangerous tendencies.

How Loading Affects Longitudinal Static Stability

You can affect the longitudinal static stability of your airplane by the way you load it. If you stay within the loading limitations as given by the POH, you'll always have a statically stable airplane.

The properly loaded airplane is analogous to the steel ball inside the bowl. It will tend to stay in the attitude and airspeed at which it was trimmed (Figure 10-16). If the CG is moved aft, the airplane becomes less statically stable and does not have as strong a tendency to return to its original position. It is as if our bowl were made shallower (Figure 10-17).

The CG can be moved aft to a point where the airplane has *no* tendency to return but remains offset if displaced. It is as if the bowl had been completely flattened (Figure 10-18). By moving the CG even farther aft, the area of *negative* static stability is encountered (Figure 10-19). The bowl has been turned inside out.

It would seem at first glance that the more statically stable an airplane is made, the better its flight characteristics. This is true—up to a point. If an airplane is so stable that a great deal of force is needed to displace it from a certain attitude, control problems arise. The pilot may not be able to maneuver the airplane and make it do its job. This is more of a problem for fighters than for transports, however.

The problem with neutral static stability is that the plane does not tend to return to its trimmed state. If you load the airplane to such a condition, you might get into trouble. In a plane with neutral static stability the feel is changed considerably. After takeoff you may ease the nose up using normal back pressure and find that the nose attitude has overshot and is too high. You ease it down and again overshoot because you have been used to fighting the airplane's natural stability, and in this case it isn't there. *This type of situation causes accidents.* Particularly dangerous is the fact that the airplane could become unstable during the flight as the fuel is burned. Designers always place the fuel tanks as near to the CG as possible. But in a neutral stability condition, a rearward movement of the CG could put you into negative static stability. It's possible that the airplane could become uncontrollable or at least be in a very dangerous condition.

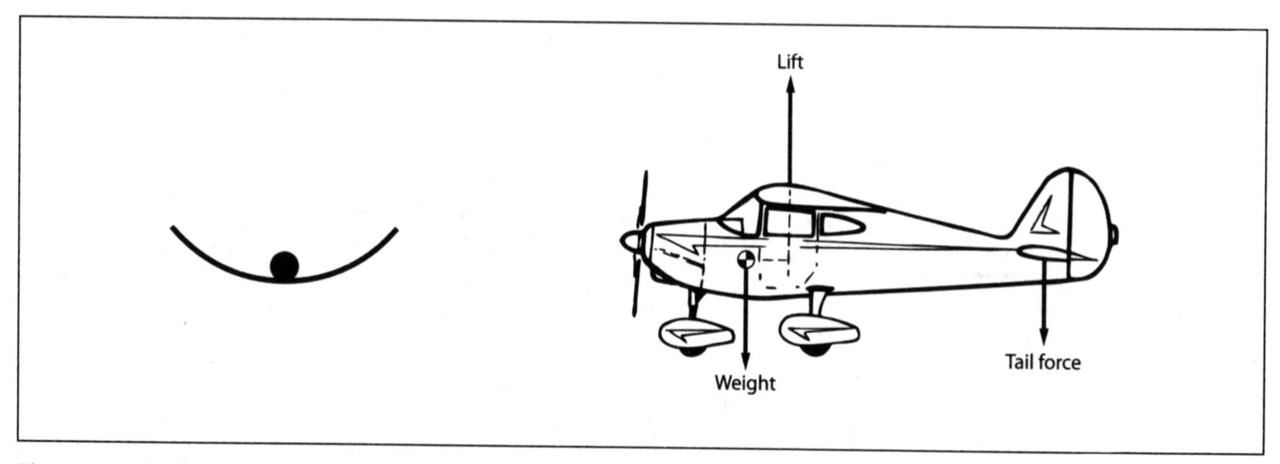

Figure 10-16. The properly loaded airplane—positive static stability (tail force exaggerated).

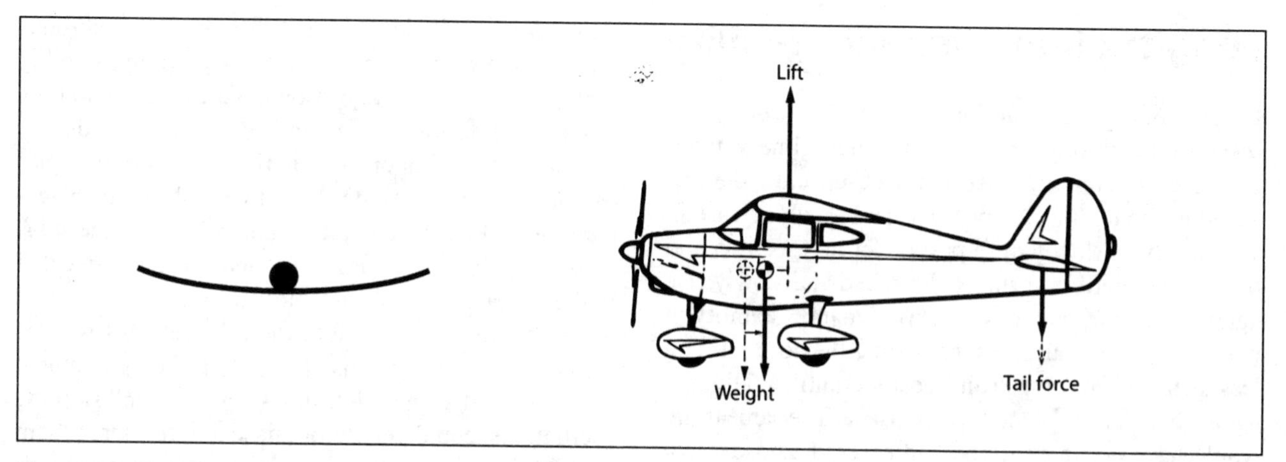

Figure 10-17. Effects of the center of gravity being moved rearward—less positive static stability.

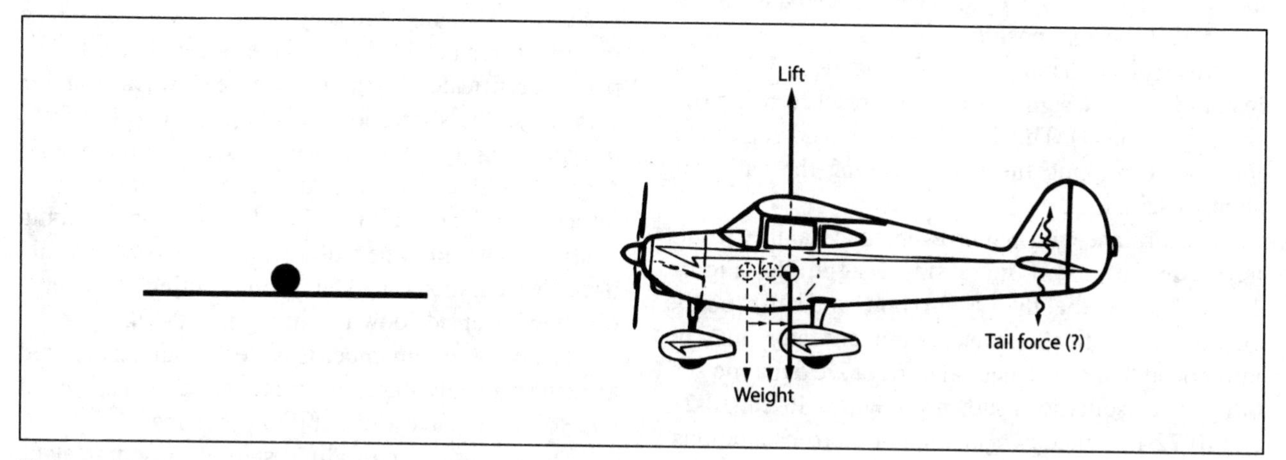

Figure 10-18. Neutral static stability.

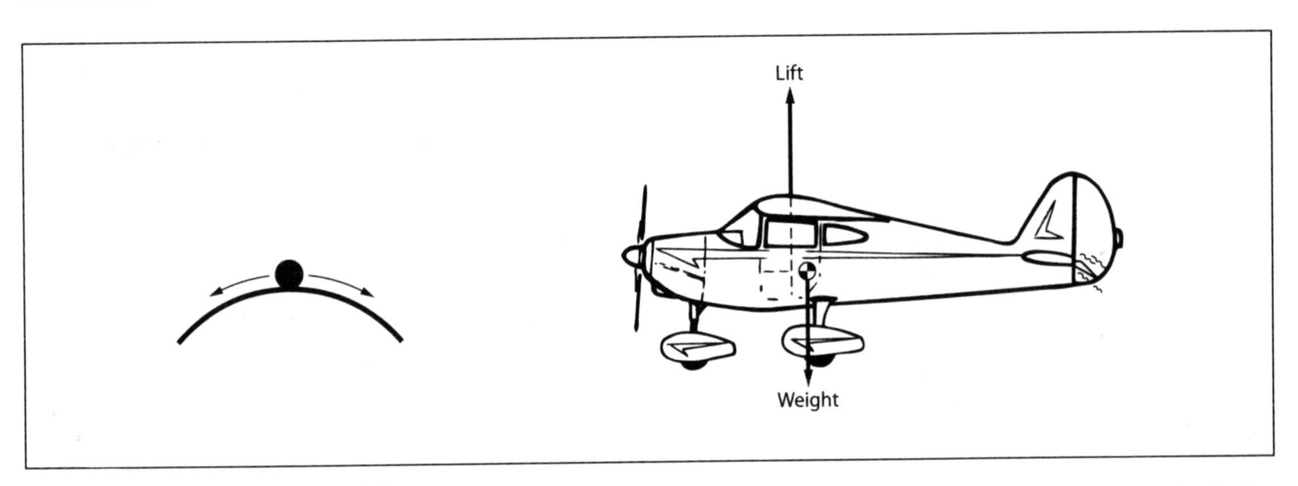

Figure 10-19. Negative static stability.

Longitudinal Dynamic Stability

Learn your plane's actions *(dynamic stability)* in response to its *static stability*. The next time you are flying cross-country, ease the nose up until the airspeed is about 20 K below cruise and slowly release it. The nose will slowly drop past the cruise position and the airplane will pick up excess speed and slowly rise again. If the airplane has *positive* dynamic stability, it may do this several times, each time the nose moving less distance from the cruise position until finally it is again flying straight and level at cruise. The same thing would have occurred if you had eased the nose down (Figure 10-20). This is like the steel ball in the bowl as cited earlier. It was dynamically stable and finally resumed its normal position.

An airplane that has *neutral* dynamic stability as a result of some design factor would react to being offset (Figure 10-21). This is as if some outside unknown force were rocking the bowl, keeping the ball constantly oscillating.

The airplane with *negative* dynamic stability would have oscillations of increasing magnitude (Figure 10-22). You see that the system (bowl and ball) and the airplane are statically stable, but other factors may be introduced that create neutral or negative dynamic stability. The oscillations shown in Figures 10-20, 10-21, and 10-22 are called *phugoid* or *long mode* oscillations. They are long enough that they can be easily controlled by the pilot and are considered of relatively little importance. The phugoid period of the C-152 is damped and is approximately 28 seconds, as an example, and it can be stopped by the pilot at any time. The airplane you are flying may have a neutrally or negatively stable phugoid oscillations and still be completely safe. (So don't be disappointed or worried if, when trying the experiment at the beginning of this section, you find these slow oscillations do not decrease in amplitude.) An airplane with neutral or negative dynamic stability in these long modes can be flown quite safely with little or no effort, for the periods may be many seconds.

Of primary importance is the *short mode* (rapid) oscillation, which can be started with abrupt displacement of stick or yoke in pitch. The periods of the short mode may be in fractions of seconds. You can see that if the short mode is unstable the oscillations could increase dangerously before the pilot realizes what is happening. Even if the oscillations are being damped, it's possible that the pilot, in trying to "help" stop the oscillations, could get out of phase and reinforce them to the point where g forces could cause structural failure. Usually such problems are caused by poor elevator design or balancing, and they are always solved by the manufacturer before the airplane is certificated. Airplanes certificated by the FAA have *positive dynamic stability* in the short mode. If the plane is offset from its path abruptly, it will return in a series of rapid, converging oscillations, or a "deadbeat" (instantaneous) return. (You can see this when flying hands-off on a gusty day.) An airplane that is *statically unstable* would have no oscillations at all but would continually diverge (the bowl is upside down as in Figure 10-19).

The point to remember is to keep your certificated airplane statically stable by correct placement of weight and you won't have any stability problems.

The dynamic longitudinal stability of an airplane is affected by *stick-fixed* or *stick-free* conditions. This means that the airplane's response is different if the elevators are "locked" by the pilot (wheel, stick, or elevators fixed) or are allowed to float free (hands off stick or wheel—or elevators free). As you probably have already guessed, the *elevator-fixed* condition is more stable and the airplane's oscillations would be more likely to dampen (Figure 10-20). Aerodynamics texts sometimes use pages of calculations to show why it is

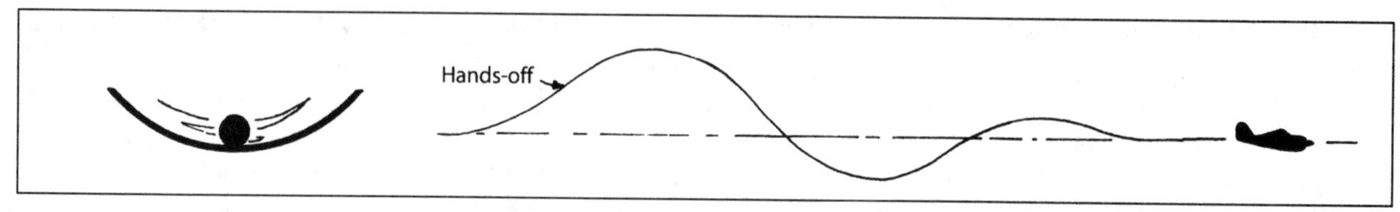

Figure 10-20. Flight path of a dynamically stable airplane (hands-off).

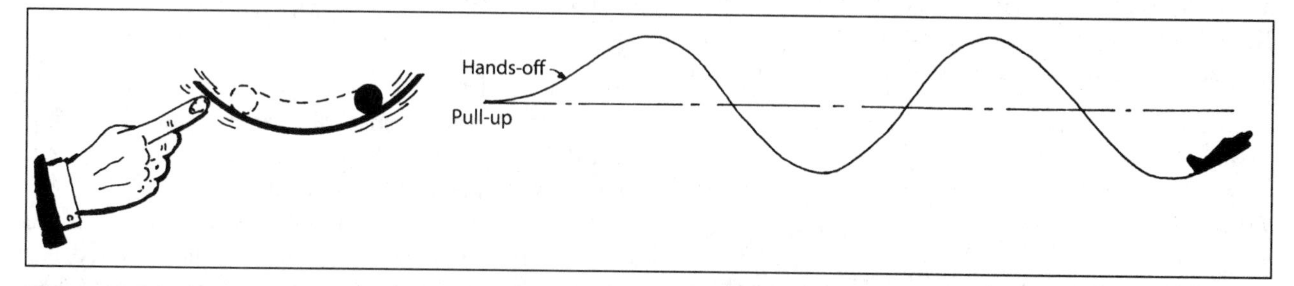

Figure 10-21. Flight path of an airplane with neutral dynamic stability (hands-off); no decrease in oscillations.

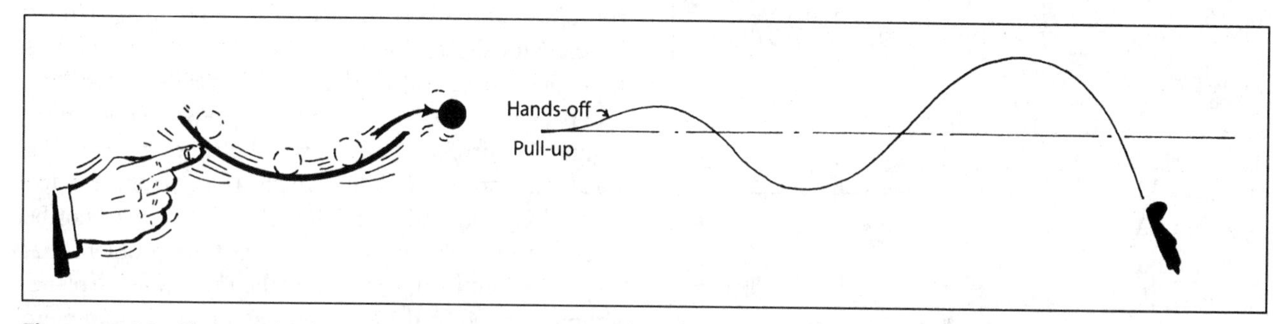

Figure 10-22. Flight path of an airplane with negative dynamic stability (hands-off); oscillation increase in amplitude.

so, but it all boils down to common sense. Look at Figure 10-23, which shows the elevator free and fixed. In Figure 10-23A, the pilot has pulled the nose up sharply and immediately released (freed) the elevator. As you can see, the aerodynamic loads tend to make the elevator position itself parallel to the airflow instead of staying parallel to the chord line (where it belongs) to help straighten the airplane out. As the airplane pitches up and down in its oscillation, the elevator follows the line of least resistance and moves itself out of the airflow.

In Figure 10-23B the pilot or autopilot has returned the elevator to the neutral position and has locked it there so that more surface is available to stabilize the situation. You might consider that the elevator-fixed condition is like an arrow with the proper amount of feather area; the elevator-free one is as if some of the feathers were clipped off, allowing the arrow to wobble more in flight. Aerodynamicists would rightly note that the elevator normally does not float the full angles shown here, but it moves up or down to a lesser degree.

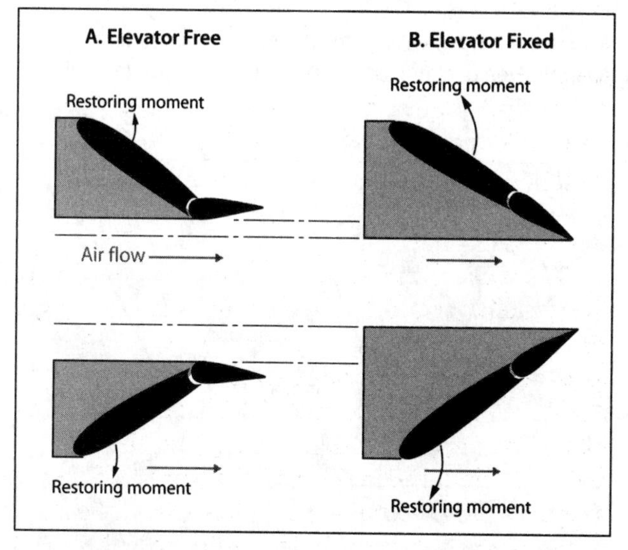

Figure 10-23. Exaggerated effects of fixed and free elevator on dynamic longitudinal stability. **A.** The elevator floats up (or down, as also shown) out of the airstream, decreasing the damping (stabilizing!) effect. **B.** The elevator is "locked" (fixed) and presents more stabilizing area to damp the oscillations. Compare the shaded areas for A and B.

Figure 10-24 is an actual trace of an airplane's dynamic stability (phugoid) at cruise power in the clean condition. Note that the elevator-free condition is basically neutrally stable while the elevator-fixed oscillations are heavily damped.

The periods from peak to peak are 30 seconds in the elevator-free configuration.

Figure 10-25 is an analysis of the airplane in Figure 10-24 showing a trace of the nose pitch attitude (degrees) versus time. In this case, the exercise started at 107 K (Figure 10-24) and a nose-up attitude of 8°. Note that in the *elevator-fixed condition the pitch attitude settled down to a value very close to the original.*

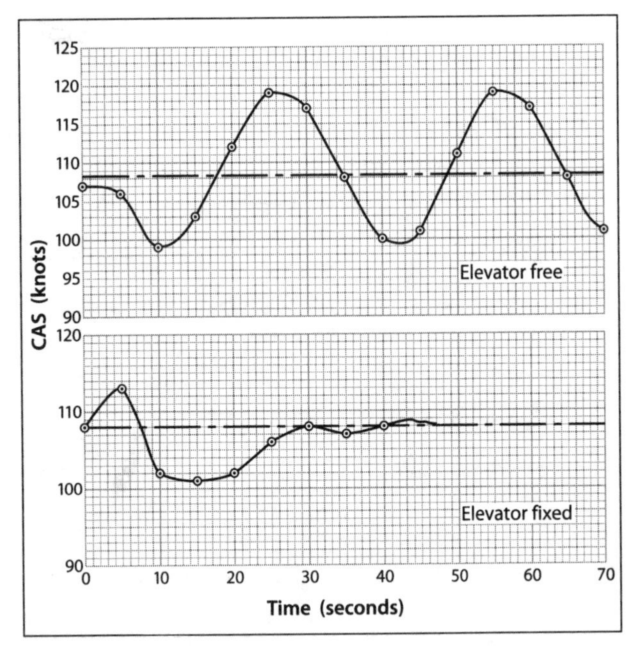

Figure 10-24. Elevator-free and -fixed oscillation (airspeed versus time) for a particular airplane in the cruise configuration.

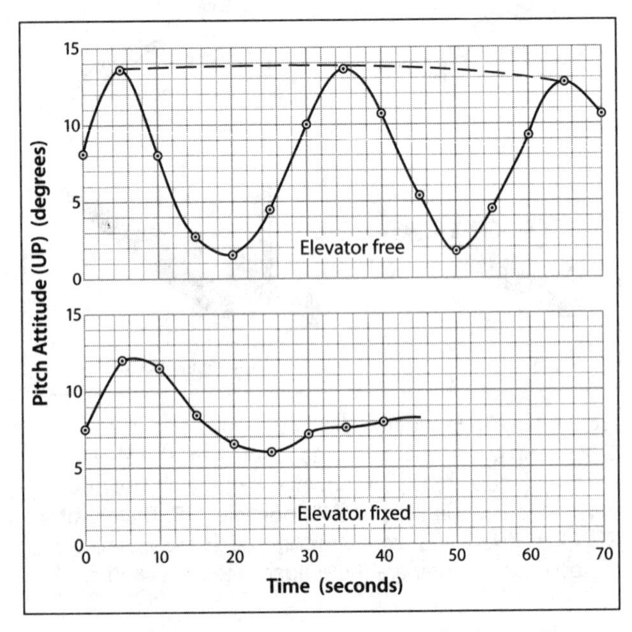

Figure 10-25. Pitch attitude versus time for the airplane in Figure 10-24.

The dashed line in the elevator-free condition in Figure 10-25 shows that the airplane might "some day" settle back down to the original pitch attitude, but, as indicated earlier, the oscillations can be quickly and easily stopped by the pilot (by "fixing" the elevators), so there's no problem.

Longitudinal Control

Elevator

You are familiar with elevators as a means of longitudinal control; airplanes also have been designed utilizing a *stabilator.* You may have trained on such an airplane. Let's review the stabilizer-elevator system.

You use the elevator to change the camber of the horizontal tail system, which changes the tail force. For the design cruise airspeed, the elevators are designed to "float" parallel with the stabilizer. Any change from this speed and power setting must be compensated for by elevator deflection. The normal airplane requires that forward pressure be held for speeds above this, and back pressure be held for any speeds below cruise. Rotate the airplane to the desired attitude by exerting fore or aft pressure on the wheel. If an airplane is too stable longitudinally, the elevator control may not be effective enough for good control. One problem that airplane manufacturers face is the too-stable airplane, although to be truthful, it's not as much of a problem to them as the unstable type. It has been found through experience that the total horizontal tail area should be 15 to 20% of the effective wing area and the elevator should make up about 35 to 45% of the total horizontal tail surface area for most general aviation propeller airplanes. The farther the horizontal tail is from the CG, the less area is necessary for the required stability (tail moment = distance × force).

The stabilizer-elevator combination is an airfoil, and you vary the tail force by positioning the elevators with the wheel or with elevator trim.

The properly designed airplane requires forward pressure for airspeed above the trim speed you have selected, and back pressure for speeds below the trim speed (this applies whether you trim it for a speed 30% above stall or at the airplane's maximum speed). This indicates *positive static stability.* You can see that this is what you've been encountering all along in your flights in FAA-certificated airplanes. A happy medium should be found; the airplane must be stable but not be too hard to displace, or maneuvering problems may arise. The greater the deviation in velocity, the more pressure is required, because the airplane is stable and resists your efforts to vary its airspeed from trim speed because of too little required down force.

As you move the CG aft you may find you can't set any particular speed as trim speed.

Stick or Wheel Forces

Figure 10-26 shows the stick (or wheel) force required to pitch the nose up (or down) at two CG positions at a particular chosen trim speed. A fictitious airplane is used, but the numbers are reasonable for a general aviation airplane (clean) trimmed for approach or holding. Assuming that push or pull forces are zero at the trim speed of 90 K, notice that the back pressure required to slow it up and hold it at 75 K is 8 pounds at forward CG and 4 pounds at a more aft CG. The stick or wheel forces will become even lighter as the CG is moved aft (dashed line) and at some point could approach zero. (The airplane may pitch up or down without help from the pilot.) The lines are curved because the dynamic pressure, q, goes up as the *square* of the airspeed. With a forward CG, the forces required to pull up or push over are much higher and the airplane would lack maneuverability. More about forward CG later in the chapter.

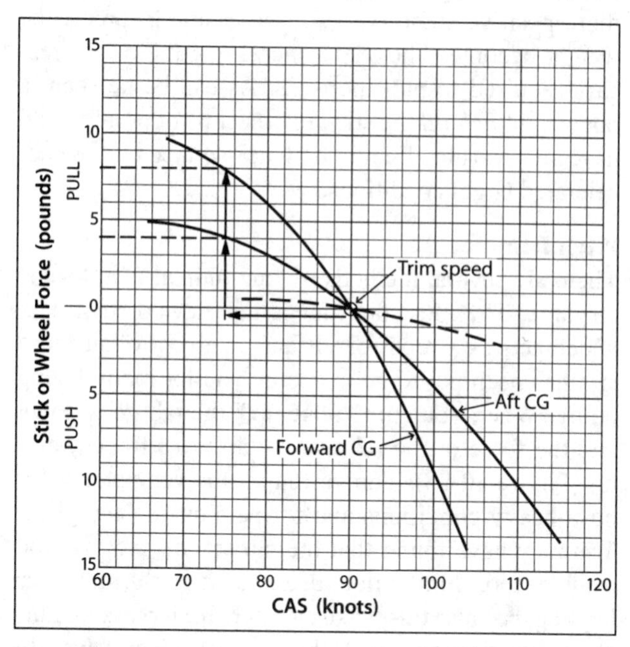

Figure 10-26. Effects of CG position on stick or wheel forces at a particular trim speed.

Suppose you are indicating 90 K and have the elevator trim tab set at what you think is the correct position. In the normal airplane this would mean that, if you applied fore or aft pressure on the wheel, the pressure necessary to hold this nose position would increase as the airspeed changed—not so in the neutrally stable airplane. You are fooling yourself by even trying to trim the airplane.

When you pull the nose up and the speed decreases, the airplane isn't fighting the back pressure and will continue in this attitude without any help from you. Wheel pressure is *not* a function of airspeed in this case and the airplane could continue to a stall, the nose would then drop, and it would maintain this nose-down attitude. This is, of course, assuming you are flying hands-off. Naturally you'll be flying the airplane and will ease the nose back down before the stall occurs. This is not to imply that the airplane is uncontrollable, but it does mean you'll have to make a conscious effort to return the nose to the proper position if it is displaced—and on a bumpy day this could get mighty tiresome. On landing, you will not be fighting the plane's stability. When you flare for the landing, you will probably overdo it because of the very light back pressure required, compared with what you've been used to. You'll probably get the nose too high, then consciously have to ease it over and may set up a cycle (Figure 10-27).

If you've trimmed the airplane for a glide, you'll normally expect the required back pressure to increase as the plane slows during the landing—that's why you could get into trouble in this situation.

The airplane with *negative* longitudinal stability will aggravate any displacement. If the nose is raised

Figure 10-27. Landing (?) a neutrally stable airplane.

in the neutrally stable airplane, it stays at that attitude until you (or some other force) lower it. The airplane that is negatively stable tends to get an even more nose-high attitude.

If you load the airplane with too much weight in the rear and get into an unstable condition, a serious accident is almost certain to occur. Take an extreme situation: You've loaded the airplane until the CG is much too far aft. You realize that there's quite a bit of weight back there and set the elevator tab to what you think is about the right amount of nose-down trim. You go roaring down the runway, ease the nose up—and it just keeps going up. This is neither the time, place, nor altitude to be practicing stalls. It may require more down-elevator than you have available—and that's that. One possibility in a case like that would be to trim nose UP, giving more elevator or stabilator area and overriding the pressure. The UP tab *might* make the elevator/stabilator more effective and save the situation. The same might apply if you can't get the nosewheel down and want to hold the nose off as long as possible on landing. You might trim it nose DOWN on the roll-out. Talk to some of the more experienced pilots you know about this, but always avoid loading beyond the aft edge of the CG envelope.

Stick Force Per G

One measure of an airplane's maneuverability is its *stick-force-per-g* factor, which is basically the pounds of pull or push necessary to change by 1 g the acceleration acting parallel to the vertical axis. A fighter or aerobatic airplane should have comparatively light control forces so that pull-ups, loops, steep turns, and other maneuvers requiring extended pilot input would not be fatiguing. The stick forces must not be so light, however, as to easily allow the pilot to overstress the airplane. In WW II, before hydraulically boosted controls were in wide use, the stick-force-per-g limits were 3 to 8 pounds for fighters and a maximum of 35 pounds for transports. This meant, for instance, that a fighter having a stick force per g of 5 pounds would require 20 pounds of stick force to pull an added 4 g's. The pilot on a transport of that era who wanted to pull those 4 extra g's from cruise would be required to exert up to 140 pounds back pressure, which discouraged an impulse to do loops in that airplane.

As far as CG position is concerned, the stick-force-per-g idea follows that of the unaccelerated longitudinal stability reactions. *As the CG is moved aft, the stick forces become lighter* and the airplane can have more g's exerted on it with less effort by the pilot. With a CG near, or at, the aft limit, what starts out as a 3-g loop pull-up could end up as a 6- or 7-g "serious situation" as the airplane continues to pitch up with little or no additional back pressure.

For a given CG position, the stick force required to pull, say, 3 g's is *higher in a turn* than in a wings-level pull-up. In a wings-level pull-up, the added lift being produced by back pressure is acting directly against weight. The pilot would not have to exert quite as much control force as in a bank where only the vertical *component* of lift is acting directly *against* weight.

Altitude reduces the stick force per g. The airplane at a higher altitude, all other factors equal, will require less push-pull force to get a certain g loading.

Manufacturers may affect the longitudinal stability and stick (or wheel) forces of the airplane by adding a weight either ahead *of* or behind the stick pivot point. This "bobweight," if placed ahead of the pivot point, under normal conditions will tend to move the stick or wheel forward, providing a nose-down effort to provide more positive stability. With increasing g forces, the weight becomes "heavier," increasing the back pressure required to pull more g's. As can be be seen, a bobweight *behind* the stick or wheel pivot point would have an opposite effect in both accelerated and nonaccelerated flight conditions.

Pitch Trim

There are several methods of longitudinal trim for the airplane. The most familiar is the elevator trim tab, which acts as a "control surface on a control surface" and has been put to good use by you for many flying hours. When you trim "nose-up," the tab goes down and the force of the relative wind moves the elevator up (Figure 10-28). You've found this very handy for nose-heavy conditions and for help during the glide. You may have found that the tab set this way caused trouble, too. Some pilots use almost full up-trim for landing, because this makes for light back pressure during the landing process. If they should suddenly have to take it around, the application of power may result in a severe tendency for the nose to rise. The slipstream hits the trim tab and elevator, which are greatly displaced at

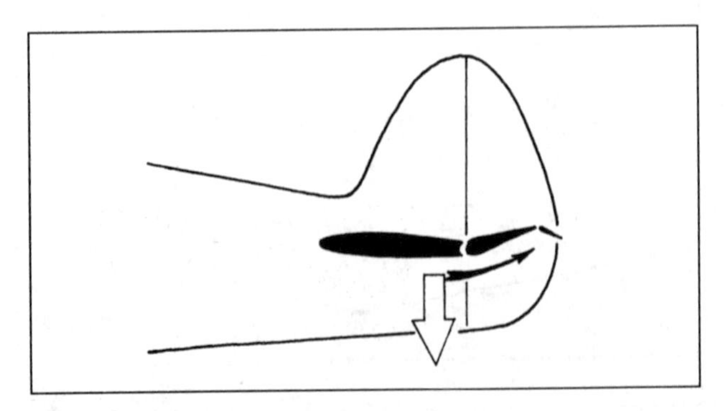

Figure 10-28. Elevator trim tab, set for nose-up.

the low-speed, power-off condition; this is particularly dangerous if the elevator tab control is geared so that it requires many turns to get back to a more nose-down setting. If the airplane were not so close to the ground, it would be amusing to watch the pilot, who can't decide whether to take one hand off the wheel (pushing forward with both hands) and make a grab for the trim control, or hold the nose down with both hands and try to get altitude first. The usual result is that the pilot does both, frantically moving the right hand from wheel to trim control and gradually getting things under control. Seen from outside the airplane, the maneuvering looks like a whale with a severe case of hiccups. This problem usually is not quite so critical in multiengine planes, because the elevators are not so much in the slipstream. In any airplane—single, multi, prop, or jet—the nose is harder to keep down as the speed increases, though the single-engine, high-powered prop plane gives the most trouble under these conditions. The airplane with an adjustable stabilizer can give the same problems, so don't think that the trim tab alone is the culprit.

Another method of elevator trimming is to use bungees. These consist of springs that tend to hold the elevator in the desired position when you set the trim control (Figure 10-29). The spring also acts as a damper for any forces that might be working through the system. You set the spring tension with the trim control. Actually you couldn't care less what the spring tension is—you move the trim handle or wheel until you get the desired result. It's doubtful that you could tell by "flight feel" that the airplane had a bungee instead of a trim tab unless you noticed it during the preflight check (and you should have).

Another method of longitudinal trimming is the movable or controllable stabilizer (Figure 10-30). The cockpit control merely turns a jack screw to position the stabilizer.

Some transports automatically trim the stabilizer to zero-out any elevator deflection, thereby reducing drag.

Special Types of Tabs

Link balance tab—If an airplane is found during flight tests to have heavy control forces, it may require a *link balance tab,* which is a tab mechanically linked so that it moves opposite to the control surface and makes the control forces much lighter. For instance, the link balance tab on an elevator moves down as the elevator moves up—a sort of mutual aid society. These tabs, by the way, also can act as trim tabs when variable length linkage is used. (You vary the linkage length when you move the trim control in the cockpit. This type of arrangement, called a *lagging tab,* is shown in Figure 10-31.

In some instances the control forces may be too light—that is, the elevator or stabilator may move so easily that in extreme conditions the pilot could inadvertently overstress the airplane. The manufacturer may use a leading link balance tab (Figure 10-32) in order to increase the control forces necessary to displace the control surface.

Servo tab—It'll probably be a long time before you use this system, for only older large planes have them. The control wheel is connected to the tab rather than to the elevator itself. When the pilot moves the wheel back, the tab is deflected downward. The impact air

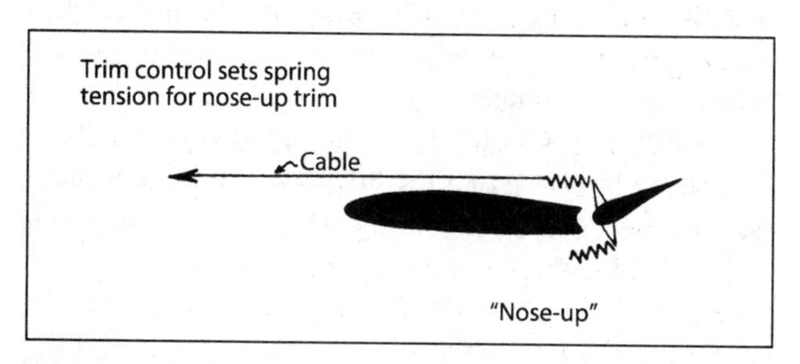

Figure 10-29. Bungees as a method of elevator trim.

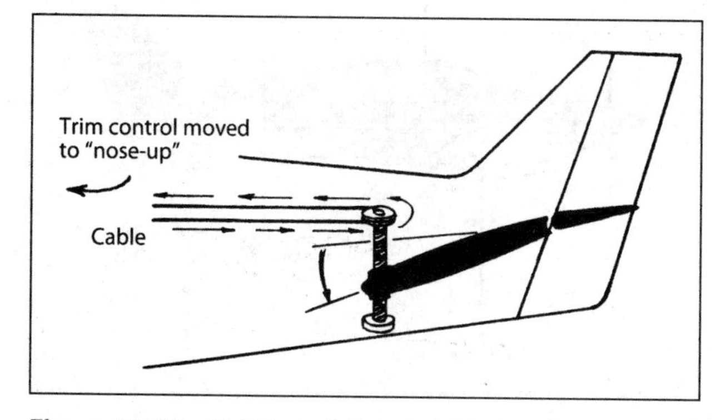

Figure 10-30. Stabilizer trim, nose-up.

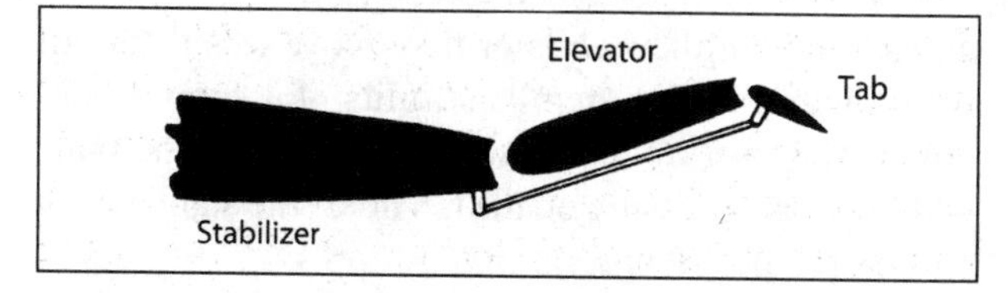

Figure 10-31. Link balance tab, lagging.

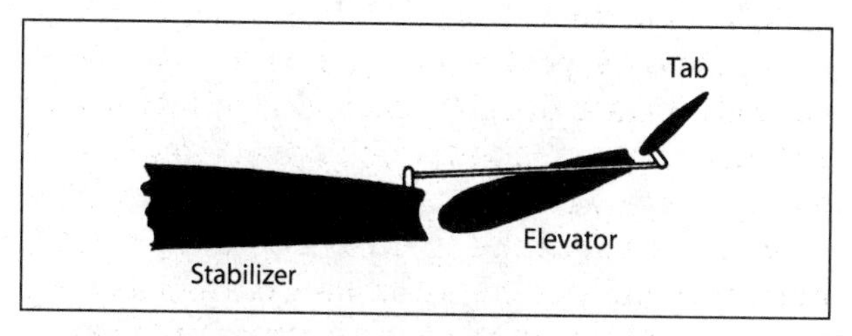

Figure 10-32. Link balance tab, leading.

pressure strikes the tab and the elevator is deflected upward. The elevator is free-floating and moves in accordance with the tab deflection.

The principle of the trim tab is simple. It uses a small area, long arm, and greater angular deflection to deflect a control surface of greater area to a lesser deflection. (Got it?)

Stabilator

The stabilator is popular as a means of longitudinal control for general aviation airplanes. It's, in effect, no more than an airfoil whose angle of attack is controlled by the control wheel and trim control. The stabilator is hinged at its aerodynamic center. In computing the tail force, use the lift equation for a wing of the stabilator's airfoil and area. You would have a C_L versus angle of attack curve and could use the equation $L = C_L S(\rho/2) V^2$; the problem would be complicated by the fact that the down wash and slipstream effects are hard to predict. But the principle is exactly the same as that for the wing.

The stabilator was first used as an effective means of control for jets in the transonic region (Mach 0.8 to 1.2). The elevator system lost effectiveness in this speed range due to shock wave effects on the stabilizer, and severe nose-down tendencies were encountered—with little control to offset these forces. In effect, the elevator was "blanketed" behind the shock wave. It was found that by moving the entire stabilizer-elevator (or stabilator) system, longitudinal control could be maintained in this critical range.

The stabilator control, when properly balanced, is quite sensitive at low speeds. (The pilot who has been flying an elevator-equipped airplane usually tends to slightly overcontrol in moving the nose up or down for the first few minutes.) Because the stabilator has more movable area, it usually does not use as much angular travel. Whereas an elevator may travel 30° up and 20° down, the stabilator may move less than half this amount. One system has limits of 18° up and 2° down. The trim tab for the stabilator works in the same way—impact pressure on the tab holds the stabilator in the desired position.

Forward CG Considerations

It would seem, from the discussion of the aft CG position, that the farther forward the CG, the better off you are. (Okay now, everybody run to the front of the airplane.) This is true for longitudinal stability but not from a control standpoint.

Let's start out with a longitudinally balanced airplane (Figure 10-8). Note in Figure 10-8 that there is no elevator deflection; the airplane is at design cruise speed and properly balanced weightwise. For our hypothetical situation, suppose that during the flight, weight is moved forward, so the CG also is moved forward another 5 inches (Figure 10-33). In order to maintain balance, the tail force must be increased, and this is done by back pressure or use of the trim tab.

Of course, you don't give a hang for the value of the tail force but would trim it until the nose stays where it belongs. If you move the CG forward another 5 inches, the required tail force would be further increased and more up-elevator would be necessary. By moving the CG forward you would soon reach a point where full up-elevator would be required. If the throttle were chopped, the loss in effectiveness of the elevators would result in a definite nosing down of the airplane. You'd be in the unhappy situation of being unable to slow down because you'd be using full elevator to maintain level flight and would have none left to ease the nose up. Of course, you couldn't chop power because control would be lost. In this exaggerated situation you'd have a tiger by the tail. The manufacturer sets forward CG limitations strict enough so that if you comply you'll never get into a dangerous situation.

You have seen that power nearly always results in a nose-up tendency, so the airplane can have a more forward CG with power on. A critical condition could

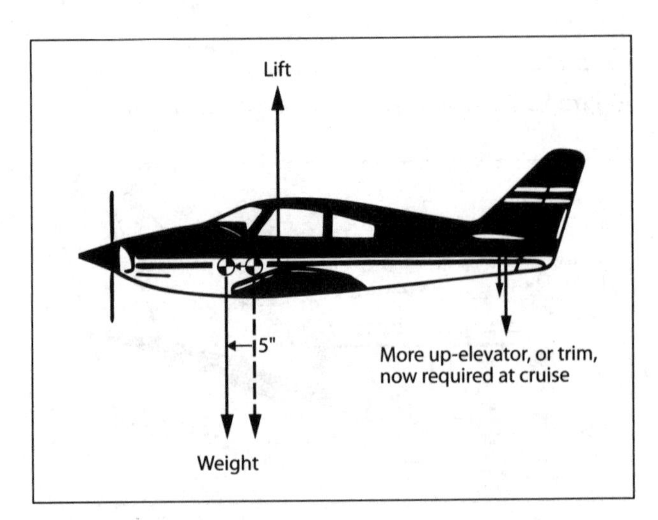

Figure 10-33. Center of gravity moved forward 5 inches.

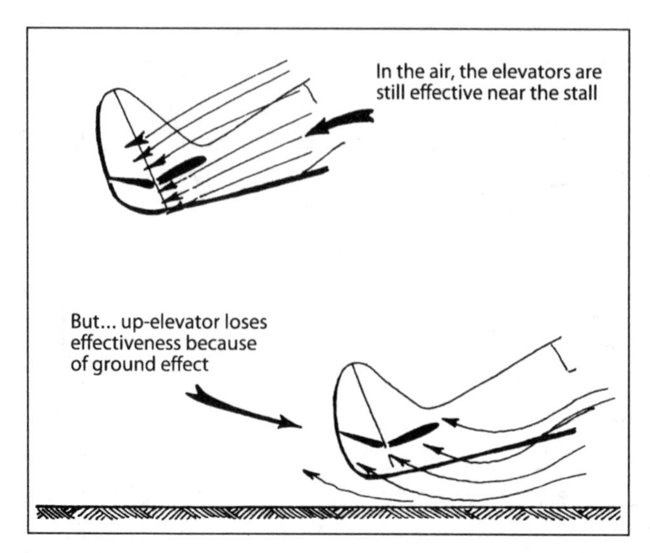

Figure 10-34. Ground effect and elevator effectiveness.

exist at very low airspeeds (approaching a stall) in the power-off condition, where the elevators are relatively inefficient due to lack of slipstream and airspeed. Such a condition would limit the most forward CG location in flight. This would also seem to be the same condition for the landing, but this is not the case. *The ground effect on landing results in a further decrease in elevator control effectiveness* (as can be seen in Figure 10-34). *In fact, it could take up to 15° more elevator deflection to get the stall (same configuration) in ground effect as at altitude, depending on the make and model. Elevator effectiveness on landing is one of the most limiting factors in establishing the forward CG of the airplane.*

Airplane Weight and Balance

The CG of an airplane must remain within certain limits for stability and control. These limits are expressed by designers in terms of percentage of the mean aerodynamic chord (Figure 10-35).

The airplane's *Weight and Balance Form* usually expresses these limits in the form of inches from the *datum* (the point from which the measurements are taken). This datum is at different points for different airplane makes and models. Some airplanes use the junction of the leading edge of the wing with the fuselage as the datum; others use the front face of the firewall. The allowable CG range is expressed in inches aft of this point, such as "allowable center of gravity range—from 13.1 to 17.5 inches aft of datum" (Figure 10-36).

Sometimes the datum is an imaginary point ahead of the airplane. This is easier to compute, in that all the moment arms are positive. The datum usually is picked so that it is an even distance ahead of a well-defined position such as the junction of the wing's leading edge with the fuselage.

Measurements are taken from a reference point and added to or subtracted from the datum to get the proper arm. In Figure 10-37, you see that the wing's leading edge is 70 inches aft of the datum. If object A, weighing 10 pounds, is placed at a point 10 inches behind the junction of the leading edge of the wing and the fuselage, its weight (10 pounds) would be multiplied by 70 + 10, or 80 inches. Its moment would be 800 lb-in. Object B, also weighing 10 pounds, 10 inches ahead of the leading edge point, would have a moment of 70 – 10, or 60 inches times its weight, or 600 lb-in.

The CG limits for the airplane in Figure 10-37 are expressed as "CG allowable range from 80 to 87 inches aft of datum."

Here's how you might run a weight and balance for the above-mentioned airplane: the manufacturer will give its Basic Empty Weight (the weight at which the airplane is actually ready to fly except for usable fuel, pilots, passengers, and baggage—in other words, with full oil and unusable fuel and not lacking any mechanical parts). Its empty CG position and/or moment are also given.

To find the empty weight and CG position for the hypothetical airplane, place each of the three wheels on a scale and level the airplane, using a bubble level on

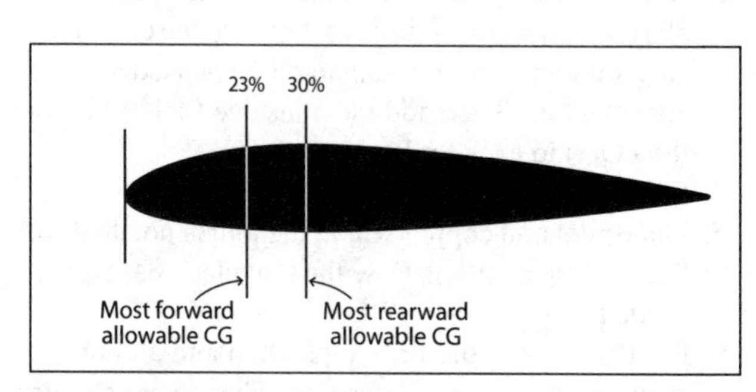

Figure 10-35. Allowable range for center of gravity, expressed as percentage of mean aerodynamic chord (average wing chord).

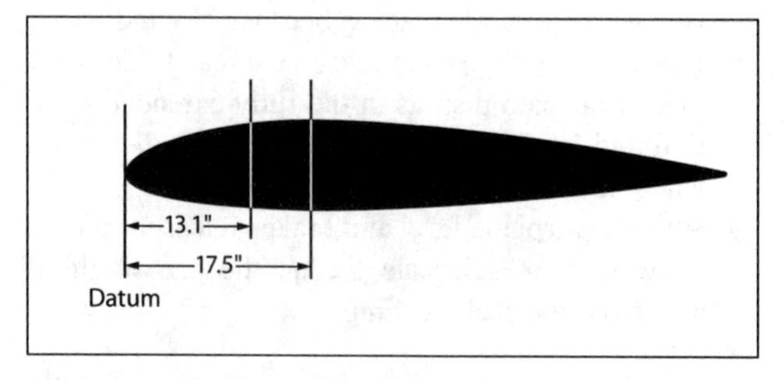

Figure 10-36. Allowable range for center of gravity, expressed as inches aft of datum.

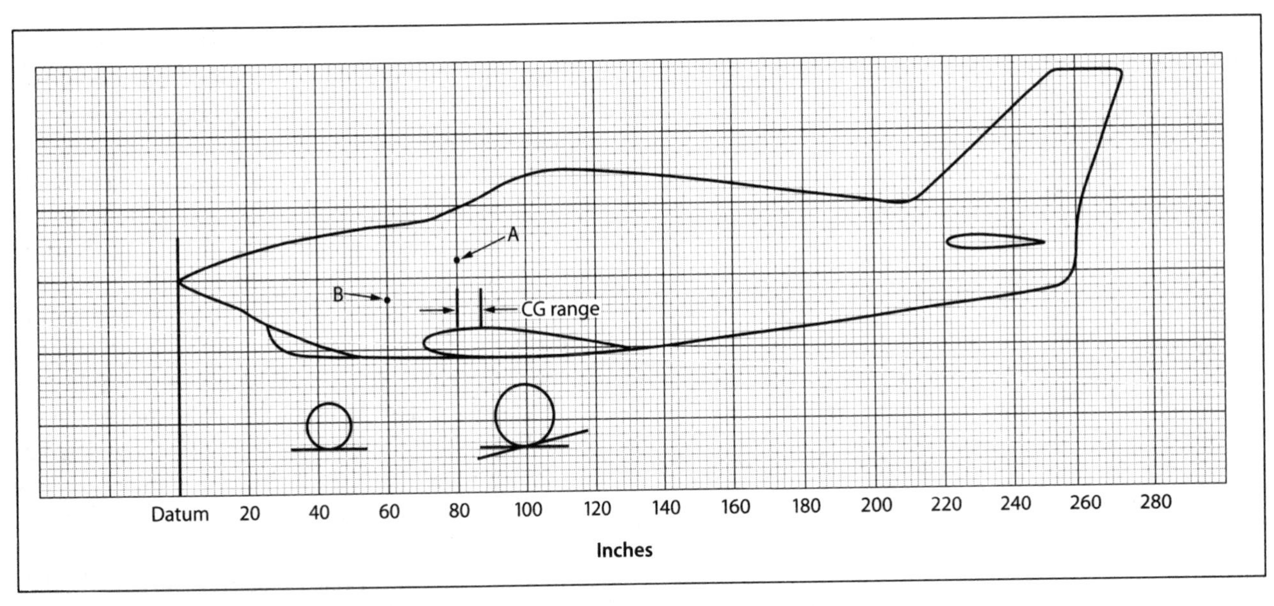

Figure 10-37. Weight and balance diagram.

the points (usually protruding screws) on the fuselage marked LEVEL. Because you'd want the Basic Empty Weight of a particular airplane, before putting it on the scales you'd do the following:

1. Be sure that items checked in the equipment list are installed in the proper location in the airplane.
2. Remove excessive dirt, grease, moisture, and foreign items such as rags, tools, sleeping passengers, or dead horses from the airplane before weighing.
3. Defuel the airplane, then open all fuel drains until all remaining fuel is drained. Operate the engine on each tank until all undrainable fuel is used and the engine stops. Then add the unusable fuel (given in the POH) to each tank.
4. Fill with oil to full capacity.
5. Place pilot and copilot seat in the fourth notch aft of the forward position. (Use the seat placement given in the POH.)
6. Put the flaps in the full-up position and all control surfaces in the neutral position. The towbar should be stowed in the proper location and all entrance and baggage doors closed.
7. Weigh the airplane inside a closed building to prevent errors in scale reading because of wind.
8. Leveling—with the airplane on the scales, block the main gear oleo pistons in the fully extended position and level the airplane by deflating the nosewheel to center the bubble in the level.
9. With the airplane level and brakes released, record the weight on each scale. Deduct the tare weight, if any, from the scale reading.

The term tare may be new to you; it means any extraneous equipment on the scale, such as chocks, or in the case of a tailwheel airplane (which must be weighed in the level flight attitude), the ladder or brace placed under the tailwheel.

The weight at the nosewheel is multiplied by its arm (44 inches in Figure 10-37) and the two totals of the main wheel weights by their arms (arm = 100 inches); the total moment is divided by the total net weight to get the Basic Empty Weight CG.

As an example, after the preparation for weighing is complete, the airplane in Figure 10-37 has a nosewheel weight of 643 pounds and the combined weight of the main gear is 1,157 pounds. Computing, the nosewheel weight (643 pounds) is multiplied by the arm of 44 inches to get a moment of 28,292 lb-in.

The total weight of the main gear is 1,157 pounds, and this is multiplied by 100 inches to get a moment of 115,700 lb-in. Adding the nosewheel and main gear, a total moment of 143,992 lb-in. is obtained (round it off to 144,000 for simplicity). Dividing this total moment by the total weight of 1,800 pounds, the Basic Empty Weight CG is found to be at 80 inches aft of datum (Figure 10-38). This airplane is a high-performance, low-wing type that carries four persons. The Basic Empty Weight is 1,800 pounds, and the empty CG position is 80 inches aft of datum. The airplane has an allowable gross weight of 3,000 pounds, leaving a useful load of 1,200 pounds (fuel, pilot, passengers, baggage). See Figure 10-38 for the calculations.

The average arm (or CG position) can then be found by dividing the total moment (258,240 lb-in.) by the

Item	Weight (lb.)		Arm Distance (in.)		Moment (lb-in.)
Basic empty weight	1,800	×	80	=	144,000
Fuel—70 gal @ 6 lb	420	×	82	=	34,440
Pilot	180	×	80	=	14,400
Passenger (front seat)	160	×	80	=	12,800
Passenger (rear seat)	170	×	115	=	19,550
Passenger (rear seat)	170	×	115	=	19,550
Baggage	100	×	135	=	13,500
Total	3,000 lb				258,240

Figure 10-38. Weight and balance table with fuel, oil, occupants, and baggage located.

Item	Weight (lb.)		Arm Distance (in.)		Moment (lb-in.)
Basic empty weight	1,015				12,640
Fuel (in wing)—20 gal	120	×	+15	=	+1,800
Pilot	170	×	+13	=	+2,210
Passenger	170	×	+13	=	+2,210
Baggage	100	×	+40	=	+4,000
Total	1,575 lb				+22,860

Figure 10-39. Weight and balance table for a two-place, side-by-side trainer. Incidentally, for positions ahead of the datum, a minus sign is used; for positions behind the datum, a plus sign.

total weight (3,000 pounds), getting an answer of 86.1 inches, which is within the allowable flying range of 80 to 87 inches. Use the above information to find the CG for various combinations, such as half fuel, pilot only, pilot and passengers, no baggage, etc. (rounded off to nearest 0.1 inch.).

Following is an example of an airplane that uses the junction of the wing's leading edge with the fuselage as a datum. The airplane is a two-place, side-by-side trainer with a Basic Empty Weight of 1,015 pounds and a gross weight of 1,575 pounds. The manufacturer has found that the empty moment is 12,640 lb-in. The allowable CG travel is from 12 to 16 inches aft of the datum (Figure 10-39). Allowable baggage is 100 pounds and usable fuel 20 gallons.

The CG = +22,860/1,575 = +14.5 inches, or 14.5 inches aft of the datum. This is well within the 12- to 16-inch CG range limitation. The moment of 22,860 lb-in. was found by adding all the moments. You could call all distances behind the datum negative and those forward positive and still arrive at the same answer. Your answer would then be a minus number, meaning that the CG is behind the datum under your new set of rules for the calculations. Or you could pick a point 10, 20, or 50 feet behind the tail as a datum and still arrive at a proper answer. The principle applies to any airplane or datum point: weight × distance = moment. You can use feet or centimeters for distance, but inches are the usual measurement so that you get moments in pound-inches. When heavier components are added to or taken from your airplane (such as radar and radios), the mechanic will show this on the airplane *Major Alteration and Repair Form* (Form FAA 337).

Some Sample Problems

(Although in the sample problems that follow the numbers are rounded off to show the principle more easily, you'll find in actual conditions that you'll be multiplying weight numbers like 1,736 times arm numbers like 43.95 so a calculator might be useful.)

Figure 10-40 is the loading graph for a four-place, high-performance airplane. A sample Basic Empty Weight for this airplane is 1,670 pounds with a moment of 63,300 lb-in. Add people, fuel, and baggage.

In Figure 10-40 the line representing the adjustable seats shows the pilot or passenger CG with the seat positioned for an average occupant, which is an arm of 37 inches (Figure 10-41). (The CG of some people is lower than others, although this would have comparatively little effect when they are sitting.)

You might work a problem using the following data (refer to Figure 10-40):

Item	Weight, lb	Moment, lb-in/1,000
Basic empty weight	1,670	63.3
Pilot	175	6.6
Front passenger	160	6.2
Rear passenger	130	9.5
Rear passenger	120	8.7
Fuel (30 gallons)	180	8.7
Baggage (area 1)	120	12.5
	2,555	115.5
		(115,500 lb-in.)

Look at Figure 10-42 to see if the results fall within the moment envelope. Figure 10-43 is a CG limit envelope for the same airplane. Check to see the CG location on it by dividing the total moment by the total weight: 115,500/2,555 = 45.2 inches aft of datum (which is the front face of the firewall).

One question you might run into is, How much weight may be added at a particular station to move the CG rearward a certain distance? For instance, a question about the problem just worked might be, How much weight can now be added to baggage area

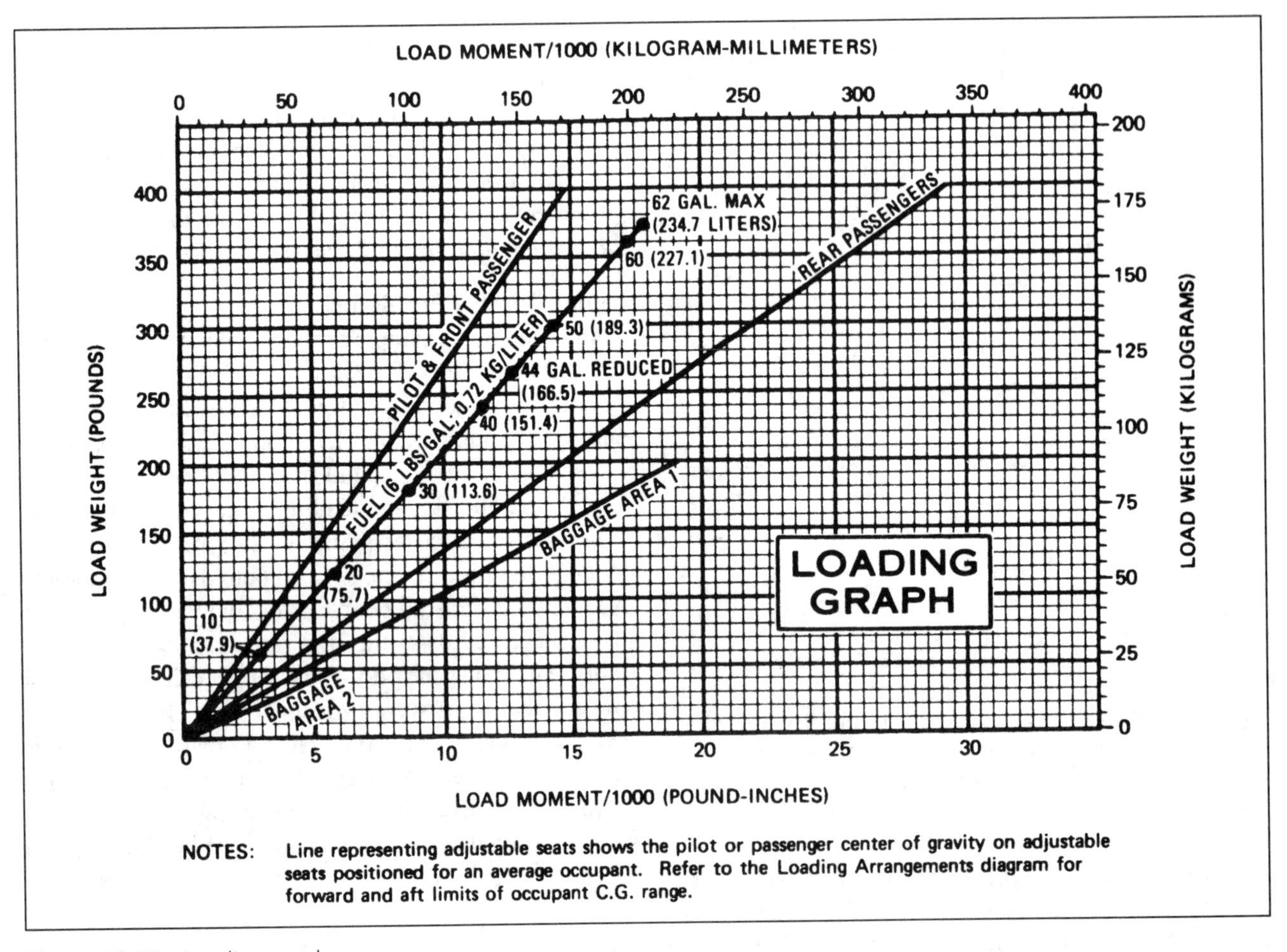

Figure 10-40. Loading graph.

2 without exceeding the rearward CG limit? Looking back at Figure 10-41 you see that the midpoint of baggage area 2 is 115 inches aft of datum. Checking Figure 10-43 you see that the CG can move rearward from its present position of 45.2 to the rear CG limit of 46.5 inches, for a total of 1.3 inches. Use this equation:

$$\frac{\text{added weight}}{\text{present weight}} = \frac{\text{CG change}}{\text{new weight arm} - \text{new CG position}}$$

$$\frac{AW}{PW} = \frac{CG}{NW_{arm} - NCG}$$

The added weight is x (to be solved), the current weight is 2,555 pounds, the change in CG is 1.3 inches, the new weight arm is 115.0 inches, and the new CG position is 46.5 inches: $x/2{,}555 = 1.3/(115.0 - 46.5) = 1.3/68.5$. Cross multiplying you'd get $68.5x = 3{,}321.5$, $x = 3{,}321.5/68.5 = 48.5$ pounds (rounded off). This addition does not exceed the maximum allowed weight.

Doublechecking and going back to the original problem, the final figures were a weight of 2,555 pounds and a moment of 115,500 lb-in. Add the weight and moment of the added baggage: 2,555 + 48.5 = 2,603.5 pounds. The added moment of the baggage is 48.5 × 115.0 = 5,577 lb-in.; 115,500 + 5,577 = 121,077 lb-in., the new total moment. Divide the new moment (121,077 lb-in.) by the new total weight: 121,077/2,603.5 = 46.5 inches. The aft limit is 46.5 inches. and the result just obtained was the result of rounding off some five- and six-figure numbers during the process. To repeat:

$$\frac{AW}{PW} = \frac{CG}{NW_{arm} - NCG}$$

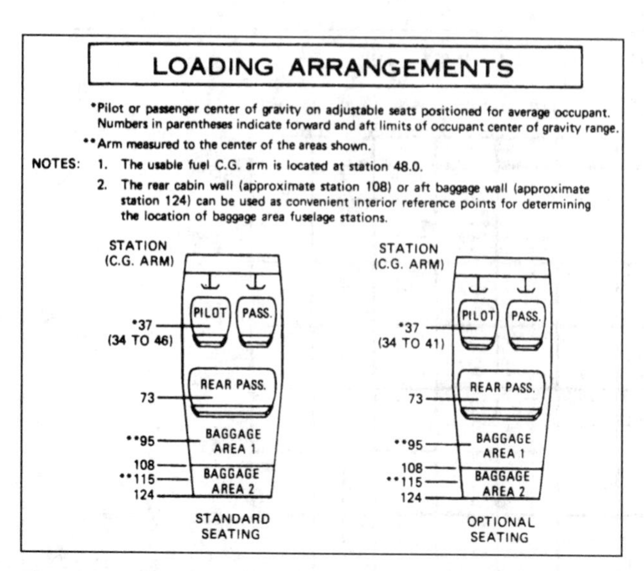

Figure 10-41. Loading arrangements. The notes are self-explanatory. This may answer some of your questions as to how the arms are derived for adjustable seats.

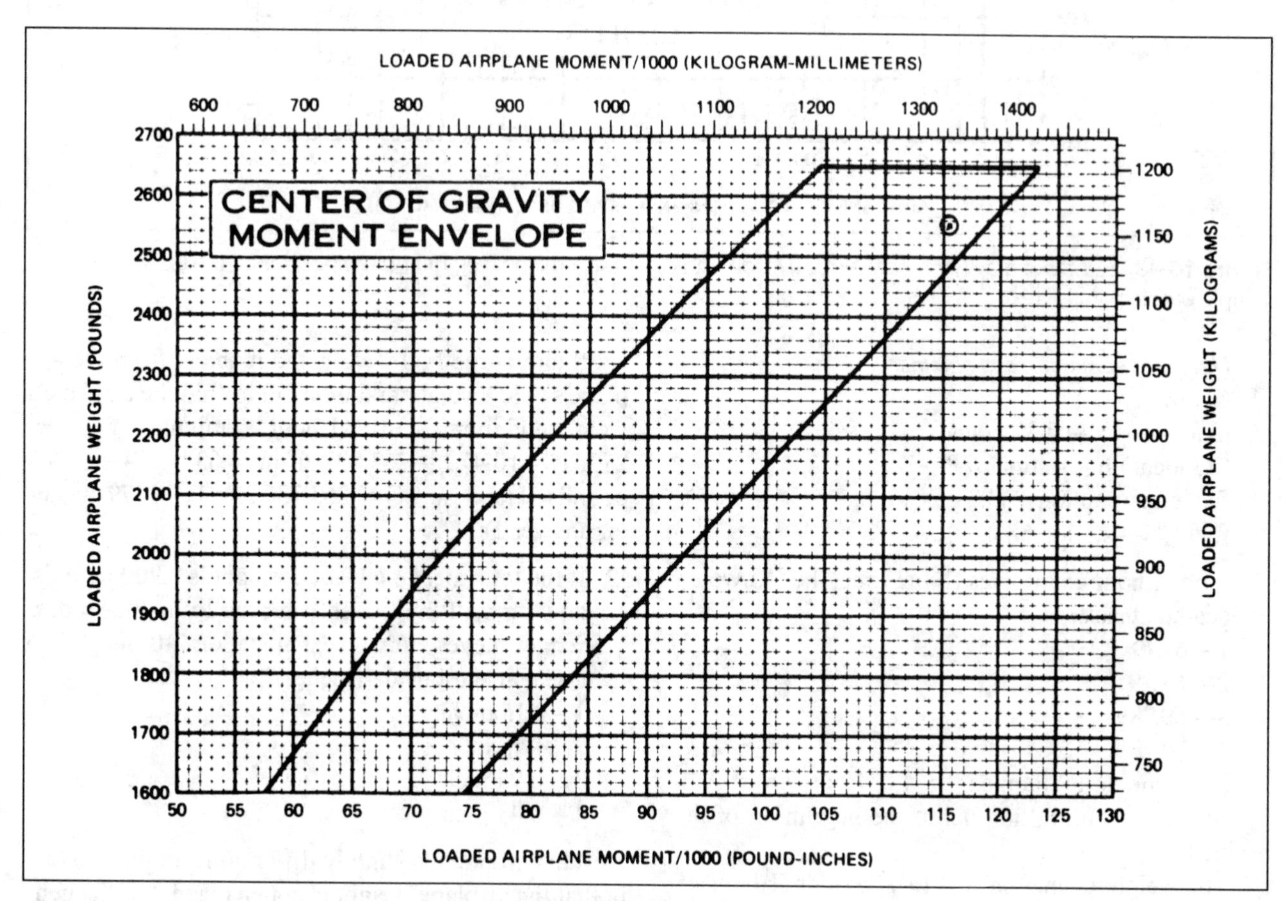

Figure 10-42. Center of gravity moment envelope. Note that moments may also be found by using the metric scale. The dot indicates that the airplane in the sample problem in the text is within the envelope.

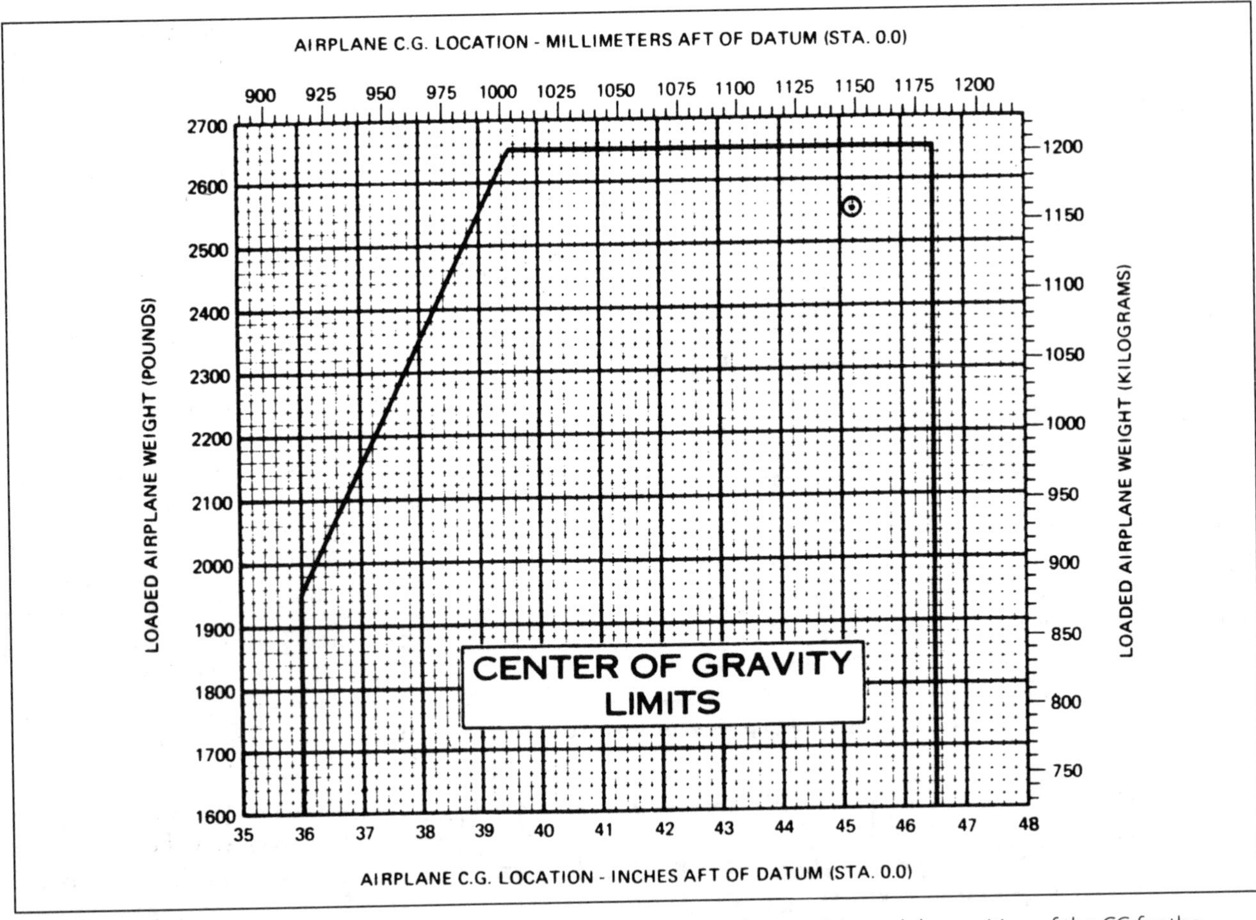

Figure 10-43. Center of gravity limit envelope. The dot indicates the airplane weight and the position of the CG for the sample problem in the text.

Here are some more problems:

1. Given:
   total weight—4,037 pounds
   CG location—station 67.8
   fuel consumption—14.7 gph
   fuel CG—station 68.0.

After 1 hour 45 minutes flying time, the CG would be located at station

1—67.79
2—68.79
3—69.78
4—70.78

Airplane total moment = 4,037 × 67.8 = 273, 709 lb-in. (including the fuel at the beginning of the problem).

The weight change in fuel in 1.75 hour (1 hour 45 minutes) × 14.7 × 6 (pounds per gallon) = 154 pounds (rounded off).

The change in the total moment is the fuel weight (154 pounds) multiplied by the fuel arm (68.0): 154 × 68.0 = 10,472 lb-in.

Subtract the fuel weight and moment from the airplane's "old" weight and moment to find the airplane's weight and moment after 1 hour 45 minutes of flying: 273,709 − 10,472 = 263,237 lb-in; 4,037 − 154 = 3,883 pounds. The new CG = 263,237/3,883 = 67.79 inches (or answer 1).

2. If the total airplane loaded weight is 8,900 pounds, how far will the CG shift forward if a 200-lb passenger moves from a seat at station 210 (inches) to a seat at station 168 (inches)?
   1—2.15 inches
   2—1.48 inches
   3—0.95 inch
   4—0.43 inch

This problem is slightly different from the last one in that the airplane weight is not changed, but the general principle is still the same. The passenger will move *forward* 42 inches.

The relationship between the passenger weight and the airplane weight and the passenger's movement and its effect on the airplane's CG change have a close relationship: 200/8,900 = CG shift (inches)/passenger shift (inches) = 200/8,900 = x/42. Cross multiplying: 8,900x = 8,400, x = 0.944 inch. The airplane CG will move forward 0.944 inch.

To check this, assume that the airplane's original CG is at station 100.0 (inches): airplane moment = 8,900 × 100.0 = 890,000 lb-in.

The 200-lb passenger, who is still part of the 8,900 pounds and has moved *forward* 42 inches, would subtract from the moment but not from the weight. The passenger moment to be subtracted from the total moment is 200 × 42 = 8,400 lb-in. To find the new CG, the new, smaller total moment is divided by the total weight: new moment = 890,000 – 8,400 = 881,600 lb-in., 881,600/8,900 = 99.056. The *new* airplane CG is at 99.056 inches, or has moved *forward* by 100.000 – 99.056 = 0.944 inch. This is closest to answer 3.

Using an airplane original CG of 80.0 inches as a check: 80.0 × 8,900 = 712,000 lb-in.; 42 × 200 = –8,400 lb-in.; total new moment = 703,600.

The new CG = 703,600/8,900 = 79.056 inches. The CG has moved *forward* 0.944 inch. (80.000 – 79.056 = 0.944).

3. Your airplane is loaded to a gross weight of 5,000 pounds with three pieces of luggage in the rear baggage compartment. The CG is 98 inches aft of datum, which is *2 inches aft of limits*. If you move two pieces of luggage that together weigh 100 pounds from the rear baggage compartment (145 inches aft of datum) to the front compartment (45 inches aft of datum), what is the new CG (inches aft of datum)?
   1—95.8
   2—96.0
   3—96.5
   4—97.0

The airplane's total moment = 98 × 5,000 = 490,000 lb-in. Subtracting the moment resulting from the luggage being moved forward: 490,000 – 10,000 = 480,000 lb-in.; the baggage is moved forward 100 inches (145 – 45 = 100); 100 × 100 = 10,000 lb-in. Dividing the new moment by the weight: 480,000/5,000 = 96.0 inches (answer 2).

It's critical that the CG limit be respected, as you've seen. On the other hand, you can use your knowledge of the CG envelope to your advantage. If you fly an airplane with a good useful load and broad CG range by yourself or just another front seat passenger, you'll spend most of your time near the front of the CG envelope. This makes for a stable airplane, but one that's a little harder to land well. You can move the CG aft a bit by carrying some weight in the aft baggage compartment, perhaps a case of oil or a bin of supplies you might find useful if you get stuck somewhere (chocks, tie-downs, etc.). Doing this makes shooting landings more enjoyable, but always honor the CG envelope and baggage weight limit and choose your ballast based on what it might do in an off-airport landing (a case of oil is better than a 25-lb steel dumbbell).

The POH of your airplane has an equipment list describing the various items (engine, propeller, battery, etc.) with their weights and arms from the datum. Each piece of equipment has a code letter indicating whether it is *required* (for certification), *optional*, or *standard* installation. You'll find that in some cases the spinner is required equipment, not because of any weight and balance factors, but because the airplane's cooling tests were done with the spinner installed and poor cooling airflow might result without it. By looking over the equipment list, you can get some idea of the weights of various items; for instance, a heavy-duty battery for a particular light twin weighs nearly 42 pounds and an ammeter hits the scale at 0.5 pound.

Figure 10-44. "I dunno, do you think we might have put too much stuff in the baggage compartment?"

The baggage compartment has weight limitations for two reasons: (1) you might move the CG too far aft by overloading it and (2) you could cause structural failure of the compartment floor if you should pull g's during the flight (Figure 10-44). For instance, you are flying a four-place airplane and are the only occupant, and the boss asks you to deliver some anvils to another town. You figure that there'll be no sweat on the CG and throw 400 pounds of anvils in the 200-lb-limit baggage compartment. For the sake of the example, let's say there is no CG problem and away you go.

En route, you suddenly see another airplane coming head-on and, without thinking, pull up abruptly. You could send 400 pounds of anvils through the bottom of the airplane down through somebody's greenhouse—or worse (Figure 10-45).

The baggage compartment floor is designed to withstand a certain number of g's with 200 pounds in it. If you pull this number of g's with 400 pounds in there, something will give.

You have a couple of early indications that maybe things are not as they should be and that maybe a dangerous condition is developing. (1) After loading a tricycle-gear airplane heavily, you will see that the airplane is in an extremely tail-low position on the ground and that taxiing is very sloppy because the nosewheel doesn't have enough weight on it for effective directional control. The nosewheel "bounces" slowly as you taxi—it doesn't know whether it wants to stay on the ground or not. (2) In the tailwheel-type airplane the tail may be extremely hard to raise during the takeoff run, even with a farther-than-normal nose-down trim setting. If this happens, chop the power before you've gone too far to stop the process.

This is all common sense. Even if you ignore rear baggage compartment placards and other rear loading limitations, maybe the fact that the airplane "just doesn't feel right, even taxiing" may give that extra warning. *But—heed those loading limitations and don't depend on "feel" to save your neck.*

You won't always run a weight and balance calculation on the airplane every time you fly it, but this discussion will give you an idea of the principles involved. Stay within the limitations on passengers and baggage as given in the POH and you'll have no fear of exceeding the CG limits or suffering in performance. *Excessive weight, poorly placed, will result in a dangerous situation both from a performance and a stability and control standpoint. Stall and spin recovery becomes more critical as the CG moves aft.* (See Figure 10-46 for a summary.)

Figure 10-45.

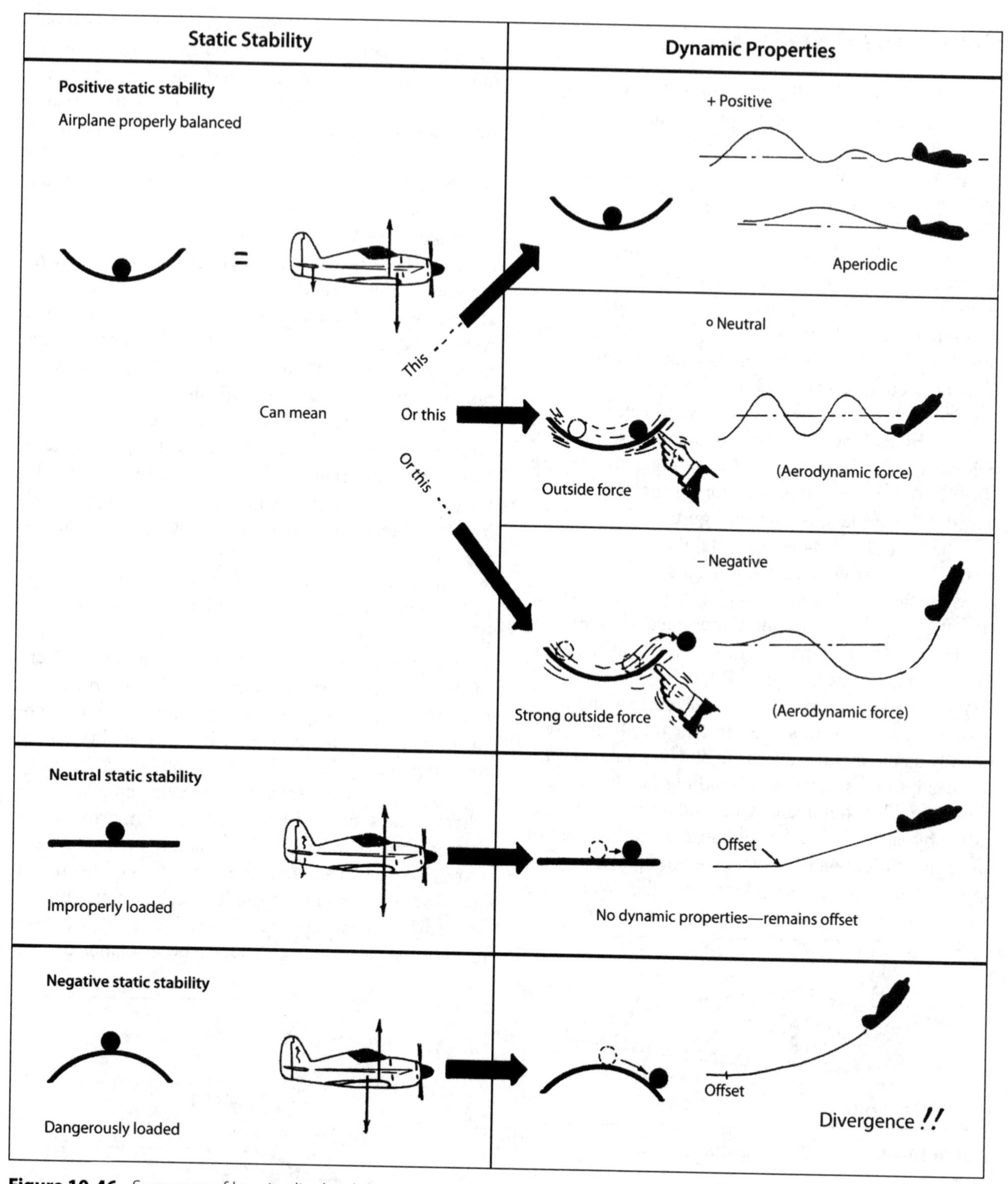

Figure 10-46. Summary of longitudinal stability.

Directional Stability

Directional stability, unlike longitudinal stability, is not greatly affected by the pilot's placement of weight in the airplane. An airplane is designed with either good or less than good directional stability. For simplification, let's consider an airplane with no fin or rudder (Figure 10-47).

You can see that if the center of side area is even with the CG, little or no directional stability is present. If this airplane were displaced in a yaw by turbulence, it would not tend to return to its original heading. If the offsetting force were strong enough, the airplane might pivot on around and fly backward for a while.

The designer must ensure positive directional static stability by making sure that this center of side area is behind the CG. This is done by adding a fin (Figure 10-48). You can see that a restoring moment is produced if the airplane is yawed (Figure 10-49).

The fin (like the horizontal stabilizer) acts like the feather on an arrow in maintaining stable flight. Naturally, the farther aft this fin is placed and the larger its size, the greater the airplane's directional stability.

The rudder, as a part of this area, is furnished to give the pilot control in yaw. If the fin is too large in comparison with the rudder area and deflection limits, poor yaw control results. The airplane may be so directionally stable that the pilot is unable to make forward or sideslips or safe crosswind landings and takeoffs.

The rudder effectiveness, or "rudder power" as it is called by engineers, is very important in the event of an engine failure on a multiengine airplane at low airspeeds. The pilot must be able to offset the asymmetric thrust of the working engine(s) at full power. For multiengine airplanes, this rudder power governs the minimum controllable speed with one engine out, or in the case of a four-engine plane, two engines out on the same side. Lateral control also enters into consideration in establishing the minimum controllable speed, but this will be covered more thoroughly in Part 2, Checking Out in Advanced Models.

Rudder deflections usually are held below 30°, because the effectiveness falls off past this amount. Another factor in rudder design is the requirement for spin recovery. However, normal category airplanes are restricted against spinning, and also, it's very rare these days that deliberate spinning is required (only in preparation for the instructor's certificate).

A properly designed airplane requires more and more rudder force to be exerted as the yaw angle is increased at any given airspeed. You've found this to be the case when steepening a forward or sideslip to land. You found that you were limited in steepness of slip by the rudder more than by the ailerons.

The rudder is considered to be an auxiliary control in flight, and in newer airplanes it is losing even this value. Its primary purpose is to overcome adverse aileron yaw and to correct for torque. With the advent of differential aileron movement and other means of overcoming adverse yaw, it is becoming less important for normal coordinated flight. It's still mighty handy for slipping and other unbalanced conditions though!

Steerable tailwheels, nosewheels, and separate wheel brakes decrease the rudder's importance for ground control. When airplanes had tail skids or free-swiveling tailwheels (and no brakes), the slipstream and relative wind on the rudder were the only means of turning on the ground. The rudder is still of primary importance for tailwheel-type airplanes during

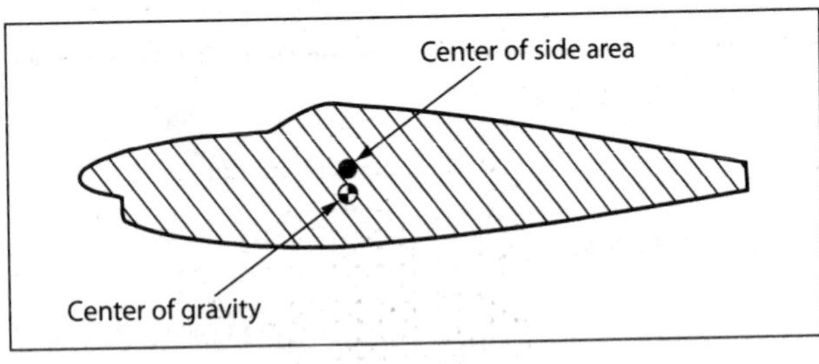

Figure 10-47. Center of side area, fuselage only.

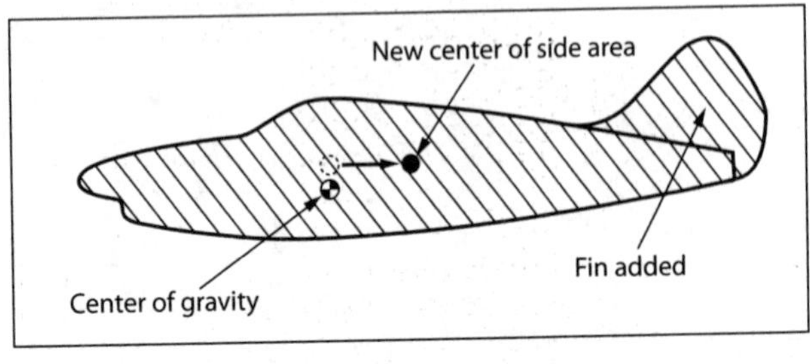

Figure 10-48. Center of side area, fin added.

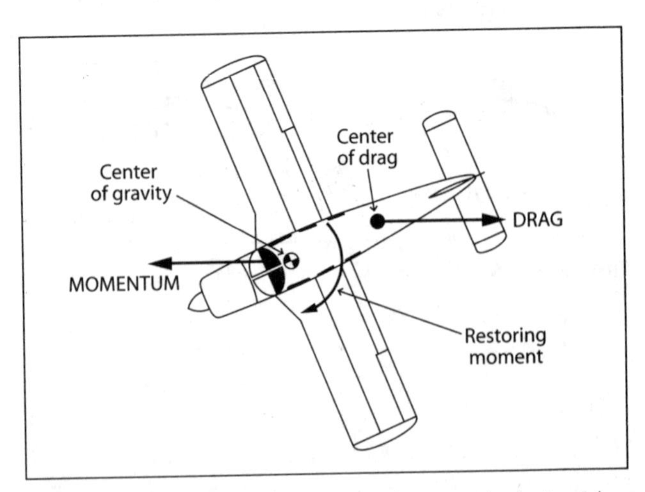

Figure 10-49. Restoring moment of a properly designed fuselage-fin combination.

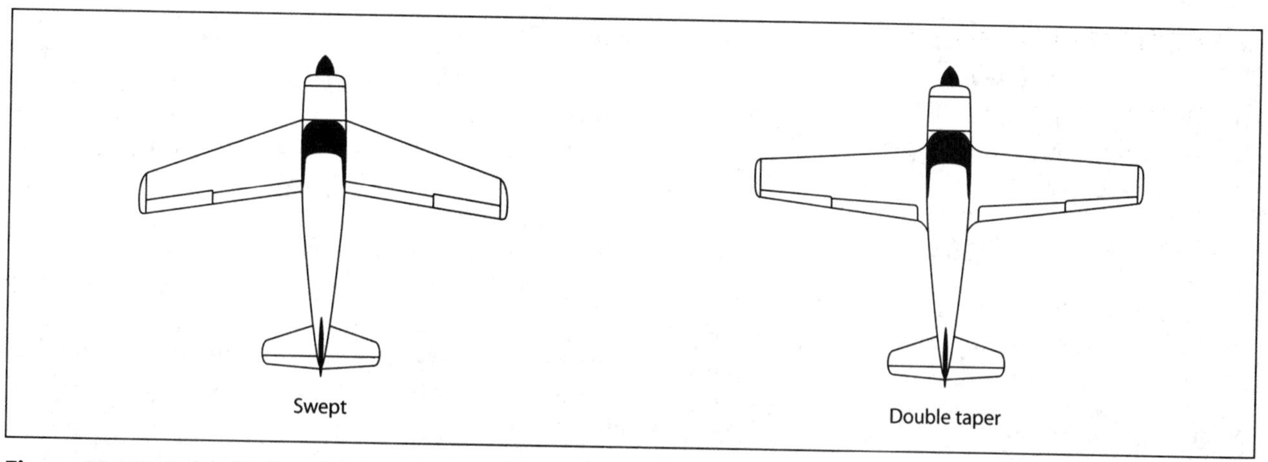

Figure 10-50. Swept-back and double-tapered wing.

takeoffs and landings—particularly in a crosswind. In fact, one of the complaints of older flight instructors is that students don't know how to use the rudder. Also, military pilots who started from scratch flying tricycle gear and jets can be surprised at how significant the rudder is when they start getting checked out in civilian tailwheel airplanes.

A swept-back wing contributes to directional stability, but very few lightplanes use this idea any more. However, a wing with double taper does help, as there is some sweep effect (Figure 10-50).

Although there are cross effects between lateral and directional stability, for simplicity's sake sweepback will be discussed here only as it affects directional stability. Take a look at an airplane in a yaw (Figure 10-51); the plane is yawed and you can see that there is a difference in drag that results in a restoring moment. Of course the fin area would be helping, too.

It's hard to separate lateral and directional control effects even though we did it to discuss sweepback. You know yourself that kicking a rudder yaws the airplane, but it also causes reactions in a roll. You know, too, that abrupt application of aileron alone normally results in adverse yaw.

Directional Dynamic Stability

With directional dynamic stability, an aerodynamic attribute called Dutch roll may result when a rudder pedal is pushed and released (not to be confused with the coordination exercise often erroneously called "Dutch rolls").

Suppose you push right rudder and quickly release it. The nose of the airplane yaws to the right initially. This speeds up the left wing (and slows down the right wing) so that a right rolling motion is effected. The airplane, having dynamic or oscillatory properties (assuming positive static directional stability), will return and overshoot, speeding up the right wing, which raises, etc. You get a combination yawing and rolling oscillation, which, putting it mildly, is somewhat disconcerting. An airplane that Dutch rolls is miserable to fly in choppy air (Figure 10-52).

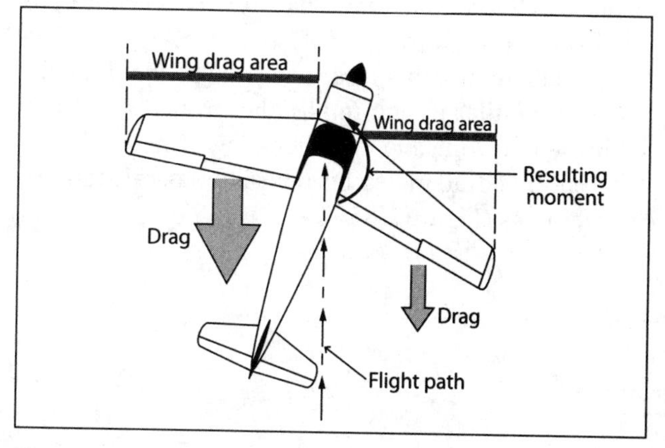

Figure 10-51. Effects of sweepback in a yaw. Sweepback increases dihedral effect and can decrease roll maneuverability.

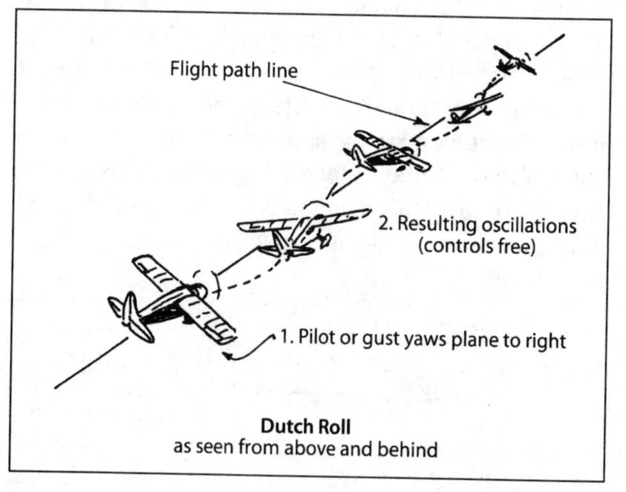

Figure 10-52. Dutch roll.

Summary of Directional Stability	
Static Stability	***Dynamic Properties***
Positive Static Stability Airplane with sufficient fin area. (Ball inside bowl) Three possibilities	**Positive Dynamic Stability** Airplane returns to straight flight after several decreasing oscillations (yaw). Rudder properly balanced.
	Neutral Dynamic Stability Airplane oscillates from side to side (yaws) when offset, neither increasing nor decreasing in amplitude.
	Negative Dynamic Stability Airplane, when offset, oscillates (yaws) with increasing amplitude. Poor rudder balance.
Neutral Static Stability Airplane with small fin. (Ball on flat plate)	**No Oscillations** When yawed, the airplane tends to stay in that position. No tendency to return to straight flight.
Negative Static Stability Airplane with critical shortage of fin area. (Ball on top of bowl)	**No Oscillations** When yawed, the airplane tends to increase the yaw. Divergence occurs.

The manufacturer tries to reach a happy medium between too great and too little directional stability (called "weathercock stability" in some texts).

Such factors as rudder balance and design have strong effects on the dynamic properties of directional stability. An airplane certificated by the FAA has positive directional stability (both dynamic and static). It's hard to separate lateral and directional control effects. Dihedral, which helps assure positive *lateral* static stability, may result in cross effects and give the airplane Dutch roll problems.

Because it is better to have a situation known as *spiral instability* than Dutch roll, nearly all airplanes are designed this way. Note in your own airplane that, if a wing lowers (controls free) and a spiral is allowed to develop, the bank increases and the spiral tightens if no effort is made by the pilot to stop it. However, the rate of increase of bank is normally slow and causes no problem in VFR conditions. This is the lesser of two evils, compared with the annoyance of Dutch roll. In situations where visual references are lost by the pilot who is not instrument qualified and/or doesn't have proper instrumentation, the tendency of the airplane is to get into a spiral of increasing tightness. (Check it sometime under VFR conditions—at a safe altitude and in an area clear of other airplanes, of course.)

Lateral Stability

Dihedral

The most common design factor for ensuring *positive static lateral stability* is dihedral. Dihedral is considered to be positive when the wingtips are higher than the roots (Figure 10-53). The effect of dihedral is to produce a rolling moment that tends to return the airplane to a balanced flight condition if sideslip occurs.

Figure 10-54 shows what forces are at work in a sideslip. You can see that a rolling moment is produced, which tends to correct the unbalanced condition.

A high-wing airplane, even though it may actually have zero dihedral, has a tendency to return to balanced condition because of its wing position. A low-wing airplane with zero dihedral will generally have negative lateral stability because of its CG position. A midwing airplane with zero dihedral usually exhibits neutral stability (Figure 10-55).

Understanding this idea, you can see that two airplanes of similar design in all other respects, but one having a high wing and the other a low wing, will have different dihedral angles for the same lateral stability requirements (Figure 10-56).

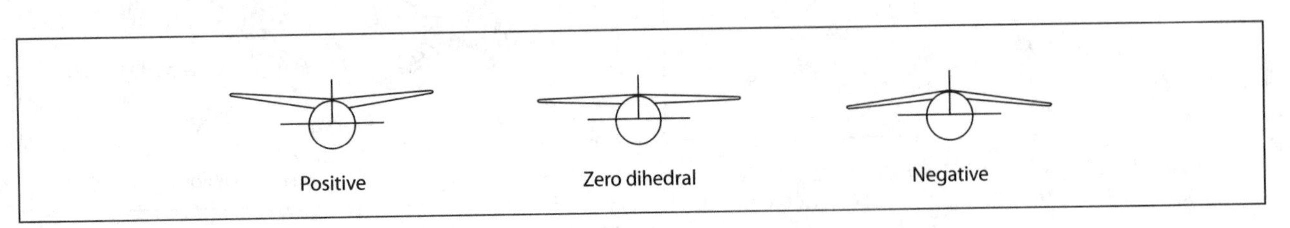

Figure 10-53. Dihedral.

Excessive dihedral makes for poor rolling qualities. The airplane is so stable laterally that it is fighting any rolling motion where slipping might be introduced (such as in a slow roll). For this reason, airplanes requiring fast roll characteristics usually have less dihedral than a less-maneuverable airplane. A fighter pilot doesn't go around doing slow rolls in combat but does need to have a high rate of roll in order to turn quickly—and sometimes in the heat of the moment may not coordinate perfectly. If the airplane has a great deal of dihedral, it may be hard to maneuver laterally, particularly if sideslipping is a factor in the roll.

Lateral and directional stability are hard to separate. For instance, the fin, which is primarily designed to aid in directional stability, may contribute to lateral stability as well. Figure 10-57 shows that the fin and rudder contribute a rolling moment as well as a yawing moment in a sideslip. In a slipping turn, the effect of the fin is to stop the slip and balance the turn, which it does through yaw *and* roll effects.

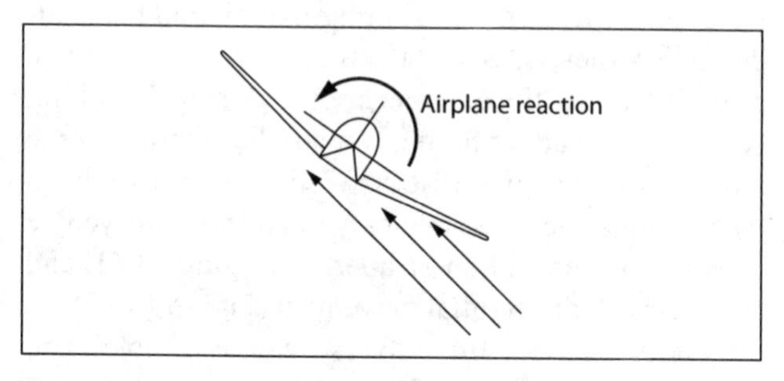

Figure 10-54. Dihedral effect in a sideslip.

Power Effects on Lateral Stability

Power is destabilizing in a sideslip for a propeller-driven airplane; that is, it may tend to counteract the effects of dihedral (Figure 10-58).

You can visualize that in an accidental slip the slipstream will tend to make the bank steeper, whereas the dihedral effect is designed to recover from the unnatural position. This slipstream effect is aggravated in the flaps-down condition.

Loading Effects

Usually the airplane loading has no effect on lateral static stability, because the fuselage is too narrow to allow offset loads. However, planes with wing tanks may present slight wing-down tendencies with asymmetric fuel load, but usually the only result is a tired arm, if there's no aileron trim.

Lateral Dynamic Stability

Dynamic stability is not a major concern in lateral stability. You recall that control surface balancing and other design factors introduced aerodynamic effects that furnished the outside force acting on the system, and the principles apply in the same way. The ailerons, if *mass balanced* (balanced around the hinge line by weight) and if comparatively free in movement, usually assure that the pure lateral movements are heavily damped. However, cross effects of yaw displacement may result in lateral oscillations, and also Dutch roll (Figure 10-59).

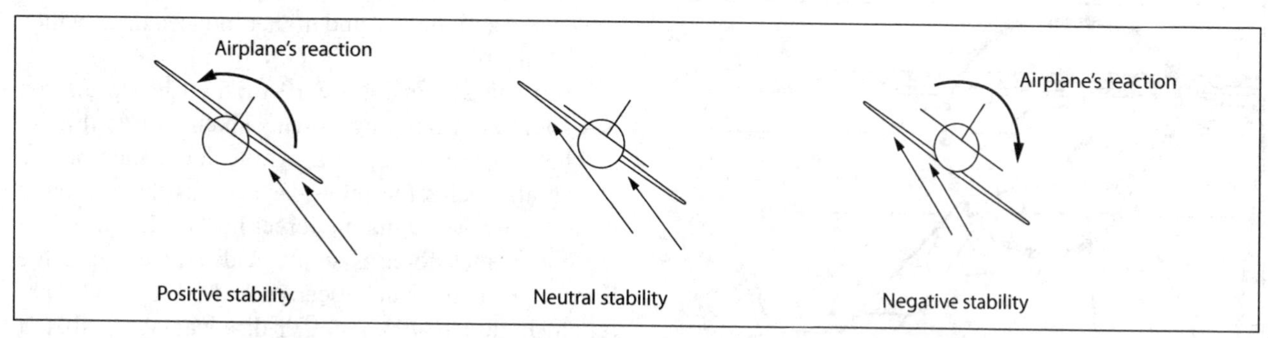

Figure 10-55. The effects of various wing positions on lateral stability; zero dihedral in each case.

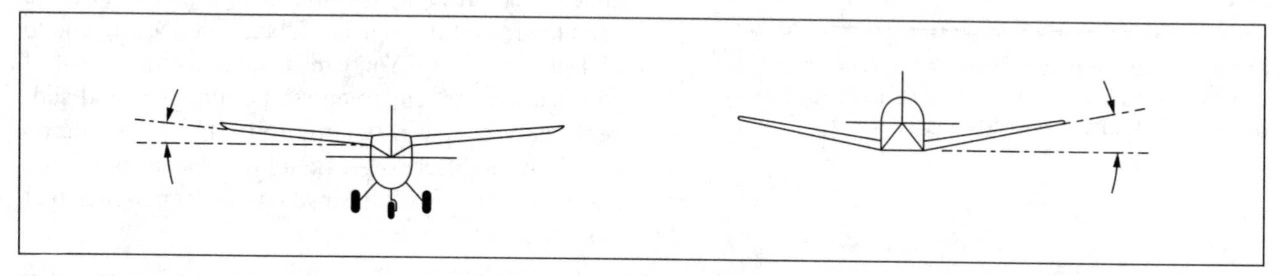

Figure 10-56. Dihedral requirements for a high- and a low-wing airplane to obtain equivalent lateral stability.

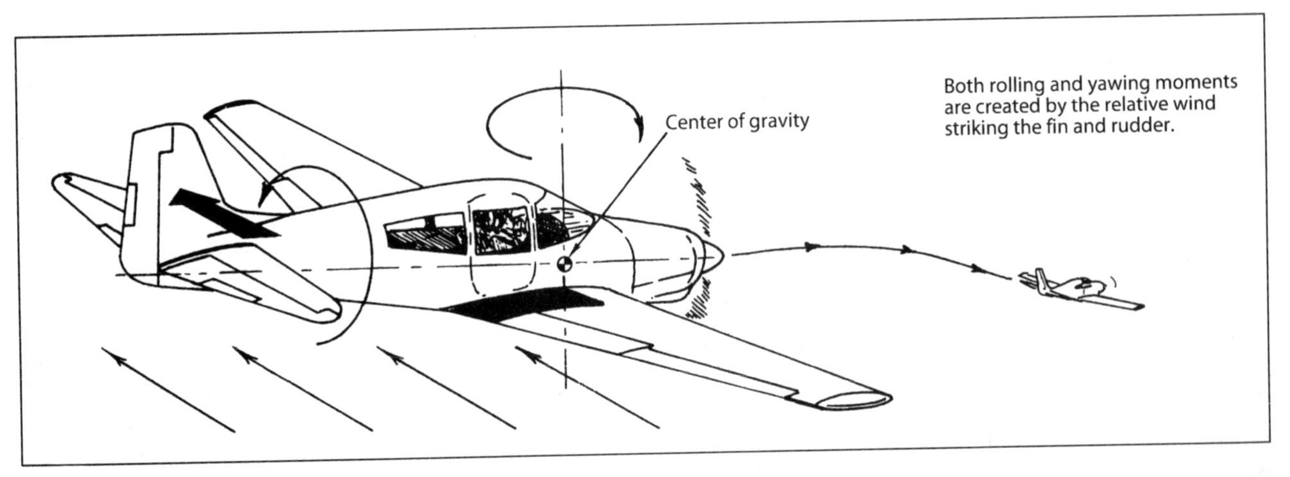

Figure 10-57. Fin effects in a slip.

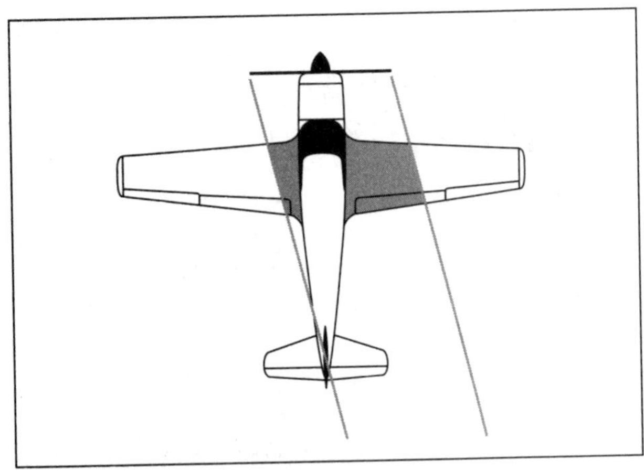

Figure 10-58. Slipstream effects on lateral stability in a left slip with power. Note that the slipstream tends to increase the lift of the high wing.

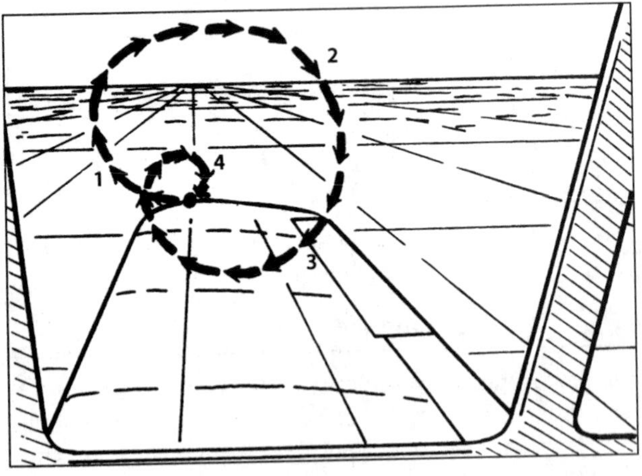

Figure 10-59. Apparent movement of a point on the wingtip during Dutch roll (damped oscillations). The pilot pressed left rudder pedal and released it.

Lateral Control

The aileron is the most widely known form of lateral control, although spoiler-type controls have been used to some extent.

A problem with ailerons is that they introduce cross effects between lateral and directional movement. You were taught from the beginning that aileron and rudder go together 99.99% of the time in the air. You were also shown that the ailerons are the principal banking control, with rudder used as an auxiliary to overcome adverse yaw (Figure 10-60). Well, everybody's been busy trying to decrease aileron yaw and no doubt you've flown airplanes with Frise ailerons (Figure 10-61) and ailerons with differential movement (Figure 10-62).

The reason for this adverse yaw is simple. You remember from Chapter 2 that induced drag is caused by lift. When you deflect the ailerons, the down aileron causes a higher C_L and higher induced drag, which results in yaw.

You can see in Figure 10-61 that the up aileron has some area hanging down, which causes drag—and helps overcome the drag of the down aileron. The design also helps the pilot—as soon as the aileron is deflected up, aerodynamic forces help deflect it so that the pilot's stick force is small. A disadvantage of the Frise-type aileron can be seen in the burbling and separation (Figure 10-61). Another disadvantage is that at high speeds the aileron may tend to overbalance. The pilot's stick force may become too light and the ailerons don't tend to return to neutral, but, if deflected, tend to deflect to the stop. You can imagine the discomfit of your passengers when you start a nice turn and suddenly do a couple of aileron rolls. The Frise aileron usually is modified to get rid of overbalance or aileron buffet by rounding off the leading edge or making other minor shape changes.

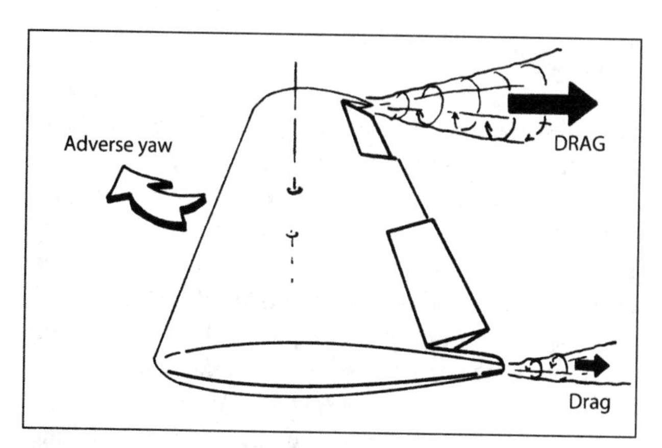

Figure 10-60. Adverse yaw.

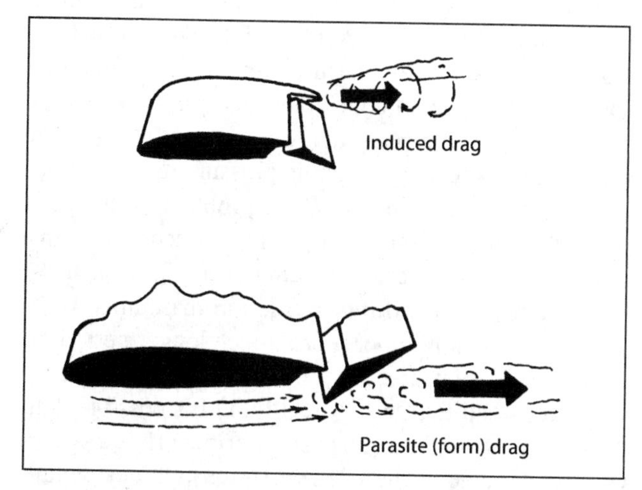

Figure 10-61. Frise-type ailerons.

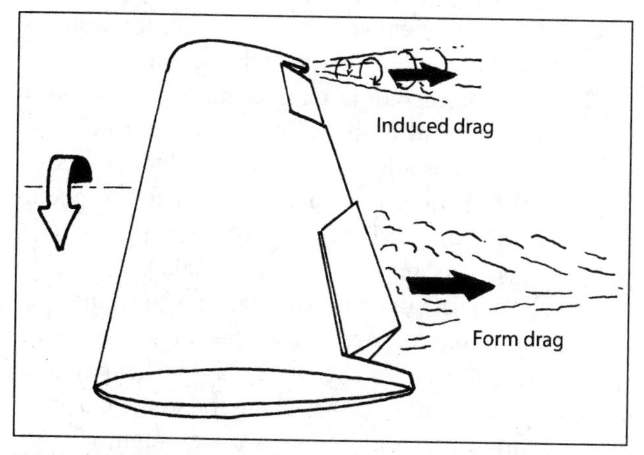

Figure 10-62. Exaggerated view of differential aileron movement.

Differential Aileron Movement

This is the most popular method today of overcoming adverse yaw, and though the control system is slightly more complicated, there are not as many aerodynamic problems to cope with. The principle involved is to balance induced drag with flat plate or form drag (Figure 10-62).

Spoiler Control

This method of control is used on airliners and corporate jets. The flight spoilers rise in conjunction with the associated aileron to lower the wing and add drag to that side—a desired combination (Figure 10-63).

A downside is that the hydraulically-actuated spoilers usually deploy based on control wheel (yoke) deflection. If they are designed to start up fairly early in the deflection, the pilot can't be in the habit of starting the takeoff with much (if any) aileron into a crosswind; the added drag of the raised spoilers can harm takeoff performance and may even add to the weathercocking tendency. If the upwind wing isn't being raised by the crosswind, the pilot waits to roll the yoke into the wind at rotation, prepared to take it out fairly quickly after lift-off and climb out in a crab or on the assigned heading.

Most transports are designed to automatically deploy all flight spoilers (both sides) on landing in addition to the higher-angled ground spoilers. This greatly reduces ground roll by killing lift and putting full weight on the wheels (and ruining many a good landing).

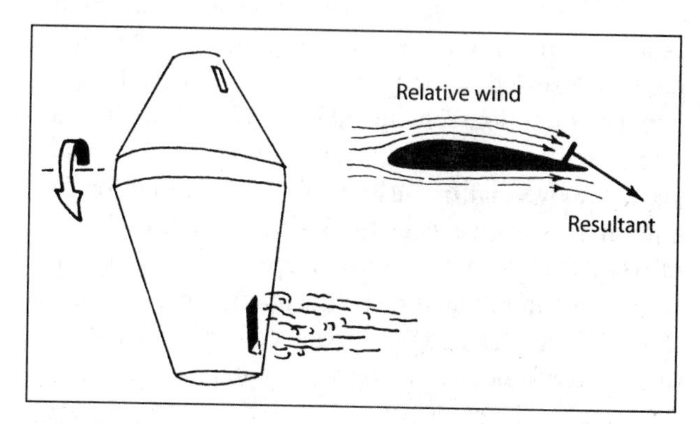

Figure 10-63. Spoiler type of lateral control.

Aileron Reversal

This is presented more for interest than anything else, because you won't be affected by it in the airplane you are flying. But earlier it was a problem for high-speed airplanes with thin wings and hydraulic (or irreversible) control systems. If an aileron is deflected by hydraulic power, the aileron may act as a trim tab, and the wing will be twisted in the opposite direction by aerodynamic forces (Figure 10-64). The application of right stick could result in a roll to the left!

Another use of the term aileron *reversal* applies to some planes—the reaction of the airplane to the sudden sharp application of ailerons near the stall. The down aileron causes added drag that results in that wing slowing and dropping—which further increases its angle of attack and stalls it. Aileron application in this case also

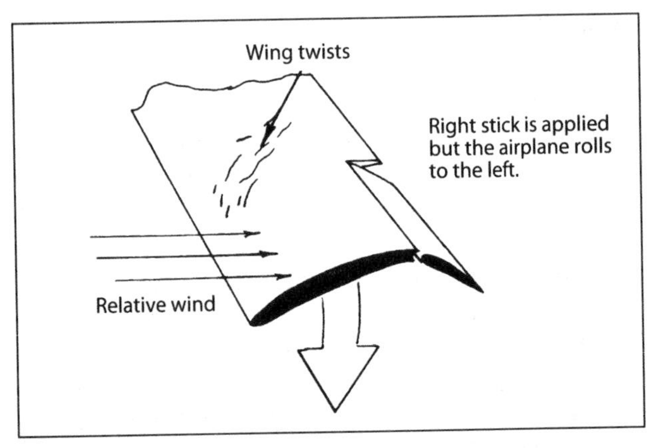

Figure 10-64. Aileron reversal for a high-speed airplane with irreversible controls.

results in the opposite effect desired. This problem will be covered more thoroughly in Chapter 21.

Figure 10-65 shows a plot of rate of roll versus calibrated airspeed for a fictitious airplane. Assuming full deflection of the ailerons, the rate of roll increases in a straight line until the point at which aerodynamic forces are such that the pilot's strength is no longer sufficient to maintain full deflection. There must be some standard of comparison among airplanes, so the FARs establish a maximum force (with a wheel control) of 50 pounds "exerted on opposite sides of the wheel and in opposite directions." Note in Figure 10-65 that the max rate of roll is 90° per second at 130 K, and it drops at speeds above that because the forces required for full aileron deflection exceed the 50-lb maximum. The rate of roll at the probable approach speed of 80 K is only slightly greater than *one-half* the maximum rate, something of interest if wingtip vortices are encountered there and you need to recover from an induced roll.

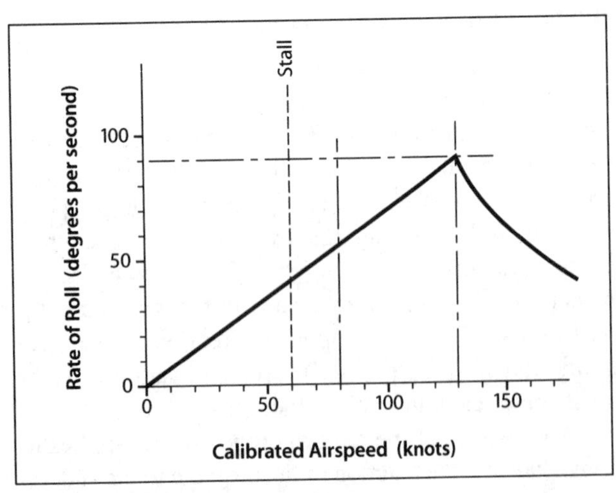

Figure 10-65. Rate of roll versus velocity for a fictitious airplane. (*Flight Instructor's Manual*)

Flutter

Control surfaces (and other components of the airplane) have natural frequencies that are a function of mass and stiffness. Aerodynamic forces of certain values may act on the structure so as to excite or negatively damp those natural modes and allow flutter. Basically, a particular control surface has a natural frequency, and the designer must keep it damped in the normal flight envelope or construct it so as to have a flutter mode well above the design dive speed (V_D).

The control surface must be aerodynamically and mass balanced or restricted so that the chances of inducing flutter are negligible (or better, impossible) in the operating range. The rigidity of the control surface may be increased to avoid flutter tendencies. Generally speaking, damping of control-surface flutter increases with increased airspeed—at lower ranges. (That makes sense—the increasing dynamic pressure tends to keep the control surface in line.) The problem is that at a particular higher airspeed the damping decreases rapidly. At the point of critical flutter speed for a particular airplane, the resulting oscillation maintains itself with a steady amplitude. (For a much longer period of steady oscillation of a whole airplane, check the elevator-free condition in Figure 10-24.) It's possible that the airplane might ease up past the critical flutter speed without damage at the edge of flutter, but accidental disturbances, such as turbulence or other factors, could trigger full-scale destructive flutter. In many cases, the onset of flutter happens so fast that damage (or destruction) occurs before the pilot can take action.

The surface, including wing or tail, can be subject to both flexing and torsional moments, and this can start or add to the aileron, elevator, or rudder flutter (Figure 10-66). Figure 10-67 shows what can occur when three factors in flutter are working on a wing. (It can get as busy as an after-Christmas sale.)

An elevator or stabilator trim tab can be an instigator of flutter, and as part of your preflight check you should check the tab for excessive play, particularly the nut and bolt attaching the actuating rod to the tab arm. Some mention has been made of a maximum play of ⅛ inch at the trailing edge of the tab (relative to the main surface). The point is that after a period of time the aerodynamic forces working on the tab can cause the hinge pin or other components to wear, and flutter could occur at airspeeds well down in the cruise area—or below.

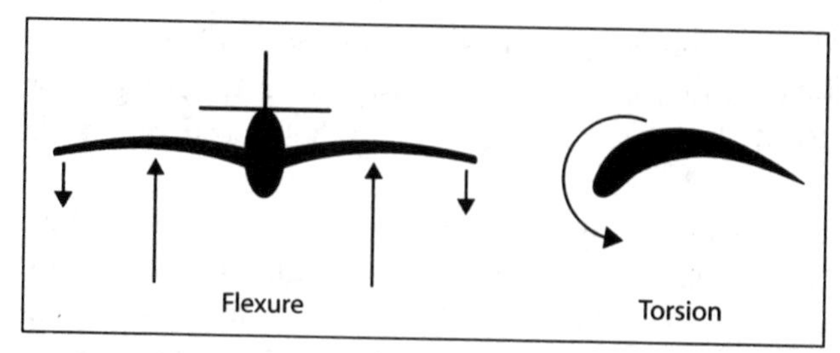

Figure 10-66. Flexure and torsion (twist) of a wing. These will not be in phase with each other, which is one cause for onset of flutter.

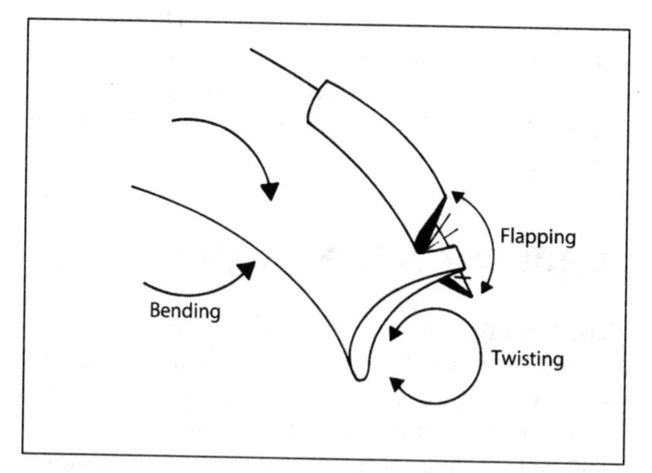

Figure 10-67. Three forces working on a wing in flutter.

Control Surfaces

It was noted earlier that a control surface (aileron, rudder, and elevator) must be mass balanced or have some other method to avoid flutter in the operating range. It depends on the airplane and control surface design, but generally a surface should not have its chordwise CG behind the hinge line (Figure 10-68 is an example).

Look at a particular elevator designed with the CG behind the hinge line (Figure 10-69). If a gust or disturbance accelerates the *tail* of the airplane *downward*, inertia of the CG of the surface causes it to move upward in relation to the fixed surfaces. The same *type* of reaction would result if the airplane tail moved upward due to a gust; the inertia of the CG of the surface would cause it to move *downward* in relation to the fixed surfaces.

If the CG is *ahead* of the hinge line, such problems will tend to be damped. If the CG is on the hinge line, no inertia effects will be noted. This idea can be used for the rudder and ailerons as well.

There have been incidents of ice creating a mass imbalance of control surfaces (ailerons) when water worked its way into the interior and froze there. The pilots were extremely surprised when flutter (and wing loss) occurred right after takeoff at a speed where flutter problems aren't supposed to exist.

Another factor, sometimes overlooked, is that excess coats of paint (applied when a control surface has been repainted) may throw off the mass balance to such a degree that flutter could occur in the normal flight regime. Owners who have refurbished airplanes have discovered this.

The mass overhang or "horn" balance is one way of keeping the control surface CG at or ahead of the hinge line and can act as a surface to decrease control forces since the surface area ahead of the hinge line is pressed on by aerodynamic forces (Figure 10-70). You may have seen some older-type airplanes that used the balance system shown in Figure 10-71. This is an external balance weight for a control surface.

The *cross-section shape* of the control surface also has an effect on flutter possibilities. The surfaces should be concave or flat, not convex (Figure 10-72). The curvature of the convex surface may allow flow past the trailing edge, setting up vortices that induce flutter. Control surfaces must be built strong enough to retain the flat or concave cross section in aerodynamic forces. This is very important to the owner of a home-built airplane (Figure 10-73).

If a control surface lacks torsional stiffness or does not have enough hinges, it may not be rigid enough along its span, and flutter may be induced as it "bows" up and down.

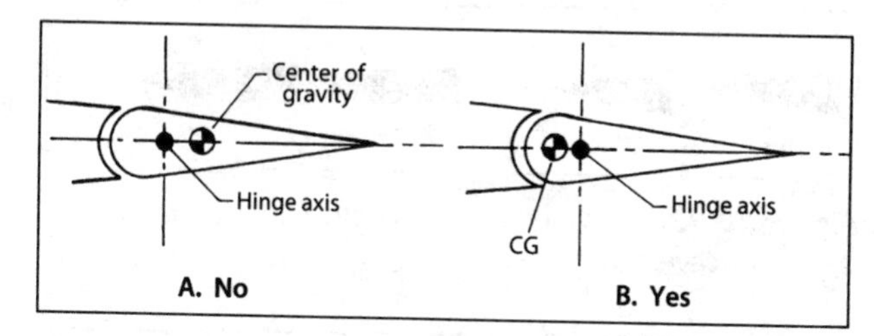

Figure 10-68. Centers of gravity for a control surface. **A.** The CG is at a bad position. **B.** A better arrangement.

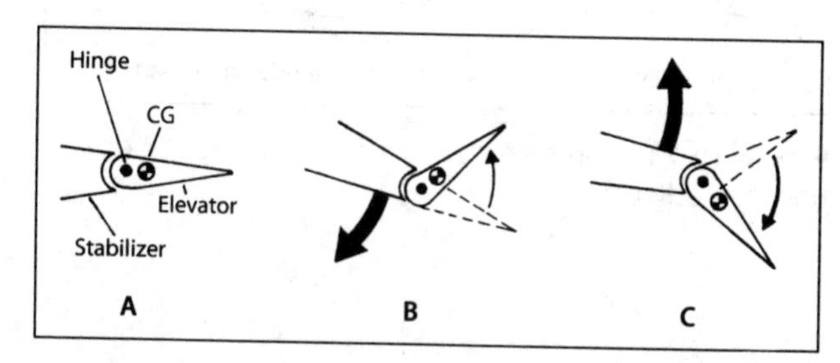

Figure 10-69. A. The CG of the elevators is behind the hinge line. **B.** A gust or disturbance moves the airplane's tail down. Because of the inertia effects of the elevators' CG, it stays "up" relative to the rest of the tail and increases the tail-down motion. **C.** The elevator may then tend to "catch up" and overshoot, exaggerating any recovery pitch motions (overrebound).

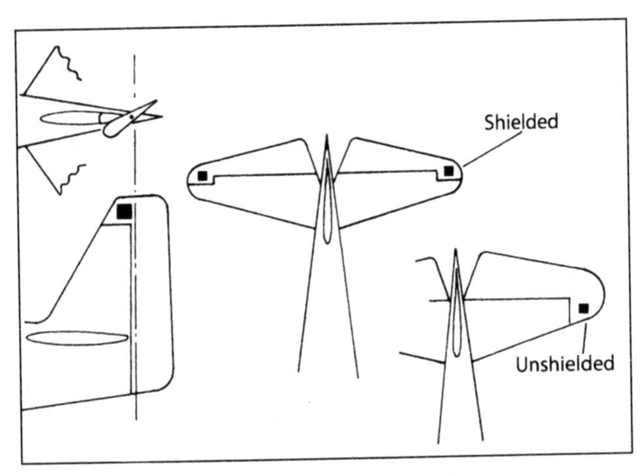

Figure 10-70. Horn-type mass and aerodynamic balancing.

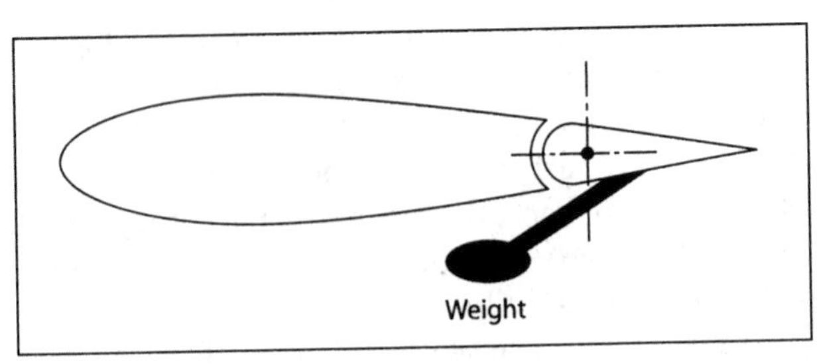

Figure 10-71. A type of control surface balance that was normally used on older, slower airplanes because the parasite drag would be very high at higher speeds.

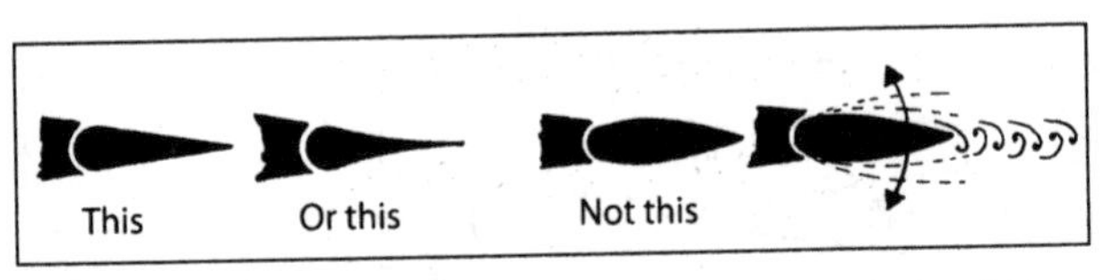

Figure 10-72. Cross sections of control surfaces should be flat or concave, not convex.

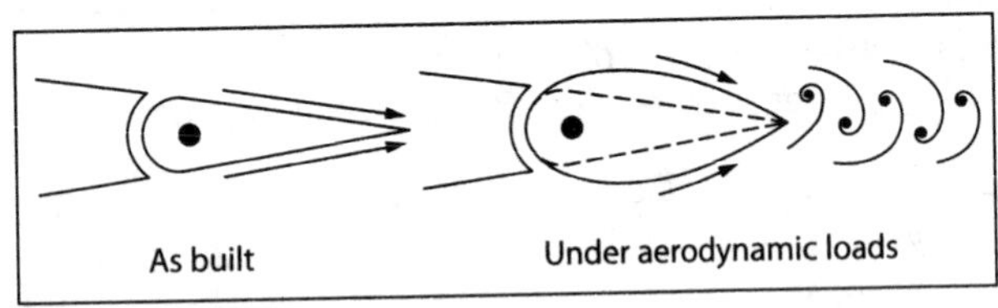

Figure 10-73. Control surface contours may be deformed under aerodynamic loading.

In some cases, ice may be more of a problem on stabilators than on the stabilizer-elevator system. Figure 10-74 shows a stabilator system, both clean and with ice.

It's important that you be aware of possible flutter problems, and during the preflight check, take an extra look at the control surfaces, balance weights, and trim systems for wear plus ice accumulation after a rain and freeze. You may be doing some charter work under some bad weather conditions and should be aware of these factors. It's very tempting on those extra-cold days to make only a cursory inspection. The main idea is for you to be alert to possible control problems if the airplane has picked up a load of ice and you are making an instrument approach when you're tired and pushing minimums.

Summary of the Chapter

Static stability is the measure of the *initial tendency* of a body to return to its original position. This initial tendency to return may further be broken down into positive, neutral, or negative static stability.

Dynamic stability is the *action* of a body caused by its static stability properties. To have oscillations, the system must have *positive* static stability. A system that has *neutral* static stability has no initial tendency to return and therefore has no oscillatory properties. Likewise, a system that has *negative* static stability diverges—it tends to leave the original position at a faster and faster rate—it cannot have oscillatory properties but diverges if offset.

The ball inside the bowl is statically stable, but outside forces may act on the system so that it may have neutral or negative dynamic stability. This outside force can be compared to aerodynamic forces set up by improper control balance or design, even though the airplane itself is properly loaded and the overall design is good.

Longitudinal stability is the most important, for it is most affected by airplane loading. If the airplane is loaded properly, as recommended by the POH, it will fall well within safe limits for longitudinal static stability.

Entire texts have been written on both airplane stability and flutter; this chapter merely hits the high points. For more thorough coverage, you are referred to the references at the end of this book.

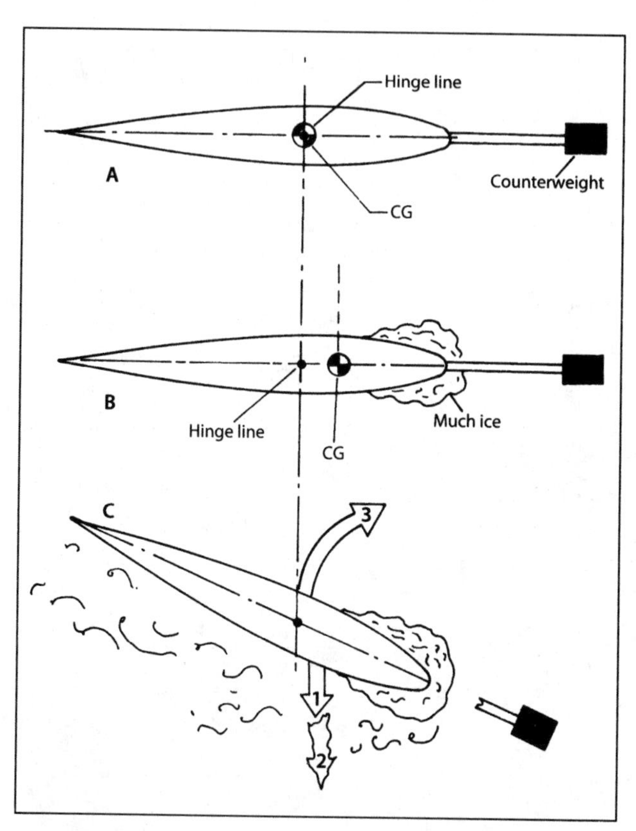

Figure 10-74. A. The clean stabilator is balanced on the hinge line and has no over- or undershooting tendencies if the airplane's tail is deflected up or down by gusts. **B.** The added weight of ice may move the CG of the system ahead of the hinge line, which is stabilizing for outside forces such as gusts but could cause overshoots of the stabilator position when pilot-induced forces are involved (the CG wants to "keep going"). **C.** In some cases, the ice could decrease the critical angle of attack (stall angle) so that, for example, when the pilot tries to raise the nose (move the tail down) as on an approach, a too-abrupt movement causes the stabilator to stall (1) and causes the tail-down force to decrease radically (2) so a nose pitch-down results (3).

11

Airplane Stress and Limits of Operation

When you run into turbulent air in VFR conditions, you slow the airplane down and probably also change altitude to try to find smoother air. In extreme conditions (such as over mountainous terrain), you might also decide to make a 180° turn. If you're on an instrument flight plan and actually on instruments, you don't have this immediate freedom of choice. You'll have to slow the airplane down to the recommended speed and notify ATC that your true airspeed has changed. Changing altitude or making a 180° turn has to be cleared with ATC, and you could be in turbulent conditions for some time without relief.

Interestingly, most pilots tend to *overrate* the amount of stress put on the airplane in rough air. A bump that is just about to tear the airplane apart (it seems) may register a miserable 2 g's on an accelerometer. Anyway, this is sort of like locking the barn after the horse is gone, and checking an accelerometer after the fact could result in notification by that instrument (if you had one) that you had just pulled 9 g's and the wings (or other parts) have departed your airplane.

Load Factors—A Review

Before getting too deeply into the subject of stress, the idea of g's might be reviewed. A g is a unit of acceleration. Your body, as you read this, has 1 g acting on it (that is, if you're just sitting motionless somewhere—if you are reading this while on a carnival ride, doing loops, etc., then this statement doesn't apply).

For an airplane, the usual measure of g (or G) forces is the lift-to-weight ratio. In straight and level flight, lift is considered to equal weight, or more properly, the up forces equal the down forces, and the airplane (and the occupants) have 1 positive g working on them. In any steady-state maneuver (climb, descent, straight and level), this is the case, except in the turn. In the level turn, you make lift greater in order for its vertical component to equal the weight of the airplane (Figure 11-1). (You might also review Chapters 1 and 3.)

As shown in Figure 11-1, the lift vector is broken down into horizontal and vertical components. The horizontal component balances the centrifugal force created by the turn, and the vertical component balances the component of weight.

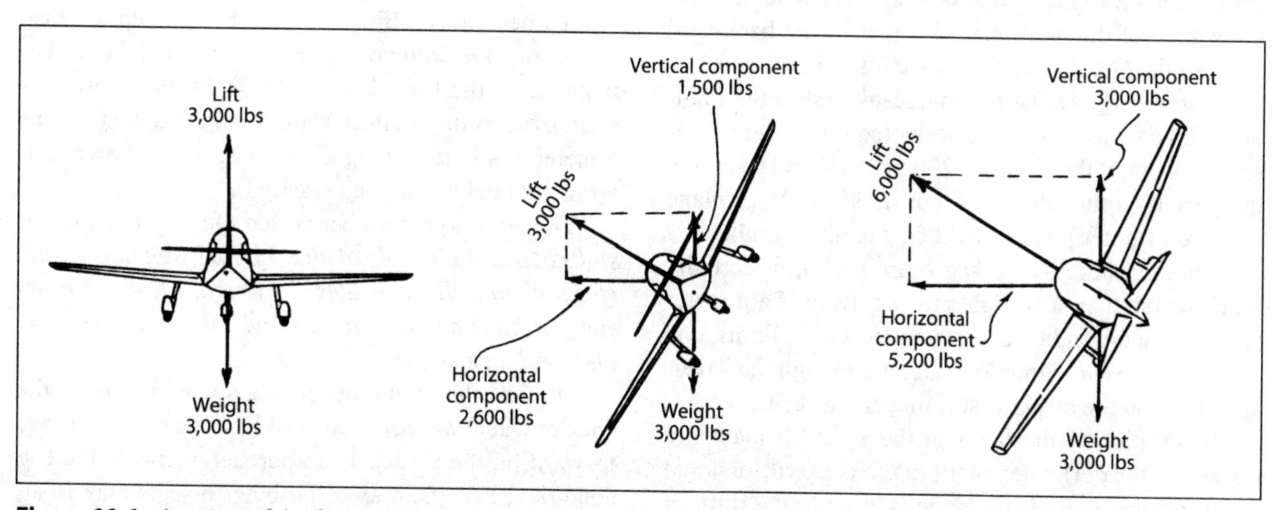

Figure 11-1. A review of the forces in the turn.

In a 30°-banked, balanced, level turn, the total lift required for a 3,000-lb airplane is 3,460 pounds, or the lift-to-weight ratio is approximately 1.15 (the airplane is pulling about 1.15 g's). At a 60° bank (Figure 11-1), the total lift required (6,000 pounds) is *twice* the weight, and the airplane is pulling 2 g's. The stall speed increases as the *square root* of the load factor (or g's pulled). The square root of 2, 1.414, is the multiple of the stall speed existing in 1-g flight. If the plane stalls at 60 K at gross weight in wings-level 1-g flight, it will stall at 1.414 × 60, or 85 K, in a 60°-banked, constant-altitude turn. Figure 11-2 indicates the effects of bank on stall speed and also shows the number of g's (positive) being pulled in a level turn at a particular angle of bank.

You can check the effects of positive g's on stall speed, or if you prefer, check in terms of bank angle. The effects of load factor on stall speed are the same for a straight pull-up as for turning flight. If you are pulling out of a dive and have a load factor of 4, your stall speed is twice normal (Figure 11-2). Or if you try to pull 4 g's in straight and level flight at 115 K (normal stall speed is 60 K at the weight in question), the airplane will stall first. Why? Because the stall speed is *doubled* at 4 g's: 2 × 60 K = 120 K. The speed of 120 K is the minimum this airplane can fly at 4 g's without stalling, and if you try to do the job at 115 K, the airplane will stall before you get the 4 g's.

Suppose your airplane normally stalls at 60 K at the weight at which you are flying, and you decide to do an accelerated stall at 150 K. You horse back on the wheel, and the stall breaks at that speed. It's likely that the stall is not the only thing that will break because you'll pull 6.25 g's, more than the limit load factor on an acrobatic airplane. Your normal stall speed at 1 g is 60 K, and the stall speed multiplier is 150/60 = 2.5. The load factor is the square of the multiplier (this is working backward now) so the $(2.5)^2 = 6.25$ g's. (See also Figure 11-2.)

A stall at 180 K (9 g's) would result in structural failure. You can see that the disoriented pilot who comes spiraling out of the clouds at 200 to 250 K and suddenly pulls back on the wheel will put stress on the airplane that even fighter planes might find hard to handle.

Another thing—a *rolling* sharp pull-up is actually much worse than a straight pull-up. Even if a g meter (accelerometer) indicates that you are within limits, one wing will have a higher load factor although the "average" load on the airplane still may not be critical.

In addition to the fact that the wing lift loads are not equal, the deflection of the ailerons exerts torsional forces on the wing. If the wing is close to the limit of its endurance when the torsional forces are introduced, you may witness an exciting event.

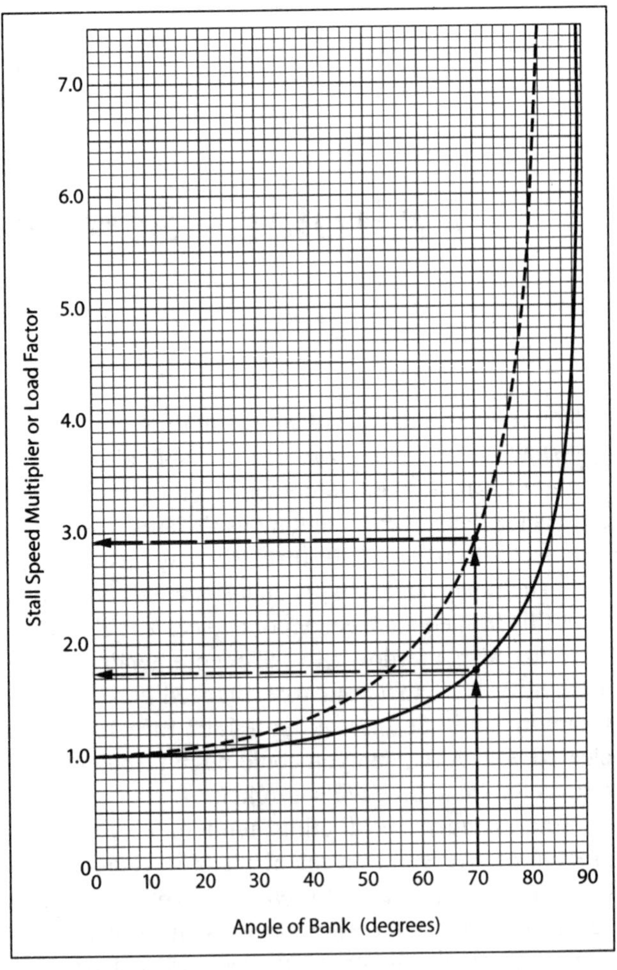

Figure 11-2. Load factors and their effects on stall speed at various bank angles. The dashed line is the load factor, the solid line is the stall speed multiplier. At a 70° bank the load factor is 2.92, the stall speed multiplier 1.71. (Old stall speed 60 K, stall speed in 70° bank = 1.71 x 60, or 103 K.) Notice the sharp increase in both load factor and stall speed at higher bank angles. This applies to all airplanes and airspeeds.

It's best on a rolling pull-up if you keep the load factor to a *maximum* of ⅔ of the limit load factor. For instance, if the limit load factor is 6.0 (acrobatic airplane), the rolling pull-up should not exceed 4.0 on the g meter. It's hard to judge, however, without an accelerometer (and when you're scared).

The point to remember is that the *airplane always stalls at a certain angle of attack for a given flap setting (from 0° to full), regardless of weight, dynamic pressure, or bank angle, and that's why the stall airspeeds and load factors vary.*

On the other hand, negative g's would result if the stick or wheel were shoved briskly forward. If you ease forward on the wheel, you approach or reach the 0-g condition. Pencils, maps, and other objects may float, and you and your passengers may feel light or tend to leave the seat.

Increased forward pressure could result in the aircraft and occupants having negative g's acting on them. Cockpit equipment, such as computers and map cases, slam to the ceiling, and the occupants are forced against the seat belts. There is a sudden awareness among the group of that chili and hot dog lunch of an hour or so ago. The airplane is designed to take less negative-g than positive-g forces.

The average healthy human usually "grays out" (starts to lose vision) at a positive 4 g's and "blacks out" (loses vision) above 6 g's. These average reactions are based on load factors sustained over a period of several seconds; the length of time has a lot to do with the effects. Extended high positive g's can cause loss of consciousness, called "G-LOC." Negative acceleration (or negative g's), as mentioned earlier, is harder on the pilot, and the average person gets pretty uncomfortable at –2 g's.

The physical symptoms of excessive negative acceleration (minus g) are called "red out." The blood rushes to the head and small blood vessels in the eyes may hemorrhage, leaving the eyes looking like road maps for several days after the occurrence.

The pilot's positive-g tolerance may be raised by wearing a *g-suit*, a tight-fitting flight suit with air bladders at the stomach and thighs. The suit is plugged into a pressure source in the airplane and the bladders are automatically inflated when positive-g forces are encountered.

The problem of raising the negative-g tolerance remains unsolved. Of course, an automatic tourniquet around the pilot's neck might stop the flow of blood to the head but this would result in a high turnover of pilots, to say the least.

The airplane, because of the physical limitations of the pilots, is designed to withstand a higher positive than negative load factor.

Airplane Categories

Just how much stress is your airplane able to take, anyway? This depends on the category in which it is certificated. The *normal* category airplane is restricted from aerobatics (acrobatics) and spins. The *utility* category may be approved to do limited aerobatics and spins. (Or it may be restricted from any spins.) The *acrobatic* category may do full aerobatics and spins. The airplane categories you'll be working with during your instrument training are most likely to be normal and utility. An acrobatic category airplane normally is not used in straight VFR flying or instrument work but will be mentioned here as a comparison with the others.

The FAA minimum-limit load factor requirements for lighter airplanes (gross weights below 12,500 pounds) are as follows:

Airplane Category	Positive g's required	Negative g's required
Normal	2.5 to 3.8	40% of the positive g's or –1.0 to –1.52
Utility	4.4	40% of the positive g's or –1.76
Acrobatic	6.0	50% of the positive g's or –3.0

Notice under the normal category that the minimum positive required g's are 2.5 to 3.8. Actually, the requirement states that the positive limit maneuvering load factor shall not be less than 2.5 g's and need not be higher than 3.8 g's. Most manufacturers design for the 3.8 figure (it actually depends on the gross weight of the model), and *this means that the pilot can pull up to 3.8 positive g's without causing permanent deformation or structural damage to that airplane.* In addition to this, a safety factor of 1.5 is built in.

A typical normal category airplane might be designed for the following load factors:

Limit load factor (no deformation): +3.8 g's and –1.52 g's

Ultimate load factor (1.5 safety factor): +5.7 g's and –2.28 g's.

When the ultimate is passed, *primary* structure (wings, engines, etc.) will start to leave the airplane. The secondary structures will have long gone. In other words, if you exceed the limit load factor, you can expect some damage to occur to the airplane. Just how *much* damage will depend on how far you exceed it. If the airplane has been damaged previously, you don't have even a 1.5 safety factor any more.

More About Limit and Ultimate Load Factors

Take a look at Figure 11-3 and the *limit* and *ultimate* load factors.

Pilot A

Figure 11-3 is for the Zephyr Six, a four-place, high-performance, low-wing airplane certificated in the normal category. Suppose that Pilot A decides to try a loop. He's not supposed to do aerobatics in a normal category airplane, but he figures he's so skillful that he won't pull over 3.8 g's.

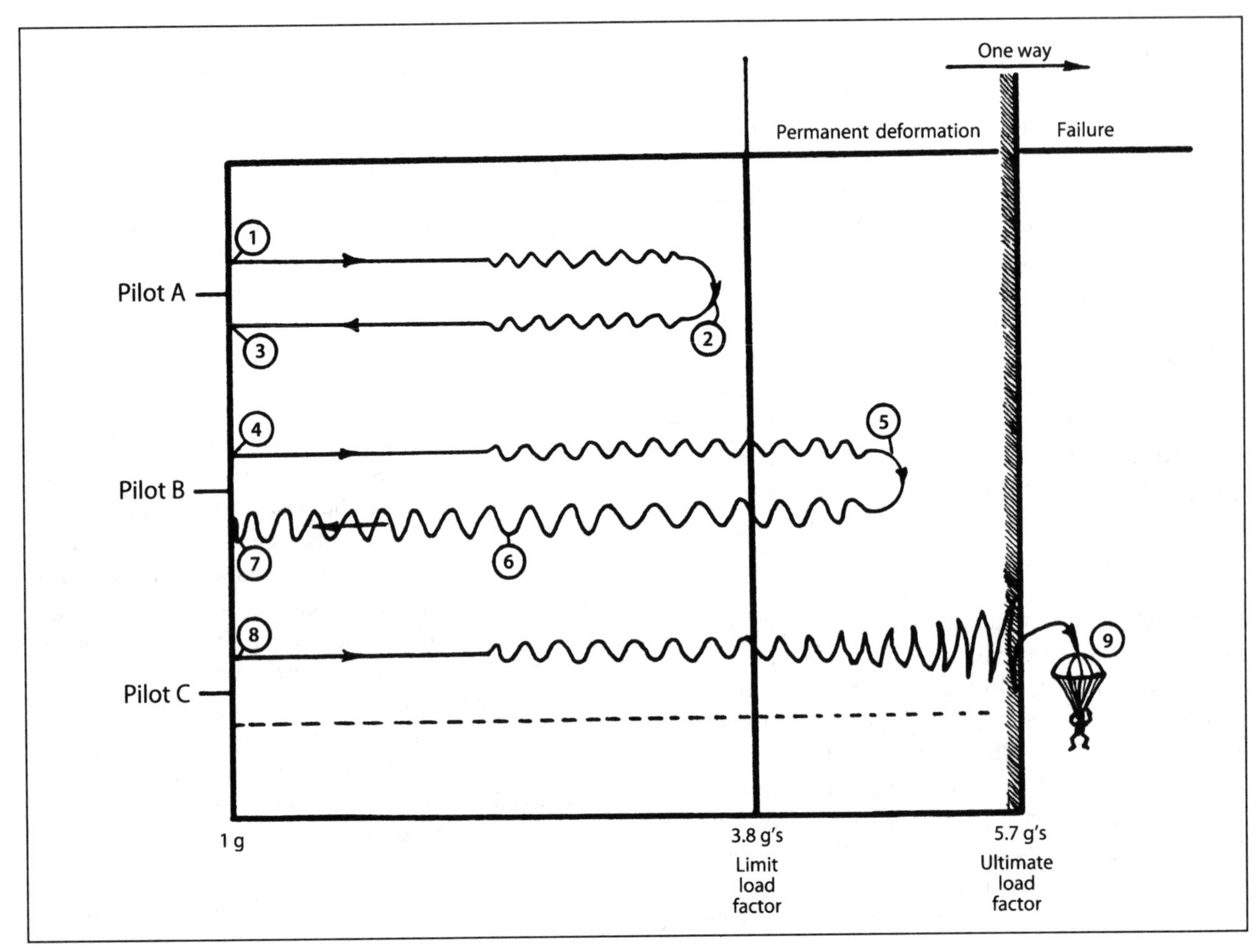

Figure 11-3. Limit and ultimate load factors for the Zephyr Six as "tested" by three pilots.

He dives to what he thinks is a good speed for a loop and pul-l-ls up *very* carefully. His route along the g trail starts at point 1. As the loop continues, he sees that the wings are wrinkled. He immediately starts easing off the back pressure. (The loop goes to pot and the airplane sort of falls out of it, but that's not his worry right now.) The airplane is at point 2 as he relaxes back pressure and the airplane moves back to the 1-g (normal) flight situation at point 3. He notices that the wrinkles disappear as the g forces are relaxed. The plane has no accelerometer and he didn't know that he had gone close to the limit load factor. It wasn't exceeded, so no permanent deformation occurred (the wrinkles disappeared). *Whew!*

Several days later in a hangar-flying session, his equanimity regained, he advises that in doing a loop in the Zephyr Six, "You can expect to see wrinkles during the loop, and you're only in trouble if they're still there after the loop is finished—ha ha." Nearly everyone is impressed.

Pilot B

Pilot B, who has visions of being an international aerobatic champion, didn't hear the last sentence of A's discussion, or it made no impression. Anyway, at the first opportunity, remembering A's description of the loop ("dive to x K and pull"), B does a loop in the Zephyr Six, starting at point 4 in Figure 11-3. Since he knows that the aircraft owner wouldn't approve of aerobatics in his normal category, favorite charter airplane, he flies well out to the far edge of the practice area before doing the loop.

He dives to x K (well, $x + 15$ K, because Pilot A did mention that he'd sorta fallen out of it; being in the process of watching the wings wrinkle and all, so maybe an extra 15 K would be better) and pulls back on the wheel with a goodly tug.

Yep, the wings start wrinkling, just like A said. (A also said that he'd heard somewhere that engineers required that they wrinkle or the wing would break off at the root.) Pilot B continues his mighty tugging and the airplane continues the loop. He doesn't know it, but he went as far as point 5. He eases the back pressure off and figures that the wrinkles ought to disappear as he comes back to point 6. They don't, and he realizes as he comes back to point 7 that, as the engineers would put it, "permanent deformation has occurred." With a large knot in his stomach he flies *carefully* back to the airport thinking of how to explain this to the owner. Maybe he could say he hit an air pocket, or something. The airplane has aged considerably in the last few minutes.

Pilot C

Sometime after the airplane has been repaired, Pilot C, having heard Pilot A's talk about the loop and wings wrinkling but not knowing of B's problems, also decides to do aerobatics in it. He thinks he's read somewhere that parachutes are required for aerobatics (he also should have read that he shouldn't do aerobatics in this airplane). So he gets a parachute, and goes out to practice for the demonstration he promised the local citizens for July Fourth. He also decides to do his practicing at a high altitude for "safety's sake."

C starts out at point 8 and decides to do a square loop as a starter. He starts his dive and pull-up (yes, the wings start wrinkling as expected). This first pull-up will have to be sharp, if the corner is going to be square. To make a long story short, C exceeds the ultimate load factor and is fortunate enough to have both a parachute and altitude. He can't fly back in the airplane to explain. But he telephones home base as soon as he is on the ground and has the parachute gathered up.

Obviously, these three stooges were lucky—no one got hurt. (Things were rounded off a bit here to avoid complications and maybe stretched a mite to make a point.) The airplane may have been previously damaged, and components would fail before reaching the ultimate load factor. Also, the airplane might not get permanent deformation at exactly 3.8001 g's. But the point is, if you *suspect* that you may have exceeded the limit load factor (not having an accelerometer on board), ease back to the airport and have a mechanic look things over.

These examples are given in a humorous vein, but remember that any damage done to the airframe may not come to light for years. It's just plain wrong to do prohibited maneuvers in an airplane.

Airspeed Indicator Markings and Important Airspeeds

In Chapter 4, it was noted that the airspeed markings gave clues to important speeds. You may have wondered just how the speeds were arrived at and why a gust could affect the airplane above or below certain speeds.

You won't need to memorize the following speeds, but they are listed for reference for your information or for ammunition in a hangar-flying session. You remember from Chapter 4 that *indicated airspeed* (IAS) is that registered by the airspeed indicator—and it could be a far-out reading. *Calibrated airspeed* (CAS) is the dynamic pressure or "real" indicated airspeed (with the instrument and system error corrected). At lower airspeeds and altitudes, the CAS is an actual measure of the dynamic pressure acting on the airplane, but at higher speeds and/or altitudes where the airplane might be nudging into compressibility effects, certain corrections must be made. This results in EAS, or CAS corrected for compressibility effects on the airspeed system.

So, to repeat a little: If the airspeed system of your airplane were perfect, the indicated and calibrated airspeeds would be the same at all times. Assume that your airplane is capable of flying at speeds and altitudes where compressibility is encountered. The effect is of "packing" in the pitot tube—the static pressure within the pitot tube and airspeed diaphragm is increased above normal, but the static pressure *outside* the diaphragm (in the instrument case) remains "normal," and therefore, the two static pressures do not cancel out. The result is an airspeed that shows a higher reading than is a measure of the actual dynamic pressure working on the airplane structure. CAS is good enough for slower, lower-flying airplanes and is to be considered the same as EAS in this book.

While we're on the subject, the stresses imposed on the airplane are a function of the dynamic pressure acting on it, so the stress envelopes are based on indicated (or calibrated or equivalent, as applicable) airspeeds, which are measurements of q ($\rho V^2/2$) working on the structure. True airspeed or groundspeed doesn't enter the picture. (For instance, a satellite in orbit has a "true airspeed" of approximately 15,200 K, but because of the extremely low density, the combination of $\rho V^2/2$, or dynamic pressure, is not enough to make a flag on it wave.)

Don't be like the private pilot who, while flying in an easterly direction at normal cruise (indicating in the green airspeed range), checked the progress with a computer and found that because of an exceptionally strong tailwind, the *groundspeed* was well over the red line speed given in the POH, throttled back, and landed immediately, thankful for the escape. Although you shouldn't exceed the red line speed, red line speed is *indicated or calibrated* (depending on the age of the airplane) *airspeed*, not true airspeed or groundspeed. The airspeed indicator hand tells you if you're in trouble in this sort of situation.

Consider CAS as a factor of $(\rho/2)V^2$. If you want to find the dynamic pressure acting on the airplane, use the equation $V^2KCAS/295$ = dynamic pressure in pounds per square foot.

Here are some of the design airspeeds (CAS) that are important in this chapter:

1. V_C—*Design cruising speed.* In designing an airplane, the manufacturer must plan for the following minimum V_C speeds in knots of at least:

a. $33\sqrt{W/S}$ for normal and utility category airplanes. The term W/S is the wing loading (gross weight divided by area) so that an airplane with a wing loading of 16 pounds per square foot (psf) would have a V_C of $33 \times \sqrt{16} = 33 \times 4 = 132$ K.

b. $36\sqrt{W/S}$ for acrobatic category airplanes. A manufacturer wanting to make a plane with a wing loading of 16 psf in the acrobatic category would have to make sure the airplane meets certain strength requirements at $36\sqrt{W/S} = 36 \times \sqrt{16} = 36 \times 4 = 144$ K.

2. V_{NO}—*Maximum structural cruising speed.* This is the limit of the green arc, where the green and yellow arcs meet. It must be no less than the minimum value of V_C just discussed. For the purpose of this book, it is shown to be the *exact* value of V_C in the markings and requirements of the figures shown.

3. V_D—*Design dive speed.* The manufacturer must prove that the airplane is capable of diving to certain speeds without coming unglued. The minimums are:

a. 1.40 V_C (min) for *normal* category airplanes. This means that the airplane with 16-psf wing loading (V_C = 132 K) would have a minimum V_D of $1.40 \times 132 = 185$ K.

b. An airplane of the same wing loading, if in the *utility* category, would have a minimum V_D of $1.50 \times 132 = 198$ K.

4. V_{NE}—*Never exceed speed.* This is the red line on the airspeed indicator and is not more than 0.9 of the V_D speed. *A test pilot flying up to the V_D speed in an airplane with a quick-jettison door wears a parachute. If you exceed the red line (V_{NE}) and search for V_D, you may discover a vital need for such equipment. Do not exceed the red line.*

5. V_A—*The maneuvering speed.* This is the maximum speed at a particular weight at which the controls may be fully deflected without overstressing the airplane. This one is not marked on the airspeed indicator and will be covered in more detail in sections following.

The Maneuver Envelope

For the normal category airplane, the *maneuver envelope* basically shows the limits of load factor and airspeed allowed for that airplane at a particular weight. Figure 11-4 is for a fictitious normal category airplane at its maximum certificated weight. Maneuver (and gust) envelopes are made up for weights down to the *minimum weight*, which is defined as the basic empty weight of the airplane with standard equipment, plus required crew at 170 pounds each, plus fuel of no more than the quantity necessary to operate for ½ hour at max continuous power. (This is a quick and dirty way of looking at the minimum weight; for more detail, check 14 CFR Part 23. Figure 11-4 matches some airspeeds with the maneuver envelope. The maneuver envelope for flaps-extended flight is drawn in with hatched lines. (The *maneuver* envelope is considered to cover the limits of *pilot-induced* load factors at various speeds.)

14 CFR Part 23 covers the strength requirements for normal and utility (and acrobatic) category airplanes, and the requirements are reasonable enough: You are not to exceed the limit load factors of +3.8 g's or –1.52 g's for the normal category airplane at any time. When flying between V_A (the maneuvering speed) and V_{NE}, (the red line speed), just make sure that your handling of the elevators does not break this rule. Note in Figure 11-4 that above V_{NO} the negative g's are further restricted in this range.

V_A, the maneuvering speed, is the dividing line between exceeding the limit load factor and stalling the airplane before getting into such a problem. Looking back a little earlier in the chapter, if you wanted to pull 4 g's in flight (and no more) with the plane that normally stalls at 60 K, you would stall the airplane at 120 K—and no faster. By pulling back abruptly at any speed less than 120 K, you'll never pull 4 g's. If you pull back abruptly at 90 K, you'll put 2.25 positive g's on the airplane (and occupants). It's the old story of squaring the ratio of stall speeds: (accelerated stall speed/normal stall speed)^2 = $(90/60)^2 = (1.5)^2 = 2.25$ g's. That's how the curved line running from the normal stall at 1 g (60 K) up to the maneuvering speed was developed. The stall speeds at various load factors were worked out. However, instead of 4 g's, the positive limit load factor for this normal category airplane is 3.8 g's, so the maneuvering speed is $\sqrt{3.8} \times 60$ K $= 1.95 \times 60 = 117$ K. If you are at the maximum certificated weight,

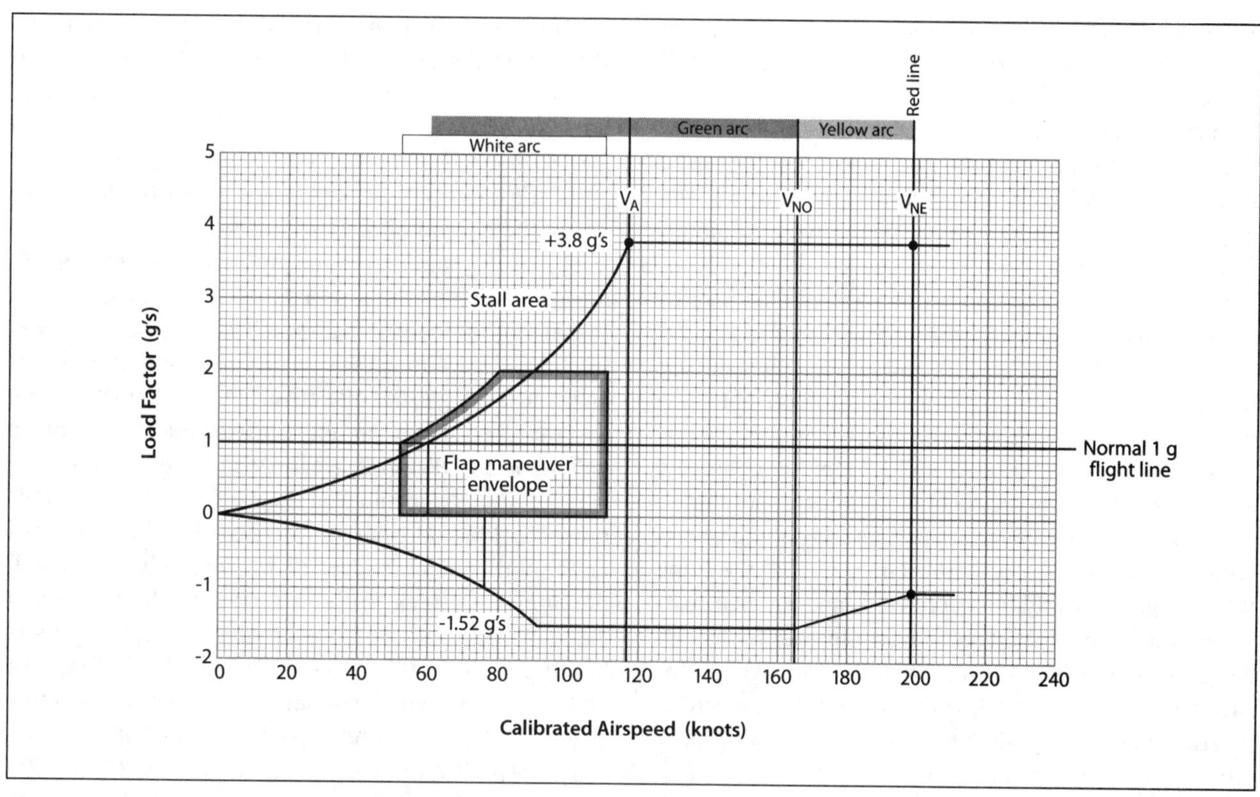

Figure 11-4. The maneuver envelope for a particular normal category airplane at max certificated weight. The envelope for flight with the flaps extended (white arc on the airspeed indicator) is shown.

you'd slow down to this airspeed (or below) in rough air so that a sharp-edged vertical gust would result in a stall rather than exceeding the limit load factor. Vertical gusts will be covered later.

So, it's agreed that at the max certificated weight (3,000 pounds in this example), the example airplane will stall before running into stress problems if the airspeed is kept below 117 K.

The stress imposed is a function of the lift-to-weight ratio. The amount of lift an airplane can suddenly produce depends on the coefficient of lift (proportional to angle of attack), wing area, air density, and TAS ($L = C_L S(\rho/2)V^2$). Since the wing area is constant for a particular airplane and its wing can only develop a certain maximum coefficient of lift before stalling, the amount of lift available varies with the square of the airspeed. Since the maneuvering speed for this fictitious airplane is established as 117 K at a gross weight of 3,000 pounds, it would be able to develop a maximum of 11,400 pounds of lift at 117 K without stalling or pulling over 3.8 g's (3.8 × 3,000 = 11,400 pounds). Check back to Figure 2-8 and note that the C_L drops rapidly after the angle of attack for stall so that a peak lift is made available by suddenly increasing the angle of attack at a specific airspeed. The peak lift at 117 K for this airplane is 11,400 pounds, which gives a load factor of 3.8, resulting from the combination of C_{LMAX}, wing area (S), air density (ρ) divided by 2, and TAS squared (V^2). The C_L used here will be C_{LMAX} (clean) since this is the factor at the stall. (You might review the section on lift in Chapter 2 if this is hazy right now.) The load factor as checked by the engineers is 11,400 (lift)/3,000 (weight) = 3.8 g's if the airplane is stalled at 117 K. So this is the maneuvering speed—or is it? It's *the* maneuvering speed for the gross weight of 3,000 pounds *but not for lower weights.* The maneuvering speed must decrease with the square root of the weight decrease, as introduced in Chapter 1.

Take the airplane at a near empty weight of 1,500 pounds. Admittedly, it's unusual for an airplane to be able to fly at a weight one-half its gross weight, but there are some models capable of this ratio and it makes for easier figuring.

Assume again that the airplane is abruptly stalled at 117 K at the light weight of 1,500 pounds. Since the maximum *lift* developed depends only on the lift factors just mentioned and has no bearing on the weight of the airplane, 11,400 pounds will be developed as before. The positive load factor will be 11,400/1,500 = 7.6 g's. The first impression is that the occupants will have 7.6 g's working on them and will probably black out (it depends on the length of time they are subjected to the load factor; this abrupt movement would result in only a very short period of 7.6 g's before the stall occurs, so let's forget them).

Okay, you say, the wings have the same load as before (11,400), so what's the problem except for a brief discomfort on the part of the pilot and passengers? The wings are all right, but there *are* "fixed-weight components," such as the engine(s), baggage, retracted landing gear, etc. The airplane's limit load factor here of 3.8 g's is based on an overall analysis of the aircraft components. The engine has gotten no lighter during the flight, and it is, as mentioned, a fixed-weight component. Because of the lighter overall weight of the airplane, the engine and other fixed-weight components are subjected to greater acceleration forces. The engine mounts may not be able to support an engine and accessories that weigh nearly 8 times normal, and the same thing might be said about retracted landing gear, batteries, and baggage. You recall from Chapter 10 that the baggage compartment is placarded for max weight for *two* reasons: (1) the CG could be moved to a dangerous position and (2) the baggage compartment floor is only stressed to take a certain number of g's with the placarded weight. For instance, the example airplane, which has a limit load factor of 3.8 positive g's, has a limit of 200 pounds weight in the baggage compartment and could have a total force up to 3.8 × 200 pounds, or 760 pounds acting on the floor without structural damage. The pilot who stalled the airplane at the light weight of the airplane at the 117-K speed has caused a force of 7.6 × 200 pounds, or 1,520 pounds, to be exerted on the floor. Figure 11-5 shows that the lighter weight at the old maneuvering speed results in load factors that can cause problems for the fixed-weight components.

Figure 11-5. Using the maneuvering speed for max certificated weight at lighter weights can put extra stress on the fixed-weight components.

If you put 400 pounds in the baggage compartment and pulled the legal 3.8 g's, the result would also be illegal, immoral, and disappointing: 1,520 pounds (temporarily) acting on a compartment floor that is stressed for 760 pounds. An effort of this nature probably will allow the taking of aerial photographs through the hole where the bottom of the compartment used to be. This is a separate matter from the problem of the maneuvering speed change but is a factor to be watched also.

A *new* maneuvering speed is necessary for the lighter weight. Since the overall limit for this fictitious airplane is 3.8 g's, the maneuvering speed must be such that that load factor cannot be exceeded—the airplane will stall first. Again, since the load factor is the lift-to-weight ratio, the airplane at the weight of 1,500 pounds must be flown at such an airspeed that the limit load factor will not be exceeded by suddenly increasing the angle of attack to the maximum. The maximum allowable lift with this lighter weight is 5,700 pounds because 5,700/1,500 = 3.8 g's. The variable is airspeed, and since airspeed is a squared function, the new airspeed (V_2) can be found: $L_1 = C_{LMAX}S(\rho/2)(V_1)^2$, $L_2 = C_{LMAX}S(\rho/2)(V_2)^2$. If L_1 = 11,400 pounds, L_2 = 5,700 pounds, and V_1 = 117 K, V_2 = ?

The maximum C_L attainable is fixed, as is the wing area, so what it boils down to is that the ratio of the two maneuvering speeds is proportional to the *square root* of the ratio of weights (because the two fixed factors of wing area and air density cancel each other): $(V_2)^2/(V_1)^2 = L_2/L_1$; $V_2/V_1 = \sqrt{L_2/L_1}$; $V_2/V_1 = \sqrt{5{,}700/11{,}400} = \sqrt{0.5} = 0.7$, or $V_2 = 0.7V_1$.

The second (lighter weight) maneuvering speed is seven-tenths of the original. Since the original was 117 K, the new one (at 1,500 pounds) is 0.7 × 117 = 82 K. Figure 11-6 compares the maneuvering envelopes at both weights. Notice that the only changes occur at the lower end of the speed range; the red line speed is the same, and the limit load factors have not changed.

The extension of the dashed curved line shows that if the airplane is abruptly stalled at the higher maneuvering speed of 117 K, a load factor of 7.6 g's will result—which is another way of looking at the comparison just discussed (Figure 11-6).

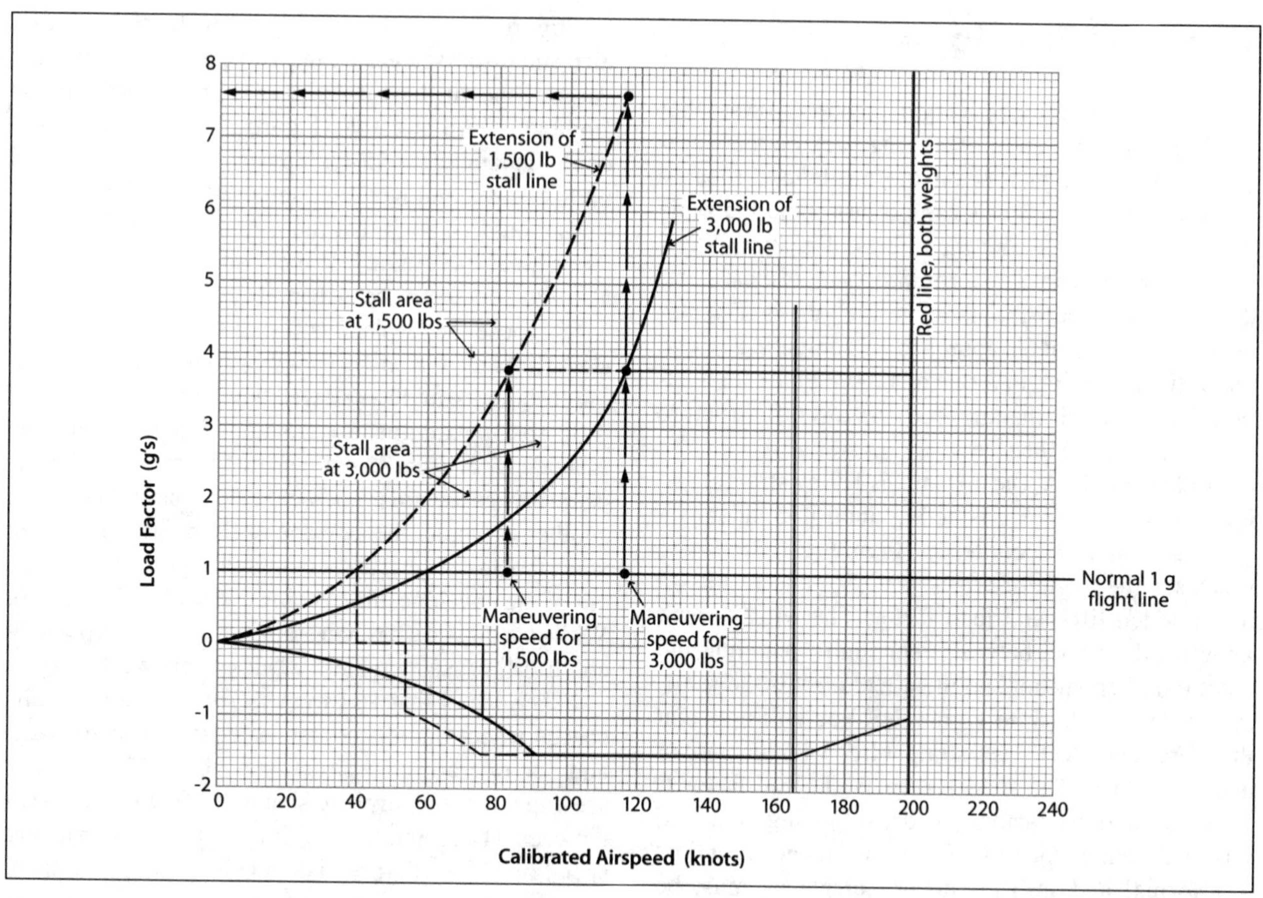

Figure 11-6. The maneuver envelope for two aircraft weights showing the two maneuvering speeds. The dashed lines show how the maneuver envelope is extended back to lower speeds as the weight decreases. (See also Figure 11-13 at the end of the chapter for weight effects on V_A for a particular airplane.)

In-Flight Failures

Airplanes are still being flown into IFR conditions by pilots who aren't qualified, and witnesses still report hearing an "explosion" in the clouds and seeing parts of an airplane falling out of the bases to the ground. Or, in VFR conditions, the pilot may let the airplane get into an airspeed and/or g's beyond its design limits. Many times witnesses hear—and see—the breakup, and the noise and breakup convince them that an internal explosion did occur and they may even convince themselves there was a fiery blast with accompanying smoke. This may throw off accident investigators for a while until a check of the wreckage shows no scorching.

Taking a hypothetical situation, assume that a normally configured airplane is in a high-speed, uncontrolled spiral. The pilot is pulling back on the wheel to pull the nose up (not realizing that the wings should be leveled first) and is increasing the download on the horizontal tail.

In this case, the wings have a very high *upload*, while the tail is being overstressed by the added download induced by the pilot's attempt to bring the nose up. If the tail fails first (it will break off "downward"), the nose will pitch down immediately and the wings, which were probably about to break off upward (and may have already been permanently bent in that direction), are now subjected to an instantaneous force in the opposite direction and fail downward. It's possible, too, that a wing (or both wings) could fail first, taking the tail with it.

The accident investigator doesn't take anything for granted, but a wings-downward failure *usually* means that the horizontal tail went first and a wing-upward failing *usually* means that that item failed first. In the earlier scenario, where the wings had high positive loads during the pull-up and then failed downward the instant the tail failed, the spars may have been deformed by the high positive (up) load before they failed downward, and this might be the *first* clue seen. It's fairly unusual for both wings to fail simultaneously but it has happened.

The current retractable-gear (and some fixed-gear) airplanes are very clean and can build up excess speed very quickly. Keep it in mind.

The Gust Envelope

The maneuver envelope is very interesting, you say, but who's going to fly around yanking back on the wheel and putting load factors on the airplane? Probably nobody, but vertical gusts can do just about the same thing. Figure 11-7 shows the effects of a sharp-edged gust on the airplane. The term *sharp-edged* means that the transition from smooth air to the gust is instantaneous—this is a safer approach in computing stress, rather than thinking in terms of a more gradual transition during which the airspeed and aircraft structure would "adjust" to the stress.

In Figure 11-7A, the airplane is flying straight and level at cruise, and 1 g is acting upon it. Suddenly, a vertical gust is encountered (Figure 11-7B), which increases the angle of attack (and C_L) and results in much added lift—and load factor. The wing doesn't know the difference between your control handling and a natural phenomenon, so the effect on it is the same. Again, looking back to Figure 2-8, you will note that the increase in the C_L is a straight line with increase of angle of attack. The sudden increase in load factor is because the other factors (air density, wing area, and airspeed) remain the same for an instantaneous action.

Normal and utility category airplanes must be able to withstand vertical gusts of 30 fps at the maximum structural cruising speed (V_{NO}, the junction of the green and yellow arcs on the airspeed) and 15-fps sharp-edged vertical gusts up to the design dive speed (models certificated under 14 CFR Part 23).

Criteria have been established in Part 23 concerning the effects of gusts on the airplane. The gusts in the design specifications are stronger, but the requirements include a "gust alleviation" factor that brings the result back pretty close to the 15- and 30-fps sharp-edged gusts. The idea of an instant change is easier to see in an example, so it is used here.

Figure 11-8 shows a gust envelope for the fictitious airplane discussed earlier (at max certificated weight). Assume the airplane is flying straight and level in 1-g flight at a CAS of 140 K (Figure 11-8, point 1). It suddenly encounters a 15-fps upward gust and is moved up to point 2 and has 2 g's imposed on it. The conditions would be such that the airplane would return to its original 1-g flight, but the load factor would have already worked on the airframe.

Suppose the airplane is flying straight and level in slow flight at 70 K at 1 g (point 3). (The pilot is expecting turbulence and has slowed down to take care of it.) A 30-fps upward gust is encountered, and the airplane is suddenly at point 4—or it should be said that the airplane moves toward point 4 but enters the stall area. As another example, the airplane is flying at the red line when the 30-fps gust is encountered at point 5; it will be out of the envelope and become overstressed (point 6). While a stall is better than losing part of the airplane, it could still cause a problem when you are on the gages.

The idea is that you want to fly in an area of airspeeds where there is no danger of stall *or* overstress, and for operating in situations where 30-fps gusts are expected, the airplane should be flown at a speed between 117 K and the maximum structural cruising speed of 165 K (Figure 11-8). (This is for the airplane at max certificated weight.)

The effects of gusts, like the earlier example of sudden full-elevator deflection, are increased at lighter weights so that the lines representing the gusts are "spread apart," and a 30-fps gust may actually result in stresses greater than that indicated by the maneuvering envelope (Figure 11-9).

The 30-fps gust has put the load factor up to 4.5 g's, but this has been justified by the manufacturer, as shown by the solid line, which indicates the *limit combined envelope boundary*. Just a minute, you say—back in the section discussing the maneuvering envelope, it

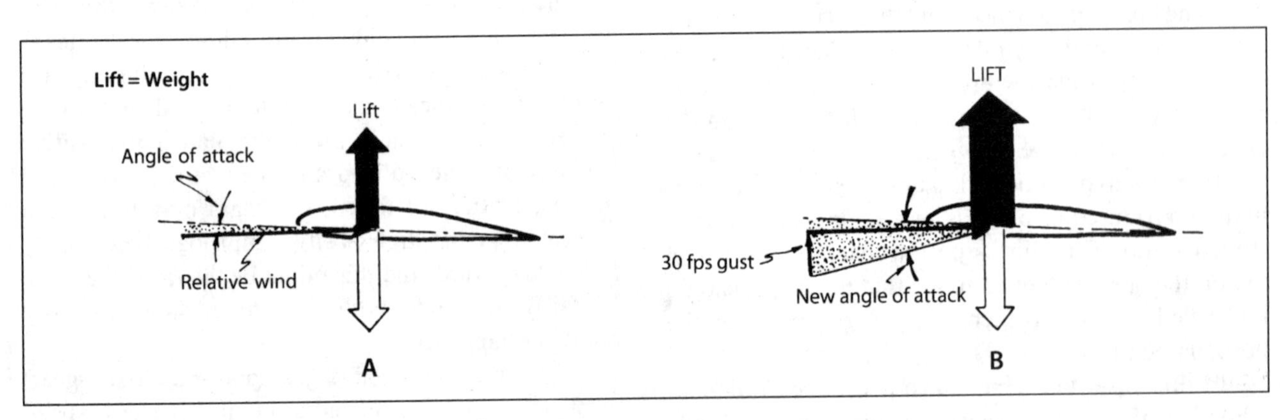

Figure 11-7. The effects of a vertical (upward) gust.

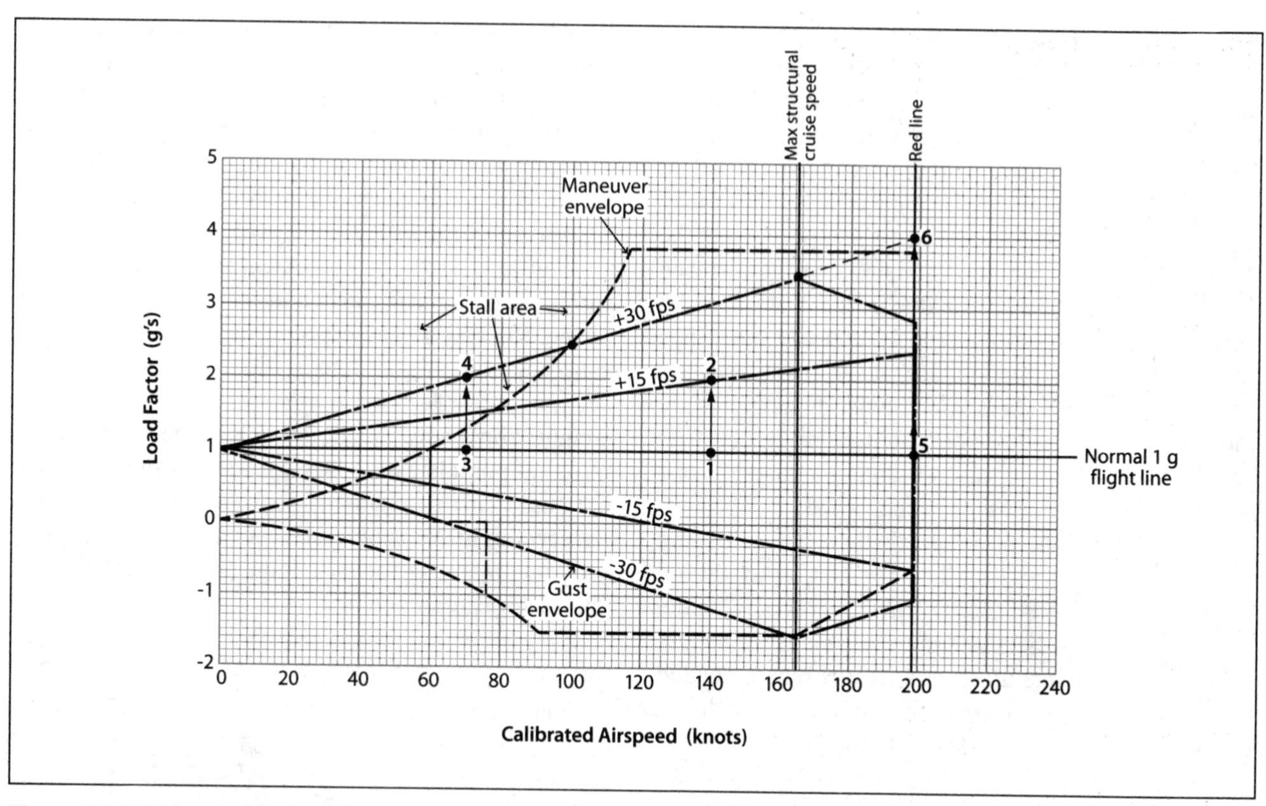

Figure 11-8. The gust envelope for the example airplane at max certificated weight. The maneuver envelope is indicated by the dashed line.

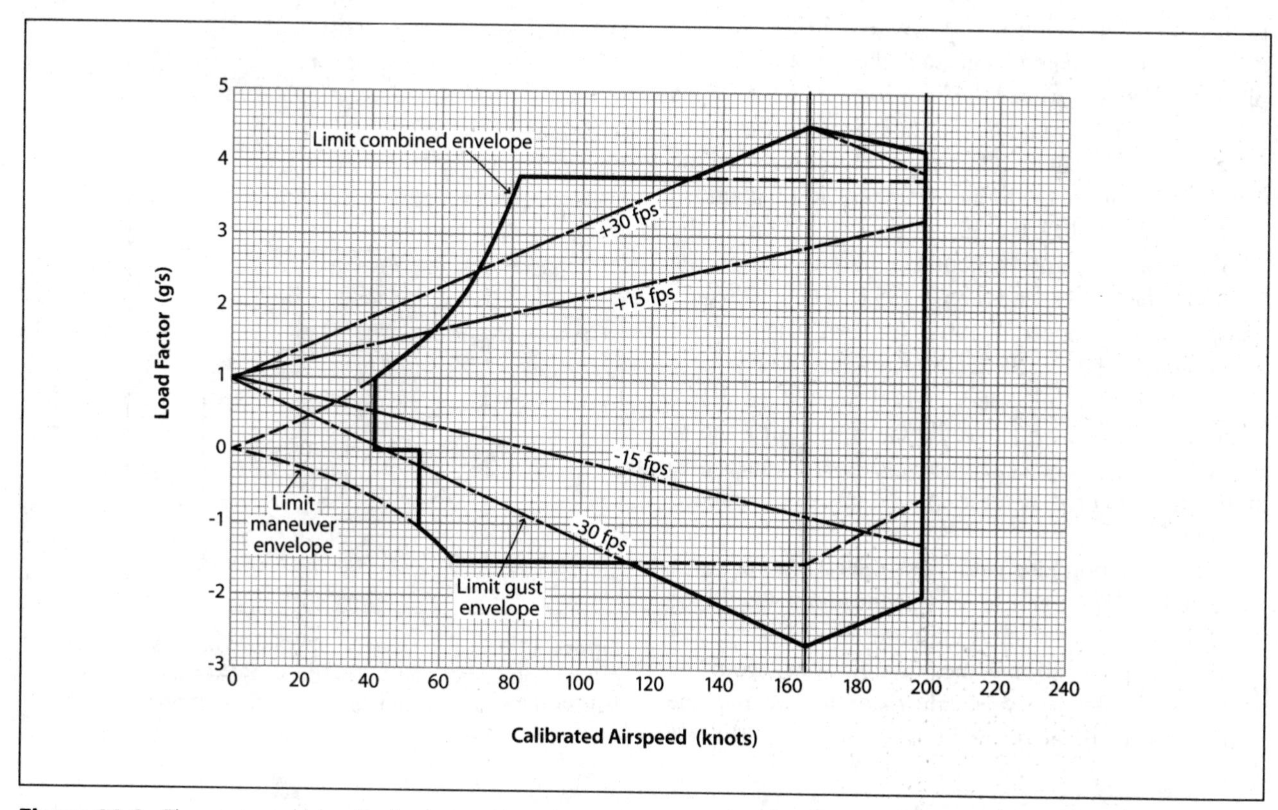

Figure 11-9. The gust envelope for the example airplane at a near-empty weight (a +30 fps gust at the V_{NO} of 164 K pulls 4.5 g's).

was noted that the pilot was not to handle the elevators in such a way that the airplane could exceed the limit load factor (in this case 3.8 g's); now, all of a sudden, the airplane can hit a 30-fps gust and exceed 3.8 g's, and it's okay. The answer is that the elevators must not be fully deflected above the maneuvering speed (it may not require full deflection at the higher speed to get the 4.5 g's). The manufacturer assumes that the airplane is flying straight and level with fixed elevators, and a vertical gust changes the angle of attack of the wings without elevator deflection. To get the same load factor by elevator deflection, strong twisting moments are introduced, and the horizontal tail could be the first part to leave your company. The manufacturer plays it safe as far as elevator usage is concerned.

Notice the range of airspeeds between exceeding the maneuvering limit load factor of 3.8 g's and stalling (even at the lower stall speed). The effect is moving the "safe" speed range back and narrowing it as the weight decreases. Some manufacturers list the recommended flight speed ranges for gross and minimum weights at various expected gust velocities in the POH.

Figure 11-10 shows the "safe speed range" (no stall or overstress) for the fictitious airplane discussed earlier at weights of 3,000 and 1,500 pounds. Assume for simplicity that the manufacturer wants to give the pilot information for flying in areas where 30-fps vertical gusts are expected and wants to make sure that the airplane does not (1) exceed the limit load factor of 3.8 g's or (2) stall at these weights. (For this example, disregard the earlier comment that the manufacturer justified the 4.5-g load factor at the lighter weight of 1,500 pounds.)

In Figure 11-10A the 30-fps gust would cause the airplane, at a weight of 3,000 pounds, to exceed the limit load factor at speeds above 185 K. The gust would cause a stall at a speed of 100 K (or less). The range of safe operation here is 85 K (185 K minus 100 K).

In Figure 11-10B, at a lighter weight of 1,500 pounds, the 30-fps gust would cause the airplane to exceed the 3.8-g load factor at 130 K and cause it to stall at a speed of 70 K (or less). The spread of airspeed would be 60 K.

At 3,000 pounds, your best operating speed in expected 30-fps vertical gust conditions would be 142.5 K. (Sure, you could maintain this exactly.) For the light weight condition, the midpoint speed would be 100 K, which is the lowest safe speed for the airplane at the max certificated weight of 3,000 pounds (Figure 11-10A).

The manufacturer may show graphs of several gust values and airplane weights and may also take into consideration any justifications of stress required in certification of the airplane. Also, the graph may have a certain (center) area of the safe airspeeds shown in green, with yellow caution areas at each end (and red lines to show the stall and overstress points).

Figure 11-11 shows a turbulent air penetration graph for an airplane at a particular weight when encountering 30- and 45-fps gusts. You might sketch in an estimated 45-fps gust line in Figures 11-8 and 11-9 to see how much leeway in airspeed you'd have at each weight. You'd have maybe 3 to 5 K at the heavy weight of 3,000 pounds as the line cuts across the V_A corner but might miss the maneuver envelope altogether at the lighter weight. You could make a graph like that in Figure 11-11 by using various airspeeds (marking them in yellow for caution, etc.).

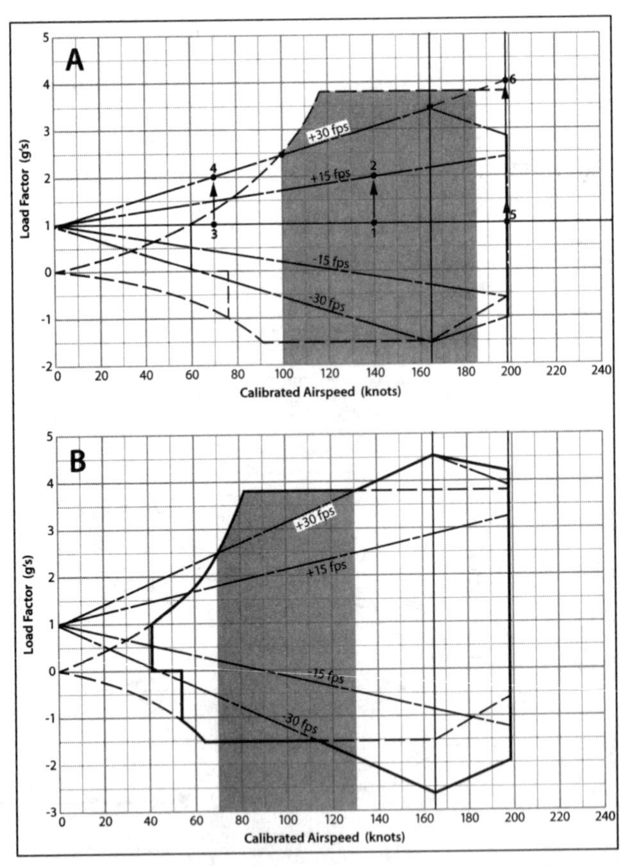

Figure 11-10. The range of operations (airspeed) for 30-fps gusts at gross weight of 3,000 pounds **(A)** and 1,500 pounds **(B)**. A 45-fps gust would cut the safe area even thinner.

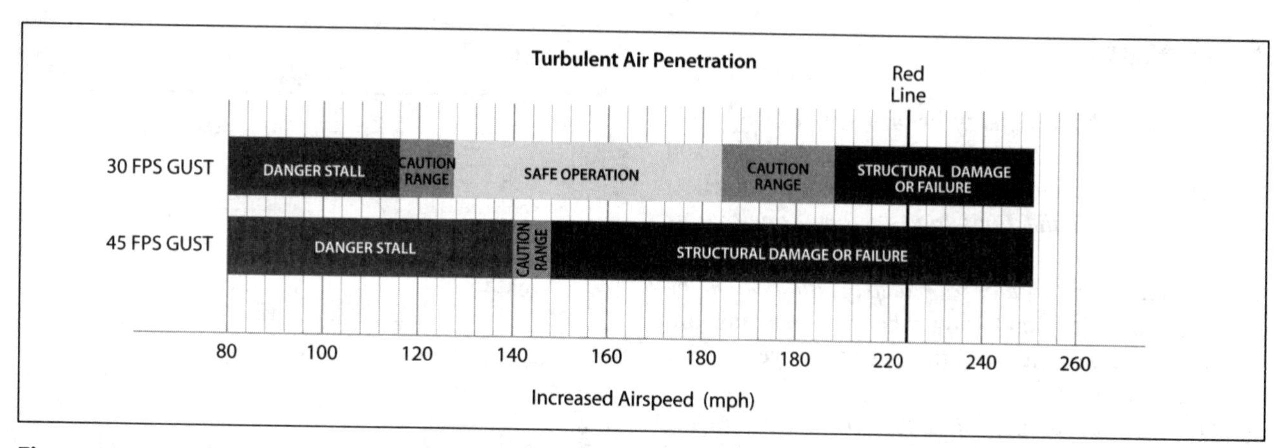

Figure 11-11. Turbulent air penetration graph. (You could make up such a chart using the gust and maneuver envelopes of the fictitious airplane of Figures 11-8, 11-9, and 11-10.)

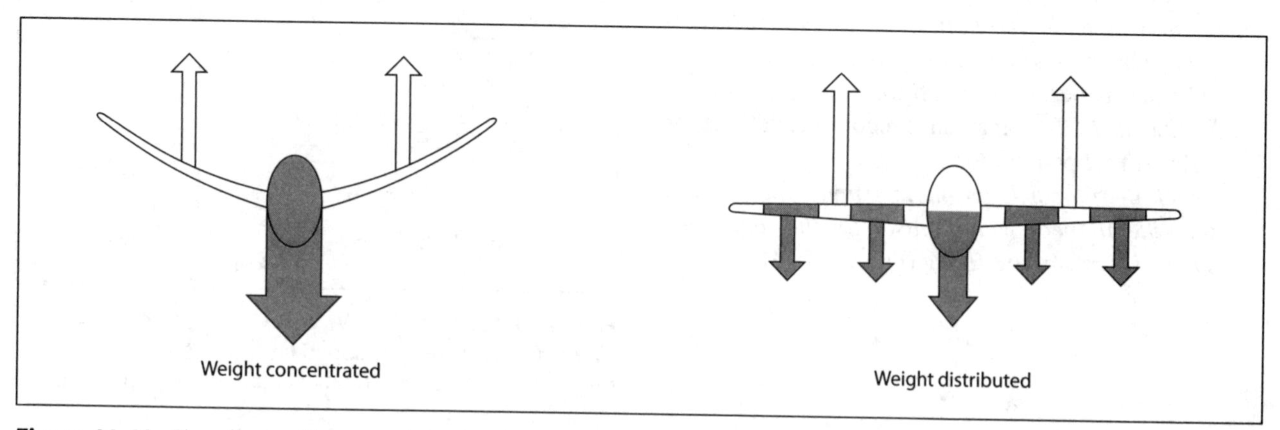

Figure 11-12. The effects of lateral weight distribution on gust- or pilot-induced stress.

Another factor in stress on the airplane is how the load is distributed. Figure 11-12 shows the effects of a vertical gust on airplanes of different wing load distributions. You can see that full tip tanks might give a better lateral weight distribution effect in gusts.

You can consider that 30-fps gusts are found *in the vicinity of* thunderstorms, 45-fps gusts are found near thunderstorms, and *inside* a cell these values can be exceeded by a wide margin.

The up-gusts were discussed first because gusts acting in this direction are more readily understood. But the down-acting gusts are more uncomfortable on the pilot and airframe. A vector system of the type illustrated in Figure 11-7 could be drawn for the down-acting gust, and the result would be a sharp decrease in angle of attack (and lift), accompanied by the sound of seat belts being stretched and heads contacting the head liner.

Summary

1. *Always look for signs of prior overstressing when you do your preflight.* And get the airplane checked out if you've accidentally flown into bad turbulence.
2. *Don't exceed the limit load factors—positive or negative.*
3. *In moderately turbulent air, keep the airspeed in the green arc.* You don't know when you may encounter severe turbulence. Stay out of the yellow arc when it's bumpy.
4. *In severe turbulence, slow the airplane below the maneuvering speed for your current weight.* Use 1.7 times the flaps-up, power-off stall speed (CAS) as a rule of thumb (again, for your current weight).
5. *If you want to do aerobatics, rent an aerobatic airplane* (chandelles and lazy eights are not considered to be acrobatics, or *aerobatics*).
6. *Read your POH.* It may have recommendations for turbulent air penetration.
7. *Check the placards on the instrument panel, and keep the airspeed within reason for the conditions under which you are flying* (Figure 11-13).

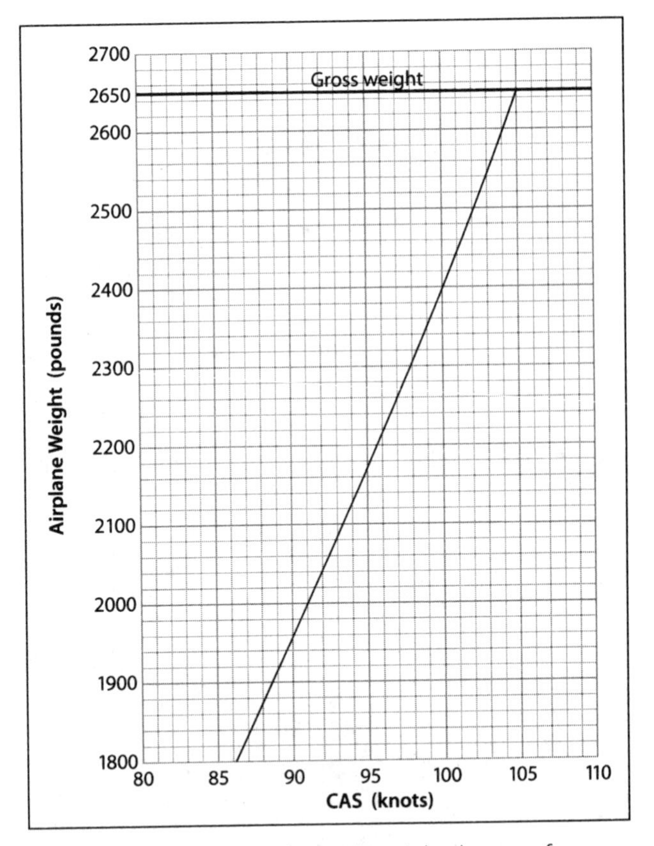

Figure 11-13. Change of V_A with weight decrease for a particular airplane, developed from Figure 1-12. Yours may have the airspeeds in tabular form for several lighter weights.

Part Two **Checking Out in Advanced Models and Types** 2

12

Airplane with Constant-Speed Propellers

The Checkout

When you first check out in an airplane with a constant-speed propeller, things can be pretty hectic. In the first place, it's a new airplane to you and the addition of the propeller control further complicates matters. After all, it's only *one* more control you say to yourself, but juggling the throttle and prop to get the right combination of power may cause some consternation for the first few tries. The check pilot who's sitting so calmly in the right seat once had the same problem. If he's grinning at your workout, it's probably because he's remembering his first struggle with throttle *and* prop controls.

The constant-speed prop allows you to get more efficiency out of the engine-propeller combination in all speed ranges. That extra control is not just put there to complicate matters, although it does impress the nonpilot to see you making adjustments with those mysterious knobs. One of the major factors is the ability to get max power on takeoff without compromising cruise performance.

The discussion of throttle and propeller controls in this chapter will cover their use with the unturbocharged or normally aspirated engine. Turbochargers will be covered in Chapter 19.

The HP developed by a particular engine depends on the manifold pressure and rpm. For instance, 65% power, often used for cruise, may be set up in several combinations of manifold pressure (mp) and rpm. The manufacturer furnishes a power setting table that allows the pilot to establish the desired HP for a particular altitude (Figure 12-1).

Another thing you might look at in Figure 12-1—the mp required at a particular rpm becomes less as altitude increases. At sea level, at 2,200 rpm, 23.3 inches of mp are required to develop 65%. At 5,000 feet, only 22 inches are required for 65% power at 2,200 rpm. There are two main reasons for this apparent inconsistency: (1) The exhaust gases have less outside pressure (back pressure) to fight at higher altitudes. Remember that the "explosion" in the cylinder is sealed, and power from the other cylinders must be used to expel

Power Setting Table — Lycoming Model O-540-A1B5, 250 HP Engine

Press. Alt. 1000 Feet	Std. Alt. Temp. °F.	138 HP 55% Rated Approx. Fuel 10.3 Gal. Hr. RPM AND MAN. PRESS.				163 HP 65% Rated Approx. Fuel 12.3 Gal. Hr. RPM AND MAN. PRESS.				188 HP 75% Rated Approx. Fuel 14.0 Gal. Hr. RPM AND MAN. PRESS.		
		2100	2200	2300	2400	2100	2200	2300	2400	2200	2300	2400
SL	59	21.6	20.8	20.2	19.6	24.2	23.3	22.6	22.0	25.8	25.1	24.3
1	55	21.4	20.6	20.0	19.3	23.9	23.0	22.4	21.8	25.5	24.8	24.1
2	52	21.4	20.4	19.7	19.1	23.7	22.8	22.2	21.5	25.3	24.6	23.8
3	48	20.9	20.1	19.5	18.9	23.4	22.5	21.9	21.3	25.0	24.3	23.6
4	45	20.6	19.9	19.3	18.7	23.1	22.3	21.7	21.0	24.8	24.1	23.3
5	41	20.4	19.7	19.1	18.5	22.9	22.0	21.4	20.8	—	23.8	23.0
6	38	20.1	19.5	18.9	18.3	22.6	21.8	21.2	20.6	—	—	22.8
7	34	19.9	19.2	18.6	18.0	22.3	21.5	21.0	20.4	—	—	—
8	31	19.6	19.0	18.4	17.8	—	—	20.5	19.9			
9	27	19.4	18.8	18.2	17.6	—	21.3	20.7	20.1			
10	23	19.1	18.6	18.0	17.4	—	—	—	19.6			
11	19	18.9	18.3	17.8	17.2	—	—	—	—			
12	16	18.6	18.1	17.5	17.0	—	—	—	—			
13	12	—	17.9	17.3	16.8							
14	9	—	—	17.1	16.5							
15	5	—	—	—	16.3							

To maintain constant power, correct manifold pressure approximately 0.17" Hg for each 10° F. variation in carburetor air temperature from standard altitude temperature. Add manifold pressure for air temperatures above standard; subtract for temperatures below standard.

Figure 12-1. Power-setting table.

the waste gases. Less back pressure means less power used to eliminate this waste—power that can be used in making the airplane go. (2) The air is cooler at higher altitudes. If you use the same mp as you carried at sea level, the mixture density and the HP developed would be greater (lower temperature means greater density if the pressure remains the same). Therefore, in order to maintain the same power, less mp is used for a given rpm with altitude increase, as Figure 12-1 shows.

The figures given in the table are for standard pressure-altitudes. The footnote shows how to correct for deviations from standard temperature, though in actual practice this is seldom done (unless you have a digital mp gage).

While we're on the subject of the power table, notice that you are unable to maintain the various percentages of power above certain altitudes. Naturally you won't be able to hold 75% power at as high an altitude as you could hold 65%—the engine can't maintain the required mp. Manufacturers generally do not recommend power settings of over 75% for cruise for reciprocating engines, because the fuel consumption and extra engine wear preclude use above this value.

Using the Throttle and Propeller Controls

The mp gage tells you of the potential power going to the engine; the tachometer tells how much is being used. With the proper throttle and prop setting, you have ideal potential *and* use of the power.

A part of the measure of an engine's power output is bmep (brake mean effective pressure) in the cylinders at the instant of combustion. If this internal pressure is too great the engine can be damaged.

The engine can efficiently use a maximum amount of fuel-air mixture at a certain rpm. A high mp means that a lot of fuel and air is available for the engine. When this higher compressed charge is shoved into the cylinders, more power should be produced. But if the prop control is set at too low an rpm, it's like putting the powder load for a cannon into a shotgun (well, maybe not quite).

If you have trouble remembering which goes first in a power change—throttle or prop—remember this: *Keep the propeller control forward more than the throttle.* If you're increasing power, the propeller control is moved forward first; in decreasing power the propeller control is moved back last. In normal usage, if it were timed, the propeller control would be forward more than the throttle (by seconds). Don't slam the throttle or prop control—the engine and propeller have inertia to overcome in changing speeds, and if you get too hasty you could damage the engine this way, too. Abrupt opening of the throttle at low speeds can cause *detonation* (Chapter 13). Rapid throttle changes in heavy engines may cause overstress.

The propeller control may be thought of as similar to an automobile (manual) gearshift. However, whereas the car just has a few set positions, you can set any "gear" combination you want with the prop control. Flat pitch, or high rpm, is comparable to low gear in a car. You set it before takeoff (prop control full forward) and "step on the gas" (open the throttle all the way). After getting off the ground you throttle back to the climb mp setting and (if the POH calls for it) pull the prop control back to the recommended rpm setting for climb.

About decreasing power: If you pull the prop control back *before* the throttle, the mp will increase because the engine isn't taking the mixture as fast any more—you're giving it more bmep than it can efficiently use, which can be bad if the difference becomes too great. (Imagine pedaling a bicycle up a steep hill and suddenly shifting to a higher gear.)

There are some geared (unturbocharged)-engine-equipped airplanes that require the pilot to reduce the rpm after takeoff and continue to use full throttle. (Pulling the throttle back with this engine would lean the mixture, a condition not conducive to long engine life in a climb.) Since the original takeoff rpm is 3,400 and the METO (maximum except take-off) rpm was (is) 3,000, the normally aspirated engine was not overboosted (28–29 inches mp and 3,000 rpm). The example engine is geared at a 120:77 ratio, or the engine turns 120 rpm to the propeller's 77 rpm. (This was mentioned so that you know that such procedures may be required for a few models of airplanes. But you'll find that in most cases, the power-changing procedures are as mentioned earlier. In any event, use the manufacturer's recommended procedure.)

To increase power, the order of engine control use is

1. Richen mixture
2. Propeller control forward
3. Increase manifold pressure-throttle forward

To reduce power (say, to level off from a climb to assume cruising flight):

1. Throttle back
2. Decrease rpm (retard the prop control)
3. Set mixture as necessary

Sometimes there's confusion concerning the prop setting. For takeoff, you'd set the prop control forward

Figure 12-2. "I guess I should have eased the prop control forward before opening the throttle." (Improper use of the throttle and prop control can cause engine indigestion.)

for *low pitch—high rpm*. For cruise, the setting would be *high pitch—low rpm*. This confusion most often occurs on an FAA knowledge test, where you know which is which but misread the question.

Some Items About Takeoff

Your first takeoff in the new airplane almost can be predicted. You take off, feeling strange and maybe a little tense because you want to be sure to do a good job. You have the prop full forward—in high rpm and the throttle wide open. Fine. The airplane lifts off and you're naturally pretty busy. Watching the runway and the area ahead, you prepare to throttle back. Glancing at the mp gage, you see it hasn't moved so you pull the power back some more. There's a power loss felt but the mp gage hasn't moved. Is it broken? The screams of the check pilot (and maybe a groan or two from the engine) direct your attention to the tachometer. Oops—it's back below cruising rpm. You pulled the prop control back first, *instead* of the throttle. You hastily shove it back up—the prop overspeeds for a couple of seconds—and you have to start the power reduction process anew for the climbout, this time pulling the throttle back *first* and *then* the prop control, as it should be. You'll feel about 6 inches high. Well, welcome to the club; you've joined a group of several hundred thousand other pilots who've done the same thing (and this includes the one in the right seat over there, who's hollering so loudly).

However, just because you didn't mean to do it doesn't lessen punishment to the engine in a deal like this. The proper procedure will come with practice.

Some pilots use their knowledge of this fact—at a constant throttle position the mp will increase if the rpm decreases—to save themselves the extra manipulation of the prop and throttle on takeoff. Suppose your airplane uses 28 inches and 2,700 rpm for takeoff at sea level, and the manufacturer recommends 24 inches and 2,400 rpm for climbout. The old pro will throttle back to about 23 inches Then, when the prop is pulled back to 2,400 rpm (moving the prop into higher pitch), the mp will rise to 24 inches and no further adjustment will be required. If the throttle had been set to 24 inches, it would have eased up to, say, 25 inches when the prop was pulled back, which would require resetting the mp. You will soon note the rise in mp with decrease in rpm after takeoff for your airplane and will do this automatically. The 1-inch rise used here is an illustration; the exact rise will depend on the difference between takeoff and climb rpm for your engine.

The Climb

You've set the power to the recommended value of 24 inches and 2,400 rpm (or whatever is set up for your particular airplane) and now feel you can relax a little. On your first flight in the new airplane, you'll want to get some altitude and just get used to it before doing anything exotic like takeoffs and landings.

As you climb it seems that after 2,000 or 3,000 feet the airplane has lost quite a bit of its go, and if the check pilot hasn't already brought it to your attention, a glance at the mp gage shows that the mp has dropped 2 (or 3) inches. A creeping throttle? No, the atmospheric pressure drops about 1 inch of mercury per 1,000 feet at lower altitudes, and the engine just isn't able to get the same amount of mp at the old throttle setting. You'll have to open the throttle of the unturbocharged engine as altitude is gained.

At the beginning of the chapter, it was mentioned that the engine of the example needed about ¼ inch less mp per 1,000 feet to maintain the same percentage of power. The mp drops 1 inch so this puts you about ¾ inch in the hole for each 1,000 feet. Some engine manufacturers recommend a constant mp for a particular engine for the climb at *all* altitudes (if you can maintain it), while for engines having limits of continuous power, they furnish tables for recommended maximum mp at various altitudes. Maintaining a constant mp to higher altitudes does mean that more power is being developed up there; this power may exceed the manufacturer's recommendation for longtime use for some engines.

Cruise

On leveling off leave the power at climb setting until the expected cruising speed is reached. This is done for two reasons: (1) The transition from climb to cruise is shorter and (2) you'll only have to set cruise power once. If you throttle back and set the power to, say, 23 inches and 2,300 rpm for cruise (or whatever the power setting chart recommends for your altitude and chosen power) immediately upon reaching the altitude, you'll find that as the airspeed picks up from climb to cruise the mp may also increase due to "ram effect" (increased dynamic pressure of the air entering the intake). You'll have to reset the mp, then lean the mixture.

Assume that you have set the prop control to maintain, for example, 2,400 rpm; if you open the throttle, the initial tendency will be for the rpm to increase (as would be the case for a fixed-pitch propeller). The propeller governor senses this and makes the pitch angle greater (higher pitch), and the added drag stops the rpm increase. Conversely, pulling the throttle back will tend to decrease the rpm, so the governor flattens the pitch as necessary so the lesser blade drag will allow the rpm to be maintained. As will be discussed shortly, if the throttle is closed, the blades reach the low pitch limit and cannot maintain the preset rpm.

During a hangar-flying session, you may hear that you don't want to be "over-square." The phrase means having an mp setting that is "bigger" than the rpm (in hundreds). The pilot who fears being over-square will fly at 22.0" mp and 2,400 rpm (65% power at sea level), thinking this stresses the engine less. Looking at Figure 12-1, you see that 24.2" mp and 2,100 rpm gives 65% at sea level, too. If it's in the POH, the engine manufacturer has warranted the engine for that mp/rpm combination. That 300 rpm makes for a lot less noise and 18,000 fewer cycles of the pistons, valves and shafts each hour.

Landing Notes

Another problem you may have the first few times is remembering to move the prop control forward to a high rpm (low pitch) during the approach to prepare for the possibility of a go-around. Some POHs recommend that the rpm be set to high cruise or climb rpm rather than for takeoff in this case, because there is a possibility of engine overspeed if throttle is suddenly applied. Others may recommend a full-high rpm setting for the landing approach.

For airplanes in which a high cruise or climb rpm is recommended for an approach, this is best done on the downwind leg when you have cruise power on. Even the constant-speed prop cannot maintain the preset rpm when you've throttled back for landing. If you have it set for 2,400 rpm at cruise, when you close or nearly close the throttle, the rpm may drop down to 2,000, or well below, when you slow up. Of course, as soon as you open the throttle past a certain mp, the rpm will increase and hold your preset value. Actually what happens when you throttle back to idle is this: the prop tries to maintain the preset rpm, and as you throttle back, the blade angle (pitch) decreases—trying to maintain the required rpm. Finally you throttle back so far that the blades are as flat as they can go but can't keep up the rpm. Moving the prop controls forward won't help—you'll have to increase power (mp, manifold pressure) before getting a reaction.

On the other hand, if the recommendation for your airplane is to set the prop to full-high rpm for the approach, *don't* do it on the downwind leg where you are developing power in the engine. The result would be a probable rpm overshoot and, at best, a noisy announcement of your presence in the area. The usual practice is to move the prop control (or controls) forward on base or after turning on final, when you're not using a lot of power. Of the four main items for landing (gear, flaps, mixture, and prop), the propeller is normally set last if a full-high-rpm setting is recommended for landing.

At any rate, you haven't been setting a propeller for landing before now and may have to be reminded a couple of times by the check pilot. Remember this: If you have to go around, you may need full power quickly and will be in bad shape if you shove the throttle wide open with the prop control back in a low rpm cruise setting.

Prop Controls

The prop control is somewhat similar to the throttle. It works the same way and may resemble the throttle, although the handle itself is usually a different shape for quick recognition by feel. The prop control for the single-engine airplane usually projects out of the instrument panel, whereas the multiengine airplane throttles, prop controls, and mixtures are usually on a quadrant. The single-engine airplane prop control usually can be moved either of two ways: (1) by pressing a manual release (lock) button and moving the control in or out in the same manner as for the throttle or (2) by using the vernier adjustment, screwing the control

Figure 12-3. 1. Using the lock button for large rpm adjustments. **2.** Using the vernier for smoother, minor adjustments. The propeller control is being turned to obtain higher rpm in the illustration.

in (clockwise) to increase rpm and turning it counterclockwise to decrease rpm. The vernier method allows for a finer setting and is used for making adjustments when the engine is developing power, such as after takeoff, cruise, or setting rpm on the downwind leg. The button lock push-pull method is good for quickly setting full-high rpm when the engine is not developing a great deal of power (before opening the throttle for takeoff or on final). See Figure 12-3.

The end result is the same. Naturally, it will take longer, for instance, to go to full-high rpm using the vernier, but many pilots prefer it and never use the button release. The *throttles* for some airplanes also may use a combination vernier and button release. *One thing to remember: the prop control moves the same way as the throttle—for more power (rpm) it's forward, for less power (rpm) it's back.*

Throttles for some *fixed-pitch* propeller planes are also of the vernier type.

More Background about Propeller Operation

If you know what type of propeller you're using on your airplane and how it works, you will be better able to analyze problems, both in flight and on the ground. Also, you should know that the constant-speed propeller needs overhauls, as does the engine. (The suggested overhaul period for some props is 1,500 hours of operation or 4 years in-service time, but more about that later.) In some cases, the prop overhaul coincides with the engine overhaul, and if it's your responsibility, you should get a factory-approved shop to do the job.

The Governor

The job of the governor is to make sure that the selected rpm is maintained, and without going into detail about the many parts involved in its construction, you might take a look at Figure 12-4. The governor is normally mounted on the front of, and geared to, the engine. The flyweights in the governor are in a constant rpm position (Figure 12-4A); the rpm is steady.

The governor has its own gear-type pump, which, like the flywheel, is geared to and driven by the engine. The governor pump boosts the oil pressure at the prop to give quick and positive response by the propeller. One type of governor pump, for example, boosts the engine oil pressure of 60 psi to 275 psi.

Possible indications of governor trouble are seen by a constant hunting for the prechosen rpm or difficulty in setting a specific rpm. The governor controls the propeller through a particular upper range of rpm (say, 2,000 to 2,600 rpm).

Some governors may be set up for single-acting operation in either direction, or double action. Governor oil pressure can be used either to increase or decrease pitch, or both. In looking at the counterweight-equipped propeller, the governor oil pressure was used to decrease, or flatten, the pitch. In the noncounterweight type it would be used to increase the pitch. *This type of system is now used on featherable propellers (not on single-engine airplanes);* further results of a loss of oil pressure will be covered in that section.

The Oil-Counterweight Propeller

This type uses oil pressure from the engine, passed through a governor to move the propeller into low pitch. Centrifugal force acting on the counterweight attached to the inner portion of each blade tends to cause the blade to twist in the hub to a higher angle of attack (higher pitch). When you select a specific rpm setting with the prop control, you're balancing oil pressure (acting on the prop piston-cylinder assembly in the hub, which moves actuating arms to "twist" the blades) against the centrifugal force acting on the prop counterweights. A loss of oil pressure in this system would have the propeller tending to go to low rpm.

Noncounterweight Propellers

This is a system with no counterweights in which oil pressure, working through the prop governor (and into the piston-cylinder system), moves the actuator arms to *increase* the pitch, opposing (1) the natural "down" pitching moment of the airfoil (blade) and (2) a spring, to maintain a prechosen rpm set by you.

So what? you ask. What can I do about it in the air anyway, if something goes wrong? If you have an idea beforehand of what a certain type of prop will do (if, for instance, all governor oil pressure was lost), you'd be able to figure how it would affect your flight now and in the immediate future. In this type of propeller, sudden and complete loss of oil pressure *in the prop hub system* at cruise would mean that the blades would go to low pitch and you'd have a noisy, high-rpm situation. You'd have no control over the propeller, but the high-rpm condition would be very handy if a go-around during that approach to the airport was required. So, the point about reviewing the system is that if the rpm suddenly goes to astounding numbers, you will know what's happening and won't hit the panic button but instead make moves to correct the situation and plan for an approach (and landing) at the nearest reasonable airport. (Assume for discussion purposes that the lack-of-oil problem is in the prop alone and the engine itself is still getting plenty of oil.) What could be done to help the situation as you head for the airport? One thing you could do is called "putting a load on the prop," or pulling the nose up to slow the airplane up (plus throttling back to decrease the power input). Basically in this condition (overspeed) you are flying a fixed-pitch prop, and it would be as if the throttle on that (very low) fixed-pitch-prop airplane were *locked* full open at a high airspeed. How could you get the rpm back down to a reasonable, low figure in that case? You'd have to slow the airplane since just throttling back wouldn't get the rpm to decrease.

Feathering Propellers

Oil-Counterweight Type

There are a couple of types of feathering propellers, and you'll have more practical interest in them when you start flying twins (Chapter 15). But the theory and operation of the system will be covered here with the other types of constant-speed props.

One type of feathering propeller has the counterweights and spring discussed earlier. You recall that in that type, oil pressure is used to put the prop into low pitch, and the counterweights (and a spring) work to increase the pitch. In the older, nonfeathering types, when the prop control was pulled back to the full-aft position, oil was let out of the hub cylinder and the pitch increased to the high-pitch limit stop, because the counterweights and spring were then in command. The high pitch was still in a "normal flying regime" but rpm was low in this setting.

The feathering prop uses the same idea only more so. (The prop, when feathered, goes to a very high pitch—going from, say, 15° to 80° to the plane of rotation.) The normal high- and low-pitch limits still stand as long as the propeller control is being moved in the normal range. But when you move the control into the feathering detent, a mechanical linkage overrides the flyweights and speeder spring. In the feather setting, the governor lever and shaft are turned beyond the normal high pitch and the pilot valve is lifted. Oil flows out of the propeller, oil pressure is lost, and it moves to feather pitch.

To unfeather (without an accumulator system), the prop control is moved to the full-forward position and the starter is engaged. When the engine is turning over, oil pressure will come up to bring the prop blades out of feather. The accumulator, which stores oil pressure for unfeathering, will be discussed in Chapter 15.

The question arises as to why the feathering props don't feather every time the engine is shut down (and the oil pressure goes to zero). The props *would* feather except that a spring-loaded centrifugal latch is inside each propeller hub system. The latch is held out of engagement by centrifugal force. When the engine is shut down in the air, the windmilling prop holds the latch *out* and the prop can be moved into feather pitch. When the prop is shut down on the ground, the propellers are in low pitch and after shutdown there is no windmilling. As soon as the propeller slows down to about 600 rpm, the spring pulls the latch into engagement before oil pressure is lost. The latch holds the blades at an angle a few degrees above low pitch so that there will be no problems with the next start.

Air-Oil Type

One type of feathering propeller uses governor oil pressure *and* the twisting movement of the blade to move the prop into low pitch (high rpm); these factors are opposed by compressed air or nitrogen trapped between the cylinder head and the piston. The compressed air takes the place of the counterweights on other types and furnishes the force for feathering when the control is moved into the feather detent.

For one air-oil propeller, the air chamber is charged with dry air or dry nitrogen gas at 175 psi at 70°F, and the servicing pressure is decreased ⅓ psi for each 1°F of reduction in temperature. (A placard giving charge pressure versus temperature is attached to the propeller cylinder.) The main reason for using *dry* air or nitrogen is that excessive moisture could cause the piston to freeze in place in very cold weather.

You can see that if the air pressure is lost or not kept up, the propeller could tend to go to and stay in flat pitch and feathering could be difficult or impossible. This type of propeller, because no counterweights are required, saves a significant amount of weight.

With the air-oil feathering type, if engine oil pressure is lost, the propeller will automatically feather. This would be better for twin performance than to have the prop going into full *flat* pitch in that situation.

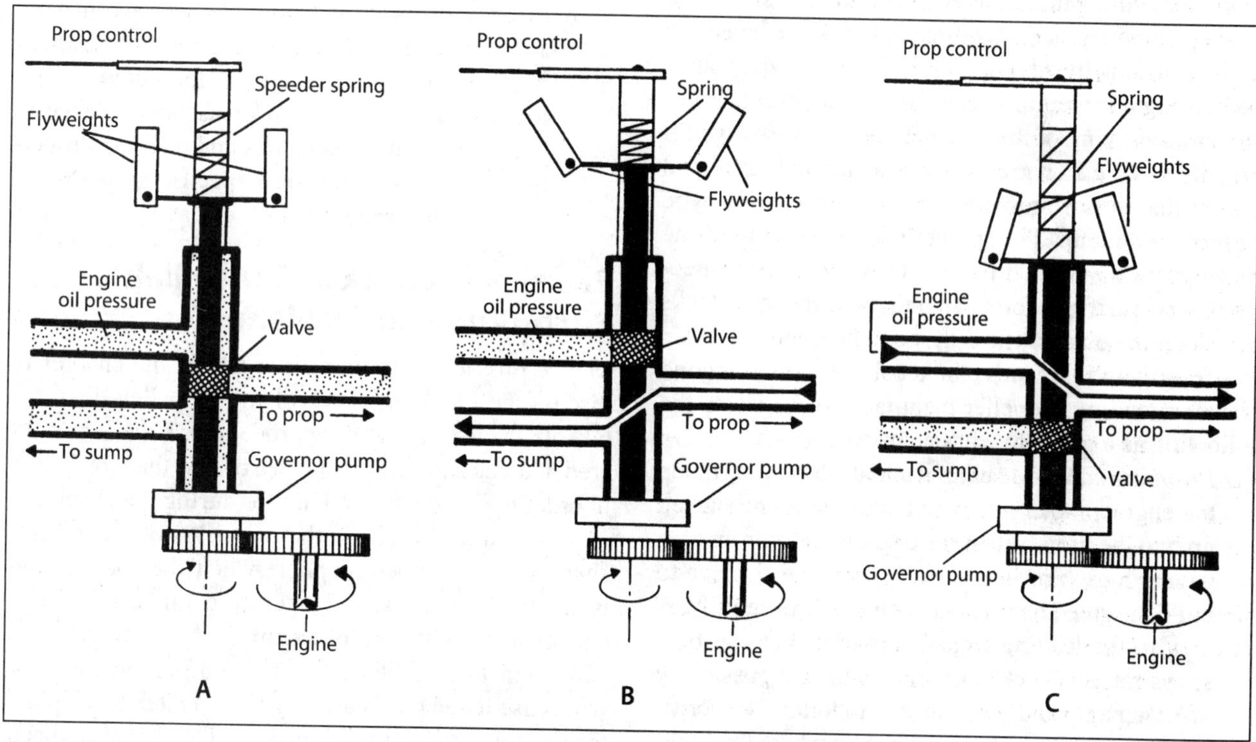

Figure 12-4. A schematic diagram of the prop governor for an oil-counterweight propeller. The flyweights are connected to the valve and shaft and are rotated by the engine through gearing. Assume that the rpm has been set to, for instance, 2,200 rpm by the prop control (which isn't moved during the sequence shown—A, B, and C). By setting the prop control, the pilot has set the compression of the speeder spring, and the counterweights (trying to increase the pitch or moving it to a *low-rpm* position) are balanced by the oil pressure (acting to decrease pitch or increase rpm), and as you will note in **A**, nothing is happening.

B. The airplane is dived, the prop gets windmilling effect, and the engine (and flyweight) rpm increases. The valve, which was doing very well earlier (in A, having shut off oil *to* or *from* the prop), is now raised as the flyweights are moved out by centrifugal force. Oil now moves from the prop hub, and the counterweights (on the prop) move the prop toward a higher pitch to increase drag and knock off the excess rpm, until equilibrium is again established at 2,200 rpm.

C. If the airplane is slowed, the engine (and flyweight) rpm decreases and the valve is lowered so that engine oil (boosted by the governor pump) goes to the hub piston assembly to decrease pitch and increase rpm back to the preset 2,200 figure.

For clarity, the *governor pump* is shown well down, out of the way of the lines and valve, but it's actually boosting the engine oil pressure to the prop in C. Also, numerous springs, valves, and other esoterica are not shown, probably causing prop engineers seeing this diagram to have a sharp rise in blood pressure; but maybe this approach will help you as a pilot to remember what's happening.

After you've read the section on *noncounterweight* props, you can see in the simplified diagram here that, by reversing the sump and engine oil pressure lines to the governor, the actions in B and C could be reversed.

With a feathering propeller with an air system and *counterweights* or *springs*, a loss of air charge may result in

1. The pretakeoff feathering check being sluggish or slow.
2. Rpm control being sluggish in flight, particularly when moved in the direction of reduced rpm.
3. A slight overspeed (or poor synchronization) in multiengine airplanes at the upper end of the prop speed range.
4. The prop overspeeding when the throttle is opened rapidly, accompanied with poor rpm recovery.

Your job, when you become a commercial pilot (or a private pilot flying more-complex airplanes), will be to keep up with what is required in checking or service of the constant-speed prop. The fixed-pitch type you've been using only required checking for nicks and security and safetying of the nuts holding it on. Now you'll also look for oil or grease leaks at the hub area and ensure that the air pressure, if your plane has that type of prop, is kept up. The spinner will cover more of the mechanism than you'd like for easy preflight inspection, but centrifugal force will move oil or grease leaks out along the blades where they can be seen.

To sum up some ideas for keeping the prop in good shape, a leading propeller manufacturer suggests the following as a guide for service instructions:

1. *Propeller care*—Be careful about where you run up the engine; loose stones and cinders can be sucked up into the prop. When starting a takeoff on an area having loose gravel or stones, allow the airplane to build up speed before you open the throttle fully. A nick in the leading edge of the propeller can be a stress raiser. Cracks can start, with the possibility of losing a tip and big problems to follow. The critical area is 5 to 9 inches from the tip where the highest vibratory stresses are found. The mechanic can file (round out) the nicks and polish the surface with fine emery cloth to assure that stresses wouldn't be concentrated at the point of the nick. Steel hub parts shouldn't be allowed to rust; use aluminum paint to touch them up as necessary, or they may be replated during the prop overhaul.
2. Daily inspection—Check the blade, spinner, and visible hub parts for damage or cracks. Check for grease or oil leakage.
3. 100-hour inspection—Generally the following is to be done on the 100-hour and/or annual inspection:
   a. Remove spinner.
   b. Check for nicks and cracks in the blades. Remove leading-edge nicks.
   c. Inspect the hub parts for cracks and all visible parts for wear and safety.
   d. Check for oil and grease leaks.
   e. Check the air pressure in the cylinder of air-oil feathering propellers. Use manufacturer's recommended figure for pressure and use dry nitrogen gas if required.
4. 1,000- or 1,500-hour inspection (this may coincide with the engine overhaul and is done at an authorized repair station, but check it for the propeller you are using)—The following steps are listed:
   a. Remove prop and completely disassemble.
   b. Magnetically inspect all steel parts. Inspect aluminum parts by the dye-penetration method.
   c. Inspect and refinish blades and if eroded or nicked, anodize.
   d. Inspect all parts for wear. Replace worn parts and replace steel parts if necessary. After plating, bake parts in oven at 375° for 3 hours.
   e. Reassemble the prop and grease and balance it. Talk to the local mechanics and read the Propeller Owner's Manual for a specific guide to the care of your propeller(s).

Pretakeoff Check of Controllable-Pitch-Propeller Airplane

Maybe this seems to be a little late in the chapter to discuss the preflight check of the propeller since the takeoff, cruise, and landing procedures have been covered, but you should have an idea of how the prop works in order to know what to look for during the check.

It's best *not* to check the magnetos of a constant-speed-prop-equipped airplane when the rpm setting is in the constant-speed operating range (the POH checklist takes this into account). If you switch to a bad magneto and the rpm starts to drop, the governor will sense it and automatically flatten pitch to keep the tachometer hand at its old reading. The constant-speed prop will, because of its inherent design, tend to mask fouled plugs, bad mags, etc. Check the magnetos before takeoff below the governor-operating range to get a true *picture*. Usually this is done somewhere between 1,700 and 2,000 rpm with the prop control full forward (high rpm).

Check the propeller operation before takeoff. Run the prop control through its range, starting with the prop in full-high rpm and at the tachometer reading recommended by the manufacturer. Pull the prop control aft to reduce rpm. Don't leave it back too long as the mp will be too high for the rpm. Most pilots pull the prop control back and immediately move it forward before the rpm drops off too far. With practice you can check the response of the propeller the instant the control is moved aft.

In really cold weather you won't get a good response the first time or two you cycle the prop. The oil that's been sitting in the hub overnight, or longer, will be thick and will need to be replaced by the warm engine oil as you cycle it. If you don't get good workable oil in the prop system, there may be problems with "hunting" (the prop not holding the preset rpm) or poor response to prop-control-setting changes. This also could be a problem if you are flying a long time in very cold weather at a constant-prop control setting. The prop wants to hunt because the oil in the hub has thickened in the cold. Periodically changing rpm (up and down) within allowed mp and rpm combination limits can help this problem. (Using multiviscosity oil or special lubricants makes matters much better in this regard.)

Summary

When you decide to check out in the airplane with a controllable-pitch prop and manifold pressure gage, give yourself a few days. Sit in the cockpit and become familiar with the new controls. Go over in your mind the various steps for takeoff, climb, cruise, and landing. Ask questions. It's hard to jump cold into a new airplane and do a good job the first time. The professional pilots realize this and spend time in the cockpit before actually flying a new type or model. You might also review Chapters 2 and 4 concerning controllable-pitch propellers and the mp gage if you plan on checking out in an airplane so equipped.

Review the POH, *Engine Manual*, and *Propeller Manual* so that you are familiar with possible problems. This keeps surprises to a minimum.

13

Advanced Fuel Systems

The information given here, of course, is general and includes representative fuel systems. For specifics, consult the POH for the airplane you are flying.

The Fuel Boost Pump

Maybe most of your flying to date has been done in high-wing airplanes using one or at most two fuel tanks and a gravity fuel system. When you start flying low-wing airplanes with wing tanks, the need for an engine-driven fuel pump will become evident. Very few cases of airplane engine-driven fuel pump failures are on record. But it *could* happen, so means are furnished to provide fuel pressure in the event of a failure. High-wing airplanes having fuel-injected engines (and also some using carburetors) require an engine-driven (constantly operating) fuel pump because of the high fuel pressure requirements, which will be discussed shortly.

In earlier days backup was provided by a "wobble pump," a mechanical lever used to pump up fuel pressure for starting and in flight if necessary. The handle usually was placed so that maximum muscle strain was needed to work it. After a long siege of pumping, the pilot "wobbled" when leaving the cockpit. (Actually the name is derived from the movement of the handle.) In older multiengine airplanes equipped with a wobble pump, the copilot stood by to use it if one of the engine-driven pumps fails on takeoff.

People being what they are—lazy—the electric boost pump came into use. It is turned on to aid in starting and again turned on to standby during the takeoff when a loss of fuel pressure is most serious. Of course, it could always be turned on if the engine-driven pump fails, but the delay during takeoff could cause serious problems. The boost pump also is turned on before landing, as it would be most embarrassing to lose the engine-driven pump if you were too low to make the runway without power. Your big problem for the first few flights will be remembering to turn it on or off at the right times.

After takeoff, turn the boost pump off as soon as a safe altitude has been reached—a lot of pilots use 500 feet as a minimum; your check pilot may have recommendations. *Always look at the fuel pressure gage as you turn the boost pump off after takeoff.* If the pressure starts going down to zero, better get the boost pump back on and get back to the airport because the indications are that the engine-driven pump has failed and the boost pump has been carrying the load. Don't just automatically flick the switch off without looking, because that way the first warning you'll have will be the engine stopping—and it may be hard to get going, even with the boost pump on again.

Assuming you use the boost for starting, turn it off temporarily sometime between starting and takeoff to see if the engine-driven pump is operating. In some airplanes with carburetors it's hard to tell the difference in fuel pressure with the boost pump on or off with the engine running; that is, its pressure is not noticeably additive to the engine-driven pump pressure. On others, it's noticeable right away. Check the operation of the boost pump (or pumps) for the carburetor-type engine *before* the engine is started, after turning the master battery switch and boost pump on. The boost pump should give a pressure reading in the normal operation range for the engine-driven pumps. With fuel-injected engines, don't indiscriminately turn on the electric fuel pump, since it's also used for priming.

Some boost pumps have three-position switches: ON, OFF, and PRIME. The PRIME position is a low-pressure position for priming and starting. The ON position also runs the pumps at low speed as long as the engine-driven pump is running. If the engine-driven pump fails with the boost pump switch ON, the boost pump will automatically switch to high-speed operation. This system, because of its complexity, normally is used on multiengine airplanes.

The POHs for some airplanes require the use of boost pumps throughout the start. Others recommended their use to build up pressure *before* the start and turning them off during the actual starting process. Still others don't suggest using boost pumps for starting or during takeoff.

Some boost pumps are located in the fuel line system; others are "submerged." The submerged boost pumps are normally only in the main fuel tanks. This is one reason why takeoffs and landings are made on the main tanks for most airplanes.

The boost pump may seem to be an additional problem to cope with, but if you remember its purpose—to furnish fuel pressure when the engine isn't running (before the start) or when the engine-driven pump has failed, or may fail—you'll have no problem with its use. Remember, it is a starting aid and/or a safety standby.

Tank Systems and Fuel Management

The airplane may have both main and auxiliary tanks. Naturally the manufacturer would prefer to have all the fuel in one tank as this would simplify the fuel system. Unfortunately, this is not possible from either a structural or a space standpoint for larger airplanes.

When you first look at the fuel system diagram of the new airplane, you'll wonder how you'll ever learn which tank should be used at what time (Figure 13-1). It may not be clear until you have actually used the tank system. After the check pilot has described the fuel management and you have flown the airplane, go back to the POH again—it'll be a lot clearer. Ask yourself WHY certain tanks are used at certain times and not at others.

Figure 13-1. Sometimes the fuel system seems a little complicated at first glance.

Fuel Systems

Figures 13-2 through 13-8 show some sample representative types of fuel systems, in a generally ascending order of complexity.

Figure 13-2, the simplest type of system, uses gravity to feed the carburetor simultaneously from both tanks. The selector (or fuel shutoff valve) in this case has two positions, ON and OFF. Note that a vent system is needed, basically for the same reason that you punch that extra hole in a can of oil to expedite the flow. (No vent would mean no fuel flow after a while.) In this case the tanks are vented together with the outlet at the left strut wing junction.

Figure 13-3 is the next step in complexity. In this high-wing, gravity-fed carburetor system, the pilot has BOTH, LEFT, RIGHT, and OFF selections available. The POH advises that the selector be on BOTH for takeoff and landing. The two tanks in this system are vented together here (as in Figure 13-2). (Note the one-way vent valves for the two airplanes.) The individual tank selections allow the pilot to compensate for unequal flow and lateral trim on longer flights.

Figure 13-4 is the fuel system for a carbureted high-wing airplane equipped with an engine-driven pump and an auxiliary (boost) pump. Fuel from each wing tank flows through the selector valve, small reservoir, and a fuel shutoff valve to the fuel strainer. From there it's routed to the engine-driven pump, which delivers fuel under pressure to the carburetor. The electric auxiliary pump, which parallels the engine-driven pump, is used when the fuel pressure drops below 2 psi. It's not necessary to have the auxiliary pump operating during normal takeoff and landing since gravity feed supplies adequate fuel flow to the carburetor with the engine-driven pump inoperative. However, this airplane has a comparatively low "high wing," and gravity flow is considerably reduced at maximum performance takeoff and climb attitudes. The auxiliary fuel pump *would* be needed if the engine-driven pump fails during those maneuvers.

Figure 13-5 shows the system for a popular low-wing trainer (carburetor). The fuel selector has three settings, LEFT, RIGHT, and OFF. The vast majority of low-wing airplanes (fuel injected or carburetor) and some high-wing airplanes with fuel injection don't have a BOTH selection. The fuller tank is used for takeoff and landing, and the selector is switched as necessary in cruise for lateral trim.

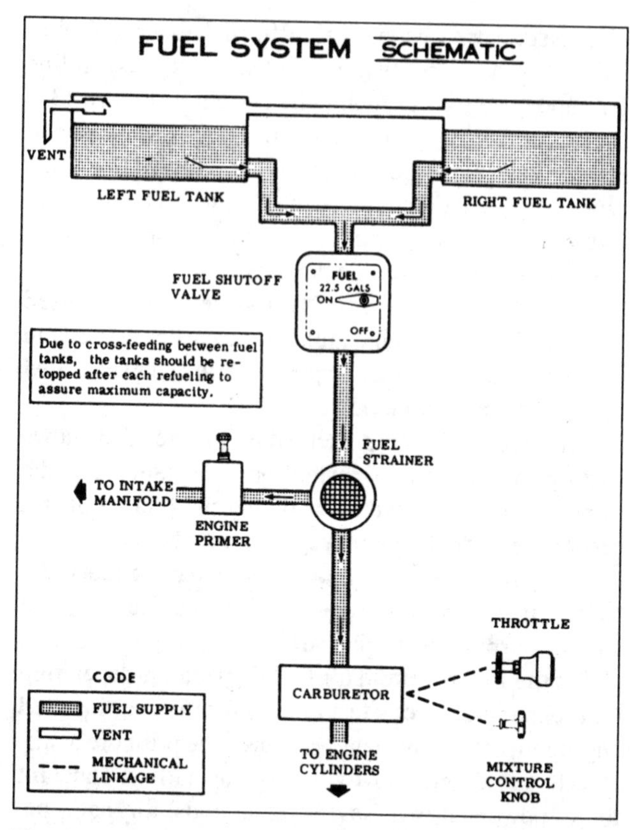

Figure 13-2. Fuel schematic of the simplest type of system; one that uses gravity to feed the carburetor simultaneously from both tanks.

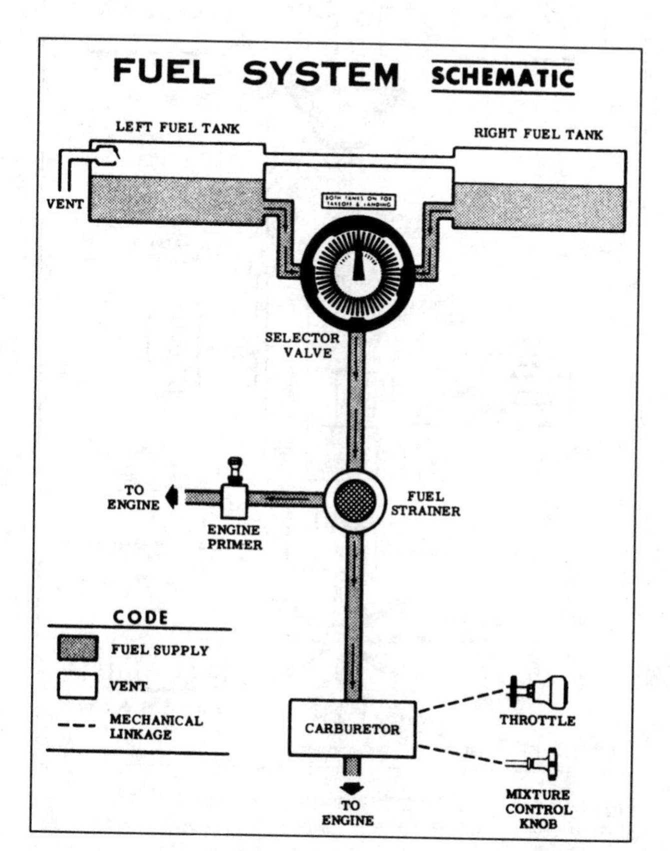

Figure 13-3. Fuel schematic of a system with BOTH, LEFT, RIGHT, and OFF selections. It still has a single vent.

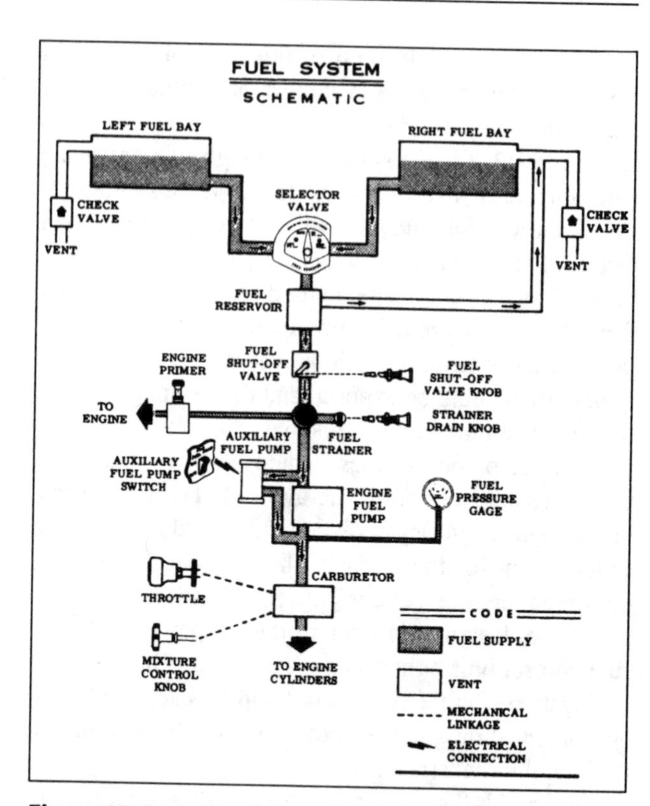

Figure 13-4. Fuel system. Note the separate fuel shut-off valve.

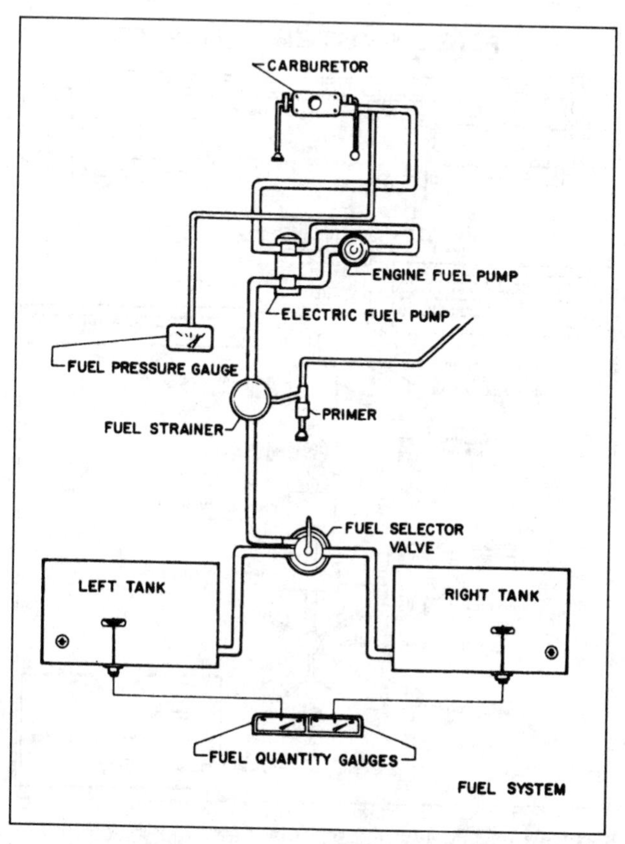

Figure 13-5. Fuel system for a low-wing trainer with a carburetor.

The electric fuel pump in this system is used as a standby for takeoff and landing and whenever the engine-driven pump fails.

Figure 13-6 is the system for a high-wing airplane (fuel injected) with two wing tanks. It looks complicated but a close study shows that everything makes sense. This is the first system shown with two reservoir tanks. This system is one method of assuring constant fuel flow for a predetermined time in fairly radical pitch or bank (slip) conditions where one of the main tank outlets might be exposed and fuel is not getting to the line when the fuel level is low.

This airplane is cross-vented (and the reservoir tanks are also vented to the system). The size of the vents in *any* fuel system depends on the fuel-flow requirement for the engine. This is a fuel injection–equipped engine (Lycoming IO-360A1B6D—more about the designation later in the chapter) and has a fuel control unit rather than a carburetor. Basically, in any system, you'll have a tank drain for each tank (this equipment should not be, but often is, *optional*) and a drain at the fuel strainer.

Figure 13-7 is a schematic for a high-wing airplane using a different fuel injection system from the one just discussed. This system design furnishes more fuel to the fuel control unit than needed and has a return line for vapor and excess fuel. (The system in Figure 13-6 is a demand-type system; it furnishes fuel as needed to mix with the air and does not require a return line. This type will be covered later in the chapter.) The returned fuel goes to the reservoir tank of the tank selected (left or right), which means that the engine is really only taking a predictable amount of fuel since what isn't used is put back into the same tank. Some earlier makes and models of single-engine airplanes returned excess fuel to the left (main) tank only.

The fuel system represented by Figure 13-8 shows two options for fuel distribution. The tanks are the same, but you'll note that following the fuel strainer a carburetor or fuel injection system may be used. Compare Figures 13-5, -6, -7, and -8. Note that the fuel pressure is taken from a point between the fuel pump(s) and the carburetor for the carburetor-equipped engine, and at the fuel manifold (or fuel distributor, depending on the manufacturer's term for it) for the fuel-injected engine. In effect, the gage measures the pressure available to the carburetor (which is normally a constant for all power settings, say, 3 to 5 pounds) for that type.

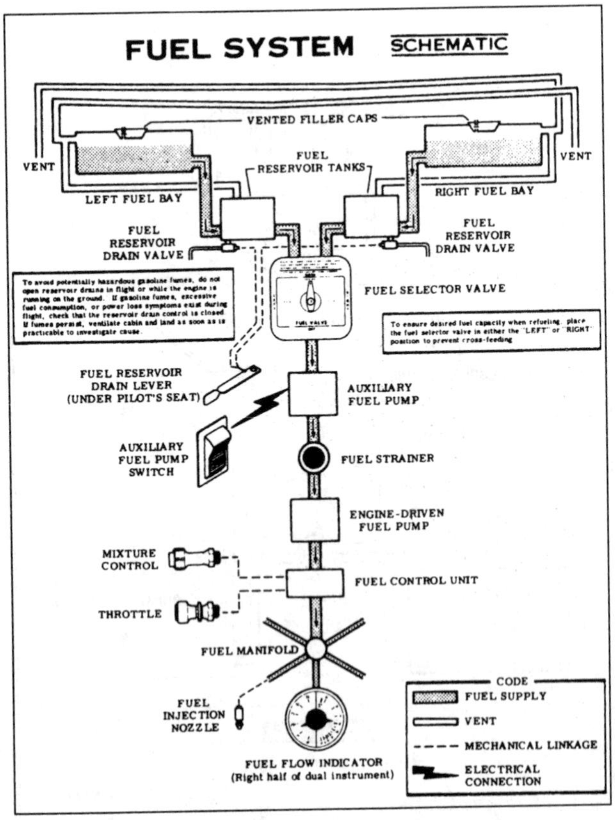

Figure 13-6. Fuel system schematic for a fuel-injected high-wing airplane that has two wing tanks. This is a demand-type system; it furnishes fuel as needed to mix with air—it does not require a return line.

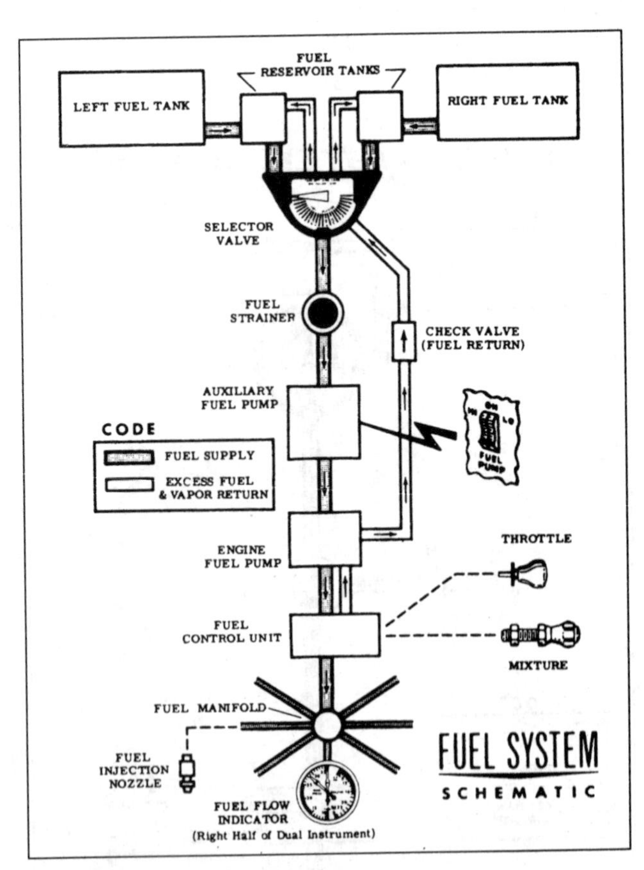

Figure 13-7. Fuel system schematic for a high-wing airplane with a return line for fuel and vapor not used.

In the injected engine, the gage measures the relative amount of fuel going through the flow distributor and so varies with mixture *and* power being used. The electric fuel pump on a carburetor engine may be energized indefinitely with the engine not running (with the fuel ON and mixture rich) without flooding (loading up) the engine. Turn on the electric fuel pump in a fuel injection engine under the conditions just cited and you'll pump fuel out on the ground.

The systems just covered include some on airplanes that are no longer in production as well as current types. In Chapter 15, the fuel systems of twins will be covered.

Fuel management includes the use of crossfeed for multiengine airplanes as well. The use of the crossfeed control will be covered in Chapter 15.

Some airplanes have an amber LOW FUEL warning light (or two lights, as required) on the annunciator panel in full view of the pilot. These are usually set to illuminate at a reasonably low fuel quantity but with enough warning for you to make other plans, such as finding a nearby convenient airport instead of completing the last thousand miles of your trip.

Leaning

As an all-around figure, gasoline engine mixtures for combustion are about 1:15, that is, about 1 pound fuel to every 15 pounds air—or about 7% fuel and 93% air by weight. For richer mixtures, an 8 to 10% fuel-air ratio is found.

For takeoff, a mixture setting of "full rich" is used. This setting assures the best combination of power *and* cooling. The full-rich setting will be slightly richer than best power, but as engine cooling also depends on a richer mixture a compromise must be made.

With the mixture in the full-rich position, you'll be using a predetermined mixture of fuel and air. As you climb, naturally the air becomes less dense (weighs less per unit volume). On the full-rich setting your carburetor is putting out about the same amount of fuel but there's less air to mix with it, so the mixture gets richer and richer. In fact, you may climb so high in full-rich that the engine will start to run rough; the fuel-air ratio is too great for smooth operation. So, you not only are losing power but are using fuel like there's no tomorrow (compared with what you should be consuming).

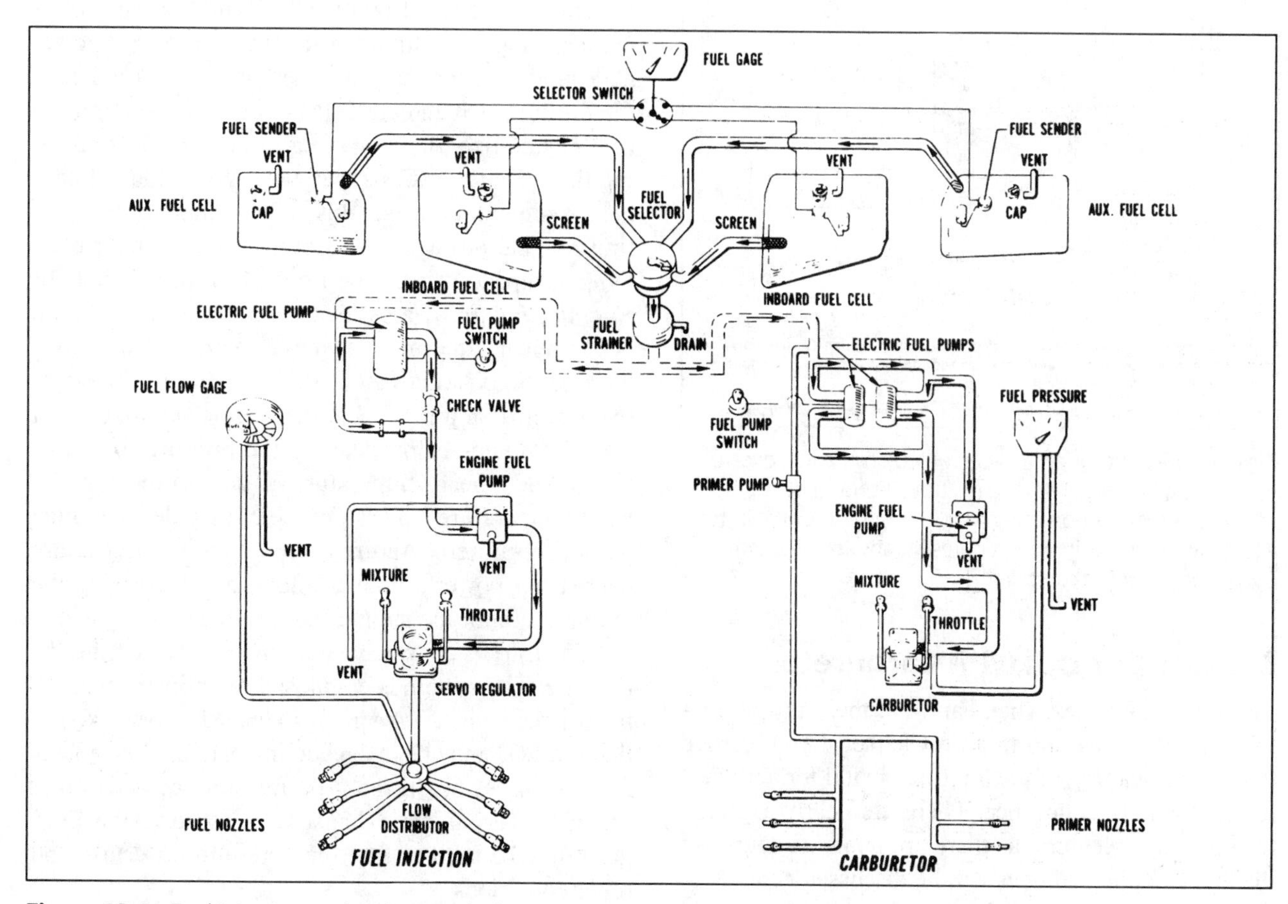

Figure 13-8. Fuel injection and carburetor fuel systems.

After reaching the desired cruise altitude, you'll level off, set cruise power, and lean the mixture. Your job with the mixture control is to establish the optimum fuel-air ratio for all conditions.

Figure 13-9 takes a general look at the effects of mixture on power, specific fuel consumption (pounds per horsepower per hour), and exhaust gas and cylinder head temperatures.

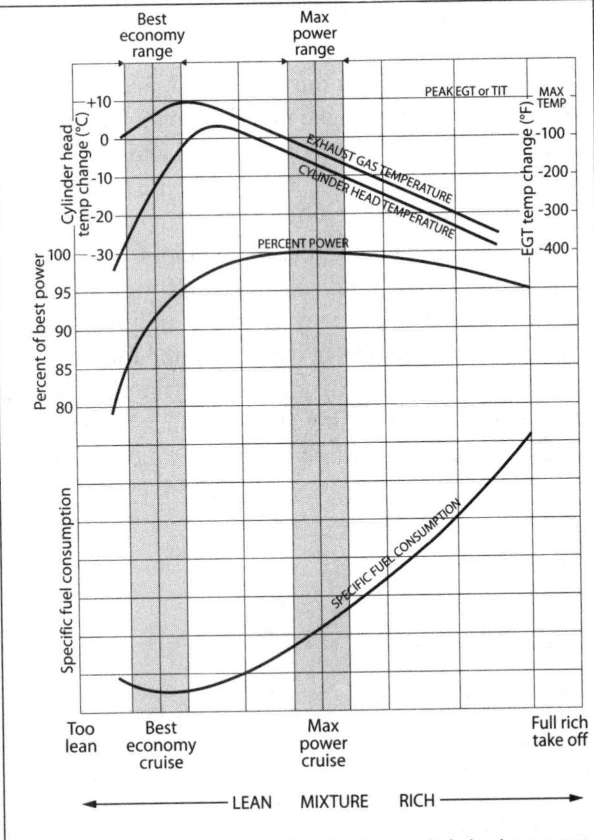

This representative diagram shows the effect of leaning on: cylinder head temperature, exhaust gas temperature or TIT, engine power, and specific fuel consumption for a constant engine RPM and manifold pressure.

Note: Textron Lycoming does not recommend operating on the lean side of peak EGT.

Figure 13-9. Although this curve depicts the response of various engine parameters to mixture, it should *not* be used as a leaning instruction for any specific engine. Consult the aircraft POH for leaning procedures for any specific aircraft. *(Lycoming, a Textron company)*

Mixture Control with Carburetor

There will be times when handling the mixture control will be very important. In Chapter 7 you learned that proper leaning of the mixture is vital for both best range and max endurance. There are nearly as many techniques for leaning as there are pilots. A couple of the less complicated ones will be discussed here.

First, it is assumed that you have neither a fuel mixture indicator (very likely you won't), a cylinder head temperature gage, nor an exhaust gas temperature (EGT) gage. In other words, you'll be leaning the mixture more or less by feel.

After leveling off and establishing the desired power setting, ease the mixture control back until the engine begins to roughen slightly. Ease it forward just until the engine smooths. This is the system most used for airplanes not equipped with an excess of gages for engine information.

A variation of the above technique is to lean the mixture with the engine operating on one magneto, as a too-lean mixture will show up more quickly than it would on BOTH. (Of course, as soon as you've set the mixture you'll go back to BOTH mags.) Most pilots don't bother to do this, and it's doubtful if a noticeable advantage is gained by using this technique (and there's some risk of not returning to BOTH).

If a cylinder head temperature gage is available, many pilots prefer to use it in leaning the mixture, particularly with a constant-speed propeller. The first method above will work with a constant-speed propeller but sometimes requires more experience because the actions of the governor tend to mask the roughness caused by the too-lean mixture.

Here is a typical method of leaning a carburetor engine using the cylinder head temperature. Set power at desired rpm and manifold pressure for cruise. Leave the mixture rich and allow the cylinder head temperature to stabilize. Begin leaning in increments, observing the cylinder head temperature. When the cylinder head temperature peaks, this is your final mixture setting for that altitude. Don't permit the cylinder head temperature to exceed the limit given in the POH or *Engine Manual.* If a sudden temperature rise should occur during the process, move the mixture control back to the position before the temperature increase. (You overdid it a little.) Let the engine stabilize for at least 5 minutes before leaning the mixture for a further cylinder head temperature reading. If the cylinder head temperature lead is on a lean cylinder, you may get a drop in temperature as you lean it out (you are decreasing power at that cylinder and decreasing the temperature for the engine as indicated by the gage).

The EGT is an excellent aid in properly setting the mixture. The system is composed of an instrument on the panel connected to a probe in the exhaust stack(s) so that the EGT may be taken and indicated. Since excess fuel or excess air in the mixture produces a cooling effect (lowering the exhaust temperature), the EGT gage may be used to find the optimum for cruise and other conditions.

As an example for one engine, to set up a cruise-leaned situation (at 75% power or less) using one of these instruments, lean the mixture until the EGT needle peaks. Then richen the mixture until the needle shows at least a 25°F temperature drop (this puts the mixture on the rich side of the highest EGT). The 25°F drop is best for fuel economy. A drop of 100°F (on the rich side) is in the area for best power. If your airplane has one of these systems, you should read the accompanying literature and talk with pilots who've used it before using it on your own. The POH for a particular airplane is the ultimate guide for EGT use.

A common erroneous idea is that an engine should not be leaned under 5,000 feet *under any circumstances.* One engine manufacturer notes that their normally aspirated, direct-drive engines with a manual mixture control should be leaned at cruise powers of 75% or less at any altitude while cruising. The 5,000-ft rule is only for climbing. In other words, in the climb use full rich to 5,000 MSL, then lean for added power and smoothness. Other airplanes have a lower limit of 3,000 feet for lean in the climb. If you're flying the type of engine(s) just described level at, say, 1,500 feet MSL at 74% power at cruise, go ahead and lean; there's no need to burn fuel you could use later. As will be noted in Chapter 19, turbocharged and other more complex engines have specified operating procedures.

To lean the carburetor-type engine at *cruise*, a leading engine manufacturer suggests the following:

1. Fixed-pitch prop—Lean to a maximum increase in rpm, or just before engine roughness.
2. Controllable prop—Lean until roughness is encountered, then richen slightly to eliminate roughness for smooth operation.

Suppose you are taking off from a field at high altitude and/or temperature (you are at a high density-altitude). It is likely that with the mixture control in the full-rich setting, the weight of fuel going into the engine is too great for the weight of the air mixed with it; that is, the mixture at that setting and altitude is so rich that the engine is not developing full power (Figure 13-10).

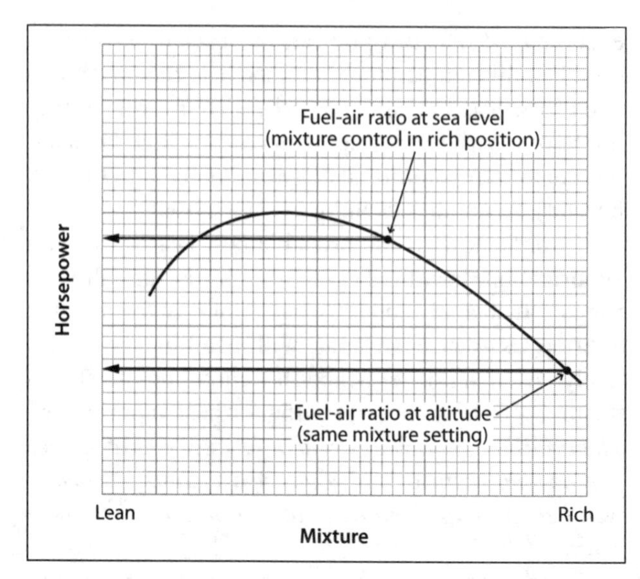

Figure 13-10. A high density-altitude and a full rich setting mean a power loss.

Under these conditions, particularly if the field is short and power is needed badly, some pilots run the engine up to some point just below prop-governor-operating speed and move the mixture control back until there is a definite pickup of rpm. The peak indicates the best power mixture setting for the density-altitude. The mixture control should be moved slightly forward of this maximum power point so the mixture will be a little on the rich side to ensure proper cooling. The mixture is normally preset to be slightly richer than best power for this reason when in the full-rich position, even at sea level conditions. It is better to be slightly on the rich side to avoid possible engine damage—even if it means a small deviation from best power. The density-altitude has to be fairly high before leaning has very much effect in increasing takeoff power.

A common error made by the pilot new to the mixture control is, after setting the mixture for best cruise at some fairly high altitude, starting the descent to the destination airport and forgetting about the mixture. During descent, the air density increases, but the carburetor is still putting out the same amount of fuel that worked so well at the higher altitude. Finally the comparable amount of fuel-air becomes so lean that the engine starts running rough and gives every sign of quitting any second. The simple remedy is to richen the mixture and all is well again. You actually have two choices in the matter of the descent. (1) You can push the mixture control all the way forward to full rich and not have to worry about it, or (2) you can richen the mixture in increments by guess as you go down. In (1) if you are very high, the engine operation may roughen slightly (it's assumed that you plan on using cruise power during the descent) but will soon smooth out as you lose altitude and you won't be as apt to forget to move it into full rich for landing.

Vaporization

It would seem that, all other things being equal, the colder the air entering the carburetor, the denser it is and the more power would be developed. However, fuel particles do not mix as well with cold air, and fuel may be wasted.

For best vaporization, a carburetor air inlet temperature of 90° to 100°F is ideal. This could mean using carburetor heat. If you are interested in maximum economy, *after* setting power, use carburetor heat to establish this temperature and then lean the mixture in one of the ways mentioned earlier. Your airplane may not have a carburetor inlet temperature gage (measuring the air temperature just *before* it goes into the carburetor), so another technique may be used.

In order to find the probable best heat setting for vaporization, lean the engine until it just starts to run rough—then apply enough carburetor heat to smooth it out (the less-dense warm air will result in a comparatively richer mixture, hence the smoothness). This is the probable heat control setting for best vaporization. *The addition of carburetor heat usually means higher engine temperatures and could be overdone in warmer weather; perhaps leading to detonation at high power settings.*

There's some confusion between *detonation* and *surface ignition* or *preignition* (people sometimes say one when they mean the other):

Detonation—As noted by FAA AC 65-9 *Airframe and Powerplant Mechanics General Handbook*, in an engine operating in a normal manner, the flame front in the cylinder traverses the charge at a *steady* velocity of about 100 ft per second. When *detonation* occurs, the first portion of the charge burns in a normal manner but the last portion burns almost instantaneously, creating an excessive momentary pressure imbalance in the combustion chamber. The cylinder head temperature will rise, engine efficiency decreases, and structural damage occurs to the piston or cylinder head. You can hear the "knock" in an automobile engine but other sounds cover it in an aircraft engine, so you'll have to depend on the instruments for indications. Normal burning or detonation might be compared with smoothly pushing the piston down (or in) with your hand or hitting the piston with a hammer to move it down.

If you suspect that detonation is occurring, throttle back, make sure the mixture is rich, open cowl flaps, and ease the nose down to assure that good cooling can occur.

Surface ignition or preignition—This is caused by hot spots or surfaces in the chamber igniting the fuel-air mixture. If this happens before the spark plugs get the chance to do their thing, it's called *preignition*. Power loss and roughness occur. It's generally attributed to overheating of spark plug electrodes (glow plugs in model airplane engines use this principle for *normal* ignition) and exhaust valves and to carbon deposits. In the days before idle shutoff systems were used for trainers, preignition was sometimes a problem and the engine would continue to run after the ignition switch was turned off. Usually opening the throttle as the switch was cut helped cool off matters, but in extreme cases the fuel had to be shut off to stop the engine.

Some mixture controls have AUTO LEAN setting positions. The more complex carburetor has an automatic altitude compensator. It contains a bellows that senses the incoming air pressure and controls the fuel metering accordingly. If you set the mixture at best economy at 5,000 feet and climb to 10,000 feet, the mixture will also be at best lean at the higher altitude—even though you haven't touched the mixture control. It is assumed here that you used a *cruise climb* and didn't need to increase the richness for the climb.

Fuel Injection

The big advantage of fuel injection is that carburetor icing is no longer present. The fuel is injected into the intake manifold just before going into the cylinder; hence, there is no temperature drop in the carburetor due to vaporization. The air temperature drops in the carburetor for two reasons: (1) vaporization and (2) the lowered pressure caused by the venturi effect—these two effects being additive.

Of course, you can get impact icing in freezing rain, etc., in either type of fuel system, but this is not the kind caused by invisible moisture.

A particular advantage of fuel injection lies in the pilot's ability to lean the mixture accurately by use of the fuel pressure or fuel-flow gage. This gage measures metered fuel pressure or the pressure of the fuel going to the spray nozzles—this being a direct measure of fuel flow. The gage usually is marked with proper fuel pressures for various power settings and/or altitudes. The lower pressure range is for various cruise power settings (45, 55, 65, or 75%). The altitude is automatically compensated for by a bellows or diaphragm within the control unit that regulates the fuel flow from the nozzles in proportion to the air pressure (volume) passing through the unit. In addition, the gage may be marked for best power for takeoff and climb for various altitudes (this will be in the higher pressure range). Whereas the fuel pressure gage in the carburetor-equipped airplane remains constant at all power settings (it measures the pressure of the fuel from the pumps to the carburetor), the pressure gage for fuel injection varies with mixture setting. To lean this engine you merely move the mixture control until the fuel pressure or fuel flow indicates that you have the correct mixture for the power setting and/or altitude.

Another advantage of fuel injection is that it theoretically gives a better fuel-air distribution to the cylinders. This does not always occur but should if the system is properly operating, because the fuel-air is mixed in a carburetor at one place for all cylinders. By the time this mixture reaches each cylinder some variation in mixture may occur among cylinders. This is not apt to occur in the fuel injection engine because the mixing is done just before entering each cylinder.

Figures 13-11 and 13-12 are two examples of fuel injection systems; one is for a fixed-pitch propeller airplane and one is for a constant-speed propeller airplane.

Disadvantages of fuel injection are

1. At low power settings on hot days (such as during prolonged taxiing), vapor lock may occur and the engine may quit.
2. A hot fuel-injected engine is often very hard to start.
3. It normally takes longer for the fuel-injected engine to get power back if a tank is run dry (more about this in Chapter 16).

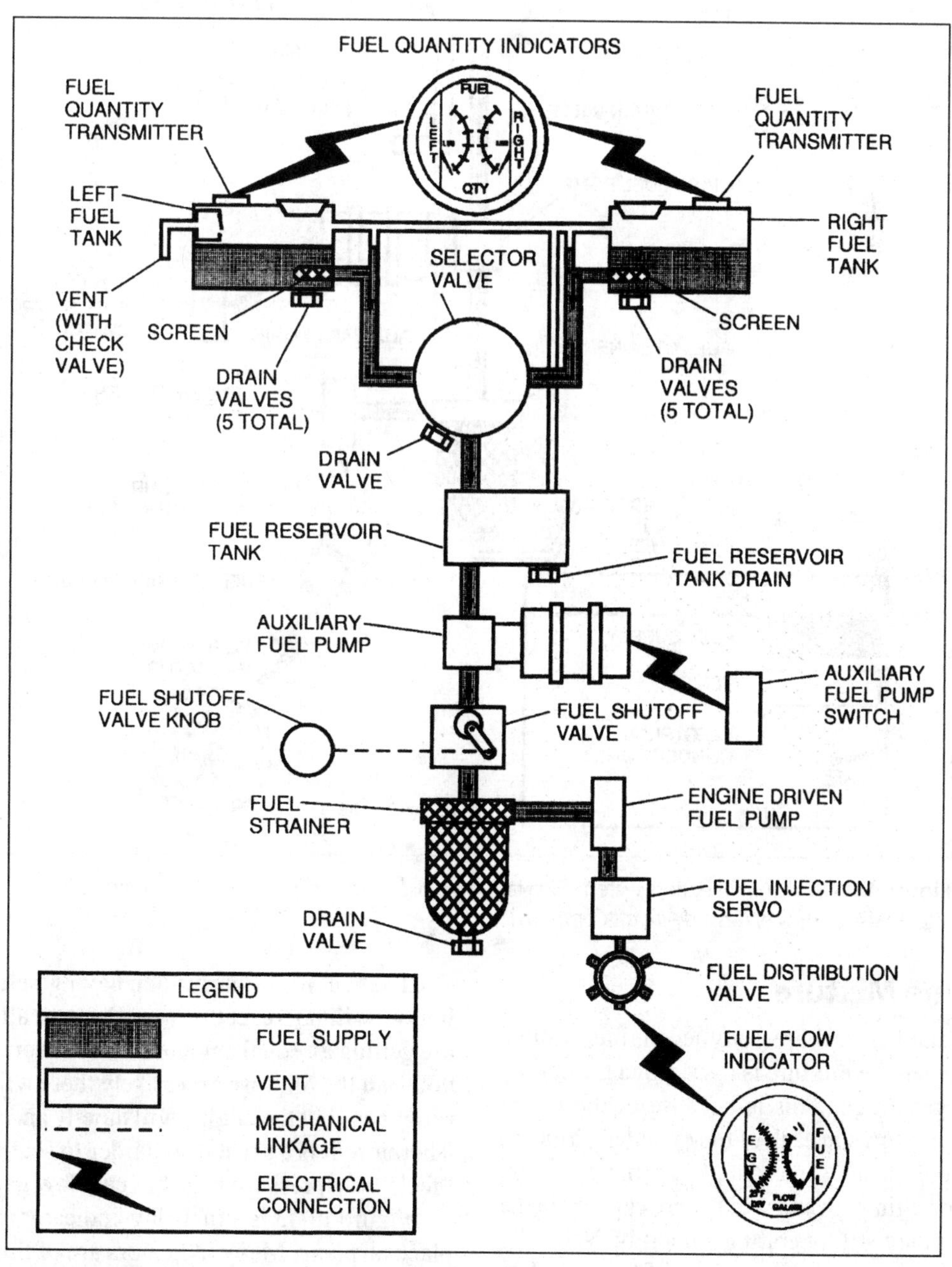

Figure 13-11. A look at the fuel injection system for a late model, four-place, fixed-pitch propeller airplane. *(Courtesy of Cessna Aircraft Company)*

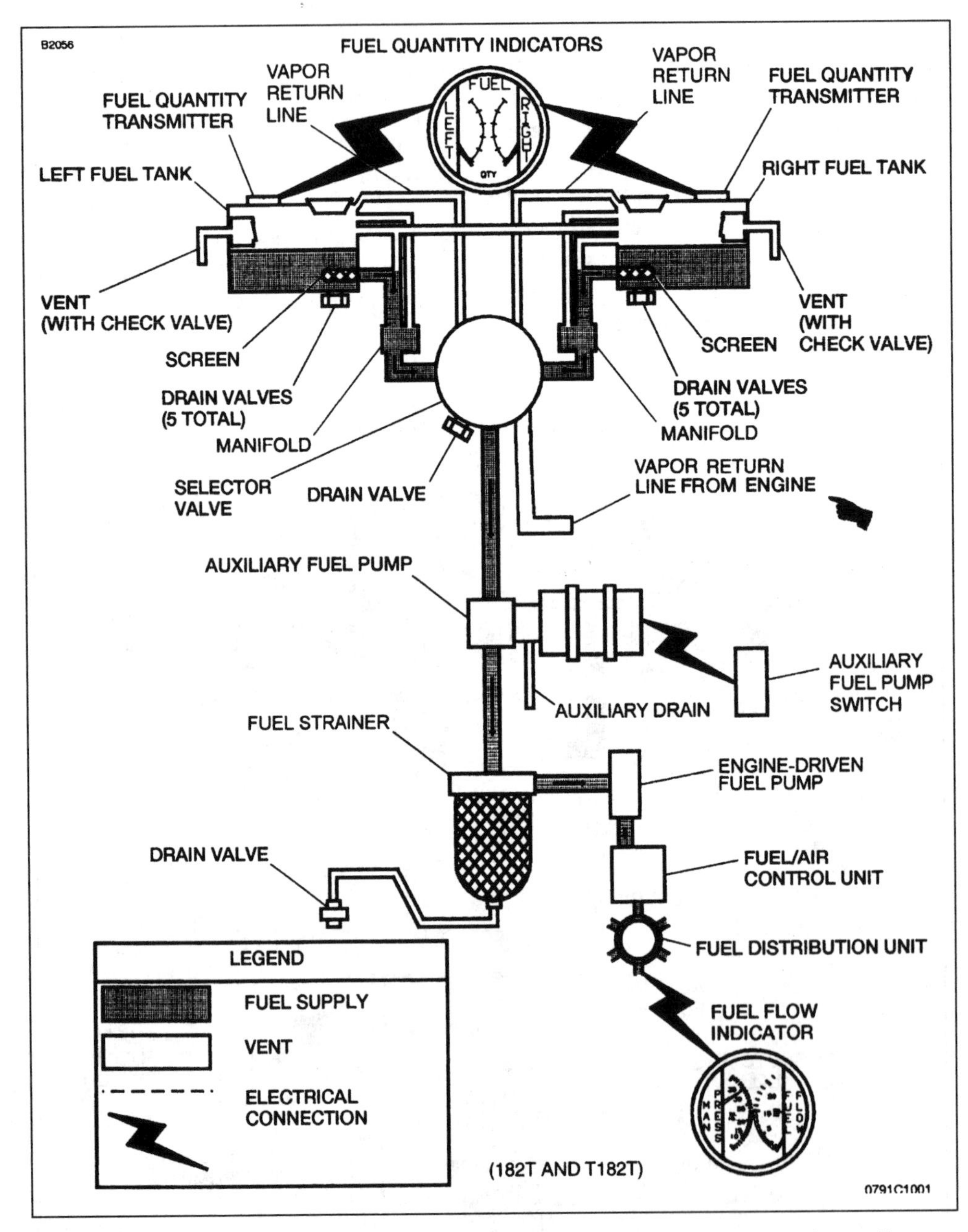

Figure 13-12. A fuel injection system for a late model, four-place, constant-speed propeller airplane. *(Courtesy of Cessna Aircraft Company)*

Leaning the Mixture

If you've leaned a carburetor-type engine, you've noticed that when the mixture is overleaned the engine will start to get rough. This is because of the initial difference in mixtures in each of the cylinders. You are leaning them all at the same rate, but some cylinders were leaner to begin with and will be too lean, while the other cylinders are still operating smoothly. Naturally the engine will run rough if only part of the cylinders are getting enough fuel. This is the idea you used in manual leaning of the carburetor.

The fuel injection system, having better fuel distribution, will not react this way. Because all the cylinders are getting an equal amount of fuel (theoretically), when you lean the mixture excessively there will be no initial roughness but the engine will quietly and smoothly die. Therefore it is a great deal harder to set the mixture by "feel," so a pressure gage or fuel-flow gage is helpful.

Figure 13-13 is a fuel-flow indicator used on a four-place airplane. Many indicators are of this type; others have a gage that measures manifold pressure and fuel flow. The outside numbers on the meter indicate the fuel flow in gallons per hour. The following procedures are used:

Starting

This is the starting procedure for this particular airplane (cold):

1. Set fuel selector on the proper tank.
2. Open the throttle approximately ½ inch.
3. Turn on the master switch and electric auxiliary fuel pump.
4. Move the mixture control to full rich until an indication of 4 to 6 gph is indicated on the flow meter; then turn the pump off (the engine is primed).
5. Move the mixture control to idle cutoff.
6. Switch ignition ON and engage starter.
7. When the engine fires, move the mixture control to full rich.

For starting hot or flooded engines the flow meter is not used, but the engine is started with the mixture in idle cutoff and fuel pump off. (The throttle is cracked ½ inch or open, respectively.) When the engine fires, move the mixture control to full rich (and retard the throttle as necessary).

Takeoff

For this fuel-injected airplane during a normal takeoff with full-rich mixture, the pointer on the fuel-flow meter will stabilize between the sea level mark and the red line (Figure 13-13). This is slightly rich to aid in fuel cooling and is recommended for normal takeoffs at sea level.

When taking off from a high-altitude field (say 4,000 feet density-altitude), the mixture should be leaned to maximum power during the pretakeoff check. Full throttle is applied and the mixture control is moved toward the lean position until the pointer has stabilized at the 4,000-ft mark (between the 19.5- and 20.0-gph marks). The takeoff is made with this mixture. The same technique can be used for obtaining maximum power at sea level, using the sea level mark. (Don't overheat the engine with prolonged climbs; richen it again after clearing any obstacles.)

Cruise

The flow meter is a good aid in setting up a cruise mixture. The example of 65% power in Figure 13-13 indicates that the two widest variations are 14.5 gph (best power) and 12.6 gph (best economy); settings should be between these limits. As you can see, 55 and 75% settings also have a range of possible settings. When you check out in a complex airplane, check out the fuel-flow gage (fuel injection). The EGT gage is a more precise method of leaning, however.

Approach and Landing

Set the mixture to full rich. (No reference to fuel-flow meter for a *precise* setting.) The POH may have some suggestions on mixture settings for approaches to high-elevation (high-density-altitude) airports.

Figures 13-14 and 13-15 show the basic differences among the fuel-metering systems just discussed.

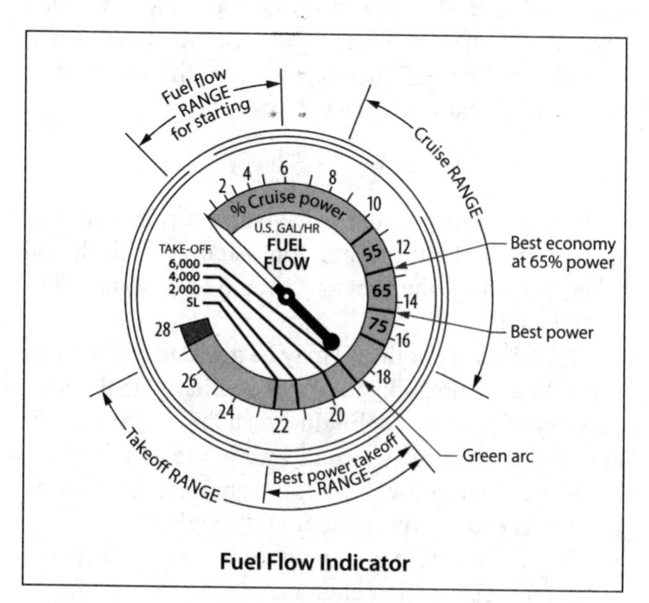

Figure 13-13. An example of a fuel flow indicator for a single-engine, fuel-injected airplane. Others may combine the manifold pressure gage and a fuel flow gage.

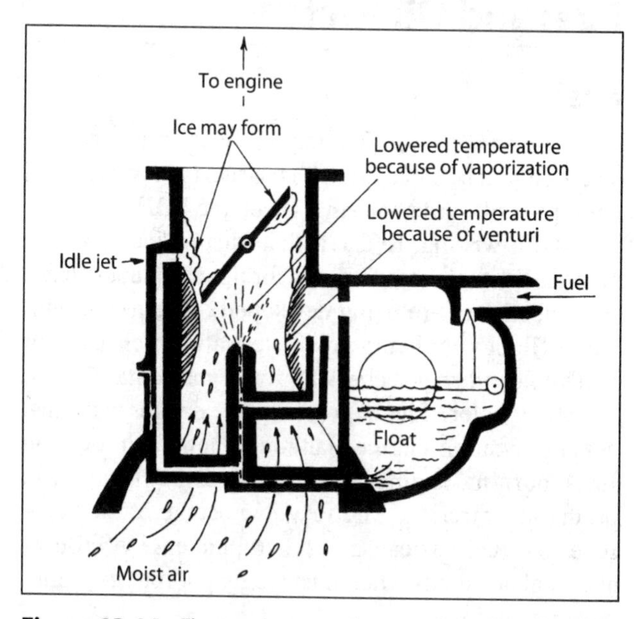

Figure 13-14. Float carburetor, showing how ice can form.

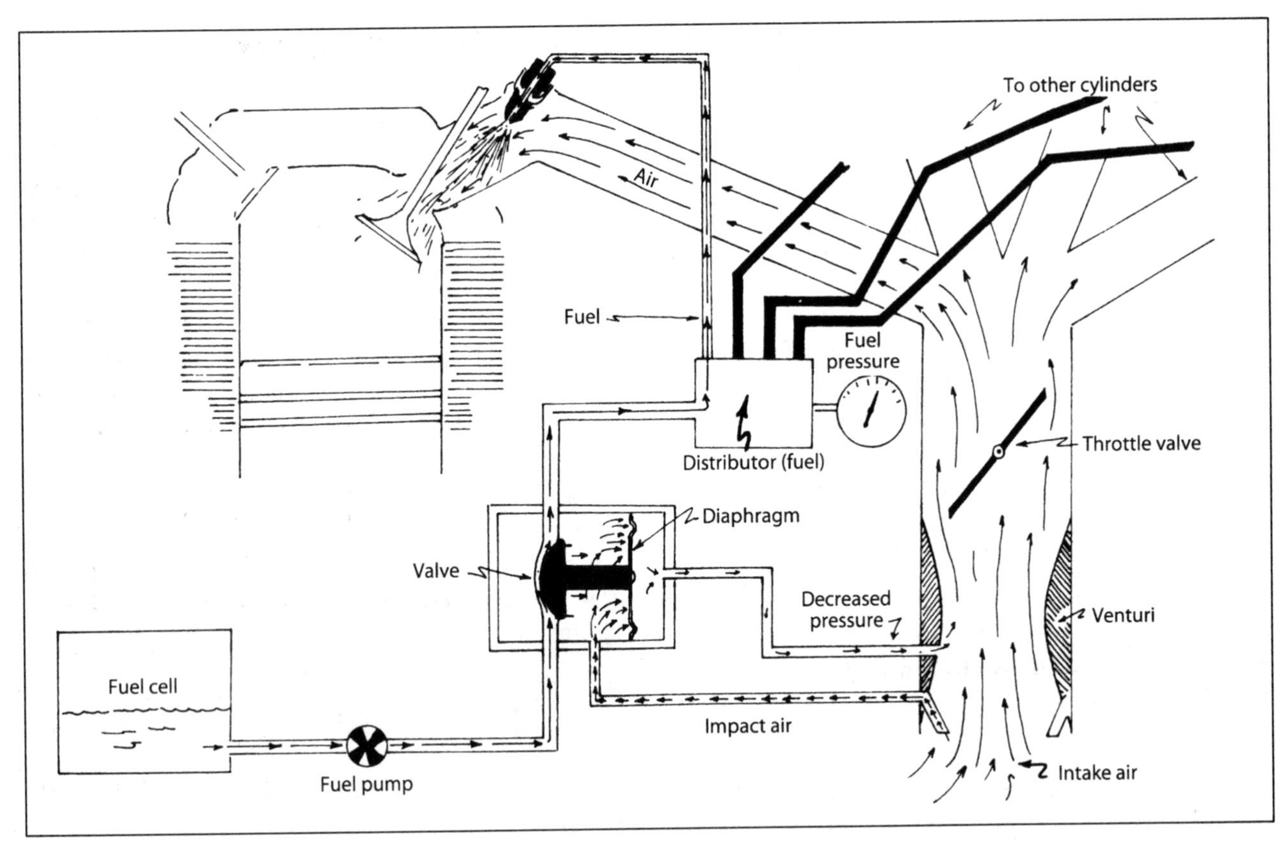

Figure 13-15. A simplified view of one type of fuel injection system.

Fuel and Oil Facts

Fuel

Only use an approved fuel for your particular airplane. There should be a placard with the fuel type at each fuel cap. If the placard's missing, check the POH.

At this writing, 100LL with its distinctive light blue color, is the fuel most common for light airplanes (lead-free substitutes are being developed). Due to the danger of flight after being mis-fueled, always check your fuel's color when you check for water and contaminates.

Straw-colored Jet-A poses a grave danger to typical general aviation engines (although new reciprocating Jet-A burning engines are starting to be installed in production aircraft). The very-low octane of the kerosene-like fuel has caused catastrophic engine failures and fatal accidents when mistakenly put into gasoline-burning engines.

You may fly an airplane that can use autogas, but it must have an STC (Supplemental Type Certificate) and many common engines are not eligible to burn the lower octane found in automobile fuel.

You'll be at a disadvantage preflighting one of those airplanes that drains the sump at a remote location, since it's hard to see water and grit in a puddle on the ramp. Try to find a way to capture the fuel so you can examine it, even if you have to find someone to help. Sometimes a rubber fuel hose can be used to guide the fuel into the sampler while you pull the handle.

You should always sample the fuel as part of your preflight, waiting a few minutes after fueling to let any water settle to the area of the drains. If you've been misfueled or have a bunch of water in the tank, it will probably make itself known just as you lift off and start across an alligator-filled swamp.

Oil

A chapter on fuel systems may seem a rather strange place to talk about oil, but you usually check the oil when you check the fuel and should have some information on it.

The viscosity of the oil may be given in one of three ways. You are probably the most familiar with the SAE (Society of Automotive Engineers) number. Oil is available in fixed viscosity or multi-weight (e.g., 15W50).

Notice that in every case, the commercial aviation number is exactly twice the SAE "weight."

There are two main types of aviation oil in use today for reciprocating engines:

1. *Straight mineral oil*—This oil is without any dispersant additives. It is a more or less inert lubricating medium.

2. *Ashless dispersant oils*—These types of detergent or compound oils (with additive) keep the foreign particles in solution without the disadvantages of ash-forming detergent additives.

Engine manufacturers generally recommend that new or newly overhauled engines should be operated on straight mineral oil during the first 50 hours of operation, or until oil consumption has stabilized. If an additive oil is used in these engines, high oil consumption might result, since the antifriction additive of some of these oils will retard the break-in of piston rings and cylinder walls.

Okay, what if you've been using straight mineral oil for several hundred hours and decide that it's to your advantage to start using a compounded oil? The least you'd better do is the following, according to one major engine manufacturer (making sure the compounded oil is approved for your engine):

1. Don't add the additive oil to straight mineral oil. Drain the straight mineral oil and then fill with additive oil.
2. Don't operate the engine longer than 5 hours before the first oil change.
3. Check all oil screens for evidence of sludge or plugging. Change oil every 10 hours if sludge conditions are evident. Resume normal oil drain periods after the sludge conditions improve.

If you are fairly close to overhaul, you might not want to go to all that trouble. The real point is that putting additive oils in an engine that has been using straight mineral oil for several hundred hours can cause problems unless you are careful.

Along these same lines, *don't* put special "antifriction" additives in the oil; the manufacturer's warranty could be voided. Don't use automotive oil in an airplane engine. In short, follow the engine manufacturer's recommendations or make a phone call to check, if you're not sure. A couple of minutes on the phone sure beats damaging an engine (and maybe damaging you and your passengers).

Since you are an "advanced pilot" and will be flying more-powerful and -complex engines, you should know *exactly* the type of fuel and oil to be used during servicing. A crew member should be available to oversee the fuel and oil servicing. Jet fuel *has* been mistakenly put in the tanks of airplanes with piston engines—with fatal accidents resulting in some cases.

Some Added Points

You will have more responsibility and authority as an advanced pilot, and you will have to know more things about the airplane and its maintenance requirements. This seems like a good place to follow with some general information (courtesy of *Avco Lycoming Flyer*), particularly in the area of engine operations.

To most private pilots, the letters and numbers that describe the engine they are using are meaningless, but you can learn a lot about your engine by looking at the model code. Figure 13-16 shows designations used.

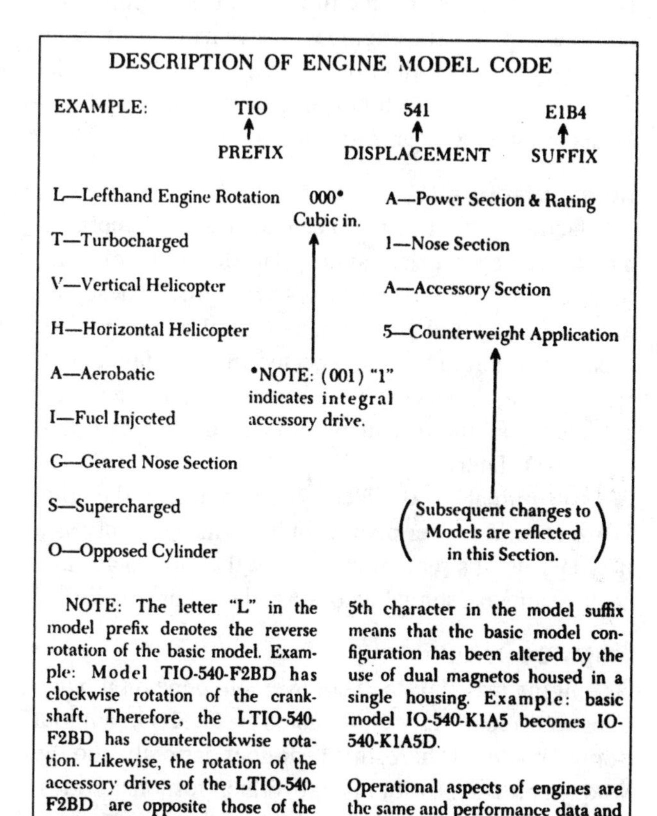

Figure 13-16. Engine model code. (*Lycoming Division, Avco Flyer*)

Definitions of Engine Maintenance and Repair

You may later need to oversee the maintenance and repair of engine(s) in the airplane you're flying and so should know the types of repair or replacement services available.

New Engine

As defined by Textron Lycoming, a new engine is the original product with all new parts and accessories, meeting all production test specifications, quality control tests, and regulations for a production certificate issued by the FAA. By the time the ultimate purchaser gets the airplane, the engine will have had the airframe manufacturer's production test time plus ferry time. The engine will have a new engine warranty and will be accompanied by an *Engine Logbook*.

Remanufacture

The factory remanufactured engine gives the benefits of a new engine at a price savings. The definition of a factory remanufactured engine is one originally designed and manufactured by a company and disassembled, repaired or altered, and inspected in accordance with that company's service bulletins, mandatory engineering changes, and any airworthiness directives (more about ADs later).

To summarize, the factory-remanufactured engine is a zero-time power plant with the same warranty as a new engine. It's remanufactured at the same place and by the same personnel who worked on it originally.

Major Overhaul

An engine may have a major overhaul done on it by an approved repair agency, as noted in FAR 43. Without going into details here, this FAR goes basically into the who, what, and how of major overhaul responsibilities. A major overhaul consists of the *complete* disassembly of the engine and its repair, reassembly, and testing to ensure proper operation. Engines are overhauled in the field and not by the manufacturer. One disadvantage of overhauling an engine is that the airplane is grounded during the process unless there's a spare available. Many owners trade in a run-out engine for a new or remanufactured one (getting credit for the old engine), thus saving a lot of downtime.

Top Overhaul

A top overhaul is defined as repair or overhaul of parts on the outside of the crankcase without completely disassembling the engine. It includes the removal of the cylinders and deglazing the cylinder walls; inspections of pistons, valve-operating mechanisms, and valve guides; and replacing the piston rings. This is done in the field; engines in earlier days had one or more top overhauls between majors.

Nitrided and Chrome Cylinders

The engine cylinders get quite a workout, and the walls have to withstand friction plus the heat of combustion; the harder the surface, the less the wear.

In 1960 Lycoming started the nitriding process to combat wear problems. This process consists of introducing an ammonia gas (NH_3) atmosphere to the practically finished part. This is done in special heat-treating, airtight furnaces at 975°F for a period of 25 to 80 hours, depending on what's required. The ammonia gas is broken down into elements of nitrogen and hydrogen. The nitrogen joins the steel and makes a very hard, wear-resistant surface. (All crankshafts and some gears are nitrided by Lycoming.) Nitrided cylinder walls increase piston ring life, giving better sealing and increased fatigue strength, compared with regular steel barrels. You can tell if your engine has nitrided barrels by (1) reading the engine manual or (2) checking for an *azure* painted band around the cylinder base (if they are painted black) or on the edges of the top cylinder head fins between the two valve push rod tubes (if the engine is painted all gray).

Some barrel walls may be chrome plated instead of nitrided (also for longer wear); the color code is orange at the places mentioned in the last paragraph.

Repair or Maintenance Notifications

The FAA states that whenever an aircraft or engine manufacturer determines through service experience that a modification is needed to extend the life of the product or for safety purposes, the manufacturer may let the owners know of impending problems or needed (or suggested) repairs. Suppose you, an owner or operator of an airplane, get a service letter—do you have to ground the airplane immediately? There are different levels of notifications by the manufacturer, and these may apply to the airplane *and/or* the engine.

Service Letter

A service letter is product information that is optional for the owner/operator, who may decide that the changes would be nice but would be too expensive.

Service Information

This is product information that the manufacturer definitely recommends compliance with. While it isn't mandatory, you'd be very wise to take advantage of the manufacturer's knowledge gained by inputs from the field.

Service Bulletin

A service letter or service instruction may be followed by a service bulletin. The bulletin outlines the trouble and tells how to remedy it. A service bulletin is technically not mandatory unless there is a time limit requirement, in which case it becomes virtually mandatory.

Airworthiness Directive (AD Note)

If an unsafe condition arises for an airframe or engine, the FAA issues an AD note, which specifies the component found to be unsafe and any conditions, limitations, or inspections under which the aircraft may continue to be operated. It's the aircraft owner/operator's mandatory responsibility to assure compliance with all AD notes. Some ADs are recurrent or repetitive, requiring certain inspections, say, every 100 hours. This must be done and recorded in the logbook each time, with the signature and certificate number of the mechanic or repair agency involved.

An AD note may have a date of effectiveness and a flight time limit for compliance. For instance, as well as giving the serial numbers of the aircraft/engines involved and referring to a service bulletin for repair procedures, the AD may basically state that "within 25 flight hours [such and such] must be done, this AD becoming effective July 10, 20____."

Know your airplane.

14

Retractable-Gear Airplanes

Background

The biggest single step forward in decreasing airplane drag was the improved design of retractable landing gear. At first the retracting systems were so complex and heavy that only large airplanes could use them. Now, through the use of electrical motors or very light hydraulic systems, nearly all high-performance, single-engine airplanes and all the light twins have retractable gear.

The advantages in speed and economy are obvious. You have no doubt already figured out the main disadvantage—the landing gear is sometimes retracted at what might be termed an "inopportune moment." Pilots also forget to put the landing gear *down* at the opportune moment. You usually can get away with forgetting to shove the prop control forward or forgetting to use flaps (you can take care of the prop on the sly as you taxi in), *but* you won't get away with forgetting to put the gear down. Three things are certain about gear-up landings: (1) they are definitely more noisy than the gear-down type; (2) the airplane does not "roll" as far; and (3) expenses are somewhat higher.

At some time in your flying career you will come close to landing gear-up—and you may go all the way if you aren't careful. The purpose of this chapter is to help keep you from going all the way.

So here's a *general* look at retractable-gear airplanes.

Pilot Stress

Believe it or not, the danger period for the pilot of a retractable-gear plane normally is not the first few hours after checkout. If you are like most new checkouts, you'll spoil the enjoyment of the first few flights by muttering to yourself over and over, "Mustn't forget to put the gear down, mustn't forget the gear, mustn't... etc." After a while you'll consider yourself an old pro and the gear check will be important but not the *only* item on the checklist as it seemed to be at first.

Back to the idea of stress: One day you'll be going into Chicago O'Hare or Atlanta Hartsfield or some other busy airport. There'll be a lot of traffic and the tower will be giving instructions at a machine gun rate. Suppose you aren't able to finish the approach because of conflicting traffic and are advised by the tower to "take it around." You pull the gear up and try to work back into the downwind leg. The traffic is heavy and the pressure is on. The tower people may seem unsympathetic, but their job is to expedite traffic flow safely. You are cleared to land again and are very busy, looking for other airplanes and setting up the pattern. *In this stressful situation you could forget to put the gear down again.* In the daytime the tower operators will probably catch you before you land gear-up. Many a pilot has been saved from a dangerous or embarrassing situation by an alert tower controller. But don't count on their doing a job that is rightfully yours. They're very busy.

At night you don't even have the possibility of a tower controller spotting the results of your memory lapse. The shower of sparks when you land will reveal your problem.

Always have the gear down before turning on base leg under normal conditions. If the tower clears you to enter base leg, have the gear *down* and *locked* before starting the descent on base. *Always check the gear indicators again after turning on final.* Some pilots point to the gear indicators so that they're sure their attention is directed there. Of course, it's possible to point to a *gear-up* light absentmindedly.

Checklist

The checklist is a valuable aid if used correctly. The trouble is that after a while you'll "know" it so thoroughly that using it becomes just a ritual done at certain times. Some pilots glance at it and don't read it. It's very easy to skip an item this way. A checklist is a liability if not used correctly—a quick glance at it may lead you to believe you've done what's necessary, giving a false sense of security. On the other hand, if you use the checklist religiously and always put the gear down at the same point, habit may save you embarrassment some time when your conscious mind is out to lunch.

GUMP (gas, undercarriage, mixture, prop) is a good back-up check, too, for landing. Use GUMPP if you have an electric fuel pump to turn on before landing.

Remember—just because you went through the motions and moved the right lever doesn't mean the gear is down. CHECK IT! Mechanical devices have their off-days too.

Landing Gear Systems

Figure 14-1 is a schematic for a landing gear system that uses an electric pump to provide pressure for the hydraulic system. The system normally operates at pressures from 1,000 to 1,500 psi. The electrical portion of the power pack is protected by a 35-amp pull-off-type circuit breaker switch (labeled GEAR PUMP) on the left switch and control panel. (See Figure 4-70, Chapter 4.) This CB may be pulled if the pump continues to run longer than 1 minute (the usual time for a cycle—up or down—is 5 to 7 seconds) to avoid pump overheating.

Figure 14-2 is a landing gear system for a twin that has an engine-driven hydraulic pump on each engine. Note that a hand pump is provided in addition to the two engine-driven pumps. Usually a hydraulic system uses a standpipe in the fluid reservoir to prevent the engine—or electric pumps—from pumping all the fluid overboard in the event of a leak. The remaining fluid may be utilized by the hand pump (Figure 14-3). The standpipe idea is found in the hydraulic systems of airliners, too.

An added point: When you first go out to the airplane to start the preflight check, confirm that the gear handle or switch is DOWN and then turn on the master switch to check for down indications.

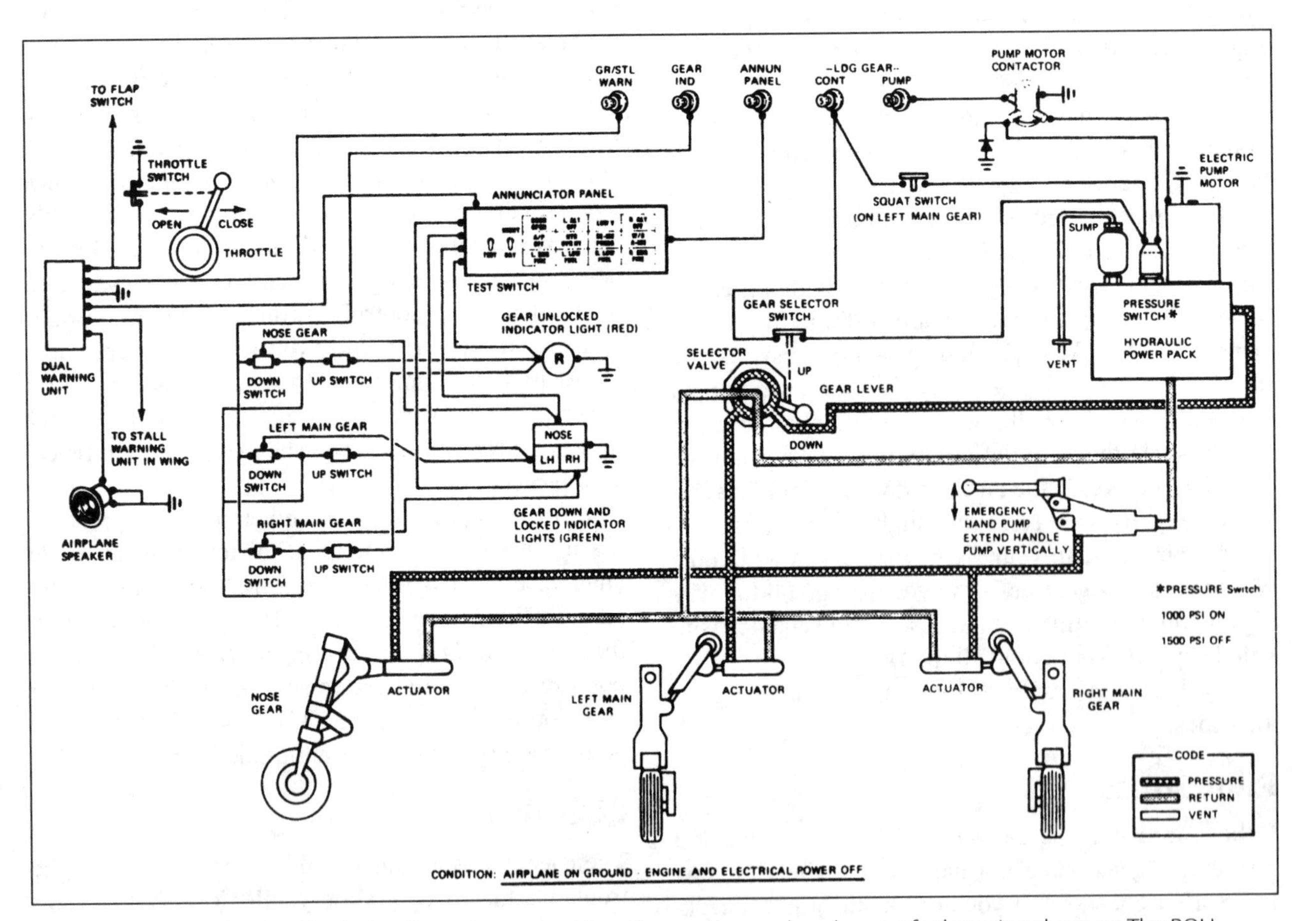

Figure 14-1. Electrical-hydraulic landing gear system. Note the emergency hand pump for lowering the gear. The POH Emergency Procedures section and the checklist detail the procedures.

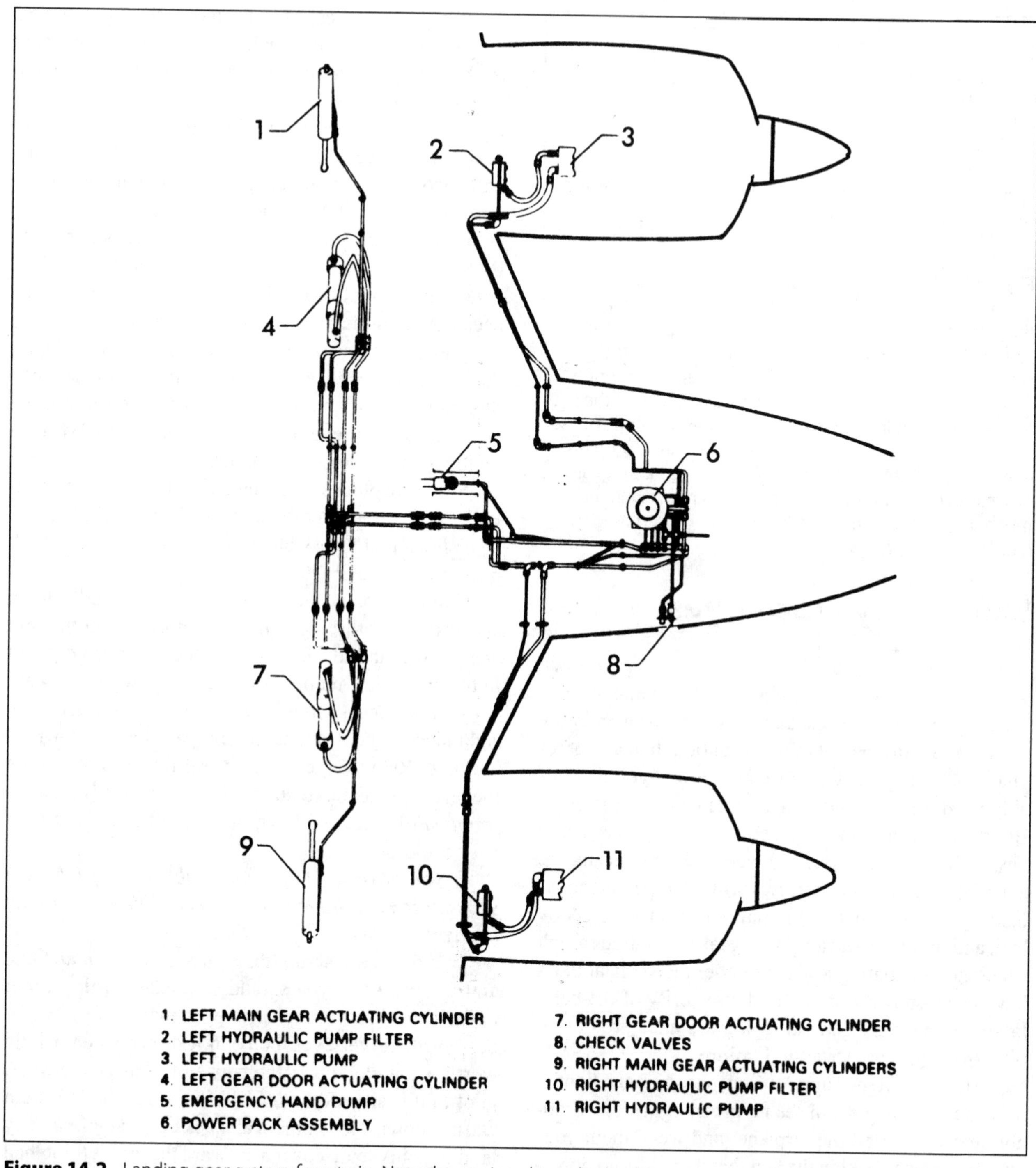

Figure 14-2. Landing gear system for a twin. Note the engine-driven hydraulic pumps on each side. This airplane has electrically operated flaps.

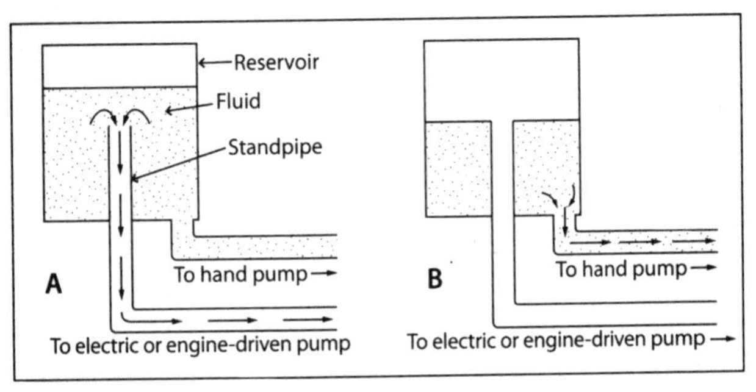

Figure 14-3. A simplified look at a standpipe principle. A. Under normal conditions (plenty of hydraulic fluid), the standpipe is the route of the fluid to the pump(s) and system. The hand pump line is essentially closed off. B. When a leak occurs, the engine-driven or electric pump(s) may pump the fluid overboard until it gets down to the top of the standpipe. The remaining fluid is available for use when the hand pump system is used. The hand pump is considered a carefully planned one-shot operation (gear-down only) because the leak may be at a point such that much or all of the remaining fluid could be lost during the hand pumping process.

Emergency Procedures

Next to the fear that you'll forget to put the gear down will be the thought, "What if it just won't come down?" The newspapers, movies, and television have probably milked more drama out of this situation than any other phase of flying. If it won't come down, you'll probably bend the prop and scrape some paint off the belly. But the cases of pilots of general aviation planes being physically unable to lower the gear by any means are extremely rare. Manufacturers frown on people belly-landing their products. This makes their airplanes look bad, and they try to arrange it so gear-up landings aren't necessary. Actuating arms and other mechanical parts have been known to fail, but the majority of the belly landings made by general aviation planes are due to pilot oversight, not structural failure.

While in flight suppose you put the gear handle or switch down and can see no green light? You probably got in, started the airplane, and went about your business—overlooking the fact that there was no down-light when you taxied out and not noticing that there was no up-light after you pulled the gear up. Here's where the ball is dropped at the beginning of the flight. *As soon as you get in the airplane, check the position of the gear handle or switch. When the master switch is turned on for start, check for a down-light.* Somebody might have tinkered around in the cockpit and moved the control to the up position. If the safety lock isn't working, the plane could slowly sink to the ground as you start to taxi. This is unlikely, but there's no need to take a chance.

In some airplanes, when the navigation lights are on, the landing gear indicator lights are dimmed because the bright lights are disconcerting at night. If the navigation lights are on in the daytime, the gear indicator lights may be so dim as to appear to be off. There have been many cases of newly checked-out pilots calling on Unicom to state that the gear isn't down. One of the first things old pilots in the airport office ask is, "Are your navigation lights off?" This usually is answered by a long pause and a rather weak, "Uh, Roger." The embarrassed pilot comes in and lands, the gear having been down all the time but the lights dimmed.

The new pilot has a red face, but this is far better than taking a chance on bellying it in. In cases like this, new pilots have been known to use the normal *and* emergency means of lowering the gear and still not seeing a down indication (naturally).

Some airplanes with electrically operated landing gear have a three-position switch (UP, OFF, and DOWN), and it's possible to stop in the middle or OFF position instead of DOWN.

Suppose you've put the gear switch or handle down and instead of three green lights (nose and both main gears down and locked) you see that there is no green light for the left main gear (the other two greens are bright and clear). Should you put passengers on the right side of the airplane and prepare for a two-wheel landing? Recycle the gear several times to try to get the left main gear extended? *Not yet. It could be a bulb problem* (the gear is down but the left gear light bulb isn't working).

If you have landing gear problems in flight, get yourself some altitude where you can think—get out of the traffic pattern.

In a four-bulb setup (three green for *down* and one amber for *all up*), you should first take out the amber up-bulb and use it to replace the left main bulb. It would be foolish to get everybody in a dither when a bulb worth a few dollars is the cause of your concern. (A pilot in this situation *could* decide, since the left main wasn't "down," to get them all back up and make a belly landing, only to discover afterward that everything had been fine except for a burned-out bulb.)

You might think, "Why not transfer one of the other green bulbs to the left main indicator?" You know each of the others *had* been showing green, but it's better to be able to confirm just before landing that all three show a *down* indication than to assume the blank bulb socket would still be showing a green light if the bulb was in it. Maybe the one spare bulb to carry is this one.

But let's say it's not the bulb. The FAA requires that the POH or its equivalent be in the airplane at all times—and this is one of the main reasons why. It's funny how blank a usually sharp mind can get sometimes. You no doubt learned the emergency gear-down procedures until you could say them in your sleep, but now the steps have eluded you. *Take your time.* Get the POH out and read the emergency procedures if you have to. Some airplanes have the step-by-step instructions printed near or on the cover plate of the emergency gear handle or switch. Follow them carefully.

Slowing the airplane down makes the landing gear extension a lot easier. Don't fly it around just above stall, but have the airspeed well below maximum gear-down speed.

In most airplanes with hydraulically actuated gear, the emergency procedure requires the gear handle to be placed in the *down* position before going on to the extension of the gear. Pilots have forgotten this and, when using a CO_2 bottle emergency extender, have wasted their one shot by having the gear handle up. They got in a hurry and didn't bother to follow the step-by-step procedure, or thought they knew the emergency procedure and didn't need to reread it. The recommendations for the emergency extension of electrically operated landing gear call for the switch to be in the DOWN position.

Getting out of the traffic pattern allows you to analyze the situation. It may be just a popped CB or a problem requiring a little hand pumping for hydraulic gear.

Don't use the emergency procedure until you are ready to land. This sounds like a rather inane statement but what it means is that the emergency gear extension is usually a one-way affair. Once the gear is put down by emergency means, you have to leave it there.

There's the case of the curious private pilot who suspected after takeoff from a strange field that he might have trouble getting the gear down by normal means because it didn't act right coming up—so he did everything wrong. Home field with a good repair station for his airplane was only 1 hour away (gear up) and he had 5 hours of fuel. On the way home he started thinking "Will it go down?" until he couldn't stand the suspense any longer and used the emergency procedure. Of course, the gear came down but he had a mighty slow trip and almost got an overheated engine.

Then there was the private pilot who did the same thing, but, being heavily loaded over mountainous terrain, decided that he had to get the gear back up. By clean living and hard work he managed to get the gear started back up (where it stuck halfway, naturally) and did a fine job of messing up his new Zephyr Six when he landed.

If you have trouble getting the gear up after takeoff, don't force the issue—leave it down. *Make sure it's down,* return, and land, unless it would be wiser to fly (gear down) to a more suitable nearby airport where the trouble can be more easily fixed after you land.

This writer on a few occasions had to blow the landing gear down on an F4U-5N for landing on a carrier. (It seemed to happen more on night landings after a long, tiring patrol.) On one occasion, after circling a downed pilot in the dark (he was picked up by a destroyer), the landing gear had to be blown down—the standpipe system had failed somehow, so a night carrier landing was made with 10° (instead of 50°) of flaps. No damage except to nerves, but it was an interesting evening.

Gear-Up Landing

If the emergency procedure doesn't work (you forgot to have the gear handle down when you pulled the CO_2 bottle as a last resort), or there has been a mechanical failure or damage that won't allow the gear to come down by any means, you might remember a few points on gear-up landings. In the majority of belly landings, (1) comparatively little damage will be done and (2) the plane's occupants won't even be shaken up (physically, that is). A quick summary of your probable procedure:

1. Choose the best runway based on length, surface winds and fuel/proximity.
2. Tighten seat belt and shoulder harness.
3. Make a normal approach; then after the field is made—
4. Battery and alternators OFF.
5. Chop the power and turn off all fuel system switches.
6. Ignition switch(es) OFF.
7. Make a normal landing.

If the runway is long enough, don't extend the flaps on the low-wing airplane. This will save a few more dollars, for extended flaps can be damaged. If the terrain is rough it would be better, though, to extend the flaps to further decrease the touchdown speed.

Figure on the prop being damaged. It will still be windmilling when you touch if you cut off the engine after the field is made. If you have any idea of killing the engine at altitude, slowing the plane up until the prop stops, and making it horizontal with the starter, forget it unless the runway is extremely long (say, 10,000 or 12,000 feet). This is no time to be practicing dead stick landings. *A bent prop is a small price to pay for assurance that the field is made.*

Your POH will cover the procedures for various gear problems, but here's an item you might consider if you have a flat nosewheel tire or the nosewheel remains up (and the main gear is down and locked). After touchdown, as you're holding the nosewheel off as long as possible, if it's not distracting, you might roll in nose-*down* trim to help keep the nose up to as slow an airspeed as possible. (Logical reasoning would assume that the elevator-stabilator trim should be rolled to a nose-up setting, but if you check the positions for nose-up or nose-down trim, you'll see that for most airplanes more *area* is available in the latter condition.) This was discussed in Chapter 10.

Summary of Emergency Procedures

The *exact* emergency procedures vary, as some airplanes use electrical power for gear actuation and others use hydraulic means.

1. Take your time and analyze.
2. Know your emergency procedures.
3. Keep the POH handy to help you remember each step.
4. Again, *take your time.*

Some More Points About Retractable Gear

Some pilots get the idea that the sooner they get the gear up on takeoff the better they look to the airport crowd. 'Tain't so!

The landing gear has a safety switch (electric gear) or a by-pass valve (hydraulically actuated gear) on one of the oleos to ensure against inadvertent retraction on the ground. As long as the weight is on this gear (the oleo is compressed), the landing gear can't be retracted (oh yeah?). Don't depend on this safety switch—it might not be working that day. Curiosity can cost money, so don't test the antiretraction safety features.

Even if the safety mechanism is working normally, don't get any ideas of putting the gear handle up during the takeoff run to "look sharp," because a gust might lift the plane enough temporarily to extend the oleo and the gear would start up before you're ready. Don't raise the gear before you are definitely airborne. Don't retract it while you could land gear-down on the runway ahead should the engine quit. (See Figure 5-12.)

Apply the brakes after takeoff before retracting the gear. Otherwise the wheels will be spinning at a good clip when they enter the wheel wells and can burn rubber that you might want to use later. Most manufacturers have buffer blocks on strips in the main wheel wells to stop the spinning, but you might as well save the tires as much as possible. Of course there's nothing you can do about a nosewheel. For larger airplanes with high takeoff speeds, this braking is frowned upon because the rapidly spinning heavy wheel has a great deal of inertia and the sudden stopping of the wheel may cause the tire to slip around the rim. Most transports automatically brake the main wheels upon retraction and have snubbers for the nose wheels.

Know your maximum gear extension speed (Figure 14-4).

If you're taking off through puddles or slush and the temperature is near freezing, leave the gear down for a while after takeoff to allow the airflow to dry the landing gear. You may want to cycle the gear a time or two to clear it before leaving it up. If the landing gear has a lot of water on it and this freezes, it might cause problems when extending the gear later.

Some retractable-gear airplanes have "automatic" gear-lowering systems designed to help the pilot who *inadvertently forgets* to put the wheels down where they belong. These systems are not intended to replace good headwork. The pilot who flies airplanes so equipped and automatically relies on the systems could be unpleasantly surprised sometime when landing the usual type of retractable-gear airplane. Also, these systems might need to be over-ridden if the engine quits and you don't want the gear down while trying to glide to that choice field.

Figure 14-4.

15

Checking Out in the Light Twin

If you're like many single-engine pilots, you may have sold yourself on the idea that twin-engine flying is strictly for people with thousands of hours and skills seldom found in lesser mortals.

Remember when you first started flying and you sometimes wondered if you'd ever really solo? (Particularly after one of those flights where everything went wrong.) Also, maybe there for a while it looked as though you'd never get the private certificate because you had to take the knowledge test again, and then had checkitis for days before the practical test. That's all behind, and now you've found a new subject to worry about—whether you'll be able to fly one of those light twins you've been admiring.

Under normal conditions the airplane is flown *exactly* as if it were a single-engine airplane. Many new pilots don't believe this, even after being told by the check pilot. It *looks* more complicated than the single-engine airplane, so they convince themselves that they'll be working a lot harder all the time.

Although there are two of each of the engine controls (throttle, prop, and mixture), think of each pair of controls as one handle—at least at the beginning. The check pilot will allow you to get well familiarized with the airplane before starting into engine-out procedures. You'll find that after a while you'll be using the controls separately as needed without any trouble.

Before flying, you and the check pilot will discuss the airplane and its systems in detail, and you'll spend a great deal of time with the POH.

This chapter takes a general look at the factors involved in checking out in the light twin; it is not intended to replace the information given by the POH and/or your instructor for a particular airplane.

Preflight Check

1. a. Ignition and master switches OFF (Figure 15-1).
   b. Check that the landing gear selector and the other controls are in their proper positions.
2. a. Check for external damage or operational interference to the control surfaces, wings, or fuselage.
   b. Check for snow, ice, or frost on the wings or control surfaces.
3. a. Visually check fuel supply.
   b. Check fuel cell caps and covers for security (adjust caps to maintain tight seal).
   c. Fuel system vents open.
4. a. Landing gear shock struts properly inflated (approximately 3 inches of piston exposed).
   b. Tires satisfactorily inflated and not excessively worn.
   c. Fuel strainers and lines drained.
   d. Cowling, landing gear doors, and inspection covers properly attached and secured.
   e. Propellers free of detrimental nicks.
   f. No obvious fuel or oil leaks.
   g. Engine oil at the proper level.
5. a. Windshield clean and free of defects.
   b. Tow bar and control locks detached and properly stowed; baggage doors secured.
6. a. Upon entering the airplane, all control operations checked.
   b. Landing gear selector and the other controls in their proper positions.
   c. Required papers in order and in the airplane.

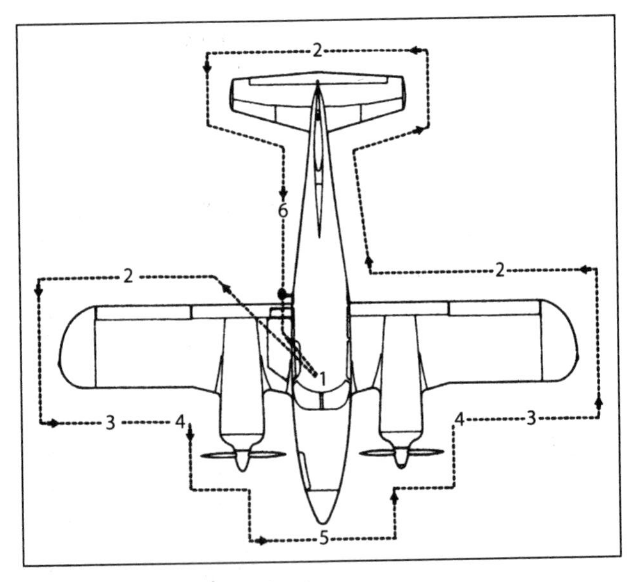

Figure 15-1. Preflight check route.

Check Before Starting Engines

1. Baggage secured.
2. Weight and CG computed.
3. Performance computed.
4. Aircraft papers in order.
5. Maps and charts checked.
6. Cabin door locked.
7. Seat belts secured.
8. Crew seats adjusted.
9. Parking brake set.
10. Altimeter set.
11. Control response checked.
12. Oxygen pressure checked for adequate supply.
13. Fuel valves ON.
14. Circuit breakers checked.
15. Switches (radio, etc.) OFF.

Except: Main voltage regulator ON. Alternators ON.

The check pilot may give you a ground briefing several days before flying to give you a chance to learn the various control locations and their use. Spend some time in the cockpit by yourself after the ground check, using the POH to mentally review the steps for starting, takeoff, etc. This generally makes the first flight a little easier for both you and the check pilot.

In addition to checking the POH for operating procedures, you should also become familiar with the various system schematics. Samples will be included as they come up for discussion in this chapter.

Starting

Normally the left (number one) engine is started first in the light twins (originally because many of the earlier light twins had a generator only on the left engine, and it could then be working to help start the right engine). The latest twins have alternators on both engines. Some light twin airplane manufacturers now recommend normally starting the left engine first because the cable from the battery to that engine is shorter, permitting more electrical power to be available. Others recommend starting the right engine first if an auxiliary power unit (APU) is used. Check the boost pumps before starting, as was discussed back in Chapter 13 (carburetor engines).

Safety is still the big item in starting. Make sure that the areas around the props are clear before engaging the starter. The tendency for new pilots is to be so busy with procedures that they sometimes forget to shout "Clear!" and get an acknowledgment before starting the engine.

After one engine has started, run it at a high enough rpm to ensure that the alternator has cut in to aid in starting the other engine. It's sometimes more than a weak battery can do to start two engines in close succession. If it's wintertime, you may not want to run the engine at higher rpm right away. If this is the case, don't be in too big a hurry to start the second engine. A short wait will allow the battery to build up again—plus the fact that you can soon run the operating engine up until it's helping.

If the engine you are starting first is cantankerous, you'd better forget it and start the other one. The alternator of the second engine can help give the boost needed to start the laggard one.

Leave all unnecessary electrical equipment OFF. This goes for starting any airplane (single- or multi-engine) with an electrical system. The sudden surge of power required for starting may damage avionics equipment. Pitot heat also causes very strong current drain and, unlike the radios and other electrically powered equipment, is less noticeable when on. Unless you happen to check the switch directly or notice the ammeter gasping at the lower end of the discharge range, the fact that the pitot heat is on may be overlooked.

If you *really* want to give the battery (or batteries) the supreme test, turn on the landing lights also. With the pitot heat, radios, and landing lights on, the chances of the engine getting started are very slim indeed (Figure 15-2).

A lot of people are awed by the idea of starting a twin-engine airplane. One way of looking at it is that you are starting a single-engine airplane twice.

Following is a checklist for starting one type of twin (fuel injected):

1. Master switch ON.
2. Cowl flaps open to proper position.
3. Throttle controls open ½ inch.
4. Propeller controls forward.
5. Electric fuel pumps ON.
6. Mixture controls set at rich until indication on fuel flow gage, then at idle cutoff.
7. Magneto switches ON.
8. Propellers clear.
9. Engage starter on the chosen engine.
10. Check oil pressure.

If engine does not fire within 5 to 10 seconds, disengage starter and reprime.

Starting engine when hot:

1. Master switch ON.
2. Magneto switches ON.
3. Electric fuel pump OFF.
4. Throttle opened ½ inch.
5. Mixture in idle cutoff.
6. Engage starter.
7. Mixture at full rich when engine fires.
8. Oil pressure checked.

Starting engine when flooded:

1. Master switch ON.
2. Magneto switches ON.
3. Electric fuel pump OFF.
4. Throttle full open.
5. Mixture in idle cutoff.
6. Engage starter.
7. Retard throttle and advance mixture when engine fires.
8. Check oil pressure.

Figure 15-2. Joshua Barnslogger, private pilot, sometimes seems to have trouble getting the prop to turn over for starting (lousy electrical system design, he figures).

Cranking periods should be limited to 30 seconds with a 2-minute interval between. Longer cranking periods shorten the life of the starter.

Remember that, for twins as for the single-engine airplanes, after each engine has started, check for proper oil pressures within 30 seconds (it will take longer if outside temperatures are 10°F or lower) and make sure the flight instruments are working and the radios are on as needed.

If you have to use an auxiliary power unit (APU) to start the engine, be sure that the avionics switches are OFF and the master switch is ON or OFF during APU use (as indicated by the POH). Don't assume that, because the airplanes you flew earlier required the master switch to be OFF during APU-assisted starts, this is the case for any twin you are checking out in. Of two current twins examined in writing this chapter, one required the master ON for APU use and the other required it OFF. In the latter case, after removal of the APU plug, you'd make sure that the master switch is ON.

Taxiing

Before taxiing, check your radios for proper functioning (this goes for single- or multiengine airplanes).

In earlier times, when nearly all multiengine airplanes had tailwheels, one of the biggest problems was learning to taxi. The new pilot was taught that the use of asymmetric power was helpful in steering the airplane. This is true, but it was sometimes overemphasized to the extent that both the check pilot and the pilot checking out became discouraged. It always started about like this: The new pilot starts taxiing and maybe the plane begins to turn to the left a little; overdoing a touch of power on the left engine to help straighten matters out, of course, then requires use of right engine power. This seesaw usually goes on until the airplane is thundering down the taxiway at ever increasing speed and in sharper and sharper S-turns. The check pilot finally has to take over and slow the airplane down, the new pilot is given back the controls, and the same procedure occurs again.

Taxi the airplane as if it were a single-engine type. It's very likely that the twin you are checking out in has a nosewheel, and the separate use of throttles will have much less effect. However, you'll soon be subconsciously using extra power on one engine whenever it's needed to make a sharper turn, so don't worry about using it right away, for it only complicates matters. One good thing about tricycle-gear and nosewheel steering—as was stated above, if you do overuse either of the throttles, the plane isn't as apt to get away from you.

Check the brakes as the airplane starts to move; you don't need any surprises when taxiing at a normal speed toward that other expensive twin (or the hangar, etc.).

Pretakeoff Check

A good checklist pays off. The same checks that applied to an advanced single-engine airplane apply here. You'll run the engines at a setting that allows the alternators to be charging well and, in the airplane with augmenter cooling, gives efficient exhaust venturi action (usually 1,200 to 1,400 rpm). Check for freedom and proper movement of controls, and check the instruments and other items as required by the checklist.

Following are some general checklist items concerning light twins:

1. *Controls free*—This is nothing new to you. Make sure the ailerons, elevators, and rudder(s) move in the right direction (it's hard to check rudder movement in some nosewheel airplanes when they're sitting still, but you can check the rudder pedal and nosewheel action while taxiing).

2. *Fuel on proper (main) tank or tanks—Always*, repeat, *always* make your run-up on the tanks you plan to use on takeoff. This gives you a chance to discover if they are furnishing fuel properly. If you make a run-up on one set of tanks and just before takeoff switch to another set, you may find that the last tank or tanks selected are not working properly. This discovery usually occurs at the most inconvenient point shortly after takeoff. It's an old aviation truism that after unknowingly switching to a dry or bad tank, there'll be just enough fuel in the fuel lines to get you into a compromising position during takeoff. Always run the engines for at least a minute at moderate (1,400 to 1,600) rpm before takeoff if you see the need for changing tanks during or after the run-up.

3. *Electric fuel pumps OFF temporarily*—This is to check the action of the engine-driven pumps. *After the check, make sure they are both ON for the takeoff if the POH calls for it.*

4. *Crossfeed checked and then OFF for takeoff*—Here's a new control for you. Normally each engine will use fuel from the tanks in its own wing. However, in the event of an engine failure, there would be a great deal of unusable fuel on the dead-engine side, limiting single-engine range as well as causing lateral trim problems as fuel is used from the operating-engine side. The crossfeed valve allows the working engine to draw fuel from the dead engine's tanks. Figure 15-3 shows a simplified schematic of the normal operation of a typical light twin fuel system.

Some airplanes do not have a separate valve for crossfeed but have a selector position on each of the two main fuel valves. If you needed to shut down the right engine in flight, for instance, you would "secure it" by throttling back, feathering it, pulling the mixture back to idle cutoff, turning off ignition switches, and putting the fuel selector to the OFF position. If you begin to run low on left-wing fuel for the good engine, you can select the crossfeed setting to allow the good engine to draw fuel from the opposite tank (Figure 15-4).

Other manufacturers have a setup whereby the pilot merely selects the tank to use fuel from—and no particular mention is made of crossfeed—which results in a great deal less confusion.

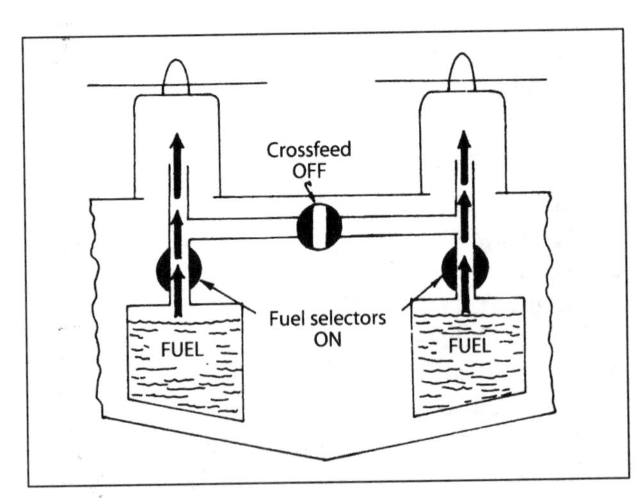

Figure 15-3. Schematic of fuel system under normal conditions, crossfeed OFF.

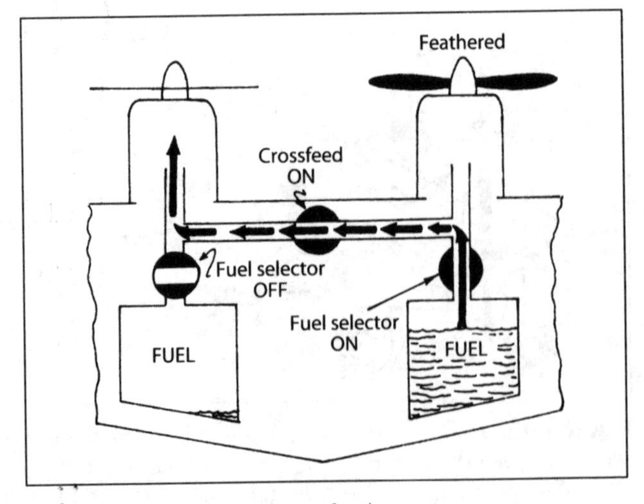

Figure 15-4. The use of crossfeed.

You could, under normal conditions on some airplanes, run the left engine from the right tank and vice versa. This is frowned upon, on general principles, because it could cause confusion at a time when instantaneous selection is necessary. The setup on most airplanes is that each engine uses its own fuel and turning off the fuel valve and selecting crossfeed allows you to operate an engine from an opposite tank (both engines running from the same wing tank). There are several combinations and learn your airplane's particular fuel system.

You might especially check which tanks the crossfeed can be operated on. The crossfeed on some airplanes works only for the main fuel tanks—auxiliary fuel in one wing cannot be used by the other engine. No matter how complicated it sounds, remember that the only purpose for crossfeed is to enable you to use fuel that would otherwise be dead weight and/or cause lateral trim problems.

Figure 15-5 shows a fuel system schematic that includes the crossfeed system. This is a next step in the fuel systems discussed in Chapter 13. Inboard or outboard tanks may be used for crossfeeding. In effect, all four tanks are "main" tanks for this airplane. The crossfeed system shown is a *pressure* crossfeed, which means the fuel is "pushed" from the dead-engine side. Since the engine-driven fuel pump isn't working with the engine stopped and the prop feathered, the *electric* boost pump on that engine must be ON to push the fuel over (the *right* engine electric pump in the situation shown in Figure 15-4).

Figure 15-6 is another light twin fuel system with a close-up of its fuel selector panel. Read the POH to ensure that you know how the crossfeed works. It's sometimes neglected in the check-out procedure.

5. *Tabs set*—You may have aileron tabs to contend with (the airplane will certainly have elevator and rudder trim controls). Make sure there's no wild setting on any of the trim controls.

6. *Flap operation checked*—If flaps are required for takeoff, or if you plan on using them, it might be better to wait until after the engine run-up before putting them down. The props, being run at high rpm on the ground, may pick up gravel and throw it into the flaps. You might find that for your particular airplane you would prefer setting the flaps just before taxiing onto the runway.

7. *All instruments checked*—You've been doing this for the single-engine airplane but now have two of each of the engine instruments to check. Be sure that oil and fuel pressures, cylinder head temperatures, and other gages are operating normally.

8. *Engine run-up*—Make sure the mixtures are full rich and the propellers are full forward (low-pitch, high-rpm). Run each engine up individually. The required rpm for prop and mag check varies with each airplane.

a. *Check the magnetos*—Here's the place where you'll realize that there are two engines instead of your

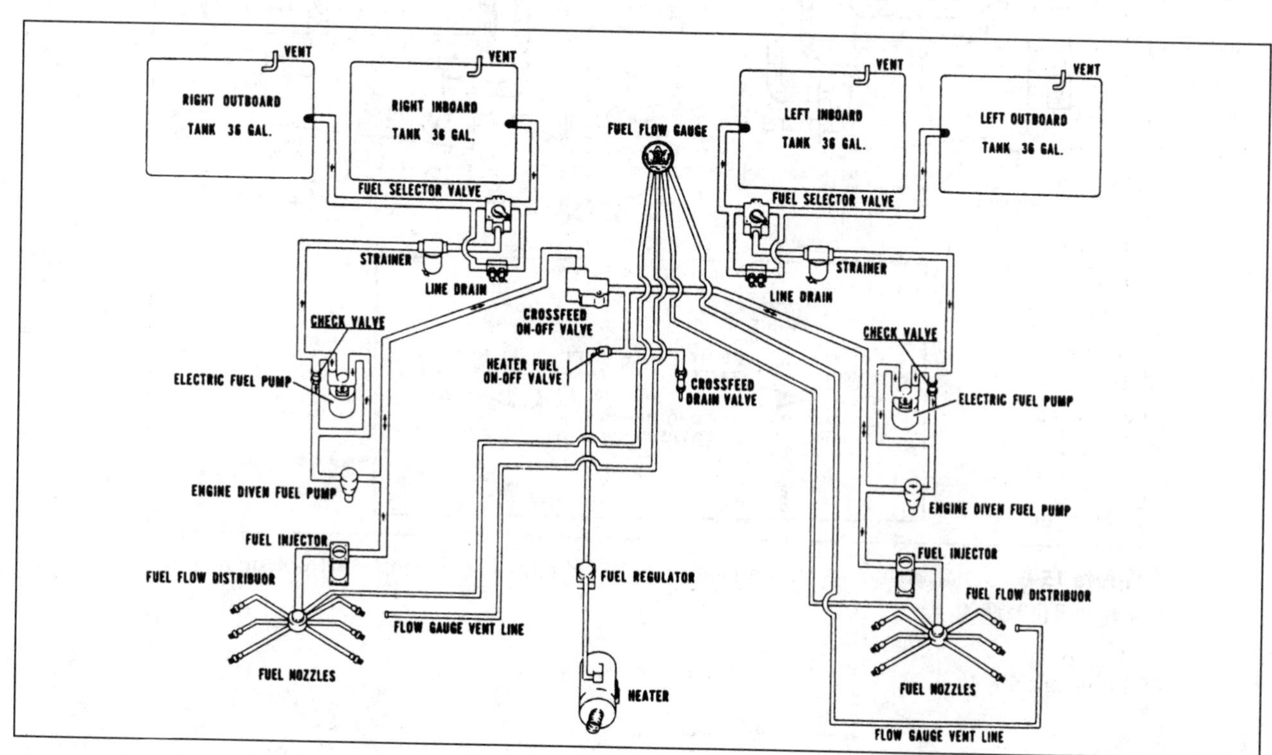

Figure 15-5. Fuel system schematic.

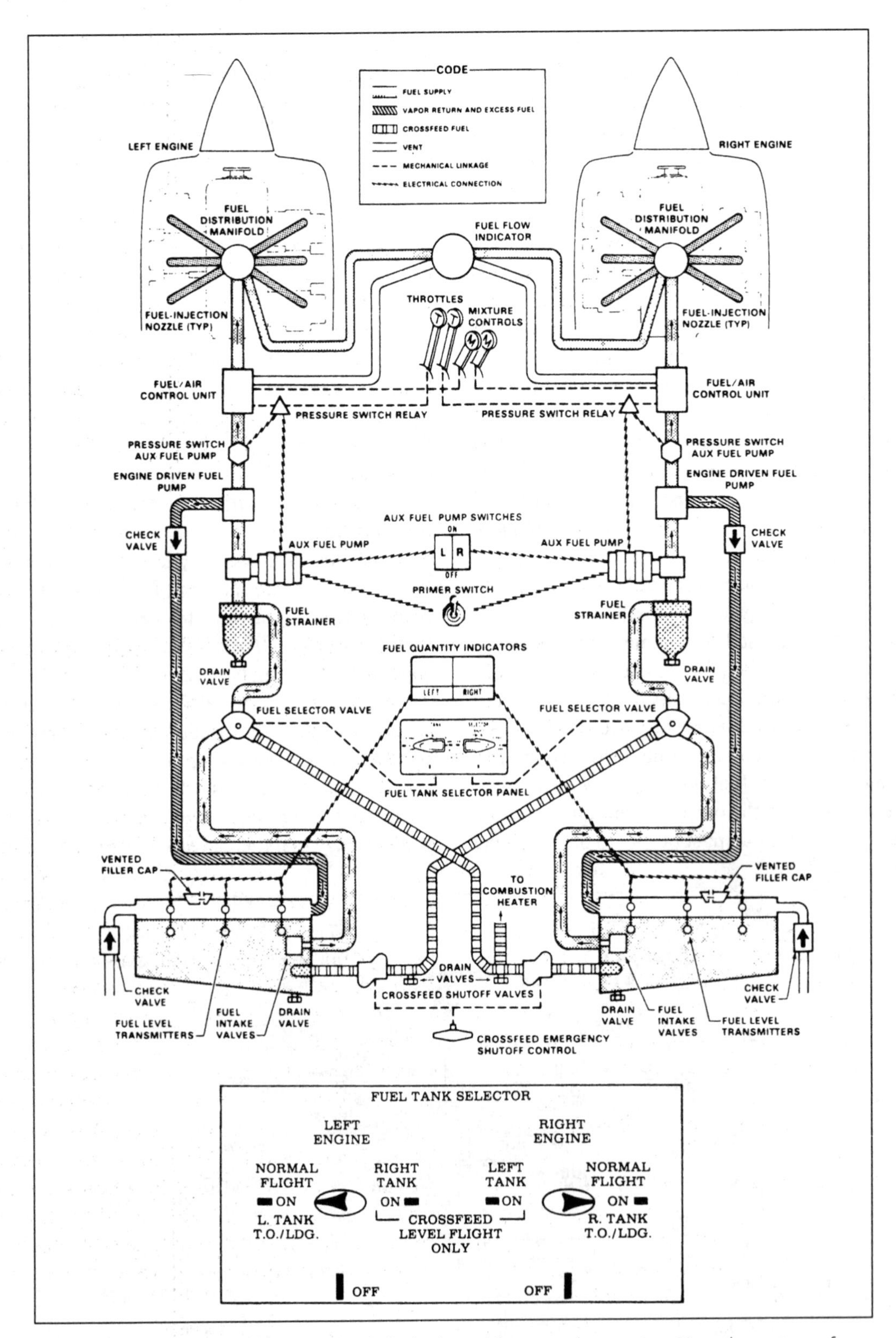

Figure 15-6. Light twin fuel system with fuel selected for normal operation. Note the system of selecting crossfeed.

usual one. It seems that checking the four mags is a good day's work. In fact, single-engine pilots have been known to get writer's cramp, or its aeronautical equivalent, checking the mags of a multiengine airplane that first time. The usual maximum allowable drop for some light twins is 150 rpm, but check to confirm this for your airplane. The usual maximum allowed difference in drop between the two magnetos is 50 rpm.

b. *Exercise the propellers*—This goes for either air-oil or oil-counterweight types. At a recommended rpm, move the propeller controls through the range from high rpm to low rpm several times (Chapter 12).

c. *Check the propeller feathering*—Multiengine airplanes have featherable propellers because it was discovered that turning the propeller blades of a dead engine edgewise to the airflow means much better engine-out performance. Naturally you'll be interested in making sure that you can feather a prop if necessary. A windmilling propeller on a dead engine cuts performance to such a degree that a critical condition could result. Most multiengine pilots would almost as soon skip checking the mags as not check the feather system. As the check pilot will tell you, don't let the prop stay in the feathered setting too long; the comparatively high manifold pressure and low rpm are not good for the engine. (One twin POH recommends a maximum drop of 500 rpm during the feather check.)

d. *Carburetor heat (carburetor engines)*—Use the carburetor air temperature gage if available, or check for a drop in manifold pressure (mp) as heat is applied. Remember that, with the fixed-pitch-prop airplane, you checked for an rpm drop when the carburetor heat was applied. A drop in rpm showed that the warmer, less-dense air was going into the engine, proof that the carburetor heat was working normally.

The constant-speed propeller, when in its operating range, will tend to cover any rpm drop. So, lacking a carburetor air temperature gage, the mp is the most positive indication that the system is working. In fact, the mp gives an *immediate* indication, whereas the carburetor air temperature gage needs a short period to indicate temperature. The mp gage is the primary indicator of the presence of carburetor ice, because you can no longer rely on rpm drop as a warning with a constant-speed propeller. You may be able to notice a very brief rpm drop, but it will immediately recover if the rpm indication is in the constant-speed-prop operating range. Remember that you'll be getting unfiltered air, and some manufacturers frown on using carburetor heat or alternate air systems during the ground run-up.

If you apply the carburetor heat with the rpm below the constant-speed operating range, you'll get an mp *and* an rpm drop that remains as long as the heat is on. The mp drop with application of full carburetor heat is not as great as you might think from the power loss involved, in some cases being about ½ inch.

Most light twins in use today have fuel-injected engines so carburetor heat, as such, isn't part of those installations. But you should know how to use alternate air systems (see Chapter 16) for your airplane.

Alternate air or carburetor heat OFF for takeoff.

e. *Electrical system*—That first look at the diagram of the electrical system can be pretty discouraging.

Current twins have two things going for them electrically, compared with the first light twins manufactured:

(1) Alternators, not generators, are used. As you are probably aware from your other flying, alternators produce voltage at lower engine rpm than do generators. (You may have never flown an airplane with a generator.)

(2) *Two* alternators, one for each engine, are used on nearly all twins these days. Back in the old days, the left engine had the *only* generator. Losing that one could mean that electrical problems would be added to your other obvious problem. In most cases, loss of one of the alternators means husbanding your electrical equipment, but you'll normally have enough voltage produced for the fundamentals. Before takeoff, check that each alternator is working properly, using the procedure suggested by the POH and your instructor.

f. *Suction or pressure systems*—Check both sources to see that the engine-driven pumps are properly operating and providing the correct suction, or pressure, in inches of mercury. It's likely that the single-engine airplanes you've been flying have been using a vacuum system; that is, the engine-driven vacuum pump *pulls* the air past the vanes on the gyro wheels in the attitude and heading indicators, and you check the suction gage for the proper reading. Many twins use a pressure or pneumatic pump (which in effect means that the air is *pushed* past the gyro wheels from the opposite direction). This system can be used also for de-icer boots, autopilots and cabin pressurization (see Chapter 19).

Takeoff and Climb

See the takeoff chart in Figure 15-7. There is very little difference in the takeoff of a single- or multiengine airplane because the throttles are normally treated as one control. However, if there is a strong crosswind you may increase the power on the upwind engine first and carry more power on that side during the initial part of the run to help offset weathercocking tendencies (Figure 15-8). As the airspeed picks up and steering improves, increase to full power on both engines. This is helpful even for airplanes with a steerable nosewheel.

You'll have to watch your throttle handling if the engines are turbocharged—you might overboost them—and the check pilot will remind you to check the mp gage as power is applied. Most instructors recommend keeping the airplane on the ground until you reach a speed of V_{MC} (single-engine minimum controllable speed) + 5 K.

Shortly after takeoff the fun begins. You raise the landing gear and set climb power (throttles back first, then props!). One of your most frustrating experiences will be trying to synchronize the propellers when you are busy getting set up for the climb. (Wait until you have 500 feet of altitude before reducing power.)

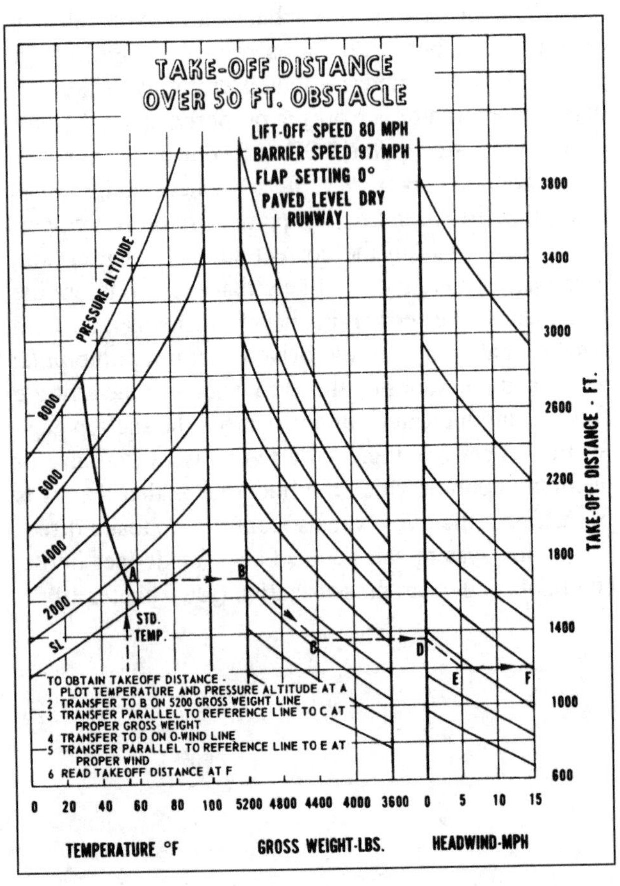

Figure 15-7. Takeoff distance chart.

One tip for synchronization is to use sound as a guide as much as possible. After throttling back to the climb mp, move the propeller controls back to the proper rpm setting. Some twins use a single tachometer with two hands, which makes the problem a little easier. In addition, there may be a "synchronizing wheel," or indicator, which tells if one engine is turning faster than the other. Other twins use two separate tachometers. When moving the prop controls back, try to keep them in the same relative position to each other (don't worry—you won't the first few times). Use one tachometer hand as a "master" and note the relative position of the other. If the other hand is at a higher rpm, ease its prop control back until the "throb" sound has disappeared. This throb is your indication of degree of synchronization—the faster the pulse, the greater the difference between the rpm of the two props. Use common sense, of course; you could pull one prop so far back that it is in feather and would have no pulsating noise at all—performance would suffer though. You'll

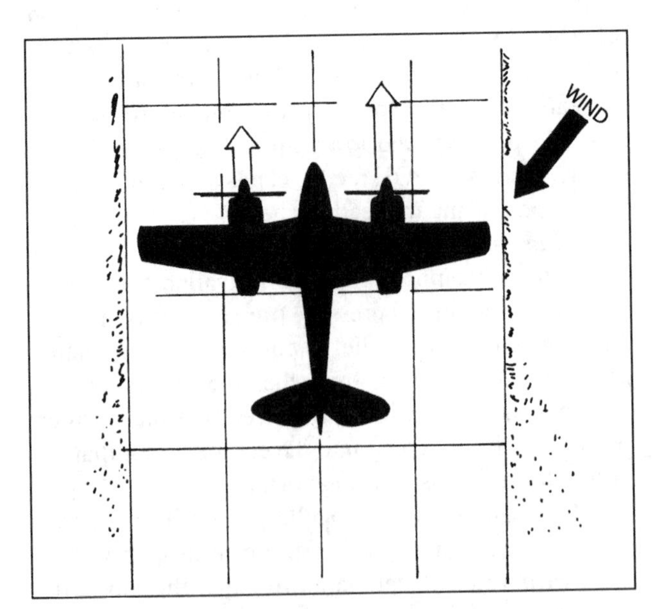

Figure 15-8. The use of asymmetric power during the beginning of a crosswind takeoff.

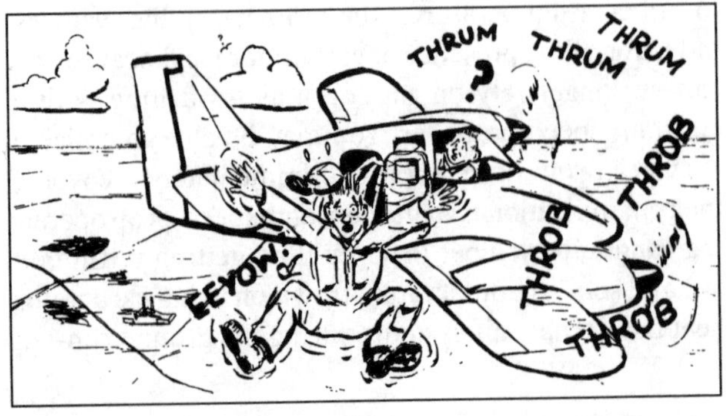

Figure 15-9. Sometimes poor prop synchronization can drive a check pilot to distraction.

soon be able to smooth out the props with a flick of the wrist (Figure 15-9).

An expression for the maximum climbing power, or maximum continuous power, is METO (maximum except takeoff). Many engines are limited in time for full-power operations; this is given in the POH and the *Engine Manual.*

Some of the engines in this class have unlimited time allowed for full-power operation. The engine manufacturer usually states that, while there is no danger of failure or immediate damage, the overhaul period may be shortened by abuse of this privilege.

Know the max rate and max angle climb speeds for your airplane—both multiengine and engine-out.

The airplane will be cleaned up and power set for proper climb, using the recommended best rate of climb speed. After reaching a safe altitude the flaps will be retracted, if used, and shortly afterward the boost pumps will be turned OFF. *Check the fuel pressure as you turn off each pump individually.*

Here is a sample checklist for takeoff and climb:

1. Parking brake OFF.
2. Mixture controls forward.
3. Propeller controls forward.
4. Throttle controls forward.
5. Accelerate to 80 K (prior to climb).
6. Retract landing gear.
7. Accelerate to best rate of climb speed.
8. Climb power set at approximately 400 AGL.
9. Electric fuel pumps OFF (one at a time if used).
10. Cowl flaps set (maintain cylinder head temperature at or below maximum).
11. Oxygen ON (above 10,000 ft or lower, as required).

Cruise and Airwork

After reaching the practice altitude, the check pilot will show you the proper cruise power setting and leaning procedure. You may have a little trouble with synchronization again, but this is to be expected. A good procedure for leveling is to ease the nose over to cruise attitude, using trim as necessary and leaving the power at climb setting to help acceleration. As the cruise airspeed is approached, throttle back to cruise mp and set the props. After getting the airplane trimmed to your satisfaction, switch tanks and lean the mixtures using the technique(s) described in Chapter 13 or those recommended by the check pilot, who may have a method particularly effective for your airplane.

The check pilot will have you do shallow, medium, and steep turns (up to 45° bank) to get the feel of the airplane. You will stall the airplane in various combinations: gear-up or -down, flaps at various settings, and at different power settings. The check pilot may demonstrate the effects of the loss of an engine when you are making a power-on stall. This practice can be dangerous and normally should be avoided. The best thing is to pull the power back on the other engine and lower the nose to pick up V_{MC} before reapplying full power.

The check pilot will throttle back or feather one engine and have you continue to slow up the airplane to V_{MC} so that you will have a graphic demonstration of the required rudder force and what can happen when you get too slow on one engine.

Single-Engine Minimum Controllable Speed

14 CFR Part 23 gives the requirements for V_{MC} as follows:

§23.149 Minimum control speed

(a) V_{MC} is the calibrated airspeed at which, when the critical engine is suddenly made inoperative, it is possible to maintain control of the airplane with that engine still inoperative, and thereafter maintain straight flight at the same speed with an angle of bank of not more than 5 degrees. The method used to simulate critical engine failure must represent the most critical mode of powerplant failure expected in service with respect to controllability.

(b) V_{MC} for takeoff must not exceed 1.2 V_{S1}, where V_{S1} is determined at the maximum takeoff weight. V_{MC} must be determined with the most unfavorable weight and center of gravity position and with the airplane airborne and the ground effect negligible, for the takeoff configuration(s) with—

(1) Maximum available takeoff power initially on each engine;

(2) The airplane trimmed for takeoff;

(3) Flaps in the takeoff position(s);

(4) Landing gear retracted; and

(5) All propeller controls in the recommended takeoff position throughout.

(c) For all airplanes except reciprocating engine-powered airplanes of 6,000 pounds or less maximum weight, the conditions of paragraph (a) of this section must also be met for the landing configuration with—

(1) Maximum available takeoff power initially on each engine;

(2) The airplane trimmed for an approach, with all engines operating, at V_{REF}, at an approach gradient equal to the steepest used in the landing distance demonstration of §23.75;

(3) Flaps in the landing position;

(4) Landing gear extended; and

(5) All propeller controls in the position recommended for approach with all engines operating.

(d) A minimum speed to intentionally render the critical engine inoperative must be established and designated as the safe, intentional, one-engine-inoperative speed, V_{SSE}.

(e) At V_{MC}, the rudder pedal force required to maintain control must not exceed 150 pounds and it must not be necessary to reduce power of the operative engine(s). During the maneuver, the airplane must not assume any dangerous attitude and it must be possible to prevent a heading change of more than 20 degrees.

(f) At the option of the applicant, to comply with the requirements of §23.51(c)(1), V_{MCG} may be determined. V_{MCG} is the minimum control speed on the ground, and is the calibrated airspeed during the takeoff run at which, when the critical engine is suddenly made inoperative, it is possible to maintain control of the airplane using the rudder control alone (without the use of nosewheel steering), as limited by 150 pounds of force, and using the lateral control to the extent of keeping the wings level to enable the takeoff to be safely continued. In the determination of V_{MCG}, assuming that the path of the airplane accelerating with all engines operating is along the centerline of the runway, its path from the point at which the critical engine is made inoperative to the point at which recovery to a direction parallel to the centerline is completed may not deviate more than 30 feet laterally from the centerline at any point. V_{MCG} must be established with—

(1) The airplane in each takeoff configuration or, at the option of the applicant, in the most critical takeoff configuration;

(2) Maximum available takeoff power on the operating engines;

(3) The most unfavorable center of gravity;

(4) The airplane trimmed for takeoff; and

(5) The most unfavorable weight in the range of takeoff weights.

You will normally want to attain this speed before taking off so that should an engine fail you'll have directional control. V_{MC} is marked as a red radial line on the airspeed indicator.

Following are some FAR 23 requirements for directional and lateral control of multiengine (smaller) airplanes.

§23.147 Directional and lateral control

(a) For each multiengine airplane, it must be possible, while holding the wings level within five degrees, to make sudden changes in heading safely in both directions. This ability must be shown at 1.4 V_{S1} with heading changes up to 15 degrees, except that the heading change at which the rudder force corresponds to the limits specified in §23.143 need not be exceeded, with the—

(1) Critical engine inoperative and its propeller in the minimum drag position;

(2) Remaining engines at maximum continuous power;

(3) Landing gear—

(i) Retracted; and

(ii) Extended; and

(4) Flaps retracted.

(b) For each multiengine airplane, it must be possible to regain full control of the airplane without exceeding a bank angle of 45 degrees, reaching a dangerous attitude or encountering dangerous characteristics, in the event of a sudden and complete failure of the critical engine, making allowance for a delay of two seconds in the initiation of recovery action appropriate to the situation, with the airplane initially in trim, in the following condition:

(1) Maximum continuous power on each engine;

(2) The wing flaps retracted;

(3) The landing gear retracted;

(4) A speed equal to that at which compliance with §23.69(a) has been shown; and

(5) All propeller controls in the position at which compliance with §23.69(a) has been shown.

(c) For all airplanes, it must be shown that the airplane is safely controllable without the use of the primary lateral control system in any all-engine configuration(s) and at any speed or altitude within the approved operating envelope. It must also be shown that the airplane's flight characteristics are not impaired below a level needed to permit continued safe flight and the ability to maintain attitudes suitable for a controlled landing without exceeding the operational and structural limitations of the airplane. If a single failure of any one connecting or transmitting link in the lateral control system would also cause the loss of additional control system(s), compliance with the above requirement must be shown with those additional systems also assumed to be inoperative.

Later you will have a chance to feather and unfeather a propeller and to fly around on one engine to check the performance. If possible, you should fly the airplane at gross weight and, at a safe altitude, simulate or actually feather a propeller to see what effect weight has on performance.

There have been cases where a plane was damaged or destroyed because commonsense rules weren't followed during a simulated engine failure. It would be mighty embarrassing to climb from the wreckage and try to explain to an irate operator/owner that you "were just practicing single-engine flight so as to avoid damaging the airplane should the real thing occur."

On two engines, you'll practice slow flight at about 10 K above the stall warning or buffet point for that configuration while holding altitude. You will also fly at landing configuration to demonstrate your ability to fly the airplane safely, maintaining altitude, speed, and a constant direction through proper use of power and the flight controls. You'll fly it long enough in each configuration to demonstrate the acceleration and deceleration characteristics of your airplane. You'll do straight and level flight, level-flight turns, and climbing and gliding turns at slow-flight speeds. The check pilot will be particularly interested in your transitions to and from slow flight. You will avoid accidental stalls, of course.

In general, this phase of your transition to multiengine flying is quite similar to the checkout in an advanced single-engine airplane (except for the engine-out demonstration). You'll find out how the airplane reacts under normal conditions. The full treatment on engine-out procedures comes later.

The procedures for leaning at cruise, rough air penetration, and use of the prop and throttle controls have been covered in earlier chapters. You might have a little problem with prop synchronization at cruise but will soon work it out. You should be able to do a good job of synchronization manually before using the automatic synchronizer installed in some airplanes.

Approach and Landing

You'll have a few more items to check than you've been used to and should use the checklist diligently, pointing to each item as you check it. Everything mentioned about mixtures, boost pumps, gear, flaps, and props for the advanced single-engine airplane still applies except that you'll have two of some of the controls to move. But, again, under normal conditions the two controls can be handled as one. (Use the main tanks for landing unless the manufacturer recommends differently.)

Note the gear- and flap-down speed and give yourself plenty of time and room on the downwind leg and approach, particularly the first few landings. Check the gear again on final.

The approach and landing will be just like a single-engine airplane except that you must keep in mind one thing: It's best to maintain an approach speed above the single-engine minimum controllable speed (V_{MC}). Because the airplane has a comparatively high wing loading, you will be making the majority of your approaches with some power. This means that, should you have a complete power failure (both engines), you probably wouldn't make the runway. The chances of both engines quitting are practically nonexistent (although it's not impossible), but one engine *could* quit on you. Suppose you get low and slow (below V_{MC}) and are dragging it in from way back. An engine fails, and as the plane starts sinking, you apply full power on the operating engine. You'll find that you made a bad mistake by being too slow—because the directional control is nil with full power on the good engine. You are too low to nose over and pick up V_{MC} (and then go to best single-engine climb speed). You might also find that the only thing to do is to chop the other throttle, turn all the switches off, and hit something soft and cheap as slowly as you can. You got caught in a trap of your own making.

Even if you are at or slightly above V_{MC}, you'll have to accelerate to best single-engine climb speed, so take this into consideration on the approach. Avoid dragged out finals (this goes for any airplane).

Many POHs suggest an approach speed above best single-engine climb speed (V_{YSE}). More about this later.

For short fields you still should have no reason to get below V_{MC}, because that speed is usually low enough to assure that you won't float before touching down. Again, dragging it around close to or below V_{MC} is taking a calculated risk, as with the short-field takeoff.

You'll be given plenty of chances to shoot normal and short-field takeoffs and landings before making single-engine approaches or go-arounds.

The landing roll, taxi, and shutdown procedures of the light twin follow closely those of advanced single-engine airplanes. The check pilot will cover any peculiarities of the checkout airplane.

Following is a landing checklist for a fictitious twin:

1. Oxygen OFF (below 10,000 feet).
2. Seat belts fastened.
3. Electric fuel pumps ON.
4. Mixture controls forward.
5. Fuel valves ON, fullest cells.
6. Landing gear (under 150 K) extended, check green.
7. Propellers set.
8. Cowl flaps as required.
9. Flaps set:
   ¼ flap—160 K max
   ½ flap—140 K max
   Full flap—125 K max
10. Heater (if used) fan ON.

And a post landing checklist:

1. Wing flaps retracted.
2. Cowl flaps open.
3. Electric fuel pump OFF.
4. Prop controls forward.
5. When completely stopped in a parking spot, check the following items for shutdown:
   a. Radio and electrical equipment OFF.
   b. Heater (if used) fan OFF.
   c. Mixture controls at idle cutoff.
   d. Magneto switches OFF.
   e. Master switch OFF.
   f. Parking brake OFF.
   g. Main volt regulator OFF.
   h. Alternators OFF.

If control locks are not available and the airplane is to be left for more than a few minutes, secure the control wheel with the safety belt strap. Chock the wheels and secure tie-downs at appropriate places.

Figures 15-10 and 15-11 are typical landing distance charts. Figure 15-11 is a graphical presentation using mph. The light twin you'll be flying will use basically the same types of performance charts as were covered in earlier chapters, and you should be able to use them with little trouble. Later in this chapter there are a couple of figures for twins only (accelerate and stop distance chart and area of decision—go or no go).

LANDING DISTANCE

SHORT FIELD

CONDITIONS:
Flaps 30°
Power Off
Maximum Braking
Paved, Level, Dry Runway
Zero Wind

NOTES:
1. Short field technique as specified in Section 4.
2. Decrease distances 10% for each 11 knots headwind. For operation with tailwinds up to 10 knots, increase distances by 10% for each 2.5 knots.
3. For operation on a dry, grass runway, increase distances by 40% of the "ground roll" figure.
4. If a landing with flaps up is necessary, increase the approach speed by 10 KIAS and allow for 35% longer distances.
5. This chart may be used for any landing weight with either standard or heavy duty main wheels, tires and brakes. (See Section 2 for landing weight limitation with standard main wheels, tires and brakes.)

WEIGHT LBS	SPEED AT 50 FT KIAS	PRESS ALT FT	0°C		10°C		20°C		30°C		40°C	
			GRND ROLL FT	TOTAL FT TO CLEAR 50 FT OBS	GRND ROLL FT	TOTAL FT TO CLEAR 50 FT OBS	GRND ROLL FT	TOTAL FT TO CLEAR 50 FT OBS	GRND ROLL FT	TOTAL FT TO CLEAR 50 FT OBS	GRND ROLL FT	TOTAL FT TO CLEAR 50 FT OBS
5150	81	S.L.	775	1395	805	1430	835	1470	865	1505	890	1545
		1000	805	1430	835	1470	865	1510	895	1550	925	1590
		2000	835	1470	865	1510	895	1555	930	1595	960	1635
		3000	865	1515	900	1555	930	1595	965	1640	995	1680
		4000	900	1555	935	1600	965	1645	1000	1690	1030	1730
		5000	935	1600	970	1650	1005	1695	1035	1740	1070	1785
		6000	970	1650	1005	1695	1040	1745	1075	1790	1110	1840
		7000	1005	1700	1045	1750	1080	1800	1120	1845	1155	1895
		8000	1045	1750	1085	1800	1125	1855	1160	1905	1200	1955

Figure 15-10. A tabular presentation of a landing distance chart for a light twin.

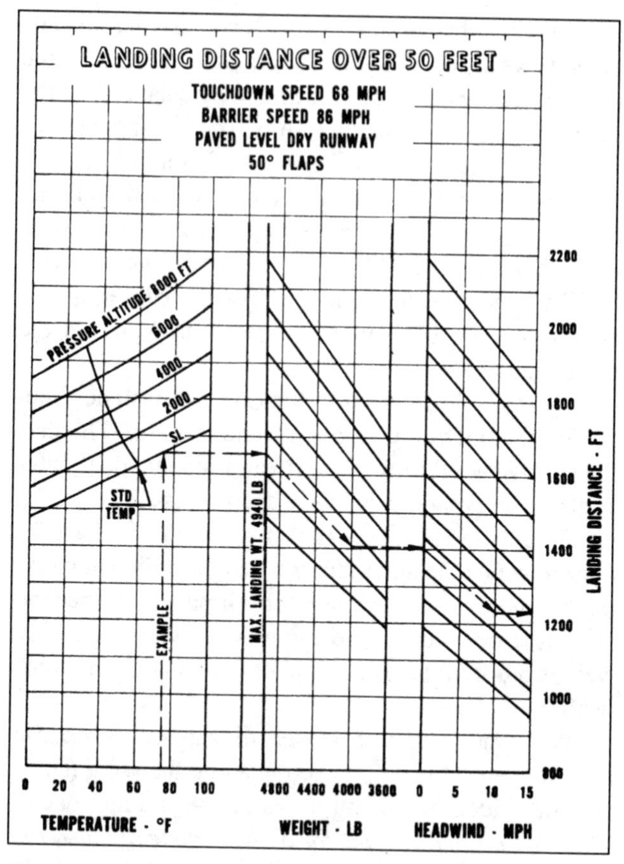

Figure 15-11. Landing distance chart.

Emergency Procedures

The nonpilot may feel that loss of an engine on a multiengine airplane is either a terrifying disaster or nothing to be concerned about. Experienced pilots know that the multiengine airplane, if properly flown with an engine out, has a strong safety factor. They also know that at certain times the airplane must be flown precisely, and in some cases it is safer to chop the other engine(s) than to try to continue. New pilots have been killed by the loss of an engine on takeoff or approach when they believed they could go around. Ironically enough, they might have survived had the engine quit at the same place in a single-engine airplane. They would have landed straight ahead in the single-engine airplane but instead attempted the impossible because of overconfidence in or ignorance of the single-engine performance of their twin.

Here's where you'll start running into the age-old problem of decisions. You may end up like the orange sorter who finally went berserk because "although the work was easy, the decisions finally got me down." As a single-engine pilot noted, one advantage to the plane with just one fan is that when the engine quits you don't have to make the decision whether to go around or not.

So, although multiengine flight is safer—you'll feel more comfortable flying over rough terrain and at night—you must realize that you earn this increased safety by learning what to do in an emergency.

One of the first things you'll find is that a windmilling prop can cause a great reduction in performance, and that gear and flaps cause a problem on a single-engine go-around.

Another point: Because you've lost half your power with one engine out doesn't mean that you'll have half the performance. *You'll have considerably less than half the performance and must take this into consideration.* For instance, you remember that the rate of climb is dependent on *excess* HP. When you cut power being produced, you'll be losing nearly all that excess HP—what you'll have left will be enough to fly the airplane plus some small amount of excess power. So, the excess HP is what suffers. (Unfortunately, there is no way for you to lose the power required to fly the airplane *and* keep the *excess* HP.)

A study of 11 current reciprocating-engine light twins, comparing multi- and single-engine climb rates at sea level, has reported differences in rates of 10 to 22%. That is, the worst performance was a rate of climb on one engine only 10% of that with both engines running; the best single-engine performer had a rate of climb 22% of that with both engines running. The others fell in between, with the average single-engine climb rate for the group about 16.5% of the multiengine rate.

Your en route performance will not suffer nearly as much as the climb or acceleration characteristics, but all phases will be affected. The single-engine rate of climb is based on a clean airplane with the inoperative prop in the minimum drag position—feathered if possible, or in high pitch (low rpm). Figure 15-12 is a thrust horsepower available and required versus airspeed curve for the light twin in Figure 2-50, with both engines operating and with one feathered at gross weight and sea level. Notice that even with a prop feathered, the THP required is greater than normal because of control deflection, loss of efficiency, etc.

Looking at the excess HP in Figure 15-12, you can see that with both engines operating there is about 240 THP in excess of that required at the best rate of climb speed of 100 K. Using the equation for rate of climb and assuming an airplane weight of 5,000 pounds, the rate of climb = (EHP × 33,000)/weight = (240 × 33,000)/5,000 = 1,584 fpm.

Checking the single-engine situation in Figure 15-12, you can see that about 45 excess THP is available at the speed for max rate of climb (90 K) in that condition: (45 x 33,000)/5,000 = 297 fpm.

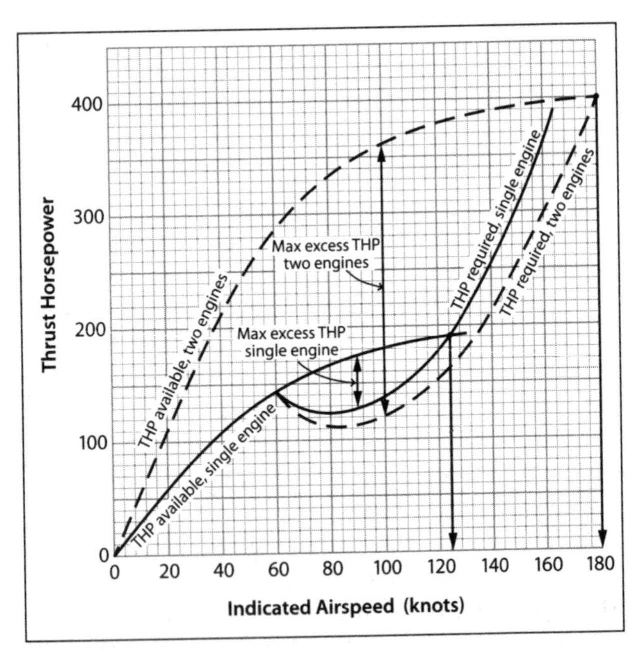

Figure 15-12. Thrust horsepower available and required versus airspeed for a light twin in both twin and single-engine flight. Gross weight at sea level.

You can climb 297 fpm in this airplane at gross weight *at sea level under ideal conditions.* (Turbulent air and/or a higher density-altitude can wreak havoc.) This gives a single-engine rate of climb of 18.75% of the rate with both engines operating. You can imagine what percentage of normal rate of climb you'd have at gross weight on a hot day with an engine out, the gear and flaps down, and a windmilling prop. You would likely end up with a negative rate of climb.

The lighter the airplane's load, the better the single-engine performance. But even an airplane at light weight doesn't have much get-up-and-go with a lot of garbage hanging out in the slipstream.

Single-Engine Control

More about V_{MC}

Single-engine minimum control speed means just that; V_{MC} has to do with control, not performance. Pilots new to twins sometimes think that as long as they maintain V_{MC} the airplane will have climb performance—not true. Also to be shown: holding the published V_{MC} does not even mean that control is maintained.

First, take a look at a situation where an airplane is clean and loses an engine. The pilot is determined to maintain control with the wings level (it seems more orderly that way); Figure 15-13 shows some of the yawing forces and moments involved.

Looking at A in Figure 15-13, you see that the airplane yaws around its CG. The moment created by the thrust of the operating engine must be balanced by the moment the pilot created by (fully?) deflecting the rudder. In B, when the CG is moved aft, the rudder arm is shortened and the airspeed required for directional control increases. *(V_{MC} gets higher with a rearward movement of CG.)* The rudder is producing sidewise "lift" when deflected, and the shorter arm requires a higher rudder "lift" (more airspeed) to maintain the same moment.

Figure 15-14 shows that banking the airplane about 5° into the operating engine results in a slip. This has the relative wind hitting the fin and rudder at a greater angle, increasing the control effectiveness.

Note that earlier in the chapter, in the Part 23 requirements, the manufacturer had the option of banking not more than 5° when establishing V_{MC}. Since the manufacturer would like a low V_{MC}, you can pretty well be assured that the test pilot used a bank in establishing that figure.

When the airplane is banked, the slip occurs because a component of weight is acting along the wing (similar to the idea of a wing-down crosswind approach). *The heavier an airplane, for a given angle of bank, the greater the weight effect and the lower the V_{MC}.* You'd figure that the lighter you fly the airplane, the lower the V_{MC}, but it doesn't work that way. Of course, the discussion here is about control; added weight would hurt performance.

Figure 15-15 shows an exaggerated example of the effects of added weight on V_{MC}. As far as the 5° bank is concerned, the greater the weight, the larger the component of weight acting toward the operating engine and the greater the sideslip (and more effective rudder and fin to help fight the turning into the dead engine). The added weight shown helps control but performance will suffer. *Best control and best performance are separate items requiring different banks.* (After the airplane is under control, you'll shallow the bank as necessary to maintain a *zero sideslip*, but more about that later.)

Increased altitude lowers V_{MC}. This makes sense because the nonturbocharged engine loses power (and thrust) with altitude, and the moment created by that operating engine is less. If you deflect the rudder fully, you'll need less dynamic pressure (lower airspeed) to counter the yawing moment created by the less-powerful engine. This, however, can be a trap. Figure 15-16 shows that while V_{MC} (IAS) decreases with altitude, the single-engine stall speed (IAS) stays the same for a given weight. The airplane will stall at the same IAS at 10,000 feet density-altitude as at sea level (see Chapter 4).

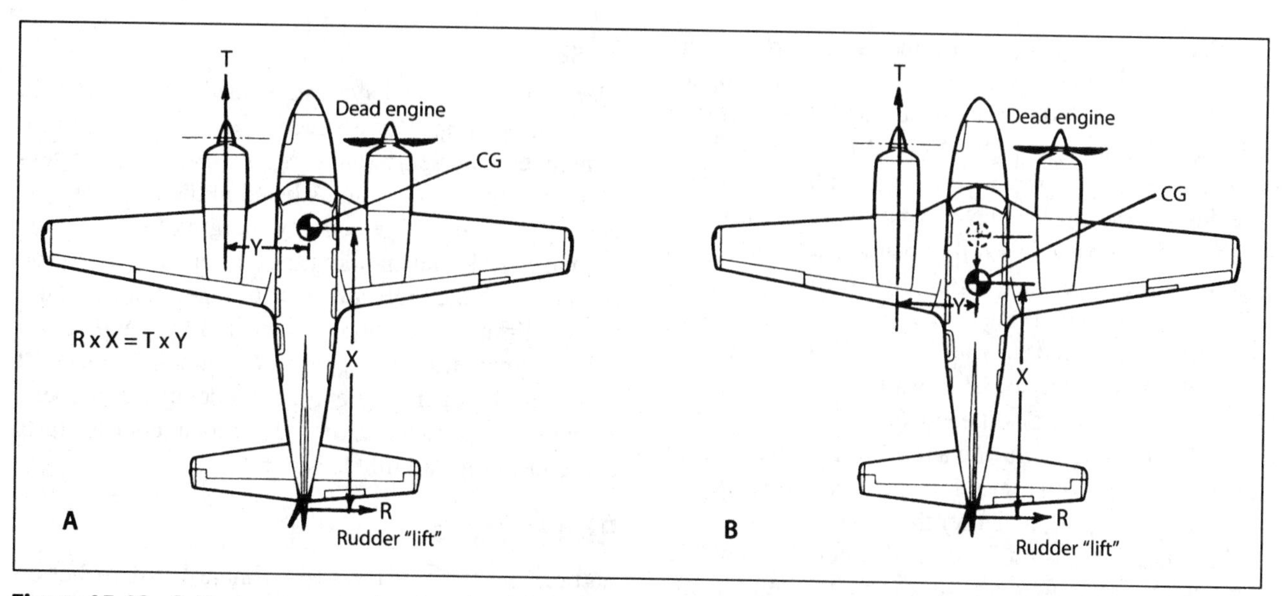

Figure 15-13. A. Yawing moments in wings-level flight. **B.** Note that moving the CG rearward hurts directional control (raises the minimum control speed).

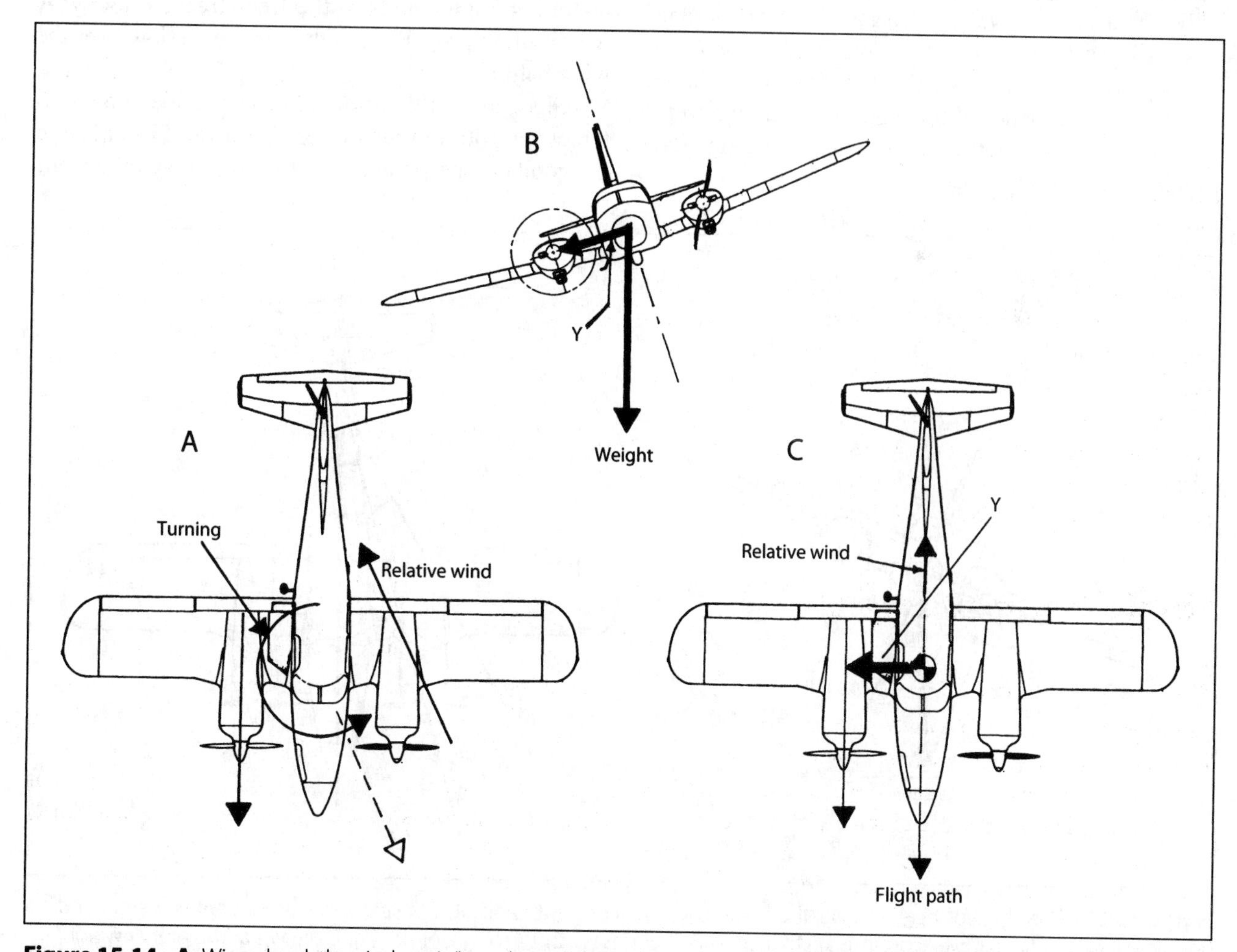

Figure 15-14. A. Wings level, the airplane is "translating" along the path shown by the dashed line. This results in the rudder being much less effective because of the relative wind direction and the airplane turns in to the dead engine. **B.** By banking in to the good engine, a component of weight is acting along the wing (the Y-axis). This is roughly the same idea as used in correcting for a crosswind with a slip. **C.** The fin and rudder are more effective because of the sideslip. (*The Flight Instructor's Manual*)

The decreasing V_{MC} soon meets and crosses the power-on stall line. You may find that, at some higher altitudes (usually 3,000 to 4,000 feet MSL), the airplane will stall before getting to V_{MC}. When you and the instructor are up there with one engined feathered, and are slowing the airplane up looking for V_{MC}, you could get a stall with very bad rolling tendencies. Fatal accidents have occurred on training flights when people got surprised. The main thing to do is get the power off that operating engine and use rudder opposite to the roll and also briskly push the wheel forward.

Accidents have also been caused by mishandling the operating engine during a real emergency. Such an instance is when full power is being used on that engine to get to the airport, and after the runway is made, you suddenly jerk the throttle back. You could be holding hard rudder and aileron as necessary to keep the airplane under control, and if the throttle of the operating engine is abruptly closed, the prop flattens out and radically increases drag on that side. Now you have a strong yawing force *in the same direction in which you are holding rudder!* You can see that the contrast would be greater if the propeller of the inoperative engine were feathered, or at its lowest drag condition, compared with having that engine carrying some power.

V_{SSE}

The manufacturers have established an "intentional one-engine inoperative speed, V_{SSE}," which can be remembered as a *safe single-engine speed.* V_{SSE} is several knots above V_{MC} and is listed in the POH. Different twins have different safety margins for V_{SSE} (one twin uses 12 K and another uses 6 K above V_{MC}, so you should check the POH for each airplane). Your instructor will limit deliberate engine cuts to V_{SSE} and above. When demonstrating V_{MC}, max continuous power will be set on the operating engine, reducing the airspeed at about 1 K per second until directional control starts being lost or a stall nibble occurs.

Roll Factors

Figure 15-17 shows the approximate lift distribution across a twin with an engine windmilling and max continuous power on the other. Induced flow from the operating engine adds to the free-stream velocity. A windmilling propeller can disturb the airflow over the wing behind it.

Okay, so you'll use aileron (with rudder) to counteract the roll and also to establish the 5° bank into the good engine, as noted earlier. This may take a fair

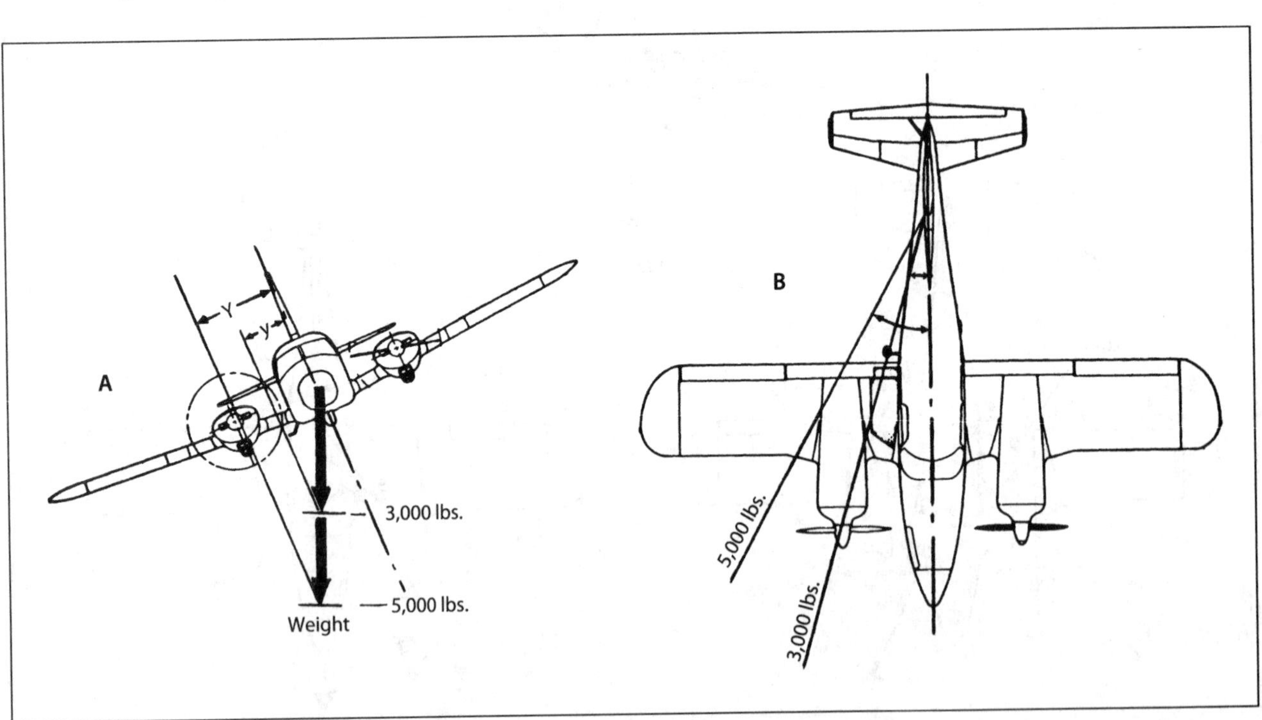

Figure 15-15. The effect of increased weight in lowering V_{MC} (constant bank). **A.** The spanwise component of weight and sideslip effect is greater at 5,000 pounds (Y) than at 3,000 pounds (y). **B.** The angle of sideslip is greater at the higher weight. (Angles of bank and sideslip exaggerated.) Note that the added weight hurts performance as does too much (or any) sideslip. (*The Flight Instructor's Manual*)

amount of aileron deflection, and you get the problem of adverse yaw. This tends to turn the airplane into the dead engine, requiring more rudder. But banking into the operating engine certainly helps in maintaining directional control. It's possible, though, to get a bank so steep, with a resulting increased angle of flow, that the rudder and fin "stall" and you'd lose control that way. Dihedral effect also will work against the bank.

Another factor working against the bank you set up is the fin and rudder above the centerline of the fuselage. You then have the airflow "striking" the side of those surfaces, tending to roll the airplane out in the opposite direction (see Figure 10-57).

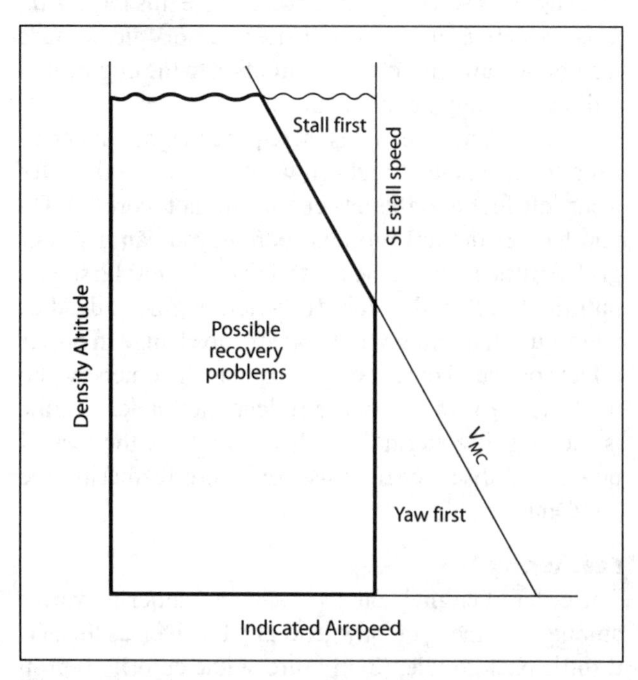

Figure 15-16. Single-engine stall speed and V_{MC} (IAS) versus density-altitude for a fictitious twin.

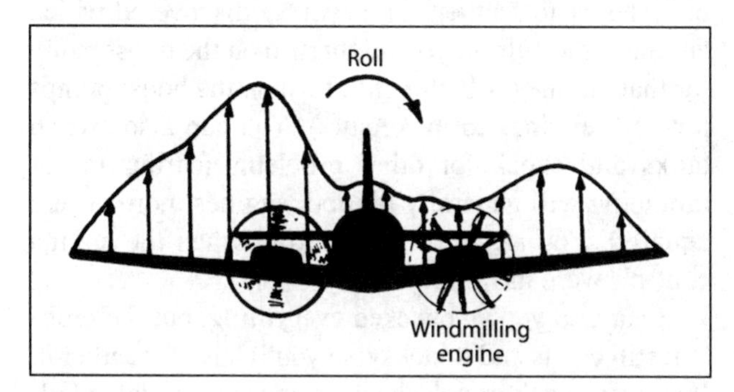

Figure 15-17. Lift distribution of a fictitious light twin with a windmilling right engine.

Single-Engine Performance

Performance

Performance will suffer from the directional and lateral *control* requirements because asymmetrical flight, such as the sideslip used for *best control*, greatly increases drag and hurts climb performance.

The bank required for best performance (climb) may be approximately half of the 5° example used for control, depending on the airplane. (Remember, get the bank in immediately to maintain control when that engine fails, because if you lose control, there won't be a need for performance.) After lateral/directional control is established, the bank is shallowed as necessary to get a zero sideslip for performance.

Your instructor might demonstrate the following at a safe altitude. Put a yaw string on the center of the nose where you both can see it. (It's best to do this on the ground *before* the flight.) At a safe altitude, feather or set zero thrust on one of the engines. After looking around for other airplanes, set up a climb at the single-engine best rate of climb speed (V_{YSE}) starting about 200 feet below your chosen altitude of, say, 4,000 feet MSL. Use max continuous power on the operating engine. The extra 200 feet allow the climb to stabilize so that as you reach the reference altitude you can start timing with a stopwatch or a sweep second hand. *Keep the ball centered and the wings level if possible.* Don't pay any attention to the yaw string. Maintain V_{YSE}, and after 200 feet of climb or 3 minutes, whichever you prefer, check the rate of climb.

Descend back to 200 feet below the starting altitude used before and start the climb sequence. Use V_{YSE}, and time the same climb segment, only this time set up a bank about one-half ball width into the operating engine and keep the yaw string centered. The immediate reaction of the ball in the turn and slip, or turn coordinator, is to move away from the dead engine as the yaw starts, and you'll be fighting this. The chances are that this second time you'll see a measurable improvement in the single-engine rate of climb. With the zero sideslip, you have set up a cleaner condition so that drag (and required HP) is at a minimum for existing conditions.

Engine Failure En Route

This is usually the least critical place for engine failure (except during taxiing or warm-up) but can lead to trouble if things are allowed to progress too far.

The check pilot will usually pull an in-flight emergency on you after you've had a chance to get the feel of the airplane. The procedure to follow in the event of an engine failure will be demonstrated and, after you have had a chance to run through it several times, the check pilot may quietly turn the fuel off on one engine in order to catch you by surprise. This is not done to see how badly you can foul up but, like the primary instructor who used to give simulated emergencies at unexpected times, it's realistic training. It's a lot different to watch the check pilot pull back one of the throttles (you'll know immediately which engine is going to be "bad") than suddenly to have one of the engines quit (which one?). You'll find that no matter how hard you've practiced or memorized the procedure, you'll be all thumbs and feet in the cockpit the first time one stops when you aren't ready for it.

Some instructors, however, argue against turning off the fuel because of possible restarting problems. (This writer agrees.) They say that the check pilot can cover the power control quadrant with a chart and pull one of the throttles.

The biggest problem at first is knowing which engine is out. In flight you'll have more time to judge and make a decision. If you feather the wrong prop on the check ride—well, you can always take the flight test again. What is needed is caution with some speed of action, but make sure that the decision is a good one. Better to be a little slow and be right, than to be fast but wrong.

To go through a typical case: an engine fails. You can't tell which one immediately by looking at the tachometers. Remember the constant-speed prop will tend to flatten pitch and maintain the chosen rpm. As long as the prop is windmilling the engine is still acting as a pump and the mp will tend to stay at the former indication. Although a slight change may immediately occur, it's hard to tell at a quick glance just which mp hand did the moving. However, as the airplane begins to slow down, the constant-speed propeller of the dead engine can no longer maintain rpm. (The governor continually flattens the blades to maintain rpm, but the low pitch limit is finally reached.) Because the dead engine is still "making the motions," movement of that throttle will still result in mp change but no feel of power variation as would normally be expected. One visual indicator is the ball in the turn and slip or turn coordinator. The ball, because things are amiss, will tend to move *away* from the engine that's causing the problem. But to be on the safe side, take the following steps before feathering.

Advance the engine controls for both engines in this order: mixtures, props, throttles. You will be needing more power on the good engine and, because you have not definitely ascertained which is good or bad, will move all engine controls forward. Some engines are limited in the time allowed for full power, and you will not want to leave the power up too long. But get in the habit of increasing power on both engines (of course, you will actually only be increasing the power of one engine, but you'll be sure this way).

Now the problem becomes one of definitely isolating the bad engine.

So, an engine has quit. Remember, *working foot—working engine.*

This means that the airplane will yaw when power is lost on one engine. You will consciously or unconsciously try to hold it straight, which requires the use of rudder—and that foot is the *working foot.* Therefore, that engine is working okay. You can use this idea: *dead foot—dead engine.* This is a better memory aid because it automatically directs your attention to the engine that will be needing the procedures.

For instance, let's say it requires right rudder to keep the airplane straight (it wants to yaw to the left). Your left foot and the left engine are not working. Do you feather the left prop as soon as you can get your grubby little hand on the control? You do not! First, you pull the left throttle back. If the left engine is dead as you figured, nothing will happen—no change in power effects or sound or feel of the airplane. If somehow you made an error in feel of the rudder and the left engine is the working engine, you'll feel and see the loss of power and discover the mistake before feathering the good engine.

Feathering

The order of engine control usage for feathering varies among airplanes but may generally be given as this: (1) throttle back to idle, (2) mixture at idle cutoff, (3) prop control into the feather detent.

In an actual engine failure at cruise, don't be in too big a hurry to feather. After you've discovered which engine is the culprit, you might turn on the boost pump for that engine (or better still, turn on the boost pumps for both engines to make sure). You can also switch tanks and check for other problems (carburetor or ram icing will generally hit both engines more or less equally). You richened the mixture when the engine controls were moved forward.

Okay, so you've checked everything, but the problem still exists and it looks like you'll have to feather it. If you make a thorough check during the simulated failure, you might discover that the check pilot has pulled the mixture to idle cut-off, but you'll go ahead with the feathering procedure for practice.

The oil-counterweight propeller must be rotating in order to be feathered. If the engine "freezes up" before the prop is feathered, you'll have some flat blades out there giving lots of drag and there won't be anything you can do about it (but it's better than a windmilling prop). If, under actual conditions, the oil pressure is dropping or has gone to zero and the oil and cylinder head temperatures are going up out of sight, you'd better feather while you can.

After the prop has stopped, trim the airplane, secure the dead engine mag and boost pump switches, and turn off the fuel to that engine.

Under actual conditions you will want to land at the nearest airport that will safely take your plane. This is no time to be landing at an extremely short field with poor approaches to the runway. On the other hand, don't figure on finishing the last 400 miles of your trip either.

Care of the Operating Engine

Now that you have feathered the propeller, you are once again a single-engine pilot. You are interested in taking care of the operating engine—you don't want to be the pilot in command of the only twin-engine glider in the area.

There are two ways to combat possible engine abuse: *airflow* and *richer mixture.* If you throttle back and slow down, you're decreasing the airflow, and *in some light twins, throttling back automatically leans the mixture as well.*

Watch the cylinder head temperature (if available) and the oil temperature carefully. It's a lot easier to keep the engine temperature within limits than to cool it *after* things have gone too far. Open the cowl flaps on the operating engine as necessary.

If you are above the single-engine ceiling, you will lose altitude after the failure of one engine. If the engine gets too hot, you also may have to ease some power and make a slight dive to get increased airflow if altitude permits. Manufacturers check their engines for cooling at gross weight, best rate of climb speed, full power, and full rich, so unless you really get wild with the good engine, you'll have no problem with it.

Landing with One Engine (Actual Emergency)

A twin-engine airplane with an engine out is an airplane in distress, no matter how glowingly the manufacturer describes its single-engine performance. You'll certainly let the tower know your status. They may see it as you enter the pattern, but give them a little advance notice so they can do some traffic planning. You'll certainly have the right-of-way—unless somebody else has *both* engines out. At an uncontrolled field you might let Unicom know that you have an engine out—other pilots in the pattern on that frequency will give you plenty of room. It's a sad fact that many pilots would literally rather die than let anybody know that they may have a problem. There have been many cases of serious or fatal accidents being caused purely by stubbornness. Don't be afraid of being joshed by fellow pilots for asking for precedence or preference in an unusual situation. Your passengers have more or less blindly entrusted their lives to YOU, and you have no right to risk them to save your pride. The pros will congratulate you for recognizing an unusual situation; the amateurs are the ones who scoff. The bottom line: never hesitate to declare an emergency.

Enough of the philosophizing. You are interested in landing on the *first* approach. Don't fly in such a manner that you get low and slow and have to apply full power to get to the runway. You might find that it will take more power than you have available to drag the airplane up to the landing area—which brings up another point: *don't lower the gear and flaps until you are pretty well assured you'll make the field.* This doesn't mean doing it all on final; you'll be better off to get the gear down on the downwind leg *and stay fairly close to the normal pattern, but you may want to be a little slower with adding flaps.*

Some older light twins that use hydraulic pressure for actuating the gear and flaps may have only one engine-driven hydraulic pump (usually on the left engine). Should this engine be the one that is secured, you'll have to remember to hand pump the gear and flaps down. This may take some time, so give yourself plenty of leeway on final. Forgetting to do this is one of the most common errors of the new twin pilot during simulated engine-out maneuvers at altitude. You make a good pattern and use good headwork until the time comes to lower the gear and flaps. You've got a good final, so you push the gear lever down but forget about the necessity for hand pumping. Valuable seconds go by before your realize that in an actual approach you would have to start pumping—and pronto! Many a new pilot, making a simulated approach at altitude with the propeller feathered on the engine-driven hydraulic pump side has "landed gear-up" at 3,000 ft. This could cause certain inconveniences in an actual landing—so do it right the first time to avoid a potentially dangerous situation if your training twin has this hydraulic pump situation.

Keep your approach speed above the single-engine minimum controllable speed (V_{MC}) until landing is assured. You can get yourself into a "coffin corner" by slowing it up too soon below V_{MC}; if full power is needed for any reason, you may lose control of the airplane. *Most twin-engine instructors and POHs recommend that the approach be made at least V_{YSE} for best chances of a successful go-around if needed.* (Not *too* fast, though.)

A good single-engine approach is one that requires gradual throttling back of the good engine as you approach the field. As you throttle back, take care of the rudder trim so that when the power is off the airplane will be in trimmed flight. Some pilots neutralize the rudder trim on final and hold the required rudder pressure with one foot. This is good except that if a sudden go-around is required things could get complicated, because the pilot will get no help at all on the rudder and must quickly trim the airplane while executing the required steps.

Another common mistake for the new twin pilot is being much too high on a single-engine approach. If you overdo the idea of not being low, you can be so high and fast that when the flaps are extended you balloon to new heights of glory and have to take it around—on *one engine.*

The perfect single-engine approach is one that allows the pilot plenty of time to correct for crosswinds and to get the airplane in the landing configuration. So, an approach that requires a slight amount of power (with gradual reduction) all the way around is much better than a high, hot, and overshot one. You'll do better if the pattern is close to normal (gear down on downwind leg)—this was said before—but flying a *slightly* closer pattern and (again) delaying flap extension as compared with a two-engine approach. *No radical maneuvering!*

This is a time when the checklist is most important. The good engine should be taken care of, so make sure that the mixture is rich, boost pump is on (if required), and fuel is on best tank. A double check of the gear is important. In the stress of the moment you may overlook it if the checklist isn't used. Make sure the prop is in high rpm (low pitch) in case you should have to go around.

As noted earlier in the chapter, abrupt throttle closing on the operating engine could cause loss of control in an *unexpected direction.* Figure 15-18 shows what could happen with a *feathered* propeller. The airplane is heavily loaded and has lost an engine. The pilot is carrying full power on the operating (right) engine and is holding full rudder and/or trim to cope with the problem. The pilot makes the approach and sees that the plane is *too* high and jerks the operating engine abruptly to idle. The right propeller goes to the flat-pitch limit in an attempt to maintain the earlier rpm, and now the drag on that side is very high. The sudden high drag plus the rudder or trim being to the right (probably *full* right) can cause an instantaneous and uncontrollable roll to the *right*, opposite to the earlier tendency. The chances of recovery in this situation would be very slim indeed.

Taking It Around on One Engine

It may be that after careful planning on your part somebody taxis out on the runway just as you are on final, or for some other reason you must go around. Once you've decided to make the big move—the sooner the better! The sooner that power is applied on final, the more airspeed and altitude you'll have.

Don't ram the throttle open because this will cause directional problems. Ease it open and retract the landing gear (you may have to pump it up). Flaps up gradually. Don't try to climb too soon—remember that you must attain and maintain the best single-engine climb speed. If you start the go-around early on final, you may use a small amount of altitude—after opening the throttle and cleaning it up—to help attain the best single-engine climb speed if you've dropped below that number. Remember that flaps require the use of vital HP, so don't be *too* slow about getting them up. The makers of several light twins recommend that the flaps be retracted *before* the gear in a go-around. Check the recommended sequence of cleaning up for your airplane. One-engine go-arounds are extremely risky, no matter what light twin you are flying. Obstructions ahead might make it better to land anyway, even if you did forget to lower the gear (and realize it at the last second).

One POH notes the following approximate *penalties* in rate of climb:

Landing gear extended—350 fpm
Flaps extended 10°—50 fpm
Flaps extended fully—450 fpm
Inoperative engine propeller windmilling—250 fpm

You can see that with gear and full flaps extended and a windmilling propeller the penalty can be 1,050 fpm.

Engine Failure on Takeoff

You may wonder why we've waited so long to be talking about engine failures on takeoff. It might seem more logical to talk about this *first* and then go into the in-flight emergencies. The fact is that you won't cover takeoff engine-out procedures until you've had plenty of practice in the air and have a good idea of the principles of single-engine flight.

There's no doubt about it, during takeoff is the most critical time to lose an engine. The plane is at its heaviest and the airspeed and altitude are low. This is the time for cautious haste. You won't have a great deal of time but will have enough to make a decision.

Use rudder to keep the plane straight and lower the good-engine wing as soon as possible to maintain control (Figure 15-14). *Control is first*, performance next.

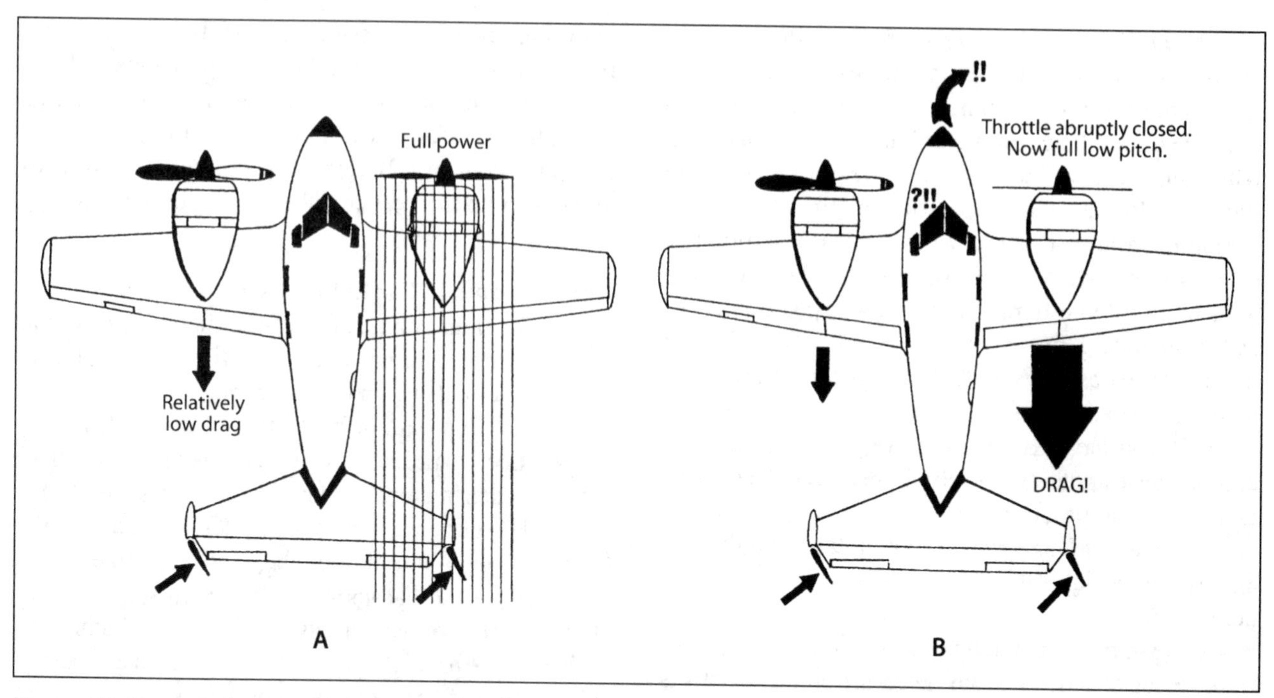

Figure 15-18. A. Full power is being carried on the operating engine. **B.** When the throttle is abruptly closed, the prop flattens into full low pitch and the drag situation is as shown. This could set up an uncontrollable roll to the right with fatal results.

In fact, if you had a yaw string on the nose, a 15° sideslip into the good engine (the string deflected about 15° from center, toward the inoperative engine) results in *best control*—but not best performance—for some light twins. When things are under control, *then* set up zero sideslip (your string straight and ball deflected approximately one-half width toward the good engine) for best performance, as in the single-engine climb experiment discussed earlier.

The check pilot will give you a single-engine emergency on takeoff by throttling one engine back to zero thrust and you will go through the necessary recovery actions. You will probably be given simulated takeoff emergencies and engine-out approaches at altitude, where you can actually feather a prop, before simulating one close to the ground with zero thrust.

On a normal takeoff, pick up the single-engine climb speed as soon as possible after takeoff, then assume the two-engine best rate-of-climb speed. Don't accelerate much above the two-engine V_Y; altitude is much more valuable than excess airspeed.

V_{YSE}, the best single-engine climb speed, is a *blue radial line* on the airspeed indicator for airplanes type-certificated under 6,000 pounds max weight [14 CFR §§23.67(b) and 23.1545(b)(5)]. V_{XSE}, the best single-engine *angle* of climb speed, is not marked on the airspeed indicator. You'd use this until obstacles were cleared and then assume V_{YSE}.

One thing is sometimes overlooked—if an engine quits on takeoff, you do not always continue the takeoff. Most new pilots have drilled themselves so thoroughly on what *to* do that they forget that there are things not to do, also:

1. If an engine quits before leaving the ground, close the throttle on the good one, use good braking, taxi back to the hangar, and complain. Directional control may be a problem if the engine quits suddenly.
2. If an engine quits after you become airborne and there is enough runway left (and your gear is still down), *always* close the throttle on the good engine, land, go back to the hangar, and complain.

Light twins on a standard sea level day at gross weight need 2,000 to 4,000 feet of runway (depending on the make and model) to accelerate to a particular airspeed and stop. Check your POH for the accelerate and stop distance information. If you are taking off from a 2,000-foot strip and your airplane requires 3,000 feet to accelerate to a predetermined engine failure speed and then stop, you are committed to continue after getting to that speed (V_1, takeoff decision speed). Remember too, that the accelerate and stop distance will *increase* with an increase in temperature and/or altitude (higher density-altitude) and wet runways (Figure 15-19).

Also included in some POHs is accelerate and go information for the airplane, if an engine is lost during takeoff. Like the accelerate and stop chart, data are given for various weights, engine failure speeds, pressure-altitudes, and temperatures. The numbers given note the total distance (feet) to clear a 50-foot obstacle under the various combinations. For instance, one twin, taking off at a particular weight, at a 6,000-ft pressure-altitude, at a temperature of 50°F (10°C) with an engine failure at 100 K, will take nearly 16,000 feet (3 SM) to clear a 50-foot obstacle. At sea level standard pressure and temperature, this airplane requires approximately 1 mile to clear 50 feet. It's likely that there will be obstacles 50 feet (or higher) within a mile of any decision point—think about it.

3. If you have lifted off above V_{MC} but have not attained best single-engine climb speed and the runway is rapidly disappearing—

a. Use aileron and rudder to maintain a bank of 5° against the initial roll and yaw. Control is number one here.

b. Clean the airplane up.

c. Keep the nose down, keep all engine controls forward, accelerate to best single-engine climb speed as soon as possible, and try to get some altitude. Don't lose control while trying to secure the bad engine right off the ground.

d. Remember, dead foot—dead engine.

e. Throttle back to check, and after making sure which engine is the culprit, feather that prop.

f. Maintain the recommended best single-engine climb speed and return and land (if possible avoid low, tight patterns).

Covering all possibilities for an engine failure on takeoff would take a set of encyclopedias. For instance, rough (high) terrain or man-made obstructions well off the end of the runway might mean it's better to belly it in, even though you have best single-engine climb speed.

Pilots have been killed when they overrated their ability and their airplanes' single-engine performance—and forgot about such things as temperature, turbulence, and altitude effects.

Figure 15-20 is a simplified look at the accelerate-stop versus accelerate-go decision. The POH for the twin you are using may have a diagram like this with specific airspeeds noted.

One thing sometimes overlooked in light twin flight training is that you *don't always immediately feather* an engine that has lost power on takeoff. You may need any power it's still producing for obstacle clearance. To exaggerate, if that sick engine is producing *one* THP, that's one more than would be working if the prop was feathered. You may decide that even though the engine is giving you some power, the sounds coming from it indicate imminent total failure and problems in feathering later, and it's best to feather right away and get on with the traffic pattern. The main things are to (1) maintain control, (2) clear any immediate obstacles, and (3) set up the best configurations for a pattern and landing.

Unfeathering in Flight Practice

Generally, if an engine is so rough that it must be shut down, it should remain so. Sometimes restarting an engine that's cutting up is asking for a fire or a situation where the prop cannot be feathered again. However, for practice purposes, it would be wise to try as much actual feathering and unfeathering as possible. Again, this will be done with the check pilot and at a safe altitude. Although you may be leery of the whole idea at first, you'll find that your confidence in single-engine flight will be immeasurably raised if *you* feather and unfeather the propeller several times and do a considerable amount of flying on one engine.

The method of unfeathering varies between models. Some use normal starting procedures (turning it over with the starter, the oil pressure unfeathering the prop as the engine starts) while others have an accumulator that stores oil or nitrogen pressure for unfeathering.

Whatever method used (which will be outlined in detail in the POH), remember that the secured engine will be cold because of the airstream passing over it. If properly primed, the engine will make an easier start in the air than on the ground because engine oil pressure will start to build up as the propeller starts turning, and the prop will move farther and farther out of feather and start windmilling.

You should take it easy in getting full power back on the engine that was shut down, particularly if you've been flying in cold conditions. Don't immediately add full power after getting it started.

After you've read the procedure and done it yourself several times, it will be quite clear (and you will feel more confident).

The Critical Engine

You may hear the term *critical engine* and will probably be asked about it when you take the check ride for the multiengine rating. First, in light twins that have both propellers turning clockwise as seen from the cockpit (which pretty well covers the U.S. light twins), the left engine is the critical one (the worse one to lose). This is because of "asymmetric disk loading" (see Figure 2-43). Figure 15-21 shows that the yawing force is greater when the left engine is out, and therefore

ACCELERATE-STOP DISTANCE

CONDITIONS:
FLAPS 10°
2400 RPM, 32.5 Inches Hg and
Mixtures Set at 160 PPH Prior to Brake Release
Cowl Flaps Open
Throttles Closed at Engine Failure
Maximum Braking During Deceleration
Paved, Level, Dry Runway
Zero Wind

NOTE:
Decrease distances 10% for each 11 knots headwind. For operation with tailwinds up to 10 knots, increase distances by 10% for each 2.5 knots.

WEIGHT LBS	ENGINE FAILURE SPEED KIAS	PRESS ALT FT	ACCELERATE - STOP DISTANCE - FEET				
			0°C	10°C	20°C	30°C	40°C
5150	77	S.L.	2965	3110	3260	3420	3595
		1000	3085	3235	3395	3570	3755
		2000	3210	3370	3540	3725	3925
		3000	3345	3515	3695	3895	4105
		4000	3490	3670	3865	4075	4305
		5000	3645	3840	4050	4275	4515
		6000	3815	4020	4245	4485	4745
		7000	3990	4210	4450	4710	4990
		8000	4180	4415	4670	4950	5250
4800	74	S.L.	2725	2845	2975	3115	3260
		1000	2830	2955	3095	3240	3400
		2000	2940	3075	3220	3375	3545
		3000	3055	3200	3355	3520	3700
		4000	3185	3340	3505	3680	3870
		5000	3320	3485	3660	3850	4055
		6000	3465	3640	3830	4030	4250
		7000	3620	3805	4010	4225	4460
		8000	3785	3985	4200	4435	4685
4400	71	S.L.	2475	2575	2680	2790	2915
		1000	2560	2670	2780	2900	3030
		2000	2655	2770	2890	3015	3155
		3000	2760	2875	3005	3140	3285
		4000	2865	2995	3130	3270	3425
		5000	2980	3120	3260	3415	3580
		6000	3105	3250	3400	3565	3745
		7000	3235	3390	3555	3730	3920
		8000	3375	3540	3715	3906	4110

Figure 15-19. Accelerate-stop distance table. At a weight of 4,800 pounds, at a pressure-altitude of 4,000 feet and 10°C, the airplane will require 3,340 feet to accelerate to 74 K and then stop.

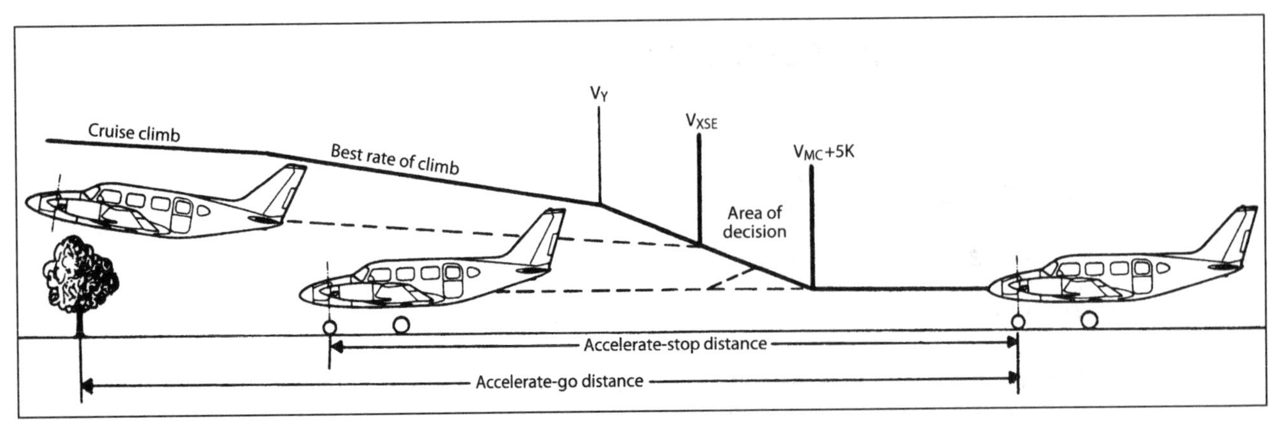

Figure 15-20. The rotation for lift-off is usually done at V_{MC} + 5 K. The area of decision is between lift-off speed and V_{XSE} (and height) and your actions in that area depend on the runway length and heights of obstacles ahead.

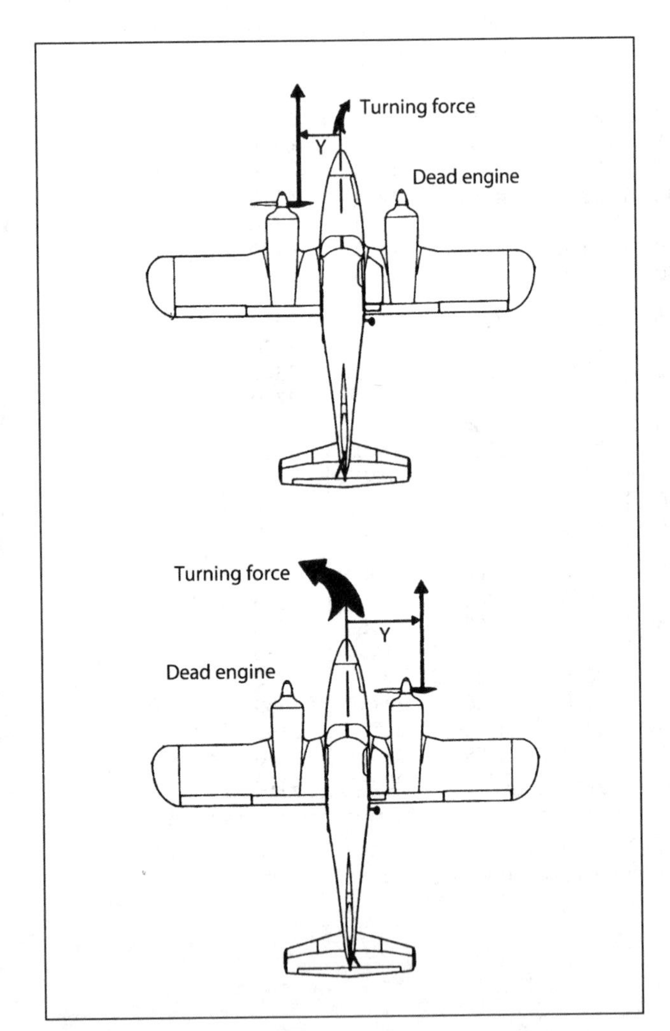

Figure 15-21. An exaggerated comparison of forces showing that from a control standpoint it's worse to lose the left engine.

directional control is more critical with the loss of that engine. Remember that asymmetric disk loading is popularly called the *P-factor.*

Don't be like some pilots who, when asked by the check pilot why the left engine is the critical one, answer, "It's because the hydraulic pump is on that engine on some light twins."

Some light twins have counter-rotating propellers—the right engine rotates "backwards," a design that eliminates the problem of a critical engine. (This does not mean that there is no longer a yaw when an engine quits but that single-engine performance is the same for either engine.) When both engines are operating normally (and equally), the "torque" forces are cancelled, with no need for rudder trim change for climbs, cruise, or dives.

Learning the Systems and Procedures

So far in this chapter, attention has been directed only to items directly concerned with flying the airplane on local flights with you and the check pilot and a light load of fuel. When you go up for the multiengine flight test and later when you get out on your own, you'll have to know about the electrical, hydraulic, and de-icing systems as avionics of your airplane, plus be able to run an accurate weight and balance, cope with electrical fires, and know engine fire control procedures. Also, the heating and ventilation system is more complicated than for the singles you've been flying. You might even find yourself unable to start the cabin gasoline heater some cold morning when you and your passengers are turning blue.

You should again take some time to really cope with flying the airplane and to start expanding your knowledge of the avionics and other systems. You might sit down in the airplane with the POH and identify various items that you've been too busy to look at closely. "Fly" a flight from start to finish in your mind, using normal procedures (but not moving any controls). Simulate start, taxi, pretakeoff check, takeoff, power change to climb, level-off with power setting and leaning, descents, patterns, approaches, landings, postlanding procedures, taxi, and shutdown. You can later (again not moving any controls) simulate an engine failure on takeoff and during climb and cruise, and go through feathering and restart procedures, plus single-engine approaches and landings. It will help you to feel at ease in the airplane if you can sit in it and make these "dry runs." (If no one is listening, you might want to make engine noises.)

If you're planning to go on and fly with the military or try for the airlines, you can set up some good attitudes about learning these more complicated systems. A light twin hydraulic system no doubt looks very complicated at this point but, compared with that of a 777, it's simple. But you can, by studying your system (and maybe reading a little on hydraulics and asking questions of the local mechanics), get information that can be used later. This is not to say that you'll have to memorize all the parts and know exactly where each line goes in order to be a good pilot (since you probably couldn't do a repair job in flight anyway), but you might have some alternate ideas for system use should a problem arise.

Sources

Thanks to Mr. Les Berven, engineer and test pilot, for his permission to use notes from his early lectures on multiengine aerodynamics at the University of Tennessee Space Institute.

Also, thanks are extended to Capt. M. R. Byington, Jr. (USN, retired), of Embry-Riddle Aeronautical University, Daytona Beach, Florida, whose report, *Optimized Engine Out Procedures for Multi Engine Airplanes,* has helped revise downward earlier estimates of the angles of bank required for zero sideslip (and best climb performance). His flight tests of the single-engine performances of a Cessna Crusader, Piper Seminole, and Beech Baron 58 at various banks have shed much light on a subject that needs to be resolved for *all* multiengine airplanes.

Part Three 3
Emergencies and Unusual Situations

16

Problems and Emergencies

When you became a private pilot you were "on your own"—no more check rides or sweating out sessions with an instructor (at least not until your Flight Review). You became free to establish as many bad habits as you pleased—and like most of us, you probably set about it very soon. If you fly your own airplane and keep up the minimum takeoffs and landings in the required period, you may legally fly for 24 months and hundreds of hours without benefit of dual. Your passengers have blind faith in your ability; they don't know whether you've been up recently with an instructor or that you haven't had a check ride since your Curtis Robin was new way back when. If everything goes normally there's no sweat, but if it doesn't, you may have a hard time finding passengers to share the expenses on your trips. If your flying is shaky enough, even the uninitiated will begin to suspect that all is not well. Gone are the days when pilots boasted of the number of planes they'd damaged during their careers.

Sure, you've been shooting landings every chance you get, and this is particularly enjoyable in the late afternoon when the air is calm. Takeoffs and landings are fun, and you can learn a lot in a good session. But there are other phases of flying, too. For instance, when was the last time you made a power-off approach? Do you have a good idea of the airplane's approximate glide ratio, clean *and* dirty?

Every once in a while you should drag out the POH and go over the emergency procedures again. You'll be surprised how much you have forgotten since the last time you reviewed them.

This chapter will bring up a few points on both low- and high-altitude emergencies and en route problems.

Rough Operation or Loss of Power

The rough running discussed here is not the "automatic rough" that the engine always jumps into when you're flying over water or rough terrain.

Okay, so the engine really starts to run rough—now what? It's a complicated piece of machinery, and the trouble could be caused by any one of a thousand things—but a large percentage of problems are caused by a very few items—namely, carburetion, fuel management, and ignition. You'll want to analyze the problem and, if possible, correct it.

Carburetion

This term covers the fuel-air mixture delivered to the engine cylinders—whether using a carburetor or fuel injection.

Carburetor Ice

One of the most common problems for carburetors is plain old-fashioned ice. However, if you've let icing go so far as to cause the engine to start running rough, you've really been asleep. You know that carburetor ice gives warning by (1) a decrease in manifold pressure (mp) in an airplane with a constant-speed prop or (2) a decrease in rpm for the fixed-pitch prop. It's quite possible that carburetor icing in a light trainer can progress to a point that *full* carburetor heat won't undo the damage. It's a vicious cycle: the heat capacity naturally depends on the engine, but the engine is sick because of the ice and the carburetor heat suffers. The engine may quit and there you sit with a windmilling propeller. So you fell asleep and now must pick a field. *Leave the carburetor heat full on as you try for the field.* There may be enough residual heat getting into the carburetor to clear out the ice before you have to land. You pulled it on and nothing happened right away, so what may be needed is a little time. This doesn't mean that you won't be picking a field and preparing for an unscheduled landing—because the residual heat may *not* do the trick. Don't count on it and sit up there with your head up and locked.

One thing of importance about carburetor ice if you don't have a carburetor air temperature gage—when you discover you have ice, use *full* carburetor heat to get the garbage cleaned out. It's suggested by a major engine manufacturer that if the airplane doesn't have any sort of induction air temperature gage (and carburetor ice is suspected), you'd best use either full heat or none, since you don't know the temperature you're setting up for the carburetor.

On some of the older higher-performance lightplanes, the carburetor or manifold heat is very effective, and the air going into the carburetor may be raised up to 200°F by applying full heat. *The use of full heat will cause a power loss and could cause detonation at high power settings.*

Remember that the ice will collect around the butterfly and jets of the float carburetor.

Your job will be to use carburetor heat and open the throttle if it looks as though the ice is getting ahead. When you open the throttle, you've made sure that the butterfly valve is opened so that the fuel-air mixture has a better chance of getting through to the engine. Icing can give you more trouble at part- or closed-throttle operation—it will take less ice to cut off the fuel-air mixture from the engine. You remember this from your student pilot days when you used carburetor heat before closing the throttle for a glide. More power means more carburetor heat available for use.

Normally, though, you'll apply heat as needed and won't increase the power. With a constant-speed propeller, you don't want to just ram the throttle wide open without thinking that you might overboost the engine.

As you know, carburetor ice is not as much a function of low temperature as it is of high humidity. If the outside air temperature is quite low the air will be so dry that carburetor ice will be a lesser problem.

Anytime you are more or less smoothly losing mp or rpm, use carburetor heat or alternate air (assuming you don't have a creeping throttle). Here's the typical situation: You notice that the mp is lower than it should be, you haven't climbed, and it looks as though you might have ice. Suppose that you were carrying 24 inches mp for cruise, but it has dropped to 22 inches. You apply heat and the mp drops to 21 inches because of the less-dense air introduced. After a few seconds the mp picks up the 2 inches it lost so that the gage registers 23 inches. When you push the heat off it will again be up to 24 inches. But if it iced once it will do it again; you'll have to experiment to get the right setting. (It may be full heat if there's no CAT gages.)

When you use full carburetor heat and send the warm, less-dense air through the engine, the mixture will be richer. *At cruise* you'll lean the mixture to smooth out operations. (Don't use carb heat for takeoff or climb except per the POH, which would be rare indeed.) After you ease the heat off, you readjust the mixture to a richer setting, as the denser cold air starts coming through again.

Some trainers' POHs suggest the use of carburetor heat throughout the approach and landing. You know by now that a go-around with full heat cuts down noticeably on performance. It's possible, too, that detonation could occur on a climb with full heat, so get heat off as full power is being applied.

If a carburetor air or induction air temperature gage is available, maintaining a minimum of 90°F CAT at cruise or letdown is seen as one way to prevent icing.

Impact Icing

The fuel injection system has the advantage of doing away with carburetor ice, but both types of systems may suffer from impact icing.

Saturated air is the culprit here. Whenever you're flying in rain, clouds, or fog, and the outside air is near freezing, impact icing may occur. As the air enters the induction system, it may be condensed and cooled to the point that ice will form at the 90° bend where the air scoop turns to enter the carburetor or fuel injection control.

Another problem is structural icing on the air intake screen. You may run into this when flying instruments later. Structural icing on the airplane may not be serious but could cause a power loss. Figure 16-1 shows a simple method of taking care of this problem. When the intake is iced over, the engine suction will open the spring-loaded trap door and the warm air from around the engine is drawn into the intake system. Naturally some power will be lost, as the warmer air is less dense than the cold outside air. But better to lose some power than all of it.

Freezing rain or drizzle may glaze over the intake also, but you will be busy trying to see through a glazed windshield and keep a heavy, waterlogged airplane flying and won't have any time to appreciate the automatic features of your airplane.

Very heavy (nonfreezing) rain may close off the air intake screen so that the engine loses partial or complete power. If this is encountered, carburetor heat or alternate air will get most of the power back. (Reset the mixture as necessary for efficient operation after applying carb heat.)

Mixture

Occasionally an engine runs rough because pilots abuse the mixture control—but usually they're aware of this misdemeanor. The two main problems are (1) a too-rich mixture at altitude or (2) descending with the mixture set for a high-altitude cruise. Occasionally there will be those who descend and try to apply full power when in the best economy setting.

You might check to see that the primer is in *and locked.* This is an often-overlooked cause of rough running, particularly at lower power settings. Notice in the fuel system schematics (carburetors) in Chapter 13 that the primer furnishes fuel to the engine at a different point. The primer fuel doesn't go through the carburetor but goes directly to the engine at the intake manifold. If the primer control (or primer pump, as it's sometimes called) is not locked, the engine may pull fuel from this source in addition to that furnished by the carburetor. The engine will run rich even though the mixture control is set properly. In rare cases, such as overenthusiastically pulling back on the mixture control and finding it pulling out in your hand (and the engine in idle cutoff at 5,000 feet AGL), the primer could be used to stretch the glide, if somewhat erratically. You leave the throttle at cruise or slightly less, pull the primer out, and give "shots" to the engine. The power will increase with each shot and decrease to a windmilling condition when you're pulling the control out for the next try. Such power surging could be pretty rough on some engines. This technique shouldn't be used for fun, but it might give you a few hundred (or thousand) feet of distance needed to make it to an airport in a jam. Check on the schematic of your airplane fuel system to see the tie-in.

Carburetor ice tends to richen the mixture, so it doesn't help to push the mixture forward if that's the problem. For all other occasions of engine roughness, moving the mixture control forward is a good idea. A richer mixture means cooler running and more power, particularly at lower altitudes. You may have overleaned the engine.

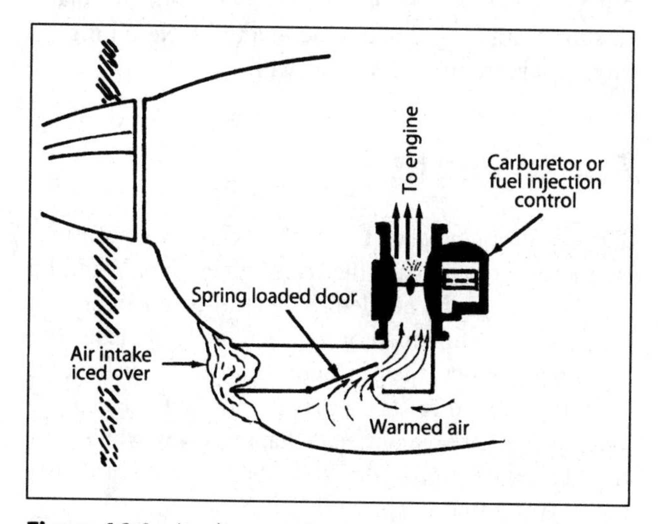

Figure 16-1. An alternate air source.

Fuel Management

Breathes there a soul so dead,
Who has not shook his head and said,
"Criminy, I forgot to switch tanks!"

There's one thing about running a tank dry—you won't get 5 minutes of frantic warning beforehand. In fact, if you haven't been watching the fuel pressure, your first warning will be a hiccup from the engine, followed by a loud silence. There is a no more active group than four pilots in a four-place airplane when a tank unexpectedly runs dry. The front-seat occupants are both scrambling for the tank selector (getting in each other's way and tripling the required time to switch tanks), while the back-seat occupants are shouting advice and maybe trying to get *their* hands into the act. Running a tank dry is a particularly effective attention getter if the three pilot-passengers are dozing when it happens. Funny as it may seem, nonpilots are not as affected by such a practice—they just sit back and quietly tremble. It's best to throttle back to prevent overspeeding of the engine when the tank change is made.

Keep up with the flying time on each tank—gages can be wrong. If the engine quits abruptly or starts losing power, you may have a leak or perhaps a stoppage. Don't get the idea because the tank(s) started at full and the consumption time isn't up that it won't do any good to switch tanks—it's worth a try. There have been too many accident reports stating, "In the wreckage it was found that the fuel selector was on an empty tank—the other tank contained fuel." This was a fuel starvation accident where mismanagement caused the crash with fuel available (fuel exhaustion means no fuel aboard).

14 CFR Part 23 states that "For reciprocating engines that are supplied from more than one tank, if engine power loss becomes apparent due to fuel depletion from the tank selected, it must be possible after switching to any full tank, in level flight, to obtain 75 percent maximum continuous power on that engine in not more than—(1) 10 seconds for naturally aspirated single-engine airplanes; (2) 20 seconds for turbocharged single-engine airplanes, provided that 75 percent, maximum continuous naturally aspirated power is regained in 10 seconds; or (3) 20 seconds for multiengine airplanes."

Some POHs advise that, should it be necessary to run a tank dry, it's best to switch at the first indication of fuel flow fluctuation or power loss and give steps for best recovery of power (fuel boost ON, etc.). Other POHs may suggest that running a tank dry be avoided. Refer to your specific handbook for suggestions as to whether a tank should be run dry and the procedures involved.

It has been found that several carburetor-equipped single-engine airplanes start 1 to 2 seconds after the fuel selector is switched from an empty to a full tank. Fuel-injected engines of the same general-type airplane took 6 to 8 seconds after the new tank was selected. While the time variance seems small, a pilot who is used to the carburetor-type reaction could decide that the fuel-injected engine won't regain power again, start switching back and forth, and get out of phase with the fuel system; 8 seconds can seem a long time—particularly if the engine has lost power and you delay analyzing the problem. The point is, the single-engine airplane must regain power within 10 seconds in either type of fuel-metering system. In the case of simply running out of fuel on one tank, you'd use the POH procedure (which may call for throttling back, turning on the boost pump, and richening the mixture) and give it a chance to work.

Ignition Problems

Plug Fouling

The most common ignition problem on the ground and at very low power settings in the air (extended glides, etc.) is plug fouling. This often occurs when using a fuel of higher lead content than recommended. The bottom plugs on a horizontally opposed engine may tend to be fouled after starting, especially if the plane has been sitting for several days. Your indication is an excessive rpm drop during a mag check. This usually can be corrected by leaning the mixture at a fairly high power setting (1,500 to 2,000 rpm). Move the mixture back until the first signs of roughness appear and leave it there for 30 to 60 seconds, You are raising the cylinder head temperature to such an extent that the oil or lead on the plug tip is burned off. Normally, fouled plugs will clean themselves out with operation, but it may be in the magneto and you just think it's in the plugs. If the treatment just described doesn't work, don't abuse the engine; richen the mixture and taxi back to the hangar to find out what's up.

This chapter is about in-flight problems. For plugs to suddenly start fouling in flight is unusual. In-flight fouling may mean serious piston ring problems, and it's best to land at the nearest airport.

Magneto Problems

If you start getting a bum mag when you're right over the center of Gitchygoomy Swamp, there's little you can do in the way of repairs. Plug or mag problems usually are characterized by almost instantaneous rough running (or not running). The engine may run smoothly and then abruptly cut in and out. Unfortunately, this instantaneous change is sometimes a characteristic of certain carburetion, as well as governor, problems. Generally speaking though, the ignition, by its very principle of operation, is more apt to cause immediate changes in engine characteristics.

So, if your purring engine suddenly starts really acting up, check the mags. Getting the bad mag out of action should smooth things out with only a small loss of power. Avoid moving the mag switch to OFF in your haste to fix the problem, though.

Loss of Oil Pressure

The average pilot tends to neglect scanning the engine instruments during flight, looking at them before takeoff and then checking them once an hour, if that often. It's quite a jarring experience to look casually at the oil pressure and find that it's gone—the hand is nestled up against ZERO and you don't know how long it's been there.

Well, take heart; for every instance of actual oil pressure loss, there are several cases where the instrument is the culprit. There's one way of telling if you're in trouble: watch the oil temperature gage (and cylinder head temperature if available). Usually a couple of minutes will tell the tale. If the temperature doesn't rise, it's just the gauge (but you may be losing oil if the line to the gauge has broken). In other words, just because you have low (or no) oil pressure doesn't mean that all is lost. But if the temperature starts a rapid rise into the red, you'd better look for a field in a single-engine plane or start feathering that engine in a twin. No oil means engine seizure in a very short while.

Fire in Flight

The smell of smoke in the cockpit can get your attention even more quickly than a rough engine. You'll be checked on your knowledge of what to do in such a case on the commercial or multiengine flight tests, but you should review the procedures for your own benefit, even if you plan to stay a private pilot for the next 50 years. When a real emergency happens, you won't have time to set up a procedure—it should be already laid out in your mind.

Electrical Fires

You're climbing out of the local airport with a full load of passengers and baggage. Suddenly you smell insulation burning and/or see smoke in the instrument panel area. Some pilots panic in this situation. Airplane control is pretty much forgotten and screaming steep turns are made back to the airport with gear-up landings following—all because maybe 20 cents worth of insulation burned. *The first requirement is to maintain control of the airplane.* Stalling and spinning at low altitudes is no way to resolve the problem.

Turn off the master switch in the case of an electrical fire for most airplanes. Then turn off all electrical and avionics equipment. If you've just lifted from an uncontrolled airport, return and land, watching for other aircraft. (Before turning off the master switch you might make a quick call on CTAF or Unicom to let your intentions be known.) At a busy, controlled field you'd want to leave the Master and one transceiver on until you are off the active runway. Otherwise you'd be gambling with the possibility of expanding the fire against a possible midair collision because no one knows your intentions.

En route, you'd turn the master switch off, turn avionics and other electrical switches off, and check circuit breakers to see if one popped as the fire started (leave the CB out). Turn the master switch back on and (if no CB had been popped) turn on essential items one by one with a short pause each time.

There are two schools of thought on opening the cabin ventilators:

1. Keep the cabin ventilators closed to avoid fanning the flames. Open them only after the fire is burned out and the system isolated.
2. Open the ventilators immediately to clear out possible toxic fumes and also to get the smoke out to expedite the isolation of the culprit. (For instance, if you turn on transceiver number two and smoke comes back, there's your problem.)

There are good arguments for both procedures; it depends on the amount of smoke and whether it is beginning to get to you. The main thing is to have considered some alternatives beforehand.

Engine Fires

Probably one of the worst situations you could encounter would be a full-fledged engine fire while on solid IFR over mountainous terrain in a single-engine airplane. One manufacturer recommends some steps in the event of an engine fire:

1. Turn mixture control to idle cutoff.
2. Turn fuel selector OFF.
3. Turn master switch OFF.
4. Establish the best glide distance airspeed.
5. Close cabin heat and cabin air controls. (Open overhead adjustable ventilators or cabin windows to get ventilation.)
6. Select a field suitable for a forced landing.
7. If the fire is not extinguished, increase the glide speed to try to find a speed at which combustion cannot occur. The usual recommendation is not to restart the engine. If one engine of a twin catches on fire you'd naturally go through the feathering procedure. Fortunately, engine fires are extremely rare, but that doesn't help when it happens to you. Review the POH.

High-Altitude Forced Landings

Picking a Field

Here's where you wish you'd practiced more power-off approaches. Set up the max distance glide speed, use carburetor heat, switch tanks, and go through the other steps previously mentioned.

Naturally you'll pick the best field available and land into the wind if possible. Maneuver so that you have a "Key Position" at a point opposite the point of intended landing, similar to the spot on the downwind leg where you've been starting the 180° power-off approaches at the airport. You are trying to turn an unusual situation into a more familiar one. The Key Position altitude should be somewhat higher above the ground than the traffic altitude you've been flying. You can S-turn or spiral to reach this position, but don't give yourself such a high margin of altitude that you overshoot—you may be so high that flaps (if available) and/or slipping won't be enough. Establish an imaginary box at the Key Position; the bottom of the box will be *at least* traffic pattern altitude and the top no more than 300 feet higher. The center of the Key Position box should be at approximately the abeam position on the downwind leg (Figure 16-2).

You may have been shooting power-on approaches throughout your recent flying career—this means that your downwind and base legs may have been much farther from the field than could be allowed for a power-off approach. *This, and the fact that a windmilling or stopped prop gives more drag than you may have counted on, could result in undershooting.* If you have a controllable-pitch prop that is still working, pull the propeller control full back to high pitch (low rpm).

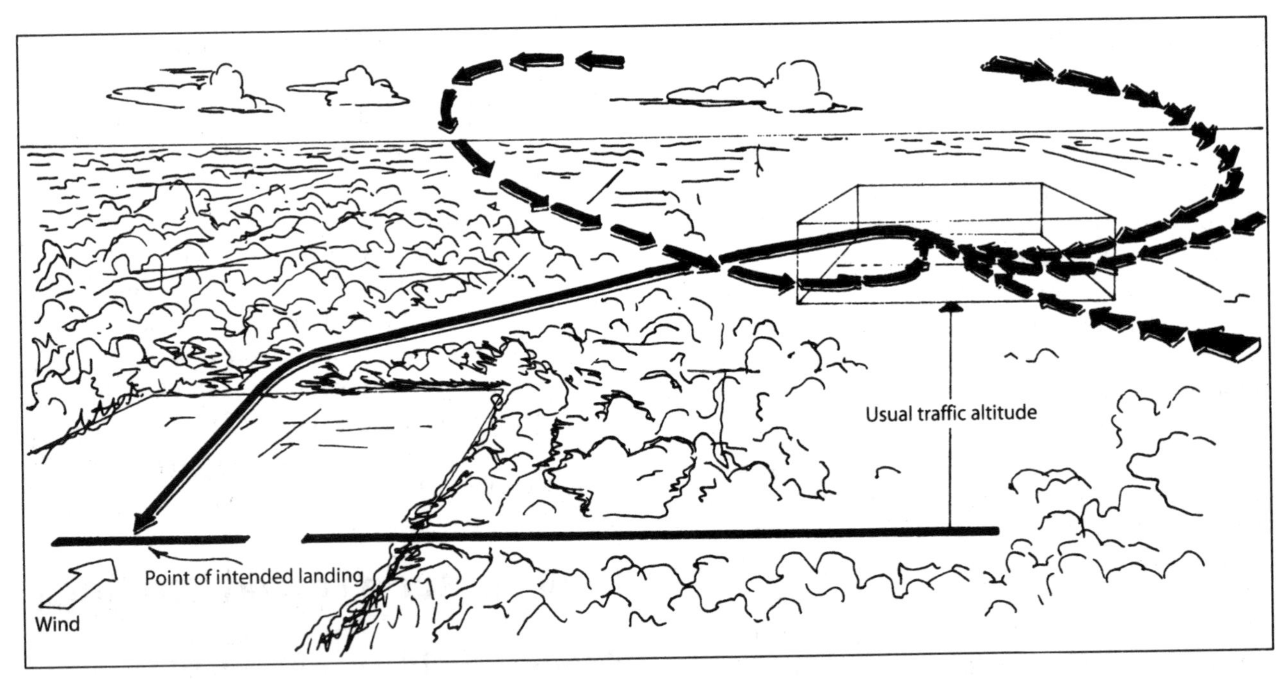

Figure 16-2. The Key Position box.

If the wind is strong, the downwind leg or Key Position box should be moved in slightly, as you would do for any power-off approach.

After you've hit the Key Position, the rest is pretty well up to you. Hitting a spot is a matter of experience and practice, and there are no printed "cribs" or "gouges" to help you. Your judgment is especially important the last 90° of turn into the field. If you are low on base, naturally you'll "cut across"; if high, you may S-turn past the wind line (Figure 16-3).

What you definitely do not want to do is get the airplane slow and wrapped up. That's the best possible way to get into serious trouble. It's a lot better to fly into something (a rougher field or bushes) with the plane under some semblance of control than to spin at a low altitude. Many fatal accidents have occurred when a pilot, under the pressure of an actual emergency, got slow and tried to rack the plane around. Some of the higher-performance planes you'll be flying are not as forgiving as the trainer you flew earlier.

There'll be times when a right-hand pattern will be better. If you don't have shoulder harnesses, have your front seat passenger hold a map case or a folded coat in front of his or her face, with the feet back—just in case. *Seats locked.* Some POHs recommend cracking the door(s) before touchdown so that they don't jam shut on impact.

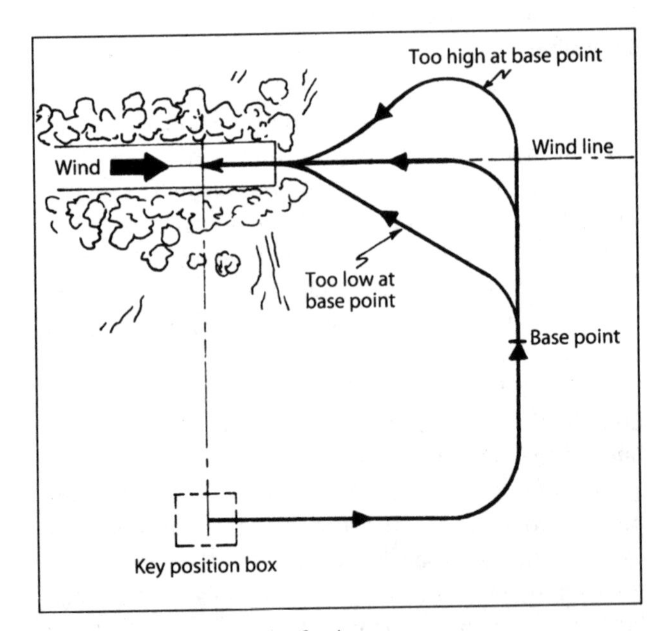

Figure 16-3. Playing the final turn.

Gear and Flaps

With a fixed-gear airplane there is no decision to be made as to whether the gear should be up or down. It's down and you can like it or lump it.

For the retractable-gear airplane, you'll have to decide whether it'll be gear-up or -down on the forced landing. There's a story that *some* years ago at a large military training base the cadets were admonished always to land gear-up in the event of an engine failure—unless they could land on a "designated military field." This rule was to ensure that the cadets did not try to land gear-down in pastures or the short civilian fields in the area; there would be less overall damage done by landing gear-up. One day on a cross-country, a cadet had an engine failure right over a busy civilian field (with 8,000-feet runways). You guessed it—he made a perfect approach and landed gear-up in the middle of the busiest runway. Needless to say, the runway wasn't of much use until the airplane was dragged off. The cadet's story? "But sir, the rules—this wasn't a designated *military* field." This left a very frustrated accident board chewing their nails and trying to broaden the regulations.

You won't have any hard-and-fast rules to go by. If the surface is either firm and smooth or extremely rough (large rocks, stumps, etc.) you'd probably be better off to put the gear *down*. If there are stumps and large rocks, the down gear will take a large amount of the shock before being torn off. You remember that the kinetic energy of your airplane is $(M/2)V^2$, or one-half the mass (weight divided by 32.2) times the square of the velocity. The longer you take to stop, the better off you are, even if it's a matter of a split second's difference. If you land gear-up on the rocky or stump-strewn field, it's possible that the obstacles may start ripping through the belly while you're at a high speed. In such a situation, forget the rest of the airplane—you'll be wanting to keep the cabin intact, so leave the gear down. As has been stated about jumping off a roof, "It's not the fall that hurts, it's the sudden stop."

The following table gives examples of impact speed versus approximate stopping distance and the longitudinal deceleration forces (g's) resulting (with g's rounded off to the nearest one-half). The stopping (skid) distance is *20 feet* in each case:

Impact Speed (K)	g's
20	1
40	3½
60	8
80	14
100	20

In another example, the stopping distance (skid) is *40 feet* in each case:

Impact Speed (K)	g's
20	Less than 1
40	2
60	4
80	7
100	10

Doubling the distance to stop cuts down on the deceleration forces by about one-half. (An airplane impacting at 100 K and stopping in 1 foot would be the victim of over 400 g's.) In a forced landing, the old idea of hitting the softest, cheapest object in the area as slowly as possible, still stands.

If you think the chosen field will be soft, generally it's a good idea to keep the gear up. And naturally for a water landing (ditching) the gear should be up.

Your decision for gear-up or -down will be based on what you see at the time. If in doubt about the firmness of a field, the usual decision is to leave the gear up. If it is soft and the wheels sink in, there's a good chance of flipping over.

All these considerations, of course, depend on whether you are *able* to get the gear down. You should have enough residual hydraulic pressure or electric power for one cycle anyway (and you may change your mind on the way down).

Flaps

Proper use of flaps can mean the difference between success or failure. A common error in practice emergencies is for the pilot to put down the gear and use full flaps right away—resulting in an undershoot. Taking off some of the flaps when undershooting may be too late to do any good—plus the fact that the sudden upping of flaps causes a temporarily increased sink rate, especially at low airspeeds. For lighter airplanes the flaps may be "upped" in increments with a noticeable extension of the glide distances (raise the nose as the flaps are retracted); for heavier airplanes at low altitude, this could get everybody's attention.

Use the flaps in this situation in increments; put a little down as you feel they are needed. If it looks as though the flaps will have to be put down by emergency means because of the no-power condition, you might be better off forgetting about them—this is no time to be fumbling around in the cockpit.

Slips

For airplanes without flaps, the slip is the big aid in hitting the field. If you are on a close base leg and are high, waiting until after turning final to slip may be too late—you may miss the field because the final leg will be too short to give you time to get set for a slip.

If it looks as though you'll be crowded, a slipping turn comes in handy. It's a good way to lose altitude in the turn without picking up excessive airspeed. You're holding a touch of top rudder and a little aileron into the turn. Don't hold so much top rudder that the turn is stopped—you still want to land in the field you picked originally (Figure 16-4).

Flaps and slips don't always mix well. Some airplanes are unforgiving this way, because the flaps may blanket the tail surfaces in a slip. You might go to altitude and try the reaction of your airplane to a flaps-down slip and also talk with some of the local pros. Check your POH, too.

Figure 16-4. The slipping turn.

Precautionary Landings

In the event of imminent fuel exhaustion, fast-deteriorating weather, or engine problems, it may be necessary to make an off-airport landing. It's always best, naturally, to be able to pick your spot while the picking is good. You should know what to do when you have to land in the hinterlands; the technique of "dragging the area" is valuable for this situation.

Basically, this technique consists of picking a field that appears to be able to take your airplane (gear-down, if possible) and flying a normal pattern and approach to the area of the field on which you plan to land. Add power and level off at about 100-ft altitude on final and fly to the right side and parallel to the landing area. Look over the landing area for holes, ditches, field condition (high grass, soft, etc.), and, in general, look for items that couldn't have been seen from altitude. If everything looks okay, open the throttle, climb out, and make a pattern with a short-field approach and landing. If you see that the field isn't for you on the first pass, repeat this technique at another one.

During the approach and pass, watch for wires or other obstructions of that nature. You can't always see the wires, but if there are poles, check which way they are running. In the case of wires, look for other poles well to both sides of the pole line; there may be other wires that would cause you trouble if you were landing parallel to the known wires.

Your decision whether to land gear-up or -down depends on the points mentioned earlier in the chapter. You'll have to decide whether things have gone so far that you may be better off to belly it in to a fairly bad field rather than take the time to find another one (if you have only a couple of minutes of fuel left, or if it looks as if the weather will soon go to zero-zero and you're practically at rock bottom altitude).

If you're not going to be able to make it to an airport, it's better to land at a field of your choice. After you're down, get on the phone and let the right people know of your plight.

Low-Altitude Problems

Engine Failure on Takeoff (Single-Engine Airplane)

One thing that has been discussed in many ways throughout this book and during your flying career is worth repeating: *Keep the airplane under control!* You can make a minor turn but keep it shallow. If you have time, cut the mixture, ignition, and fuel. Turn off the master switch after you've used flaps (electric). Have the airplane as slow as possible when you touch down. If you are going into trees, don't stall it out above them but fly into them at the lowest possible speed, still with control.

If the engine starts running rough after passing the airport boundary (or any point where it's too late to try to land again), fly straight ahead (if the terrain and populated area allow) and try to gain altitude without getting too slow. The engine may quit at any time and at least you'll be headed more or less into the wind. *Ease* your way back to the airport. Maintain a safe airspeed.

Open Door

A door opening suddenly during takeoff or in flight is quite an experience. There can be a loud bang as it opens, and the noise of the air moving past the crack is enough to set up a good case of combat fatigue in a short while. In addition to the sundry noises associated with such a problem, the airplane may have tail buffeting or the wing on that side may tend to drop because of the disturbed airflow.

The usual situation is that the pilot has forgotten to lock the door (it should be on the checklist) and no problem occurs until the airspeed is such that the drop in pressure caused by the air moving past the door is enough to pull it from the latching mechanism—then the fun begins. It seems that the airspeed required for this is reached just after lift-off; the usual setting for a door opening episode is on a short runway, in turbulent air, with obstacles ahead, the airplane at gross weight, and your nervous maiden aunt sitting by the door.

If the door opens on the takeoff run and there is room to stop, naturally this is the thing to do. If it opens after lift-off and there isn't room left to land, keep *full* power and climb at the normal climb airspeed. In some cases performance will suffer but the airplane can be flown. Fly a normal pattern (don't wrack it around), make your approach at a slightly faster airspeed, and carry the airplane closer to the ground before starting the transition—more or less fly it on. As was mentioned, the wing on that side may tend to drop out early. It would help if your passenger would hold the door as closely shut as possible to minimize the effects. (You may be able to close the door of some airplanes after you climb to a safe altitude.)

Your biggest problem will be plain old-fashioned fear. It's a nerve-shattering occurrence and between the noise and the buffeting, plus occasional screams from distraught passengers, you could be fatally distracted. Fatalities have occurred in airplanes that were perfectly capable of flying with the door open, when the pilot tried to cut corners and spun in.

If you're at altitude and your Aunt Minerva catches her knitting bag on the handle and suddenly presents you with fresh air in copious quantities, you may be able to shut the door in flight. Generally, the procedure is to throttle back to idle, slow and trim the airplane to a speed just above the stall, open the small storm window on the pilot's side to help equalize the pressure, and shut the door—and lock it. On some airplanes the storm window can be held open with your left elbow while holding the control wheel with your left hand. You can reach over and shut the door with your right hand if you're by yourself. Needless to say, you don't want to be trying this at low altitude.

You may have to land the airplane with the door ajar and should expect some buffeting during the approach and landing. Usually, of its own accord, the door will settle on a position of 3 to 6 inches open. If there isn't a passenger available to hold it shut, add 5 to 10 K to the approach speed *using a normal approach pattern.*

There may be different techniques for your airplane; the main idea is to bring this possible problem to your attention. Check on your airplane with other pilots and/or your POH and go over in your mind what to do in such an event. Better to set up a plan now than to have to work something out in all that noise and confusion.

Seat Belt and Shoulder Harness

There may be a time when you lift off and are committed (the runway is behind you) and you suddenly hear what sounds like the engine destroying itself. There is a bang, bang, bang, and you're sure that a complete power loss is imminent. Check the engine instruments and maintain control of the airplane as you gain altitude and decide what the problem might be.

There have been instances of pilots chopping power at the end of the runway and landing in bad terrain (damaging their airplanes and injuring themselves) when the only problem was a seat belt or shoulder harness hanging out the door and whacking against the fuselage. Such noises could be engine problems, of course, but you want to maintain control of the airplane while you check things. When you are flying solo, fasten that empty seat belt and harness so that this can't happen. (If you have passengers you should certainly oversee fastening their belts and harnesses.)

The sound of a rampaging seat belt or harness is usually a steady banging that may sound like an engine problem but is isolated as to its general position. Sure, the straps will probably cause minor paint or fabric damage, but you'd be a lot better flying a normal pattern and landing rather than opening the door and pulling the straps and/or belt in. The main point, anyway, is to remind you that control of the airplane is primary in case you hear such sounds.

Gusty Air, Turbulence, and Gradient Winds

Wind velocities and directions vary with altitude—this is expected—but what's not always expected is the fact that the wind may change velocity and/or direction with only a small altitude change. On a gusty day the wind velocity may change almost instantly; you might be in a tight spot if you're flying the airplane too close to the stall.

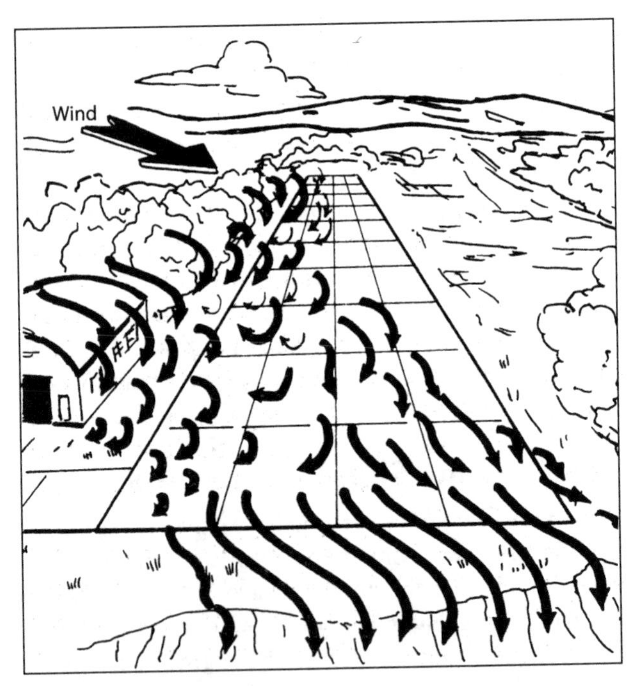

Figure 16-5. The effects of obstacles on the wind.

A problem to watch closely is the effect on the wind of obstacles such as trees or buildings on the windward side of the runway (Figure 16-5).

Even if the wind is steady and you've been holding the same crosswind correction all the way down on final, things can go to pot pretty fast when you get close to the ground. Not only obstacles cause trouble—but the wind itself could change velocity abruptly. The airplane feels as if the bottom were dropping out and the air may be extremely choppy. Adding power (fast!) usually keeps things under control.

There may be a time when you are racing a thunderstorm to the field. Remember something here, too—the wind may shift abruptly; it can be very strong one way and when you get all set up for landing, you find that you are now trying to land cross-downwind. Keep a close eye on the wind indicator on final when there are thunderstorms in the vicinity or when a cold front passage is expected momentarily.

Wake Turbulence

You may not have had the dubious pleasure of encountering wake turbulence, but chances are good that sometime you will.

Naturally, the most critical place to fly into wake turbulence is at a low altitude, and the most likely place for trouble is on takeoff or landing. Give the big planes plenty of room. Take it around again or ask for another runway if you think there might be wake turbulence hanging around; the turbulence may be around for several minutes after the instigator has made its getaway.

If there is a crosswind, always take off or land on the upwind side of the runway. After taking off, stay on the upwind side of the big airplane that's causing the hazard. One hazard in a light crosswind condition (3 to 7 K) is that one of the vortices is kept over the same position relative to the runway. (The downwind vortex will be moved even faster laterally.) One vortex may move over to a parallel runway and cause mischief over there.

If the wind is straight down the runway or calm and you *must* take off, the following steps are best: (1) don't lift the airplane off until you have plenty of flying speed—hold it on a little longer than usual but plan to get off before the point of the big plane's lift-off, since its vortices will begin at the point of rotation for lift-off and (2) after lifting off make a shallow turn to one side and then turn back to parallel the runway (Figure 16-6).

Even an immediate turn may not help if you take off directly behind the other plane with no waiting time. Although you will get out of the way as soon as possible, there may be a period when you will be in the turbulence. Whether you'll have enough airspeed to get through it safely is a matter for conjecture—so it's best to wait.

If you are landing behind another plane and the wind is directly down the runway or calm, you'd be better off to land past the spot it touched down, making a slightly steeper approach than usual. Of course, if it overshoots and lands so far down the runway that reverse thrust was the only thing that saved it, you'd better take your airplane around rather than land long. Even on the go-around, stay to the upwind side.

The best thing is to avoid wake turbulence, but you may be caught unprepared. Again, the most exciting place to get caught is during takeoff or landing; you're low and slow and don't have very good control effectiveness.

Wake Turbulence on Takeoff or Landing

You've just lifted off and suddenly turbulence makes the airplane go berserk; it rolls violently, and opposite aileron and rudder have little effect in stopping it. In addition to the roll, the turbulence may try to pick the airplane up or slam it back on the ground.

Keep full power on and do not try to climb up through it. Keep the nose down. You need airspeed. If you are slow when hitting the disturbance you'll make more trouble by hauling back on the wheel. Don't let it put you into the ground (if you can help it), but don't get to thinking that you can pop up through it either—you might end up on your back at 20 feet and get socked with a violation of Federal Aviation Regulations for putting on an airshow without permission. Besides, you wouldn't want to land this way as there are no wheels on the top of the airplane.

When the airplane rolls, try to stop the bank from becoming too steep, but don't attempt to level the wings completely. A turn is needed right now, and some bank will help you get out of the choppy area. Turn in the direction that the turbulence tends to roll you.

You may cut some fancy capers at a low altitude and end up flying 45° from your takeoff heading for a few seconds but you want to get into smooth air—and stay there. After doing all sorts of graceful and not so graceful rolling and maneuvering right off the ground because of wake turbulence one day, a private pilot was asked by the tower if he were in trouble. His answer became a classic in radio communication, although it resulted in an FCC violation for "improper language over the air." Tower folks realize that wake turbulence is a definite menace to lightplanes and warn pilots if there is a chance of it during takeoff or landing.

On takeoff or landing, airspeed is insurance when wake turbulence is encountered. You may have to deliberately fly a few feet off the ground for a few seconds until clear of the disturbance.

Wake turbulence is unpredictable; the airplane's reaction will depend on how you fly into it. Seen from behind, its motion is rotational, but you may fly into only one side of the vortex.

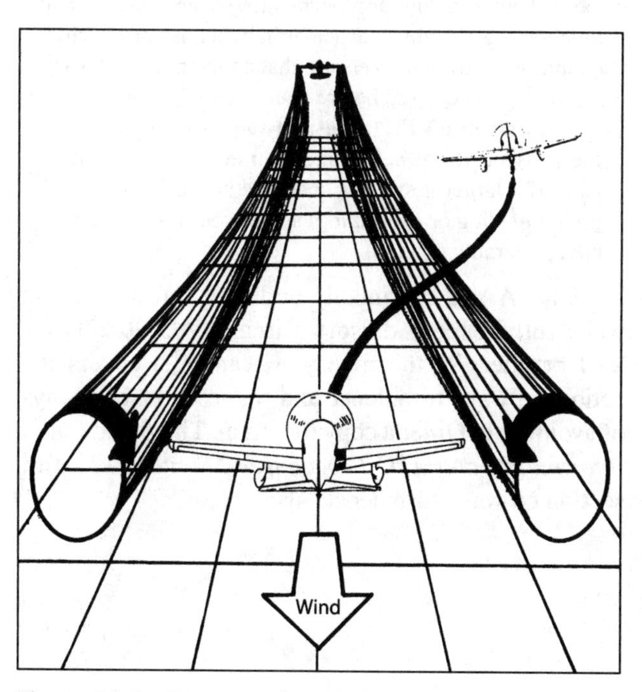

Figure 16-6. Clearing wake turbulence on takeoff.

If turbulence is encountered on approach, the best answer is full power. Keep the nose down, turn out of the area, and go around.

If you suspect there will be wake turbulence during an approach and landing, keep your airspeed up and literally fly the airplane on. *Better yet, if you suspect that there'll be turbulence on approach or landing, take it around—always.* When you take off or land into a known area of turbulence, you're betting a large repair bill (or worse) against a couple of minutes saved. Anytime you think there may be wake turbulence on landing, you can request another runway—a crosswind usually is much easier to cope with.

Wingtip vortices have a direct tie-in with induced drag. You remember that induced drag was a function of a high coefficient of lift. This means that induced drag is greatest at low airspeeds (high angles of attack). Wing tip vortices are the worst for an airplane with a high span loading (pounds of weight per foot of span) and at low speeds with flaps up.

Avoid flying into wake turbulence at high speeds—enough stress may be imposed on the airplane to cause structural failure. Avoid crossing directly behind a large airplane. If you encounter wake turbulence at altitude, *don't pull up sharply to climb out of it.* Throttle back but don't try to slow up too quickly, because you will be adding stress to the airplane. The most aggressive maneuver you should try is a *shallow* climbing turn. If you are crossing the turbulence at a 90° angle, you'll probably be through it before you have a chance to do anything.

You can see that at altitude the greatest danger is at high speeds where the sudden encountering of turbulence results in overstressing the airplane. On takeoff and landing, the problem is that the airspeed is low and control may be marginal.

If you must cross directly behind a large airplane, go above it if possible (this is assuming that you have time to make up your mind) because (1) the downwash of the wings tends to carry the disturbances downward and (2) you'll be slowing up as you start to climb (Figure 16-7). There's no need to add further stress on the airplane by sharp pull-ups or other radical maneuvers.

Wake turbulence moves downward (and outward as it gets close to the ground). You may encounter downward flows of several hundred feet per minute. Here's an excerpt from the AIM on the subject:

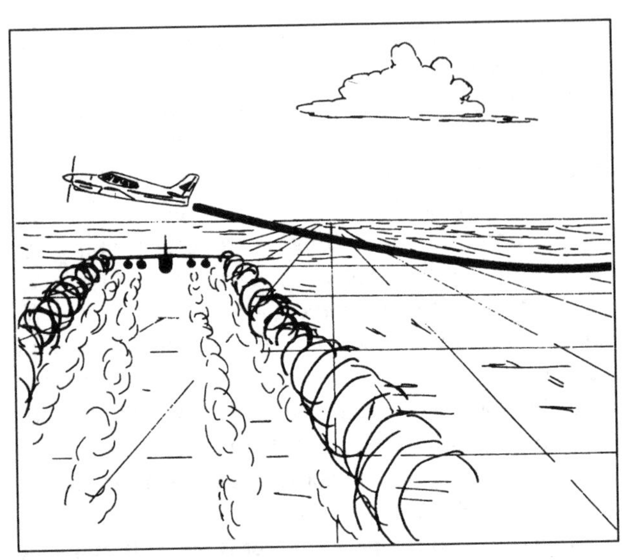

Figure 16-7. If you have time to decide, when crossing behind a large airplane always go above it.

Aeronautical Information Manual— Wake Turbulence Avoidance Procedures

a. Under certain conditions, airport traffic controllers apply procedures for separating IFR aircraft. If a pilot accepts a clearance to visually follow a preceding aircraft, the pilot accepts responsibility for separation and wake turbulence avoidance. The controllers will also provide to VFR aircraft, with whom they are in communication and which in the tower's opinion may be adversely affected by wake turbulence from a larger aircraft, the position, altitude and direction of flight of larger aircraft followed by the phrase "CAUTION—WAKE TURBULENCE." After issuing the caution for wake turbulence, the airport traffic controllers generally do not provide additional information to the following aircraft unless the airport traffic controllers know the following aircraft is overtaking the preceding aircraft. **Whether or not a warning or information has been given, however, the pilot is expected to adjust aircraft operations and flight path as necessary to preclude serious wake encounters.** When any doubt exists about maintaining safe separation distances between aircraft during approaches, pilots should ask the control tower for updates on separation distance and aircraft groundspeed.

b. The following vortex avoidance procedures are recommended for the various situations:

1. Landing behind a larger aircraft—same runway. Stay at or above the larger aircraft's final approach flight path-note its touchdown point-land beyond it.

2. Landing behind a larger aircraft—when parallel runway is closer than 2,500 feet. Consider possible drift to your runway. Stay at or above the larger aircraft's final approach flight path—note its touchdown point.

3. Landing behind a larger aircraft—crossing runway. Cross above the larger aircraft's flight path.

4. Landing behind a departing larger aircraft—same runway. Note the larger aircraft's rotation point—land well prior to rotation point.

5. Landing behind a departing larger aircraft—crossing runway. Note the larger aircraft's rotation point—if past the intersection—continue the approach—land prior to the intersection. If larger aircraft rotates prior to the intersection, avoid flight below the larger aircraft's flight path. Abandon the approach unless a landing is ensured well before reaching the intersection.

6. Departing behind a larger aircraft. Note the larger aircraft's rotation point and rotate prior to the larger aircraft's rotation point. Continue climbing above the larger aircraft's climb path until turning clear of the larger aircraft's wake. Avoid subsequent headings which will cross below and behind a larger aircraft. Be alert for any critical takeoff situation which could lead to a vortex encounter.

7. Intersection takeoffs—same runway. Be alert to adjacent larger aircraft operations, particularly upwind of your runway. If intersection takeoff clearance is received, avoid subsequent heading which will cross below a larger aircraft's path.

8. Departing or landing after a larger aircraft executing a low approach, missed approach, or touch-and-go landing. Because vortices settle and move laterally near the ground, the vortex hazard may exist along the runway and in your flight path after a larger aircraft has executed a low approach, missed approach, or a touch-and-go landing, particular in light quartering wind conditions. You should ensure that an interval of at least 2 minutes has elapsed before your takeoff or landing.

9. En route VFR (thousand-foot altitude plus 500 feet). Avoid flight below and behind a large aircraft's path. If a larger aircraft is observed above on the same track (meeting or overtaking) adjust your position laterally, preferably upwind.

The FAA is continually updating information on wake turbulence; Advisory Circular AC 90-23G (or 23H or later, by the time you read this) covers the actions of wake turbulence and suggests the best ways of avoiding it. Order a copy (it's free). The *Basic Flight Information and ATC Procedures Manual* has a full section on wake turbulence, also.

Personal Note

This writer has encountered serious (is there any other kind?) wake turbulence three times:

1. As the pilot of a Stinson Voyager on final at Memphis, competing with several transports in the pattern, I found myself inverted—I pushed and rolled to recover. (I had been teaching aerobatics that summer.) I chose another runway for landing after that.

2. I crossed the wake turbulence of a B-52 (both of us at cruise), and the up-and-down shaking of my Aztec was memorable, indeed. Fortunately, there was no damage (to the Aztec). I didn't see the B-52 until after the encounter (it was 15 miles away when I hit the wake).

3. Approaching a straight-deck carrier at about 6 K above a stall, I got the benefit of the wake turbulence of another Corsair as it took a wave-off. My airplane hit the deck, fortunately catching a cable with the hook, but ended up gearless (it broke off) in the starboard wingwalk. It was not my finest hour.

Wake turbulence can be a menace to your health.

Summary

Every so often break out the POH of the airplane(s) you are flying, and look through Section 3, Emergency Procedures, to review the steps to take in the event of various problems. You'll be surprised how procedures may have slipped a bit in your mind. You're on the way to becoming a professional pilot and need to be able to make the right moves when needed.

Part Four **Advanced Navigation and Airplane Systems** 4

17 Advanced Navigation

A Review

You may have been flying cross-country primarily by use of navaids or GPS since getting the private certificate (and some pilots carry nothing but IFR en route low-altitude charts on VFR cross-countries—which could pose a problem if the avionics fail), but as an aspiring advanced or professional pilot, you should have more than just the bare bones of VFR navigation. This chapter discusses some points that will help with the commercial certificate knowledge test as well as some techniques to use in actual operations.

In this day of Global Positioning Systems (GPS), it may seem strange to go back to the basics of navigation again. This is appropriate because (1) a pilot should have the basics to fall back on should the latest airplane systems fail and (2) the navigation information in this chapter is gradually being lost because progressions of textbooks drop more of the basics.

It's assumed here that you remember the factors of variation (East is Least and West is Best) and can still read a compass deviation card, but you might get your computer and review a couple of wind triangle problems. For instance,

GIVEN:

True course (TC)—150°
True airspeed (TAS)—120 K
Wind—340° at 15 K
(Winds aloft are given in knots and true directions.)

Find the true heading and groundspeed:

True heading (TH)—149°
Groundspeed (GS)—135 K

The wind is about 10° from being directly on the tail and, remembering the trigonometry from Chapter 1, you can see that the tailwind component is 98.5% (the cosine of 10°) of the wind's value, or 14.77 K (call it 15 K).

Here's another problem:

GIVEN:

True course—276°
True airspeed—157 K
Wind—from 170° at 20 K

Find the true heading and groundspeed:

True heading—269°
Groundspeed—161 K

When you're working a wind triangle, try to visualize the situation. The true course is 276° and the wind is from 170° (true), giving about a 16° advantage behind the wing (Figure 17-1).

The wind triangle is three legs (naturally), consisting of (1) the E-W (earth-wind) line (the wind's path in relation to the earth), (2) the E-P (earth-plane) line, or the true course and groundspeed (what the airplane is doing in relation to the earth), and (3) the W-P (wind-plane) line, or the true airspeed and true heading (what

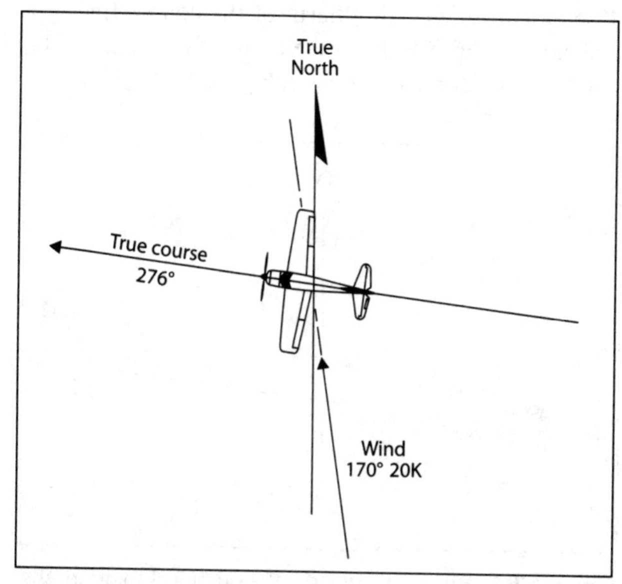

Figure 17-1. Visualizing the problem just cited, you'll note that you'll have a slight tailwind component and will have to correct to the left. The computer can find the details.

the airplane is doing in relation to the air mass it is flying through). If you know the values of two of the lines, the third may be found (Figure 17-2).

The usual navigation problem is like the two just worked: given the true course and wind, you have to find the true heading and groundspeed. As you'll see, in some problems you may be required to work backward to find the wind.

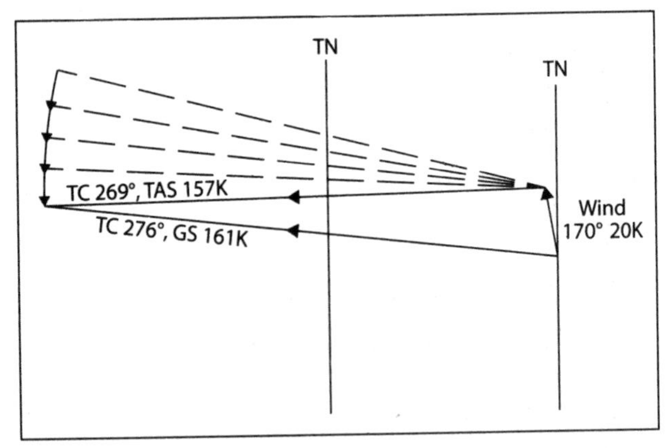

Figure 17-2. The wind triangle. The TAS value (157 K) is swung down to intersect the TC line to get the TH and GS. (TN = True North)

Finding the Wind

For instance, you are on a cross-country and, having no knowledge of the wind, keep the heading indicator (corrected to the compass) exactly on the selected TC of 083°0. The TAS at your altitude is 148 K and after exactly 1 hour of flight, you find yourself over a town 20 nautical miles (NM) north of the course line at a distance of 156 NM from the point of departure. The wind can be found as shown in Figure 17-3.

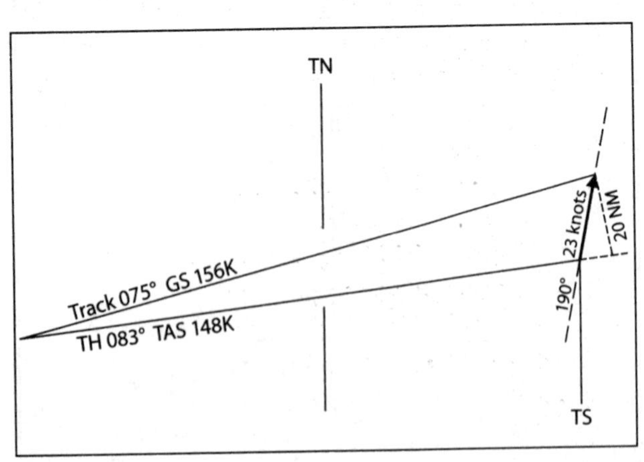

Figure 17-3. Finding the wind—the graphical solution. The implication here is that you've been sitting with your head in the cockpit and haven't looked out since departing an hour ago, but for Pete's sake, it's only an example. TS means True South.

Naturally, you can use your electronic computer, or E-6B computer to find the wind; here is how the problem might look on the knowledge test:

(Question) **01. GIVEN:**
True course (track) .... 075°
Groundspeed .... 156 K
True heading .... 083°
True airspeed .... 148 K

Determine the approximate wind direction and speed:
1—240° at 25 K
2—140° at 12 K
3—190° at 23 K
4—320° at 22 K

You will note that the TH is 8° to the right of the true course, or track, and the GS is 8 K greater than the TAS, so the wind is from the right and slightly behind the airplane. This would eliminate answers 2 and 4 immediately, but the best way to get the answer is to work the problem (Figure 17-4).

You would set up the GS and TC using the permanent-etched circle on the E-6B. To more easily remember: The permanent circle on the wind side of the computer always has to do with the factors that apply to the (solid) ground, such as TC and GS. *You* draw in the penciled circle for the more nebulous air factors such as TAS and TH. The TH is 8° more (right) than the true course, so somewhere along line 1 will be the wind's origin. Also, the TAS is 148 K and where value 2 intersects the drift line is the origin of the wind. Looking at both the drift correction angle and TAS you can keep the length of the intersecting lines to a minimum. The arrow drawn in represents the relative bearing and wind velocity.

Rotate the compass rose until the line intersections are lined up with the TRUE INDEX and slide the grommet to an even number (150 K in Figure 17-4C) to be able to read the wind speed more easily. The result is 190° at 23 K (answer 3).

In any navigation problems be sure the various factors use the same criteria (knots with nautical miles; true headings with other true directions, etc.).

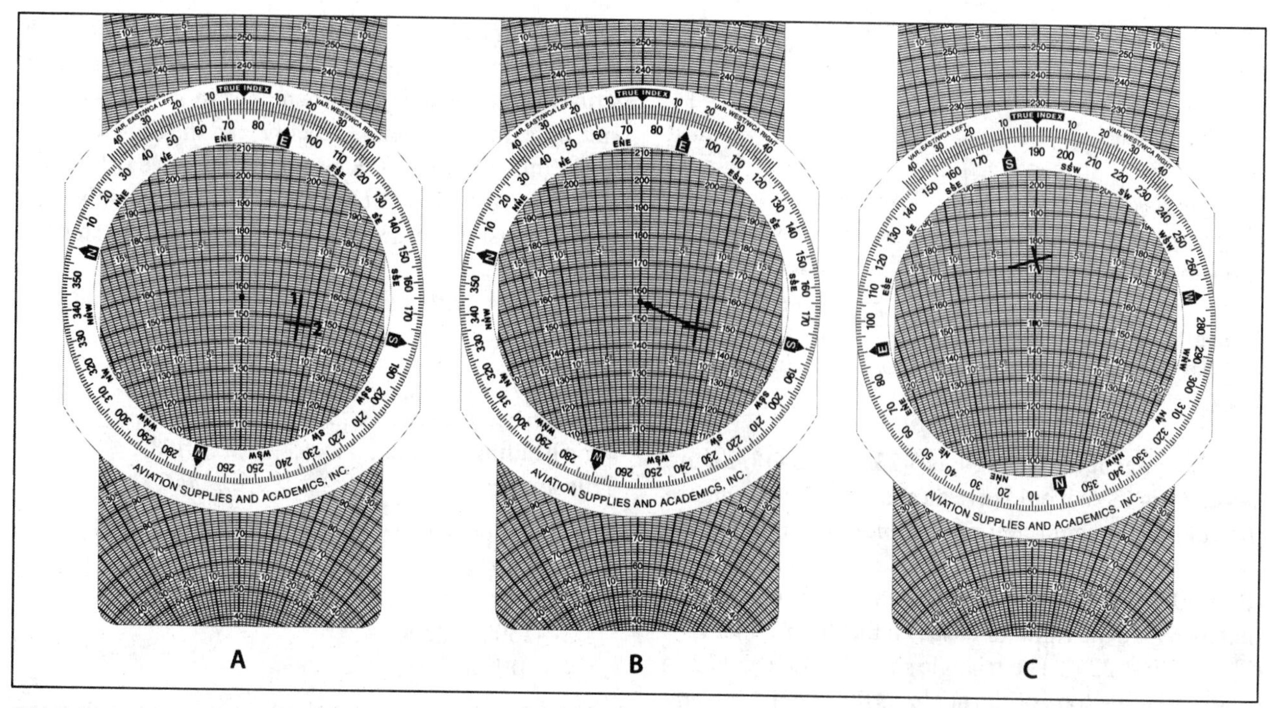

Figure 17-4. Finding the wind speed and direction on the ASA-E6B. **A.** Set up the true course (075°) and groundspeed (156 K) and then draw in the lines representing the drift correction (8° right, 1) and true airspeed (148 K, 2). Their intersection (the cross) is the wind's origin. **B.** You are "filling out" the third side of the triangle when the wind is inserted. **C.** Turn the compass rose until the intersection is lined up with the TRUE INDEX to read the wind speed and direction (190° at 23 K).

Looking at another problem:

02. GIVEN:

True course .... 155°
Groundspeed.................................... 174 K
True heading .... 163°
True airspeed .... 182 K

Determine the approximate wind direction and speed:

1—050° at 20 K
2—080° at 24 K
3—230° at 26 K
4—260° at 28 K

The TC is 155° and the TH is 8° farther right (163°). The GS is 8 K less than the TAS so that a headwind component exists (Figure 17-5).

If you are sharp at trigonometry, you could probably figure out a rough answer before using the computer. For instance, an airplane's GS is 174 K and it has to correct 8° for wind. The ratio between the correction angle (8°) and 60° is the same as the relationship between the GS and the component of wind acting perpendicular to the flight path.

For a rule of thumb in finding angles, use the "rule of 60"—for every mile the airplane is off course at 60 miles, it will be 1° off the course line. (Or for every degree off course at 60 miles, it will be a 1-mile distance from the center line.) Figure 17-6 shows the idea. (Your navigation problems don't usually come out in even 60s, but the relationship still stands.) See Figure 17-5 again: 8°/60 (the correction in degrees) = x/174 K, or, cross-multiplying, the component is 60x = 8 × 174; 60x = 1,392; x = 23.2 K (call it 23 K).

The headwind component is the difference between the TAS and GS, as given, or 8 K. You could solve for the hypotenuse (the wind speed) in the manner shown back in Figure 1-3—squaring the two sides, adding the results, and then taking the square root of that: $(23)^2 + (8)^2 = (\text{wind speed})^2$; $529 + 64 = 593$; wind speed = $\sqrt{593} = 24$ K. As far as the wind speed is concerned, it splits answers 2 and 3, but only 3 requires a correction to the right.

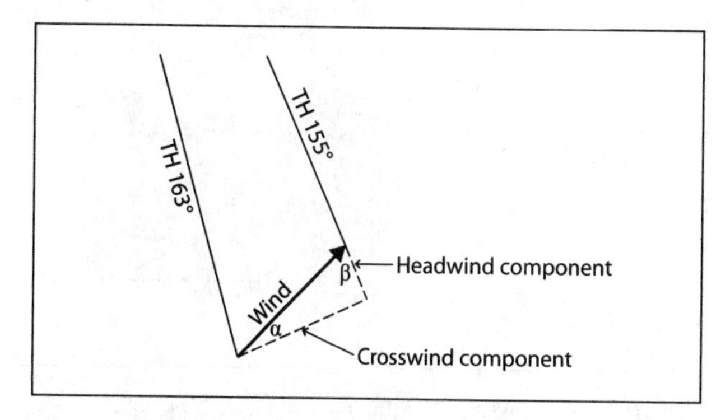

Figure 17-5. A quick sketch shows that the wind is probably from the southwest (around 230°).

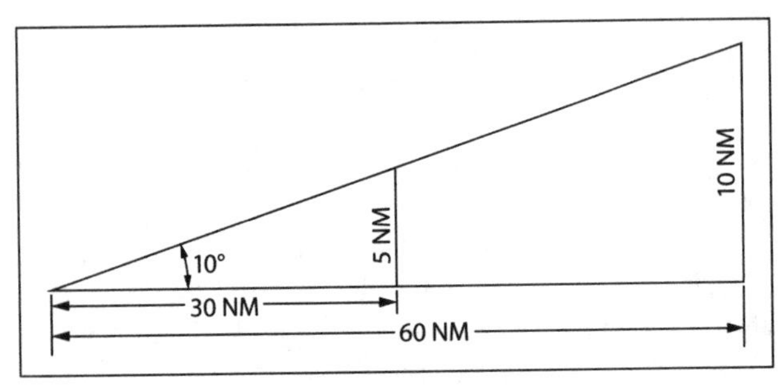

Figure 17-6. The rule of 60: the angle = (10/60) x 60 = 10°, 10° = (10/60) x 60; for 30 miles, 10° = (5/30) x 60 (the angle is exaggerated).

The tangent of the angle is 8/23.2 = 0.3448. Figure 1-8 or a trig table would give an answer, but you can use the rule of 60 again and *approximate* the *small* angle (α): $\alpha = 0.3448 \times 60 = 20.7°$ (call it 21°). The large angle (β) is $90 - \alpha = 90 - 21 = 69°$. The wind is from approximately 69° to the right, or based on the thumb rule, 155° (TC) + 69° = 224°. The triangle shown in Figure 17-5 is a right triangle (one of the angles is 90°), and since any triangle has interior angles totaling 180°, the two other angles must add up to 90°. One angle (α) is 21°, so the other angle (β) must be 69° (rounded off).

The answer by the rule of thumb is wind from 224° at 24 K, which is closest to answer 3. The rule of thumb becomes less and less accurate as an angle of 30° is approached, but it works well for smaller angles as a quick estimate.

Of course, this method is for background purposes and too long and involved for working in a practical situation, but as will be shown later in the chapter, the rule of 60 may be used to quickly find the time required to fly inbound to a VOR or NDB and solve off-course correction problems. Using a computer to solve the problem just discussed, Figure 17-7 shows the steps to take.

Solving another problem for finding the wind:

03. GIVEN:

True course .... 027°
Groundspeed...................................... 138 K
True heading .... 018°
True airspeed .... 146 K

Find the approximate wind direction and speed:

1—040° at 22 K
2—100° at 24 K
3—150° at 22 K
4—312° at 24 K

An analysis shows that the TH (018°) is *less* than the TC (027°), so a left correction for wind is required. This would eliminate the first three answers since in each of those choices the wind is from the *right* of the TC.

Also, since the GS is *less* than the TAS, a headwind component exists, which could be either 1 or 4. Since the wind of 040° is too close on the nose to require 9° correction (and it's on the wrong side to require a left correction), the answer must be 4.

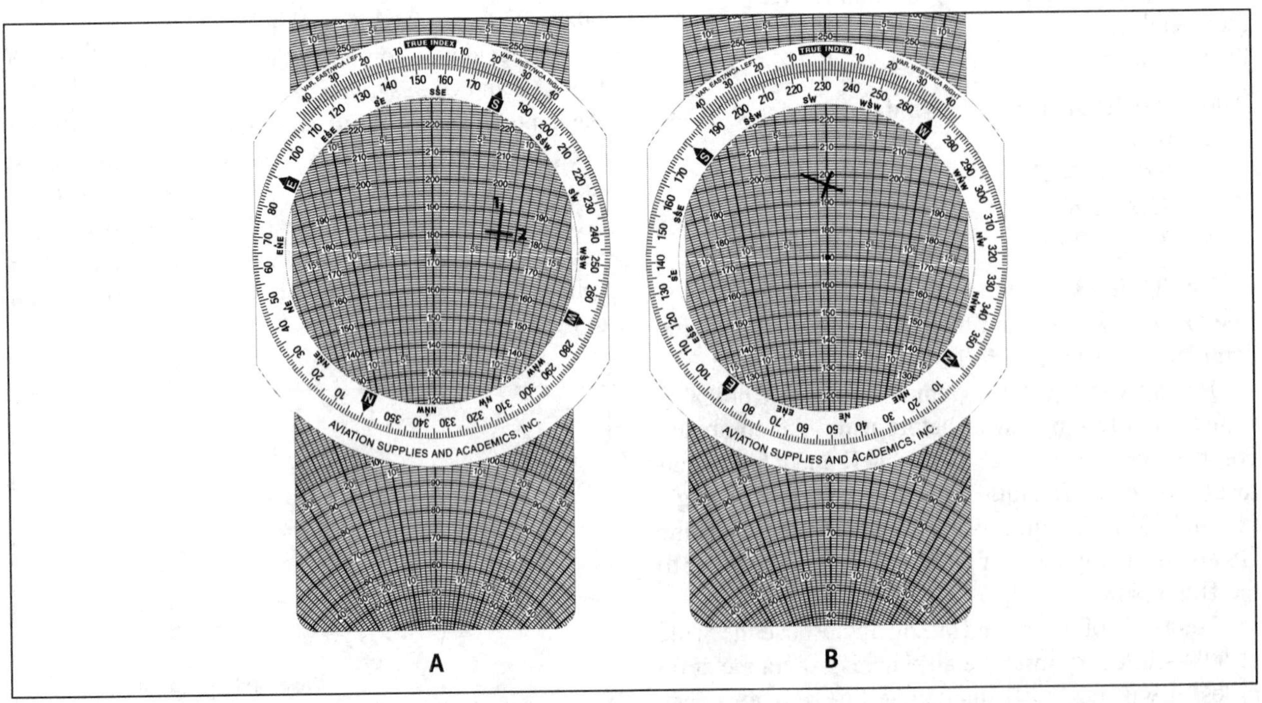

Figure 17-7. Solving for wind. **A.** The TC (155°) and GS (174 K) are set under the grommet and the lines representing an 8° right correction (1) and a TAS of 182 K (2) are drawn in. **B.** The compass rose is rotated to center the cross on the TRUE INDEX to get a wind from 231° at 26 K, which is closest to answer 3.

Answers to all the numbered problems are at the end of this chapter.

04. GIVEN:

TC .... 230°
GS .... 168 K
TH .... 221°
TAS .... 162 K

Determine the approximate wind direction and speed:

1—100° at 28 K
2—123° at 27 K
3—135° at 24 K
4—335° at 28 K

05. GIVEN:

TC .... 335°
GS .... 144 K
TH .... 324°
TAS .... 158 K

The wind is from approximately

1—190° at 36 K
2—220° at 30 K
3—280° at 34 K
4—265° at 32 K

06. GIVEN:

TC .... 295°
GS .... 174 K
TH .... 308°
TAS .... 164 K

Determine the approximate wind direction and speed:

1—046° at 40 K
2—150° at 35 K
3—185° at 40 K
4—350° at 35 K

Radius of Action (Fixed Base)

The problem is basically to determine the time to turn back to the point of departure after flying outbound as far as possible, as might be done on a search mission. The simplest problem is that of a no-wind situation: an airplane cruising at 150 K TAS (and GS) with a fuel supply for 4 hours (plus reserve) can fly how far out before turning back? The simple answer is that the airplane can fly out for 2 hours (300 NM) and fly back the same distance. Of course, the wind complicates the matter somewhat.

The point is that the airplane must fly the same ground distance out and back (it's still the same distance from "here" to "there" as it is from "there" to "here"). The relationship is that of GS out to distance out and GS back to distance back; for the times required outbound and back (without hitting the details), the formula turns out to be

$$TO = \frac{TT \times GSB}{GSO + GSB}$$

(TO = time out, TT = total time, GSO = groundspeed out, GSB = groundspeed back, TB = time back, which equals TT minus TO.)

In the following example, the wind, TAS, and total fuel (or total time) are given. The GS is solved for both legs, and the problem is set up:

TT—4 hours of fuel (not including reserves)
GSO—146 K
GSB—166 K
Departure time—1107Z

Problem: Find the time to turn back toward the departure point (home base) and the distance of that point from the base: TO = (TT × GSB)/(GSO + GSB) = (240 minutes × 166)/(146 + 166) = 39,840/312 = 127.7 minutes (call it 128 minutes). The time to turn back is 2 hours and 8 minutes (2:08) after takeoff, or 1315Z.

You might prefer to work the problem using hours and tenths of hours: 10 = (4.0 × 166)/312 = 664/312 = 2.128 hours, = 2 hours and 8 minutes (rounded off). You would fly out for 2.128 hours at 146 K (GSO) for a distance of 311 NM. Since the distance back should be the same, a check would be as follows: 4.0 hours (TT) – 2.128 hours = 1.872 hours back at 166 K = 311 NM. (The out and back distances don't always come out exactly the same because of rounding off.)

If you use hours and tenths of hours for time, instead of minutes, be sure to convert the decimal to minutes. One of the following questions has a departure time of 1440Z and an answer of 2.27 hours (rounded off) for time outbound. One of the choices is 1707Z (2 hours and 27 minutes later). The 2.27 hours should be converted to 2:16 (0.27 × 60 = 16.2 minutes) for an answer of 1656Z.

07. GIVEN:

TC out .... 065°
TAS .... 180 K
Fuel available .... 3 hr plus reserve
Wind velocity .... 290° at 30 K
Takeoff time 1021Z

Determine the time to turn back toward the departure point:

1—1128Z
2—1140Z
3—1152Z
4—1216Z

Figure 17-8 shows the procedure: TO = (TT × GSB)/(GSO + GSB) = (180 minutes × 158)/(200 + 158) = 28,440/358 = 79.44 minutes (call it 79 minutes, or 1 hour and 19 minutes). Departing at 1021Z, the turn should be made at 1140Z (answer 2). As a double check, see that the distances out and back are the same: time out = 79 minutes at 200 K = 263 NM; time back = 3:00 – 1:19 = 1:41 minutes at 158 K = 265 NM. The slight difference is caused by rounding off to the nearest minute earlier, but you can tell that the answer is correct.

One more example:

08. GIVEN:

TC out .... 300°
TAS .... 150 K
Fuel available .... 4 hr plus reserve
Wind velocity.................................. 250° at 30 K
Takeoff time.................................... 1323Z

Determine the time to turn back toward the departure point:

1—1453Z
2—1507Z
3—1539Z
4—1545Z

Figure 17-9 illustrates the solution: The GS is found to be 129 K outbound and 168 K inbound. Solving: TO = (TT × GSB)/(GSO + GSB) = 40,320/297 = 135.76 minutes (rounded off to 136 minutes). Takeoff time = 1,323 + 2:16 = 1539Z (answer 3). A double check on distances: distance out = 2 hours 16 minutes (or 2.27 hours) at 129 K = 293 miles; distance back = 1:44 at 168 K = 291 miles. Again, the slight difference is caused by rounding off to the nearest minute.

09. GIVEN:

TC out .... 215°
TAS .... 190 K
Fuel available .... 4 hr 30 min plus reserve
Wind velocity.................................. 130° at 20 K
Takeoff time.................................... 1440Z

Determine the time to turn back toward the departure point:

1—1549Z
2—1618Z
3—1656Z
4—1707Z

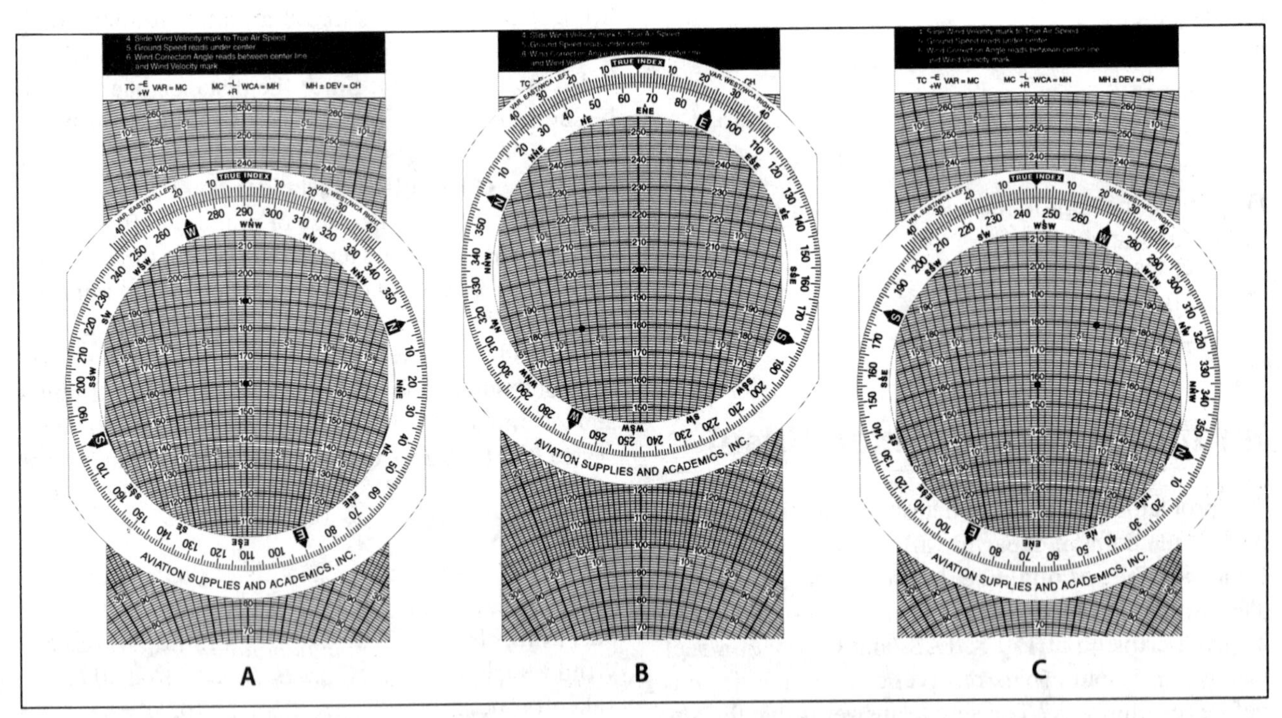

Figure 17-8. Radius of action from a fixed base. **A.** Set up the wind (290° at 30 K). **B.** The wind triangle is solved for the outbound leg (065° TC), getting a TH of 058° and a GS of 200 K. **C.** The return leg, the reciprocal of the outbound leg, is 245°. The TH back is 252° and the GS 158 K.

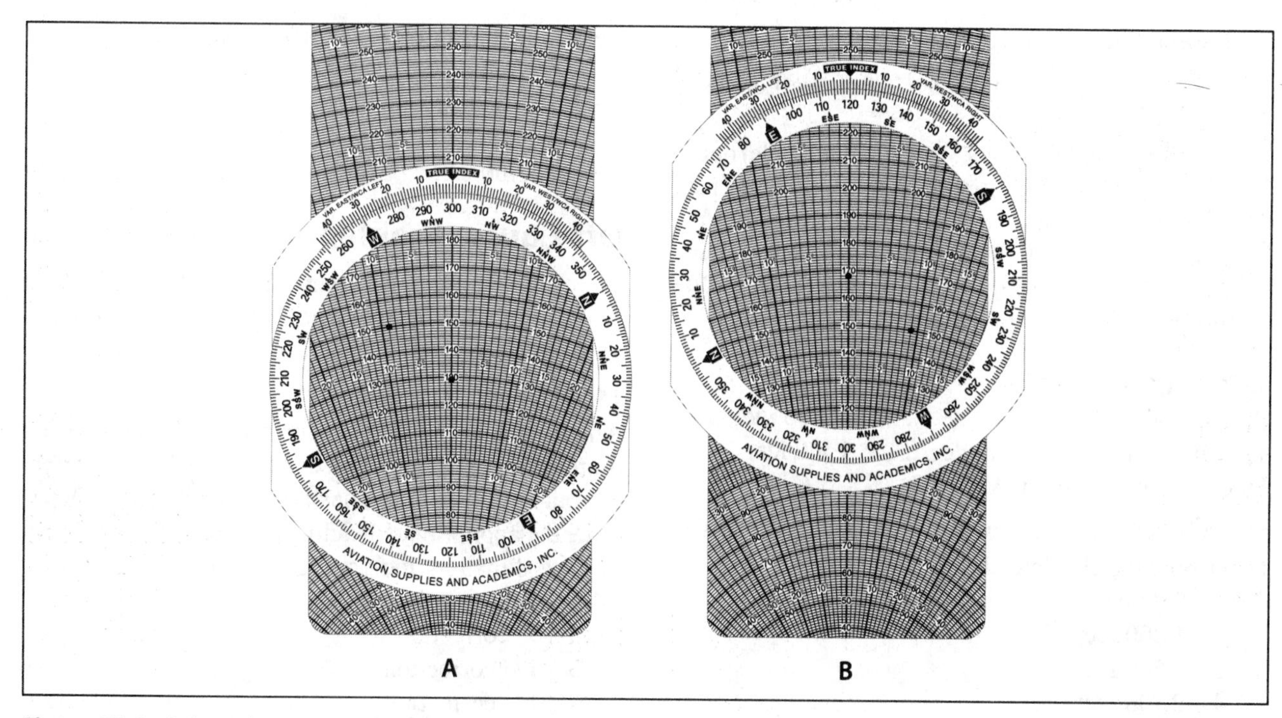

Figure 17-9. Solving for time to turn back toward the departure point. The wind of 250° at 30 K has already been set in. **A.** The groundspeed out (GSO) is 129 K. **B.** The groundspeed back is 168 K. TO = (240x168)/(129+168) = 40,320/297; TO = 136 minutes (rounded off); TO = 2 hours and 16 minutes.

10. GIVEN:

TC out .... 155°
TAS .... 200 K
Fuel available .... 3 hr 30 min plus reserve
Wind velocity.................................. 100° at 15 K
Takeoff time.................................... 0940Z

Determine the time to turn back toward the departure point:

1—1129Z
2—1159Z
3—1217Z
4—1243Z

Correcting for True and Absolute Altitude

Using the circular slide rule side of the E-6B, you can solve for true and absolute altitudes *(true altitude = height above sea level; absolute altitude = height above terrain).*

Several problems follow (indicated altitude equals calibrated altitude for these problems).

11. GIVEN:

Pressure-altitude .... 12,000 feet
Indicated altitude .... 11,500 feet
Free air temperature (OAT) .... -10°C
Terrain elevation .... 10,500 feet

From the conditions given, determine the approximate absolute altitude:

1—500 feet
2—950 feet
3—1,000 feet
4—1,500 feet

Refer to Figure 17-10:

1. Set up the pressure altitude (12,000 feet) opposite the OAT (–10°C).
2. Read the *true* altitude (11,450 feet) on the outer scale opposite the indicated (calibrated) altitude of 11,500 feet on the inner scale.
3. Subtract the terrain elevation (10,500 feet) from the true altitude (11,450 feet) to get 950 absolute altitude (answer 2).

Another problem of the same type:

12. GIVEN (a very hot day):

Pressure-altitude .... 10,000 ft
Indicated (and calibrated) altitude ..... 8,500 ft
Free air temperature (OAT) .... +20°C
Terrain elevation .... 6,500 ft

Determine the approximate absolute altitude:

1—1,500 ft
2—2,795 ft
3—3,150 ft
4—3,375 ft

Refer to Figure 17-11:

1. Set up the pressure altitude (10,000 feet) opposite the OAT (+20°C).
2. Read the *true* altitude of 9,300 feet (outer scale) opposite the indicated (calibrated) altitude of 8,500 feet.
3. Subtract the terrain elevation (6,500 feet) from the true altitude (9,300 feet) to get 2,800 feet (answer 2). You could read the true altitude closer (9,295 feet) to come up with the exact answer.

13. GIVEN:

Pressure-altitude .... 11,000 feet
Indicated (calibrated) altitude .... 9,500 feet
Free air temperature (OAT) .... -15°C
Terrain elevation .... 8,300 feet

Determine the absolute altitude:

1—920 feet
2—1,200 feet
3—1,500 feet
4—2,700 feet

14. GIVEN:

Pressure-altitude .... 13,000 feet
Indicated (calibrated) altitude .... 11,500 feet
Free air temperature (OAT) .... -25°C
Terrain elevation .... 9,600 feet

Determine the absolute altitude:

1—970 feet
2—1,300 feet
3—2,600 feet
4—3,400 feet

Off-Course Problems

The rule of 60 is a good aid for solving this type of problem in its simplest form. For instance, consider a situation as follows:

15. GIVEN:

An airplane is 15 NM off course from the 125-NM en route course position. The distance from that original en route position to the destination is 200 NM. Determine the approximate heading change necessary to fly to the destination (look at Figure 17-12).

1—5° correction
2—7° correction
3—12° correction
4—14° correction

Using the rule of 60, the angle at which the airplane has departed the original course line can be found. Remember that at 60 NM, 1° = 1 NM (and vice versa), and though the numbers here are not even factors of 60, the rule applies. Therefore, if the airplane was 15 NM off the course line at 60 NM, the angle would be

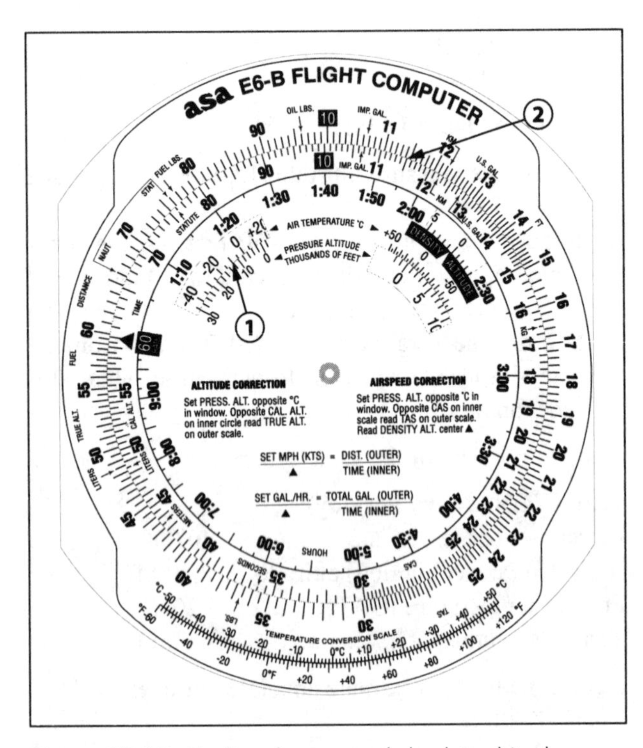

Figure 17-10. Finding the true and absolute altitudes.

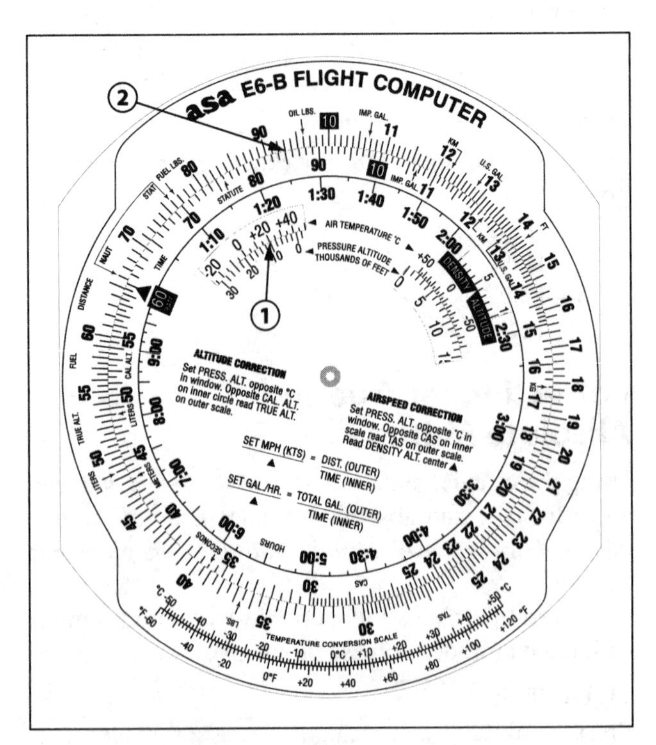

Figure 17-11. Another true altitude problem.

15°, or $\alpha = (15/60) \times 60 = 15°$. However, it's off 15 NM in 125 NM, so the equation would be $(15/125) \times 60 = 7.2°$. This makes sense because if it were off 15 NM at the 120-NM point, the angle would be 7.5°, or $(15/120) \times 60 = 7.5°$. The airplane is off 15 NM at 125 NM so the angle would be slightly less than 7.5°, or in this case 7.2°. The airplane would have to turn this amount *toward* the course to *parallel* it. To return to the course at the destination (or fly directly to the destination), the airplane would have to turn another angle in addition to the 7.2° (Figure 17-13).

To find α_1 (α_1 and α_2 are equal in Figure 17-13 so you can work backward from α_2 if you prefer), the same rule of 60 procedure is applied. Angle β_1 is a function of the ratio of the distance off course (15 NM) to the distance to the destination (200 NM) times 60: $\beta_1 = (15/200) \times 60 = 4.5°$. The total heading change required is $\alpha_2 + \beta_1 = 7.2 + 4.5 = 11.7°$. The correct answer from the four choices listed earlier would be 3.

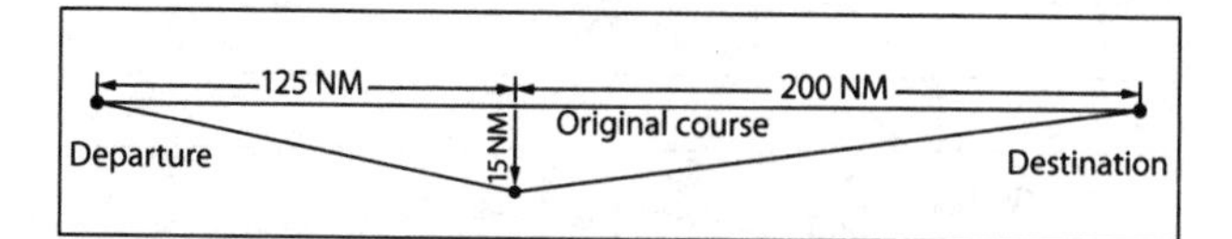

Figure 17-12. An off-course correction problem. The airplane is 15 NM off course from the 125-NM course position (drawing not to scale).

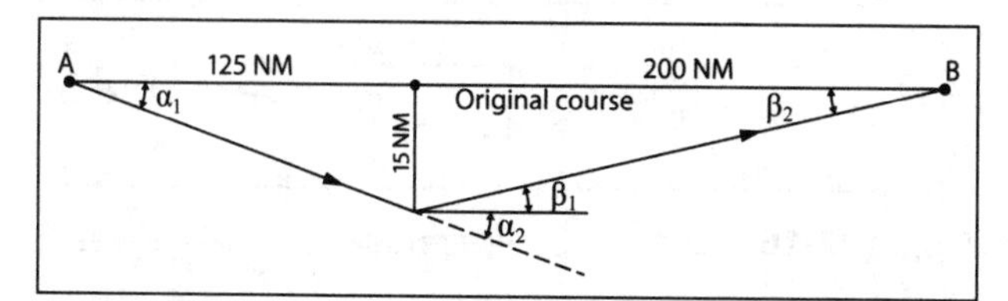

Figure 17-13. Angle α_1 is the off-course angle. Angle α_2, the change in heading required to parallel the original course, equals α_1. Angle β_1 is the additional change in heading to fly to the destination (angles exaggerated and not to scale). $\beta_1 = \beta_2$.

For Math Buffs Only

You could work it out trigonometrically using a calculator and/or trig table: $\tan \alpha_2 = 15/125 = 0.12 = 6.8427734°$; $\tan \beta_1 = 15/200$, $\beta_1 = 4.2891534°$; total change $= 11.131927°$. The answer is closest to choice 3.

At small angles, the sine and tangent are very close and the argument might be that, because of the way the question is stated (leg x is 125 NM), the other leg distance should be found by using the sine of the angle: $\sin \alpha_1 = 15/125$, $\alpha_1 = 6.8921026°$; $\sin \beta_1 = 15/200$, $\beta_1 = 4.301224°$; total heading change $= 11.193325°$, which is still the closest answer to choice 3. Okay, fun's fun—but let's get back to the practical side.

Using the Navigation Computer

You can set up the off-course problem on the circular slide rule side of the computer (Figure 17-14):

16. GIVEN:

At the point where you should be 134 NM along the true course line you find that you are 13 NM off course.

1. How many degrees correction are required to *parallel* the course?
2. If the destination is 104 miles farther, what additional correction is required to fly to the destination?

Set up the problem with the distance (134 NM) on the inner scale opposite the distance off course (13 NM) on the outer scale. The answer, which is read at the 60 index, is approximately 5.8°. How do you know that the answer shouldn't be 58° or 580° or 0.58°? The answer can be approximated by the rule of 60. The 13 NM is slightly less than one-tenth of 134 NM so the angle should be 60/10, or roughly 6° (slightly less). Doing the same for the remaining distance of 104 NM, you find that the angle is 7.5°, for a total of 13.3° heading change to fly to the destination.

Checking it with the rule of 60: $(13/134) \times 60 = 5.8°$ and $(13/104) \times 60 = 7.5°$; $5.8 + 7.5 = 13.3°$. It's not likely that you'll fly this close an angle. One last off-course problem:

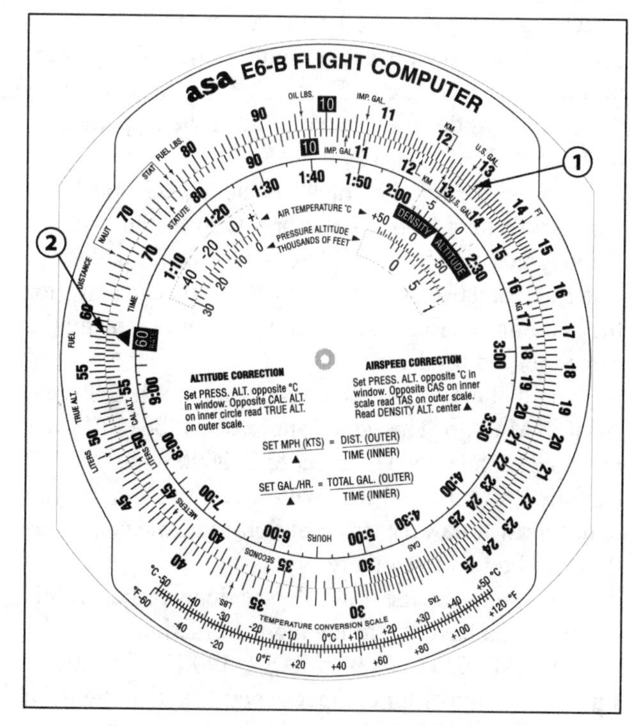

Figure 17-14. Setting up an off-course problem: Set up the distance (134, on the inner scale) opposite the off-course value (13, on the outer scale); then read the degrees (5.8) at the 60 index.

17. GIVEN:

Distance flown .... 160 NM
Distance off course .... 20 NM
Distance to destination .... 220 NM

Determine the total heading correction necessary to fly to the destination:

1—5° correction
2—8° correction
3—13° correction
4—17° correction

Using the rule of 60: to parallel the course, (20/160) × 60 = 7.5°; additional heading change required, (20/220) × 60 = 5.5°; total heading change, 7.5 + 5.5 = 13° (answer 3).

A variation on this is the computation of wind correction required to fly from the point off course to the destination. For instance (a simple approach):

TC from A to B is 090°, TAS is 120 K, total distance (straight line) from A to B is 230 NM.

The wind was predicted to be calm at the (lower) altitude of cruise. After carefully holding the compass heading required to maintain the TH *and* TC of 090°, you find 55 minutes after takeoff that you are over the town of Shiloh, which is 10 miles south of course and a straight line distance of 90 NM from the departure point A (Figure 17-15).

Using the rule of 60 you can estimate that the ground track flown is angled south of the TC by a certain number of degrees. First solve for the GS (using the circular slide rule): in 55 minutes the airplane has traveled 90 NM, for a GS of 98 K.

Next solve for the track or "new" TC you flew, which will be added (in *this* problem) to the original TC: degrees off course = (10/90) × 60 = 6.67° (call it 7°). The track or TC was 090 + 7° = 097°. You can solve for the heading required to get to B (no-wind) by using the same method used earlier.

The distance from the correction point is 230 – 90 = 140 NM to go. The *added* angle would be (10/140) × 60 = 4.3°. The new TC to get to B is 90° – 4.3° = 86° (rounded off). In real life, with a sectional chart, you could draw a new TC from Shiloh to B, measure it as 086°, and go on from there.

First solve for the wind as was done earlier in this chapter. You have the following information:

GS = 98 K, TC = 097°, TAS = 120 K, TH = 090°. Putting this into your computer, you find that the *wind is from 062° at 26 K.*

The next problem is to compute the TH and GS to the destination (B). If you were over Shiloh at 1107Z, at what time should you be over the destination? Putting the wind of 062° at 26 K into the computer, using a TC of 086° and a TAS of 120 K, you find the TH and GS in flying to B: TH = 081°, GS = 96K.

At what time, assuming no change in TAS, should you be over B? The straight-line distance from Shiloh to B is 140 NM. (Working out the trigonometry you'd find that it's really 140.35 mi from Shiloh to B; the angle from the original course is so shallow that the new distance is practically the same.)

The time required at 96 K to travel 140 NM is 88 minutes, or 1:28; 1107Z + 1:28 = 1235Z. You'd be over B at 1235Z.

You can see that over- or undercorrecting for wind could be worked out the same way.

Summing it all up, look at Figure 17-16. If the off-course angle is 10° or less, for practical purposes assume that leg 1 and leg 2 are equal—and the same applies for legs 3 and 4. In the problem just worked, the angles are 7° and 4°, respectively (rule of thumb), so the assumption could be used. (The computer would give closer tolerances than these estimates.)

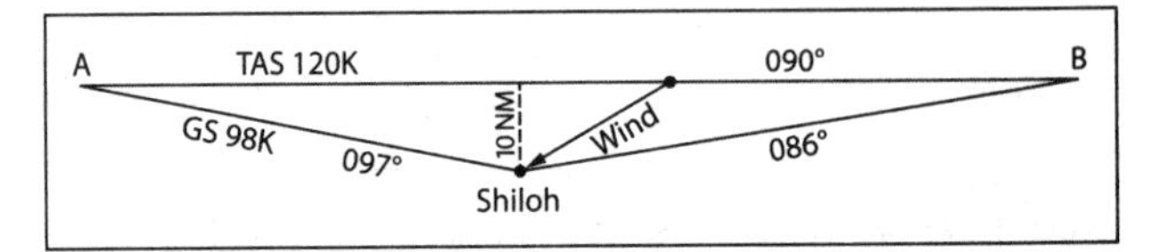

Figure 17-15. Off-course wind correction problem.

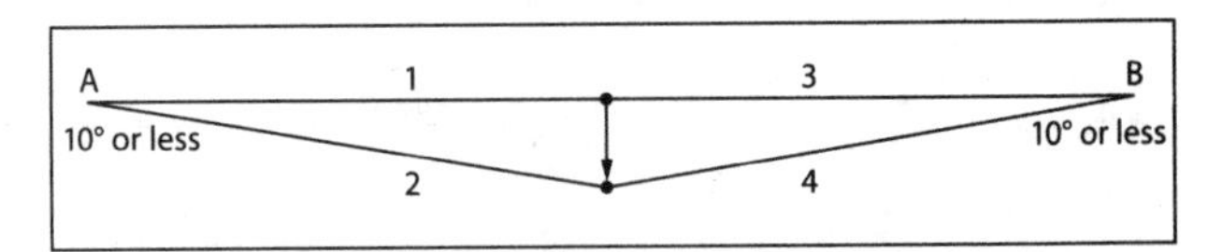

Figure 17-16. Legs 1 and 2 are considered equal here, as are legs 3 and 4.

Computing Climb and Descent Factors

The Climb

There's nothing complicated about computing climb factors (time, fuel, miles covered, TH, GS, magnetic heading, compass heading). Climbs were discussed in Chapter 5, and *The Student Pilot's Flight Manual*, Chapter 24, covers just such a problem as follows:

18. GIVEN:

An airplane departs an airport under the following conditions:

Airport elevation .... 900 feet
Cruise altitude .... 8,500 feet
Rate of climb .... 500 fpm
Average TAS (during climb) .... 130 K
True course .... 220°

Average wind velocity .... 300° at 30 K
Variation... 3°W
Deviation.. –2°
Average fuel consumption
during climb.................................. 14 gal./hour

Determine the approximate time, compass heading, distance, and fuel consumption during the climb:

1—15 min, 242°, 31 NM, 3.5 gal.
2—15 min, 234°, 31 NM, 3.5 gal.
3—15 min, 234°, 26 NM, 3.9 gal.
4—12 min, 234°, 31 NM, 4.2 gal.

First, start at the beginning (always a good idea, if slightly overstated here). The time required to climb from 900 feet to 8,500 feet at 500 fpm is (8,500 – 900)/500 = 7,600/500 = 15.2 minutes. Let that sit for a while.

Work the wind triangle with the known facts and find the TH and GS. The computer finds that TH = 233° and GS = 121 K. The magnetic heading (MH) is TH ± variation = 233° + 3° = 236°. The compass heading is MH ± deviation = 236° – 2° = 234°. The time in climb = 15.2 minutes, the compass heading = 234°, the distance = 15.2 minutes at 121 K = 31 NM (rounded off), and fuel consumption = 15.2 minutes at 14.0 gph = 3.5 gallons. It looks like *choice 2* of the answers gets the nod.

Descent Factors

The descent problem is basically the same except that you must realize that the descent is normally made to the traffic pattern; you might have a set-up such as cruising altitude = 6,500 feet, airport elevation = 700 feet, and traffic pattern altitude = 800 feet.

You'll be letting down to 1,500 MSL (700 + 800) for a descent of 5,000 feet at a given descent rate. You'll be given the average wind and you will work a wind triangle to find the time, compass heading, distance, and fuel consumption during the descent (as was done for the climb problem).

Time Between Bearings

It's likely that you will have an instrument rating before getting the commercial certificate and will have worked on time-and-distance problems using the VOR and/or ADF, but a review might be in order.

The rule of 60 works for both time and distance, since the ratios would be the same in a given situation. Here's a typical problem: Find the time and fuel required to fly to the station after flying perpendicularly through a certain number of degrees of bearing change (Figure 17-17). Using the rule of 60, you'd find that if the airplane in Figure 17-17 took 7 minutes to fly the 10° from A to B, it would require (60/10) × 7 = 42 minutes to fly from B to C, or time between bearings/time to station = bearing change (degrees)/60.

As an example: An airplane changes bearing 10° (Figure 17-17) in 7 minutes. Substituting the numbers in the above formula: 7 minutes/time to station = 10/60. Cross-multiplying: 42 minutes = time to station × 10 = 420/10 = 42 minutes; time to station = 42 minutes.

It's easier to divide 60 by degrees of bearing change and multiply by the result: 60°/10° = 6; 6 × 7 minutes = 42 minutes. For a 15° bearing change, the time multiplier is 60/15 = 4. For a 20° bearing change, the multiplier is 3, etc. Accuracy is lost as angles reach 30°, as indicated earlier.

An airplane using 14.3 gph, flying a time-and-distance problem, has a bearing change of 10° in 8 minutes and 36 seconds. It has just completed its turn and has just headed into the station at exactly 1122:00Z. When is station passage expected and how much fuel will be required to fly to the station under *no-wind conditions?*

The multiplier is 60°/10° = 6. It will take 6 times as long to fly into the station as it did to fly the 10° bearing change (no-wind): 6 × 8.6 = 51.6 = 51 minutes and 36 seconds. At a fuel consumption of 14.3 gph, 52 minutes (rounded off) would require 12.4 gallons of fuel. The time over the station would be 1122:00 + 51:36 = 1213:36Z (1213 + 36 seconds) Z.

There's a lot wrong with calling the time to the station to the nearest second with a wind, and that's why *no-wind conditions* were cited earlier. Figure 17-18 shows why there might be a discrepancy between the predicted and actual time to station. In Figure 17-18 the wind effect shortens the time required to fly the 10° bearing change (because of tailwind) and lengthens the time-to-station figure (because of headwind). You'd get there later than predicted.

Using the rule of 60, if the airplane in Figure 17-18 takes 6 minutes to fly the 10° bearing change, it should get to the station in (60/10) × 6 = 36 minutes. This is the estimate for no-wind conditions, or if the wind is not known. Looking at Figure 17-18, you can see that with

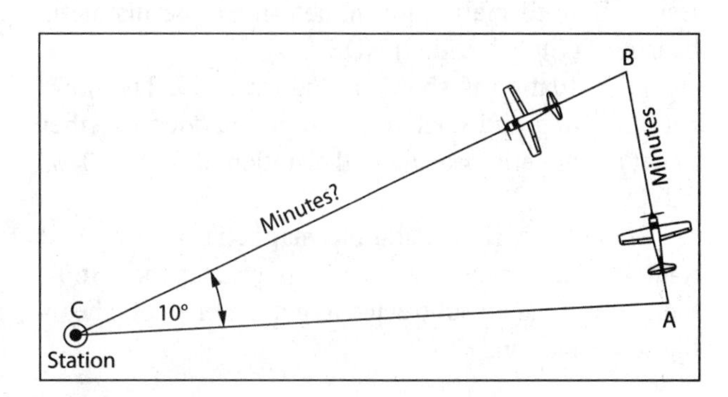

Figure 17-17. Time-to-station problem.

a wind from the opposite direction, the time required to fly the bearing change would be greater and hence the time to fly to the station would be overestimated. (You'd get there earlier than predicted.)

Here's a problem you might find on an advanced FAA knowledge test:

19. GIVEN:
Time between bearings...................... 8 minutes
Bearing change .... 5°
Rate of fuel consumption................... 14 gal. per hr

Calculate the approximate fuel required to fly to the station: 60/5 = 12; 12 × 8 minutes = 96 minutes to the station at 14.0 gallons per hour; fuel consumed = 22.4 gallons.

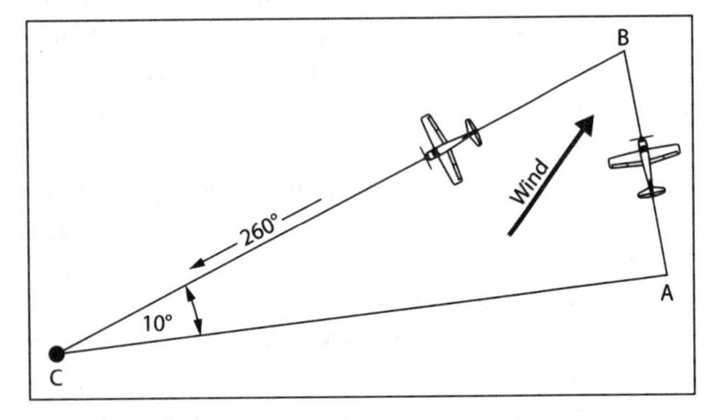

Figure 17-18. The wind can affect time-to-station predictions.

The ADF and Relative Bearings

As you know, ADF problems are usually tougher than VOR work because of the need to include the *relative* bearing of the station in solving magnetic bearings *to* or *from* the station.

A typical problem: You are inbound to VOR A on the 270 radial. (This first sentence is enough to shoot some people out of the saddle when they think that they are inbound on a *course* of 270°.) Your magnetic heading = 078°, your relative bearing to NDB B = 070°. Using the information given, determine the magnetic bearing *to* (italics added) NDB B.

The situation is shown in Figure 17-19. The magnetic heading and relative bearing are added together to get a magnetic bearing to the station of 078° + 070° = 148°.

Remember, if you add the magnetic heading and relative bearing and the answer is greater than 360°, then 360° must be subtracted to get the magnetic bearing to the station.

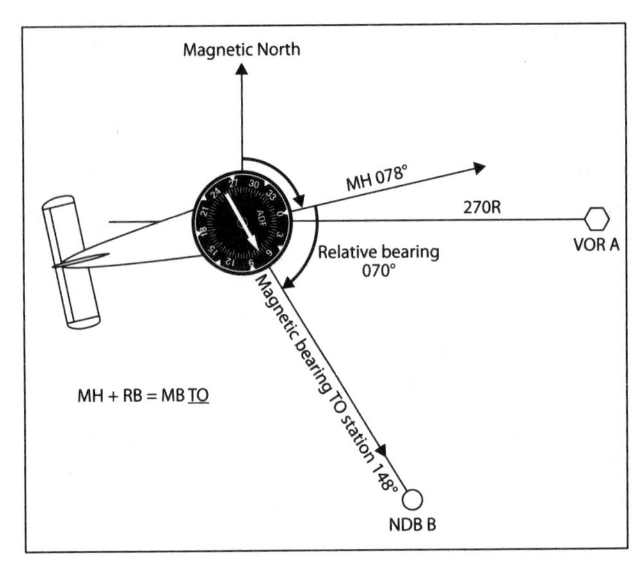

Figure 17-19. Visualizing an ADF problem.

Here's another problem:

20. GIVEN:
Inbound to VOR A............................ 130 radial
Magnetic heading .... 317°
Relative bearing to NDB B
(fixed dial ADF).............................. 215°

Using the information given, determine the magnetic bearing from NDB B (sketch it).

1—165°
2—172°
3—345°
4—352°

The magnetic heading 317° plus the relative bearing 215° = 532°. Subtracting 360°, 532 – 360 = 172° to the NDB. Looking at the answers, 2 has this value, so problem solved—*not at all!*

The requirement was to find the bearing *from* the station as might be used in getting cross-bearings for locating the airplane's position. It's necessary to add or subtract 180° to or from the airplane's bearing to the station to get the answer: 172° + 180° = 352°. Answer 4 is correct.

Carefully read all questions on knowledge tests.

Other Navigation Techniques

No-Wind Plot

If a number of course changes are required during a flight (say, on an overwater search), it would be inconvenient to run a wind triangle for each short leg; a log should be kept of true headings and true airspeeds, however, so that the *air track* may be combined with the known or estimated wind to find the ground position.

Your log might read as follows (Figure 17-20):

You would note the compass heading for each leg and then convert it to TH. After laying out the legs of the air plot to point F, you would extend the wind *from* there—100° for a distance of 40 NM. The wind (air mass) of 280° at 30 K has been acting on the airplane for 81 minutes and has moved the airplane 40 NM, 100° from the no-wind (air) plot at F. If you had worked a wind triangle for each leg and plotted the ground points on the chart, the answer should have been the same. (Distances are rounded off to the nearest mile here.)

Landfall Navigation

This is the technique used if fuel is an important consideration and there are no airports near the destination. During WW II, airplanes ferried from Brazil to Dakar (Africa) didn't have enough fuel for an extended search up and down the barren coastline if landfall was made out of sight of the destination airport. After a very long flight over the ocean with generally poor wind information, at landfall with no references the question was, Which way should I turn to go to the airport—north or south? A wrong turn could mean fuel exhaustion and bellying in on a deserted beach with its attendant problems. One answer was to *make* sure that the airplane was north (or south, as the crew chose) of the desired landfall (Figure 17-21).

The problem was either turning downwind in a strong wind (A) and drifting so far (south in Figure 17-21) that the flight up the coast or river (leg B) was slow (so that the airplane runs out of fuel before getting to the destination), or turning upwind in a strong wind and *not* compensating enough for the wind (leg

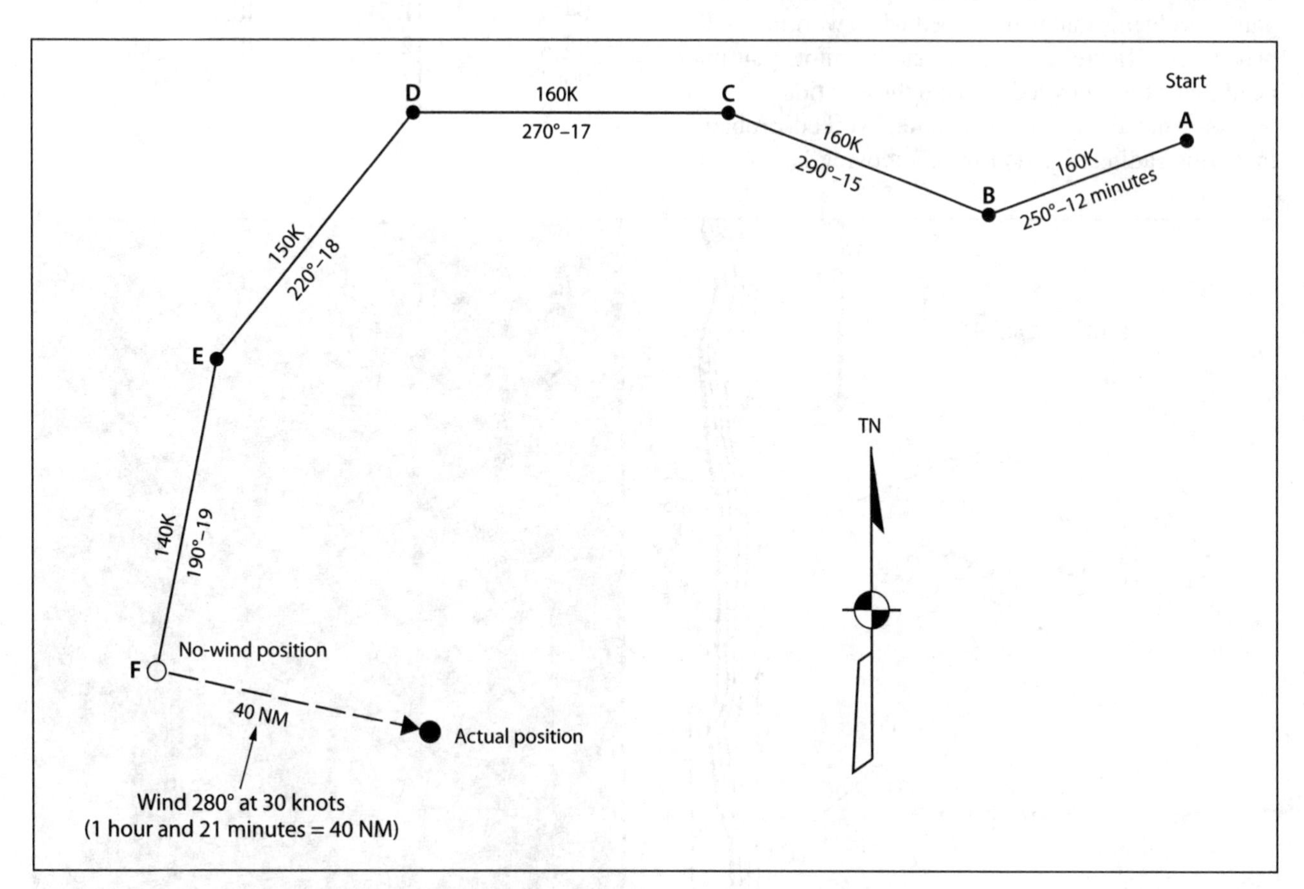

Figure 17-20. No-wind or air plot. The numbers on each leg (12, 15, 17, etc.) are the minutes.

C) (so that the airplane still makes landfall south—out of sight—of the airport and the pilot, because of the "northerly" heading change, turns south and flies away from it). The choice of which way to make the cut would depend on best wind or drift information.

You can use this procedure in finding an airport by a road or river in lowered visibility and in strange territory: Turn to one side or the other, and then after hitting the road or river turn and fly up or down it until reaching the airport (Figure 17- 21, right). Keep the road or river in sight.

Summary

Once in a while review the aspects of navigation you don't normally use, such as making one of your shorter cross-countries using sectional charts and keeping the nav radios and GPS turned off. Also, one of these nights, when there's nothing on TV, you might break out the instruction book for your E-6B or electronic computer and work some of the "other" types of navigation problems that you skipped when working on the private certificate. As a professional pilot, you may need that extra knowledge in a tight situation.

As a naval aviator, this writer worked problems involving radius of action from a moving base (which could also be an alternate airport problem) on a Mark III plotting board. The current computers do not lend themselves so well to this problem, but a graphical solution is described in *Practical Air Navigation* by Lyons (see the Bibliography); though the knowledge is useful at times, it is not critical for the commercial aspirant and is left for study in that book.

It has been noted over the past few years that the basic navigation skills of the average U.S. pilot have slipped and should a nav-radio or GPS receiver fail, in some cases a bona fide emergency would exist even in good VFR conditions. You, of course, are not included with that group. I've used four choices for these problems, unlike the A, B, C choices you'll run into for the FAA Knowledge Test.

Answers to Problems in This Chapter

Answers to problems here include those answers already given as a part of the explanation process.)

01. 3	08. 3	15. 3
02. 3	09. 3	16. 5.8°, 7.5°
03. 4	10. 1	17. 3
04. 2	11. 2	18. 2
05. 4	12. 2	19. 22.4 gal.
06. 1	13. 1	20. 4
07. 2	14. 2	

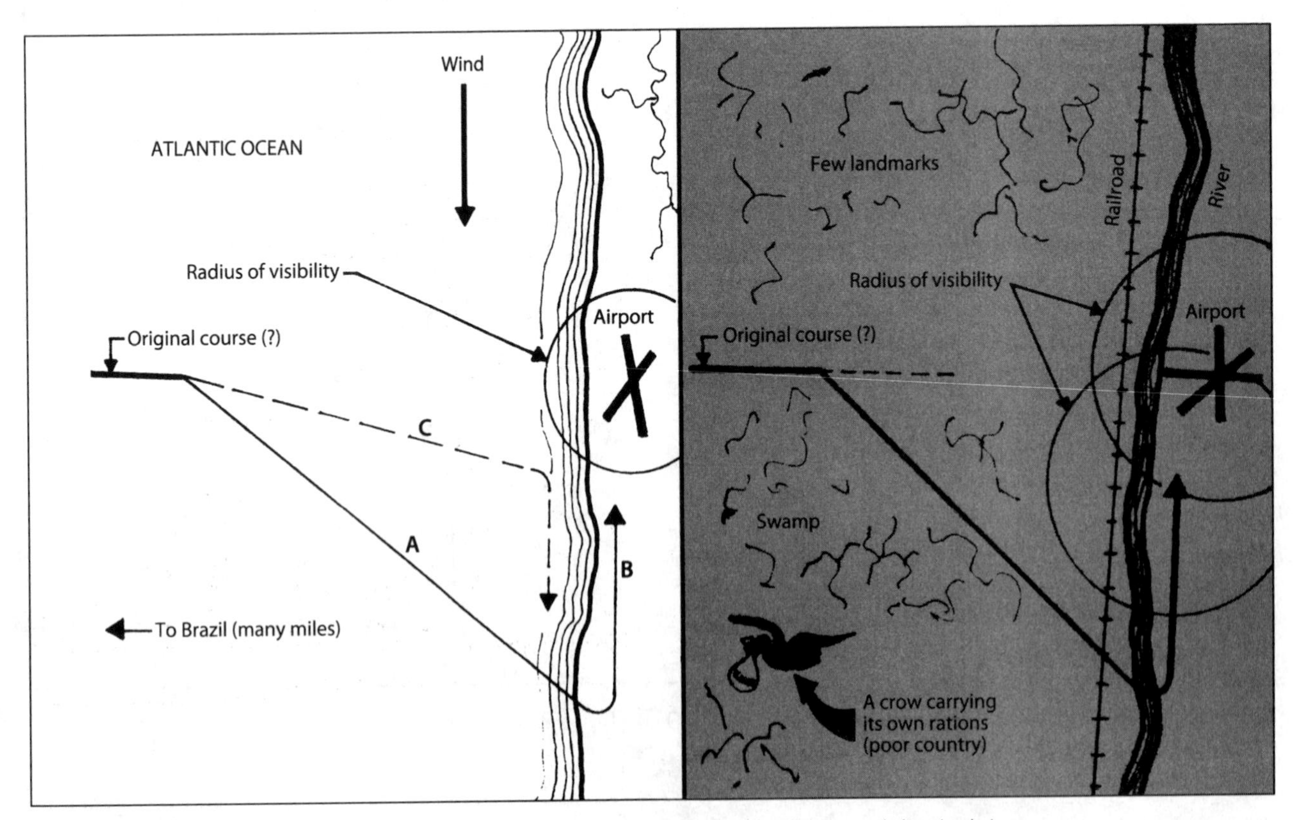

Figure 17-21. Landfall navigation. This is particularly important in periods of poor visibility (right).

18

Altitude and the Pilot

Most of the world's population lives somewhere between 6,000 feet and sea level. Although residents of the Himalayas and Andes perform well above 10,000 feet, most persons' physical and mental performances deteriorate as that altitude is approached and passed. The rate of deterioration naturally depends on the physical condition of the individual.

As Figure 18-1 shows, the troposphere goes up to an average of about 35,000 feet. It varies from about 28,000 feet at the geographic poles to 55,000 feet at the equator and varies with the seasons, being highest in the summer. The troposphere provides most of the weather problems because it contains moisture and has temperature changes and turbulence.

The tropopause is a comparatively narrow band between the troposphere and the stratosphere, and its lower altitude boundary naturally varies with that of the troposphere. The tropopause, on average, is considered to extend from approximately 35,000 to 45,000 feet and be approximately 10,000 feet thick.

Above the tropopause lie the stratosphere and ionosphere, as yet relatively uncrowded with flight traffic. There the normal temperature lapse rate of 3½°F or 2°C no longer exists, and the temperature remains a constant –67°F above 35,000 feet. The jet stream is found in the upper tropopause and in the stratosphere.

Oxygen Requirements

Oxygen makes up about 21% of the atmosphere, nitrogen is 78%, and various inert gases such as argon fill out the rest of the mixture.

This ratio of gases remains constant up to about 70,000 feet. However, physiologists are more interested in the partial *pressures* of the air acting on the pilot. At sea level, the total pressure is 760 mm of mercury. The lung air sacs are 100% saturated with water vapor at a body temperature of 98.6°F. Physiologists have determined that a water vapor pressure of 47 mm of mercury is present in the lungs with this body temperature and does not vary with the altitude at which the pilot is operating. This vapor pressure has to be subtracted from the pressure of inhaled air. The available atmospheric pressure at sea level is 760 mm. When the lung water vapor pressure is considered, there will be a loss of about 6.2% of the available intake (47/760 = 6.2%). At 12,000 feet the available atmospheric air pressure is 483 mm, and the constant lung water vapor pressure of

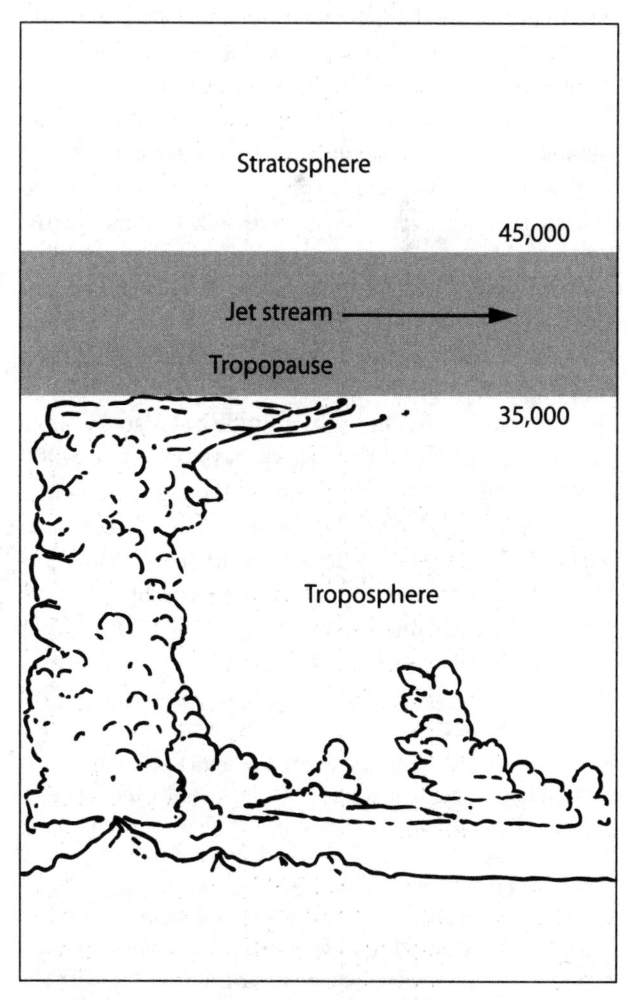

Figure 18-1. The atmosphere.

47 mm takes a relatively bigger bite out of the available air pressure (about 9.8%).

Figure 18-2 shows a good summary of the usable atmosphere oxygen (O_2) at sea level and at 12,000 feet pressure-altitude. (The O_2 pressure available is rounded off to 20% for each altitude.)

The lungs clear the blood of carbon dioxide (CO_2, which is the gaseous by-product of metabolism). Under resting conditions, the lung air sacs contain 40 mm CO_2 pressure. Note that this is another constant regardless of altitude and takes a comparatively greater amount of the available atmospheric pressure at 12,000 feet.

The brain needs a continuous irrigation of 96% O_2 saturation for peak mental function. A saturation of 87% allows acceptable mental performance in a normal individual but is getting close to marginal. (Sometimes it feels as if you're mentally operating at 18,000 feet when sitting on the ground if you've had a full day of flying or not enough rest lately.) So 12,000 feet is as high as you should go without supplemental O_2.

The CO_2 pressure (40 mm) is in an at-rest condition. When you're flying you'll be performing some activity, if only adjusting the autopilot, and the CO_2 level might be higher than 40 mm. Your physical condition has a great deal to do with your reaction to altitude operations. If you're tired, have been partying too much the last few nights, are a heavy smoker, or have been taking antihistamines, you can expect that your tolerance to altitude operations will be lowered, at least temporarily. You should consider your passengers' health also; they may have heart disease, poor circulation, or lung problems such as emphysema or asthma. If you do charter work after getting your commercial certificate, you'll find that a dependable O_2 system can not only give you more flexibility in choice of altitude but also can be a valuable aid if one of your passengers finds that 8,000 or 9,000 feet is *his* or *her* limit without supplemental O_2. Of course, it depends on the size of the airplane and the type of trips you'd be making as to the economics of installing a permanent type of O_2 system, but portable systems are available for specific trips. 14 CFR §91.211 (Supplemental Oxygen) states:

(a) *General.* No person may operate a civil aircraft of U.S. registry—

(1) At cabin pressure altitudes above 12,500 feet (MSL) up to and including 14,000 feet (MSL), unless the required minimum flight crew is provided with and uses supplemental oxygen for that part of the flight at those altitudes that is of more than 30 minutes duration;

(2) At cabin pressure altitudes above 14,000 feet (MSL) unless the required minimum flight crew is provided with and uses supplemental oxygen during the entire flight time at those altitudes; and

(3) At cabin pressure altitudes above 15,000 feet (MSL) unless each occupant of the aircraft is provided with supplemental oxygen.

(b) *Pressurized cabin aircraft.*

(1) No person may operate a civil aircraft of U.S. registry with a pressurized cabin—

(i) At flight altitudes above flight level 250 unless at least a 10-minute supply of supplemental oxygen, in addition to any oxygen required to satisfy paragraph (a) of this section, is available for each occupant of the aircraft for use in the event that a descent is necessitated by loss of cabin pressurization; and

(ii) At flight altitudes above flight level 350 unless one pilot at the controls of the airplane is wearing and using an oxygen mask that is secured and sealed and that either supplies oxygen at all times or automatically supplies oxygen whenever the cabin pressure altitude of the airplane exceeds 14,000 feet (MSL), except that the one pilot need not wear and use an oxygen mask while at or below flight level 410 if there are two pilots at the controls and each pilot has a quick-donning type of oxygen mask that can be placed on the face with one hand from the ready position within 5 seconds, supplying oxygen and properly secured and sealed.

(2) Notwithstanding subparagraph (b)(1)(ii) of this section, if for any reason at any time it is necessary for one pilot to leave the controls of the aircraft when operating at flight altitudes above flight level 350, the remaining pilot at the controls shall put on and use an oxygen mask until the other pilot has returned to that crewmember's station.

UTILIZABLE ATMOSPHERIC OXYGEN

	Sea Level	*12,000 feet*
Available Atmospheric Air Pressure	760 mm Mercury	483 mm Mercury
Lung Air Sac Water Vapor	−47	−47
Pressure of Remaining Lung Gases	713	436
Oxygen Portion (20%)	x0.20	x0.20
Oxygen Pressure in Air Sac	143	87
Minus Air Sac Carbon Dioxide	40	40
Oxygen Pressure in Lung Air Sacs	103 mm Mercury	47 mm Mercury
Provides Arterial Blood Oxygen % of	96%	87%

Figure 18-2. Utilizable atmospheric oxygen. *(FAA AM 66-28 Oxygen in General Aviation, Stanley R. Mohler, M.D.)*

If your airplane is unturbocharged, operations above 12,000 feet will be rather disappointing anyway. (Note that the regulations say 12,500 up to 30 minutes.)

Some Physiological Facts

Okay, now you're convinced that it's not wise to fly in an environment higher than 12,000 feet pressure-altitude without supplemental oxygen. (Note the use of the term *environment*—if your cabin is pressurized to an altitude of 12,000 feet or below, you can be flying at an actual altitude of, say, 45,000 feet and doing just fine as long as the system works—but more about the airplane systems requirements in the next chapter.)

Each time you *inhale* (at 12 to 16 times per minute) you pull in about 1 pint of air (500 cc), bringing O_2 into your body. Each *exhalation* is getting rid of CO_2. The inhaled O_2 passes into the blood, and CO_2 is released, moving from the blood to the lung air sacs. The blood continually takes the fresh O_2 to the tissues and carries the CO_2 back to the lungs for exhalation.

Gases tend to move from high to low pressures. Blood entering the lung has a comparatively high CO_2 pressure, so the CO_2 is passed out through the lung membrane and exhaled. The incoming air has a high O_2 pressure and is absorbed through the membrane to join the blood.

The balance between O_2 and CO_2 in the body is maintained by sensing devices in the brain that react to CO_2 partial pressure. If the CO_2 partial pressure is too high, the rate of breathing (and the volume of air intake) is increased so that more CO_2 is exhaled. If the CO_2 partial pressure is too low the opposite occurs. Another system located in the large arteries near the heart checks the partial pressure of O_2.

If you get anxious or scared, you could develop hyperventilation—breathing too fast or too deeply and losing an excessive amount of CO_2. You might feel dizzy, drowsy, or lightheaded and experience tingling of the fingers and toes, increased feelings of body heat, blurred vision, a rapid heart rate, muscle spasm, nausea, and even unconsciousness. Except for the last two items, hyperventilation has much the same symptoms as an extreme case of teenage love, but hyperventilation is the more dangerous of the two when flying an airplane. The word is to slow down your rate of breathing. In extreme cases, breathing into a paper bag will build up the CO_2 again, reusing the CO_2 you just breathed out.

Oxygen Equipment Types

Continuous flow—This is considered the simplest system and is normally used from ground level to 25,000 feet (or higher, with more advanced mask and regulator designs, according to the FAA pamphlet "O_2 over 10".) This system may consist of a carry-on O_2 bottle with a control knob for setting a predetermined O_2 flow rate, and, of course, an oxygen mask. Much of the O_2 was lost around the edges of the earlier general aviation "disposable" masks, but designs have improved considerably.

The continuous-flow system could be a fixed-type regulator with the console in the cabin (the O_2 bottle is *usually* in the baggage compartment or an area where it can easily be replenished on the ground). The regulator may have several outlets for plugging in hoses and masks (Figure 18-3).

The *diluter-demand system*, which was first widely used in WW II fighters, is designed to give different amounts of air and O_2, as required by altitude (Figure 18-4). As the cabin altitude increases (cabin air pressure, without pressurization, is the same as that outside) or the atmospheric pressure decreases, whichever way you want to look at it, the pilot's inhalation will bring in a higher percentage of O_2 until, at 30,000 feet, it reaches 100% O_2. Usually the system has two settings: NORMAL, for the condition just discussed, and 100% OXYGEN, for use anytime the pilot thinks it's necessary (for instance, getting fumes through the cabin air-O_2 mix on the normal setting). There is usually an emergency valve on the system that turns on a steady flow of O_2 for emergency use (if you're about to pass out from lack of O_2 on the other two settings and need

Figure 18-3. Continuous-flow system. This is generally used from ground level to 25,000 feet (or higher with more advanced masks and regulator designs).

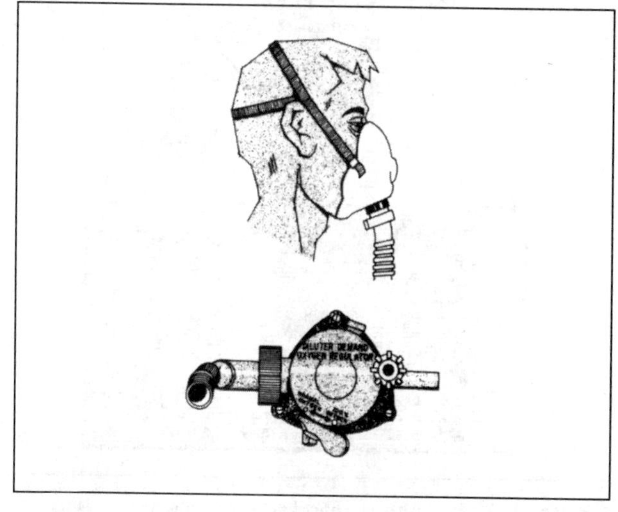

Figure 18-4. The diluter-demand system. This is suggested for operations at 25,000 to 35,000 feet. *(FAA pamphlet "O_2 over 10")*

to get perked up before it's too late—but more about that later).

The *pressure-demand* system is used for operations in the 35,000- to 45,000-ft level (unpressurized cabin) where the diluter-demand system is unable to keep up the pressure for O_2 absorption into the lungs and also blood O_2 saturation (Figure 18-5). You'd need this type of equipment in case of decompression when operating a pressurized airplane at this altitude range.

You don't necessarily have to use all three systems for sea level to 45,000-ft operations. But the top altitude listed for each is the maximum at which it would normally be used.

When breathing normally without an oxygen mask, or using the demand-diluter O_2 system, you do the work when you inhale; the air is pulled in and the normal elasticity of the lungs forces it out. The first time you use a pressure-demand system, you almost have to learn to breathe again, consciously breathing out against the pressure coming into the mask. For some people the first encounter can be claustrophobic, one pilot describing his introduction to the system said, "It seemed that every time I relaxed a little, I got a lungful of oxygen, whether I needed it or not!" Some of your passengers may get a closed-in feeling or one of being unable to get their breath when using the oxygen mask the first time with any system. You may have to do some extra reassuring and tell them that this feeling does happen to some people and with familiarity the feeling should pass. Their worry should be whether they are getting sufficient (or any) O_2; depending on the type or model of equipment you're using, an indicator showing that O_2 is flowing can be an aid.

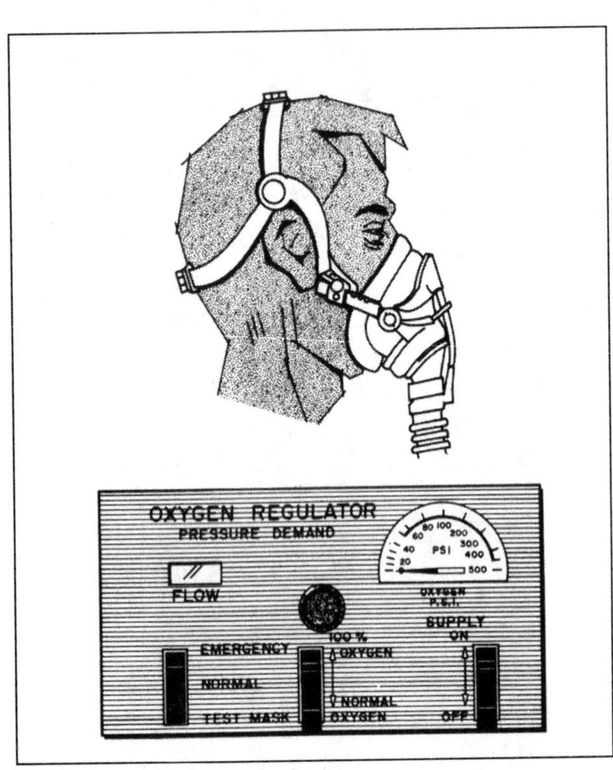

Figure 18-5. Pressure-demand system. This system is for operations from 35,000 to 45,000 ft. *(FAA pamphlet "O_2 over 10")*

Cannulas—If you've ever been in a hospital using oxygen or ever visited a patient who is on oxygen, you are familiar with the cannula system. Its use for aircraft oxygen systems is a fairly recent innovation, and it is light and simple. There are restrictions to its use as indicated in 14 CFR §23.1447, and the FAA requires that there is a standby face mask on the aircraft for each cannula device used.

The system is basically a face piece with nostril inserts and a tube to the oxygen source. The same warnings apply to cigarette smoking and mixing oil and oxygen. Usually there is a warning about using the cannula above 18,000 feet and in high stress situations where the breathing rate increases with work load. One well-known oxygen equipment manufacturer and supplier suggests that during actual IFR operations above 15,000 feet a cannula device not be used, but a normal face mask be worn because of its higher flow rate. (See the Bibliography for the address for more information on this.)

If your airplane has permanent O_2 equipment, it should be a part of the preflight check even if you are only planning a trip on a CAVU day at lower altitudes. If you make checking it a habit, you won't get caught short sometime when you need to go high to avoid turbulent weather.

Carbon Monoxide

Carbon monoxide (CO) is produced by incomplete burning of the engine exhaust and is most commonly found in aircraft cockpits when there is a leak in the exhaust manifold inside the cabin heater shroud. If the cabin heat is on, the CO is piped into the cockpit and, since it has no smell, it can be detected only by special equipment.

CO is concentrated in the blood as a carboxyhemoglobin complex that cannot transport oxygen. Since CO binds the hemoglobin 200 times greater than oxygen, it is essential to avoid toxic levels. One of the first symptoms (a slight headache) of CO intoxication occurs at 10% blood level; at 20% you develop a throbbing headache, and at 30% a severe headache. Vision starts to decrease and you become irritable, dizzy, or nauseous.

The possibility of detecting these symptoms before they impair your judgment on a long high-altitude flight are slight. If, however, you are on 100% oxygen you shorten the half-life of carboxyhemoglobin from 6 hours to 1 hour. Furthermore, if the mask is tight fitting you will not be breathing any CO. So if your passengers complain of headaches, dizziness, and/or nausea, you should all go on 100% oxygen at once.

Know your O_2 system. A full bottle won't do you any good at altitude if the valve is OFF—and it's in the baggage compartment or some other inaccessible place.

Know the hours of O_2 available for the number of passengers for various pressures for your system. Figure 18-6 is a table of the duration of a particular full system for various pilot and passenger combinations.

Crew	Passengers	Oxygen Supply Range in Hours
1	0	25.76
1	1	14.72
1	2	10.30
1	3	7.93
1	4	6.44
1	5	5.42
1	6	4.68
1	7	4.12
2	0	12.88
2	1	9.37
2	2	7.36
2	3	6.07
2	4	5.15
2	5	4.48
2	6	3.96

Figure 18-6. Oxygen duration chart.

Problems at High Altitudes

Your general health should be good if you are going to fly at high altitudes; a person who is overweight and never exercises can expect problems.

Tobacco and alcohol can raise your "apparent" altitude by several thousand feet:

Actual Altitude (ft)	Physiological Altitude (ft)
Sea level	7,000 (+7,000)
10,000	14,000 (+4,000)
20,000	22,000 (+2,000)

From this information it would seem that smokers and non-smokers are the same at altitudes above 20,000 feet, but physiological evidence doesn't back this up.

For night flying, it's suggested that O_2 be used from 5,000 feet for better vision. (Night fighters go on 100% O_2 from the surface up.)

If you're tired or stressed or using certain drugs, your tolerances to hypoxia will be low or practically nonexistent.

Hypoxia

The problem you'd most expect is hypoxia, or lack of O_2 at the tissue level. There are several types of hypoxia, one being caused by an *anemic* condition, so an individual can have trouble even at sea level. Anemia may be caused by a disease or by loss of blood through accident or overenthusiastic blood donating. The average healthy person recovers from a blood donation in a few hours, but as a rule 72 hours is the minimum time after a donation before flying as pilot in command.

Hypoxic hypoxia is the type that could occur at high altitudes. Some of your passengers might need more O_2 than you are using because of lung problems such as emphysema, bronchitis, or other conditions.

If your O_2 system goes haywire or pressurization is lost, you'll have a certain amount of useful-consciousness time in which to put on an oxygen mask or open another valve, descend, etc. (Figure 18-7). The rate of change for useful-consciousness time starts to level off as higher altitudes are reached. For instance, the 3,000-ft change between 22,000 and 25,000 feet shortens the time by about 180 seconds, whereas the 25,000-ft change from 40,000 to 65,000 feet only shortens it an additional 6 seconds.

How do you recognize the symptoms of hypoxia (Figure 18-8)? People react differently, but a person's particular symptoms are much the same each time, so once you've experienced hypoxia you can recognize it later (assuming, of course, that the first time was under controlled conditions such as in an altitude chamber so you survived to experience it again.)

The problem is that once hypoxia is well developed, a feeling of lethargy or well-being may cause you to ignore the warning signs such as added difficulty in computing ETAs or reading back clearances. One jet

Altitude	Useful Consciousness
22,000 feet	5 minutes
25,000 feet	2 minutes
28,000 feet	1 minute
30,000 feet	45 seconds
35,000 feet	30 seconds
40,000 feet	18 seconds
65,000 feet	12 seconds

Figure 18-7. Time of useful consciousness at various altitudes, based on O_2 circulation time plus the amount necessary in the brain to keep it functioning. *(Aircraft Division United States Steel)*

Symptoms of Hypoxia		
Altitude	Time of Exposure	Symptoms
10,000 to 14,000 feet	several hours	Headache, fatigue, listlessness, nonspecific deterioration of physical and mental performance
15,000 to 18,000 feet	30 minutes	Impairment of judgment and vision, high self-confidence, euphoria, disregard for sensory perceptions, poor coordination, sleepiness, dizziness, personality changes as if intoxicated, cyanosis (bluing)
20,000 to 35,000 feet	5 minutes	Same symptoms as "15,000 to 18,000 feet" only more pronounced with eventual unconsciousness.
35,000 to 40,000 feet	15 to 45 seconds	Immediate unconsciousness (with little or no warning!)

Figure 18-8. Some common symptoms of hypoxia. *(Aircraft Division United States Steel)*

fighter pilot who had a close shave at 35,000 feet when his oxygen hose inadvertently became disconnected noted that he saw the "blinker" (the indicator of proper O_2 flow) wasn't working but "it didn't seem to make much difference." His erratic flying showed problems, his wingman's radio calls alerted him to go on emergency O_2, and things then got back to normal. There have been cases of fighter pilots in an advanced stage of hypoxia who haven't responded to such calls and crashed. While you can make a rapid recovery from hypoxia after the proper O_2 flow is established (15 seconds), there may be some disorientation and dizziness for a time. A person who has had a bad case of hypoxia may not remember being unconscious.

If you are going to be a pilot in command of an airplane capable of operating a high altitudes, it's a good idea to get a checkout in the altitude chamber at the FAA Center at Oklahoma City or a military installation near you. Check with your local Flight Standards District Office for a list of these military facilities and the procedure in scheduling a checkout.

If possible, while under supervision in the chamber, take off your mask and see the effects of hypoxia on *you*. The supervisors may have you name the suits of various playing cards or have you write your name and address several times in succession to check the deterioration of your mental and physical processes. (You'll start well but soon will forget how to spell your name or will stare at a big black ace of spades trying to figure out the suit.) The supervisor will put your mask on before things go too far. The thing about hypoxia is that generally it's not an uncomfortable feeling and can induce a euphoria that interferes with the instinct for survival. You'll have to *reason* that O_2 is needed, even though you "feel fine."

Hypoxia increases fatigue even after recovery.

Dysbarism

Dysbarism is a big nonspecific word used earlier for body gas problems, whether trapped in the blood or in body cavities, such as sinuses, intestines, stomach, or middle ear.

You've probably had some trouble at one time or another with clearing your ears on a letdown, particularly if you had a cold. In extreme conditions, you may have had trouble in a climb, even in the low-powered types of airplane you flew as a student or private pilot. You can well imagine the ear problem if decompression occurred in a pressurized airplane. It has been said that the Stuka pilots of WW II had their eardrums pierced to facilitate pressure equalization. The U.S. dive bomber pilots did not follow suit but made sure the passages (eustachian and ear tubes) were clear when diving. Pilots with colds or other sources of stoppages have had ruptured eardrums in glide or dive bombing on the first run and then the "pleasure" of making several more runs in this condition—it is extremely painful.

Decompression sickness (the bends)—is the result of nitrogen and other gases being dissolved in the blood and other fluids. When the surrounding pressure fails (as would be the case in failure of cabin pressure or flying at an altitude of 35,000 to 45,000 feet without any pressurization), these gases—nitrogen mostly—form gas bubbles, particularly in the joints. The pain is severe. Although advice is often given to "not exercise the area, it makes more bubbles form," you'll find yourself bending your wrists or other joints in an attempt to ease the pain. Bubble formation in the lungs can also cause pain and disability. Bends can be fatal. Scuba and other divers who've been down to depths of 35 feet or more (where the pressure on them is at least twice that of the sea level atmosphere) and come up too fast can suffer the bends, as can a pilot in an unpressurized airplane at high altitudes. You should not fly or ride in an airplane too soon after SCUBA diving. Check the AIM for recommendations. Suffering a sudden loss of cabin pressure after having been diving could be catastrophic.

Bends at altitude (35,000 to 40,000 feet) may take up to 20 minutes to develop severe symptoms. But if you were scuba diving and then flew within a few hours, it's possible that you could get the bends at 8,000 feet cabin altitude or lower. This writer got the bends when flying an F4U-5N Corsair with a *dilutor-demand* system at 41,000 feet. (See Figure 18-4.) Not too smart!

Summary

Know your O_2 equipment and pressurization system thoroughly. Work out beforehand the procedures to be used in the event of O_2 system failures, loss of pressurization, or other problems. Get a checkout on altitude effects in a chamber before acting as pilot in command of an airplane capable of operating at high altitudes.

19

Turbocharging and Pressurization

Background

This chapter is intended only to give some general information on turbocharging. You'll get a thorough checkout when you start to fly any new turbo system because of the different pilot techniques and requirements, compared with normally aspirated engines.

You'll find that some older systems have a separate control for the turbo waste gate (more about that later) and others are automatic; in the latter, the pilot uses the throttle(s) alone to set up the desired manifold pressure (mp).

Turbocharging allows the engine to develop more HP at sea level (ground-boosted engines) and at altitude (ground-boosted and altitude-turbocharged). But the primary purpose of such systems is to develop and maintain better high-altitude engine operations at a small cost in weight.

Some of the turbochargers used in the older light twins with radial engines are driven by the crankshaft, but at a much higher speed through gearing. These turbochargers are single-stage, single-speed. The single compressor always operates at the same gear ratio, and the pilot does not "shift gears" as altitude is gained.

The number of "stages" of an engine turbocharging system indicates the number of compressing cycles it goes through. The air, or mixture, may be compressed several times through a series of compressor sections, but most light general aviation airplane systems have only one stage. The terms *single-speed* or *two-speed* are used in conjunction with mechanically driven *superchargers* (part of the original engine, hooked up with the crankshaft through a gear train). The single speed is at a fixed-gear ratio, and there's nothing the pilot can do about it. The two-speed type allowed the system to change from low blower to high blower as altitude was gained (this shifting was done at altitudes varying from 7,000 to 12,000 feet, depending on the airplane/engine combinations). (See the FAA's *Aviation Maintenance Technician Handbook–Powerplant.*)

Turbosupercharging

Basically, *turbocharging* is accomplished by using the exhaust gases of the engine to turn a turbine wheel directly connected to a compressor wheel that compresses intake air and routes it to the carburetor for mixing with the fuel. In the fuel-injection engine, the compressed air is sent on to the engine for mixing at the cylinder intake. If you were going to design a system, you might start as shown in Figure 19-1. The turbo is always "on" in that example. At sea level the internal pressures in the engine (brake mean effective pressure) could be too high.

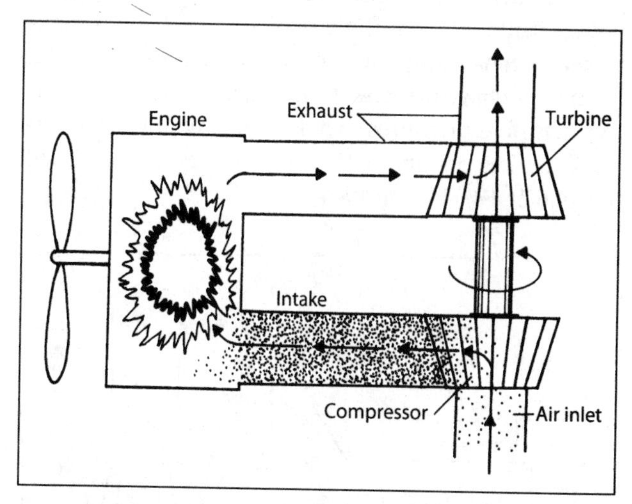

Figure 19-1. A view of the turbocharging principle. There are, of course, a *few* other factors to consider.

Altitude Turbocharging

Assuming that an engine being turbocharged is not allowed to exceed, say, 29 inches of mp at its maximum rpm, some means of getting the compressed air at altitude is needed. In other words, in order to get 29 inches of mp at 16,000 feet might require starting off with 43 inches at sea level. This won't work for our fictitious engine—it may not take the pressure.

The best thing is to add a "waste gate" to the system so that a choice is available (Figure 19-2). The pilot can control the waste gate position as altitude is gained, finally closing it completely to route all the exhaust gases through the turbine wheel. When the waste gate is completely closed, the available mp drops with further altitude gain (Figure 19-3).

In Chapter 12 it was noted that as altitude is increased, the cooler outside air and lower exhaust back pressure result in more HP per inch of mp. This was also shown in Figure 12-1, a power-setting chart. But another practical consideration is involved in the operation of the turbocharger. As the air is compressed in the process, it becomes hotter. As the airplane goes higher the turbo wheel must turn faster to do the job and so some heat (and loss of efficiency) is involved. With some models of equipment, a *higher* mp is required to get the same HP at altitude to offset this. This is mentioned because some turbocharged airplanes you'll be flying may have power-setting charts that call for relative manifold pressures that don't jibe with your previous experience with nonboosted engines (as discussed in Chapter 12) (Figure 19-4).

Ground-Boosted Engines

The Lycoming TIO-541 model engine, which permits 38 inches to 43 inches for takeoff, has a larger and stronger crankshaft, lower compression ratio to protect the combustion chamber, special exhaust valves and guides to protect against hotter exhaust gas temperatures (EGTs), and oil squirts in the crankcase that direct a stream of oil at the pistons to help cool them.

It's extremely important that the proper octane fuel be used—detonation can be much more of a menace for boosted engines.

Waste Gates Again

To get back to the turbocharging system you're designing, look again at Figures 19-2 and 19-3. You've decided that the waste gate idea is the best way to go, and now need to design a way to control it. Oil pressure from the engine could be used to actuate the waste gate and also lubricate the turbine shaft.

Like a constant-speed propeller (which has a combination of oil pressure and counterweight, oil versus air pressure, or oil versus a spring and the normal pitching moment of the prop), maybe here an oil pressure and spring combination would be a good system for controlling the waste gate operation. The most logical approach would be to use oil pressure to *close* the waste gate, fighting a spring that wants to open it. The waste gate control, which is separate from the other engine controls in the older manual system, is adjusted for the desired mp altitude. This control is usually a vernier

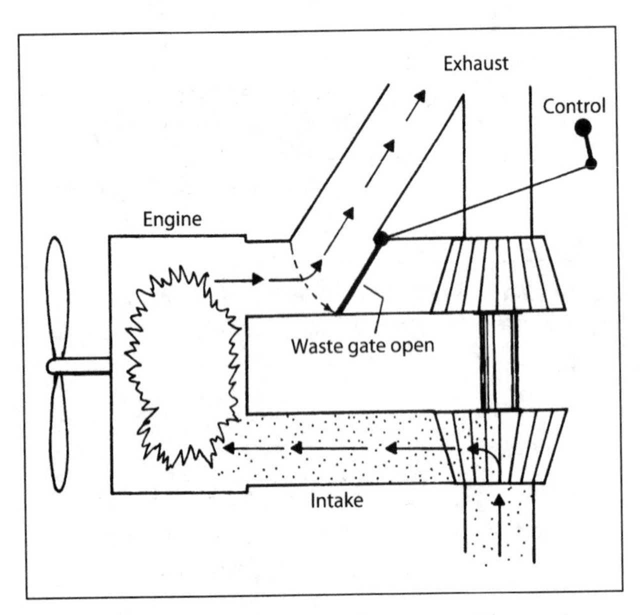

Figure 19-2. A simplified view of a system with a waste gate added. The gate is open so the engine is normally aspirated (the turbo isn't working).

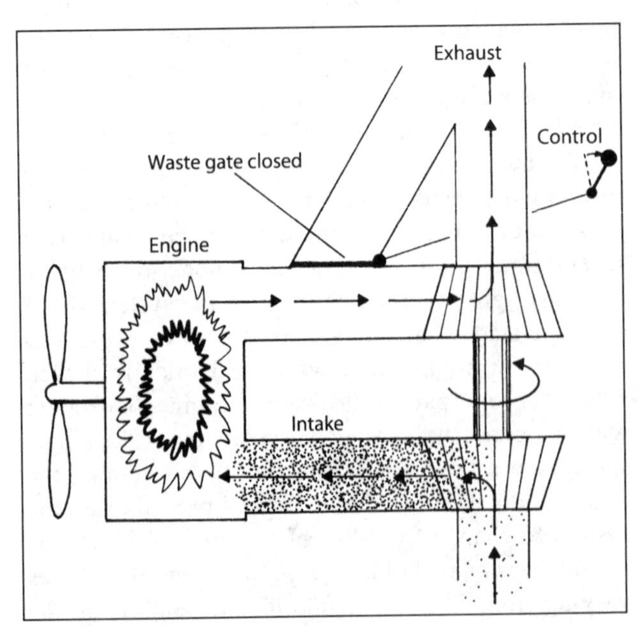

Figure 19-3. The waste gate is completely closed; any further increase in altitude will result in a drop in manifold pressure.

A Power Setting Table (Cruise) - Lycoming Model IO-540-C4B5, 250 HP Engine

Normal Cruise Approx 210 HP RPM	MP	Intermediate Cruise Approx 190 HP RPM	MP	Economy Cruise Approx 175 HP RPM	MP	Long Range Cruise Approx 140 HP RPM	MP
2400	26.0	2200	26.0	2200	24.0	2100	21.0
		2300	25.0	2300	23.2	2200	20.0
		2400	24.0	2400	22.4	2300	19.3

B Power Setting Table (Cruise) - Lycoming Model TIO-540-C1A, 250 HP Engine

Turbo Cruise Approx 232 HP RPM	MP	Intermediate Cruise Approx 200 HP RPM	MP	Economy Cruise Approx 173 HP RPM	MP	Long Range Cruise Approx 140 HP RPM	MP
2400	34.0	2300	31.0	2200	28.0	2100	25.0
		2400	30.0	2300	27.0	2200	24.0
		2500	29.0	2400	26.0	2300	23.0

Figure 19-4. Power setting charts for **(A)** a normally aspirated engine and **(B)** the boosted version. Comparing manifold pressures for long-range cruise power settings for both types, you can see (underlined) that the boosted engine requires higher manifold pressure for a given rpm. The full chart carries information on mp limits for various altitudes for different propellers and corrective factors. (Example only, not to be used for flight purposes.)

type, and in the multi, there'll be one for each engine. With this oil pressure-spring arrangement, a loss of oil pressure in the system would result in the spring opening the waste gate and the engine becoming normally respirating—unboosted—again. The airplane, if at altitudes requiring boosting to sustain flight, would descend until power was available for straight and level and other operations. This setup is better than having the waste gate closed when oil pressure is lost in the turbo system, which could mean, at low altitudes, overboosting an engine designed for a maximum of 29 inches of mercury or thereabouts. Figure 19-5 shows a schematic of a turbocharged engine.

The next step is to install an *automatic absolute pressure control system*. With it the pilot uses the throttle at altitude to set up the mp desired without adjusting a separate control. The automatic control system adjusts for pressure, and the turbocharger is operated so that the mp follows throttle movements. This automatic feature is normally set at the factory and shouldn't be worked on in the field.

Operation of a Turbocharged Engine

You'll naturally use the POH for the exact word on the particular airplane/engine setup, but a few general items on operations should be covered.

First, while you're careful in changing power with the nonboosted constant-speed prop, even more care must be taken with the turbocharged engine. An abrupt or improper sequence of power adjustments can damage the engine. The following items apply to both manual and automatic systems when in operation:

1. The throttle(s) must be operated smoothly or the engines will surge. Since the turbo(s) will react to power input, this is bad for the turbocharger(s) and the engine(s).
2. Figure 12-2 (engine indigestion) shows what can happen if you get out of sequence in using the prop control and throttle in a nonboosted engine. So, to increase power, increase rpm first. To decrease power, decrease mp first. Handle the power controls very carefully.
3. The cylinder head temperatures (CHTs) will run hotter at high altitudes because of the higher turbine speeds. You'll need to closely monitor that instrument. Keep temperatures within prescribed limits. (The CHT will tend to average at least 30°F higher at altitude.)
4. Cruise control at altitude is to be in accordance with specific instructions for that airplane and engine combination.
5. A power setting of 75% is used by most pilots for cruise. Consult charts for the most utility.

Manually Controlled Turbocharger

The waste gate(s) will be open (turbo turned OFF) for takeoffs at field density-altitudes below 4,000 to 5,000 feet. Always make sure that the manual control is in the waste-gate-open position before starting the engine. You may have brought things back to normal as

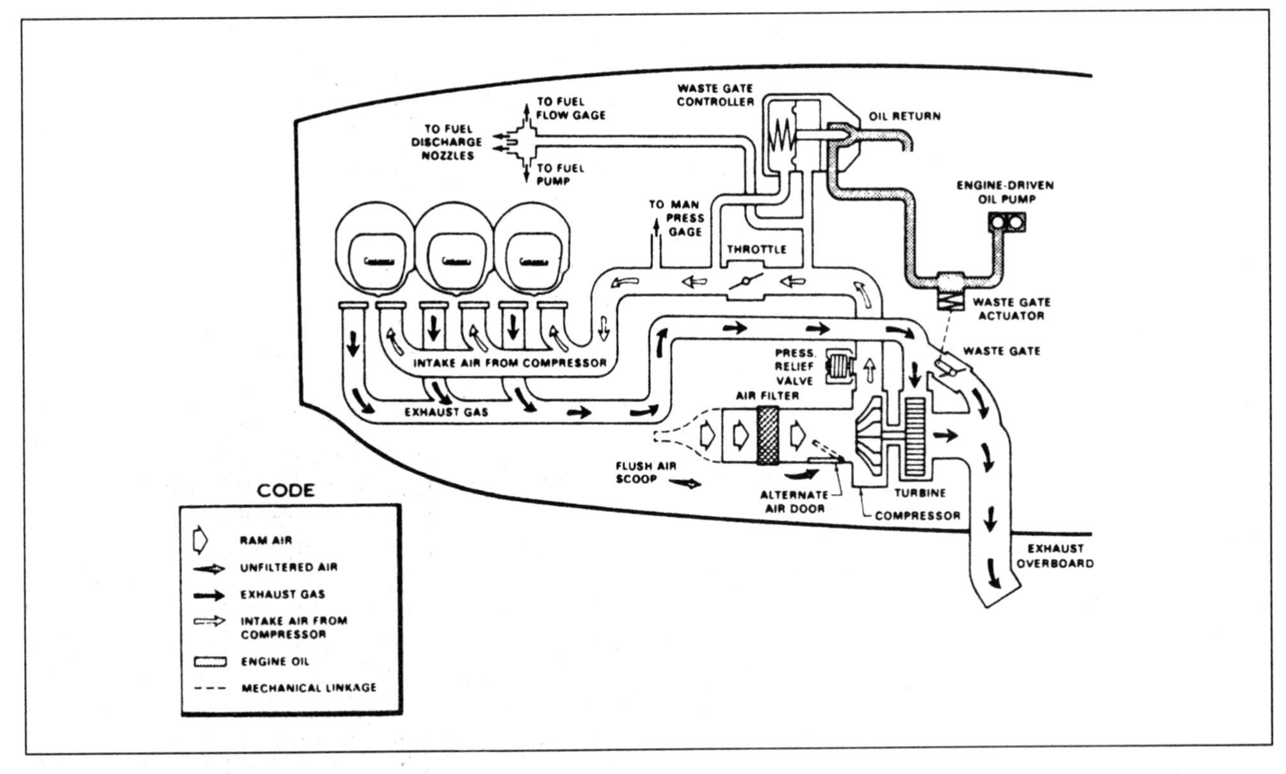

Figure 19-5. Turbocharger system.

you descended on that last flight, but somebody might have closed the waste gate in the meantime. Using 60+ inches of mp on takeoff or go-around, in an engine limited to 29 inches or so, could get everybody's attention and cost you thousands of dollars.

Takeoff and Climb

This type of system is left OFF (waste gate open) for takeoff and climb until 4,000 to 5,000 feet (density-altitude) is reached, at which point you'll be using full throttle to maintain required climb mp. (Takeoff and climb at *full rich* mixture.) As altitude is gained, the manual waste gate control, usually a vernier type, is gradually closed to maintain the required mp.

Cruise Control

Use the power chart for your airplane/engine to set power at the particular altitude chosen. As far as leaning by reference to the EGT is concerned, use the recommended proper leaning procedures.

Temperatures, particularly CHT, are higher at altitude and can be a critical factor, if ignored. One of the first light twins equipped with turbochargers could not fly level on one engine above a certain altitude because *cooling was the critical factor.* It could maintain altitude on one engine at 90- to 100-mph CAS but 120-mph CAS was necessary to keep the temperatures down, and it was going downhill at that speed. Some manufacturers use a turbine inlet temperature (TIT) gage as standard equipment.

Descent

Descent with a *manually* controlled turbocharger is the reverse of the climb in that the waste gates are gradually opened as altitude is lost, so the airplane passes through the 4,000- to 5,000-ft level as a normal aspirating engine type. Suppose you *forget* to open the waste gates (after closing the throttle to make a fast descent) and then suddenly apply full throttle(s) for a quick go-around. The ensuing noise and activity would be very interesting to those on the ground observing, but you would probably be so busy trying to land a no-powered airplane that you wouldn't appreciate it.

Always reduce power with the turbo controls first.

Automatic Control

One type of automatic turbocharging system is described as follows:

1. Engine induction air taken in through a flush scoop on the inboard side of the nacelle is filtered and passed into the compressor.
2. The compressed (or pressurized) air then passes through the throttle system and induction manifold into the engine. (The air and fuel are mixed as normally for a fuel-injection system.)

3. The exhaust is routed to the turbine, which drives the compressor, and the cycle continues (Figures 19-1, -2, and -3).

To avoid exceeding the maximum allowed manifold pressure, the waste gate in this system allows some of the exhaust to bypass the turbine and exit via the tailpipe. The waste gate position changes to hold a constant compressor discharge pressure.

When the waste gate is *fully closed* (as might be the case at or above the critical altitude—see Figure 19-3), any change in turbine speed will directly affect the mp (the more turbine rpm, the more mp, etc.).

When the waste gate is *fully open* (see Figure 19-2), the engine will respond as does a normally aspirated engine in rpm changes. If you move the prop control forward (*increase* rpm) the mp will *decrease* slightly and vice versa, just like that constant-speed-prop-equipped, normally aspirating engine you've been flying. When the *waste gate is fully closed* (see Figure 19-3 again) the mp reacts the opposite of a normally aspirated engine. An increase in rpm (and the resulting increase in turbine and compressor speed) *increases* the mp. A decrease in rpm decreases mp because of these factors.

When the waste gate is closed, the mp will also vary with airspeed (impact air). The turbocharger operates with pressure ratios of up to 3:1, and any change in intake pressure is multiplied—with a result that the exhaust and turbine (and compression) are affected.

Check the POH for details on how the turbocharging system works on *your* airplane, including monitoring the EGT (Exhaust Gas Temperature) gages for the various regimes of flight.

Cabin Pressurization

Turbocharged airplanes may also use the system for cabin pressurization. Probably the optimum shape for pressurization would be a sphere, which would have no sharp angles or possible stress areas. Since crowding crewmen and passengers into such an arrangement would be uncomfortable, the next best and most logical move is to pressurize a cylindrical section (Figure 19-6). Note that some variation from a pure sealed cylinder is necessary because of the airplane's geometry, but that basically the pressure cabin might be considered an environment cylinder in the airplane. Sealing the windows and particularly the door is of great importance.

Turboprop airplanes or jets usually take air from the earlier stages of the compressor section. This would seem simple enough except that the air is very hot (normally much too hot for a comfortable cabin) and must be routed through the airplane's air conditioning system. The pilot sets the cabin temperature controls. The result is the mixture of pressurized (hot) air from the compressor and cold air from the air conditioner necessary to get the right temperature. In some cases, a failure of the air conditioner means that depressurization (to get some cooler outside air so that the people in the airplane don't get overheated) and descent (so that those same people don't get hypoxia) are necessary.

Some cabin pressurization systems are tied in with the engine gear-driven pneumatic pumps (as opposed to vacuum pumps). To review a little, you've had plenty of experience with flight instruments being operated by the engine-driven vacuum pumps. You know that in some twins each of the two vacuum pumps has the capacity to operate the flight instruments, plus the de-icer boots on the wings and horizontal tail. Since the instrument gyro wheels operate because of air moving across the vanes, how this flow is obtained (whether by suction at one end of the system or pressure at the other) doesn't matter. A pneumatic pump, or pumps, may be tied in with pressure from the turbocharger compressor section(s) so that each may supplement the other for cabin pressurization or running the de-icers or flight instruments. A series of check valves and controls are used to make sure that each system is contributing as necessary. For instance, you'd need the instruments and maybe the de-icers at lower altitudes during IFR

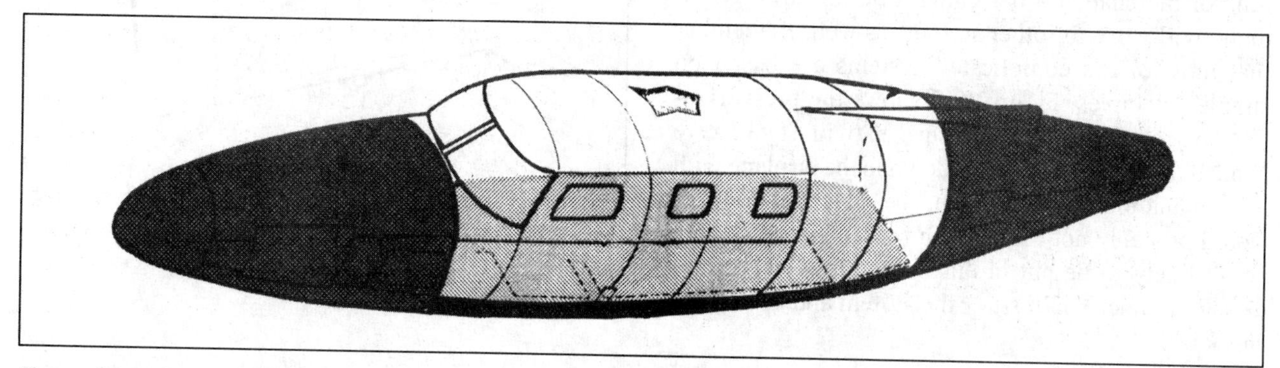

Figure 19-6. Pressurized cabin area for a light twin. The floor is the bottom pan of the pressurized cabin area.

operations when neither turbocharging nor cabin pressurization is required—and the engine-driven pneumatic pumps are then doing the job. At higher altitudes, air from the compressor section(s) may be working hard to pressurize and do the other chores required by the various systems.

The pressurization system for one current reciprocating-engine twin depends totally on the pneumatic pumps for cabin pressurization when the manifold pressures are below 17 to 18 inches. There is no turbocharger pressure used in this power regime. In cruise conditions the cabin pressurization is split 50-50 between the pneumatic pump and the turbochargers.

If it comes to which system (de-icers or cabin pressurization) has first choice with the pneumatic pump(s), the de-icers get the nod.

A detailed description of the various high-altitude systems would take up too much space here. Besides, the POH will give all the operating details needed. The idea here is to take an overall look so that you can understand the principles of systems for different airplanes and thus make better use of them. If you memorize the operating steps (push button 1, pull knob 2, etc.) without knowing how the system works generally, you wouldn't be as able to correct serious problems at, say, 29,000 feet when action is needed now. Or if you have a gripe about the system and need to talk to a mechanic, it's not considered professional to say something like, "Gee, it sure doesn't work right"—if that's all you can contribute.

Basically, when introduced to a system new to you, ask *what, why,* and *how.*

What is the system? Think about its description. What should it do? This will help start you thinking about how it works.

Why is it needed, or *why* is its addition advantageous? This also pins down the idea of its principle of operation.

How should it work? How will you make it function both normally and under emergency conditions?

You might find that the approach used in the beginning of the chapter—designing a turbocharging system—will work for other systems as well. Remember that most of the complicated systems are based on simple principles. Figure 19-7 shows the pressurization controls for an older pressurized twin. If you were handed this illustration or sat down in the airplane with no explanation or preparation, the dials and controls would probably not make much sense. Of course, you aren't likely to be put in this spot unless you're in a disaster movie. You'll study the system and get a good check out.

To continue with our example—in looking at Figure 19-7 you might examine the various items and ask, *why?* For example, it would be useful to know the cabin altitude when you are well above the altitude requiring O_2 for survival. The gage is handier and more accurate than turning around to check the various shades of blue in the passengers' faces. Don't be afraid to ask why something is a part of the system.

If you design your "own" system for a turbocharged, pressurized airplane, you might at first come up with a very simple one. You'd then expand it for various component controls. The first design would be close to the one in Figure 19-1. You'd soon see that a continuously operating turbocharging, pressurizing, and de-icing system wouldn't work. You would then start adding controls to operate the de-icers, or turbochargers, or pressurization when needed. While you need to avoid any unauthorized cabin air leaks, you'd have controlled, adjustable leakage using an outflow valve to get the desired cabin pressure. Besides, who wants to breathe the same air over and over?

You'd soon find yourself adding all the "complicated" controls and instruments as you progressed in designing a system. When each is added as necessary, it's easy to understand, but if you are faced with the whole conglomerate at once, it can be overpowering.

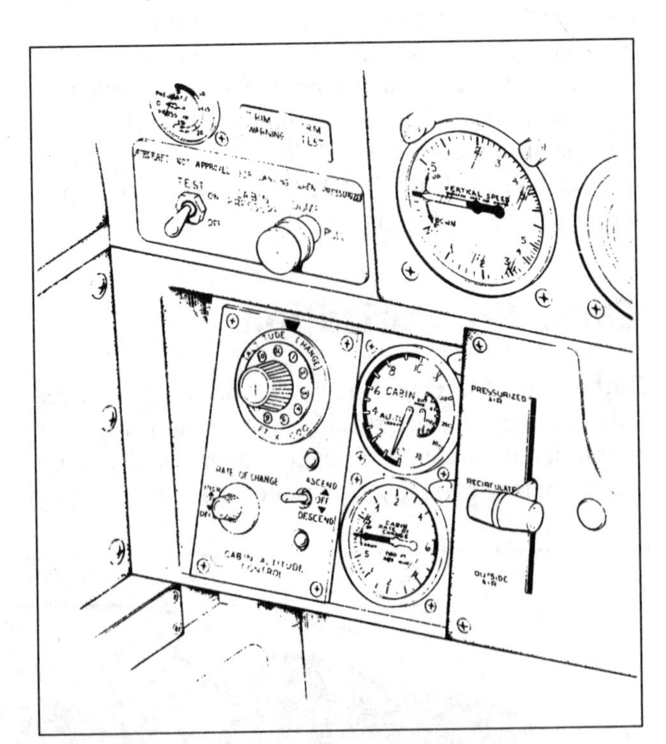

Figure 19-7. Pressurized cabin console.

Summary

This chapter has taken a general look at turbocharging and cabin pressurization so that you'll understand the principles when you are first introduced to the systems (and the controls) for a specific airplane. Once you understand what the system is to do, the POH instructions will make more sense.

Following are some terms you should be familiar with concerning turbocharging (as given by the Lycoming *Flyer*):

Turbocharge and *turbocharger*—The term *turbocharge* means to increase the air pressure (density) above or higher than ambient conditions. A *turbocharger* is any device that accomplishes this.

Turbo-supercharger—More commonly referred to as a *turbocharger;* this device is a supercharger driven by a turbine. The turbine is spun by energy extracted from engine exhaust gas.

Compressor—A compressor is the portion of a turbocharger that takes in ambient air and compresses it before discharging it to the engine. This compressor is a high-speed radial outflow wheel that accelerates the air as it passes through the wheel passages. Then the collector around the wheel transforms the velocity energy to a pressure head.

Turbine—A turbocharger turbine operates almost in reverse of the compressor. Hot exhaust gases of the engine are ducted into the turbine housing where the velocity is increased prior to passing through the turbine wheel. The expansion of these gases releases energy to drive the turbine wheel.

Waste gate and *waste gate actuator*—In a turbocharger system, the term waste gate refers to a valve (usually a butterfly type) that dumps engine exhaust gases before they reach the turbocharger. The valve may be actuated by a hydraulic piston and cylinder with the piston linked to an arm on the butterfly valve shaft.

Absolute pressure controller—This is an automatic control that senses compressor discharge pressure in an aneroid bellows attached to a poppet valve. This poppet valve in turn controls the amount of engine oil bled to the crankcase, thereby modulating the waste gate as necessary to maintain a constant compressor discharge pressure.

Adjustable absolute pressure controller—This controller is similar to the absolute pressure controller except that the desired compressor discharge pressure can be varied by the pilot. Each time a new pressure is selected, that pressure will hold automatically.

Manual controls—With manual controls the waste gate position and subsequent turbocharger output are controlled and modulated by the pilot rather than by an automatic control device.

Automatic controls—Unlike manual controls, the automatic controls perform the necessary functions to maintain preselected operating conditions without the pilot's attention.

Density controller—This device has the same general construction as an absolute pressure controller, except the bellows are filled with a temperature-sensitive dry nitrogen. These bellows will cause the controller to maintain a constant density, rather than pressure, by allowing the pressure to increase as the temperature increases, holding a constant of pressure over the square root of a temperature: $C = P/\sqrt{T}$ where C = constant, P = pressure, and T = temperature.

Ground-boosted or *ground turbocharged*—These phrases indicate that the engine depends on a certain amount of turbocharging at sea level to produce the advertised HP. An engine that is so designed will usually include a lower compression ratio to avoid detonation.

Deck pressure—This is the pressure measured in the area downstream of the turbo compressor discharge and upstream of the engine throttle valve. This should not be confused with manifold pressure.

Manifold pressure—This is the pressure measured downstream of the engine throttle valve. It is almost directly proportional to the engine power output.

Differential pressure controller—This controller uses a diaphragm rather than the bellows found in the absolute pressure controller. It is usually used in conjunction with a density controller. Its function is to override the density controller so that the compressor discharge pressure is not held at an unnecessarily high level when lower manifold pressures are being used. The differential controller will usually maintain a compressor discharge approximately 2 inches to 4 inches of mercury above the selected mp. In this system, the density controller is only effective at wide-open engine throttle conditions.

Normalizing—If a turbocharger system is used only to regain power losses caused by decreased air pressure of high altitude, it is considered that the engine has been normalized.

Overboost—An overboost condition means that mp is exceeding the limits at which the engine was tested and FAA certified. This can be detrimental to the life and performance of the engine. Overboost can be caused by malfunctioning controllers or an improperly operating waste gate in the automatic system or by pilot error in a manually controlled system.

Overshoot—This is a condition in which the automatic controls do not have the ability to respond quickly enough to check the inertia of the turbocharger speed increase with rapid engine throttle advance. Overshoot differs from overboost in that the high mp lasts for only a few seconds. This condition can usually be overcome by smooth throttle advance.

Sonic nozzle—Sonic nozzles are used in turbocharger systems where bleed air is used for cabin pressurization. This is a flow-limiting device that works on the principle of controlling flow by passing the air through a smooth orifice. They are sized so that, at sonic velocity, the maximum desired flow is achieved. The sonic nozzle prevents too much air from going to the cabin and thereby starving the engine of its needed supply.

Bootstrapping—This is a term used in conjunction with turbo machinery. If you were to take all the air coming from a turbocharger compressor and duct it directly back into the turbine of that turbocharger, it would be called a *bootstrap system.* If no losses were encountered, it theoretically would run continuously. It would also be very unstable because if for some reason the turbo speed changed, the compressor would pump more air to drive the turbine faster, etc. A turbocharged engine above critical altitude (waste gate closed) is similar to the example mentioned above, except there is an engine placed between the compressor discharge and turbine inlet. Slight system changes cause the exhaust gas to change slightly, which causes the turbine speed to change slightly, which causes the compressor air to the engine to change slightly, which in turn again affects the exhaust gas, etc.

Critical altitude—A turbocharged engine's (auto) waste gate is in a partially open position at sea level. As the aircraft is flown to higher altitudes (lower ambient pressures), the waste gate closes gradually to maintain the preselected mp. At the point where the waste gate reaches its fully closed position, the preselected mp starts to drop. This is the critical altitude for that engine.

Part Five **Preparing for the Commercial Knowledge and Practical Tests** 5

20

The Knowledge Test

You have, at this stage, taken the private pilot knowledge test (and others) and so have a good idea of what to expect in getting ready for an FAA test. It could be that it's been a little while since you really hit the theory, so this chapter has some suggestions for home study. It's suggested that you fly more complex airplanes and, if possible, actually use oxygen systems and turbocharged airplanes before taking the test—it will help you remember.

Home Study and Review

You may prefer to study at your pace rather than attend a formal ground school. *Aviation Weather* should be in the library of every pilot; the weather questions in the *Commercial Pilot Knowledge Test* are based on *Aviation Weather* and *Aviation Weather Services*. You should know the weather information available, such as Hourly Weather Reports (METARs), Terminal Aerodrome Forecast (TAFs), Pilot Reports, and Winds and Temperatures Aloft Forecasts.

Be familiar with charted data and their symbols as given on Radar Summary Charts, Low and High Level Significant Weather Prognosis Charts, Constant Pressure Prog Charts, Observed Winds and Temperature Aloft Charts, Weather Depiction Charts, and Convective Weather Outlooks.

In weather theory, know the various types of fog and how they are formed. What are the initial indications of wind shear? Know the various stages of thunderstorms and the characteristics of each. On the commercial test you'll be expected to know much more about high-altitude meteorology and jet stream theory.

You should be able to estimate the height of the bases of local convective type (summertime) clouds when given the surface temperature and the dewpoint. (The difference between the surface temperature and the dewpoint [Celsius] should be divided by 2.2 to get the height in thousands of feet.) Remember that 59°F and 15°C are sea level standard temperatures, and the normal lapse rates are –3½°F and –2°C per 1,000 feet.

There are copies of FARs and AIM available from commercial publishers and you should have the latest copies to study for the questions in the knowledge test here (as well as references for your day-to-day operations).

Following are some suggested study areas that not only apply as a review for the commercial knowledge test but also as a review of the material covered in this book.

Chapter 2

Laws of motion—Newton's laws of motion should be reviewed and understood.

Principles of airfoils—As noted in this chapter, Bernoulli's theorem and Newton's law (for every action there is an equal and opposite reaction) go here. Have a good knowledge of the general pressure distribution around an airfoil and what happens to the center of pressure as angle to attack is increased (see Figure 2-3). Make sure that you have a good picture of coefficient of lift versus angle of attack, and the effects of flaps on the coefficient of lift and drag (and how pitch and trim are affected by the use of flaps). Review the effects of ice, snow, or frost on airfoils. Also know the effects of air density on lift and thrust.

Wing planforms—The planform of the wing affects stall characteristics (rectangular planforms give best lateral control characteristics if other factors are equal). Be familiar with such terms as aspect ratio, taper, sweep, span, and area, and how they affect airplane aerodynamics and performance.

Drag—Review the types of drag and how airspeed and/or angle of attack affect each.

Gyroscopic precession—This and the other factors of torque should be well familiar to you.

Stalls—What happens to the airflow when the critical (stall) angle of attack is reached? Stalls are a function of angle of attack, not airspeed. Know the effects of CG position on stall speed and recovery characteristics. What are the effects of flaps on stall speed? Of weight?

Power—Brake and thrust horsepower and the effect of THP on performance (climbs, descents, and straight and level) should be understood. Be aware of the airplane's actions on the front and back sides of the power curve and how a change in airspeed requires more (or less) power to maintain a constant altitude.

Ground effect—Know that ground effect is the result of a change in downwash and a decrease in induced drag and be able to analyze its effects on the airplane performance and longitudinal stability during takeoff or landing. What happens to induced drag as the airplane flies out of ground effect?

Chapter 3

The Four Forces—Know that the axis of reference in flight mechanics is the airplane's flight path and that the Four Forces are measured parallel and perpendicular to that axis. Weight must be broken down into two components in climbing or descending flight, in order to see what proportion is acting perpendicular or parallel to the line of flight. Analyze the forces at level slow flight and at cruise, climbs, descents, and turns.

Particularly review Figures 3-15, -16, and -17. Check these equations (The V is in knots):

$$\text{radius (r)} = \frac{V^2}{11.26 \tan \phi}$$

$$\text{rate of turn} = \frac{1{,}091 \tan \phi}{V}$$

The point is not necessarily to memorize the equations but to realize that the radius goes up as a function of the velocity squared for a given bank angle (ϕ). (If you double the airspeed when flying at a particular angle of bank, the radius goes up 4 times.) For turn rate, the slower the airspeed, the greater the rate of turn for a particular bank angle (halve the airspeed and the turn rate doubles).

Chapter 4

Be sure that you can answer questions on the flight instruments and their errors. Be well versed on vacuum and pressure pump systems, including the principles of gyroscopic operations and aircraft acceleration effects on the attitude indicator. Review the pitot/static system and how those instruments may be affected by icing and other factors. (Also know the effects on the instruments of using the alternate air source.) You should take another very good look at the magnetic compass and its operational errors, including acceleration (ANDS), northerly turning (NOSE), deviation, and variation. Know the various types of altitudes (indicated, density, pressure, true, and absolute) and how pressure and temperature affect the indicated-altitude and true-altitude relationships. Understand how the various engine instruments obtain their readings. Know the various airspeeds (IAS, CAS, EAS, and TAS) and how each is found. (Be able to work both ways through each type of airspeed and understand what a Mach number is.) What are the airspeed indicator markings (V speeds)?

Chapter 5

Be able to work with the various types of takeoff and obstacle-clearance charts, as given in the chapter and for airplanes you're flying. Know the effects of headwind component (and crosswind component limits), weight, runway surface, density-altitude (pressure altitude, temperature, and humidity) and approximate runway slope effects. Remember that **H**igh, **H**ot, and **H**umid **H**urt (takeoff performance). Be able to use a crosswind/headwind component chart. Also be able to answer questions on normal and crosswind takeoff techniques, and short- and soft-field takeoffs and landings. Review in your mind the techniques you use in taxiing in strong surface winds.

Chapter 6

Review this chapter well and understand the difference between max rate and max angle, and obstacle clearance climbs and how they are derived. Wind affects *angle* of climb but *not rate* (assume no turbulence). Be able to read—quickly and accurately—the various rate of climb charts available. Know that excess *thrust horsepower* controls the *rate* of climb and excess *thrust* controls *angle* of climb. Be able to accurately use time, fuel, and distance-to-climb information—both tabular and graphic.

Chapter 7

Review this chapter, with emphasis on being able to read cruise power setting charts; understand that the maximum range speeds and power settings are lower than for "normal" cruise (65 to 75%) and that maximum endurance is found at even lower speed/power settings. Max endurance is greatest at lower altitudes. Note that airplanes close to the max range airspeed can fly at a "high" or "low" airspeed, and pilots may not realize that they are flying the lower one and may think they've gotten it "on the step" (see Figure 7-2).

Chapter 8

Understand how max distance and minimum sink glides are different. Note that the wind affects the glide *angle* but not the *rate* of sink. (This is the same condition as max angle and max rate climbs and, like them, it's assumed that there is no turbulence to affect performance.)

Review how density-altitude affects the maximum distance glide angle and sink rate, and how the indicated (calibrated) airspeed for the max distance glide must be reduced with weight decrease. Look at the maximum glide distance charts again.

Chapter 9

The theory and techniques of normal and crosswind landings and short- and soft-field approaches and landings should be well established in your mind. This is a good time to review the various flap operations and systems you've encountered in your practical flying experience (electrical, hydraulic, and manual systems and their idiosyncrasies) so that you'll be able to answer any questions from a pilot's standpoint. Know the factors (wind, density-altitude, slope, runway surface, and braking) that affect the landing roll. Check out your use of graphic and tabular landing distance data. Read about the different types of hydroplaning and the minimum hydroplaning speed.

Chapter 10

As a commercial pilot you'll be expected to go more deeply into the theory of stability and control so that you can generally predict an airplane's reaction to a new weight placement or a design change.

Take a good look at Figure 10-46 and be sure that you are knowledgeable about the principles of longitudinal static and dynamic stability. Know what effects sweepback and dihedral have on directional and lateral stability. It should go without saying that you will be expected to be familiar with the various types of weight and balance envelopes and be able to accurately work any weight and balance problems on the test. Also know the effects that weight and balance have on performance (forward CG means a higher stall speed in most cases because the down force on the tail makes it "weigh" more—see Figure 7-4). What is gross weight and useful load? What is included in the Basic Empty weight of the airplane? How can the pilot affect the longitudinal stability of the airplane? As you fly larger airplanes with greater cargo capacity, you'll have to be aware of such factors as cargo shifting and complete management of weight and balance. Know how ground effect affects longitudinal stability.

Chapter 11

Take another good look at this chapter for aircraft limitations (airspeeds, load factors, and weights). Remember that the definition of the maneuvering speed is that maximum airspeed (calibrated) at which abrupt and complete control travel may be accomplished without exceeding the limit load factor. The maneuvering speed (CAS) is a multiple of the stall speed times the square root of the limit load factor. Since the stall speed decreases with the *square root* of the weight (the limit load factor is required to be constant), the maneuvering speed used must decrease with the square root of the weight change. Note that stresses due to gusts depend on the weight, lift slope of the airfoil, velocity of the airplane, and the gust velocity. Review Figures 11-8 and 11-9 and be able to find on similar charts the load factor imposed by a 15- or 30-psf (vertical) gust at a chosen airspeed. Know the limit (design) and ultimate positive and negative load factors for normal, utility, and acrobatic category airplanes. Remember that the load factor is the lift to weight ratio (LF = L/W), and these can be shuffled around to solve for each value (if you know the other two). Be able to find the increase in stall speed and/or load factors for a given angle of bank as shown in Figure 11-2. *The load factor imposed in a balanced, constant-altitude turn is the same at a given bank for all airplanes at all airspeeds.* In a 60° bank the C-152 pilot will have the same 2 g's imposed as will an F-16 pilot at that bank.

What are the *differences* in stall speed and load factors as a bank is changed?

Chapter 12

Know the basics of manifold pressure/rpm relationships and the theory of the constant-speed propeller (review also Chapter 2 in the section on thrust to see *why* the constant-speed propeller is more efficient than the fixed-pitch type). Remember the different types of constant-speed propellers and their principles of operation (also covered in Chapter 2).

Chapter 13

There will be questions on fuel injection and carburetor principles and the use of mixture/throttle and boost pumps. And, elementary as it may seem, know the principles of the reciprocating engine (general ideas of carburetion, ignition, and the fuel and oil types available and how they are designated). Understand detonation and preignition, including their causes and effects, and general engine starting and shutdown procedures. You might also review the operations of the various fuel systems you've used. Know the point(s) in the carburetor where icing would most likely occur. Be able to describe the symptoms of carburetor icing in fixed-pitch-prop and constant-speed-prop airplanes. Remember that the term *induction icing* covers both carburetor and fuel injection systems. What temperatures are "best" (worst?) for carb ice? Fuel vaporization and lowered pressure in the venturi are the two big factors in forming carb ice. What are the advantages and disadvantages of carburetor and fuel injection systems? Note that the carburetor or air mixture temperature gage becomes more important for high-powered and turbocharged engines. What does carburetor heat do to the mixture?

Chapter 14

Know the various types of retractable landing gear systems used, plus safety additions and general emergency procedures for the two main types {electrically and hydraulically actuated). Also review the systems you've had practical experience with.

Chapter 15

Look at this chapter for the definition of the single-engine minimum controllable speed and for a further review of airplane performance as indicated by the graph of twin- and single-engine THP available and required. You might review the section on engine starting for some reminders on general engine starting and run-up procedures. How is V_{YSE} shown on the airspeed indicator?

Chapter 16

There will likely be questions on the knowledge test on emergency landings. You should go over some general ideas on rough-running engines, fire in flight (both engine and electrical), and techniques for landing on various types of terrain. For further study, order NTSB Report No. AAS-72-3, *Emergency Landing Techniques in Small Fixed-Wing Aircraft.*

Wake turbulence and procedures to avoid it should be gone over in your mind again, both for this test *and* for your day-to-day flying, in case you hadn't thought about it for a while. Have you worked out a procedure for your airplane if a door comes open on takeoff or en route? Run over in your mind the possible effects of turbulence and gradient winds.

Chapter 17

Rework some of the navigation and performance problems in this chapter and affirm that your work with the computer is quick and accurate. Review the equation for radius of action from a moving base, time out (TO) = (TT × GSB)/(GSO + GSB), and if you use hours and tenths be sure that you don't confuse fractions of hours with minutes (2.28 hours is not 2 hours and 28 minutes but 2 hours and 16.8 minutes). In the off-course problems, the flight to the destination will require two steps in heading corrections: (1) the change required to parallel the original course plus (2) the turn to fly to the destination. Review the "rule of 60" so that you can double-check your computer work on off-course and time- or fuel-to-station problems.

Chapter 18

You'll have some questions on the physiological effects of high-altitude flying. Know the general theory of the different types of O_2 systems. Be able to recognize the symptoms of hypoxia, the bends, and hyperventilation (the latter is not necessarily a problem caused by altitude, but it could happen at altitude and be confused with hypoxia, which might result in more anxiety and more hyperventilation). Review the latest Part 91 O_2 requirements.

Chapter 19

Have a good grasp of the theory and operation of turbocharged engines and how cabin pressurization is generally used. Some people get confused as to whether the waste gate is open or closed when the turbocharger is in action. Review the illustrations, and, if your mind goes blank on the knowledge, "redesign" a system.

Federal Aviation Regulations

Be familiar with 14 CFR Parts 1, 61, 71, 91, 119, and 135, plus National Transportation Safety Board Part 830. You'll be expected to have a very good knowledge of these parts and the following FAA Advisory Circulars:

Series 00—General
Series 20—Aircraft
Series 60—Airmen
Series 70—Airspace
Series 90—ATC and General Operations
Series 120—Air Carrier and Commercial Operators
Series 150—Airports
Series 170—Air Navigation Facilities

AIM and Other Publications

Review the *Aeronautical Information Manual* (AIM), *Notices to Airmen,* and *Airport/Facility Directory* (A/FD) to bring yourself up to date on the latest requirements.

Summary of the Home Study and Review

Don't try to memorize a lot of information, but use your time to cover the required areas. It's better if you use a couple of weeks for review (a comparatively small amount each evening) than to try to cram at the last minute.

The Commercial Pilot Knowledge Test

Introduction

The FAA has available hundreds of computer testing centers nationwide. These testing centers offer the full range of airman knowledge tests including military competence, instrument foreign pilot, and pilot examiner predesignated tests.

Commercial Pilot—Airplane
Commercial Pilot—Rotorcraft–Helicopter
Commercial Pilot—Rotorcraft–Gyroplane
Commercial Pilot—Glider
Commercial Pilot—Free Balloon–Hot Air
Commercial Pilot—Lighter-Than-Air-Airship
Military Competency—Airplane
Military Competency—Helicopter

What is required to become a skilled and effective commercial pilot? Although some individuals possess more knowledge and skills than others, no one is born a natural pilot. Competent commercial pilots become so through study, hard work, and experience.

This book is not offered as a quick and easy way to obtain the necessary information for passing the knowledge tests. There is no quick and easy way to obtain this knowledge in addition to the skills needed to transform a student into a pilot capable of operating safely in our complex national airspace system. Rather, the intent of this book is to define and narrow the field of study, as much as possible, to the required knowledge areas for obtaining a commercial pilot certificate.

Even though you can obtain the test questions on the Internet, *rote memorization of test questions may render good test scores, but a correlative understanding of the subject matter may be lacking. This correlative understanding of the entire aviation schema is what produces a safe and effective pilot.*

Eligibility Requirements

The general prerequisites for a commercial pilot certificate require that the applicant have a combination of experience, knowledge, and skill. For specific information pertaining to certification, an applicant should carefully review the appropriate sections of 14 CFR Part 61 for commercial pilot certification.

Knowledge Areas on the Tests

Commercial pilot tests are comprehensive because they must test an applicant's knowledge in many subject areas. Applicants for a commercial pilot certificate or added rating should review the appropriate information pertinent to the category sought. The information includes NTSB Part 830, 14 CFR Parts 23, 61, 67, 71, 91, 125, 135, Principles of Flight, Weather, Navigation, Operations, and in the case of Airship applicants, Instrument Procedures. Additionally, Free Balloon and Airship applicants must review Fundamentals of Instruction.

The applicant for a commercial pilot certificate must have received and logged (recorded) ground instruction from an authorized instructor, or must present evidence showing satisfactory completion of a course of instruction or home study course, in at least the following areas of aeronautical knowledge appropriate to the category of aircraft for which a rating is sought.

Aeronautical Knowledge Areas

1. The Federal Aviation Regulations that apply to commercial pilot privileges, limitations, and flight operations.
2. Accident reporting requirements of the National Transportation Safety Board.
3. Basic aerodynamics and the principles of flight.
4. Meteorology, including recognition of critical weather situations, wind shear recognition and avoidance, and the use of aeronautical weather reports and forecasts.
5. The safe and efficient operation of the aircraft.
6. Weight and balance computation.
7. Use of performance charts.
8. Significance and effects of exceeding aircraft performance limitations.
9. Use of aeronautical charts and magnetic compass for pilotage and dead reckoning.
10. Use of air navigation facilities.
11. Aeronautical decision making and judgment.
12. Principles and functions of aircraft systems.
13. Maneuvers, procedures, and emergency operations appropriate to the aircraft.
14. Night and high-altitude operations.
15. Descriptions of and procedures for operating within the National Airspace System.

Description of the Tests

All test questions are the objective, multiple-choice type, with three choices of answers. Each question can be answered by the selection of a single response. Each test question is independent of other questions, that is, a correct response to one does not depend upon or influence the correct response to another.

The maximum time allowed for taking each test is either 2, 2.5, or 3 hours. The times vary depending on the number of questions assigned to each test and are based on previous experience and educational statistics. This amount of time is considered more than adequate for the applicant with proper preparation and instruction. The minimum passing score is 70 percent.

The following tests each contain 100 questions to be completed in 3 hours:

Commercial Pilot—Airplane
Commercial Pilot—Rotorcraft–Helicopter
Commercial Pilot—Rotorcraft–Gyroplane
Commercial Pilot—Glider
Commercial Pilot—Free Balloon–Hot Air
Commercial Pilot—Lighter-Than-Air-Airship

The following test contains 60 questions to be completed in 2.5 hours:

Commercial Pilot—Free Balloon–Gas

The following tests each contain 50 questions to be completed in 2 hours:

Military Competency—Airplane
Military Competency—Helicopter

Communication between individuals through the use of words is a complicated process. In addition to being an exercise in the application and use of aeronautical knowledge, a commercial pilot knowledge test is also an exercise in communication because it involves the use of the written language. Because the tests involve written rather than spoken words, communication between the test writer and the person being tested may become a difficult matter if care is not exercised by both parties. Consequently, considerable effort is expended to write each question in a clear, precise manner. Make sure you read carefully the instructions given with each test, as well as the statements in each test item.

When taking a test, keep the following points in mind:

1. Answer each question in accordance with the latest regulations and procedures.

2. Read each question carefully before looking at the possible answers. You should clearly understand the problem before attempting to solve it.

3. After formulating an answer, determine which test answer most nearly corresponds with your answer. The answer chosen should completely resolve the problem.

4. From the answers given, it may appear that there is more than one possible answer. However, there is only one answer that is correct and complete. The other answers are either incomplete, erroneous, or represent common misconceptions.

5. If a certain question is difficult for you, it is best to mark it for RECALL and proceed to the next question. After you answer the less difficult questions, return to those that you marked for recall and answer them. The recall procedure will be explained to you prior to starting the test. Although the computer should alert you to unanswered questions, make sure every question has an answer recorded. This procedure will enable you to use the available time to the maximum advantage.

6. When solving a calculation problem, select the answer that is closest to your solution. The problems have been checked manually and with various types of calculators. If you have solved it correctly, your answer will be closer to the correct answer than any of the other choices.

Taking a Knowledge Test by Computer

You should determine what authorization requirements are necessary before going to the computer testing center. Testing center personnel cannot begin the test until you provide the proper authorization, if one is required. A limited number of tests require no authorization. In the case of retesting, you must present either a passed, expired passed (24 months), or failed test report for that particular test. This policy is covered in the *Commercial Pilot Knowledge Test Guide* (FAA-G-8082-5). However, you should always check with your instructor or your local Flight Standards District Office if you are unsure of what kind of authorization to bring to the testing facility.

The next step is the actual registration process. Most computer testing centers require that all applicants contact a central 1-800 phone number. At this time, you should select a testing center, schedule a test date, and make financial arrangements for test payment. Applicants may register for tests several weeks in advance of the proposed testing date. You may cancel your appointment up to 2 business days before test time, without financial penalty. After that time, you may be subject to a cancellation fee as determined by the testing center.

Your actual test is under a time limit, but if you know your material, there should be sufficient time to complete and review your answers. Within moments of completing the test, you will receive an airman test report, which contains your score. It also lists those subject matter knowledge areas where questions were answered incorrectly. *The total number of subject matter knowledge codes shown on the airman test report is not necessarily an indication of the total number of questions answered incorrectly.*

You can study these knowledge areas to improve your understanding of the subject matter. Your instructor is required to review each of these areas listed on your airmen test report with you, and complete an endorsement that remedial instruction was conducted. Also, the pilot examiner may quiz you on the areas of deficiency during the practical test.

The airman test report, which must show the computer testing company's embossed seal, is an important document. DO NOT LOSE THE AIRMAN TEST REPORT because you will need to present it to the examiner before taking the practical test. Loss of this report means that you will have to request a duplicate copy from the FAA in Oklahoma City. This will be costly and time consuming.

Check with your local Flight Standards District Office if you are in doubt about the latest information on the requirements just covered.

Cheating or Other Unauthorized Conduct

Computer testing centers follow rigid testing procedures established by the FAA. This includes test security. When entering the test area, you are permitted to take only scratch paper furnished by the test administrator and an authorized aviation computer, plotter, etc., approved for use in accordance with FAA Order 8080.6, Conduct of Airmen Knowledge Testing via the Computer Medium, and AC 60-11C, Test Aids and Materials That May Be Used by Airman Knowledge Testing Applicants. The FAA has directed testing centers to stop a test any time a test administrator suspects a cheating incident has occurred.

An FAA investigation will then follow. If the investigation determines that cheating or other unauthorized conduct has occurred, any airman certificate that you hold may be revoked, and you may not be allowed to take a test for 1 year.

Retesting Procedure

If the score on the airman test report is 70 or above, in most cases the report is valid for 24 calendar months. You may elect to retake the test, in anticipation of a better score, after 30 days from the date your last test was taken. Prior to retesting, you must give your current airman test report to the computer testing administrator. Remember, the score of the *latest* test you take will become your official test score. The FAA will not consider allowing anyone to retake a valid test before the 30-day remedial study period.

A person who fails a knowledge test may apply for retesting before 30 days of the last test providing that person presents the failed test report and an endorsement from an authorized instructor certifying that additional instruction has been given and the instructor finds the person competent to pass the test. A person may retake a failed test after 30 days without an endorsement from an authorized instructor.

Note: Be sure to check with your CFI, the FSDO, or at FAA.gov for the very latest information on knowledge test procedures and requirements.

21

The Practical Test

Background

This chapter is for the private pilot with an instrument rating who is taking the practical test in a single-engine land airplane. Figure 21-1 is a checklist to be used to get ready; add or delete items as they apply to your particular situation.

You should have the latest *Practical Test Standards* available to you because there may have been some minor changes since *this* book was printed; for instance, certain maneuvers may have been combined or altitude or heading limits may have been increased or decreased. The information here is intended to give a general look at the requirements of the practical test so you can see what will be expected.

The descriptions have been paraphrased and additional information is included. Also included is information from older *Practical Test Standards*, which will be of help to you. Some of the orders of presentation have been changed for easier transitions.

The practical test will have Areas of Operation, which are phases of flight arranged in logical sequences from the preparation to the conclusion of the flight. (The examiner may, however, conduct the practical test in any sequence that results in a complete and efficient test.)

Tasks are procedures and maneuvers appropriate to an Area of Operation. The tasks are set up for each aircraft category and class (Airplane Single-Engine Land, Airplane Multiengine Land, Rotorcraft Helicopter, Lighter-Than-Air Airship, etc.). As noted earlier, this chapter is aimed at the ASEL applicant.

The references for this practical test (in addition to this book) are:

14 CFR Part 39—Airworthiness Directives
14 CFR Part 43—Maintenance, Preventive Maintenance, Rebuilding and Alteration
14 CFR Part 61—Certification: Pilots, Flight Instructors and Ground Instructors
14 CFR Part 91—General Operating and Flight Rules
14 CFR Part 93—Special Air Traffic Rules
AC 00-6—Aviation Weather
AC 00-45—Aviation Weather Services
AC 61-65—Certification: Pilots and Flight Instructors
AC 61-67—Stall and Spin Awareness Training
AC 61-84—Role of Preflight Preparation
AC 90-48—Pilot's Role in Collision Avoidance
AC 90-66—Recommended Standard Traffic Patterns and Practices for Aeronautical Operations at Airports without Operating Control Towers
AC 91-13—Cold Weather Operation of Aircraft
AC 91-73—Part 91 and 135 Single-Pilot Procedures During Taxi Operations
AC 120-51—Crew Resource Management Training
AC 120-74—Parts 91, 121, 125, and 135 Flightcrew Procedures During Taxi Operations
AC 150-5340-18—Standards for Airport Sign Systems
FAA-H-8083-1—Aircraft Weight and Balance Handbook
FAA-H-8083-3—Airplane Flying Handbook
FAA-H-8083-2—Risk Management Handbook
FAA-H-8083-6—Advanced Avionics Handbook
FAA-H-8083-25—Pilot's Handbook of Aeronautical Knowledge
FAA-P-8740-19—Flying Light Twins Safely
AIM—Aeronautical Information Manual
A/FD—Airport/Facility Directory
NOTAMs—Notices to Airmen
Other—Pilot's Operating Handbook, FAA-Approved Flight Manual, and latest Navigation Charts

Refer to the latest available issuance of the above references (for example, AC 00-6A, -B, -C, or -L).

Each Objective lists in sequence the important elements that must be satisfactorily performed to demonstrate competency in a task. The Objective includes:

1. Specifically what you as an applicant should be able to do;
2. Conditions under which the task is to be performed; and

3. Acceptable performance standards. (You may be required to do some of the tasks in a complex airplane on the flight test.)

Example of a PTS Task:

Task D: Taxiing (ASEL)
References: FAA-H-8083-3; POH/AFM.
Objective: To determine that the applicant:

1. Exhibits satisfactory knowledge of the elements related to safe taxi procedures at towered and non-towered airports.
2. Performs a brake check immediately after the airplane begins moving.
3. Positions the flight controls properly for the existing wind conditions.
4. Controls direction and speed without excessive use of brakes.
5. Exhibits procedures for steering, maneuvering, maintaining taxiway, runway position, and situational awareness to avoid runway incursions.
6. Exhibits proper positioning of the aircraft relative to hold lines.
7. Exhibits procedures to insure clearances/instructions are received and recorded/read back correctly.
8. Exhibits situational awareness/taxi procedures in the event the aircraft is on a taxiway that is between parallel runways.
9. Uses a taxi chart during taxi.
10. Complies with airport/taxiway markings, signals, ATC clearances, and instructions.
11. Utilizes procedures for eliminating pilot distractions.
12. Taxiing to avoid other aircraft/vehicles and hazards.

You'll complete the appropriate checklist. When the examiner determines during the performance of a task that the knowledge and skill objective of a similar task has been met, it may not be necessary to require the performance of that similar task.

When the demonstration of a task is not practicable, such as operating over a congested area or unsuitable terrain or a demonstration that does not conform to the manufacturer's recommendations, competency can be evaluated by oral testing.

The examiner may not follow the precise order in which the areas of operation and tasks appear in each standard. The examiner may change the order, or in some instances combine tasks to conserve time. Examiners should develop a plan of action that includes the order and combination of tasks to be demonstrated by the applicant in a manner that results in an efficient and valid test. It is of utmost importance that the examiner accurately evaluate the applicant's ability to perform safely as a pilot and also recognize the applicant's weaknesses as well as satisfactory performance.

Examiners place special emphasis on the areas of aircraft operation that are most critical to flight safety, such as positive aircraft control and sound judgment in decision making. Although these areas may not be listed under each task, they are essential to flight safety and will receive careful evaluation throughout the practical test. If they are shown in the objective, additional emphasis is placed on them. The examiner will also emphasize positive exchange of the flight controls procedure (who is flying the airplane), stall/spin awareness, spatial disorientation, collision avoidance, wake turbulence avoidance, low-level wind shear, Land and Hold Short (LAHSO), runway incursion avoidance, controlled flight into terrain (CFIT), aeronautical decision making, and checklist usage (other areas will be determined by future revisions of the test standard).

When you get the latest copy you'll find that practical test standards will also refer to the metric equivalent of various altitudes throughout. The metric altimeter

APPLICANT'S PRACTICAL TEST CHECKLIST

APPOINTMENT WITH EXAMINER:

EXAMINER'S NAME____________________

LOCATION____________________

DATE/TIME____________________

ACCEPTABLE AIRCRAFT

- ☐ Aircraft Documents:
  Airworthiness Certificate
  Registration Certificate
  Operating Limitations
- ☐ Aircfaft Maintenance Records:
  Logbook Record of Airworthiness Inspections and AD Compliance
- ☐ Pilot's Operating Handbook, FAA-Approved Airplane Flight Manual

PERSONAL EQUIPMENT

- ☐ View-Limiting Device
- ☐ Current Aeronautical Charts
- ☐ Computer and Plotter
- ☐ Flight Plan Form
- ☐ Flight Logs
- ☐ Current AIM, Airport Facility Directory, and Appropriate Publications

PERSONAL RECORDS

- ☐ Identification - Photo/Signature ID
- ☐ Pilot Certificate
- ☐ Current and Appropriate Medical Certificate
- ☐ Completed FAA Form 8710-1, Airman Cerftificate and/or Rating Application with Instructor's Signature (if applicable)
- ☐ Computer Test Report
- ☐ Pilot Logbook with appropriate Instructor Endorsements
- ☐ FAA Form 8060-5, Notice of Disapproval (if applicable)
- ☐ Approved School Graduation Certificate (if applicable)
- ☐ Examiner's Fee (if applicable)

Figure 21-1.

is arranged in 10-meter increments, so the numbers are rounded off to the nearest 10-m increment for simplicity.

Use of Distractions during Practical Tests

Numerous studies indicate that many accidents have occurred when the pilot was distracted during phases of flight. And many accidents have resulted from engine failure during takeoffs and landings where safe flight would have been possible if the pilot had used correct control technique and proper attention. Distractions that have been found to cause problems are:

1. Preoccupation with situations inside or outside the cockpit.
2. Maneuvering to avoid other traffic.
3. Maneuvering to clear obstacles during takeoffs, climbs, approaches, or landings.

To strengthen this area of pilot training and evaluation, the examiner will provide realistic distractions throughout the flight portion of the practical test in order to evaluate the applicant's ability to divide attention while maintaining safe flight:

1. Simulating engine failure.
2. Simulating radio tuning and communication.
3. Identifying a field suitable for emergency landings.
4. Identifying features or objects on the ground.
5. Reading the outside air temperature gage.
6. Removing objects from the glove compartment or map case.
7. Questioning by the examiner.

(Note: the above items are not in the current *Practical Test Standards* [PTS] but were borrowed from older ones to give an idea of specific distractions.)

Practical Test Prerequisites

As an applicant for the commercial practical test, you are required by 14 CFR Part 61 to:

1. Be at least 18 years if age;
2. Be able to read, speak, write, and understand the English language. If in doubt, the Administrator may put operating limitations on the certificate;
3. Possess a private pilot certificate with an airplane rating, if a commercial pilot certificate with an airplane rating is sought, or meet the flight experience required for a private pilot certificate (airplane rating) and pass the private plot airplane knowledge and practical test;
4. Possess an instrument rating (airplane) or the following limitation shall be placed on the commercial pilot certificate: "Carrying passengers in airplanes for hire is prohibited at night or on cross-country flights of more than 50 nautical miles";
5. Have passed the appropriate commercial pilot knowledge test since the beginning of the 24th of the month before the month in which he or she takes the practical test (Get that?);
6. Have satisfactorily accomplished the required training and obtained the aeronautical experience prescribed;
7. Possess at least a current third class medical certificate;
8. Have an endorsement from an authorized instructor certifying that the applicant has received and logged training time within 60 days preceding the date of application in preparation for the practical test, and is prepared for the practical test; and
9. Also have an endorsement certifying that the applicant has demonstrated satisfactory knowledge of the subject areas in which the applicant was deficient on the airman knowledge test.

The airplane must be a complex airplane furnished by you for the performance of takeoffs, landings, and appropriate emergency procedures. A complex landplane has retractable gear, flaps, and controllable propeller or turbojet propulsion.

Use of FAA-approved flight simulator or flight training device: You may be authorized to use an FAA-qualified and FAA-approved flight simulator or flight training device (FTD) for certain requirements on the practical test, as given in the *Practical Test Standards* book. You should check with your flight instructor to confirm whether a flight simulator or FTD at the flight school (if so equipped) meets FAA standards for the practical test.

Aircraft and Equipment Requirements for the Practical Test

You are required to provide an appropriate and airworthy aircraft for the practical test. This aircraft must be capable of, and its operating limitations must not prohibit, the pilot operations required on the test. It must have fully functioning controls except as provided in 14 CFR sections 61.45(c) and (e).

Flight Instructor Responsibility

An appropriately rated flight instructor is responsible for training you as a commercial pilot applicant to acceptable standards in all subject matter areas, procedures, and maneuvers included in the tasks within the appropriate commercial pilot practical test standard. Because of the impact of their teaching activities in developing safe, proficient pilots, flight instructors should exhibit a high level of knowledge, skill, and the ability to impart that knowledge and skill to students. Additionally, your flight instructor must certify that you are able to perform safely as a commercial pilot and are competent to pass the required practical test.

Throughout your training, the flight instructor is responsible for emphasizing the performance of effective visual scanning, collision avoidance, and runway incursion avoidance procedures.

Satisfactory Performance

Satisfactory performance to meet the requirements for certification is based on your ability to safely:

1. Perform the approved areas of operation for the certificate or rating sought within the approved standards.
2. Demonstrate mastery of the aircraft with the successful outcome of each task performed never seriously in doubt.
3. Demonstrate satisfactory proficiency and competency within the approved statndards.
4. Demonstrate sound judgment.
5. Demonstrate single-pilot competence if the aircraft is type certificated for single-pilot operations.

Unsatisfactory Performance

If, in the judgment of the examiner, you don't meet the standards of performance for any task performed, the associated area of operation is failed and therefore the practical test is failed. The examiner or you may discontinue the test any time after the failure of an area of operation makes you ineligible for the certificate or rating sought. The test will be continued *only* with your consent. If the test is either continued or discontinued, you are entitled credit for only those tasks satisfactorily performed. However, during the retest and at the discretion of the examiner, any task may be re-evaluated, including those previously passed.

Typical areas of unsatisfactory performance and grounds for disqualification are:

1. Any action or lack of action by you that requires corrective intervention by the examiner to maintain safe flight.
2. Failure to use proper and effective visual scanning techniques to clear the area before and while performing maneuvers.
3. Consistently exceeding tolerances stated in the Objectives.
4. Failure to take prompt corrective action when tolerances are exceeded.

When a disapproval notice is issued, the examiner will record your unsatisfactory performance in terms of area of operation appropriate to the practical test conducted.

Crew Resources Management (CRM)

CRM refers to the effective use of all available sources: human resources, hardware, and information. Human resources include all groups routinely working with the cockpit crew or pilot who are involved with decisions that are required to operate a flight safely. CRM is not a single task but a set of competencies that must be evident in all tasks in this practical test standard as applied to single pilot operations or crew.

Use of Checklist

Throughout the practical test, you'll be evaluated on the use of an appropriate checklist. Proper use depends on the specific task being evaluated. It may be that (for instance in a single pilot operation) a checklist should be reviewed *after* the elements have been accomplished. Division of your attention and proper visual scanning should be considered when using a checklist.

Positive Exchange of Flight Controls

Before the flight make sure that there is a clear understanding of who has control of the aircraft. Review this before the flight. When the instructor or examiner wants you to take the controls, he or she will say, "You have the flight controls." You say, "I have the flight controls." You'll follow the same procedure giving them back. Don't let there be a question as to *who is flying the aircraft.*

Preflight Preparation

Certificates and Documents

You should understand and be able to explain commercial pilot certificate privileges and limitations applicable to flights for compensation or hire, medical certificates, personal logbooks, or flight records.

Documents That Stay in the Airplane

Airplane Registration

The certificate of registration contains the name and address of the owner, the aircraft manufacturer, the model, the registration number, and the manufacturer's serial number. The registration number is painted on the airplane. You can change the registration number of your airplane by applying to the FAA and paying a small fee, assuming that the number and letter combination you have chosen is not already in use. Many corporation planes use this system; for instance, the Jones Machinery Corporation may decide that the registration "N1234P" is too ordinary so they apply for, and get, "N100JM" or some other "more suitable" number-letter combination.

The manufacturer's serial number, however, is permanent and a means of identifying the airplane even when the registration number has been changed several times. The serial number 6-1050 means that the airplane is a Zephyr model 6, the 1,050th airplane of that model manufactured. The manufacturer's serial number is used for establishing the airplanes affected by new service notes or bulletins ("Zephyr Sixes, serials 6-379 through 6-614, must comply with this bulletin"); you can check the registration certificate for the manufacturer's serial number to see if your airplane is affected. If you own an airplane, you should know the serial number.

When an airplane changes owners, or the registration number is changed, a new registration certificate must be obtained.

Certificate of Airworthiness

The certificate of airworthiness is a document showing that the airplane has met the safety requirements of the Federal Aviation Administration and is "airworthy." It remains in effect indefinitely, or as long as the aircraft is maintained in accordance with the requirements of the FAA. Unlike the certificate of registration, it must be displayed so that it can be readily seen by pilot or passenger. The airworthiness certificate itself will stay in the airplane indefinitely, but in order for it to be valid, the following must be complied with:

1. *Privately owned aircraft* (not operated for hire)—The aircraft must have had a periodic (annual) inspection within the preceding 12 calendar months in accordance with the FARs. The logbooks and inspection forms will be a voucher for this.

2. *Aircraft used for hire*—In addition to the periodic (annual) inspection, an airplane used for hire to carry passengers or for flight instruction must have had an inspection within the last 100 hours of flight time in accordance with the FARs. This interval may be exceeded by not more than 10 hours when necessary to reach a point at which the inspection may be accomplished. In any event, such time must be included in the next 100-hour interval. The annual inspection is accepted as a 100-hour inspection. Both the annual and 100-hour inspections are complete inspections of the aircraft and identical in scope. In order to perform an annual inspection, however, the mechanic or facility must have inspection authorization.

3. *Progressive inspection*—The airplane you're flying may use the progressive inspection system. The owner or operator provides or makes arrangements for continuous inspection of the aircraft, so the inspection work load can be adjusted or equalized to suit the operation of the aircraft or the need of the owner. This plan permits greater utilization of the aircraft. The owner using progressive inspections must provide proper personnel, procedures, and facilities. Progressive inspections eliminate the need for periodic and 100-hour inspections during the period that this procedure is followed.

Check the logbooks and the inspection forms before taking the flight test to make sure that the airplane is airworthy. It would be plenty embarrassing for the flight examiner to find that the airplane has not been inspected as required and is not airworthy. No matter whether you begged, borrowed, hired, or stole the airplane, the final responsibility rests on you at the flight test. The owner/operator will be in trouble too, but this won't make it any easier on you.

If there is no record of the required inspections, then the airworthiness certificate is null and void. For information on Airworthiness Directives, service letters, and service bulletins, see the section "Repair of Maintenance Notifications" at the end of Chapter 13 of this book.

Airplane Flight Manual or Pilot's Operating Handbook

The POHs for general aviation airplanes are laid out as follows for standardization purposes:

Section 1—General

This section contains a three-view of the airplane and descriptive data on engine, propeller, fuel and oil, dimensions, and weights. It contains symbols, abbreviations, and terminology used in airplane performance.

Section 2—Limitations

This section includes airspeed limitations. The primary airspeed limitations are given in knots and in both indicated and calibrated airspeeds (although some manufacturers furnish mph data as well), and the markings are in knots and indicated airspeeds.

The maneuvering speed, which is the maximum indicated airspeed at which the controls may be abruptly and fully deflected without overstressing the airplane, depends on the stall speed, which decreases as the airplane gets lighter. (Review Chapter 11.)

Included here also are power plant limitations (engine rpm limits, maximum and minimum oil pressures, and maximum oil temperature and rpm range). Weight and CG limits are included for the particular airplane.

Maneuver and flight load factor limits are listed, as well as operations limits (day and night, VFR, and

IFR), fuel limitations (usable and unusable fuel), and minimum fuel grades. An airplane may not be able to use some of the fuel in flight; this is listed as "unusable fuel." For example, one airplane has a total fuel capacity of 24 U.S. gallons with 22 U.S. gallons being available in flight (2 gallons unusable).

Copies of composite or individual aircraft placards are included.

Section 3—Emergency Procedures

Here are checklists for such things as engine failures at various portions of the flight; forced landings, including ditching; fires during start and in flight; icing; electrical power supply malfunctions; and airspeeds for safe operation.

Included are amplified procedures for dealing with these "problems," such as how to recover from inadvertently flying into instrument conditions, recovering after a vacuum system failure, spin recoveries, rough engine operations, and electrical problems.

Section 4—Normal Procedures

This section has checklist procedures from preflight through climb, cruise, landing, and securing the airplane. It's followed by amplified procedures of the same material. Recommended speeds for normal operation are summarized, as well as given in the amplified procedures. Noise characteristics of the airplane may be included here.

Section 5—Performance

Performance charts (takeoff, cruise, landing) with sample problems are included, with range and endurance information, airspeed and altimeter calibration charts for normal and alternate static sources, and stall speed charts.

Section 6—Weight and Balance and Equipment List

Airplane weighing procedures are given here, as well as a loading graph and an equipment list with weights and arms of the various airplane components.

Section 7—Airplane and Systems Descriptions

The airframe, with its control systems, is described and diagrammed. The landing gear, engine and engine controls, etc., and fuel, brake, electrical, hydraulic, instrument, anti-icing, ventilation, and heating systems are covered here.

Section 8—Airplane Handling, Service, and Maintenance

Here is the information you need for preventive maintenance, ground handling, servicing and cleaning, and care for a particular airplane.

Section 9—Supplements

This covers optional systems, with descriptions and operating procedures of the electronics, oxygen, and other nonrequired equipment.

Other Aircraft Documents—Airframe, Engine, and Propeller Maintenance Records

The FARs state that the registered owner or operator must maintain a maintenance record in a form and manner prescribed by the FAA administrator, including a current and accurate record of the total time in service on the aircraft and on each engine, propeller, and appliance of the aircraft, and a record of inspections and the record of required maintenance. Such records shall be:

1. Presented for required entries each time inspection or maintenance is accomplished on the aircraft or engine.
2. Transferred to the new registered owner or operator upon disposition of the aircraft or engine involved.
3. Made available for inspection by authorized representatives of the FAA administrator or NTSB.

Number 3 is the reason you should have the logbooks and inspection reports with you for the flight test.

Logbooks

The logbook entry must include the type and extent of maintenance, alterations, repair, overhaul, or inspection and reflect the time in service and date when completed. The logbook should have entries when mandatory notes, service bulletins, and airworthiness directives are complied with. The regulations call for a separate, current, and permanent record of maintenance accomplished on the airframe, engine, and propeller, and the logbook is the record. You could carve the information on a piece of granite, but this would be unhandy to haul around, so the usual procedure is to use a logbook.

The airframe and each engine and propeller must have separate records.

Before taking the flight test, make sure your logbooks are the right ones and are up to date.

Record of Major Repairs and Alterations.

This is FAA form 337, a special form for major changes done after the plane leaves the manufacturer. The owner/operator keeps a copy, and an entry is made in the logbook with a reference to the date or work order by number and approving agency. The FAA 337 notes the new empty weight, useful load, and empty CG (as in the logbook) and is normally attached to the weight and Balance form in the airplane. Review Chapter 13 for information on service bulletins and other maintenance requirements.

Be able to locate and explain airworthiness directives, compliance records, maintenance/inspection requirements, and appropriate record keeping.

Summary of the Aircraft Documents

You can accomplish a great deal by going over the documents with the owner/operator of the airplane you plan to use on the flight test. Examiners can ask embarrassing questions that would have been simple to answer had you just spent a few minutes checking the airplane's papers (Figure 21-2). By the way, be sure you can explain limitations imposed on airplane operations with inoperative instruments or equipment, when a special flight permit is required, and procedures for obtaining a special flight permit. Know the required instruments and equipment for day/night VFR and whether your aircraft has a Minimum Equipment List (MEL).

Weather Information

Be able to obtain weather information pertinent to a proposed flight. Know what is pertinent and be able to interpret and understand the significance.

You'll be graded on reading actual information at the time of the practical test. If you haven't dealt with the workings of the National Weather Service lately, you'd better call an FSS or Weather Service Office and get up to date on what information is currently available and the best way to interpret it.

Figure 21-2.

Break out your copies of *Aviation Weather* and *Aviation Weather Services* beforehand for a good review of weather theory and how to interpret the information provided by the National Weather Service.

There will be emphasis on PIREPs, SIGMETs, and AIRMETs. Know how to use wind shear reports. Make a quick checklist to be sure that you can answer questions on METARs, TAFs, and FAs, the surface analysis chart, radar summary chart, wind and temperature aloft chart, significant weather prognostic chart, convective outlook chart, AWOS, ASOS, and ATIS reports. You'll make a competent go/no-go decision based on available weather information.

Cross-Country Flight Planning

Your knowledge and ability to plan a cross-country flight may be based on the most complex airplane used for the practical test. In-flight demonstrations of cross-country procedures will be tested under the area of operation "Navigation." You'll have a preplanned VFR cross-country flight (with a flight plan to the first fuel stop) considering maximum payload and fuel. (For Pete's sake, select and use current and appropriate aeronautical charts.) You'll plot a course with fuel stops, available alternates, and a suitable course of action for various situations.

You'll pick the best checkpoints and the most favorable altitude or flight level considering weather and equipment capabilities. You'll be expected to select appropriate radio aids for navigation and get pertinent information from the *Airport/Facility Directory* and other flight publications, including NOTAMs. You'll fill out a navigation log and simulate filing a VFR flight plan. When you select the route, check the airspace, obstructions, and terrain features—planning on flying through a TFR can cost points.

National Airspace System

Know the basic weather minimums for all classes of airspace and be able to prove your knowledge of Class A, B, C, D, E, and G airspace. You'll probably be asked questions on special use airspace and other airspace areas.

Performance and Limitations

You'll be expected to know the limits of your airplane, such as limit load factors and airspeeds (see Chapter 11) and to demonstrate proficient use of the appropriate performance charts, tables, and data—including cruise control, range, and endurance (Chapter 7).

You'll be expected to determine the airplane's performance in all phases of flight, so Chapters 5 to 9 of this book might be reviewed.

You'll be expected to refer to the approved weight and Balance data for the airplane. You might review the section on Airplane Weight and Balance in Chapter 10. You'll probably be asked for some practical computations of permissible fuel and payload (baggage and passenger) distributions. The FAA considers the following as standard for weight and balance computations:

Fuel—6 pounds per gallon
Oil—7½ pounds per gallon
Actual weights of persons

Remember that the baggage compartment is placarded for two reasons: (1) structural and (2) CG considerations.

You'll be expected to be able to work a weight and balance for the airplane being used, to determine that the weight and CG are within limits. You'll naturally use the charts and graphs furnished by the manufacturer. Don't use the sample empty weight, as given in the POH, unless the examiner just wants a general example. At least know that you'd use the actual empty weight and empty CG of the airplane you're flying.

Review Chapter 10, particularly with respect to the effect of CG positions on stability and control. Also note the effects of weight on performance and airplane stresses (Chapter 11).

Know the effects of seasonal and atmospheric conditions on the airplane's performance (for instance, High, Hot, and Humid Hurts). You'll be expected to use sound judgment in making a competent decision on whether the required performance is within the airplane's capabilities and operating limitations. (If you come back after the flight test with a wrinkled airplane, don't expect to get a commercial certificate that trip.)

Operation of Systems

You'll have to be familiar with the primary flight controls and trim, wing flaps, spoilers, and leading edge devices (Chapter 2).

Know the *pitot-static system* and the associated flight instruments (Chapter 4) as well as the *vacuum/pressure* systems and associated instruments that may have possible problems associated with the flight instruments and systems (Chapters 4 and 19).

Be aware of the foibles of *retractable landing gear* with particular emphasis on the retraction system (normal and emergency), the indicators, the brakes and tires, and the nosewheel steering (Chapter 14).

As far as the *power plant* is concerned, know the controls and indicators as well as the induction, carburetor/fuel injection, exhaust and turbocharging, and cooling and fire detection systems (Chapters 4, 12, and 19).

Be very familiar with the *propeller* type and controls (Chapters 2 and 12).

As far as the *fuel system* is concerned, you'd better have full knowledge of its capacity, pumps, control, and indicators, plus fueling procedures (approved grade, color, and additives) and the low-level warning system. For Pete's sake, know where the fuel drain valves are and in what order they should be used (Chapter 13).

The *oil system* information includes capacity, grade, and indicators (Chapters 4 and 13).

The *hydraulic system* will be discussed with attention paid to the controls and indicators plus pumps and regulators (Chapter 14).

You might review Chapter 4 and the *Pilot Operating Handbook* for the *electrical system* of your airplane. [Does your airplane have an alternator(s) or generator(s), and what are the advantages and disadvantages of each?] You might check Figure 4-70 to see a simple electrical system. Know where the battery is located and note if your airplane has an auxiliary power plug. What circuit breakers or fuses protect what components? If you lost all electrical power, what systems and instruments would you lose? Be very familiar with the internal and external lighting and controls.

You might review Chapter 18 and your POH for the *environmental system* of your airplane, including heating, cooling and ventilation, oxygen and pressurization, and the controls and indicators for all this.

Check out the *ice prevention and elimination systems* for your airplane (Chapter 19).

Avionics is a most important system. Which antenna (top or bottom) is for what communications system?

Aeromedical Factors

The *Airman's Information Manual* has an excellent chapter on "Medical Facts for Pilots," and there you can get information on hypoxia, hyperventilation, middle ear and sinus problems, spatial disorientation, motion sickness, the effects of alcohol and drugs, carbon monoxide poisoning, dehydration, stress and fatigue. (Review Chapter 18 of this book, also.) If you scuba dive and then fly too soon afterward, you could get the bends.

Night Operations

Review night visual perception, including functions of rods and cones, how the eyes adapt to changing light conditions, and how to cope with illusions created by various light conditions. Know about aids for increasing vision effectiveness.

Be aware of personal and required airplane lighting and equipment and how a pilot can judge another airplane's probable path by light interpretation. Review airport and navigation lighting, including pilot-controlled lighting.

If you had to, could you explain the steps of a night flight from preflight to landing, including possible emergencies?

Preflight Procedures

Preflight Check or Visual Inspection

Be prepared to answer *why* you are checking certain things on the airplane.

Start the line check in the cockpit. Make sure the ignition switch (or switches) and battery (master) switch are OFF.

Use the manufacturer's recommended procedure checklist. A pilot who finally makes up a line check only in order to pass a flight check doesn't deserve to get a higher certificate or rating. Of course, *you* have used a thorough line check for every flight since the student pilot days, so the only difference on the flight test will be explaining why each item is inspected.

It's amazing how little some pilots know about the internal workings of their airplanes. This is more often the case when the pilot has rented airplanes all along and has a blind faith in the operator. It may be possible that the pilot has never drained fuel strainers, always assuming that "the operator did it this morning." These pilots may not even know where to drain the fuel to check for water or dirt. It has happened. Know by feel where all the switches, circuit breakers, and spare fuses are hidden for both day *and* night operations.

When you become a commercial pilot or buy your own airplane you'll be carrying more of the preflight responsibility. As a commercial pilot you may operate away from the home base for days or weeks on a charter operation. Good ol' Joe, the mechanic, won't be around to drain the fuel strainer and check the oil for you. It'll be up to you to decide whether repair work should be done and whom to contact at the strange field. (Review Chapters 12, 13, 14, and 15.)

Airplane Servicing

You'd better know the proper grade and type of fuel and oil for your airplane and determine that there is an adequate supply of both on board. The examiner could ask questions about possible types of fuel contamination and how to eliminate it. If your airplane has oxygen equipment, know how to check the adequacy of the supply and how to use it (Chapter 18).

Cockpit Management

You'll show that you know good procedures in cockpit management by making sure that passengers and cargo are secure and full-control movement is possible. Brief passengers (the examiner) on safety belt use, doors, and emergency procedures. Make sure that your material (charts, etc.) and equipment are readily available. Ensure that loose (and dangerous) items are secured. Discuss with your instructor beforehand the factors of crew resource management.

Engine Starting

Use the checklist! Be able to explain the correct starting procedures, including use of external power sources and the effects of incorrect starting procedures. Don't abuse the equipment. You'll be judged on positioning the airplane to avoid creating hazards, determining that the area is clear, setting up the engine controls properly, setting (holding) the brakes, avoiding excessive engine rpm and/or allowing the airplane to move too soon, and checking the engine instruments after the start. Also, be able to explain the use of an external power source, hand propping hazards, and starting in hot or cold engine and/or weather conditions.

Taxiing

Be able to discuss all aspects of safe taxiing procedures, including the effect of wind on the airplane and the other elements in the flight test taxiing excerpts at the beginning of this chapter.

Runway Incursion Avoidance

You'll be asked to describe (and demonstrate) proper methods of avoiding runway incursions. Make sure you have a good knowledge of airport markings, especially runway hold short lines. Use the taxi diagram, write down taxi instructions as they are given, don't spend time "heads-down" while you are moving, and if you have any doubt about a clearance, ask for clarification as you bring the airplane to a stop. A good practice is the "sterile cockpit" concept required of the air carrier pilots—if you are moving on the ground, keep your activities restricted to "safety of flight." Also, if you aren't 100% sure of your location, immediately confess and ask for help. After you pass the checkride, you need to keep the good habits up—runway incursions happen at airports of all sizes.

Before Takeoff Check

Use the manufacturer's, or a recommended, checklist. If you start and make a run-up without a checklist, the examiner will terminate the flight (and is right to do so). You are now working to become a *professional* pilot and probably have used a checklist during every flight anyway. If your chandelles or lazy eights aren't so hot but your other flying has been good, and if you've been conscientious about using a checklist, you're much more apt to pass than if you have outstanding chandelles but no checklist.

If you position the airplane improperly (blasting other airplanes), run up over sand or gravel (sandblasting *your* airplane's propeller), or make a long run-up headed downwind (maybe overheating the engine), you could fail this task.

Touch each control or switch or adjust it to the prescribed position after calling it out from the checklist. Pay attention to both inside and outside the cockpit.

Recognize any discrepancy and determine that the airplane is ready for flight. ("The left mag *always* drops 600 rpm.") Review critical takeoff performance, airspeeds, and distances and describe emergency procedures. Catch the takeoff and departure clearances and note the takeoff time. *Don't* have a runway incursion or conflict with traffic prior to taxiing into the takeoff position.

Airport Operations

Radio Communications and ATC Light Signals

Be sure to think before transmitting (or listening for) a particular service and to transmit and report correctly using the recommended standard phraseology (no CB chatter). You'll be expected to be sharp in receiving, acknowledging, and complying with communications and to follow prescribed procedures for a simulated or actual communications failure. Be able to interpret and comply with ATC light signals.

Traffic Patterns

You'll be judged on your professionalism in the traffic pattern operations at airports with or without operating control towers. You also will be expected to use proper collision avoidance procedures and established traffic pattern procedures and to stick to instructions and rules. *Avoid wake turbulence!* Fly a precise pattern and make good corrections for wind drift.

Maintain adequate spacing from other traffic (formation flying is out) and maintain the traffic pattern altitude within ±100 feet and the desired airspeed within ±10 K. Don't forget the checklist, don't land on the wrong runway, and don't have any runway incursions.

Airport Taxiway and Runway Signs, Markings, and Lighting

You'll be expected to identify, interpret, and conform to airport, runway, and taxiing marking aids. To land on the *wrong* side of a displaced threshold or ignore the taxiway hold line could result in some disappointment.

Know and comply with airport lighting aids.

Takeoffs, Landings, and Go-Arounds/ Rejected Landings

Normal and Crosswind Takeoff and Climb

Review Chapters 5 and 6 for takeoff and climb factors. Be able to explain the elements of normal and crosswind takeoffs and climbs, including airspeeds, configurations, and emergency procedures. Adjust the mixture control as recommended (manufacturer or other reliable sources) for the existing conditions.

Note obstructions or other hazards and make sure the airplane is capable of performing the takeoff. Other factors to be considered are wind, alignment, necessary aileron deflection at the start and during the takeoff run, engine instrument check, smooth throttle operation, positive directional control (on center line), rotation at proper airspeed, maintaining V_Y ±5 K, good wind drift correction on climbout, retraction of gear and flaps at the proper point and airspeed in climb (after a positive rate of climb is indicated), setting desired climb power at safe altitude, maintaining a straight track over the extended center line until a turn is required, and completion of an after-takeoff checklist. If you pull the prop control back first (if the manufacturer insists that it should be the other way around) or forget to retract the gear and climb laboriously up to altitude, it could result in disqualification. Use proper noise abatement procedures. (Refer to your airplane's POH and Chapters 5, 6, 12, and 14.)

Normal and Crosswind Approach and Landing

You'll be asked to explain the elements of normal and crosswind approaches and landings, including airspeeds, configurations, performance, and related safety factors. Maintain a stabilized approach and recommended airspeed, or in the absence of a recommended airspeed, not more than 1.3 V_{S0} ±5 K with the wind gust factor applied.

For normal landings, the tailwheel-type airplane should touch down all three wheels simultaneously at or near the power-off stall speed. In strong gusty surface winds, you should be prepared to use a wheel landing. In the nosewheel-type airplane, the touchdowns should be on the main gear with little or no weight on the nosewheel.

Your crosswind corrections should be made throughout the final approach and touchdown. (Don't think you can wander all over creation on final, make a last second "save" and be given a lot of credit for headwork.) Don't relax your guard during the landing roll while congratulating yourself after an extra-smooth touchdown. Don't exceed the crosswind controlability of the airplane and don't ground loop. If a crosswind condition does not exist, be prepared for oral questions on the subject.

Figure 21-3. The mark used for power-off accuracy landings is considered to be a deep ditch—don't undershoot.

You'll be judged on takeoff and landing technique, judgment, drift correction, coordination, power technique, and smoothness. Keep the final approach speed within ±5 K with a gust correction applied and touchdown within 200 feet beyond a line or mark specified by the examiner.

For review purposes, take a look at these points on *power-off* accuracy landings. In a power-off approach to hit a spot, it is always better to be slightly high. If there's any question, you may slip or use flaps. Things may work out so that neither slipping nor flap application is necessary. Nothing is more embarrassing on a flight test than to think you're high, apply full flaps or make a steep slip, and discover that enthusiasm caused you to *undershoot*. The line or mark that you are required to land within 200 feet beyond is considered to be a ditch (Figure 21-3). If you are going to undershoot, recognize the fact and apply power. An examiner who catches you trying to "stretch the glide" may get a bad impression of your flying ability.

About correcting for overshooting: Although the rate of sink will increase considerably by slowing up the airplane in the glide, this is not the place to get cocked up and dangerously slow. Violent maneuvering, excessive slips, or dangerously low airspeeds will be disqualifying. One aid in telling whether you'll hit the spot or not is to watch its apparent movement as you glide toward it on final. If it moves toward you, an overshoot may occur; away, you may undershoot the spot.

Ground effect will tend to carry you farther down the field than you can determine by the apparent movement of the spot (Figure 21-4).

Every approach will have some small amount of "float." The amount depends on the approach speed. If you approach at 140 K (normal approach speed 80 K), the float distance will be extremely long. If you should approach at 61 K (stall speed 60 K), the float distance will be quite short (the airplane kind of "squashes" onto the ground).

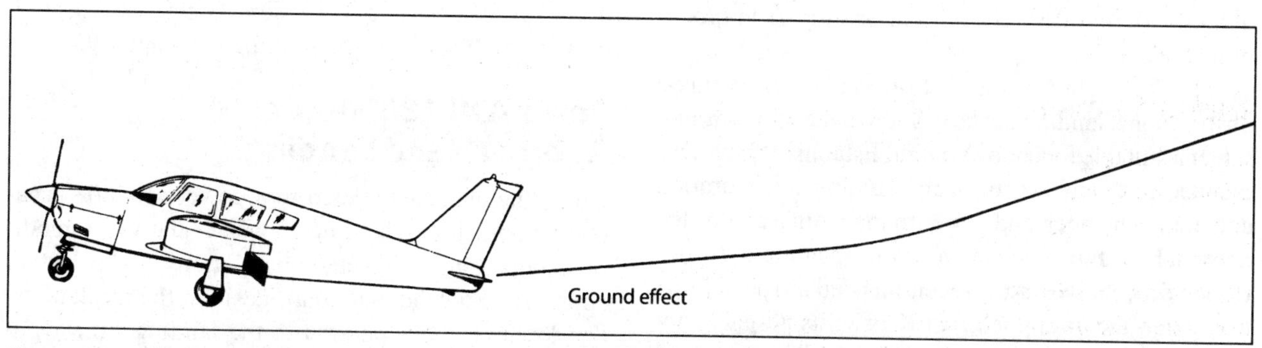

Figure 21-4. Ground effect.

Don't get so engrossed in the accuracy landing that you forget to put the wheels down, or skip other checklist items.

For points on various takeoffs and landings review Chapters 5 and 9.

A last note on the flight test landings: Improper or incomplete prelanding procedures, touching down with an excessive side load on the landing gear, and poor directional control will be disqualifying. Although it's not specifically mentioned, landing gear-up will terminate the flight test (probably this would be considered a result of improper or incomplete prelanding procedures).

Be aware of the possibility of wind shear or wake turbulence and carefully survey the touchdown point and area.

Soft-Field Takeoff and Climb

Know *why* you are using specific techniques, configurations, and airspeeds for this TASK. You should also be able to explain the emergency procedures and hazards associated with attempting to climb at airspeeds less than V_X.

Taxi onto the takeoff surface at a speed consistent with safety, align the airplane on the takeoff path without stopping, and advance the throttle to full power smoothly. Check the engine instruments and maintain a pitch attitude that transfers the weight from the wheels to the wings as soon as possible. Maintain directional control, lift off at the lowest possible airspeed, and stay in ground effect while accelerating. Accelerate to V_X ±5 K, if obstructions are to be cleared, otherwise to V_Y ±5 K. Retraction of flaps, gear, power use, and the flight track after takeoff will be judged. Checklist requirements are the same as for the short-field takeoff just covered (Chapters 5, 6, 12, and 14).

Soft-Field Approach and Landing

You'll be judged on your knowledge of what's involved in a soft-field approach and landing and why techniques different from the normal or short-field procedures must be used.

On the flight (practical) test, you are to evaluate obstructions, landing surface, and wind conditions and select a suitable touchdown point. Establish the recommended soft-field approach and landing configuration and adjust the pitch and power to maintain a controlled approach to the touchdown point. (Maintain a controlled descent rate at the recommended airspeed [gust correction factor applied], ±5 K or in its absence, not more than 1.3 V_{SO}.) Be aware of the possibility of wind shear and/or wake turbulence. Make smooth and timely corrections as necessary throughout the procedure and touch down smoothly at minimum descent rate and airspeed with no drift or misalignment of the longitudinal axis. Don't ground loop. Keep the airplane moving so that you wouldn't bog down (in an actual situation).

Short-Field Takeoff and Climb

Be able to explain *why* special techniques are required, the significance of specific airspeeds and configurations, and the expected performance for existing operating conditions. Know your emergency procedures for this phase of flight. Use the recommended flap setting and adjust the mixture control as recommended. (Start at the very beginning of the takeoff surface.) Use smooth throttle, check the engine instruments, and keep it straight on the runway. Rotate and lift off at the recommended airspeed and accelerate to V_X +5, -0 K until any obstacle is cleared or until at least 50 feet above the surface, then accelerate to V_Y and maintain it within ±5 K. Retract the flaps and landing gear as recommended. (Don't retract the gear until you can no longer land on the runway.) Set desired power at a safe maneuvering altitude, maintain a straight track (correct for any crosswind) until a turn is required, and complete the after-takeoff checklist (Chapters 5, 6, 12, and 14).

Short-Field Approach and Landing

Know the elements related to a short-field approach and landing. You'll be expected to touch down smoothly and within 100 feet of a specified point, with little or no float, no drift, and with the airplane's longitudinal axis aligned with the runway center line. Maintain a stabilized approach, controlled rate of descent, and recommended airspeed (or in its absence not more than 1.3 V_{SO}) with gust correction applied, ±5 K. (Remain aware of wind shear and/or wake turbulence.) Use that checklist! Figure 21-4 shows ground effect. You will be expected to maintain positive directional control and apply smooth braking, as necessary to stop in the shortest distance consistent with safety. (Review the section on short-field landing and braking in Chapter 9.)

Power-Off 180° Accuracy Approach and Landing

Know the elements related to a power-off 180° accuracy approach and landing. Consider the wind conditions, landing surface, and obstructions, and select an appropriate touchdown point. Position the airplane on the downwind leg, parallel to the landing runway, at not more than 1,000 feet AGL. Abeam the specified touchdown point, close the throttle (don't forget carb heat, if called for), and establish the appropriate glide speed. Complete the final airplane configuration and touch down in a normal landing attitude, at or within 200 feet beyond the specified touchdown point. Make sure you use an appropriate checklist! (Review Chapters 8, 9, and 16 in this book.)

Go-Around/Rejected Landing

You will likely have to explain the go-around procedure, including the recognition of the need to make a go-around, the importance of making a timely decision, the use of recommended airspeeds, the drag effects of landing gear and flaps (retract the gear after a positive rate-of-climb indication), and properly coping with undesirable pitch and yaw tendencies. Trim the airplane to accelerate to V_Y before the final flap retraction and climb at V_Y ±5 K. Watch that wind drift and obstruction clearances and use that checklist. The examiner may present a situation on the flight check in which a go-around from a rejected landing is required and check that you recognize it and that your performance is acceptable. (The main requirement is to maintain good control of the airplane during the cleaning-up process and establishment of climb.)

Slow Flight and Stalls

Note: As of this writing, the only stalls required by the Commercial PTS are power-off, power-on and accelerated stalls with recovery at the "onset" (buffeting).

Maneuvering During Slow Flight

This may not be the place for slow flight and stalls in the practical test, but the main thing is to know the subject. The examiner is *not* required to follow the precise order of the test. You will do slow flight at a safe altitude and will maneuver at an airspeed at which controllability is minimized to the point that further increasing the angle of attack or load factor (g force) or reducing power would result in an immediate stall.

For good practice beforehand, do slow flight in medium-banked level, climbing, and descending turns, and straight and level flight with various flap settings in both cruising and landing configurations.

You'll be checked on your competence in establishing the minimum controllable airspeed and positive control of the airplane and in recognizing incipient stalls. Your straight and level flight should be held within limits of ±50 feet altitude and ±10° of the assigned heading. If you don't look around before and during the maneuver, or if you stall the airplane, the examiner will disqualify you. Primary emphasis will be placed on airspeed control.

You might review the following while getting ready for the flight test:

Remember to keep turns shallow because the stall speed increases with angle of bank. You may have to use more power to maintain altitude in the turns.

The problem that most pilots have in the straight portions is that of maintaining heading. They concentrate so hard on airspeed that the airplane is allowed to turn at will.

The following tolerances are suggested for straight and level and turning flight:

Heading—±10°

Altitude—no change of altitude in excess of ±50 ft

Airspeed—Stabilize and maintain the airspeed at which an increase in angle of attack or g force or reduction in power would result in an immediate stall. (Airspeed +5/–0 K)

Bank—±5° in coordinated flight

A good exercise for you to practice for airplane cruise configuration is as follows:

1. Throttle back to less than the estimated power required to maintain altitude at the maximum endurance speed. Maintain altitude and heading as the airplane slows and adjust power as necessary. Fly straight and level for 2 minutes.
2. Increase power for climb as you raise the nose. Don't let the airspeed change. Maintain your heading—torque will now be more of a problem. Climb straight ahead for 1 minute. Make shallow climbing turns in each direction (15° to 20° banks).
3. Throttle back and resume level slow flight.
4. Carburetor heat ON, throttle closed. Set up a glide, maintain the slow flight airspeed. Don't jerk the throttle closed but ease it back as the nose is lowered to the glide position (Figure 21-5).
5. Make shallow gliding turns (20° to 30° banks) in each direction.

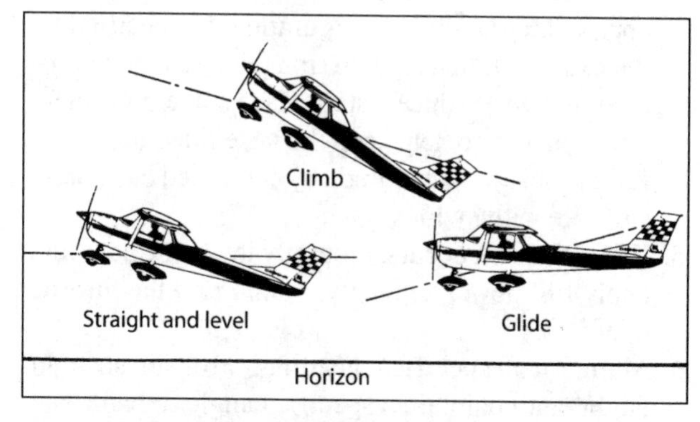

Figure 21-5. Slow-flight attitudes.

Repeat the exercise with the airplane in landing configuration, in straight and level flight, and in constant altitude turns. The transition to the various attitudes will give you the most trouble. The stall warner may be sounding off throughout the exercise. Roll out on specified headings within ±10°.

Common Errors

1. Poor altitude control during the transition from cruise to slow flight.
2. Heading problems during straight and level and during climb.
3. Stalling the airplane.
4. Excessive changes of speed during transition from straight and level to climb or glide.
5. Failure to maintain a continuous surveillance of the area before and during the procedure. (Don't stare at the airspeed indicator or altimeter.)
6. Getting below 1,500 feet AGL.

Straight-Ahead Stalls

Always clear the area by making two 90° turns in opposite directions, or one 180° turn before doing stalls straight ahead. There will be a blind spot over the nose during the stall. Some pilots mechanically make these turns but don't look around. This is not only unsafe but a waste of time. If you don't look around during the turns it's as bad as no attempt to clear the area at all.

Be sure in all stalls that you have recovered at least 1,500 feet above the ground.

Power-Off Stalls

You will maintain a heading ±10° in straight stalls.

Procedure

1. Clear the area.
2. Carburetor heat ON (if your airplane requires it), allow about 10 seconds for any ice to be cleared, then set power to approach configuration. (Practice clean and/or in the landing configuration as specified by the examiner.)
3. Raise the nose from the stabilized descent in the approach or landing configuration, as specified by the examiner, in a smooth transition to a pitch attitude that will induce a stall. Have some prominent object picked to help keep the nose lined up.
4. Pin the nose at that attitude by continued back pressure. Keep the wings level.
5. When the stall occurs, promptly lower the nose and apply full power smoothly—don't ram the throttle open.
6. Maintain a specified heading, ±10° in straight flight, and maintain a specified angle of bank, not to exceed 20° ±5° in turning flight when inducing the stall.
7. Retract the flaps to the recommended setting and retract landing gear (as it applies) after a positive rate of climb is established.

The check pilot could ask you to make a power-off recovery, which only means that the recovery is not quite as quick as that using power but is still positive. The reason for a no-power recovery would be to simulate a dead stick glide during an emergency when you've let it get too slow and are approaching a stall (with no power available to help recover). Keep looking around during the stall process, even though you cleared the area before starting.

After the recovery, allow the airplane to accelerate to V_X or V_Y approach speed and return to the altitude, heading, and airspeed specified by the examiner.

Power-On Stalls

The only difference between this stall and the power-off version is that cruise power (or more) is used throughout, which makes it necessary for you to raise the nose slightly higher in order to get stall indications without too much delay. Power makes a difference in nose attitude and stall speed because of the added slipstream over the wings and the airplane's vertical component of thrust. Figure 21-6 shows a comparison of the nose positions for the power-on and power-off approaches to a stall (pitch angles exaggerated).

The recovery for the stall consists of promptly reducing the pitch attitude and applying full throttle. Get in the habit of automatically applying full power on all stalls unless you are told otherwise by the check pilot.

Keep the following points in mind when flying the power-on stalls portion of the practical test:

1. Know what you are talking about when explaining this stall.
2. Be sure to start (and stay) above 1,500 feet AGL.
3. Establish the takeoff or departure configuration. Set the power to no less than 65 percent available power.

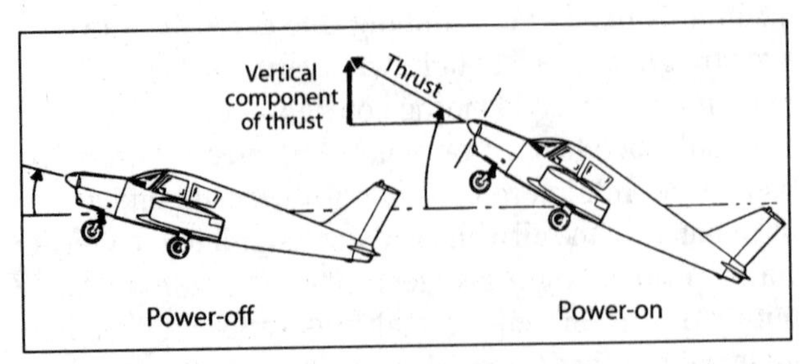

Figure 21-6. A comparison of the attitudes of the power-off and power-on versions of a stall.

4. Make that transition smoothly from the takeoff or departure attitude to a pitch attitude that will induce a stall.
5. Maintain a specified heading ±5°, in straight flight; maintain a specified angle of bank, not to exceed 20°, ±10° in turning flight, while inducing the stall.
6. Recognize and recover promptly as the stall occurs by simultaneously reducing the angle of attack, increasing power to maximum allowable, and leveling the wings to return to the straight and level flight attitude, with a minimum loss of altitude appropriate for the particular airplane.
7. Retract flaps to the recommended setting, retract the landing gear (if available) after a positive rate of climb is established.
8. Accelerate to V_X or V_Y before the final flap retraction; return to the altitude, heading, and airspeed specified by the examiner.

You'll be expected to recover to the point where adequate control effectiveness is regained with the minimum loss in altitude. Allow the airplane to accelerate to the best angle of climb with simulated obstacles, or the best rate of climb without simulated obstacles, and resume the climb. (See Takeoff and Departure Stalls.)

Common Errors (straight stalls portion)

1. Failure to clear the area.
2. Lowering the nose before there are definite indications of the stall.
3. Not keeping the wings level throughout.
4. Letting the nose wander.
5. Not maintaining the heading within ±5°.

Complete or Full Stall

This stall is a good exercise for keeping the wings level—and little else—but you should be familiar with it, if only for academic interest. The maneuver may be done at cruise power or at idle, as with the first stall types mentioned.

In performing this stall, pull the nose up higher than for the normal stall (up to about 30° above the horizon) and continue easing the control wheel back until the break occurs. In the complete stall, do not start a recovery until the nose has fallen to the horizon (keep that wheel all the way back!) at which point you release back pressure and apply full power.

You'll find that the power-on version may give you a little trouble in keeping the wings level and that the nose tends to wander. As you can see, this is an exercise—you certainly wouldn't deliberately wait until the nose had fallen through to the horizon before starting recovery in an accidental stall at low altitudes!

Summary of Some Straight-Ahead Stalls

Approach to a stall—Recover before the break. (Not required on the practical test.)

Normal stall—Recover immediately at the onset (buffet) or when full up-elevator travel has occurred.

Complete stall—The nose is higher; recover after the break when the nose has moved down to the horizon. (Not required on the practical test.)

Always clear the area.

Note that there are six possible combinations of the above stalls—each one with and without power.

Keep the wings level with coordinated controls as the nose is lowered and don't let the nose wander.

Turning Stalls

The heading of this section may be a little misleading because you should also practice the takeoff and departure stalls and approach to landing stalls straight ahead. However, in most cases, pilots seem to get into trouble in climbing or gliding turns at low altitudes—hence the heading.

Takeoff and Departure Stalls

These stalls simulate a situation that happens too often—a stall occurring during the takeoff or climbout. It may be caused by the pilot's distraction at a critical time or by just showing off.

The maneuver should be done at slightly above takeoff speed, in takeoff configuration (this means flaps if you normally use them for takeoff and, of course, gear down) and at recommended takeoff power. They should be done from straight climbs and climbing turns of 20°, ±10° constant bank.

You may find that the "high" wing will stall first in most airplanes and the airplane will roll in that direction, because as the stall is approached, the wings start losing lift and the airplane mushes and starts to slip. The highest wing gets interference from the fuselage and quits first. You can check this by watching the ball throughout the approach and stall; if you can no longer keep the ball centered (it will indicate a slip), the high wing will stall first. Don't blindly expect this to happen because if you stall at a higher airspeed and are skidding, the bottom wing may be slowed to a point where it might stall first. There is one model trainer on the market that has a tendency in a balanced climbing right turn to have the inside (right wing) drop first (the left turns are as expected). Also, your particular airplane may have been rigged laterally after leaving the manufacturer so that funny things happen in the stall. Of course, that's why you practice them anyway—to see what *your* airplane does and to find the best method of recovery. But normally, you can count on an "over the top" type of stall (the airplane rolls away from the ball).

To recover, get the nose down and level the wings with coordinated controls. Unless the roll is particularly vicious, you can usually recover by merely relaxing back pressure.

Procedure

1. Gently slow the airplane to about 5 K above the stall in the takeoff configuration (lift-off speed).
2. Apply climbing power and start a shallow-banked turn in either direction, pulling the nose up steeply. (Practice them from straight climbs, also.) Note the altitude at the "lift-off."
3. When the stall breaks, relax back pressure, use opposite rudder if necessary to stop any roll, and then level the wings with coordinated controls.

When practicing these stalls, you'll find that if the bank is steep you'll have trouble getting a clean break. The nose may drop, causing the airplane to descend in a tight circle, shuddering and buffeting—with no stall break.

Keep your head swiveling all during the approach and stall.

Practice the stall in both directions as well as straight ahead.

Common Errors

1. Too steep a bank in the turning stalls—no definite stall break. The bank angle must be 20°, ±10°.
2. Too early a recovery—recovering before a definite break.
3. Too late a recovery—the airplane is allowed to rotate too far before recovery is started.
4. Failure to make a steep climb and thereby delaying the stall as the airplane mushes.
5. Overeagerness to get the nose down; abrupt forward pressure on the wheel or stick, with the result that the nose is pushed too low and excessive altitude is lost during recovery.

Approach-to-Landing, or Gliding-Turn Stalls

These stalls might be considered a power-off version of the departure stalls. The airplane will be in the landing configuration and the engine throttled back. This stall demonstrates what *could* happen if the airplane is allowed to get too slow during a landing approach. This type of stall will be harder to get to break cleanly, particularly if you are practicing solo. Of course, you may have a great deal of trouble getting the airplane to stall cleanly during practice and then be complacent someday and find that the airplane *can* stall if you get sloppy and distracted. Practicing these stalls is intended to help you recognize what could happen and learn how to recover as quickly and safely as possible.

Procedure

Keep looking around throughout the approach and stall.

1. With the airplane in landing configuration, establish a normal gliding turn of 20°, ±10°, bank in either direction (after applying carburetor heat if called for). Be sure to practice the stalls in both directions—not all approaches are made from left-hand patterns. For straight-ahead versions, keep the heading within ±10° of that selected.
2. Flatten the glide through continued back pressure until the stall occurs.
3. Stop any roll with rudder and aileron as you simultaneously release back pressure and apply *full* power.
4. Clean up the airplane and establish a climb or continue the approach as required.

Practice this stall from straight glides as well as from moderately banked (20°) turns.

It requires no will power to lower the nose when you're practicing stalls at 3,000 feet. It's very easy up there—you just get the nose down and don't pay any attention to it. *But* at 200 feet or so you'd have to force yourself to release back pressure to recover from a stall. Fatal accidents have occurred because pilots have gone back to their instincts and ignored training when under stress.

Practice with your instructor recoveries without power—note the difference.

Common Errors

1. Too steep a bank in the turning stall.
2. Allowing the wings to become level through inattention during the stall approach. You wouldn't have this problem during an actual landing approach because you'd be watching the runway and would be turning as necessary to line up.
3. Too early a recovery; not allowing the stall to break.
4. Overeagerness in getting the nose down; excessive forward pressure during the recovery.

Accelerated Stalls

Here is proof positive that a stall is a matter of angle of attack, not airspeed.

You don't do any of the accelerated stalls at an airspeed of more than 1.25 times the unaccelerated stall speed because of the possibility of overstressing the airplane, particularly in gusty air. The flaps will be retracted for this same reason.

Accelerated stalls are done from a turn of 45° bank. There are two reasons for this: (1) this is the condition under which most pilots actually encounter the accelerated stall in flight—when they try to tighten the turn by pulling back on the wheel or by trying to maintain altitude without sufficient power and (2) this avoids inadvertently pulling the nose straight up abruptly in practice, getting a whip stall (the airplane stalls with the nose up so steeply that it tends to slide backward).

Unless you are skidding, the high wing will usually stall first, as in the departure and approach stalls, but the roll will be faster. The recovery is standard; release back pressure and return to level flight through use of coordinated controls. Plan on adding power during recovery.

In practice, recover (1) immediately upon stall recognition and (2) after a full stall develops and the nose falls below level flight attitude.

In situation 1 the recovery is simple. Relaxing the back pressure at the right time can result in the airplane's recovering in straight and level flight, if the high wing stalled first and roll occurred.

In situation 2 the nose will be low, and the airplane will probably have rolled over into a steep bank. Relax back pressure and then bring the airplane back to straight and level flight through use of coordinated controls.

Recover quickly with a minimum loss of altitude, but don't get overeager and restall it.

Don't get over cruise speed at any time during the recovery.

Procedure

1. Using power as needed to maintain altitude, make a 45° (or more)-banked turn. Slow the airplane to no more than 1.25 times the normal stall speed.
2. Increase the angle of attack in a moderate climb or constant altitude until a stall occurs. Power may be reduced below cruising to aid in producing the stall, but any decrease in the rate of climb or loss of altitude will relieve the load factor (and the stall is not "accelerated"). Remember the term "accelerated" means that above-normal load factors are present at the stall.
3. Release back pressure, open the throttle, and recover to straight and level flight using coordinated controls.

The 1.25 factor does not apply to an aerobatic category airplane, but keep it below the maneuvering speed or recommended speed for accelerated maneuvers.

Incidentally, some airplanes do *not* give a sharp stall break and, with these, when the wheel or stick is full back, initiate your recovery.

Common Errors

1. Jerking the wheel or stick back.
2. The opposite—timid application of back pressure.
3. Too brisk forward pressure on recovery, which hangs occupants on seat belts and puts undue negative stress on the airplane.

Cross-Control (Skidding) Stalls

This stall is most likely to occur during the turn onto the final approach but, as such, is not required on the commercial practical test. A typical situation might be as follows:

You see that in the turn onto final you will go past the runway unless your turn rate is increased. Now, everybody knows that the stall speed increases with an increase in bank, so you figure that the best way to turn is by skidding around—and not increasing the bank. You start applying inside rudder, which increases the turn rate, but the outside wing is speeded up and the bank starts to increase. You take care of this by using aileron against the turn, which actually helps drag the inside wing back farther. Because the airplane is in a banked attitude, application of inside rudder (and opposite aileron) tends to make the nose drop, which is counteracted by increased back pressure. The situation is perfect—for having one wing stall before the other, that is, true, the wing with the down aileron has more coefficient of lift (the down aileron acts as a flap, increasing the coefficient of lift), but the drag of that wing increases even more sharply, which slows it more. So the inside wing starts dropping, which increases the angle of attack—and it stalls before the outside wing. Another term for this stall is "under-the-bottom stall"—an apt description.

Look back at Figure 2-11 (the NASA 0006 airfoil) to see the theory behind *why* the wing with the down aileron stalls first. The coefficient of lift (C_L) versus angle of attack curve, without flaps, stalls at about 9°. When flaps are used, the stall occurs at about 6° angle of attack. The C_L is higher at the stall, but that flapped wing stalls "sooner" because both wings' angle of attack is increased from some point of reference. The down aileron acts as a flap and the lift of each wing is about equal, since lift is a combination of calibrated airspeed (dynamic pressure, q) and angle of attack, or C_L, for a given airplane (the use of inside rudder speeds up the outside, unflapped wing). The stall occurs as the critical angle of attack is reached first for the wing with the down aileron.

You should be familiar with this stall and know that it *could* happen and note the best means of recovery.

Figure 21-7. The pilot sees on approach that, unless the rate of turn is increased, he'll fly past the runway and have to turn back to it.

Figure 21-8. This is sloppy flying and the other pilots will notice. He knows that the stall speed increases with a steeper bank so he decides to cheat by using inside rudder and skidding it around (and maybe using just a *touch* of opposite aileron).

Figure 21-9. Inside rudder means that the outside (left) wing will speed up, steepening the right bank. He applies more opposite (left) aileron. The cycle continues until he is in a shallow, banked skid with well-crossed controls at a very low speed (he is using added back pressure to keep the nose up).

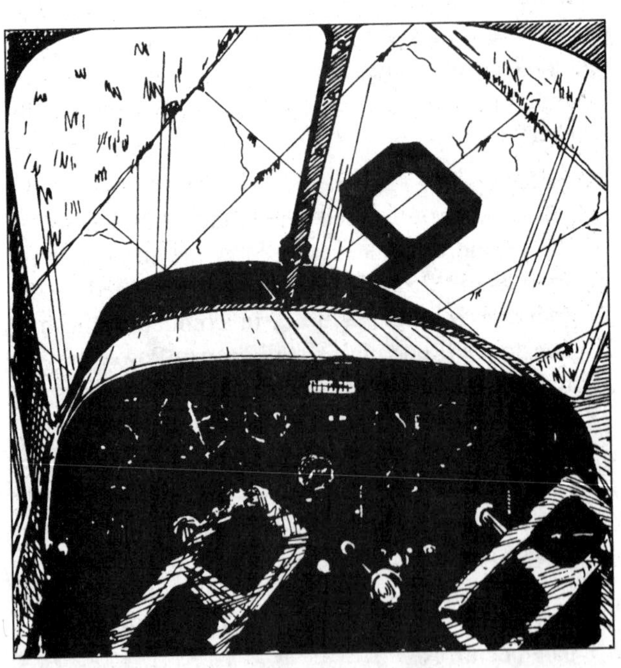

Figure 21-10. A view of the runway as seen from a near inverted position just after the stall occurs. Another statistic!

Figures 21-7 through 21-10 show the probable sequence of such an actual stall at a low altitude. The series shows a *right-hand* approach—an even more likely setup for such a stall, as you would be more apt to misjudge the turn.

Anytime you find yourself with a tailwind on the base leg, you should be alert for the overshoot and the temptation of trying to salvage the approach. If in doubt, take it around.

Procedure

1. Practice these stalls at a safe altitude and keep an eye out for other traffic. Use carburetor heat, if required. Make a shallow gliding turn in either direction. You may have to carry some power during the practice sessions to help get a good break. Sometimes it seems it is easily accomplished only when you *don't* want to stall. In practice stalls it's probably best not to use flaps because of the possibility of exceeding the max flaps-down speed during the recovery. In an actual stall on an approach turn, you'd have the flaps down but wouldn't be worrying particularly about the max flaps-down speed during the recovery.
2. Apply more and more inside rudder to cheat on the turn. Use opposite aileron as necessary to keep the bank from increasing.
3. Keep the nose up by increasing the back pressure.
4. When the stall break occurs, the roll will be rapid. Neutralize the ailerons; stop any further rotation with opposite rudder as you relax the back pressure. Get the flaps up before reaching V_{FE} if they were used.
5. Then return to normal flight with coordinated controls and add power as the recovery progresses.

As the roll is fast, the bank may be vertical or past vertical. The nose will be low and speed will build up quickly. The usual error in practice is allowing the airspeed to build up too high during recovery, which wastes altitude. Recover to straight and level flight with coordinated controls as soon as possible without overstressing the airplane or getting a secondary stall.

The bad thing is that this stall is most likely to occur at lower altitudes where recovery is less sure. Practice it until you are able to recognize the conditions leading up to it—and then avoid those conditions. Another bad thing is that the feeling you get as the stall is approached is like that you feel when turning a corner in a car; it feels "natural" (you've felt this thousands of times when driving and turning corners). It is suggested that the first turn from downwind to base have a 30° bank. This gets you around to see the runway and only raises the stall speed of *any airplane* by a factor of 1.07. This stall is not required to be demonstrated on the commercial practical test but is included for information.

Common Errors

1. Not neutralizing the ailerons at the start of the recovery.
2. Using too much opposite (top) rudder to stop rotation, causing the airplane to slip badly.
3. Hesitation in recovering, with a greater than necessary altitude loss.

Spin Awareness

Although spins are not required on the commercial practical test, you're required to have some idea of the theory behind them. *A spin is an aggravated stall resulting in autorotation.*

The airplanes that you've been flying are generally spin resistant; you have to make them spin. They should show no uncontrollable spin characteristics no matter how you use the controls. Some of the older light trainers would come out of a spin of their own accord with the pilot's hands and feet removed from the controls, but this is not the most effective spin recovery method. You remember in the departure and approach stalls and the cross-control stall that one wing stalled before the other and a rolling moment was produced. If you had held the wheel back and used rudder in the direction of roll, a spin would have likely followed. The whole theory of the spin can be understood by realizing that one wing is stalled before the other, producing an imbalance of lift and drag (autorotation). If you continue to hold back pressure and hold rudder into the roll, this stalled condition remains and the roll continues as the nose "falls off" downward.

Background

Spins and spirals are sometimes confused. The spiral is a high-speed, low-angle-of-attack, descending turn; *normal control pressures* are used to recover. The spin is at low airspeed and a high angle of attack; *mechanical control movements* are used for recovery. (More about spin recovery procedures later.)

The following factors about upright (normal) spins aren't generally known.

Rate of Descent

In the developed spin, the average two-place trainer has a rate of descent of from 5,500 to 8,000 fpm, depending on the spin mode. (Usually, the flatter spin mode has the lower rate of descent, but even a "mere" 5,500 fpm can be fatal.)

One question often asked is, How much altitude is lost per turn? There's not a simple answer because the greater the number of turns, the less the loss per turn. For instance, you'd probably do well to allow for a loss of 1,000 to 1,500 feet for a 1-turn spin, because altitude is also required for entry and recovery from that one turn. On the other hand, a 21-turn spin in a current trainer resulted in a total altitude loss of 4,100 feet from start to level-off after recovery—an average of 195 feet per turn. In that longer spin, the altitude used for entry and recovery is spread out among the 21 turns instead of being a major factor, as for the 1-turn spin.

Rate of Rotation

One popular trainer averages 1.3 seconds per turn (277° per second) in the first five or six turns, then pitches up slightly from the 6th to 9th (or 10th) turn with the rotation rate slowing to about 170° per second. You may find that the engine quits (the prop stops) in prolonged spins, but this does not affect the effectiveness of recovery. After the airplane is out of the spin, the starter can be used to get things going again. (Holler "Clear!" before using the starter, naturally.)

Instrument Indications

The airspeed will be low and remain so if the airplane stays in the spin. If, as the rotation progresses, the airspeed continues to increase from stall or near-stall indications, the airplane is easing into a spiral and recovery should be effected immediately to avoid high-airspeed and/or high-stress problems. As mentioned, one light trainer in an extended spin changed modes (back and forth), that is, moved from a comparatively steep nose-down attitude to a more pitched-up one; and the airspeed varied from 45 K in the steep mode to zero in the more pitched-up attitude.

The turn and slip needle, or the small airplane in the turn coordinator, is always leaning in the direction of the spin, but the ball is normally unreliable. For instance, the reaction of the ball depends on its relative position to the CG. (The airplane is rotating around its CG, which is moving around the spin axis, which in turn is moving in relation to a vertical, or earth-related, axis. If you think about this in a spin you may get confused enough to forget how to recover—a procedure that will be discussed shortly. On several side-by-side airplanes, with the turn and slip or turn coordinator located on the left (pilot's) side of the panel, the ball always goes to (and stays on) the left side of the instrument for both *left and right developed spins*. (A slip indicator placed on the *right* side of the panel moved over to and stayed on the *right* side of the instrument in spins in both directions.) It has been noted in some sources that the ball always goes to the outside of the spin, and for recovery the pilot should "step on the ball." In some airplanes with the slip indicator in the center of the panel, a slight tendency for the ball to move outside of the spin has been noted, *but don't "predict" it for your airplane.*

In a current tandem military basic trainer, the ball in the front cockpit (near the CG) has a reaction different from the one in the rear cockpit. (In one experiment spinning in either direction, the ball in the front cockpit T/S had very small oscillations on each side of neutral and the rear cockpit ball deflected slightly *into* the spin.)

Practice Spin to the Left

1. Before doing any spins in an airplane you haven't spun before, it would be wise to have an instructor experienced in spinning it ride with you to demonstrate the entry and recovery procedures. Even if you've spun earlier models of an airplane, you'd better review the recovery procedure and either talk to some of the local instructors or get them to ride with you. In later models, the manufacturer may have changed the geometry of the airplane or added other factors that affected the airplane's recovery characteristics. Such changes can surprise you on that first spin.

Of course, you should make sure that the airplane is certificated for spinning and is properly loaded. The control cables should have the proper tension because it would be "interesting," after getting into the spin, to discover that full-opposite rudder pedal deflection used for recovery only moves the rudder a few degrees.

2. Get enough altitude so that you'll be recovered by 3,000 feet above the ground.

3. Clear the area and start a normal power-off stall (use carburetor heat if recommended).

4. Just as the stall break occurs, apply—and hold—full left rudder; keep the wheel or stick full back. Some airplanes require a blast of power to get the spin started; the prop blast gives the rudder added effectiveness to yaw the airplane.

5. The nose drops as the airplane rolls, but the full up-elevator does not allow the airplane to recover from the stall. The unequal lift of the wings gives the airplane its rotational motion.

The spin is continued as long as the rudder and wheel are held as above. The rotation of the airplane tends to continue the imbalance of lift; the "down-moving" wing keeps its high angle of attack and remains well stalled. The "up-moving" wing maintains a lower angle of attack (and more lift).

If you should unconsciously relax back pressure before the developed spin, a spiral will result.

The properly executed spin is no harder on the airplane than a stall. A sloppy recovery puts more stress on the airplane than the spin itself.

Don't have the flaps down when practicing spins because it might change the airplane's spin characteristics, plus the fact that you might exceed the maximum flaps-down speed during the recovery.

Spin Recovery

It would be well to take the recovery step-by-step from a theoretical standpoint first, and then bring in some practical recovery procedures.

1. You used the rudder to induce the yaw in the spin entry, so opposite rudder should be applied to stop the yaw, equalize the lift of the two wings, and stop autorotation. If the rudder effectively does this, it should be neutralized as soon as rotation stops or a spin in the opposite direction (a progressive spin) could be started.

2. At this instant, in a theoretical look at recovery procedures, the rudder is neutral (the rotation has stopped) but you're still holding the wheel or stick full back and the airplane is still stalled, even though the nose appears to be pointed almost straight down. If you continued to hold the wheel full back the airplane would be buffeting and could, because of rigging, tend to whip off into a new spin in either direction.

The autorotation, or imbalance of lift and drag, has been broken, and now the stall recovery is initiated by relaxing the back pressure *or* giving a brisk forward motion of the wheel or stick (depending on the airplane). For older and lighter trainers such as the J-3 Cub, Aeronca Champion, Taylorcrafts, or Cessna 120-140s, a slight relaxing of the back pressure was enough to assure that the stall (and spin) was broken. In some later airplanes with higher wing loadings, the wheel or stick must be *briskly* moved forward, well ahead of neutral, to get the nose farther down and break the stall.

3. The third step is recovery from the dive after the autorotation and stall are broken. Sometimes the airspeed is allowed to get too high or too much back pressure is used on the pull-out (or both). Sometimes a pilot in a hurry to recover relaxes back pressure (or uses a brisk forward motion as required) and immediately pulls back on the control wheel to "get it out of the dive," which results in a quick restalling of the airplane and possibly setting off a progressive (or new) spin. You've had this experience with plain everyday stalls—a too-quick recovery can put the airplane back into a stalled condition, and the process has to be started again.

Okay, the three steps mentioned were just that, a listing of required control movements for discussion purposes. You'll find that with some airplanes the use of rudder alone won't stop the rotation, so you wouldn't wait for it to take effect before applying forward pressure, which would help not only to break the stall but also to aid the rudder in stopping the yaw and unbalanced lift-drag condition. In other words, you would apply full opposite rudder followed immediately by brisk forward movement of the wheel, holding the controls this way until rotation stops. Usually in this procedure, because of the almost simultaneous application of elevator with the rudder, the nose is down and the airspeed starts picking up as soon as the rotation stops; at this point the rudder is neutralized and back pressure is again applied to ease the airplane from the dive. (Some POHs suggest simultaneous use of rudder and elevator in the recovery.)

For some airplanes, ailerons against the spin speed it up, but for others the rate of rotation slows if ailerons are used opposite to the roll. *A suggested all-around procedure, however, is to leave the ailerons neutral throughout the spin and recovery to avoid adding some unknown factors to the recovery.*

Usually, the steeper spin modes are more easily recoverable and have a faster rate of rotation, as was discussed earlier in this section. If in extended spins the airplane moves into a flatter mode (which usually means more time and turns required for recovery), the recovery process may move it back through the earlier, faster rotation mode as it goes back to the normal flight regime. The initial reaction by the pilot is to think that the recovery inputs are making things worse (the rotation speeded up!) when actually this is a good sign for many airplanes. Fortunately the airplane often moves through the increased rotation rate and on to recovery before the pilot has time to "start thinking" and back off from this proper recovery technique. Sometimes it seems to take longer to recover than anticipated. There's always the temptation to Try Something Else. If you are using the POH-recommended recovery, give it a chance, although it may seem a long time before good things start happening.

In theory, it would seem that adding power during recovery would increase the slipstream by the rudder, thereby increasing its effectiveness. The problem is that in a standard configuration, pitch-up results from added power—and *that* you don't need. A NASA study has shown that even in jets of high thrust-to-weight ratios, addition of power has little measurable effect in aiding recovery and in some cases may be detrimental. Also, in an extended spin, the engine may stop completely, as noted earlier, which would make academic the subject of power helping or hurting the recovery.

Summary of Spins

The POH will take precedence over the general look at spins given here, but you might keep in mind the following notes about spin recoveries.

1. Most airplanes recover more promptly if the throttle is closed before using the aerodynamic controls. Neutralize the ailerons. Then,

2. A general recovery procedure is to use full rudder opposite to the spin, followed almost immediately by a brisk forward movement, well ahead of neutral, of the wheel or stick. (Don't violently *jam* the wheel full forward—the airplane could be overstressed or an inverted spin entered.) For some airplanes the rate of rotation appears to speed up as the recovery starts, which could fool you into thinking that things are getting worse.

3. As soon as rotation has stopped, neutralize the rudder and use the elevator to help further break the stall or ease the airplane from the dive. One error made by pilots with comparatively little spin recovery experience is continuing to hold opposite rudder after the rotation has stopped and airspeed builds up; this can cause heavy side loads on the vertical tail.

4. Normally docile airplanes can bite back if the CG is near or at the aft limits of the envelope. Of course, you would not deliberately spin an airplane with people in the rear seats or with baggage back there; if you get into a stall situation with this type of loading, don't let a rotation get started. For most airplanes, the first two turns are an incipient spin condition and the spin can be stopped relatively easily. After that, moments of inertia can be such in the developed spin that recovery is impossible. If it looks like the stall is getting out of hand, get that nose down farther with a brisk forward movement of the wheel (and you may decide that opposite rudder and wheel action is the best move to make—you can apologize to the passengers later).

For the oral part of the Practical Test, you should know the following:

1. Aerodynamic conditions required for a spin: One wing is stalled before the other; both wings are stalled in the developed spin but have a different angle of attack with resulting differences in lift and drag, thus maintaining autorotation.
2. Flight situations and conditions where unintentional spins may occur. Pilot distraction and uncoordinated flight are the most likely culprits.
3. Instrument indications during spin or spiral. Check the "Instrument Indications" section under Spin Awareness in this chapter.
4. Techniques and Procedures used to recognize and recover from unintentional spins. See the "Spin Recovery" section under Spin Awareness in this chapter.

Performance Maneuvers

Steep Turns

Maximum performance maneuvers are required on the commercial flight test so that you may demonstrate your ability to fly in a precise manner. These maneuvers are a measure of airmanship and are specifically planned so you fly the airplane through all speed ranges and in varying attitudes. The precision maneuvers are practice maneuvers and are seldom used in normal flying.

The maneuvers done at higher altitudes (1,500 feet above the surface or higher) are considered "high work" and are normally all done at the beginning of the flight test, although there is no written law about it. High work and low-altitude maneuvers are grouped as such here to give a clearer picture of the probable sequence of the flight test. The stall series and slow flight have been covered as a separate unit.

Here's a suggestion for any climbs or glides during the flight test (or anytime). Don't climb or glide straight ahead for extended periods. Remember that there is a blind spot under the nose. Make all climbing turns *shallow* and keep a sharp lookout for other airplanes (a steeply banked climbing turn results in a lot of turn and little climb).

You've done steep turns before but now have closer limits to stay within. To review the maneuver briefly:

The steep turn required on the commercial flight test is a steep turn with a bank of at least 50°. Remember though that a 60° bank or more is conceived as aerobatics. Your airplane may not be certificated to legally do that. You will be allowed up to a ±100-ft altitude lapse, a ±10-K entry airspeed variation, and a rollout ±10° of the entry heading.

Establish the manufacturer's recommended airspeed or, if one is not stated, a safe airspeed not to exceed V_A (see Chapter 11).

No slip or skid will be maintained.

You may use climb power in the turns to help maintain altitude at the steep angle of bank.

Procedure

You may have to do a steep turn in either direction, and the check pilot will require that you roll directly from one into another.

At a safe altitude and clear area, pick a road or a prominent landmark on the horizon to use as a reference point. Don't just peer ahead when looking for a point—an outstanding one may be off the wingtip. Head toward the reference point and get settled on the chosen altitude.

Choose the direction of the first steep turn and, after looking to make sure that you aren't turning into another airplane, start rolling into the turn and smoothly open the throttle to climb power. You should use a 50° bank and have climb power established before you have turned the first 45°. Your job will be to maintain a near-constant bank.

A bank of 50° is pretty steep and the usual tendency is to lose altitude. If this occurs, you know that the bank must be shallowed in order to regain altitude. If you have a tendency to climb, a slight steepening of the bank may help you—but you only have about 5° of bank to vary on each side of the 50°.

In several places in earlier chapters it was mentioned that the load factor was 2 in a 60° bank and that the stall speed was increased by the factor of the $\sqrt{2}$, or 1.414. The stall speed increases by 41% in a 60°-banked, constant-altitude turn. The stall speed increases because of the bank. The airplane slows because the angle of attack is increased to maintain altitude, and you are being squeezed in the middle even at the slightly lesser bank here of 50°. The power you are using helps to lower the stall speed as well as allowing you to maintain a constant altitude at a higher airspeed.

Check the nose, wing, and altimeter as you turn. Keep a sharp eye out for the reference point and keep up with your turn. The earlier you catch deviations, the fewer problems you'll have.

If the airplane is holding the bank and altitude, don't do anything. The most common problem is that the pilot spoils the ideal setup by trying to be doing *something* at all times.

Remember "torque" effects: the airplane is slower than cruise and you are using climb power. The tendency is to skid slightly in the left turns and slip in the right turns. Slight right rudder may be needed to keep the ball centered. There's no need to go into detail about the fallacy of trying to hold up the nose with top rudder during the turn—*don't!*

The ±100-ft altitude allowance means that at *no time* during the maneuver may you exceed those limits. Some pilots figure that it doesn't matter how far they are off the original altitude during the turns as long as they are within 100 feet of it when they roll out. They find that the check pilot disagrees.

As you roll out, throttle back to cruise power, even if you plan on rolling right back into a steep turn in the opposite direction. The biggest problem most pilots have is keeping the nose from rising during the roll-out even if they have started throttling back. Imagine how tough it would be to keep from gaining altitude with excess power being used. Smoothly apply climb power as you roll into the opposite bank.

Common Errors

1. Too much back pressure at the beginning of the roll-in; the nose rises and the airplane climbs.
2. Improper throttle handling; rough throttle operation at the beginning and end of the maneuver.
3. Attempting to use back pressure alone to bring the nose up, if it drops; forgetting that the bank must be shallowed.
4. Failure to keep up with the checkpoint.
5. Letting the nose rise on roll-out, causing the airplane to climb.
6. Slipping or skidding throughout the turns.

Summing up the check pilot's expectations for the steep power turns: you'll be asked to enter a 360° turn maintaining a bank angle of at least 50°, ±5° in smooth, stabilized, coordinated flight. Keep the altitude within ±100 feet and the desired airspeed within ±10 K. Keep your attention divided between orientation and airplane control. After rolling out within ±10° of the initial heading, you are to immediately set up a steep turn of at least 360° in the opposite direction, with the same limits. Avoid indications of an approaching stall or a tendency to exceed the structural limits of the airplane during the turns.

Chandelles

The chandelle is a maximum performance climbing turn with a 180° change in direction (Figure 21-11). It is a good training maneuver because of the speed changes and the requirement for careful planning. Clear the area.

Procedure

Use the recommended entry speed given in the POH or on the appropriate placard. Stay below the maneuvering speed, if you aren't sure about the entry speed. Cruise plus 10% is a quick and dirty figure for chandelle entry for many airplanes. However, for some complex airplanes, the maneuvering speed is lower than the usual cruise CAS, and the airplane should be slowed to V_A before starting the chandelle. As the proper speed is reached, set up a medium bank (approximately 30°). The ailerons are then neutralized. You may have to hold slight left rudder in the dive because of offset fin effect, but check it for your airplane. Apply back pressure smoothly. The airplane's bank will tend to *steepen slightly* as the nose moves up and around because of the pitch change, but the examiner will want you to maintain a constant bank. You'll be changing rudder pressure because of the torque effects as the speed changes.

The airplane will be turned slightly before you get the back pressure started—this is expected. The wrong thing to do during the initial dive and bank is to try

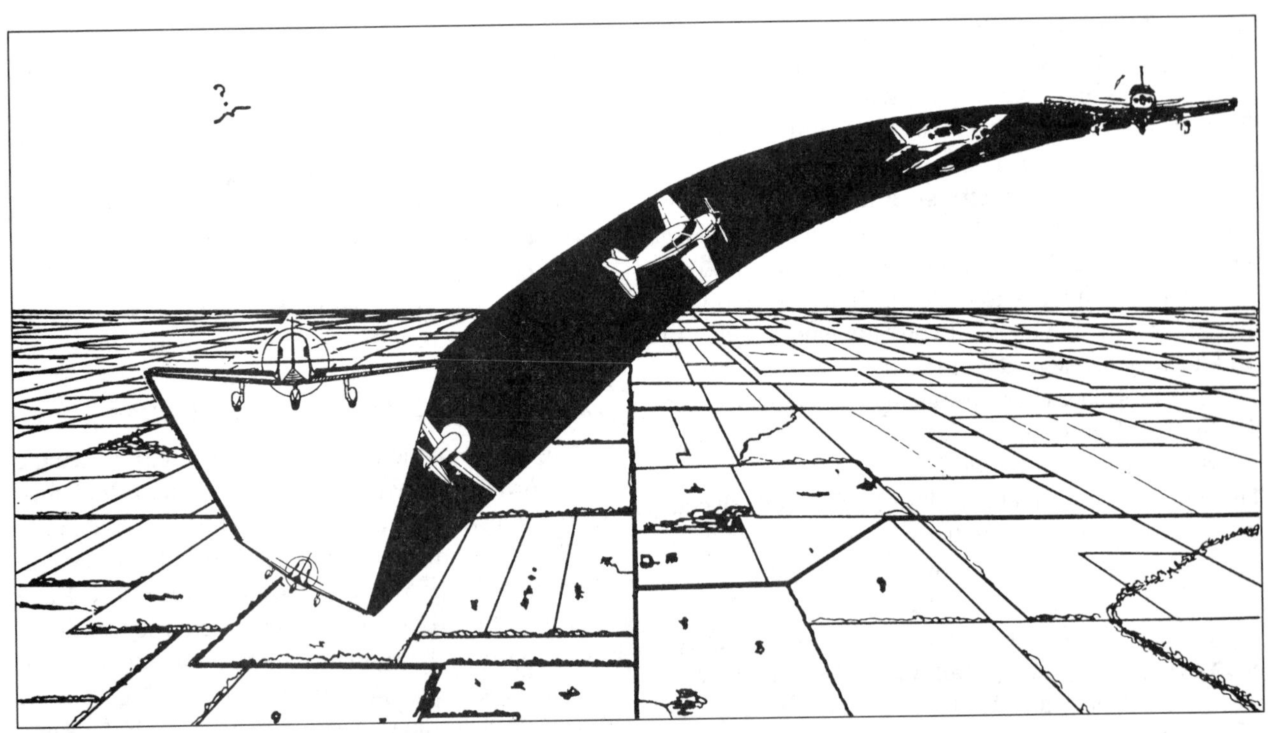

Figure 21-11. A chandelle to the right. During the transition back to cruise, don't vary ±50 feet from the final altitude attained.

to keep the airplane headed for the reference point by holding top rudder. Expect the slight turn and don't worry about it.

As the climb is started and the airspeed drops, smoothly increase power to full throttle but don't cause the engine to overspeed. It's better to start the dive at cruise rpm (assuming a fixed-pitch prop) and try to maintain this by opening the throttle as the airspeed decreases in the climb.

At the 90° turn position, the roll-out is started; the airplane should be in a wings-level attitude with the airspeed just above the stall at the 180° position. The nose is then lowered and the airplane returned to cruise attitude. (The nose should not be raised or lowered further after the 90° position; the first 90° is used to bring it up to the proper pitch attitude, which is maintained during the roll-out.) The throttle is eased back to maintain cruise rpm as the speed picks up. Use whatever right rudder is necessary to take care of torque during this part of the maneuver.

Your main problem will be setting up the proper bank; too shallow and the airplane will stall before completing the turn; too steep and little climb is attained. You can visualize this by exaggeration—the effect of a 0° bank or a 90° bank in the dive portion. The exact amount of bank depends on your airplane's characteristics, but for most trainers the initial bank should fall between 25° and 30°.

It's best to do chandelle turns into the wind so you won't drift so far. The initial dive is done crosswind, and the turn is made into the wind. Pilots practicing chandelles have made the turns downwind and after several maneuvers have found themselves a considerable distance from the practice area. This is a very slow way to go cross-country but is fast enough to get you to a new area before you realize it. Remember that the check pilot is interested in your *planning* as well as smoothness in the maneuver.

A straight stretch of highway, railroad, or power line right-of-way is the best aid in doing a precise chandelle. You may prefer to start (and end) the maneuver parallel to the highway, but some pilots find that starting and ending perpendicularly to the reference gives them a better check at the 90°-of-turn point.

Basically the first 90° of the chandelle is the pitch change (constant 30° bank), with the pitch at the 90° point held through the rest of the maneuver. (Don't let the nose move up or down after that point.) The second 90° is the constant changing (reduction) of the bank, so that, with perfect timing (it says here), the roll-out is completed and the airplane is at the final airspeed (within +5 K of the power-on stall speed, as an example) just as the 180° point is reached. Incidentally, make certain that the airplane is always at least 1,500 feet AGL in the chandelle or lazy eight. If you have a reliable safety pilot, it's fun to do chandelles under the hood.

Common Errors

1. A too-shallow initial bank, resulting in the airplane's stalling before 180° of turn is reached.
2. A too-steep initial bank, resulting in all turn and little climb.
3. Poor coordination throughout, particularly failing to compensate for torque during the last 90° of turn.
4. Failing to roll out at 180° of turn; becoming so engrossed in the nose attitude and airspeed that the turn is neglected. You are expected to roll out within ±10° of the desired heading.
5. Excessive back pressure, stalling the airplane, or too weak back pressure, resulting in the airplane "dragging" itself around with little evidence of a high-performance maneuver.

With underpowered airplanes you may be lucky to finish the chandelle at the same altitude you started, much less gain a great deal of altitude. This will be understood by the check pilot, who is more interested in your technique than in outstanding performance—which the underpowered airplane does not have—and who knows that if you have the skill, when you do get a chance to fly a more powerful airplane you'll get the extra performance.

You'd better perform chandelles consistently within 10° of the desired heading and recover within +5 K of the power-on stall speed. (Note: The PTS indicates that the recovery is made "...just above a stall airspeed..." with no specific airspeed lead mentioned. This makes sense because you shouldn't be staring at the airspeed indicator anyway. The stall speed decreases as a function of the square root of the weight change and would be hard to compute. The airspeed indicator *may* have a large error at low speeds. This is a "fly-by-feel" maneuver if done properly.)

Lazy Eights

The lazy eight is one of the best maneuvers for finding out if a pilot has the feel of the airplane. It requires constantly changing airspeed and bank, and because of this, is more difficult than the chandelle.

The lazy eight gets its name from the figure the nose apparently transcribes on the horizon—a figure 8 lying on its side (a "lazy" eight) (Figure 21-12). For the sake of clarity you can consider the lazy eight as a series of wingovers. Unlike the wingovers, however, it has no transition between maneuvers.

The turns of the lazy eights, like the chandelles, should be done into the wind to avoid drifting too far from the original area.

The airspeed should vary from cruise, or the recommended entry speed, to just above a stall at the 90° turn (max bank) point. The maximum bank at the 90° turn point should be 30°. (Divide your attention and keep an eye out for other airplanes.)

Remember that you'll want a constant change of pitch, bank, and turn rate, and the altitude and airspeed should be consistent at the 180° points, ±100 feet and ±10 K. Your heading tolerance is ±10° at each 180° point.

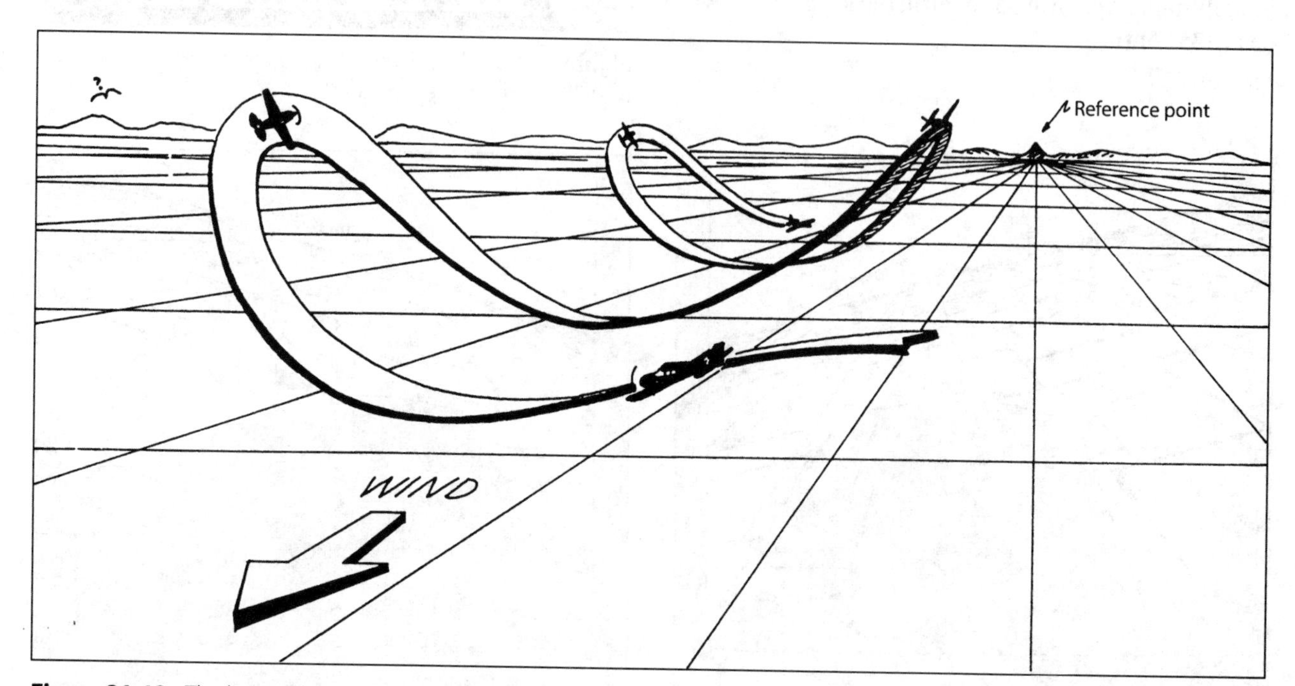

Figure 21-12. The lazy eight.

Procedure

Pick a well-defined reference point off the wingtip, preferably one that is into the wind. A point on the horizon is best so you won't be moving in on it and distorting your pattern. *Clear the area.*

Leaving the throttle at cruise setting, lower the nose and pick up an airspeed at cruise or V_A, whichever is lower (use the recommended entry speed, if available). Pull up smoothly and as the nose moves through the level-flight pitch position, start rolling into a bank toward the reference point (say, to the right). The maximum bank should be at the 90° point of turn. The airspeed should be just above a stall.

An extension of your line of sight over the nose should pass through the reference point at the 90° point of turn. The second 90° of turn consists of a shallow diving turn, rolling out until at the completion of 180° the wings are level and the reference point is off the left wing. Ease the nose up smoothly and make a climbing turn to the left, following through as before. You may continue the maneuver indefinitely.

To sum up: The maneuver is a climbing turn of ever steepening bank until the 90° point of turn is reached, after which it becomes a descending turn of ever shallowing bank until the 180° point is reached, at which the wings are level. This is followed by a 180° combination climb and descending turn in the opposite direction. Figures 21-13, -14, and -15 show how the reference point would appear as seen from the cockpit at different parts of the first 180° of the maneuver. The nose should have its highest pitch at 45° of turn; the lowest pitch will be at 135° of turn.

Keep the maneuver "lazy." One of the faults of most pilots is that as they get further into the series of turns, the faster and more frantic their movements. You may have to make yourself relax as the series progresses.

You should always be at the same altitude (±100 feet) at the bottom of the dive. If you tend to climb, decrease power slightly. If you tend to lose altitude, increase power as necessary. The maneuver should be symmetrical; that is, the nose should go the same distance below the horizon as above it. By judicial use of the power, you'll attain starting altitude and airspeed at the completion of the maneuver, ±100 feet and ±10 K, respectively.

You may have to consciously apply bottom rudder (and maybe opposite aileron) at the top of the "loop" to keep the ball centered at all times. Back pressure

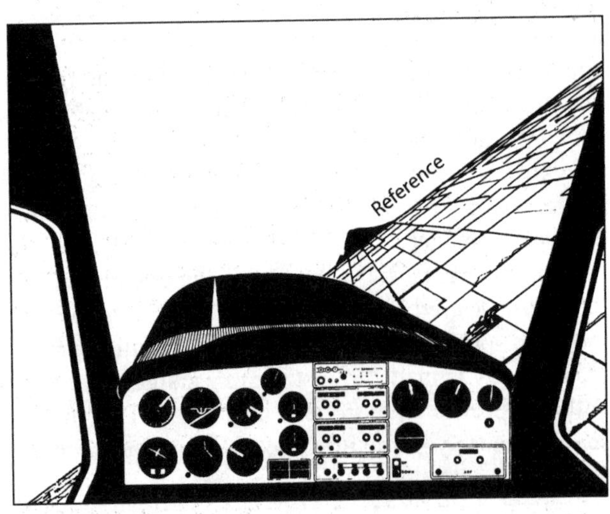

Figure 21-14. The reference as seen at the 90° point of turn (30°-bank) in the lazy eight.

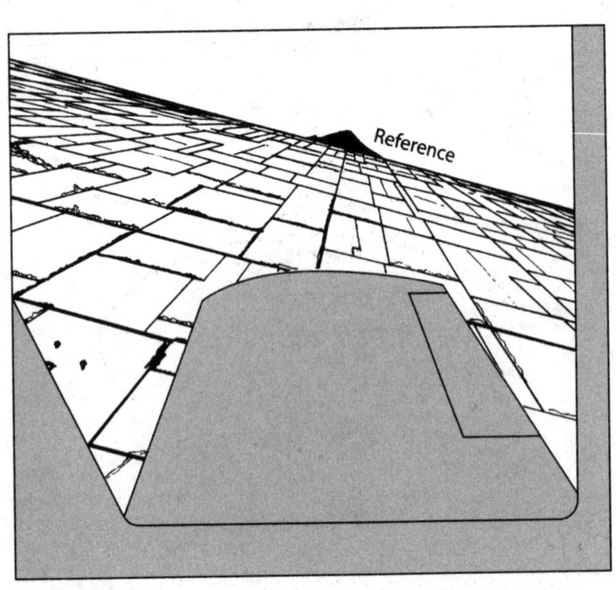

Figure 21-13. The reference point as seen during the initial dive (lazy eight).

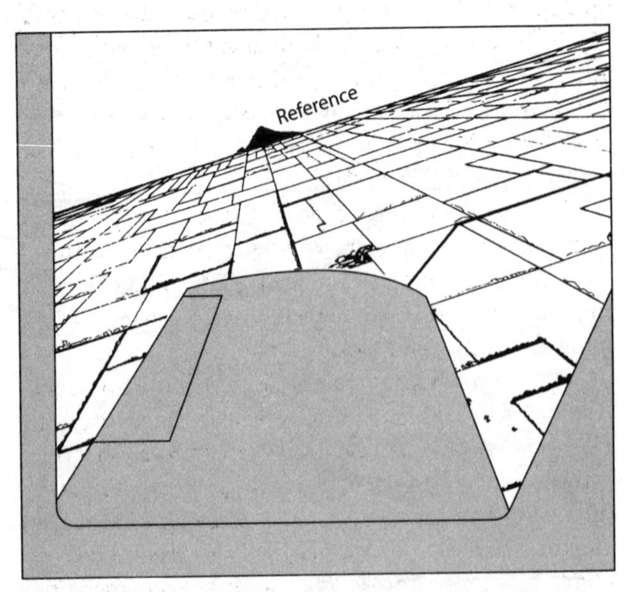

Figure 21-15. The point as seen in the shallow dive after 180° of turn (lazy eight).

usually is needed at the peak to make sure your line of sight goes through the point without the airplane slipping.

You'll continue the maneuver through the number of symmetrical loops specified and resume straight and level flight.

Common Errors

1. Poor coordination; slipping and skidding.
2. Too steep a bank at the peak of the maneuver.
3. Failing to maintain the same altitude at the bottom of the descents.
4. Losing the reference point.

You will be judged on planning, orientation, coordination, smoothness, altitude control, and airspeed control.

Steep Spirals

This maneuver has the same principles and is close to the turns-around-a-point maneuvers you did earlier in your flying career; that is, you have to vary the bank to correct for wind effects and maintain a constant radius about the point on the ground.

This maneuver is more difficult and so is more advanced than turns around a point because it requires steeper banks and the airplane is descending (power at idle), which changes the perspective of the point. Also you'll be expected to (1) look around for other airplanes, (2) correct for wind drift, (3) keep the airplane from getting too fast in the spiral, and (4) level off at a safe altitude.

Your attention will be outside the cockpit most of the time (with occasional checks of airspeed and altimeter). Your directional orientation will be on trial here.

The required maneuver is a several-turn spiral in either direction with a bank of up to 60° at the steepest sector of each turn. *You know that the point of steepest bank will be when you are headed directly downwind. The shallowest bank will be when you are headed directly upwind in the turn.*

You will be evaluated on drift correction, airspeed control, coordination, and vigilance for other traffic.

Your tolerances are airspeed ±10 K and bank of up to 60° maximum at the steepest point. Keep up with the number of turns and look around!

Make sure that you have sufficient altitude to complete at least three 360° turns. It wouldn't look too good from a headwork standpoint if you expected to start a 3-turn spiral at 1,000 feet above the ground—the check pilot might wonder a little. If you aren't sure there's enough altitude to do the job, tell the check pilot and climb to a better altitude. You should be recovered from the spirals at 1,000 feet or better.

Practice three turns in each direction. Use carburator heat as recommended in the POH. Figure 21-16 is the spiral from a side perspective.

Figure 21-17 shows part of the steep spiral as seen by an observer directly above the point. The 360° turns are treated separately; perspective requires that the lowest turn appear to be of a smaller radius, but *all turns should be of equal radius.*

The check pilot normally will require the spirals as the last maneuver of the high work, since you can also use them to get down for the low-work maneuvers. He may say "forced landing" during one of the turns, requiring you to set up a simulated "dead stick" (power-off) pattern to a nearby field. Because you have been correcting for the wind, you should know its direction, but it's funny how blank your mind can go sometimes.

Back to the spiral itself—watch your coordination. Pilots who normally make extra-smooth gliding turns sometimes get so engrossed in the reference point that they'll do anything to keep it where they want it, and the ball in the turn and slip instrument just barely stays in the cockpit.

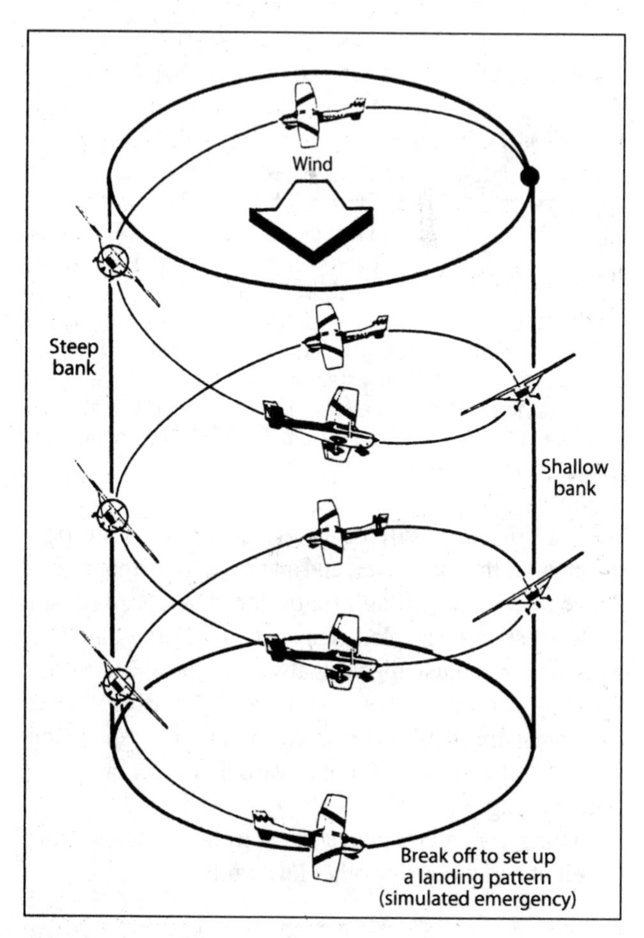

Figure 21-16. The spiral. The maneuver can be used to stay over a chosen landing spot for simulated or actual emergency landings. (*Student Pilot's Flight Manual*)

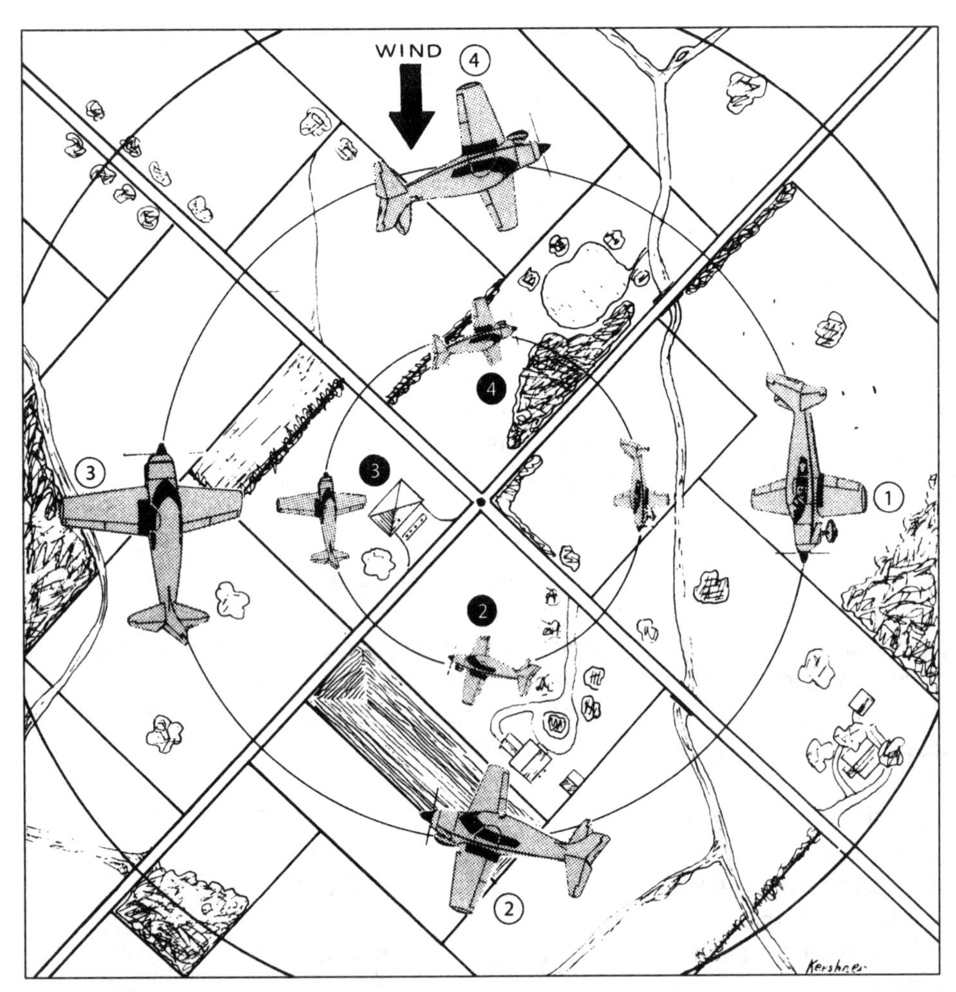

Figure 21-17. Steep gliding spirals about a point. The turns would actually be a descending helix rather than the "separate" turns shown. Consider the need for varying the bank to maintain a constant radius; point 1 on the circle will require the steepest bank (headed directly downwind) and point 3 will require the shallowest bank in order to follow the circle. At points 2 and 4, the airplane will have comparable banks, but you will actually have a crab set up. (The turns will be balanced and the ball centered at all times.) The required bank and crab will vary smoothly around the circle.

Since the airplane must start at a fairly high altitude in order to complete the turns, the point is harder to see (and hold) at the beginning of the maneuver. In fact you'll find that things start really falling into place during that lowest, final, 360° turn. Because of the required higher initial altitude, this maneuver is more difficult than turns around a point, which are done at a constant lower altitude.

The airplane will be in the clean configuration throughout the maneuver, and an airspeed of about 50% above the stall is a rough figure for glide speed. Don't get too fast or the airplane may get out of hand for a few seconds (or at least appear that way to the check pilot). If you are too slow, you could stall by pulling excess back pressure in the steep bank. Maintain the specified airspeed ±10 K and roll out toward an object or specified heading, ±10°.

This is a good maneuver for spiraling down to start the eights on pylons or other low work.

Common Errors

1. Poor correction for wind drift.
2. Poor coordination; slipping or skidding.
3. Airspeed too fast in the spiral.
4. Failure to keep up with the number of turns.
5. Failure to look around for other traffic (fixating on the point).
6. Poor planning; not being able to complete the maneuver without getting excessively low.
7. *Not clearing the engine.*

Ground Reference Maneuver

Eights on Pylons

This maneuver (also called on-pylon eights) is a ground reference maneuver, but in this case, rather than flying a constant *path* with respect to the pylons, the airplane is flown so that the wing maintains a constant *reference* to them. While in the turning part of the maneuver, you should see the pylon remaining at a constant spot with reference to the airplane's lateral axis (or more properly, your line of sight). If you had a fixed telescopic sight at your eye level, pointing at 90° to the airplane center line, the cross hairs should stay centered on the pylon as the airplane turns on it, although, as will be noted later, the pylon will be closer or farther away as the wind affects the pattern. The examiner could require an emergency descent (covered later) to get you down to the eights-on-pylon altitude.

At cruising airspeed (assuming no wind), you'll find that at a certain altitude you'll be able to lay the wing on an object and keep it there indefinitely as you circle in a balanced turn. This pivotal altitude (PA) is a function of the *square* of the airspeed and can be found by the equation PA = TAS^2 (mph)/15, or TAS^2(K)/11.3. (The number 11.3 is easier to work with than the more accurate 11.26.) A trainer flying at a TAS of 100 K would have a pivotal altitude of $100^2/11.3 = 10{,}000/11.3 = 885$ feet above the surface.

The pivotal altitude depends on the relative speed (squared) of the airplane to the pylon, and if wind is a factor (as it normally is), the *groundspeed* is the value to be used in the formula. An airplane flying on a pylon with a wind existing would have to change altitudes around the "circle" in order to keep the reference line (the pilot's line of sight) on the pylon. With a 10-K wind for a 100-K trainer, the pivotal altitude could vary from 717 feet when traveling directly upwind to 1,071 feet when headed directly downwind. Check this with the equation. The angle of bank has nothing to do with the pivotal altitude; a 15° bank has the same pivotal altitude as a 60° bank for a given TAS (or groundspeed) (Figure 21-18).

Figure 21-19A shows the eights on pylons in a no-wind condition at a constant TAS. The airplane is circling each pylon at a constant bank and altitude and the circles are symmetrical. Note the "circles" in the maneuver in a wind (Figure 21-19B) are more egg shaped than round, and the line of elongation is 90° to what would be "predicted"; it would seem that the longest part of the "eggs" should be pointed downwind but this is not the case, as you will see when you do the maneuver.

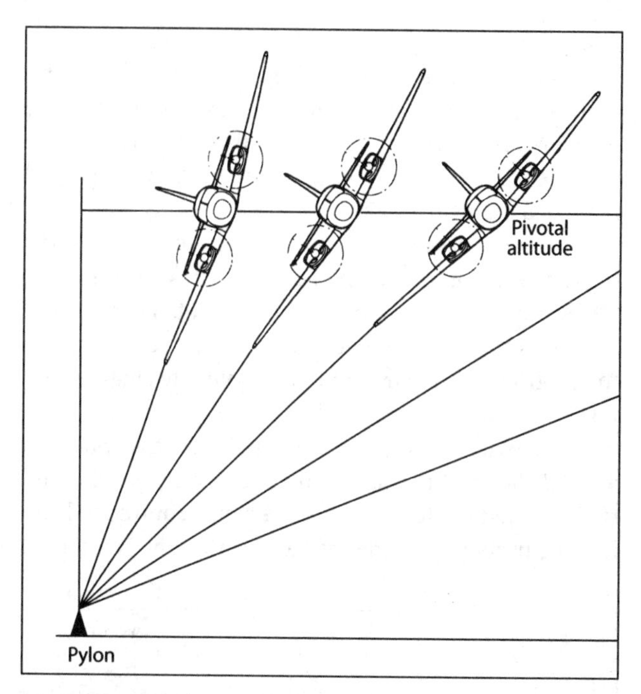

Figure 21-18. The angle of bank does not affect the pivotal altitude if the airspeed (or more accurately, the speed relative to the pylon) is constant. The chances are very great that you would not be doing eights on pylons in a twin, particularly at such steep banks—this is only an example.

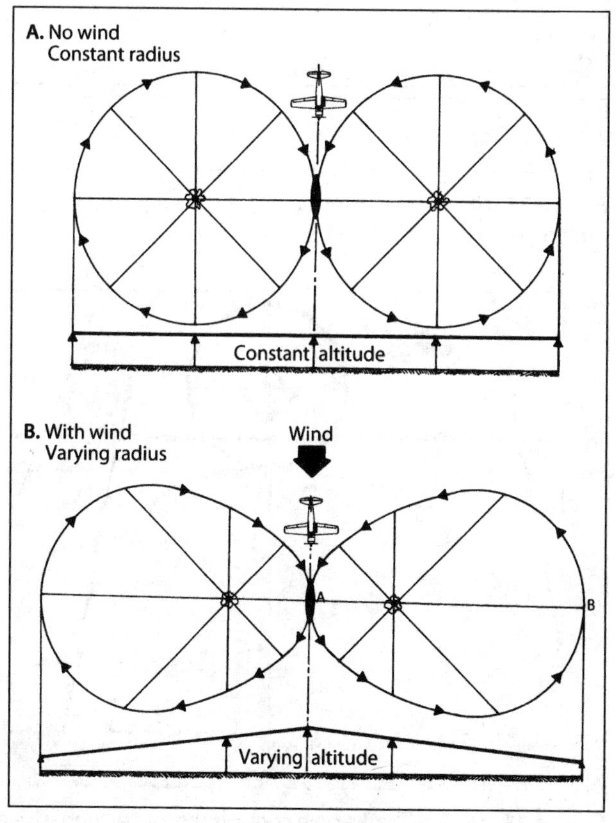

Figure 21-19. A. A no-wind eights-on-pylons pattern. **B.** The same pattern in a moderate to high wind (wind effect exaggerated to make a point). The arrows indicate the path in both cases but do not represent the heading in the on-pylon eights with wind.

Procedure

Pick the pylons as shown in Figure 21-20. A medium-banked (30°–40°) pylon eight is best for getting the idea of the maneuver. A short straightaway may be used between circles, and with a wind, those legs will require a crab correction.

Enter the pattern at cruise power (or less, for the higher-performance airplanes) and make the roll-in. Generally it's better to time it so that the roll-in is started comparatively late and is a positive one, rather than rolling in too early and then having to shallow out, resteepen, etc.

The pylon is kept at the same *relative* position around the circling part of the maneuver, but the distance from the reference (and the bank required to keep it at the proper spot) changes as the airplane is affected by the wind. When the airplane is flying downwind, it will be closer to the pylon (and more steeply banked) than when flying directly upwind (Figure 21-19B). Also, the altitude must change to maintain the proper pivotal altitude for the speed relative to the pylon (groundspeed).

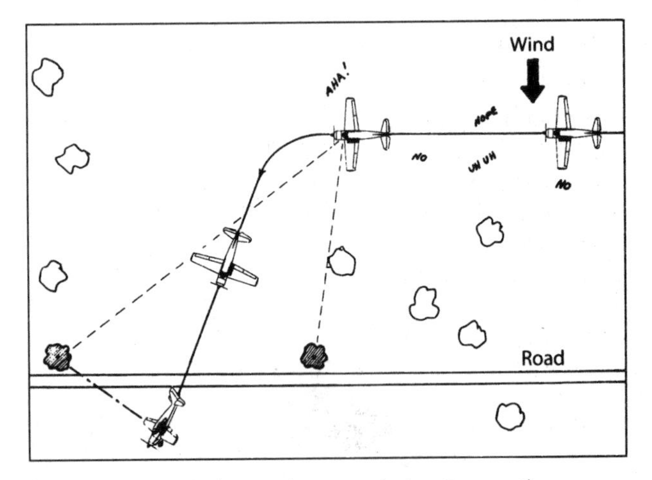

Figure 21-20. Picking pylons precisely prevents the prolonging of practice periods.

You might think of it as keeping the pylon centered in the cross hairs (Figure 21-21). All flying must be coordinated and the bank varied to keep the pylon "centered." As the airplane moves into the pylon (flying downwind), the bank must be steepened (or the reference will move down, out of the proper position), and as it moves away from the pylon the bank must be shallowed. You control the relative "up" and "down" motion of the pylon with *bank angle change.*

Note in Figure 21-21 that you are looking along the imaginary dashed line along the wing; the right-seat occupant in a side-by-side trainer would use that same line (if the person in the left seat isn't in the way). However, a rear-cockpit occupant of a tandem trainer who tried to use that same point on the wingtip would be turning into the pylon (Figure 21-22).

The correct pivotal altitude must be maintained (varied with groundspeed), or the pylon cannot be held. If the altitude is too high for the groundspeed, that is, the airplane is above that particular pivotal altitude, the airplane will fall "behind" the pylon. If the airplane is too low it will gain on the pylon, or the pylon will start dropping behind.

In the first case (the airplane falling back), the tendency is to use outside rudder to keep the wing on the point, with a slip resulting. On the other hand, if the

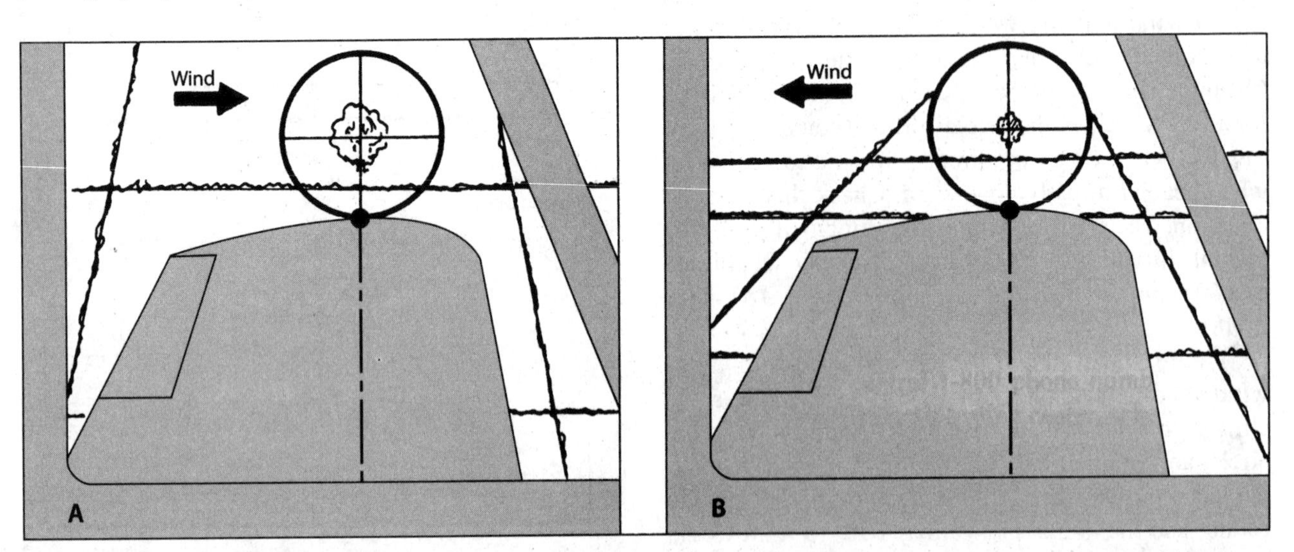

Figure 21-21. The bank angle controls the "up" or "down" relative motion of the reference; A and B show what would be seen at positions A and B in Figure 21-19B. The relative positions of the pylon are the same at both positions, as shown by the crosshairs, but the wind effect has changed the distances to the pylon—and the bank required to maintain the "bulls-eye." A is the closest point, steepest bank, and highest altitude, and B is the farthest point from the pylon, the shallowest bank, and the lowest altitude in Figure 21-19B (slightly exaggerated).

airplane is gaining on the pylon, you'll want to hold inside rudder (skid) to move the wing back to "where it belongs." The maneuver should, in theory, be perfectly coordinated throughout (it says here), but in turbulence it's more easily said than done.

So the problem of fore or aft motion of the pylon must be corrected by an altitude change. Suppose that the pylon is apparently moving ahead of the wingtip reference. The problem is either that the altitude is too high for the groundspeed or that the groundspeed is too low for the altitude. You would ease the nose over (no power change) and gain on the pylon, because (1) the increased airspeed (groundspeed) raises the pivotal altitude and (2) the loss of altitude brings you closer to the required pivotal altitude. You are bringing the airspeed and altitude requirements together with one move and would adjust altitude as the airspeed decays back to normal. As the airplane descends in the pattern, the bank must be decreased to keep the pylon at the same relative position.

If the airplane is too low and is gaining on the pylon, back pressure is used to (1) gain altitude and (2) slow the airplane up; this combination hastens the correction. The bank will have to be increased as the new, proper altitude is reached so that the correct relative position of the pylon is maintained. (Use a model and a desktop "pylon" to see the relationship.) Check Figure 21-23.

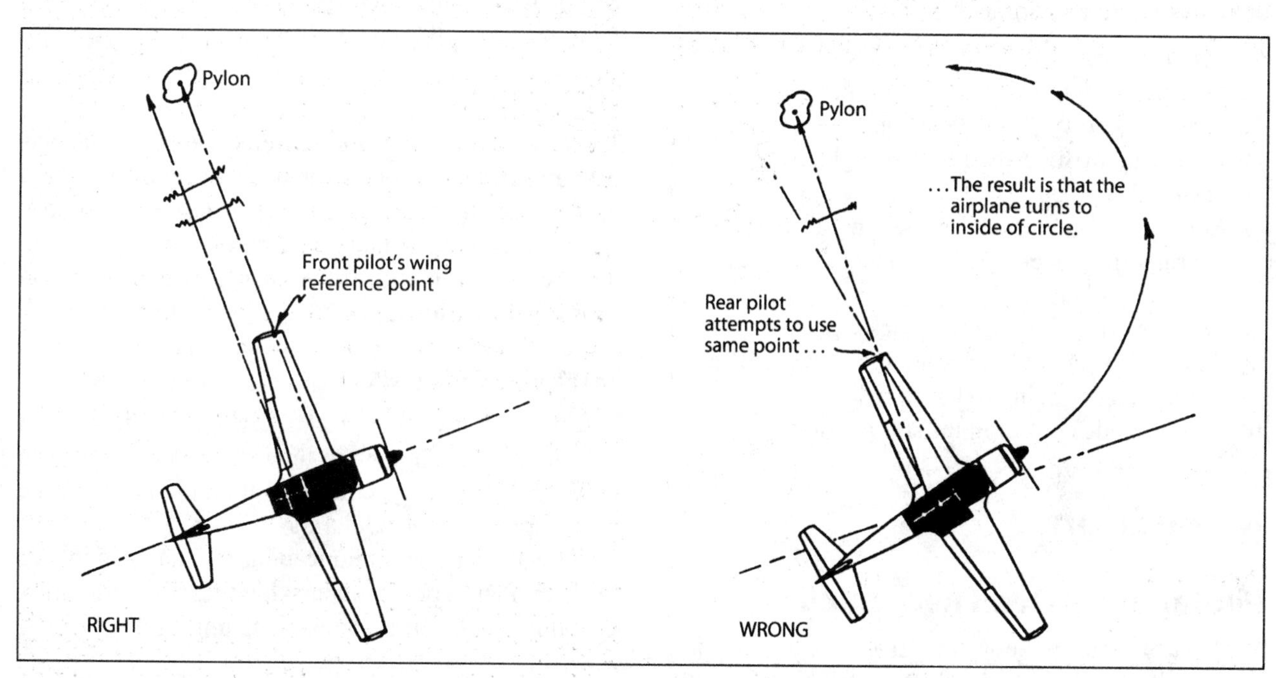

Figure 21-22. The rear-cockpit occupant has to use a different wing tip reference or he will turn into the pylon.

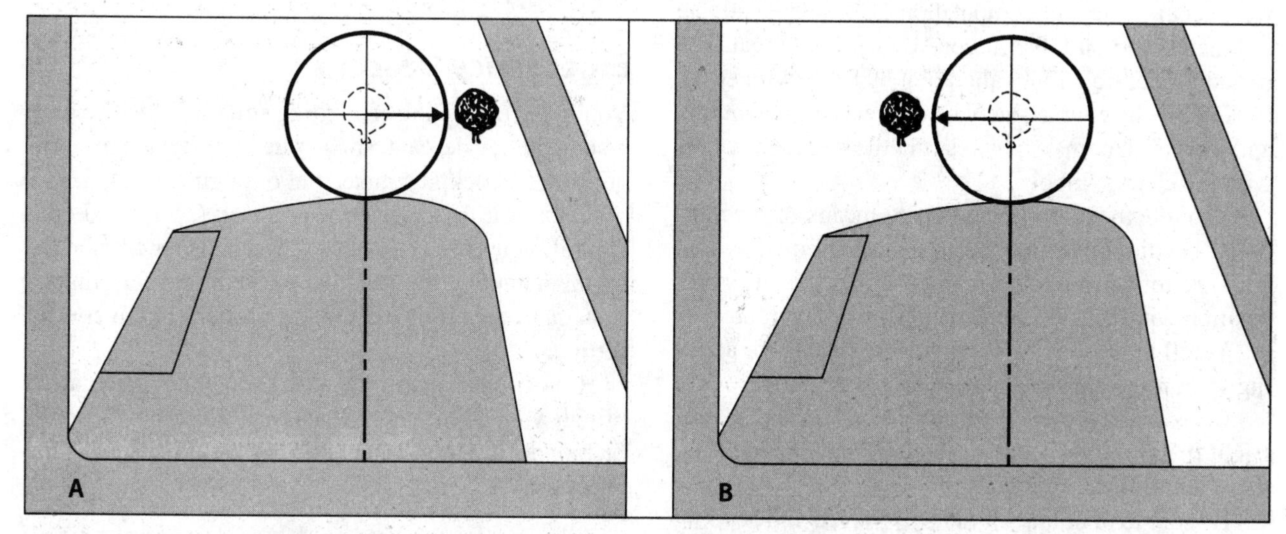

Figure 21-23. Effects of being above or below the proper altitude for the groundspeed. **A.** Above the pivotal altitude the pylon moves ahead of the airplane. **B.** Below it the pylon appears to be falling behind.

Steep eights on pylons may be easier than medium or shallow ones because the circle portion is complete before you have a chance to get too far off the proper path. (A shallow eight can be a real challenge to some people, and as they slowly move around the larger circles, altitude and bank can vary considerably.) If you aren't organized on the roll-in of the steep eight, however, you won't catch up until that part of the maneuver is over. There's always hope for that *other* pylon, though.

Eights on pylons are excellent for learning to fly the airplane only by outside references. An airspeed or altimeter watcher will have problems with these maneuvers. By watching the pylon, the pilot can maintain the proper pivotal altitude all the way around without reference to the altimeter.

Common Errors

1. Poor pylon picking; too close, too far, or easily lost.
2. Overconcentration on one pylon.
3. Poor wind drift correction in straightaways.
4. "Losing" a pylon.
5. Rolling in too soon, particularly when the pylon is on the right (in a side-by-side airplane) and is hidden.
6. Poor bank control.
7. Too-slow rollout in back-to-back eights.
8. Failure to keep looking around for other traffic.
9. Skidding or slipping to hold a pylon.
10. Poor altitude control in the straightaway.

Navigation

Pilotage and Dead Reckoning

You'll be expected to know the elements related to pilotage and dead reckoning. You'll correctly fly at least to the first planned checkpoint, to demonstrate that you were accurate in your computations. Consider available alternates and suitable action for various situations, including possible route alteration by the examiner.

Follow the course solely by reference to landmarks and identify landmarks by relating the surface features with the chart symbols.

You're expected to navigate by means of precomputed headings, groundspeed, and elapsed time, and you'd better be able to verify at all times the airplane's position within 2 NM of the flight's planned route.

You'll have an ETA margin of 3 minutes for arriving at en route checkpoints and the destination.

Correct and record the differences between the preflight fuel, groundspeed, and heading calculations and those determined en route.

Be sure to maintain altitude (±100 feet) and heading (±10°) during the level portion of the flight.

Don't forget to use the checklist.

Navigation Systems and Radar Services

You'll demonstrate a knowledge of radio navigation and radar services and select and identify the appropriate facilities. You will locate the airplane's position relative to the navigation facility and intercept and track on a given radial or bearing. Recognize and describe the indication of a station passage if appropriate.

You'll locate your position using cross radials or bearings and will recognize and describe the indication of a station passage.

You will be expected to recognize signal loss, take appropriate action, and use proper communications whenever utilizing radar services.

Limits are ±100 feet, heading ±10°.

Diversion

The examiner may ask for a diversion route to an alternate airport and you'll divert to that airport promptly. You'll give an accurate estimate of heading, groundspeed, arrival time, and fuel consumption to that point. Stay within ±100 feet of the appropriate altitude and ±10° of your heading.

Lost Procedures

Select the best course of action when you're given a lost situation and maintain the original or appropriate heading. If necessary, climb and attempt to identify the nearest prominent landmark(s).

Use available communications and navigation aids for help. Plan a precautionary landing if deteriorating visibility and/or fuel exhaustion is impending.

Emergency Operations

Emergency Descent

You'll be required to recognize situations that require an emergency descent, such as decompression, passenger illness, cockpit smoke, and/or engine fire.

Establish the prescribed airspeed (±5 K) and configuration for the emergency descent as recommended by the manufacturer, without exceeding safety limitations, and be sure to know the proper engine control settings.

Use proper planning and keep your orientation (divide your attention as necessary). Keep positive load factors during the descent and, for Pete's sake, use the checklist.

Emergency Approach and Landing (simulated)

You'll be expected to know and be able to explain approach and landing procedures to be used in various emergencies. When the examiner sets up the simulated emergency, you are to establish and maintain the best glide airspeed (±10 K) and the configuration required for the various parts of this problem. (One of the common errors in this exercise is to let the airspeed get too fast, above the best glide speed.) You are to pick a suitable landing area within gliding distance. Bank and look directly under the airplane; many a pilot has headed off to the far horizon, ignoring a 640-acre pasture right below. Keep the airplane in the clean configuration until the landing area (pattern) is made. Set up an emergency pattern (see Chapter 16), considering altitude, wind, terrain, obstructions, and other factors. You'll be expected to follow an appropriate checklist. You should work out your own procedure, perhaps moving across the cockpit from right to left (or vice versa) to set up the most logical sequence. One airplane is set up so that a right-to-left sequence works well:

1. Fuel management (on floor between seats). Depending on the altitude of the emergency and the system, it could mean switching tanks or turning the fuel off.
2. Mixture RICH (on panel).
3. Carburetor heat ON.
4. Ignition switch—check mags or turn them OFF if the landing is inevitable.
5. Master OFF after needed electrical components (flaps, radio, etc.) are used, but before touchdown.

Review Chapter 16 for ideas on gear-up or -down landings.

After the glide is established and the landing site selected, you are to try to determine the reason for the simulated malfunction and try to remedy it. *You must remain in coordinated control of the airplane at all times.*

On the Practical Test be prepared for a landing or go-around, as specified by the examiner.

You'll be checked on your judgment, planning procedures, and positive control during the simulated emergencies.

Systems and Equipment Malfunctions

You'll be expected to explain indications and courses of actions for various systems and equipment malfunctions. Review the POH for your airplane and Chapters 12, 13, 14, 16, and 19 of this book (and Chapter 15, too, if you're taking the test in a twin).

You'll analyze the situation for simulated emergencies:

1. Partial or complete power loss (Chapter 16 and POH).
2. Rough-running engine or overheating (Chapter 16 and POH).
3. Carburetor or induction icing (Chapter 16 and POH).
4. Fuel starvation (Chapter 16 and POH).
5. Smoke or fire in flight (Chapter 16 and POH).
6. Electrical malfunctions (POH).
7. Landing gear or flap malfunction (including asymmetrical flap position) (Chapter 16 and POH).
8. Door, window, or emergency exits opening in flight. (Chapter 16 and POH).
9. Trim inoperative (POH).
10. Loss of pressurization (Chapter 19 and POH).
11. Loss of oil pressure (POH).
12. Structural icing (POH).
13. Pitot-static/vacuum system and associated flight instruments malfunction (POH).
14. Any other emergency unique to the airplane flown.
15. And, very important, make sure that there is an emergency checklist available.

Emergency Equipment and Survival Gear

You'd better know the following about the emergency equipment for your airplane by describing its

1. Location.
2. Method of operation.
3. Servicing requirements.
4. Method of safe storage.

In addition, you should be well familiar with the facts of survival gear that are appropriate for operation in various climatological and topographical environments.

High Altitude Operations

Supplemental Oxygen

Know the FARs concerning use of supplemental oxygen in non-pressurized airplanes for the flight crew and passengers and the distinctions between "aviators breathing oxygen" and other types. How can you determine availability of oxygen service? Know (and be able to describe) the operational characteristics of continuous flow, demand, and pressure demand systems. Are you familiar with the care and storage of high-pressure oxygen bottles?

Review 14 CFR §91.211, Chapter 18, and your POH.

Pressurization

Review Chapter 19, the FARs, and your POH so that you know the regulatory requirements for the use of pressurized airplane systems. Review the operational characteristics of the cabin pressure control system. What are the hazards associated with high-altitude flight and decompression?

How about the operational and physiological reasons for completing emergency descents? Be able to describe the need for wearing safety belts and shoulder harnesses and for rapid access to supplemental oxygen. What are the supplemental requirements when operating airplanes with pressurized cabins?

Can you operate the system properly and react promptly and accurately to pressurization malfunctions?

If the test airplane is not equipped with supplemental oxygen and/or pressurization, these two tasks will be knowledge tasks only and no demonstration is required. (Makes sense.)

Postflight Procedures

Parking and Securing After Landing

Know thoroughly the after-landing procedures, including local and ATC procedures. Pick a good parking spot and check your wind correction technique and watch for obstacles. (If you taxi into another airplane or the gas pump, you'll likely flunk the practical test.)

Review ramp safety factors such as taxiing and parking signals and proper shutdown, securing, and postflight inspection. Be careful not to damage persons or property as you park and secure the airplane.

Use the checklist for sequence of shutdown, but get the engine shut down without undue delay; don't sit in the cockpit with the engine running and your head down in the cockpit, reading a complicated shutdown procedure. You should be able by now to do a good job of chocking and/or tying down the airplane and setting the control lock(s) as applicable. Perform a careful postflight inspection using a prescribed checklist.

After the Practical Test

After you've passed the practical test and are a commercial pilot, you'll find a new attitude toward flying. You are a professional and will have to maintain closer standards than before. You are on your own and will have to make decisions on maintenance, weather, and airport operations—maybe in situations where there is no one else to discuss it with. *Don't let passengers or other pilots talk you into flying when you don't feel right about it.* You know your limitations better than anybody else, and as a professional you shouldn't let outside pressures push you. Maybe you're thinking of going with the airlines or corporate flying; don't let a poorly planned charter trip (with passenger pressure) get you into a spot that could result in a violation or an accident, which could affect your chances for later advances in your career. You'd be surprised how a firm *No* to a bad situation lets passengers know who is in command of the airplane.

At the beginning of this chapter on the Practical Test Standards (PTS), information was added to help. This is not intended to replace the Test but to help with the requirements and let you get a look at what to expect. There is *no* substitute for an up-to-date PTS when you get ready for your commercial certificate.

Keep up your proficiency and you'll find that you're starting on the most rewarding career possible.

Happy (and safe) flying.

Bibliography

Aerodynamics for Naval Aviators. NAVWEPS 00-80T-80. 1965. Naval Air Systems Command, U.S. Navy (reprinted with permission by ASA).

Berven, Lester H., 1978. *Engine-Out Characteristics of Multiengine Aircraft.* Staff Study. Washington, D.C.; FAA.

Byington, Melville R., Jr., 1988. *Optimized Engine Out Procedures for Multi Engine Airplanes.* Embry-Riddle Aeronautical University, Daytona Beach, FL.

Dommasch, Daniel O., et al. 1967. *Airplane Aerodynamics, 4th ed.* New York; Pitman.

Flyer. Williamsport, PA.; AVCO-Lycoming.

Fung, Y. C., 1969. *An Introduction to the Theory of Elasticity.* New York; Dover.

Kershner, W. K. (edited by W.C. Kershner), 2012. *The Flight Instructor's Manual, 5th ed.* Newcastle, WA; ASA.

Kershner, W. K. (edited by W.C. Kershner), 2012. *The Instrument Flight Manual, 7th ed.* Newcastle, WA; ASA.

Kershner, W. K. (edited by W.C. Kershner), 2010. *The Student Pilots Flight Manual, 10th ed.* Newcastle, WA; ASA.

Liston, Joseph, 1953. *Power Plants for Aircraft.* New York; McGraw-Hill.

Lyon, Thoburn C., 1972. *Practical Air Navigation, 11th ed.* Denver, CO; Jeppesen-Sanderson.

Perkins, C. D., and Hage, R. E., 1949. *Airplane Performance, Stability and Control.* New York; Wiley.

FAA Handbook and Advisory Circulars reprinted by ASA:

Aviation Maintenance Technician Handbook – General (FAA-H-8083-30). 2008. Washington, D.C.; FAA.

Aviation Maintenance Technician Handbook – Airframe, Volumes 1 & 2 (FAA-H-8083-31). 2012. Washington, D.C.; FAA.

Aviation Maintenance Technician Handbook – Powerplant, Volumes 1 & 2 (FAA-H-8083-32). 2012. Washington, D.C.; FAA.

Aviation Weather Services (AC 00-45). 2010. Washington, D.C.; FAA/NWS.

Practical Test Standards for Commercial Pilot, Airplane (FAA-S-8081-12). 2012. Washington, D.C.; FAA.

FAA Advisory Circulars published by the GPO:

Aeronautical Decision Making (AC 60-22). 1991. Washington, D.C.; FAA.

Aircraft Wake Turbulence (AC 90-23). 2014. Washington, D.C.; FAA.

(continued)

Companies supplying Pilot's Operating Handbooks, products, or other information:

Barfield Instrument Corp., Miami, FL.

Bendix Products, Aerospace Div., Bendix Aviation Corp., South Bend, IN.

Castleberry Instruments and Avionics, Austin, TX.

Cessna Aircraft Co., Wichita, KS (for models 150, 172, 180, 182, 210, 310).

Continental Development Corp., Ridgefield, CT (instantaneous vertical speed indicator).

Hartzell Propeller, Inc., Piqua, OH.

Lycoming, a Textron company, Williamsport, PA (detailed engine specifications and flyers).

McCauley Propeller Systems, Vandalia, OH.

Precise Flight, Inc., Bend, OR (Nelson Oxygen System, speed brakes).

Sigma-Tek, Inc., Wichita, KS (aircraft instruments).

Acknowledgments and Notes from Previous Editions

W.K. Kershner

Seventh Edition Notes

The reader of the sixth edition will note that I have removed the questions and answers and explanations for the commercial knowledge test. This title and edition thus completes the removal of the test material from all of my texts.

There are several reasons for the removal, but primarily, a book is updated and reprinted every 6 months to 1 year. The FAA questions are changed more often than that, and the reader has access to the latest questions by several means. The removal of the questions and answers and explanations has not compromised the quality of information in the text. The areas of knowledge required to be a safe pilot are still here.

With this edition I again owe thanks to Lynne Bishop who caught errors (technical and grammatical) and kept me on the straight and narrow. I also owe much to my wife of 49 years for her patience and help with typing.

Acknowledgments from Previous Editions

The writer has been fortunate in having knowledgeable people available to comment on the manuscripts for each edition and would like to thank the following people for their help (these acknowledgments are not meant to imply endorsement of *The Advanced Pilot's Flight Manual* by any of the organizations mentioned and should not be construed as such).

American Aviation Publications for permission to take parts of articles I wrote for *Skyways* magazine.

Harold Andrews of the Stability and Control Section of the Bureau of Naval Weapons, Washington, D.C., for his pertinent comments on the chapter on Stability and Control and other parts.

Merritt Bailey, my editor at Iowa State University Press, who was instrumental in assuring that this book, like the *Student Pilot's Flight Manual*, was published in a manner more readable than that evidenced by my sometimes rambling discussions in the manuscript.

Michael Beaumont, of Houston, Texas, who sent information on gyro instruments.

Don Bigbee, of Castleberry Instruments and Avionics, who sent photos and data on gyro instruments and gave permission for them to be used in Chapter 4.

Lynne Bishop, editor at Iowa State University Press, for her work on the sixth edition.

Business/Commercial Aviation magazine for permission to use material from some of my articles on airplane performance.

Capt. M. R. Byington, Jr., of the Aeronautical Science Department at Embry-Riddle Aeronautical University, who made suggestions for improvement of later printings of the fifth edition and who gave me permission to include references to his report, *Optimized Engine Out Procedures for Multi Engine Airplanes* (May 1988).

Bill Carlon, of Sigma-Tek, Inc., who furnished brochures and data and gave permission to use photos of gyro instruments that were a great aid in Chapter 4.

Bernard Carson, instructor in the Aeronautical Engineering Department at Pennsylvania State University, who reviewed parts of the manuscript and made helpful comments on flight limitations.

Cessna Aircraft Company, for furnishing actual curves of Drag and Thrust horsepower required and available and other information on Cessna airplanes and for allowing me to insert copyrighted material (performance charts, schematics of systems, and placards).

Leighton Collins, Editor of *Air Facts*, who reviewed parts of the manuscript and whose suggestions on methods of presenting some of the more technical parts were of particular value.

Joe Diblin, of Avco Lycoming, who furnished very valuable information on Lycoming engines and let me use material from the Avco Lycoming *Flyer.* His easy-to-understand writing style makes learning about engines a pleasure.

Employees at Aero Design, Beech, Mooney, and other companies, who helped me in quests for sometimes obscure reports and information.

Dudley C. Fort, Jr., M.D., of Sewanee, who gave me added information on carbon monoxide for Chapter 18.

Hartzell Propeller Inc., of Piqua, Ohio, and McCauley Industrial Corp. of Dayton, Ohio, for furnishing much-needed data on propellers.

Allen W. Hayes, veteran flight instructor of Ithaca, N.Y., whose cogent arguments on the subject of flight mechanics were the greatest factor in researching and inserting a chapter on that subject.

John Paul Jones, Chief of the Engineering and Manufacturing Branch of the FAA Training Center, and H. E. Smith, Jr., engineering pilot of the Center, who reviewed the complete manuscript and made valuable comments and suggestions.

Ralph Kimberlin of the University of Tennessee Space Institute, who provided general data on stability and control for Chapter 10.

Arthur L. Klaastad, of Kent, Washington, whose letters on analysis of flight mechanics were most useful in revising Chapter 3.

T. M. Koenig, of Bolivar Aviation (Tennesee), who provided a very good analysis, with drawings, of the forces and moments acting on a light twin with an engine out.

Ken Landis, Chief Controller at the Williamsport, Pennsylvania, airport, who kindly reviewed that part of the manuscript dealing with communications procedures.

Dr. Robert Langel, Goddard Space Flight Center, NASA, who furnished charts of magnetic variation and changes in variation for Chapter 4.

Jack LeBarron, of the Navy's *Approach* magazine, who always managed to find and furnish performance information when it was most needed.

Capt. Arthur Lippa, Jr., General Manager, Aircraft Division of U.S. Steel, who gave permission to use material from the booklet "Medical Factors in Flight."

Audrey J. Little, flight instructor of Nashville, whose reviews and many suggestions were useful.

Stanley R. Mohler, M.D., Chief, Aeromedical Applications, FAA, who furnished information on the use of oxygen.

Piper Aircraft employees who reviewed parts of the manuscript that covered their special areas and who made valuable suggestions and comments, including Clyde R. Smith, Flight Test Supervisor; Calvin Wilson, Aerodynamicist; Elliot Nichols, Design Engineer, Power Plants Installation; and Richard Wible.

Hampton Pitts, of Nashville, Tennesee, who sent an excellent analysis of gyro precession and who also recommended books and papers for further reading on the subject.

Robert M. Potter for suggestions and information on hydroplaning.

Delbert W. Robertson, W. R. Wright, and Hugh Pritchard of the Chattanooga Weather Bureau Airport Station and Jack Merryman of the Nashville WBAS, who answered questions and furnished actual sequence reports and other weather data for publication.

William Schmedel, Director of Training, National Aviation Academy, St. Petersburg, Flordia, who pointed out errors in earlier printings.

Robert Scripture, Jennie A. Smith, and G. M. Yerkes, of Safetech, Inc., who allowed me to make photos of E-6B models FDF-47 and FDF-57-B for the navigation problems in Chapter 17.

Hugh R. Skinner, Jr., of Barfield Instrument Corporation, who sent material on the pressure instruments, including a print of his informative paper, "The Altimeter Credibility Gap."

Fred C. Stashak, Chief Stress Engineer of Piper Aircraft Corporation, who furnished information on Piper airplanes.

Dr. Mervin Strickler, of the FAA Public Affairs Office, who aided in getting the manuscript to the right people in the FAA.

F. C. Taylor, of Mooney Aircraft Corporation, who furnished detailed power-required and -available curves on the Mooney 231.

W. D. (Bill) Thompson, of Precise Flight, Inc., who furnished information on descent rate control, mentioned in Chapter 8, information concerning the use of thumb rules for performance, in addition to furnishing answers to specific questions concerning Cessna aircraft.

Eleanor Ulton, who typed the smooth copy of the manuscript and smoothed, as well, some of the rougher edges of my writing.

Harry Weisberger, of Sperry, who sent material on gyroscopes that was of great help in writing Chapter 4.

Calvin Wilson, Aerodynamicist, of Piper Aircraft Corporation, who furnished data on Piper airplanes. Also, Cal furnished speed-power information and gave permission to use information from the Aztec E *Pilot's Operating Handbook.*

Bob Kruse, an FAA specialist and former Air Force fighter pilot, gave much valued advice that helped to ensure accuracy of information.

Special thanks to my wife, whose encouragement has never faltered and who has furnished practical help in the form of typing or keyboarding the manuscripts. Without her help, these editions could not have been completed. And special thanks also to my son, Bill, who flies for American Airlines, for help with the answers and explanations to the questions for airplanes on the *Commercial Pilot Knowledge Test* that were included in an earlier edition.

Index

V

W

Y

Z

Preparing for the Praxis

Your Guide to Licensure

Learning about the Praxis Series™ Statewide Testing Licensure

Many states require prospective teachers to take standardized tests for licensure. The following questions and answers will help you learn more about this important step to becoming a teacher.

What kinds of tests do states require for certification?

Some tests assess students' competency in basic skills of reading, writing, and mathematics, often prior to admission to a professional teacher education program. Many states also require standardized tests at the end of a teacher education program; these tests assess prospective teachers' competency and knowledge in their subject area and about teaching and learning.

Do all states use the same test for certification?

No. The most commonly used test is the *Praxis Series*™, published by the Educational Testing Service (ETS); as of January 2003, 35 states required some form of the *Praxis Series*™ for certification. You can also see a list of states requiring the Praxis tests on the ETS home page (http://www.ets.org/praxis). You can learn about each state's testing requirements by checking its department of education website or contacting the state department of education by mail or telephone. The University of Kentucky has developed a website with the web addresses for all 50 states' certification requirements (http://www.uky.edu/Education/TEP/usacert.html).

What is the *Praxis Series*™, and what is the difference between Praxis I, Praxis II, and Praxis III?

The *Praxis Series*™ is a set of three levels of standardized tests developed by the Educational Testing Service.

Praxis I assesses reading, writing, and mathematics skills. ny states require minimum passing scores on the three s I subtests (also sometimes called the **Preprofessional est,** or **PPST**) prior to admission to a teacher educaram.

I measures prospective teachers' knowledge of the earning process and the subjects they will teach. Praxis II includes tests on Principles of Learning and Teaching, specific subject assessments, and multiple subject assessments. Many states require that prospective teachers pass both a subtest on principles of teaching and learning appropriate to the grade level to be taught and either a single-subject or multiple-subject test appropriate to the area of certification. It is important to check with an advisor, testing center, or state certification office about the appropriate Praxis II tests to take for certification.

Praxis III focuses on classroom performance assessment and is usually taken by teachers in their first year of teaching. Prospective teachers who are applying for initial certification are not required to take Praxis III.

If my state uses the *Praxis Series*™, how do I know which tests to take?

Contact your advisor or student services center if you are currently a student in a teacher education program. If you are applying for certification through an alternative certification program, contact the state department of education's certification office.

What is the format of the Principles of Learning and Teaching (PLT) test?

The Principles of Learning and Teaching Tests are two hours in length, and consist of 45 multiple choice questions and six constructed-response (short-answer) questions. Each test includes three case histories followed by seven multiple-choice and two short-answer questions and 24 additional multiple choice questions.

What does the PLT test cover?

The PLT covers four broad content categories:

- Organizing Content Knowledge for Student Learning
- Creating an Environment for Student Learning
- Teaching for Student Learning
- Teacher Professionalism

ETS provides descriptions of topics covered in each category on their Website (http://www.ets.org/praxis) and in their free *Test at a Glance* booklet.

What courses in my teacher preparation program might apply to the PLT?

Almost all of your teacher preparation courses relate to the PLT in some way. This book, *Becoming a Teacher,* addresses many concepts that are assessed in the PLT tests, particularly in the areas of Creating an Environment for Student Learning and Teacher Professionalism. You have probably studied or will study concepts and knowledge related to the four content categories in courses such as educational foundations, educational psychology or human growth and development, classroom management, curriculum and methods, and evaluation and assessment. You may have had or will have field experiences and seminars that provide knowledge about these concepts.

How should I prepare for the PLT?
Test-taking tips are provided in the next section.

Test-Taking Tips for the Praxis Series™ and State Certification Tests

Test-Taking Tip 1: Know the Test

- **Review the topics covered in the exam.** For the *Praxis Series*™, the ETS booklet *Test at a Glance* (available online at http://www.ets.org/praxis or free by mail) includes detailed descriptions of topics covered in each of the four content categories.
- **Take the sample tests.** The ETS provides samples tests for the *Praxis Series*™ on their website and in their print materials. Analyze the kinds of questions asked, the correct answers, and the knowledge necessary to answer the questions correctly.
- **Analyze the sample questions and the standards used for scoring the responses to open-ended (constructed response) questions.** Read the scoring guides carefully; the test readers will use these criteria to score your written response. Write your own responses to the sample questions and analyze them using the test-scoring guide. If your responses do not meet all the criteria for a score of 3 on Praxis (or the highest score for your test), revise them.

Test-Taking Tip 2: Know the Content

- **Plan ahead.** You can begin preparing for Praxis and other standardized teacher certification tests early in your program. Think about how each of your courses relate to the concepts and content of the exam.
- **Review what you learned in each course in relation to the topics covered in the test.** Review course textbooks and class notes for relevant concepts and information. At the end of each course, record reminders of how the course's content and knowledge relate to concepts on the test.
- **Think across courses.** The Praxis case studies draw upon knowledge from several courses. As you prepare for the exam, think about how knowledge, skills, and concepts from the courses that you took relate to each other. For example, you might have learned about aspects of working with parents in a foundations course, an educational psychology course, and a methods course. Be prepared to integrate that knowledge.
- **Review the content with others.** Meet with a study group and review the test and your coursework together. Brainstorm about relevant content using the ETS descriptions or other descriptions of each test's categories and representative topics as a guideline.

Test-Taking Tip 3: Apply Good Test-Taking Strategies

- **Read the test directions carefully.** Even though you have previewed the test format and directions as part of learning about the test, make sure you understand the directions for this test.

For multiple choice questions:

- **Read each question carefully.** Pay attention to key words such as *not, all, except, always,* or *never.*
- **Try to anticipate the answer to the question before looking at the possible responses.** If your answer is among the choices, it is likely to be correct. Before automatically choosing it, however, carefully read the alternative answers.
- **Answer questions you are certain of first.** Return to questions you are uncertain about later.
- **If you are unsure of the answer, eliminate obviously incorrect responses first.**

For short open-ended response questions:

- **Read the directions carefully.** Look for key words and respond directly to exactly what is asked.
- **Repeat key words from the question to focus your response.** For example, if you are asked to list two advantages of a method, state "Two advantages are (1) . . . and (2) . . ."
- **Be explicit and concrete.** Short-answer responses should be direct and to the point.

For essay questions:

- **Read the question carefully and pay close attention to key words, especially verbs.** Make sure you understand all parts of the question. For example, if the question asks you to list advantages and disadvantages, be sure to answer both parts.
- **Before you write your response, list key points or make an outline.** The few minutes you take to organize your thoughts will pay off in a better-organized essay.
- **Use the question's words in your response.** For example, if the question asks for three advantages, list each in a sentence, "The first advantage is . . .", "The second advantage is . . . ," and "The third advantage is . . .". Make it easy for the reader to score your response.
- **Stay on topic.** Answer the question fully and in detail, but do not go beyond what the question asks or add irrelevant material.

Sample State Licensure Test Questions

The following sample questions illustrate the kinds of questions in the *Praxis Series*™ Principles of Learning and Teaching tests and other state licensure tests. The case study focuses on elementary education, which is the focus on Principles of Learning and Teaching: Grades K–6 (0522). Praxis tests for Principles of Learning and Teaching: Grades 5–9 (0523) and Principles of Learning and Teaching: Grades 7–12 (0524) would include case histories appropriate to those grade levels.

The Principles of Learning and Teaching tests focus on four broad content categories:

- Organizing Content Knowledge for Student Learning
- Creating an Environment for Student Learning
- Teaching for Student Learning
- Teacher Professionalism

The sample questions that follow include one case study followed by three related multiple-choice questions, two short-answer constructed-response questions, and three additional discrete multiple-choice questions. An actual Praxis Principles of Learning and Teaching test would include three case histories, each with seven related multiple-choice questions, two constructed-response questions, and 24 additional discrete multiple-choice questions. It would draw from many courses and field experiences in your teacher education program.

These sample questions focus only on content and issues presented in *Becoming a Teacher*; they are not representative of the actual test in scope, content, or difficulty. Learn more about Praxis and try more sample questions on the Educational Testing Service website at http://www.ets.org/praxis.

Following the sample questions are answers with explanations and references to Praxis topics and appropriate parts of this book.

Sample Case Study and Related Questions

Case History: K–6

Columbus, New Mexico, is an agricultural community near the international boundaries separating Mexico and the United States. It's a quiet town where traditional views of community and territory are being challenged. Just three miles from the border is Columbus Elementary School, a bilingual school for kindergarten through fifth grade students. Of the some 340 students enrolled at Columbus Elementary, approximately 97% are on free or reduced price lunches. The school is unique because about 49% of the students live in Mexico and attend Columbus Elementary at U.S. taxpayer expense. Columbus Elementary is a fully bilingual school. In the early grades, basic skills are taught in Spanish, but by the third-grade level, students have begun to make the transition to English. Most of the teachers at Columbus Elementary School are English speakers; some have limited Spanish skills. The school also employs teaching assistants who are fluent in Spanish and can assist the teachers in these bilingual classrooms.

Dennis Armijo, the principal of Columbus Elementary School, describes the unique relationship between Columbus and its neighboring community, Palomas, Mexico. "Most of the people who live in Columbus, New Mexico have relatives in Palomas, Mexico. At one point or another, many Columbus residents were Mexican residents and they came over and established a life here. And so they still have ties to Mexico and a lot of uncles and aunts and grandparents still live in Palomas. They have a kind of family togetherness, where they just go back and forth all the time. The kids that are coming over from Mexico, most of those are American citizens who have been born in the United States. Now the parents may not be able to cross because of illegal status, but the kids are U.S. citizens; they have been born in U.S. hospitals."

Columbus Elementary School's international enrollment poses special challenges for family and parental involvement. Mr. Armijo notes that parental contact is often not as frequent as he would like it to be. The school occasionally runs into problems reaching parents because many don't have telephones and must be reached through an emergency number in Mexico that might be as far as three blocks away or through a relative on the United States side of the border. In many cases, school personnel go into Mexico and talk to the parents or write them a letter so they can cross the border legally to come to the school. Despite these barriers, however, Mr. Armijo says that cooperation from the parents is great. "They'll do anything to help out this school."

The parents who send their children across the border to Columbus Elementary are willing to face the logistical difficulties of getting their children to Columbus each day because they want their children to have the benefits of a bilingual education. Mr. Armijo notes that the only reason that many parents from across the border send their kids to Columbus is to learn English. He describes a potential conflict that sometimes arises from this expectation:

"There's—I wouldn't call it a controversy, but there's some misunderstanding, mainly because parents don't understand what a bilingual program is. Some of them don't want their children to speak Spanish at all; they say they are sending the children to our school just to learn English. A true bilingual program will take kids that are monolingual speakers of any language and combine them together. At Columbus Elementary, for example, if you have a monolingual English speaker and a monolingual Spanish speaker, if they are in a true bilingual program you hope that the Spanish speaker will learn English and the English speaker will learn Spanish. And if they live here for the rest of their lives, they will be able to communicate with anybody. So when the students from Mexico come over, they need, as far as I know, they need to learn the skills or the way of life, the American way of life, the American dream, if you will, of an education. Because at some point or another, they might want to come over. Remember, these students are United States citizens, even though they live with their parents in Mexico. I'm almost sure that most of those kids are going to come over across to the United States and live here and so they need to have this education.

Perspective of Linda Lebya, Third Grade Teacher

Linda Lebya is [in] her third year of teaching third grade at Columbus Elementary School. She lives nearby on a ranch with her husband, who is a deputy sheriff. She speaks conversational Spanish, although she is not a native Spanish speaker. About 95% of her third-grade students are Spanish-speaking.

Lindas classroom is small but inviting. Colorful posters and pictures on the wall reflect the students culture and many words and phrases are posted in Spanish and English. Desks are grouped in clusters of four so students can sit together facing one another. A list of vocabulary words, written in English and Spanish, is on the blackboard.

Linda describes her teaching approaches and some of the challenges she faces. First, she describes a typical spelling lesson:

> *On Monday as an introduction for spelling vocabulary we have 10 vocabulary words written in English and Spanish. The intent is for* [students] *to learn it in English; I also put up the Spanish words with the intent of helping them to learn what the English word means. We discuss the words in English and Spanish, then use them in sentences in each language.*

Columbus Elementary is a poor school, and Linda reports that resources are limited:

> *Lack of books is a problem because we re supposed to be teaching in Spanish for part of the day but the only thing we have in Spanish are the readers. All the other materials are in English so that is a problem.*

One resource that Ms. Lebya does have is a Spanish-speaking instructional assistant. She describes the assistant s role in her classroom:

> *All of the teachers here at Columbus K 3 have an instructional assistant to help out with different things. My assistant this year is really wonderful; she helps out a great deal. She teaches the Spanish reading to the students because I m not as fluent to teach it. I can speak it and I can understand, but to actually teach it, I wouldn t know how; my Spanish is not strong enough.*

Linda describes her understanding of multicultural education:

> *Multicultural education here means that most of the students are from a different culture. We have a few Anglos but most of the students are Mexicans or Hispanics, and when you are*

teaching multicultural education, you want to make sure that the students understand that their culture is just as important as the dominant culture. For example, one of our vocabulary words was fiesta or party. Some of our students were not in school that day because they were making their First Holy Communion and their families were having a big celebration. We talked about official fiestas like Cinco de mayo *and family or traditional fiestas like today and the students made English and Spanish sentences about fiestas and parties. It all helps them to value their culture while they learn about the culture of the United States.*

And as far as the Spanish sentences, thats just giving them an opportunity to do something well because they already know it in Spanish. They have the vocabulary in Spanish, so theyre able to do a good job in making the sentences, and thats something they can feel good about and help their self-esteem. (Kent, Larsen, and Becker 1998)

DIRECTIONS: Each of the multiple-choice questions below is followed by four choices. Select the one that is best in each case.

1. Which approach best describes the philosophy of the bilingual program at Columbus Elementary School?
   - **A.** Children should receive instruction in both English and their native language and culture throughout their school years, making a gradual transition to English.
   - **B.** Students should make the transition to English through ongoing, intensive instruction in English as a Second Language.
   - **C.** Students should be removed from their regular classes to receive special help in English or in reading in their native language.
   - **D.** Students should be immersed in English, then placed in English-speaking classes.

2. Sleeter and Grant describe five approaches to multicultural education. Which approach best characterizes the Columbus Elementary School program, based on the comments of Ms. Lebya?
   - **A.** Human Relations Approaches
   - **B.** Single-Group Studies
   - **C.** Teaching the Exceptionally and Culturally Different
   - **D.** Education that Is Multicultural and Social Reconstructionist

3. Ms. Lebya's instructional approach to teaching vocabulary could best be described as
   - **A.** individualized instruction
   - **B.** cooperative learning
   - **C.** inquiry learning
   - **D.** direct instruction

Sample Short-Answer Questions

The Principles of Learning and Teaching tests include two open-ended short-answer questions related to the case study. A well-constructed short-answer response demonstrates an understanding of the aspects of the case that are relevant to the question, responds to all parts of the question, supports explanations with relevant evidence, and demonstrates a strong knowledge of appropriate concepts, theories, or methodologies relevant to the question. Two readers who are practicing teachers will score the responses according to an ETS scoring guide. (To view the scoring guide, go to the ETS web page: (http://www.ets.org/praxis).

The following sample open-ended questions draw from knowledge and concepts covered in this book only. In an actual Praxis Principles of Learning and Teaching test, respondents should use knowledge and concepts derived from all parts of their teacher education program.

4. Ms. Lebya says that she relies on her instructional assistant to teach reading in Spanish because "I'm not fluent enough to teach it. I can speak it and understand it, but to actually teach it, I wouldn't know how." List at least one positive and one negative possible consequence of this teaching arrangement.

5. Is it possible to teach well without textbooks? If so, in what situations? If not, why not?

Sample Discrete Multiple-Choice Questions

The Principles of Learning and Teaching tests include 24 discrete multiple-choice questions that cover an array of teaching and learning topics. In an actual Praxis Principles of Learning and Teaching test, respondents would draw from knowledge and concepts learned in all aspects of an undergraduate teacher preparation program. In this sample test, items are drawn from concepts discussed in *Becoming a Teacher*.

6. On the first day of school, Mr. Jones told his eighth-grade class that all students must arrive at class on time and with all their materials. He posted the same rule on the bulletin board by the door.

On Tuesday of the second week of school, a classroom visitor observed the following: two students arrived about five minutes late for class and took their seats without any comment from Mr. Jones; one student received permission to go his locker to get an assignment the class was reviewing; another student borrowed a pen from Mr. Jones so she could complete an in-class activity.

The student actions and teacher response suggest which of the following:

A. Mr. Jones did not establish a set of expectations at the beginning of the year.
B. Mr. Jones did not make consequences clear and apply them consistently.
C. Mr. Jones taught and retaught desired behaviors.
D. Mr. Jones demonstrated "with-it-ness" when working with the students.

7. Mr. Williams placed a pitcher of water and several containers of different sizes and shapes on a table. He asked a small group of students, "Which container holds the most water? Which holds the least? How can you figure it out?"

Mr. Williams' philosophical orientation probably is:

A. behaviorism
B. perennialism
C. constructivism
D. essentialism

8. Ms. Jackson was planning a unit of study for her eleventh-grade American history class. She wanted to determine what students already know and want to know about the topic prior to beginning the unit. Which forms of pre-assessment would be most useful?

A. a norm-referenced test
B. a teacher-made assessment
C. a criterion-referenced test
D. a summative assessment

Answers

1. The best answer is A. In the Columbus School's bilingual program, children learn primarily in Spanish during their first few grades, then begin the transition to English in the third grade. They are not experiencing an intensive English instruction or pullout program, nor are they immersed in English.
Related Praxis Topics: I. Organizing Content Knowledge for Student Learning/Needs and characteristics of students from diverse populations; II. Creating an Environment for Student Learning/Appropriate teacher responses to individual and cultural diversity; III. Teaching for Student Learning/Needs and characteristics of students from diverse populations
Related material in this book: Chapter 7: Teaching Diverse Learners

2. The best answer is C. Both Mr. Armijo and Ms. Lebya emphasize that the purpose of their bilingual program is to help the students assimilate into American culture and acquire language and skills that will help them be successful if they choose to live in the United States.
Related Praxis Topics: I. Organizing Content Knowledge for Student Learning/Needs and characteristics of students from diverse populations; II. Creating an Environment for Student Learning/Appropriate teacher responses to individual and cultural diversity
Related material in this book: Chapter 7: Teaching Diverse Learners

3. The best answer is D. Ms. Lebya uses a teacher-directed approach, in which she asks specific questions of the students and provides praise or corrective feedback.
Related Praxis Topics: I. Organizing Content for Student Learning/Creating or selecting teaching methods, learning activities, and instructional for the students and are aligned with the goals of the lesson; III. Teaching for Student Learning/Repertoire of flexible teaching and learning strategies
Related material in this book: Chapter 9: Authentic Instruction and Curricula for Creating a Community of Learners; Chapter 11: Teaching with Technology

4. A strong response to this open-ended question will explicitly state at least one potential positive consequence and one potential negative consequence to the teaching arrangement. The respondent will use or paraphrase the question and answer explicitly in complete sentences.
Sample Response: One potential positive consequence of having the Spanish-speaking teaching assistant teach reading in Spanish is that the students will acquire better reading skills in Spanish. If they become good readers in Spanish, they may find it easier to become good readers in English later. One potential negative conse-

quence of having the Spanish-speaking teaching assistant teach reading in Spanish is that she may not have the knowledge or skills to teach reading. (Many teaching assistants have not had the educational preparation that licensed teachers have.) Ms. Lebya's Spanish may not be strong enough to pick up on those problems or correct them. Thus, the children may not become strong readers in Spanish.
Related Praxis Topic: III. Teaching for Student Learning/Making content comprehensible to students; IV. Teacher Professionalism/Reflecting on the extent to which learning goals were met
Related material in this book: Chapter 7: Teaching Diverse Learners

5. A strong response to this open-ended question will explicitly take a position on the necessity of textbooks and will defend that position. The respondent will use or paraphrase the question and answer explicitly in complete sentences.
Sample Response: It is entirely possible to teach well without textbooks. Although textbooks can be an invaluable resource for teachers, they are only one kind of resource that can be used for instruction. Instead of textbooks, teachers could use a collection of printed materials, such as articles or primary resources, or Web sites from the Internet. The teacher could also use multimedia resources, such as films, videotapes, or audiotapes. To teach well without textbooks, however, the teacher must have clear goals and spend time looking for good alternative materials.
Related Praxis Topic: I. Organizing Content Knowledge for Student Learning/Creating or selecting teaching methods, learning activities, and instructional materials or other resources that are appropriate for the students and are aligned with the goals of the lesson
Related material in this book: Chapter 9: Authentic Instruction and Curricula for Creating a Community of Learners; Chapter 11: Teaching with Technology

6. **The best answer is B.** Although Mr. Jones established and posted classroom procedures at the beginning of the school year, he did not make consequences clear. When students did not follow the procedures, he did not correct the students or remind them of the established classroom expectations.
Related Praxis Topic: II. Creating an Environment for Student Learning/Establishing and maintaining consistent standards of classroom behavior
Related material in this book: Chapter 9: Authentic Instruction and Curricula for Creating a Community of Learners

7. **The best answer is C.** Mr. Williams encouraged the students to construct meaning or make sense of information for themselves, one of the characteristics of constructivism.
Related Praxis Topic: I. Organizing Content Knowledge for Student Learning/Major theories of human development and learning; III. Teaching for Student Learning/Stages and patterns of cognitive and cultural development
Related material in this book: Chapter 3: Ideas and Events That Have Shaped Education in the United States

8. **The best answer is B.** Ms. Jackson can best find out what students know and want to know by designing her own instrument.
Related Praxis Topic: I. Organizing Content Knowledge for Student Learning/Structuring lessons based on the knowledge, experiences, skills, strategies, and interests of the students in relation to the curriculum.
Related material in this book: Chapter 9: Authentic Instruction and Curricula for Creating a Community of Learners; Chapter 10: Curriculum Standards, Assessment, and Students' Learning

References

Educational Testing Service (2002). *Tests at a Glance: Praxis II Subject Assessments/Principles of Learning and Teaching.* Available online: http://www.ets.org/praxis/prxtest.html

Kent, T.W., Larsen, V.A., & Becker, F.J. (1998). *Educational Border Culture in New Mexico.* Boston: Allyn and Bacon.

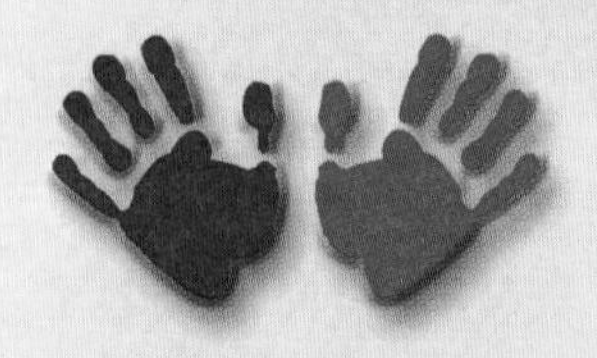

Becoming a Teacher

Sixth Edition

Forrest W. Parkay
Washington State University

Beverly Hardcastle Stanford
Azusa Pacific University

Allyn and Bacon
Boston • New York • San Francisco
Mexico City • Montreal • Toronto • London • Madrid • Munich • Paris
Hong Kong • Singapore • Tokyo • Cape Town • Sydney

Executive Editor and Publisher: Stephen D. Dragin
Senior Developmental Editor: Mary Kriener
Senior Editorial Assistant: Barbara Strickland
Marketing Manager: Tara Whorf
Senior Production Editor: Annette Pagliaro
Editorial Production Service: Modern Graphics, Inc.
Photo Research: PoYee Oster/Photoquick Research
Composition Buyer: Linda Cox
Manufacturing Buyer: Andrew Turso
Cover Administrator: Linda Knowles
Text Design: Studio Montage
Electronic Composition: Modern Graphics, Inc.

For related titles and support materials, visit our online catalog at www.ablongman.com.

Between the time Website information is gathered and then published, it is not unusual for some sites to have closed. Also, the transcription of URLs can result in unintended typographical errors. The publisher would appreciate notification where these errors occur so that they may be corrected in subsequent editions.

Library of Congress Cataloging-in-Publication Data

Parkay, Forrest W.
Becoming a teacher / Forrest W. Parkay, Beverly Hardcastle Stanford.—6th ed.
p. cm.
ISBN 0-205-38854-X
1. Teaching—Vocational guidance. 2. Education—Study and teaching—United States.
3. Teachers—United States—Attitudes. 4. Teaching—Computer network resources.
I. Stanford, Beverly Hardcastle- II. Title.

LB1775 .P28 2003
371.1'0023'73—dc21

2003043707

Printed in the United States of America
10 9 8 7 6 5 4 3 2 1 WC 08 07 06 04 03

PHOTO CREDITS

Page 4, © Ariel Skelley/CORBIS; 7, © Jim Cummins/Getty Images; 21, Will Hart; 31, © Michael Newman/PhotoEdit; 36, Will Hart; 39, © Jose Luis Pelaez/CORBIS; 45, © Bill Aaron/PhotoEdit; 55, © Grantpix/Monkmeyer; 61, © Lon C. Dieh/Photo Edit; 76, © Meyers/Monkmeyer; 83, © Jim Cummins/CORBIS; 85 both, 86 top, Lyrl Ahern; 86 bottom, Will Hart; 87, Courtesy of Special Collections, Milbank Memorial Library, Teachers College, Columbia University; 88, Peter McLaren; 90, © Ellen Senisi/The Image Works; 92, Will Hart; 93, North Wind Picture Archives; 96 top, Library of Congress; 96 bottom, 97, North Wind Picture Archives; 100, © Bettmann/CORBIS; 101, Lyrl Ahern; 102 top, © Bettmann/CORBIS; 102, bottom, Lyrl Ahern; 104, Courtesy of the authors; 107, © Syracuse Newspapers/The Image Works; 118, © Spencer Platt/Getty Images; 121, © Specner Airsley/The Image Works; 122, © David Young-Wolff/PhotoEdit; 131, © Bob Daemmrich/The Image Works; 141, © Jack Kurtz/The Image Works; 156, © Mark Wilson/Getty Images; 166, Courtesy of the authors; 168, © Michael Newman/PhotoEdit; 173, © Mary Kate Denny/Photo Edit; 176, © William Thomas Cain/Getty Images; 192, © Richard Hutchings/Photo Edit; 195, Will Hart; 205, Brian Smith; 212, © Meyers/Monkmeyer; 217, © Bob Daemmrich/The Image Works; 228, AP/Wide World Photos; 238, © David Zelick/Getty Images; 243, Will Hart; 251, Library of Congress; 254, © Robert E. Daemmrich/Getty Images; 260, AP/Wide World Photos; 269, Will Hart; 276, © Ellen Serisi/The Image Works; 278, CORBIS; 279 top left, © Goodman/Monkmeyer; 279 top right, © Dreyfuss/ Monkmeyer; 279 bottom left, © Forsyth/Monkmeyer; 279 bottom right, © Byron/Monkmeyer; 282, Photo Courtesy of Carol Gilligan; 289, © Bonnie Kamin/PhotoEdit; 298, © Mark Harmel/Getty Images; 308, 309, Will Faller; 316, © Will Hart/PhotoEdit; 320, Will Hart; 324, Courtesy of the authors; 340, Will Hart; 344, © Spencer Grant/Photo Edit; 346, © Paul Howell/ Liaison/Getty Images; 356, © Zephyr Picture/IndexStock; 362, © Bob Daemmrich/The Image Works; 366, © Tribune Media Services, Inc. All Rights Reserved. Reprinted with permission; 368 left, © Alan Carey/The Image Works; 368 right, © David Young-Wolff/Photo Edit; 370, AP/Wide World Photos; 375, © Tony Freeman/Photo Edit; 386, © Arthur Tilley/Getty Images; 394, © Bachmann/PhotoEdit; 400, Courtesy of the authors; 410, 416, © A. Ramey/Photo Edit; 430, © Chip Henderson/IndexStock; 440, © Elena Rooraid/Photo Edit; 446, © Michael Newman/PhotoEdit; 454, Will Hart; 468, © David Young-Wolff/PhotoEdit; 474, © Andrew Halbrooke/The Image Works; 485, © Michael Newman/PhotoEdit; 491, © David Young-Wolff/Photo Edit; 495, Will Hart. On the Frontlines, Shadow of a girl on a swing, Andersen Ross/PhotoDisc; Children, Playground, Rommel/Masterfile; Technology Highlights, Teacher helping student with computer, Eyewire/Eyewire Collection; Praxis guide, T. Lindfors.

Contents

part one
The Teaching Profession 2

Preface

We hope you share our belief that teaching is the world's most important profession. With the recent push for standards and accountability and the announcement of the new education initiative, "No Child Left Behind," becoming a teacher has never required more professionalism than it does today. Succeeding in the early years has always been a daunting challenge for new teachers, but never more than now. Ask any experienced teacher to identify the secrets to success and most, if not all, will cite the importance of mentors. To facilitate your students' journey to becoming professional educators, the sixth edition of *Becoming a Teacher* continues a strong tradition of mentorship. **Dear Mentor** features at the start of every Part and **Keepers of the Dream** features in various chapters provide thoughtful feedback and guidance from accomplished teachers addressing the questions and concerns raised by preservice teachers much like the students who will be using this book.

In addition to its strong "mentor" message, *Becoming a Teacher,* Sixth Edition takes a no-nonsense approach toward helping students make that all-important first decision about becoming a teacher. We confront contemporary issues in education head-on and provide students with practical guidance for wending their way through the education maze. New features present your students with a realistic picture of the world of teaching and assist them with their career decisions and professional options.

New Features of the Sixth Edition

Becoming a Teacher, Sixth Edition has taken bold steps in addressing two of the biggest issues facing teachers today—standards-based education and career resiliency.

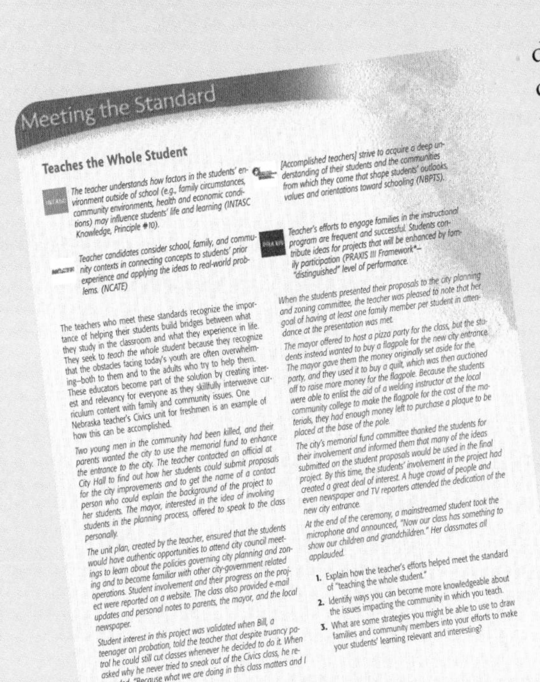

Meeting the Standard

Teaches the Whole Student

The teacher understands how factors in the students' environment outside of school (e.g., family circumstances, community environments, health and economic conditions) may influence students' life and learning (INTASC Knowledge, Principle #10).

Teacher candidates consider school, family, and community contexts in connecting concepts to students' prior experience and applying the ideas to real-world problems. (NCATE)

[Accomplished teachers] strive to acquire a deep understanding of their students and the communities from which they come that shape students' outlooks, values and orientations toward schooling (NBPTS).

Teacher's efforts to engage families in the instructional program are frequent and successful. Students contribute ideas for projects that will be enhanced by family participation (PRAXIS III Framework—"distinguished" level of performance.*

The teachers who meet these standards recognize the importance of helping their students build bridges between what they study in the classroom and what they experience in life. They seek to *teach the whole student* because they recognize that the obstacles facing today's youth are often overwhelming—both to them and to the adults who try to help them. These educators become part of the solution by creating interest and relevancy for everyone as they skillfully interweave curriculum content with family and community issues. One Nebraska teacher's Civics unit for freshmen is an example of how this can be accomplished.

Two young men in the community had been killed, and their parents wanted the city to use the memorial fund to enhance the entrance to the city. The teacher contacted an official at City Hall to find out how her students could submit proposals for the city improvements and to get the name of a contact person who could explain the background of the project to her students. The mayor, interested in the idea of involving students in the planning process, offered to speak to the class personally.

The unit plan, created by the teacher, ensured that the students would have authentic opportunities to attend city council meetings to learn about the policies governing city planning and zoning and to become familiar with other city-government related operations. Student involvement and their progress on the project were reported on a website. The class also provided e-mail updates and personal notes to parents, the mayor, and the local newspaper.

Student interest in this project was validated when Bill, a teenager on probation, told the teacher that despite truancy patrol he could still cut classes whenever he decided to do it. When asked why he never tried to sneak out of the Civics class, he responded, "Because what we are doing in this class matters and I want to be part of that."

When the students presented their proposals to the city planning and zoning committee, the teacher was pleased to note that her goal of having at least one family member per student in attendance at the presentation was met.

The mayor offered to host a pizza party for the class, but the students instead wanted to buy a flagpole for the new city entrance. The mayor gave them the money originally set aside for the party, and they used it to buy a quilt, which was then auctioned off to raise more money for the flagpole. Because the students were able to enlist the aid of a welding instructor at the local community college to make the flagpole for the cost of the materials, they had enough money left to purchase a plaque to be placed at the base of the pole.

The city's memorial fund committee thanked the students for their involvement and informed them that many of the ideas submitted on the student proposals would be used in the final project. By this time, the students' involvement in the project had created a great deal of interest. A huge crowd of people and even newspaper and TV reporters attended the dedication of the new city entrance.

At the end of the ceremony, a mainstreamed student took the microphone and announced, "Now our class has something to show our children and grandchildren." Her classmates all applauded.

1. Explain how the teacher's efforts helped meet the standard of "teaching the whole student."
2. Identify ways you can become more knowledgeable about the issues impacting the community in which you teach.
3. What are some strategies you might be able to use to draw families and community members into your efforts to make your students' learning relevant and interesting?

Standards-based education is addressed directly in a new separate chapter and two pedagogical features that provide students with a clearer understanding of how the standards and assessment movement affects them. An entirely new chapter, **Curriculum Standards, Assessment, and Student Learning** (Chapter 10), examines the role that standards and new approaches to assessing student learning have in today's classrooms. This chapter will help your students understand the implications of high-stakes testing, formal and informal assessments, and standards-based curricula. A new feature within each chapter, **Meeting the Standard,** supports this instruction by providing your students with

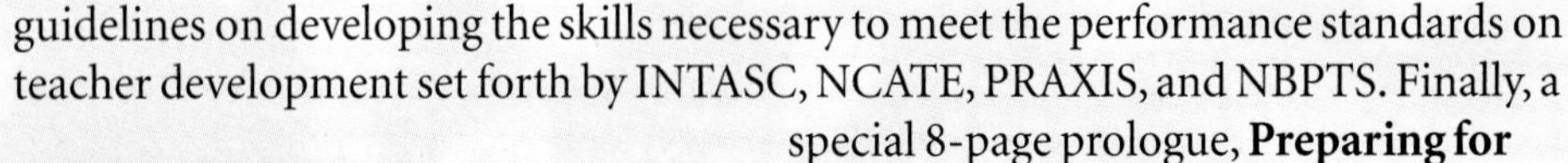

guidelines on developing the skills necessary to meet the performance standards on teacher development set forth by INTASC, NCATE, PRAXIS, and NBPTS. Finally, a special 8-page prologue, **Preparing for the Praxis: Your Guide to Licensure** provides students with a brief tutorial of FAQs, test-taking tips, and sample test questions intended to remove some of the intimidation of this important professional step. Correlations to content in the book demonstrate why *Becoming a Teacher,* Sixth Edition is the ideal preparation guide for taking the Praxis.

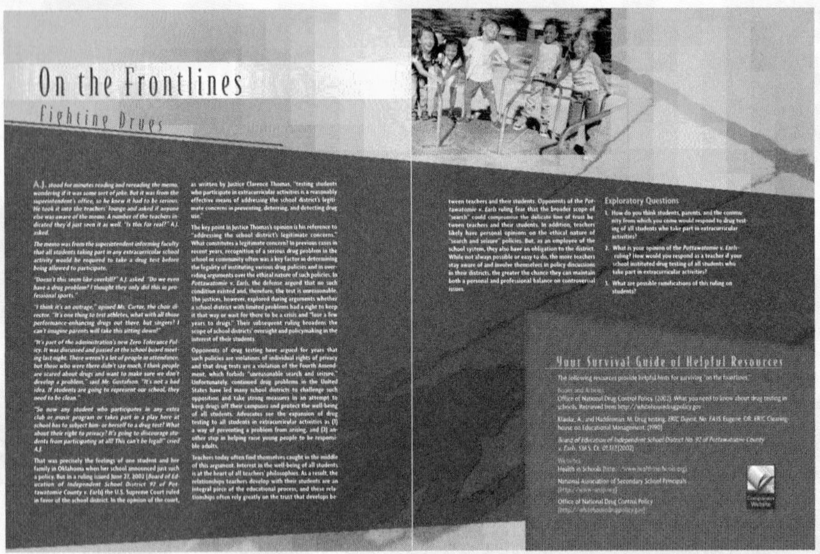

In response to concerns raised by instructors over the issue of better preparing tomorrow's teachers for the real issues in the classroom, **On the Frontlines** features in every chapter examine contemporary issues many teachers must deal with on a daily basis but with little training. Sample cases provide students with firsthand insights into real-world challenges and practical solutions for meeting those challenges. An accompanying "Survival Guide" of recommended print and online resources will help students with all classroom practicums and student teaching experiences.

Reflections on Education features at the end of each Part provide a scholarly examination of key issues that must be addressed as education moves forward in the twenty-first century. Penned by contributing academics, these features provide closure to larger questions raised in the **Dear Mentor** features that open each unit.

Expand your knowledge of the concepts discussed in this chapter by reading current and historical articles from the *New York Times* by visiting the **"Themes of the Times"** section of the Companion Website (**www.ablongman.com/parkay6e**).

Special **Themes of the Times** and **Where Do You Stand?** icons refer students to a robust Companion Website (www.ablongman.com/parkay6e) that allows students to interact with subject matter beyond the general text. A direct link to specially selected *New York Times* articles through the "Themes of the Times" connection on the Companion Website offers students the opportunity to read differing perspectives on contemporary education topics. Bonus articles entitled "Where Do You Stand?" provide opportunities to reflect on the realities of teaching and on controversial trends and issues that have aroused public opinion and attracted media attention. Upon reading each article, students are then asked to take a stand and vote on each issue, comparing their responses to hundreds of respondents across the country.

Where Do You Stand? Visit the Companion Website to Voice Your Opinion.

Organization of the Book

The text maintains the organization established in the previous edition that divided the book into four parts:

Part One: The Teaching Profession (Chapters 1–2) focuses on the theme of teachers and teaching. After reading these chapters students will be better able to determine whether teaching is a good career choice for them. Among the topics we address are why people choose to teach, the challenges and realities of teaching, the knowledge and skills needed to become a teacher, and how to establish mentoring relationships.

Part Two: Foundations of Teaching (Chapters 3–6) explores the foundations of education, a requisite for every professional teacher. These foundational areas include the philosophical, historical, social, cultural, political, financial, and legal dimensions of U.S. education.

Part Three: The Art of Teaching (Chapters 7–11) examines student characteristics and the worlds of the classroom and the school. Here, readers learn about characteristics of students at different stages of development, students as learners, the dynamics of classroom life, the curricula that are taught in schools, and teaching with technology. A new Chapter 9 on **Authentic Instruction and Curricula for Creating a Community of Learners** highlights proven strategies for creating positive learning environments and well-managed classrooms.

Part Four: Your Teaching Future (Chapters 12–13) discusses issues and trends that will impact each student's quest to become an effective teacher, especially the expanding leadership role of teachers, planning for a successful first year of teaching, and the teacher's role in shaping the future of education.

In addition, we explore four overriding issues in education that need to be addressed—teacher perseverance, countering a socially toxic environment, education in a nation of changing demographics, and preparing a literate populace. Each of these issues is raised in the questions posed and answered in the **Dear Mentor** features that begin each part and then addressed further in scholarly **Reflections on Education** features that close out each part.

Reflections on Education

The Rewards and Challenges of Those First Years of Teaching
by Jan Richards

Internet Resources

References

Becoming a Teacher 71

Additional Features and Learning Aids

Included in *Becoming a Teacher,* Sixth Edition are many additional features we believe will help prepare students for rewarding futures as professional teachers.

To guide study, **Focus Questions** at the beginning of each chapter reflect the questions posed in the main headings of the text. **Opening scenarios** present decision-making or problem-solving situations to reflect upon and resolve. These situations are referred to again in the chapter and provide readers an opportunity to apply new learning in specific problem-solving contexts.

To inspire preservice teachers with the experiences of outstanding teachers, a **Keepers of the Dream** feature in each odd-numbered chapter profiles an individual in education whose philosophies and professional contributions reflect a commitment to touching others' lives through teaching. **Technology Highlights** features in even-numbered chapters relate educational technology to chapter content. A **Professional Reflection** feature in each chapter provides readers an opportunity to reflect on their beliefs and values and issues teachers face. This feature is designed to give practice in the applied reflective inquiry that should characterize every teacher's professional life.

In addition, chapter-ending material includes a **Teacher's Database** feature with **online activities** for using the vast resources of the World Wide Web and the Internet to facilitate professional growth. Cyberspace has transformed teaching and learning in many schools and classrooms; and advanced telecommunications will continue to change the way teachers teach and assess students' learning.

This edition of *Becoming a Teacher* continues the popular **Professional Portfolio** feature that will enable preservice teachers to document their growth and accomplishments over time. Each chapter includes guidelines for creating a portfolio entry that readers can actually use when they begin teaching; in addition, students may wish to use selected portfolio entries during the process of applying for a first teaching position.

As a further study aid, **Key Terms and Concepts** are boldfaced in the text and listed with page cross-references at the ends of chapters. An expanded **Glossary** at the end of the book helps readers quickly locate the definitions of key terms and concepts and the text pages on which they appear.

Optional end-of-chapter critical thinking questions closely correlate the text with the videoclips on the **VideoWorkshop** CD-ROM that assist students with applying general concepts to the classroom. (VideoWorkshop is available as a value pack item with this book.)

Other end-of-chapter learning aids in this edition include a concise **Summary** and suggested **Applications and Activities.** Applications and activities include journal-writing opportunities in **Teacher's Journal** and field experiences in **Observations and Interviews.** In "Teacher's Journal," we continue a feature that has proved useful and popular with instructors who ask students to keep a teacher's journal to encour-

Video**Workshop Extra!**

If the Video Workshop package was included with your textbook, go to Chapter 1 of the Companion Website (http://www.ablongman.com/parkay6e) and click on the Video Workshop button. Follow the instructions for viewing videoclip 1 and completing this exercise. Consider this information along with what you've read in Chapter 1 while answering the following questions.

1. Teachers face many challenges in and out of the classroom. The text presents five challenges: classroom management, social problems that impact students, need for family and community support, long working hours and job stress, and need for professional empowerment. Explain how students' perceptions of teachers affect each of these challenges and how teachers might prepare for students' expectations.
2. Society holds teachers accountable for students' achievement. How do teachers send students the message that they (teachers) have confidence in students' abilities to succeed? Create a motto that teachers could present to students on the first day of school that conveys a strong relationship between teachers' expectations of and confidence in students' abilities.

age active reflection as they learn about teaching. The short, optional journal-writing activities are based on the "writing-to-learn" and "writing-across-the-curriculum" concepts.

Supplements for Students

- Students who visit the **Companion Website** that accompanies the text (ablongman.com/parkay6e) will find many features and activities to help them in their studies: web links, learning activities; practice tests; video and audio clips, and vocabulary flash cards. In addition, a **Teacher's Resource Guide** provides a rich and varied array of materials, sources, strategies, contacts, and data that beginning teachers can rely on for support. These materials—from a checklist for evaluating a school's effectiveness at integrating technology into the teaching-learning process to sample questions to ask during a job interview—will prove extremely valuable in preparing for, and beginning, a first teaching position. The website also features an interactive **Education Timeline** that highlights the people and events that have shaped education through history plus connections to the **Themes of the Times** articles described earlier. The website also features **Syllabus Manager**, an online syllabus creation and management tool. Instructors can easily create syllabi with direct links to the companion website, links to other online resources, and student assignments. Students may access the syllabus at any time to help them with research projects and to complete the assignments.
- **VideoWorkshop for Foundations of Education** is a new way to bring video into your course for maximized learning! This total teaching and learning system includes quality video footage on an easy-to-use CD-ROM plus a Student Learning Guide and an Instructor's Teaching Guide—both with textbook-specific Correlation Grids. The result? A program that brings textbook concepts to life with ease and that helps your students understand, analyze, and apply the objectives of the course. VideoWorkshop is available for your students as a value-pack option with this textbook.
- **Research Navigator™ (with ContentSelect Research Database) (Access Code Required)** Research Navigator™ (researchnavigator.com) is the easiest way for students to start a research assignment or research paper. Complete with extensive help on the research process and three exclusive online databases of credible and reliable source material including EBSCO's ContentSelect™ Academic Journal Database, New York Times Search by Subject Archive, and "Best of the Web" Link Library, Research Navigator™ helps students quickly and efficiently make the most of their research time. Research Navigator™ is free when packaged with the textbook and requires an access code.
- **iSearch Guide for Education (with Research Navigator™)** This free reference guide includes tips, resources, activities, and URLs to help students use the Internet for their research projects. The first part introduces students to the basics of the Internet and the World Wide Web. Part II includes many Net activities that tie into the content of the text. Part III lists hundreds of education Internet resources. Part IV outlines how to use the Research Navigator™ resources. The guide also includes information on how to correctly cite research, and a guide to building an online glossary, Includes access code for Research Navigator™.

Supplements for the Instructor

- The **Instructor's Resource Manual** includes a wealth of interesting ideas and activities designed to help instructors teach the course. Each chapter includes: a chapter-at-a-glance organizer that correlates chapter outlines, learning objectives, and teaching supplements; an annotated lecture outline that provides examples, discussion questions, and student activities; suggestions for additional resources; and handout masters that provide additional lecture support materials. In addition the *Manual* includes Web-based student activities correlated to the Companion Website for the text.
- A **Test Bank** of more than 1,000 questions, including multiple choice items, essay questions, case studies, and authentic assessments, plus text page references and answer feedback. (Including optional VideoWorkshop test items that may be included.)
- **Computerized Test Bank** The printed Test Bank is also available electronically through our computerized testing system: TestGen EQ. Instructors can use TestGen EQ to create exams in just minutes by selecting from the existing database of questions, editing questions, or writing original questions.
- The **Allyn & Bacon Interactive Video: Issues in Education**, features news reports from around the country on topics covered in the text. The VHS video contains ten modules of up-to-date news clips exploring current issues and debates in education. Some of the topics include: teacher shortages, alternative schools, community-school partnerships, standardized testing and bilingual classrooms. An accompanying instructor's guide outlines teaching strategies and discussion questions to use with the clips.
- **Allyn & Bacon Transparencies for Foundations of Education/Introduction to Teaching, 2002** a set of 100 acetate transparencies related to topics in the text.
- **Digital Media Archive for Foundations of Education/Introduction to Teaching** This CD-ROM contains a variety of media elements that instructors can use to create electronic presentations in the classroom. It includes hundreds of original images, as well as selected art from Allyn and Bacon foundations and introduction to teaching texts, providing instructors with a broad selection of graphs, charts, and tables. For classrooms with full multimedia capability, it also contains video segments and Web links.
- **Online Course Management Systems** Powered by Blackboard™ and hosted nationally, Allyn and Bacon's own course management system, **CourseCompass,** helps you manage all aspects of teaching your course. It features preloaded content to support Foundations of Education and Introduction to Teaching courses (your sales rep can give you additional information). For colleges and universities with **Blackboard™** licenses, special course management packages are available in this format as well.

Acknowledgments

Many members of the Allyn and Bacon team provided expert guidance and support during the preparation of the Sixth edition of *Becoming a Teacher.* Clearly, Mary Kriener, our developmental editor, heads the list. From suggestions for revision, feedback on draft manuscripts, and skillful coordination of the revision process, from beginning to end, to coordination of the book's supplements, Mary's hard work is deeply appreciated. Additionally, the first author was a visiting professor at Assumption University in Bangkok, Thailand, during the final stages of the revision process, and he extends a heartfelt "khorp khun maak khrup" ("thank you very much," in Thai) to Mary for the extra effort required to keep the project moving ahead and on schedule. In spite of thousands of miles that separate Bangkok and Boston, Mary provided continuous, expert support and guidance. Her positive attitude, clear communication skills, remarkable productivity, and sense of humor made the work of revising the book surprisingly enjoyable. In addition, the authors benefited from excellent suggestions made by Steve Dragin, Executive Editor and Publisher. His extensive understanding of textbook publishing enriched the sixth edition immeasurably.

The authors extend a special thanks to Tom Jefferies, Associate Development Editor, for his coordination of the book's supplements; and to Paul A. Smith, Vice President and Editor-in-Chief; Tara Whorf, Marketing Manager; and Annette Pagliaro, Senior Production Editor; all of whom were steadfast in their support of the sixth edition.

The authors extend a special thanks to contributing writers Julie Jantzi and Nancy Brashear of Azusa Pacific University for their research on and authorship of the Meeting the Standard pieces.

Julie Jantzi and Nancy Brashear

The authors extend a special thanks to Steven Million of Winthrop University and Mary Harris for their outstanding work on the Interactive Companion Website. Additional thanks go to Steven Million, Jessican Little, and David Vawter of Winthrop University for writing the Test Bank; Julie Jantzi and Nancy Brashear for preparing the Instructor's Resource Manual; Lisa Fiore of Lesley University for preparing VideoWorkshop questions and activities that appear in the text and throughout the supplements; and Mary K. Ducharme for writing the special Preparing for the Praxis guide.

We are also grateful to the many people throughout the United States who have used the previous edition and provided suggestions and materials for this edition, including our students. We also wish to thank the following reviewers, who provided concise, helpful suggestions during the developmental stages of this book: Tim Anderson, Nebraska Wesleyan University; Patricia Bason, Elon University; Tim Fiegen, Dakota State University; Dwight C. Holliday, Indiana University Northwest; Michael Jacobs, University of Northern Colorado; Courtney Moffatt, Edgewood College; Barbara Slater Stein, James Madison University; and Judy Wilkerson, University of South Florida.

Forrest W. Parkay appreciates the support of his family, friends, and colleagues during the intensive, months-long revision process. In particular, Judy N. Mitchell, Dean of the College of Education at Washington State University; Dennis Warner, Associate Dean; Donald B. Reed, Chair of the Department of Educational Leadership and Counseling Psychology; and the faculty, teaching assistants, and research assistants in the Department of Educational Leadership and Counseling Psychology that gave him much-appreciated encouragement and support. In addition, the following colleagues provided Dr. Parkay with ideas, resources, and suggestions for this edition—Linda Chaplin, Scott Walter, and Chris Sodorff, all of Washington State University; Robert Leahy, Stetson University; Ralph Karst, Northeastern Louisiana University; Satnam Singh Bhugra, Lansing Community College; Lyn Middleton, University of Wollongong, Australia; Liping Liu, Brevard College; and Soren Wheeler, American Association for the Advancement of Science. And, for demonstrating the power of professional inquiry, he owes a profound debt to a great teacher, mentor, and friend, Herbert A. Thelen, Professor Emeritus, University of Chicago.

Finally, the personal support Dr. Parkay received from his family was invaluable. During the revision process, the time he spent with his daughters Anna, Catherine, and Rebecca were very special and brought much-needed balance back into his life. To Arlene, his wife, friend, and helper, he gives a deep thanks. She was always there to provide the support that made the sixth edition possible. Moreover, she made many valuable contributions to the project, not the least of which was obtaining and keeping track of letters of permission. Since the first edition of *Becoming a Teacher* was published in 1990, Arlene's encouragement, patience, and understanding have been remarkable.

Forrest W. Parkay

Beverly Hardcastle Stanford expresses appreciation to her Azusa Pacific University colleagues and students for their contributions to the sixth edition of this textbook. Dean Emeritus Alice V. Watkins, Dr. Maria Pacino, and Dr. Paul A. Flores, and former student Dr. Jan Richards shared their thoughts on current concerns in education in the **Reflections on Education** pieces at the end of each section of the book. Along with Dr. Nancy Brashear and Dr. Julie Jantzi, the perspectives of these colleagues enrich the text.

Dr. Stanford is also grateful to the Azusa Pacific University students who wrote the **Dear Mentor** letters, Catherine Solorio, Jerry Fincher, Mark Hasson, and Lyndie J. Okura. She thanks the experienced teachers who responded to the letters, doctoral students Gilbert Navarro, William M. Gillum, and Jenny L. Hite, and masters student Alonia P. Alexander. The voices of these beginning and veteran teachers help ground the book in today's teaching realities.

For their inspiration as **Keepers of the Dream,** Dr. Stanford gives special thanks to Dr. Marcia McVey and Ms. Betsy McIntire. The former is an admirable administrator, and the latter a teacher who enriches the lives of her students with special needs.

Beverly Hardcastle Stanford

As with the past revisions, Dr. Stanford gives her greatest thanks to her husband, Dick, for his enduring enthusiasm and support of this endeavor. During the months of this revision, he underwent major heart surgery, a shoulder replacement, and had two additional extended hospital stays because of medical complications. His positive attitude and courage confronting and recovering from those challenges while at the same time encouraging those around him, including his wife, were inspiring and put into perspective what matters most, the relationships in our lives.

Relationships are a theme in this book, in the way it was created and in what it seeks to accomplish. It is a team attempt to mentor new teachers. Dr. Stanford thanks her past and present students, colleagues, the Allyn and Bacon team, and her co-author and his colleagues for their teamwork in this endeavor. The hope of all of us is that the book will not only ease teachers' entry into the profession but will enable them to remain in the field to serve children and youth wisely and well.

Forrest W. Parkay

Beverly Hardcastle Stanford

This book is dedicated to our students—their spirit continually renews us and inspires confidence in the future of teaching in America

The Teaching Profession

Dear Mentor

Promoting Teacher Resiliency

Dear Mentor,

After earning a B.A. in business administration and working in the industry for the past twenty-five years, I have decided to return to school to obtain my certification to teach and one day teach technology at the middle school level. What do I need to know to make this move into teaching a successful career change? I've heard stories about teacher burnout. What can I do to make the first few years successful for the students and the teacher alike? What challenges should I expect to face the first year, and how should I react? What measures do I need to take to realize my dream, especially in light of the recent political focus on core subject areas and high-stakes testing? How important is it to integrate my personal experiences in business into the curriculum and lesson plans?

Sincerely,
Jerry A. Fincher

Dear Jerry,

I have had the pleasure of teaching social studies at an urban high school for the last seven years, as well as teaching an instructional methods course for the University of Phoenix. I am presently pursuing a doctorate in education. It is always exciting to see a professionally experienced and enthusiastic person entering the field of education. Each individual comes into the classroom with experiences and attributes that make the person unique; these attributes will be your key to success. All teachers, especially those transitioning from another career, should build off of their valuable traits and strengthen their weaknesses. As an experienced professional, you undoubtedly recognize what special skills and talents you possess. Your students will be best served by your bringing those skills into the classroom.

As in most professions, teaching requires a great deal of preparation and commitment. My first three years of teaching were primarily spent developing my curriculum and teaching style. New teachers generally enter the classroom with a great deal of uncertainty. It is important that teachers expect these challenges and go into the classroom with a lot of flexibility and determination. Although I entered the classroom with a certain set of personality and professional characteristics, I was not sure how those traits would translate into teaching. My teaching style and classroom structure continue to develop as I become more confident in my teaching abilities. Give yourself an opportunity to make mistakes and learn from your experiences. All teachers benefit from revising their curriculum and classroom activities on a regular basis. Allow yourself some time and flexibility—experiment in the classroom. Creativity and patience in the classroom will help you to further develop the characteristics needed to become the most comfortable and efficient teacher possible. It was not until several years into my teaching career that I felt I had found my "style" in the classroom.

New teachers also must concern themselves with the recent increase in political and social pressures on accountability in the classroom. Although this added emphasis on the core subjects takes some focus off of elective courses, technology remains an integral part of the education curriculum. All teachers and students are better served by a greater focus on preparing students for the technological changes that our society is experiencing. This knowledge of technology should be used to help students and faculty deal with the high-stakes testing that is facing all schools.

Best of luck in your educational career.

Sincerely,
William M. Gillum
Adjunct Professor
Teacher, Chaffey High School; Ontario, California

1 Teaching: Your Chosen Profession

People have an overwhelming interest in teaching as a potential career. . . . They are considering teaching for the most noble of reasons—the high esteem they place on education and their desire to influence and inspire young minds.

—Bob Chase
past president of the National Education Association, commenting on the 2002 Teacher Day online ballot conducted by the NEA

Three years ago you decided to become a teacher—it hardly seems possible that today you're going to have your first job interview. Walking from the parking lot toward the school, you think about your readiness for teaching. "Am I ready? Do I have what it takes to become a good teacher? Can I handle the stress? Will my students learn a lot from me?"

Approaching the main entrance, you look at the dozens of students playing on the open field next to the building. Their joyful, exuberant sounds this warm late-August morning remind you of your own school days. Some children are moving constantly, running in tight circles and zig-zags as they yell and motion to friends who are also on the move. Others stand near the entrance in groups of two or three, talking and milling about as they wait for the bell signaling the start of the first day of school.

At the bottom of the long stairs leading up to a row of green metal doors, you overhear the conversation of three students.

"It's a great movie. What time should we meet?" the taller of two girls asks. Before her friends can respond, she adds, "My aunt's going to pick me up at four o'clock, so I should be home by four-thirty."

"Let's meet at five o'clock," the other girl says. "I can be ready by then."

"Si, pero no creo que pueda hacerlo para las cinco," the boy says. "Tengo que llevar a mi hermanita a la clinica. ¿Podermos hacerlo después?"

"Bueno, pero no muy tarde," the tall girl says, switching effortlessly to Spanish. "Tenemos que reunirnos con los otros chicos."

"Si, además no quiero perder el comienzo de la película," says the other girl.

Reaching the top of the stairs, you open a door and walk through the vestibule out into a brightly lit hallway. The main office is directly in front of you. To the right of the office door is a bulletin board proclaiming in large red block letters, "Welcome back, students!" Beneath that greeting, in smaller black letters, is another message: "It's going to be a great year!"

Inside the office, you approach the counter on which sits a plastic sign that says "Welcome" in five languages: English, Spanish, Swahili, Chinese, and Russian. You introduce yourself to the school's head secretary. He remains seated behind a gray steel desk covered with loose papers.

"I have an appointment with Ms. Wojtkowski," you inform him. "It's about a replacement for Mr. Medina."

"Good. She's expecting you. Why don't you have a seat over there?" He motions for you to sit on the couch across from the teachers' mailboxes. "She's working with some teachers on setting up a meeting of our Site-Based Council. She ought to be finished in just a few minutes."

While waiting for Ms. Wojtkowski, you think about questions you might be asked. Why did you choose to become a teacher? What is your philosophy of education? How would you use technology in your classroom? What is your approach to classroom management? How would you meet the needs of students from different cultural and linguistic backgrounds? How would you set up a program in your major teaching area? How would you involve parents in the classroom? What are your strengths? Why should the district hire you?

Reflecting on these questions, you admit they are actually quite difficult. Your answers, you realize, could determine whether you get the job.

Focus Questions

1. **Why do you want to teach?**
2. **What are the challenges of teaching?**
3. **What is teaching really like?**
4. **What does society expect of teachers?**
5. **How do good teachers view their work?**

Expand your knowledge of the concepts discussed in this chapter by reading current and historical articles from the *New York Times* by visiting the "**Themes of the Times**" section of the Companion Website (**www.ablongman.com/parkay6e**).

The interview questions just posed are not easily answered. Why did you decide to become a teacher? How will you meet the needs of all students? What do you have to offer students? The answers to these and similar questions depend, in large measure, on the personality and experiences of the person responding. However, they are questions that professional teachers recognize as important and worthy of careful consideration.

The primary purpose of this book is to orient you to the world of education and to help you begin to formulate answers to such questions. In addition, this book will help you answer your own questions about the career you have chosen. What is teaching really like? What kind of rewards do teachers experience? What are the trends and issues in the profession? What problems can you expect to encounter in the classroom? What will you need to know and be able to do to meet the challenges of the teaching profession?

We begin this book by asking you to examine why you want to become a teacher because we believe that effective teachers know why they want to teach. They examine their motives carefully, are aware of what draws them to teaching, and acknowledge what makes them uncertain about choosing teaching as a profession.

Why Do You Want to Teach?

People are drawn to teaching for many reasons. For some, the desire to teach emerges early and is nurtured by positive experiences with teachers during the formative years of childhood. For others, teaching is seen as a way of making a significant contribution to the world and experiencing the joy of helping others grow and develop. And for others, life as a teacher is attractive because it is exciting, varied, and stimulating.

Desire to Work with Children and Young People

The desire to work with young people is the most frequently cited reason teachers give for choosing their profession, according to the National Education Association (NEA) research report, *Status of the American Public School Teacher* (2002a). Though the conditions under which teachers work may be challenging, their salaries modest, and segments of their communities unsupportive, most teach simply because they care about students.

The day-to-day interactions between teachers and students build strong bonds. Daily contact also enables teachers to become familiar with the personal as well as the academic needs of their students, and this concern for students' welfare and growth outweighs the difficulties and frustrations of teaching. As the following quotations from highly accomplished individuals illustrate, the teacher's potential to make a difference in students' lives can be profound:

> *The dream begins, most of the time, with a teacher who believes in you, who tugs and pushes and leads you on to the next plateau, sometimes poking you with a sharp stick called truth.*
> *—Dan Rather, national news commentator*

> *Compassionate teachers fill a void left by working parents who aren't able to devote enough attention to their children. Teachers don't just teach; they can be vital personalities who help young people to mature, to understand the world and to understand themselves.*
> *—Charles Platt, science fiction novelist*

> *One looks back with appreciation to the brilliant teachers who touched our human feelings. The curriculum is so much necessary raw material, but warmth is the vital element for the growing plant and for the soul of the child.*
> *—Carl Jung, world-renowned psychoanalyst*

Teachers can play a critical role in shaping the future of young people. What positive effect might this teacher have on this student?

Most teachers appreciate the unique qualities of youth. They enjoy the liveliness, curiosity, freshness, openness, and trust of young children or the abilities, wit, spirit, independence, and idealism of adolescents. Like the following teacher, they want to be connected to their students: "I now know that I teach so I can be involved in my students' lives, in their real life stories" (Henry et al. 1995, 69).

Teachers also derive significant rewards from meeting the needs of diverse learners. Although students from the United States' more than one hundred racial and ethnic groups and students with special needs are increasing in number, effective teachers recognize that their classrooms are enriched by the varied backgrounds of students. To enable you to experience the satisfaction of helping all students learn, significant portions of this book are devoted to **student variability** (differences among students in regard to their developmental needs, interests, abilities, and disabilities) and **student diversity** (differences among students in regard to gender, race, ethnicity, culture, and socioeconomic status). An appreciation for such diversity, then, will help you to experience the rewards that come from enabling each student to make his or her unique contribution to classroom life.

Companion Website

Where Do You Stand? Visit the Companion Website to Voice Your Opinion.

The opportunity to work with young people, whatever their stage of development and whatever their life circumstances, is a key reason people are drawn to teaching and remain in the profession.

A Passion for Teaching

The 2001 *MetLife Survey of the American Teacher: Key Elements of Quality Schools* reported that 79 percent of teachers "strongly agree" that they are passionate about teaching (Harris Interactive 2001). Elementary and secondary teachers, as well as new and experienced teachers, were equally likely to describe themselves as passionate about teaching. Why do teachers find teaching so satisfying? What does it mean to be *passionate* about teaching?

A Passion for the Subject Some teachers who report that they are passionate about teaching may mean that they are passionate about teaching in their discipline. As an inner-city teacher who responded to the *MetLife Survey* put it: "Teaching is my purpose in life. I am very passionate about learning and think that I was placed here on this earth to teach. I feel good about being a teacher. I have enthusiasm, knowledge, and love to teach the children" (Harris Interactive 2001, 26).

A Passion for the Teaching Life For those teachers who always enjoyed school, it is often the life of a teacher that has appeal—to be in an environment that encourages a high regard for education and the life of the mind, and to have daily opportunities to see students become excited about learning. Albert Einstein, for example, regretted that he did not devote his career to the teaching life:

> *Believe it or not, one of my deepest regrets [is that I didn't teach]. I regret this because I would have liked to have had more contact with children. There has always been something about the innocence and freshness of young children that appeals to me and brings me great enjoyment to be with them. And they are so open to knowledge. I have never really found it difficult to explain basic laws of nature to children. When you reach them at their level, you can read in their eyes their genuine interest and appreciation (quoted in Bucky 1992, 99).*

A Passion for the Teaching–Learning Process To be passionate about teaching can also mean to be passionate about the act of teaching and the learning that follows. Many teachers focus on the process rather than on the subject or even the students. Persons with this orientation are attracted by the live, spontaneous aspects of teaching and are invigorated by the need to think on their feet and to capitalize on teachable moments when they occur. "[T]hey possess a variety of schemata for seeing what is important, [and they] have a broad repertoire of moves with which to quickly and gracefully act on the situation that they see" (Eisner 1998, 200).

Influence of Teachers

It seems reasonable to assume that the process of becoming a teacher begins early in life. Although it is not true that some people are born teachers, their early life experiences often encourage them to move in that direction. Since some of the adults who have the greatest influence on children—beyond their parents or guardians—are their teachers, a teacher's influence during the formative years is often the catalyst for deciding to become a teacher. For example, of the respondents to the NEA 2002 Teacher Day online ballot who reported that they would consider becoming a teacher (eight out of ten), 22 percent identified the influence of a teacher in elementary or secondary school as the principal reason for considering a teaching career (National Education Association 2002b).

Evidence also suggests that those who become teachers were often more influenced by their teachers as people than as subject-matter experts. "It is the human dimension that gives all teachers . . . their power as professional influences" (Zehm and Kottler 1993, 2). Behind the decision to become a teacher is often the inspirational memory of earlier teachers to whom one continues to feel connected in a way that goes beyond the subjects they taught.

Desire to Serve

Many choose to teach because they want to serve others; they want the results of their labor to extend beyond themselves and their families. Some decide to select another major or leave teaching to earn more money elsewhere, only to return to teaching, confiding that they found the other major or work lacking in meaning or significance. Being involved in a service profession is their draw to the field.

For many teachers, the decision to serve through teaching was influenced by their experiences as volunteers. Nearly half of the teachers surveyed by the New York City School Volunteer Program, for example, reported that they had served as volunteers in an educational setting before deciding to become a teacher, and 70 percent of these teachers reported that this experience contributed to their decision to become a teacher (Educational Testing Service 1995). As one New York teacher said, "I always wanted to be a teacher, and all of my volunteer experiences contributed to this career choice" (8).

The desire to serve others and give something back to society is a key attraction of the **Teach for America** program developed in 1989 by Wendy Kopp as an outgrowth of her senior thesis at Princeton University. Teach for America volunteers, recent graduates from some of the United States' best colleges and universities, are assigned to teach for a minimum of two years in urban and rural school districts with severe shortages of science, math, and language arts teachers. Volunteers complete five weeks of intensive training at the Teach for America Institute in Houston. After two years of teaching, being monitored by state and school authorities, and taking professional development courses, Teach for America teachers can earn regular certification. Upon completion of their two-year assignment, volunteers then return to their chosen careers in other fields, though more than half remain in education as teachers, principals, and educational administrators (Teach for America 1999).

Explore more deeply your reasons for becoming a teacher. The Professional Reflection focuses on several characteristics that may indicate your probable satisfaction with teaching as a career.

Practical Benefits of Teaching

Not to be overlooked as attractions to teaching are its practical benefits. Teachers' hours and vacations are widely recognized as benefits. Though the number of hours most teachers devote to their work goes far beyond the number of hours they actually spend at school, their schedules do afford them a measure of flexibility not found in other professions. For example, teachers with school-age children can often be at home when their children are not in school, and nearly all teachers, regardless of their years of experience, receive the same generous vacation time: holiday breaks and a long summer vacation. On the other hand, with the continued growth of year-round schools—3,011 schools in forty-four states were on year-round schedules in 2001–02—many teachers have three or four "mini vacations" throughout the year and welcome the flexibility of being able to take vacations during off-peak seasons (National Association for Year-Round Education 2002).

Salaries and Benefits Although intangible rewards represent a significant attraction to teaching, teachers are demanding that the public acknowledge the value and professional standing of teaching by supporting higher salaries. According to a 2002 poll, *A National Priority: Americans Speak on Teacher Quality* (Hart and Teeter 2002), 83 percent of the public favors increased salaries for teachers, even if it means paying higher taxes. As a result, teacher salaries have increased steadily since the 1990s. The average salaries of all teachers in 1990 was $31,367; for 2001, the average was approximately $43,000 (National Center for Education Statistics 2002a). In 1999–2000, nineteen school districts serving the nation's one

Professional Reflection

Assessing Your Reasons for Choosing to Teach

For each of the following characteristics, indicate on a scale from 1 to 5 the extent to which it applies to you.

	Very applicable				Not at all applicable
1. A passion for learning	1	2	3	4	5
2. Success as a student	1	2	3	4	5
3. Good sense of humor	1	2	3	4	5
4. Positive attitudes toward students	1	2	3	4	5
5. Tolerance toward others	1	2	3	4	5
6. Patience	1	2	3	4	5
7. Good verbal and writing skills	1	2	3	4	5
8. Appreciation for the arts	1	2	3	4	5
9. Experiences working with children (camp, church, tutoring, etc.)	1	2	3	4	5
10. Other teachers in family	1	2	3	4	5
11. Encouragement from family to enter teaching	1	2	3	4	5
12. Desire to serve	1	2	3	4	5
			Total score		

Now that you have completed the self-assessment, calculate your total score; the highest score = 60, the lowest = 12. Interpret the results of your self-assessment with caution. A high score does not necessarily mean that you will be dissatisfied as a teacher, nor does a low score mean that you will be highly satisfied.

Table 1.1 Average salaries of public school teachers, 2000–01

State	Average Salary	State	Average Salary
1 New Jersey	53,281*	27 Texas	38,361
2 Connecticut	52,693	28 New Hampshire	38,301
3 California	52,480	29 Vermont	38,254
4 New York	52,040	30 Florida	38,230
5 Michigan	50,694*	31 Alabama	37,956*
6 Pennsylvania	48,528	32 South Carolina	37,938
7 District of Columbia	48,704	33 Tennessee	37,431
8 Rhode Island	48,474*	34 Missouri	36,722
9 Alaska	48,123	35 Kentucky	36,589
10 Illinois	47,847	36 Iowa	36,479
11 Massachusetts	47,789	37 Utah	36,441
12 Delaware	47,047	38 Idaho	36,375
13 Maryland	45,963	39 Maine	36,373
14 United States	43,335*	40 Arizona	36,302*
15 Indiana	43,311	41 Kansas	35,901
16 Ohio	42,764	42 West Virginia	35,888
17 Georgia	42,216	43 Wyoming	34,678
18 Minnesota	42,212	44 Arkansas	34,641
19 Washington	42,137	45 Oklahoma	34,499
20 Wisconsin	42,122	46 Nebraska	34,175
21 Oregon	41,711	47 New Mexico	33,785
22 North Carolina	41,151	48 Louisiana	33,615
23 Nevada	40,443*	49 Montana	33,249
24 Virginia	40,197	50 Mississippi	31,954
25 Hawaii	40,052	51 North Dakota	30,891
26 Colorado	39,184	52 South Dakota	30,265

*estimated

Source: National Education Association. Washington, DC: National Education Association, 2001. http://www.nea.com

hundred largest cities had maximum salaries exceeding $60,000, and thirty-eight districts had maximum salaries greater than $50,000. Yonkers had the highest maximum salary ($74,951), followed by Jersey City ($73,500), Pittsburgh ($65,100), Newark ($64,677), and Rochester ($62,888). Table 1.1 shows a state-by-state ranking of salaries for public school teachers for 2000–01.

Though the general consensus is still that teachers are underpaid, teacher salaries are becoming more competitive with other occupations; in fact, salaries are becoming one of the attractions for the profession. For example, based on the fact that 884 teachers were paid more than $70,000 during 1997–98 in New Jersey, John Challenger, a job placement specialist and CEO, predicted that New Jersey would see its first $100,000 teacher before the next millennium. According to Challenger, occupations typically stereotyped as moderate-to-low paying will experience a "windfall" in the twenty-first century. As private businesses invest in public schools to help develop tomorrow's skilled workforce, teachers will be "able to contract their skills and wares to the highest corporate bidder, yet remain on the payroll at their school" (United Press International 1998).

When we are comparing teacher salaries state-by-state, it is important to remember that higher salaries are frequently linked to a higher **cost of living,** a more experienced teaching force, and a more desirable location. In addition, many districts have developed salary policies to attract high-quality graduates of teacher education programs, to encourage the best teachers to remain in the classroom, or to draw teachers into subjects and geographic areas in which there are shortages. These policies can increase a teacher's salary by thousands of dollars; for example, the Southern Regional Education Board reported that states in the region offered annual quality-based incentives that ranged from $1,000 to $7,500 during 2000 (Grimes 2000).

Teachers' salaries are typically determined by years of experience and advanced training as evidenced by graduate credit hours or advanced degrees. Additional duties, such as coaching an athletic team, producing the yearbook and school newspaper, sponsoring clubs, or directing the band, bring extra pay for many teachers. Most districts offer at least limited summer employment for teachers who wish to teach summer school or develop curriculum materials. Additionally, about one-fourth of the nation's three million public school teachers **"moonlight"** (i.e., hold a second job) to increase their earnings.

Teachers also receive various **fringe benefits,** such as medical insurance and retirement plans, which are usually given in addition to base salary. These benefits vary from district to district and are determined during collective bargaining sessions. When considering a school district for your first position, carefully examine the fringe benefits package as well as the salary schedule and opportunities for extra pay.

Job Security and Status Periods of economic recession and a need to cut costs to remain competitive in a global economy often result in layoffs for workers in other sectors of U.S. society; however, teachers tend to enjoy a higher level of job security during such times. Not surprisingly, 77 percent of teachers surveyed in 1995 rated job security as better in teaching than in other occupations they had considered (Louis Harris and Associates 1995). In addition, the widespread practice of **tenure** (job security granted to teachers after satisfactory performance for a specified period, usually two to five years) contributes to job security for teachers.

Clearly, there will be many job opportunities for teachers in the near future. As a result of what researchers call a demographic "echo" of the baby boom, the school-age population in the United States is expected to reach 47.2 million by 2011, an increase of 11 percent since 1992 (National Center for Education Statistics 2001). In addition, the combined effects of enrollment increases, retirements, and attrition rates between 20 and 30 percent for teachers with three to five years of experience indicate that the nation will need 2 million new public school teachers by 2008–09 (American Federation of Teachers, 2001).

One view of the status accorded teachers comes from the NEA 2002 Teacher Day online ballot. Seventy-nine percent of respondents reported that they would consider a teaching career, and 68 percent would recommend teaching as a career choice to their children (National Education Association 2002b). However, perhaps the most accurate view of the status accorded teachers comes from the teachers themselves. In 1984, 47 percent of the 1,981 teachers responding to *The Metropolitan Life Survey of the American Teacher* agreed with the statement, "As a teacher, I feel respected in today's society." According to the 1995 survey of 1,011 teachers, the number of teachers agreeing with the statement had increased to 53 percent (Louis Harris and Associates 1995, 16). (NOTE: The question was not asked in the 2001 survey. The complete findings of the 2001 and 2002 MetLife Surveys of American Teachers can be accessed through the MetLife homepage at www.metlife.com.)

Companion Website

Job Opportunities for Teachers from Diverse Groups During the first part of the twenty-first century, there will be exceptional job opportunities for teachers from diverse racial and ethnic backgrounds and for teachers with disabilities. Clearly, students from diverse racial, ethnic, and cultural backgrounds and students with disabilities benefit from having role models with whom they can easily identify. In addition, teachers from diverse groups and teachers with disabilities may have, in some instances, an enhanced understanding of student diversity and student variability that they can share with other teachers.

Data released in 2001 by the National Center for Education Statistics indicate that 38 percent of public school students were considered part of a minority group during 1999, an increase of 16 percent from 1972. African American and Hispanic students accounted for 16.5 and 16.2 percent of the public school enrollment, an increase of 2 and 10 percent, respectively, from 1972. The percentage of students from other racial or ethnic groups also increased from 1 percent in 1972 to 6 percent (National Center for Education Statistics 2002a). When contrasted with the diverse mosaic of student enrollments, the backgrounds of today's teachers reveal less diversity.

The typical undergraduate candidate preparing to teach is a young, white female who recently graduated from high school and is attending college full-time. Postbaccalaureate-level individuals preparing to teach tend to be older, to include slightly more people of color and more males, to be transitioning into teaching from an occupation outside the field of education, to have prior teaching-related experience, and to be attending college part-time (Feistritzer 1999). Figure 1.1 illustrates the differences between the racial and ethnic compo-

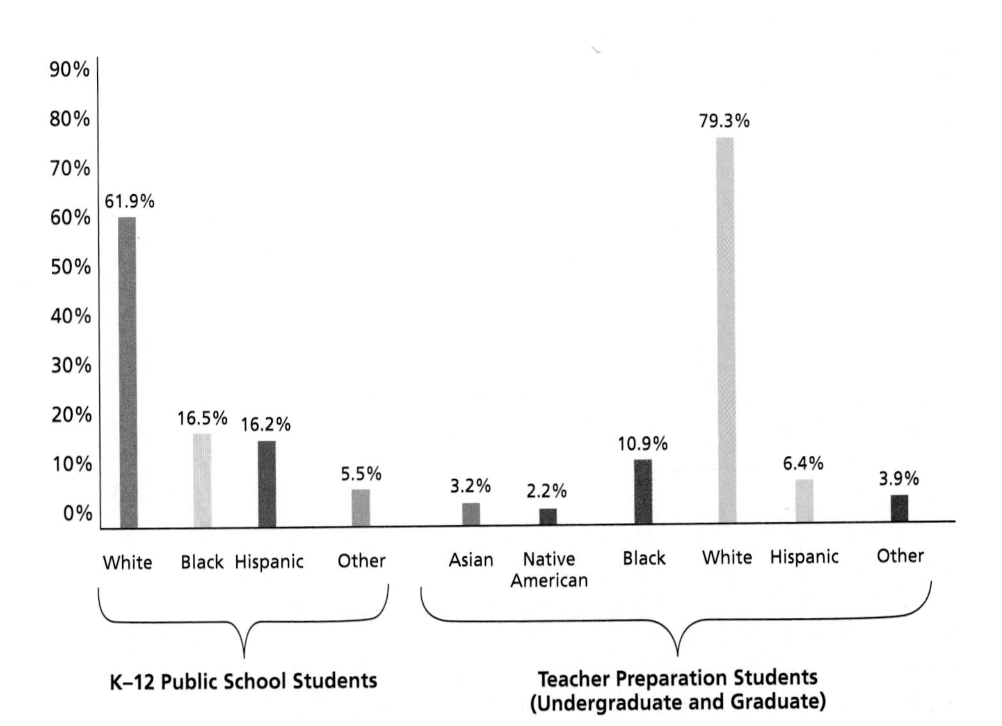

Figure 1.1 Racial and ethnic distribution of K–12 public school and teacher preparation students
Source: Based on data from (1) U.S. Department of Education, National Center for Education Statistics, The Condition of Education 2001. Washington, DC: National Center for Education Statistics, 2001. (2) C. Emily Feistritzer, A Report on Teacher Preparation in the U.S. Washington, DC: National Center for Education Information, 1999.

sition of students enrolled in U.S. public schools and that of teacher preparation students in undergraduate and graduate programs.

Research indicates that people with disabilities can be effective educators (Anderson, Keller, and Karp 1998; Karp and Keller 1998). "They hold positions in a variety of educational professions, such as all types of teaching, counseling, administration, and speech therapy, and have a variety of disabilities, such as learning disabilities, physical disabilities, visual impairments, deafness and hearing loss, medical conditions, and brain injuries" (Keller, Anderson, and Karp 1998, 8).

The percentage of children with disabilities receiving special education in public preK–12 schools is approximately 10 percent (Hardman, Drew, and Egan 2002), and the current critical need for special education teachers is expected to continue well into the twenty-first century. Nevertheless, there is an apparent lack of information on the number of educators with disabilities—a situation that leads Keller, Anderson, and Karp (1998, 8) to suggest that our need to "approach the question of how many educators have disabilities so tentatively and circumspectly is perhaps telling."

What Are the Challenges of Teaching?

Like all professions, teaching has undesirable or difficult aspects. As one high school social studies teacher put it: "Teaching is not terrible. It's great. I love it. It just feels terrible sometimes" (Henry et al. 1995, 119).

Prospective teachers need to consider the problems as well as the pleasures they are likely to encounter. You need to be informed about what to expect if you are to make the most of your professional preparation program. With greater awareness of the realities of teaching, you can more purposefully and meaningfully (1) reflect on and refine your personal philosophy of education, (2) acquire teaching strategies and leadership techniques, and (3) develop a knowledge base of research and theory to guide your actions. In this manner, you can become a true professional—free to savor the joys and satisfactions of teaching and confident of your ability to deal with its frustrations and challenges. Table 1.2 shows that teachers must deal with a variety of problems in the schools.

Classroom Management and Increasing School Violence

Not surprisingly, discipline and increased crime and violence among youth are strong concerns for education majors. Before teachers can teach they must manage their classrooms effectively. Even when parents and the school community are supportive and problems are relatively minor, dealing with discipline can be a disturbing, emotionally draining aspect of teaching. Twenty-two percent of teachers surveyed in the MetLife Survey of the American Teacher 2001 identified "students with discipline problems" as a "big problem" (Harris Interactive 2001).

Though acts of violence in schools are rare, the possibility of experiencing such events can cause additional job-related stress for teachers. The last few years of the 1990s were marked by frequent reports of random, horrific violence in and around schools. Several communities previously immune to such tragedies were thrust into the national spotlight as a result of violent incidents: Littleton, Colorado; Paducah, Kentucky; Moses Lake, Washington; Springfield, Oregon; and Jonesboro, Arkansas, to name a few.

In addition, many schools have high **teacher–student ratios,** which can make classroom management more difficult. Feeling the press of overcrowding and valiantly resisting the realization that they cannot meet the needs of all their stu-

Table 1.2 What do you think are the biggest problems with which the public schools of this community must deal?

	1999 Teachers %	1996 Teachers %	1989 Teachers %	1984 Teachers %
Parents' lack of support/interest	18	22(1T)	34(1)	31(1)
Pupils' lack of interest/attitudes/truancy	13	16(3)	26(3)	20(3)
Lack of financial support/funding/money	9	22(1T)	27(2)	21(2)
Lack of discipline/more control	7	20(2)	25(4T)	19(4)
Lack of family structure/problems of home life	6	15(4)	8(8)	4(13)
Overcrowded school	4	7(5T)	7(9T)	4(10)
Use of drugs/dope	2	7(5T)	13(7)	5(7)
Fighting/violence/gangs	1	7(5T)	–	–
Moral standards/dress code/sex/pregnancy	*	7	4(15T)	2(22)

*Less than 1 percent.

Note: Figures add to more than 100 percent because of multiple answers, except 1999 figures, which add to less than 100 percent because all answers are not reported. Parenthetical figures indicate rankings. *T* indicates a response tied for a given rank.

Source: From Carol A. Langdon, "Sixth Poll of Teachers' Attitudes toward the Public Schools: Selected Questions and Responses," Bloomington, IN: Phi Delta Kappa Center for Education, Development, and Research, *Research Bulletin,* April 2000, No. 26 (http://www.pdkintl.org/edres/resbul26.htm).

dents, teachers may try to work faster and longer to give their students the best possible education. All too often, however, they learn to put off, overlook, or otherwise attend inadequately to many students each day. The problem of high teacher–student ratios becomes even more acute when complicated by the high **student-mobility rates** in many schools. In such situations, teachers have trouble not only in meeting students' needs but also in recognizing students and remembering their names! As you will see, developing a leadership plan, a learning environment, and communication skills will help you face the challenges of classroom management.

Social Problems That Impact Students

Many social problems affect the lives and learning of many children and youth, such as substance abuse, teen pregnancy, homelessness, child abuse and neglect, violence and crime, suicide, and health problems such as HIV/AIDS and fetal alcohol syndrome. Twenty-one percent of teachers surveyed in the MetLife Survey of the American Teacher 2001 reported that "problems such as hunger, poverty or troubled family lives" were a "big problem" in their schools. These problems were reported more frequently by urban teachers (29 percent) than by teachers in suburban/rural schools (18 percent) (Harris Interactive 2001).

The social problems that place students at risk of school failure are not always easy to detect. Students' low productivity, learning difficulties, and attitude problems demand teacher attention; yet teachers may be unaware of the source of those difficulties. Even when teachers do recognize the source of a problem, they may lack the resources or expertise to offer help. Teachers feel frustrated by the wasted potential they observe in their students. In addition, when the public calls for schools to curb or correct social problems, that expectation can increase the stress teachers experience.

On the Frontlines

What Teachers Need to Know

"My teacher preparation program was the best, but the real thing [teaching] is so different! Nothing can get you ready for it. You have to do it to understand."

This thought is common for first-year teachers, and they're right. Experience really is the best teacher. However, this is not to say that simply gaining teaching experience is the best way to learn to teach well, just as jumping into the deep end of a pool is not the best way to develop an exemplary swimming stroke. Unfortunately, potentially outstanding teachers are lost each year because they jumped into teaching unprepared.

Entering the teaching field can be much smoother than that, and preparation for that entry is the key. A rigorous teacher education program—one that mixes theory and practice well, incorporates extensive field experiences in schools, and requires a student teaching practicum with an exemplary mentor teacher and a skilled and perceptive university student teacher supervisor—is the first step in the ideal preparation. The next step is to smooth the first-year experience by providing school-based mentors who regularly advise, scaffold, and support novice teachers as they continue with their learning "on the job." This ideal is not far-fetched and indeed, to the benefit of fortunate teachers and students alike, can be found in many places throughout the country.

Even with the ideal, however, the realities of teaching can be startling and even unbalancing for the new teacher. A poll on public opinion regarding improving education, conducted by David Haselkorn of Recruiting New Teachers (RNT) and Louis Harris, found that respondents regarded important public school problems as being "student drug use" (68 percent), "school violence" (65 percent), "student drinking" (64 percent), "lack of parent involvement" (59 percent), "teenage pregnancy" (58 percent) and "students' lack of basic skills" (51 percent) (RNT 2001). The authors of the report sum up the overall finding this way: "In the end, most Americans believe that the promise of top-quality education can be achieved in the public schools, but only if we recruit, train, and develop a teaching corps capable of doing the job".

For this reason, our text is incorporating in each chapter glimpses of some of the surprises new teachers might encounter. We call these pieces "On the Frontlines" to convey their newsworthiness and their on-the-scene reality dimension. In each we describe a challenge, look at the larger issues connected with it, and suggest strategies for responding to it. We also offer resources that can help you learn more about the issues and the ways teachers respond to them.

Though the hurdles are high, they are also inviting. In recent years the public has become more appreciative of something experienced teachers have known all along: Teachers can make a difference. In the RNT and Harris poll, "when asked which of eight professions they felt 'provides the most important benefit to society,' the public put teachers first by more than a 3–1 margin over physicians (62% vs. 17%)". And "when asked about a career they would recommend to a family member, people ranked teaching (39%) a close second to medicine (40%), despite the well-established differences in pay". This contrasts markedly with previous polls.

Is the new respect due to the publicity on school shootings and violence? Is it due to distress over young people's easy access to alcohol, drugs, and guns? Is it due to their knowledge of the increased linguistic diversity in schools and the obvious demands placed on teachers? Whatever the cause, the public now values teachers more than in the recent past. Many would say the appreciation directly connects to teachers' requirements to handle today's tougher school realities. We hope that On the Frontlines assists you in anticipating how you will handle some of the realities of teaching—and that that, in turn, will increase your desire to teach.

Exploratory Questions

1. What does the public regard as the biggest problems for public schools today? Locate the most recent Phi Delta Kappan annual poll (http://www.pdkintl.org/kappan/k0109gal.htm) to find your answer.
2. What strategies are effective in retaining new teachers? Visit the Recruiting New Teachers website (http://www.rnt.org) and read the reports on strategies for teacher retention.

Your Survival Guide of Helpful Resources

The following resources provide helpful hints for surviving "on the frontlines." In addition to online access, the resources below offer individual subscriptions. Look for more resources on the Companion Website for this book.

Teacher Magazine
(http://www.teachermagazine.org/)

Instructor Magazine
(http://teacher.scholastic.com/products/instructor.htm)

Harvard Education Letter
(http://www.edletter.org/)

Weekly Reader
(http://www.weeklyreader.com/)

Companion Website

Need for Family and Community Support

Support from parents and the community can make a significant difference in the teacher's effectiveness in the classroom. Increasingly, there has been a realization that school, parents, and community must work together so that children and youth develop to their maximum potential academically, socially, emotionally, and physically. For example, 53 percent of the student leaders who attended the 1999 United States Senate Youth Program said "parental support" was the biggest factor in their success at high school (William Randolph Hearst Foundation 1999). Parents who talk with their children, help with homework, read to them, monitor their television viewing, and attend meetings of the Parent Teacher Organization (PTO) and school open houses can enhance their children's ability to succeed in school (Fuligni and Stevenson 1995; Henry 1996; Moore 1992). Similarly, communities can support schools by providing essential social, vocational, recreational, and health support services to students and their families. As Figure 1.2 shows, teachers included in the MetLife Survey of the American Teacher 2001 believe that, on average, 44 percent of their students have parents who need to be more involved in their children's education. In schools with more than two-thirds of students from families with below-average income, this figure increases to 69 percent (Harris Interactive 2001).

Long Working Hours and Job Stress

The official working hours for teachers are attractive, but the real working hours are another matter. Not built into contracts are the after-hours or extra assignments found at all levels of teaching—from recess duty and parent conferences to high school club sponsorships and coaching. Also not obvious are the hours of preparation that occur before and after school—frequently late into the night and over the weekend. Over 90 percent of teachers work more than forty hours per week, with the largest percentage working more than fifty-five hours per week (Louis Harris and Associates 1995).

The need to complete copious amounts of paperwork, including record keeping, may be the most burdensome of the teacher's nonteaching tasks. On average, teachers spend ten hours per week on school-related responsibilities not

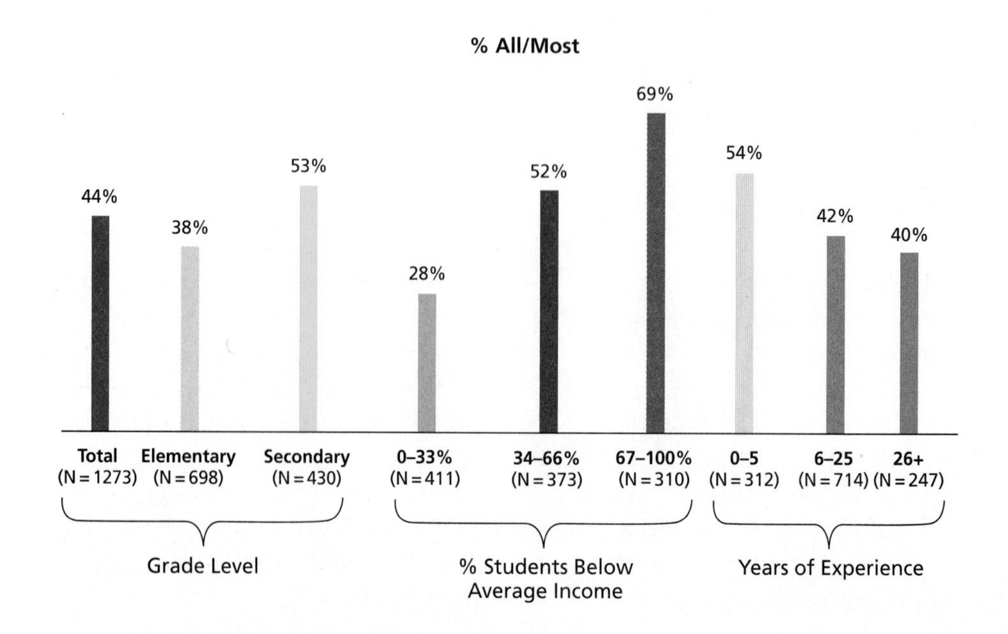

Figure 1.2 Teachers' views on parental involvement
How many of your students have parents who need to be more involved in what their children are learning in school–all, most, some, very few, or none at all? *Source: The MetLife Survey of the American Teacher: Key Elements of Quality Schools.* New York: Harris Interactive, Inc., 2001, p. 105.

directly related to teaching (Louis Harris and Associates 1995, 68). Other non-teaching tasks include supervising student behavior on the playground, at extracurricular events, and in the halls, study halls, and lunchrooms; attending faculty meetings, parent conferences, and open houses; and taking tickets or selling at concessions for athletic events. Individually, such assignments and responsibilities may be enjoyable; too many of them at once, however, become a burden and consume the teacher's valuable time.

In addition to long working hours, factors such as students' lack of interest, conflicts with administrators, public criticism, overcrowded classrooms, lack of resources, and isolation from other adults cause some teachers to experience high levels of stress. Unchecked, acute levels of stress can lead to job dissatisfaction, emotional and physical exhaustion, and an inability to cope effectively—all classic symptoms of teacher **burnout.** To cope with stress and avoid burnout, teachers report that activities in seven areas are beneficial: social support, physical fitness, intellectual stimulation, entertainment, personal hobbies, self-management, and supportive attitudes (Gmelch and Parkay 1995, 46–65).

Gaining Professional Empowerment

In an interview with journalist Bill Moyers, noted Harvard educator Sara Lawrence Lightfoot eloquently describes why teachers desire **professional empowerment:**

> *[Teachers are] saying, "I haven't had the opportunity to participate fully in this enterprise." Some teachers are speaking about the politics of teachers' voice. They're saying, "We want more control over our lives in this school." Some of them are making an even more subtle point—they're talking about voice as knowledge. "We know things about this enterprise that researchers and policy makers can never know. We have engaged in this intimate experience, and we have things to tell you if you'd only learn how to ask, and if you'd only learn how to listen" (Moyers 1989, 161).*

Although some teachers may experience frustration in their efforts to gain professional empowerment, efforts to empower teachers and to "professionalize" teaching are leading to unprecedented opportunities for today's teachers to extend their leadership roles beyond the classroom. In fact, "Teachers in the U.S. today are developing leadership skills to a degree not needed in the past . . . the continuing professional development of teaching as a profession requires that teachers exercise greater leadership at the school level and beyond" (Parkay et al. 1999, 20–21).

What Is Teaching Really Like?

In this section we examine six basic **realities of teaching** that illustrate why teaching is so demanding and why it can be so exciting, rewarding, and uplifting. And when we say that teaching is demanding, we mean more than the fact that Mr. Smith's third-period plane geometry students just can't seem to learn how to compute the area of a triangle; or that Ms. Ellis's sixth-grade composition class can't remember whether to use *there* or *their;* or even that 21 percent of the teacher respondents to the MetLife Survey of the American Teacher 2001 reported that "all" or "most" of their students need, but are not receiving, social support services (Harris Interactive 2001). Although there are many frustrating, stressful events with which teachers must cope, the difficulty of teaching goes much further, or deeper, than these examples suggest.

Reality 1: The Unpredictability of Outcomes

The outcomes of teaching, even in the best of circumstances, are neither predictable nor consistent. Any teacher, beginner or veteran, can give countless examples of how the outcomes of teaching are often unpredictable and inconsistent. Life in most classrooms usually proceeds on a fairly even keel—with teachers able to predict, fairly accurately, how their students will respond to lessons. Adherence to the best laid lesson plans, however, may be accompanied by students' blank stares, yawns of boredom, hostile acting out, or expressions of befuddlement. On the other hand, lack of preparation on the teacher's part does not necessarily rule out the possibility of a thoroughly exciting class discussion, a real breakthrough in understanding for an individual student or the entire class, or simply a good, fast-paced review of previously learned material. In short, teachers are often surprised at students' reactions to classroom activities.

Students' Responses Contrary to the popular notion that teaching consists entirely of specific competencies or observable behaviors that have predetermined effects on students, the reactions of students to any given activity cannot be guaranteed. Furthermore, teachers, unlike other professionals, cannot control all the results of their efforts.

One example of the unpredictability of teaching is given in a teacher intern's description of setting up an independent reading program in his middle school classroom. Here we see how careful room arrangement and organization of materials do not ensure desired outcomes and how a teacher learned to adjust to one reality of teaching.

> *I wanted everything looking perfect. For two more hours, I placed this here and stuffed that in there. . . . There were stacks of brand-new books sitting on three odd shelves and a metal display rack. . . . I coded the books and arranged them neatly on the shelves. I displayed their glossy covers as if the room was a B. Dalton store.*

A few weeks after setting up the reading program, however, this teacher observes that

> *The orderly environment I thought I had conceived was fraught with complications. For example, the back rows of the classroom were inaccessible regions from which paper and pencil pieces were hurled at vulnerable victims, and there were zones where, apparently, no teacher's voice could be heard. . . . The books . . . remained in chaos. Novels turned up behind shelves, on the sidewalks outside, and in the trash can. And still, at least once a week, I dutifully arranged them until I was satisfied. But something was happening. It was taking less and less for me to be satisfied. . . . [I] loosened up (Henry et al. 1995, 73–76).*

Contrary to the preceding example, unpredictability in the classroom is not always bad. Another teacher intern describes her unexpected success at setting up a writing workshop at an urban middle school with a large population of at-risk students. One day she began by telling her students that

> *"We're going to be starting something new these six weeks. . . . We will be transforming this classroom into a writing workshop." What was I trying to do here? They're not writers. . . . Raymond stared down at Where's Waldo. Michael was engrossed in an elaborate pencil drum solo. Edwina powdered her nose and under her eyes.*
>
> *"Listen to me, you guys," I said, trying not to lose it before we even started. "We're starting something completely different, something you never get a chance to do in your other classes."*

A few heads turned to face me. Veronica slugged Edwina, and Edwina slid her compact into her back pocket.

"What, Miss . . . chew gum?"

In spite of her initial reservations, this teacher made the following observations the next day—the first day of the writing workshop.

Today, it's all clicking.

"Aw, man, I told you I don't understand that part. Why does that guy in your story . . . Chris . . . say that it's too early to rob the store?" David pleads. "It doesn't make sense."

Raymond tips his desk forward and smiles. "It's too early because they want to wait until the store's almost closed."

"Well, then, you've got to say that. Right, Miss?"

I lean against the door frame and try not to laugh. I listen to the conversations around me. Yes, they're loud and they're talking and they're laughing. But they're learning. My students are involved in their writing, I say to myself and shake my head (Henry et al. 1995, 54–55).

Philip Jackson describes the unpredictability of teaching in his well-known book *Life in Classrooms:* "[As] typically conducted, teaching is an opportunistic process. . . . Neither teacher nor students can predict with any certainty exactly what will happen next. Plans are forever going awry and unexpected opportunities for the attainment of educational goals are constantly emerging" (Jackson 1990, 166).

Results in the Future Teachers strive to effect changes in their students for the future as well as for the here and now. In *Life in Classrooms,* Jackson labels this the preparatory aspect of teaching. In addition to having students perform better on next Monday's unit exam or on a criterion-referenced test mandated by the state, teachers expect students to apply their newly acquired skills and knowledge at some indeterminate, usually distant, point in the future.

Just as months or years may pass before the results of teaching become clear, teachers may wait a long time before receiving positive feedback from students.

In what ways must this classroom teacher face the reality of unpredictable outcomes? What are five other basic realities that all teachers face in their work?

The following note one teacher received from a student she had many years ago illustrates the delayed satisfaction that can characterize teaching:

> *Dear Mrs. Gilday,*
>
> *I am one of many students who fondly remembers you. I was very fortunate to have you as my fifth-grade teacher. In you we saw dignity, respect, and true caring. Your manner was gentle, your time always given freely. Your lessons were interesting and you had a sense of humor. You did not always call on the waving hands or dismiss incorrect answers or embarrass your students. Rather, you coaxed them along, enabling them to succeed.*
>
> *We were all individuals to you and were treated with respect. I never said it then, but thank you—for everything.*
>
> *Sincerely,*
>
> *Grace*
>
> *(Paul and Colucci 2000, 51)*

Reality 2: The Difficulty of Assessing Students' Learning

It is difficult to assess what students learn as a result of being taught. The ultimate purpose of teaching is to lead the student to a greater understanding of the things and ideas of this world. But, as even the most casual appraisal of human nature will confirm, it is very difficult, perhaps impossible, to determine precisely what another human being does or does not understand. Although the aims or intentions of teaching may be specified with exacting detail, one of the realities of teaching, as the following junior high school teacher points out, is that some of what students learn may be indeterminate and beyond direct measurement:

> *There is no clear end result. . . . That frustrates me. I want so badly for my joy [of teaching] to be neatly tied up so that I can look at it admiringly. . . . I want so badly to see my successes—I don't know, give me certificates or badges or jelly beans. Then I can stack them up, count them, and rate myself as a teacher* (Henry et al. 1995, *68–69).*

In spite of state-by-state efforts to institute standardized tests of basic skills and thereby hold teachers accountable, the conventional wisdom among teachers is that they are often uncertain about just what their students learn. We have miles of computer printouts with test data, but very little knowledge of what lies behind a child's written response, little understanding of how the child experiences the curriculum. As one educational researcher concludes: "The inaccessibility of data is similar both in science and in learning. We cannot directly 'see' subatomic particles, nor can we 'see' the inner-workings of the mind and emotions of the child. Both are inferential: both are subject to human interpretation" (Costa 1984, 202).

On the one hand, then, teachers must recognize their limited ability to determine what students actually learn; on the other, they must continuously work to become aware of the latest approaches to assessing students' learning. Figure 1.3 presents a set of guiding principles for teachers to follow in developing a student-centered approach to classroom assessment.

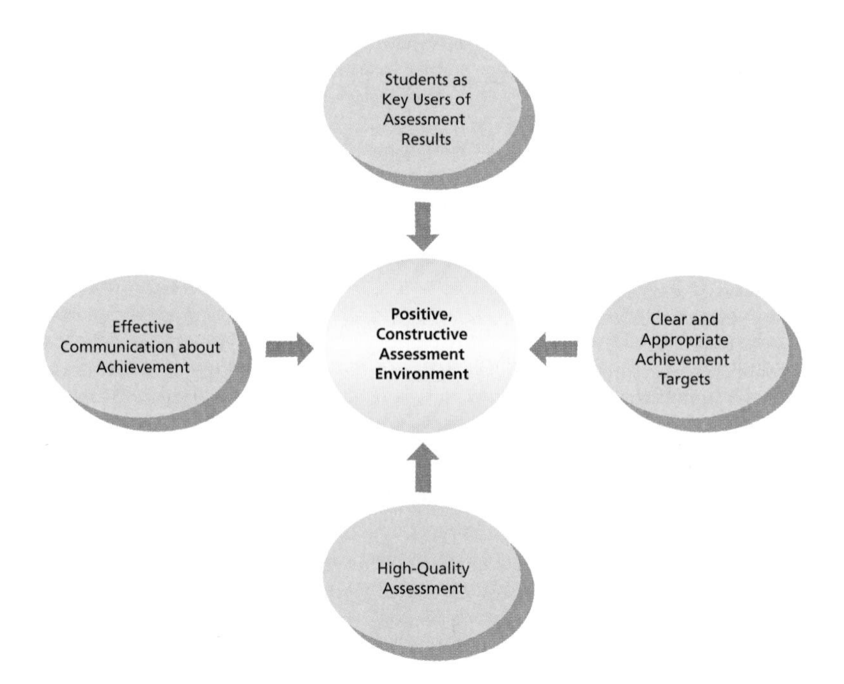

Figure 1.3 **The principles of sound assessment: a critical blend**
Source: Adapted from Richard J. Stiggins, Student-Involved Classroom Assessment, 3rd ed. Upper Saddle River, NJ: Merrill, 2000, p. 18.

Reality 3: The Need for Teacher–Student Partnership

The teacher's ability to influence student behavior is actually quite limited. The very fact that we refer to the teaching–learning process indicates the extent to which classroom events are "jointly produced" (Doyle 1986, 395) and depend on a teacher–student partnership. According to Arthur Combs (1979, 234–35) in a book aptly titled *Myths in Education: Beliefs That Hinder Progress and Their Alternatives:*

> *A teacher's influence on all but the simplest, most primitive forms of student behavior, even in that teacher's own classroom, cannot be clearly established. The older children get, the less teachers can influence even those few, primitive forms of behavior. The attempt to hold teachers responsible for what students do is, for all practical purposes, well nigh impossible.*

At best, a teacher tries to influence students so that they make internal decisions to behave in the desired manner—whether it be reading the first chapter of *The Pearl* by Friday or solving ten addition problems during a mathematics lesson. Teaching is a uniquely demanding profession, therefore, because the work of teachers is evaluated not in terms of what teachers do but in terms of their ability "to help the students become more effective as learners," to "become active seekers after new development" (Joyce, Weil, and Calhoun 2000, 408, 399). This reality underscores the need for a partnership between teacher and learners, including learners who are culturally diverse.

Reality 4: The Impact of Teachers' Attitudes

With the role of teacher also comes the power to influence others by example. Educational psychologist Jeanne Ellis Ormrod (2003, 342) states that "as teachers, we 'teach' not only by what we say but also by what we do. It is critical that we model appropriate behaviors and *not* model inappropriate ones." Clearly, students learn much by imitation, and teachers are models for students. In the primary grades, teachers are idolized by their young students. At the high school level, teachers have the potential to inspire students' emulation and establish the classroom tone by modeling expected attitudes and behaviors.

In *Listening to Urban Kids: School Reform and the Teachers They Want* (Wilson and Corbett 2001), students express the following views about teachers' attitudes:

> *I heard teachers talking about people, saying "Those kids can't do nothing." Kids want teachers who believe in them (86).*
>
> *A good teacher to me is a teacher who is patient, willing to accept the fact that she might be dealing with students who have problems (87).*
>
> *Since this is one of his first year's teaching, I give him credit. He relates, but he also teaches. . . . He advises us. He not only tries to teach but gets involved with us (88).*

A high school teacher offers a teacher's perspective on the importance of developing positive relationships with students: "[The] relationship between teachers and students is becoming one of the most important aspects of teaching. [In] a world of broken homes and violence, the encouragement of their teachers may be the only thing students can hold onto that makes them feel good about themselves" (Henry et al. 1995, 127).

Teachers also model attitudes toward the subjects they teach and show students through their example that learning is an ongoing, life-enriching process that does not end with diplomas and graduations. Their example confirms the timeless message of Sir Rabindranath Tagore that is inscribed above the doorway of a public building in India: "A teacher can never truly teach unless he is still learning himself. A lamp can never light another lamp unless it continues to burn its own flame."

Reality 5: The Drama and Immediacy of Teaching

Interactive teaching is characterized by events that are rapid-changing, multidimensional, and irregular. We have already discussed how the outcomes of teaching are unpredictable and inconsistent. Yet the challenges of teaching go beyond this. The face-to-face interactions teachers have with students—what Jackson (1990, 152) has termed **interactive teaching**—are themselves rapid-changing, multidimensional, and irregular. "Day in and day out, teachers spend much of their lives 'on stage' before audiences that are not always receptive. . . . Teachers must orchestrate a daunting array of interpersonal interactions and build a cohesive, positive climate for learning" (Gmelch and Parkay 1995, 47).

When teachers are in the **preactive teaching** stages of their work—preparing to teach or reflecting on previous teaching—they can afford to be consistently deliberate and rational. Planning for lessons, grading papers, reflecting on the misbehavior of a student—such activities are usually done alone and lack the immediacy and sense of urgency that characterize interactive teaching. While actually working with students, however, you must be able to think on your feet and respond appropriately to complex, ever-changing situations. You must be flexible and ready to deal with the unexpected. During a discussion, for example, you must operate on at least two levels. On one level, you respond appropriately to students' comments, monitor other students for signs of confusion or comprehension, formulate the next comment or question, and be alert for signs of misbehavior. On another level, you ensure that participation is evenly distributed among students, evaluate the content and quality of students' contributions, keep the discussion focused and moving ahead, and emphasize major content areas.

During interactive teaching, the awareness that you are responsible for the forward movement of the group never lets up. Teachers are the only professionals who practice their craft almost exclusively under the direct, continuous gaze of up to thirty or forty clients. Jackson (1990, 119) sums up the experience: "The *immediacy* of classroom events is something that anyone who has ever been in charge of a roomful of students can never forget."

Reality 6: The Uniqueness of the Teaching Experience

Teaching involves a unique mode of being between teacher and student—a mode of being that can be experienced but not fully defined or described. On your journey to become a teacher, you will gradually develop your capacity to listen to students and to convey an authentic sense of concern for their learning. Unfortunately, there is no precise, easy-to-follow formula for demonstrating this to students. You will have to take into account your personality and special gifts to discover your own best way for showing this concern.

One reason it is difficult to describe teaching is that an important domain of teaching, **teachers' thought processes,** including professional reflection, cannot be observed directly. Figure 1.4 shows how the unobservable domain of the teacher's "interior reflective thinking" interacts with and is influenced by the observable domain of the teacher's "exterior reflective action." Teachers' thought processes include their theories and beliefs about students and how they learn, their plans for teaching, and the decisions they make while teaching. Thought processes and actions can be constrained by the physical setting of the classroom or external factors such as the curriculum, the principal, or the community. On the other hand, teachers' thought processes and actions may be influenced by unique opportunities, such as the chance to engage in curriculum reform or school governance. The model also illustrates a further complexity of teaching—namely, that the relationships between teacher behavior, student behavior, and student achievement are reciprocal. What teachers do is influenced not only by their thought processes before, during, and after teaching but also by student behavior and student achievement. This complexity contributes to the uniqueness of the teaching experience.

What Does Society Expect of Teachers?

The prevailing view within our society is that teachers are public servants accountable to the people. As a result, society has high expectations of teachers—some would say too high. Entrusted with our nation's most precious resource, its children and youth, today's teachers are expected to have advanced knowledge and skills and high academic and ethical standards. Although promoting students' academic progress has always been their primary responsibility, teachers are also expected to further students' social, emotional, and moral development and to safeguard students' health and well-being. Increasingly, the public calls on teachers and schools to address social problems and risk factors that affect student success.

The Public Trust

Teaching is subject to a high degree of public scrutiny and control. The level of trust that the public extends to teachers as professionals varies greatly. The public appears to have great confidence in the work that teachers do. Because of its faith in the teaching profession, the public invests teachers with considerable power over its children. For the most part, parents willingly allow their children to be influenced by teachers and expect their children to obey and respect teach-

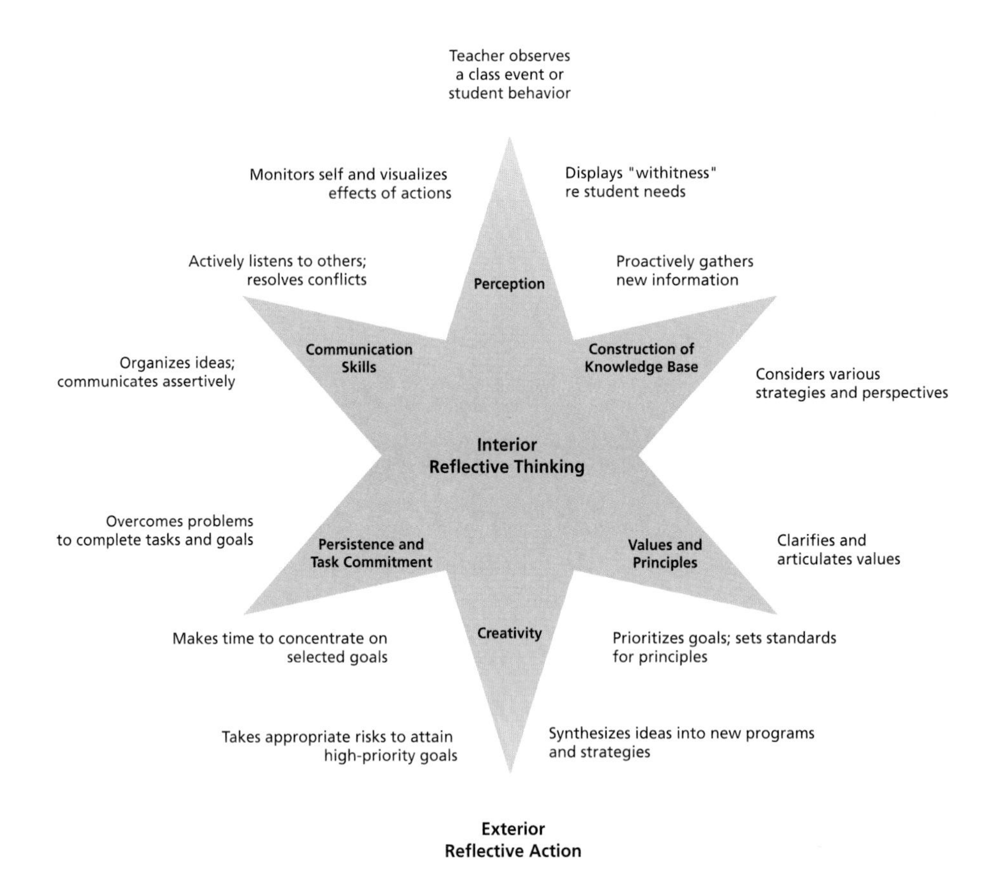

Figure 1.4 A model of reflective action in teaching
Source: Judy W. Eby, Reflective Planning, Teaching, and Evaluation: K–12, 2nd ed. Upper Saddle River, NJ: Merrill, 1998, p. 14. © 1998. Reprinted by permission of Prentice-Hall, Inc., Upper Saddle River, NJ.

ers. However, the public trust increases and decreases in response to social and political changes that lead to waves of educational reform.

In the 1970s, for example, teachers were portrayed as incompetent, unprofessional, unintelligent, and generally unable to live up to the public's expectations. Calls for higher standards and minimum competency testing were an expression of diminished public trust. Further professionalization of teaching has been the response. During the 1980s, the image of teachers was battered by ominous sounding commission reports, a negative press, and public outcries for better schools. National reports, such as ***A Nation at Risk,*** declared that U.S. education was shockingly inadequate, if not a failure.

In the 1990s, however, deliberate efforts were made to restore dignity to the profession of teaching. To highlight the important work of teachers, public and commercial television stations aired programs with titles such as "Learning in America: Schools That Work," "America's Toughest Assignment: Solving the Education Crisis," "The Truth about Teachers," "Why Do These Kids Love School?", "Liberating America's Schools," and "America's Education Revolution: A Report from the Front." The Learning Channel began to air *Teacher TV,* a news-style program that explores education trends and issues and features teachers, schools, and communities around the country. Many national corporations initiated award programs to recognize excellence among teachers. Disney Studios, for example, initiated Disney's American Teacher Awards in 1991. As a tribute to countless outstanding teachers, a major media campaign to recruit new teachers in the early 1990s was formed around the slogan, "Be a Teacher. Be a Hero." Table 1.3 shows how people rated their public schools in selected years between 1983, just after the release of *A Nation at Risk,* and 2002.

Table 1.3 Ratings given the local public schools (in percent)

	2002	2001	1999	1998	1995	1993	1991	1989	1987	1985	1983
A&B	47	51	49	46	41	47	42	43	43	43	31
A	10	11	11	10	8	10	10	8	12	9	6
B	37	40	38	36	33	37	32	35	31	34	25
C	34	30	31	31	37	31	33	33	30	30	32
D	10	8	9	9	12	11	10	11	9	10	13
Fail	3	5	5	5	5	4	5	4	4	4	7
Don't know	6	6	6	9	5	7	10	9	14	13	17

Source: Alec M. Gallup, Lowell C. Rose, and Stanley M. Elan, "The 24th Annual Gallup Poll of the Public's Attitudes toward the Public Schools," *Phi Delta Kappan,* September 1992, p. 32; Stanley M. Elam and Lowell C. Rose, "The 27th Annual Phi Delta Kappa/Gallup Poll of the Public's Attitudes toward the Public Schools," *Phi Delta Kappan,* September 1995, p. 42; Lowell C. Rose and Alec M. Gallup, "The 30th Annual Phi Delta Kappa/Gallup Poll of the Public's Attitudes toward the Public Schools," *Phi Delta Kappan,* September 1999, p. 45; and Lowell C. Rose and Alec M. Gallup, "The 34th Annual Phi Delta Kappa/Gallup Poll of the Public's Attitudes toward the Public Schools," *Phi Delta Kappan,* September 2002, p. 43 (http://www.pdkintl.org/kappan/k0209pol.htm#1a).

Teacher Competency and Effectiveness

Society believes that competent, effective teachers are important keys to a strong system of education. Accordingly, teachers are expected to be proficient in the use of instructional strategies, curriculum materials, advanced educational technologies, and classroom management techniques. They are also expected to have a thorough understanding of the developmental levels of their students and a solid grasp of the content they teach. To maintain and extend this high level of skill, teachers are expected to be informed of exemplary practices and to demonstrate a desire for professional development.

Teacher competency and effectiveness includes the responsibility to help all learners succeed. Though today's students come from a diverse array of backgrounds, society expects teachers to hold strong beliefs about the potential for all children. Regardless of their students' ethnicity, language, gender, socioeconomic status, family backgrounds and living conditions, abilities, or disabilities, teachers have a responsibility to ensure that all students develop to their fullest potential. To accomplish this, teachers are expected to have a repertoire of instructional strategies and resources to create meaningful learning experiences that promote students' growth and development. In each chapter of this book, a Meeting the Standards feature illustrates the role that professional standards can play in your journey toward becoming a competent, effective teacher.

Teacher Accountability

Teachers must "be mindful of the social ethic—their public duties and obligations—embodied in the practice of teaching." (Hansen 1995, 143). Society agrees that teachers are primarily responsible for promoting students' learning, though it is not always in agreement about what students should learn. In any case, society expects teachers to understand how factors such as student backgrounds, attitudes, and learning styles can affect achievement; and it expects that teachers will create safe and effective learning environments. Society also believes that teachers and schools should be accountable for equalizing educational opportunity and maintaining high professional standards.

Meeting the Standard

Sorting through the Maze

As someone entering the field of education, you soon will become immersed in the world of *standards,* the outcome of a push in recent years for accountability and excellence in education. To ensure that all students are taught by competent and effective teachers, several professional associations and state departments of education have developed standards that reflect what teachers should know and be able to do. Most likely, the teacher education program in which you are enrolled will use one or more of these sets of standards to evaluate your progress toward becoming an effective teacher. During your training, you are sure to hear repeatedly about plans instituted by state departments of education to assess teachers and students alike on an ongoing basis.

The professional standards that have had the greatest impact on teacher education programs nationally (as well as on teachers' ongoing professional growth and development) are those developed by the Interstate New Teacher Assessment and Support Consortium (INTASC), the National Council for Accreditation of Teacher Education (NCATE), the Praxis Series: Professional Assessments for Beginning Teachers, and the National Board for Professional Teaching Standards (NBPTS). The following figure provides a brief mission statement of each group and an overview of their standards. How have these standards influenced the teacher education program in which you are enrolled? Does your state have a set of professional standards that also applies to your teacher education program? To help you get the most out of your teacher education program, each chapter of this book includes a Meeting the Standard feature that illustrates how selected professional standards developed by each of these four groups are related to chapter content. The focus of this feature is on your development of sound teaching skills–and perhaps to make some sense of the "standards maze." Therefore, selections from each group's list of standards are identified and organized around common themes. In some chapters, the discussion is organized around a case study to illustrate the standards in action; in other chapters, the feature provides general analysis to provide a deeper understanding of the standards theme. Application exercises provide opportunities to measure how well you might meet the "generic" standard and to develop the skills necessary to "meet the standards."

Teacher accountability also means meeting high standards of conduct. Teachers are no longer required to sign statements such as the following, taken from a 1927 contract: "I promise to sleep at least eight hours a night, to eat carefully, and to take every precaution to keep in the best of health and spirits, in order that I may be better able to render efficient service to my pupils" (Waller 1932, 43). Nevertheless, society does expect teachers to hold high standards of professional ethics and personal morality and to model behaviors that match those standards.

How Do Good Teachers View Their Work?

As Table 1.4 on page 30 shows, teachers' overall satisfaction with their careers has increased since 1984. In 1984, 40 percent of teachers reported that they were "very satisfied" with teaching; in 2001, this figure had increased to 52 percent.

Good teachers derive greatest satisfaction when they are effective in promoting students' learning—when they "make a difference" in students' lives. When you recall your most effective teachers, you probably think of particular individuals, not idealizations of the teacher's many roles. What good teachers do can be described in terms of five **modes of teaching,** which are more general and significant than a discussion of roles. You may recognize these modes in your observations of teachers and in the writings of gifted teachers when they reflect on their work. You may even acknowledge these modes of teaching as deeper reasons for becoming a teacher.

INTASC Standards

INTASC is a consortium of more than thirty states that has developed standards and an assessment process for initial teacher certification. INTASC model core standards are based on ten principles evident in effective teaching regardless of subject or grade level. The principles are based on the realization that effective teachers integrate content knowledge with pedagogical understanding to assure that all students learn (INTASC 1993).

1. Knowledge of Subject Matter
2. Knowledge of Human Development and Learning
3. Adapting Instruction for Individual Needs
4. Multiple Instructional Strategies
5. Classroom Motivation and Management
6. Communication Skills
7. Instructional Planning Skills
8. Assessment of Student Learning
9. Professional Commitment and Responsibility
10. Partnerships

NCATE Standards

NCATE standards are for the accreditation of colleges and universities with teacher preparation programs. Currently, fewer than half of the 1,300 institutions that prepare teachers are accredited by NCATE. While NCATE standards apply to teacher education programs, not to teacher education students per se, NCATE believes that "the new professional teacher who graduates from a professional accredited school, college, or department of education should be able to" do the following (NCATE 2002):

- Help all prekindergarten through twelfth grade (P–12) students learn
- Teach to P–12 student standards set by specialized professional associations and the states
- Explain instructional choices based on research-derived knowledge and best practice
- Apply effective methods of teaching students who are at different developmental stages, have different learning styles, and come from diverse backgrounds
- Reflect on practice, act on feedback, and integrate technology into instruction effectively

What should teachers know and be able to do?

NBPTS Standards

This board issues professional certificates to teachers who possess extensive professional knowledge and the ability to perform at a high level. Certification candidates submit a portfolio including videotapes of classroom interactions and samples of student work plus the teacher's reflective comments. Trained NBPTS evaluators who teach in the same field as the candidate judge all elements of the assessments. NBPTS has developed five "core propositions" on which voluntary national teacher certification is based (NBPTS 1994):

1. Teachers are committed to students and their learning.
2. Teachers know the subjects they teach and how to teach those subjects to students.
3. Teachers are responsible for managing and monitoring student learning.
4. Teachers think systematically about their practice and learn from experience.
5. Teachers are members of learning communities.

Praxis Series

Based on knowledge and skills states commonly require of beginning teachers, the Praxis Series assesses individual development as it corresponds to three steps in becoming a teacher. These three areas of assessment are Academic Skills Assessments: entering a teacher education program (Praxis I); Subject Assessments: licensure for entering the profession (Praxis II); and Classroom Performance Assessments: the first year of teaching (Praxis III). Praxis III involves the assessment of actual teaching skills in four areas (Danielson 1996):

1. Planning and Preparation
   - Demonstrating knowledge of content and pedagogy
   - Demonstrating knowledge of students
   - Selecting instructional goals
   - Demonstrating knowledge of resources
   - Designing coherent instruction
2. The Classroom Environment
   - Creating an environment of respect and rapport
   - Establishing a culture for learning
   - Managing classroom procedures
   - Managing student behavior
   - Organizing physical space
3. Instruction
   - Communicating clearly and accurately
   - Using questioning and discussion techniques
   - Engaging students in learning
   - Providing feedback to students
   - Demonstrating flexibility and responsiveness
4. Professional Responsibilities
   - Reflecting on teaching
   - Maintaining accurate records
   - Communicating with families
   - Contributing to the school and district
   - Growing and developing professionally

Table 1.4 Teachers' job satisfaction: 1984–2001

All in all, how satisfied would you say you are with teaching as a career—very satisfied, somewhat satisfied, somewhat dissatisfied, or very dissatisfied?

Base: All teachers

	1984	1985	1986	1987	1988	1989	1995	2001*
Base	1981	1846	1602	1002	1208	2000	1011	1273
	%	%	%	%	%	%	%	%
Very satisfied	40	44	33	40	50	44	54	52
Somewhat satisfied	41	35	48	45	37	42	33	40
Somewhat dissatisfied	16	16	15	12	11	11	10	7
Very dissatisfied	2	5	4	2	2	3	2	1

Source: The MetLife Survey of the American Teacher: Key Elements of Quality Schools. New York: Harris Interactive, Inc., 2001, p. 117.

A Way of Being

In becoming a teacher, you take on the role and let it become a part of you. Increasingly, the learning of facts can be achieved easily with good books, good TV, CD-ROMs, and access to the Internet. What cannot be done in these ways is teaching styles of life, teaching what it means to be, to grow, to become actualized, to become complete. The only way a teacher can teach these qualities is to possess them. As Jane Danielewicz (2001, 3) states in a book aptly titled *Teaching Selves,* "What makes someone a good teacher is not methodology, or even ideology. It requires engagement with identity, the way individuals conceive of themselves so that teaching is a state of being, not merely ways of acting or behaving."

A Creative Endeavor

Teaching is a creative endeavor in which teachers are continually shaping and reshaping lessons, events, and the experiences of their students. In *The Call to Teach,* David Hansen (1995, 13) describes the creative dimensions of teaching this way: "In metaphorical terms, teaching is . . . more than carrying brick, mortar, and shovel. Rather, it implies being the architect of one's classroom world."

With careful attention to the details of classroom life, effective teachers artistically develop educative relationships with their students; they "read" the myriad events that emerge while teaching and respond appropriately. One high school teacher, identified as highly successful by her principal, reported: "I have to grab the kids that don't want to do math at all and somehow make them want to do this work. I'm not sure how I do it, but kids just want to do well in my class. For some mysterious reason, and I don't care why, they really want to do well."

A Live Performance

Teaching is a live performance with each class period, each day, containing the unpredictable. Further, teachers are engaged in live dialogues with their classes and individual students. The experience of teaching is thus an intense, attention-demanding endeavor—an interactive one that provides minute-to-minute challenges.

Some teachers embrace the live performance aspect of teaching more than others, believing that within it lies true learning. They recognize that teaching "... is full of surprises; classroom lessons that lead to unexpected questions and insights; lessons that fail despite elaborate planning; spur-of-the-moment activities that work beautifully and that may change the direction of a course; students who grow and learn; students who seem to regress or grow distant" (Hansen 1995, 12).

What are the modes of teaching that define the essence of good teaching and distinguish gifted teachers? Which mode of teaching might this photo represent?

A Form of Empowerment

Power is the dimension of teaching most immediately evident to the new teacher. It is recognized in the first-grader's awed "Teacher, is this good?" on through the high school senior's "How much will this paper count?" Customarily, teachers get respect, at least initially; the deference derives from their power to enhance or diminish their students' academic status and welfare.

Even in the most democratic classrooms, teachers have more influence than students because they are responsible for what happens when students are with them, establishing the goals, selecting the methods, setting the pace, evaluating the progress, and deciding whether students should pass or fail. How you use this power is critical. As you know, students at any level can be humiliated by teachers who misuse their power or convey negative expectations to students. A student teacher in a fifth-grade class comments on the impact negative expectations can have on students:

> *They [students] can sense how a teacher feels, especially how she feels about them personally. Students often find themselves locked into a role that they have played for so long they don't know how to get out of it. Students deserve the right to have an education. They should not have to worry about what negative comments their teachers are saying about them (Rand and Shelton-Colangelo 1999, 107).*

An Opportunity to Serve

To become a teacher is to serve others professionally—students, the school, the community, and the country, depending on how broad the perspective is. Most who come to teaching do so for altruistic reasons. The altruistic dimension of teaching is at the heart of the motivation to teach. The paycheck, the public regard, and the vacations have little holding power compared to the opportunity to serve. As the authors of *On Being a Teacher* observe:

> *Very few people go into education in the first place to become rich or famous. On some level, every teacher gets a special thrill out of helping others. . . . The teachers who flourish, those who are loved by their students and revered by their colleagues, are those who feel tremendous dedication and concern for others—not just because they are paid to do so, but because it is their nature and their ethical responsibility (Zehm and Kottler 1993, 8–9).*

Whatever form the altruistic rewards of teaching take, they ennoble the profession and remind teachers of the human significance of their work.

Keepers of the Dream

Caroline Bitterwolf, National Board Certified Teacher

Caroline Bitterwolf remembers sitting at her typewriter, completing her application for national certification, with a fellow teacher helping her assemble the final materials. They just made the 9:00 A.M. deadline. At least one hundred hours of preparation preceded that moment, and, according to Bitterwolf, she could not have done it without the support of family, friends, her school colleagues, students, and their parents. Later, with the rigorous evaluation behind her, she would become the first Idaho teacher and one of the first 81 (of 289) national candidates to be certified by the National Board for Professional Teaching Standards (NBPTS).

"I was amazed at what I found."

Bitterwolf's telephone inquiry to the NBPTS in Detroit marked what she describes as "the beginning of a wonderful relationship." The staff's friendliness encouraged her, but when the board's directions and standards arrived, she found them daunting. "I'll never do it. The expectations are so high. No way I'll measure up," she thought, and she put the box of information on a back shelf.

She tried to forget the box but couldn't. So she began working through the materials and discovered that nothing was required that she was not already doing. The directions guided the seventh-grade study skills teacher to constantly reflect on and write about what she was doing, why, and how it fit her students. She also needed to document her practices with lesson plans, videotapes of her teaching, and written analyses. The time-consuming effort proved to be of real value. "I was amazed at what I found. Who I was, why I was teaching, what my goals were–it consolidated everything for me."

For the final phase of the review, the Moscow, Idaho, teacher traveled to the Vancouver, Washington, assessment center where she participated in two 12-hour days of activities, developing curriculum, evaluating materials, responding to videos of others teaching, writing essays, and being interviewed. She regards the overall application and assessment process as "the best professional development activity I have ever experienced."

Bitterwolf's involvement in national certification did not stop with her achieving national certification. She also participated in a video promoting the national standards and was elected to the National Board for Professional Teaching Standards.

That she came so far she attributes to the wonderful teachers she knew and met along the way. In addition to the teachers in her family and in her own schooling experience, Bitterwolf gives credit to a woman she regards as her professional mentor, Sally Borghart, "a four-foot ten-inch English lady who wore wedgies," who helped her teach ninth-grade inner-city remedial reading in Annapolis, Maryland. It was the only job Bitterwolf was able to get–a teaching assistantship through CETA (Comprehensive Employment Training Act). The transition from a southern church preschool to the tough vocabulary of inner-city youths caused the young teacher to spend most of the first semester in tears. "But Sally had a way with these young adults and through her I learned, really learned, how to communicate with my students–to empathize with them. She literally taught me how to diagnose student problems and set up programs to meet their individual needs, how to set up thematic units. She was way ahead of her time."

For a teacher who moved from "no way, I'll never measure up" to being a nationally certified teacher and member of the NBPTS, Bitterwolf's words of advice for teachers fit well: "Constantly strive to keep learning. . . . Do not be afraid to try new things," and be active in your profession so that we "can be the best we can be."

As Keepers of the Dream

Many of our country's most talented youth and dedicated veterans in the teaching field retain the desire to teach. In part, the desire endures because teachers have been positively influenced by one or more teachers of their own, who enriched, redirected, or significantly changed their lives. The desire also endures because teachers recognize the many joys and rewards the profession offers.

Reflecting on dedicated teachers and their contributions to our lives, we are guided to teaching for the benefit it brings to others. In doing so, we become keepers of a part of the American dream—the belief that education can improve the quality of life. That dream, more powerful than all our images of teachers, is alive throughout the country. This textbook acknowledges teachers and others in education who are making a difference in a special feature called Keepers of the Dream.

Summary

Why Do You Want to Teach?

- An important reason for becoming a teacher is a desire to work with children and young people.
- Other reasons include a passion for teaching based on a passion for the subject, the teaching life, or the teaching–learning process; the influence of teachers in one's past; and a desire to serve others and society.
- Practical benefits of teaching include on-the-job hours at school, vacations, increasing salaries and benefits, job security, and a feeling of respect in society.
- In contrast to the diversity of student enrollments, the backgrounds of today's teachers are less diverse; thus teachers from diverse racial and ethnic backgrounds and teachers with disabilities will experience exceptional job opportunities for the foreseeable future.

What Are the Challenges of Teaching?

- Working conditions for teachers can be difficult and stressful; however, for most teachers satisfactions outweigh dissatisfactions.
- Though problems in schools vary according to size of community, location, and other factors, teachers face five challenges: classroom management, social problems that impact students, need for family and community support, long working hours and job stress, and need for professional empowerment.
- Maintaining discipline and avoiding school-based violence are major concerns among preservice teachers.
- Social problems that impact the lives of many children and youth include substance abuse, teen pregnancies, homelessness, poverty, family distress, child abuse, violence and crime, suicide, and health problems such as HIV/AIDS and fetal alcohol syndrome.
- Though hours in the teacher's work day may appear attractive, over 90 percent of teachers work more than forty hours per week and spend an average ten hours per week on work not directly related to teaching assignments.
- Though job-related factors cause some teachers to experience high levels of stress, stress-reduction activities can help teachers cope and avoid burnout.
- As a consequence of nationwide efforts to improve schools, teachers are assuming new leadership roles and experiencing higher levels of professional empowerment.

What Is Teaching Really Like?

- The outcomes of teaching, even in the best of circumstances, are neither predictable nor consistent.
- It is difficult to assess what students learn as a result of being taught.

- The teacher's ability to influence student behavior is actually quite limited.
- With the role of teacher also comes the power to influence others by example.
- Interactive teaching is characterized by events that are rapid-changing, multidimensional, and irregular.
- Teaching involves a unique mode of being between teacher and student—a mode of being that can be experienced but not fully defined or described.

What Does Society Expect of Teachers?

- Society has high expectations of the teachers to whom it entrusts its children and youth.
- The public's image of teachers and its attitudes toward schools have improved since the 1980s.
- Society expects teachers to be competent and effective, and it holds teachers accountable for student achievement, for helping all learners succeed, and for maintaining high standards of conduct.

How Do Good Teachers View Their Work?

- Teachers' overall satisfaction has increased significantly since the mid-1980s.
- Helping students learn and making a difference in students' lives provide teachers with their greatest satisfaction.
- The essence of good teaching can be described in terms of modes of teaching illustrating what good teachers do.
- Five modes of teaching are teaching as a way of being, a creative endeavor, a live performance, a form of empowerment, and an opportunity to serve.

Key Terms and Concepts

burnout, **19**
cost of living, **12**
fringe benefits, **12**
interactive teaching, **24**
modes of teaching, **28**
moonlight, **12**
A Nation at Risk, **26**
preactive teaching, **24**
professional empowerment, **19**
realities of teaching, **19**
student diversity, **8**
student-mobility rates, **15**
student variability, **8**
Teach for America, **9**
teacher accountability, **28**
teacher–student ratios, **14**
teachers' thought processes, **25**
tenure, **12**

Applications and Activities

Teacher's Journal

1. Consider your reasons for deciding to become a teacher. How do they compare with those described in this chapter?
2. Describe a former teacher who has had a positive influence on your decision to teach. In what ways would you like to become like that teacher?
3. What is your impression of the public's image of teachers in your state or community today? What factors might be contributing to the kind of attention or lack of attention teachers are receiving?
4. Think about a time when a teacher truly motivated you to learn. What did that teacher do to motivate you? Do you believe other students in the class had the same reaction to this teacher? Why or why not?
5. Recall and describe specific experiences you had with teachers in elementary school, middle school or junior high school, or high school. Were you ever made uncomfortable because of a teacher's power over you? Were you ever ridiculed or diminished by a teacher? Or have you experienced the opposite—being elevated by a teacher's regard for you?

Teacher's Database

1. Make a list of recent portrayals of teachers in movies, television, and other media. Analyze the portrayals in terms of the type of teacher image they present—positive, neutral, or negative.
2. Clip articles in a major newspaper that relate to one of the focus questions in this chapter. Analyze the clippings as

sources of information and examples you can use to develop an answer to that question.

3. While you are on the Web, use your favorite search engine and search for information by key words or topics such as: teacher burnout, cost of living, moonlighting, Teach for America, accountability, teacher–student ratios, and tenure.

Observations and Interviews

1. As a collaborative project with classmates, visit a local school and interview teachers to learn about their perceptions of the rewards and challenges of teaching. Share your findings with other groups in your class.
2. Arrange to observe a teacher's class. During your observation, note evidence of the five modes of teaching discussed in this chapter. Ask your instructor for handout master 1.1, "Observing Modes of Teaching," which has been developed for this activity.
3. Ask your instructor to arrange group interviews between students in your class and students at the local elementary, middle, junior, and senior high schools. At each interview session, ask the students what characterizes good and not so good teachers. Also, ask the students what advice they would give to beginning teachers.
4. During an observation of a teacher's class, note evidence of the six realities of teaching discussed in this chapter. How many realities are evident during your observation? Which reality is most prevalent? Least prevalent? To help you record your observations, ask your instructor for handout master 1.2, "Observing Realities of Teaching."
5. Visit a first-year teacher (possibly a graduate from your institution) and ask about his or her first impressions of becoming a teacher. What aspects of teaching were difficult? Which easy? What surprises did this first-year teacher encounter? How would this person have prepared differently?

Professional Portfolio

To help you in your journey toward becoming a teacher, each chapter in this textbook includes suggestions for developing your **professional portfolio,** a collection of evidence documenting your growth and development while learning to become a teacher. At the end of this course you will be well on your way toward a portfolio that documents your knowledge, skills, and attitudes for teaching and contains valuable resources for your first teaching position.

For your first portfolio entry, expand on Teacher's Journal entry #1, which asks you to consider your reasons for becoming a teacher. In your entry (or videotaped version), identify the rewards of teaching for you. Identify the satisfactions. Also, describe the aspects of teaching that you will find challenging.

Video**Workshop Extra!**

If the Video Workshop package was included with your textbook, go to Chapter 1 of the Companion Website (http://www.ablongman.com/parkay6e) and click on the Video Workshop button. Follow the instructions for viewing videoclip 1 and completing this exercise. Consider this information along with what you've read in Chapter 1 while answering the following questions.

1. Teachers face many challenges in and out of the classroom. The text presents five challenges: classroom management, social problems that impact students, need for family and community support, long working hours and job stress, and need for professional empowerment. Explain how students' perceptions of teachers affect each of these challenges and how teachers might prepare for students' expectations.
2. Society holds teachers accountable for students' achievement. How do teachers send students the message that they (teachers) have confidence in students' abilities to succeed? Create a motto that teachers could present to students on the first day of school that conveys a strong relationship between teachers' expectations of and confidence in students' abilities.

2 Learning to Teach

The knowledge base for teaching is growingly steadily. Professional consensus and research findings have begun to provide authoritative support of knowledge related to many of the tasks, responsibilities and results of teaching. But much remains to be learned.

—National Board for Professional Teaching Standards, *What Teachers Should Know and Be Able to Do*

One day early in the year Ms. D. posed the following problem to her first graders: "Jenny had 4 pieces of gum and Esther had 7 pieces of gum. How many pieces did they have together?" After students had worked a few minutes, the class discussed what they found.

Ms. D.: Luis, how did you solve that problem?

Luis: I counted the blocks.

Ms. D.: But how did you count them?

Luis: I counted Jenny's pieces 1, 2, 3, 4 and then I counted the other girl's 5, 6, 7, 8, 9, 10, 11.

Ms. D.: Thanks, Luis. Sarah, how did you do it?

Sarah: I counted in my head.

Ms. D.: OK. Do you remember what numbers you said?

Sarah: I started at 5 and said 5, 6, 7, 8, 9, 10, 11.

Ms. D.: How did you know to stop at 11?

Sarah: I don't know. I guess I just counted seven times and stopped.

Ms. D.: How did you keep track that you counted seven times?

Sarah: I don't know.

Ms. D.: Did anyone else do it Sarah's way? I'm trying to figure out how she kept track of seven when she was counting.

Juan: I did it like that. Sometimes I keep track on my fingers and sometimes I just keep track in my head.

Ms. D.: OK. I'm going to keep thinking about that. Did anyone else do it a different way?

Rasheed: I started at 8 and went 8, 9, 10, 11.

Mira: I knew that 4 and 6 is 10 so 4 and 7 would be 11.

As she watched her students solve simple addition and subtraction problems, listened to their descriptions, and discussed what she was hearing with her colleagues, Ms. D. began learning a good deal about how her students solved these problems. She learned that many of her students moved through a progression of methods for solving the same kind of problem. For addition problems, the progression looked much like the sequence of methods presented by students in the classroom episode presented above.

Ms. D. learned that the methods themselves contained important properties of numbers and operations. For example, the fact that Sarah's method and Rasheed's method both produced the correct answer was an early encounter with commutativity, but with a form of this property that Ms. D. had not thought of before. The question of whether this would always work became a rich question for students to explore. Mira's method contained a decomposition and recomposition of numbers that Ms. D. began to recognize as an essential character of numbers, especially as students began adding and subtracting two- and three-digit numbers (Hiebert, Gallimore, and Stigler 2002, 5–6).

Focus Questions

1. **What essential knowledge do you need to teach?**
2. **What are five ways of viewing the teacher knowledge base?**
3. **How do reforms in teacher education affect you?**
4. **What can you learn from observing in classrooms?**
5. **How can you gain practical experience for becoming a teacher?**
6. **How can you develop your teaching portfolio?**
7. **How can you benefit from mentoring relationships?**
8. **What opportunities for continuing professional development will you have?**

Expand your knowledge of the concepts discussed in this chapter by reading current and historical articles from the *New York Times* by visiting the "**Themes of the Times**" section of the Companion Website (www.ablongman.com/parkay6e).

In the opening scenario, Ms. D., an experienced first-grade teacher at a racially and economically diverse school in the Midwest, is learning about the solution strategies her students use. Ms. D.'s ability to reflect on her teaching experiences for the purpose of developing professional knowledge is the hallmark of a professional teacher. Furthermore, her reflections are reminders that teaching is a complex act—one that requires thoughtfulness, insight into the motivations of others, and good judgment.

What Essential Knowledge Do You Need to Teach?

Students preparing to become teachers must have three kinds of knowledge before they can manage effectively the complexities of teaching: knowledge of self and students, knowledge of subject, and knowledge of educational theory and research. It is to this essential knowledge that we now turn.

Self-Knowledge

Effective teachers are aware of themselves and sensitive to the needs of their students. Although it is evident that teachers should understand their students as fully and deeply as possible, it is less evident that this understanding depends on their level of self-knowledge. If teachers are knowledgeable about their needs (and, most important, able to take care of those needs), they are better able to help their students. As Arthur Jersild (1955, 3), one of the first educators to focus attention on the connection between the teacher's personal insight and professional effectiveness, pointed out, a teacher's self-understanding and self-acceptance are prerequisites for helping students to know and accept themselves.

Teachers' self-evaluations often are influenced by emotions that teachers may experience when they teach, such as anxiety or loneliness. Promoting anxiety are the realities of teaching outlined in Chapter 1. For example, three conditions that cloud teachers' efforts are (1) the interminable nature of teaching (i.e., their work is never completed), (2) the intangible and often unpredictable characteristics of teaching results, and (3) the inability to attribute learning results to specific teachers' instruction. Unlike architects, lawyers, and doctors, teachers can never stand back and admire their work. If a student does well, that success rightfully belongs to the student.

Teachers thus need to develop the ability to tolerate ambiguities and to reduce their anxieties about being observably effective. Without this ability, a teacher "can feel that one is 'wrong,' 'missing something,' a 'bad fit' with students and with teaching itself. One can feel that one's circumstances are unfair, that one is giving but not receiving. One can feel helpless, not knowing what to do, not even knowing how to get the frustration out of mind let alone how to resolve it in practice" (Hansen 1995, 60).

Teachers can also experience loneliness or psychological isolation, since most of their time is spent interacting with children and youth, not adults. Though increased opportunities for professional collaboration and networking are reducing teacher isolation, teachers are behind classroom doors most of the day, immersed in the complexities of teaching and trying to meet the diverse needs of their students. Most teachers would welcome more interaction with their colleagues, especially time to observe one another. Without opportunities to receive feedback from one's peers, teachers are deprived of an important catalyst for professional growth. As Elliot Eisner puts it: "The result of professional isolation is the difficulty that teachers encounter in learning what they themselves do in their own classrooms when they teach. [How] can a teacher learn that he or she is talking too much, not providing suffi-cient time for student reflection, raising low-order questions, or is simply boring students? Teachers unaware of such features of their own performance are in no position to change them" (1998, 160–161). Additionally, by observing how a colleague responds to the challenges of teaching, the observer has an opportunity to reflect on his or her approaches to meeting those same challenges. For example, a fourth-grade teacher came to the following insight as a result of observing his teaching partner: "Being a teacher is so much more than an extensive repertoire of strategies and techniques. [To] be a teacher is to find a way to live within an environment filled with dilemmas" (Hole 1998, 419).

What kinds of basic knowledge and skills do teachers need to do their jobs well? Why is it important that you stay in touch with student culture?

Knowledge of Students

Knowledge of students is also important. Student characteristics such as their aptitudes, talents, learning styles, stage of development, and their readiness to learn new material are among the essential knowledge teachers must have. The importance of this knowledge is evident in comments made by an intern at a middle school: "To teach a kid well you have to know a kid well. . . . Teaching middle school takes a special breed of teachers who understand the unique abilities and inabilities . . . [of] those undergoing their own metamorphosis into teenagers" (Henry et al. 1995, 124–125). As Ms. D. illustrated in the opening scenario, teachers gain this

Professional Reflection

Inventorying Your Knowledge of Children and Youth

To be accepted into a teacher preparation program, you may be required by your college or university to have prior experiences working with children and youth. The knowledge of children and youth acquired through such experiences provides an excellent foundation on which to begin your preparation for becoming a teacher.

Use the following outline to inventory your experiences working with children and youth. Your experiences might include working with service clubs such as Girl Scouts or Boy Scouts, 4-H, Campfire, and youth groups; volunteering at a child care center; coaching a sport as part of a parks and recreation program; or tutoring young children in reading or mathematics.

After completing your inventory, reflect on your experiences. During which experiences were you functioning, at least partially, in the role of "teacher"? For example, did you have to demonstrate the skills involved in a particular sport? As a member of a club in high school, did you explain club activities to new members or to parents? While holding a leadership position in a group, were you expected to function as a "role model" to other members of the group?

Setting	Activity	Participants' Age and Sex	Your Role	Date
Example:				
Summer sports program	Taught swimming	Coed, ages 6–8	Camp counselor	Summer 2002
1.				
2.				
3.				

kind of knowledge through study, observation, and constant interaction. Without considerable understanding of children and youth, teachers' efforts to help students learn and grow can be inappropriate and, in some cases, counterproductive. Teachers' expectations of students directly affect student achievement. The Professional Reflection activity is designed to guide you in reflecting on opportunities you have already had to acquire knowledge about learners.

Knowledge of Subject

With the title of *teacher* comes an assumption of knowledge. Those outside the field of education expect a teacher to be a ready reference for all sorts of information. Clearly, teachers who have extensive knowledge of their subjects are better equipped to help their students learn. However, knowledge of subject matter does not translate into an understanding of *how* to share that knowledge with students—a point illustrated in a case study conducted by a team of researchers at the National Center for Research on Teacher Learning. The case focused on "Mary," an undergraduate literature major enrolled in a teacher education program at a major university. By any standards, Mary was a subject-matter expert—she was valedictorian of a large, urban high school; had straight A's in the literature courses she had taken; and had a sophisticated understanding of literature, especially poetry. The case study revealed that Mary had little understanding of classroom activities that would show her students *how* to read with sophistication and concluded that "some prospective teachers may come to teacher education unaware of how they have learned the processes they use and that render them expert. Unaided by their disciplines in locating the underpinnings of their expertise, these skilled, talented, and desirable recruits may easily become, ironically, those who can *do* but who cannot *teach*" (Holt-Reynolds 1999, 43).

Extensive knowledge of subject matter, as the National Board for Professional Teaching Standards (1994, 19–20) puts it, "entails more than being able to recite lists of dates, multiplication tables, or rules of grammar. [Accomplished] teachers possess what is sometimes called **'pedagogical content knowledge.'** Such understanding is the joint product of wisdom about teaching, learning, students and content. It includes knowledge of the most appropriate ways to present the subject matter to students through analogies, metaphors, experiments, demonstrations and illustrations."

Knowledge of Methods for Applying Educational Theory and Research

Theories about learners and learning guide the decision making of professional teachers. Not only do such teachers know that a certain strategy works, but they also know *why* it works. Because they recognize the importance of theories, they have at their disposal a greater range of options for problem solving than teachers who have not developed their repertoire of theories. Your ultimate goal as a professional is to apply theoretical knowledge to the practical problems of teaching.

Where Do You Stand? Visit the Companion Website to Voice Your Opinion.

To illustrate the usefulness of research on students' learning, we present six teaching strategies that Barak Rosenshine (1995, 267) recommends, based on his and others' research on cognitive processing, studies of teachers whose students have higher achievement gains than students of other teachers, and research on cognitive strategies.

1. Present new material in small steps so that the working memory does not become overloaded.
2. Help students develop an organization for the new material.
3. Guide student practice by (a) supporting students during initial practice and (b) providing for extensive student processing.
4. When teaching higher level tasks, support students by providing them with cognitive strategies.
5. Help students to use cognitive strategies by providing them with procedural prompts (e.g., questions students ask themselves while learning new material—"who," "what," "why," "when," etc.) and modeling the use of procedural prompts.
6. Provide for extensive student practice.

Research on students' learning is not intended to set forth, in cookbook fashion, exactly what teachers should do to increase students' learning. Instead, it may be helpful to think of educational research as providing teachers with rules of thumb to guide their practice. For example, Rosenshine, Meister, and Chapman (1996, 198) point out that, in spite of extensive research on the effectiveness of procedural prompts, "at the present time, developing procedural prompts appears to be an art. [It] is difficult to derive any prescriptions on how to develop effective procedural prompts for cognitive strategies in reading, writing, and subject matter domains." Finally, noted educational psychologist Lee Cronbach (quoted in Eisner 1998, 112) may have put it best when he said "[educational research] is to help practitioners use their heads."

What Are Five Ways of Viewing the Teacher Knowledge Base?

Just as people hold different expectations for schools and teachers, there are different views on the knowledge and abilities teachers need to teach well. The complexities of teaching make it difficult to describe in exact detail the **knowledge base** on which teaching as a profession rests. This difficulty results, in part, because there is no universally accepted definition of what good teaching is. Educational researchers are still learning *what* good teachers know and *how* they use that knowledge.

In addition, many people believe that a knowledge base for teaching should consist not only of what educational researchers have learned about teaching but also what teachers themselves "know" about teaching—often called *teachers' craft knowledge* or *practitioner knowledge* (Hiebert, Gallimore, and Stigler 2002; Kennedy 1999; Leinhardt 1990). **Teachers' craft knowledge,** as this chapter's opening scenario based on Ms. D.'s first-grade classroom illustrates, is developed by teachers in response to specific problems of practice. Five widespread views of the knowledge and abilities teachers must possess are portrayed in Figure 2.1.

A Personal Development View

One view of what teachers need to know and be able to do places primary emphasis on who the teacher is as a person. According to this view, teachers should be concerned with developing themselves as persons so that they may learn to use themselves more effectively. The importance of personal develop-

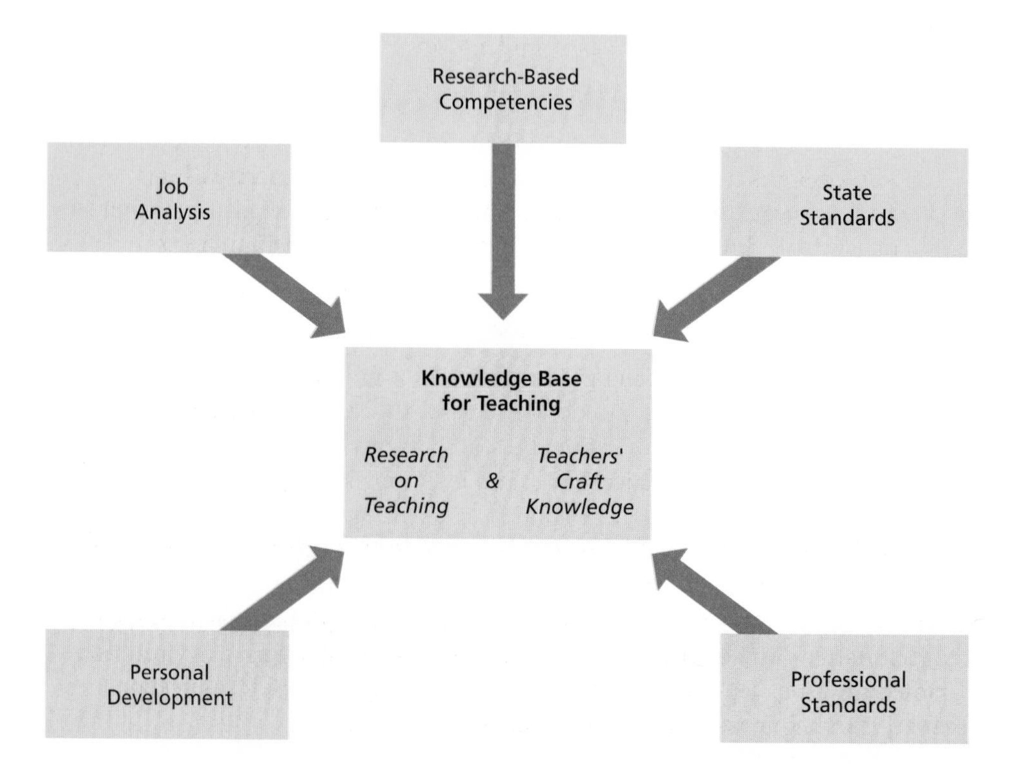

Figure 2.1 Five views of the knowledge base for teaching

ment is described as follows by the authors of *On Being a Teacher:* "Teachers who appear in charge of their own lives, who radiate power, tranquility, and grace in their actions, are going to command attention and respect. People will follow them anywhere. . . . What we are saying is that you have not only the option, but also the imperative, to develop the personal dimensions of your functioning, as well as your professional skills" (Zehm and Kottler 1993, 15).

What this approach requires, then, is that teachers continually develop their powers of observation and reflection so that they can most effectively respond to the needs of students. Teaching becomes an authentic, growth-oriented encounter between teacher and students. An important dimension of this **personal development view** is the teacher's need for self-knowledge, particularly in regard to oneself as a learner.

Research-Based Competencies

Since the late 1980s, several states and a few large cities have developed their own lists of **research-based competencies** that beginning teachers must demonstrate. These competencies are derived from educational research that has identified what effective teachers do. Typically, the states have developed *behavioral indicators* for each competency, which trained observers from universities and school districts use to determine to what extent teachers actually exhibit the target behaviors in the classroom.

The Florida Performance Measurement System (FPMS) was the first research-based performance system to be implemented on a statewide basis. Beginning teachers in Florida must now demonstrate behaviors in six domains: planning, management of student conduct, instructional organization and development, presentation of subject matter, verbal and nonverbal communication, and testing (student preparation, administration, and feedback). Appendix 2.1 presents the Summative Observation Instrument for the FPMS and the "effective" and "ineffective" behavioral indicators for four of those domains.

State Standards

In addition to sets of research-based competencies for evaluating practicing teachers, several states have developed performance-based standards for what new teachers should know and be able to do. Known as **outcome-based** or **performance-based teacher education**, the new approach is based on several assumptions:

- Outcomes are demonstrations of learning rather than a list of teaching specializations, college courses completed, or concepts studied.
- Outcomes are performances that reflect the richness and complexity of the teacher's role in today's classrooms—not discrete, single behaviors.
- Demonstrations of learning must occur in authentic settings—that is, settings similar to those within which the teacher will teach.
- Outcomes are culminating demonstrations of what beginning teachers do in real classrooms.

Typically, outcome-based standards are developed with input from teachers, teacher educators, state department of education personnel, and various professional associations. To illustrate state standards for teacher preparation, we present Kentucky's New Teacher Standards in Appendix 2.2.

A Job-Analysis Approach

Another view of what teachers need to know and be able to do is based on the job analyses that some school districts conduct. Typically, a **job analysis** begins with a review of existing job descriptions and then proceeds to interviews with those currently assigned to the job and their supervisors regarding the activities and responsibilities associated with the job. These data are then analyzed to identify the dimensions of the job. Finally, interview questions based on the dimensions are developed and used by district personnel responsible for hiring.

To illustrate the job-analysis view of the knowledge, skills, and attitudes needed by teachers, we present the thirteen dimensions used for selecting "star" urban teachers. By comparing the behaviors and beliefs of outstanding urban teachers with those of quitters and failures, Martin Haberman (1995, 779–780) and his colleagues at the University of Wisconsin, Milwaukee, identified thirteen characteristics of successful teachers of low-income urban students. These characteristics, identified by principals, supervisors, other teachers, parents, and the teachers themselves, include the following:

- *Persistence*
- *Protecting learners and learning*—Star teachers see protecting and enhancing students' involvement in learning activities as their highest priority. . . .
- *Application of generalizations*—[Stars are] able to take principles and concepts from a variety of sources (i.e., courses, workshops, books, and research) and translate them into practice.
- *Approach to students "at-risk"*—Star teachers believe that, regardless of the life conditions their students face, they as teachers bear a primary responsibility for sparking their students' desire to learn.
- *Professional versus personal orientation to students*—[Stars] use such terms as *caring, respect,* and *concern,* and they enjoy the love and affection of students when it occurs naturally. But they do not regard it as a prerequisite for learning.
- *Burnout: its causes and cures*—[Star teachers] recognize that even good teachers will eventually burn out if they are subjected to constant stress, so they learn how to protect themselves. . . .
- *Fallibility*—[Stars] can accept their own mistakes.

The remaining six dimensions are *organizational ability, physical/emotional stamina, teaching style* modeled on coaching, *explanation of success* based on students' effort rather than ability, *rapport* with students, and *readiness* to believe that education will provide students with the best chance of "making it" in American society.

Professional Views

As the Meeting the Standards feature in Chapter 1 points out, various professional associations have outlined what teachers should know and be able to do. For example, the **National Board for Professional Teaching Standards (NBPTS)** was created so that teachers, like professionals in other fields, can achieve distinction by demonstrating that they meet high, rigorous standards for their profession. In addition to demonstrating their knowledge and skills through a series of performance-based assessments, teachers must complete written exercises that

Technology Highlights

What technology-related knowledge and skills do teachers need?

Today, thousands of teachers and students routinely use desktop and laptop computers with built-in modems, faxes, and CD-ROM players; camcorders; optical scanners; speech and music synthesizers; laser printers; digital cameras; and LCD projection panels. In addition, they use sophisticated software for e-mail, word processing, desktop publishing, presentation graphics, spreadsheets, databases, and multimedia applications.

To prepare teachers to use these new technologies, many teacher education programs and state departments of education have developed technology competency guidelines for classroom teachers. For example, Colorado teachers are now required to have technology skills in three areas: basic computer/technology operations and concepts, personal and professional use of technology, and integration of technology into a standards-based curriculum. The following competencies are included in the Colorado guidelines. How many of these competencies do you possess, and what steps can you take to acquire those you do not have?

1. Media Communications and Integration
   - Set up and operate video media [e.g., videotape recorders, laser disc players and digital video disc (DVD)]
   - Connect video output devices and other presentation systems to computers and video sources for large-screen display
   - Use painting, drawing, and authoring tools
   - Plan, create and use linear and nonlinear multimedia presentations
   - Use imaging devices such as scanners, digital cameras, and/or video cameras with computer systems and software
2. Telecommunications
   - Connect to the Internet or an online service
   - Use Internet search engines
   - Use a web browser to access and use resources on Internet and World Wide Web (WWW)
   - Download and print resources from the WWW
   - Use URL management tools (e.g., "bookmarks" and/or "favorite sites")
   - Telnet to a remote computer on the Internet
   - Connect to, and use resources from, the Access Colorado Library and Information Network (ACLIN) and the CDE website
   - Use electronic mail (compose, send, retrieve, read, reply to sender, reply to all and forward)
   - Attach files to e-mail messages
   - Retrieve and use attachments (e.g., view, read, save and print)
   - Configure and use specialized e-mail lists relevant to professional information needs
   - Create and use group addresses for electronic mail
   - Collaborate with peers through available tools (e.g., e-mail, websites, threaded and other online discussions)

Source: Adapted from *Colorado Technology Competency Guidelines for Classroom Teachers and School Library Media Specialists,* Educational Telecommunications Unit, Colorado Department of Education, January 1999.

probe the depth of their subject-matter knowledge and their understanding of how to teach those subjects to students. In November 2001, the NBPTS awarded National Board Certification to 6,509 teachers, bringing the total number of board-certified teachers to 16,044 (National Board for Professional Teaching Standards 2002). The goal of the NBPTS is to have 100,000 board-certified teachers by 2006. Examples of NBPTS portfolio activities and assessment center activities for the early childhood generalist and early adolescence/English lan-

Figure 2.2 INTASC Model Standards for Beginning Teacher Licensing, Assessment, and Development

INTASC Model Standards for Beginning Teacher Licensing, Assessment, and Development

Principle #1: Knowledge of Subject Matter
The teacher understands the central concepts, tools of inquiry, and structures of the discipline(s) he or she teaches and can create learning experiences that make these aspects of subject matter meaningful for students.

Principle #2: Knowledge of Human Development and Learning
The teacher understands how children learn and develop, and can provide learning opportunities that support their intellectual, social, and personal development.

Principle #3: Adapting Instruction for Individual Needs
The teacher understands how students differ in their approaches to learning and creates instructional opportunities that are adapted to diverse learners.

Principle #4: Multiple Instructional Strategies
The teacher understands and uses a variety of instructional strategies to encourage students' development of critical thinking, problem solving, and performance skills.

Principle #5: Classroom Motivation and Management
The teacher uses an understanding of individual and group motivation and behavior to create a learning environment that encourages positive social interaction, active engagement in learning, and self-motivation.

Principle #6: Communication Skills
The teacher uses knowledge of effective verbal, nonverbal, and media communication techniques to foster active inquiry, collaboration, and supportive interaction in the classroom

Principle #7: Instructional Planning Skills
The teacher plans instruction based upon knowledge of subject matter, students, the community, and curriculum goals.

Principle #8: Assessment of Student Learning
The teacher understands and uses formal and informal assessment strategies to evaluate and ensure the continuous intellectual, social, and physical development of the learner.

Principle #9: Professional Commitment and Responsibility
The teacher is a reflective practitioner who continually evaluates the effects of his/her choices and actions on others (students, parents, and other professionals in the learning community) and who actively seeks out opportunities to grow professionally.

Principle #10: Partnerships
The teacher fosters relationships with school colleagues, parents, and agencies in the larger community to support students' learning and well-being.

guage arts are presented in Appendix 2.3 and in "NBPTS Assessment Center Activities" on this book's website.

Standards proposed by the **Interstate New Teacher Assessment and Support Consortium (INTASC)** reflect a trend toward performance-based or outcome-based assessment of essential knowledge and abilities for teachers. The INTASC model core standards for licensing teachers are based on ten principles (see Figure 2.2) that should be present in all teaching regardless of the subject or grade level taught. Each principle includes *knowledge, dispositions,* and *performance* statements that identify the qualities on which a prospective teacher is assessed. For example, Principle #1, Knowledge of Subject Matter, includes the following statements:

> **Principle #1:** The teacher understands the central concepts, tools of inquiry, and structures of the discipline(s) he or she teaches and can create learn-

ing experiences that make these aspects of subject matter meaningful for students.

Knowledge: The teacher understands major concepts, assumptions, debates, processes of inquiry, and ways of knowing that are central to the discipline(s) s/he teaches.

Disposition: The teacher realizes that subject matter knowledge is not a fixed body of facts but is complex and ever-evolving. S/he seeks to keep abreast of new ideas and understandings in the field.

Performance: The teacher effectively uses multiple representations and explanations of disciplinary concepts that capture key ideas and link them to students' prior understandings.

In light of the five differing views of what teachers ought to know and be able to do, it seems clear that becoming a teacher is complex and demanding. We believe that effective teachers use six kinds of knowledge and skills to meet the challenges of the profession. As Figure 2.3 shows, effective teachers are guided by **reflection** and a **problem-solving orientation.** On the basis of reflection and problem solving, they use knowledge of self and students (including cultural differences), craft knowledge, knowledge of subject matter, and knowledge of educational theory and research to create optimum conditions for student learning.

How Do Reforms in Teacher Education Affect You?

Since the publication in 1983 of *A Nation at Risk: The Imperative for Educational Reform,* the United States has experienced an unprecedented push for reform in education. During that time, numerous commissions were established and scores of reports were written outlining what should be done to improve U.S. schools. Most of these reports called for changes in the education of teachers. In fact, the preparation program you are now involved in probably has been influenced by this **educational reform movement**. Calls for reform in teacher education have emphasized increased academic preparation, an expanded role for schools, and state standards boards.

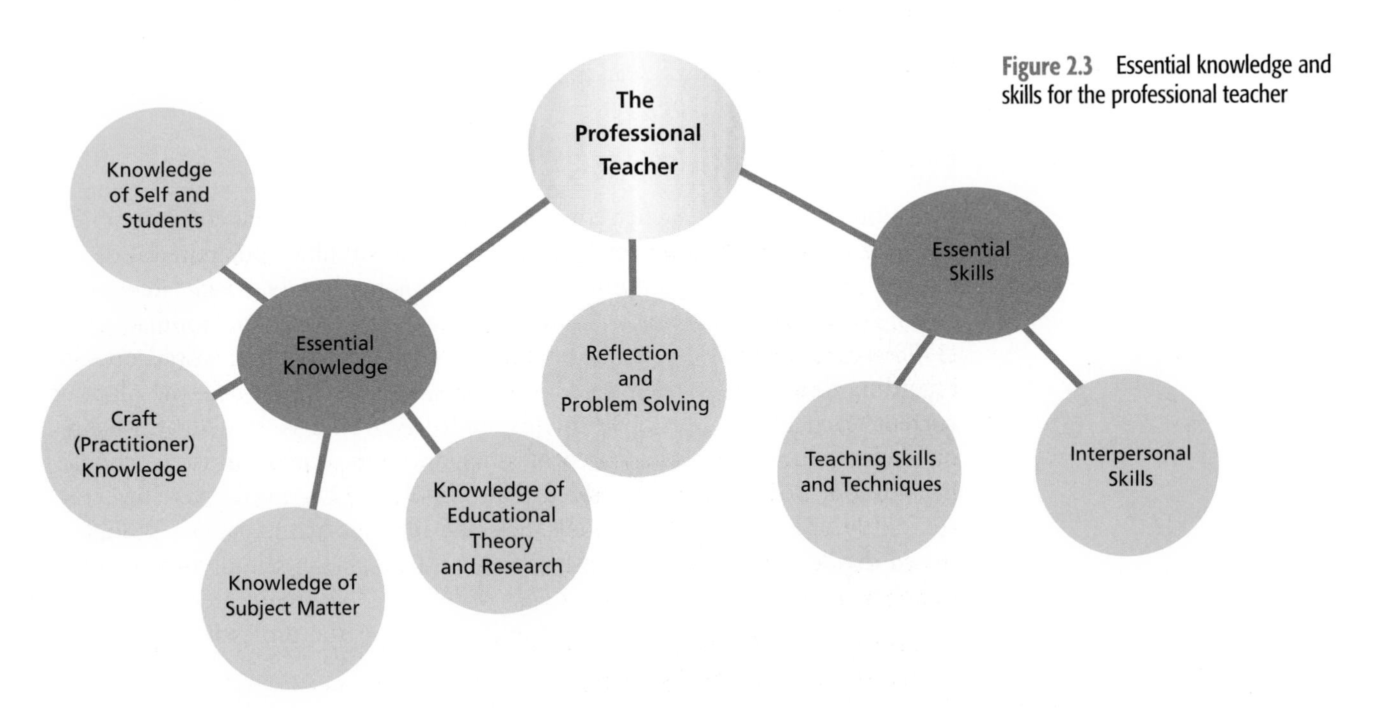

Figure 2.3 Essential knowledge and skills for the professional teacher

Increased Academic Preparation

One call for the reform of teacher education was made by the **Holmes Group,** named after Henry W. Holmes, dean of the Harvard Graduate School of Education during the 1920s. The Holmes Group was initially made up of ninety-six major universities. In *Tomorrow's Teachers,* a 1986 report written by thirteen deans of education and one college president, the Holmes Group recommended that all teachers have a bachelor's degree in an academic field and a master's degree in education. Although the Holmes Group viewed additional academic preparation as a means of enhancing the professional status of teachers, critics maintained that students' education would be delayed and be more expensive, with no assurance that students who spent five years obtaining a teaching certificate would be paid more.

The Holmes Group held an action summit in 1993 to develop a comprehensive plan for redesigning the schools of education at Holmes Group member institutions. The plan outlined steps for creating Tomorrow's School of Education (TSE)—an institution that has put into practice the Holmes Group agenda for the reform of teacher education. In early 1995, the Holmes Group released the TSE plan, which recommended that teacher educators become more involved with schools and that students move through a five-year program in cohorts. The report also urged colleges of education to establish **professional development schools (PDSs)** that are linked to colleges or universities and operate on the same principle as teaching hospitals. Students act as intern teachers, and college faculty and school staff develop new teaching methods and collaborate on educational research projects.

In 1996, after a decade of what it described as "uneven progress" in the reform of teacher education and a realization that "the reform of professional education is so complicated and difficult that it has not yielded to any one reform group's efforts to improve it," the Holmes Group joined with other professional organizations—including the NBPTS, the National Education Association (NEA), and the American Federation of Teachers (AFT)—to create the **Holmes Partnership.** The Holmes Partnership adopted six principal goals: high-quality professional preparation; simultaneous renewal (of public K–12 schools and pre- and in-service education); equity, diversity, and cultural competence; scholarly inquiry and programs of research; faculty development; and policy initiation (Holmes Partnership 2001).

Expanded Role for Schools

Based on his study of teacher education programs around the country, noted educator John Goodlad set forth his plan for the simultaneous renewal of schools and teacher preparation programs in his book, *Educational Renewal: Better Teachers, Better Schools.* To improve teacher preparation, Goodlad (1998) recommended the creation of Centers of Pedagogy that would operate according to a specific set of principles. These centers would take the place of current teacher education departments, and they would be staffed by a team of teacher educators, liberal arts professors, and educators from local schools. In addition, Goodlad recommended that school districts and universities create jointly operated partner schools. Selected teachers at the partner school would divide their time between teaching students at the school and supervising beginning teachers. Partner schools would thus become centers for the renewal of education as well as laboratory schools for the professional development of beginning teachers.

State Standards Boards

To regulate and improve the professional practice of teachers, administrators, and other education personnel, states have established **professional standards boards.** In some states, standards boards have the authority to implement standards; in others, they serve in an advisory capacity to educational policymakers. In Washington state, for example, the Washington Advisory Board for Professional Teaching Standards recently made a recommendation to the State Board of Education calling for a three-level teacher certification system. Candidates, on completion of an approved program, would receive a Residency Certificate. With demonstration of successful teaching and a recommendation from the employing school district, a candidate then would be eligible for a renewable, five-year Professional Certificate. Finally, persons who hold national certification from the NBPTS or who hold a combination of advanced degrees, experience, and proficiency in performance-based standards would be eligible for the optional Professional Career Certificate.

In the wake of national reports such as *What Matters Most: Teaching for America's Future* (National Commission on Teaching and America's Future 1996) and *Quality Counts 2000: Who Should Teach?* (*Education Week* 2000), which highlighted the common practice of teachers teaching "out-of-field," professional standards boards in many states have launched extensive reviews of their teacher certification standards. Also, some standards boards have addressed whether education students' subject-matter preparation should continue to be separate from professional preparation and whether alternative routes to certification such as school district-controlled internship programs should be encouraged.

What Can You Learn from Observing in Classrooms?

Classroom observations are a vital element of many **field experiences.** Students report that these experiences aid them greatly in making a final decision about entering the teaching field. Most become more enthusiastic about teaching and more motivated to learn the needed skills; a few decide that teaching is not for them. Recognizing the value of observations, many teacher education programs are increasing the amount of field experiences and placing such fieldwork earlier in students' programs. For example, at Washington State University (WSU), students preparing to become elementary teachers complete one week of classroom observations as part of their first education course. Later in their program, WSU students complete two 45-hour blocks of observations in K–8 classrooms and a five-week advanced practicum (or field experience) that requires several hours of classroom observation each week.

Technology and Classroom Observations

Currently, many universities and school districts are cooperating on the use of two-way interactive compressed video technology to enable preservice teachers on campus to observe live coverage in school classrooms off campus. Compressed video can be transmitted over existing telephone lines or the Internet in a relatively inexpensive, unobtrusive, and time-efficient way. **Distance learning**—the use of technology such as video transmissions that enables students to receive instruction at multiple, often remote sites—now enables teacher education programs to use the power of models for learning how to teach. For example, distance learning enables students at Texas A & M University and the

University of Memphis to observe inner-city classrooms and afterwards to discuss their observations with the teachers. One of the designers of the interactive video program at Memphis comments on its benefits: "Previously everyone visited different schools and saw very different things. [This] shared clinical experience will lead to a more focused discussion of teaching methods" (University of Memphis 1994/95, 2).

Focused Observations

Observations are more meaningful when they are focused and conducted with clear purposes. Observers may focus on the students, the teacher, the interactions between the two, the structure of the lesson, or the setting. More specifically, for example, observers may note differences between the ways boys and girls or members of different ethnic groups communicate and behave in the classroom. They may note student interests and ability levels, study student responses to a particular teaching strategy, or analyze the question and response patterns in a class discussion.

Observations may also be guided by sets of questions related to specific areas. For instance, since beginning teachers are frequently frustrated by their lack of success in interesting their students in learning, asking questions specifically related to motivation can make an observation more meaningful and instructive. Figure 2.4 presents a helpful set of focused questions on motivation. Similar questions can be generated for other focus areas such as classroom management, student involvement, questioning skills, evaluation, and teacher–student rapport.

Observation Instruments

A wide range of methods can be used to conduct classroom observations, ranging from informal, qualitative descriptions to formal, quantitative checklists. With reform efforts to improve education in the United States has come the development of instruments to facilitate the evaluation of teacher performance, a task now widely required of school administrators. Students preparing to teach can benefit by using these evaluative instruments in their observations. An example is the "Formative Observation of Effective Teaching Practices Instrument" on this book's website.

How Can You Gain Practical Experience for Becoming a Teacher?

A primary aim of teacher education programs is to give students opportunities to experience, to the extent possible, the real world of the teacher. Through field experiences and carefully structured experiential activities, preservice teachers are given limited exposure to various aspects of teaching, from curriculum development to classroom management. Observing, tutoring, instructing small groups, analyzing video cases, operating instructional media, performing student teaching, and completing various noninstructional tasks are among the most common experiential activities.

Classroom Experiences

Because of the need to provide opportunities to put theory into practice before student teaching, many teacher education programs enable students to participate in microteaching, teaching simulations, analyses of video cases, field-based practica and clinical experiences, and classroom aide programs.

Directions: *As you observe, note the ways that students are motivated intrinsically (from within) and extrinsically (from factors outside themselves).*

Intrinsic Motivation

What things seem to interest students at this age?

Which activities and assignments seem to give them a sense of pride?

When do they seem to be confused? Bored? Frustrated?

What topics do they talk about with enthusiasm?

In class discussions, when are they most alert and participating most actively?

What seems to please, amuse, entertain, or excite them?

What do they joke about? What do they find humorous?

What do they report as being their favorite subjects? Favorite assignments?

What do they report as being their least favorite subjects and assignments?

How do they respond to personalized lessons (e.g., using their names in exercises)?

How do they respond to activity-oriented lessons (e.g.,fieldwork, project periods)?

How do they respond to assignments calling for presentations to groups outside the classroom (e.g., parents, another class, the chamber of commerce)?

How do they respond to being given a choice in assignments?

Extrinsic Motivation

How do teachers show their approval to students?

What phrases do teachers use in their praise?

What types of rewards do teachers give (e.g., grades, points, tangible rewards)?

What reward programs do you notice (e.g., points accumulated toward free time)?

What warnings do teachers give?

What punishments are given to students?

How do teachers arouse concern in their students?

How do students motivate other students?

What forms of peer pressure do you observe?

How do teachers promote enthusiasm for an assignment?

How do teachers promote class spirit?

How do teachers catch their students' interest in the first few minutes of a lesson?

Which type of question draws more answers—recall or open-ended?

How do teachers involve quiet students in class discussions?

How do teachers involve inactive students in their work?

In what ways do teachers give recognition to students' accomplishments?

Figure 2.4 Guiding questions for observing motivation

Microteaching Introduced in the 1960s, **microteaching** was received enthusiastically and remains a popular practice. The process calls for students to teach brief, single-concept lessons to a small group of students (five to ten) while concurrently practicing a specific teaching skill, such as positive reinforcement. Often the microteaching is videotaped for later study.

As originally developed, microteaching includes the following six steps.

1. Identify a specific teaching skill to learn about and practice.
2. Read about the skill in one of several pamphlets.
3. Observe a master teacher demonstrate the skill in a short movie or on videotape.
4. Prepare a three- to five-minute lesson to demonstrate the skill.
5. Teach the lesson, which is videotaped, to a small group of peers.
6. Critique, along with the instructor and student peers, the videotaped lesson.

On the Frontlines

Discipline Challenges

In the second week of your first teaching assignment, you are confronted with a discipline challenge. You, Mrs. Clark, and Mr. Taylor have begun rotating classes for science, social studies, and language arts. Your science lesson went smoothly for the first two groups, but when Mr. Jones's students enter your classroom you sense trouble.

Their loud talking, physical jostling, taunts, and derisive laughter put you on edge. As they sit down, several look inside your students' desks and put things into their pockets. You stop them and announce, "Do not to disturb the contents of the desks."

After you introduce your lesson, you notice a row of boys smiling and looking from left to right at each other. You realize they have taken one of your student's backpacks off the back of the chair and are passing it under their desks to the outside. When it reaches the person nearest the window, before you can intercede, he stands up and drops the bag out the second-story window. "Now what?" you ask yourself.

"The biggest barriers to new teachers' success are poor classroom-management skills (82 percent) and disruptive students (57 percent)," reports David Gordon, editor of the *Harvard Education Letter* (1999). The statistics result from responses of 118 school districts to a poll conducted by Recruiting New Teachers (RNT) (http://www.rnt.org).

The annual Phi Delta Kappa/Gallup Poll of public attitudes toward education found in 2001 that "lack of discipline, more control" was ranked as "the biggest problem public schools face," as it had been in numerous earlier polls. A related poll found that students are now bothered by classroom discipline problems as well. As Gordon reports, "In a survey of 1200 teenagers . . . 43 percent of public school students said the behavior of other students interferes with their school performance" (1991b, p. 1).

While these statistics are alarming, new teachers can take comfort in the fact that teachers have always worried initially about how they would manage disruptive behavior and control a roomful of students. Most veteran teachers can share classroom discipline stories they survived and the lessons they learned.

The wisdom of veterans should surely be tapped, but novice teachers can learn even more from their own experiences. Professor Nancy Martin, who teaches classroom management courses, observes, "Training doesn't mean anything until teachers get in the classroom. It's like swimming—you can never really know what it's like just by reading about it" (Gordon, 1999). An RNT survey found that one of the qualities the public regarded as "very important for an excellent teacher to have" was "at least one semester's experience in a classroom as a student teacher", Experience matters.

In his article "Rising to the Discipline Challenge," Gordon (1999) summarizes tried-and-true guidelines for classroom management: (1) "Get students involved"; (2) "Establish rules and be consistent"; (3) "Take care of the little things"; (4) "Involve community and parents"; and (5) "Report incidents."

In a study of elementary and secondary classroom environments during the first month of the school year, Edward Emmer, Carolyn Evertson and Murray Worsham (1999, 2002) discovered that teachers who fared best in terms of classroom management were those who spent considerable time in the first few days "teaching" the classroom rules and procedures. A month later these teachers had significantly fewer management and discipline problems than their colleagues who had not spent similar time working with students on classroom rules and procedures.

A common theme in classroom management literature is the importance of the teacher's relationship with students. Respect and regard are basic to the development of a well-managed classroom environment in which quality learning can thrive. Ninety percent of the respondents to an RNT survey ranked as very important a teacher's "ability to establish good relationships with children and adolescents".

New teachers will fare best from a multifaceted preparation for classroom challenges: reading theorists' proposed approaches and programs; taking courses in classroom management, child and adolescent development, and group dynamics; tapping the wisdom of veteran teachers; and gaining their own classroom experience. Researchers also recommend new teachers learn to trust their own intuition. This recommendation is a welcome recognition and valuing of the gifts that people drawn to teaching bring with them.

Exploratory Questions

1. How would you respond to the students' misbehavior described in the opening scene?
2. Why do you think the first month of school is so important for determining the management tone for the rest of the school year?
3. What "rules of the room" would you establish in your first two days of a school year?

Your Survival Guide of Helpful Resources

The following resources provide helpful hints for surviving "on the frontlines."

Books and Articles

Emmer, E. T., Evertson, C. M., and Worsham, M. E. (2002). *Classroom management for secondary teachers,* 6th ed. Boston: Allyn and Bacon.

Evertson, C. M., Emmer, E. T., and Worsham, M. E. (2002). *Classroom management for elementary teachers,* 6th ed. Boston: Allyn and Bacon.

Gordon, D. T. (1999, September/October). Rising to the discipline challenge. *Harvard Education Letter, 15*(5), 1–4.

Warger, C. (1999, September). Positive behavior support and functional assessment. Retrieved from http://www.ed.gov/databases/ERIC_Digests/ed434437.html

Websites

Recruiting New Teachers (http://www/rnt.org)

Technical Assistance Center on Positive Behavioral Interventions and Supports (PBIS) (http://www.pbis.org/english/)

Simulations As an element of teacher training, **teaching simulations** provide opportunities for vicarious practice of a wide range of teaching skills. In simulations, students analyze teaching situations that are presented in writing, on audiotape, in short films, or on videotape. Typically, students are given background information about a hypothetical school or classroom and the pupils they must prepare to teach. After this orientation, students role-play the student teacher or the teacher who is confronted with the problem situation. Following the simulation, participants discuss the appropriateness of solutions and work to increase their problem-solving skills and their understanding of the teacher's multifaceted role as a decision maker.

With recent advances in computer technology, some teacher education programs are experimenting with computer-based simulations that enable students to hone their classroom planning and decision-making skills. Students at Nova Southwestern University in Florida, for example, learn to diagnose learning disabilities among children and youth by analyzing computer-simulated cases (Brown 1994). In some cases, computer simulations are also being used for teacher professional development. For example, a three-dimensional virtual reality (VR) simulation model proved more effective than a workshop method for training kindergarten teachers to understand children's needs and perceptions (Katz 1999), and a computer-based simulation has been used to train school personnel in crisis management (Degnan and Bozeman 2001).

While progress is being made in the development of VR technology, "it is not possible to say how great the potential may actually be in the realm of teacher education" (Brown 1999, 318). Current simulations are limited to specific skills such as classroom management or tutoring highly motivated individuals. As VR technology improves, however, one day we may see simulations of classrooms that show a variety of students with differing needs as learners.

Video Cases Teacher education students who view, analyze, and then write about video cases have an additional opportunity to appreciate the ambiguities and complexities of real-life classrooms, to learn that "there are no clear-cut, simple answers to the complex issues teachers face" (Wasserman 1994, 606). Viewing authentic video cases enables students to see how "teaching tradeoffs and dilemmas emerge in the video 'text' as do the strategies teachers use, the frustrations they experience, the brilliant and less-brilliant decisions they make" (Grant, Richard, and Parkay 1996, 5).

Practica A **practicum** is a short-term field-based experience (usually about two weeks long) that allows teacher education students to spend time observing and assisting in classrooms. Though practica vary in length and purpose, students are often able to begin instructional work with individuals or small groups. For example, a cooperating teacher may allow a practicum student to tutor a small group of students, read a story to the whole class, conduct a spelling lesson, monitor recess, help students with their homework, or teach students a song or game.

Classroom Aides Serving as a teacher's aide is another popular means of providing field experience before student teaching. A teacher aide's role depends primarily on the unique needs of the school and its students. Generally, aides work under the supervision of a certified teacher and perform duties that support the teacher's instruction. Assisting teachers in classrooms familiarizes college students with class schedules, record-keeping procedures, and students' performance levels, and provides ample opportunity for observations. In exchange, the classroom teacher receives much needed assistance.

Student Teaching

The most extensive and memorable field experience in teacher preparation programs is the period of student teaching. "Student teaching provide[s] student teachers with realistic evaluations of their strengths and weaknesses as prospective teachers and help[s] them to develop competencies in classroom management" (Wentz 2001, 73). States require students to have a five-week to semester-long student teaching experience in the schools before certifying them as teachers. The nature of student teaching varies considerably among teacher education programs. Typically, a student is assigned to a cooperating (or master) teacher in the school, and a university supervisor makes periodic visits to observe the student teacher. Some programs even pay student teachers during the student teaching experience.

What strategies can you use to make your student teaching experience truly valuable to you in becoming a teacher? In what sense will you remain a student teacher throughout your career?

Student teaching is a time of responsibility. As one student teacher put it, "I don't want to mess up [my students'] education!" It is also an opportunity for growth, a chance to master critical skills. During a typical student teaching assignment, a student teacher will spend about half of his or her time teaching, with the remaining time devoted to observing and participating in classroom activities. The amount of time actually spent teaching, however, is not as important as the student teacher's willingness to reflect carefully on his or her experience. Two excellent ways to promote reflection during student teaching are journal writing and maintaining a reflective teaching log.

Student Teacher Journal Writing Many supervisors require student teachers to keep a journal of their classroom experiences so that they can engage in reflective teaching and begin the process of criticizing and guiding themselves. The following two entries—the first written by a student teacher in a fourth-grade classroom, the second by a student teacher in a high school English class—illustrate how journal writing can help student teachers develop strategies for dealing with the realities of teaching.

> Today I taught a lesson on the geography of the Northeast, and the kids seemed so bored. I called on individuals to read the social studies text, and then I explained it. Some of them really struggled with the text. Mr. H. said I was spoon-feeding them too much. So tomorrow I am going to put them into groups and let them answer questions together rather than give them the answers. This ought to involve the students in the learning a bit more and enable some of the better readers to help out those who have difficulty, without the whole class watching. I feel bad when I see those glazed looks on their faces. I need to learn how to be more interesting (Pitton 1998, 120).

> I had good feedback on small groups in their responses to questions on *Of Mice and Men.* They were to find a paragraph that might indicate theme and find two examples of foreshadowing. We found five!

> The short story unit was awful during fourth hour. The kids just didn't respond. I quickly revamped my approach for the next hour. Fifth hour did seem to go better. (Mostly though, I think it was just that I was more prepared, having had one class to try things out.) I can see how experience really helps. Now that I've tried the story "The Tiger or the Lady," I would use the same material, but I would know HOW to use it more effectively! (Pitton 1998, 143).

Relatively unstructured, open-ended journals, such as the ones from which these entries were selected, provide student teachers with a medium for subjectively exploring the student teaching experience.

Reflective Teaching Logs To promote the practice of reflecting more analytically, some supervisors ask their student teachers to use a more directed and structured form of journal keeping, the **reflective teaching log.** In this form a student lists and briefly describes the daily sequence of activities, selects a single episode to expand on, analyzes the reason for selecting it and what was learned from it, and considers the possible future application of that knowledge.

To illustrate the reflective teaching approach to keeping a log, we share here a partial entry for one episode. The entry is of particular interest because it illustrates how a college student can disagree with a supervising teacher's response to a classroom situation.

Log for December 1—Erin Tompkins

Sequence of Events

1. Arrival—end of eighth period
2. Ninth period—helped Sharad study science
3. After-school program—worked on science with Ricki, P.K., and Tom
4. Late bus duty with Ms. Soto
5. Departure

Episode

I was helping Ricki and P.K. fill out a table about the location and function of the different cell parts. P.K. asked me a question and two other students laughed at him. I began to answer his question when Ms. Soto came over to the table where we were working and yelled at P.K. She said, "P.K. I don't need you distracting other students who are trying to get their work done." He started to tell her what he asked me and she said, "I don't care. You can leave the room if you don't knock it off. Just do your work and be quiet or you're out!" She then apologized to me and went back to helping another student.

Analysis

I was very frustrated after this episode. This is the first time I've seen Ms. Soto raise her voice with a student and accuse him of causing problems when he was getting his work done and other students were being disruptive. P.K. had asked me a legitimate question; the other students who laughed at him were the problem. I was frustrated because Ricki and P.K. were working hard and asking me good questions. I was annoyed that P.K. was being reprimanded for asking a question that was relevant to the topic we were working on. I also felt helpless because I wanted to tell Ms. Soto that it wasn't P.K. who was the problem. I didn't feel it was my place to correct her in front of her students and kept quiet. I decided that my saying something would only make things worse because it would encourage P.K. to continue arguing with Ms. Soto and he would be in more trouble (Posner 2000, 137–138).

Though student teaching will be the capstone experience of your teacher education program, the experience should be regarded as an *initial* rather than a terminal learning opportunity—your first chance to engage in reflection and self-evaluation for a prolonged period.

Gaining Experiences in Multicultural Settings

The enrollment in schools in the United States of students from diverse cultural backgrounds will continue to increase dramatically during the twenty-first century. As this trend continues, it is vitally important that those entering the teaching profession achieve an understanding of children's differing backgrounds. For example, students in Washington State University's teacher education program must document how they have met the following "administrative code" for teacher certification: "All candidates for teacher certification must demonstrate in their field experience their ability to work effectively with students of various backgrounds including (1) students from racial and or ethnic populations other than the candidate's, and (2) students with exceptional needs (i.e., those with handicapping conditions and the highly capable)."

As a teacher you can be assured that you will teach students from backgrounds that differ from your own—including students from the more than one hundred racial and ethnic groups in the United States and students who are poor, gifted, or have disabilities. You will have the challenge of reaching out to all students and teaching them that they are persons of worth and can learn. You will also be confronted with the difficult challenge of being sensitive to differences among students while at the same time treating all equally and fairly. To prepare for these realities of teaching, you should make every effort to gain experiences in multicultural settings.

Induction and Internship Programs

In response to widespread efforts to improve education, many states and local school districts, often in collaboration with colleges and universities, have begun teacher induction or internship programs. Among the programs that have received national attention are the Florida Beginning Teacher Program, the California Mentor Teacher Program, the Virginia Beginning Teacher Assistance Program, and the Kentucky Beginning Teacher Internship Program.

Induction programs provide beginning teachers with continued assistance at least during the first year. **Internship programs** also provide participants with support, but they are usually designed primarily to provide training for those who have not gone through a teacher education program. In some instances, however, the terms *induction* and *internship* are used interchangeably.

Most induction and internship programs serve a variety of purposes:

1. To improve teaching performance
2. To increase the retention of promising beginning teachers during the induction years
3. To promote the personal and professional well-being of beginning teachers by improving teachers' attitudes toward themselves and the profession
4. To satisfy mandated requirements related to induction and certification
5. To transmit the culture of the system to beginning teachers (Huling-Austin 1990, 539)

To accomplish these purposes, induction programs offer resources such as workshops based on teacher-identified needs, observations by and follow-up conferences with individuals not in a supervisory role, support from mentor (or buddy) teachers, and support group meetings for beginning teachers.

School-Based Teacher Education

A new model of teacher preparation that provides students with extensive practical field experiences and often uses practicing teachers as instructors or mentors is known as **school-based teacher education.** In some cases, school-based programs are designed for students who have received a bachelor's degree and then wish to obtain teacher certification; in other cases, programs are designed for adults who are employed by a school district as teacher assistants but who don't have a bachelor's degree. Examples of each type are the Teachers for Chicago Program and the Northern Arizona University (NAU)-Nogales Unified School District program.

To select, train, and retain effective teachers for Chicago's schools, a group of schools, the Chicago Teachers Union, deans of education at area universities, and the Golden Apple Foundation for Excellence in Teaching created the Teachers for Chicago Program. Candidates, selected through a rigorous interview process, enroll in a graduate education program at one of nine area colleges and universities. After a summer of coursework, they begin a two-year paid internship under the guidance of a mentor teacher. Interns fill vacant teacher positions in the schools and are responsible for the academic progress of their students. On completion of the program, interns have earned a master's degree and have met state certification requirements.

The NAU-Nogales Unified School District program prepares special education teachers to work in rural schools. Students in the program are employed as teacher assistants or serve as volunteer interns. The nontraditional program integrates individual courses into a fifteen-hour block of coursework per semester and includes a supervised internship in an inclusive elementary classroom or a special education setting. Courses are taught by NAU faculty at a Nogales school and are enriched by resource specialists and guest speakers from area schools (Ver Velde et al. 1999).

Substitute Teaching

On completion of a teacher education program and prior to securing a full-time teaching assignment, many students choose to gain additional practical experience in classrooms by **substitute teaching.** Others, unable to locate full-time positions, decide to substitute, knowing that many districts prefer to hire from their pool of substitutes when full-time positions become available. Substitute teachers replace regular teachers who are absent due to illness, family responsibilities, personal reasons, or professional workshops and conferences. Each day, approximately 270,000 substitutes are employed in schools across the United States, and one full year of a student's K–12 education is taught by substitute teachers (Substitute Teaching Institute 2002).

Qualifications for substitutes vary from state to state and district to district. An area with a critical need for subs will often relax its requirements to provide classroom coverage. In many districts, it is possible to substitute teach without regular certification. Some districts have less stringent qualifications for short-term, day-to-day substitutes and more stringent ones for long-term, full-time ones. In many districts, the application process for substitutes is the same as that for full-time applicants; in others, the process may be somewhat briefer. Often, substitutes are not limited to working in their area of certification; however, schools try to avoid making out-of-field assignments. If you decide to substitute teach, contact the schools in your area to learn about the qualifications and procedures for hiring substitutes.

In spite of the significant role substitutes play in the day-to-day operation of schools, "research tells us that they receive very little support, no specialized training, and are rarely evaluated. . . . In short, the substitute will be expected

Advantages and Disadvantages of Substitute Teaching

Advantages
- Gain experience without all the nightly work and preparation
- Compare and contrast different schools and their environments
- Be better prepared for interviews by meeting administrators and teachers
- Teach and learn a variety of material
- Get to know people—network
- See job postings and hear about possible vacancies
- Gain confidence in your abilities to teach
- Practice classroom management techniques
- Learn about school and district politics—get the "inside scoop"
- Choose which days to work—flexible schedule

Disadvantages
- Pay is not as good as full-time teaching
- No benefits such as medical coverage, retirement plans, or sick days
- Lack of organized representation to improve wages or working conditions
- May receive a cool reception in some schools
- Must adapt quickly to different school philosophies
- Lack of continuity—may be teaching whole language one day; phonetics the next

Figure 2.5 Advantages and disadvantages of substitute teaching
Source: John F. Snyder, "The Alternative of Substitute Teaching." In *1999 Job Search Handbook for Educators.* Evanston, IL: American Association for Employment in Education, p. 38.

to show up to each class on time, maintain order, take roll, carry out the lesson, and leave a note for the regular teacher about the classes and events of the day without support, encouragement, or acknowledgment" (St. Michel 1995, 6–7). While working conditions such as these are certainly challenging, substitute teaching can be a rewarding, professionally fulfilling experience. Figure 2.5 presents several advantages and disadvantages of substitute teaching.

How Can You Develop Your Teaching Portfolio?

Now that you have begun your journey toward becoming a teacher, you should acquire the habit of assessing your growth in knowledge, skills, and attitudes. Toward this end, you may wish to collect the results of your reflections and self-assessment in a **professional portfolio.** A professional portfolio is a collection of work that documents an individual's accomplishments in an area of professional practice. An artist's portfolio, for example, might consist of a résumé, sketches, paintings, slides and photographs of exhibits, critiques of the artist's work, awards, and other documentation of achievement. Recently, new approaches to teacher evaluation have included the professional portfolio. The NBPTS, for example, uses "portfolios [and] other evidence of performance prepared by the candidate" (National Board for Professional Teaching Standards 1994, 55) as one way of assessing whether teachers have met the high standards for board certification. Teacher education programs at several universities now use portfolios as one means of assessing the competencies of candidates for teacher certification. Also, many school districts are beginning to ask applicants to submit portfolios that document their effectiveness as teachers.

Portfolio Contents

What will your portfolio contain? Written materials might include the following: lesson plans and curriculum materials, reflections on your development as a teacher, journal entries, writing assignments made by your instructor, sample tests you have prepared, critiques of textbooks, evaluations of students' work at the level for which you are preparing to teach, sample letters to parents, and a résumé. Nonprint materials might include video- and audiotapes featuring you in simulated teaching and role-playing activities, audiovisual materials (transparencies, charts, or other teaching aids), photographs of bulletin boards, charts depicting room arrangements for cooperative learning or other instructional strategies, sample grade book, certificates of membership in professional organizations, and awards.

Your portfolio should represent your *best work* and give you an opportunity to become an advocate of *who you are* as a teacher. Because a primary purpose of the professional portfolio is to stimulate reflection and dialogue, you may wish to discuss what entries to make in your portfolio with your instructor or other teacher education students. In addition, the following questions from *How to Develop a Professional Portfolio: A Manual for Teachers* (Campbell et al. 2001) can help you select appropriate portfolio contents:

> Would I be proud to have my future employer and peer group see this? Is this an example of what my future professional work might look like? Does this represent what I stand for as a professional educator? If not, what can I revise or rearrange so that it represents my best efforts? (6)

Using a Portfolio

In addition to providing teacher education programs with a way to assess their effectiveness, portfolios can be used by students for a variety of purposes. A portfolio may be used as

1. A way to establish a record of quantitative and qualitative performance and growth over time
2. A tool for reflection and goal setting as well as a way to present evidence of your ability to solve problems and achieve goals
3. A way to synthesize many separate experiences; in other words, a way to get the "big picture"
4. A vehicle for you to use to collaborate with professors and advisors in individualizing instruction
5. A vehicle for demonstrating knowledge and skills gained through out-of-class experiences, such as volunteer experiences
6. A way to share control and responsibility for your own learning
7. An alternative assessment measure within the professional education program
8. A potential preparation for national, regional, and state accreditation
9. An interview tool in the professional hiring process
10. An expanded résumé to be used as an introduction during the student teaching experience

How Can You Benefit from Mentoring Relationships?

When asked "[what] steps might be taken to attract good people into teaching and to encourage good teachers to remain in teaching," 82 percent of respondents to the MetLife Survey of the American Teacher 2001 said "providing mentoring and ongoing support for new teachers" would "help a lot" (Harris Interactive 2001, 125). Like the following first-year suburban high school

What questions might you ask a mentor teacher that might help you develop as a professional?

teacher, the teachers surveyed realized the value of a **mentor:** "I wish I had one [a mentor] here. . . . There are days that go by and I don't think I learn anything about my teaching, and that's too bad. I wish I had someone" (Dollase 1992, 138).

In reflecting on how a mentor contributed to his professional growth, Forrest Parkay defined **mentoring** as

> an intensive, one-to-one form of teaching in which the wise and experienced mentor inducts the aspiring protégé [one who is mentored] into a particular, usually professional, way of life. . . . [T]he protégé learns from the mentor not only the objective, manifest content of professional knowledge and skills but also a subjective, nondiscursive appreciation for *how* and *when* to employ these learnings in the arena of professional practice. In short, the mentor helps the protégé to "learn the ropes," to become socialized into the profession (Parkay 1988, 196).

An urban middle school intern's description of how his mentor helped him develop effective classroom management techniques exemplifies "learning the ropes": " 'You've got to develop your own sense of personal power,' [my mentor] kept saying. 'It's not something I can teach you. I can show you what to do. I can model it. But I don't know, it's just something that's got to come from within you' " (Henry et al. 1995, 114).

Those who have become highly accomplished teachers frequently point out the importance of mentors in their preparation for teaching. A mentor can provide moral support, guidance, and feedback to students at various stages of professional preparation. In addition, a mentor can model for the protégé an analytical approach to solving problems in the classroom. Table 2.1 shows several problem-solving approaches a mentor can demonstrate to a novice teacher.

What Opportunities for Continuing Professional Development Will You Have?

Professional development is a life-long process; any teacher, at any stage of development, has room for improvement. Indeed, "the continual deepening of knowl-

Table 2.1 Problem-solving approaches used by a mentor

Prescription giving	Remedy given by the mentor with a rationale, examples, alternatives, parameters of use, or rules
Personal storytelling	The mentor gives an example of his or her own classroom experiences to set a context for the prescription
Rehearsal	Verbal practice or rehearsal by the mentor and novice teacher of a strategy to be implemented in the classroom the next day, together with problem anticipation and troubleshooting
Role-playing	Playing and reversal of roles by the mentor and novice teacher reflecting problem situations or concerns of the novice teacher; both teacher and student roles are played
Modeling	Verbalization by the mentor of a teaching strategy or interaction technique with demonstration
Oral blueprinting	Oral planning by the novice teacher with critique and refinement by the mentor
Replay	Reconstruction of the day's events by the novice teacher with probing and clarifying questions and feedback from the mentor

Source: J. A. Ponticel and S. J. Zepeda, "Making Sense of Teaching and Learning: A Case Study of Mentor and Beginning Teacher Problem Solving," in D. J. McIntyre and D. M. Byrd (eds.), *Preparing Tomorrow's Teachers: The Field Experience: Teacher Education Yearbook IV.* Thousand Oaks, CA: Corwin Press, p. 127. Copyright © 1996 by Corwin Press. Reprinted by permission of Corwin Press, Inc.

edge and skills is an integral part of any profession [and] teaching is no exception" (Garet et al. 2001, 916). To meet the need for professional development, many school systems and universities have programs in place for the continuing professional development of teachers.

Self-Assessment for Professional Growth

Self-assessment is a necessary first step in pursuing opportunities for professional growth. A teacher comments on the importance of self-assessment after being certified by the NBPTS: "Serious reflection and self-examination [were necessary] as I gauge[d] my skills and knowledge against objective, peer-developed, national standards in specific teaching areas" (National Board for Professional Teaching Standards 1995, 13).

Several questions can help you make appropriate choices as a teacher: In which areas am I already competent? In which areas do I need further development? How will I acquire the knowledge and skills I need? How will I apply new knowledge and practice new skills? Answers to such questions will lead you to a variety of sources for professional growth: teacher workshops, teacher centers, professional development schools, the opportunity to supervise and mentor student teachers, and graduate programs. Figure 2.6 illustrates the relationship of these professional development experiences to your teacher education program.

Teacher Workshops

The quality of **in-service workshops** is uneven, varying with the size of school district budgets and the imagination and knowledge of the administrators and teachers who arrange them. It is significant that the most effective in-service pro-

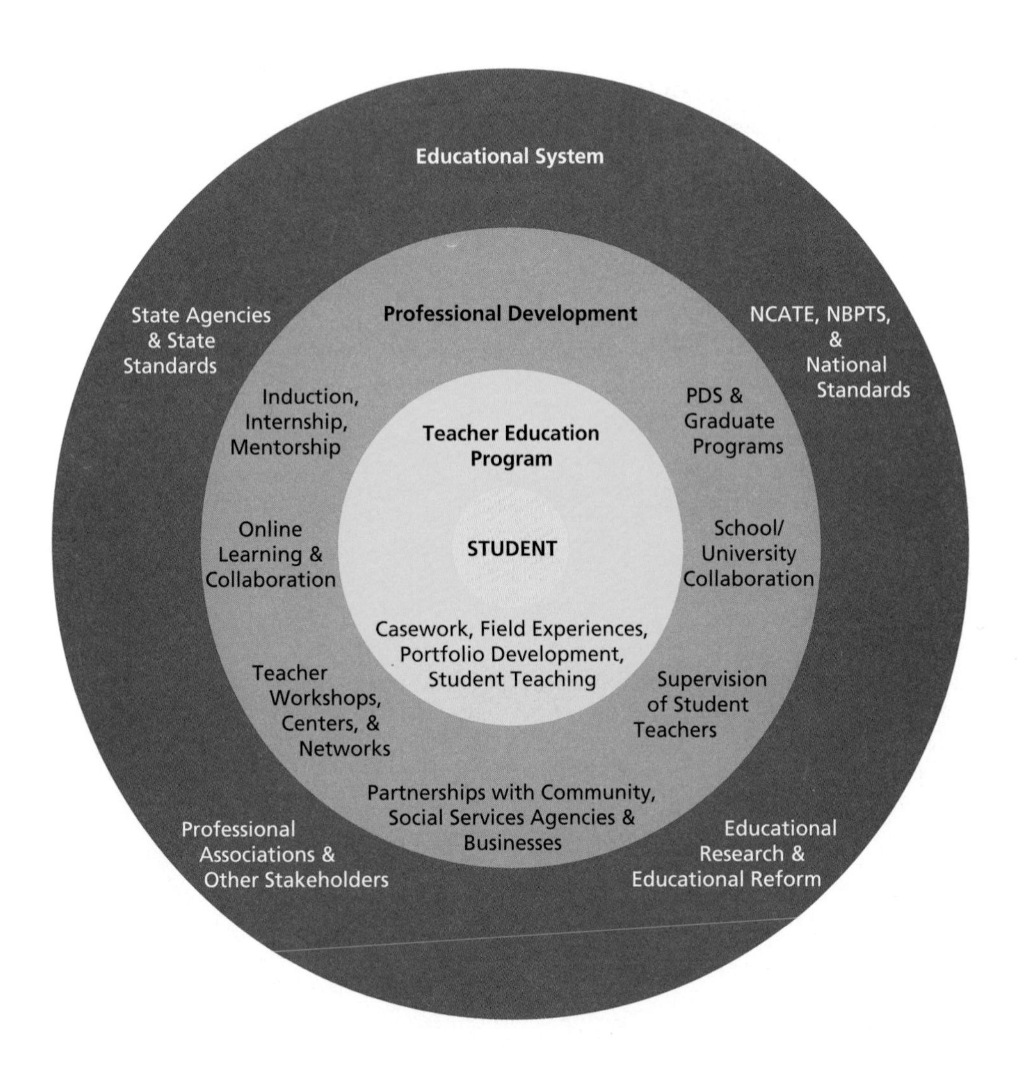

Figure 2.6 Professional development: from teacher education student to practitioner

grams tend to be the ones that teachers request—and often design and conduct. In addition, a national study of 1,027 mathematics and science teachers found that professional development activities such as workshops are most effective if they "(a) focus on content knowledge, (b) [provide] opportunities for active learning, and (c) [have] coherence with other learning activities" (Garet et al. 2001, 916).

Some workshops focus on topics that all teachers (regardless of subject or level) can benefit from: classroom management, writing-across-the-curriculum, multicultural education, and strategies for teaching students with learning disabilities in the general education classroom, for example. Other workshops have a sharper focus and are intended for teachers of a subject at a certain level—for example, whole-language techniques for middle school students, discovery learning for high school science students, and student-centered approaches to teaching literature in the high school classroom.

Teacher Centers

Teacher centers provide opportunities for teachers "to take the lead in the decision making and implementation of staff development programs based on the needs of teachers. [They] provide the structure for teachers to take charge of their own professional growth" (Teacher Centers of New York State 1999). In contrast to in-service programs, these are more clearly initiated and directed by

Meeting the Standard

Researches Effectiveness of Own Teaching

The teacher is committed to continuous learning and engages in professional discourse about subject matter knowledge and children's learning of the discipline (INTASC Disposition, Principle #1).

NCATE *Candidates preparing to work in schools as teachers or other professional school personnel know and demonstrate the content, pedagogical, and professional knowledge, skills, and dispositions necessary to help all students learn (NCATE, Standard 1: Candidate Knowledge, Skills and Dispositions).*

Teachers think systematically about their practice and learn from experience (NBPTS, Proposition 4).

Teacher seeks out opportunities for professional development and makes a systematic attempt to conduct action research in his/[her] classroom (PRAXIS III Framework–"distinguished" level of performance).*

Even the most experienced and effective teachers realize that teaching is complex and can never be mastered fully. This is why veterans of twenty or thirty years still find teaching fascinating. Teachers who meet the standards articulated above continuously evaluate their own teaching, sometimes informally in the moments immediately following a lesson, sometimes in the evenings through a reflective journal, and at other times through an intentional, focused process known as action research. They assess what is working and what needs to work better in their teaching and designing of learning experiences. They stretch their knowledge about teaching through studying in a graduate program, reading professional journals, talking with experienced colleagues, and participating in professional development opportunities. They also continually update their content knowledge and enliven it by gathering current, student-relevant illustrations from the world outside their classrooms–in newspapers, films, music, fiction, sports events, and personal experiences. Test yourself in terms of this standard by completing one of the following:

1. Conduct an action research exercise in a simulation or actual teaching situation. Begin by selecting a teaching or learning challenge that concerns you (for instance, teaching students how to add fractions with 2, 4, and 8 as denominators). Propose two ways to teach the concept. You might use a demonstration approach to teach the concept for one strategy and use an inductive, hands-on approach to teach for the second strategy. In both cases, use mock and real Hershey Bars, the former for the teaching or learning activity, the latter for rewards when the concept is mastered.
2. Evaluate the results of the above action research exercise or a similar comparative teaching or learning exercise. Reflect on what you thought worked well and on which parts of the lesson seemed to falter, and consider how you think students responded to it. Then examine the students' work you assigned to access how well they understood the concept. Finally, provide an evaluation form for the students to complete anonymously, asking questions regarding their response to the lesson. Explain the benefits to them of completing the form thoughtfully. Consider what you learned from the three sources of information–your personal reflection, student performance, and student feedback. Decide on the approach you intend to use the next time you work on the same concept.

Teachers increase their effectiveness by actively evaluating their instruction and their students' responses to it. Formal action research endeavors and informal, ongoing reflective analyses are promising ways teachers use to evaluate teaching efforts and learning designs.

teachers. Some centers cooperate with a local or neighboring college of education and include members of the faculty on their planning committees.

Many teachers find teacher centers stimulating because they offer opportunities for collegial interaction in a quiet, professionally oriented setting. The busy, hectic pace of life in many schools, teachers often find, provides little time for professional dialogue with peers. Furthermore, in the teacher center, teachers are often more willing to discuss openly areas of weakness in their performance. As one teacher put it:

> At the teacher center I can ask for help. I won't be judged. The teachers who have helped me the most have had the same problems. I respect them, and I'm willing to learn from them. They have credibility with me.

Professional Development Schools

Professional development schools (PDSs) have emerged recently as a way to link school restructuring and the reform of teacher education in the United States. These school–university partnerships offer teachers the following opportunities:

- Fine learning programs for diverse students
- Practical, thought-provoking preparation for novice teachers
- New understanding and professional responsibilities for experienced educators
- Research projects that add to all educators' knowledge about how to make schools more productive (Holmes Group n.d., 1).

For example, a teacher at a PDS might team with a teacher education professor and teach a university-level course, participate in a collaborative research project, offer a professional development seminar for other teachers, arrange for the teacher educator to demonstrate instructional strategies in his or her classroom, or jointly develop relevant field experiences for prospective teachers.

Supervision and Mentoring of Student Teachers

After several years in the classroom, teachers may be ready to stretch themselves further by supervising student teachers. Some of the less obvious benefits of doing so are that teachers must rethink what they are doing so that they can explain and sometimes justify their behaviors to someone else, learning about themselves in the process. Furthermore, because they become a model for their student teachers, they continually strive to offer the best example. In exchange, they gain an assistant in the classroom—another pair of eyes, an aid with record keeping—and more than occasionally, fresh ideas and a spirit of enthusiasm.

Graduate Study

A more traditional form of professional development is to do graduate study. With the recent reforms, most states now require teachers to take some graduate courses to keep their certifications and knowledge up to date. Some teachers take only courses that are of immediate use to them; others use their graduate study to prepare for new teaching or administrative positions; and still others pursue doctoral work to teach prospective teachers or others in their discipline at the college level.

Study on the Internet

If you have access to the Internet, you can locate many possibilities for continuing professional development. Teachers use the Internet to exchange ideas and experiences and to acquire additional expertise in teaching or to share their expertise with others. See the Appendix "Professional Development Opportunities on the Internet," on this book's website. In addition, at the website for *Becoming a Teacher,* you will find a periodically updated list of professional development opportunities available for teachers on the Web. If you decide to visit any of these sites, remember that websites are frequently changed or withdrawn from the Internet. The web addresses given throughout this book were active at the time of printing. Also, because it is estimated that 10,000 websites are added each day, periodically you should use key words related to education and your favorite search engine to gather the latest information and resources.

Summary

What Essential Knowledge Do You Need to Teach?

- Professional teachers reflect on their classroom experiences.
- Teachers need three kinds of knowledge: knowledge of self and students, knowledge of subject, and knowledge of educational theory and research.
- Teachers' self-knowledge influences their ability to understand students.
- The ambiguities of teaching can cause teachers to experience anxiety.
- Elementary teachers can experience loneliness because they are isolated from adults; secondary teachers can experience loneliness because of departmentalization.
- Teachers must know their students' aptitudes, talents, learning styles, stage of development, and readiness to learn new material.
- Teachers must understand their subjects deeply so they can modify instructional strategies based on students' perception of content.
- Knowledge of educational theory enables professional teachers to know why certain strategies work.
- Educational research provides teachers with rules of thumb for practice.

What Are Five Ways of Viewing the Teacher Knowledge Base?

- There is no universally accepted definition of "good" teaching.
- Many people believe that a knowledge base for teaching should consist not only of what educational researchers have learned about teaching but also what teachers themselves "know" about teaching—often called *teachers' craft knowledge* or *practitioner knowledge.*
- The teacher knowledge base (essential knowledge and abilities) can place primary emphasis on personal development, research-based competencies, state standards, job analyses, or the views of professional organizations.
- Many states have developed standards for outcome-based or performance-based teacher education. Outcomes are based on what beginning teachers do in real classrooms.
- The job-analysis view of teaching is based on identifying job dimensions—the knowledge, skills, and attitudes teachers need.
- The National Board for Professional Teaching Standards (NBPTS) has developed standards for voluntary national certification.
- Effective teachers are guided by reflection and a problem-solving orientation.

How Do Reforms in Teacher Education Affect You?

- As part of the educational reform movement, the Holmes Group recommends that teachers obtain a bachelor's degree in an academic field and a master's degree in education.
- The Holmes Group recommends establishing professional development schools linked to colleges of education.
- In *Teachers for Our Nation's Schools,* John Goodlad recommends the creation of Centers of Pedagogy.
- State-level professional standards boards set criteria for the certification and professional development of education personnel in some states; in others, state standards boards are limited to advising educational policymakers.

What Can You Learn from Observing in Classrooms?

- The opportunity to observe in classrooms helps some students make a final decision about becoming a teacher.
- Many teacher education programs are providing students with more and earlier opportunities to observe in classrooms.
- Distance-learning classrooms, using compressed video, link teacher education programs to schools off campus.
- Observations can focus on a particular aspect of classroom life or be guided by a set of questions related to a specific area, such as how the teacher motivates students.
- Observation instruments range from informal, qualitative descriptions to formal, quantitative checklists.

How Can You Gain Practical Experience for Becoming a Teacher?

- Teacher education students can gain practical experience through focused classroom observations, microteaching, teaching simulations, analyses of video cases, field-based practica and clinical experiences, and classroom aide programs.
- In microteaching, students practice specific skills by teaching brief lessons that are later analyzed.
- Computer simulations and virtual reality—as well as written, videotaped, and audiotaped cases—are being used for teaching simulations.
- Journal writing and reflective teaching logs increase the benefits of the student teaching experience.

- To prepare to teach students from diverse backgrounds, teacher education students should actively seek field experiences in multicultural settings.
- Induction programs provide assistance to beginning teachers. Internship programs and school-based teacher education programs provide extensive practical experiences.
- Substitute teaching provides additional practical experience after completing a teacher education program.

How Can You Develop Your Teaching Portfolio?

- A portfolio documents professional growth and development over time.
- A portfolio can be organized around specific outcomes or standards.
- Portfolio contents should represent one's best work.
- Professional portfolios can be used in teacher evaluation, self-evaluation, and hiring.

How Can You Benefit from Mentoring Relationships?

- Ask for advice from teachers you admire.
- Mentoring can be a source of professional growth for experienced teachers.
- Mentoring enables the protégé to "learn the ropes."

What Opportunities for Continuing Professional Development Will You Have?

- Self-assessment is necessary to select appropriate professional development experiences.
- Opportunities for professional development include teacher workshops, teacher centers, professional development schools, supervision and mentoring of student teachers, graduate study, and the Internet.

Key Terms and Concepts

Applications and Activities

Teacher's Journal

1. What does self-knowledge mean to you? Why is self-knowledge important in teaching? What steps can you take to achieve greater self-knowledge?
2. As a teacher, you will encounter challenges related to student variability (differences in developmental needs, interests, abilities, and disabilities) and student diversity (differences in gender, race, ethnicity, culture, and socioeconomic status). To begin thinking about how you will acquire and use knowledge about your students, write a brief profile of yourself as a student in elementary school, in middle school or junior high school, and in high school.
3. Reflect on your education as a teacher. What are your primary concerns about the preparation you are receiving? What experiences do you think will be most helpful to you as you move toward becoming a teacher? What qualities would you look for in a mentor?
4. On the basis of your field experiences to date and the information in Chapters 1 and 2, ask yourself these questions and respond in your journal: Do I have the aptitude to be-

come a good teacher? Am I willing to acquire the essential knowledge and skills teachers need? Do I really want to become a teacher?

Teacher's Database

1. Find out more about Tech Corps, a national network of volunteers that uses technology to enhance teaching and learning. Each of these leaders share his or her knowledge and expertise by mentoring five colleagues.

2. Instead of using "outside experts" to deliver professional development workshops to teachers, some states are implementing teacher networks in which teachers address problems of mutual concern. For example, to help teachers implement portfolio assessments of fourth- and eighth-grade student learning in mathematics and eighth-grade writing, Vermont's Department of Education has developed a teacher network. Teacher leaders from the state's educational regions meet periodically with state department personnel to plan three to four teacher network meetings each year. To learn more about the Vermont network, visit the Vermont Department of Education website at http://www.state.vt.us/educ

3. Investigate the California State Telemation Program, a statewide network of teachers who mentor one another. The program focuses on integrating online resources into site-level planning, curriculum development, learning strategies, and student-centered activities.

Observations and Interviews

1. Think about areas for focused observations of teaching, such as classroom management, student involvement, questioning techniques, evaluation, or teacher–student rapport. For one or more areas, brainstorm and order in logical sequence a set of questions you could use to guide your next observations. Include a list of questions to ask the teacher whom you will observe.

2. As a collaborative project with classmates, interview students who have completed student teaching at your college or university. What tips do they have for developing a positive relationship with a cooperating teacher? For establishing rapport with students? For developing confidence in presenting lessons?

3. Arrange to interview a school administrator about the knowledge, skills, and aptitude he or she thinks teachers must have. To help you plan for the interview, ask your instructor for handout master M2.2, "Interviewing School Administrators about Teachers' Knowledge and Skills." Which of the knowledge and skills discussed in this chapter does the administrator mention? Does he or she mention knowledge and skills not discussed in this chapter?

4. Observe a teacher in the classroom for the purpose of identifying examples that help to answer the following questions. How does the teacher demonstrate or use knowledge of self and students? Knowledge of subject matter? Knowledge of educational theory and research?

5. Observe a classroom in which there is likely to be some teacher–student interaction (for example, questions and answers, discussion, or oral review and feedback). On the basis of the data you collect, what conclusions can you draw about life in this classroom? To help record your observations, ask your instructor for handout master M2.1, "Recording Classroom Interactions."

Professional Portfolio

1. Create a plan for developing your portfolio. What specific outcomes or standards will you use to organize your portfolio entries? What artifacts will you use to demonstrate your professional growth and development?

2. Evaluate the products of your studies in education so far in your preparation for becoming a teacher. Identify a few examples of your best work to include in your portfolio. Also, evaluate your Teacher's Journal, Teacher's Database, and Observations and Interviews for possible inclusions in your portfolio.

Video**Workshop Extra!**

If the Video Workshop package was included with your textbook, go to Chapter 2 of the Companion Website (http://www.ablongman.com/parkay6e) and click on the Video Workshop button. Follow the instructions for viewing videoclip 1 and completing this exercise. Consider this information along with what you've read in Chapter 2 while answering the following questions.

1. Reforms in teacher education are necessary to ensure optimal training for classroom teachers. What can you infer about society's expectations of teachers from such reforms (e.g., mandatory teacher exams)? Write a brief analysis of how society's expectations are manifest in the classroom context.

2. Explain the relationship between a teacher's self-knowledge and knowledge of students. How does this knowledge affect everyday practice?

Appendix 2.1

FLORIDA PERFORMANCE MEASUREMENT SYSTEM SCREENING/SUMMATIVE OBSERVATION INSTRUMENT

FRAME FACTOR INFORMATION (PLEASE PRINT)

Teacher's Name

______________ (Last) ______________ (First) ______________ (Middle)

SS# _ _ _ - _ _ - _ _ _ _

Institution of Graduation ________ Inst. # ________

Graduated from a College of Education ☐1. Yes ☐2. No

Number of Complete Years of Teaching Experience ______

District Name ______________ Number ______

School Name ______________ Number ______

Observer's Name

______________ (Last) ______________ (First) ______________ (Middle) ☐

SS# _ _ _ - _ _ - _ _ _ _

Position ☐1. Principal ☐2. Ass't Principal ☐3. Teacher ☐4. Other

Class _____ Grade Level (Specify one level only–For Adult Ed. mark level 13 For Kindergarten or Preschool mark Level 00.)

Subject Area Observed

- ☐1. Language Arts
- ☐2. Foreign Language
- ☐3. Social Sciences
- ☐4. Mathematics
- ☐5. Science
- ☐6. Physical Education, ROTC
- ☐7. Business Education, DCT, CBE
- ☐8. Industrial Arts/Education
- ☐ 9. Home Economics
- ☐10. Other Vocational Ed.
- ☐11. Arts
- ☐12. Music
- ☐13. Exceptional Stud. Ed.
- ☐14. Other (Specify) ______________

Type of Classroom/Facility in Which the Observation Occurred

- ☐ 1. Regular Classroom—Self-contained, Open, Pod
- ☐ 2. Laboratory or Shop
- ☐ 3. Field, Court, Gymnasium
- ☐ 4. Media Room or Library

Total Number of Students in Class ______

Observation Information Date __/__/__

Type of Observation ☐ 1. Prof. Orien. ☐ 2. Dis. Assess ☐ 3. Other (Specify) ______________

Screening Obs. ☐ 1. ☐ 2. ☐ 3. ☐ 4.

Summative Obs. ☐ 1. ☐ 2. ☐ 3. ☐ 4.

Time Observation Begins _ _:_ _ Observation Ends _ _:_ _

Test Begins _ _:_ _ Test Ends_ _:_ _

Methods Used in the Observed Lesson

- ☐ 1. Lecture
- ☐ 2. Interactive/Discussion
- ☐ 3. Independent Study/Lab or Shop Work

Teacher's Signature ______________

Observer's Signature ______________

Number of Students Not Engaged

1☐ 2☐ 3☐ 4☐

DOMAIN	EFFECTIVE INDICATORS		TOT. FREQ.	FREQUENCY	FREQUENCY	TOT. FREQ.	INEFFECTIVE INDICATORS
3.0 Instructional Organizatrion and Development	1. Begins instruction promptly						1. Delays
	2. Handles materials in an orderly manner						2. Does not organize materials systematically
	3. Orients students to classwork/maintains academic focus						3. Allows talk/activity unrelated to subject
	4. Conducts beginning/ending review						4.
	5. Questions: academic comprehension/ lesson development	a. single factual (Domain 5.0)					5a. Allows unison response
		b. requires analysis/reasons					5b. Poses multiple questions asked as one
							5c. Poses nonacademic questions/nonacademic procedural questions
	6. Recognizes response/amplifies/gives correct feedback						6. Ignores student or response/expresses sarcasm, disgust, harshness
	7. Gives specific academic praise						7. Uses general, nonspecific praise
	8. Provides practice						8. Extends discourse, changes topic with no practice
	9. Gives directions/assigns/checks comprehension of homework, seatwork assignments/gives feedback						9. Gives inadequate directions on homework/no feedback
	10. Circulates and assists students						10. Remains at desk/circulates inadequately
4.0 Presentation of Subject Matter	11. Treats concepts—definition/attributes/examples/ nonexamples						11. Gives definition or example only
	12. Discusses cause-effect/uses linking words/applies law or principle						12. Discusses either cause or effect only/uses no linking word(s)
	13. States and applies academic rule						13. Does not state or does not apply academic rule
	14. Develops criteria and evidence for value judgment						14. States value judgment with no criteria or evidence
5.0 Communication: Verbal and Nonverbal	15. Emphasises important points						15.
	16. Expresses enthusiasm verbally/challenges students						16.
	17.						17. Uses vague/scrambled discourse
	18.						18. Uses loud, grating, high pitched, monotone, or inaudible talk
	19. Uses body behavior that shows interest—smiles, gestures						19. Frowns, deadpan or lethargic
2.0 Management of Student Conduct	20. Stops misconduct						20. Delays desist/doesn't stop misconduct/desists punitively
	21. Maintains instructional momentum						21. Loses momentum—fragments nonacademic directions, over dwells

Observer's Notes: ______________

Appendix 2.2

MODELS OF PROFESSIONAL STANDARDS: KENTUCKY'S NEW TEACHER STANDARDS

Preamble to the New Teacher Standards

The New Teacher Standards describe what first-year teachers should know and be able to do in authentic teaching situations and the academic content, teaching behaviors, and instructional processes that are necessary to promote effective student learning. They imply more than the mere demonstration of teaching competencies. They imply a current and sufficient academic content understanding that promotes consistent quality performance on teaching tasks. Authentic teaching tasks provide opportunities and contexts for performances by beginning teachers. In Kentucky, all teaching and learning tasks address Kentucky's academic expectations. These identify what students need to be successful in the world of the future. Thus, teachers design and implement instruction and assess learning that develops students' abilities to:

1. **Use basic communication and mathematics skills** in finding, organizing, expressing, and responding to information and ideas.
2. **Apply core concepts and principles** from science, arts and humanities, mathematics, practical living studies, social studies, and vocational studies.
3. **Become a self-sufficient individual** who demonstrates high self-esteem, a healthy lifestyle, flexibility, creativity, self-control, and independent learning.
4. **Become a responsible group member** who demonstrates consistent, responsive, and caring behavior; interpersonal skills; respect for the rights and responsibilities of others; world views; and an open mind to other perspectives.
5. **Think and solve problems** including the ability to think critically and creatively, develop ideas and concepts, and make rational decisions.
6. **Connect and integrate experiences and new knowledge** throughout the curriculum, question and interpret ideas from diverse perspectives, and apply concepts to real-life situations.

New Teacher Standards

I. **Designs/Plans Instruction** The teacher designs/plans instruction and learning climates that develop students' abilities to use communication skills, apply core concepts, become self-sufficient individuals, become responsible team members, think and solve problems, and integrate knowledge.

II. **Creates/Maintains Learning Climates** The teacher creates learning climates that support the development of students' abilities to use communication skills, apply core concepts, become self-sufficient individuals, become responsible team members, think and solve problems, and integrate knowledge.

III. **Implements/Manages Instruction** The teacher introduces/implements/manages instruction that develops students' abilities to use communication skills, apply core concepts, become self-sufficient individuals, become responsible team members, think and solve problems, and integrate knowledge.

IV. **Assesses and Communicates Learning Results** The teacher assesses learning and communicates results to students and others with respect to student abilities to use communication skills, apply core concepts, become self-sufficient individuals, become responsible team members, think and solve problems, and integrate knowledge.

V. **Reflects/Evaluates Teaching/Learning** The teacher reflects on and evaluates specific teaching/learning situations and/or programs.

VI. **Collaborates with Colleagues/Parents/Others** The teacher collaborates with colleagues, parents, and other agencies to design, implement, and support learning programs that develop students' abilities to use communication skills, apply core concepts, become self-sufficient individuals, become responsible team members, think and solve problems, and integrate knowledge.

VII. **Engages in Professional Development** The teacher evaluates his/her overall performance with respect to modeling and teaching Kentucky's Learning Goals and implements a professional development program that enhances his/her own performance.

VIII. **Knowledge of Content** The teacher demonstrates a current and sufficient academic knowledge of certified content areas to develop student knowledge and performance in those areas.

IX. **Demonstrates Implementation of Technology** The teacher uses technology to support instruction; access and manipulate data; enhance professional growth and productivity; communicate and collaborate with colleagues, parents, and the community; and conduct research.

Source: Kentucky Education Professional Standards Board, Kentucky's New Teacher Standards.

Appendix 2.3

SAMPLE NBPTS PORTFOLIO ENTRIES

Early Childhood Generalist Portfolio, for Teachers of Students Ages 3–8

The National Board for Professional Teaching Standards has suggested portfolio entries to give candidates (or potential candidates) a clear picture of the kinds of entries to include in a portfolio. The entries below are for the Early Childhood Generalist certificate for the 2002–2003 cycle.

Entries Based on Student Work Samples

Entry 1: Examining Children's Literacy Development In this entry, you select two children to feature as examples of your work with children in fostering literacy development. Your approach to assessment of the children's abilities and needs, response to that assessment in the design and implementation of instruction, and selected work samples demonstrating the children's literacy development are the focus of this entry.

Entries Based on Videotape

Entry 2: Building a Classroom Community In this entry, you submit a videotape and instructional materials that demonstrate your knowledge and ability to deepen students' knowledge of a social studies topic/concept/theme, your ability to integrate the arts, and your interaction with children during group discussion/activities that illustrates your approach to creating a climate in the classroom that promotes children's development of social and interpersonal skills.

Entry 3: Integrating Mathematics and Science In this entry, you submit a videotape and instructional materials of an integrative learning experience designed to deepen children's understanding of mathematics and science concepts through a "Big Idea" in science and develop skills in using mathematical and scientific ways of observing, thinking, and communicating.

Entries Based onDocumented Accomplishments

Entry 4: Documented Accomplishments: Contributions to Student Learning In this entry, you illustrate your partnerships with students' families and community, and your development as a learner and collaborator with other profession-als by submitting descriptions and documentation of your activities and accomplishments in those areas.

Source: National Board for Professional Teaching Standards, *Early Childhood Generalist Portfolio, for Teachers of Students Ages 3–8*. Arlington, VA: National Board for Professional Teaching Standards, 2002, pp. 5–7.

Reflections on Education

The Rewards and Challenges of Those First Years of Teaching

by Jan Richards

The rewards of teaching are unique and immeasurable. A teacher's gratification knowing that he or she has made a difference in a child's life, rekindling hope and awakening curiosity about the world, cannot be captured in words. A teacher contributes to a child's character every day, building confidence and enhancing self-esteem. Great teaching is an act of lighting a candle in the darkness, of modeling tolerance and compassion, and of offering hope for the future. Such are the rewards mentioned most by successful teachers. But the increasing challenges of teaching are also a very real part of the package—challenges that have contributed to the problem of teacher attrition. Studies have shown that teachers are most at risk for leaving the profession in their first five years (Johnson et al. 2001).

Teacher shortages, attrition, and retention are growing problems in education today. Education researchers have warned of a severe teacher shortage in the next ten years, largely due to the fact that most teachers are in the forty-five to fifty-five age groups and may plan to retire during this period. At the same time, the nation's school enrollment is projected to increase by one million children. This means that approximately 50,000 additional teachers will be needed to fill the gap (U.S. Department of Education 1999, ¶ 8).

In a day when retaining enough teachers to do the job of educating our nation's young has become a persistent problem and the stress of teaching has markedly increased, many teachers are leaving the profession. The ills of society are entering the classroom. Children often come to school unprepared (academically and emotionally), and teachers sometimes sense that their roles have shifted to that of social workers and counselors as well as instructors. According to Richard Ingersoll (2001, 14), many new teachers who enter the classroom drop out within the first five years (up to 50 percent in some school districts)—a far greater rate than that of other occupations. The average employee turnover in the United States is 11 percent while teacher turnover is closer to 14 percent. Teacher retention is an ongoing problem. Teachers report they are leaving the profession because of a lack of money, administrative support, and respect, as well as a lack of discipline support in school.

But with or without ideal working conditions, many teachers choose to stay. Studies of experienced, resilient teachers suggest what attitudes new teachers might learn and implement. Beverly H. Stanford (2001), Gerard J. Brunetti (2001), and Gloria Ladson-Billings (1994) interviewed resilient teachers who stayed for many years in schools where they were needed most—among children who were often poor, educationally disadvantaged, and minority. Reported reasons for staying in such challenging school environments were the teachers' commitment to children and the satisfaction they found knowing they had made a great difference in these children's lives. They cared deeply about their students.

Even for a new teacher determined to make a difference and to successfully persevere through the pressures of those first five years, learning to handle the challenges of teaching is not easy. Just taking the required education courses and participating in discussions on classroom management or the effects of poverty on children's academic performance is little preparation for the sudden realities new teachers encounter. Not surprisingly, beginning teachers often report feeling anxious and inadequate for the task.

Adopting three attitudes modeled by successful, experienced teachers may help a beginning teacher stay focused on the big picture rather than becoming sidetracked by trivial irritations or minor setbacks. *First, successful teachers allow for mistakes and view them as a part of their professional growth.* All teachers have days they do not feel well, when a lesson falls flat, or when they are short-tempered because the class behavior is less than ideal. Teachers also enjoy those shining moments when a grateful student smiles in appreciation because a new concept suddenly becomes clear. Reflecting on both days of disaster and moments of success is a practice that strengthens and builds confidence. Persevering teachers reflect continuously on why a discipline plan is not working or on the best way to arrange the classroom, walk to the library, or implement cooperative learning groups. They often keep a journal as a record of their insights.

Second, persevering teachers look for sources of help, opportunities for in-services or workshops that will strengthen their skills and increase their knowledge of teaching strategies. Other sources of help take the form of experienced teachers willing to share their expertise on classroom management options or success dealing with students or parents. Often a principal will arrange a time new teachers can observe talented teachers in action. Another wonderful source of information and help is the Internet. The websites listed at the end of the feature are just a few of the many that offer lesson plans, ideas for math or science projects, or ways to handle behavior problems.

Third, persevering teachers create a support system, knowing they need the support of others to help them succeed. Many new teachers have reported that they formed their own support group, sharing their successes and failures with other new struggling teachers who understand their frustrations firsthand. The group may eat lunch together or plan on a weekly get-together after school. Most schools have some form of mentoring program as added support as well. New teachers who do not have the luxury of a mentor in their school may find an experienced teacher close by who is willing to offer help when needed. It is important that beginning teachers seek professional models who demonstrate positive attitudes and obviously love their work.

Maintaining emotional well-being is critical because as a teacher, your moods, attitudes, humor, and morale spill over to the students in your care. Students are watching, and they depend on and often reflect the attitudes their teachers project. No job requires more flexibility, patience, tolerance, and desire to make a difference in the lives of so many as that of a teacher. And no job offers the sense of deep satisfaction and reward. When asked about how satisfied she was with the experience of being in the classroom, one second-year teacher named Abby responded:

> I love working with my kids and I'm really satisfied when I look at them at the beginning of the year, and the wonderful individuals that they've become at the end of the year. That's my satisfaction—just being in that classroom with those kids because I know nothing else matters but what I do in there (Richard 2002).

Jan Richards is currently an Assistant Professor at National University in San Diego, CA after twenty years of teaching in public schools, grades 1–8. Her published writings and reviews about teaching have appeared in Principal, Educational Horizons, KDPi Record, New Teacher Advocate, Educational Forum, and Childhood Education.

References

Brunetti, G. J. (2001). Why do they teach?: A study of job satisfaction among long-term high school teachers. *Teacher Education Quarterly, 28*(3), 49–74.

Ingersoll, R. M. (2001). Teacher turnover, teacher shortages, and the organization of schools. Supported under the Educational Research and Development Centers Program, U.S. Department of Education. Document R-01-1. Retrieved November 17, 2001, from http://tcrecord.org/Collection.asp?CollectionsID=73

Johnson, S. M., Birkeland, S., Kardos, S. M., Kauffman, D., Liu, E., & Peske, H. G. The Project on the Next Generation of Teachers at the Harvard Graduate School of Education. (September/October 2001). Retaining the next generation of teachers: The importance of school-based support. *Harvard Education Letter* Retrieved October 28, 2001, from http://www.edletter.org/current/support.shtml

Ladson-Billings, G. (1994). *The dreamkeepers: Successful teachers of African American children.* San Francisco, CA: Jossey-Bass.

Richards, J. S. (2002). Principal behaviors that encourage teachers to stay in the profession: Perceptions of K–8 teachers in their second to fifth year of teaching. Interview of Abby from a dissertation in progress.

Stanford, B. H. (2001). Reflections of resilient, persevering urban teachers. *Teacher Education Quarterly, 28*(3), 75–87.

U.S. Department of Education. (1999). No end in sight: A back to school special report on the baby boom echo. Retrieved November 17, 2001 from http://www.ed.gov/pubs/bbecho99

Internet Resources

Carol Hurst's Children's Literature Site
(http://www.carolhurst.com/)

This site offers reviews of children's books and ideas for using them in the classroom. Recommended books and activities are also integrated into other subjects such as math and history for creating thematic units. "Themes and Other Subjects" will connect you to literature, art, and history as they relate to your subject as well as to dozens of other valuable sites that can enhance the lesson. This is the site to visit when you are putting together a thematic unit.

Enchanted Learning (Grades K–6)
(http://www.enchantedlearning.com)

This wonderful site for students provides information on a variety of subjects and includes a rich collection of pictures and information on the rain forest, dinosaurs, and many other topics. Your students will enjoy exploring their own interests in the computer lab or at a learning center, or they can use the site as a resource for writing research reports.

Kathy Shrock's Guide for Educators
(http://school.discovery.com/schrockguide/)

Sponsored by the Discovery Channel, this is one of the best online sites providing teachers with a variety of resources, practical tools, and materials. Many subjects are covered: history and social studies, mathematics, language arts, science, and special education resources, to name just a few. There is also a section on lesson plans for any grade level. Just go to the lesson plan section (http://school.discovery.com/lessonplans/), copy a plan that fits your needs, then modify it for your particular students. If you are desperate for a bulletin board idea on a specific topic, go to http://school.discovery.com/schrockguide/bulletin/elembrd.html and look at "Bulletin Board Ideas."

The Learning Page: Historical Photographs from the American Memory Collection, Library of Congress
(http://rs6.loc.gov/ammem/ndlpedu/index.html)

This site offers access to millions of copyright-free photographs for classroom use. For example, these well-known images can be used when presenting information about the Great Depression. This site offers some great possibilities. The page American Memory Timeline helps teachers use primary sources in their lesson planning. The links are arranged in chronological order with listings such as *Civil War and Reconstruction, 1861–1877; Rise of Industrial America, 1876–1900;* or *Great Depression/World War II, 1929–1945.* Teacher-created lessons are offered as well.

Lesson Plans Page
(http://www.lessonplanspage.com)

This website offers valuable lesson plan ideas for students of all ages, with over 1,500 lesson plans on math, science, social studies, art, physical education and health, language arts, computers and the Internet, and many others. It includes lessons for special holidays and back-to-school ideas.

Mars Exploration (Grades 3–8)
(http://mars.jpl.nasa.gov/)

This terrific site offers many opportunities for interactive fun while learning about Mars. It includes classroom activities with step-by-step instructions. Exploring this site is a great way to introduce your unit on the solar system.

Math Goodies
(http://www.mathgoodies.com/)

This award-winning site has over four hundred pages of math lessons, puzzles, and worksheets for teachers, students, and parents. Interactive lessons include such topics as geometry, number theory, percent, integers, probability, pre-algebra, and introductory statistics. There is an answer key as well. In the "Math Fact Café," you can build your own worksheets for grades 1 through 4 or print out flash cards for grades 1 through 3. When your students need added practice on a math concept, this site will keep their interest.

Teacher Talk
(http://education.indiana.edu/cas/tt/tthmpg.html)

This online publication is devoted specifically to the questions and needs of beginning secondary teachers. It offers tips for creative teaching and ideas for understanding the needs of adolescents. *Teacher Talk* addresses the concerns of new teachers such as student teaching and classroom management.

Foundations of Teaching

Dear Mentor

Teaching in Socially Toxic Environments

Dear Mentor,

As a first-year teacher working in a low income, low-performing school district where there is little parental involvement, I have concerns about the negative social environment in which my students live and the effect it has on them. They live in multiple family homes, have dealt with broken marriages, have bounced in and out of foster care, or have been victims of abuse. Some are involved in gangs and some are single parents trying to earn a living. For these students school is not their number one priority. As a teacher, how can I create a safe and healthy environment for my students? Is forty-five minutes a day enough to make a difference in a student's life? As a first-year teacher I am concerned with how I am going to teach curriculum to students who are being challenged with greater issues. How is it possible to meet the needs of students who come from such different home environments? How can I free their minds of their troubles? How do I invest in all 130 kids while teaching curriculum? What role do I play? A friend, or a teacher?

Sincerely,
Catherine Solorio

Dear Catherine,

First-year teachers are often overwhelmed when they realize that from day one of their teaching careers they become more than just educators to the students who fill the seats of their classrooms. Many students look to their teachers for guidance and counseling on topics that should be addressed by parents or caretakers, but unfortunately, as you have mentioned in your letter, children are often faced with multiple risk factors that subject them to hardships that may often turn the children away from those who are the closest to them. One caring teacher can make a difference.

There is no single factor or thing that makes an individual resilient. A person's resilience is made up of three major components:

1. *Factors within the individual*
2. *Factors associated with the family*
3. *Factors associated with the community*

As a teacher, the influence you have over what happens in the household may be very limited; however, the potential to influence components one and three is vast. Helping your students become resilient individuals is possible even within the time constraint of a forty-five-minute class period. As a history teacher, you have the luxury of using historical figures as role models for your troubled teens. Many great leaders of the past had to overcome great adversities to help change the world for the better. Plan and conduct lessons about the lives of such leaders as Cesar Chavez, Martin Luther King Jr., or Rosa Parks. Include in the lessons role playing so that the students act out the lives of these leaders. During the process of role playing, the students may connect with the material and realize that they share similar experiences with those who have helped mold this country. Role playing is a very powerful tool to help you teach values such as empathy, tolerance, perseverance, and respect. By means of providing the students with the opportunity to learn values, you are consequently improving their emotional intelligence. An emotionally intelligent person is prepared to combat the hardships of a "toxic environment."

Along with helping the students strengthen the factors within themselves, you may also be of great service to them if you lead by example. Teachers are role models whether or not they choose to be. The question is, "What type of role model do you want to be?" You asked what would be more helpful for the troubled students, if you were to be a teacher or a friend to them? Children who are exposed to abuse or other risks at home look to you more for structure and guidance than for friendship. If you are a compassionate teacher and make a sincere effort to reach out to the students, they will know and feel that. With this in mind, help them understand that it is necessary to reach out to someone in their times of need and, more important, that you are someone whom they can trust. They need to know that they are not responsible for many of the hardships they are exposed to!

By virtue of your position, you are one of the integral figures of the community. For many students, you are the most important factor. I wish you the best of luck with your students.

Sincerely,
Gil Navarro
Teacher, Rowland Unified School District
La Puente, California

3 Ideas and Events That Have Shaped Education in the United States

We educate and we are educated for some purpose we consider good. We teach what we think is a valuable set of ideas. How else could we construct education?

—Jack L. Nelson, Kenneth Carlson, and Stuart B. Palonsky
Critical Issues in Education: A Dialectic Approach, 4th ed., 2000

Two weeks after the September 11th terrorist attack on the World Trade Center, you are talking with five other teachers in the faculty lounge. The conversation is about yesterday's staff meeting, during which the principal said teachers should stress to students the importance of not blaming Arab Americans, Muslims, or others who appear to be of the same ethnic or religious background as the suspected terrorists. About twenty Arab American and fifteen Muslim students attend your school.

"I think schools have a critical role in modeling principles of freedom, justice, and democracy," says Mary.

"I agree," says Juan. "For example, I like the idea that we teach the kids about the internment of Japanese Americans during the World War II. Today, it's the same thing . . . people taking out their anger on people because they share an ethnicity with the attackers."

"Right," says Karen. "History repeats itself. Did you hear that an Islamic center in Washington state received calls suggesting that Muslims be interned, just like Japanese citizens and Japanese Americans were during World War II?"

Frank, who has taught at your school for fifteen years, says, "Don't get me wrong, but this is another example of how the curriculum is weakened by having to teach nonacademic subjects—sex and drug education, how to balance the family budget, current events, whatever. I say, if discrimination happens at our school, then we deal with it—but we don't need to make it part of the curriculum."

"I don't agree," says Nong. "Schools must play a part to assure that freedom is not denied to anyone at this critical moment in our nation's history."

"Right," says Mary. "We have an obligation to prevent discrimination, not just react to it *after* it happens. Kids need to see how education is the key to understanding themselves and others. If we can't get along as human beings on this planet, we're in trouble. Look at the attack on the World Trade Center, suicide bombers in Israel, the killing in Northern Ireland. Sure, we've got the Internet and all this technology, but as a species we haven't evolved at all."

"We have to learn from our past," says Karen. "That's one of the main purposes of education, to see how the great ideas—freedom, justice, equality—can help us improve things. Like I tell my students, there isn't one problem today that Shakespeare didn't have tremendous insights into four hundred years ago—war, racism, poverty."

"Well, all I know is that when I started teaching, we just taught the basics," Frank says. "It was as simple as that. We were there to teach, and the kids, believe it or not, were there to learn. Nowadays, we have to solve all of society's problems—eliminate poverty, racism, war, or whatever."

Do you agree or disagree with Frank's beliefs about teaching? What do you think the purposes of education should be?

Focus Questions

1. **What determines your educational philosophy?**
2. **What are the branches of philosophy?**
3. **What are five modern philosophical orientations to teaching?**
4. **What psychological orientations have influenced teaching philosophies?**
5. **How can you develop your educational philosophy?**
6. **What were teaching and schools like in the American colonies (1620–1750)?**
7. **What were the goals of education during the Revolutionary Period (1750–1820)?**
8. **How was the struggle won for state-supported common schools (1820–1865)?**
9. **How did compulsory education change schools and the teaching profession (1865–1920)?**
10. **What were the aims of education during the Progressive Era (1920–1945)?**
11. **How did education change during the modern postwar era (1945–present)?**

Expand your knowledge of the concepts discussed in this chapter by reading current and historical articles from the *New York Times* by visiting the "**Themes of the Times**" section of the Companion Website (**www.ablongman.com/parkay6e**).

As the above scenario suggests, teachers must answer several vital questions about their work. What should the purposes of education be? What knowledge is of most worth? Also, as Karen suggests, teachers must learn from the past. We cannot understand schools today without a look at what they were yesterday. The current system of public and private education in the United States is an ongoing reflection of its philosophical and historical foundations and of the aspirations and values brought to this country by its founders and generations of settlers. Developing an appreciation for the ideas and events that have shaped education in the United States is an important part of your education as a professional.

Still, you may wonder, what is the value of knowing about the philosophy and history of U.S. education? Will that knowledge help you to be a better teacher? First, knowledge of the ideas and events that have influenced our schools will help you evaluate more effectively current proposals for change. You will be in a better position to evaluate changes if you understand how schools have developed and how current proposals might relate to previous change efforts. Second, awareness of ideas and events that have influenced teaching is a hallmark of professionalism in education.

The first half of this chapter presents several basic philosophical concepts that will help you answer five important questions that teachers must consider as they develop an educational philosophy:

- What should the purposes of education be?
- What is the nature of knowledge?
- What values should students adopt?
- What knowledge is of most worth?
- How should learning be evaluated?

The second half presents brief overviews of six periods of education in the United States. For each period, we discuss the philosophical concepts, social forces, events, and persons that, in our judgment, have had the greatest impact on education in our country.

What Determines Your Educational Philosophy?

In simplest terms, **educational philosophy** consists of what you believe about education—the set of principles that guides your professional action. Every teacher, whether he or she recognizes it, has a philosophy of education—a set of beliefs about how human beings learn and grow and what one should learn in order to live the good life. Teachers differ, of course, in regard to the amount of effort they devote to the development of their personal philosophy or educational platform. Some feel that philosophical reflections have nothing to contribute to the actual act of teaching. (This stance, of course, is itself a philosophy of education.) Other teachers recognize that teaching, because it is concerned with *what ought to be*, is basically a philosophical enterprise.

Your behavior as a teacher is strongly connected to your personal beliefs and your beliefs about teaching and learning, students, knowledge, and what is worth knowing (see Figure 3.1). Regardless of where you stand in regard to these five dimensions of teaching, you should be aware of the need to reflect continually on *what* you believe and *why* you believe it.

Figure 3.1 The influence of the teacher's educational beliefs on teaching behavior

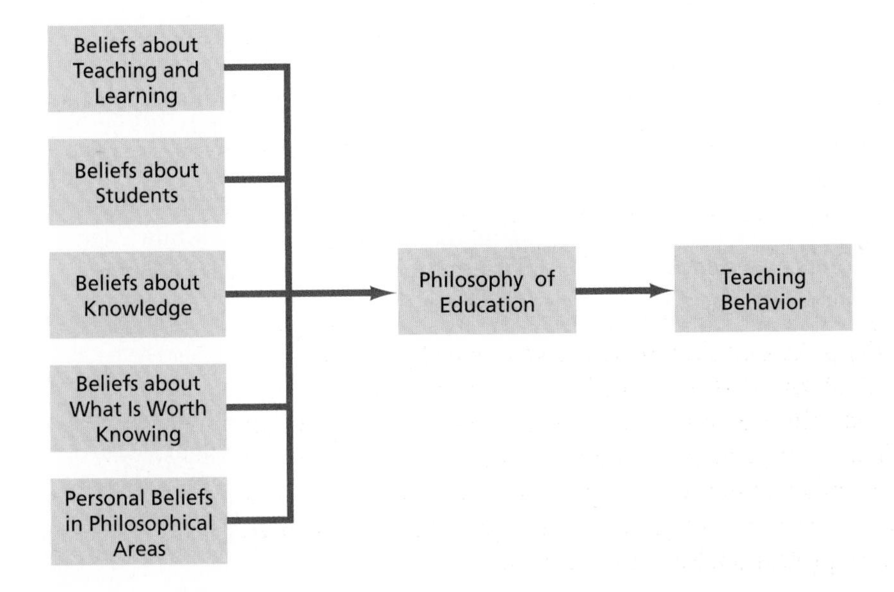

Beliefs about Teaching and Learning

One of the most important components of your educational philosophy is how you view teaching and learning. In other words, what is the teacher's primary role? Is the teacher a subject matter expert who can efficiently and effectively impart knowledge to students? Is the teacher a helpful adult who establishes caring relationships with students and nurtures their growth in needed areas? Or is the teacher a skilled technician who can manage the learning of many students at once?

Some teachers emphasize the individual student's experiences and cognitions. Others stress the student's behavior. Learning, according to the first viewpoint, is seen as the changes in thoughts or actions that result from personal experience; that is, learning is largely the result of internal forces within the individual. In contrast, the other view defines learning as the associations between various stimuli and responses. Here, learning results from forces that are external to the individual.

Beliefs about Students

Your beliefs about students will have a great influence on how you teach. Every teacher formulates an image in his or her mind of what students are like—their dispositions, skills, motivation levels, and expectations. What you believe students are like is based on your unique life experiences, particularly your observations of young people and your knowledge of human growth and development.

Negative views of students may promote teacher–student relationships based on fear and coercion rather than on trust and helpfulness. Extremely positive views may risk not providing students with sufficient structure and direction and not communicating sufficiently high expectations. In the final analysis, the truly professional teacher—the one who has a carefully thought-out educational philosophy—recognizes that, although children differ in their predispositions to learn and grow, they all *can* learn.

Beliefs about Knowledge

How a teacher views knowledge is directly related to how he or she goes about teaching. If teachers view knowledge as the sum total of small bits of subject matter or discrete facts, their students will most likely spend a great deal of time learning that information in a straightforward, rote manner.

Other teachers view knowledge more conceptually, that is, as consisting of the big ideas that enable us to understand and influence our environment. Such teachers would want students to be able to explain how legislative decisions are made in the state capital, how an understanding of the eight parts of speech can empower the writer and vitalize one's writing, and how chemical elements are grouped according to their atomic numbers.

Finally, teachers differ in their beliefs as to whether students' increased understanding of their own experiences is a legitimate form of knowledge. Knowledge of self and one's experiences in the world is not the same as knowledge about a particular subject, yet personal knowledge is essential for a full, satisfying life.

Beliefs about What Is Worth Knowing

As we saw in this chapter's opening scenario, teachers have different ideas about what should be taught. Frank believes it is most important that students learn the basic skills of reading, writing, and computation. These are the skills they will need to be successful in their chosen occupations, and it is the school's responsibility to prepare students for the world of work. Karen believes that the

Meeting the Standard

Models and Promotes Intellectual Growth

INTASC *The teacher understands major concepts, assumptions, debates, processes of inquiry, and ways of knowing that are central to the discipline(s) s/he teaches (INTASC Knowledge, Principle #1).*

Accomplished teachers are models of educated persons . . . and the capacities that are prerequisites for intellectual growth: the ability to reason and take multiple perspectives to be creative and take risks, and to adopt an experimental and problem-solving orientation (NBPTS).

NCATE *Candidates learn to contextualize teaching and to draw upon representations from the students' own experiences and knowledge. They know how to challenge students toward cognitive complexity and engage all students, including students with exceptionalities, through instructional conversation (NCATE).*

PRAXIS *Not only are the goals valuable, but teacher can also clearly articulate how goals establish high expectations and relate to curriculum frameworks and standards (PRAXIS III Framework*–"distinguished" level of performance).*

Teachers who meet these standards have developed a philosophy of how the teaching and learning process takes place, as well as how to challenge students to perform at high levels of achievement. With an understanding of the role that prior knowledge plays in learning new concepts, a variety of effective strategies in hand, and a strong understanding of the curriculum, teachers can match learning opportunities to student needs to model and encourage continuing cognitive growth over the course of the school year. Consider the following example:

> Josephine was recently hired to begin her first year of teaching. Although she had just completed her student teaching in two different grade levels, she was hired to teach at another grade level. Excited about the prospect of beginning what she hoped would be a long and rewarding teaching career, she was nervous about what she was responsible for teaching in this new assignment, as well as how she would be able to stimulate learning in her classroom.
>
> Josephine knew that she had acquired the basics of academics through the completion of her bachelor's degree, and she was excited that she would be responsible for designing the curriculum that would help her students grow intellectually. Part of what she'd be teaching included the study of the U.S. Constitution. She considered herself very knowledgeable in this area and was excited that she would be introducing her students to the "checks and balances" of the governmental branches. She had also completed the requirements to become a credentialed teacher. But was this enough preparation for the responsibilities she was facing?
>
> After calling on her former master teacher for emotional support and receiving reassurance from her mentor, Josephine felt more up to the task. She contacted the grade level leader at her new school and requested a meeting with her so that she could learn about school and district curriculum guidelines and check out school textbooks and other materials to review during the final weeks of summer before school began. Before the meeting with her new colleague, however, she decided to review resources that would prepare her for understanding the specifics of the disciplines she would be teaching, as well as provide her with a sure-fire strategy for quickly identifying prior learning students would be bringing to each new learning experience.
>
> Since she now knew which grade level and subjects she would be teaching, the first task at hand was to identify the national, state, and district curriculum frameworks and standards for not only her grade level, but also the ones below and above so that she would understand the expected paths of learning for her new students. She knew that as time allowed, she would have to cultivate a broader view of the curriculum expectations, but this seemed a good place to begin. She was able to locate some of this information online, and she already had some of the frameworks and standards in booklet form from her credential program.
>
> Josephine also reviewed a successful technique she had learned in one of her methods courses for identifying the assumptions and past knowledge students would bring to the learning process so that she would be better able to challenge them with new ideas and creative projects. She decided to use the "K-W-L" chart at the beginning of each unit. In the left-hand column of a large sheet of butcher paper, she would record student responses to the question "What do you think you already **k**now about this subject?" In the middle column, she would write down responses to the question "**W**hat would you like to learn about this topic?" so that she could incorporate their interests into the unit. At the conclusion of the unit, she would debrief them by writing their responses to the question "What did you **l**earn?" in the right-hand column of the chart. This activity would let her correct misconceptions that students brought with them at the beginning of the unit, as well as give the students closure to the learning that had taken place during the unit.
>
> Josephine was now ready to meet with her new colleague to begin planning the curriculum that would challenge her students to learn more about the world around them.

Through a variety of strategies that would help her identify and organize major areas of learning, Josephine prepared herself for her new year of teaching. Additionally, she was ready to apply these areas of knowledge to the specific and individual backgrounds of her students. By modeling and promoting growth in her students, Josephine was setting high expectations for learning from the beginning.

1. Refer to your state and national standards for specific guidelines in one specific content area and grade level for which you will be responsible to teach. Highlight these major areas with a classmate.
2. Using a K-W-L chart, anticipate what responses students might give you in each column as you teach a unit based on a particular content area.

most worthwhile content is to be found in the classics or the Great Books. Through mastering the great ideas from the sciences, mathematics, literature, and history, students will be well prepared to deal with the world of the future. Last, Mary is concerned with developing the whole child and teaching students to become self-actualizing. Thus, the curriculum should be meaningful and contribute to the student's efforts to become a mature, well-integrated person.

What Are the Branches of Philosophy?

To provide you with further tools to formulate and clarify your educational philosophy, this section presents brief overviews of six areas of philosophy that are of central concern to teachers: metaphysics, epistemology, axiology, ethics, aesthetics, and logic. Each area focuses on one of the questions that have concerned the world's greatest philosophers for centuries: What is the nature of reality? What is the nature of knowledge and is truth ever attainable? According to what values should one live? What is good and what is evil? What is the nature of beauty and excellence? What processes of reasoning will yield consistently valid results?

Metaphysics

Metaphysics is concerned with explaining, as rationally and as comprehensively as possible, the nature of reality (in contrast to how reality *appears*). What is reality? What is the world made of? These are metaphysical questions. Metaphysics also is concerned with the nature of being and explores questions such as, What does it mean to exist? What is humankind's place in the scheme of things? Metaphysical questions such as these are at the very heart of educational philosophy. As two educational philosophers put it: "Our ultimate preoccupation in educational theory is with the most primary of all philosophic problems: metaphysics, the study of ultimate reality" (Morris and Pai 1994, 28).

Metaphysics has important implications for education because the school curriculum is based on what we know about reality. And what we know about reality is driven by the kinds of questions we ask about the world. In fact, any position regarding what schools should teach has behind it a particular view of reality, a particular set of responses to metaphysical questions.

Epistemology

The next major set of philosophical questions that concerns teachers is called **epistemology.** These questions focus on knowledge: What knowledge is true? How does knowing take place? How do we know that we know? How do we decide between opposing views of knowledge? Is truth constant, or does it change from situation to situation? What knowledge is of most worth?

How you answer the epistemological questions that confront all teachers will have significant implications for your teaching. First, you will need to determine what is true about the content you will teach; then you must decide on the most appropriate means of conveying this content to students. Even a casual consideration of epistemological questions reveals that there are many ways of knowing about the world, at least five of which are of interest to teachers:

1. *Knowing Based on Authority*—for example, knowledge from the sage, the poet, the expert, the ruler, the textbook, or the teacher.
2. *Knowing Based on Divine Revelation*—for example, knowledge in the form of supernatural revelations from the sun god of early peoples, the many gods of the ancient Greeks, or the Judeo-Christian god.

By bringing content to life, teachers can pique the interest of their students. How is this teacher helping students connect with the content?

3. *Knowing Based on Empiricism (Experience)*—for example, knowledge acquired through the senses, the informally gathered empirical data that direct most of our daily behavior.
4. *Knowing Based on Reason and Logical Analysis*—for example, knowledge inferred from the process of thinking logically.
5. *Knowing Based on Intuition*—for example, knowledge arrived at without the use of rational thought.

Axiology

The next set of philosophical problems concerns values. Teachers are concerned with values because "school is not a neutral activity. The very idea of schooling expresses a set of values" (Nelson, Carlson, and Palonsky 2000, 304).

Among the axiological questions teachers must answer for themselves are: What values should teachers encourage students to adopt? What values raise humanity to our highest expressions of humaneness? What values does a truly educated person hold?

Axiology highlights the fact that the teacher has an interest not only in the *quantity* of knowledge that students acquire but also in the *quality* of life that becomes possible because of that knowledge. Extensive knowledge may not benefit the individual if he or she is unable to put that knowledge to good use. This point raises additional questions: How do we define quality of life? What curricular experiences contribute most to that quality of life? All teachers must deal with the issues raised by these questions.

Ethics While axiology addresses the question "What is valuable?", **ethics** focuses on "What is good and evil, right and wrong, just and unjust?"

A knowledge of ethics can help the teacher solve many of the dilemmas that arise in the classroom. Frequently, teachers must take action in situations where they are unable to gather all of the relevant facts and where no single course of action is totally right or wrong. For example, a student whose previous work was above average plagiarizes a term paper: Should the teacher fail the student for the course if the example of swift, decisive punishment will likely prevent other students from plagiarizing? Or should the teacher, following her hunches about what would be in the student's long-term interest, have the student redo the term paper and risk the possibility that other students might get the mistaken notion that plagiarism has no negative consequences? Another ethical dilemma: Is an elementary mathematics teacher justified in trying to increase achievement for the whole class by separating two disruptive girls and placing one in a mathematics group beneath her level of ability?

Aesthetics The branch of axiology known as **aesthetics** is concerned with values related to beauty and art. Although we expect that teachers of music, art, drama, literature, and writing regularly have students make judgments about the quality of works of art, we can easily overlook the role that aesthetics ought to play in *all* areas of the curriculum.

Aesthetics can also help the teacher increase his or her effectiveness. Teaching, because it may be viewed as a form of artistic expression, can be judged according to artistic standards of beauty and quality. In this regard, the teacher is an artist whose medium of expression is the spontaneous, unrehearsed, and creative encounter between teacher and student.

Logic **Logic** is the area of philosophy that deals with the process of reasoning and identifies rules that will enable the thinker to reach valid conclusions. The two kinds of logical thinking processes that teachers most frequently have students master are *deductive* and *inductive* thinking. The deductive approach requires the thinker to move from a general principle or proposition to a specific conclusion that is valid. By contrast, inductive reasoning moves from the specific to the general. Here, the student begins by examining particular examples that eventually lead to the acceptance of a general proposition. Inductive teaching is often referred to as discovery teaching—by which students discover, or create, their own knowledge of a topic.

Perhaps the best-known teacher to use the inductive approach to teaching was the Greek philosopher Socrates (ca. 470–399 B.C.). His method of teaching, known today as the Socratic method, consisted of holding philosophical conversations (dialectics) with his pupils. The legacy of Socrates lives in all teachers who use his questioning strategies to encourage students to think for themselves. Figure 3.2 presents guidelines for using **Socratic questioning** techniques in the classroom.

Figure 3.2 The spirit and principles of Socratic questioning

Source: Richard Paul and Linda Elder, "The Art of Socratic Questioning," *Critical Thinking,* Fall 1995, 16.

The Spirit and Principles of Socratic Questioning

- Treat all thoughts as in need of development.
- Respond to all answers with a further question (that calls on the respondent to develop his or her thinking in a fuller and deeper way).
- Treat all assertions as a connecting point to further thoughts.
- Recognize that any thought can only exist fully in a network of connected thoughts. Stimulate students—by your questions—to pursue those connections.
- Seek to understand—where possible—the ultimate foundations for what is said or believed.
- Recognize that all questions presuppose prior questions and all thinking presupposes prior thinking. When raising questions, be open to the questions they presuppose.

What Are Five Modern Philosophical Orientations to Teaching?

Five major philosophical orientations to teaching have been developed in response to the branches of philosophy we have just examined. These orientations, or schools of thought, are perennialism, essentialism, progressivism, existentialism, and social reconstructionism. The following sections present a brief description of each of these orientations, moving from those that are teacher-centered to those that are student-centered (see Figure 3.3).

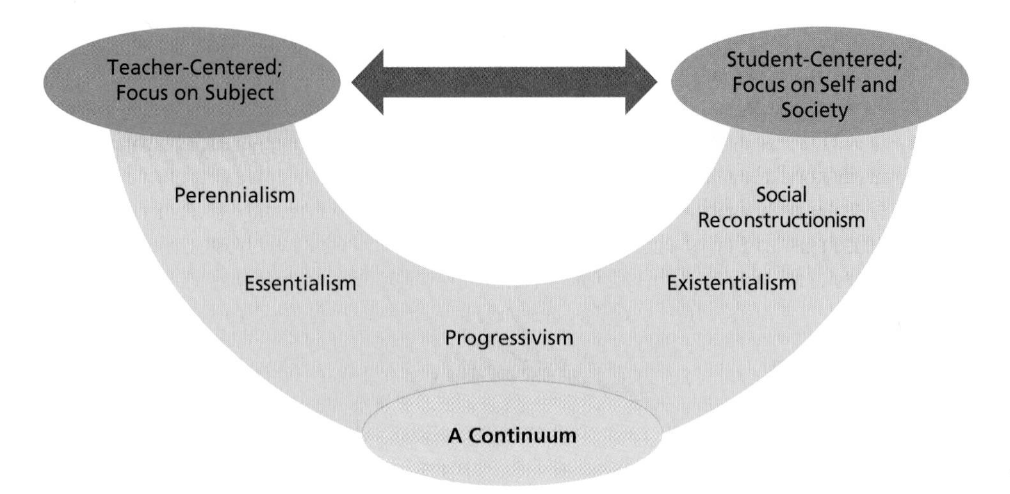

Figure 3.3 Five philosophical orientations to teaching

Perennialism

Perennialism, as the term implies, views truth as constant, or perennial. The aim of education, according to perennialist thinking, is to ensure that students acquire knowledge of unchanging principles or great ideas. Like Karen, whom you met briefly in this chapter's opening scenario, perennialists believe that the great ideas continue to have the most potential for solving the problems of any era.

The curriculum, according to perennialists, should stress students' intellectual growth in the arts and sciences. To become "culturally literate," students should encounter in these areas the best, most significant works that humans have created. Thus, a high school English teacher would require students to read Melville's *Moby Dick* or any of Shakespeare's plays rather than a novel on the current best-seller list. Similarly, science students would learn about the three laws of motion or the three laws of thermodynamics rather than build a model of the space shuttle.

Perennialist Educational Philosophers Two of the best known advocates of the perennialist philosophy have been Robert Maynard Hutchins (1899–1977) and, more recently, Mortimer Adler. As president of the University of Chicago from 1929 to 1945, Hutchins (1963) developed an undergraduate curriculum based on the study of the Great Books and discussions of these classics in small seminars. Noted educational philosopher Mortimer Adler, along with Hutchins, was instrumental in organizing the Great Books of the Western World curriculum. Through focusing study on over one hundred enduring classics, from Plato to Einstein, the Great Books approach aims at the major perennialist goal of teaching students to become independent and critical thinkers. It is a demanding curriculum, and it focuses on the enduring disciplines of knowledge rather than on current events or student interests.

Robert Maynard Hutchins (1899–1977)

Essentialism

Essentialism, which has some similarities to perennialism, is a conservative philosophy of education originally formulated as a criticism of progressive trends in schools by William C. Bagley (1874–1946), a professor of education at Teachers College, Columbia University. Essentialists, like Frank whom you met in this chapter's opening scenario, believe that human culture has a core of common knowledge that schools are obligated to transmit to students in a systematic, disciplined way. Unlike perennialists, who emphasize a set of external truths, essen-

William C. Bagley (1874–1946)

tialists stress what they believe to be the essential knowledge and skills (often termed "the basics") that productive members of our society need to know.

According to essentialist philosophy, schooling should be practical and provide children with sound instruction that prepares them to live life; schools should not try to influence or set social policies. Critics of essentialism, however, charge that such a tradition-bound orientation to schooling will indoctrinate students and rule out the possibility of change. Essentialists respond that, without an essentialist approach, students will be indoctrinated in humanistic and/or behavioral curricula that run counter to society's accepted standards and need for order.

John Dewey (1859–1952)

Progressivism

Progressivism is based on the belief that education should be child-centered rather than focused on the teacher or the content area. The writing of John Dewey (1859–1952) in the 1920s and 1930s contributed a great deal to the spread of progressive ideas. Briefly, Deweyan progressivism is based on three central assumptions:

1. The content of the curriculum ought to be derived from students' interests rather than from the academic disciplines.
2. Effective teaching takes into account the whole child and his or her interests and needs in relation to cognitive, affective, and psychomotor areas.
3. Learning is essentially active rather than passive.

Progressive Strategies The progressive philosophy also contends that knowledge that is true in the present may not be true in the future. Hence, the best way to prepare students for an unknown future is to equip them with problem-solving strategies that will enable them to discover meaningful knowledge at various stages of their lives.

Educators with a progressive orientation give students a considerable amount of freedom in determining their school experiences. Contrary to the perceptions

How might you explain what is happening in this classroom from the perspective of progressivism? From the perspective of perennialism? From the perspective of essentialism?

of many, though, progressive education does not mean that teachers do not provide structure or that students are free to do whatever they wish. Progressive teachers begin where students are and, through the daily give-and-take of the classroom, lead students to see that the subject to be learned can enhance their lives.

In a progressively oriented classroom, the teacher serves as a guide or resource person whose primary responsibility is to facilitate student learning. The teacher helps students learn what is important to them rather than passing on a set of so-called enduring truths. Students have many opportunities to work cooperatively in groups, often solving problems that the group, not the teacher, has identified as important.

Existentialism

Existential philosophy is unique in that it focuses on the experiences of the individual. Other philosophies are concerned with developing systems of thought for identifying and understanding what is common to *all* reality, human existence, and values. **Existentialism,** on the other hand, offers the individual a way of thinking about *my* life, what has meaning for *me,* what is true for *me.* In general, existentialism emphasizes creative choice, the subjectivity of human experiences, and concrete acts of human existence over any rational scheme for human nature or reality.

The writings of Jean-Paul Sartre (1905–1980), well-known French philosopher, novelist, and playwright, have been most responsible for the widespread dissemination of existential ideas. According to Sartre (1972), every individual first exists and then he or she must decide what that existence is to mean. The task of assigning meaning to that existence is the individual's alone; no preformulated philosophical belief system can tell one who one is. It is up to each of us to decide who we are.

Life, according to existential thought, has no meaning, and the universe is indifferent to the situation humankind finds itself in. Moreover, "existententialists [believe] that too many people wrongly emphasize the optimistic, the good, and the beautiful—all of which create a false impression of existence" (Ozmon and Craver 1999, 253). With the freedom that we have, however, each of us must commit him- or herself to assign meaning to his or her *own* life. As Maxine Greene, who has been described as "the preeminent American philosopher of education today" (Ayers and Miller 1998, 4), states: "We have to know about our lives, clarify our situations if we are to understand the world from our shared standpoints." (1995b, 21). The human enterprise that can be most helpful in promoting this personal quest for meaning is the educative process. Teachers, therefore, must allow students freedom of choice and provide them with experiences that will help them find the meaning of their lives. This approach, contrary to the belief of many, does not mean that students may do whatever they please; logic indicates that freedom has rules, and respect for the freedom of others is essential.

Maxine Green (b. 1917)

Existentialists judge the curriculum according to whether or not it contributes to the individual's quest for meaning and results in a level of personal awareness that Greene (1995b) terms "wide-awakeness." As Greene (1995a, 149–150) suggests in the following, the ideal curriculum is one that provides students with extensive individual freedom and requires them to ask their own questions, conduct their own inquiries, and draw their own conclusions: "To feel oneself en route, to feel oneself in a place where there are always possibilities of clearings, of new openings, this is what we must communicate to the young if we want to awaken them to their situations and enable them to make sense of and to name their worlds."

Social Reconstructionism

As the name implies, **social reconstructionism** holds that schools should take the lead in changing or reconstructing society. Theodore Brameld (1904–1987), acknowledged as the founder of social reconstructionism, based his philosophy on two fundamental premises about the post–World War II era: (1) We live in a period of great crisis, most evident in the fact that humans now have the capability of destroying civilization overnight, and (2) humankind also has the intellectual, technological, and moral potential to create a world civilization of "abundance, health, and humane capacity" (Brameld 1959, 19). In this time of great need, then, social reconstructionists like Mary, whom we met in this chapter's opening scenario, believe that schools should become the primary agent for planning and directing social change. Schools should not only *transmit* knowledge about the existing social order; they should seek to *reconstruct* it as well.

Social Reconstructionism and Progressivism Social reconstructionism has clear ties to progressive educational philosophy. Both provide opportunities for extensive interactions between teacher and students and among students themselves. Furthermore, both place a premium on bringing the community, if not the entire world, into the classroom. Student experiences often include field trips, community-based projects of various sorts, and opportunities to interact with people beyond the four walls of the classroom.

According to Brameld and social reconstructionists such as George Counts, who wrote *Dare the School Build a New Social Order?* (1932), the educative process should provide students with methods for dealing with the significant crises that confront the world: war, economic depression, international terrorism, hunger, inflation, and ever-accelerating technological advances. The logical outcome of such education would be the eventual realization of a world-wide democracy (Brameld 1956). Unless we actively seek to create this kind of world through the intelligent application of present knowledge, we run the risk that the destructive forces of the world will determine the conditions under which humans will live in the future.

George Counts (1889–1974)

What Psychological Orientations Have Influenced Teaching Philosophies?

In addition to the five philosophical orientations to teaching described in previous sections of this chapter, several schools of psychological thought have formed the basis for teaching philosophies. These psychological theories are comprehensive world views that serve as the basis for the way many teachers approach teaching practice. Psychological orientations to teaching are concerned primarily with understanding the conditions that are associated with effective learning. In other words, what motivates students to learn? What environments are most conducive to learning? Chief among the psychological orientations that have influenced teaching philosophies are humanistic psychology, behaviorism, and constructivism.

Humanistic Psychology

Humanistic psychology emphasizes personal freedom, choice, awareness, and personal responsibility. As the term implies, it also focuses on the achievements, motivation, feelings, actions, and needs of human beings. The goal of education, according to this orientation, is individual self-actualization.

Humanistic psychology is derived from the philosophy of **humanism,** which developed during the European Renaissance and Protestant Reformation and is based on the belief that individuals control their own destinies through the application of their intelligence and learning. People "make themselves." The term "secular humanism" refers to the closely related belief that the conditions of human existence relate to human nature and human actions rather than to predestination or divine intervention.

In the 1950s and 1960s, humanistic psychology became the basis of educational reforms that sought to enhance students' achievement of their full potential through self-actualization (Maslow 1954, 1962; Rogers 1961). According to this psychological orientation, teachers should not force students to learn; instead, they should create a climate of trust and respect that allows students to decide what and how they learn, to question authority, and to take initiative in "making themselves." Teachers should be what noted psychologist Carl Rogers calls "facilitators," and the classroom should be a place "in which curiosity and the natural desire to learn can be nourished and enhanced" (1982, 31). Through their nonjudgmental understanding of students, humanistic teachers encourage students to learn and grow.

Behaviorism

Behaviorism is based on the principle that desirable human behavior can be the product of design rather than accident. According to behaviorists, it is an illusion to say that humans have a free will. Although we may act as if we are free, our behavior is really *determined* by forces in the environment that shape our behavior. "We are what we are and we do what we do, not because of any mysterious power of human volition, but because outside forces over which we lack any semblance of control have us caught in an inflexible web. Whatever else we may be, we are not the captains of our fate or the masters of our soul" (Power 1982, 168).

Founders of Behavioristic Psychology John B. Watson (1878–1958) was the principal originator of behavioristic psychology and B. F. Skinner (1904–1990) its best-known promoter. Watson first claimed that human behavior consisted of specific stimuli that resulted in certain responses. In part, he based this new conception of learning on the classic experiment conducted by Russian psychologist Ivan Pavlov (1849–1936). Pavlov had noticed that a dog he was working with would salivate when it was about to be given food. By introducing the sound of a bell when food was offered and repeating this several times, Pavlov discovered that the sound of the bell alone (a conditioned stimulus) would make the dog salivate (a conditioned response). Watson came to believe that all learning conformed to this basic stimulus-response model (now termed classical or type S conditioning).

Skinner went beyond Watson's basic stimulus-response model and developed a more comprehensive view of conditioning known as operant (or type R) conditioning. Operant conditioning is based on the idea that satisfying responses are conditioned, unsatisfying ones are not. In other words, "The things we call pleasant have an energizing or strengthening effect on our behaviour" (Skinner 1972,

What are some ways in which parents and teachers of young children might employ behaviorism strategies for teaching skills?

74). Thus the teacher can create learners who exhibit desired behaviors by following four steps:

1. Identify desired behaviors in concrete (observable and measurable) terms.
2. Establish a procedure for recording specific behaviors and counting their frequencies.
3. For each behavior, identify an appropriate reinforcer.
4. Ensure that students receive the reinforcer as soon as possible after displaying a desired behavior.

Constructivism

In contrast to behaviorism, constructivism focuses on processes of learning rather than on learning behavior. According to **constructivism,** students use cognitive processes to *construct* understanding of the material to be learned—in contrast to the view that they *receive* information transmitted by the teacher. Constructivist approaches support student-centered rather than teacher-centered curriculum and instruction. The student is the key to learning.

Unlike behaviorists who concentrate on directly observable behavior, constructivists focus on the mental processes and strategies that students use to learn. Our understanding of learning has been extended as a result of advances in **cognitive science**—the study of the mental processes students use in thinking and remembering. By drawing from research in linguistics, psychology, anthropology, neurophysiology, and computer science, cognitive scientists are developing new models for how people think and learn.

Teachers who base classroom activities on constructivism know that learning is an active, meaning-making process, that learners are not passive recipients of information. In fact, students are continually involved in making sense out of activities around them. Thus the teacher must *understand students' understanding* and realize that students' learning is influenced by prior knowledge, experience, attitudes, and social interactions.

How Can You Develop Your Educational Philosophy?

As you read the preceding brief descriptions of five educational philosophies and three psychological orientations to teaching, perhaps you felt that no single philosophy fit perfectly with your image of the kind of teacher you want to become. Or, there may have been some element of each approach that seemed compatible with your own emerging philosophy of education. In either case, don't feel that you need to identify a single educational philosophy around which you will build your teaching career. In reality, few teachers follow only one educational philosophy, and, as Figure 3.4 shows, educational philosophy is only one determinant of the professional goals a teacher sets.

Most teachers develop an *eclectic* philosophy of education, which means they develop their own unique blending of two or more philosophies. To help you identify the philosophies most consistent with your beliefs and values about educational goals, curriculum, and teachers' and students' roles in learning, complete the Philosophic Inventory found in the Professional Reflection on pp. 115–117. The self-knowledge you glean from completing the inventory and the philosophical constructs presented in the first half of this chapter provide a useful framework for studying the six periods in the historical development of schools that follow. For example, you will be able to see how philosophical orientations to education waxed and waned during each period—whether it was the perennialism and essentialism that characterized colonial schools, the progressivism of the 1920s and 1930s, the essentialism of the 1950s and 1980s, the humanism and social reconstructionism of the 1960s, or the constructivism of the 1990s.

What Were Teaching and Schools Like in the American Colonies (1620–1750)?

Education in colonial America had its primary roots in English culture. The settlers of our country initially tried to develop a system of schooling that paralleled the British two-track system. If students from the lower classes attended

Figure 3.4 The relationship of philosophy to educational practice
Source: George R. Knight, *Issues & Alternatives in Educational Philosophy,* 3rd ed. Berrien Springs, MI: Andrews University Press 1998, p. 34.

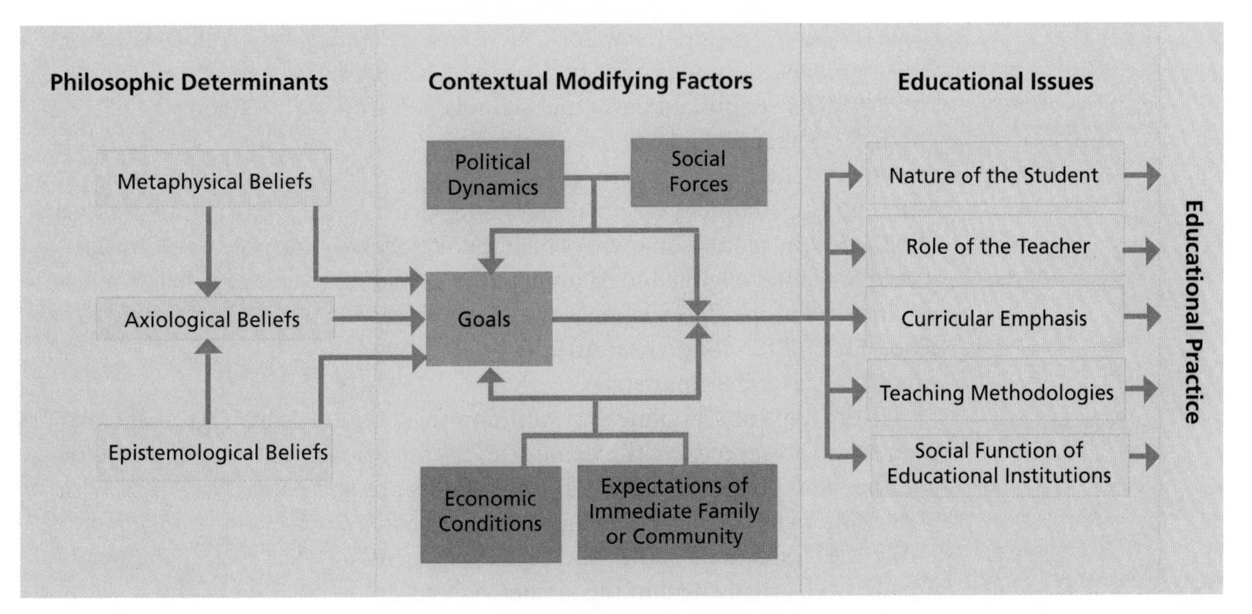

These children are active learners in a real or relevant context, constructing their own meanings through direct experience. How might this lesson be seen as an eclectic blend of progressive, existential, and constructivist ideals?

school at all it was at the elementary level for the purpose of studying an essentialist curriculum of reading, writing, and computation and receiving religious instruction. Students from the upper classes had the opportunity to attend Latin grammar schools, where they were given a college-preparatory education that focused on perennialist subjects such as Latin and Greek classics.

Above all, the colonial curriculum stressed religious objectives. Generally, no distinction was made between secular and religious life in the colonies. The religious motives that impelled the Puritans to endure the hardships of settling in a new land were reflected in the schools' curricula. The primary objective of elementary schooling was to learn to read so that one might read the Bible and religious catechisms and thereby receive salvation.

Colonial Schools

In the New England colonies (Massachusetts Bay, New Hampshire, and Connecticut), there was a general consensus that church, state, and schools were interrelated. As a result, town schools were created throughout these colonies to teach children the basics of reading and writing so they could learn the scriptures. The Puritan view of the child included the belief that people are inherently sinful. Even natural childhood play was seen as devil-inspired idleness. The path to redemption lay in learning to curb one's natural instincts and behave like an adult as quickly as possible. To bring about this premature growth, the teacher had to correct the child constantly and try to curb his or her natural instincts. As one historian put it, "In colonial New England the whole idea of education presumed that children were miniature adults possessed of human degeneracy. The daily school routine was characterized by harshness and dogmatism. Discipline was strict, and disobedience and infractions of rules were often met with severe penalties meted out by quick-tempered, poorly qualified instructors" (Rippa 1997, 30).

The middle colonies (New York, New Jersey, Pennsylvania, and Delaware) were more diverse, and groups such as the Irish, Scots, Swedes, Danes, Dutch, and Germans established **parochial schools** based on their religious beliefs. Anglicans, Lutherans, Quakers, Jews, Catholics, Presbyterians, and Mennonites in the Middle Colonies tended to establish their own schools. In the largely Protestant southern colonies (Virginia, Maryland, Georgia, and North and South Carolina), wealthy plantation owners believed the primary purpose of education was to promote religion and to prepare their children to attend colleges and universities in Europe. The vast majority of small farmers received no formal schooling and the children of African slaves received only the training they needed to serve their masters.

No one type of schooling was common to all the colonies. The most common types, however, were the dame schools, the reading and writing schools, and the Latin grammar schools. **Dame schools** provided initial instruction for boys and, often, the only schooling for girls. These schools were run by widows or housewives in their homes and supported by modest fees from parents. Classes were usually held in the kitchen, where children learned only the barest essentials of reading, writing, and arithmetic during instruction lasting for a few weeks to one year. Females might also be taught sewing and basic homemaking skills. Students often began by learning the alphabet from a **horn book.** Developed in medieval Europe, the horn book was a copy of the alphabet covered by a thin transparent sheet made from a cow's horn. The alphabet and the horn covering were attached to a paddle-shaped piece of wood.

Reading and writing schools offered boys an education that went beyond what their parents could teach them at home or what they could learn at a dame school. Reading lessons were based on the Bible, various religious catechisms, and the *New England Primer,* first printed in 1690. The Primer introduced children to the letters of the alphabet through the use of illustrative woodcuts and rhymed couplets. The first couplet began with the pronouncement that

In Adam's fall
We sinned all.

And the final one noted that

Zaccheus he
Did climb the Tree
His Lord to see.

The *Primer* also presented children with large doses of stern religious warnings about the proper conduct of life.

The **Latin grammar school,** comparable to today's secondary school, was patterned after the classical schools of Europe. Boys enrolled in the Latin grammar schools at the age of seven or eight, whereupon they began to prepare to enter Harvard College (established in 1636). Following graduation from Harvard, they would assume leadership roles in the church.

The Origins of Mandated Education

Universal compulsory education had its origins in the **Massachusetts Act of 1642.** Prior to this date, parents could decide whether they wished their children to be educated at home or at a school. Church and civic leaders in the colonies,

N NOAH did view
The old world & new

O Young OBADIAS,
DAVID, JOSIAS
All were pious.

P PETER deny'd
His Lord and cry'd.

Q Queen ESTHER ſues
And ſaves the *Jews*.

R Young pious RUTH,
Left all for Truth.

S Young SAM'L dear
The Lord did fear.

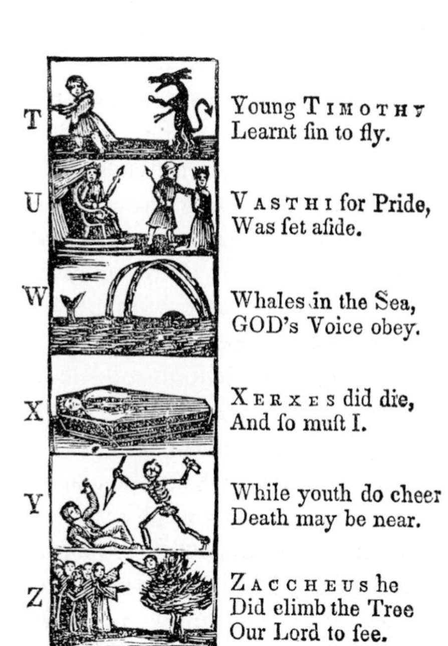
T Young TIMOTHY
Learnt ſin to fly.

U VASTHI for Pride,
Was ſet aſide.

W Whales in the Sea,
GOD's Voice obey.

X XERXES did die,
And ſo muſt I.

Y While youth do cheer
Death may be near.

Z ZACCHEUS he
Did climb the Tree
Our Lord to ſee.

What do these two pages from a 1727 edition of *The New England Primer* suggest about the curriculum and aims of education in early schools in the United States?

Where Do You Stand? **Visit the Companion Website to Voice Your Opinion.**

however, decided that education could no longer remain voluntary. They saw that many children were receiving inadequate training. Moreover, they realized that organized schools would serve to strengthen and preserve Puritan religious beliefs.

The Puritans decided to make education a civil responsibility of the state. The Massachusetts General Court passed a law in 1642 that required each town to determine whether young people could read and write. Parents and apprentices' masters whose children were unable "to read and understand the principles of religion and the capital laws of the country" (Rippa 1997, 36) could be fined and, possibly, lose custody of their children.

Although the Act of 1642 did not mandate the establishment of schools, it did make it clear that the education of children was a direct concern of the local citizenry. In 1648, the Court revised the 1642 law, reminding town leaders that "the good education of children is of singular behoof and benefit to any commonwealth" and that some parents and masters were still "too indulgent and negligent of their duty" (Cohen 1974, 394–395). As the first educational law in this country, the Massachusetts Act of 1642 was a landmark.

The **Massachusetts Act of 1647,** often referred to as the Old Deluder Satan Act (because education was seen as the best protection against the wiles of the devil), mandated the establishment and support of schools. In particular, towns of fifty households or more were to appoint a person to instruct "all such children as shall resort to him to write and read." Teachers were to "be paid either by the parents or masters of such children, or by the inhabitants in general" (Rippa 1997, 36).

Education for African Americans and Native Americans

At the close of the American Revolution, nearly all of the half million African Americans were slaves who could neither read nor write (Button and Provenzo 1989). In most cases, those who were literate had been taught by their masters or through small, church-affiliated programs. Literate Native Americans and Mexican Americans usually had received their training at the hands of missionaries. One of the first schools for African Americans was started by Elias Neau in New York City in 1704. Sponsored by the Church of England, Neau's school taught African and Native Americans how to read as part of the Church's efforts to convert students.

Other schools for African and Native Americans were started by the Quakers, who regarded slavery as a moral evil. Though Quaker schools for African Americans existed as early as 1700, one of the best known was founded in Philadelphia in 1770 by Anthony Benezet, who believed that African Americans were "generously sensible, humane, and sociable, and that their capacity is as good, and as capable of improvement as that of white people" (Button and Provenzo 1989, 45). Schools modeled on the Philadelphia African School opened elsewhere in the Northeast, and "Indian schools" also were founded as philanthropic enterprises.

From the seventeenth to the late-twentieth centuries, schools were segregated by race. The first recorded official ground for school segregation dates back to a decision of the Massachusetts Supreme Court in 1850. When the Roberts family sought to send their daughter Sarah to a white school in Boston, the court ruled that "equal, but separate" schools were being provided and that the Roberts therefore could not claim an injustice (*Roberts v. City of Boston* 1850). From the beginning, however, schools were not equal, and students did not have equal educational opportunity.

What Were the Goals of Education during the Revolutionary Period (1750–1820)?

Education in the United States during the Revolutionary period was characterized by a general waning of European influences on schools. Though religious traditions that had their origins in Europe continued to affect the curriculum, the young country's need to develop agriculture, shipping, and commerce also exerted its influence on the curriculum. By this time, the original settlers who had emigrated from Europe had been replaced by a new generation whose most immediate roots were in the new soil of the United States. This new, exclusively American, identity was also enhanced by the rise of civil town governments, the great increase in books and newspapers that addressed life in the new country, and a turning away from Europe toward the unsettled west. The colonies' break with Europe was most potently demonstrated in the American Revolution of 1776.

Following independence, many leaders were concerned that new disturbances from within could threaten the well-being of the new nation. To preserve the freedoms that had been fought for, a system of education became essential. Through education, people would become intelligent, participating citizens of a constitutional democracy. Among these leaders were Benjamin Franklin, Sarah Pierce, Thomas Jefferson, and Noah Webster.

Benjamin Franklin's Academy

Benjamin Franklin (1706–1790) designed and promoted the Philadelphia Academy, a private secondary school, which opened in 1751. This school, which replaced the old Latin grammar school, had a curriculum that was broader and more practical and also focused on the English language rather than Latin. The academy was also a more democratically run institution than previous schools had been. Though academies were largely privately controlled and privately financed, they were secular and often supported by public funds. Most academies were public in that anyone who could pay tuition could attend, regardless of church affiliation (Rippa 1997, 65).

In his *Proposals Relating to the Education of Youth in Pennsylvania,* written in 1749, Franklin noted that "the good Education of youth has been esteemed by wise men in all ages, as the surest foundation of the happiness both of private families and of commonwealths" (Franklin 1931, 151).

Franklin's proposals for educating youth called for a wide range of subjects that reflected perennialist and essentialist philosophical orientations: English grammar, composition, and literature; classical and modern foreign languages; science; writing and drawing; rhetoric and oratory; geography; various kinds of history; agriculture and gardening; arithmetic and accounting; and mechanics.

Sarah Pierce's Female Academy

English **academies,** often called people's colleges, multiplied across the country, reaching a peak of 6,185 in 1855, with an enrollment of 263,096 (Spring 1997, 22). Usually, these academies served male students only; a notable exception was Sarah Pierce's Litchfield Female Academy in Litchfield, Connecticut. Pierce (1767–1852) began her academy in the dining room of her home with two students; eventually, the academy grew to 140 female students from nearly every state and from Canada (Button and Provenzo 1989, 87).

For the most part, however, girls received little formal education in the seventeenth and eighteenth centuries and were educated for entirely different purposes than were boys. As the following mission statement for Pierce's Academy suggests, an essentialist, rather than perennialist, curriculum was appropriate for girls:

> Our object has been, not to make learned ladies, or skillful metaphysical reasoners, or deep read scholars in physical science: there is a more useful, tho' less exalted and less brilliant station that woman must occupy, there are duties of incalculable importance that she must perform: that station is home; these duties, are the alleviation of the trials of her parents; the soothing of the labours & fatigues of her partner; & the education for time and eternity of the next generation of immortal beings . . . (Button and Provenzo 1989, 88).

Emma Willard (1787–1870)

Some women enrolled in **female seminaries,** first established in the early nineteenth century to train women for higher education and public service outside of the home. Educational opportunities for women expanded in conjunction with social reform movements that gradually led to greater political equality for women, including the right to vote in the twentieth century. For example, Troy Seminary, founded in 1821 by educator and poet Emma Willard (1787–1870), became one of the first women's colleges in the country.

Thomas Jefferson's Philosophy

Thomas Jefferson (1743–1826), author of the Declaration of Independence, viewed the education of common people as the most effective means of preserving liberty. As historian S. Alexander Rippa put it, "Few statesmen in American history have so vigorously strived for an ideal; perhaps none has so consistently viewed public education as the indispensable cornerstone of freedom" (1997, 55).

For a society to remain free, Jefferson felt, it must support a continuous system of public education. He proposed to the Virginia legislature in 1779 his Bill for the More General Diffusion of Knowledge. This plan called for state-controlled elementary schools that would teach, with no cost to parents, three years of reading, writing, and arithmetic to all white children. In addition, twenty state grammar schools would be created in which selected poor students would be taught free for a maximum period of six years.

Jefferson was unsuccessful in his attempt to convince the Virginia House of Burgesses of the need for a uniform system of public schools as outlined in his bill. Jefferson was, however, able to implement many of his educational ideas through his efforts to found the University of Virginia. He devoted the last years of his life to developing the university, and he lived to see the university open with forty students in March 1824, one month before his eighty-first birthday.

Noah Webster's Speller

In the years following the Revolution, several textbooks were printed in the United States. Writers and publishers saw the textbook as an appropriate vehicle for promoting democratic ideals and cultural independence from England. Toward this end, U.S. textbooks were filled with patriotic and moralistic maxims. Among the most widely circulated books of this type were Noah Webster's *Elementary Spelling Book* and *The American Dictionary.*

Noah Webster (1758–1843)

Webster (1758–1843) first introduced his speller in 1783 under the cumbersome title, *A Grammatical Institute of the English Language.* Later versions were titled the *American Spelling Book* and the *Elementary Spelling Book*. Webster's speller earned the nickname "the old blue-back" because early copies of the book were covered in light blue paper and later editions covered with bright blue paper.

In the introduction to his speller, Webster declared that its purpose was to help teachers instill in students "the first rudiments of the language, some just ideas of religion, morals and domestic economy" (Button and Provenzo 1989, 65). Throughout, the little book emphasized patriotic and moralistic virtues. Short, easy-to-remember maxims taught pupils to be content with their lot in life, to work hard, and to respect the property of others.

How Was the Struggle Won for State-Supported Common Schools (1820–1865)?

The first state-supported high school in the United States was the Boston English Classical School, established in 1821. The opening of this school, renamed English High School in 1824, marked the beginning of a long, slow struggle for state-supported **common schools** in this country. Those in favor of free common schools tended to be city residents and nontaxpayers, democratic leaders, philanthropists and humanitarians, members of various school societies, and working people. Those opposed were rural residents and taxpayers, members of old aristocratic and conservative groups, owners of private schools, members of conservative religious sects, Southerners, and non-English-speaking residents. By far the most eloquent and effective spokesperson for the common school was Horace Mann.

Horace Mann's Contributions

Horace Mann (1796–1859) was a lawyer, Massachusetts senator, and the first secretary of a state board of education. He is best known as the champion of the common school movement, which has led to the free, public, locally controlled elementary schools we know today. Mann worked tirelessly to convince people that their interests would be well served by a system of universal free schools for all:

Horace Mann (1796–1859)

> It [a free school system] knows no distinction of rich and poor, of bond and free, or between those, who, in the imperfect light of this world, are seeking, through different avenues, to reach the gate of heaven. Without money and without price, it throws open its doors, and spreads the table of its bounty, for all the children of the State (Mann 1868, 754).

Improving Schools In 1837, Mann accepted the position of Secretary of the Massachusetts State Board of Education. At the time, conditions in Massachusetts schools were deplorable, and Mann immediately began to use his new post to improve the quality of schools. Through the twelve annual reports he submitted while secretary and through *The Common School Journal,* which he founded and edited, Mann's educational ideas became widely known in this country and abroad.

In his widely publicized *Fifth Report* (published in 1841), Mann told the moneyed conservative classes that support of common public schools would provide them "the cheapest means of self-protection and insurance." Where could they find, Mann asked, "any police so vigilant and effective, for the protection of all the rights of person, property and character, as such a sound and comprehensive education and training, as our system of Common Schools could be made to impart?" (Rippa 1997, 95).

In his *Seventh Report* (published 1843), Mann extolled the virtues of schools he had visited in Prussia that implemented the humanistic approaches of noted Swiss educator Johann Heinrich Pestalozzi (1746–1827). "I heard no child ridiculed, sneered at, or scolded, for making a mistake," Mann wrote (Rippa 1997, 96).

The Normal School During the late 1830s, Mann put forth a proposal that today we take for granted. Teachers, he felt, needed more than a high school education to teach; they should be trained in professional programs. The French had established the *école normale* for preparing teachers, and Mann and other influential educators of the period, such as Catherine Beecher (1800–1878), whose sister, Harriet Beecher Stowe (1811–1896), wrote *Uncle Tom's Cabin,* believed that a similar program was needed in the United States. Through her campaign to ensure that women had access to an education equal to that of men and her drive to recruit women into the teaching profession, Beecher contributed significantly to the development of publicly funded schools for training teachers (Holmes and Weiss 1995).

The first public **normal school** in the United States opened in Lexington, Massachusetts, on July 3, 1839. The curriculum consisted of general knowledge courses plus courses in pedagogy (or teaching) and practice teaching in a model school affiliated with the normal school. In 1849, Electa Lincoln Walton (1824–1908), an 1843 graduate of the normal school, became acting head administrator and the first woman to administer a state normal school. Walton was energetic and determined to succeed, as her journal reveals:

> Many people think women can't do much. I'd like to show them that they can keep a Normal School and keep it well too. . . . I will succeed. . . . I will never be pointed at as an example of the incompetency of woman to conduct a large establishment well" (Holmes and Weiss 1995, 42).

When Mann resigned as secretary in 1848, his imprint on education in the United States was broad and deep. As a result of his unflagging belief that education was the "great equalizer of the conditions of men—the balance wheel of the social machinery" (Mann 1957, 87), Massachusetts had a firmly established system of common schools and led the way for other states to establish free public schools.

Reverend W. H. McGuffey's Readers

Reverend William Holmes McGuffey (1800–1873) had perhaps the greatest impact on what children learned in the new school. Far exceeding Noah Webster's speller in sales were the famous **McGuffey readers.** It has been estimated that 122 million copies of the six-volume series were sold after 1836. The six readers ranged in difficulty from the first-grade level to the sixth-grade level. Through such stories as "The Wolf," "Meddlesome Matty," and "A Kind Brother," the readers emphasized virtues such as hard work, honesty, truth, charity, and obedience.

Absent from the McGuffey readers were the dour, pessimistic views of childhood so characteristic of earlier primers. Nevertheless, they had a religious, moral, and ethical influence over millions of American readers. Through their reading of the "Dignity of Labor," "The Village Blacksmith," and "The Rich Man's Son," for example, readers learned that contentment outweighs riches in this world. In addition to providing explicit instructions on right living, the McGuffey readers also taught countless children and adults how to read and study.

Justin Morrill's Land-Grant Schools

The common school movement and the continuing settlement of the West stimulated the development of public higher education. In 1862, the **Morrill Land-Grant Act,** sponsored by Congressman Justin S. Morrill (1810–1898) of Vermont, provided federal land for states either to sell or to rent in order to raise funds for the establishment of colleges of agriculture and mechanical arts. Each state was given a land subsidy of 30,000 acres for each representative and senator in its congressional delegation. Eventually, seven and a half million dollars from the sale of over seventeen million acres was given to land-grant colleges and state universities. The Morrill Act of 1862 set a precedent for the federal government to take an active role in shaping higher education in the United States. A second Morrill Act in 1890 provided even more federal funds for land-grant colleges.

How Did Compulsory Education Change Schools and the Teaching Profession (1865–1920)?

From the end of the Civil War to the end of World War I, publicly supported common schools steadily spread westward and southward from New England and the Middle Atlantic states. Beginning with Massachusetts in 1852, compulsory education laws were passed in thirty-two states by 1900 and in all states by 1930.

Because of compulsory attendance laws, an ever-increasing proportion of children attended school. In 1869–70, only 64.7 percent of five- to seventeen-year-olds attended public school. By 1919–20, this proportion had risen to 78.3 percent; and in 1995–96, it was 91.7 percent (National Center for Education Statistics 1999, 50). The growth in enrollment on the high school level was exceptional. Historical data from the National Center for Education Statistics (1999) enable us to determine that between 1880 and 1920, the population in the United States increased 108 percent, and high school enrollment increased 1,900 percent!

As common schools spread, school systems began to take on organizational features associated with today's schools: centralized control; increasing authority for state, county, and city superintendencies; and a division of labor among teachers and administrators at the individual school site. Influenced by the work of Frederick W. Taylor (1856–1915), an engineer and the founder of **scientific management,** school officials undertook reforms based on management principles and techniques from big business. For example, they believed that top-down management techniques should be applied to schools as well as factories.

Higher Education for African Americans

In *Up from Slavery,* Booker T. Washington (1856–1915) recounts how he walked part of the five hundred miles from his home in West Virginia to attend the Hampton Normal and Agricultural Institute of Virginia, one of the country's first institutions of higher education for African Americans. Four years after graduating from Hampton, Washington returned to be the school's first African American instructor.

Washington had a steadfast belief that education could improve the lives of African Americans just as it had for white people: "Poverty and ignorance have affected the black man just as they affect the white man. But the day is breaking, and education will bring the complete light" (Rippa 1997, 122). In 1880, Washington helped to found the Tuskegee Institute, an industrial school for African Americans in rural Alabama. According to Washington, the Institute would play a key role in bringing about racial equality:

> The Tuskegee idea is that correct education begins at the bottom, and expands naturally as the necessities of the people expand. As the race grows in knowledge, experience, culture, taste, and wealth, its wants are bound to become more and more diverse; and to satisfy these wants there will be gradually developed within our ranks—as already has been true of the whites—a constantly increasing variety of professional and business men and women (Button and Provenzo 1989, 274).

W.E.B. DuBois (1868–1963)

Not all African Americans shared Washington's philosophy and goals. William E. Burghardt DuBois (1868–1963), the first African American to be awarded a Ph.D. and one of the founders of the National Association for the Advancement of Colored People (NAACP), challenged Booker T. Washington's views on education. In his book *The Souls of Black Folks,* DuBois criticized educational programs that seemed to imply that African Americans should accept inferior status and develop manual skills. DuBois called for the education of the most "talented tenth" of the African American population to equip them for leadership positions in society as a whole.

The Kindergarten

Early childhood education also spread following the Civil War. Patterned after the progressive, humanistic theories of the German educator Friedrich Froebel (1782–1852), the **kindergarten,** or "garden where children grow," stressed the motor development and self-activity of children before they began formal schooling at the elementary level. Through play, games, stories, music, and language activities, a foundation beneficial to the child's later educational and social development would be laid. After founding the first kindergarten in 1837, Froebel developed child-centered curriculum materials that were used in kindergartens in the United States and throughout the world.

Margarethe Schurz (1832–1876), a student of Froebel, opened the first U.S. kindergarten in her home at Watertown, Wisconsin, in 1855. Her small neighborhood class was conducted in German. In 1860, Elizabeth Palmer Peabody (1804–1891), sister-in-law of Horace Mann and the American writer Nathaniel Hawthorne, opened the first private English-speaking kindergarten in this country in Boston. Initially, kindergartens were privately supported, but in St. Louis in 1873, Susan Blow (1843–1916) established what is commonly recognized as the first successful public kindergarten in the United States. She patterned her kindergarten after one she visited while in Germany. So successful was her program that by 1879, a total of 131 teachers were working in fifty-three kindergarten classes (Button and Provenzo 1989, 169). The U.S. Bureau of Education recorded a total of twelve kindergartens in the country in 1873, with seventy-two teachers and 1,252 students. By 1997, enrollments had mushroomed to 2,847,000 in public kindergartens and 575,000 in private kindergartens (National Center for Education Statistics 1999, 61).

The Professionalization of Teaching

During the later 1800s, professional teacher organizations began to have a great influence on the development of schools in America. The National Education Association (NEA), founded in 1857, and the American Federation of Teachers (AFT), founded in 1916, labored diligently to professionalize teaching and to increase teachers' salaries and benefits.

By the early 1900s, the demand for teachers had grown dramatically. An increasing number of women entered the teaching field at this time, beginning a trend often referred to as the "feminization of teaching." Female teachers were given less respect from the community than their male predecessors, though they were still more highly regarded than women who worked in factories or as domestics. In addition, they were expected to be of high moral character. They were subjected to a level of public scrutiny hard to imagine today.

Women became influential in shaping educational policies during the early 1900s, in part through the women's suffrage movement that led to the right to vote. Women such as Ella Flagg Young (1845–1918), superintendent of Chicago schools from 1909 to 1915, and Catherine Goggin and Margaret Haley, leaders of the Chicago Teachers Federation, played important roles in the governance of Chicago schools (Holmes and Weiss 1995; Button and Provenzo 1989). Another Chicagoan and visionary educational leader, Jane Addams (1860–1935), founded Hull House, a social and educational center for poor immigrants. In *Democracy and Social Ethics* (published in 1902), Addams drew from her training as a social worker and developed a philosophy of socialized education that linked schools with other social service agencies and institutions in the city. At the ceremony to present her the Nobel Peace Prize in 1931, Addams was described as "the foremost woman of her nation" (Rippa 1997, 142).

Margaret Haley

What Were the Aims of Education during the Progressive Era (1920–1945)?

The philosophy of progressivism had a profound influence on the character of education in the United States from the end of World War I to the end of World War II. During the late nineteenth and early twentieth centuries, supporters of the **progressive movement** were intent on social reform to improve the quality of American life. As pointed out earlier, educational progressives believed that the child's interests and practical needs should determine the focus of schooling. In 1919, the Progressive Education Association was founded and went on to devote the next two decades to implementing progressive theories in the classroom that they believed would lead to the improvement of society.

Teachers in progressive schools functioned as guides rather than taskmasters. They first engaged students through providing activities related to their natural interests, and then they moved students to higher levels of understanding. To teach in this manner was demanding: "Teachers in a progressive school had to be extraordinarily talented and well educated; they needed both a perceptive understanding of children and a wide knowledge of the disciplines in order to recognize when the child was ready to move through an experience to a new understanding, be it in history or science or mathematics or the arts" (Ravitch 1983, 47).

John Dewey's Laboratory School

As pointed out earlier in this chapter, progressive educational theories were synthesized most effectively and eloquently by John Dewey (1859–1952). Born in the year that Darwin's *Origin of Species* was published, Dewey graduated from the University of Vermont when he was twenty. He later earned a doctorate at Johns Hopkins University, where his thinking was strongly influenced by the psychologist William James.

From 1894 to 1904, Dewey served as head of the departments of philosophy, psychology, and pedagogy at the University of Chicago. From 1904 until he re-

What hallmarks of progressive education are evident in this photograph of one of the first classrooms in the country operated according to Dewey's philosophy? How would a progressive classroom look today?

tired in 1930, Dewey was a professor of philosophy at Columbia University. Dewey's numerous writings have had a profound impact on U.S. schools. In his best-known works, *The School and Society* (1900) and *The Child and the Curriculum* (1902), Dewey states that school and society are connected and that teachers must begin with an understanding of the child's world, the psychological dimension, and then progress to the logical dimension represented by the accumulated knowledge of the human race.

While at the University of Chicago, Dewey and his wife, Alice, established a Laboratory School for testing progressive principles in the classroom. The school opened in 1896 with two instructors and sixteen students and by 1902 had grown to 140 students with twenty-three teachers and ten university graduate students as assistants. The children, four to fourteen years old, learned traditional subjects by working cooperatively in small groups of eight to ten on projects such as cooking, weaving, carpentry, sewing, and metalwork (Rippa 1997).

Maria Montessori's Method

Maria Montessori (1870–1952)

While Dewey's ideas provided the basis for the development of progressive education in the United States, progressive educators in Europe were similarly developing new approaches that would also impact American education. Chief among these was Maria Montessori (1870–1952), an Italian physician who was influenced by Rousseau and believed that children's mental, physical, and spiritual development could be enhanced by providing them with developmentally appropriate educational activities.

At Montessori's school for poor preschool-age children in Rome, teachers created learning environments based on students' levels of development and readiness to learn new material. According to the **Montessori method,** prescribed sets of materials and physical exercises are used to develop students' knowledge and skills, and students are allowed to use or not use the materials as they see fit. The materials arouse students' interest, and the interest motivates them to learn. Through highly individualized instruction, students develop self-discipline and self-confidence. Montessori's ideas spread throughout the world; by 1915, almost one hundred Montessori schools were operating in the United States (Webb, Metha, and Jordan 1999). Today, Montessorian materials and activities are a standard part of the early childhood and elementary curricula in public schools throughout the nation.

Education of Immigrants and Minorities

The diversity of America's school population increased dramatically during the late nineteenth and early twentieth centuries. Latin Americans, Eastern Europeans, and Southern Europeans followed earlier waves of Western- and Northern-European immigrants such as the Irish and Germans. As with Native American education, the goal of immigrant education was rapid assimilation into an English-speaking Anglo-European society that did not welcome racially or ethnically different newcomers.

Also at stake was the preservation or loss of traditional culture. In some areas, school policies included the punishment of Cuban and Puerto Rican children, for example, for speaking Spanish in school, and children learned to mock their unassimilated parents. In other areas, efforts were made to exclude certain groups, such as Asians, and ethnic enclaves established separate schools for the purpose of preserving, for example, traditional Chinese culture.

By the time Native Americans were granted U.S. citizenship in 1924, confinement on reservations and decades of forced assimilation had devastated Native American cultures and provided few successful educational programs. In 1928, a landmark report titled *The Problem of Indian Administration* recommended that Native American education be restructured. Among the recommendations were the building of day schools in Native American communities and the reform of boarding schools for Native American children. In addition, the report recommended that school curricula be revised to reflect tribal cultures and the needs of local tribal communities. Another fifty years passed before the recommendations began to be implemented.

How Did Education Change during the Modern Postwar Era (1945–present)?

Throughout the twentieth century and into the new century, many long-standing trends in U.S. education continued. These trends may be grouped and summarized in terms of three general patterns, shown in Figure 3.5 on page 104. At the same time, the decades since the end of World War II have seen a series of profound changes in U.S. education. These changes have addressed three as yet unanswered questions: (1) How can full and equal educational opportunity be extended to all groups in our culturally pluralistic society? (2) What knowledge and skills should be taught in our nation's schools? (3) How should knowledge and skills be taught?

The 1950s: Defense Education and School Desegregation

Teachers and education were put in the spotlight in 1957 when the Soviet Union launched the first satellite, named *Sputnik,* into space. Stunned U.S. leaders immediately blamed the space lag on inadequacies in the education system. The Soviet Union was first into space, they maintained, because the progressive educational philosophy had undermined academic rigor. For example, students

Three General Patterns of Trends in U.S. Education

Americanization

- Americanizing of European educational institutions and instructional models
- Americanizing of English language textbooks and curriculum
- Cultural assimilation of immigrants and others through education
- Aims of education based on moral didacticism and pragmatism
- Aims of education relating to child development and child welfare
- Aims of education relating to success in a society based on capitalism
- Aims of education relating to citizenship in a democracy

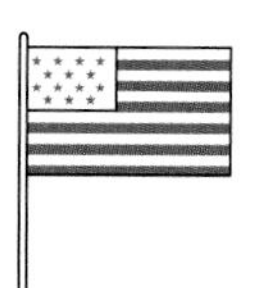

Democratization

- Steady growth of compulsory, free, secular, publicly funded education
- Preservation of state, local, and parental control of schooling and schools
- Protection of teachers' and students' rights under the U.S. Constitution
- Shifts in educational reform initiatives that reflect a two-party electoral system
- Continual expansion of early childhood education
- Continual expansion of opportunities for higher education and adult education
- Traumatic periodic extensions of educational opportunity to "other" Americans (women; racial, ethnic, and language minorities; people with disabilities)

Professionalization

- Professionalizing of teaching as an occupation
- Professionalizing of teacher organizations and associations
- Growth in scientific and bureaucratic models for the management of schools
- Rising standards for qualifications to teach
- Continual development of institutions and programs for teacher education
- Greater application of theory and research on teaching and learning
- Generally rising status and salaries for teachers as members of a profession

Figure 3.5 Three general patterns of trends in U.S. education

in the United States were taught less science, mathematics, and foreign language than their European counterparts.

The federal government appropriated millions of dollars over the next decade for educational reforms that reflected the essentialist educational philosophy. Through provisions of the **National Defense Education Act of 1958,** the U.S. Office of Education sponsored research and innovation in science, mathematics, modern foreign languages, and guidance. Out of their work came the new math; new science programs; an integration of anthropology, economics, political science, and sociology into new social studies programs; and renewed interest and innovations in foreign language instruction. Teachers were trained in the use of new methods and materials at summer workshops, schools were given funds for new equipment, and research centers were established. In 1964, Congress extended the act for three years and expanded Title III of the act to include money for improving instruction in reading, English, geography, history, and civics.

The end of World War II also saw the beginning of school **desegregation.** On May 17, 1954, the U.S. Supreme Court rejected the "separate but equal" doctrine that had been used since 1850 as a justification for excluding African Americans from attending school with whites. In response to a suit filed by the NAACP on behalf of a Kansas family, Chief Justice Earl Warren declared that to segregate school children "from others of similar age and qualifications solely because of their race generates a feeling of inferiority as to their status in the community that may affect their hearts and minds in a way unlikely ever to be undone" (***Brown v. Board of Education of Topeka* 1954**).

The Supreme Court's decision did not bring an immediate end to segregated schools. Though the court one year later ordered that desegregation proceed with "all deliberate speed," opposition to school integration arose in school districts across the country. Some districts, whose leaders modeled restraint and a spirit of cooperation, desegregated peacefully. Other districts became battlegrounds, characterized by boycotts, rallies, and violence.

The 1960s: The War on Poverty and the Great Society

The 1960s, hallmarked by the Kennedy administration's spirit of action and high hopes, provided a climate that supported change. Classrooms were often places of pedagogical experimentation and creativity reminiscent of the progressive era. The open-education movement, team teaching, individualized instruction, the integrated-day concept, flexible scheduling, and nongraded schools were some of the innovations that teachers were asked to implement. These structural, methodological, and curricular changes implied the belief that teachers were capable professionals.

The image of teachers in the 1960s was enhanced by the publication of several books by educators who were influenced by the progressivist educational philosophy and humanistic psychology. A. S. Neill's *Summerhill* (1960), Sylvia Ashton-Warner's *Teacher* (1963), John Holt's *How Children Fail* (1964), Herbert Kohl's *36 Children* (1967), James Herndon's *The Way It Spozed to Be* (1969), and Jonathan Kozol's *Death at an Early Age* (1967)—a few of the books that appeared at the time—gave readers inside views of teachers at work and teachers' perceptions of how students learn.

The administrations of Presidents Kennedy and Johnson funneled massive amounts of money into a War on Poverty. Education was seen as the key to breaking the transmission of poverty from generation to generation. The War on Poverty developed methods, materials, and programs such as subsidized breakfast and lunch programs, Head Start, Upward Bound, and the Job Corps that would be appropriate to children who had been disadvantaged due to poverty.

The War on Poverty has proved much more difficult to win than imagined, and the results of such programs nearly forty years later have been mixed. The three- to six-year-olds who participated in Head Start did much better when they entered public schools; however, academic gains appeared to dissolve over time. Although the Job Corps enabled scores of youth to avoid a lifetime of unemployment, many graduates returned to the streets where they eventually became statistics in unemployment and crime records. The education of low-income children received a boost in April 1965 when Congress passed the **Elementary and Secondary Education Act.** As part of President Johnson's Great Society program, the act allocated funds on the basis of the number of poor children in school districts. Thus schools in poverty areas that frequently had to cope with such problems as low achievement, poor discipline, truancy, and high teacher turnover rates received much needed assistance in addressing their problems.

In 1968, the Elementary and Secondary Education Act was amended with Title VII, the Bilingual Education Act. This act provided federal aid to low-income children "of limited English-speaking ability." The act did not spell out clearly what bilingual education might mean other than to say that it provided money for local school districts to "develop and carry out new and imaginative elementary and secondary school programs" to meet the needs of non-English-speaking children. Since the passing of Title VII, debate over the ultimate goal of

Keepers of *the Dream*

Marian Wright Edelman, Founder of Children's Defense Fund

Marian Wright Edelman knew discrimination even as a child. When she was five she was scolded by a friend for drinking from a water fountain reserved for whites only in a downtown department store in her hometown of Bennettsville, South Carolina. When she went to the movies there, she was not permitted to sit in seats on the first floor—they, too, were reserved for whites only. But the incident that angered her the most was seeing discrimination in the rescue workers at the scene of an accident on the highway near her home. The ambulance picked up the slightly injured white truck driver and left behind the seriously hurt black migrant workers who had been in the car the truck had hit. "I remember watching children like me bleeding," she recalls, "I remember the ambulance driving off. You never, ever forget" (Terry 1993, 4).

When she was fourteen, her father suffered a heart attack and was rushed to a hospital. Riding in the ambulance with him, Edelman listened to his dying wish for her, "Don't let anything get in the way of your education." Ten days after his death the Supreme Court outlawed school segregation in its *Brown v. Board of Education* decision.

"You never, ever forget."

Edelman followed her father's advice, graduating first from Spelman College and then from Yale Law School. When she obtained her law degree she returned to Mississippi, where she became the first African American woman to be admitted to the state's bar. After the Voting Rights Act of 1965 was passed, Edelman took up the cause of the poor.

Recognizing the need for a lobbying agency for children, she founded the Children's Defense Fund in Washington D.C. As its president she seeks "to educate the nation about the needs of children and encourage preventive investment in children before they get sick, drop out of school, suffer too-early pregnancy or family breakdown, or get into trouble."

Edelman's message for teachers is to see that all children, especially those who are poor, are taught how to read, write, and compute so that they can have positive and healthy options in their future. She believes strongly that

> all Americans must commit personally and as voters to a national crusade of conscience and action that will ensure that no child is left behind. Only we—individually and collectively—can transform our nation's priorities and assure its future as we face a new century and begin a new millennium. (Edelman 1992, 20)

bilingual education has been intense: Should it help students to make the *transition* to regular English-speaking classrooms, or should it help such students *maintain* their non-English language and culture?

The 1970s: Accountability and Equal Opportunity

The 1970s was a mixed decade for U.S. education, marked by drops in enrollment, test scores, and public confidence, as well as progressive policy changes that promoted a more equal education for all in the United States. Calls for "back to basics" and teacher accountability drives initiated by parents, citizens groups, and politicians who were unhappy with the low academic performance level of many students dominated this troubled decade at the height of the Vietnam conflict. For the first time in polling history, more than half of the U.S. adults polled in 1975 reported that they regarded themselves as better educated than the younger generation (Gallup 1975).

Financial difficulties also confronted the schools. National Center for Education Statistics data reveal that, instead of increasing as it had since 1940, the enrollment of children in prekindergarten through grade 8 in public and private schools declined by nearly five million during the 1970s (National Center for Education Statistics 1999, 12). Schools found themselves with a reduction in state aid, which was determined on the basis of pupil attendance figures. Financial problems were exacerbated by reduced support from local taxpayers, who resisted tax increases for the schools because they were stressed by their own economic problems, or had lost confidence in the schools, or because fewer of them had children in school. Consequently, this further reduced the ability to meet the needs of students.

Many parents responded to the crisis by becoming education activists, seeking or establishing alternative schools, or joining the home education movement led by John Holt, who by then had given up on reforming schools. These parents held a poor image of teachers and schools; they believed that they could provide a better education for their children than public school teachers could. Those who kept their children in the public schools demanded teacher **accountability,** which limited teachers' instructional flexibility and extended their evaluation paperwork. Basal readers and teacher-proof curricular packages descended on teachers, spelling out with their cookbook directions the deeper message that teachers were not to be trusted to teach on their own. Confidence in teachers reached a low point.

In addition, during the late 1960s and early 1970s increasing numbers of young people questioned what the schools were teaching and how they were teaching it. Thousands of them mobilized in protest against an establishment that, in their view, supported an immoral, undeclared war in Vietnam and was unconcerned with the oppression of minorities at home. In their search for reasons why these and other social injustices were allowed to exist, many militant youth groups singled out the schools' curricula. From their perspective, the schools taught subjects irrelevant to finding solutions to pressing problems.

Responding in good faith to their critics' accusations, schools greatly expanded their curricular offerings and instituted a wide variety of instructional strategies. In making these changes, however, school personnel gradually realized that they were alienating other groups: taxpayers who accused schools of extravagant spending; religious sects who questioned the values that children were being taught; **back-to-basics** advocates who charged that students were not learning how to read, write, and compute; and citizens who were alarmed at steadily rising school crime, drugs, and violence.

What impact has Title IX had on the education of females? What does equal educational opportunity for female and male students really mean?

On the Frontlines

Meeting Today's Cultural Challenges

For a field assignment for your credential program you are to teach a lesson in the subject you plan to teach. You meet with the assigned high school math teacher who selects the algorithm you'll teach. He also tells you about the class: eighteen Hispanic students—"seven speak little English"; three Chinese—"they speak some English but are very shy"; and five Anglos—"have to watch a couple of them—they laugh at the students struggling with English." You grew up in a part of the country and attended schools where everyone spoke English, so the linguistic diversity is new to you, exciting, but also a bit challenging.

You ask how you should work with the students who speak little English, and he explains that they decide for themselves if they want extra help. If they do, they move to the back of the room and sit at a table at which the bilingual aide sits. Shaking his head he adds, "Some who should get help don't, because they're embarrassed and don't want the others to see they need help." He assures you that students who are bilingual often step in and help out and promises that he will be in the room in case you need him. However, it's clear he intends to stay in the background to give you a sense of teaching on your own.

The time of your lesson has arrived. You are about to begin, and you want everyone, all twenty-six students, to learn, enjoy, and benefit from the lesson you have planned.

One of the greatest changes shaping U.S. education today and into the future is the changing demographic of its students. The 2000 census supported what had long been suspected and what educators have known for some time: that minority populations were becoming far less of a minority every year. This changing demographic challenges schools as they struggle to address the needs of *all* students. In her book, *Made in America: Immigrant Students in Our Public Schools,* Laurie Olsen shares the school experiences of adolescent students—immigrant and U.S.-born—and their perspectives on what she calls the Americanization project in our public schools. The problem for immigrant students is threefold: "(1) the marginalizing and separating of immigrant students academically; (2) requiring immigrant students to become English-speaking . . . in order to participate in the academic and social life of the high school; and (3) pressuring one to find and take his or her place in the racial hierarchy in the United States". The response of U.S.-born Americans to immigrants is similarly complex, as Olsen observes: "All of us engage in a massive struggle over the values of this nation, the meaning of diversity, the content of our race and language relations, and our visions of fairness, democracy, and inclusion".

Teachers find themselves in the midst of these challenges and soon realize that, because of their positions as teachers, they are key leaders, for good or ill, in navigating through them. As a teacher, your thoughts about diversity and inclusiveness, your personal biases and prejudices, your beliefs regarding each group of students, and your expectations and goals for them will be conveyed, consciously or unconsciously, through your words and actions. And your students will read them well. That is why as you prepare to teach, you need to examine your beliefs honestly, to work to overcome your prejudices, and to develop an overall teaching philosophy that can be a guiding compass when you encounter cross-cultural dilemmas.

New teachers need practical, detailed guidance immediately: What are "newcomer programs," and does your school or district have them? What school resources are available to help you communicate with parents who speak languages other than English? Fortunately, advice regarding teaching immigrant students is increasingly accessible. For instance, the Northwest Regional Educational Laboratory provides a booklet, *Meeting the Needs of Immigrant Students,* that contains helpful guidelines and checklists to

measure how immigrant-friendly your classroom is, with items such as—"Am I knowledgeable about the immigration experience of my students' families?" and "Do I use peer teaching, where limited-English proficient students can participate and practice English-language skills in small groups?" Finally, your own efforts to extend your understanding of the ethnic groups you will be teaching, combined with what you learn from sources like those noted below, can help increase your ability to teach and serve your immigrant students well

Exploratory Questions

1. How might you promote parent involvement in conferences, class activities, and school events with parents who speak little English?
2. How might you individualize your instruction to accommodate the learning styles and needs of students with limited English skills?
3. What are some ways to make immigrant students feel at home in your classroom?

Your Survival Guide of Helpful Resources

The following resources provide helpful hints for surviving "on the frontlines."

Books and Articles

Beykont, Z. F. (Ed.). (2002). *The power of culture: Teaching across language difference.* Cambridge, MA: Harvard Education Publication Group.

Gonzalez, J. M., and Darling-Hammond, L. (2000). Programs that prepare teachers to work effectively with students learning English (ERIC Digest: EDO-FL-00-09). Retrieved from http://www.cal.org/ericcll/digest/0009programs.html

Northwest Regional Educational Laboratory. (2001). *Meeting the needs of immigrant students.* Retrieved from http://www.nwrel.org/cnorse/booklets/immigration/5.html

Olsen, L. (1997). *Made in America: Immigrant students in our public schools.* New York: The New Press.

Walqui, A. (2000). Strategies for success: Engaging immigrant students in secondary schools (ERIC Digest: ED442300). Retrieved from http://www.ed.gov/databases/ERIC_Digests/ed442300.html

Companion Website

Despite the siege on teachers and schools, however, the reforms of the 1960s and 1970s did result in a number of improvements that have lasted into the present. More young people graduate from high school now than in previous decades, more teachers have advanced training, school buildings are better equipped, and instructional methods and materials are both more relevant to learners and more diverse.

For those people who had been marginalized by the educational system, the federal acts that were passed in the 1970s brought success and encouragement: the Title IX Education Amendment prohibiting sex discrimination (1972), the Indian Education Act (1972), the Education for All Handicapped Children Act (1975), and the Indochina Migration and Refugee Assistance Act (1975).

Title IX of the Education Amendments Act, which took effect in 1975, stated that "no person in the United States shall, on the basis of sex, be excluded from participation in, be denied the benefits of, or be subjected to discrimination under any education program or activity receiving Federal financial assistance."

The **Education for All Handicapped Children Act** (Public Law 94–142), passed by Congress in 1975, extended greater educational opportunities to children with disabilities. This act (often referred to as the **mainstreaming** law) specifies extensive due process procedures to guarantee that children with special needs will receive a free, appropriate education in the least restrictive educational environment. Through the act's provisions, parents are involved in planning educational programs for their children.

The 1980s: A Great Debate

The first half of the 1980s saw a continuation, perhaps even an escalation, of the criticisms aimed at the schools during the two previous decades. In fact, Lee Shulman (1987) characterized much of the 1980s as an era of "teacher bashing." With the publication in 1983 of the report by the National Commission on Excellence in Education, *A Nation at Risk: The Imperative for Educational Reform,* a great national debate was begun on how to improve the quality of schools. *A Nation at Risk* and dozens of other national reports on U.S. schools gave evidence to some that the schools were failing miserably to achieve their goals.

Responses included more proposals for curriculum reform. Mortimer Adler's *Paideia Proposal* (1982) called for a perennialist core curriculum based on the Great Books. *High School: A Report on Secondary Education in America* (1983), written by Ernest Boyer for the Carnegie Foundation for the Advancement of Teaching, suggested strengthening the academic core curriculum in high schools, a recommendation that was widely adopted. In 1986, former Secretary of the U.S. Department of Education William Bennett advocated a perennialist high school curriculum that he described in *James Madison High* (1987). Educators at the middle school level began to create small learning communities, eliminate tracking, and develop new ways to enhance student self-esteem as a result of the Carnegie Council on Adolescent Development report *Turning Points: Preparing American Youth for the 21st Century* (1989). These and other reform reports that swept the nation during the 1980s made a lasting imprint on education in the United States.

The 1990s: Teacher Leadership

The push to reform schools begun in the 1980s continued throughout the 1990s, and teaching was transformed in dramatic ways. In response to challenges such

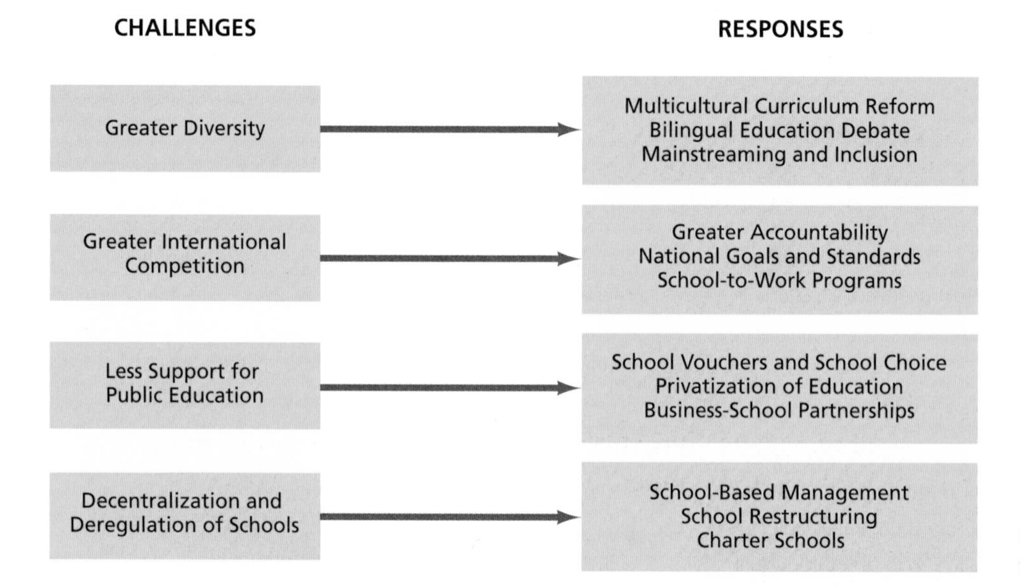

Figure 3.6 The 1990s: A sampler of trends in education

as greater diversity, greater international competition, less support for public education, and decentralization and deregulation of schools, innovative approaches to teaching and learning were developed throughout the United States (see Figure 3.6). Teachers went beyond the classroom and assumed leadership roles in school restructuring and educational reform—roles that we examine more fully in Chapters 12 and 13. Through collaborative relationships with students, principals, parents, and the private sector, teachers changed the nature of their profession. As one high school teacher said in the late 1990s: "I see it [change] happening. Not overnight, but I think it's going to. When I first started teaching in the early sixties, I would never have envisioned things changing as much as they have" (Grant and Murray 1999, 212).

The New Century: Continuing the Quest for Excellence

An excerpt from the mission statement of the International Centre for Educational Change at the Ontario Institute for Studies in Education captures well the world of teaching during the first decade of the new century—it is a "a world of intensifying and rapid change . . . [characterized by] new technologies, greater cultural diversity, restructured approaches to administration and management, and a more sophisticated knowledge-base about teaching and learning." As educators work within this complex, exciting environment, their work will be enhanced if they acknowledge the ideas and events described in this chapter. In effect, they will be students of our educational past to improve our educational future.

The United States has set for itself an education mission of truly ambitious proportions. To realize fully this mission during the new century will be difficult, but an examination of our history shows that it is not impossible. In little more than 380 years, our education system has grown from one that provided only a minimal education to an advantaged minority to one that now provides maximal educational opportunity to the majority. Clearly, the beginning of the new century provides ample evidence that our nation will not waver from its longstanding commitment to ensuring that all children have equal access to educational excellence.

Summary

What Determines Your Educational Philosophy?

- An educational philosophy is a set of beliefs about education, a set of principles to guide professional action.
- A teacher's educational philosophy is made up of personal beliefs about teaching and learning, students, knowledge, and what is worth knowing.

What Are the Branches of Philosophy?

- The branches of philosophy and the questions they address are (1) metaphysics (What is the nature of reality?), (2) epistemology (What is the nature of knowledge and is truth attainable?), (3) axiology (What values should one live by?), (4) ethics (What is good and evil, right and wrong?), (5) aesthetics (What is beautiful?), and (6) logic (What reasoning processes yield valid conclusions?).

What Are Five Modern Philosophical Orientations to Teaching?

- *Progressivism*—The aim of education should be based on the needs and interests of students.
- *Perennialism*—Students should acquire knowledge of enduring great ideas.
- *Essentialism*—Schools should teach students, in a disciplined and systematic way, a core of "essential" knowledge and skills.
- *Social reconstructionism*—In response to the significant social problems of the day, schools should take the lead in creating a new social order.
- *Existentialism*—In the face of an indifferent universe, students should acquire an education that will enable them to assign meaning to their lives.

What Psychological Orientations Have Influenced Teaching Philosophies?

- *Humanism*—Children are innately good, and education should focus on individual needs, personal freedom, and self-actualization.
- *Behaviorism*—By careful control of the educational environent and with appropriate reinforcement techniques, teachers can cause students to exhibit desired behaviors.
- *Constructivism*—Teachers should "understand students' understanding" and view learning as an active process in which learners construct meaning.

How Can You Develop Your Educational Philosophy?

- Instead of basing their teaching on only one educational philosophy, most teachers develop an eclectic educational philosophy.
- Professional teachers continually strive for a clearer, more comprehensive answer to basic philosophical questions.

What Were Teaching and Schools Like in the American Colonies (1620–1750)?

- Colonial education was patterned after the British two-track system and its primary objective was to promote religion.
- Puritans believed children were naturally corrupt and sinful and should be disciplined sternly at the dame schools, reading and writing schools, and Latin grammar schools common to the colonies.
- Mandated education in the United States had its origins in t wo colonial laws: the Massachusetts Acts of 1642 and 1647.
- At the end of the American Revolution, the few African and Native Americans who were literate were taught at church-sponsored schools that were segregated by race.

What Were the Goals of Education during the Revolutionary Period (1750–1820)?

- During the Revolutionary period, characterized by a declining European influence on American education, education in the new democracy was shaped by the ideas of Benjamin Franklin, Thomas Jefferson, and Noah Webster.
- Educational opportunities for women were often limited to preparing them for family life.

How Was the Struggle Won for State-Supported Common Schools (1820–1865)?

- Horace Mann, a strong advocate for state-supported, free common schools, believed that teachers should receive post secondary training in normal schools.
- The six-volume McGuffey reader, with its moral lessons and emphasis on virtue, determined much of what children learned at school.
- The Morrill Land-Grant Act, passed in 1862, provided federal land for colleges and set a precedent for federal involvement in education.

How Did Compulsory Education Change Schools and the Teaching Profession (1865–1920)?

- The spread of common schools and dramatic increases in their enrollments led to the use of scientific management techniques for their operation.
- Booker T. Washington, founder of the Tuskegee Institute, believed education could prepare African Americans to live peaceably with whites, while W. E. B. DuBois believed African Americans should educate themselves for leadership positions and not accept inferior status.
- Kindergartens became common and used child-centered curricula patterned after German educator Friedrich Froebel's ideas.
- The National Education Association (NEA) and the American Federation of Teachers (AFT) were founded to professionalize teaching and increase teachers' salaries and benefits.

What Were the Aims of Education during the Progressive Era (1920–1945)?

- John Dewey's Laboratory School at the University of Chicago, a model of progressive education, offered a curriculum based on children's interests and needs.
- Progressive educator Maria Montessori developed age-appropriate materials and teaching strategies that were implemented in the United States and throughout the world.
- Public criticism of progressive education led to its decline at the start of World War II. School enrollments became increasingly diverse as a result of immigration, and a goal of education was the rapid assimilation of all groups into an English-speaking Anglo-European culture.

How Did Education Change during the Modern Postwar Era (1945–present)?

- The Soviet Union's launching of *Sputnik* in 1957 sparked educational reform, particularly in science, mathematics, and foreign language education. Schools were ordered to desegregate with "all deliberate speed" as a result of a 1954 decision by the Supreme Court in *Brown v. Board of Education of Topeka.*
- Innovative curricula and instructional strategies were used in many classrooms of the 1960s. The Elementary and Secondary Education Act of 1965, part of President Johnson's Great Society and War on Poverty programs, provided federal money to improve the education of poor children.
- Alarmed by declining test scores, the public became critical of schools during the 1970s and demanded accountability. An array of federal legislation was passed to provide equal educational opportunity for all students.
- *A Nation at Risk* and other reports during the 1980s addressed weaknesses in U.S. schools and sparked a "Great Debate" on how to improve U.S. education.
- In response to continuing challenges to education, teachers during the 1990s took leadership roles in school restructuring, school governance, curriculum change, and other aspects of educational reform.

Key Terms and Concepts

Applications and Activities

Teacher's Journal

1. Imagine that you are a colleague of Frank, who was profiled in this chapter's opening scenario. Write a memo to him in which you react to his philosophical orientation to teaching.
2. Recall one of your favorite teachers in grades K–12. Which of the educational philosophies or psychological orientations to teaching described in this chapter best captures that teacher's approach to teaching? Write a descriptive sketch of that teacher "in action."
3. Based on what you have read in this chapter, identify several broad or long-term trends in the development of U.S. education that continue even today. How are those trends reflected in educational policies and practices through the decades? How is this trend evident at different points in the past and now? How might this trend be manifested in the future?
4. Write a personal history of your experience as a student, focusing on the age or grade level of the students you plan to teach. Conclude with an analysis of how you expect your experience as a student will influence you as a teacher.
5. Reflect on the "daily school routine" you experienced as an elementary-aged child. How does that routine differ from that experienced by children in colonial schools? Recall how your teachers handled classroom discipline; how do those approaches differ from those used by colonial teachers? How do your views of children differ from those held by Puritan teachers during the colonial era? Do "remnants" of the Puritan influence on U.S. education still exist today?

Teacher's Database

1. Visit the home page of the American Philosophical Association (APA), Philosophy in Cyberspace, The History of Education Site, or another professional organization devoted to educational philosophy or history and compile a list of online publications, associations, and reference materials you could use in developing your educational philosophy further.

Companion Website

2. Explore encyclopedias, bibliographies, periodicals, news sources, and online reference works to research in greater detail the contributions of a pioneer in education or a historical development described in Chapter 3.

Observations and Interviews

1. Interview a teacher for the purpose of understanding his or her educational philosophy. Formulate your interview questions in light of the philosophical concepts discussed in this chapter. Discuss your findings with classmates.
2. Administer a philosophical inventory (see Professional Reflection, "Using a Philosophic Inventory") to a group of teachers at a local school. Analyze the results and compare your findings with classmates. To guide you in this school-based activity, ask your instructor for handout master M3.2, "Administering an Educational Philosophy Inventory."
3. Observe the class of a teacher at the level at which you plan to teach. Which of the five philosophies or three psychological orientations to teaching discussed in this chapter most characterizes this teacher? To help you with this activity, ask your instructor for handout master M3.3, "Identifying Educational Philosophies in Action."
4. Visit a school and interview the principal about the school's educational philosophy. Ask him or her to comment on what is expected of teachers in regard to achieving the goals contained in the statement of philosophy.
5. Interview veteran teachers and administrators at a local school and ask them to comment on the changes in education that they have observed and experienced during their careers. In particular, compare their remarks to this chapter's discussion of education during the post–World War II era, using this chapter's descriptions of the era to guide your questions. What events do respondents identify as having had the greatest impact on their teaching?
6. As a collaborative project with classmates, conduct on-site interviews and observations for the purpose of researching the history of a particular school and its culture. You might also collaborate with teachers and students of history or social studies at the school to help you in your investigation. For more specific guidelines, ask your instructor for handout master M3.4, "Researching the History of a School."

Professional Portfolio

1. Prepare a written (or videotaped) statement in which you describe a key element of your educational philosophy. To organize your thoughts, focus on *one* of the following dimensions of educational philosophy:

- Beliefs about teaching and learning
- Beliefs about students
- Beliefs about knowledge
- Beliefs about what is worth knowing
- Personal beliefs about the six branches of philosophy

Develop your statement of philosophy throughout the course, covering all dimensions. On completion of your teacher-education program, review your portfolio entry and make any appropriate revisions. Being able to articulate your philosophy of education and your teaching philosophy will be an important part of finding your first job as a teacher.

2. Prepare a video- or audiotaped oral history of the school experiences of older members of the community. Focus on a topic or issue of special interest to you and prepare some questions and probes in advance. For instance, you might be interested in an aspect of curriculum or student relations. Analyze the oral histories in relation to the development of education in the United States and record your analysis.

VideoWorkshop Extra!

If the Video Workshop package was included with your textbook, go to Chapter 3 of the Companion Website (www.ablongman.com/parkay6e) and click on the Video Workshop button. Follow the instructions for viewing videoclip 5 and completing this exercise. Consider this information along with what you've read in Chapter 3 while answering the following questions.

1. An example of a teaching philosophy mentioned in videoclip 5 is that "students should be allowed to work at their own developmental level." Compare the different psychological orientations (humanism, behaviorism, constructivism) that influence teaching philosophies, and decide which orientation best supports the above philosophical notion.
2. Movements in education and educational aims have been strongly influenced by historical events. Which recent events might have an important influence on current educational practice, and how would educational standards change to reflect such philosophical development?

Using a Philosophic Inventory

Professional Reflection

The following inventory is to help identify your educational philosophy. Respond to the statements on the scale from 5 "Strongly Agree" to 1 "Strongly Disagree" by circling the number that most closely fits your perspective.

Strongly agree				**Strongly disagree**	
5	4	3	2	1	1. The curriculum should emphasize essential knowledge, *not* students' personal interests.
5	4	3	2	1	2. All learning results from rewards controlled by the external environment.
5	4	3	2	1	3. Teachers should emphasize interdisciplinary subject matter that encourages project-oriented, democratic classrooms.
5	4	3	2	1	4. Education should emphasize the search for personal meaning, *not* a fixed body of knowledge.
5	4	3	2	1	5. The ultimate aim of education is constant, absolute, and universal: to develop the rational person and cultivate the intellect.
5	4	3	2	1	6. Schools should actively involve students in social change to reform society.
5	4	3	2	1	7. Schools should teach basic skills, *not* humanistic ideals.
5	4	3	2	1	8. Eventually, human behavior will be explained by scientific laws, proving there is no free will.
5	4	3	2	1	9. Teachers should be facilitators and resources who guide student inquiry, *not* managers of behavior.

Strongly agree			**Strongly disagree**		
5	4	3	2	1	10. The best teachers encourage personal responses and develop self-awareness in their students.
5	4	3	2	1	11. The curriculum should be the same for everyone, the collective wisdom of Western culture delivered through lecture and discussion.
5	4	3	2	1	12. Schools should lead society toward radical social change, *not* transmit traditional values.
5	4	3	2	1	13. The purpose of schools is to ensure practical preparation for life and work, *not* to encourage personal development.
5	4	3	2	1	14. Good teaching establishes an environment to control student behavior and to measure learning of prescribed objectives.
5	4	3	2	1	15. Curriculum should emerge from students' needs and interests; therefore, it *should not* be prescribed in advance.
5	4	3	2	1	16. Helping students develop personal values is more important than transmitting traditional values.
5	4	3	2	1	17. The best education consists primarily of exposure to great works in the humanities.
5	4	3	2	1	18. It is more important for teachers to involve students in activities to criticize and transform society than to teach the Great Books.
5	4	3	2	1	19. Schools should emphasize discipline, hard work, and respect for authority, *not* encourage free choice.
5	4	3	2	1	20. Human learning can be controlled: Anyone can be taught to be a scientist or a thief; therefore, personal choice is a myth.
5	4	3	2	1	21. Education should enhance personal growth through problem solving in the present, *not* emphasize preparation for a distant future.
5	4	3	2	1	22. Because we are born with an unformed personality, personal growth should be the focus of education.
5	4	3	2	1	23. Human nature is constant–its most distinctive quality is the ability to reason; therefore, the intellect should be the focus of education.
5	4	3	2	1	24. Schools perpetuate racism and sexism camouflaged as traditional values.
5	4	3	2	1	25. Teachers should efficiently transmit a common core of knowledge, *not* experiment with curriculum.
5	4	3	2	1	26. Teaching is primarily management of student behavior to achieve the teacher's objectives.
5	4	3	2	1	27. Education should involve students in democratic activities and reflective thinking.
5	4	3	2	1	28. Students should have significant involvement in choosing what and how they learn.
5	4	3	2	1	29. Teachers should promote the permanency of the classics.
5	4	3	2	1	30. Learning should lead students to involvement in social reform.
5	4	3	2	1	31. On the whole, school should and must indoctrinate students with traditional values.
5	4	3	2	1	32. If ideas cannot be proved by science, they should be ignored as superstition and nonsense.
5	4	3	2	1	33. The major goal for teachers is to create an environment in which students can learn on their own by guided reflection on their experiences.
5	4	3	2	1	34. Teachers should create opportunities for students to make personal choices, *not* shape their behavior.
5	4	3	2	1	35. The aim of education should be the same in every age and society, *not* differ from teacher to teacher.
5	4	3	2	1	36. Education should lead society toward social betterment, *not* confine itself to essential skills.

Philosophic Inventory Score Sheet

In the space available, record the number you circled for each statement (1–36) from the inventory. Total the number horizontally and record it in the space on the far right of the score sheet. The highest total indicates your educational philosophy.

Essentialism

Essentialism was a response to progressivism and advocates a conservative philosophic perspective. The emphasis is on intellectual and moral standards that should be transmitted by the schools. The core of the curriculum should be essential knowledge and skills. Schooling should be practical and not influence social policy. It is a back-to-basics movement that emphasizes facts. Students should be taught discipline, hard work, and respect for authority. Influential essentialists include William C. Bagley, H. G. Rickover, Arthur Bestor, and William Bennett: E. D. Hirsch's *Cultural Literacy* could fit this category.

_____ + _____ + _____ + _____ + _____ + _____ = _____
1 7 13 19 25 31 Total

Behaviorism

Behaviorism denies free will and maintains that behavior is the result of external forces that cause humans to behave in predictable ways. It is linked with empiricism, which stresses scientific experiment and observation; behaviorists are skeptical about metaphysical claims. Behaviorists look for laws governing human behavior the way natural scientists look for empirical laws governing natural events. The role of the teacher is to identify behavioral goals and establish reinforcers to achieve goals. Influential behaviorists include B. F. Skinner, Ivan Pavlov, J. B. Watson, and Benjamin Bloom.

_____ + _____ + _____ + _____ + _____ + _____ = _____
2 8 14 20 26 32 Total

Progressivism

Progressivism focuses on the child rather than the subject matter. The students' interests are important; integrating thinking, feeling, and doing is important. Learners should be active and learn to solve problems by reflecting on their experience. The school should help students develop personal and social values. Because society is always changing, new ideas are important to make the future better than the past. Influential progressivists include John Dewey and Francis Parker.

_____ + _____ + _____ + _____ + _____ + _____ = _____
3 9 15 21 27 33 Total

Existentialism

Existentialism is a highly subjective philosophy that stresses the importance of the individual and emotional commitment to living authentically. It emphasizes individual choice over the importance of rational theories. Jean Paul Sartre, the French philosopher, claimed that "existence precedes essence." People are born, and each person must define him- or herself through choices in life. Influential existentialists include Jean Paul Sartre, Soren Kierkegaard, Martin Heidegger, Gabriel Marcel, Albert Camus, Carl Rogers, A. S. Neill, and Maxine Greene.

_____ + _____ + _____ + _____ + _____ + _____ = _____
4 10 16 22 28 34 Total

Perennialism

The aim of education is to ensure that students acquire knowledge about the great ideas of Western culture. Human beings are rational, and it is this capacity that needs to be developed. Cultivation of the intellect is the highest priority of an education worth having. The highest level of knowledge in each field should be the focus of curriculum. Influential perennialists include Robert Maynard Hutchins, Mortimer Adler, and Allan Bloom.

_____ + _____ + _____ + _____ + _____ + _____ = _____
5 11 17 23 29 35 Total

Reconstructionism

Reconstructionists advocate that schools should take the lead to reconstruct society. Schools have more than a responsibility to transmit knowledge, they have the mission to transform society as well. Reconstructionists go beyond progressivists in advocating social activism. Influential reconstructionists include Theodore Brameld, Paulo Friere, and Henry Giroux.

_____ + _____ + _____ + _____ + _____ + _____ = _____
6 12 18 24 30 36 Total

(*Source:* Prepared by Robert Leahy for *Becoming a Teacher: Accepting the Challenge of a Profession,* 3d ed., 1995. Used by permission of the author.)

Social Realities Confronting Today's Schools

As society changes, so change the dimensions of the teacher's task.

—Steven E. Tozer, Paul C. Violas, and Guy B. Senese
School & Society: Educational Practice as Social Expression

Jeff Banks, a history teacher at Southside High School, enters the faculty lunchroom and sees his friends, Sue Anderson, Nancy Watkins, and Bret Thomas, at their usual table in the corner. Southside is located in a medium-size city in the Southeast. The school, in the center of a low- to middle-income area known as Lawndale, has an enrollment of almost 1,900 students. About 70 percent of these self-identify as Anglo-European Americans, with the remaining 30 percent about evenly divided between African Americans and Mexican Americans. Southside has a reputation for being a "good" school—for the most part, students are respectful of their teachers. Parents, many of whom work in the several small factories found in Lawndale, generally support the school and are involved in school activities in spite of their heavy work schedules. The consensus among teachers is that most Southside parents recognize that education is the key if their children are to "better themselves" and move out of Lawndale.

As soon as Jeff is within earshot of his friends, he knows they are talking about yesterday's tragic shooting at a high school in Germany. During a rampage that lasted several hours at the school, an expelled student killed fifteen adults, two students, and then himself. The incident is eerily reminiscent of the carnage that took place at a high school in Colorado a few years ago. In that instance, two boys killed twelve fellow students, one teacher, and then themselves.

"It's so scary," Sue says, "Who knows, something like that could happen right here at Southside. We have no idea what kids have to deal with today."

"Yeah, we have no idea who might snap," says Bret. "With a lot of these school shootings lately, it seems to be a kid that no one would have expected. Quiet, polite, good student—you just never know."

"In some cases, that's true," Jeff says, placing his lunch tray on the table and then sitting down between Sue and Bret. "But a lot of time there are signs. A lot of these kids are loners and outcasts; they're into violent video games, cults, drugs, guns, you name it."

"What I want to know," says Sue, "is how we can prevent something like that from happening here? Since the Colorado shootings, there have been bomb scares, threats, guns confiscated at dozens of schools around the country."

"Well, I don't think metal detectors, more police in schools, and stiffer penalties for kids who bring guns to school are necessarily the answers," says Bret. "The question is, Why are kids doing this?"

"Right, how can we prevent things like this?" says Jeff.

"If we're going to change things," says Sue, "we've got to figure out ways to identify and help kids who feel so desperate that they turn to violence."

"Well, that's all well and good," says Nancy with a sigh. "But I don't see where all of this is going to lead. Our responsibility as teachers is to educate our kids. We're not psychiatrists or social workers. We can't change society. Besides, we've got youth agencies, centers for families in crisis, and all kinds of social service agencies."

What is the role of schools during the first decade of the twenty-first century? Should teachers play a role in addressing social problems such as violence in our society? What would you say to a teacher who expresses views such as Nancy's?

Focus Questions

1. **What is the role of schools in today's society?**
2. **How can schools be described?**
3. **What are schools like as social institutions?**
4. **What characteristics distinguish successful schools?**
5. **What social problems affect schools and place students at risk?**
6. **What are schools doing to address societal problems?**
7. **How can community-based partnerships address social problems that hinder students' learning?**

Expand your knowledge of the concepts discussed in this chapter by reading current and historical articles from the *New York Times* by visiting the **"Themes of the Times"** section of the Companion Website (www.ablongman.com/parkay6e).

The discussion among Jeff and his fellow teachers highlights the expectation of much of the public that schools (and teachers) have a responsibility to address problems that confront modern society. Those who agree with Nancy's point of view tend to believe that schools should teach only content to students. Others, however, believe that teachers have an obligation to address domestic social problems.

What Is the Role of Schools in Today's Society?

In the United States, people agree that the role of schools is to educate. Unlike other institutions in society, schools have been developed exclusively to carry out that very important purpose. That we are not always in agreement about what the role of schools should be, however, is illustrated by the fact that we disagree about what it means to be an educated person. Is a person with a college degree educated? Is the person who has overcome, with dignity and grace, extreme hardships in life educated?

Schools and Prosocial Values

Although there is widespread debate about what academic content the schools should teach, the public agrees that schools should teach **prosocial values** such as honesty, patriotism, fairness, and civility. The well-being of any society requires support of such values; they enable people from diverse backgrounds to live together peacefully. One poll of the public, for example, revealed that 90 percent or more of the public believed that the following values should be taught in public schools: respect for others, industry or hard work, persistence or the ability to follow through, fairness in dealing with others, compassion for others, and civility and politeness (Elam, Rose, and Gallup 1994). The strong support for these prosocial values reflects the public's belief that the schools should play a key role in promoting the democratic ideal of equality for all.

Schools and Socialization of the Young

Schools are places where the young become socialized—where they learn to participate intelligently and constructively in the nation's society. This purpose is contained in the national educational goal that calls for schools to prepare students for "responsible citizenship, further learning, and productive employment in our nation's modern economy." The 1998 Phi Delta Kappa/Gallup Poll revealed that 79 percent of the public believed that the practice of good citizenship was a "very important" measure of school effectiveness, even more important than going on to postsecondary education, getting a job, or scoring well on standardized tests (Rose and Gallup 1998).

Additionally, schools, more than any other institution in our society, assimilate persons from different ethnic, racial, religious, and cultural backgrounds and pass on the values and customs of the majority. The Los Angeles Unified School District, for example, recently reported that its students represented nine major language groups and 171 languages. It is through the schools that persons from such diverse backgrounds learn English and learn about the importance Americans attach to the Fourth of July or Veterans Day; about the contributions of George Washington, Abraham Lincoln, or Dr. Martin Luther King Jr.; and about the basic workings of capitalism and democracy.

In what ways do schools serve a socialization function for students and communities alike? How do they reflect their communities and the wider American society?

Schools and Social Change

Schools also provide students with the knowledge and skills to improve society and the quality of life and to adapt to rapid social change. Naturally, there exists a wide range of opinion about how society might be improved. Some teachers, like Jeff, Sue, and Bret in this chapter's opening scenario, believe that one purpose of schooling is to address social problems such as violence in society; while other teachers, such as their friend, Nancy, believe schools should teach academic content and not try to change society. Less controversial have been efforts to prepare students to serve others through volunteerism and to participate actively in the political life of the nation. During the early 1990s, some high schools began to direct every student to complete a service requirement to help students see that they are not only autonomous individuals but also members of a larger community to which they are accountable. Other schools began to introduce service-learning activities into their curricula. **Service learning** provides students with opportunities to deliver service to their communities while engaging in reflection and study on the meaning of those experiences. Service learning brings young people into contact with the elderly, the sick, the poor, and the homeless, as well as acquaints them with neighborhood and governmental issues.

Schools and Equal Educational Opportunity

Ample evidence exists that certain groups in U.S. society are denied equality of opportunity economically, socially, and educationally. For example, if we look at the percentage of children three to four years old who participate in early childhood programs such as Head Start, nursery school, and prekindergarten—experiences that help children from less advantaged backgrounds start elementary school on an equal footing with other children—we find that children from lower-income families are less likely to have such opportunities (National Center for Education Statistics 2002a). In addition, there is a positive relationship between parents' educational attainment and their children's enrollment in early childhood programs; also, Latino children are less likely to be enrolled than white or African American children (National Center for Education Statistics 2002a).

Technology Highlights

Are up-to-date technologies being used effectively in low-income urban schools?

According to two recent reports (Education Writers Association 2001; Lonergan 2001), the gap in the availability of computers and Internet access between affluent and poor schools has decreased dramatically since the early 1990s. For example, federal funding has enabled low-income schools in Chicago, Milwaukee, Detroit, and Cleveland to acquire extensive telecommunications networks and high-speed bandwidth to support audio, video, and data transmissions.

In poorer urban school districts, however, funding and time to train teachers to use technology are often lacking. Furthermore, teachers in low-income schools often use computers for drill and practice only, rather than for research and inquiry as do teachers in wealthier schools. Teachers assume that children need to learn basic skills through drill and practice before they can move on to higher-order problem solving. In addition, pressure to do well on standardized tests has led teachers to use drill-and-practice software rather than software that promotes critical thinking and reasoning.

What technologies do you think should be available to *all* students to enhance their learning? What technologies should be available to *all* teachers? What would be the impact on *your* current ability to learn if you had access only to outdated equipment, or none at all? What leadership roles can teachers in urban schools take to increase their students' access to advanced technologies?

Source: Education Writers Association, *New Networks, Old Problems: Technology in Urban Schools.* Washington, DC: Education Writers Association, 2001. Available from the Education Writers Association, 1331 H Street NW #307, Washington, DC 20005, (202) 637-9700; fax (202) 637-9707; ewa@ewa.org. James M. Lonergan, "Preparing Urban Teachers to Use Technology for Instruction," *ERIC Digest, No. 168,* October 2001.

Extensive programs at the federal, state, and local levels have been developed to provide equity for all in the United States—regardless of race, ethnicity, language, gender, or religion. The United States has always derived strength from the diversity of its people, and all students should receive a quality education so that they may make their unique contributions to society.

The goal of providing equal educational opportunity for all has long distinguished education in the United States from that found in most other countries. Since the 1850s, schools in the United States have been particularly concerned with providing children from diverse backgrounds the education they need to succeed in our society. As James Banks (1999, 4) suggests, "Education within a pluralistic society should affirm and help students understand their home and community cultures. [To] create and maintain a civic community that works for the common good, education in a democratic society should help students acquire the knowledge, attitudes, and skills needed to participate in civic action to make society more equitable and just."

How Can Schools Be Described?

Given the wide variation in schools and their cultures, many models have been proposed for describing the distinguishing characteristics of schools. Schools can be categorized according to the focus of their curricula; for example, high schools may be college prep, vocational, or general. Another way to view schools is according to their organizational structure; for example, open schools or magnet schools. A **magnet school** allows students from an entire district to attend a school's specialized program. Some magnet schools are organized around specific academic disciplines such as science, mathematics, or the basic skills; others focus on the performing and visual arts, health professions, computers, or international studies and languages.

Metaphors for Schools

Other models view schools metaphorically; that is, what is a school like? Some schools, for example, have been compared to factories; students enter the school as raw material, move through the curriculum in a systematic way, and exit the school as finished products. Terrence Deal and Kent Peterson (1999, 21) have suggested that exemplary schools "become like tribes or clans, with deep ties among people and with values and traditions that give meaning to everyday life." Others have suggested that schools are like banks, gardens, prisons, mental hospitals, homes, churches, families, and teams.

In the school-as-family metaphor, for example, the effective school is a caring community of adults who attend to the academic, emotional, and social needs of the children and youth entrusted to their care.

Schools and Social Class

In spite of a general consensus that schools should promote social change and equal opportunity, some individuals believe that schools "reproduce" the existing society by presenting different curricula and educational experiences to students from different socioeconomic classes. Students at a school in an affluent suburb, for example, may study chemistry in a well-equipped lab and take a field trip to a high-tech industry to see the latest application of chemical research, while students at a school in an impoverished inner-city neighborhood learn chemistry from out-of-date texts, have no lab in which to conduct experiments, and take no field trips because the school district has no funds. Schools, in effect, preserve the stratification within society and maintain the differences between the "haves" and the "have-nots." As Joel Spring puts it: "The affluent members of U.S. society can protect the educational advantages and, consequently, economic advantages, of their children by living in affluent school districts or by using private schools. [T]heir children will attend the elite institutions of higher education, and their privileged educational background will make it easy for them to follow in the footsteps of their parent's financial success" (Spring 1999, 290–291).

A useful way to talk about the relationship between schooling and social class in the United States is suggested by the four categories of schools Jean Anyon (1996) found in her study of several elementary schools in urban and suburban New Jersey. Anyon maintains that schools reproduce the existing society by presenting different curricula and educational experiences to students from different socioeconomic classes.

Anyon studied a small group of schools in one metropolitan area and her criteria are linked almost exclusively to socioeconomic status. Few schools actually fit the categories in all ways.

The first kind of school she calls the *working-class school.* In this school, the primary emphasis is on having students follow directions as they work at rote, mechanical activities such as completing dittoed worksheets. Students are given little opportunity to exercise their initiative or to make choices. Teachers may make negative, disparaging comments about students' abilities and, through subtle and not-so-subtle means, convey low expectations to students. Additionally, teachers at working-class schools may spend much of their time focusing on classroom management, dealing with absenteeism, and keeping extensive records.

The *middle-class school* is the second type identified by Anyon. Here, teachers emphasize to students the importance of getting right answers, usually in the form of words, sentences, numbers, or facts and dates. Students have slightly more opportunity to make decisions, but not much. Most lessons are textbook based. Anyon points out that "while the teachers spend a lot of time explaining and expanding on what the textbooks say, there is little attempt to analyze how or why things happen. . . . On the occasions when creativity or self-expression is requested, it is peripheral to the main activity or it is 'enrichment' or 'for fun' " (Anyon 1996, 191).

The *affluent professional school,* unlike the previous two types of schools, gives students the opportunity to express their individuality and to make a variety of choices. Fewer rules govern the behavior of students in affluent professional schools, and teacher and student are likely to negotiate about the work the student will do.

Anyon provides the following definition of the fourth type of school she identified, the *executive elite school:*

> In the executive elite school, work is developing one's analytical intellectual powers. Children are continually asked to reason through a problem, to produce intellectual products that are both logically sound and of top academic quality (Anyon 1996, 196).

In the affluent professional and executive elite schools, teacher–student relationships are more positive than those in the working-class and middle-class schools. Teachers are polite to their students, seldom give direct orders, and almost never make sarcastic or nasty remarks. However schools are categorized, it seems clear that they reflect the socioeconomic status of the communities they serve.

What Are Schools Like as Social Institutions?

Schools are social institutions. An **institution** is an organization established by society to maintain and improve its way of life. Schools are the institutions our society has established for the purpose of educating the young. For the last two hundred years, American schools have developed complex structures, policies, and curricula to accomplish this mission.

The School as a Reflection of Society

As you might expect, schools mirror the national culture and the surrounding local culture and other special interests. Private, parochial, and religious schools, for example, are often maintained by groups that see the school as a means of perpetuating their preferred way of life. One example of how schools reflect contemporary priorities in life in the United States is the growing number of public schools located in shopping malls. In commenting on his experiences at a school located in the Landmark Shopping Mall in Northern Virginia, a student is able to say that the goal of countless students around the country is his reality: "As well as getting an education, I get a job" (Spring 1997, 4). Nevertheless, as Mary Henry (1993, 29) points out, "Schools are . . . not simply puppets of the dominant mainstream society. They have their own unique concerns and their own 'poetry' of people and events. Whether public or private, all schools are not the same."

Rural, Suburban, and Urban Schools Schools also reflect their location. Schools in rural, urban, and suburban settings often have significantly different cultures. Rural schools are often the focal point for community life and reflect values and beliefs that tend to be more conservative than those associated with urban and suburban schools. While the small size of a rural school may contribute to the development of a family-like culture, its small size may also make it difficult to provide students with an array of curricular experiences equal to that found at larger schools in more populated areas. In contrast, large suburban or urban schools may provide students with more varied learning experiences, but these schools may lack the cohesiveness and community focus of rural schools.

Schools and Community Environments The differences among the environments that surround schools can be enormous. Urban schools found in or near decaying centers of large cities often reflect the social problems of the surrounding area, such as drug abuse, crime, and poverty. One of the most serious problems confronting education in the United States is the quality of such schools. Across the country—in Chicago, New York, Los Angeles, St. Louis, Detroit, and Cleveland—middle-class families who can afford to, move away from urban centers or place their children in private schools. As a result, students in urban school districts are increasingly from low-income backgrounds.

In *Savage Inequalities*, Jonathon Kozol documents the startling contrast between the neighborhoods that surround impoverished inner-city schools and those that surround affluent suburban schools. In comparing New Trier High School in affluent Winnetka, Illinois, and Chicago's DuSable High School, an inner-city school at which the first author of this textbook taught for eight years, Kozol points out that New Trier is in a neighborhood of "circular driveways, chirping birds and white-columned homes" (1991, 62). In contrast, DuSable's surroundings are "almost indescribably despairing"; across the street from the school is "a line of uniform and ugly 16-story buildings, the Robert Taylor Homes, which constitute . . . the city's second-poorest neighborhood" (1991, 68, 71).

Though the extreme poverty found in some communities may impact their schools in undesirable ways, effective teachers at such schools communicate to students that they are "rich" in ways that go beyond material wealth—as one adult wrote to her second-grade teacher (Paul and Smith 2000, 53):

> *Dear Mrs. Smith,*
>
> *This letter is to thank you for your kindness and support when I was in your second grade class. . . . My family was receiving public assistance and people were always coming to the school to check my shoes or my coat to see if I qualified for new ones. . . . You never drew attention to me when I needed to go into the hall to see one of the public assistance workers and you were always adding little things to my lunches. You even did a lesson about having real wealth and I knew that you were talking to me. You were a wonderful, caring teacher and I will never forget you.*
>
> *THANK YOU!*
>
> *Jenny*

The Culture of the School

Although schools are very much alike, each school is unique. Each has a culture of its own—a network of beliefs, values and traditions, and ways of thinking and behaving that distinguishes it from other schools.

Much like a community, a school has a distinctive culture—a collective way of life. Terms that have been used to describe **school culture** include *climate, ethos, atmosphere,* and *character.* Some schools may be characterized as community-like places where there is a shared sense of purpose and commitment to providing the best education possible for all students. Other schools lack a unified sense of purpose or direction and drift, rudderless, from year to year. Still others are characterized by internal conflict and divisiveness and may even reflect what Deal and Peterson (1999) term a "toxic" school culture; students, teachers, administrators, and parents may feel that the school is not sufficiently meeting their needs. The following excerpt from the mission statement of an award-winning school in the high desert of Northern Arizona illustrates several qualities of a school culture that nurtures students:

> *The Ganado Primary School's mission is to provide opportunities for children to make sense of their world, to respect themselves and others, to respect their environment, and to appreciate and understand their cultural and linguistic heritage. [Our] mission is to help everyone [children, teachers, and administrators] negotiate their experiences with the content of the classroom, instructional style, and the social, emotional, physical and professional interactions of school life. We believe that a relaxed atmosphere [characterized by] surprise, challenge, hard work, celebration, humor, satisfaction, and collegiality is the natural order of the day for all (Deal and Peterson 1999, 17).*

The Physical Environment The physical environment of the school both reflects and helps to create the school's overall culture. "Whether school buildings are squeezed between other buildings or located on sprawling campuses, their fenced-in area or other physical separation distinguishes them from the community-at-large" (Ballantine 1997, 210). Some schools are dreary places or, at best, aesthetically bland. The tile floors, concrete block walls, long, straight corridors, and rows of fluorescent lights often found in these schools contribute little to their inhabitants' sense of beauty, concern for others, or personal comfort.

Other schools are much more attractive. They are clean, pleasant, and inviting; and teachers and students take pride in their building. Overall, the physical environment has a positive impact on those who spend time in the school; it encourages learning and a spirit of cohesiveness.

Formal Practices of Schools The formal practices of schools are well known to anyone who has been educated in U.S. schools. With few exceptions, students attend school from six years of age through sixteen at least, and usually to eighteen, Monday through Friday, September through May, for twelve years. For the most part, students are assigned to grade level on the basis of age rather than ability or interest. Assignment to individual classes or teachers at a given grade level, however, may be made on the basis of ability or interest.

Teachers and students are grouped in several ways in the elementary school and in one dominant pattern in junior and senior high school. At the elementary school level, the **self-contained classroom** is the most traditional and prevalent arrangement. In this type of classroom, one teacher teaches all or nearly all subjects to a group of about twenty-five children, with the teacher and students remaining in the same classroom for the entire day. Often art, music, physical education, and computer skills are taught in other parts of the school, so students may leave the classroom for scheduled periods. Individual students may also attend special classes for remedial or advanced instruction, speech therapy, or instrumental music and band lessons.

In **open-space schools,** students are free to move among various activities and learning centers. Instead of self-contained classrooms, open-space schools have large instructional areas with movable walls and furniture that can be rearranged easily. Grouping for instruction is much more fluid and varied. Students do much of their work independently, with a number of teachers providing individual guidance as needed.

In middle schools and junior and senior high schools, students typically study four or five academic subjects taught by teachers who specialize in them. In this organizational arrangement, called **departmentalization,** students move from classroom to classroom for their lessons. High school teachers often share their classrooms with other teachers and use their rooms only during scheduled class periods.

School Traditions **School traditions** are those elements of a school's culture that are handed down from year to year. The traditions of a school reflect what students, teachers, administrators, parents, and the surrounding community believe is important and valuable about the school. One school, for example, may have developed a tradition of excellence in academic programs; another school's traditions may emphasize the performing arts; and yet another may focus on athletic programs. Whatever a school's traditions, they are usually a source of pride for members of the school community.

Ideally, traditions are the glue that holds together the diverse elements of a school's culture. They combine to create a sense of community, identity, and trust among people affiliated with a school. Traditions are maintained through stories that are handed down, rituals and ceremonial activities, student productions, and trophies and artifacts that have been collected over the years. For example, Joan Vydra, now principal of Briar Glen Elementary School in Wheaton, Illinois, initiated Care Week as part of the fall tradition at her former school, Hawthorne Elementary. Vydra believed that a tradition of care would nurture student success. On the first day of Care Week, students learned the importance of caring for themselves; on Tuesdays, caring for their families; on Wednesdays, caring for each other; on Thursdays, caring for the school; and on Fridays, caring for those served by local charities (Deal and Peterson 1999).

The Culture of the Classroom

Just as schools develop their unique cultures, each classroom develops its own culture or way of life. The culture of a classroom is determined in large measure by the manner in which teacher and students participate in common activities. In addition, "the environment of the classroom and the inhabitants of that environment—students and teachers—are constantly interacting. Each aspect of the system affects all others" (Woolfolk 2001, 434).

The quality of teacher–student interactions is influenced by the physical characteristics of the setting (classroom, use of space, materials, resources, etc.) and the social dimensions of the group (norms, rules, expectations, cohesiveness, distribution of power and influence). These elements interact to shape **classroom culture.** Teachers who appreciate the importance of these salient elements of classroom culture are more likely to create environments that they and their students find satisfying and growth-promoting. For example, during the second month of student teaching in the second grade, "Miss Martin" reflects on her efforts to create a classroom culture characterized by positive teacher–student interactions:

> *I started off with a big mistake. I tried to be their friend. I tried joining with them in all the jokes and laughter that cut into instruction time. When this didn't work, I overcompensated by yelling at them when I needed them to quiet down and get to work. I wasn't comfortable with this situation. I did not think it was like me to raise my voice at a child. I knew I needed to consider how they felt. I realized that if I were them, I'd hate me, I really would. In desperation, I turned to my education textbooks for advice.*
>
> *This was a huge help to me, but a book can only guide you. It can't establish a personality for you or even manage your classroom for you. You have to do that yourself and as lovingly and effectively as possible. But I had so much trouble finding a middle ground: love them, guide them, talk to them, manage them, but don't control them (Rand and Shelton-Colangelo 1999, 8–9).*

Similarly, students believe that effective teachers develop positive, task-oriented classroom cultures, while ineffective teachers develop negative cultures. At one inner-city school, for example,

> *[sixth-grade] students saw their social studies/language arts teacher as someone they could learn from and relate to well, while they seemed to constantly do battle with their math and science teacher. Students portrayed [the math and science teacher] as overdemanding, impatient, and insensitive; [the social studies/language arts teacher] seemed to be just the opposite. [The math and science teacher], according to one student, "has an attitude problem. She wants us to be so good the*

> *first time. She wants us to always be perfect. She has us walk in a line in the hallway. We are the only class in the school to do that. . . . She is the only [teacher] who won't go over things. She never comes in with a smile; she is always evil. By not going over it, we got a bad attitude. I haven't learned nothing in her class" (Wilson and Corbett 2001, 54–55).*

Clearly, the math and science teacher has developed an adversarial, counterproductive relationship with students. The social studies/language arts teacher, on the other hand, recognizes the importance of developing positive relationships with students and understands how such relationships pave the way for student learning.

What Characteristics Distinguish Successful Schools?

Like Miss Martin referenced above, you may be uncertain at this point in your professional education of your ability to develop a positive classroom climate at a school. However, a great many schools in all settings and with all kinds of students are highly successful, including inner-city and isolated rural schools and schools that serve pupils of all socioeconomic, racial, and ethnic backgrounds. What are the characteristics of these schools? Do they have commonalities that account for their success?

Measures of Success

First, we must define what we mean by a *successful school.* One measure of success, naturally, is that students at these schools achieve at a high level and complete requirements for graduation. Whether reflected in scores on standardized tests or other documentation of academic learning gains, students at these schools are learning. They are achieving literacy in reading, writing, computation, and computer skills. They are learning to solve problems, think creatively and analytically, and, most importantly, they are learning to learn.

Another valid measure of success for a school is that it achieves results that surpass those expected from comparable schools in comparable settings. The achievement of students goes beyond what one would expect. In spite of surrounding social, economic, and political forces that impede the educative process at other schools, these schools are achieving results.

Finally, successful schools are those that are improving, rather than getting worse. School improvement is a slow process, and schools that are improving—moving in the right direction rather than declining—are also successful.

Research on School Effectiveness

During the 1980s and early 1990s, much research was conducted to identify the characteristics of successful (or effective) schools. The characteristics of successful schools were described in different ways in several research projects. The following is a synthesis of those findings.

- *Strong leadership*—Successful schools have strong leaders—individuals who value education and see themselves as educational leaders, not just as managers or bureaucrats. They monitor the performance of everyone at the school—teachers, staff, students, and themselves. These leaders have a vision of the school as a more effective learning environment, and they take decisive steps to bring that about.

- *High expectations*—Teachers at successful schools have high expectations of students. These teachers believe that all students, rich or poor, can learn, and they communicate this to students through realistic, yet high, expectations.

- *Emphasis on basic skills*—Teachers at successful schools emphasize student achievement in the basic skills of reading, writing, and mathematical computation.
- *Orderly school environment*—The environments of successful schools are orderly, safe, and conducive to learning. Discipline problems are at a minimum, and teachers are able to devote greater amounts of time to teaching.
- *Frequent, systematic evaluation of student learning*—The learning of students in successful schools is monitored closely. When difficulties are noticed, appropriate remediation is provided quickly.
- *Sense of purpose*—Those who teach and those who learn at successful schools have a strong sense of purpose. From the principal to the students, everyone at the school is guided by a vision of excellence.
- *Collegiality and a sense of community*—Teachers, administrators, and staff at successful schools work well together. They are dedicated to creating an environment that promotes not only student learning but also their own professional growth and development.

Research has also focused on strategies for making schools more effective. Since the early 1990s, school districts across the nation have been participating in school restructuring that changes the way students are grouped, uses of classroom time and space, instructional methods, and decision making. A synthesis of research (Newmann and Wehlage 1995) conducted between 1990 and 1995 on restructuring schools identified four characteristics of successful schools:

1. *Focus on student learning*—Planning, implementation, and evaluation focus on enhancing the intellectual quality of student learning. All students are expected to achieve academic excellence.
2. *Emphasis on authentic pedagogy*—Students are required to think, to develop in-depth understanding, and to apply academic learning to important, realistic problems. Students might, for example, conduct a survey on an issue of local concern, analyze the results, and then present their findings at a town council meeting.
3. *Greater school organizational capacity*—The ability of the school to strive for continuous improvement through professional collaboration is enhanced. For example, teachers exchange ideas to improve their teaching; they seek feedback from students, parents, and community members; and they attend conferences and workshops to acquire new materials and strategies.
4. *Greater external support*—The school receives critical financial, technical, and political support from outside sources.

In short, the cultures of effective schools encourage teachers to grow and develop in the practice of their profession.

What Social Problems Affect Schools and Place Students at Risk?

A complex and varied array of social issues impact schools. These problems often detract from the ability of schools to educate students. Furthermore, schools are often charged with the difficult (if not impossible) task of providing a front-line defense against such problems.

One of the most vocal advocates of the role of schools in solving social problems was George S. Counts, who said in his 1932 book *Dare the School Build a New Social Order?* that "if schools are to be really effective, they must become centers for the building, and not merely the contemplation, of our civilization" (12). Many people, however, believe that schools should not try to build a new social order. They should be concerned only with the academic and social development of students—not with solving society's problems. Nevertheless, the debate over the role of schools in regard to social problems will continue to be vigorous. For some time, schools have served in the battle against social problems by offering an array of health, education, and social service programs. Schools provide breakfasts, nutritional counseling, diagnostic services related to health and family planning, after-school child care, job placement, and sex and drug education, to name a few. In the following sections we examine several societal problems that directly influence schools, teachers, and students.

Identifying Students at Risk

An increasing number of young people live under conditions characterized by extreme stress, chronic poverty, crime, and lack of adult guidance. As James Garbarino (1999, 19) points out in *Lost Boys: Why Our Sons Turn Violent and How We Can Save Them:* "In almost every community in America, growing numbers of kids live in a socially toxic environment." Frustrated, lonely, and feeling powerless, many youths escape into music with violence-oriented and/or obscene lyrics, violent video games, cults, movies and television programs that celebrate gratuitous violence and sex, and cruising shopping malls or "hanging out" on the street. Others turn also to crime, gang violence, promiscuous sex, or substance abuse. Not surprisingly, these activities place many young people at risk of dropping out of school. In fact, it is estimated that the following percentages of fourteen-year-olds are likely to exhibit one or more at-risk behaviors (substance abuse, sexual behavior, violence, depression, or school failure) and to experience serious negative outcomes as a result: 10 percent at very high risk, 25 percent at

Increased incidents of aggression and bullying among young people has school authorities and parents alike worried about the long-term effects of such behavior on individual students, as well as the climate of schools. How does violence—of all levels—affect the educational environments of schools and their communities?

Table 4.1 Event dropout rates and number and distribution of fifteen- through twenty-four-year-olds who dropped out of grades 10–12, by background characteristics: October 2000

Characteristic	Event Dropout Rate (percent)	Number of Event Dropouts (thousands)	Population Enrolled (thousands)	Percent of All Dropouts	Percent of Population Enrolled
Total	4.8	488	10,126	100.0	100.0
Sex					
Male	5.5	280	5,087	57.4	50.2
Female	4.1	208	5,039	42.6	49.8
Race/ethnicity[1]					
White, non-Hispanic	4.1	276	6,786	56.6	67.0
Black, non-Hispanic	6.1	91	1,510	18.6	14.9
Hispanic	7.4	100	1,351	20.5	13.3
Asian/Pacific Islander	3.5	13	379	2.7	3.7
Family income[2]					
Low income	10.0	141	1,408	28.9	13.9
Middle income	5.2	298	5,728	61.1	56.6
High income	1.6	48	2,990	9.9	29.5
Age[3]					
15–16	2.9	84	2,924	17.2	28.9
17	3.5	121	3,452	24.8	34.1
18	6.1	165	2,721	33.8	26.9
19	9.6	70	724	14.3	7.1
20–24	16.1	49	305	10.0	3.0
Region					
Northeast	3.9	73	1,849	15.0	18.3
Midwest	4.4	109	2,481	22.3	24.5
South	6.2	220	3,543	45.1	35.0
West	3.8	86	2,253	17.6	22.2

[1]Due to small sample sizes, American Indians/Alaska Natives are included in the total but are not shown separately.
[2]Low income is defined as the bottom 20 percent of all family incomes for 2000; middle income is between 20 and 80 percent of all family incomes; and high income is the top 20 percent of all family incomes.
[3]Age when a person dropped out may be one year younger, because the dropout event could occur at any time over a twelve-month period.
Note: Because of rounding, detail may not add to totals.

Source: U.S. Department of Commerce, U.S. Census Bureau, Current Population Survey, October 2000.

high risk, 25 percent at moderate risk, 20 percent at low risk, and 20 percent at no risk (Dryfoos 1998).

Grouped by gender, race, ethnicity, family income, age, and region, students drop out of school at varying rates. Table 4.1, for example, shows that the dropout rate for Hispanic students in 2000 was higher than the rates for other groups. Also, African American students dropped out of school more frequently than their white peers. Lastly, the data reveal that students from low-income families are more likely to drop out than their counterparts from middle- and high-income families. **Students at risk** of dropping out tend to get low grades, perform below grade level academically, are older than the average student at their grade level because of previous retention, and have behavior problems in school.

Many youth take more than the typical four years to complete high school, or they eventually earn a high school equivalency certificate (GED). If these alternative routes to high school completion are considered, however, there are still significant differences among racial/ethnic groups. For example, in 2000, 91.8 percent of whites between the ages of eighteen and twenty-four had completed high school, compared to 83.7 percent of African Americans and 64.1 percent of Latinos (U.S. Census Bureau 2000).

Many children in the United States live in families that help them grow up healthy, confident, and skilled, but many do not. Instead, their life settings are characterized by problems of alcoholism or other substance abuse, family or gang violence, unemployment, poverty, poor nutrition, teenage parenthood, and a history of school failure. Such children live in communities and families that have many problems and frequently become dysfunctional, unable to provide their children with the support and guidance they need. According to *Kids Count Data Book, 1999*, "13 percent, or 9.2 million, of our children are growing up with a collection of disadvantages that could curtail, if not scuttle, their chances to become productive adult participants in the mainstream of America's future" (Annie E. Casey Foundation 1999, 1).

Children who experience the negative effects of poverty are from families of all ethnic and racial groups. As Marian Wright Edelman (November 9, 1997, B5), founder and president of the Children's Defense Fund, said:

> *Since 1973, families headed by someone younger than 30 have suffered a collapse in the value of their incomes, a surge in poverty, and a stunning erosion of employer-provided health benefits for their children. . . . Virtually every category of young families with young children has suffered major losses in median incomes: whites (22 percent), Hispanics (28 percent), and blacks (46 percent). . . . Low-income children are two or three times more likely to suffer from health problems, including infant death, iron deficiency, stunted growth, severe physical or mental disabilities, and fatal accidental injuries. . . . [T]he risk of students falling behind in school goes up by 2 percentage points for every year spent in poverty.*

The life experiences of students who are at risk of dropping out can be difficult for teachers to imagine; and, as the following comments by a student teacher in an inner-city third-grade classroom illustrate, encountering the realities of poverty for the first time can be upsetting:

> *Roughly 85 percent of [students are] living in poverty. The entire school population is eligible for free or reduced lunch. I was horrified. I guess I was a little ignorant of other people's situations.*
>
> *[Some] students came in wearing the same clothes for a week. Others would come in without socks on. No pencils, crayons, scissors, or glue. Some without breakfast, lunch, or a snack. My heart bled every day. I found myself becoming upset about their lives. I even found myself thinking about them at night and over the weekend. [I] noticed that they were extremely bright students, but their home life and economic status hindered them from working to their potential. Some of my students couldn't even complete their homework because they had no glue, scissors, or crayons at home (Molino 1999, 55).*

Children and Poverty

Although the United States is one of the richest countries in the world, it has by no means achieved an enviable record in regard to poverty among children (see Table 4.2 on page 134). According to the *Kids Count Data Book, 2002*, almost 20 percent of children live in families below the poverty line, and 25 percent live

Table 4.2 Profile of children in the United States

	Trend Data 1990	1999
Indicators of child well-being		
Percent low birth-weight babies	7.0%	7.6%
Infant mortality rate (deaths per 1,000 live births)	9.2	7.1
Child death rate (deaths per 100,000 children ages 1–14)	31	24
Rate of teen death rate by accident, homicide, and suicide (deaths per 100,000 teens ages 15–19)	71	53
Teen birth rate (births per 1,000 females ages 15–17)	37	29
Percent of teens who are high school dropouts (ages 16–19)	10%	10%
Percent of teens not attending school and not working (ages 16–19)	10%	8%
Percent of children living with parents who do not have full-time, year-round employment	30%	25%
Percent of children in poverty (data reflect poverty in the previous year)	20%	19%
Percent of families with children headed by a single parent	24%	27%
Economic condition of families		
Median income of families with children		$47,900
Children in extreme poverty (income below 50% of poverty level)		7%
Female-headed families receiving child support or alimony		35%
Child health		
Children without health insurance: 1999		14%
2-year-olds who were immunized: 2000		78%
Children in low-income working families		
Number of children under age 18 in low-income working families		10,054,000
Percent of children under age 18 in low-income working families		15%
Children in low-income working families receiving food stamps		24%
Children in low-income working families without health insurance		24%

Source: *Kids Count Data Book, 2002.* Baltimore: Annie Casey Foundation, 2002.

with parents who do not have full-time, year-round employment. In the District of Columbia, 31 percent live in poverty, 27 percent in New Mexico, and 26 percent in Louisiana (Annie E. Casey Foundation 2002).

Despite the high standards of living in the United States, each year about 1 percent of the U.S. population, some two to three million people, experience homelessness. Sixty percent of homeless women and 41 percent of homeless men have minor children (U.S. Department of Health and Human Services 2002). And, not surprisingly, the incidence of child abuse, poor health, underachievement in school, and attendance problems is higher among these children than it is among children with homes.

Family Stress

The stress placed on families in a complex society is extensive and not easily handled. For some families, such stress can be overwhelming. The structure of families who are experiencing the effects of financial problems, substance abuse, or violence, for example, can easily begin to crumble.

The National Clearinghouse on Child Abuse and Neglect (NCCAN) reported that Child Protective Service (CPS) agencies investigated three million reports of alleged child maltreatment, involving five million children in 2000. Of these children, CPS determined that about 879,000 were victims of child maltreatment. Almost two-thirds of child victims (63 percent) suffered neglect (including medical neglect); 19 percent were physically abused; 10 percent were sexually abused; and 8 percent were psychologically maltreated (National Clearinghouse on Child Abuse and Neglect 2002). Clearly, the burden of having to cope with such abuse in the home environment does not prepare a child to come to school to learn.

Stress within the family can have a significant negative effect on students and their ability to focus on learning while at school. Such stress is often associated with health and emotional problems, failure to achieve, behavioral problems at school, and dropping out of school.

With the high rise in divorce and women's entry into the workforce, family constellations have changed dramatically. No longer is a working father, a mother who stays at home, and two or three children the only kind of family in the United States. The number of single-parent families, stepparent families, blended families, and extended families has increased dramatically during the last decade. Table 4.2 shows that 27 percent of families with children were headed by a single parent in 1999.

Just as there is diversity in the composition of today's families, so, too, there is diversity in the styles with which children are raised in families. Because of the number of working women and single-parent homes, an alarming number of children are unsupervised during much of the day. It has been estimated that there may be as many as six million such **latchkey children** younger than thirteen (Hopson, Hopson, and Hagen 2002). To meet the needs of latchkey children, many schools offer before- and after-school programs.

In addition, many middle-class couples are waiting longer to have children. Although children of such couples may have more material advantages, they may be "impoverished" in regard to the reduced time they spend with their parents. To maintain their life-style, these parents are often driven to spend more time developing their careers. As a result, the care and guidance their children receive is inadequate, and "Sustained bad care eventually leads to a deep-seated inner sense of insecurity and inadequacy, emotional pain, and a troublesome sense of self" (Comer 1997, 83). To fill the parenting void that characterizes the lives of an increasing number of children from all economic classes, schools and teachers are being called on to play an increased role in the socialization of young people.

Substance Abuse

One of the most pressing social problems confronting today's schools is the abuse of illegal drugs, tobacco, and alcohol. Though drug abuse by students moved from the top-ranked problem facing local schools according to the 1996 Gallup Poll of the public's attitudes toward the public schools to the fifth-ranked problem in the 2001 poll, drug use among students remains at alarming levels. The University of Michigan's Institute for Social Research (2002) reported that, in 2001, 54 percent of students had tried an illicit drug by the time they finished high school. Figure 4.1 on page 136 shows trends in illicit drug use among eighth, tenth, and twelfth graders between 1976 and 2000. The Institute also found that alcohol use remains extremely widespread among today's youth. Eighty percent of students have consumed alcohol (more than just a few sips), and 51 percent have done so by eighth

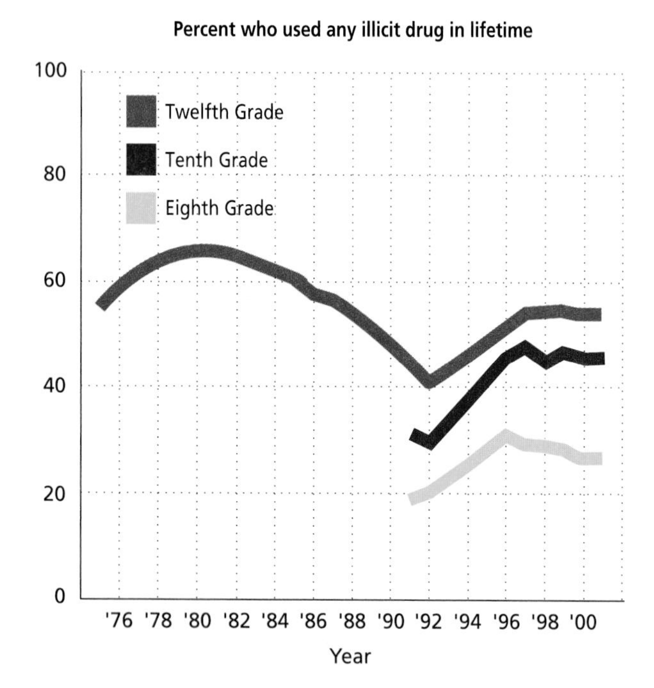

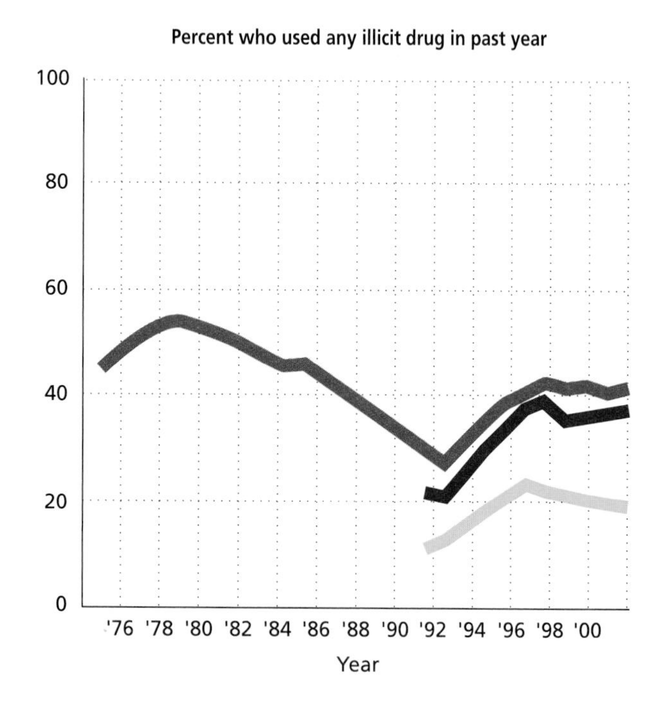

Figure 4.1 Trends in illicit drug use: eighth, tenth, and twelfth graders.
Source: Monitoring the Future: National Results on Adolescent Drug Use. The University of Michigan: Institute for Social Research, 2002.

grade. Sixty-four percent of the twelfth-graders and 23 percent of the eighth-graders report having been drunk at least once in their life.

The use of drugs among young people varies from community to community and from year to year, but overall it is disturbingly high. Mind-altering substances used by young people include the easily acquired glue, white correction fluid, and felt marker, as well as marijuana, amphetamines, and cocaine. The abuse of drugs not only poses the risks of addiction and overdosing, but is also related to problems such as HIV/AIDS, teenage pregnancy, depression, suicide, automobile accidents, criminal activity, and dropping out of school.

For an alarming number of young people, drugs are seen as a way of coping with life's problems.

Violence and Crime

While the rate of victimization in U.S. schools has decreased since 1992, according the Justice Department's *Indicators of School Crime and Safety, 2001,* students are victims of about 2.5 million crimes each year (U.S. Department of Justice 2001). During 1999, there were 1.6 million thefts in schools and 880,000 nonfatal violent crimes, including about 186,000 serious violent crimes (rape, sexual assault, robbery, and aggravated assault). Between 1993 and 1999, the percentage of ninth- through twelfth-grade students who were threatened or injured with a weapon remained constant between 7 and 8 percent; on the other hand, the percentage of students who reported carrying a gun, knife, or club on school property during the previous thirty days dropped from 12 percent to 7 percent. Figure 4.2 shows the number of nonfatal crimes against students by type of crime and selected student characteristics.

In addition, the U.S. Department of Justice estimates that there are more than 30,500 gangs and approximately 816,000 gang members (Moore and Terrett 1999). According to *Indicators of School Crime and Safety, 2001,* the percentage of students who reported that street gangs were present at their schools decreased from 29 percent in 1995 to 17 percent in 1999. In 1999, urban students were more likely to report street gangs at their schools (26 percent) than were suburban and rural students (16 percent and 11 percent, respectively). During the same year, public school students were more likely to report street gangs than were students at private schools (19 percent and 4 percent, respectively).

Gang membership is perceived by many youth as providing them with several advantages: a sense of belonging and identity, protection from other gangs, opportunities for excitement, or a chance to make money through selling drugs or participating in other illegal activities. Though few students are gang members, a small number of gang-affiliated students can disrupt the learning process, create disorder in a school, and cause others to fear for their physical safety. Strategies for reducing the effect of gang activities on schools include the identification of gang members, implementing dress codes that ban styles of dress identified with gangs, and quickly removing gang graffiti from the school.

Since 1996, the nation's concern about school crime and safety heightened as a result of a string of school shootings. Among the communities that had

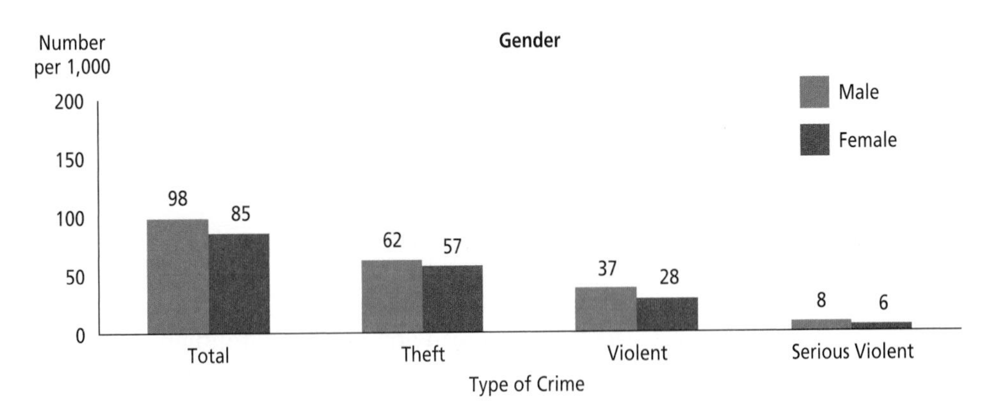

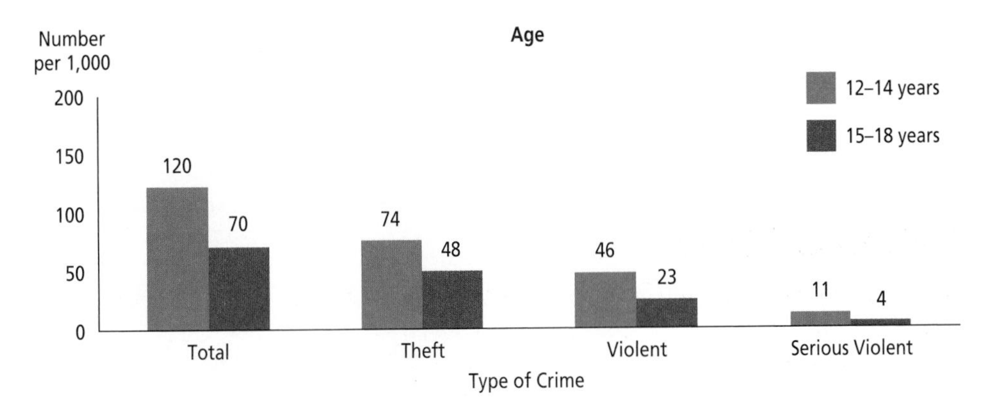

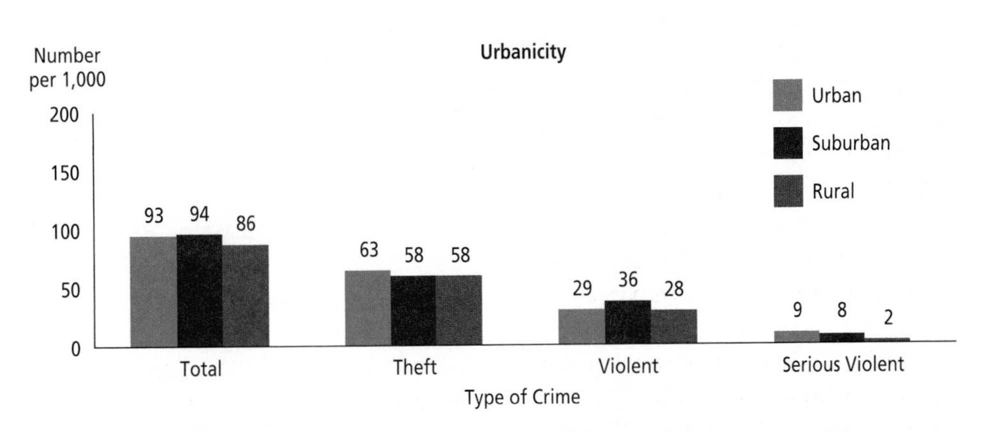

Note: Serious violent crimes include rape, sexual assault, robbery, and aggravated assault. Violent crimes include serious violent crimes and simple assault. Total crimes include violent crimes and theft. "At school" includes inside the school building, on school property, or on the way to or from school. Detail may not add to totals because of rounding.

Figure 4.2 Number of nonfatal crimes against students ages twelve through eighteen occurring at school or going to or from school per 1,000 students, by type of crime and selected student characteristics: 1999.
Source: Reported in *Indicators of School Crime and Safety, 2001.* Washington, DC: U.S. Department of Justice, p. 6.

to cope with such tragic incidents were Moses Lake, Washington (1996); Pearl, Mississippi (1997); West Paducah, Kentucky (1997); Jonesboro, Arkansas (1998); Springfield, Oregon (1998); and Littleton, Colorado (1999). Since the recurring question after each instance of horrific school violence was "Why?" there was a renewed effort to understand the origins of youth violence. Indeed, the entire nation debated gun control measures; the influence of violence in television, movies, and point-and-shoot video games; and steps that parents, schools, and communities could take to curb school crime and violence. Figure 4.3 shows the percentage of schools reporting various types of security measures.

The increased use of guns by children and youth to solve conflicts is one consequence of the "gun culture" in the United States, in which it is estimated that nearly 40 percent of homes have at least one gun (Garbarino 1999). On the issue of television violence, the American Psychological Association reviewed research studies and concluded that television violence *alone* is responsible for up to 15 percent of all aggressive behavior by children and youth (Garbarino 1999). Lastly, David Grossman, a military psychologist, and his colleague pointed out that violent point-and-shoot video games are similar to those used to "desensitize" soldiers to shoot at human figures (Grossman and Siddle 1999).

As a result of the school shootings listed earlier and the public's concern with school crime and violence, many schools developed crisis management plans to cope with violent incidents on campus. Schools also reviewed their ability to provide students, faculty, and staff with a safe environment for learning; for example, Appendix 4.1 presents a "School Safety Checklist" excerpted from the National Education Association's *School Safety Check Book.* Additionally, to help troubled youth *before* they commit violence, the Ameri-

Figure 4.3 Security measures.
Source: Indicators of School Crime and Safety, 2001. Washington, DC: U.S. Department of Justice.

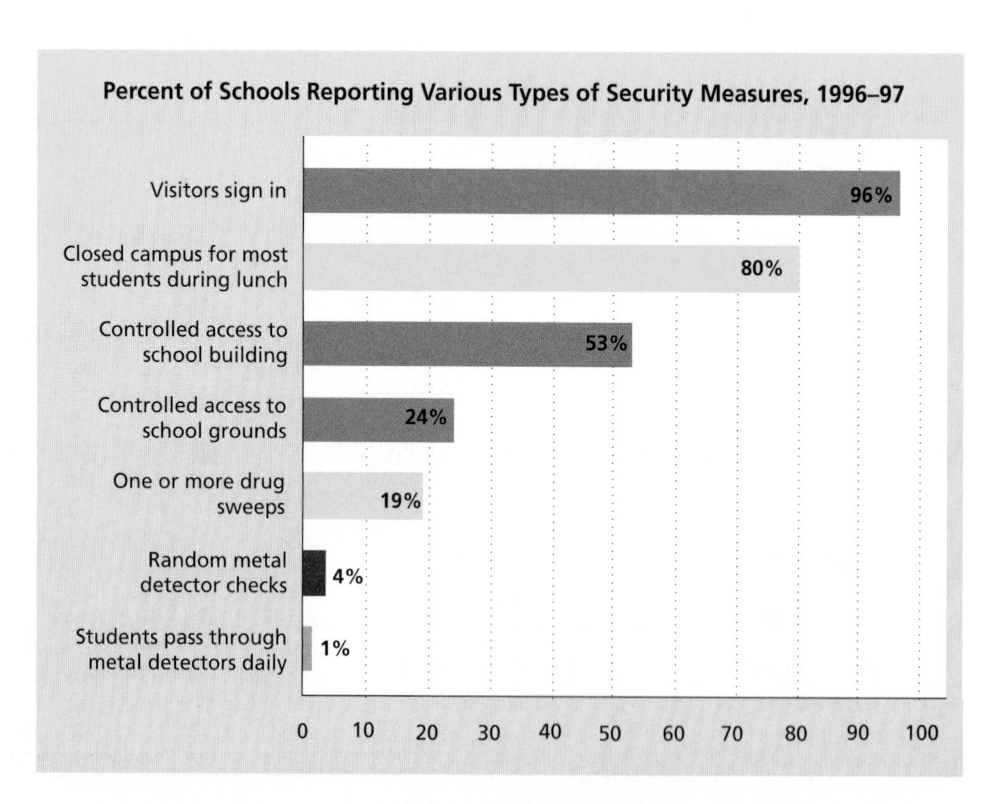

can Psychological Association, in collaboration with MTV, developed a set of warning signs, as shown in Figure 4.4.

Teen Pregnancy

Each year more than one million U.S. teenagers (one in nine women between the ages of fifteen and nineteen) become pregnant, and about 85 percent of these pregnancies are unintended. This figure includes about 18 percent of all African American women ages fifteen to nineteen, 16 percent of Latina women, and 8 percent of Anglo-European women (Alan Guttmacher Institute 1999). Indeed, most teachers of adolescents today may expect to have at least some students who are, or have been, pregnant.

Since peaking in 1990, the teenage pregnancy, birth, and abortion rates have declined, largely the result of more effective contraceptive practices among sexually active teenagers (Alan Guttmacher Institute 1999). Nevertheless, teen pregnancies remain a serious problem in society. Because the physical development of girls in adolescence may not be complete, complications can occur during pregnancy and in the birthing process. Also, adolescents are less likely to receive prenatal care in the crucial first trimester; they tend not to eat well-balanced diets; and are not free of harmful substances such as alcohol, tobacco, and drugs, which are known to be detrimental to a baby's development. These young mothers "are at risk for chronic educational, occupational, and financial difficulties, and their offspring are also at risk for medical, educational, and behavioral problems" (Durlak 1995, 66). Because most teen mothers drop out of school, forfeiting their high school diplomas and limiting their access to decent, higher-paying job opportunities, they and their children stay at the bottom of the economic ladder.

Suicide among Children and Youths

The increase in individual and multiple suicides is alarming. The National Institute for Mental Health (1999) reported that suicide is the third leading cause of death among youth ages fifteen to twenty-four and accounts for more than four thousand deaths yearly for this group. The Institute also estimated that there are eight to twenty-five attempted suicides for one completion.

Although female students are almost two times more likely than male students to have seriously considered attempting suicide during the preceding twelve months, about six times as many male students as females actually commit suicide. Latino students are about two times more likely than white students to attempt suicide, and students in grade nine are about four times more likely than students in grade twelve to make a suicide attempt that requires medical attention (Centers for Disease Control and Prevention 1998). Also, lesbian and gay youth are two to three times more likely to attempt suicide than their heterosexual peers, and they account for up to 30 percent of all completed suicides among youth (Besner and Spungin 1995).

Figure 4.4 Recognizing violence warning signs in others.
Source: MTV and American Psychological Association, *Warning Signs: A Violence Prevention Guide for Youth from MTV and APA.* New York: MTV. Washington, DC: American Psychological Association, n.d.

Recognizing Violence Warning Signs in Others

If you see these immediate warning signs, violence is a serious possibility:

- Loss of temper on a daily basis
- Frequent physical fighting
- Significant vandalism or property damage
- Increase in use of drugs or alcohol
- Increase in risk-taking behavior
- Detailed plans to commit acts of violence
- Announcing threats or plans for hurting others
- Enjoying hurting animals
- Carrying a weapon

If you notice the following signs over a period of time, the potential for violence exists:

- A history of violent or aggressive behavior
- Serious drug or alcohol use
- Gang membership or strong desire to be in a gang
- Access to or fascination with weapons, especially guns
- Threatening others regularly
- Trouble controlling feelings like anger
- Withdrawal from friends and usual activities
- Feeling rejected or alone
- Having been a victim of bullying
- Poor school performance
- History of discipline problems or frequent run-ins with authority
- Feeling constantly disrespected
- Failing to acknowledge the feelings or rights of others

What Are Schools Doing to Address Societal Problems?

Responding to the needs of at-risk students will be a crucial challenge for schools, families, and communities during the twenty-first century. Since most children attend school, it is logical that this pre-existing system be used for reaching large numbers of at-risk children (and, through them, their families). During the last decade, many school districts have taken innovative steps to address societal problems that impact students' lives.

Though programs that address social problems are costly, most of the public believes that schools should be used for the delivery of health and social services to students and their families. However, there has been disagreement about the extent to which school facilities should be used for anything but meeting students' educational needs. For example, the Committee for Economic Development (1994, 1) stated, "Schools are not social service institutions; they should not be asked to solve all our nation's social ills and cultural conflicts." In isolated instances, community groups and school boards have resisted school-based services such as family planning clinics and mental health services. However, increases in state funding and foundation support to provide school-based health, mental health, and social services have tended to dissipate most of this resistance (Dryfoos 1998).

Under pressure to find solutions to increasing social problems among children and adolescents, educators have developed an array of intervention programs. In general, the aim of these programs is to address the behavioral, social, and academic adjustment of at-risk children and adolescents so they can receive maximum benefit from their school experiences.

Professional Reflection

Identifying the Factors Behind Youth Violence

In *Lost Boys: Why Our Sons Turn Violent and How We Can Save Them,* James Garbarino presents ten "facts of life" for violent boys. After reading the list, consider the following questions: What steps can teachers and other adults take to reduce the influence of these factors on individual youth? What kinds of academic and counseling services might be helpful for students prone to violence? How should schools involve the parents and/or guardians of violence-prone youth?

1. Child maltreatment leads to survival strategies that are often antisocial and/or self-destructive.
2. The experience of early trauma leads boys to become hypersensitive to arousal in the face of threat and to respond to such threats by disconnecting emotionally or acting out aggressively.
3. Traumatized kids require a calming and soothing environment to increase the level at which they are functioning.
4. Traumatized youth are likely to evidence an absence of future orientation.
5. Youth exposed to violence at home and in the community are likely to develop juvenile vigilantism, in which they do not trust an adult's capacity and motivation to ensure safety, and as a result believe they must take matters into their own hands.
6. Youth who have participated in the violent drug economy or chronic theft are likely to have distorted materialistic values.
7. Traumatized youth who have experienced abandonment are likely to feel life is meaningless.
8. Issues of shame [and humiliation] are paramount among violent youth. [They] share a common sense of inner crisis, a crisis of shame and emptiness. These boys are ashamed of who they are inside, and their efforts to compensate for that shame drive their violence.
9. Youth violence is a boy's attempt to achieve justice as he perceives it.
10. Violent boys often seem to feel they cannot afford empathy.

Source: James Garbarino, *Lost Boys: Why Our Sons Turn Violent and How We Can Save Them.* New York: The Free Press, 1999, pp. 217–230.

In the following sections, we describe five intervention strategies that have proven effective in addressing academic, social, and behavioral problems among children and adolescents: peer counseling, full-service schools, school-based interprofessional case management, compensatory education, and alternative schools and curricula. Also see the Appendix "Selected Resources for Meeting Needs of Students Placed at Risk" on this book's website—a list of publications, organizations, and online locations that are good sources of information on the problems children and youth may encounter.

Peer Counseling

To address the social problems that affect students, some schools have initiated student-to-student **peer counseling** programs—usually monitored by a school counselor or other specially trained adult. In peer counseling programs, students can address problems and issues such as low academic achievement, interpersonal problems at home and at school, substance abuse, and career planning. Evidence indicates that both peer counselors and students experience increased self-esteem and greater ability to deal with problems.

When peer counseling is combined with cross-age tutoring, younger students can learn about drugs, alcohol, premarital pregnancy, delinquency, dropping out, HIV/AIDS, suicide, and other relevant issues. Here the groups are often college-age students meeting with those in high school, or high school students meeting with those in junior high school or middle school. In these preventative programs, older students sometimes perform dramatic episodes that portray students confronting problems and model strategies for handling the situations presented.

Full-Service Schools

In response to the increasing number of at-risk students, many schools are serving their communities by integrating educational, medical, social and/or human services. **Full-service schools** tend to be in low-income urban areas and involve collaborative partnerships among school districts, departments of public health, hospitals, and various nonprofit organizations. At full-service schools, students

The Thomas J. Pappas School in Phoenix, AZ (www.tjpappasschool.org) was established for the sole purpose of meeting the educational needs of homeless children. What might be the potential benefits of helping these at-risk students?

On the Frontlines

Making Schools Safe

As you make plans for the first month of the school year, mixed in with the preparations for using the new reading program, integrating computer lab work with your math program, and selecting a good book to read to class during your after-lunch literature period, are pressing questions about what you should do or say, if anything, about the violence in your students' worlds. You wonder about how you should handle the anniversary of September 11th. You wonder whether your fourth graders have followed the news reports on the search for a missing child, a search that ended last week with the discovery of her body. You wonder how aware your students are of events around them. With the Oklahoma City terrorism, school shooting tragedies, the September 11th horrors, local gang violence and drive-by murders, and the random and often fatal child kidnappings, you as an adult see the frightening dimensions of the world today. You hope your students have been sheltered, but you know how hard that is with the heavy media coverage of the tragedies. How much time should you devote to these issues, if any? Do you, or does the school, have a responsibility to address such issues? What can you do to make your students feel safe? What can you do as their teacher to assure their safety at school?

"All the reforms in the world won't mean a thing if we don't have safe classrooms for students to learn and teachers to teach," U.S. Secretary of Education, Rod Paige, told a gathering of seven hundred school leaders and school safety and violence prevention experts at a safe schools conference in Washington, D.C., in August 2002. Emphasizing President George W. Bush's concerns about homeland security, Paige issued four directives to his audience:

1. *"We must create a comprehensive, coordinated national strategy for greater school preparedness."* Secretary Paige reminded school leaders that being in the middle of a crisis is not the time to develop a school readiness safety plan. Recognizing that most schools have emergency plans in place, he urged others to prepare them. He also announced that a model plan was being prepared that could serve as a rubric to test the completeness of their plans. The model would "address everything from shootings to suicides—from accidents to large-scale emergencies like we saw on 9/11. It will encourage districts to form partnerships with local law enforcement and other emergency responders." Consulting on the model plan were experts from countries that have experienced extensive terrorism: Northern Ireland, Turkey, and Spain. Paige noted that Turkey's expertise was sorely gained: "Over a 13-year period, they saw 146 teachers killed by terrorists and 370 schools destroyed by terrorists."
2. The second directive is to use insights gained from the *Safe School Initiative*, the Department of Education and Secret Service's investigation of thirty-seven student-instigated incidents of school violence between 1974 and 2000. Specifically, Paige emphasized a key preventative step: *"We as adults—in our homes, our schools and our communities—must do a better job of listening to kids, paying attention and connecting on a personal level."* He told of schools in San Juan, California, that use a unique strategy to care for students who might need help.

   During training before school opens, they post the name of every child on the walls and ask the teachers to put a mark by the names of the kids they know well. The children nobody knows—those with no marks by their names—get assigned a silent mentor. That mentor is a caring adult who makes it his or her business to get to know that child and help in any way possible—a sort of guardian angel who's available to play basketball, offer homework help or just listen.
3. His third directive addressed creating a culture of respect at schools: *"We must change the culture in our schools to a culture that says every individual has worth—everyone deserves to be treated with dignity and respect."* He expressed dismay over the researchers' discovery that students of schools where shootings occurred knew of the impending shootings but didn't tell anyone. When questioned, their responses were similar to that of one friend of a shooter: "Calling someone would have been a betrayal. It just didn't seem right to tell." The effort to

create a culture of respect, among students and among students and adults, would counter what the investigators referred to as "the code of silence."

4. Finally, Paige urged that *"educators—at the local, state, and federal levels—must be included at the table at every step of the emergency planning process."* The effort to keep our students and schools safe needs to be a coordinated one to be most effective."

Teachers at all levels of the K–12 school system can find ways to help keep their students safe and help them feel safe. They can begin by listening, seeing what their students are concerned about, being sensitive to their drawings, journal writings, conversations, and essays. Then they will know more about how to proceed.

Exploratory Questions

1. What responsibilities do you feel schools have in helping students deal with social realities around them? Should schools incorporate lessons on addressing social issues into their curricula, as recommended by Secretary Paige, or should schools address the issues as they arise?
2. Complete a search on the Internet of "safe school initiatives" to explore what advice is being given about talking to children about potential dangers.

Your Survival Guide of Helpful Resources

The following resources provide helpful hints for surviving "on the frontlines."

Books and Articles

Paige, R. (2002, August). *All the reforms in the world won't mean a thing if we don't have safe classrooms for students to learn and teachers to teach.* Press release from the Department of Education, Washington, DC. Retrieved from http://www.ed.gov/PressReleases/08-2002/08052002.html

Threat assessment in schools: A guide to managing threatening situations and to creating safe school climates. Available at 1-877-4ED-PUBS or http://www.nochildleftbehind.gov. Use the search tool to locate the report.

Websites

National Alliance for Safe Schools (http://www.safeschools.org)

National Center for Missing & Exploited Children (http://www.missingkids.com/.)

Safe Communities-Safe Schools (http://www.colorado.edu/cspv/safeschools/)

and their families can receive health screening, psychological counseling, drug prevention counseling, parent education, and family planning information. See the Appendix "Family Needs Assessment" on this book's website.

One example of a full-service school is award-winning Salome Urena Middle Academy (SUMA), a middle school serving a Dominican community in Washington Heights, New York. Open six days per week, fifteen hours per day, year round, SUMA offers before-school and after-school child care. Through seventy-five partnerships with various community groups and agencies, SUMA offers a comprehensive, integrated array of programs and services to children and their families. Students may enroll in their choice of four academies—business; community service; expressive arts; and mathematics, science, and technology. A Family Institute offers English as a second language, Spanish, aerobics, and entrepreneurial skills. At a Family Resource Center, social workers, paraprofessionals, parents, and other volunteers offer help with immigration, employment, and housing. Next to the Family Resource Center, a clinic provides dental, medical, and mental health services. Each year, the school's more than 1,200 students, their parents, and siblings are served at a cost significantly less than the per-pupil expenditures in most suburban schools. Moreover, according to an evaluation conducted by Fordham University, the school has realized a significant increase in attendance, a major reduction in misbehavior, and a modest increase in test scores (Dryfoos 1994, 1998; Karvarsky 1994).

School-Based Interprofessional Case Management

In responding to the needs of at-risk students, it has been suggested that schools "will need to reconceptualize the networks of community organizations and public services that might assist, and they will need to draw on those community resources" (Edwards and Young 1992, 78). One such approach to forming new home/school/community partnerships is known as **school-based interprofessional case management.** The approach uses professionally trained case managers who work directly with teachers, the community, and the family to coordinate and deliver appropriate services to at-risk students and their families. The case management approach is based on a comprehensive service delivery network of teachers, social agencies, and health service agencies.

One of the first case-management programs in the country is operated by the Center for the Study and Teaching of At-Risk Students (C-STARS) and serves twenty school districts in the Pacific Northwest. Center members include Washington State University, the University of Washington, a community-based organization, and Washington State's Department of Social and Health Services. Working with teachers and other school personnel, an interprofessional case management team fulfills seven functions to meet the needs of at-risk students: assessment, development of a service plan, brokering with other agencies, service implementation and coordination, advocacy, monitoring and evaluation, and mentoring. Program evaluation data have shown significant measurable improvements in student's attendance, academic performance, and school behavior.

Compensatory Education

To meet the learning needs of at-risk students, several federally funded **compensatory education programs** for elementary and secondary students have been developed, the largest of which is Title I. Launched in 1965 as part of the Elementary and Secondary Education Act (ESEA) and President Lyndon Johnson's Great Society education program, Title I (called Chapter I between

1981 and 1994) was designed to improve the basic skills (reading, writing, and mathematics) of low-ability students from low-income families. Each year, more than five million students (about 10 percent of enrollments) in nearly all school districts benefit from Title I programs. The Educational Excellence for All Children Act of 1999, former President Clinton's plan for reauthorizing the Elementary and Secondary Education Act, including Title I, called for dramatic new steps to improve education for at-risk students. The $8 billion program called for an end to "social promotion" in schools and higher standards for teacher quality and training.

Students who participate in Title I programs are usually taught through "pullout" programs, in which they leave the regular classroom to receive additional instruction individually or in small groups. Title I teachers, sometimes assisted by an aide, often have curriculum materials and equipment not available to regular classroom teachers.

Research on the effectiveness of Title I programs has been inconclusive, with some studies reporting achievement gains not found in other studies. Recent research has found positive effects on students' achievement in the early grades, but these gains tend to dissipate during the middle grades. The pattern of short-lived gains is strongest for students attending urban schools that serve a high proportion of families in poverty (Levine and Levine 1996). Some critics of Title I and other compensatory education programs such as Head Start for preschool children, Success for All for preschool and elementary children, and Upward Bound for high school students argue that they are stopgap measures at best. Instead, they maintain, social problems such as poverty, the breakdown of families, drug abuse, and crime that contribute to poor school performance should be reduced.

Alternative Schools and Curricula

To meet the needs of students whom social problems place at risk, many school districts have developed alternative schools and curricula. Usually, an **alternative school** is a small, highly individualized school separate from the regular school; in other cases, the alternative school is organized as a **school-within-a-school.** Alternative school programs usually provide remedial instruction, some vocational training, and individualized counseling. Since they usually have much smaller class sizes, alternative school teachers can monitor students' progress more closely and, when problems do arise, respond more quickly and with greater understanding of student needs.

One exemplary alternative school is the Buffalo Alternative High School serving at-risk seventh to twelfth grade students in the Buffalo, New York, Public School District. To reach students who are not successful at regular schools, the Buffalo program offers individualized instruction, small class sizes, and various enrichment programs delivered in what school staff describe as a "supportive, noncoercive, nontraditional setting." Most students are expected to return to their regular schools after a minimum of four weeks. Students must earn six hundred "points" (based on attendance, punctuality, attitude, behavior, and performance) to return to their regular school.

In addition, the Buffalo Alternative High School operates eight satellite schools in nonschool buildings throughout Buffalo. Among these programs are:

- *SAVe (Suspension Avoidance Vehicle)*—a two-week program students complete before returning to their sending school or enrolling in the Alternative High School

- *City-as-School*—students serve as interns in the public and private sectors and earn academic credit
- *SMART (Students Moving Ahead Through Remediation Testing)*—seventh- and eighth-grade students held behind can qualify for promotion to the appropriate grade
- *Bilingual Satellite*—educational services provided to Spanish-speaking students

While they don't work in alternative school settings, many highly effective regular teachers have developed alternative curricula to meet the unique learning needs of students at risk. Many teachers, for example, link students' learning to the business, civic, cultural, and political segments of their communities. The rationale is that connecting at-risk students to the world beyond their schools will enable them to see the relevance of education.

How Can Community-Based Partnerships Address Social Problems That Hinder Students' Learning?

In the previous section, we looked at *intervention* programs schools have developed to ensure the optimum behavioral, social, and academic adjustment of at-risk children and adolescents to their school experiences. Here, we describe innovative, community-based partnerships that some schools have developed recently to *prevent* social problems from hindering students' learning.

The range of school-community partnerships found in today's schools is extensive. For example, as the "Interactive Organizational Model" in Figure 4.5 illustrates, Exeter High School in suburban Toronto has developed partnerships with 13 community organizations and more than 100 employers. Through Exeter's Partners in Learning program, business, industry, service clubs, and social service agencies make significant contributions to students' learning.

The Community as a Resource for Schools

To assist schools in addressing the social problems that impact students, many communities are acting in the spirit of a recommendation made by the late Ernest Boyer: "Perhaps the time has come to organize, in every community, not just a *school* board, but a *children's* board. The goal would be to integrate children's services and build, in every community, a friendly, supportive environment for children" (Boyer 1995, 169). In partnerships between communities and schools, individuals, civic organizations, or businesses select a school or are selected by a school to work together for the good of students. The ultimate goals of such projects are to provide students with better school experiences and to assist students at risk.

Civic Organizations To develop additional sources of funding, many local school districts have established partnerships with community groups interested in improving educational opportunities in the schools. Some groups raise money for schools. The American Jewish Committee and the Urban League raised funds for schools in Pittsburgh, for example. Other partners adopt or sponsor schools and enrich their educational programs by providing funding, resources, or services.

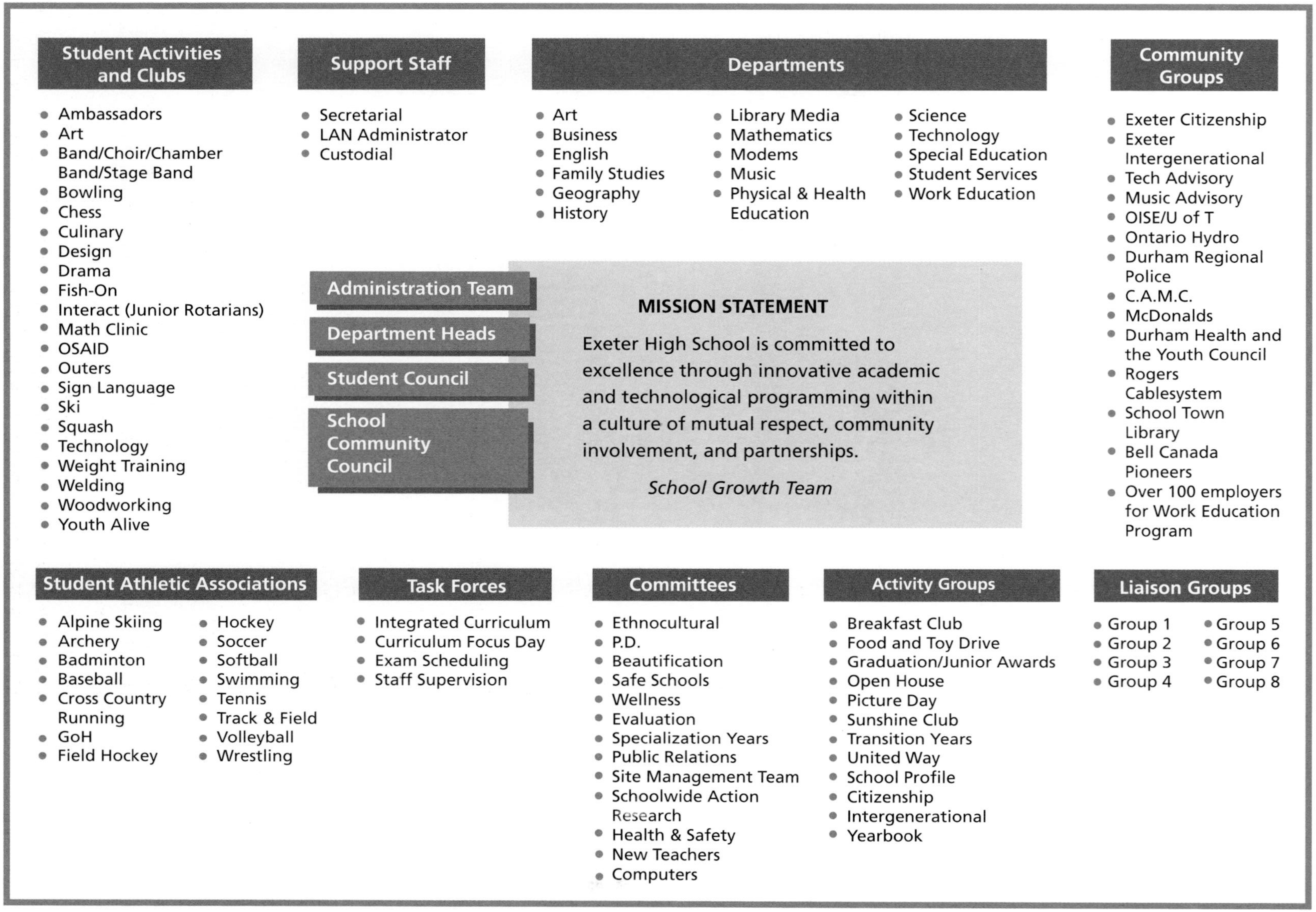

Student Activities and Clubs

- Ambassadors
- Art
- Band/Choir/Chamber Band/Stage Band
- Bowling
- Chess
- Culinary
- Design
- Drama
- Fish-On
- Interact (Junior Rotarians)
- Math Clinic
- OSAID
- Outers
- Sign Language
- Ski
- Squash
- Technology
- Weight Training
- Welding
- Woodworking
- Youth Alive

Support Staff

- Secretarial
- LAN Administrator
- Custodial

Departments

- Art
- Business
- English
- Family Studies
- Geography
- History
- Library Media
- Mathematics
- Modems
- Music
- Physical & Health Education
- Science
- Technology
- Special Education
- Student Services
- Work Education

Community Groups

- Exeter Citizenship
- Exeter Intergenerational
- Tech Advisory
- Music Advisory
- OISE/U of T
- Ontario Hydro
- Durham Regional Police
- C.A.M.C.
- McDonalds
- Durham Health and the Youth Council
- Rogers Cablesystem
- School Town Library
- Bell Canada Pioneers
- Over 100 employers for Work Education Program

Administration Team

Department Heads

Student Council

School Community Council

MISSION STATEMENT

Exeter High School is committed to excellence through innovative academic and technological programming within a culture of mutual respect, community involvement, and partnerships.

School Growth Team

Student Athletic Associations

- Alpine Skiing
- Archery
- Badminton
- Baseball
- Cross Country Running
- GoH
- Field Hockey
- Hockey
- Soccer
- Softball
- Swimming
- Tennis
- Track & Field
- Volleyball
- Wrestling

Task Forces

- Integrated Curriculum
- Curriculum Focus Day
- Exam Scheduling
- Staff Supervision

Committees

- Ethnocultural
- P.D.
- Beautification
- Safe Schools
- Wellness
- Evaluation
- Specialization Years
- Public Relations
- Site Management Team
- Schoolwide Action Research
- Health & Safety
- New Teachers
- Computers

Activity Groups

- Breakfast Club
- Food and Toy Drive
- Graduation/Junior Awards
- Open House
- Picture Day
- Sunshine Club
- Transition Years
- United Way
- School Profile
- Citizenship
- Intergenerational
- Yearbook

Liaison Groups

- Group 1
- Group 2
- Group 3
- Group 4
- Group 5
- Group 6
- Group 7
- Group 8

Figure 4.5 Exeter High School interactive organizational model.

Source: Gordon Cawelti, *Portaits of Six Benchmark Schools: Diverse Approaches to Improving Student Achievement.* Arlington, VA: Educational Research Service, 1999, p. 32. Used with permission.

Meeting the Standard

Teaches the Whole Student

The teacher understands how factors in the students' environment outside of school (e.g., family circumstances, community environments, health and economic conditions) may influence students' life and learning (INTASC Knowledge, Principle #10).

Teacher candidates consider school, family, and community contexts in connecting concepts to students' prior experience and applying the ideas to real-world problems. (NCATE)

[Accomplished teachers] strive to acquire a deep understanding of their students and the communities from which they come that shape students' outlooks, values and orientations toward schooling (NBPTS).

Teacher's efforts to engage families in the instructional program are frequent and successful. Students contribute ideas for projects that will be enhanced by family participation (PRAXIS III Framework– "distinguished" level of performance.*

The teachers who meet these standards recognize the importance of helping their students build bridges between what they study in the classroom and what they experience in life. They seek to *teach the whole student* because they recognize that the obstacles facing today's youth are often overwhelming–both to them and to the adults who try to help them. These educators become part of the solution by creating interest and relevancy for everyone as they skillfully interweave curriculum content with family and community issues. One Nebraska teacher's Civics unit for freshmen is an example of how this can be accomplished.

Two young men in the community had been killed, and their parents wanted the city to use the memorial fund to enhance the entrance to the city. The teacher contacted an official at City Hall to find out how her students could submit proposals for the city improvements and to get the name of a contact person who could explain the background of the project to her students. The mayor, interested in the idea of involving students in the planning process, offered to speak to the class personally.

The unit plan, created by the teacher, ensured that the students would have authentic opportunities to attend city council meetings to learn about the policies governing city planning and zoning and to become familiar with other city-government related operations. Student involvement and their progress on the project were reported on a website. The class also provided e-mail updates and personal notes to parents, the mayor, and the local newspaper.

Student interest in this project was validated when Bill, a teenager on probation, told the teacher that despite truancy patrol he could still cut classes whenever he decided to do it. When asked why he never tried to sneak out of the Civics class, he responded, "Because what we are doing in this class matters and I want to be part of that."

When the students presented their proposals to the city planning and zoning committee, the teacher was pleased to note that her goal of having at least one family member per student in attendance at the presentation was met.

The mayor offered to host a pizza party for the class, but the students instead wanted to buy a flagpole for the new city entrance. The mayor gave them the money originally set aside for the party, and they used it to buy a quilt, which was then auctioned off to raise more money for the flagpole. Because the students were able to enlist the aid of a welding instructor at the local community college to make the flagpole for the cost of the materials, they had enough money left to purchase a plaque to be placed at the base of the pole.

The city's memorial fund committee thanked the students for their involvement and informed them that many of the ideas submitted on the student proposals would be used in the final project. By this time, the students' involvement in the project had created a great deal of interest. A huge crowd of people and even newspaper and TV reporters attended the dedication of the new city entrance.

At the end of the ceremony, a mainstreamed student took the microphone and announced, "Now our class has something to show our children and grandchildren." Her classmates all applauded.

1. Explain how the teacher's efforts helped meet the standard of "teaching the whole student."
2. Identify ways you can become more knowledgeable about the issues impacting the community in which you teach.
3. What are some strategies you might be able to use to draw families and community members into your efforts to make your students' learning relevant and interesting?

Volunteer Mentor Programs Mentorship is a trend in community-based partnerships today, especially with students at risk. Parents, business leaders, professionals, and peers volunteer to work with students in neighborhood schools. Goals might include dropout prevention, high achievement, improved self-esteem, and healthy decision making. Troubleshooting on lifestyle issues often plays a role, especially in communities plagued by drug dealing, gang rivalry, casual violence, and crime. Mentors also model success.

Some mentor programs target particular groups. For instance, the Concerned Black Men (CBM), a Washington, DC-based organization with fifteen chapters around the country, targets inner-city African American male youth. More than five hundred African American men in diverse fields and from all walks of life participate as CBM mentors to students in area schools. Their goal is to serve as positive adult male role models for youth, many of whom live only with their mothers or grandmothers and lack male teachers in school. To date, CBM has given cash awards and scholarships to more than four thousand youth selected on the basis of high academic achievement, motivation, leadership in academic and nonacademic settings, and community involvement.

Corporate-Education Partnerships Business involvement in schools has taken many forms, including, for example, contributions of funds or materials needed by a school, release time for employees to visit classrooms, adopt-a-school programs, cash grants for pilot projects and teacher development, educational use of corporate facilities and expertise, employee participation, student scholarship programs, and political lobbying for school reform. Extending beyond advocacy, private sector efforts include job initiatives for disadvantaged youths, inservice programs for teachers, management training for school administrators, minority education and faculty development, and even construction of school buildings.

Business-sponsored school experiments focus on creating model schools, laboratory schools, or alternative schools that address particular local needs. In Minneapolis, for example, the General Mills Foundation has provided major funding to create the Minneapolis Federation of Alternative Schools (MFAS), a group of several schools designed to serve students who have not been successful in regular school programs. The goals for students who attend MFAS schools include returning to regular school when appropriate, graduating from high school, and/or preparing for postsecondary education or employment.

In addition to contributing more resources to education, chief executive officers and their employees are donating more time; 83 percent of the top managers surveyed by a recent *Fortune* poll said they "participate actively" in educational reform, versus 70 percent in 1990. At Eastman Kodak's Rochester, New York, plant, for example, hundreds of employees serve as tutors or mentors in local schools. In some dropout prevention programs, businessmen and businesswomen adopt individual students, visiting them at school, eating lunch with them once a week, meeting their families, and taking them on personal field trips.

Schools as Resources for Communities

A shift from the more traditional perspective of schools is the view that schools should serve as multipurpose resources *for* the community. By focusing not only on the development of children and youth, but on their families as well, schools ultimately enhance the ability of students to learn. As Ernest Boyer (1995, 168) put it, "No arbitrary line can be drawn between the school and life outside. Every [school] should take the lead in organizing a *referral service*—a community safety net for children that links students and their families to support agencies in the region—to clinics, family support and counseling centers, and religious institutions."

Beyond the School Day Many schools and school districts are serving their communities by providing educational and recreational programs before and after the traditional school day and during the summers. Increasingly, educational policymakers recognize that the traditional school year of approximately 180 days is not the best arrangement to meet students' learning needs. As the RCM Research Corporation, a nonprofit group that studies issues in educational change, points out: "Historically, time has been the glue that has bonded the traditions of our public school system—i.e., the Carnegie units, equal class periods, no school during summer months, 12 years of schooling, etc.—and, as a result, the use of time has become sacrosanct, 'We have always done it this way!' How time is used by schools often has more to do with administrative convenience than it does with what is best educationally for the student" (RCM Research Corporation 1998).

Proposals for year-round schools and educationally oriented weekend and after-school programs address the educational and developmental needs of students impacted by social problems. According to the National Association for Year-Round Education, 1,646 year-round schools served 1.3 million students in 1992; by 2002, 3,011 year-round schools served 2.2 million students. In Austin, Texas, for example, schools can participate in an Optional Extended Year (OEY) program that allows them to provide additional instruction in reading and mathematics to students at risk of being retained a grade. Schools participating in OEY can choose from among four school day options: (1) extended day, (2) extended week, (3) intersession of year-round schools, and (4) summer school (Idol 1998; Washington 1998).

Programs that extend beyond the traditional school day also address the needs of parents and the requirements of the work world. As an elementary teacher in Missouri said, "Many of my students just hang around at the end of every day. They ask what they can do to help me. Often there's no one at home, and they're afraid to go home or spend time on the streets" (Boyer 1995, 165).

After-school educational and recreational programs are designed to (1) provide children with supervision at times when they might become involved in antisocial activities, (2) provide enrichment experiences to widen children's perspectives and increase their socialization, and (3) improve the academic achievement of children not achieving at their potential during regular school hours (Fashola 1999). Ernest Boyer argued that schools should adapt their schedules to those of the workplace so that parents could become more involved in their children's education, and that businesses, too, should give parents more flexible work schedules. Drawing on the model of Japan, Boyer suggested that the beginning of the school year could be a holiday to free parents to attend opening day ceremonies and celebrate the launching and continuation of education in the same way that we celebrate its ending.

For several years, the After-School Plus (A+) Program in Hawaii has operated afternoon enrichment programs from 2:00 to 5:00 for children in kindergarten through sixth grade. The children, who are free to do art, sports, drama, or homework, develop a sense of *ohana,* or feeling of belonging. Currently, 178 program sites serve nearly 22,000 students (National Governors' Association & NGA Center for Best Practices 2002). Since the mid-1970s, schools in Buena Vista, Virginia, have operated according to a Four Seasons Calendar that includes an optional summer enrichment program. Buena Vista's superintendent estimates that the district saves more than $100,000 a year on retention costs; though some students take more time, they are promoted to the next grade (Boyer 1995).

Although some research indicates that extended school days and school calendars have a positive influence on achievement (Center for Research on Effective Schooling for Disadvantaged Students 1992; Gandara and Fish 1994), the Center for Research on the Education of Students Placed at Risk (CRESPAR) at Johns Hopkins University concluded that "there is no straightforward answer to the question of what works best in after-school programs" (Fashola 1999). According to CRESPAR, few studies of the effects of after-school programs on measures such as achievement or reduction of antisocial behavior meet minimal standards for research design. Nevertheless, CRESPAR found that after-school programs with stronger evidence of effectiveness had four elements: training for staff, program structure, evaluation of program effectiveness, and planning that includes families and children (Fashola 1999).

Social Services In response to the increasing number of at-risk and violence-prone children and youth, many schools are also providing an array of social services to students, their families, and their communities. The following comments by three female students highlight the acute need for support services for at-risk youth who can turn to aggression and violence in a futile attempt to bolster their fragile self-esteem and to cope with the pain in their lives. All three girls have been involved in violent altercations in and around their schools, and all three frequently use alcohol and illegal drugs. Fifteen-year-old "Mary" has been physically abused by both her father and mother, and she was raped when she was fourteen. "Linda," also fifteen years old, was sexually molested during a four-year period by a family acquaintance, and she endures constant physical and psychological abuse from her father. Fourteen-year-old "Jenny" is obsessed with death and suicide, and she aspires to join a gang.

> *When you're smoking dope, you just break out laughing, you don't feel like punching people because it's just too hard. It takes too much. . . . You're mellow. . . . You just want to sit there and trip out on everybody. . . . It's even good for school work. When I used to get stoned all the time last year, I remember, I used to sit in class and do my work because I didn't want the teacher to catch me, and this year I'm getting failing marks 'cause I'm not doing my work 'cause I'm never stoned (Mary).*
>
> *I just know I got a lot of hatred. . . . And there's this one person [Jenny], and it just kinda happened after she mouthed me off, I was just like totally freaked with her and now I just want to slam her head into something. I wanna shoot her with a gun or something. I wanna kill her. . . . If I could get away with it I'd kill her. I wouldn't necessarily kill her, but I'd get her good. I just want to teach her a lesson. I'd beat the crap out of her. She's pissed me off so badly. I just want to give her two black eyes. Then I'd be fine. I'd have gotten the last word in (Linda).*
>
> *I like fighting. It's exciting. I like the power of being able to beat up people. Like, if I fight them, and I'm winning, I feel good about myself, and I think of myself as tough. . . . I'm not scared of anybody, so that feels good. My friends are scared of a lot of people, and I go "Oh yeah, but I'm not scared of them. . . . All these people in grade eight at that junior high are scared of me, they don't even know me, and they're scared of me. It makes me feel powerful (Jenny) (Artz 1999, 127, 136, 157).*

Although some believe that schools should not provide social services, an increase in the number of at-risk students like Mary, Linda, and Jenny suggest that the trend is likely to continue. In Seattle, a referendum required that a percentage of taxes be set aside to provide services to elementary-age children. In Florida, Palm Beach County officials created the Children's Services Council to address sixteen areas, from reducing the dropout rate to better child care. From parent support groups, to infant nurseries, to programs for students with special needs, the council has initiated scores of projects to benefit the community and its children.

Summary

What Is the Role of Schools in Today's Society?

- Though debate about the role of schools continues, the public believes that schools have a responsibility to address problems confronting U.S. society.
- The public also believes that schools should teach prosocial values such as honesty, patriotism, fairness, and civility.
- Schools socialize students to participate intelligently and constructively in society.
- Schools in the United States, in contrast to those in most other countries, are committed to providing equal educational opportunity.

How Can Schools Be Described?

- Schools can be categorized according to the focus of their curricula and according to their organizational structures.
- Metaphors for schools have suggested that schools are like families, tribes or clans, banks, gardens, prisons, and so on, with the school-as-family metaphor often describing schools that are successful.
- Some people believe that schools reproduce the existing social class structure, that they maintain the differences between the "haves" and "have-nots." For example, Anyon's four categories of schools—working-class schools, middle-class schools, affluent professional schools, and executive elite schools—illustrate the relationship between schooling and social class.

What Are Schools Like as Social Institutions?

- As social institutions that contribute to the maintenance and improvement of society, schools mirror the national U.S. culture and the surrounding local culture.
- Schools develop their own unique cultures, and the community environment that surrounds a school can impact it positively or negatively.
- Elements of a school's physical environment such as self-contained classrooms, open-space arrangements, and departmentalization contribute to a school's character and culture. Similarly, each classroom develops its own culture, which is influenced by the physical setting and the social dimensions of the group.

What Characteristics Distinguish Successful Schools?

- Three aspects of successful schools have been suggested: (1) their students manifest a high level of learning; (2) their results surpass those for comparable schools; and (3) they are improving rather than getting worse.
- Research has identified seven characteristics of effective schools; strong leadership, high expectations, emphasis on basic skills, orderly school environment, frequent and systematic evaluation of student learning, sense of purpose, and collegiality and a sense of community.
- Research indicates that successfully restructured schools emphasize student learning, authentic pedagogy, building organizational capacity, and external support.

What Social Problems Affect Schools and Place Students at Risk?

- Among the many social problems that impact the school's ability to educate students are poverty, family stress, substance abuse, violence and crime, teen pregnancy, and suicide.
- Children at risk, who represent all ethnic and racial groups and all socioeconomic levels, tend to get low grades, underachieve, be older than other students at the same grade level, and have behavior problems at school.

What Are Schools Doing to Address Societal Problems?

- Schools have developed intervention and prevention programs to address social problems. Three effective intervention programs are peer counseling, full-service schools, and school-based interprofessional case management.
- Since 1965, an array of federally funded compensatory education programs has provided educational services to improve the basic skills of low-ability students from low-income families.
- Many school districts have developed alternative schools or schools-within-a-school that provide highly individualized instructional and support services for students who have not been successful in regular schools. Also, highly effective teachers modify their techniques and develop alternative curricula to meet the needs of students at risk.

How Can Community-Based Partnerships Address Social Problems That Hinder Students' Learning?

- Communities help schools address social problems that hinder students' learning by providing various kinds of support.
- Civic organizations raise money for schools, sponsor teams, recognize student achievement, award scholarships, sponsor volunteer mentor programs, and provide other resources and services to enrich students' learning.
- Corporate–education partnerships provide schools with resources, release time for employees to visit schools, scholar-

ships, job initiatives for disadvantaged youth, in-service programs for teachers, and management training for school administrators.

- Schools serve as resources for their communities by providing educational and recreational programs before and after the school day, and by providing health and social services.

Key Terms and Concepts

alternative school, **145**
classroom culture, **128**
compensatory education programs, **144**
departmentalization, **127**
full-service schools, **141**
institution, **125**
latchkey children, **135**
magnet school, **123**
open-space schools, **127**
peer counseling, **141**
prosocial values, **120**
school-based interprofessional case management, **144**
school culture, **126**
school traditions, **127**
school-within-a-school, **145**
self-contained classroom, **127**
service learning, **122**
students at risk, **132**

Applications and Activities

Teacher's Journal

1. Collect and summarize several newspaper and magazine articles that contain references to social problems that impact the schools. To what extent do the articles address prevention or intervention strategies discussed in this chapter?
2. Reflect on your experiences with the impact of social problems on teaching and learning at the elementary, middle, or high school levels. Select one of the social issues or problems discussed in this chapter and describe its influences on you or your peers.

Teacher's Database

1. Join or start an interactive online discussion on one or more of the following topics discussed in this chapter. You might join a newsgroup already in progress or request discussion partners via an e-mail mailing list or via any one of the message board opportunities that are offered at many of the sites you have already explored. You might also establish a communication link among your classmates or with students in other schools who are taking a similar course.

   alternative schools
   at-risk students
   children in poverty
   crime and violence in schools
   family stress
   latchkey children
   school-based clinics
   substance abuse
   teen pregnancies
   youth suicide

   Formulate a research question concerning demographic aspects of students and their families, and go online to gather current national and state statistics on topics related to your question. For example, your question might relate to one or more of the above topics.
2. Develop a collaborative project with classmates to investigate and report on issues in drug abuse prevention, at-risk intervention, or violence prevention. Begin by exploring two sites maintained by the U.S. government: Children, Youth and Families Education and Research Network (CYFERNet); and Children, Youth, and Families at Risk (CYFAR). Both sites have extensive resources, databases, and services for at-risk children, youth, and their families.

Companion Website

Observations and Interviews

1. Reflect on your experiences relating to social problems at the elementary, middle, or high school levels. Then gather statistics and information about how a local school or local school district is responding to the social problems discussed in this chapter. To help you identify the kind of information to gather, ask your instructor for handout master M4.2, "Analyzing Impacts of Social Problems on Schools."
2. Obtain at least one statement of philosophy, or mission statement, from a school with which you are familiar. Analyze the statement(s), identifying and highlighting portions that refer to the role of schools discussed in this chapter (prosocial values, socialization, social change, and equal educational opportunity).

Professional Portfolio

1. Analyze a school as a social institution. How is the school organized in terms of roles and statuses? How does the school's organization and functioning reflect the wider society as well as the community in which it is located? What characteristics of the school and its people relate to the urban, rural, or suburban nature of the school environment? Does the school match one of the four categories of schools identified by Jean Anyon on the basis of social class?

2. Develop a case study of a school's culture. Visit a local school or base your study on a school you have attended. Organize your case in terms of the following categories of information:

   Environment—How would you describe the school facility or physical plant and its material and human resources? How is space organized? What is the climate of the school?

   Formal Practices—What grades are included at the school? How is the school year organized? How is time structured? How are students and teachers grouped for instruction?

   Traditions—What events and activities and products seem important to students, teachers, and administrators? What symbols, slogans, and ceremonies identify membership in the school? How do community members view and relate to the school?

   Draw conclusions from your case study: What aspects of the school culture seem to support learning and academic achievement? On the basis of your case study, draft a position statement on the kind of culture you would like to create or promote in your classroom.

Video**Workshop Extra!**

If the Video Workshop package was included with your textbook, go to Chapter 4 of the Companion Website (www.ablongman.com/parkay6e) and click on the VideoWorkshop button. Follow the instructions for viewing videoclip 3 and completing this exercise. Consider this information along with what you've read in Chapter 4 while answering the following questions.

1. Schools often reflect problems and prosperity in the surrounding area. Quality of schools is affected accordingly. Design an after-school program that could energize students and foster a relationship with those in the community.
2. Compare rural, urban, and suburban schools in terms of their potential for promoting self-worth in the student population. What types of activities could help teachers encourage students' risk-taking and problem-solving in the classroom?

Appendix 4.1

SCHOOL SAFETY CHECKLIST

Give your school a thorough crime prevention inspection now. Use this checklist as a guideline to determine your school's strengths and weaknesses.

	Yes	No
1. Is there a policy for dealing with violence and vandalism in your school? (The reporting policy must be realistic and strictly adhered to.)	____	____
2. Is there an incident reporting system?	____	____
3. Is the incident reporting system available to all staff?	____	____
4. Is there statistical information available as to the scope of the problems at your school and in the community?	____	____
5. Have the school, school board, and administrators taken steps or anticipated any problems through dialogue?	____	____
6. Does security fit into the organization of the school? (Security must be designed to fit the needs of the administration and made part of the site.)	____	____
7. Are the teachers and administrators aware of laws that pertain to them? To their rights? To students' rights? Of their responsibility as to enforcement of and respect for rules, regulations, policies, and the law?	____	____
8. Is there a working relationship with your local law enforcement agency?	____	____
9. Are students and parents aware of expectations and school discipline codes?	____	____
10. Are there any actual or contingency action plans developed to deal with student disruptions and vandalism?	____	____
11. Is there a policy as to restitution or prosecution of perpetrators of violence and vandalism?	____	____
12. Is there any in-service training available for teachers and staff in the areas of violence and vandalism and other required reporting procedures?	____	____
13. Is there a policy for consistent monitoring and evaluation of incident reports?	____	____
14. Is the staff trained in standard crime prevention behavior?	____	____

Source: Excerpted from *The School Safety Check Book* by the National School Safety Center, 141 Duesenberg Dr., Suite 16, Westlake Village, CA, 91362, http://www.nsscl.org.

5 Struggles for Control of Schools in the United States

Among the 14,000 school districts of the nation, it seems as if everyone is trying something new in the way of curriculum, organization, finances and so on. But the impression left to the observer is that of disorganized focus on problems and remedies.

—Frederick W. Wirt and Michael W. Kirst
The Political Dynamics of American Education

On entering the teachers' lounge during your planning period, you can tell immediately that the four teachers in the room are having a heated discussion.

"I don't see how you can say that teachers have much control over the schools," says Kim, a language arts teacher. "It's all so political. The feds, our legislators, the school board—it's the politicians who really control the schools. This April all my kids have to take a test based on the new state standards—we didn't write the standards, it was the politicians. They exploit the schools just so they can get elected."

"If you want to know who *really* controls the schools," Enrique, a mathematics teacher, says, "it's big business. The politicians are actually their pawns. Big business is concerned about international competition—so, they exert tremendous pressure on the politicians who, in turn, lean on the teachers. And then . . ."

"Just a minute," says Hal, raising his hand to silence Enrique. Hal is one of the school's lead teachers and chair of the site-based council. "Maybe that's the way things were in the past, but things *are* changing. I'm not saying that politics or big business doesn't influence the schools, but we have a lot of influence over what we teach and how. Look at our site-based council and all the decisions we've made during the last two years—block scheduling, teaching teams, a common planning time, integrated curricula, and a school-wide assessment program."

"Right, teaching really is changing," says Roberta, a science teacher and multimedia coordinator for the school. "Just think about the National Board for Professional Teaching Standards—now we've got the option of becoming board certified, just like lawyers have the bar exam and architects have their licensing exam. Also, the majority of the board is made up of teachers, and they helped to develop the standards."

"Good example," Hal says. "Already there's a few thousand board-certified teachers, and there's supposed to be more than 100,000 by 2005. I'm working on my portfolio so I can apply next year."

"It's just a matter of time before board-certified teachers come to have more leverage in controlling the schools," says Roberta. "With more and more districts moving to some sort of school choice, the school that has more board-certified teachers is going to attract more students. So, teachers with board certification will be able to set the conditions under which they work. The market value of board certification is going to rise."

"Exactly," says Hal. "Right now in North Carolina, board-certified teachers get a 12 percent increase in pay."

"Well, I don't quite share your optimism about how teachers are going to have all this influence," says Kim. "Look at every presidential election—the Democrats and Republicans always try to exploit education. So, they talk about all the changes they'd make . . . higher standards, more accountability for teachers, more input for parents, and so on. Plus all politicians—whether they're running for president, governor, or whatever—they use education to build their political careers, and teachers are the ones who have to implement their utopian ideas."

"I agree to some extent," says Roberta. "Politicians will always use education for their own ends. But that's just rhetoric; what's really happening, bit by bit, is that teachers are becoming much more influential."

"Let's just ask this new teacher here," says Hal as he smiles and nods in your direction. "Don't you think teachers have a lot of influence over how schools are run? During the rest of your career, you'll be involved in school governance, won't you?"

Hal, Roberta, Enrique, and Kim look at you, awaiting your response. What do you say?

Focus Questions

1. **Who is involved in the struggles for control of schools in the United States?**
2. **What is the role of the local community in school governance?**
3. **What powers and influence do states have in governing schools?**
4. **What assistance do regional education agencies provide?**
5. **How does the federal government influence education?**
6. **How are schools financed in the United States?**
7. **What are some trends in funding for equity and excellence?**
8. **How will the privatization movement affect equity and excellence in education?**

Expand your knowledge of the concepts discussed in this chapter by reading current and historical articles from the *New York Times* by visiting the "**Themes of the Times**" section of the Companion Website (www.ablongman.com/parkay6e).

Who Is Involved in the Struggles for Control of Schools in the United States?

Professional teachers recognize the need to understand the many complex political forces that currently influence schools in the United States (see Figure 5.1). For example, the opening scenario for this chapter illustrates how teachers and various political interest groups seek to influence policies related to school governance. Clearly, teachers have much to gain from becoming politically involved; and, as the title of a guide to political action for teachers suggests, *You Can Make a Difference* (Keresty, O'Leary, and Wortley 1998).

During the twenty-first century, struggles for control of schools in the United States will continue. Among the groups that will continue to have a keen concern for shaping educational policies, at least nine can be identified:

1. *Parents*—Concerned with controlling local schools so that quality educational programs are available to their children

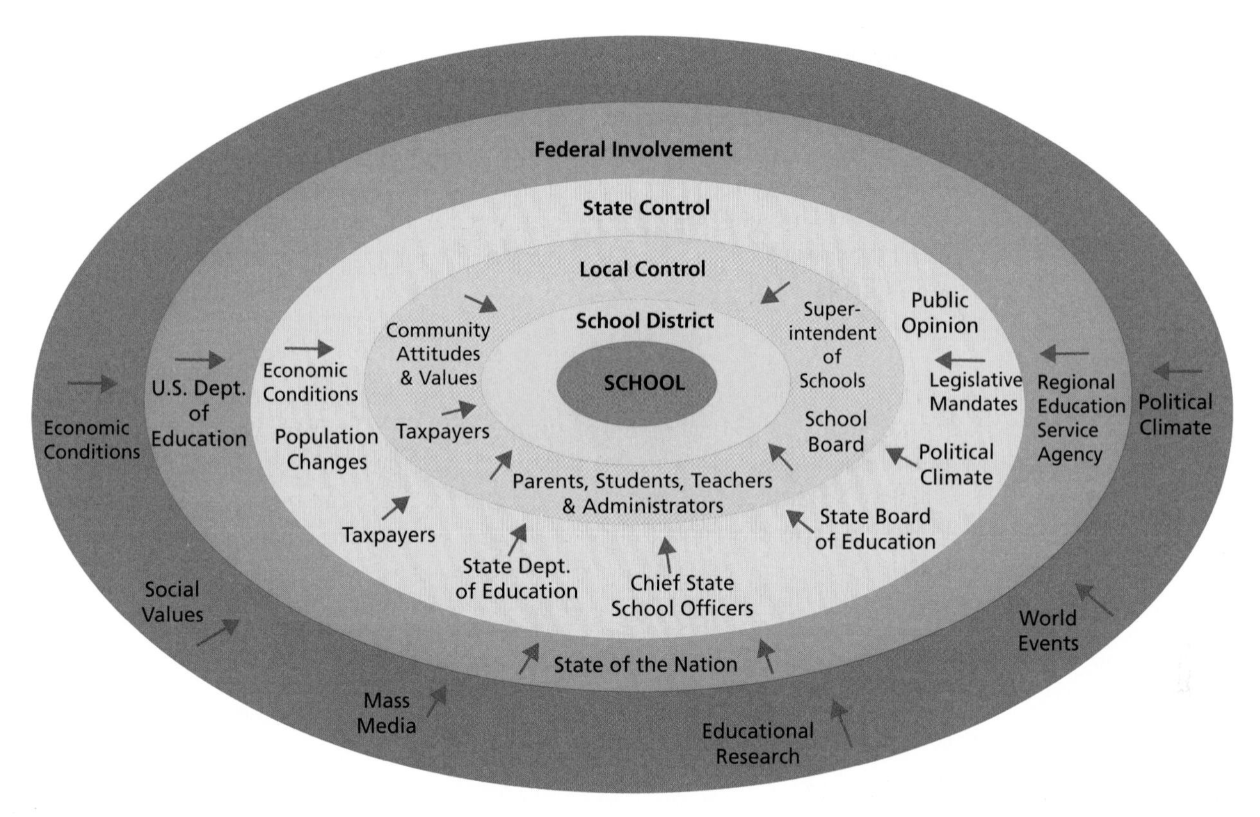

Figure 5.1 Political influences on the schools

2. *Students*—Concerned with policies related to freedom of expression, dress, behavior, and curricular offerings
3. *Teachers*—Concerned with their role in school reform, improving working conditions, terms of employment, and other professional issues
4. *Administrators*—Concerned with providing leadership so that various interest groups, including teachers, participate in the shared governance of schools and the development of quality educational programs
5. *Taxpayers*—Concerned with maintaining an appropriate formula for determining local, state, and federal financial support of schools
6. *State and federal authorities*—Concerned with the implementation of court orders, guidelines, and legislative mandates related to the operation of schools
7. *Minorities and women*—Concerned with the availability of equal educational opportunity for all and with legal issues surrounding administrative certification, terms of employment, and evaluation
8. *Educational theorists and researchers*—Concerned with using theoretical and research-based insights as the bases for improving schools at all levels
9. *Businesses and corporations*—Concerned with receiving from the schools graduates who have the knowledge, skills, attitudes, and values to help an organization realize its goals

Out of the complex and often turbulent interactions of these groups, school policies are developed. And, as strange as it may seem, no one of these groups can be said to control today's schools. As Seymour Sarason (1997, 36), author of several books on the complexities of educational change, points out, education in the United States "*is a system in which accountability is so diffused that no one is accountable*" (italics in original). Those who we might imagine control schools—principals, superintendents, and boards of education—are in reality responding to shifting sets of conditions created by those who have an interest in the schools. In addition, schools are influenced by several out-of-school factors—what sociologists have termed *environmental press.* Because schools reflect the society they serve, they are influenced directly and indirectly by factors such as those illustrated in Figure 5.1.

Clearly, it is difficult to untangle the web of political forces that influence schools. Figure 5.2 shows graphically how school authorities are confronted with the difficult task of funneling the input from various sources into unified, coherent school programs. In the next four sections of this chapter, we examine the many political forces that impinge on the schools by looking at how they are influenced at the local, state, federal, and regional levels.

Figure 5.2 School politics.
Source: Adapted from Frederick M. Wirt and Michael W. Kirst, *The Political Dynamics of American Education,* 2d ed. Berkeley, CA: McCutcheon, 1997, p. 34. Used with permission.

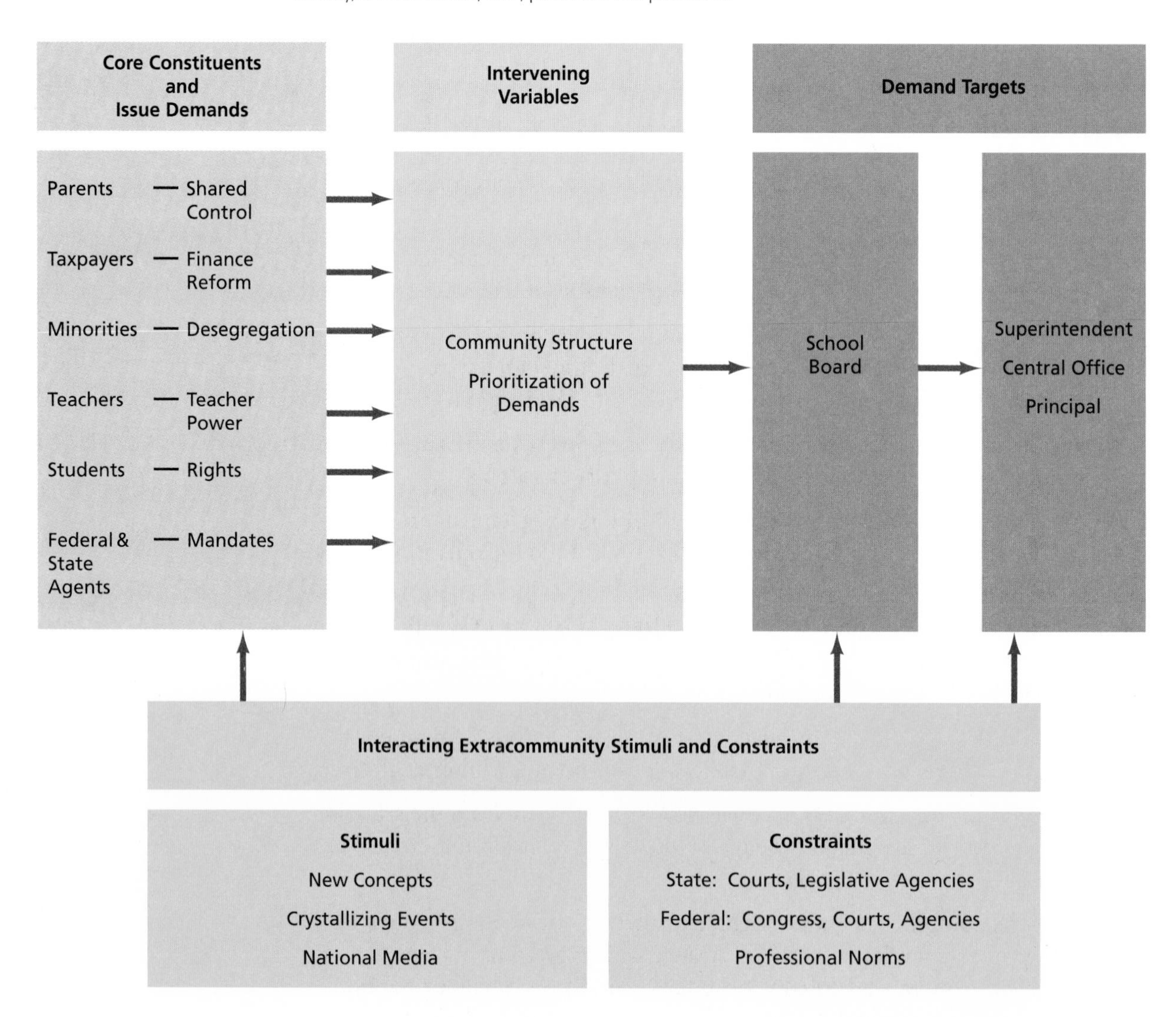

What Is the Role of the Local Community in School Governance?

The Constitution does not address the issue of public education, but the Tenth Amendment is used as the basis for giving states the responsibility for the governance of education, that is, the legal authority to create and manage school systems. In addition, as seen in Figure 5.2, various individuals and groups, though not legally empowered, do exercise local control over schools by trying to influence those legally entitled to operate the schools.

The Tenth Amendment gives to the states all powers not reserved for the federal government and not prohibited to the states. The states have, in turn, created local school districts, giving them responsibility for the daily operation of public schools. As a result of efforts to consolidate districts, the number of local public school districts has declined from 119,001 in 1937–38 to 14,928 in 1999–2000 (National Center for Education Statistics 2002a).

Local School District

Local school districts vary greatly in regard to demographics such as number of school-age children; educational, occupational, and income levels of parents; operating budget; number of teachers; economic resources; and number of school buildings. Some serve ultrawealthy communities, others impoverished ghetto neighborhoods or rural areas. Their operations include 423 one-teacher elementary schools in this country (National Center for Education Statistics 2002a) as well as scores of modern, multi-building campuses in heavily populated areas. The largest school districts are exceedingly complex operations with multi-million-dollar-a-year operating budgets (see Table 5.1) The largest—the New York City school system—has more than a million pupils (from 190 countries), nearly 64,000 teachers (a number that exceeds the number of *students* in

Table 5.1 Selected data for the ten largest public school systems, 1999

School System	Total Enrollment	Number of Teachers[1]	Pupil/Teacher Ratio	Number of Schools	Total Expenditures in Thousands[2]	Expenditure per Pupil[2]
New York City	1,075,710	63,989	16.8	1,207	$10,799,265	$8,106
Los Angeles Unified	710,007	33,754	21.0	655	$4,618,160	$6,010
City of Chicago	431,750	23,455	18.4	597	$3,446,592	$6,617
Miami-Dade County	292,023	18,104	19.9	350	$2,501,659	$5,952
Broward County, FL	241,094	11,322	21.3	234	$1,470,830	$5,453
Clark County, NV	217,526	10,838	20.1	246	$1,356,279	$5,108
Houston Independent School District	209,716	11,638	18.0	296	$1,231,086	$5,340
Philadelphia	205,199	11,423	18,0	259	$1,510,785	$5,702
Hawaii Public Schools	185,860	10,866	17.1	256	$1,266,378	$5,859
Detroit Public Schools	167,124	9,148	18.3	268	$1,345,361	$7,326

[1]Data exclude teachers reported as working in school district offices rather than in schools.
[2]Data are for 1997–98.

Source: U.S. Department of Education, National Center for Education Statistics, Common Core of Data survey. (Table prepared October 2001.) Adapted from *Digest of Education Statistics 2002.* Washington, DC: National Center for Education Statistics, U.S. Department of Education, Tables 92 and 93.

On the Frontlines

Sex Education in the Schools

As her seventh-grade students filed out of her room at the end of the day, Mary stood at the door saying goodbye. She also monitored the hallway around her classroom, as the principal had asked all teachers to do in an effort to help maintain some order in between classes and at the start and end of the days. As she looked around, Mary noticed two eighth-graders about twenty feet away saying goodbye to each other for the day. They were the latest "item" among students—and faculty, for that matter. They had their arms around each other and were getting a little carried away as they kissed. Mary knew the school had a policy about "public displays of affection," but it was very ambiguous and students often got very defensive when teachers said something, feeling it was "none of their business."

Before Mary said anything, the two students gathered their books and left, but the incident revived an ongoing conflict Mary had with herself. She knew that students were much more sexually aware and active than many people realized or are willing to admit. As the middle school health education teacher, she also knew that the students weren't very realistic about the dangers they faced if they weren't fully informed or aware of the consequences of their actions. She'd spoken with colleagues at the elementary schools in the district who told her they saw disturbing signs at their level as well, such as students wearing skimpy and revealing clothing and sexual comments they'd heard students make to each other. Mary's educational training prepared her to teach a comprehensive health education curriculum that included open discussions on sexuality, but she wondered just how much she could cover. What is her responsibility? She taught in a somewhat conservative community and she wondered whether she'd run into opposition if she opened up her curriculum.

Sex education in U.S. schools has become a lightning rod of controversy in the past fifteen years and is one area of the curriculum that draws the most interest and feedback by parents and community members. At the heart of the issue is the recognition that young people are sexually active and, as a result, put themselves at risk for a number of social problems—including HIV infection and AIDS, sexually transmitted diseases (STDs), unplanned pregnancies, sexual abuse, and rape. According to the Alan Guttmacher Institute, more than half of seventeen-year-olds in the United States have had intercourse; each year 10 percent of women fifteen to nineteen become pregnant; and each year one in four sexually active teenagers acquires an STD. While the rates of sexual activity among teens has declined slightly since the peak years of the 1980s, data from the Centers for Disease Control and Prevention (CDC) indicate that as recently as 2000, nearly 469,000 children were born to teen mothers. Because children born to teen mothers are more likely to be low-birth-weight and have recurring health problems, the long-term consequences of teen pregnancies are serious. In the not-so-distant past, many young mothers dropped out of school to take care of their children. Today some school districts provide onsite day care programs in an effort to help teen mothers stay in school and receive an education.

The consequences for teens who contract STDs can be much more fatal. According to the CDC, in 1999 HIV was the fifth-leading cause of death for U.S. adults between the ages of twenty-five and forty-four. Because HIV infection can be symptom-free for years, many of these young adults likely were infected in their teens. While data do show a decline in the overall number of new cases of AIDS each year, there has not been a decline in the number of newly diagnosed HIV cases among youth. Of other STDs, rates for chlamydia gonorrhea are higher among teens than for adults. If left untreated, each can lead to infertility or even fatality.

The controversy lies in the fight over control of the health education curriculum, and particularly the sex education curriculum—a fight that rages on in school districts throughout the country. The overriding question is, "Who should be responsible for the sexual education of students—schools or families?" National health specialists recommend a program that recognizes the diversity of values and that complements the education received at home: one that reflects a synergy of school, community, and home. Comprehensive school health educators feel schools play an important role in providing complete information about sexual health, including alternative lifestyles and thoughts on sexual activity. Because sexuality can be a sensitive subject for families to discuss openly and completely, schools offer an objective environment that allows students to explore and express their feelings on the subject. But many people feel that sexual beliefs are rooted in reli-

gious and moral values and therefore should be the prime responsibility of families and churches. They prefer that health education curricula be limited in its topics of discussion. Advocates of limited curricula prefer abstinence-only, which teaches sex in marriage only, or abstinence-based curricula, which acknowledges alternative behaviors but stresses abstaining until marriage.

The question each school district and community has to answer is, "What in the curriculum do you limit, if anything?" The controversy over what can or cannot be included varies greatly by school districts, depending on a number of factors including the perceived need within a given community. The controversy is a challenge for health education teachers trying to help their students grow to be healthy adults. However, because the issue of teen sexuality is not limited to the health classroom, all teachers need to be aware of the policies of their districts and the "temperature" of the communities. In addition, teachers need to be aware of the support they can expect to get from administrators when attempting to make a risky change to the curriculum.

Exploratory Questions

1. To whom does Mary have the greatest responsibility on the issue of sex education—her students or the community? What internal conflict might Mary be experiencing?
2. What would you do to determine how well a community might accept your inclusion of controversial subjects in your instruction? What could you do to ease any conflict over such inclusion?
3. Visit the SIECUS Sexuality Education site (listed below) and find the "State Mandates for Sexuality Education." What does your state require or recommend be included in sex education?

Your Survival Guide of Helpful Resources

The following resources provide helpful hints for surviving "on the frontlines."

Books and Articles

The Alan Guttmacher Institute. (1999, September). Teen sex and pregnancy: Facts in brief. Retrieved from http://www.agi-usa.org/pubs/fb_teen_sex.html on September 18, 2002.

Centers for Disease Control and Prevention. (2002, March 11). Young people at risk: HIV/AIDS among America's youth. Retrieved from http://www.cdc.gov/hiv/pubs/facts/youth.htm on September 18, 2002.

Websites

Sexuality Information and Education Council of the United States (http://www.siecus.org/school/sex_ed/)

Centers for Disease Control and Prevention, Division of Adolescent and School Health (http://www.cdc.gov/nccdphp/dash/)

National Center for Health Statistics, Centers for Disease Control and Prevention (http://www.cdc.gov/nchs)

Cincinnati; Minneapolis; Portland, Oregon; Sacramento; Seattle; and St. Louis), 1,200 schools, and total annual expenditures of almost $11 billion. The New York system, overseen by a Schools Chancellor, consists of thirty-two community school districts, each with its own superintendent.

School districts also differ in regard to their organizational structures. Large urban systems, which may contain several districts, tend to have more complex distribution of roles and responsibilities than do smaller districts. Appendix 5.1 presents a typical organizational structure for a school district of about 20,000 pupils, while the Appendix "New York City Board of Education" on this book's website presents the organizational structure for the New York City Board of Education.

School Board

A **school board,** acting as a state agent, is responsible for the following important activities: approving the teachers, administrators, and other school personnel hired by the superintendent; developing organizational and educational policies; and determining procedures for the evaluation of programs and personnel.

In most communities, school board members are elected in general elections. In some urban areas, however, board members are selected by the mayor. Board members typically serve a minimum of three to five years, and their terms of office are usually staggered. School boards usually range in size from five to fifteen members, with five or seven frequently suggested as the optimum size. Board members in urban areas usually are paid, but in most other areas are not.

A 2001 national survey of school board members revealed that women constituted 39 percent of school boards and men 61 percent. The survey also revealed that board membership does not reflect the growing diversity of students in the United States—minority membership on school boards was 13.6 percent, an increase of 2.7 percent compared to 1998. The survey also revealed that school board members were more affluent than the general population: 24 percent of board members had annual incomes of $50,000 to $74,999; 22 percent $75,000 to $99,000; and 21.3 percent $100,000 to $149,000 (*American School Board Journal* 2001).

Nearly all school board meetings are open to the public; in fact, many communities even provide radio and television coverage. Open meetings allow parents and interested citizens an opportunity to express their concerns and to get more information about problems in the district.

School boards play a critical role in the U.S. education system, as Rod Paige, U.S. Secretary of Education, points out: "The quality of school board governance effectiveness is the single most important determinant of school district success or failure" (*School Board News* 2002). However, school boards have been criticized recently by authorities for not educating themselves about issues and education policymaking, being reluctant to seek input from their communities, not communicating a shared vision of educational excellence to their communities, and not developing positive, productive relationships with superintendents.

Some states have taken steps to reform school boards. For example, Arkansas provides school board members with training in developing partnerships with their communities, creating a vision of educational excellence, and teambuilding (*School Board News* 2002). West Virginia implemented legislation in 1994 to restructure school boards "so that they become well-informed, responsive, policy-making bodies." Board members now serve for four years rather than six, and they must complete training focused on "boardmanship and governing effectiveness" (Danzberger 1994, 394).

Superintendent of Schools

Though school boards operate very differently, the **superintendent** is invariably the key figure in determining a district's educational policy. The superintendent is the chief administrator of the school district, the person charged with the responsibility of seeing to it that schools operate in accord with federal and state guidelines as well as policies set by the local school board. Though the board of education delegates broad powers to the superintendent, his or her policies require board approval.

How the superintendent and his or her board work together appears to be related to the size of the school district, with superintendents and school boards in larger districts more likely to be in conflict. School boards in smaller districts, however, are more effective when they do oppose the superintendent. In large districts, the board's own divisiveness makes it less likely that the board will successfully oppose the superintendent (Wirt and Kirst 1997).

Superintendents must have great skill to respond appropriately to the many external political forces that demand their attention, and conflict is inevitable. Effective superintendents demonstrate that they are able to play three roles simultaneously: politician, manager, and teacher. It is a demanding position, and turnover is high; for example, between 1980 and 1995, the New York City school system had ten chancellors (Hurwitz 1999).

The Role of Parents

Parents may not be involved legally in the governance of schools, but they do play an important role in education. One characteristic of successful schools is that they have developed close working relationships with parents. Additionally, children whose parents or guardians support and encourage school activities have a definite advantage in school.

Through participation on school advisory and site-based councils, parents are making an important contribution to restructuring and school reform efforts around the country. In addition, groups such as the Parent-Teacher Association (PTA), Parent-Teacher Organization (PTO), or Parent Advisory Council (PAC) give parents the opportunity to communicate with teachers on matters of interest and importance to them. Through these groups, parents can become involved in the life of the school in a variety of ways—from making recommendations regarding school policies to providing much-needed volunteer services, or to initiating school-improvement activities such as fund-raising drives.

Many parents are also influencing the character of education through their involvement with the growing number of private, parochial, for-profit, and charter schools. In addition, many parents are activists in promoting school choice, voucher systems, and the home schooling movement. In their effort to influence schools in the United States, some parents even join well-funded conservative think tanks that launch sophisticated national campaigns to remove from public schools practices and materials that they believe have links to secular humanist or New Age beliefs. According to a book titled *School Wars: Resolving Our Conflicts over Religion and Values,* educational reform initiatives targeted by activist parents have included "outcome-based education, the whole language approach [to teaching reading], thinking skills programs, imagery techniques, self-esteem programs, the teaching of evolution, global education and multiculturalism, and sex education" (Gaddy, Hall, and Marzano 1996, 93).

Keepers of *the Dream*

Marcia McVey, School District Superintendent

On the shelves in Marcia McVey's office are dozens of statues of elephants. They vary in size and material—wood, ceramic, cloth, and crystal. The collection began when she was named superintendent of the Duarte, California, Independent School District. In her interview with the school board, the body that selects the superintendent, she had used an elephant metaphor to convey her vision for the district's future. She explained that most people in a school district are like people who focus on only one part of the elephant instead of the whole animal. As a consequence, different people have different pictures of the elephant—or the school district. However, she personally enjoys having the big picture and seeing the elephant whole.

In her extended metaphor, the personnel office of the school district is the heart of the elephant, the school board its head, the principals and teachers its legs, and the children the body. "It takes all parts to make the body move ahead," she told the board. Then she suggested that this elephant was ailing and that she saw herself as an elephant doctor.

The board unanimously selected her to be superintendent and, during their first closed session, presented her with a beautiful statue of an elephant. Later they gave her a matching elephant in recognition of one of her early accomplishments as superintendent. She soon discovered that elephants were the gift of choice whenever someone at work wanted to celebrate her birthdays and achievements or simply to thank her. Over the five years of McVey's superintendency her unplanned collection grew to over 100 elephants, a tangible expression of appreciation from the board members, district office administrators, principals, teachers, clerks, parents, and custodians whose lives she touched.

McVey's career path in education is like a tour through a school district's organization chart. She began as a classroom teacher and for ten years taught grades 4 through 11. Then she worked for three years as a school counselor in an intermediate school and as its assistant principal for a year. Over the next ten years she served as principal at two elementary schools. During that time, she took a year's leave of absence to work at the state level on the California State Department of Education Task Force on Conflict Resolution in the Secondary Schools. Then she left elementary school administration to work in the district office as the Director of Curriculum and Instruction K–12. Four years later she began what, in retrospect, seems like a march to the superintendency—three years as assistant superintendent in one district, four years as assistant superintendent in another, two years as deputy superintendent, and then the superintendency that launched her elephant collection! After retiring from the superintendency, having served thirty-six years in K–12 education, she began teaching future principals and superintendents in the Education Administration Department of a local university. Her graduate students say that she challenges them, pushes them to do their best, and cares about them as people, taking their concerns seriously and helping them locate the right administration position for them. The fifteen students in her first university class continue to communicate with her by e-mail.

". . . getting involved in the community . . ."

When she is asked which of the education positions she has held she liked best, she replies that *each* was the best: "I've always loved what I was doing. As a counselor, I could be a spokesperson for the students; as a principal, I loved working with a team—the parents, teachers, students, everyone. The work as director of curriculum was challenging, and it impacted a whole school district. We decided what the curriculum should be, developed it, and helped see that it was implemented. That was fun. As the superintendent I worked with teams again, empowering principals, getting involved in the community, and communicating regularly with the school board."

Discussing key issues she dealt with as superintendent, McVey noted three areas—money, people, and instruction. Challenges in the first area included, "seeing that positive collective bargaining agreements were negotiated in a timely and fair manner and having to communicate to employees why there wasn't sufficient funding for salary increases. Secondary and integral to this one was building a team, so valued employees didn't leave the district." And of course, balancing the budget was always a challenge.

People-related challenges were "establishing and maintaining credible personnel procedures and practices; keeping the board and all the stakeholders of a school district and the larger community up to date on all of the issues; and being accountable for the progress of the students."

In the area of instruction, McVey had to keep up with the textbook selection process, staff development, and budgets related to new textbook adoptions. A particular challenge in this area was implementing technology and instructional programs. McVey was involved in every aspect, from overseeing the wiring in all the aging buildings for new technology, acquiring hardware, gaining clerical support for the new programs, and implementing staff training and evaluation, to "finding money, establishing consortia and partnerships to make it all work."

Woven throughout McVey's comments is her appreciation of the human dimension of her work. She clearly enjoyed her superintendency—and all the education positions she has held—because of the people. "Helping people be the best that they can be has been the whole purpose of my work."

School Restructuring

At many schools across the country exciting changes are taking place in regard to how schools are controlled locally. To improve the performance of schools, to decentralize the system of governance, and to enhance the professional status of teachers, some districts are **restructuring** their school systems. Restructuring goes by several names: shared governance, administrative decentralization, teacher empowerment, professionalization, bottom-up policymaking, school-based planning, school-based management, and shared decision making. What all these approaches to school governance have in common is allowing those who know students best—teachers, principals, aides, custodians, librarians, secretaries, and parents—greater freedom in deciding how to meet students' needs.

In a synthesis of research on school restructuring at more than 1,500 schools, the Center on Organization and Restructuring of Schools at the University of Wisconsin found that the following structural conditions enhance a school's "professional community" and increase students' learning:

- Shared governance that increases teachers' influence over school policy and practice
- Interdependent work structures, such as teaching teams, which encourage collaboration
- Staff development that enhances technical skills consistent with school missions for high-quality learning
- Deregulation that provides autonomy for schools to pursue a vision of high intellectual standards
- Small school size, which increases opportunities for communication and trust
- Parent involvement in a broad range of school affairs (Newmann and Wehlage 1995, 52)

School-Based Management

One of the most frequently used approaches to restructuring schools is **school-based management (SBM).** Most SBM programs have three components in common:

1. Power and decisions formerly made by the superintendent and school board are delegated to teachers, principals, parents, community members, and students at local schools. At SBM schools, teachers can become directly involved in making decisions about curriculum, textbooks, standards for student behavior, staff development, promotion and retention policies, teacher evaluation, school budgets, and the selection of teachers and administrators.
2. At each school, a decision-making body (known as a board, cabinet, site-based team, or council)—made up of teachers, the principal, and parents—implements the SBM plan.
3. SBM programs operate with the whole-hearted endorsement of the superintendent of schools.

Chicago School Reform A pioneer in school-based management has been the City of Chicago Public Schools. For years, the Chicago Public School System has been beset by an array of problems: low student achievement, periodic teacher strikes, budget crises, a top-heavy central bureaucracy, and schools in the decaying inner city that seemed beyond most improvement efforts. In response to these problems, the late Mayor Harold Washington appointed a fifty-five-member committee of business, education, and community leaders to develop a school reform proposal. Among the group's recommendations was the creation of a **local school council (LSC)** for each of the city's more than 550 schools, with the majority of council members being parents of schoolchildren.

In December 1988, the Illinois state legislature passed the Chicago School Reform Act, "an undertaking of enormous scope" (Bryk et al. 1998, 28) and believed by some to be "the most fundamental restructuring since the early part of the twentieth century" (Moore 1992, 153). Among the provisions of the act were the following:

- School budgets would be controlled by a local school council made up of six parents, two community members, two school employees, and the principal.
- The council had the authority to hire and fire the principal.
- The council, with input from teachers and the principal, had the authority to develop an improvement plan for the local school.
- New teachers would be hired on the basis of merit, not seniority.
- Principals could remove teachers forty-five days after serving them official notice of unsatisfactory performance.
- A Professional Personnel Advisory Committee of teachers would have advisory responsibility for curriculum and instruction.

The first six years of the Chicago Reform Act produced few concrete improvements. In 1995, frustrated with the district's chronic fiscal problems and inability to increase student achievement, the Illinois legislature gave Mayor Richard M. Daley control over Chicago's schools. Daley created a five-member "reform board of trustees" and appointed a chief executive officer (CEO) who advocated "a balance between local control and central-office control" (Hendrie 1999).

What are the goals of school restructuring? In school-based management, who participates in the governance and management of schools? How is school-based management different from the school board model of local governance?

By many accounts, the Chicago reform efforts during the last half of the 1990s were a continuing "struggle about how to improve an urban school system" (Hendrie 1999). Friction between the mayor's management team and the parent-dominated LSCs intensified with each report that an LSC member had abused his or her authority.

In spite of ongoing conflicts over the governance of Chicago schools, the program resulted in modest increases in student achievement. In 1990, less than a quarter of the city's third- through eighth-graders read at the national norm; by 2000, more than a third (36.4 percent) did so (Hess 2000). Mathematics scores improved even more—from just over a quarter of elementary students at the national norm in 1990 to just under half in 2000 (Hess 2000). At the high school level, graduation rates for nineteen-year-olds increased slightly, and dropout rates for nineteen-year-olds decreased slightly (Miller, Allensworth, and Kochanek 2002).

The preceding gains, however, were not uniform in schools across the city; for example, the city's lowest-performing schools showed little improvement (Rosenkranz 2002). In addition, the Reform Act's goal for Chicago schools to reach national norms within five years was not reached. In spite of modest results, however, the Chicago experiment is clearly one of the more dramatic efforts to empower parents and make them full partners in school governance.

What Powers and Influence Do States Have in Governing Schools?

Above the level of local control, states have a great influence on the governance of schools. Since the 1990s, the influence of the state on educational policy has increased steadily. For example, every state (except Iowa) has statewide academic standards, and every state has mandated a standardized test to assess students' mastery of academic standards. Currently, seventeen states require students to pass exit or end-of-course exams to receive a high school diploma, and seven more plan to do so in the future (Olson 2002). In addition, more than twenty states give state boards of education the authority to intervene in academically "bankrupt" schools whose students score too low as a group.

In response to criticisms of U.S. education, many of which pointed to the nation's frequent low ranking in international comparisons of achievement, many states launched extensive initiatives to improve education, such as the following:

- Increased academic standards
- Greater accountability for teachers
- Testing students in teacher education programs prior to graduation
- Frequent assessments of students' mastery of basic skills
- Professional development as a criterion for continued employment of teachers
- Recertification of experienced teachers

As mentioned previously, the Tenth Amendment to the Constitution allows the states to organize and to administer education within their boundaries. To meet the responsibility of maintaining and supporting schools, the states have assumed several powers:

- The power to levy taxes for the support of schools and to determine state aid to local school districts
- The power to set the curriculum and, in some states, to identify approved textbooks
- The power to determine minimum standards for teacher certification
- The power to establish standards for accrediting schools
- The power to pass legislation necessary for the proper maintenance and support of schools

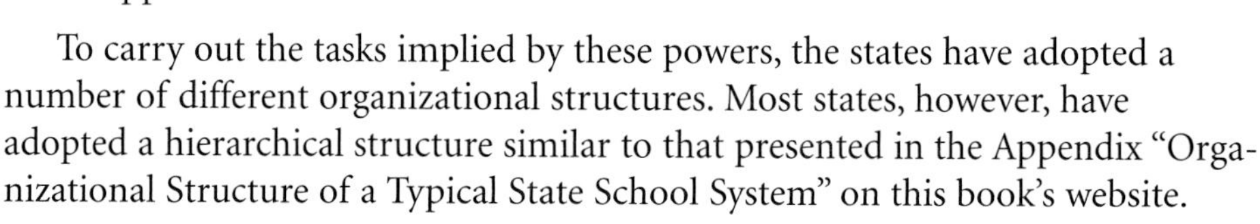

To carry out the tasks implied by these powers, the states have adopted a number of different organizational structures. Most states, however, have adopted a hierarchical structure similar to that presented in the Appendix "Organizational Structure of a Typical State School System" on this book's website.

The Roles of State Government in Education

Various people and agencies within each state government play a role in operating the educational system within that state. Though state governments differ in many respects, the state legislature, the state courts, and the governor have a direct, critical impact on education in their state.

The Legislature In nearly every state, the legislature is responsible for establishing and maintaining public schools and for determining basic educational policies within the state. To accomplish these ends, the legislature has the power to enact laws related to education. Among the policies that the state legislature may determine are the following:

- How the state boards of education will be selected and what their responsibilities will be
- How the chief state school officer will be selected and what his or her duties will be
- How the state department of education will function
- How the state will be divided into local and regional districts
- How higher education will be organized and financed
- How local school boards will be selected and what their powers will be

In addition, the legislature may determine how taxes will be used to support schools, what will or will not be taught, the length of the school day and school year, how many years of compulsory education will be required, and whether or not the state will have community colleges and/or vocational/technical schools. Legislatures may also make policies that apply to such matters as pupil attendance, admission, promotion, teacher certification, teacher tenure and retirement, and collective bargaining.

The Courts From time to time, state courts are called on to uphold the power of the legislature to develop laws that apply to schools. The state courts must determine, however, that this power does not conflict with the state or federal constitution. It is important to remember, too, that the role of state courts is not to develop laws but to rule on the reasonableness of laws that apply to specific educational situations.

Perhaps no state court had a greater impact on education during the first half of the 1990s than the Kentucky Supreme Court. In 1989, the Court ruled that

Meeting the Standard

Recognizes and Uses School Governance Structure

The teacher understands schools as organizations within the larger community context and understands the operations of the relevant aspects of the system(s) within which s/he works (INTASC Knowledge, Principle #10).

Accomplished teachers can evaluate school progress and the allocation of school resources in light of their understanding of state and local educational objectives (NBPTS).

Teacher candidates reflect a thorough understanding of pedagogical content knowledge delineated in professional, state, and institutional standards (NCATE).

Teacher is highly proactive in serving students, seeking out resources when necessary (PRAXIS III Framework–"distinguished" level of performance).*

Although teaching can sometimes appear to be a "lonely" activity, teaching itself doesn't occur in a vacuum. The teacher must recognize that while he or she is the central force in the classroom that the students, school, community, and school board all support the local learning experience. In addition, both state and national structures govern curriculum, laws, and behaviors. The wise teacher soon learns to enlist the aid of all possible resources to aid in the effective learning environment.

Mario was the newest teacher in his grade level, and next week was "Back-to-School Night." He was excited that he would be meeting some of the parents, but he was also insecure that they might ask him something he didn't know about the school, the subjects he was teaching, or even how they could participate in making decisions at the school or district level.

In preparation for the evening, he decided to prepare a packet of information to give to the parents. He spoke with his colleagues about what types of materials would be useful to share as he anticipated questions. He also included a brief description of the state curriculum guidelines, the school district guidelines for his grade level, and a brief explanation of what he would be doing in class to address those guidelines during the course of the school year. This preparation gave him the opportunity to personalize his welcome to parents and guardians and to let them know what their children would be learning during the year. He was also able to incorporate a parent volunteer form into the packet. He shared his information with his principal, who contributed some additional information including the dates of school board meetings, PTA meetings, and school holidays.

When the evening arrived, Mario was well prepared and confident. He discovered that he was the "expert" in the classroom and that the parents were looking to him for guidance about how they could bridge the learning that was taking place in the classroom with family support. The evening was so successful that Mario and his colleagues decided to plan a cooperative grade-level presentation next year during the "Back-to-School Night."

By preparing the welcome packet with information about curriculum, student learning outcomes, and community involvement, Mario learned much about the structure of his new school and the needs and expectations of the community. In addition, he effectively demonstrated the role the teacher plays in providing resources to serve students, as well as their families.

1. What role can parents and community members play in helping a teacher meet local and state education requirements?
2. Write a welcome letter to parents that includes a description of the major curriculum and behavioral goals you will be implementing in the classroom, as well as inviting them to participate as classroom volunteers, school site volunteers, and committee members on school projects (e.g., the Halloween Carnival).
3. Design a sign-up sheet for parents to volunteer in your classroom. Be sure to include all of the follow-up information you will need (e.g., name of child in class, phone number, e-mail address). On the top of the form, include a brief description of what the activity entails (e.g., date, time, purpose of the activity, participation by parents).

the state's entire school system was "inadequate." Naming the state superintendent and the state education agency as part of the problem and pointing out that Kentucky schools were ineffective and inequitable, the Court labeled the school system "unconstitutional." The Court called on the governor and the legislature to develop an entirely new system of education for the state. A twenty-two-member task force, appointed by the governor and the legislature, then developed the 906-page **Kentucky Education Reform Act (KERA)** passed in 1990. KERA required each school to form a school-based management council by 1996 with authority to set policy in eight areas: curriculum, staff time, student assignment, schedule, school space, instructional issues, discipline, and extracurricular activities. Three teachers, two parents (elected by their peers), and the principal comprised each council.

Since its adoption, KERA has dramatically equalized funding across the state, and some school districts have made substantial gains in funding for students. Though variations among district spending on education still exist, these are no longer based on "the traditional determinants of educational financing . . . local income and property wealth. Now districts with low incomes or little property value per student are just as likely to have high educational spending as are wealthy districts" (Hoyt 1999, 36). In addition, teacher salaries and student/ teacher ratios have improved compared to national averages. However, student achievement, as measured by test score gains or graduation rates, has not improved (The Kentucky Institute for Education Research 2001).

The Governor Though the powers of governors vary greatly from state to state, a governor can, if he or she chooses, have a far-reaching impact on education within the state. The governor may appoint and/or remove educators at the state level, and in some states the governor may even appoint the chief state school officer. Furthermore, in every state except North Carolina, the governor may use his or her veto power to influence the legislature to pass certain laws related to education. Governors are also extremely influential because they make educational budget recommendations to legislatures, and, in many states, they may elect to use any accumulated balances in the state treasury for education. Governors can also have a significant impact on matters related to curriculum and instruction within the state and, indeed, across the nation. For example, Roy Romer, former governor of Colorado, was instrumental in organizing ACHIEVE, an effort by U.S. governors and corporate leaders to raise academic standards and develop accountability systems for schools. In addition, the **National Governors' Association (NGA)** is active in teacher education and school reforms.

State Board of Education

The **state board of education,** acting under the authority of the state legislature, is the highest educational agency in a state. Every state, with the exception of Wisconsin, has a state board of education. In most states there are two separate boards, one responsible for elementary through secondary education, the other for higher education.

The method of determining board members varies from state to state. In some states, the governor appoints members of the state board; in other states, members are selected through general elections. Two states have *ex officio* members who, by virtue of the positions they hold, automatically serve on the board. Most states have either seven- or nine-member boards.

People disagree on which is better: electing or appointing board members. Some believe that election to the state board may cause members to be more concerned with politics than with education. Others argue that elected board members are more aware of the wishes of the public whom the schools are supposed to serve. People in favor of appointing members to the state board suggest that appointment increases the likelihood that individuals will be chosen on the basis of merit rather than politics.

The regulatory and advisory functions generally held by state boards are as follows:

- Ensuring that local school districts adhere to legislation concerning educational policies, rules, and regulations

Education is often at the center of the issues during election campaigns. Why is education such an important focal point for candidates and communities alike?

- Setting standards for issuing and revoking teaching and administrative certificates
- Establishing standards for accrediting schools
- Managing state monies appropriated for education
- Developing and implementing a system for collecting educational data needed for reporting and program evaluation
- Advising the governor and/or the state legislature on educational issues
- Identifying both short- and long-range educational needs in the state and developing plans to meet those needs
- Hearing all disputes arising from the implementation of its educational policies

State Department of Education

The educational program of each state is implemented by the state's department of education, under the leadership of the chief state school officer. State departments of education have a broad set of responsibilities, and they affect literally every school, school district, and teacher education program in a state. In general, the state board of education is concerned with policymaking, the **state department of education** with the day-to-day implementation of those policies. Perhaps the greatest boost for the development of state departments of education came with the federal government's Elementary and Secondary Education Act of 1965 (see Chapter 3). This act and its subsequent amendments required that local applications for federal funds to be used for innovative programs and for the education of disadvantaged, disabled, bilingual, and migrant students first receive approval from state departments of education.

Today, the responsibilities of state departments of education include (1) certifying teachers, (2) distributing state and federal funds to school districts, (3) reporting to the public the condition of education within the state, (4) ensuring that school districts adhere to state and federal guidelines, (5) accrediting schools, (6) monitoring student transportation and safety, and (7) sponsoring research and evaluation projects to improve education within the state.

Perhaps the most significant index of the steady increase in state control since the 1980s is the fact that the states now supply the majority of funding for schools. During the twenty-first century, the power and influence of state departments of education will continue to be extensive.

Chief State School Officer

The **chief state school officer** (known as the commissioner of education or superintendent of public instruction in many states) is the chief administrator of the state department of education and the head of the state board of education. In twenty-five states, the state board of education appoints the chief state school officer; in fifteen, the office is filled through a general election; and in the remaining ten, the governor appoints an individual to that position (personal communication, Council of Chief State School Officers June 7, 1999).

Though the specific responsibilities of the chief state school officer vary from state to state, most individuals in this position hold several responsibilities in common:

1. Serving as chief administrator of the state department of education and state board of education
2. Selecting state department of education personnel
3. Recommending educational policies and budgets to the state board
4. Interpreting state school laws and state board of education policies
5. Ensuring compliance with state school laws and policies
6. Mediating controversies involving the operation of schools within the state
7. Arranging for studies, committees, and task forces to address educational problems and recommend solutions
8. Reporting on the status of education to the governor, legislature, state board, and public

What Assistance Do Regional Education Agencies Provide?

When one thinks of how schools are governed and the sources of political pressure applied to them, one typically thinks of influences originating at three levels: local, state, and federal. There is, however, an additional source of control—the regional, or intermediate, unit. The intermediate unit of educational administration, or the **Regional Educational Service Agency (RESA),** is the least understood branch of the state public school system. Through the intermediate unit, local school districts can receive supportive services that, economically and logistically, they could not provide for themselves.

Presently, about half of the states have some form of intermediate or regional unit. The average unit is made up of twenty to thirty local school districts and covers a fifty-square-mile area. The intermediate or regional unit has many different names: educational service district (in Washington), county education office (in California), education service center (in Texas), intermediate school district (in Michigan), multicounty educational service unit (in Nebraska), and board of cooperative educational services (in New York).

The primary role of the intermediate unit is to provide assistance directly to districts in the areas of staff development, curriculum development, instructional media, and program evaluation. Intermediate or regional units also help school districts with their school improvement efforts by providing help in targeted areas such as bilingual education, vocational education, educational technology, and the education of gifted and talented students and students with disabilities. Although intermediate units do monitor local school districts to see that they follow state educational guidelines, local districts, in fact, exert great influence over RESAs by identifying district-level needs that can be met by the intermediate unit.

How Does the Federal Government Influence Education?

Since the birth of the United States, the federal government has played a major role in shaping the character of schools. This branch of government has always recognized that the strength and well-being of the country are directly related to the quality of its schools. The importance of a quality education, for example, has been highlighted by many U.S. Supreme Court rulings supporting the free speech rights of teachers and students under the First Amendment and the right of all citizens to equal educational opportunity under the Fourteenth Amendment. During the twenty-first century it is clear that the nation will face unprecedented levels of both global competition and the need for greater international cooperation. A rapidly changing, increasingly complex society will require a better-educated workforce to compete and cooperate successfully.

The federal government has taken aggressive initiatives to influence education at several points in U.S. history, such as the allocation of federal money to improve science, mathematics, and foreign language education after Russia launched the world's first satellite. During World War II, the federal government funded several new educational programs. One of these, the Lanham Act (1941), provided funding for (1) the training of workers in war plants by U.S. Office of Education personnel, (2) the construction of schools in areas where military personnel and workers on federal projects resided, and (3) the provision of child care for the children of working parents.

Another influential and extensive federal program in support of education was the Servicemen's Readjustment Act, popularly known as the **G.I. Bill of Rights.** Signed into law by President Franklin D. Roosevelt in 1944, the G.I. Bill has provided millions of veterans with payments for tuition and room and board at colleges and universities and at technical schools. Similar legislation was later passed to grant educational benefits to veterans of the Korean and Vietnam conflicts. Not only did the G.I. Bill stimulate the growth of colleges and universities in the United States, but it also opened higher education to an older and nontraditional student population.

The executive, legislative, and judicial branches of the federal government influence education in four ways:

1. *Exert moral suasion*—develop a vision and promote educational goals for the nation; for example, to honor public and private K–12 schools that are

either academically superior in their states or that demonstrate dramatic gains in student achievement, Rod Paige, Secretary of Education under the George W. Bush administration, launched the *No Child Left Behind—Blue Ribbon Schools Program* (U.S. Department of Education 2002).

2. *Provide categorical aid*—assist school systems with funding if they adopt federally endorsed programs, methods, or curricula
3. *Regulate*—withhold federal funds if a school system fails to follow legal statutes related to equal educational opportunity
4. *Fund educational research*—identify and then fund research projects related to federal goals for education

The Impact of Presidential Policies

Presidential platforms on education often have a profound effect on education. Ronald Reagan's two terms of office (1980–88) and George H. W. Bush's term (1988–92), for example, saw a significant shift in the federal government's role in education. In general, these two administrations sought to scale back what some viewed as excessive federal involvement in education. During Bill Clinton's two terms of office (1992–2000), the federal government assumed a more active role in ensuring equal educational opportunity. As George W. Bush stated in his address to the nation (January 19, 2002), his educational platform would reflect a strong emphasis on standards and accountability:

> We are insisting on high standards for all our children. We're putting a new emphasis on reading as the first step toward achievement. We're offering teachers new training, and states and localities new flexibility. And we're going to measure and test how everyone is doing in our new accountability system, so we can get help to children before it is too late.

U.S. Department of Education

In addition to supporting educational research, disseminating the results of research, and administering federal grants, the U.S. Department of Education

How do federal education initiatives influence schools at the local level? How does federal funding help reduce inequalities among schools?

advises the president on setting a platform for his educational agenda. For example, U.S. Secretary of Education Rod Paige released a five-year strategic plan for the Department of Education, setting six goals for the agency and for the nation.

1. *Create a culture of achievement*—create a culture of achievement throughout the nation's education system by effectively implementing the new law, the No Child Left Behind Act of 2001, and by basing all federal education programs on its principles: accountability, flexibility, expanded parental options, and doing what works
2. *Improve student achievement*—improve student achievement for all groups of students by putting reading first, expanding high-quality mathematics and science teaching, reforming high schools, and boosting teacher and principal quality, thereby closing the achievement gap
3. *Develop safe schools and strong character*—establish disciplined and drug-free education environments that foster the development of good character and citizenship
4. *Transform education into an evidence-based field*—strengthen the quality of education research
5. *Enhance the quality of and access to postsecondary and adult education*—increase opportunities for students and the effectiveness of institutions
6. *Establish management excellence*—create a culture of accountability throughout the Department of Education (Press release, March 7, 2002)

How Are Schools Financed in the United States?

To provide free public education to all school-age children in the United States is a costly undertaking. Schools must provide services and facilities to students from a wide range of ethnic, racial, social, cultural, linguistic and individual backgrounds. Expenditures for these services and facilities have been rising rapidly and are expected to continue rising through 2008 (see Figure 5.3 on page 178). Total expenditures for public elementary and secondary schools in 2000–01 were $422.7 billion, and the total **expenditure per pupil** was $8,194 (in constant 1997–98 dollars) (National Center for Education Statistics 2001). Figure 5.4 on page 178 shows how the education dollar for public schools is allocated.

Financing an enterprise as vast and ambitious as the United States system of free public schools has not been easy. It has proved difficult both to devise a system that equitably distributes the tax burden for supporting schools and to provide equal educational services and facilities for all students. And, "rather than one national education system [in the United States], there are fifty state systems that raise revenues from local, state, and federal sources. Dollars are distributed quite unequally across the states, districts, and schools. And only a small fraction of the education dollar supports regular classroom instruction—significant proportions are spent in schools, but outside of the classroom" (Odden and Busch 1998, 4). Moreover, there has been a tendency for the financial support of schools to be outpaced by factors that continually increase the cost of operating schools, such as inflation, rising enrollments, and the need to update aging facilities. According to the 2001 Gallup Poll of the public's attitudes toward the public schools, "lack of financial support/funding/money" (along with "lack of discipline/more control") was

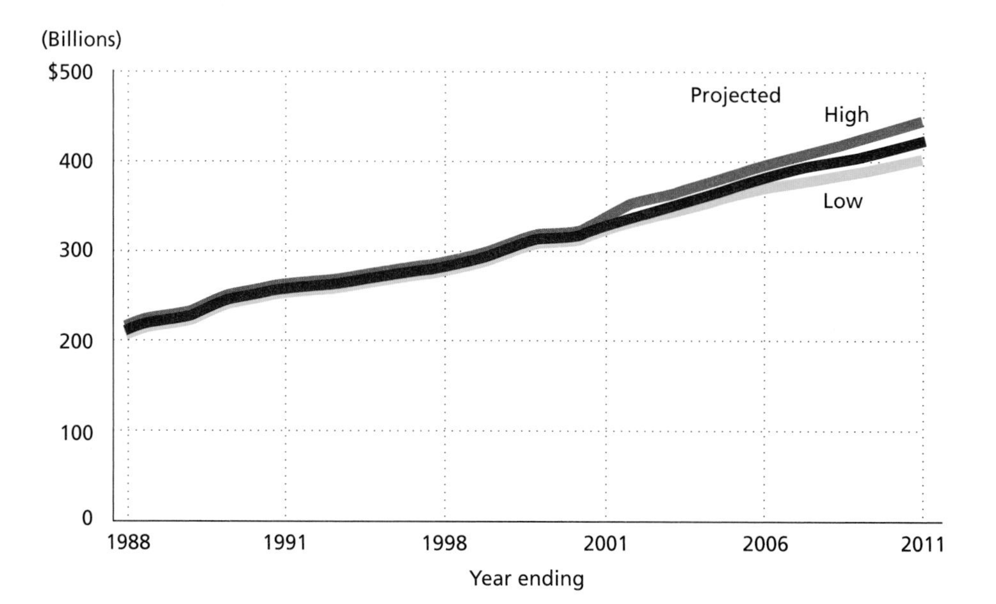

Figure 5.3 Current expenditures of public schools (in constant 1999–2000 dollars), with alternative projections: 1985–86 to 2010–11.
Source: Projections of Education Statistics to 2011, Figure 53. Washington, DC: National Center for Education Statistics, 2001.

seen as the number one problem confronting local schools. Moreover, almost 60 percent of the public believed that the amount of money spent on public schools in their state differs from school district to school district "a great deal" (28 percent) or "quite a lot" (29 percent).

A combination of revenues from local, state, and federal sources is used to finance public elementary and secondary schools in the United States. As Table 5.2 shows, schools received almost half of their 1998–99 funding from the state, 44.2 percent from local and other sources, and 7.1 percent from the federal government. Since 1980, schools have received almost equal funding from local and state sources; prior to that date, however, schools received most of their revenues from local sources, and early in the twentieth century, nearly all school revenues were generated from local property taxes.

Revenues for education are influenced by many factors, including the apportionment of taxes among the local, state, and federal levels; the size of the tax

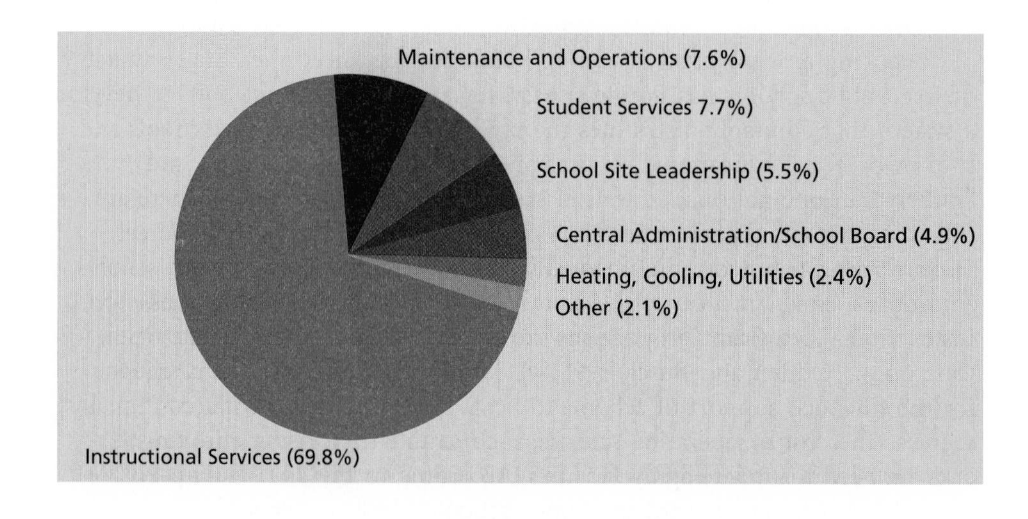

Figure 5.4 Average allocation of the 2001–02 school district operating budget.
Source: Educational Research Service (ERS) National Survey of School District Budgets, 2001–02. Copyright © by Educational Research Service. Used with permission.

Table 5.2 Revenues for public elementary and secondary schools, by source of funds: 1919–20 to 1998–99

	Percentage Distribution		
School Year	Federal	State	Local (including intermediate)[1]
1919–20	0.3	16.5	83.2
1929–30	0.4	16.9	82.7
1939–40	1.8	30.3	68.0
1949–50	2.9	39.8	57.3
1959–60	4.4	39.1	56.5
1969–70	8.0	39.9	52.1
1979–80	9.8	46.8	43.4
1989–90	6.1	47.1	46.8
1996–97	6.6	48.0	45.4
1997–98[2]	6.8	48.4	44.8
1998–99	7.1	48.7	44.2

[1]Includes a relatively small amount from nongovernmental private sources (gifts and tuition and transportation fees from patrons). These sources accounted for 2.5 percent of total revenues in 1998–99.
[2]Revised from previously published figures.
Note: Beginning in 1980–81, revenues for state education agencies are excluded. Beginning in 1988–89, data reflect new survey collection procedures and may not be entirely comparable with figures for earlier years. Details may not sum to totals due to rounding.

Source: Excerpted from U.S. Department of Education, National Center for Education Statistics, *Statistics of State School Systems: Revenues and Expenditures to Public Elementary and Secondary Education;* and Common Core of Data surveys. (Table prepared May 2001.)

base at each level; and competing demands for allocating funds at each level. In addition, funding for education is influenced by the following factors:

- The rate of inflation
- The health of the national economy
- The size of the national budget deficit
- Taxpayer revolts to limit the use of property taxes to raise money, such as Proposition 13 in California and Oregon's property tax limitation
- Changes in the size and distribution of the population
- School-financed lawsuits to equalize funding and ensure educational opportunity

Local Funding

At the local level, most funding for schools comes from **property taxes** that are determined by the value of property in the school district. Property taxes are assessed against real estate and, in some districts, also against personal property such as cars, household furniture and appliances, and stocks and bonds. Increasing taxes to meet the rising costs of operating local schools or to fund needed improvements is often a heated issue in many communities.

Although property taxes provide a steady source of revenue for local school districts, there are inequities in the ways in which taxes are determined. By locating in areas where taxes are lowest, for example, businesses and industries often avoid paying higher taxes while continuing to draw on local resources and services. In addition, the fair market value of property is often difficult to assess, and groups within a community sometimes pressure assessors to keep taxes on their property as low as possible. Most states specify by law the minimum property tax rate for local school districts to set. In many districts, an increase in the tax rate must have the approval of voters. Some states place no cap, or upper limit, on tax rates, and other states set a maximum limit.

State Funding

Most state revenues for education come from sales taxes and income taxes. Sales taxes are added to the cost of items such as general goods, gasoline, amusements, alcohol, and insurance. Income taxes are placed on individuals (in many states) and on business and industry.

As mentioned previously, states contribute nearly 50 percent of the resources needed to operate the public schools. The money that a state gives to its cities and towns is known as **state aid.** Table 5.3 compares selected states on the percent of education funds received from federal, state, local and intermediate, and private sources in relation to total expenditures for 1998–99.

Federal Funding

The role of the federal government in providing resources for education has been limited. As shown in Table 5.2, the federal share of funding for public elementary and secondary schools peaked in 1979–80 at 9.8 percent and had declined to 6.6 percent by 1996–97. Prior to 1980 the federal government had in

Table 5.3 Revenues for public elementary and secondary schools by source and state: 1998–99

		Percent of Total Revenues 1998–99			
State	**Revenues**	**Federal**	**State**	**Local and Intermediate**	**Private**[1]
Alaska	$1,290,358	13.8	61.0	22.5	2.7
California	$40,002,760	8.6	59.3	30.9	1.1
Connecticut	$5,607,014	4.0	39.0	54.4	2.7
District of Columbia	$760,592	16.5	–	83.1	0.4
Louisiana	$4,697,639	11.5	50.4	35.8	2.3
Nebraska	$2,168,308	6.9	37.1	50.8	5.2
New York	$29,874,220	6.0	42.2	50.9	0.9
Oregon	$4,047,900	7.0	56.8	32.7	3.5
Texas	$25,647,339	8.5	42.4	46.7	2.5
Washington	$7,212,175	6.8	64.6	25.3	3.3

[1]Includes revenues from gifts, and tuition and fees from patrons.
Note: Excludes revenues for state education agencies. Detail may not sum to totals due to rounding.

Source: U.S. Department of Education, National Center for Education Statistics, Common Core of Data survey. (Table prepared May 2001.)

effect bypassed the states and provided funding for local programs that were administered through various federal agencies, such as the Office of Economic Opportunity (Head Start, migrant education, and Follow Through) and the Department of Labor (Job Corps and the Comprehensive Employment Training Act [CETA]). Since the Reagan administration (1980–88), federal aid has increasingly been given directly to the states in the form of **block grants,** which a state or local education agency may spend as it wishes with few limitations. The 1981 **Education Consolidation and Improvement Act (ECIA)** gave the states a broad range of choices in spending federal money. The ECIA significantly reduced federal aid to education, however, thus making state aid to education even more critical.

Though a small proportion of the funds for schools comes from the federal level, the federal government has enacted supplemental programs to help meet the educational needs of special student populations. Such programs are often referred to collectively as **entitlements.** The most significant is the Elementary and Secondary Education Act of 1965, which President George W. Bush reauthorized in 2002 as the No Child Left Behind Act. Title I of the act allocates a billion dollars annually to school districts with large numbers of students from low-income families. Among the other funded entitlement programs are the Vocational Education Act (1963), the Manpower Development and Training Act (1963), the Economic Opportunity Act (1964), the Bilingual Education Act (1968), the Indian Education Act (1972), and the Education for All Handicapped Children Act (1975).

The federal government also provides funding for preschool programs such as Project Head Start. Originally started under the Economic Opportunity Act of 1964 to provide preschool experiences to poor children, Head Start was later made available to children whose parents were above the poverty level. Funding for Head Start was $4.66 billion in 1999. Reauthorized by Congress in 1998, Head Start served an estimated 830,000 children and their families that year. The Head Start Act Amendments of 1994 also established the Early Head Start program, designed to serve pregnant women and children under three from low-income families.

What Are Some Trends in Funding for Equity and Excellence?

The fact that schools have had to rely heavily on property taxes for support has resulted in fiscal inequities for schools. Districts with higher property wealth are able to generate more money per pupil than districts with lower property values. The degree of inequity between the wealthiest and the poorest districts, therefore, can be quite large. In some states, for example, the ability of one district to generate local property tax revenues may be several times greater than another district's. Moreover, unequal educational funding in the United States makes it one of the most inequitable countries in the world (Odden and Busch 1998).

In *Savage Inequalities: Children in America's Schools,* noted educator Jonathan Kozol (1991) presents a compelling analysis of the inequities in school funding. He found that the amount of money spent on each school age child ranged from $1,500 to $15,000, depending on where the child lived. Disputing those who claim that parental values, not high spending on education, determines how much children learn, Kozol points out that high spending on education in affluent districts does coincide with high achievement.

Tax Reform and Redistricting

To correct funding inequities, several court suits were initiated during the 1970s. In the 1971 *Serrano v. Priest* case in California, it was successfully argued that the relationship between spending and property wealth violated the state's obligation to provide equal protection and education. The California Supreme Court ruled in a six-to-one decision that the quality of a child's education should not be dependent on the "wealth of his parents and neighbors." The court also recognized that communities with a poor tax base could not be expected to generate the revenues of more affluent districts. Nevertheless, the Court did not forbid the use of property taxes to fund education.

Then, in 1973, the U.S. Supreme Court decided in *San Antonio Independent School District v. Rodriguez* that fiscal inequities stemming from unequal tax bases did not violate the Constitution. That court's decision reversed a lower court's ruling claiming that school financing on the basis of local property taxes was unconstitutional.

Regardless of the mixed outcomes of court challenges, many state legislatures have enacted school finance equity reforms during the last fifteen years. A few states (California, Hawaii, New Mexico, Washington, and West Virginia, for example) have led the way by developing programs to ensure statewide financial equality. These states have **full-funding programs** in which the state sets the same per-pupil expenditure level for all schools and districts.

Other states have adopted new funding formulas to try to broaden their revenue base. Level funding augmented by sales taxes, cigarette taxes, state lottery revenues, property taxes on second homes, and school-choice plans are among the solutions tried. One of the most dramatic changes in educational funding occurred in Michigan in 1993 with the passage of Proposal A, a plan that greatly reduced school funding from local property taxes and increased funding from the state's sales tax.

Since each state has been free to determine the number of districts within its boundaries, a common approach to achieving equal funding is **redistricting,** redrawing school district boundaries to reduce the range of variation in the ability of school districts to finance education. Redistricting not only equalizes funding; it can also reduce the cost of maintaining and operating schools if smaller districts are combined. The per-pupil cost of instruction, supplies, and equipment is usually lower in large districts. In addition, greater resources often allow larger districts to offer a broader curriculum and higher salaries to attract more qualified teachers.

Vertical Equity

Other states have developed various mechanisms for providing **vertical equity,** that is, for allocating funds according to legitimate educational needs. Thus, additional support is given to programs that serve students from low-income backgrounds; those with limited English proficiency, or special gifts and talents; and those who need special education or vocational programs.

Additional state-appropriated funds to cover the costs of educating students with special needs are known as **categorical aid.** Funding adjustments are also made to compensate for differences in costs within a state—higher expenses due to rural isolation or the higher cost of living in urban areas, for example. Some states even conduct periodic regional cost-of-living analyses, which are then used to determine adjustments in per-pupil funding.

School Choice

One of the most bitter struggles for control of schools in the United States is centered around **school choice,** the practice of allowing parents to choose the schools their children attend. According to the 2001 Phi Delta Kappa/Gallup Poll of the public's attitudes toward the public schools, 44 percent were in favor of allowing parents to send their school-age children to any public, private, or church-related school they choose, with the government paying all or part of the tuition, and 54 percent were opposed (Rose and Gallup 2001, 45).

Debate continues about whether school choice programs will, in fact, promote equity and excellence. Advocates of school choice believe that giving parents more options will force public schools to adjust to free-market pressures—low-performing schools would have to improve or shut down. Moreover, they contend that parents whose children must now attend inferior, and sometimes dangerous, inner-city schools would be able to send their children elsewhere. In addition, some supporters see choice as a way to reduce the influence of top-heavy school bureaucracies and teachers' unions.

On the other hand, opponents believe that school choice would have disastrous consequences for public schools and lead to students being sorted by race, income, and religion. School choice, they argue, would subsidize the wealthy by siphoning money away from the public schools and further widen the gap between rich and poor districts. Other critics contend that school choice could lead to the creation of segregated schools and schools that would be more committed to competing for education dollars and the most able, manageable students. Moreover, a study of the impact of competition on three urban school systems concluded that "competition did not force [the districts] to substantially alter system, governance, management, or operations." And, in the words of an observer at two schools, "teachers have thirty kids in their classroom just like they did last year, just like they did ten years ago. They still teach the same way. [Vouchers] haven't affected what they do" (Hess 2002, 198).

Voucher Systems

One approach to providing educational equity that has generated considerable controversy is the **voucher system** of distributing educational funds. Although various plans have been proposed, one of the most common would give states the freedom to distribute money directly to parents in the form of vouchers. Parents

Reflecting on School Choice

Imagine that you are given vouchers to send your child to any school in your state. What factors would you consider in making your choice? Compare your list with the following list, most important coming first, from a recent survey of parents:

- Quality of teaching staff
- Maintenance of school discipline
- Courses offered
- Size of classes
- Test scores of students

What are the similarities and differences between the lists? What do the differences reveal about your view of education and schools?

would then use the vouchers to enroll their children in schools of their choice. The most controversial voucher proposals would allow parents to choose from among public as well as private (secular, parochial, for-profit, and charter) schools; others would limit parents' choice to public schools. As the Professional Reflection illustrates, voucher programs require that parents and guardians reflect on the kind of educational experiences they want for their children.

Where Do You Stand? Visit the Companion Website to Voice Your Opinion.

Debates about vouchers regularly make the national news. New Mexico's pro-voucher governor clashed with the state's legislature over private school vouchers (*Education Week* 1999a). In 1999, Florida became the first state to offer state-paid tuition to children in failing public schools to attend a public, private, or religious school of choice; however, a Florida judge ruled in 2002 that the program violated the Florida Constitution because it gave tax money to religious schools (*Los Angeles Times* 2002). And, for months, the media covered New York City Schools Chancellor Rudolph Crew's opposition to Mayor Rudolph W. Giuliani's plan to "give poorer parents the same opportunity to make choices about their children's education that the richest and most affluent parents in New York City have" (*Education Week* 1999b).

It is clear that the debate over school choice will continue for the foreseeable future. Gradually, support for school choice appears to be increasing—currently, almost half of the states allow some form of "interdistrict" transfer, which would allow students to attend public schools outside of their home district. In fact, Grant and Murray (1999, 235) suggest that "it is conceivable that by 2020 as many as a quarter of all students could be enrolled in some 'school of choice,' whether private or public." While support for vouchers may be increasing slightly, support drops significantly if it means less money for public schools. As Figure 5.5 shows, a 2002 survey shows that the public favors vouchers by a fifty-one-to-forty margin; but when asked if they still support the idea if it means less money for public schools, they oppose vouchers by a 2-to-1 margin.

Corporate-Education Partnerships

To develop additional sources of funding for equity and excellence, many local school districts have established partnerships with the private sector. Businesses may contribute funds or materials needed by a school, sponsor sports teams, award scholarships, provide cash grants for pilot projects and teacher development, and even construct school buildings. One example of a corporate-education partnership is Thomas Jefferson High School for Science and Technology, a college preparatory magnet school in Alexandria, Virginia. Twenty-five local and multinational businesses, including AT&T, Mobil, Boeing, Honeywell, and Exxon, raised almost a million dollars for the school. State-of-the-art facilities include a $600,000 telecommunications lab with a television studio, radio station, weather station, and a satellite earth station. The school has a biotech laboratory for genetic engineering experiments in cloning and cell fission as well as labs for research on energy and computers.

Corporate contributions to education total more than $2 billion annually, with about 9 percent going to elementary and secondary education and the rest to colleges, including grants to improve teacher preparation. A survey of Fortune 500 and Service 500 companies found that 78 percent contributed money to education, 64 percent contributed materials or equipment, 26 percent offered teachers summer employment, and 12 percent provided executives-on-loan to schools (Hopkins and Wendel 1997, 15).

If schools in the United States are to succeed in meeting the challenges of the twenty-first century, they will need to be funded at a level that provides quality

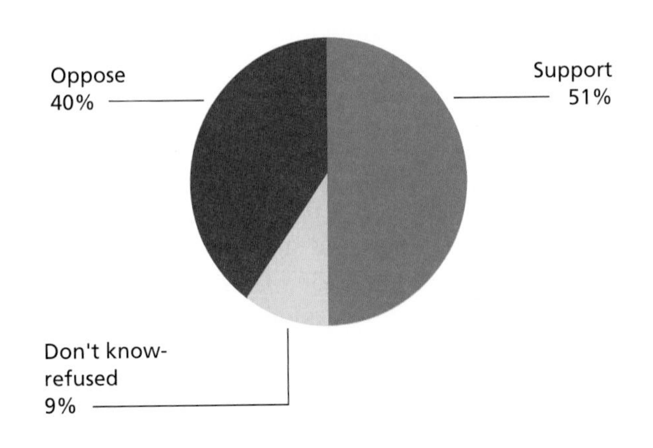

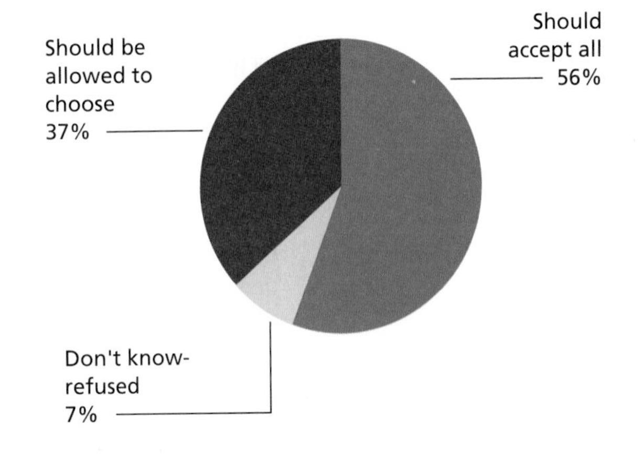

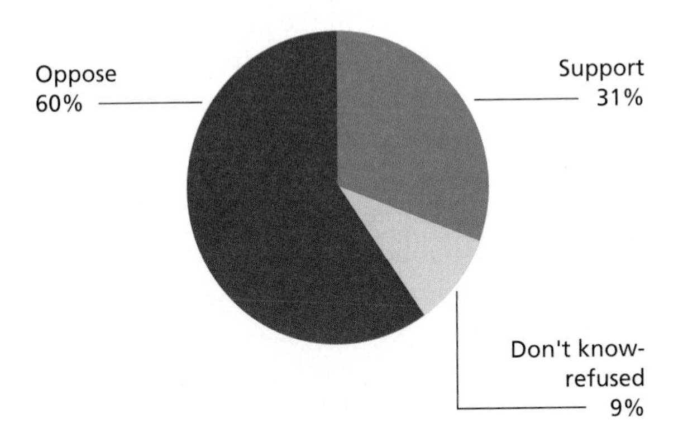

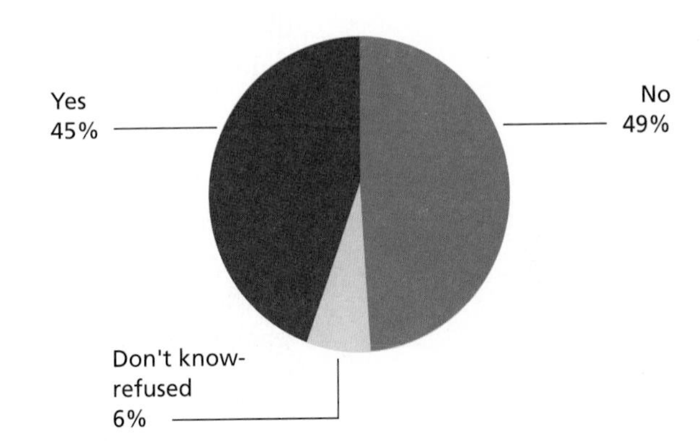

Note: Only those with children in the home were asked if they would accept vouchers to send their children to private school, and only a third of all in the poll had children in their home.

The poll of 1,011 people was taken July 17–21, 2002, and has an error margin of plus or minus 3 percentage points, larger for subgroups.

Figure 5.5 Americans weigh in on school vouchers.
Source: ICR/International Communications Research for the Associated Press, 2002.

educational experiences to students from a diverse array of backgrounds. Though innovative approaches to school funding have been developed, much remains to be done before both excellence and equity characterize all schools in the United States.

How Will the Privatization Movement Affect Equity and Excellence in Education?

One of the most dramatic reforms in U.S. education during the last decade has been the development of charter schools and for-profit schools, both of which were developed to provide an alternative to the perceived inadequacies of the public schools. On many different levels—governance, staffing, curricula, funding, and accountability—the **privatization movement** is a radical departure from schools as most people have known them.

Where Do You Stand? Visit the Companion Website to Voice Your Opinion.

Charter Schools

In 1991, Minnesota passed the nation's first charter school legislation calling for up to eight teacher-created and -operated, outcome-based schools that would be free of most state and local rules and regulations. When the St. Paul City Academy opened its doors in September 1992, it became the nation's first charter school.

Charter schools are independent, innovative, outcome-based, public schools. "The charter school concept allows a group of teachers, parents, or others who share similar interests and views about education to organize and operate a school. Charters can be granted by a local school district, by the state, or by the national government. In effect, charter schools offer a model for restructuring that gives greater autonomy to individual schools and promotes school choice by increasing the range of options available to parents and students within the public schools system" (Wohlstetter and Anderson 1994, 486). Currently, thirty-six states, Puerto Rico, and the District of Columbia have adopted charter school legislation. Of the nation's nearly 2,400 charter schools, about 10 percent are operated on a for-profit basis (Keller 2002). Charter schools in Arizona range from those focusing on the fine arts to charter schools in remote regions of the state that serve Native American communities.

To open a charter school, an original charter (or agreement) is signed by the school's founders and a sponsor (usually the local school board). The charter specifies the learning outcomes that students will master before they continue their studies. Charter schools, which usually operate in the manner of autonomous school districts (a feature that distinguishes them from the alternative schools that many school districts operate), are public schools and must teach all students. If admission requests for a charter school exceed the number of available openings, students are selected by drawing.

Because charter schools are designed to promote the development of new teaching strategies that can be used at other public schools, they can prove to be an effective tool for promoting educational reform and the professionalization of teaching in the future. Moreover, as Milo Cutter, one of the two teachers who founded St. Paul City Academy points out, charter schools give teachers unprecedented leadership opportunities and the ability to respond quickly to students' needs:

> [We had] the chance to create a school that takes into account the approaches we know will work. We listen to what the students want and need, because we ask them. And each day we ask ourselves if we are doing things the best way we can. We also have the flexibility to respond. We can change the curriculum to meet these needs as soon as we see them. Anywhere else it would take a year to change. It is much better than anything we have known in the traditional setting (North Central Regional Education Laboratory 1993, 3).

In a report titled *Do Charter Schools Measure Up? The Charter School Experiment after 10 Years,* the American Federation of Teachers (AFT) suggested that, by mid-2002, charter schools had not lived up to the claims of their advocates. The following are among the shortcomings of charter schools, according to the AFT report:

- Charter schools contribute to the racial and ethnic isolation of students.
- Charter school teachers are less experienced and lower paid than teachers in other public schools.
- Charter schools generally score no better (and often do worse) on student achievement tests than other comparable public school students.

- Charter schools have not been held to the "bargain" they made—trading freedom from rules for increased accountability.
- Charter schools were supposed to experiment with new curricula and classroom practices, but they have proven no more innovative than other public schools (American Federation of Teachers 2002, 5–6).

For-Profit Schools

One of the most controversial educational issues for the twenty-first century is the practice of turning the operation of public schools over to private, for-profit companies. Advocates of privatization believe privately operated schools are more efficient; they reduce costs and maximize "production"—that is, student achievement. Opponents, however, are concerned that profit, rather than increasing student achievement, is the real driving force behind **for-profit schools.** For-profit education companies focusing on the preK–12 level had revenues of $58 billion in 2001 (Eduventures 2002). Critics of for-profit schools are also concerned that school districts may not be vigilant enough in monitoring the performance of private education companies.

Concerned about the slow pace of educational reform in the United States, Christopher Whittle, the originator of Channel One, launched the $3 billion Edison Project in 1992—an ambitious plan to develop a national network of more than one thousand for-profit secondary schools by 2010. As of 2001–02, the Edison Project, now named Edison Schools, Inc., had become the largest company involved in the for-profit management of K–12 schools, and it served 74,000 students in 133 schools located in twenty-two states and the District of Columbia (Edison Schools, Inc. 2002).

In 1999, Edison Schools, Inc., reported that achievement was steadily moving upward at the "vast majority" of Edison schools. At seventeen of the Edison schools that had been able to establish achievement trends, fourteen had records the company labeled "positive" or "strongly positive," and three had records that were labeled "weak" (Walsh 1999b). However, in a report analyzing the results reported by Edison the previous year, the American Federation of Teachers claimed that the company exaggerated achievement gains at many schools and downplayed negative results at others. "On the whole, Edison results were mediocre," the report claimed (American Federation of Teachers 1998).

Another approach to for-profit schools was developed by Education Alternatives, Inc. (EAI), a company that negotiates with school districts to operate their public schools. Participating school districts give the company the same per-pupil funding to operate the school that the district would have used. The company, using its own curricula and cost-saving techniques, agrees to improve student performance and attendance in return for the opportunity to operate schools at a profit. Education Alternatives, Inc., which began operating its first for-profit school in Dade County, Florida, in 1991, became the first private company to run an entire school district when the Duluth, Minnesota, School Board awarded the company a three-month contract in 1992 to serve as interim superintendent for the district. In Baltimore and Hartford, Connecticut, where EAI operated several schools in the mid-1990s, critics challenged the achievement gains the company reported and accused the company of mismanaging finances. After numerous disputes over the management of schools, both school systems eventually terminated their contracts with the company. In 1999, EAI moved its headquarters from Bloomington, Minnesota, to Scottsdale, Arizona, and became the Tesseract Group, Inc. At that time, the company operated forty schools serving more than six thousand students.

Summary

Who Is Involved in the Struggles for Control of Schools in the United States?

- Parents, students, teachers, administrators, taxpayers, state and federal authorities, minorities and women, educational theorists and researchers, and businesses and corporations are among the groups that exert political influence on education.
- Schools reflect the society they serve and thus are influenced by out-of-school factors such as the mass media, demographic shifts, international events, and social issues.

What Is the Role of the Local Community in School Governance?

- Local school districts, which vary greatly in size, locale, organizational structure, demographics, and wealth, are responsible for the management and operation of schools.
- Local schools boards, whose members are usually elected, set educational policies for a district; however, many people believe that boards should be reformed to be more well informed and responsive.
- The superintendent, the chief administrator of a local district, has a complex array of responsibilities and must work cooperatively with the school board and others in an environment that is often politically turbulent.
- Through groups like the PTA or PTO, some parents are involved in local school activities and reform efforts; others are involved with private schools; and some actively promote alternative approaches to education such as school choice, voucher systems, and home schooling.
- As part of the restructuring movement, schools are changing their policies for governance, curricula, and community collaboration; the Chicago School Reform Act is one example of restructuring based on school-based management that empowers teachers, principals, parents, community members, and students at local schools.

What Powers and Influence Do States Have in Governing Schools?

- The state legislature, state courts, and the governor significantly influence education by setting policies related to the management and operation of schools within a state; many states have even passed legislation allowing them to take over academically failing school districts or individual schools.
- The state board of education, the highest educational agency in a state, regulates education and advises the governor and others on important educational policies.
- The state department of education implements policies related to teacher certification, allocation of state and federal funds, enforcement of state and federal guidelines, school accreditation, and research and evaluation projects to improve education.
- The chief state school officer oversees education within a state and, in collaboration with the governor, legislature, state board of education, and the public, provides leadership to improve education.

What Assistance Do Regional Education Agencies Provide?

- The Regional Educational Service Agency (RESA), an intermediate unit of educational administration in about half of the states, provides assistance to two or more school districts for staff development, curriculum development, instructional media, and program evaluation.

How Does the Federal Government Influence Education?

- The federal government influences education at the state level through funding general and categorical programs, establishing and enforcing standards and regulations, conducting and disseminating educational research, providing technical assistance to improve education, and encouraging equity and excellence for the nation's schools.
- The national legislature, federal and Supreme courts, and the president significantly influence education by exerting moral suasion for the improvement of schools, providing categorical aid for federal programs, ensuring that school systems follow legal statutes, and funding educational research.
- The U.S. Department of Education supports and disseminates educational research through ERIC, administers federal grants in education, and assists the president in developing and promoting a national agenda for education.
- At times, the roles of the federal and state governments in education are in conflict.

How Are Schools Financed in the United States?

- Schools are supported with revenues from the local, state, and federal levels, with most funding now coming from the state level.
- Local funding is provided through property taxes, which in many instances result in inequitable funding for schools located in areas with an insufficient tax base.
- One challenge to financing schools has been the development of an equitable means of taxation for the support of education.

What Are Some Trends in Funding for Equity and Excellence?

- Many state legislatures have enacted tax reforms including full-funding programs which set the same per-pupil expenditures for all schools and districts. Some states have achieved greater equity through redistricting–redrawing district boundaries to reduce funding inequities.

- Some states achieve vertical equity by providing additional funding, or categorical aid, to educate students with special needs. Also, many local districts and schools receive additional funding through partnerships with the private sector.
- School choice and voucher programs are two controversial approaches to providing parents the freedom to select the schools their children attend.

How Will the Privatization Movement Affect Equity and Excellence in Education?

- Charter schools and for-profit schools, both part of the privatization movement, were developed in response to perceived inadequacies of the public schools.
- Charter schools are independent, innovative, outcome-based public schools started by a group of teachers, parents, or others who obtain a charter from a local school district, a state, or the federal government.
- Edison Schools, Inc. (formerly the Edison Project) and the Tesseract Group, Inc. (formerly Education Alternatives, Inc.) are examples of for-profit schools operated by private corporations.

Key Terms and Concepts

block grants, **181**
categorical aid, **182**
charter schools, **186**
chief state school officer, **174**
Education Consolidation and Improvement Act (ECIA), **181**
entitlements, **181**
expenditure per pupil, **177**
for-profit schools, **187**
full-funding programs, **182**
G.I. Bill of Rights, **175**
Kentucky Education Reform Act (KERA), **171**
local school council (LSC), **168**
local school districts, **161**
National Governors' Association (NGA), **172**
privatization movement, **185**
property taxes, **179**
redistricting, **182**
Regional Educational Service Agency (RESA), **174**
restructuring, **167**
school-based management (SBM), **167**
school board, **164**
school choice, **183**
state aid, **180**
state board of education, **172**
state department of education, **173**
superintendent, **165**
vertical equity, **182**
voucher system, **183**

Applications and Activities

Teacher's Journal

1. In *Conflict of Interests: The Politics of American Educaion*, 3rd ed., Joel Spring (1998, 50) points out the following:

> Differing political groups struggle to have their ideas emphasized in schools. Politicians attempt to win votes by claiming that their educational policies will improve schools and society. Ethnic politicians demand language and cultural policies in schools that will maintain the cohesiveness of their particular constituencies. And a long-standing conflict exists between business interests and workers over the content of education. Many workers want schools to be avenues of economic mobility for their children, while many businesspeople want the schools to focus on job training to meet corporate needs.

Describe some examples of how politicians, workers, and business people are currently using schools to promote their interests within your state. Which actions do you support? Which do you oppose?

2. From the many political forces that influence schools (see Figure 5.1, page 159), select one factor and describe how it is currently influencing education at the national level. How is this factor influencing schools at the local level in your area?
3. Think of businesses and agencies in your community that might be good partners for a school. Select one of them and develop a proposal outlining the nature, activities, and benefits (to both) of the partnership you envision.

Teacher's Database

1. Use the Internet to gather information about the structure of education and school funding in your state. How many districts are in your state? Which is the largest? What are enrollment figures, trends, and projections for your state? What are the figures for household income and poverty rate? What proportion of school funding in your state is from the local, state, and federal levels? What are the total expenditures and per-pupil expenditures?

Begin your data search at the U.S. Department of Education's National Center for Education Statistics (NCES) where you will find NCES data from the *Digest of Education Statistics,* the *Condition of Education, Youth Indicators, Projections of Education Statistics,* the *Directory of Department of Education Publications,* the *Directory of Current OERI-Funded Projects,* and the *Directory of Computer Data Files.*

2. Find information on sources of funding for education, education budgets, and issues of education finance. Begin at the U.S. Department of Education and then go to the Budget home page of the Department.

Observations and Interviews

1. Visit a private (secular, parochial, for-profit, or charter) school. Find out how teachers and other staff members are hired and how the school is organized and governed. How does the management and operation of this school differ from public schools?
2. Interview a school superintendent and ask him or her to comment on how federal, state, and local forces affect education in the district. To what extent do influences at these three levels help (and/or hinder) the district in accomplishing its goals?
3. Interview a teacher and ask how legislation at the federal and state levels affects the teacher's work. Would the teacher like to see the federal government more or less involved in education? Report your findings to the rest of the class.
4. Attend a meeting of a local school board and observe the communication and decision-making process at that meeting. To help you make this observation, ask your instructor for handout master M5.1, "Observing Community-Based Decision Making on Education."
5. To understand how school-based decision making works, observe a meeting of a site-based council (SBC) or local school council (LSC). For guidance in making this observation, ask your instructor for handout master M5.2, "Observing School-Based Decision Making."

Professional Portfolio

Prepare a profile of a school district. The district may be in your hometown, your college or university community, or a community in which you would like to teach. Information on the district may be obtained from your university library, public library, school district offices, state board of education, or professional teacher associations.

Keeping in mind that school district statistics are more readily available in some cases than in others, your profile might include the following types of information:

- Organizational chart showing (if possible) personnel currently assigned to each position
- Tables showing numbers of school buildings, students, teachers, administrators, support personnel, and so forth
- Graduation/dropout rate
- Scores on standardized achievement tests
- Total annual budget
- Expenditures per pupil
- Entitlement programs
- Demographic characteristics of population living in the area served by the district–age, race or ethnicity, socioeconomic status, unemployment rate, and so forth
- Volunteer groups serving schools in the district
- Pupil-teacher ratio
- Percent of ethnic minority students, students with disabilities, and so forth
- Percent of students going on to college

Video**Workshop Extra!**

If the VideoWorkshop package was included with your textbook, go to Chapter 5 of the Companion Website (www.ablongman.com/parkay6e) and click on the VideoWorkshop button. Follow the instructions for viewing videoclip 12 and completing this exercise. Consider this information along with what you've read in Chapter 5 while answering the following questions.

1. Educational technology is described in videoclip 12 as the "process of bringing together tools, resources, and strategies." Compare the roles of students, parents, community members, and government officials in terms of control of schools. Which group of individuals has the greatest potential impact on educational technology, and why?
2. The debate over funding for schools and school systems inevitably brings up the issue of "haves" versus "have-nots" in our society. What can you infer from the idea that equity is sometimes achieved through partnerships with private corporations or individuals? How does this affect schools and school systems?

Appendix 5.1

TYPICAL ORGANIZATIONAL STRUCTURE FOR A MEDIUM-SIZE SCHOOL DISTRICT (20,000 PUPILS)

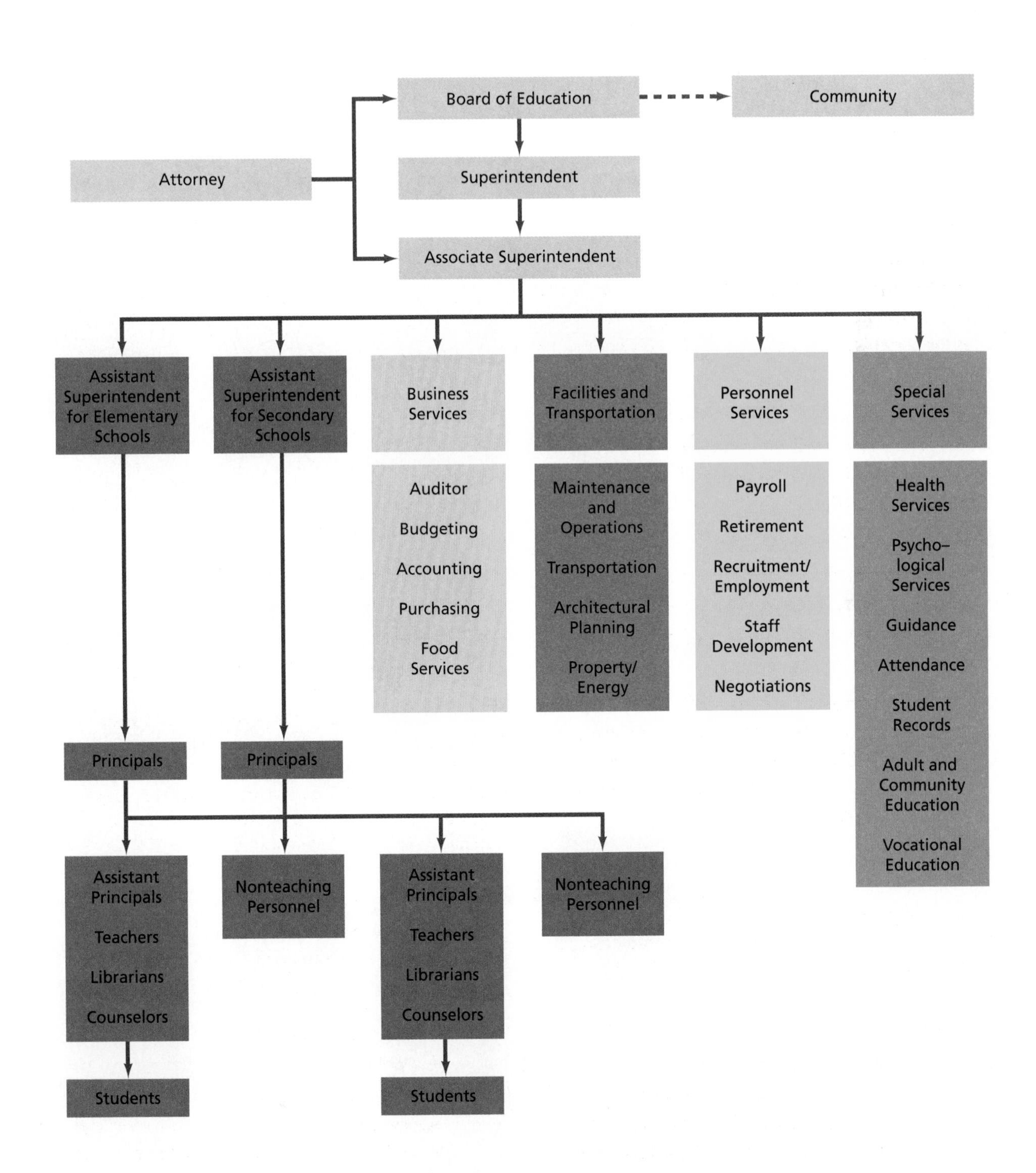

6 Ethical and Legal Issues in Education in the United States

Teachers perform their duties within a network of laws—laws that both empower and constrain.

—Michael Imber and Tyll van Geel
A Teacher's Guide to Education Law, 2nd ed., 2001

The day has ended and you are grading papers while waiting to meet with Cassandra, one of your fifth-grade students, and her mother. Cassandra's mother called you at home yesterday to arrange the meeting. When you asked her about the purpose of the meeting, she was vague and offered only that Cassandra had recently had "some trouble" with one of her classmates, Robert.

A quick glance at the clock tells you they should arrive at any moment. To prepare for the meeting, you stop grading papers and reflect on what you know about the situation between Cassandra and Robert.

Because he was held back in the third grade, Robert is almost two years older than his classmates. Though physically more mature than the other boys in your class, Robert's social skills are less developed. Although he acts silly and immature from time to time, Robert has not been a behavior problem . . . at least not until a week ago, when Cassandra told you what happened on the playground.

Last Monday at the end of the day, Cassandra told you that Robert had "talked mean" to her during recess on the playground. When you questioned Cassandra to find out exactly what Robert said, her answers were hard to follow. At first, it seemed that, whatever words were exchanged, they were not unlike the taunts boys and girls hurl back and forth daily on playgrounds across the country. As you continued to press for details, however, Cassandra began to talk, again vaguely, about how Robert had "talked dirty" to her. Further questioning of Cassandra still failed to give you a clear picture of what happened on the playground.

Based on what you learned from talking with Cassandra, you decided to give Robert a stern reminder about appropriate ways of talking to other people. The following morning you did just that.

Robert listened respectfully and seemed genuinely contrite. He promised to leave Cassandra alone while they were on the playground. The conversation ended with you telling Robert that his behavior on the playground and in the classroom would be monitored closely.

During the following week, it appeared that the friction between Robert and Cassandra had ended. As far as you could tell, the matter was over.

When Cassandra and her mother entered the room, you knew immediately that both were upset. Cassandra looked like she was on the verge of tears, and her mother looked angry.

"Tell your teacher what you told me," Cassandra's mother began, as she and her daughter seated themselves at two student desks in front of your desk.

"Well," Cassandra began slowly, almost whispering, "Robert bothered me on the playground yesterday." Cassandra started breathing more deeply as she struggled to continue. "He came over to me and. . . ." Cassandra stared at the top of her desk while searching for additional words to express what she wanted to say.

"What she means to tell you," said Cassandra's mother, "is that Robert rubbed up against her and said he wanted to have sex with her. She was sexually harassed."

On hearing what Robert is alleged to have done, you are shocked. What should you do? How does a teacher tell the difference between sexual harassment and the teasing and name calling that are an inescapable part of growing up? Should you try to determine the truth of the allegations before involving the principal? What are your responsibilities to Cassandra and her mother? What are your responsibilities to Robert? How should your school handle the matter?

Focus Questions

1. **Why do you need a professional code of ethics?**
2. **What are your legal rights as a teacher?**
3. **Do student teachers have the same rights?**
4. **What are your legal responsibilities as a teacher?**
5. **What are the legal rights of students and parents?**
6. **What are some issues in the legal rights of school districts?**

Expand your knowledge of the concepts discussed in this chapter by reading current and historical articles from the *New York Times* by visiting the "**Themes of the Times**" section of the Companion Website (**www.ablongman.com/parkay6e**).

The preceding scenario, based partially on actual events that culminated with the filing of a lawsuit against a school board (*Davis v. Monroe County Board of Education* 1999) and a U.S. Supreme Court ruling in 1999, highlights the role that legal issues can play in the lives of teachers and students. In this instance, a fifth-grade Georgia girl said she endured a five-month "barrage of sexual harassment and abuse" from a classmate. The boy allegedly touched the girl's breasts, rubbed against her suggestively, and repeatedly said he wanted to have sex with her. The lawsuit claimed that the girl's mother reported each incident to school officials but the boy was never disciplined; as a result, the girl's grades fell and she became mentally and emotionally upset. The sharply divided Supreme Court (five majority and four dissenting) ruled that school districts can be sued under Title IX in cases involving student-on-student sexual harassment, if the district acts with "deliberate indifference" to the harassment. (Title IX prohibits discrimination on the basis of sex in programs that receive federal money.)

In this chapter we examine significant ethical and legal issues that affect the rights and responsibilities of teachers, administrators, students, and parents. Teachers must act in accordance with a wide range of federal and state legislation and court decisions. As a teacher, you may need to deal with such legal issues as the teacher's responsibility for accidents, discriminatory employment practices, freedom of speech, desegregation, student rights, and circumstances related to job termination or dismissal. Without knowledge of the legal dimensions of such issues, you will be ill-equipped to protect your rights and the rights of your students.

What ethical dilemmas might this experiment pose for a teacher? How might you respond? On what moral or ethical grounds would you base your response? What legal concerns might be involved?

Why Do You Need a Professional Code of Ethics?

The actions of professional teachers are determined not only by what is legally required of them, but also by what they know they *ought* to do. They do what is legally right, and they *do the right thing.* A specific set of values guides them. A deep and lasting commitment to professional practice characterizes their work. They have adopted a high standard of professional ethics and they model behaviors that are in accord with that code of ethics.

At present, the teaching profession does not have a uniform **code of ethics** similar to the Hippocratic oath, which all doctors are legally required to take when they begin practice. However, the largest professional organization for teachers, the National Education Association (NEA), has a code of ethics for its members that includes the following statement: "The educator accepts the responsibility to adhere to the highest ethical standards."

Ethical Teaching Attitudes and Practices

Teaching is an ethical enterprise—that is, a teacher has an obligation to act ethically, to follow what he or she knows to be the most appropriate professional action to take. The best interests of students, not the teacher, provide the rule of thumb for determining what is ethical and what is not. Behaving ethically is more than a matter of following the rules or not breaking the law—it means acting in a way that promotes the learning and growth of students and helps them realize their potential.

Unethical acts break the trust and respect on which good student-teacher relationships are based. An example of unethical conduct would be to talk publicly about Cassandra's allegations against Robert (described in this chapter's opening scenario). Other examples would be using grades as a form of punishment, expressing rage in the classroom, or intentionally tricking students on tests. You could no doubt think of other examples from your own experience as a student.

Ethical Dilemmas in Classroom and School

Teachers routinely encounter **ethical dilemmas** in the classroom and in the school. They often have to take action in situations in which all the facts are not known or for which no single course of action can be called *right* or *wrong.* At these times it can be quite difficult to decide what an ethical response might be. Dealing satisfactorily with ethical dilemmas in teaching often requires the ability to see beyond short-range consequences to consider long-range consequences.

Consider, for example, the following three questions based on actual case studies. On the basis of the information given, how would you respond to each situation?

1. Should the sponsor of the high school literary magazine refuse to print a well-written story by a budding writer if the piece appears to satirize a teacher and a student?

Professional Reflection

Identifying the Consequences of Responding to an Ethical Dilemma

Based on your own experiences, describe an ethical dilemma that you have confronted. Then answer each of the following questions:

- What about the situation made it an ethical dilemma?
- What actions did you take in response to the dilemma?
- What were the short-range consequences of your actions? Long-range consequences?
- Were there unanticipated negative consequences of your actions? Unanticipated positive consequences?
- If confronted with the same dilemma today, how would you respond differently?
- Why would you respond differently?
- In general, what steps should a person take to ensure that his or her response to an ethical dilemma is the "best" course of action to take?

2. Is a reading teacher justified in trying to increase achievement for an entire class by separating two disruptive students and placing one in a reading group beneath his reading level?
3. Should a chemistry teacher punish a student (on the basis of circumstantial, inconclusive evidence) for a laboratory explosion if the example of decisive, swift punishment will likely prevent the recurrence of a similar event and thereby ensure the safety of all students?

As the Professional Reflection suggests, an important part of responding to an ethical dilemma is identifying possible consequences of one's actions.

What Are Your Legal Rights as a Teacher?

It is frequently observed that with each freedom comes a corresponding responsibility to others and to the community in which we live. As long as there is more than one individual inhabiting this planet, there is a need for laws to clarify individual rights and responsibilities. This necessary balance between rights and responsibilities is perhaps more critical to teaching than to any other profession. As education law experts Martha McCarthy, Nelda Cambron-McCabe, and Stephen Thomas (1998, 309) point out: "Although public educators do not shed their constitutional rights as a condition of public employment, under certain circumstances restrictions on these freedoms are justified by overriding governmental interests."

While schools do have limited "power over" teachers, teachers' rights to **due process** cannot be violated. Teachers, like all citizens, are protected from being treated arbitrarily by those in authority. A principal who disagrees with a teacher's methods cannot suddenly fire that teacher. A school board cannot ask a teacher to resign merely by claiming that the teacher's political activities outside of school are "disruptive" of the educational process. A teacher cannot be dismissed for "poor" performance without ample documentation that the performance was, in fact, poor and without sufficient time to meet clearly stated performance evaluation criteria.

Certification

Karla Brown is a junior high school English teacher and lives in a state with a law specifying that a teacher must show proof of five years of successful teaching experience for a teaching certificate to be renewed. Last year was Karla's fifth year of teaching, and her principal gave her an unsatisfactory performance rating. Karla's principal told her that her teaching certificate cannot be renewed. Is the principal correct?

Karla's principal is mistaken about the grounds for nonrenewal of a teaching certificate. According to the state's law, *unsuccessful* performance, or a failure to complete the school year, is grounds for nonrenewal of a certificate—not performance that is judged to be *unsatisfactory.* Because state laws vary and unsuccessful performance is defined differently in different states, however, Karla's principal might have been correct if she taught in another state.

No teacher who meets all of a state's requirements for initial certification can arbitrarily be denied a certificate. "However, obtaining a certificate does not guarantee the right to retain it" (Imber and van Geel 2001, 192). For a certificate to be revoked, the reason must be job-related and demonstrably impair the teacher's ability to perform satisfactorily. In this regard, the case of a California teacher whose certificate was revoked because someone admitted to having a homosexual relationship with the teacher is often cited. The court determined that the teacher's homosexual conduct was not an impairment to the teacher's performance and ordered the certificate restored (*Morrison v. State Board of Education* 1969). When courts have upheld the refusal to hire and the right to terminate homosexual teachers, these decisions have been influenced by factors such as sexual involvement with students or public acts of indecency (McCarthy, Cambron-McCabe, and Thomas 1998). Several states (California, Connecticut, Hawaii, Massachusetts, Minnesota, New Jersey, and Wisconsin) and the District of Columbia have laws that prohibit discrimination on the basis of sexual orientation in regard to employment, housing, and education. States that have such antidiscrimination laws "make it difficult, if not impossible . . . to uphold the denial of employment or the discharge of homosexuals" (LaMorte 2002, 227).

Teachers' Rights to Nondiscrimination

George, who pled guilty to possession of marijuana and cocaine in a criminal trial, was not reinstated to his teaching position after his criminal record was expunged. George claims that he is being discriminated against because of his past. Is he right?

States may impose certain limitations on initial certification as long as those limitations are not discriminatory in regard to race, religion, ethnic origin, sex, or age. Nearly all the states, for example, require that applicants for a teaching certificate pass a test that covers basic skills, professional knowledge, or academic subject areas. Qualifications for initial certification may also legally include certain personal qualities. The case of George at the beginning of this section, for example, is based on a Louisiana case involving a man who was not reinstated to his teaching position even though his criminal record had been expunged. The court maintained that he had committed the act, and that expungement did not erase that fact, nor did it erase the "moral turpitude" of the teacher's conduct (*Dubuclet v. Home Insurance Company* 1995).

The right to **nondiscrimination** in regard to employment is protected by Title VII of the Civil Rights Act of 1964, which states:

It shall be an unlawful employment practice for an employer (1) to fail or refuse to hire or to discharge any individual, or otherwise to discriminate against any individual with respect to his compensation, terms, conditions, or privileges of employment, because of such individual's race, color, religion, sex, or national origin; or (2) to limit, segregate, or classify his employees or applicants for employment in any way which would deprive or tend to deprive any individual of employment opportunities or otherwise adversely affect his status as an employee, because of such individual's race, color, religion, sex, or national origin.

Teaching Contracts

A **teaching contract** represents an agreement between the teacher and a board of education. For a contract to be valid, it must contain these five basic elements:

1. *Offer and acceptance*—The school board has made a formal offer and the employee has accepted the contract terms.
2. *Competent parties*—The school board is not exceeding the authority granted to it by the state and the teacher meets the criteria for employment.
3. *Consideration*—Remuneration is promised to the teacher.
4. *Legal subject matter*—The contract terms are neither illegal nor against public policy.
5. *Proper form*—The contract adheres to state contract laws.

Before you sign a teaching contract, it is important that you read it carefully and be certain that it is signed by the appropriate member(s) of the board of education or board of trustees. Ask for clarification of any sections you don't understand. It is preferable that any additional nonteaching duties be spelled out in writing rather than left to an oral agreement. Because all board of education policies and regulations will be part of your contract, you should also read any available teacher handbook or school policy handbook.

The importance of carefully reading a contract and asking for clarification is illustrated in the following case:

> *Victor Sanchez had just begun his first year as an English teacher at a high school in a city of about 300,000. Victor became quite upset when he learned that he had been assigned by his principal to sponsor the poetry club. The club was to meet once a week after school. Victor refused to sponsor the club, saying that the contract he had signed referred only to his teaching duties during regular school hours. Could Victor be compelled to sponsor the club?*

Certain assignments, though not specified in a contract, may be required of teachers in addition to their regular teaching load, as long as there is a reasonable relationship between the teacher's classroom duties and the additional assignment. Furthermore, such assignments can include supervision of school events on weekends as well. Though Victor's contract did not make specific reference to club sponsorship, such a duty would be a reasonable addition to his regular teaching assignment.

When school authorities have assigned teachers to additional duties not reasonably related to their teaching, the courts have tended to rule in favor of teachers who file suit. For example, a school's directive to a tenured teacher of American history to assume the additional role of basketball coach was not upheld by a court of appeals (*Unified School District No. 241 v. Swanson* 1986).

Due Process in Tenure and Dismissal

Tenure is a policy that provides the individual teacher with job security by (1) preventing his or her dismissal on insufficient grounds and (2) providing him or her with due process in the event of dismissal. Tenure is granted to teachers by the local school district after a period of satisfactory teaching, usually two to five years. In most cases, tenure may not be transferred from one school district to another.

The following case highlights the importance of tenure to a teacher's professional career:

A teacher was dismissed from his teaching position by the school board after it learned that the teacher was a homosexual. The teacher filed suit in court, claiming that his firing was arbitrary and violated the provisions of tenure that he had been granted. The school board, on the other hand, maintained that his conduct was inappropriate for a teacher. Was the school board justified in dismissing the teacher?

The events in this case were actually heard by a court, which ruled that the teacher was unfairly dismissed (*Burton v. Cascade School District Union High School No. 5* 1975). The court said that the board violated the teacher's rights as a tenured employee by failing to show "good and just cause" for dismissal. The teacher was awarded the balance due under his contract and an additional one-half year's salary. In a similar case, however, a court upheld the dismissal of a teacher whose sexual orientation was the target of parents' complaints and students' comments. The court ruled that the teacher could no longer effectively carry out his teaching duties (*Gaylord v. Tacoma School District No. 10* 1977).

The practice of providing teachers with tenure is not without controversy. Some critics point out that tenure policies make it too difficult to dismiss incompetent teachers and that performance standards are high in many other fields that do not provide employees with job security. Generally, however, the courts have held the position that tenure is a property right "from which students ultimately benefit" (Essex 1999, 179).

Just about every state today has a tenure law that specifies that a teacher may be dismissed with good cause; what counts as a good cause varies from state to state. The courts have ruled on a variety of reasons for **dismissal:** (1) insubordination, (2) incompetence or inefficiency, (3) neglect of duty, (4) conduct unbecoming a teacher, (5) subversive activities, (6) retrenchment or decreased need for services, (7) physical and/or mental health, (8) age, (9) causing or encouraging disruption, (10) engaging in illegal activities, (11) using offensive language, (12) personal appearance, (13) sex-related activities, (14) political activities, and (15) use of drugs or intoxicants.

For a tenured teacher to be dismissed, a systematic series of steps must be followed so that the teacher receives due process and his or her constitutionally guaranteed rights are not violated. Due process involves a careful, step-by-step examination of the charges brought against a teacher. Most states have outlined procedures that adhere to the following nine steps:

1. The teacher must be notified of the list of charges.
2. Adequate time must be provided for the teacher to prepare a rebuttal to the charges.
3. The teacher must be given the names of witnesses and access to evidence.
4. The hearing must be conducted before an impartial tribunal.
5. The teacher has the right to representation by legal counsel.
6. The teacher (or legal counsel) can introduce evidence and cross-examine adverse witnesses.
7. The school board's decision must be based on the evidence and findings of the hearing.
8. A transcript or record must be maintained of the hearing.
9. The teacher has the right to appeal an adverse decision.

These steps notwithstanding, it should be noted that "the definition [of due process] in each instance depends largely on a combination of the specific facts in a situation, the law governing the situation, the particular time in history in which judgment is being rendered, and the predilections of the individual judge(s) rendering the decision" (LaMorte 2002, 6), as the following case illustrates:

Near the start of his fifth year of teaching at an elementary school in a small city, and two years after earning tenure, Mr. Mitchell went through a sudden and painful divorce. A few months later a woman whom he had met around the time of his divorce moved into the house he was renting.

For the remainder of the school year he and the woman lived together. During this time, he received no indication that his lifestyle was professionally unacceptable, and his teaching performance remained satisfactory.

At the end of the year, however, Mr. Mitchell was notified that he was being dismissed because of immoral conduct; that is, he was living with a woman he was not married to. The school board called for a hearing and Mr. Mitchell presented his side of the case. The board, nevertheless, decided to follow through with its decision to dismiss him. Was the school board justified in dismissing Mr. Mitchell?

Though at one time teachers could readily be dismissed for living, unmarried, with a member of the opposite sex, a lifestyle such as Mr. Mitchell's is not that unusual today. Because the board had not shown that Mr. Mitchell's alleged immoral conduct had a negative effect on his teaching, his dismissal would probably not hold up in court, unless the community as a whole was upset by his behavior. Moreover, Mr. Mitchell could charge that his right to privacy as guaranteed by the Ninth Amendment to the Constitution had been violated. Overall, it appears that the decision to dismiss Mr. Mitchell was arbitrary and based on the collective bias of the board. Nevertheless, teachers should be aware that courts frequently hold that teachers are role models, and the local community determines "acceptable" behavior both in school and out of school.

Teachers also have the right to organize and to join teacher organizations without fear of dismissal. In addition, most states have passed **collective bargaining** laws that require school boards to negotiate contracts with teacher organizations. Usually, the teacher organization with the most members in a district is given the right to represent teachers in the collective bargaining process.

An important part of most collective bargaining agreements is the right of a teacher to file a **grievance,** a formal complaint against his or her employer. A teacher may not be dismissed for filing a grievance, and he or she is entitled to have the grievance heard by a neutral third party. Often, the teachers' union or professional association that negotiated the collective bargaining agreement will provide a teacher who has filed a grievance with free legal counsel.

One right that teachers are not granted by collective bargaining agreements is the right to strike. Like other public employees, teachers do not have the legal right to strike in most states. Although teachers have a limited right to strike in a few states, "extensive restrictions have been placed on its use" (McCarthy, Cambron-McCabe, and Thomas 1998, 433). Teachers who do strike run the risk of dismissal (*Hortonville Joint School District No. 1 v. Hortonville Education Association* 1976), though when teacher strikes occur a school board cannot possibly replace all the striking teachers.

Academic Freedom

A teacher of at-risk students at an alternative high school used a classroom management/motivational technique called "Learnball." The teacher divided the class into teams, allowed students to elect team leaders and determine class rules and grading exercises, and developed a system of rewards that included listening to the radio and shooting baskets with a foam ball in the classroom. The school board ordered the teacher not to use the Learnball approach. Did the teacher have the right to continue using this teaching method?

This case is based on actual events involving a teacher in Pittsburgh. The teacher brought suit against the board to prevent it from imposing a policy that banned Learnball in the classroom. The teacher cited the principle of **academic freedom** and claimed that teachers have a right to use teaching methods and materials to which school officials might object. A U.S. District Court, however, upheld the school board policy against Learnball (*Murray v. Pittsburgh Board of Public Education* 1996).

Although the courts have held that teachers have the right to academic freedom, it is not absolute and must be balanced against the interests of society. In fact, education law expert Michael LaMorte (2002, 200) suggests that the concept of academic freedom "is no longer as strong a defense as it once was"; for this defense to prevail "it must be shown that the teacher did not defy legitimate state and local curriculum directives; followed accepted professional norms for that grade level and subject matter; discussed matters which were of public concern; and acted professionally and in good faith when there was no precedent or policy."

Famous Cases A landmark case involving academic freedom focused on John Scopes, a biology teacher who challenged a Tennessee law in 1925 that made it illegal to teach in a public school "any theory which denies the story of the Divine Creation of man as taught in the Bible, and to teach instead that man is descended from a lower order of animals." Scopes maintained that Darwin's theory about human origins had scientific merit and that the state's requirement that he teach the biblical account of creation violated his academic freedom.

Scopes's trial, which came to be known as the Monkey Trial, attracted national attention. Prosecuting Scopes was the "silver-tongued" William Jennings Bryan, a famous lawyer, politician, and presidential candidate. The defending attorney was Clarence Darrow.

Scopes believed strongly in academic freedom and his students' right to know about scientific theories. He expressed his views in his memoirs, *Center of the Storm:*

> *Especially repulsive are laws restricting the constitutional freedom of teachers. The mere presence of such a law is a club held over the heads of the timid. Legislation that tampers with academic freedom is not protecting society, as its authors piously proclaim. By limiting freedom they are helping to make robot factories out of schools; ultimately, this produces nonthinking robots rather than the individualistic citizens we desperately need—now more than ever before (1966, 277).*

The Monkey Trial ended after eleven days of heated, eloquent testimony. Scopes was found guilty of violating the Butler Act and was fined $100. The decision was later reversed by the Tennessee Supreme Court on a technicality.

Since the Scopes trial, controversy has continued to surround the teaching of evolution. In many states during the 1980s, for example, religious fundamentalists won rulings that required science teachers to give equal time to both creationism and evolutionism in the classroom. The Supreme Court, however, in *Edwards v. Aguillard* (1987) ruled that such "balanced treatment" laws were unconstitutional. In the words of the Court: "Because the primary purpose of the [Louisiana] Creationism Act is to advance a particular religious belief, the Act endorses religion in violation of the First Amendment." In 1996, controversy over evolution again emerged in Tennessee when lawmakers defeated, by a 20 to 13 vote, legislation that would allow districts to dismiss teachers for "insubordination" if they taught evolution as fact.

Another case suggesting that a teacher's right to academic freedom is narrow and limited is *Krizek v. Cicero-Stickney Township High School District No. 201* (1989). In this instance, a District Court ruled against a teacher whose contract was not renewed because she showed her students an R-rated film (*About Last Night*) as an example of a modern-day parallel to Thornton Wilder's play *Our Town.* Although the teacher told her students that they would be excused from viewing the film if they or their parents objected, she did not communicate directly with their parents. The teacher's attempt to consider the objections of students and parents notwithstanding, the Court concluded that

> *the length of the film indicates that its showing was more than an inadvertent mistake or a mere slip of the tongue, but rather was a planned event, and thus indicated that the teacher's approach to teaching was problematic.*

Though concerned more with the right of a school to establish a curriculum than with the academic freedom of teachers per se, other cases have focused on the teacher's use of instructional materials. In *Mozert v. Hawkins County Board of Education* (1987, 1988), for example, a group of Tennessee parents objected to "secular humanist" reading materials used by their children's teachers. In *Smith v. Board of School Commissioners of Mobile County* (1987), 624 parents and teachers initiated a court suit alleging that forty-four history, social studies, and home economics texts used in the Mobile County, Alabama, public schools encouraged immorality, undermined parental authority, and were imbued with the "humanist" faith. In both cases, the courts supported the right of schools to establish a curriculum even in the face of parental disapproval. In *Smith v. Board of School Commissioners of Mobile County* (1987), the Eleventh Circuit Court stated that "[i]ndeed, given the diversity of religious views in this country, if the standard were merely inconsistency with the beliefs of a particular religion there would be very little that could be taught in the public schools."

States' Rights The preceding cases notwithstanding, the courts have not set down specific guidelines to reconcile the teacher's freedom with the state's right to require teachers to follow certain curricular guidelines. The same federal court, for example, heard a similar case regarding a high school teacher who wrote a vulgar word for sexual intercourse on the blackboard during a discussion of socially taboo words. The court actually sidestepped the issue of academic freedom and ruled instead that the regulations authorizing teacher discipline were unconstitutionally vague and, therefore, the teacher could not be dismissed. The court did, however, observe that a public school teacher's right to traditional academic freedom is "qualified," at best, and the "teacher's right must yield to compelling public interests of greater constitutional significance." In reviewing its decision, the court also said, "Nothing herein suggests that school authorities are not free after they have learned that the teacher is using a teaching method of which they disapprove, and which is not appropriate to the proper teaching of the subject, to suspend him [or her] until he [or she] agrees to cease using the method" (*Mailloux v. Kiley* 1971).

Although some teachers have been successful in citing academic freedom as the basis for teaching controversial subjects, others have been unsuccessful. Teachers have been dismissed for ignoring directives regarding the teaching of controversial topics related to sex, polygamy, race, and religion. Though the courts have not been able to clarify just where academic freedom begins and ends, they have made it clear that the state does have a legitimate interest in what is taught to impressionable children.

Do Student Teachers Have the Same Rights?

Do student teachers have the same legal status as certified teachers? Read the following case:

> *Meg Grant had really looked forward to the eight weeks she would spend as a student teacher in Mrs. Walker's high school English classes. Meg knew that Mrs. Walker was one of the best supervising teachers she might have been paired with, and she was anxious to do her best.*
>
> *In Mrs. Walker's senior class, Meg planned to teach* Brave New World. *Mrs. Walker pointed out to Meg that this book was controversial and some parents might object. She asked Meg to think about selecting an additional title that students could read if their parents objected to* Brave New World. *Meg, however, felt that Mrs. Walker was bowing to pressure from conservative parents, so she decided to go ahead and teach the book.*
>
> *Two weeks later Meg was called down to the principal's office where she was confronted by an angry father who said, "You have no right to be teaching my daughter this Communist trash; you're just a student teacher." What should Meg do? Does she have the same rights as a fully certified teacher?*

In some states, a student teacher such as Meg might have the same rights and responsibilities as a fully certified teacher; in others, her legal status might be that of an unlicensed visitor. The most prudent action for Meg to take would be to apologize to the father and assure him that if any controversial books are assigned in the future, alternative titles would be provided. In addition, Meg should learn how important it is for a student teacher to take the advice of his or her supervising teacher.

"The legal status of the student teacher is a perennial question with both student teachers and cooperating teachers" (Wentz 2001, 55). One study found that the authority of student teachers to teach was established by law in only forty states, and no state had a statutory provision regulating the dismissal of a student teacher, the assignment of a student teacher, or the denial of the right to student teach (Morris and Curtis 1983). Nevertheless, student teachers should be aware that a potential for liability exists with them just as it does with certified teachers.

One area of debate regarding student teachers is whether they can act as substitutes for their cooperating teachers or even other teachers in a school building. Unfortunately, many school districts have no policy regarding this practice. Depending on statutes in a particular state, however, a student teacher may substitute under the following conditions:

- A substitute teacher is not immediately available.
- The student teacher has been in that student teaching assignment for a specified minimum number of school days.
- The supervising teacher, the principal of the school, and the university supervisor agree that the student teacher is capable of successfully handling the teaching responsibilities.
- A certified classroom teacher in an adjacent room or a member of the same teaching team as the student teacher is aware of the absence and agrees to assist the student teacher if needed.

Legal Advice for Student Teachers

1. Read the teacher's handbook, if one is available, and discuss its contents with the cooperating teacher. Be sure you understand its requirements and prohibitions.

2. Thoroughly discuss school safety rules and regulations. Be certain you know what to do in case of emergency, before assuming complete control of the classroom.

3. Be aware of the potential hazards associated with any activity and act accordingly to protect children from those dangers.

4. Be certain you know what controls the district has placed on the curriculum you will be teaching. Are there specific texts and/or methodologies that district policy requires or prohibits?

5. Be certain that student records are used to enhance and inform your teaching. Make certain that strict confidentiality is respected.

6. Document any problems you have with students, or as a teacher, in case you are called upon to relate details at a later time.

Figure 6.1 Legal advice for student teachers.
Source: Julie Mead and Julie Underwood, "A Legal Primer for Student Teachers," in Gloria Slick (Ed.), *Emerging Trends in Teacher Preparation: The Future of Field Experiences.* Thousand Oaks, CA: Corwin Press, 1995, pp. 49–50.

- The principal of the school or the principal's representative is readily available in the building.
- The student teacher is not paid for any substitute service. (This matter is negotiable in some jurisdictions.) (Dunklee and Shoop 2002, 89–90)

Given the ambiguous status of student teachers, it is important that you begin your student teaching assignment with a knowledge of the legal aspects of teaching and a clear idea of your rights and responsibilities. To accomplish this, follow the recommendations in Figure 6.1 made by school law experts Julie Mead and Julie Underwood.

What Are Your Legal Responsibilities as a Teacher?

Teachers are, of course, responsible for meeting the terms of their teaching contracts. As noted previously, teachers are responsible for duties not covered in the contract if they are reasonably related to teaching. Among these duties may be club sponsorship; lunchroom, study hall, or playground duty; academic counseling of students; and record keeping.

Teachers are also legally responsible for the safety and well-being of students assigned to them. Although it is not expected that a teacher be able to control completely the behavior of young, energetic students, a teacher can be held liable for any injury to a student if it is shown that the teacher's negligence contributed to the injury.

Should this teacher/coach have any concerns about tort liability? How might this teacher reduce the risk of liability?

Avoiding Tort Liability

An eighth-grade science teacher in Louisiana left her class for a few moments to go to the school office to pick up some forms. While she was gone, her students continued to do some laboratory work that involved the use of alcohol-burning devices. Unfortunately, one girl was injured when she tried to relight a defective burner. Could the teacher be held liable for the girl's injuries?

The events described above actually occurred in 1974 (*Station v. Travelers Insurance Co.*). The court that heard the case determined that the teacher failed to provide adequate supervision while the students were exposed to dangerous conditions. Considerable care is required, the court observed, when students handle inherently dangerous objects, and the need for this care is magnified when students are exposed to dangers they don't appreciate.

At times, teachers may have concerns about their liability for damages as a result of their actions. The branch of law concerned with compensating an individual who suffers losses resulting from another's negligence is known as tort law. "A tort is a civil wrong in which one suffers loss as a result of the improper conduct of another" (LaMorte 2002, 383). The harm inflicted on the injured party may be the result of "intentional wrongdoing, recklessness, or simple carelessness" (Imber and van Geel 1993, 575). According to **tort liability** law, an individual who is negligent and at fault in the exercise of his or her legal duty may be required to pay monetary damages to an injured party. Generally, the standard of behavior applied by the courts is that the injury "must be avoidable by the exercise of reasonable care" (McCarthy, Cambron-McCabe, and Thomas 1998, 436). However, teachers are held to a higher standard than ordinary citizens, and certain teachers (e.g., physical education and chemistry teachers) are held to an even higher standard because of the increased risk of injury involved in the classes they teach. Table 6.1 on page 206 presents several examples of cases in which students were injured and educators were found to have breached their duty of care.

Negligence In contrast to the decision reached by the Louisiana court mentioned earlier, the courts have made it clear that there are many accidents that

Table 6.1 Selected court decisions in which school personnel were found negligent for failure to meet a "standard of care"

1. A woodworking instructor allowed a student to operate a table saw without the use of a safeguard, which resulted in serious damage to his proximal interphalangeal joint. *Barbin v. State,* 506 So. 2d 88 (1st Cir. 1987).
2. A student dislocated his shoulder during an intramural football game, when the school provided no protective equipment and improper supervision of the game. *Locilento v. John A. Coleman Catholic High School,* 523 N.Y.S. 2d 198 (A.D. 3d Dept. 1987).
3. An eleven-year-old student suffered serious head injuries from a blow in the head during a kick game and was without medical attention for more than an hour. The one-hour delay caused a hematoma to grow from the size of a walnut to that of an orange. *Barth v. Board of Education,* 490 N.E. 2d 77 (Ill. App. 186 Dist. 1986).
4. An eight-year-old girl was seriously burned when her costume caught fire from a lighted candle on her teacher's desk. *Smith v. Archbishop of St. Louis,* 632, S.W. 2d 516 (Mo. App. 1982).
5. A twelve-year-old boy was killed when he fell through a skylight at school while retrieving a ball. *Stahl v. Cocalico School District,* 534 A. 2d 1141 (Pa. Cmwlth. 1987).
6. A boy was seriously injured while playing on school grounds when he fell into a hole filled with glass, trash, and other debris, due to the absence of school officials to warn him of the dangerous condition. *Dean v. Board of Education,* 523 A. 2d 1059 (Md. App. 1987).
7. A female student was in route to class when she pushed her hand through a glass panel in a smoke-colored door, causing severe and permanent damage. *Bielaska v. Town of Waterford,* 491 A. 2d 1071 (Conn. 1985).
8. A high school student was seriously injured when he was tackled and thrown to the ground during a touch football game in gym class, based on inadequate supervision when the players began to use excessive force. *Hyman v. Green,* 403 N.W. 2d 597 (Mich. App. 1987).

Source: From Nathan L. Essex, *School Law and the Public Schools: A Practical Guide for Educational Leaders.* Boston: Allyn and Bacon, 1999, pp. 110, 126. Copyright © 1999 by Allyn and Bacon. Reprinted by permission.

teachers cannot reasonably foresee that do result in student injuries. For example, a teacher on playground duty was found to be not negligent when a student threw a rock that struck another student in the eye. After the teacher walked past a group of boys, one boy threw a small rock that hit a larger rock on the ground and then bounced up to hit the other boy in the eye. The court ruled that "[w]here the time between an act of a student and injury to a fellow student is so short that the teacher had no opportunity to prevent injury, it cannot be said that negligence of the teacher is a proximate cause of the injury" (*Fagen v. Summers* 1972). In another case, the court ruled that a New York teacher could not have anticipated that the paper bag she asked a student to pick up contained a broken bottle upon which the student cut herself (*West v. Board of Education of City of New York* 1959). In two almost identical cases, the courts ruled that a teacher of a class with a good behavior record could not reasonably be expected to anticipate that a student would be injured by a pencil thrown by a classmate while the teacher was momentarily out of the room attending to her usual duties (*Ohman v. Board of Education* 1950; *Simonetti v. School District of Philadelphia* 1982).

When a court considers a case involving tort liability, evidence is examined to determine whether the responsible party (the school district, the administrator, or the teacher) acted negligently. For a school official to be considered liable, the following must be shown to be present:

1. A legal duty to conform to a standard of conduct for the protection of others
2. A failure to exercise an appropriate standard of care

3. A causal connection, often referred to as "proximate cause," between the conduct and the resultant injury
4. Actual loss or damage as a result of the injury (LaMorte 2002, 406)

As a teacher, you should be especially alert when conditions exist that might lead to accidental injury of one or more students. You will have a duty in regard to your pupils, and you could be held liable for injuries that students incur as a result of your **negligence.** This does not mean, however, that your liability extends to any and all injuries your students might suffer; only if you fail to provide the same degree of care for pupils that a reasonable and prudent person would have shown in similar circumstances can you be held liable. Our review of court cases involving the tort liability of teachers suggests that most cases involve at least one of the following:

- Inadequate supervision
- Inadequate instruction
- Lack of or improper medical treatment of pupils
- Improper disclosure of defamatory information concerning pupils—for example, release of school records that contain negative statements about a student

Teachers' concern about their potential monetary liability for failing to act reasonably and prudently in preventing injury to their students has been lessened by the availability of liability insurance. Many professional organizations for teachers offer liability coverage as part of their membership benefits, and teachers may also purchase individual liability insurance policies. In addition, some states that provide school districts with full or partial immunity from tort liability are considering extending the same protection to school employees. Georgia, for example, has extended immunity to teachers and principals (La Morte 2002).

Educational Malpractice Since the mid-1970s several plaintiffs have charged in their **educational malpractice** suits that schools should be responsible for a pupil whose failure to achieve is significant. In the first of such cases, the parents of Peter W. Doe charged that the San Francisco Unified School District was negligent because it allowed him to graduate from high school with a fifth-grade reading level and this handicap would not enable him to function in adult society. In particular, they charged that the "defendant school district, its agents and employees, negligently and carelessly failed to provide plaintiff with adequate instruction, guidance, counseling and/or supervision in basic academic skills such as reading and writing, although said school district had the authority, responsibility, and ability [to do so]." They sought $500,000 for the negligent work of the teachers who taught Peter.

In evaluating the claim of Peter W. Doe and his parents, the court pointed out that the alleged injury was not within the realm of tort law and that many factors beyond a school's responsibility or control can account for lack of achievement. The court did not hold the school responsible for Peter's lack of achievement and made it clear that to do so would be to set a precedent with potentially drastic consequences: "To hold [schools] to an actionable duty of care, in the discharge of their academic functions, would expose them to the tort claims—real or imagined—of disaffected students and parents in countless numbers. . . . The ultimate consequences, in terms of public time and money,

Table 6.2 Physical and behavioral indicators of child abuse and neglect

Type of Child Abuse/Neglect	Physical Indicators	Behavioral Indicators
Physical abuse	Unexplained bruises and welts: • on face, lips, mouth • on torso, back, buttocks, thighs • in various stages of healing • clustered, forming regular patterns • reflecting shape of article used to inflict (electric cord, belt buckle) • on several different surface areas • regularly appear after absence, weekend, or vacation • human bite marks • bald spots Unexplained burns: • cigar, cigarette burns, especially on soles, palms, back, or buttocks • immersion burns (sock-like, glove-like, doughnut-shaped on buttocks or genitalia) • patterned like electric burner, iron, etc. • rope burns on arms, legs, neck, or torso Unexplained fractures: • to skull, nose, facial structure • in various stages of healing • multiple or spiral fractures Unexplained lacerations or abrasions: • to mouth, lips, gums, eyes • to external genitalia	Wary of adult contacts Apprehensive when other children cry Behavioral extremes: • aggressiveness • withdrawal • overly compliant Afraid to go home Reports injury by parents Exhibits anxiety about normal activities, e.g., napping Complains of soreness and moves awkwardly Destructive to self and others Early to school or stays late as if afraid to go home Accident prone Wears clothing that covers body when not appropriate Chronic runaway (especially adolescents) Cannot tolerate physical contact or touch
Physical neglect	Consistent hunger, poor hygiene, inappropriate dress Consistent lack of supervision, especially in dangerous activities or long periods Unattended physical problems or medical needs Abandonment Lice Distended stomach, emaciated	Begging, stealing food Constant fatigue, listlessness, or falling asleep States there is no caretaker at home Frequent school absence or tardiness Destructive, pugnacious School dropout (adolescents) Early emancipation from family (adolescents)

would burden them—and society—beyond calculation" (*Peter Doe v. San Francisco Unified School District* 1976).

Reporting Child Abuse

Teachers, who are now *required* by law to report any suspected child abuse, are in positions to monitor and work against the physical, emotional, and sexual abuse and the neglect and exploitation of children. Teachers' professional journals and information from local, state, and federal child welfare agencies encourage teachers to be more observant of children's appearance and behavior in order to detect symptoms of child abuse. Such sources often provide lists of physical and behavioral indicators of potential child abuse, similar to that shown in Table 6.2.

Table 6.2 Continued

Type of Child Abuse/Neglect	Physical Indicators	Behavioral Indicators
Sexual abuse	Difficulty in walking or sitting	Unwilling to participate in certain physical activities
	Torn, stained, or bloody underclothing	Sudden drop in school performance
	Pain or itching in genital area	Withdrawal, fantasy, or unusually infantile behavior
	Bruises or bleeding in external genitalia, vaginal, or anal areas	Crying with no provocation
	Venereal disease	Bizarre, sophisticated, or unusual sexual behavior or knowledge
	Frequent urinary or yeast infections	Anorexia (especially adolescents)
	Frequent unexplained sore throats	Sexually provocative
		Poor peer relationships
		Reports sexual assault by caretaker
		Fear of or seductiveness toward males
		Suicide attempts (especially adolescents)
		Chronic runaway
		Early pregnancies
Emotional maltreatment	Speech disorders	Habit disorders (sucking, biting, rocking, etc.)
	Lags in physical development	Conduct disorders (antisocial, destructive, etc.)
	Failure to thrive (especially in infants)	Neurotic traits (sleep disorders, inhibition of play)
	Asthma, severe allergies, or ulcers	Behavioral extremes:
	Substance abuse	• compliant, passive
		• aggressive, demanding
		Overly adaptive behavior:
		• inappropriately adult
		• inappropriately infantile
		Developmental lags (mental, emotional)
		Delinquent behavior (especially adolescents)

Source: Adapted from Cynthia Crosson Tower, *The Role of Educators in the Prevention and Treatment of Child Abuse and Neglect*, The User Manual Series, 1992. Washington, DC: U.S. Department of Health and Human Services. Derry Koralek, *Caregivers of Young Children: Preventing and Responding to Child Maltreatment*, The User Manual Series, 1992. Washington, DC: U.S. Department of Health and Human Services.

Many communities, through their police departments or other public and private agencies, provide programs adapted for children to educate them about their rights in child-abuse situations and to show them how to obtain help.

On occasion, parents and guardians have alleged a Fourth Amendment (protection against search and seizure) violation, claiming that school personnel should not have questioned or examined a student to determine if child abuse had occurred. In a Pennsylvania case, the court concluded that the Fourth Amendment had not been violated as a result of school personnel questioning a student about suspected abuse. According to the court, Pennsylvania's Child Protective Services Law required teachers and administrators to determine if there was "reason to believe" that a student had been abused (*Picarella v. Terrizzi* 1995).

Schools usually have a specific process for dealing with suspected abuse cases, involving the school principal and nurse as well as the reporting teacher. Because a child's physical welfare may be further endangered when abuse is reported, caution and sensitivity are required. Teachers are in a unique position to help students who are victims of child abuse, both because they have daily contact with them and because children learn to trust them.

Observing Copyright Laws

The continuing rapid development of technology has resulted in a new set of responsibilities for teachers in regard to observing **copyright laws** pertaining to the use of photocopies, videotapes, and computer software programs. In 1976 Congress revised the Copyright Act by adding the doctrine of **fair use.** Although the fair use doctrine cannot be precisely defined, it is generally interpreted as it was in *Marcus v. Rowley* (1983)—that is, one may "use the copyrighted material in a reasonable manner without [the copyright holder's] consent" as long as that use does not reduce the demand for the work or the author's income. To "move the nation's copyright law into the digital age," the Digital Millennium Copyright Act (DMCA) amended the Copyright Act in 1998. The DMCA makes it illegal to circumvent copy-blocking measures (encryption and encoding, for example) that control access to copyrighted works. However, according to the statute, educational institutions may circumvent access control measures "solely for the purpose of making a good faith determination as to whether they wish to obtain authorized access to the work."

With the vast amount of material (in text, audio, video, and graphic formats) now distributed in digital form over the Internet, teachers must consider copyright laws and restrictions that apply to the use of this material. Unfortunately, the Copyright Act does not provide guidelines for the use of intellectual property found on the Internet. In any case, teachers should understand that "when [their] computer displays a home page on the Internet, [the] computer is presenting a copy of the page that 'exists' on a remote computer. . . . [They] are viewing a published copy of an original document" (Schwartz and Beichner 1999, 199), and the doctrine of fair use applies to the use of such materials.

Photocopies To clarify the fair use doctrine as it pertained to teachers photocopying instructional materials from books and magazines, Congress endorsed a set of guidelines developed by educators, authors, and publishers. These guidelines allow teachers to make single copies of copyrighted material for teaching or research but are more restrictive regarding the use of multiple copies. The use of multiple copies of a work must meet the tests of brevity, spontaneity, and cumulative effect.

- *Brevity* means that short works can be copied. Poems or excerpts cannot be longer than 250 words, and copies of longer works cannot exceed 1,000 words or 10 percent of the work (whichever is less). Only one chart or drawing can be reproduced from a book or an article.
- The criterion of *spontaneity* means that the teacher doing the copying would not have time to request permission from the copyright holder.
- The criterion of *cumulative effect* limits the use of copies to one course and limits the material copied from the same author, book, or magazine during the semester. Also, no more than nine instances of multiple copying per class are allowed during a semester.

Companion Website

Videotapes Guidelines for the use of videotapes made by teachers of television broadcasts were issued by Congress in 1981 (see the Appendix "Guidelines for Off-Air Recordings" on this book's website). Videotaped material may be used in the classroom only once by the teacher within the first ten days of taping. Additional use is limited to reinforcing instruction or evaluation of student learning, and the tape must be erased within forty-five days.

Computer Software Computer software publishers have become concerned about the abuse of their copyrighted material. Limited school budgets and the high cost of computer software have led to the unauthorized reproduction of software. To address the problem, the Copyright Act was amended in 1980 to apply the fair use doctrine to software. Accordingly, a teacher may now make one backup copy of a program. If a teacher were to make multiple copies of software, the fair use doctrine would be violated because the software is readily accessible for purchase and making multiple copies would substantially reduce the market for the software. Software publishers have several different options for licensing their software to schools (see Table 6.3), and teachers should be aware of the type of license that has been purchased with each software program they use.

The increased practice of networking computer programs—that is, storing a copy of a computer program on a network file server and serving the program to a computer on the network—is also of concern to software publishers. As yet, the practice has not yet been tested in the courts. As more public schools develop computer networks, however, the issue of networked software will most likely be debated in the courts.

Electronic Mail and the Internet With the huge increase in the transmission of documents via electronic mail (e-mail) and the Internet, copyright laws have been extended to cyberspace. Material "published" online may include a statement by the author(s) that the material is copyright protected and may not be duplicated without permission. In other cases, the material may include a statement such as the following: "Permission is granted to distribute this material freely through electronic or by other means, provided it remains completely intact and unaltered, the source is acknowledged, and no fee is charged for it." If the material is published without restrictions on the Internet, one may assume that the author waives copyright privileges; however, proper credit and a citation should accompany the material if it is reproduced.

Table 6.3 Common types of commercial software licenses

License Type	What Is Permitted	Suitability for Schools
Single-user license	Permits installation on one and only one computer.	Not usually economical for schools.
Multiple-user license (sometimes called a "Lab Pack")	Permits installation on up to a specified number of computers (typically 5, 10, 50, etc.).	Economical and commonly found in K–12 schools.
Network license	Permits installation on a network. License will specify the maximum number of simultaneous users.	Economical and commonly found in larger K–12 schools if they are networked.
Site license	Permits installation on any and all computers owned by the institution.	Not typically used in K–1 2 schools. More common for college campuses.

Source: From James E. Schwartz and Robert J. Beichner, *Essentials of Educational Technology.* Boston: Allyn and Bacon, 1999, p. 195. Copyright © 1999 by Allyn and Bacon.

Technology Highlights

What ethical and legal issues will you face regarding the use of computer software?

With the explosion of computer-based technology in schools, teachers face a new ethical and legal issue–adhering to copyright laws as they relate to computer software. Making an illegal copy of software on a computer hard drive–in effect, stealing another person's "intellectual property"–is quite easy. In fact, "It is very common for otherwise ethical and moral people to ask for and/or offer illegal copies of software to one another" (Schwartz and Beichner 1999, 193). It is therefore important that, as a teacher, you be an exemplar of ethical behavior regarding copyrighted computer software. Just as you would not allow students to plagiarize written material or submit work that was not their own, you should follow the same standard of behavior regarding the use of computer software.

Currently, the Copyright Act is being revised to reflect how the doctrine of fair use should be applied to digital data. "Revisions to the Copyright Act will require a balancing of authors' interests in compensation for intellectual work and educators' continuing concern for 'fair use' " (McCarthy, Cambron-McCabe, and Thomas 1998, 265–266). Two questions currently not answered by copyright law as it pertains to the educational use of computer software are the legality of (1) installing a single program on several computers in a laboratory and (2) modifying the program for use in a computer network.

Imagine that during your first year of teaching a colleague suggests using a software program in one (or both) of the preceding ways. Analyze your colleague's suggestion in light of the following excerpt from the Copyright Act, which presents four factors that are considered to determine whether use of copyrighted material constitutes fair use or an infringement:

> (1) the purpose and character of the use, including whether such use is of a commercial nature or is for nonprofit educational purposes; (2) the nature of the copyrighted work; (3) the amount and substantiality of the portion used in relation to the copyrighted work as a whole; and (4) the effect of the use on the potential market for or value of the copyrighted work.

How do you respond to your colleague's suggestion? What is the rationale for your response?

Publishing on the Internet Thousands of teachers and their students around the globe are publishing material at their home pages on the Internet. Teacher- and student-produced materials can be copyright protected by including a statement that the materials may not be duplicated without permission. In addition, teachers should be careful not to include information that would enable someone to identify children in a class. Children's last names should never be published, nor should photos of children be published with any identifying information.

What Are the Legal Rights of Students and Parents?

As a prospective teacher, you have an obligation to become familiar with the rights of students. Since the 1960s students have increasingly confronted teachers and school districts with what they perceived to be illegal restrictions on their behavior. In this section we discuss briefly some of the major court decisions that have clarified students' rights related to freedom of expression, suspension and expulsion, search and seizure, privacy, and nondiscrimination.

Freedom of Expression

The case of *Tinker v. Des Moines Independent Community School District* (1969) is perhaps the most frequently cited case concerning students' **freedom of expression.** The Supreme Court ruled in *Tinker* that three students, ages thirteen, fifteen, and sixteen, had been denied their First Amendment freedom of expression when they were suspended from school for wearing black arm bands in protest of the Vietnam War. The court ruled that neither teachers nor students "shed their rights to freedom of speech or expression at the schoolhouse gate." In addition, the court found no evidence that the exercise of such a right interfered with the school's operation.

Censorship One area of student expression that has generated frequent controversy is that of student publications. Prior to 1988, the courts generally made it clear that student literature enjoyed constitutional protection, and it could only be regulated if it posed a substantial threat of school disruption, if it was libelous, or if it was judged vulgar or obscene *after publication.* However, school officials could use "prior **censorship**" and require students to submit literature before publication if such controls were necessary to maintain order in the school.

Within these guidelines, students frequently successfully defended their right to freedom of expression. For example, the right of high school students to place in the school newspaper an advertisement against the war in Vietnam was upheld (*Zucker v. Panitz* 1969). Students were also upheld in their right to distribute information on birth control and on laws regarding marijuana (*Shanley v. Northeast Independent School District* 1972). And other cases upheld the right of students to publish literature that was critical of teachers, administrators, and other school personnel (*Scoville v. Board of Education of Joliet Township High School District 204* 1970, 1971; *Sullivan v. Houston Independent School District* 1969).

In January 1988, however, the Supreme Court, in a five-to-three ruling in *Hazelwood School District v. Kuhlmeier,* departed from the earlier *Tinker* decision and gave public school officials considerable authority to censor school-sponsored student publications. The case involved a Missouri high school principal's censorship of articles in the school newspaper, the *Spectrum,* on teenage pregnancy and the impact of divorce on students. The principal believed the articles were inappropriate because they might identify pregnant students and because references to sexual activity and birth control were inappropriate for younger students. Several students on the newspaper staff distributed copies of the ar-ticles on their own and later sued the school district, claiming that their First Amendment rights had been violated.

Writing for the majority in *Hazelwood School District v. Kuhlmeier,* Justice Byron White (who had voted with the majority in *Tinker*) said school officials could bar "speech that is ungrammatical, poorly written, inadequately researched, biased or prejudiced, vulgar or profane, or unsuitable for immature audiences." White also pointed out that *Tinker* focused on a student's right of "personal expression," and the Missouri case dealt with school-sponsored publications that were part of the curriculum and bore the "imprimatur of the school." According to White, "Educators do not offend the First Amendment by exercising editorial control over the style and content of student speech in school-sponsored expressive activities so long as their actions are reasonably related to legitimate pedagogical concerns."

A case involving an attempt to regulate an "underground" student newspaper entitled *Bad Astra,* however, had a different outcome. Five high school students in Renton, Washington, produced a four-page newspaper at their expense, off school property, and without the knowledge of school authorities. *Bad Astra* contained articles that criticized school policies, a mock poll evaluating teachers, and several poetry selections. The students distributed 350 copies of the paper at a senior class barbecue held on school grounds.

After the paper was distributed, the principal placed letters of reprimand in the five students' files, and the district established a new policy whereby student-written, non-school-sponsored materials with an intended distribution of more than ten were subject to predistribution review. The students filed suit in federal district court, claiming a violation of their First Amendment rights. The court, however, ruled that the new policy was "substantially constitutional." Maintaining that the policy was unconstitutional, the students filed an appeal in 1988 in the Ninth Circuit Court and won. The court ruled that *Bad Astra* was not "within the purview of the school's exercise of reasonable editorial control" (*Burch v. Barker* 1987, 1988).

Where Do You Stand? **Visit the Companion Website to Voice Your Opinion.**

Dress Codes Few issues related to the rights of students have generated as many court cases as have dress codes and hairstyles. The demand on the courts to hear such cases prompted Supreme Court Justice Hugo L. Black to observe that he did not believe "the federal Constitution imposed on the United States Courts the burden of supervising the length of hair that public school students should wear" (*Karr v. Schmidt* 1972). In line with Justice Black's observation, the Supreme Court has repeatedly refused to review the decisions reached by the lower courts.

In general, the courts have suggested that schools may have dress codes as long as such codes are clear, reasonable, and students are notified. However, when the legality of such codes has been challenged, the rulings have largely indicated that schools may not control what students wear unless it is immodest or is disruptive of the educational process.

Students in private schools, however, do not have First Amendment protections provided by *Tinker v. Des Moines Independent Community School District* because private schools are not state affiliated. As a result, students at private schools can be required to wear uniforms, and "[d]isagreements over 'student rights' . . . are generally resolved by applying contract law to the agreement governing the student's attendance" (LaMorte 2002, 105).

At one time, educators' concerns about student appearance may have been limited to hairstyles and immodest dress; however, today's educators, as Michael LaMorte (2002, 156) points out, may be concerned about "T-shirts depicting violence, drugs (e.g., marijuana leaves), racial epithets, or characters such as Bart Simpson; ripped, baggy, or saggy pants or jeans; sneakers with lights; colored bandannas, baseball or other hats; words shaved into scalps, brightly colored hair, distinctive haircuts or hairstyles, or ponytails for males; exposed underwear; Malcolm X symbols; Walkmen, cellular phones, or beepers; backpacks; tatoos, unusual-colored lipstick, pierced noses, or earrings; and decorative dental caps."

Since gangs, hate groups, and violence in and around public schools have become more prevalent during the last decade, rulings that favor schools are becoming more common when the courts "balance the First Amendment rights of students to express themselves against the legitimate right of school authorities to maintain a safe and disruption-free environment" (LaMorte 2002, 156). This balance is clearly illustrated in *Jeglin v. San Jacinto Unified School District* (1993). In this instance, a school's dress code prohibiting the wearing of clothing with writing, pictures, or insignia of professional or college athletic teams was challenged on the grounds that it violated students' freedom of expression. The court acknowledged that the code violated the rights of elementary and middle school students, but not those of high school students. Gangs, known to be present at the high school, had intimidated students and faculty in connection with the sports-oriented clothing. The court ruled that the curtailment of students' rights did not "demand a certainty that disruption will occur, but only the existence of facts which might reasonably lead school officials to forecast substantial disruption."

After the Colorado high school shootings in 1999, which left fourteen students and a teacher dead—including the two gunmen who were members of a clique called the "Trench Coat Mafia"—many school districts made their rules for student dress more restrictive. Ten days after the shootings, a federal judge who upheld a school's decision to suspend a student for wearing a T-shirt that said "Vegan" (a vegetarian who doesn't eat animal products), said "gang attire has become particularly troubling since two students wore trench coats in the Colorado shooting." And, in Jonesboro, Arkansas, where four students and a teacher were shot and killed the previous year, a group of boys and girls identifying themselves as the "Blazer Mafia" were suspended for ten days (Portner 1999).

To reduce disruption and violence in schools, some school districts now require younger students to wear uniforms. In 1994, the 90,000-student Long Beach, California, school system became the first in the nation to require K–8 students to wear uniforms. Currently, the Birmingham, Alabama; Chicago; Dayton, Ohio; Oakland, California; and San Antonio public schools require elementary-age students to wear uniforms. At the beginning of the 2002–03 school year, Memphis took steps to become the nation's first large urban district to require all students to wear uniforms when school commissioners voted eight to one to implement a school uniform policy for the district's 175 schools (Richard 2002).

Currently, half the states have school districts with mandatory school uniform requirements, and "estimates suggest that over the next several years, one in four public school students may be wearing uniforms" (LaMorte 2002, 158). Courts have upheld mandatory school uniform policies. For example, a court ruled against a parent who challenged New York City's school uniform policy for pre-K through eighth-grade students. The parent claimed that the opt-out provision would make his daughter "stick out," while the New York City Board of Education stated that the policy would "promote a more effective learning climate; foster school unity and pride; improve student performance; foster self-esteem; eliminate label competition; simplify dressing and minimize costs to parents; teach children appropriate dress and decorum in the 'workplace'; and help to improve student conduct and discipline" (*Lipsman v. New York City Board of Education* 1999).

Due Process in Suspension and Expulsion

In February and March 1971, a total of nine students received ten-day suspensions from the Columbus, Ohio, public school system during a period of city-wide unrest. One student, in the presence of his principal, physically attacked a police officer who was trying to remove a disruptive student from a high school auditorium. Four others were suspended for similar conduct. Another student was suspended for his involvement in a lunchroom disturbance that resulted in damage to school property. All nine students were suspended in accordance with Ohio law. Some of the students and their parents were offered the opportunity to attend conferences prior to the start of the suspensions, but none of the nine was given a hearing. Asserting that their constitutional rights had been denied, all nine students brought suit against the school system.

In a sharply divided five-to-four decision, the Supreme Court ruled that the students had a legal right to an education, and that this "property right" could be removed only through the application of procedural due process. The court maintained that suspension is a "serious event" in the life of a suspended child and may not be imposed by the school in an arbitrary manner (*Goss v. Lopez* 1975).

As a result of cases such as *Goss v. Lopez,* every state has outlined procedures for school officials to follow in the suspension and expulsion of students. In cases of short-term suspension (defined by the courts as exclusion from school for ten days or less), the due process steps are somewhat flexible and determined by the nature of the infraction and the length of the suspension. As Figure 6.2 shows, however, long-term suspension (more than ten days) and expulsion require a more extensive due process procedure. The disciplinary transfer of a disruptive student to an alternative school, designed to meet his or her needs, is not considered an expulsion (LaMorte 2002).

In response to an increase of unruly students who disrupt the learning of others, a few districts and states have granted teachers the authority to sus-

Figure 6.2 Due process in suspension and expulsion.
Source: Adapted from Martha M. McCarthy, Nelda H. Cambron-McCabe, and Stephen B. Thomas, *Public School Law: Teachers' and Students' Rights.* Boston: Allyn and Bacon, 1998, pp. 205, 301.

At minimum, students should be provided with:

Suspension for 10 days or fewer

- Oral or written notification of the nature of the violation and the intended punishment.
- An opportunity to refute the charges before an objective decisionmaker (such a discussion may immediately follow the alleged rule infraction).
- An explanation of the evidence on which the disciplinarian is relying.

Long-term suspension and expulsion

- Written notice of the charges, the intention to expel, and the place, time, and circumstances of the hearing, with sufficient time for a defense to be prepared.
- A full and fair hearing before an impartial adjudicator.
- The right to legal counsel or some other adult representation.
- The right to be fully apprised of the proof or evidence.
- The opportunity to present witnesses or evidence.
- The opportunity to cross-examine opposing witnesses.
- Some type of written record demonstrating that the decision was based on the evidence presented at the hearing.

What are students' rights with regard to their persons, lockers, personal property, and records in school and on school grounds? How are school districts' rights of search and seizure decided? In what ways have students' rights to privacy been upheld?

pend students for up to ten days. Teachers in Cincinnati and Dade County, Florida, for example, have negotiated contracts that give them authority to remove disruptive students from their classrooms; however, district administrators decide how the students will be disciplined. In 1995, Indiana became the first state to grant teachers the power to suspend students, and the following year New York's governor proposed legislation to allow teachers to remove students from their classrooms for up to ten days for "committing an act of violence against a student, teacher, or school district employee; possessing or threatening to use a gun, knife, or other dangerous weapon; damaging or destroying school district property; damaging the personal property of teachers or other employees; or defying an order from a teacher or administrator to stop disruptive behavior" (Lindsay 1996, 24).

Reasonable Search and Seizure

As a teacher you have reason to believe that a student has drugs, and possibly a dangerous weapon, in his locker. Do you have the right to search the student's locker and seize any illegal or dangerous items? According to the Fourth Amendment, citizens are protected from **search and seizure** conducted without a search warrant. With the escalation of drug use in schools and school-related violence, however, cases involving the legality of search and seizure in schools have increased. These cases suggest guidelines that you can follow if confronted with a situation such as that described here.

The case of *New Jersey v. T.L.O.* (1985) involved a fourteen-year-old student (T.L.O.) whom a teacher found smoking a cigarette in a rest room. The teacher took the student to the principal's office, whereupon the principal asked to see the contents of her purse. On opening the purse, the principal found a pack of cigarettes and what appeared to be drug paraphernalia and a list titled "People who owe me money." T.L.O. was arrested and later found guilty of delinquency charges.

After being sentenced to one year's probation, T.L.O. appealed, claiming that the evidence found in her purse was obtained in violation of the Fourth Amend-

On the Frontlines

Fighting Drugs

A.J. stood for minutes reading and rereading the memo, wondering if it was some sort of joke. But it was from the superintendent's office, so he knew it had to be serious. He took it into the teachers' lounge and asked if anyone else was aware of the memo. A number of the teachers indicated they'd just seen it as well. "Is this for real?" A.J. asked.

The memo was from the superintendent informing faculty that all students taking part in any extracurricular school activity would be required to take a drug test before being allowed to participate.

"Doesn't this seem like overkill?" A.J. asked. "Do we even have a drug problem? I thought they only did this in professional sports."

"I think it's an outrage," opined Ms. Carter, the choir director. "It's one thing to test athletes, what with all those performance-enhancing drugs out there, but singers? I can't imagine parents will take this sitting down!"

"It's part of the administration's new Zero Tolerance Policy. It was discussed and passed at the school board meeting last night. There weren't a lot of people in attendance, but those who were there didn't say much. I think people are scared about drugs and want to make sure we don't develop a problem," said Mr. Gustafson. "It's not a bad idea. If students are going to represent our school, they need to be clean."

"So now any student who participates in any extra club or music program or takes part in a play here at school has to subject him- or herself to a drug test? What about their right to privacy? It's going to discourage students from participating at all! This can't be legal!" cried A.J.

That was precisely the feelings of one student and her family in Oklahoma when her school announced just such a policy. But in a ruling issued June 27, 2002 (*Board of Education of Independent School District 92 of Pottawatomie County v. Earls*) the U.S. Supreme Court ruled in favor of the school district. In the opinion of the court, as written by Justice Clarence Thomas, "testing students who participate in extracurricular activities is a reasonably effective means of addressing the school district's legitimate concerns in preventing, deterring, and detecting drug use."

The key point in Justice Thomas's opinion is his reference to "addressing the school district's legitimate concerns." What constitutes a legitimate concern? In previous cases in recent years, recognition of a serious drug problem in the school or community often was a key factor in determining the legality of instituting various drug policies and in overriding arguments over the ethical nature of such policies. In *Pottawatomie v. Earls*, the defense argued that no such condition existed and, therefore, the test is unreasonable. The justices, however, explored during arguments whether a school district with limited problems had a right to keep it that way or wait for there to be a crisis and "lose a few years to drugs." Their subsequent ruling broadens the scope of school districts' oversight and policymaking in the interest of their students.

Opponents of drug testing have argued for years that such policies are violations of individual rights of privacy and that drug tests are a violation of the Fourth Amendment, which forbids "unreasonable search and seizure." Unfortunately, continued drug problems in the United States have led many school districts to challenge such opposition and take strong measures in an attempt to keep drugs off their campuses and protect the well-being of all students. Advocates see the expansion of drug testing to all students in extracurricular activities as (1) a way of preventing a problem from arising, and (2) another step in helping raise young people to be responsible adults.

Teachers today often find themselves caught in the middle of this argument. Interest in the well-being of all students is at the heart of all teachers' philosophies. As a result, the relationships teachers develop with their students are an integral piece of the educational process, and these relationships often rely greatly on the trust that develops be-

tween teachers and their students. Opponents of the *Pottawatomie v. Earls* ruling fear that the broader scope of "search" could compromise the delicate line of trust between teachers and their students. In addition, teachers likely have personal opinions on the ethical nature of "search and seizure" policies. But, as an employee of the school system, they also have an obligation to the district. While not always possible or easy to do, the more teachers stay aware of and involve themselves in policy discussions in their districts, the greater the chance they can maintain both a personal and professional balance on controversial issues.

Exploratory Questions

1. How do you think students, parents, and the community from which you come would respond to drug testing of all students who take part in extracurricular activities?
2. What is your opinion of the *Pottawatomie v. Earls*- ruling? How would you respond as a teacher if your school instituted drug testing of all students who take part in extracurricular activities?
3. What are possible ramifications of this ruling on students?

Your Survival Guide of Helpful Resources

The following resources provide helpful hints for surviving "on the frontlines."

Books and Articles

Office of National Drug Control Policy. (2002). What you need to know about drug testing in schools. Retrieved from http://whitehousedrugpolicy.gov

Klauke, A., and Hadderman, M. Drug testing. *ERIC Digest, No. EA35*. Eugene, OR: ERIC Clearinghouse on Educational Management. (1990)

Board of Education of Independent School District No. 92 of Pottawatomie County v. Earls. 536 S. Ct. *01.332* (2002).

Websites

Health in Schools (http://www.healthinschools.org)

National Association of Secondary School Principals (http://www.nassp.org)

Office of National Drug Control Policy (http://whitehousedrugpolicy.gov)

Companion Website

ment and that her confession to selling marijuana was tainted by an illegal search. The U.S. Supreme Court found that the search had been reasonable. The Court also developed a two-pronged test of "reasonableness" for searches: (1) A school official must have a reasonable suspicion that a student has violated a law or school policy and (2) the search must be conducted using methods that are reasonable in scope.

Another case focused on the use of trained dogs to conduct searches of 2,780 junior and senior high school students in Highland, Indiana. During a two-and-a-half- to three-hour period, six teams with trained German shepherds sniffed the students. The dogs alerted their handlers a total of fifty times. Seventeen of the searches initiated by the dogs turned up beer, drug paraphernalia, or marijuana. Another eleven students singled out by the dogs, including thirteen-year-old Diane Doe, were strip searched in the nurse's office. It turned out that Diane had played with her dog, who was in heat, that morning and that the police dog had responded to the smell of the other dog on Diane's clothing.

Diane's parents later filed suit, charging that their daughter was searched illegally. The court ruled that the use of dogs did not constitute an unreasonable search, nor did holding students in their homerooms constitute a mass detention in violation of the Fourth Amendment. The court did, however, hold that the strip searches of the students were unreasonable. The court pointed out that the school personnel did not have any evidence to suggest that Diane possessed contraband because, prior to the strip search, she had emptied her pockets as requested. Diane was awarded $7,500 in damages (*Doe v. Renfrow* 1980, 1981).

Court cases involving search and seizure in school settings have maintained that school lockers are the property of the schools, not students, and may be searched by school authorities if reasonable cause exists. In addition, students may be sniffed by police dogs if school authorities have a reasonable suspicion that illegal or dangerous items may be found. Lastly, courts have tended not to allow strip searches; however, as *Cornfield v. Consolidated High School District No. 230* (1993) illustrates, strip searches may be constitutional depending upon the circumstances giving rise to the search, the age of the student, and the severity of the suspected infraction. In *Cornfield,* the court allowed a strip search of a sixteen-year-old student suspected of "crotching" drugs. The court's decision was influenced by "allegations of several recent prior incidents such as dealing in drugs, testing positive for marijuana, possession of drugs, having 'crotched' drugs during a police raid at his mother's house, failing a urine analysis for cocaine, unsuccessful completion of a drug rehabilitation program, and a report by a bus driver that there was a smell of marijuana where the student sat on the bus" (LaMorte 2002, 153).

In general, the courts have tried to balance the school's need to obtain information and the student's right to privacy. To protect themselves from legal challenges related to searches, educators should follow guidelines that have been suggested by school law experts:

- Inform students and parents at the start of the school year of the procedures for conducting locker and personal searches.
- Base any search on "reasonable suspicion."
- Conduct any search with another staff member present.
- Avoid strip searches or mass searches of groups of students.

- Require that police obtain a search warrant before conducting a search in the school.

Some schools use drug testing as a requirement for either attendance or interscholastic participation, including sports competition, or as a means of discipline. A 1988 court case upheld a urinalysis drug test for randomly selected student athletes because those who tested positively were suspended only from participating in sports for a period of time and no disciplinary or academic penalties were imposed (*Schaill v. Tippecanoe School Corp.* 1988). Similarly, the U.S. Supreme Court reversed a lower court's ruling and stated that a school district's desire to reduce drug use justified the degree of intrusion required by random tests of student athletes' urine (*Acton v. Vernonia School District* 1995). A few school districts have attempted to implement mandatory drug testing of teachers. So far the courts have upheld the decision rendered in *Patchogue-Medford Congress of Teachers v. Board of Education of Patchogue-Medford Union Free School District* (1987) that drug testing of teachers violates the Fourth Amendment's prohibition of unreasonable searches.

Privacy

Prior to 1974 students and parents were not allowed to examine school records. On November 19, 1974, Congress passed the Family Educational Rights and Privacy Act (FERPA), which gave parents of students under eighteen and students eighteen and older the right to examine their school records. Every public or private educational institution must adhere to the law, known as the **Buckley Amendment,** or lose federal money.

Under the Buckley Amendment, schools must do the following:

1. Inform parents and students of their rights.
2. Provide information to parents and students about the type of educational records available and how to obtain access to them.
3. Allow parents or students to review records, request changes, request a hearing if changes are not allowed, and, if necessary, add their own explanation about the records.
4. Not give out personally identifiable information without prior written, informed consent of a parent or students.
5. Allow parents and students to see the school's record of disclosures.

The Buckley Amendment actually sets forth the minimum requirements that schools must adhere to, and many states and school districts have gone beyond these minimum guidelines in granting students access to their records. Most high schools, for example, now grant students under eighteen access to their educational records, and all students in Virginia, elementary through secondary, are guaranteed access to their records.

A number of exceptions are allowed by the Buckley Amendment. The teacher's gradebook, psychiatric or treatment records, notes or records written by the teacher for his or her exclusive use or to be shared with a substitute teacher, or the private notes of school law enforcement units, for example, are not normally subject to examination.

The provisions of FERPA came to the nation's attention in 2000 when Kristja Falvo challenged the practice of having students grade one another's papers (peer grading) on the grounds that it was embarrassing to her three children and resulted in grading errors. A district court disagreed and ruled in favor of the school district, maintaining that peer grading is a common school practice. However, the Tenth Circuit Court of Appeals reversed that decision and ruled that the practice of peer grading violated students' privacy since grades are entered into teachers' gradebooks and thus fit the definition of "educational records" (*Falvo v. Owasso Independent School District* 2000). Eventually, however, the case reached the Supreme Court, which ruled nine to zero that the privacy law was not intended to protect grades on day-to-day classroom assignments and that students could grade one another's work (*Owasso Independent School District v. Falvo* 2002).

Students' Rights to Nondiscrimination

Schools are legally bound to avoid discriminating against students on the basis of race, sex, religion, disability, marital status, or infection with a noncommunicable disease such as HIV/AIDS. One trend that has confronted schools with the need to develop more thoughtful and fair policies has been the epidemic in teenage pregnancies.

In regard to students who are married, pregnant, or parents, the courts have been quite clear: Students in these categories may not be treated differently. A 1966 case in Texas involving a sixteen-year-old mother established that schools may provide separate classes or alternative schools on a *voluntary* basis for married and/or pregnant students. However, the district may not *require* such students to attend separate schools, nor may they be made to attend adult or evening schools (*Alvin Independent School District v. Cooper* 1966).

The courts have made an about-face in their positions on whether students who are married, pregnant, or parents can participate in extracurricular activities. Prior to 1972 participation in these activities was considered a privilege rather than a right, and restrictions on those who could participate were upheld. In 1972, however, cases in Tennessee, Ohio, Montana, and Texas established the right of married students (and, in one case, a divorced student) to participate (*Holt v. Sheldon* 1972; *Davis v. Meek* 1972; *Moran v. School District No. 7* 1972; and *Romans v. Crenshaw* 1972). Since then, restrictions applicable to extracurricular activities have been universally struck down.

During the 1980s, many school districts became embroiled in controversy over the issue of how to provide for the schooling of young people with HIV/AIDS and whether school employees with HIV/AIDS should be allowed to continue working. In rulings on HIV/AIDS-related cases since then, the courts have sided with the overwhelming medical evidence that students with AIDS pose no "significant risk" of spreading the disease. "To date, courts have revealed a high degree of sensitivity to students with HIV or AIDS and to their being included in the public school mainstream" (LaMorte 2002, 335). In 1987, for example, a judge prevented a Florida school district from requiring that three hemophiliac brothers who were exposed to HIV/AIDS through transfusions be restricted to homebound instruction (*Ray v. School District of DeSoto County* 1987).

To stem the spread of HIV/AIDS, school systems in many large cities—New York, Los Angeles, San Francisco, and Seattle, to name a few—have initiated programs to distribute condoms to high school students. New York's condom-distribution program, which initially did not require parental consent, was challenged in 1993 (*Alfonso v. Fernandez*). The court ruled that

Meeting the Standard

Acts Legally and Ethically and with Compassion

INTASC The teacher understands and implements laws related to students' rights and teacher responsibilities (e.g., for equal education, appropriate education for handicapped students, confidentiality, privacy, appropriate treatment of students, reporting in situations related to possible child abuse) (INTASC Knowledge, Principle #10).

Candidates work with students, families, and communities in ways that reflect the dispositions expected of professional educators as delineated in professional, state, and institutional standards (NCATE).

Teachers employ technical knowledge and skill, yet must be ever mindful of teaching's ethical dimensions (NBPTS).

Teacher demonstrates genuine caring and respect for individual students. Students exhibit respect for teacher as an individual beyond that for the role (PRAXIS III Framework*–"distinguished" level of performance).

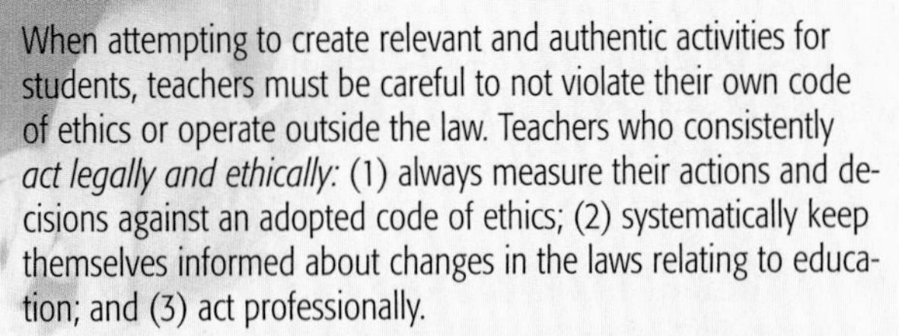

When attempting to create relevant and authentic activities for students, teachers must be careful to not violate their own code of ethics or operate outside the law. Teachers who consistently *act legally and ethically:* (1) always measure their actions and decisions against an adopted code of ethics; (2) systematically keep themselves informed about changes in the laws relating to education; and (3) act professionally.

In the following true example, a teacher wanted to make the learning process relevant for her students, but notice how many legal and ethical risks she may have taken in this pursuit.

Before a field trip to the police department, county jail, and the courthouse, a ninth-grade civics teacher let the students have thirty minutes to walk around in a small shopping mall. Imagine the students' surprise when they returned to their school bus and saw three of their classmates sitting in the back seat of a police car. Apparently the three students, who were often in trouble in class, had tried to sneak some items out of a store without paying for them. Later, these same three students were spotted in a brightly lit stage area of the line-up room at the police station. After the tour guide explained how the room was used, the lights went out and the class was ushered from the jail to the courtroom. As the courtroom door opened, there sat the three apprehended classmates. By this time, the entire class realized that the teacher had staged the arrests; however, she had certainly succeeded in focusing the students' attention. She watched with pleasure as these fifteen- and sixteen-year-olds took copious notes while the judge explained the trial process. Later the judge invited some of the students to serve as the attorneys, witnesses, bailiff, and court reporter in a mock trial for their classmates.

1. Review the professional code of ethics located on the National Education Association's (NEA) website (http://www.nea.org/code.html). At what points do you think the civics teacher may have acted outside the principles of the NEA code when she had students arrested to create a relevant and authentic learning experience? At what point might she have broken some laws? What would be required to ensure that such an experience would be carried out within the boundaries of the laws and the code of ethics provided by the NEA?

Companion Website

2. How well formed is your professional code of ethics? Have you adopted one? If not, take some time now, review the resources in this chapter and at the Companion Website, and then write out your own principles.
3. Based on your understanding of the laws and standards of professional ethics, what are the student privacy and child endangerment issues related to requiring students to create and display student learning portfolios on the Web?
4. There are many legal and ethical areas that impact educators and their students such as civil rights, tort liabilities, copyright laws, child abuse laws, search and seizure, privacy, and nondiscrimination. Having up-to-date legal resources handy can be quite useful. Take some time and organize the resources found in this chapter, the Companion Website, and other sources so you can access them quickly when you need to use them. Which resources should you revisit routinely to keep current with the changes? What plan of action might you follow to ensure that you stay informed?

the program was a "health issue" and that the district could not dispense condoms without prior parental approval. The court maintained that the program violated parents' due process rights under the Fourteenth Amendment to raise their children as they see fit; however, the program did not violate parents' or students' freedom of religion. Three years later, however, the U.S. Supreme Court declined to review a Massachusetts high court ruling that upheld a school board's decision to place condom machines in high school restrooms and allow junior- and senior-level students to request condoms from the school nurse (*Curtis v. School Committee of Falmouth* 1995, 1996).

What Are Some Issues in the Legal Rights of School Districts?

Clearly, the law touches just about every aspect of education in the United States today. Daily, the media remind us that ours is an age of litigation; no longer are school districts as protected as they once were from legal problems. Corporal punishment, sexual harassment, religious expression, and home schooling are among the issues in the legal rights of school districts.

Corporal Punishment

The practice of **corporal punishment** has had a long and controversial history in education in the United States. Currently, policies regarding the use of corporal punishment vary widely from state to state, and even from district to district.

Critics believe that corporal punishment "is neither a necessary nor an effective response to misbehavior in school" (Slavin 2000, 391), and some believe the practice is "archaic, cruel, and inhuman and an unjustifiable act on the part of the state" (LaMorte 2002, 137). In spite of such arguments against its effectiveness, corporal punishment continues to be widespread. Nevertheless, almost half of the states and many school districts currently ban corporal punishment, and many others restrict its use (LaMorte 2002).

The most influential Supreme Court case involving corporal punishment is *Ingraham v. Wright,* decided in 1977. In Dade County, Florida, in October 1970, junior high school students James Ingraham and Roosevelt Andrews were paddled with a wooden paddle. Both students received injuries as a result of the paddlings, with Ingraham's being the most severe. Ingraham, who was being punished for being slow to respond to a teacher's directions, refused to assume the "paddling position" and had to be held over a desk by two assistant principals while the principal administered twenty "licks." As a result, Ingraham "suffered a hematoma requiring medical attention and keeping him out of school for several days."

The court had two significant questions to rule on in *Ingraham:* Does the Eighth Amendment's prohibition of cruel and unusual punishment apply to corporal punishment in the schools? And, if it does not, should the due process clause of the Fourteenth Amendment provide any protection to students before punishment is administered? In regard to the first question, the Court, in a sharply divided five-to-four decision, ruled that the Eighth Amendment was not applicable to students being disciplined in school, only to persons convicted of crimes. On the question of due process, the Court said, "We conclude that the

Due Process clause does not require notice and a hearing prior to the imposition of corporal punishment in the public schools, as that practice is authorized and limited by the common law." The Court also commented on the severity of the paddlings in *Ingraham* and said that, in such cases, school personnel "may be held liable in damages to the child and, if malice is shown, they may be subject to criminal penalties."

Though the Supreme Court has upheld the constitutionality of corporal punishment, many districts around the country have instituted policies banning its use. Where corporal punishment is used, school personnel are careful to see that it meets criteria that have emerged from other court cases involving corporal punishment:

- Specific warning is given about what behavior may result in corporal punishment.
- Evidence exists that other measures attempted failed to bring about the desired change in behavior.
- Administration of corporal punishment takes place in the presence of a second school official.
- On request, a written statement is provided to parents explaining the reasons for the punishment and the names of all witnesses.
- [The punishment meets] the reasonableness standard—punishment must be within the bounds of reason and humanity.
- [The punishment meets] the good faith standard—the person administering the punishment is not motivated by malice and does not inflict punishment wantonly or excessively (Dunklee and Shoop 2002, 127).

Sexual Harassment

Though few victims report it, sexual harassment affects about four out of every five teenagers in schools across the nation, according to surveys of eighth- through eleventh-graders conducted by the American Association of University Women (AAUW) in 1993 and 2001. Students' responses were based on the following definition: "Sexual harassment is unwanted and unwelcome sexual behavior which interferes with your life. Sexual harassment is not behaviors that you like or want (for example wanted kissing, touching, or flirting)" (American Association of University Women 1993, 2001).

The 2001 survey revealed that the percentage of boys experiencing harassment "often" or "occasionally" increased from 49 percent in 1993 to 56 percent in 2001. On the other hand, the percentage of students reporting that their school has a policy on **sexual harassment** increased from 26 percent in 1993 to 69 percent in 2001. Although most teens report that they are harassed by their schoolmates, 7 percent of boys and girls experiencing physical or nonphysical harassment report being harassed by a teacher. Table 6.4 highlights the results of the 2001 AAUW survey.

As our discussion of this chapter's opening scenario pointed out, a landmark Supreme Court Case (*Davis v. Monroe County Board of Education* 1999) ruled by a narrow five-to-four margin that educators can be held liable if they fail to take steps to end peer sexual harassment. In their majority opinion, five justices disagreed with the claim by the other four justices that "nothing short of ex-

Table 6.4 Sexual harassment in the nation's schools (Based on a national survey of 2,064 public school students, eighth through eleventh grades)

- 83% of girls and 79% of boys report having ever experienced harassment.
  - The number of boys reporting experiences with harassment often or occasionally has increased since 1993 (56% vs. 49%), although girls are still somewhat more likely to experience it.
  - For many students sexual harassment is an ongoing experience: over 1 in 4 students experience it "often."
  - These numbers do not differ by whether the school is urban or suburban or rural.
- 76% of students have experienced nonphysical harassment while 58% have experienced physical harassment. Nonphysical harassment includes taunting, rumors, graffiti, jokes or gestures. One-third of all students report experiencing physical harassment "often or occasionally."
- There has been a sea change in awareness of school policies about harassment since 1993. Seven in 10 students (69%) say that their school has a policy on sexual harassment, compared to only 26% of students in 1993.
- Substantial numbers of students fear being sexually harassed or hurt in school.
  - A substantial number of students—both boys and girls—fear being hurt by someone in their school life. 18% are afraid some or most of the time, and less than half (46%) are "never" afraid in school.
  - One-third of students fear being sexually harassed in school. Hispanic boys and girls are more likely than African American students to feel afraid.
- According to the new report, harassment has many facets:
  - Peer-on-peer harassment is most common for both boys and girls, although 7% of boys and girls experiencing physical or nonphysical harassment report being harassed by a teacher.
  - Boys are more likely than girls to report nonphysical harassment in locker rooms (28% v. 15%) or restrooms (15% to 9%).
  - Half of boys reporting harassment have been nonphysically harassed by a girl or woman, and 39% by a group of girls or women. In contrast, girls are most likely to report harassment by one boy or man (73% in nonphysical harassment; 84% in physical harassment).
  - Over one-third (35%) of students who have been harassed report that they first experienced it in elementary school.
  - Most harassment occurs under teachers' noses in the classroom (61% for physical harassment and 56% for nonphysical) and in the halls (71% for physical harassment and 64% for nonphysical).
  - Students are perpetrators, too. Slightly more than half of students (54%) say that they have sexually harassed someone during their school life. This represents a decrease from 1993, when 59% admitted as much. In particular, boys are less likely than in 1993 to report being a "perpetrator" (57% to 66%).

Source: Excerpted from American Association of University Women Educational Foundation, ***Hostile Hallways: Bullying, Teasing, and Sexual Harassment in School.*** New York: Harris Interactive, 2001.

pulsion of every student accused of misconduct involving sexual overtones would protect school systems from liability or damages." Instead, their ruling was intended "only for harassment that is so severe, pervasive, and objectively offensive that it effectively bars the victim's access to an educational opportunity or benefit."

The dissenting justices, however, expressed concern about the "avalanche of liability now set in motion" and the "potentially crushing financial liability" for schools.

> *A female plaintiff who pleads only that a boy called her offensive names, that she told a teacher, that the teacher's response was unreasonable, and that her school performance suffered as a result, appears to state a successful claim. . . . After today, Johnny will find that the routine problems of adolescence are to be resolved by invoking a federal right to demand assignment to a desk two rows away.*

To highlight their concern about the effects of the ruling, the dissenting Justices also noted that shortly after a U.S. Department of Education warning that schools could be liable for peer sexual harassment, a North Carolina school suspended a six-year-old boy who kissed a female classmate on the cheek.

In addition to harassment by the opposite sex, same-sex harassment, usually against gay and lesbian students, is a problem at some schools. Since the mid-1990s, several school districts have faced lawsuits filed by gay and lesbian students who claimed that school officials failed to protect them from verbal and physical antigay harassment. For example, in 1999 six gay and lesbian teenagers in Morgan Hill, California, filed a complaint in a U.S. District Court charging that school officials failed to protect them from years of antigay harassment. One of the complainants alleged that teachers regularly witnessed the harassment but did nothing to stop it: "Most [teachers] just don't want the hassle; others will acknowledge that they are homophobic, that they just don't like gays and lesbians." Moreover, the student found that administrators also refused to get involved: "Taking these things [i.e., complaints about antigay harassment] to the administrators and having them, my protectors, say 'Go back to class and stop talking about it' affected me more than anything. I learned that teachers won't do anything for you if they don't get any backup from the administration" (Ruenzel 1999). A 1996 verdict awarding almost $1 million to a gay student by a U.S. District Court was the first time a federal jury found school officials responsible for antigay harassment committed by students (Jacobson 1996). Currently, at least five states and several school districts have education policies that prohibit discrimination based on sexual orientation.

Increased reports of sexual harassment of students by educators and a Supreme Court ruling in 1992 (*Franklin v. Gwinnett County Public Schools*) that students could sue and collect damages for harassment under Title IX of the Education Act of 1972 are causing some teachers to be apprehensive about working closely with students, and a small number of teachers even report that they fear being falsely accused by angry, disgruntled students. As a school superintendent put it, "There's no question but that the attitudes of personnel in schools are changing because of the many cases [of sexual harassment] that have come up across the country. I think all of us are being extremely cautious in how we handle students and in what we say and do with students and employees" (*Spokesman Review* 1993, 1A). To address the problem, many school districts have suggested guidelines that teachers can follow to show concern for students, offer them encouragement, and congratulate them for their successes.

Religious Expression

Conflicts over the proper role of religion in schools are among the most heated in the continuing debate about the character and purposes of education in the United States. Numerous school districts have found themselves embroiled in legal issues related to school prayer, Bible reading, textbooks, creationism, singing of Christmas carols, distribution of religious literature, New Age beliefs, secular humanism, religious holidays, use of school buildings for religious meetings, and the role of religion in moral education, to name a few. On the one hand, conservative religious groups wish to restore prayer and Christian religious practices to the public schools; on the other, secular liberals see religion as irrele-

What are the rights of schools with regard to religious expression? What are the rights of students? What kinds of challenges do schools whose students come from mixed religious backgrounds face?

vant to school curricula and maintain that public schools should not promote religion. In addition, somewhere between these two positions are those who believe that, while schools should not be involved in the *teaching of* religion, they should *teach about* religion.

During the last fifty years, scores of court cases have addressed school activities related to the First Amendment principle of separation of church and state. As Michael Imber and Tyll van Geel put it: "By far the most common constitutional objection raised against a school program is that it fails to respect the wall of separation between church and state" (2001, 21). In one of these landmark cases (*Engel v. Vitale* 1962), the U.S. Supreme Court ruled that recitation of a prayer said in the presence of a teacher at the beginning of each school day was unconstitutional and violated the First Amendment which states: "Congress shall make no law respecting an establishment of religion, or prohibiting the free exercise thereof." Justice Hugo Black, who delivered the opinion of the Court, stated "it is no part of the business of government to compose official prayers for any group of the American people to recite as a part of a religious program carried on by government."

The following year, the U.S. Supreme Court ruled that Bible reading and reciting the Lord's Prayer in school were unconstitutional (*School District of Abington Township v. Schempp* 1963). In response to the district's claim that unless these religious activities were permitted a "religion of secularism" would be established, the Court stated that "we agree of course that the State may not establish a 'religion of secularism' in the sense of affirmatively opposing or showing hostility to religion, thus 'preferring those who believe in no religion over those who do believe.' We do not agree, however, that this decision in any sense has that effect."

To determine whether a state has violated the separation of church and state principle, the courts refer to the decision rendered in *Lemon v. Kurtzman* (1971). In this instance, the U.S. Supreme Court struck down an attempt by the Rhode Island legislature to provide a 15 percent salary supplement to teachers of secular subjects in nonpublic schools and Pennsylvania legislation to provide financial supplements to nonpublic schools through reimbursement for teachers' salaries, texts, and instructional materials in certain secular subjects. According to the three-part test enunciated in *Lemon v. Kurtzman,* governmental practices "must first, have a secular legislative purpose; second, its principal or primary effect must be one that neither advances nor inhibits religion; and, third, it must not foster an excessive government entanglement with religion" (LaMorte 2002, 377). Though criticized vigorously by several Supreme Court justices since 1971, the so-called **Lemon test** has not been overruled.

Since the mid-1990s, the courts heard several cases addressing the question of whether parents' right to direct their children's upbringing meant they could demand curricula and learning activities that were compatible with their religious beliefs. Without exception, the courts have rejected "parent-rights" cases against the schools; those rights, according to a U.S. Court of Appeals ruling in support of a schoolwide assembly on HIV/AIDS, "do not encompass a broad-based right to restrict the flow of information in the public schools" (*Brown v. Hot, Sexy and Safer Productions, Inc.* 1996). In a similar case, parents objected to a Massachusetts school district's policy of distributing condoms to junior and senior high school students who requested them. The state's Supreme Judicial Court rejected the parental rights argument and their argument that the program infringed on their First Amendment right to free exercise of religion: "Parents have no right to tailor public school programs to meet their individual religious or moral preferences" (*Curtis v. School Committee of Falmouth* 1996).

Home Schooling

One spinoff of the public's heightened awareness of the problems that schools face has been the decision by some parents to educate their children in the home. While most home-schoolers view home schooling as an opportunity to provide their children with a curriculum based on religious values, many home-schoolers are motivated not by religious doctrine but by concern about issues such as school violence, poor academic quality, or peer pressure. The U.S. Department of Education reported in 2001 that there were 850,000 home-schooled children nationwide. Many observers of home schooling estimate the number to be at least one million and definitely growing. In addition, it is estimated that home-schooling parents spend about $700 million a year on instructional materials (Walsh 2002).

Home schooling is legal in all the states and the District of Columbia; however, how it is regulated, and whether resources are allocated, vary greatly. In 1999, NHERI reported that forty-one states had no minimum academic requirements for parents who decided to home-school their children. More than 60 percent of the states have home-schooling statutes or regulations, and half of the states require that home-schooled students participate in standardized testing (LaMorte 2002). In most states, home-schoolers must demonstrate that their instruction is "equivalent" to that offered in the public schools, a standard set in *New Jersey v. Massa* (1967).

Legal support for home schools has been mixed. In 1998, a Massachusetts court ruled that home visits by a local superintendent were not a valid requirement for approval by school officials of a home-school program (*Brunelle v. Lynn Public Schools* 1998). In 1993 and 1994, legislation to require home-school teachers to be state certified were defeated in South Dakota and Kansas, and similar laws were overturned in Iowa and North Dakota. However, a federal district court upheld a West Virginia statute making children ineligible for home schooling if their standardized test scores fell below the 40th percentile (*Null v. Board of Education* 1993). In Iowa, mandatory home-schooling reports to the state were upheld in *State v. Rivera* (1993); home-schoolers in that state must submit course outlines, weekly lesson plans, and provide the amount of time spent on areas of the curriculum. A Maryland law requiring the state's monitoring of home schooling was upheld despite a parent's claim that the state's curriculum promoted atheism, paganism, and evolution (*Battles v. Anne Arundel County Board of Education* 1996). And courts have not been sympathetic to home-schoolers who would like to have their children participate in extracurricular activities or other after-school activities (for example, *Swanson v. Guthrie Independent School District No. 1* 1998).

Table 6.5 Educator's rights and responsibilities

Legislation or Court Ruling	How It Affects Educators
Application of Bay v. State Board of Education, 1963	A past criminal conviction is grounds for being denied a teaching certificate.
Title VII of the Civil Rights Act of 1964	Educators are guaranteed nondiscrimination in hiring situations.
Morrison v. State Board of Education, 1969	An educator's conduct in his/her personal life is not an impairment to professional performance or grounds for revoking a teaching certificate.
Mailloux v. Kiley, 1971	School authorities are free to suspend teachers who use teaching methods of which they disapprove.
Station v. Travelers Insurance Co., 1974	Teachers must provide adequate supervision while students are exposed to dangerous conditions.
Burton v. Cascade School District Union High School, 1975	A tenured teacher cannot be dismissed unless the employer shows "good and just cause."
Hortonville Joint School District No. 1 v. Hortonville Education Association, 1976	Teachers working under collective bargaining agreements may be dismissed for striking.
Peter Doe v. San Francisco Unified School District, 1976	A school cannot be held responsible for a student's lack of achievement.
Copyright Act of 1980	The fair use doctrine applies to software as well as print materials.
Marcus v. Rowley, 1983	Teachers can make "fair use" of copyrighted material.
Unified School District No. 241 v. Swanson, 1986	Schools cannot assign duties to teachers that are not reasonably related to their teaching.
Edwards v. Aguillard, 1987	"Balanced treatment" laws that mandate curricula that advance particular religious beliefs are unconstitutional.
Mozert v. Hawkins County Board of Education, 1987, 1988, and *Smith v. Board of School Commissioners of Mobile County,* 1987	A school may establish a curriculum despite parental disapproval.
Krizek v. Cicero-Stickney Township High School District No. 20, 1989	Teachers must notify students' parents before using materials that might be found objectionable in the classroom.
Murray v. Pittsburgh Board of Public Education, 1996	Teachers may not have the right to use teaching methods and materials to which school officials object.
Davis v. Monroe County Board of Education, 1999	School districts can be sued in cases involving student-on-student sexual harassment, if the district acts with "deliberate indifference."

Table 6.5 lists chronologically and summarizes the key legislation and court decisions affecting educators that are discussed in this chapter.

As the preceding cases related to home schooling show, school law is not static—instead, it is continually evolving and changing. In addition, laws pertaining to education vary from state to state. Therefore, it is important for the beginning teacher to become familiar with current publications on school law in his or her state.

Summary

Why Do You Need a Professional Code of Ethics?

- A professional code of ethics guides teachers' actions and enables them to build relationships with students based on trust and respect.
- A code of ethics helps teachers see beyond the short-range consequences of their actions to long-range consequences, and it helps them respond appropriately to ethical dilemmas in the classroom.

What Are Your Legal Rights as a Teacher?

- The right to due process protects teachers from arbitrary treatment by school districts and education officials regarding certification, nondiscrimination, contracts, tenure, dismissal, and academic freedom.
- Several court rulings have illustrated how the constitutional rights of teachers must be balanced against a school's need to promote its educational goals.

Do Student Teachers Have the Same Rights?

- Many states have not clarified the legal status of student teachers to teach. However, student teachers should be aware that a potential for liability exists for them just as it does with certified teachers, and they should clarify their rights and responsibilities prior to beginning student teaching.
- Depending on state statutes, a student teacher may substitute under certain conditions for a cooperating teacher.

What Are Your Legal Responsibilities as a Teacher?

- Teachers are responsible for meeting the terms of their teaching contracts, including providing for their students' safety and well-being.
- Three legal responsibilities that concern teachers are avoiding tort liability (specifically, negligence and educational malpractice), recognizing the physical and behavioral indicators of child abuse and then reporting suspected instances of such abuse, and observing copyright laws as they apply to photocopies, videotapes, computer software, and materials published on the Internet.

What Are the Legal Rights of Students and Parents?

- Students' rights related to freedom of expression, suspension and expulsion, search and seizure, privacy, and nondiscrimination are based on several landmark legal decisions.
- Generally, students' freedom of expression can be limited if it is disruptive of the educational process or incongruent with the school's mission.
- Students can be neither suspended nor expelled without due process.
- Courts have developed a two-pronged test for search and seizure actions involving students: (1) School officials must have "reasonable" suspicion that a student has violated a law or school policy, and (2) the search must be done using methods that are reasonable and appropriate, given the nature of the infraction.
- Under the Buckley Amendment, students have the right to examine their school records, and schools may not give out information on students without their prior written consent.
- Schools may not discriminate against students on the basis of race, sex, religion, disability, marital status, or infection with a noncommunicable disease such as HIV/AIDS.

What Are Some Issues in the Legal Rights of School Districts?

- In spite of its proven ineffectiveness, corporal punishment has been upheld by the Supreme Court; however, almost half of the states and many school districts ban it, and many others restrict its use.
- About four out of five teenagers are affected by sexual harassment. According to a landmark Supreme Court decision in 1999, school officials can be held responsible if they fail to act on reports of sexual harassment of students by their peers. Schools can also be held responsible for the sexual harassment of students by professional staff, according to a 1992 Supreme Court decision.
- Courts have ruled that school officials can be held responsible if they fail to take steps to protect gay and lesbian students from antigay harassment.
- The First Amendment principle of separation of church and state has been applied to numerous court cases involving religious expression in the public schools. Court rulings banning school prayer, Bible reading, and other religious activities are often based on the three-part test developed in *Lemon v. Kurtzman* (1971). The courts have ruled consistently against parents who demand curricula and learning activities that are compatible with their religious beliefs.
- Home schooling is legal in all states, though most require home-schoolers to demonstrate that their instruction is "equivalent" to that in public schools.

Key Terms and Concepts

academic freedom, **201**
Buckley Amendment, **221**
censorship, **213**
code of ethics, **195**
collective bargaining, **200**
copyright laws, **210**
corporal punishment, **224**
dismissal, **199**
due process, **196**
educational malpractice, **207**
ethical dilemmas, **195**
fair use, **210**
freedom of expression, **213**
grievance, **200**
Lemon test, **228**
negligence, **207**
nondiscrimination, **197**
search and seizure, **217**
sexual harassment, **225**
teaching contract, **198**
tenure, **198**
tort liability, **205**

Applications and Activities

Teacher's Journal

1. Record in your journal examples of situations you observed or experienced in which you feel a teacher may have violated ethical principles. Include one example pertaining to a teacher's commitment to students and one example pertaining to a teacher's commitment to the profession. Conclude your analysis of these cases with a personal statement about your goals for ethical conduct as a teacher.
2. What limits do you believe should be placed on *what* teachers teach? On *how* they teach? Which of the legal cases on academic freedom discussed in this chapter support your views?
3. A California school district suspended a fourteen-year-old student for writing two essays with violent content for an English assignment. In one essay titled "Goin' Postal," a boy goes to school with a gun and shoots the principal seven times (Walsh 1999c). How should teachers respond to student work—essays, creative writing, videos, and so forth—that has violent content?
4. What is your position regarding corporal punishment? Are there circumstances under which its use is justified?
5. Review the section on the legal rights of students (pp. 212–224). Can you recall a time when you believe your rights as a student (or the rights of a classmate) were denied? Describe those events. What court cases and parts of the U.S. Constitution would apply to the events you describe?

Teacher's Database

1. Conduct an Internet search on one or more of the topics listed below or on another topic from Chapter 6. Narrow your search to issues and information relating to school law and the legal rights and responsibilities of school districts and schools, teachers and administrators, and students and parents. Include a search of news sources, such as *Education Week* on the Web, for summaries of recent court rulings pertaining to education and school law. The texts of many policies, laws, and U.S. Supreme Court decisions are also available online. You may wish to select a particular court case from Chapter 6 to investigate.

   Topics on legal issues to search from Chapter 6:

   academic freedom
   censorship
   collective bargaining
   copyright law
   corporal punishment
   creation science
   dress codes
   due process
   expulsion
   free speech
   gay and lesbian rights
   home schooling
   nondiscrimination
   privacy
   professional ethics
   school prayer
   school uniforms
   search and seizure
   sexual harassment
   suspension
   teacher dismissal
   teacher tenure

2. Using an index system or a keyword search engine, locate and visit the websites of three or more of the following educational journals and publications. At each site, download or record information related to one or more of the education law issues discussed in Chapter 6.

   American Educator
   American School Board Journal
   Childhood Education
   Educational Leadership
   Elementary School Journal

High School Journal

Instructor

Kappa Delta Phi Record

Phi Delta Kappan

PTA Today

Teacher Magazine

Young Children

Observations and Interviews

1. Interview several students at a middle school or high school to get their views regarding the legal rights of students. You may wish to develop a questionnaire that explores students' opinions in depth on a particular issue, such as freedom of expression or religion in the schools. Or you might get students' reactions to one of the legal cases summarized in this chapter. Present the results of your interview or survey to your classmates.
2. During an observation of a teacher's day, identify an ethical dilemma that the teacher confronts. Describe the dilemma and the teacher's response in a journal entry. To help you with this activity, ask your instructor for handout masters M6.1, "Identifying Ethical Dilemmas in Teaching," and M6.2, "Analyzing Teachers' Responses to Ethical Dilemmas."
3. Interview a school superintendent or principal to find out about any instances of actual or threatened litigation that occurred in the district during the last year or so. Ask him or her to identify procedures the district has in place to ensure due process for teachers and students. Report your findings.

Professional Portfolio

Survey a group of students, teachers, and/or parents regarding a legal issue in education. Among the legal issues and questions you might address are the following:

- Should tenure for teachers be abolished? Does tenure improve the quality of education students receive?
- Under what circumstances should restrictions be placed on what teachers teach and how they teach?
- Should parents be allowed to provide home schooling for their children?
- Are parents justified in filing educational malpractice suits if their children fail to achieve in school?
- Under what circumstances should restrictions be placed on students' freedom of expression?
- Should schools have the right to implement dress codes? Guidelines for students' hairstyles? School uniforms?
- Should corporal punishment be banned? If not, under what circumstances should it be used?
- How should schools combat the problem of sexual harassment?
- To combat drug abuse, should schools implement mandatory drug testing of students? Of teachers?
- Should students have access to their educational records? Should their parents or guardians?
- As part of an HIV/AIDS prevention program, should condoms be distributed to high school students? Should parental approval be required for participation?

The report summarizing the results of your survey should include demographic information such as the following for your sample of respondents: gender, age, whether they have children in school, level of education, and so on. When you analyze the results, look for differences related to these variables.

Video**Workshop Extra!**

If the VideoWorkshop package was included with your textbook, go to Chapter 6 of the Companion Website (www.ablongman.com/parkay6e) and click on the VideoWorkshop button. Follow the instructions for viewing videoclip 6 and completing this exercise. Consider this information along with what you've read in Chapter 6 while answering the following questions.

1. The text states that a professional code of ethics guides teachers' actions and affects their relationships with students. Videoclip 6 presents the issue of student self-esteem, specifically in terms of non-English-speaking students. What steps could a teacher take to ensure that non-English-speaking students feel valued and respected in a classroom that is part of a predominantly English-speaking school?
2. The legal rights of students and parents affect children's educational experiences. Which rights discussed in the text have the most potential to foster a student's sense of self-efficacy?

Reflections on Education

Countering Our "Socially Toxic Environment"

by Alice Watkins

In late summer 2002, the *Los Angeles Times* carried a heartbreaking photograph of a young boy standing amid litter and squalor of what appeared to be a filthy room. With him was a uniformed Los Angeles policewoman assigned to escort him to a county shelter for protective custody. The child's mother had been arrested for drug violations, and he was living with adult addicts.

That innocent victim of drug abuse and physical and emotional neglect would spend his weekend in a county shelter. However, on Monday, with the start of a new school year, he likely would find himself in a classroom with a new teacher. No grief counselor would wait to help him mourn the loss of his mother. He likely would not find himself surrounded by friends, neighbors, or professionals who could help him understand his loss of childhood, family, and security.

A generally held belief is that every child has the right to grow and develop in an environment made safe and protected by healthy, loving, and nurturing adults committed to the development of the child. Unfortunately, in the twenty-first-century United States thousands of children are innocent victims of poverty, hunger, physical abuse, and sexual abuse. For many of those children, including the young boy in the *Los Angeles Times* story, perhaps the only constant variable in their environments is the classroom teachers they encounter in school.

In a 1989 interview, Marian Wright Edelman challenged the United States to address the problem of children in poverty and expressed alarm that people were not upset:

> "The work force of the year 2000 is our preschoolers today. . . . [O]ne in seven is going to drop out of school. This is a recipe for national catastrophe.
>
> We lose about ten thousand children every year to poverty. That's [*a higher number*] over a five-year period than we lost in the Vietnam War. But where is the outrage?" (Lanker, 1989, p. 121).

Sadly, her message still applies today, a decade and a half later.

What has happened to one of the world's greatest superpowers? When did the United States lose its will to protect and guard the well-being of our children? President George W. Bush has challenged the nation to "leave no child behind." For educators, this is a powerful mandate that should "drive" the design of the classroom curriculum, influence the selection of leadership personnel, and dramatically reform public education nationwide.

If we truly accept the president's challenge, we must begin by ensuring that every child has access to an educational environment that is physically safe, and psychologically and intellectually challenging. We must offer all children a place where they can grow and mature into healthy school achievers. This can happen if every classroom is staffed by a teacher who is:

- Intellectually bright, well educated, and well prepared
- Expert in the content areas offered
- Knowledgeable of the critical stages of developmental growth of children and youth
- Aware of the latest research on how children learn, effective methods of stimulating learning, and intellectual achievement

Becoming a teacher is a dream shared by talented young men and women across our nation. They carry with them a passion for impacting, in a significant way, the lives of the children and youth whom they will meet in the classroom. Unfortunately, one of the grim realities that they confront immediately is the recognition of the frightening challenges that confront many children growing up in the United States. As millions of children struggle to succeed academically in U.S. schools, countless millions of them must also overcome the challenges of dealing with physical and sexual abuse, homelessness, dysfunctional families, poverty, and violence in their homes, communities, and schools.

Consequently, beginning teachers must understand and accept the need to motivate students and capture their minds and hearts even when these students face incredible obstacles to school achievement. Understanding the condition of "childhood" in too many U.S. communities is a harsh reality for beginning teachers in public schools.

Fortunately, resources are available to support beginning teachers as they prepare to meet the needs of children and youth who confront the social problems of the twenty-first-century United States. James Garbarino (1995) in *Raising Children in a Socially Toxic Environment* provides a comprehensive list of specific resources, agencies, and suggestions that professionals and parents can use to assist and protect children and youth in our society. His book provides an outstanding summary of the challenges facing children and teacher in the United States today. It is recommended reading for every beginning teacher.

In summary, beginning teachers must understand the external variables that affect the students in their classrooms. Further, they must prepare themselves to provide the best care and quality of instruction to assist all of their students. The social challenges facing U.S. children and youth have profound implications for classroom teachers. As young men and women contemplate "becoming a teacher," they must seek to understand the communities, families, and children that they will serve.

Alice V. Watkins, Ph.D. is the Associate Dean Emeritus at California State University—Los Angeles and Dean Emeritus at Azusa Pacific University. She has enjoyed a distinguished career in teacher education that spans 33 years.

References

Garbarino, J. (1995). *Raising children in a socially toxic environment.* San Francisco: Jossey-Bass.

Lanker, B. (1989). *I dream a world.* New York: Stewart, Tabori, & Chang, Inc.

part 3

The Art of Teaching

Dear Mentor

Teaching to Today's Changing Demographic

Dear Mentor,

I am currently enrolled in a student teaching program. I will be teaching business and computer applications to high school students. The school in which I have been placed has the following demographics: 45 percent Hispanic, 25 percent African American, 20 percent Caucasian, 5 percent Asian, and 5 percent Pacific Islander.

I see this assignment as a dream come true. I want to create a learning environment that enables students with different learning styles and non-English-speaking students to thrive academically. However, I do have some concerns. First, how do I reach non-English-speaking students in a computer lab? Second, how do I communicate with non-English-speaking parents? Finally, how do I reward at-risk students when their peers view academic success negatively?

Regards,
W. Mark Hasson

Dear Mark,

Congratulations on your upcoming business and computer class assignment. I have been teaching for more than thirteen years and presently teach high school students. I found your questions to represent common concerns for an incoming teacher.

In response to your first question, a computer lab involves a lot of hands-on application, in that the students first observe and then perform the activity. In providing directions to your classes, make sure your instructions are given slowly, clearly, and precisely, and avoid using idioms. Another successful tool for non-English-speaking students is the buddy system, where you take a student whose comprehension of the English language is stronger and pair him or her with a student whose English language skills are weaker. Finally, place a lot of printed computer visuals throughout your computer lab.

In answer to how best to communicate with non-English-speaking parents, develop a bilingual student progress form that has both positive and negative comments and statements that you want to convey to the parents about their son's or daughter's behavior or progress in your class. Parents appreciate such additional informational updates from teachers, especially between grading periods. Student progress forms allow parents to work with their sons or daughters in rectifying a problem before the next grading period. Positive comments inform the parents and students that they are doing things correctly and motivate them to remain on task. Also, the bilingual coordinator at your school site is a great resource in helping you to communicate verbally with your non-English-speaking parents.

Finally, how do you motivate and reward at-risk students when their peers view academic success negatively? Students, teachers, and adults all enjoy some form of recognition and praise. Although there are students who are intrinsically motivated, the majority are extrinsically motivated. One way of rewarding at-risk students is to have an open discussion with your students and to solicit their input about implementing a reward system within their computer class. In this way, you find out what might motivate them. You also could send your students e-mailed messages of praise, encouragement, and positive feedback if they have their own personal computers and passwords. Personal e-mails are great student motivators because they are private, interpersonal communications between only teacher and student. Good luck!

Sincerely,
Alonia P. Alexander
Westchester High School
Westchester, CA

7 Teaching Diverse Learners

The highest result of education is tolerance.

—Helen Keller

Today I strolled into Sojourner Truth High School with a bit of concern. I had been student teaching for the spring semester at the same high school I had attended myself as a teenager and was really enjoying the experience, looking forward to it every day. Since February, I have been responsible for teaching five freshman world history classes to a group of inner-city students. The classes are made up of mostly African Americans like myself as well as a small percentage of Caribbean, Hispanic, Asian, and Polish American students. I care for these students and am committed to making a difference in their lives.

Ms. Callaway, my cooperating teacher, puts a lot of faith and trust in my approach to teaching. She told me that the students sorely need African American males in positions of authority who can relate to their problems. She stressed that the students look up to me and enjoy my innovative lessons.

I know that I have in fact reached some of the students, and I am proud of my teaching successes. The students seem to be really learning by relating history to their everyday lives. I have spent many long hours trying to make history come alive for them. I want the students to see history as *theirs,* and I believe that I am meeting with much success, at least on the academic front.

But my zeal and eagerness are nevertheless starting to wear down. My growing lack of enthusiasm, I have realized, is due to the daily blatant disregard and disrespect that students have for themselves and others.

I find it difficult to teach a lesson without constantly reminding my class, "Watch your mouth!" "Take your hat off, please," and "Please be respectful of other folks' differences." All day long, in and out of class, I directly and indirectly hear conversations heavily laced with profanity, disrespect, and insults. I know that this kind of talk will not help my students advance themselves in the outside world. I know that for them to succeed, I need to help them gain self-esteem and to project a better image to others.

At first, I thought that maybe if I set a good example each and every day by using proper speech, not wearing my hat in the building, and respecting my peers and all of the students, I could help. After all, I had graduated from this same school and could serve as a role model of someone who had gone to college and gained a profession. But without fail, there was little improvement.

My failure to reach my students has caused me many sleepless nights. I worry that knowledge and love for history is not enough. So much is stacked against my students that they need every edge they can get. I remember Ms. Jefferson, a teacher at this very school, now retired, who inspired me to make profound changes in my own life. I want to do for my students what Ms. Jefferson did for me, but I feel that I am reaching a dead end.

One day, out of frustration, I simply asked the students, "Why do you think that it is so necessary to use profanity in the classroom?"

I listened to their answers: "It's a habit!" "It's the way I express myself!" "I can't help it!" "I don't know; it's the way I talk!"

So I went on to ask, "Why do guys wear their hats in the building?" They pretty much all agreed that it was done "to be cool" and as a "habit."

"But how," I responded, "are you guys going to go to college if you are trying so hard to be cool all the time and can't control your mouths or your dress?'"

They said they liked the way they talked and dressed and didn't need college.

Then I asked, "Well, why do you think that it's a must to insult or hurt someone's feelings?"

Everyone agreed that it was done because "it's fun."

"But what happens when someone's feelings are really hurt or the insults get out of hand?" I persisted.

"Well, I guess I got to kick his #@@###*!" was the only response.

Deep down inside, I know there must be some hope for these kids, but I do not know where to begin or what else to do. I feel helpless (Curtis Parker quoted in Rand and Shelton-Colangelo, 1999, 87–88).

Focus Questions

1. **How is diversity embedded in the culture of the United States?**
2. **What does equal educational opportunity mean?**
3. **What is meant by bilingual education?**
4. **What is multicultural education?**
5. **How is gender a dimension of multicultural education?**

Expand your knowledge of the concepts discussed in this chapter by reading current and historical articles from the *New York Times* by visiting the **"Themes of the Times"** section of the Companion Website (**www.ablongman.com/parkay6e**).

The above reflections by Curtis Parker on his student teaching experience highlight how important it is for teachers to be able to communicate with students from diverse cultural backgrounds. Although Curtis is momentarily discouraged by his inability to get his students to stop using profanity and to improve their behavior, he may actually be influencing his students more than he realizes. It is possible, for example, that some of Curtis's students really do understand the important lesson in life he is trying to teach them; however, their strong need not to risk disapproval of their peers prevents them from changing their behavior at this time. At the very least, Curtis's students know that he cares genuinely about their education, that he wants to learn about their lives, and, though he disapproves of some of their behavior, he does not disapprove of them. Finally, as Curtis notes, his students are "relating history to their everyday lives" and he is "meeting with much success"—two solid indicators that he is building positive relationships with his students and will continue to become an increasingly influential role model in their lives.

This chapter looks at cultural diversity in the United States and the challenges of equalizing educational opportunity for all students. Professional teachers, such as Curtis is well on his way toward becoming, see cultural diversity as an asset to be preserved and valued, not a liability. The United States has always derived strength from the **diversity** of its people, and *all* students should receive a high-quality education so that they may make their unique contributions to society.

How Is Diversity Embedded in the Culture of the United States?

The percentage of ethnic minorities in the United States has been growing steadily since the end of World War II. As Figure 7.1 shows, 28.4 million foreign-born people lived in the United States in 2000. The Census Bureau estimates that there is a net increase of one international migrant every thirty seconds. Twenty percent of U.S. senators are grandchildren of immigrants, a claim that can be made by no other nation in the world about its leading legislative body (Wirt and Kirst 1997). In addition, the Census Bureau estimates that

- By 2010, blacks and Hispanics will equal the number of whites.
- By 2025, half of U.S. youth will be white and half "minority."
- By 2050, no one group will be a majority among adults.

In 2000, 39 percent of public school students were considered to be part of a minority group, an increase of 17 percentage points from 1972. This increase was largely due to the growth in the proportion of Hispanic students. In 2000, Hispanic students accounted for 17 percent of the public school enrollment, up by 11 percentage points from 1972. African Americans were 17 percent of the public school enrollment in 2000, up by 2 percentage points from 1972. The percentage of students from other racial and ethnic minority groups also increased,

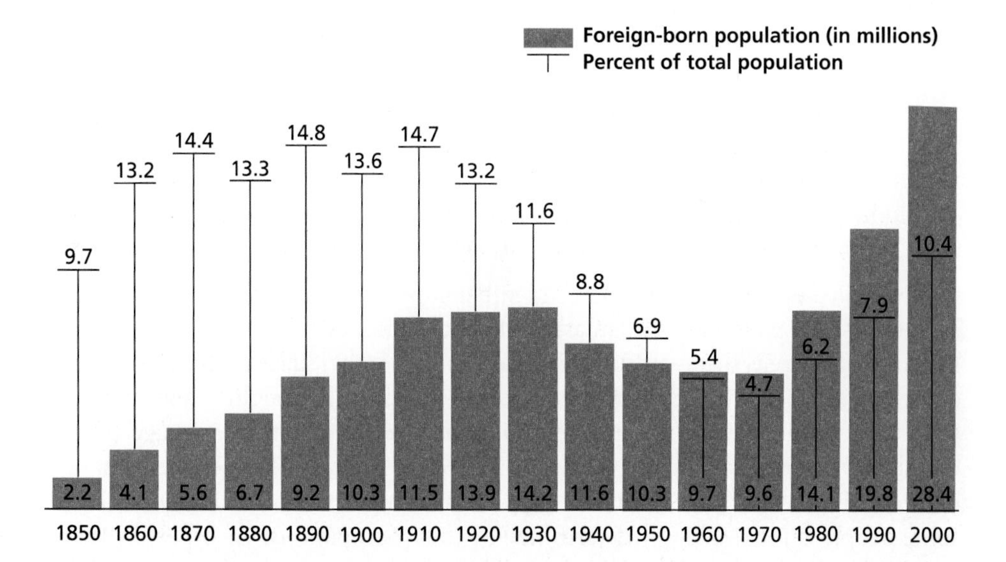

Figure 7.1 Foreign-born population and percent of total population for the United States: 1850–2000.
Source: U.S. Census Bureau (2001), "Profile of the Foreign-born Population in the United States: 2000. Washington, D.C.: U.S. Census Bureau, p. 9.

from 1 percent in 1972 to 5 percent in 2000 (National Center for Education Statistics 2002).

Changes in the racial and ethnic composition of student enrollments are expanding the array of languages and cultures found in the nation's public schools. Though differences in student backgrounds offer opportunities to enhance the learning environment, these differences also raise challenges for schools. There is, for example, an increased demand for bilingual programs and teachers. All but a few school districts face a critical shortage of minority teachers. And, there is a need to develop curricula and strategies that address the needs and backgrounds of all students—regardless of their social class, gender, sexual orientation, or ethnic, racial, or cultural identity.

The Meaning of Culture

As we suggested in Chapter 4, one mission of schools is to maintain the culture of the United States. But what is the U.S. culture? Is there a single culture to which everyone in the country belongs? Before we can answer that question we must define the term *culture.* Simply put, **culture** is *the way of life* common to a group of people. It consists of the values, attitudes, and beliefs that influence their traditions and behavior. It is also a way of interacting with and looking at the world. Though at one time it was believed that the United States was a "melting pot" in which ethnic cultures would melt into one, ethnic and cultural differences have remained very much a part of life in the United States. A "salad-bowl" analogy captures more accurately the **cultural pluralism** of U.S. society. That is, the distinguishing characteristics of cultures are to be preserved rather than blended into a single culture.

Dimensions of Culture Within our nation's boundaries, we find cultural groups that differ according to other distinguishing factors, such as religion, politics, economics, and geographic region. The regional culture of New England, for example, is quite different from that of the Southeast. Similarly, Californians are culturally different from Iowans.

However, everyone in the United States does share some common dimensions of culture. James Banks, an authority on multicultural education, has termed this shared culture the "national macroculture" (2002). In addition to being members of the national macroculture, people in the United States are members of ethnic groups. An **ethnic group** is made up of individuals within a larger culture who share a self-defined racial or cultural identity and a set of beliefs, attitudes, and values. Members of an ethnic group distinguish themselves from others in the society by physical and social attributes. In addition, you should be aware that the composition of ethnic groups can change over time, and that there is often as much variability within groups as between them.

Cultural Identity In addition to membership in the national macroculture, each individual participates in an array of subcultures, each with its customs and beliefs. Collectively, these subcultures determine an individual's **cultural identity,** an overall sense of who one is. Other possible elements that might shape a person's cultural identity include age, racial identity, exceptionalities, language, gender, sexual orientation, income level, and beliefs and values. These elements have different significances for different people. For example, the cultural identity of some people is most strongly determined by their occupations; for others by their ethnicity; and for others by their religious beliefs.

Remember that your future students will have their own complex cultural identities, which are no less valid for being different. For some of them, these identities may make them feel "disconnected" from the attitudes, expectations, and values conveyed by the school. For example,

> *Students who come from homes where languages other than English are the medium of communication, who share customs and beliefs unique to their cultural community and/or home countries, or who face the range of challenges posed by economic insecurity will not often find much of their family, community, or national existence reflected in the school setting. Often these students feel that school is itself foreign, alienating, and unrelated to their beliefs and concerns (Rice and Walsh 1996, 9).*

As a teacher, you will be challenged to understand the subtle differences in cultural identities among your students and to create a learning environment that enables all students to feel comfortable in school and "connected to" their school experiences.

Language and Culture Culture is embedded in language, a fact that has resulted in conflict among different groups in our society. Some groups, although they support the preservation of ethnic cultures, believe that members of non-English-speaking groups must learn English if they are to function in U.S. society. There is also conflict between those who wish to preserve linguistic diversity and those who wish to establish English as a national language.

Much of the debate has focused on **bilingual education,** that is, using two languages as the medium of instruction. Bilingual education is designed to help students maintain their ethnic identity and become proficient in both English and the language of the home, to encourage assimilation into the mainstream culture and integrate the home language and culture with a new one. Some people are staunchly opposed to any form of bilingual education, and others support it as a short-term way to teach English to students.

Students in today's classrooms have diverse cultural identities. As a teacher, what steps will you take to integrate *all* students into the classroom?

Language diversity is an important dimension of U.S. cultural diversity regardless. Many students come from homes where English is not spoken. The National Clearinghouse for English Language Acquisition reported that there were about 4.4 million **limited English proficient (LEP)** students—those with limited ability to understand, read, or speak English and who have a first language other than English—in public schools in 1999–2000, or about 9.3 percent of the total enrollment (National Clearinghouse for English Language Acquisition 2002). This number represents a 27.3 percent increase over the reported 1997–98 public school LEP enrollment. Among the states, California enrolled the largest number of public school LEP students, with 1.48 million, followed by Texas (0.55 million), Florida (0.24 million), New York (0.23 million), Illinois (0.14 million), and Arizona (0.13 million). In 1999–2000, states reported over four hundred languages spoken by LEP students nationwide, with 76 percent claiming Spanish as their native language. For the 1998–99 school year, thirty-six urban school districts enrolled ten thousand or more students identified as LEP (see Table 7.1).

Students differ among themselves not only regarding the first language spoken in the home, but also in the *language patterns* they acquire from the culture within which they are raised. Researchers have found that children from working-class backgrounds tend to develop "restricted" language patterns with their use of English, while children from middle-class backgrounds tend to develop more "elaborated" language patterns (Bernstein 1996; Heath 1983). In many cases, children encounter a mismatch between the language patterns used in the home and those they are expected to use in school, and this mismatch can be "a serious stumbling block for working-class and nonwhite pupils" (MacLeod 1995, 18).

Students' language patterns became a topic of national debate in late 1996 when the Oakland, California, school district passed a resolution on "ebonics" (a blend of the words *ebony* and *phonics*), also known as "black English." The resolution, which recognized ebonics as the "primary language" of many of the district's 28,000 African American students, called for them to be taught in their primary language and suggested that some students might be eligible for state and federal bilingual education or ESL money. Critics of the resolution pointed out that "black English" is a nonstandard form of English or a dialect of English and not a foreign language. Other critics were concerned that students and teachers would be taught ebonics. In the midst of intense national debate, the district revised the resolution so that it no longer called for students to be taught in their "primary language"; instead, the district would implement new programs to move students from the language patterns they bring to school toward proficiency in standard English. Other dialects of English and their use in the classroom have been debated from time to time—for example, "Chicano English," "Cajun English," or Hawaiian Creole English (more popularly known as "pidgin English").

The Concept of Multiculturalism **Multiculturalism** is a set of beliefs based on the importance of seeing the world from different cultural frames of reference and on recognizing and valuing the rich array of cultures within a nation and within the global community. For teachers, multiculturalism affirms the need to create schools where differences related to race, ethnicity, gender, disability, and social class are acknowledged and all students are viewed as valuable members and as human resources for enriching the teaching–learning process. Furthermore, a central purpose of teaching, according to the multiculturalist view, is to prepare

Table 7.1 Which urban school districts in the U.S. have high LEP enrollments?

Rank	District	No. LEPs	Total Enrollment	% LEP
1	Los Angeles, CA[1]	310,955	688,574	45.2%
2	New York City, NY[1]	148,399	972,606	15.3%
3	Chicago, IL[1]	62,865	430,841	15.0%
4	Dallas, TX[1]	52,290	159,908	32.7%
5	Houston, TX[1]	49,345	191,765	25.7%
6	Miami-Dade, FL[1]	46,365	352,595	13.1%
7	Santa Ana, CA[2]	39,133	56,071	69.8%
8	San Diego, CA[1]	38,484	138,433	27.8%
9	Long Beach, CA[1]	31,225	89,214	35.0%
10	Clark County, NV[1]	26,896	203,579	13.0%
11	Fresno, CA[1]	25,473	78,258	32.6%
12	Garden Grove, CA[2]	22,972	46,916	49.0%
13	Broward County, FL[1]	20,091	225,619	8.9%
14	San Francisco, CA[1]	19,370	63,823	30.3%
15	Palm Beach, FL[2]	19,055	162,029	11.8%
16	Fort Worth, TX[1]	18,652	70,627	26.4%
17	Oakland, CA[1]	17,742	54,256	32.7%
18	Montebello, CA[2]	16,647	33,999	49.0%
19	Hillsborough, FL[1]	16,162	156,908	10.3%
20	Pomona, CA[2]	15,461	32,819	47.1%
21	El Paso, TX[2]	15,106	62,945	24.0%
22	Sacramento City, CA[1]	15,054	51,378	29.3%
23	Fairfax County, VA[2]	14,809	149,029	9.9%
24	St. Paul, MN[1]	14,783	45,325	32.6%
25	Denver, CO[3]	14,385	68,790	20.9%
26	Compton, CA[2]	13,175	29,409	44.8%
27	Glendale, CA[2]	12,790	30,312	42.2%
28	Ontario-Montclair, CA[2]	12,531	25,151	49.8%
29	Tucson, AZ[2]	12,345	66,234	18.6%
30	Anaheim, CA[2]	12,183	20,927	58.2%
31	San Bernardino, CA[2]	11,283	48,907	3.1%
32	Philadelphia, PA[2]	10,710	207,333	5.2%
33	Orange County, FL[1]	10,554	138,866	7.6%
34	Stockton City, CA[2]	10,401	36,124	28.8%
35	Salt Lake City, UT[1]	10,034	61,498	16.3%
36	Fontana, CA[2]	10,023	34,339	29.2%

[1]Data obtained from the Council of Great City Schools (www.cgcs.org).
[2]Data obtained from State Education Agency.
[3]Data obtained from Local Education Agency.

Source: Barron, V. (2001). National Clearinghouse for English Language Acquisition, September 2001. Retrieved at http://www.ncela.gwu.edu/aslencela/02districts.htm

students to live in a culturally pluralistic world—a world that "contrasts sharply with cultural assimilation, or 'melting pot' images, where ethnic minorities are expected to give up their traditions and blend in or be absorbed by the mainstream society or predominant culture" (Bennett 2003, 14).

For teachers, multiculturalism also means actively seeking out experiences within other cultures that lead to increased understanding of and appreciation for those ways of life. To provide such cross-cultural experiences for their students, several teacher education programs have developed "cultural immersion" experiences that enable prospective teachers to live in their students' neighborhoods and communities while student teaching. The University of Alaska-Fairbanks Teachers for Alaska Program, for example, enables students to live in remote Alaskan Native villages during their year-long student teaching experience. In the Urban Education Program of the Associated Colleges of the Midwest, prospective teachers live in a former convent in a multiracial, economically diverse neighborhood in Chicago. There the students teach and participate in structured activities that take them into the city's other ethnic neighborhoods. Students at Indiana University can choose among three unique student teaching experiences: the Native American Reservation Project, the Overseas Project, and the Bilingual/Bicultural Project. Through student teaching on a reservation, in another country, or on the Rio Grande border, students have a life-altering cultural immersion experience. As a student who participated in the Native American Reservation Project and now teaches high school in Indianapolis put it: "Before we went to the reservation, people [came] back to IU who said that it would change your life. We thought, 'Oh yeah, sure.' But it really does. A day doesn't go by when I don't think of those students, of that place" (Indiana University 1999).

Ethnicity and Race

Your understanding of the distinction between ethnicity and race will enable you to provide students with educational experiences that reflect ethnic and racial diversity in meaningful ways. **Ethnicity** refers to a shared identity based on a "common national or geographic origin, religion, language, sense of peoplehood, common values, separate institutions, and minority or subordinate status" (Banks 2001, 84).

On the other hand, **race** is a subjective concept that is used to distinguish among human beings on the basis of biological traits and characteristics. Numerous racial categories have been proposed, but because of the diversity among humans and the mixing of genes that has taken place over time, no single set of racial categories is universally accepted. Since many genetic factors are invisible to the naked eye (DNA, for example), noted anthropologist Ashley Montagu has suggested that there could be as few as three "races" (Negroid, Caucasoid, and Mongoloid) or as many as three hundred, depending on the kind and number of genetic features chosen for measurement. In his classic book, *Man's Most Dangerous Myth: The Fallacy of Race,* Montagu pointed out that

> *It is impossible to make the sort of racial classification which some anthropologists and others have attempted. The fact is that all human beings are so . . . mixed with regard to origin that between different groups of individuals . . . "overlapping" of physical traits is the rule (1974, 7).*

To reflect the realities of racial identities in the United States, the questionnaire for Census 2000 was changed so that people with a "mixed race" background could select "one or more races" for their racial identity. In addition, the

"Spanish/Hispanic/Latino" category allowed respondents to choose among the following: Mexican, Mexican American, and Chicano; Puerto Rican; Cuban; and "other" Spanish/Hispanic/Latino. Similarly, respondents who self-identified as "Asian or Pacific Islander" had the following choices: Asian Indian, Chinese, Filipino, Japanese, Korean, Vietnamese, "other" Asian, Native Hawaiian, Guamanian or Chamorro, Samoan, and "other" Pacific Islander.

There are many ethnic groups in U.S. society, and everyone belongs to at least one. However, as James Banks points out:

> *An individual is ethnic to the extent that he or she shares the values, behavioral patterns, cultural traits, and identification with a specific ethnic group. Many individuals have multiple ethnic attachments; others consider themselves "American" rather than ethnic.*
>
> *An individual's identity with his or her ethnic group varies significantly with the times in his or her life, with economic and social status, and with the situations and/or settings (Banks 2003, 15).*

It is also clear that racial and ethnic identities in the United States are becoming more complex. We now know that "racial and ethnic identities derive their meanings from social and historical circumstances, that they can vary over time, and that they can sometimes even be slipped on and off like a change of clothing" (Coughlin 1993, A7). For example, a third-generation descendent of a Japanese immigrant may choose to refer to him- or herself as a Japanese American, an American, or an Asian American. Furthermore, it is evident that "specific racial categories acquire and lose meaning over time" (Coughlin 1993, A7), and the use of ethnic and racial labels and expressions of group membership is largely self-selected and arbitrary.

The Concept of Minorities

To understand the important concept of **minorities,** it may help to remember that even though the term *minority* technically refers to any *group* numbering less than half of the total population, in certain parts of the country "minorities" are actually the majority. However, more important than the numbers themselves is an appreciation of how many groups of people have continuously struggled to obtain full educational, economic, political, and social opportunities in society. Along with minority racial and ethnic groups, others who have traditionally lacked power in U.S. public life are immigrants, the poor, children and the elderly, non-English speakers, members of minority religions, and women. Groups that have been most frequently discriminated against in terms of the quality of education they have received include African Americans, Spanish-speaking Americans, Native Americans, Asian Americans, exceptional learners, people with disabilities, and females. There is mounting evidence that many students from these groups continue to receive a substandard education that does not meet their needs or help empower them to participate fully and equally in life in the United States.

Minority Groups and Academic Achievement Minority-group students are disproportionately represented among students who have failed to master minimum competencies in reading, writing, and mathematics. It has been estimated that ethnic minority students are two to four times more likely than others to drop out of high school. In addition, "in many schools across the nation, racial and language minority students are overrepresented in special education and experience disproportionately high rates of suspension and expulsion" (Bennett 2003, 18). Nevertheless, there has been a trend of "modest growth in achievement among students from minority groups and from 'less advantaged' backgrounds" (Berliner and Biddle 1995, 27).

When we consider the lower achievement levels of minority students, it is important to note the much higher incidence of poverty among minority families and the research showing that socioeconomic status—not race, language, or culture—contributes most strongly to students' achievement in school (Coleman et al. 1966; Jencks et al. 1972; Jencks and Phillips 1998; National Center for Education Statistics 1980). Understandably, it is difficult for poor children to learn well if they endure the stress of living in crime-ridden neighborhoods, dwelling in dilapidated homes, or going to school hungry.

Stereotyping and Racism

Although teachers should expand their knowledge of and appreciation for the diverse cultural backgrounds of their students, they should also guard against forming stereotypes or overgeneralizations about those cultures. **Stereotyping** is the process of attributing behavioral characteristics to all members of a group. In some cases, stereotypes are formed on the basis of limited experiences with and information about the group being stereotyped, and the validity of these stereotypes is not questioned.

Within any cultural group that shares a broad cultural heritage, however, considerable diversity exists. For example, two Puerto Rican children who live in the same community and attend the same school may appear alike to their teachers when, in reality, they are very different. One may come from a home where Spanish is spoken and Puerto Rican holidays are observed; the other child may know only a few words of Spanish and observe only the holidays of the majority culture.

In addition to being alert for stereotypes they and others may hold, teachers should learn to recognize **individual racism,** the prejudicial belief that one's ethnic or racial group is superior to others. They should also be able to recognize **institutional racism,** which occurs when institutions "behave in ways that are overtly racist (i.e., specifically excluding people-of-color from services) or inherently racist (i.e., adopting policies that while not specifically directed at excluding people-of-color, nevertheless result in their exclusion)" (Randall 2001).

In light of the arbitrariness of the concept of race, James A. Banks points out, "In most societies, *the social significance of race is much more important than the presumed physical differences among groups*" (2003, 72, italics in original). Unfortunately, many people attach great importance to the concept of race. If you believe "that human groups can be validly grouped on the basis of

Professional Reflection

Reflecting on Your Cultural Identity

In a Teacher's Journal entry, describe your cultural identity. Who are you? What beliefs, customs, and attitudes are part of your culture? Which of these are most important to your cultural identity?

Next, think of the ethnic and cultural groups in the United States with which you are unfamiliar. When you become a teacher, some of your students may be from these groups. What are some stereotypes about these groups that you tend to believe? How might these stereotypes influence your teaching and teaching effectiveness? How will you test or change your beliefs as part of the process of becoming a teacher?

their biological traits and that these identifiable groups inherit certain mental, personality, and cultural characteristics that determine their behavior" (Banks 2003, 73) then you hold racist beliefs. When people use such beliefs as a rationale for oppressing other groups, they are practicing racism. The activity "Can You Recognize Racism?" on this book's website presents a checklist for a small-group activity that can help you become more aware of individual and institutional racism.

As a teacher, you will not be able to eliminate stereotypic thinking or racism in society. However, you have an obligation to all your students to see that your curriculum and instruction are free of any forms of stereotyping or racism. The Professional Reflection will help you examine, and possibly reassess, your cultural attitudes and values and determine whether you have stereotypes about other cultural groups.

What Does Equal Educational Opportunity Mean?

To provide equal educational opportunity to all students means that teachers and schools promote the full development of students as individuals, without regard for race, ethnicity, gender, sexual orientation, socioeconomic status, abilities, or disabilities. More specifically, educators fulfill this important mission by continually evaluating the appropriateness of the curricular and instructional experiences they provide to each student.

In the following sections, we review the progress that has been made to provide students from diverse groups with equal educational opportunity, and we focus on strategies for teaching in diverse classrooms. The strategies we present for each group draw from research that suggests that particular learning styles *may be* associated with specific ethnic groups in U.S. society (Bennett 2003; Hale-Benson 1986; Shade 1982). These strategies should not lead you to assume, however, that *all* students from a certain group learn in a particular way. As Christine I. Bennett, an expert on multicultural education, points out:

> *The notion that certain learning styles are associated with different ethnic groups is both promising and dangerous. Promise lies in the realization that low academic achievement among some ethnic minorities may sometimes be attributed to conflicts between styles of teaching and learning, not low intelligence. This leads to the possibility that teachers will alter their own instructional styles to be more responsive to the learning needs of students. Danger lies in the possibility that new ethnic stereotypes will develop while old ones are reinforced, as in "Blacks learn aurally," "Asians excel in math," "Mexican American males can't learn from female peer tutors," and "Navajos won't ask a question or participate in a discussion" (2003, 67).*

We omit Anglo-European Americans from our review, not because students from this very diverse group always have had equal educational opportunities, but because this group represents the historically dominant culture. To a great extent, it has determined the curricular and instructional practices found in schools.

Like the groups we discuss, however, "Anglo-European American" is not a single, monolithic culture. Americans whose ethnic heritage is English, Polish, German, Italian, Irish, Czechoslovakian, Russian, or Swedish, for example, often differ greatly in religious and political traditions, beliefs, and values. Their individual ethnic identity may or may not be strengthened by recent immigrants from their country of origin. European ethnics have, nevertheless, assimilated into the mainstream U.S. society more completely than others.

Keepers of *the Dream*

Betsy McIntire, 2002 Teacher of the Year Finalist for Los Angeles County

Her youthful, ready-to-learn-more attitude belies the fact that Betsy McIntire has taught for thirty-three years, a tenure long enough to include two major transitions in U.S. education: racial integration of public schools and Public Law 94.142. In contrast to many of her colleagues, McIntire embraced both changes with enthusiasm from their inception.

McIntire experienced the heat of integration in Meridian, Mississippi, in 1967, her first year of teaching and the first year schools there were integrated. The process was slow. One African American child was assigned to McIntire's second-grade class of otherwise all white children. "He was the star of the class," she recalls, "which was wonderful." The school also hired one African American teacher to "integrate" the faculty. Arriving late to a faculty meeting, McIntire sat down next to the young African American woman at an otherwise empty table in the corner of the room, drawing stares from her fellow faculty. The African American teacher stared at her, too. Both reactions startled her. Exclusion never occurred to McIntire.

"... shares with parents her love for their children and a desire to help them."

That same attitude served McIntire well in 1975 when Public Law 94.142 was passed while she was teaching in Alabama. The law sought to assure that "all handicapped children have available to them, a free appropriate public education." It opened classrooms to thousands of students who previously were either underserved or not served at all by our public education system. McIntire recalls the changes small communities like hers had to make to develop a program for children with special needs and to provide a setting that was accessible to them.

Over the years, as the faces of her classroom have changed, McIntire has continued to embrace that change and promote inclusion of all forms. Reflecting the trend throughout much of the nation, she now works with children from Mexico, Taiwan, China, and India. The K–5 children in her school represent twelve language groups, and over half of the children McIntire works with in her special education classes are English language learners.

One of McIntire's biggest challenges has been communicating with parents. How can monolingual teachers communicate with parents who don't speak English? McIntire uses the school's home-school coordinator to make phone calls, translate her letters to students' home, and assist in parent-teacher conferences. Other parents who are bilingual, older brothers and sisters, and fellow teachers who speak the needed language are additional sources of help.

Communicating with the parents of children with special needs presents a different challenge. "These parents come in with many different ideas on what they want for their children. For some parents the discovery that their child has a learning disability is almost a relief. They are grateful to have an explanation for something they had sensed," McIntire explains. A few others, however, are in denial and angry over their child's placement in a special education classroom. They often insist on getting a second opinion, and McIntire always encourages them to do so. In some cases, parents have the same problems as their son or daughter. Past negative schooling experiences cause them to regard school with distrust. "They don't see school as an inviting place," McIntire observes.

Breaking through that mistrust is critical. For IEP (Individual Educational Plan) meetings, McIntire tries to have the child who is the focus of the meeting attend it as well. She explains, "When children sit in they see that I respect their parents and that makes them feel better about the situation." In addition, McIntire works hard to create a sense of community among all the parents of her students. She invites families in to celebrate holidays with the class, asks them to bring in artifacts or food, and frequently has "tasting parties" with ethnic foods. She also draws parents in to see their children perform in a readers' theater and lets students take classroom books home to read to their parents and siblings. Each effort reduces the barriers that separate school and home.

Most of all, McIntire shares with parents her love for their children and a desire to help them. In the past, she was openly, even angrily, protective of her students when other students made fun of them. However, in recent years she has approached the problem proactively. With her students' permission, she visits other classes to show videos about various learning and physical disabilities. She also teaches her students how to respond effectively when others taunt them. Taking a tip from Bill Cosby, she tells students to say "So?" when they are called names and to repeat "So?" each time something derogatory is said to them. Through role playing and practice, her students learn to turn taunts into humor or to simply ignore them.

In 2002, McIntire was selected as the outstanding teacher of the year in her school, then in her school district, and finally as one of the finalists for all of Los Angeles County. Her caring spirit and desire to continue to learn ways to better serve her students are hallmarks for her. The quote on her classroom wall aptly conveys her regard for all students: "You will learn here, you will grow here, you will amaze yourself here."

Education and African Americans

Of the more than 287 million persons living in the United States, approximately 13 percent are African Americans. According to U.S. Census Bureau projections, the African American population in the United States is expected to increase from 36 million (13 percent of the total population) in 2001 to 45 million (14 percent of the total) in 2020, and then to 55 million (15 percent of the total) in 2040. The incidence of social problems such as unemployment, crime, drug abuse, poverty, inadequate housing, and school dropouts is proportionally greater for African Americans than for whites. The struggle of African Americans to improve their quality of life after the end of slavery has been hampered for generations by persistent racism, discrimination, poverty, crime, unemployment, and underemployment.

The civil rights movement of the 1960s and 1970s made it clear that African Americans had been denied full access to many aspects of U.S. life, including the right to a good education. A 1976 report by the United States Commission on Civil Rights, for example, revealed that a Southern school district in the 1930s spent nearly eighteen times as much for the education of white pupils as it did for the education of African Americans.

The Desegregation Era Perhaps the most blatant form of discrimination against African Americans has been school segregation and unequal educational opportunity. As you learned in Chapter 3, the attempt was made to justify segregation by the idea of separate-but-equal schools. It was not until the National Association for the Advancement of Colored People (NAACP) brought suit on behalf of a Kansas family (*Brown v. Board of Education of Topeka, Kansas*) in 1954 that the concept of separate-but-equal schools was decidedly struck down.

The parents of Linda Brown felt that the education their fourth-grader was receiving in the segregated Topeka schools was inferior. When their request that she be transferred to a white school was turned down, they filed suit. In a landmark decision, the U.S. Supreme Court ruled that segregated schools are "inher-

What is the legacy of school desegregation today? What are some outcomes of education research and curriculum reform related to the African American experience?

ently unequal" and violate the equal protection clause of the Fourteenth Amendment. U.S. citizens, the justices asserted, have a right to receive an equal opportunity for education.

As a result of opportunities created during the civil rights movement, a substantial number of African Americans are now members of the middle class. Affirmative action programs have enabled many African Americans to attain high-ranking positions in the business, medical, legal, and educational professions. Such gains lead James Banks to point out that

> *[A]ny accurate and sophisticated description of the status of African Americans on the threshold of the twenty-first century must describe not only the large percentage of Blacks who are members of the so-called underclass, but also the smaller and significant percentage of African Americans who have entered the middle and upper classes and who function in the mainstream society. Many of the children of the new middle class are not only unacquainted with poverty, but also have been socialized in mainstream middle- and upper-class communities. They have little first-hand experience with traditional African American culture (Banks and Banks 1997, 228–29).*

Resegregation of Schools in the United States As the United States continues to become more ethnically and racially diverse, there is evidence that schools have been "resegregating" since 1990, according to *Resegregation in American Schools,* a Harvard University report released in June 1999 (Orfield and Yun 1999). The report included the following findings:

- Latinos attend the most severely segregated schools (see Figure 7.2).
- Since the late 1980s, schools in the South have been resegregating.
- As African Americans and Latinos move to the suburbs, they are attending segregated schools, especially in urban areas.
- States with a high proportion of African American students made progress toward desegregation in the 1970s; however, all showed increases in school segregation between 1980 and 1996.
- Segregated schools, with the exception of those for white students, tend to have a high concentration of poverty, which has a negative influence on student achievement.

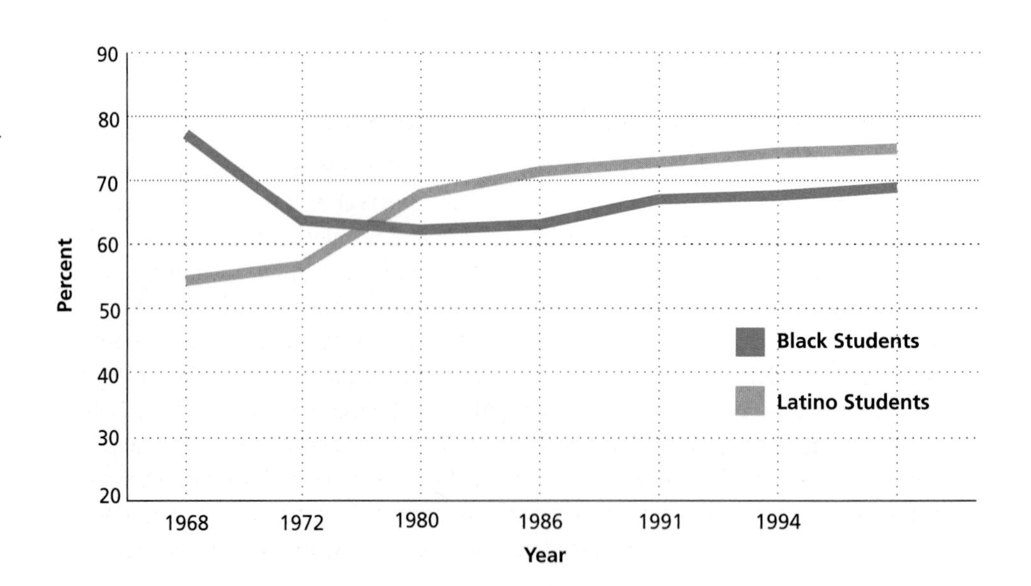

Figure 7.2 Percent of African American and Latino students in 50–100% minority schools, 1968–96.
Source: Gary Orfield and John T. Yun, *Resegregation in American Schools.* Cambridge, MA: The Civil Rights Project, Harvard University, June 1999. Used by permission of the publisher.

One reason for the trend back to resegregation has been Supreme Court rulings that removed judicial supervision of school districts' efforts to desegregate—for example, *Board of Education of Oklahoma City Public Schools v. Dowell,* 1991; *Freeman v. Pitts,* 1992; and *Brown v. Unified School District No. 501,* 1999. In addition, the Supreme Court ruled in *Missouri v. Jenkins,* 1995, that Kansas City schools did not have to maintain desegregation through a magnet school approach until actual benefits for African American students were shown. Such rulings by the Supreme Court prompted the filing of many lawsuits to end desegregation in several large school districts.

The Learning Needs of African American Students Research on factors related to students' success in school suggests that schools are monoethnic and do not take into account the diverse needs of ethnic minority-group students (Bennett 2003). In the case of African American students, the failure of the school curriculum to address their learning needs may contribute to high dropout rates and below-average achievement. For example, research indicates that teaching strategies that emphasize cooperation—not competition—often result in higher achievement among African American (and Mexican American) students (Aronson and Gonzalez 1988). In addition, it has been suggested that because many African Americans have grown up in an oral tradition, they may learn better through oral/aural activities—for example, reading aloud and listening to audiotapes (Bennett 2003). However, one should not assume that all African Americans learn better aurally.

Afrocentric Schools To address the educational inequities that African American and other minority-group students may experience as a result of segregation, many communities have tried to create more ethnically and racially diverse classrooms through the controversial practice of busing students to attend schools in other neighborhoods. Also, some African Americans have recently begun to call for **Afrocentric schools**—that is, schools that focus on African American history and cultures for African American pupils. Proponents believe that the educational needs of African American students can be met more effectively in schools that offer Afrocentric curricula.

Private Afrocentric schools, or "black academies," have sprung up across the country in recent years, many supported by the growing number of African Americans who practice Islam, a religion based on the teachings of the prophet Mohammed. Curricula in these schools emphasize the people and cultures of Africa and the history and achievements of African Americans. Teaching methods are often designed for culture-based learning styles, such as choral response, learning through movement, and sociality.

Education and Latino and Hispanic Americans

Hispanic Americans, the fastest growing minority group in the United States, account for about 10 percent of the population, and it has been estimated that an additional five million illegal aliens who speak Spanish may be in the country. By 2010, the Hispanic population is expected to be 14 percent, surpassing African Americans as the nation's largest minority group. The U.S. Census Bureau estimates that the Hispanic American population in the United States will increase from 32 million (12 percent of the total population) in 2001 to 52 million (16 percent of the total) in 2020, and then to 80 million (22 percent of the total) in 2040.

Included in the category of Hispanic Americans are people who call themselves Latinos and Chicanos and who report their ancestry as Mexican, Puerto Rican, Cuban, Central American, or South American. Five states have populations that are more than 10 percent Hispanic: California, Texas, New Mexico,

Arizona, and Colorado. Many states have passed English-only laws and made efforts to restrict Hispanic immigrants' access to education. Prior to 1983, six states had English-language laws; however, efforts by political action groups such as U.S. English, founded by the late Senator S. I. Hayakawa of California in 1983, were instrumental in getting English-only laws passed in 25 states by 1999, including California and Colorado. Arizona's 1988 Official English amendment was overturned by the Arizona State Supreme Court in 1998. In addition, California voters approved Proposition 187 in 1994, which prevents public schools from educating the children of illegal aliens.

Socioeconomic Factors Although some Spanish-speaking immigrants come to the United States hoping to escape a life of poverty in their home country, many others come because they have relatives in the United States or they wish to take advantage of business opportunities in this country. For those Spanish-speaking immigrants who lack job skills and have little education, however, adjusting to the complexities and demands of life in the United States may be difficult.

Socioeconomic factors affect the education of some Hispanics, such as the children of migrant farm workers. Among the estimated one million or so migrant farm workers in this country, more than 70 percent are Spanish-speaking. The dropout rate among all migrant workers is 90 percent, and 50 percent leave school before finishing the ninth grade (Bennett 2003). Migrant children are handicapped by the language barrier, deprivation resulting from poverty, and irregular school attendance. Some states have educational intervention programs in place for reaching this group.

The Learning Needs of Spanish-Speaking Students What can easily happen to Spanish-speaking learners if they are taught by teachers who are not sensitive to their learning needs is illustrated in Christine I. Bennett's portrait of Jesús, an LEP student:

> *Jesús Martinez was a bright, fine-looking six-year-old when he migrated with his family from Puerto Rico to New York City. At a time when he was ready to learn to read and write his mother tongue, Jesús was instead suddenly thrust into an English-only classroom where the only tool he possessed for oral communication (the Spanish language) was completely useless to him. Jesús and his teacher could not communicate*

What effects has the growing Hispanic population in the U.S. had on schools both throughout the country as well as in some states in particular? Why might some Hispanic Americans prefer assimilation over bilingual education for their children?

Meeting the Standard

Respects Student Diversity

The teacher understands how students differ in their approaches to learning and creates instructional opportunities that are adapted to diverse learners (INTASC Knowledge, Principle #3).

Accomplished teachers recognize that in a multicultural nation students bring to the schools a plethora of abilities and aptitudes that are valued differently by the community, the school and the family (NBPTS, Proposition #1).

The unit designs, implements, and evaluates curriculum and experiences for candidates to acquire and apply the knowledge, skills, and dispositions necessary to help all students learn. These experiences include working with diverse higher education and school faculty, diverse candidates, and diverse students in P–12 schools (NCATE, Standard 4: Diversity).

Teacher displays knowledge of the interests or cultural heritage of each student (PRAXIS III Framework–"distinguished" level of performance).*

Teachers who meet these standards challenge themselves to value not only the strength of "differences" of groups (such as cultural, linguistic, gender, and learning styles), but also the uniqueness of the individual. By establishing a "safe" learning environment that promotes respect for all students, as well as designing and implementing creative learning opportunities, teachers provide a foundation for academic excellence.

Edith looked over her class roster. Class would begin in three weeks, and she recognized several family names. She had been at the school for three years, which was long enough to have already taught several brothers and sisters. She enjoyed getting to know the families in the community in which her school was located.

She already knew that in addition to a majority of Hispanic students, she would have Native American, Taiwanese, African American, and Caucasian students. It also appeared that more than half of her students were boys. Since her school mainstreamed students with learning challenges, as well as gifted students, she knew that her class would feature multiple levels of learning. Already her mind was spinning in anticipation of "building a community" based on both the commonalities and the differences of her new students. She knew that a classroom that valued a variety of strengths through varied backgrounds was a classroom that could truly encourage all students to succeed.

To prepare for the first week of class, Edith prepared two ongoing activities, the "Me Box" and the "Real World Table," both designed to begin building a "safe environment" for learning that would draw on the backgrounds of her students.

- The "Me Box" Activity: In the first activity, students are asked to design a personalized "Me Box" to share with each other in pairs. Shoe boxes are ideal for this activity and easy to collect; however, paper lunch bags can also be used. Students may draw or paste pictures and/or words from magazines on the outside to represent their interests and strengths, and they will be asked to share the outsides of their boxes with each other. Students should also put items in the box that describe special goals, attributes, or experiences they have had. They don't have to share these with their partner unless they want to and feel that they have built "trust" with each other.
- The "Real World Table" Activity: Students are asked to bring items on an identified topic (e.g., "things that grow on trees") to be shared on a "Real World Table," which will be filled with "realia" (including such "real things" as flower blossoms, lemons, pictures of products from trees, etc.).

Through the deliberate implementation of specific community-building activities during the first weeks of school, Edith will promote inclusion of all her students, thus setting the tone for a healthy, diversified, respectful classroom. Using the "Me Box" and giving students several opportunities to share during the first month of school, they get to know each other personally and learn to respect each other's differences. The "Real World Table" encourages students to connect with each other on a variety of topics, and it strengthens the vocabulary of students who speak English as a second language.

1. Edith's activities will help build a healthy and respectful classroom environment. How will this environment enhance the learning environment of the classroom? How might the school as a whole benefit?
2. What are some other ways a teacher might create "instructional opportunities that are adapted to diverse learners," as stated in INTASC Principle #3?

> *with each other because each spoke a different language and neither spoke the language of the other. Jesús felt stupid, or retarded; his teacher perceived him to be culturally disadvantaged and beyond her help. However, she and the school officials agreed to allow him to "sit there" because the law required that he be in school (2003, 8).*

Bennett also captures well the dilemma that many Spanish-speaking LEP students find themselves in: "Students with limited English proficiency are often caught up in conflicts between personal language needs—for example, the need to consolidate cognitive skills in the native language—and a sociopolitical climate that views standard English as most desirable and prestigious" (2003, 271). The degree to which students from Spanish-speaking backgrounds are motivated to learn English varies from group to group. Mexican American students who live in the southwest may retain the Spanish language to maintain ties with family and friends in Mexico. Recently arrived Cubans, on the other hand, may have a stronger motivation to learn the language of their new country. In regard to what they wish to learn, children take their cues from the adults around them. If their parents or guardians and friends and relatives have learned English and are bilingual, then they will be similarly motivated. Many Hispanic Americans who value assimilation over their traditional culture favor English-only education.

However, the limited English proficiencies of many children raised in native Spanish-speaking families contribute significantly to the difficulties they have in school. To address the needs of these students, federally funded bilingual-bicultural programs encourage teachers to view bicultural knowledge as a bridge to the school's curriculum. Bilingual education is examined in detail later in this chapter.

Education and Asian Americans and Pacific Islanders

Asian Americans and Pacific Islanders represent about 4 percent of the total population of the United States. The U.S. Census Bureau estimates that the Asian and Pacific Islander population in the United States will increase from 11.6 million (4 percent of the total population) in 2001 to 19.6 million (6 percent of the total) in 2020, and then to 29 million (8 percent of the total) in 2040. This group, comprising at least 34 ethnic groups that speak more than 300 languages and dialects (Asian Americans/Pacific Islanders in Philanthropy 1997), is tremendously diverse and includes people from South Asia, primarily Bangladesh, India, and Pakistan; Southeast Asia, including Indochina (Laos, Thailand, Indonesia, Malaysia, and Vietnam) and the Philippines; East Asia, including China, Hong Kong, Japan, Korea, and Taiwan; and the Pacific Islands, including Hawaii, Guam, and Samoa. About 55 percent of the total Asian American and Pacific Islander population lives in the western United States, compared to 22 percent of the total population (U.S. Census Bureau 2002).

Historical, Cultural, and Socioeconomic Factors The three largest Asian American groups are Chinese (23.8 percent of Asian Americans), Filipinos (20.4 percent), and Japanese (12.3 percent) (U.S. Census Bureau 1998). Although these groups differ significantly, each "came to the United States seeking the American dream, satisfied important labor needs, and became victims of an anti-Asian movement designed to prevent their further immigration to the United States. [They] also experienced tremendous economic, educational, and social mobility and success in U.S. society" (Banks 2003, 413).

The California gold rush of 1849 brought the first immigrants from Asia, Chinese men who worked in mines, on railroads, and on farms, and who planned to return to their families and homeland. Early Chinese immigrants encountered widespread discrimination in their new country, with anti-Chinese riots occurring in San Francisco, Los Angeles, and Denver between 1869 and 1880. In 1882, Congress passed the Immigration Act, which ended Chinese immigration until 1902. The Chinese were oriented toward maintaining traditional language and religion and established tight-knit urban communities, or "Chinatowns." Recently, many upwardly mobile, professional Chinese Americans have been assimilated into suburban communities, while newly arrived, working-class immigrants from China and Hong Kong are settling in redeveloped Chinatowns.

Japanese immigrants began to arrive in Hawaii and the U.S. mainland in the late 1800s; most worked in agriculture, fisheries, the railroads, or industry and assimilated rapidly despite racial discrimination. The San Francisco Board of Education, for example, began to segregate all Japanese students in 1906, and the Immigration Act of 1924 ended Japanese immigration until 1952. During World War II, the United States was at war with Japan. In response to war hysteria over the "yellow peril," the United States government interned 110,000 Japanese Americans, most of them American-born, in ten detention camps from 1942 to 1946. Since World War II, Japan has developed into one of the world's leading economic and technological powers—an accomplishment that has contributed, no doubt, to a recent decline in Japanese immigration to the United States.

Filipinos began to immigrate to Hawaii and the mainland as field laborers during the 1920s. They, too, encountered racism; in 1934 Congress passed the Tydings-McDuffie Act, which limited Filipino immigration to the United States to 50 persons annually. The following year, President Franklin Roosevelt signed the Repatriation Act, which provided free transportation to Filipinos willing to return to the Philippines. While most early Filipino immigrants had little education and low income, recent immigrants have tended to be professional, technical workers who hope to obtain employment in the United States more suitable for their education and training than they could in the Philippines (Banks 2003).

Teacher's Concerns about Asian American Students Asian Americans are frequently stereotyped as hard-working, conscientious, and respectful of authority, what Sue and Sue (1999) term a "model minority." In fact, 42.2 percent of Asian Americans 25 years and over have a bachelor's degree or more, compared to 23.9 percent of the total population (U.S. Census Bureau 1999). The unreliability of such stereotypes notwithstanding, Asian American parents do tend to require their children to respect authority and value education. However, "for many Asian American students, this image is a destructive myth," according to a report titled *An Invisible Crisis: The Educational Needs of Asian Pacific American Youth.* "As their schools fail them, these children become increasingly likely to graduate with rudimentary language skills, to drop out of school, to join gangs, or to find themselves in the low-paying occupations and on the margins of American life" (Asian Americans/Pacific Islanders in Philanthropy 1997). Families often pressure children to be successful academically through sacrifice and hard work. At the same time, there has been an increase in the number of Asian American youth who are in conflict with their parents' way of life. Leaders in Asian American communities have expressed concern about increases in dropout rates, school violence, and declining achievement. Some Indochinese Americans, for example, face deep cultural conflict in schools. Values and practices that are accepted in U.S. culture, such as dating and glorification of the individual, are sources of conflict between many Indochinese students and their parents.

Teachers need to be sensitive to cultural conflicts that may contribute to problems in school adjustment and achievement for Asian American students and realize that

> *Stereotypes about Asian "whiz kids" and jealousy over the relatively high percentages of Asian Americans in the nation's colleges and universities may blind some non-Asian parents, fellow students, and teachers to the deep cultural conflict many Southeast Asian Americans face in our schools (Bennett 2003, 157).*

To help Asian American students adjust to the U.S. culture, Qiu Liang offers teachers the following advice based on his school experiences as a Chinese immigrant:

> *They [teachers] should be more patient [with an immigrant child] because it is very difficult for a person to be in a new country and learn a new language. Have patience.*
>
> *If the teacher feels there is no hope in an immigrant child, then the child will think, "Well, if the teacher who's helping me thinks that I can't go anywhere, then I might as well give up myself" (Igoa 1995, 99–100).*

Similarly, Dung Yoong offers these recommendations based on her educational experiences as a Vietnamese immigrant:

> *Try to get them to talk to you. Not just everyday conversation, but what they feel inside. Try to get them to get that out, because it's hard for kids. They don't trust—I had a hard time trusting and I was really insecure because of that.*
>
> *[P]utting an immigrant child who doesn't speak English into a classroom, a regular classroom with American students, is not very good. It scares [them] because it is so different. [Teachers] should start [them] slowly and have special classes where the child could adapt and learn a little bit about American society and customs (Igoa 1995, 103).*

Education and Native Americans and Alaskan Natives

Native Americans and Alaskan Natives peopled the Western hemisphere more than 12,000 years ago. Today, they represent less than 1 percent of the total U.S. population, or about two million people (U.S. Census Bureau 2002). This group consists of 517 federally recognized and 365 state-recognized tribes, each with its own language, religious beliefs, and way of life. The four largest groups are the Cherokee Nation of Oklahoma, over 308,000 members; the Navajo Nation, 219,000; the Chippewa Nation, 104,000; and the Sioux Nation of the Dakotas, 103,000 (U.S. Census Bureau 1993). Approximately 760,000 Native Americans live on 275 reservations located primarily in the West. More than half of the Native American and Alaskan Native population lives in six states: Alaska, Arizona, California, New Mexico, Oklahoma, and Washington (Manning and Baruth 1996). Though most Native Americans live in cities, many are establishing connections with reservation Indians as a means of strengthening their cultural identities.

Native Americans are an example of the increasing ambiguity of racial and ethnic identities in the United States. For example, controversy exists over who is Native American. "Some full-blooded native people do not regard a person with one-quarter native heritage to qualify, while others accept $^1/_{128}$" (Bennett 2003, 138). While most Native Americans consider a person with one-quarter or more tribal heritage to be a member, the U.S. Census Bureau considers anyone who claims native identity to be a member. An expert on Native Americans and Alaskan Natives, Arlene Hirschfelder (1986), points out that fifty-two legal definitions of Native Americans have been identified. Native Americans were declared U.S. citizens in 1924, and native nations have been recognized as independent, self-governing territories since the 1930s (Bennett 2003).

Historical, Cultural, and Socioeconomic Factors Perhaps more than any other minority group, Native Americans have endured systematic long-term attempts to eradicate their languages and cultures. Disease, genocide, confinement on reservations, and decades of forced assimilation have devastated Native American cultures. In 1492, native people used 2 billion acres of land; currently, they own about 94 million acres of land, or about 5 percent of U.S. territory (Bennett 2003). Today, the rates of unemployment, poverty, and lack of educational attainment among Native Americans are among the nation's highest. Since the 1970s, however, there has been a resurgence of interest in preserving or restoring traditional languages, skills, and land claims.

There are hundreds of Native American languages, which anthropologists have attempted to categorize into six major language families (Banks 2002). Older tribal members fluent in the original tribal language and younger members often speak a form of so-called "reservation English." The challenge of educating Native Americans from diverse language backgrounds is further complicated by the difference in size of various Native American populations. These range from the more than 300,000 Cherokee to the 200 or so Supai of Arizona. As a result of the extreme diversity among Native Americans, it has even been suggested that "There is no such thing as an 'Indian' heritage, culture, or value system. [N]avajo, Cherokee, Sioux, and Aleut children are as different from each other in geographic and cultural backgrounds as they are from children growing up in New York City or Los Angeles" (Gipp 1979, 19).

Education for Native American children living on reservations is currently administered by the federal government's Bureau of Indian Affairs (BIA). The **Indian Education Act of 1972** and its **1974 amendments** supplement the BIA's educational programs and provide direct educational assistance to tribes. The act seeks to improve Native American education by providing funds to school districts to meet the special needs of Native American youth, to Indian tribes and state and local education agencies to improve education for youth and adults, to colleges and universities for the purpose of training teachers for Indian schools, and to Native American students to attend college.

Research on Native American Ways of Knowing Considerable debate has occurred over the best approaches for educating Native Americans. For example, Banks points out that "since the 1920s, educational policy for Native Americans has vacillated between strong assimilationism to self-determination and cultural pluralism" (2001, 22). In any case, the culture-based learning styles of many Native Americans and Alaskan Natives differ from that of other students. The traditional upbringing of Native American children generally encourages them to develop a view of the world that is holistic, intimate, and shared. "They approach tasks visually, seem to prefer to learn by careful observation which precedes performance, and seem to learn in their natural settings experientially" (Swisher and Deyhle 1987, 350). Bennett suggests the following guideline to ensure that the school experiences of Native American students are in harmony with their cultural backgrounds: "An effective learning environment for Native Americans is one that does not single out the individual but provides frequent opportunities for the teacher to interact privately with individual children and with small groups, as well as opportunities for quiet, persistent exploration" (2003, 212).

Increasingly, Native Americans are designing multicultural programs to preserve their traditional cultures and ways of knowing. Although these programs are sometimes characterized as emphasizing separatism over assimilation, for many Native Americans they are a matter of survival. The Heart of the Earth Survival School in Minneapolis, for example, was created to preserve the languages and cultures of the northern Plains Indians. Native American teachers at the school provide bilingual instruction in Ojibwe and Dakota. Students are encouraged to wear traditional dress and practice traditional arts, such as drumming and dancing.

Cultural preservation is also the primary concern at Alaskan Native schools in remote parts of western Alaska and Cherokee schools in the Marietta Independent School District of Stillwell, Oklahoma. In Alaska, elders come into the classroom to teach children how to skin a seal, an education that few Alaskan Native children receive today at home. In Oklahoma, schools try to keep alive the diverse languages of peoples forced to relocate to reservations there from the Southwestern United States in the last century. Students of mixed Cherokee, Creek, and Seminole descent become fluent and literate in the Cherokee language.

What Is Meant by Bilingual Education?

Bilingual education programs are designed to meet the learning needs of students whose first language is not English by providing instruction in two languages. Regardless of the instructional approach used, one outcome for all bilingual programs is for students to become proficient in English. Additionally, students are encouraged to become **bicultural,** that is, able to function effectively in two or more linguistic and cultural groups.

In 1968, Congress passed the Bilingual Education Act, which required that language-minority students be taught in both their native language and English. In response to the Act, school districts implemented an array of bilingual programs that varied greatly in quality and effectiveness. As a result, many parents filed lawsuits, claiming that bilingual programs were not meeting their children's needs. In 1974, the Supreme Court heard a class action suit (*Lau v. Nichols*) filed by 1,800 Chinese students in San Francisco who charged that they were failing to learn because they could not understand English. The students were enrolled in all-English classes and received no special assistance in learning English. In a unanimous ruling, the Court asserted that federally funded schools must "rectify the language deficiency" of students who "are certain to find their classroom experiences wholly incomprehensible." That same year, Congress adopted the

In recent elections, education has been at the forefront of candidate debates, with bilingual education at the center of many candidates' platforms. Why do you think bilingual education creates such a schism among Americans?

Four Types of Bilingual Education Programs

Immersion programs: Students learn English and other subjects in classrooms where only English is spoken. Aides who speak the first language of students are sometimes available, or students may also listen to equivalent audiotaped lessons in their first language.

Transition programs: Students receive reading lessons in their first language and lessons in English as a Second Language (ESL). Once they sufficiently master English, students are placed in classrooms where English is spoken and their first language is discontinued.

Pull-out programs: On a regular basis, students are separated from English-speaking students so that they may receive lessons in English or reading lessons in their first language. These are sometimes called sheltered English programs.

Maintenance programs: To maintain the student's native language and culture, instruction in English and instruction in the native language are provided from kindergarten through twelfth grade. Students become literate.

Figure 7.3 Four types of bilingual education programs.

Equal Educational Opportunity Act (EEOA), which stated in part that a school district must "take appropriate action to overcome language barriers that impede equal participation by its students in its instructional programs."

Bilingual programs, most of which serve Latino and Hispanic American students, are tremendously varied and reflect "extreme differences in student composition, program organization, teaching methodologies and approaches, and teacher backgrounds and skills" (Griego-Jones 1996, 115). Generally, however, four types of bilingual education programs are currently available to provide special assistance to the 3.5 million language-minority students in the United States (see Figure 7.3). Only about 315,000 students actually participate in some kind of bilingual program.

Research and Debate on Bilingual Programs

Research on the effectiveness of bilingual programs is mixed (Rothstein 1998). Some who have examined the research conclude that bilingual programs have little effect on achievement (Baker 1991; Rossell 1990; Rossell and Baker 1996). Others have found that well-designed bilingual programs do increase students' achievement and are superior to monolingual programs (Cziko 1992; Nieto 1992; Schmidt 1991; Trueba, Cheng, and Kenji 1993; Willig 1987).

Where Do You Stand? Visit the Companion Website to Voice Your Opinion.

Considerable debate surrounds bilingual programs in the United States. Those in favor of bilingual education make the following points:

- Students are better able to learn English if they are taught to read and write in their native language.
- Bilingual programs allow students to learn content in their native language rather than delaying that learning until they master English.
- Further developing competencies in students' native languages provides important cognitive foundations for learning English and academic content.
- Second-language learning is a positive value and should be as valid for a Spanish-speaker learning English as for an English-speaker learning Spanish.
- Bilingual programs support students' cultural identity, social context, and self-esteem.

On the other hand, those opposed to bilingual programs make the following points:

- Public schools should not be expected to provide instruction in all the first languages spoken by their students, nor can schools afford to pay a teacher who might teach only a few students.
- The cost of bilingual education is high. Bilingual programs divert staff and resources away from English-speaking students.
- If students spend more time exposed to English, they will learn English more quickly.
- Bilingual programs emphasize differences among and barriers between groups; they encourage separateness rather than assimilation and unity.
- Bilingual education is a threat to English as the nation's first language.

Advice for Monolingual Teachers

Although the future of bilingual education in the United States is uncertain, teachers must continue to meet the needs of language-minority students. These needs are best met by teachers who speak their native language as well as English. However, this is often not possible, and monolingual teachers will find increasing numbers of LEP students in their classrooms. See the Appendixes "Creating Classroom Environments That Support Second-Language Learners," and "Strategies for Enhancing the Learning and Literacy of Second-Language Learners" on this book's website. Developed by bilingual/ESL education expert Gisela Ernst and her colleagues, these strategies can be used whether or not a teacher is bilingual.

What Is Multicultural Education?

Multicultural education is committed to the goal of providing all students—regardless of socioeconomic status, gender, sexual orientation or ethnic, racial, or cultural backgrounds—with equal opportunities to learn in school. Multicultural education is also based on the fact that students do not learn in a vacuum—their culture predisposes them to learn in certain ways. And finally, multicultural education recognizes that current school practices have provided, and continue to provide, some students with greater opportunities for learning than students who belong to other groups. The suggestions in the Appendixes referenced above are examples of multicultural education in practice.

As multiculturalism has become more pervasive in U.S. schools, controversy over the need for multicultural education and its purposes has emerged. Carl Grant has identified as "myths" the following six arguments against multicultural education: "(1) It is both divisive and so conceptually weak that it does little to eliminate structural inequalities; (2) it is unnecessary because the United States is a melting pot; (3) multiculturalism—and by extension multicultural education—and political correctness are the same thing; (4) multicultural education rejects the notion of a common culture; (5) multicultural education is a 'minority thing'; and (6) multicultural education will impede learning the basic skills" (1994, 5). Though multicultural education is being challenged by those who promote these beliefs, we believe that public dialogue and debate about how schools can more effectively address diversity is healthy—an indicator that our society is making real progress toward creating a culture that incorporates the values of diverse groups.

Dimensions of Multicultural Education

According to James A. Banks, "Multicultural education is a complex and multidimensional concept" (Banks 2001, 5). More specifically, Banks suggests that multicultural education may be conceptualized as consisting of five dimensions: (1) content integration, (2) knowledge construction, (3) prejudice reduction, (4) an equity pedagogy, and (5) an empowering school culture (see Figure 7.4). As you progress through your teacher-education program and eventually begin to prepare curriculum materials and instructional strategies for your multicultural classroom, remember that integrating content from a variety of cultural groups is just one dimension of multicultural education. Multicultural education is not "something that is done at a certain time slot in the school day where children eat with chopsticks or listen to Peruvian music. . . . [It is] something that is infused throughout the school culture and practiced daily" (Henry 1996, 108).

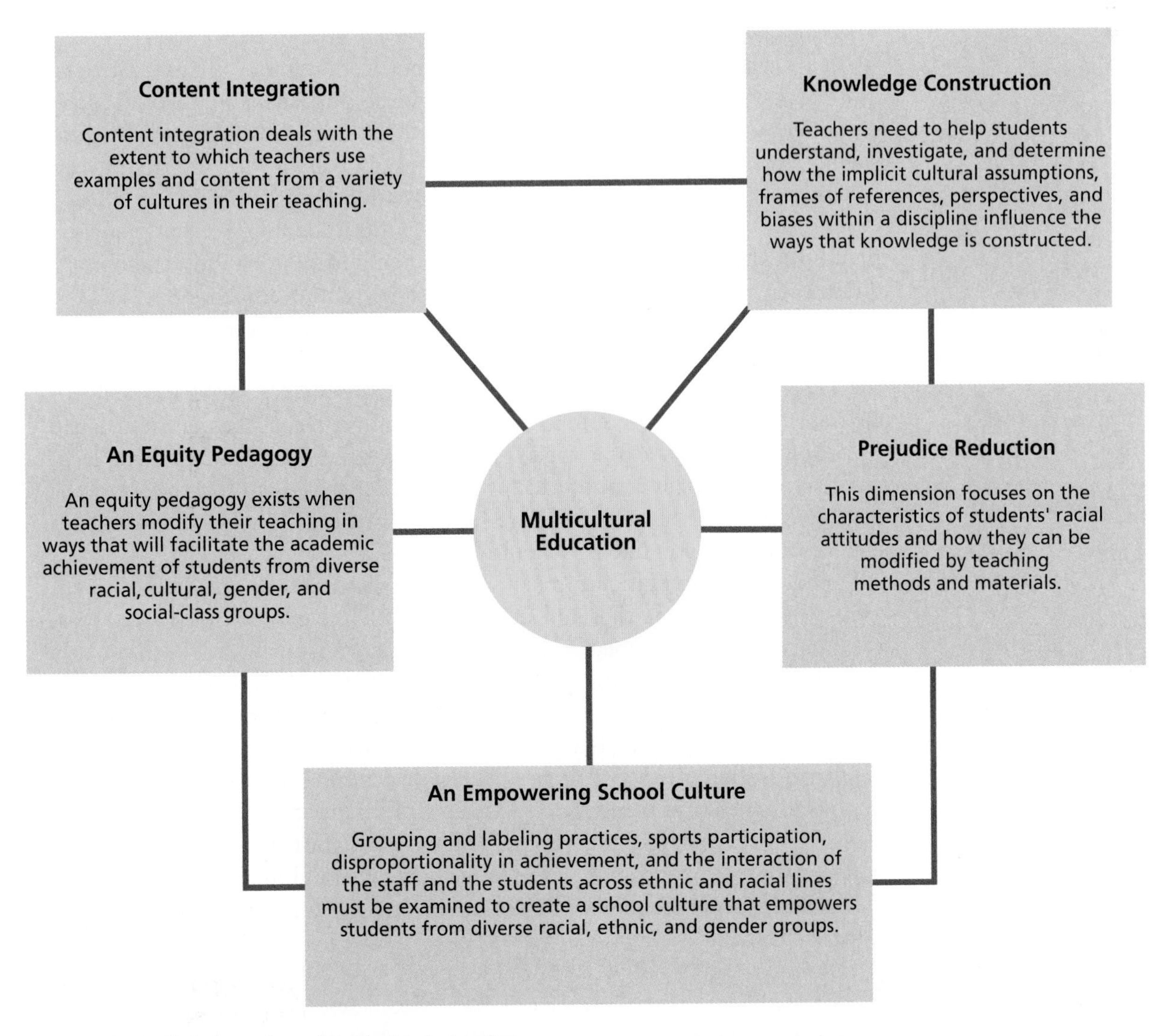

Figure 7.4 Banks's dimensions of multicultural education.
Source: From James A. Banks and Cherry A. McGee Banks, *Multicultural Education: Issues and Perspectives,* 3d ed. Boston: Allyn & Bacon, 1997, p. 24. Copyright © 1997 by Allyn & Bacon. Reprinted by permission.

Multicultural education promotes students' positive self-identity and pride in their heritage, acceptance of people from diverse backgrounds, and critical self-assessment. In addition, multicultural education can prompt students, perhaps with guidance from their teachers, to take action against prejudice and discrimination within their school. Indeed, as Joel Spring says, "multicultural education should create a spirit of tolerance and activism in students. An understanding of other cultures and of differing cultural frames of reference will . . . spark students to actively work for social justice" (1998, 163). For example, students might reduce the marginalization of minority-group students in their school by inviting them to participate in extracurricular and after-school activities.

Multicultural Curricula

As a teacher you will teach students who historically have not received full educational opportunity—students from the many racial and ethnic minority groups in the United States, students from low-income families or communities, students with exceptional abilities or disabilities, students who are gay or lesbian, and students who are male or female. You will face the challenge of reaching out to all students and teaching them that they are persons of worth who can learn.

In your diverse classroom your aim is not to develop a different curriculum for each group of students—that would be impossible and would place undue emphasis on differences among students. Rather, your curriculum should help increase students' awareness and appreciation of the rich diversity in U.S. culture. A **multicultural curriculum** addresses the needs and backgrounds of all students regardless of their cultural identity. As Banks suggests, the multicultural curriculum "enable[s] students to derive valid generalizations and theories about the characteristics of ethnic groups and to learn how they are alike and different, in both their past and present experiences. . . . [It] focus[es] on a range of groups that *differ* in their racial characteristics, cultural experiences, languages, histories, values, and current problems" (2003, 16). Teachers who provide multicultural education recognize the importance of asking questions such as those posed by Valerie Ooka Pang: "Why is a child's home language important to keep? What strengths does culture give children? What impact does culture have on learning? What does racism, sexism, or classism look like in schools?" (1994, 292).

In developing a multicultural curriculum, you should be sensitive to how your instructional materials and strategies can be made more inclusive so that they reflect cultural perspectives, or "voices," that previously have been silent or marginalized in discussions about what should be taught in schools and how it should be taught. "Non-dominant groups representing diversity in the school whose voices traditionally have not been heard include those defined by race, language, gender, sexual orientation, alternative family structures, social class, disability, bilingualism, and those with alien or refugee status" (Henry 1996, 108). Effective teachers attend to these previously unheard voices not as an act of tokenism but with a genuine desire to make the curriculum more inclusive and to "create space for alternative voices, not just on the periphery but in the center" (Singer 1994, 286).

Multicultural Instructional Materials and Strategies

To create classrooms that are truly multicultural, teachers must select instructional materials that are sensitive, accurately portray the contributions of ethnic

groups, and reflect diverse points of view. (See the Appendix "Selected Resources for Multicultural Education" on this book's website.) Teachers must also recognize that "[s]ome of the books and other materials on ethnic groups published each year are insensitive, inaccurate, and written from mainstream and insensitive perspectives and points of view" (Banks 2003, 111). Some guidelines for selecting multicultural instructional materials follow:

- Books and other materials should accurately portray the perspectives, attitudes, and feelings of ethnic groups.
- Fictional works should have strong ethnic characters.
- Books should describe settings and experiences with which all students can identify and yet should accurately reflect ethnic cultures and lifestyles.
- The protagonists in books with ethnic themes should have ethnic characteristics but should face conflicts and problems universal to all cultures and groups.
- The illustrations in books should be accurate, ethnically sensitive, and technically well done.
- Ethnic materials should not contain racist concepts, clichés, phrases, or words.
- Factual materials should be historically accurate.
- Multiethnic resources and basal textbooks should discuss major events and documents related to ethnic history (Banks 2003, 127).

Yvonne Wilson, a first-grade teacher in Talmoon, Minnesota, and an Ojibwe Indian, points out that a teacher's willingness to learn about other cultures is very important to students and their parents:

> *People in the community know if you are trying to understand their culture. Students also see it. Becoming involved—going to a powwow or participating in other cultural events—shows people that here is a teacher who is trying to learn about our culture.*

Participating wholeheartedly in cross-cultural experiences will help you to grow in the eight areas outlined in Figure 7.5 as essential for successful teaching in a diverse society.

How Is Gender a Dimension of Multicultural Education?

Though it may be evident that gender affects students' learning in many ways, it may not be evident that gender is an important dimension of multicultural education. However, as Tozer, Violas, and Senese point out:

> *Traditional definitions of culture have centered around the formal expression of a people's common existence—language, art, music, and so forth. If culture is more broadly defined to include such things as ways of knowing, ways of relating to others, ways of negotiating rights and privileges, and modes of conduct, thought, and expression, then the term "culture" applies not only to ethnic groups but to people grouped on the basis of gender. [G]ender entails cultural as well as physiological dimensions (1993, 310).*

On the Frontlines

Connecting with Families

For a fieldwork project you observe Mr. Rocha, a well-regarded educator who has taught third grade for over thirty years. You are quickly impressed by the high respect he receives from and gives to his students and their parents. The children seem to try harder and behave better when they are in his presence. Parents seek him out, defer to him, ask his advice, and volunteer to help. He regularly includes parents in class activities, asks them to share favorite books with the class, and invites them and their preschool children to join him on class walks to the town library.

One day you ask if he would mind telling you how he establishes his special relationship with students and their families. He seems to welcome the request and speaks quickly, earnestly, and with some urgency:

> *Before school begins each year I go to the home of each child in my class. I greet the child and say that I'm going to be his or her teacher, and I tell the child's parents how honored I am to be their child's teacher. Next I sit down with them, usually at the kitchen table, all of us—child, parents, and teacher—and we discuss the goals we each have for the coming school year. I tell them that how well the child does in meeting all the goals is a three-way responsibility—the child's, the parents', and mine.*
>
> *When the year starts, I already know the children. In the first few days, I talk to them about respect and what it means. I explain that teachers deserve respect, and that they should listen to me, as their teacher, with their ears, eyes, and heart. Then I tell them that they deserve respect, and I commit myself to listening to them with my ears, eyes, and heart. Finally, I explain that everyone in the room deserves respect, no matter who they are. So when any student talks to the class, everyone needs to listen to him or her with their ears, eyes, and heart. . . . That always seems to work well.*

Driving home that evening you think about your conversation with Mr. Rocha and imagine yourself visiting your future students' homes before the school year begins. Where you hope to teach many of your students will be Hispanic. Will you be welcome in their homes? You don't speak very much Spanish. How can you have a good goal-setting talk with your limited Spanish? You will have just moved to the community. Will the parents accept a newcomer? How safe is it to go alone into some of the neighborhoods? The questions come faster than answers.

The worlds of teachers and parents may seem far apart, but as Sara Lawrence Lightfoot (1978) observes in *Worlds Apart: Relationships Between Families and Schools*, the development of a trusting relationship can bridge the distance between them. When parents see teachers as committed partners working with them for the good of their children, the best form of parent involvement emerges.

While connecting between worlds has always been complex—developing relationships is never formulaic—today the challenge is greater, the worlds to bridge more varied. Teachers now need to know family structures, roles, hierarchies, and values in a variety of cultures. Research about their students' worlds must be more extensive. And they will need to adapt their ways of connecting and relating to parents in general to the specific parents of their students.

Joyce Epstein, Director of the Center on School, Family, and Community Partnerships at Johns Hopkins University, provides a helpful framework for connecting with families that consists of six types of involvement.

The first is *Parenting*, offering information on parenting and child or adolescent development, and helping schools learn about families. This can be done by sharing articles with parents, conducting workshops, and offering school programs that feature experts in the field.

The second is *Communicating*, having an effective school-to-home and home-to-school exchange of information. The use of personal letters, visiting, class and teacher newsletters, and dialogic homework assignments that call for parent responses are common means for communicating.

The third is *Volunteering*, eliciting the assistance of families in school with ongoing school needs and special events.

Children especially appreciate having their parents volunteer.

The fourth is *Learning at Home,* involving parents in homework activities.

The fifth is *Decision Making,* including families in school governance, parent organizations, superintendent circles.

The sixth is *Collaborating with the Community,* coordinating "resources and services *for* families, students, and the school with businesses, agencies, and other groups, and providing services to the community."

In any effort to involve parents and connect with families, the key ingredient is respect. When parents are convinced that you respect their child and respect them, a promising relationship can begin.

Exploratory Questions

1. You have a very diverse classroom, with a number of foreign-born students from Mexico, China, England, and Pakistan. What challenges would you face in trying to connect with your students' parents? What challenges would you face in the classroom?
2. Using the websites listed here, identify at least one strategy for connecting with parents and creating a healthy learning "community" in your classroom.

Your Survival Guide of Helpful Resources

The following resources provide helpful hints for surviving "on the frontlines."

Books and Articles

Bruns, D. A. (2001). Working with culturally and linguistically diverse families (ERIC Digest ED455972). Retrieved from http://www.ed.gov/databases/ERIC_Digests/ed455972.html

Hiatt-Michael, D. (2001). Preparing teachers to work with parents (ERIC Digest ED460123). Retrieved from http://www.ed.gov/databases/ERIC_Digests/ed460123.html

Lightfoot, S. L. (1978). *Worlds apart: Relationships between families and schools.* New York: Basic Books.

Websites

The Institute for Responsive Education: Connecting School, Family, and Community (http://www.responsiveeducation.org/)

National Network of School Partnerships located at Johns Hopkins University (http://www.csos.jhu.edu/p2000/sixtypes.htm)

Partnership for Family Involvement in Education (http://pfie.ed.gov/)

Companion Website

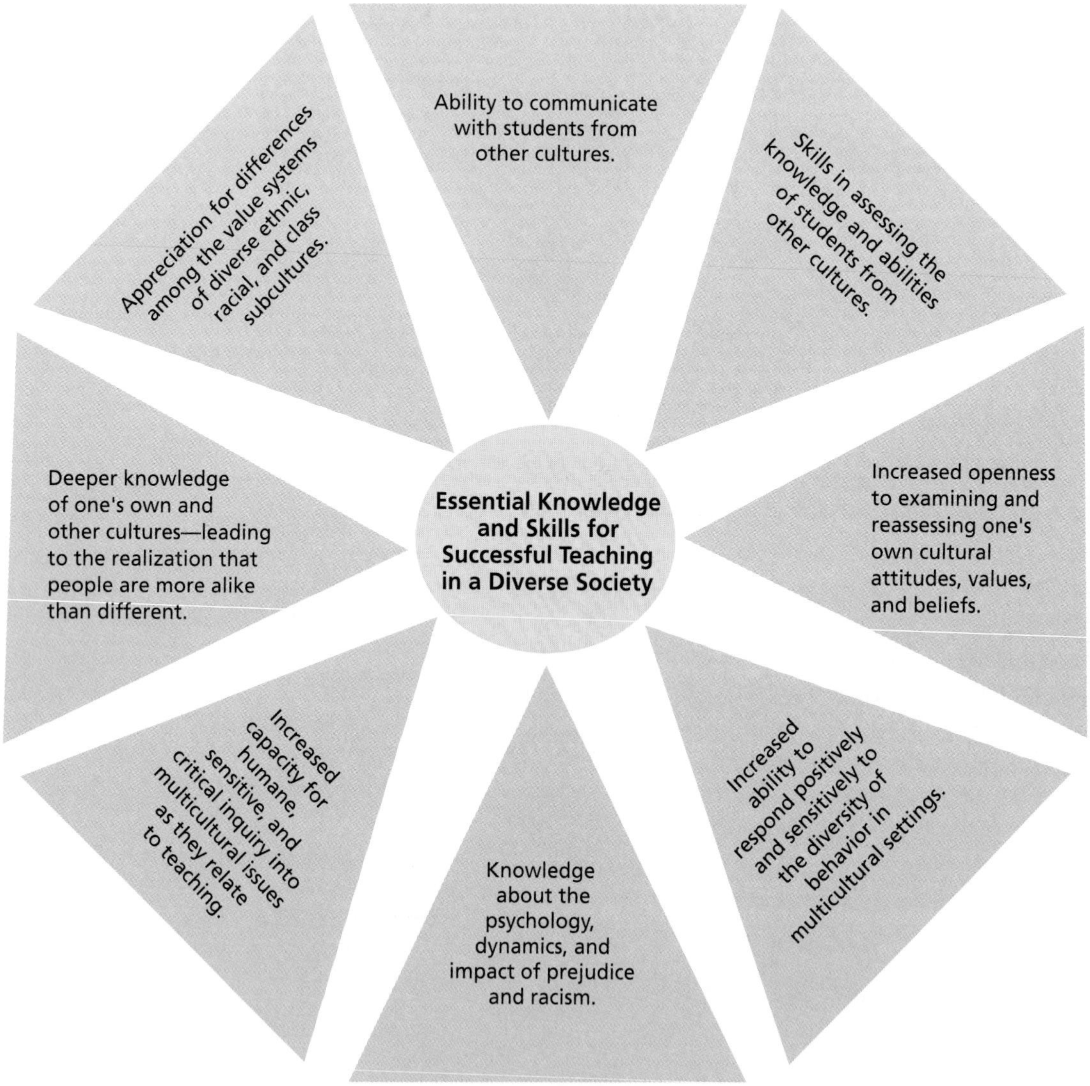

Ability to communicate with students from other cultures.

Skills in assessing the knowledge and abilities of students from other cultures.

Increased openness to examining and reassessing one's own cultural attitudes, values, and beliefs.

Increased ability to respond positively and sensitively to the diversity of behavior in multicultural settings.

Knowledge about the psychology, dynamics, and impact of prejudice and racism.

Increased capacity for humane, sensitive, and critical inquiry into multicultural issues as they relate to teaching.

Deeper knowledge of one's own and other cultures—leading to the realization that people are more alike than different.

Appreciation for differences among the value systems of diverse ethnic, racial, and class subcultures.

Essential Knowledge and Skills for Successful Teaching in a Diverse Society

Figure 7.5 Essential knowledge and skills for successful teaching in a diverse society.
Source: Adapted from Forrest W. Parkay and Henry T. Fillmer, "Improving Teachers' Attitudes toward Minority-Group Students: An Experiential Approach to Multicultural Inservice," *New Horizons Journal of Education,* November 1984, pp. 178–179.

Gender Differences

Cultural differences between males and females are partially shaped by society's traditional expectations of them. Through **sex role stereotyping** families, the media, the schools, and other powerful social forces condition boys and girls to act in certain ways regardless of abilities or interests. As we mentioned in Chapter 4, one of the aims of schools is to socialize students to participate in society. One dimension of the **sex role socialization** process conveys to students certain expectations about the way boys and girls are "supposed" to act. Girls are supposed to play with dolls, boys with trucks. Girls are supposed to be passive, boys active. Girls are supposed to express their feelings and emotions when in pain, boys to repress their feelings and deny pain.

Students may be socialized into particular gender-specific roles as a result of the curriculum materials they use at school. By portraying males in more dominant, assertive ways and portraying females in ways that suggest that they are passive and helpless, textbooks can subtly reinforce expectations about the way girls and boys "should" behave. Within the last few decades, though, publishers of curriculum materials have become more vigilant about avoiding these stereotypes.

Gender and Education

As noted in Chapter 3, it was not until Title IX of the Education Amendments Act was passed in 1972 that women were guaranteed equality of educational opportunity in educational programs receiving federal assistance. Title IX has had the greatest impact on athletic programs in schools. On the thirtieth anniversary of Title IX, U.S. Secretary of Education Roderick Paige stated: "Without a doubt, Title IX has opened the doors of opportunity for generations of women and girls to compete, to achieve, and to pursue their American dreams. In 1971, before Title IX went into effect, more than 294,000 girls participated in high school sports. Last year, that number exceeded 2.7 million—an 847 percent increase" (Press Release, U.S. Department of Education, June 27, 2002). The law requires that both sexes have equal opportunities to participate in and benefit from the availability of coaches, sports equipment, resources, and facilities. For contact sports such as football, wrestling, and boxing, sports that were not open to women, separate teams are allowed.

The right of females to equal educational opportunity was further enhanced with the passage of the **Women's Educational Equity Act (WEEA)** of 1974. This act provides the following opportunities:

What impact has civil rights legislation had on the education of females? Why and in what ways does gender bias persist in many U.S. classrooms and schools?

- Expanded math, science, and technology programs for females
- Programs to reduce sex-role stereotyping in curriculum materials
- Programs to increase the number of female educational administrators
- Special programs to extend educational and career opportunities to minority, disabled, and rural women
- Programs to help school personnel increase educational opportunities and career aspirations for females
- Encouragement for more females to participate in athletics

Despite reforms stemming from WEEA, several reports in the early 1990s criticized schools for subtly discriminating against girls in tests, textbooks, and teaching methods. Research on teacher interactions in the classroom seemed to point to widespread unintentional gender bias against girls. Two of these studies, *Shortchanging Girls, Shortchanging America* (1991) and *How Schools Shortchange Girls* (1992), both commissioned by the American Association of University Women (AAUW), claimed that girls were not encouraged in math and science and that teachers favored boys' intellectual growth over that of girls.

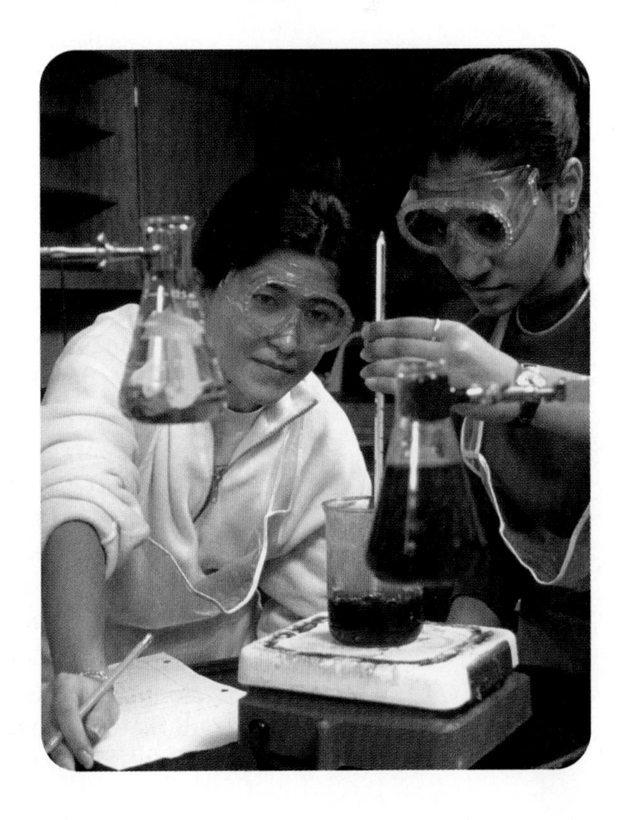

In the mid-1990s, however, some gender equity studies had more mixed findings. In their analysis of data on achievement and engagement of 9,000 eighth-grade boys and girls, University of Michigan researchers Valerie Lee, Xianglei Chen, and Becky A. Smerdon (1996) concluded that "the pattern of gender differences is inconsistent. In some cases, females are favored; in others males are favored." Similarly, University of Chicago researchers Larry Hedges and Amy Nowell found in their study of thirty-two years of mental tests given to boys and girls that, while boys do better than girls in science and mathematics, they were "at a rather profound disadvantage" in writing and scored below girls in reading comprehension (Hedges 1996, 3).

Additional research and closer analyses of earlier reports on gender bias in education were beginning to suggest that boys, not girls, were most "shortchanged" by the schools (Sommers 1996). Numerous articles as well as a 1999 PBS series that began with a program titled "The War on Boys" challenged the conclusions of the earlier AAUW report, *How Schools Shortchange Girls.* Other commentary discounted gender bias in the schools as a fabrication of radical feminism; among the first to put forth this view was Christina Hoff Sommers's (1994) controversial book, *Who Stole Feminism? How Women Have Betrayed Women;* and, more recently, Judith Kleinfeld's (1998) *The Myth That Schools Shortchange Girls: Social Science in the Service of Deception* and Cathy Young's (1999) *Ceasefire! Why Women and Men Must Join Forces to Achieve True Equality.*

To examine gender issues in the public schools, *The Metropolitan Life Survey of the American Teacher, 1997* surveyed 1,306 students in grades 7–12 and interviewed 1,035 teachers in grades 6–12. The analysis of data indicated that:

> *(1) contrary to the commonly held view that boys are at an advantage over girls in school, girls appear to have an advantage over boys in terms of their future plans, teachers' expectations [see Figure 7.6], everyday experiences at school and interactions in the classroom; (2) minority girls [African Americans and Hispanics only] hold the most optimistic views of the future and are the group most likely to focus on education goals; (3) minority boys are the most likely to feel discouraged about the future and the least interested in getting a good education; and (4) teachers nationwide view girls as higher achievers and more likely to succeed than boys. [These] findings appear to contradict those from other studies which conclude that girls have lower expectations than boys, feel less confident, perceive competitiveness as a barrier to learning and believe that society discourages them from pursuing their goals (Louis Harris and Associates 1997, 3).*

To shed light on gender differences in academic achievement, Warren Willingham and Nancy Cole (1997) conducted a seminal study of the scores of 15 million students in the fourth, eighth, and twelfth grades on hundreds of standardized exams used by schools and college placement exams such as the SAT. Contrary to long-standing assumptions that there are pronounced differences between the performance of males and females on standardized tests, their study found that "there is not a dominant picture of one gender excelling over the other and, in fact, the average performance difference across all subjects is essentially zero." Boys and girls, Willingham and Cole found, were fairly evenly matched in verbal and abstract reasoning, math computation, and the social sciences. The superiority of boys in math and science was found to be surprisingly slight and "significantly smaller than 30 years ago." Boys were found to have a clear advantage in mechanical and electronic ability and knowledge of economics and history, while girls had a clear advantage

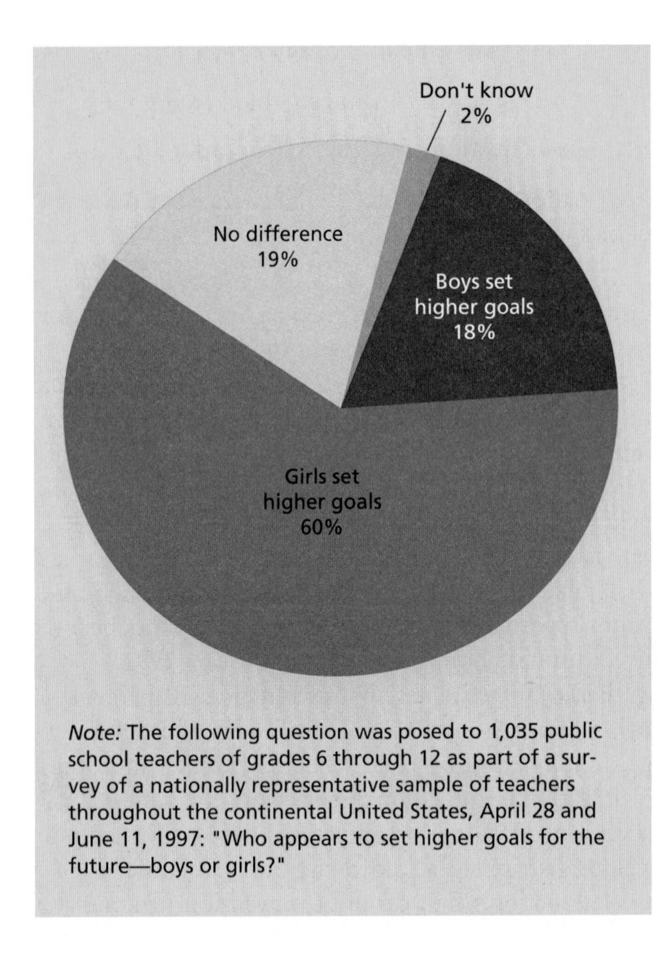

Figure 7.6 Teachers' opinions on who aims higher: boys or girls.
Source: The Metropolitan Life Survey of the American Teacher 1997: Examining Gender Issues in Public Schools. New York: Louis Harris and Associates, Inc., 1997, p. 52.

in language skills, especially writing, and a "moderate edge" in short-term memory and perceptual speed. Furthermore, the authors concluded that gender differences in test scores are not the result of bias in the exams; instead, the differences are genuine and would be reflected also in more carefully designed tests.

Gender-Fair Classrooms and Curricula

Although research and debate about the bias boys and girls encounter in school will no doubt continue, it is clear that teachers must encourage girls and boys to develop to the full extent of their capabilities and provide them an education that is free from **gender bias**—subtle favoritism or discrimination on the basis of gender.

Following is a list of basic guidelines for creating a **gender-fair classroom.** Adherence to these guidelines will help teachers "address the inequities institutionalized in the organizational structure of schools, the curriculum selected to be taught, the learning strategies employed, and their ongoing instructional and informal interactions with students" (Stanford 1992, 88).

- Become aware of differences in interactions with girls and boys.
- Promote boys' achievement in reading and writing and girls' achievement in mathematics and science.

- Reduce young children's self-imposed sexism.
- Teach about sexism and sex role stereotyping.
- Foster an atmosphere of collaboration between girls and boys.

See the Appendix "Selected Resources for Achieving Gender Equity" on this book's website.

Sexual Orientation In addition to gender bias, some students experience discrimination on the basis of their sexual orientation. To help all students realize their full potential, teachers should acknowledge the special needs of gay, lesbian, and bisexual students for "there is an invisible gay and lesbian minority in every school, and the needs of these students [a]re often unknown and unmet" (Besner and Spungin 1995, xi). One study of 120 gay and lesbian students ages fourteen to twenty-one found that only one-fourth said they were able to discuss their sexual orientation with school counselors, and less than one in five said they could identify someone who had been supportive of them (Tellijohann and Price 1993). Moreover, a similar study of lesbian and gay youth reported that 80 percent of participants believed their teachers had negative attitudes about homosexuality (Sears 1991).

Based on estimates that as much as 10 percent of society may be homosexual, a high school with an enrollment of 1,500 might have as many as 150 gay, lesbian, and bisexual students (Besner and Spungin 1995; Stover 1992). The National Education Association, the American Federation of Teachers, and several professional organizations have passed resolutions urging members and school districts to acknowledge the special needs of these students.

The nation's first dropout prevention program targeting gay, lesbian, and bisexual students was implemented in the Los Angeles school system. Known as Project 10, the program focuses on education, suicide prevention, dropout prevention, creating a safe environment for homosexual students, and HIV/AIDS education (Uribe and Harbeck 1991). In 1993, Massachusetts became the first state to adopt an educational policy prohibiting discrimination against gay and lesbian students and teachers. At one Massachusetts high school, gay and straight students created the Gay-Straight Alliance (GSA), a school-sanctioned student organization that gives students a safe place to discuss sexual orientation issues (Bennett 1997).

Homosexual students can experience school-related problems and safety risks. The hostility gay, lesbian, and bisexual youth can encounter may cause them to feel confused, isolated, and self-destructive (Alexander 1998; Anderson 1997; Edwards 1997; Jones 1999; Jordan, Vaughan, and Woodworth 1997). Teachers and other school personnel can provide much-needed support. Informed, sensitive, and caring teachers can play an important role in helping all students develop to their full potential. Such teachers realize the importance of recognizing diverse perspectives, and they create inclusive classroom environments that encourage students to respect differences among themselves and others and to see the contributions that persons from all groups have made to society.

Summary

How Is Diversity Embedded in the Culture of the United States?

- The percentage of ethnic minorities in the United States has been growing steadily since World War II. By 2025, half of U.S. youth will be white and half "minority"; and by 2050, no one group will be a majority among adults in the United States. Currently, the majority of students in several states and many urban districts are from groups traditionally thought of as minority.
- Culture is defined as the way of life common to a group of people, including beliefs, attitudes, habits, values, and practices.
- Dimensions of cultural identity include beliefs, attitudes, and values; racial identity; exceptionalities; language; gender; ethnicity; income level; and occupation.
- Ethnicity refers to a commonly shared racial or cultural identity and a set of beliefs, values, and attitudes. The concept of *race* is used to distinguish among people on the basis of biological traits and characteristics. A minority group is a group of people who share certain characteristics and are fewer in number than the majority of a population.
- The lower achievement levels of certain minority-group students compared to those of their Anglo-European American and Asian American counterparts reflect the strong connection between socioeconomic status (SES) and achievement, since the incidence of poverty is highest among minority families.
- Stereotyping is the process of attributing certain behavioral characteristics to all members of a group, often on the basis of limited experiences with and information about the group being stereotyped. Individual racism is the prejudicial belief that one's own ethnic or racial group is superior to others, and institutional racism refers to laws, customs, and practices that lead to racial inequalities.

What Does Equal Educational Opportunity Mean?

- Equal educational opportunity means that teachers promote the full development of students without regard for race, ethnicity, gender, sexual orientation, socioeconomic status, abilities, or disabilities.
- Past evidence indicates that four minority groups in the United States have been denied equality of educational opportunity through various forms of racism, discrimination, and neglect: African Americans, Latino and Hispanic Americans, Asian Americans and Pacific Islanders, and Native Americans and Alaskan Natives. Teachers can meet the needs of students from these groups by becoming familiar with their cultural and linguistic backgrounds and learning styles.
- In spite of increasing diversity in the United States, there has been a trend since 1990 for schools to "resegregate," perhaps as a result of Supreme Court rulings that removed judicial supervision of school district efforts to desegregate.

What Is Meant by Bilingual Education?

- Bilingual education programs provide instruction in a student's first language and English. The goal of bilingual programs is for students to learn English and become bicultural, able to function effectively in two or more linguistic/cultural groups. Four approaches to bilingual education are immersion, maintenance, pull-out, and transition programs.
- Some research has found that bilingual programs have a positive effect on achievement, while others have found little effect. In light of inconclusive outcomes and mixed support, there has been a continuing debate over bilingual education in the United States.

What Is Multicultural Education?

- Five dimensions of multicultural education have been suggested: content integration, knowledge construction, prejudice reduction, an equity pedagogy, and an empowering school culture.
- A multicultural curriculum addresses the needs and backgrounds of all students—regardless of their cultural identity—and expands students' appreciation for diversity. Effective multicultural materials and instructional strategies include the contributions of ethnic groups and reflect diverse points of view or "voices" that previously may have been silenced or marginalized in society.

How Is Gender a Dimension of Multicultural Education?

- Gender includes ways of knowing and "modes of conduct, thought, and expression"; these are dimensions of culture.
- The behavior of boys and girls in our society is influenced by *sexism, sex role socialization,* and *sex role stereotyping.*
- Both boys and girls experience inequities in the classroom; teachers, however, can provide both sexes with an education free of *gender bias* by creating gender-fair classrooms and curricula.
- Teachers should acknowledge the special needs of students who are gay, lesbian, or bisexual, and provide them with safe, supportive learning environments.

Key Terms and Concepts

Afrocentric schools, **253**
bicultural, **260**
bilingual education, **243**
cultural identity, **242**
cultural pluralism, **242**
culture, **242**
diversity, **241**
ethnic group, **242**
ethnicity, **246**
gender bias, **271**
gender-fair classroom, **271**
Indian Education Act of 1972 and 1974 Amendments, **259**
individual racism, **248**
institutional racism, **248**
limited English proficiency (LEP), **244**
minorities, **247**
multicultural curriculum, **264**
multicultural education, **262**
multiculturalism, **244**
race, **246**
sex role socialization, **268**
sex role stereotyping, **268**
stereotyping, **248**
Women's Educational Equity Act (WEEA), **269**

Applications and Activities

Teacher's Journal

1. Reflecting on your experiences in schools and the five dimensions of multicultural education (see Figure 7.4 on page 263), describe the steps your teachers took to create an empowering school culture and social climate.
2. During your school years, did you ever experience discrimination as a member of a "different" group? Write about one outstanding incident that you feel affected your performance as a student.
3. As a teacher, what activities and materials might you use in a specific learning context to reduce the prejudices of students toward groups different from theirs?
4. Describe an example of sex role stereotyping or gender bias that you experienced or observed in a school setting and how you felt about it.

Teacher's Database

1. Conduct an online keyword search for sources of information on one or more of the following diversity topics from Chapter 7. Share your findings with classmates before narrowing your search:

   bilingual education

   cultural diversity

   English as a Second Language (ESL)

   English for Students of Other Languages (ESOL)

   gender equity

   multicultural education

2. Using one of the diversity topics listed above, go online to gather current national and state statistics related to that topic. For example, you may gather relevant data at one or more of the following sites:

   National Assessment of Educational Progress

   National Center for Education Information

   National Center for Education Statistics

   National Data Resource Center

   U.S. Bureau of the Census

Observations and Interviews

1. If possible, visit a school that has an enrollment of students whose cultural or socioeconomic backgrounds differ from your own. What feelings and questions about these students emerge as a result of your observations? How might your feelings affect your teaching and teaching effectiveness? How might you go about finding answers to your questions?
2. Interview a teacher at the school identified in the above activity. What special satisfactions does he or she experience from teaching at the school? What significant problems relating to diversity does he or she encounter, and how are they dealt with?

Professional Portfolio

Prepare an annotated directory of local resources for teaching students about diversity, implementing multicultural curricula, and promoting harmony or equity among diverse groups. For each entry, include an annotation–that is, a brief description of the resource materials and their availability.

Resources for your personalized directory should be available through local sources such as your university library, public library, community agencies, and so on. Among the types of resources you might include are the following:

- Films, videos, audiocassettes, books, and journal articles
- Simulation games designed to improve participants' attitudes toward diversity
- Motivational guest speakers from the community
- Ethnic museums and cultural centers
- Community groups and agencies dedicated to promoting understanding among diverse groups
- Training and workshops in the area of diversity

VideoWorkshop Extra!

If the VideoWorkshop package was included with your textbook, go to Chapter 7 of the Companion Website (www.ablongman.com/parkay6e) and click on the VideoWorkshop button. Follow the instructions for viewing videoclip 2 and completing this exercise. Consider this information along with what you've read in Chapter 7 while answering the following questions.

1. A stimulating classroom environment engages students' senses and strengths. Design a classroom environment for students in grades K–5, 6–8, or 9–12, and be able to discuss the following: why you chose to arrange the classroom in such a way; which materials would be readily accessible to students; and how the environment engages students' senses.
2. The students you teach are diverse in terms of ethnic and socioeconomic backgrounds. Devise a plan for how you would address a national holiday (e.g., Thanksgiving) in your classroom of eighth-grade students.

8 Addressing Learners' Individual Needs

My child will never be considered a poster child. She does not give professionals the satisfaction of making great progress, nor is she terribly social. But I need the same type of investment by professionals as any other parents of children with disabilities. The most important thing any educator can do for me is to love my Mary.

—Carol, mother of daughter with Rett syndrome, quoted in *Very Young Children with Special Needs* (Howard et al. 2001).

It's late Friday afternoon, the end of the fourth week of school, and you've just finished arranging your classroom for the cooperative learning groups you're starting on Monday. Leaning back in the chair at your desk, you survey the room and imagine how things will go on Monday. Your mental image is positive, with one possible exception—eleven-year-old Rick. Since the first day of school, he's been very disruptive. His teacher last year described him as "loud, aggressive, and obnoxious."

Since school began, Rick has been belligerent and noncompliant. For the most part, he does what he wants, when he wants. As far as you know, he has no close friends; he teases the other kids constantly and occasionally gets into fights.

Rick's parents divorced when he was in the second grade. His father was given custody of Rick and his younger sister. Two years later, Rick's father married a woman with three children of her own. You've heard that Rick's two new half-brothers, thirteen and fifteen years old, are "out of control," and the family has been receiving counseling services from the local mental health clinic.

Rick's school records indicate that other teachers have had trouble with him in the past. Academically, he's below his classmates in all subjects except physical education and art. Comments from two of his previous teachers suggest Rick has a flair for artwork. Last year, Rick was diagnosed with mild learning and behavior disorders.

Mr. Chavez, the school psychologist, and Ms. Tamashiro, the school's inclusion facilitator, have been working with you on developing an individualized education program (IEP) for Rick. In fact, before school on Monday, you're meeting with Ms. Tamashiro to discuss how to involve Rick in the cooperative learning groups. You're anxious to get her suggestions, and you're confident that with her help and Mr. Chavez's, you can meet Rick's learning needs.

Focus Questions

1. **How do students' needs change as they develop?**
2. **How do students vary in intelligence?**
3. **How do students vary in ability and disability?**
4. **What are special education, mainstreaming, and inclusion?**
5. **How can you teach all learners in your inclusive classroom?**

Expand your knowledge of the concepts discussed in this chapter by reading current and historical articles from the *New York Times* by visiting the **"Themes of the Times"** section of the Companion Website (www.ablongman.com/parkay6e).

As the preceding scenario about Rick suggests, teachers must understand and appreciate students' unique learning and developmental needs. They must be willing to learn about students' abilities and disabilities and to explore the special issues and concerns of students at three broad developmental levels—childhood, early adolescence, and late adolescence. The need to learn about the intellectual and psychological growth of students at the age level you plan to teach is obvious. In addition, understanding how their interests, questions, and problems will change throughout their school years will better equip you to serve them in the present. In this chapter, we look at how students' needs change as they develop and how their needs reflect various intelligences, abilities, and disabilities.

How Do Students' Needs Change as They Develop?

Development refers to the predictable changes that all human beings undergo as they progress through the life span—from conception to death. Although developmental changes "appear in orderly ways and remain for a reasonably long period of time" (Woolfolk 2001, 24), it is important to remember that students develop at different rates. Within a given classroom, for example, some students will be larger and physically more mature than others; some will be socially more sophisticated; and some will be able to think at a higher level of abstraction.

As humans progress through different **stages of development,** they mature and learn to perform the tasks that are a necessary part of daily living. There are several different types of human development. For example, as children develop physically, their bodies undergo numerous changes. As they develop cognitively, their mental capabilities expand so that they can use language and other symbol systems to solve problems. As they develop socially, they learn to interact more effectively with other people—as individuals and in groups. And, as they develop morally, their actions come to reflect a greater appreciation of principles such as equity, justice, fairness, and altruism.

Because no two students progress through the stages of cognitive, social, and moral development in quite the same way, teachers need perspectives on these three types of development that are flexible, dynamic, and, above all, useful. By becoming familiar with models of cognitive, social, and moral development, teachers at all levels, from preschool through college, can better serve their students. Three such models are Piaget's theory of **cognitive development,** Erikson's stages of **psychosocial development,** and Kohlberg's stages of **moral reasoning.**

Jean Piaget (1896–1980)

Piaget's Model of Cognitive Development

Jean Piaget (1896–1980), the noted Swiss biologist and epistemologist, made extensive observational studies of children. He concluded that children reason differently from adults and even have different perceptions of the world. Piaget surmised that children learn through actively interacting with their environments, much as scientists do, and proposed that a child's thinking progresses through a sequence of four cognitive stages (see Figure 8.1). According to Piaget's theory of cognitive development, the rate of progress through the four stages varies from individual to individual.

During the school years, students move through the **preoperational stage,** the **concrete operations stage,** and the **formal operations stage;** yet, because of individual interaction with the total environment, each student's perceptions and learning will be unique. According to Piaget,

> *The principal goal of education is to create [learners] who are capable of doing new things, not simply repeating what other generations have done—[learners] who are creative, inventive, and discoverers. [We] need pupils who are active, who learn early to find out by themselves, partly by their own spontaneous activity and partly through material we set up for them; who learn early to tell what is verifiable and what is simply the first idea to come to them (quoted in Ripple and Rockcastle 1964, 5).*

Figure 8.1 Piaget's stages of cognitive growth

1. **Sensorimotor Intelligence (birth to 2 years):** Behavior is primarily sensory and motor. The child does not yet "think" conceptually; however, "cognitive" development can be observed.

2. **Preoperational Thought (2–7 years):** Development of language and rapid conceptual development are evident. Children begin to use symbols to think of objects and people outside of their immediate environment. Fantasy and imaginative play are natural modes of thinking.

3. **Concrete Operations (7–11 years):** Children develop ability to use logical thought to solve concrete problems. Basic concepts of objects, number, time, space, and causality are explored and mastered. Through use of concrete objects to manipulate, children are able to draw conclusions.

4. **Formal Operations (11–15 years):** Cognitive abilities reach their highest level of development. Children can make predictions, think about hypothetical situations, think about thinking, and appreciate the structure of language as well as use it to communicate. Sarcasm, puns, argumentation, and slang are aspects of adolescents' speech that reflect their ability to think abstractly about language.

Guidelines for Teaching School-Age Children at Piaget's Stages of Cognitive Growth

Teaching the Child at the Preoperational Stage

1. Use concrete props and visual aids whenever possible.
2. Make instruction relatively short, using actions as well as words.
3. Don't expect the students to be consistent in their ability to see the world from someone else's point of view.
4. Be sensitive to the possibility that students may have different meanings for the same word or different words for the same meaning. Students may also expect everyone to understand words they have invented.
5. Give children a great deal of hands-on practice with the skills that serve as building blocks for more complex skills such as reading comprehension.
6. Provide a wide range of experiences in order to build a foundation for concept learning and language.

Teaching the Child at the Concrete-Operational Stage

1. Continue to use concrete props and visual aids, especially when dealing with sophisticated material.
2. Continue to give students a chance to manipulate and test objects.
3. Make sure presentation and readings are brief and well organized.
4. Use familiar examples to explain more complex ideas.
5. Give opportunities to classify and group objects and ideas on increasingly complex levels.
6. Present problems that require logical, analytical thinking.

Teaching the Child at the Formal Operations Stage

1. Continue to use concrete-operational teaching strategies and materials.
2. Give students the opportunity to explore many hypothetical questions.
3. Give students opportunities to solve problems and reason scientifically.
4. Whenever possible, teach broad concepts, not just facts, using materials and ideas relevant to the students' lives.

Figure 8.2 Guidelines for teaching school-age children at Piaget's stages of cognitive growth.
Source: Excerpted from Anita e. Woolfolk, *Educational Psychology,* 7th ed. Boston: Allyn and Bacon, 1998, pp. 33, 36, 39. Copyright © 1998 by Allyn and Bacon. Reprinted by permission.

Figure 8.2 presents guidelines for teaching children at the preoperational stage, the concrete operations stage, and the formal operations stage.

Erikson's Model of Psychosocial Development

Erik Erikson's model of psychosocial development delineates eight stages, from infancy to old age (see Table 8.1). For each stage a **psychosocial crisis** is central in the individual's emotional and social growth. Erikson expresses these crises in polar terms; for instance, in the first stage, that of infancy, the psychosocial crisis is trust versus mistrust. Erikson explains that the major psychosocial task for the infant is to develop a sense of trust in the world but not to give up totally a sense of distrust. In the tension between the poles of trust and mistrust, a greater pull toward the more positive pole is considered healthy and is accompanied by a virtue. In this case, if trust prevails, the virtue is hope. Shortly before his death in 1994 at the age of 91, Erikson postulated a ninth stage in the human life cycle, *gerotranscendence,* during which some people mentally transcend the reality of their deteriorating bodies and faculties. In the final chapter of an extended version of Erikson's *The Life Cycle Completed,* first published in 1982, his wife and lifelong colleague, Joan M. Erikson (1901–1997), described the challenge of the ninth stage:

> *Despair, which haunts the eighth stage, is a close companion in the ninth, because it is almost impossible to know what emergencies and losses of physical ability are im-*

minent. As independence and control are challenged, self-esteem and confidence weaken. Hope and trust, which once provided firm support, are no longer the sturdy props of former days. To face down despair with faith and appropriate humility is perhaps the wisest course (1997, 105–106).

When we examine the issues and concerns of students in childhood and early and late adolescence later in this chapter, we will return to Erikson's model of psychosocial development. For further information on this significant and useful theory of development, we recommend that you read Erikson's first book, *Childhood and Society* (1963).

Kohlberg's Model of Moral Development

According to Lawrence Kohlberg (1927–1987), the reasoning process people use to decide what is right and wrong evolves through three levels of development. Within each level, Kohlberg has identified two stages. Table 8.2 on page 282 shows that at Level I, the preconventional level, the individual decides what is right on the basis of personal needs and rules developed by others. At Level II,

Table 8.1 Erikson's eight stages of psychosocial development

Stage	Psychosocial Crisis	Approximate Age	Important Event	Description
1. Infancy	Basic trust versus basic mistrust	Birth to 12–18 months	Feeding	The infant must form a first loving, trusting relationship with the caregiver or develop a sense of mistrust.
2. Early childhood	Autonomy versus shame/doubt	18 months to 3 years	Toilet training	The child's energies are directed toward the development of physical skills, including walking, grasping, controlling the sphincter.
3. Play age	Initiative versus guilt	3 to 6 years	Independence	The child learns control but may develop shame and doubt if not handled well.
4. School age	Industry versus inferiority	6 to 12 years	School	The child continues to become more assertive and to take more initiative but may be too forceful, which can lead to guilt feelings.
5. Adolescence	Identity versus role confusion	Adolescence	Peer relationships	The child must deal with demands to learn new skills or risk a sense of inferiority, failure, and incompetence.
6. Young adult	Intimacy versus isolation	Young adulthood	Love relationships	The teenager must achieve identity in occupation, gender roles, politics, and religion.
7. Adulthood	Generativity versus stagnation	Middle adulthood	Parenting/Mentoring	The young adult must develop intimate relationships or suffer feelings of isolation. Each adult must find some way to satisfy and support the next generation.
8. Mature love	Ego integrity versus despair	Late adulthood	Reflection on and acceptance of one's life	The culmination is a sense of acceptance of oneself as one is and a sense of fulfillment.

Source: Adapted from Lester A. Lefton and Linda Brannon, *Psychology,* 7th ed. Boston: Allyn and Bacon, 2003. Copyright © 2003. Reprinted by permission.

the conventional level, moral decisions reflect a desire for the approval of others and a willingness to conform to the expectations of family, community, and country. At Level III, the postconventional level, the individual has developed values and principles that are based on rational, personal choices that can be separated from conventional values.

Kohlberg suggests that "over 50 percent of late adolescents and adults are capable of full formal reasoning [i.e., they can use their intelligence to reason abstractly, form hypotheses, and test these hypotheses against reality], but only 10 percent of these adults display principled (Stages 5 and 6) moral reasoning" (2000, 138–139). In addition, Kohlberg found that maturity of moral judgment is not highly related to IQ or verbal intelligence.

Carol Gilligan (1936–)

Some individuals have criticized Kohlberg's model as being too systematic and sequential, limited because it focuses on moral reasoning rather than actual behavior, or biased because it tends to look at moral development from a male perspective (Bracey 1993). Carol Gilligan, for example, suggests that male moral reasoning tends to address the rights of the individual while female moral reasoning addresses the individual's responsibility to other people. In her book, *In a Different Voice: Psychological Theory and Women's Development* (1993), Gilligan

Table 8.2 Kohlberg's theory of moral reasoning

I. Preconventional Level of Moral Reasoning

Child is responsive to cultural rules and labels of good and bad, right or wrong, but interprets these in terms of consequences of action (punishment, reward, exchanges of favors).

Stage 1: Punishment-and-obedience orientation
Physical consequences of action determine its goodness or badness.
Avoidance of punishment and deference to power are valued.

Stage 2: The instrumental-relativist orientation
Right action consists of that which satisfies one's own needs and occasionally the needs of others. Reciprocity is a matter of "You scratch my back and I'll scratch yours."

II. Conventional Level of Moral Reasoning

Maintaining the expectations of the individual's family, group, or nation is perceived as valuable, regardless of consequences.

Stage 3: The interpersonal concordance or "good boy-nice girl" orientation
Good behavior is that which pleases or helps others and is approved by them.

Stage 4: The "law and order" orientation
Orientation toward fixed rules and the maintenance of the social order. Right behavior consists of doing one's duty and showing respect for authority.

III. Postconventional, Autonomous, or Principled Level of Moral Reasoning

Effort to define moral principles that have validity and application apart from the authority of groups.

Stage 5: The social-contract, legalistic orientation
Right action defined in terms of rights and standards that have been agreed on by the whole society. This is the "official" morality of the American government and Constitution.

Stage 6: The universal-ethical-principle orientation
Right is defined by conscience in accord with self-chosen ethical principles appealing to logic and universality.

Source: Adapted from Lawrence Kohlberg, "The Cognitive-Developmental Approach to Moral Education," Forrest W. Parkay and Glen Hass (eds.), in Curriculum Planning: A Contemporary Approach, 7th ed. Boston: Allyn and Bacon, 2000, p. 137. The original version appeared in Journal of Philosophy, 70(18), 1973, pp. 631–632.

refers to women's principal moral voice as the "ethics of care," which emphasizes care of others over the more male-oriented "ethics of justice." Thus, when confronted with a moral dilemma, females tend to suggest solutions based more on altruism and self-sacrifice than on rights and rules (Gilligan 1993).

The question remains, can moral reasoning be taught? Can teachers help students develop so that they live according to principles of equity, justice, caring, and empathy? Kohlberg suggests the following three conditions that can help children internalize moral principles:

1. Exposure to the next higher stage of reasoning
2. Exposure to situations posing problems and contradictions for the child's current moral structure, leading to dissatisfaction with his [her] current level
3. An atmosphere of interchange and dialogue combining the first two conditions, in which conflicting moral views are compared in an open manner (Kohlberg 2000, 144).

One approach to teaching values and moral reasoning is known as **character education,** a movement that stresses the development of students' "good character." In remarks at the opening of the 2002 White House Conference on Character and Community, President George W. Bush stressed the importance of building character in our nation's schools:

Where Do You Stand? Visit the Companion Website to Voice Your Opinion.

> *We've got to do more than just teach our children skills and knowledge. We also want to make sure they're kind and decent, compassionate and responsible, honest and self-disciplined. Our children must learn to make a living, but even more, they must learn how to live . . . [as] Martin Luther King, Jr. said: "Intelligence is not enough. Intelligence plus character, that is the goal of true education" (White House press release, June 19, 2002).*

There is no single way for teachers to develop students' character; however, in comments made shortly after the shooting deaths of fourteen students and a teacher at Columbine High School in Colorado, well-known sociologist and organizer of several White House conferences on character education Amitai Etzioni (1999) said, "What schools should help youngsters develop—if schools are going to help lower the likelihood of more Columbines—are two crucial behavior characteristics: the capacity to channel impulses into prosocial outlets, and empathy with others." In addition, Figure 8.3 on p. 286 illustrates twelve strategies Thomas Lickona suggests teachers can use to create moral classroom communities.

Many schools, such as the Hyde Schools in Bath, Maine, and Woodstock, Connecticut, emphasize specific moral values in their curricula. The character-based educational program at the Hyde Schools focuses on five words: *curiosity, courage, concern, leadership,* and *integrity* (Gauld and Gauld 2002). Kennedy Middle School in Eugene, Oregon, implemented the "Second Step" program, described by a teacher as "a school-wide curriculum that teaches students skills such as how to communicate, problem-solve, and work together in a community. They learn the importance of responsibility and honesty . . . [and] a large section at the beginning of each unit emphasizes empathy" (DeRoche and Williams 2001, 163).

Maslow's Model of a Hierarchy of Needs

Students' developmental levels also vary according to how well their biological and psychological needs have been satisfied. Psychologist Abraham Maslow

On the Frontlines

Character Education

You're in your first week of playground duty at an elementary school. Your first concern is safety—you want to be certain that no one gets hurt. With only two teachers to monitor the 160 or so children, that task in itself is challenging. But a second concern surfaces as you hear how the kids talk and play with each other. Some children are blatantly mean to each other. Others are friendly but have awful nicknames for each other.

A week of playground duty leaves you disheartened and full of questions. The children seem to have so little regard for each other. Having caught some of your students cheating recently, you wonder about today's value systems. "Do kids not know the difference between right and wrong?" you ask yourself. How can you make children treat each other with respect? Is it your responsibility to develop their characters? Should you be the one to teach students not to call people names or take things from others against their will? Is it your job to tell students it's wrong to borrow money and not pay it back? Why do you have to worry about closely monitoring your students' papers? Are you, as their teacher, responsible for teaching children basic moral values—what's right and what's wrong? Isn't that the parents' job?

Fortunately, serious incidents that call character into question don't take place in every school every day; but character development does. Teachers need to accept their role as a powerful influence on students' behavior outside the home. Judith Rich Harris, author of *The Nurture Assumption,* writes that when children go astray "too much attention [is] paid to the home and not enough to the child's other environments . . . the world outside the home. And the most important part of that world is the school." Teachers play a crucial role in that environment. As Harris observes, "They can influence the attitudes and behaviors of the entire group. And they exert this influence where it is likely to have long-term effects: in the world outside the home, the world where children will spend their adult lives."

"Teachers haven't a clue about what goes on at recess. They stay near the classrooms and don't walk around and see what's happening," one fifth grader confides.

Problems on the playground or in the hallways have a way of seeping into the classroom and contaminating the learning climate. When students are angry, hurt, or fearful, they have trouble learning. So teachers need to *listen* to children; and they need to be proactive about bringing to an end students' unkind, disrespectful, and dishonest behavior. By partnering with other adults—other teachers, staff members, administrators, and parents—teachers can help bring about systemic change.

Within the classroom, teachers can find natural ways to incorporate value lessons into their existing curricula—lessons that promote integrity and honor. In the book *Bringing in a New Era of Character Education,* (2002) Arthur Schwartz suggests that young children study maxims to live by, and high school students develop an honor code culture. Older students can also study the moral messages in films such as *The Magestic* and *K-19 The Widowmaker* or they can explore the ethical issues that arise in lessons and discuss them openly. Of course, teachers play a critical role as models as well. They need to continually remind themselves that the words they use and the attitudes and actions they display are ongoing moral lessons for their students. Showing students respect can go a long way.

The number of books, curricula, programs, organizations, conferences, and centers focused on moral and character education has increased in recent years, largely due to the increase in student and societal violence. With access to timely resources, teachers can work to enhance an essential of their students' educations and lives, their moral and character development.

Exploratory Questions

1. How would you work with others to bring about change in the way children interact on the playground?
2. What are some causes of children's mean treatment of others and how might a teacher address those causes in the classroom?
3. What would be your argument in favor of integrating character education into your classroom?

Your Survival Guide of Helpful Resources

The following resources provide helpful hints for surviving "on the frontlines."

Books and Articles

Damon, W. (Ed.). (2002). *Bringing in a new era in character education.* Stanford, CA: Hoover Institution Press.

Harris, J. D. (May/June 1999). How many environments does a child have? *Harvard Education Letter, 15*(3), 8.

Noddings, N. (2002). *Educating moral people: A caring alternative to character education.* New York: Teachers College Press.

Schwartz, A. J. (2002). *Bringing in a New Era in Character Education.* Stanford, CA: Stanford University, Hoover Institution Press.

Websites

Center for the Advancement of Ethics and Character (http://www.bu.edu/education/caec/)

Character Education Partnership (http://www.character.org)

International Center for Character Education (http://www.teachvalues.org/icce)

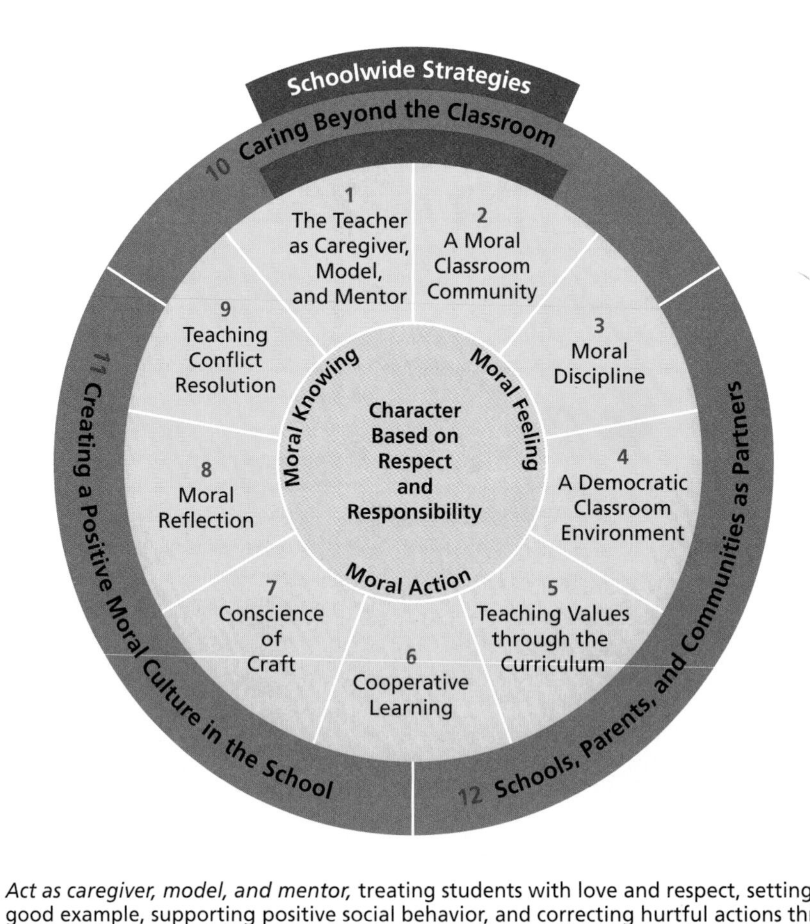

1. *Act as caregiver, model, and mentor,* treating students with love and respect, setting a good example, supporting positive social behavior, and correcting hurtful actions through one-on-one guidance and whole-class discussion.
2. *Create a moral community,* helping students know one another as persons, respect and care about one another, and feel valued membership in, and responsibility to, the group.
3. *Practice moral discipline,* using the creation and enforcement of rules as opportunities to foster moral reasoning, voluntary compliance with rules, and a respect for others.
4. *Create a democratic classroom environment,* involving students in decision making and the responsibility for making the classroom a good place to be and learn.
5. *Teach values through the curriculum,* using the ethically rich content of academic subjects (such as literature, history, and science) as vehicles for teaching values and examining moral questions.
6. *Use cooperative learning* to develop students' appreciation of others, perspective taking, and the ability to work with others toward common goals.
7. *Develop the "conscience of craft"* by fostering students' appreciation of learning, capacity for hard work, commitment to excellence, and sense of work as affecting the lives of others.
8. *Encourage moral reflection* through reading, research, essay writing, journal keeping, discussion, and debate.
9. *Teach conflict resolution,* so that students acquire the essential moral skills of solving conflicts fairly and without force.
10. *Foster caring beyond the classroom,* using positive role models to inspire altruistic behavior and providing opportunities at every grade level to perform school and community service.
11. *Create a positive moral culture in the school,* developing a schoolwide ethos that supports and amplifies the values taught in classrooms.
12. *Recruit parents and the community as partners in character education,* letting parents know that the school considers them their child's first and most important moral teacher.

Figure 8.3 A comprehensive approach to values and character education.
Source: Thomas Lickona, *Educating for Character: How Our Schools Can Teach.* New York: Bantam Books, 1991, p. 69.

(1908–1970) formulated a model of a **hierarchy of needs** (see Figure 8.4) that suggests that people are motivated by basic needs for survival and safety first. When these basic needs have been met sufficiently, people naturally seek to satisfy higher needs, the highest of which is self-actualization—the desire to use one's talents, abilities, and potentialities to the fullest. Students whose needs for safety have been fairly well satisfied will discover strong needs for friendship, affection, and love, for example. If efforts to satisfy the various needs are thwarted, the result can be maladjustment and interruption or delay in the individual's full and healthy development.

The hierarchy of needs model has particular relevance for teachers because students differ markedly in terms of where they are on Maslow's hierarchy of needs. Many families lack the resources to provide adequately for children's basic needs. Children from families that are concerned with day-to-day survival may not receive the support that could help them succeed in school. They come to school tired and hungry and may have trouble paying attention in class. Others may be well fed and clothed but feel unsafe, alien, or unloved; they may seek to protect themselves by withdrawing emotionally from activities around them.

Developmental Stresses and Tasks of Childhood

During Erikson's school-age stage, children strive for a sense of industry and struggle against feelings of inferiority. If successful, they gain the virtue of competence, believing in their abilities to do things. If children find evidence that they are inferior to others, if they experience failure when they try new tasks, and if they struggle without ever gaining a sense of mastery, then they feel incompetent.

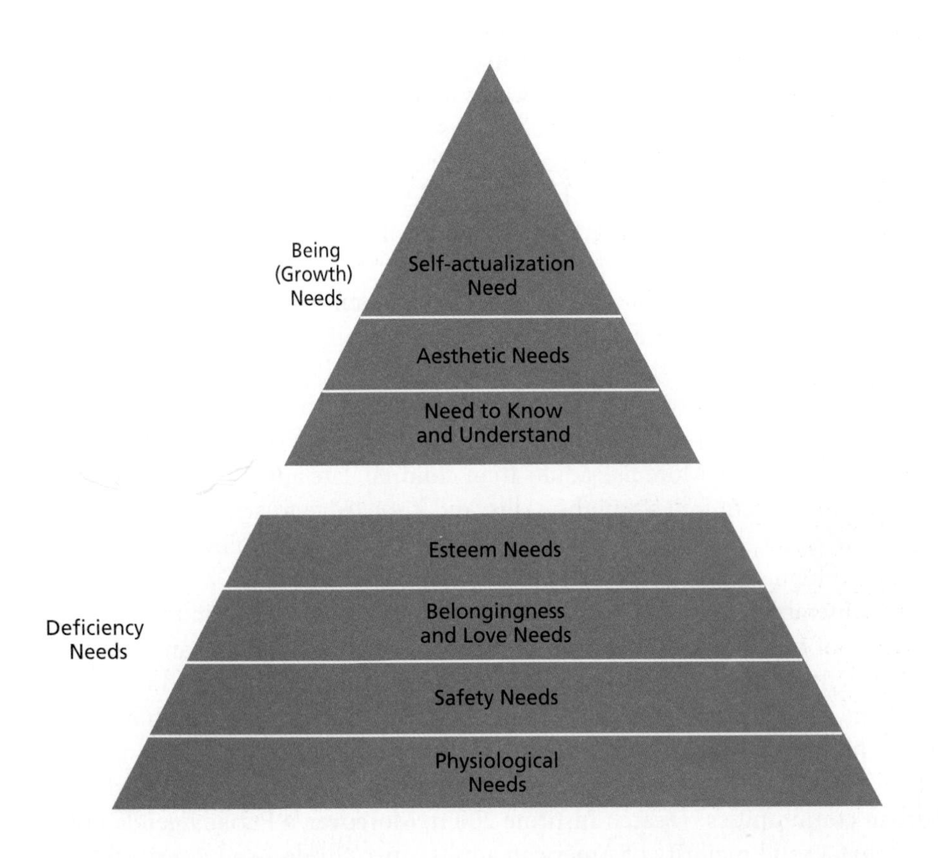

Figure 8.4 Maslow's hierarchy of needs. Note: The four lower-level needs are called deficiency needs because the motivation to satisfy them decreases when they are met. On the other hand, when being (growth) needs are met, motivation to fulfill them increases.

Source: Based on Abraham H. Maslow, *Toward a Psychology of Being,* 3rd ed. New York: John Wiley & Sons, 1999; and *Motivation and Personality,* 3rd ed. Boston: Addison-Wesley Publishing Company, 1987.

Children gain the sense of industry needed at this age by playing seriously, mastering new skills, producing products, and being workers. When they first go to school they are oriented toward accomplishing new things (some kindergartners expect to learn to read on their first day of school and are disappointed when they don't). For young schoolchildren, the idea of work is attractive; it means that they are doing something grown-up.

Is childhood a time of carefree play or a period of stress? Certainly the answer depends on the life circumstances and personality of the individual child. In a study of stressful events in the lives of more than 1,700 children in the second through the ninth grades in six countries, Karou Yamamoto and his associates found that the most stressful events "threaten[ed] one's sense of security and occasion[ed] personal denigration and embarrassment" (1996, 139). Other studies have shown that serious stress is experienced by latchkey children, for example, who are left on their own or in each others' care for part or all of the day.

Developmental Stresses and Tasks of Adolescence

Many psychologists believe that adolescence contains two distinct stages: an early period covering the ages of ten to twelve through the ages of fourteen to sixteen, and a late period from approximately fifteen to sixteen through nineteen. Although a continuity exists in each individual's life, the psychosocial issues of adolescence—coping with change and seeking identity—vary in form and importance as individuals progress through the transition from childhood to adulthood.

In Erik Erikson's model of the eight stages of humans, identity versus role diffusion is the psychosocial crisis for the adolescent years. Although the quest for identity is a key psychosocial issue for both early and late adolescence, many believe that Erikson's identity-versus-role diffusion stage fits best for early adolescence. During this time, young adolescents, using their new thinking abilities, begin integrating a clearer sense of personal identity. Erikson's role diffusion refers to the variety of roles that adolescents have available to them.

According to Erikson's theory, when adolescents identify themselves with a peer group, with a school, or with a cause, their sense of fidelity—the "virtue" of this stage—is clear and strong. At this stage adolescents are loyal and committed, sometimes to people or ideas that may dismay or alarm their parents, sometimes to high ideals and dreams.

In late adolescence, the quest for identity shifts from relying on others to self-reliance. Young people continue to work on strengthening their sense of identity in late adolescence, but as they do so they draw less on the reactions of their peers and more on their own regard for what matters. Although late adolescents possess an array of interests, talents, and goals in life, they share a desire to achieve independence. More like adults than children, late adolescents are anxious to use newly acquired strengths, skills, and knowledge to achieve their own purposes, whether through marriage, parenthood, full-time employment, education beyond high school, a career, or military service.

The vulnerability of today's adolescents is dramatically evident in the results of a survey of one thousand schools and one million students based on forty "developmental assets" (positive relationships, opportunities, skills, and values) adolescents need to become healthy, mature adults: "[O]n average, youth have less than half of the 40 assets they need to grow up healthy, caring, and responsible. . . . [T]his statistic remains relatively consistent among urban, rural, and suburban communities" (Search Institute 2002). Moreover, a Public Agenda poll "found that a solid majority of American adults—two thirds—spontaneously

What needs must this child satisfy for healthy development? What childhood stresses does she face? What developmental tasks must she accomplish in her psychosocial development? What needs, stresses, and developmental tasks will affect this child as an adolescent? Why is information about development important to teachers?

describe adolescents in starkly negative terms: wild, rude, irresponsible. Half give those descriptions even to younger children" (Scales 2001, 64). The list of alarming concerns in adolescence includes academic failure and retention, accidents, anorexia, assaultive behavior, criminal activity, cultism, depression, discipline problems, dropouts, drug abuse, homicides, incest, prostitution, runaways, school absenteeism, suicide, teenage pregnancy, vandalism, and the contraction of sexually transmitted diseases.

What can teachers do to help children and adolescents develop to their full potential? To help prevent the problems that place them at risk, an energetic, creative, and multifaceted approach is necessary. Figure 8.5 presents several strategies for helping students develop competence, positive self-concepts, and high esteem and for intervening to prevent or address problems that place them at risk.

How Do Students Vary in Intelligence?

In addition to developmental differences, students differ in terms of their intellectual capacity. Unfortunately, test scores, and sometimes intelligence quotient (IQ) scores, are treated as accurate measurements of students' intellectual ability because of their convenience and long-time use. What is intelligence and how has it been redefined to account for the many ways in which it is expressed? Though many definitions of intelligence have been proposed, the term has yet to be completely defined. One view is that **intelligence** is the ability to learn. As David Wechsler, the developer of the most widely used intelligence scales for children and adults, said: "Intelligence, operationally defined, is the aggregate or global capacity to act purposefully, to think rationally, and to deal effectively with the environment" (1958, 7). Other definitions of intelligence that have been proposed are the following:

- Goal-directed adaptive behavior
- Ability to solve novel problems
- Ability to acquire and think with new conceptual systems
- Problem-solving ability

1. **Provide opportunities and encouragement for students to develop competence.**
    - Provide a learning environment in which students can risk making mistakes.
    - Assign work that students can perform successfully and still be challenged.
    - Have realistic but high expectations for students.
    - Express belief in students' ability to succeed.
    - Encourage industry by letting students work on goals or projects of their choosing.
    - Provide opportunities for students to take special responsibility.
    - Assign older students to work with younger ones.
    - Reward industry and competence.
2. **Promote the development of positive self-concept and high self-esteem.**
    - Give praise more than criticism.
    - Take students and their work seriously.
    - Respect students' dignity.
    - Plan individual and group activities that boost morale.
    - Provide opportunities for students to interact and work cooperatively.
    - Teach and model acceptance of human diversity and individuality.
    - Develop systems for the recognition and reward of individual and group achievement.
    - Support students' efforts to achieve and appropriately express independence.
3. **Intervene to prevent or address problems that place students at risk.**
    - Provide a safe and structured learning environment where students feel secure.
    - Practice effective leadership and classroom management.
    - Provide opportunities to discuss preferences, values, morals, goals, and consequences.
    - Teach and model critical thinking, decision making, and problem solving.
    - Teach and model prosocial attitudes and behaviors and conflict resolution strategies.
    - Provide information on subjects of special concern to students and parents.
    - Cultivate family involvement.
    - Collaborate, consult, network, and refer on behalf of students.

Figure 8.5 What teachers can do to help children and adolescents develop

- Planning and other metacognitive skills
- Memory access speed
- What people think intelligence is
- What IQ tests measure
- The ability to learn from bad teaching (Woolfolk 2001, 108)

Intelligence Testing

The intelligence tests that we now use can be traced to the 1905 Metrical Scale of Intelligence designed by French psychologists Alfred Binet and Theodore Simon, who were part of a Paris-based commission that wanted a way to identify children who would need special help with their learning. Binet revised the scale in 1908, which was adapted for American children in 1916 by Lewis Terman, a psychologist at Stanford University. Terman's test was, in turn, further adapted, especially by the U.S. Army, which transformed it into a paper-and-pencil test that could be administered to large groups. The use of such intelligence tests has continued throughout the years. Approximately 67 percent of the population have an IQ between 85 and 115—the range of normal intelligence.

Individual intelligence tests are presently valued by psychologists and those in the field of special education because they can be helpful in diagnosing a student's strengths and weaknesses. However, group intelligence tests given for the purpose of classifying students into like-score groups have received an increasing amount of criticism.

The most significant and dramatic criticism of group IQ tests has been that test items and tasks are culturally biased, drawn mostly from white middle-class experience. Thus the tests are more assessments of how informed students are about features in a specific class or culture than of how intelligent they are in general. This complaint became a formal, legal challenge when, on the basis of their IQ test scores, a group of African American children were put into special classes for mentally retarded children. Their parents brought the complaint to the courts in 1971 and persisted with it all the way to the federal appellate court, where a decision was eventually made in their favor in 1984. In that well-known case, *Larry P. v. Riles* (1984), the court decided that IQ tests were discriminatory and culturally biased. However, in another case, *PASE v. Hannon* (1980), an Illinois district court ruled that when IQ tests were used in conjunction with other forms of assessment, such as teacher observation, they were not discriminatory for placement purposes. Although the criticism continues, a number of psychometricians are seeking other solutions by attempting to design culture-free intelligence tests.

Multiple Intelligences

Many theorists believe that intelligence is a basic ability that enables one to perform mental operations in the following areas: logical reasoning, spatial reasoning, number ability, and verbal meaning. However, other theorists believe "that conventional notions of intelligence are incomplete and hence inadequate. [One's] ability to achieve success depends on capitalizing on one's strengths and correcting or compensating for one's weaknesses through a balance of analytical, creative, and practical abilities" (Sternberg 2002, 447–448). For example, Howard Gardner believes that human beings possess at least eight separate forms of intelligence; "each intelligence reflects the potential to solve problems or to fashion products that are valued in one or more cultural settings. [Each] features its own distinctive form of mental representation" (1999, 71–72). Drawing on the theories of others and research findings on savants, prodigies, and other exceptional individuals, Gardner originally suggested in *Frames of Mind* (1983) that human beings possessed seven human intelligences: logical-mathematical, linguistic, musical, spatial, bodily-kinesthetic, interpersonal, and intrapersonal. In the mid-1990s, he identified an eighth intelligence, that of the naturalist; and in his book *The Disciplined Mind,* he suggests that "it is possible that human beings also exhibit a ninth, existential intelligence—the proclivity to pose (and ponder) questions about life, death, and ultimate realities" (1999, 72). According to Gardner, every person possesses the eight intelligences (see Figure 8.6 on page 292), yet each person has his or her particular blend of the intelligences.

Gardner's theory of **multiple intelligences** is valuable for teachers. As Robert Slavin suggests, "Teachers must avoid thinking about children as smart or not smart because there are many ways to be smart (2000, 130). Some students are talented in terms of their interpersonal relations and exhibit natural leadership abilities. Others seem to have a high degree of what some researchers have termed *emotional intelligence*—awareness of and ability to manage their feelings (Salovey and Feldman-Barrett 2002; Salovey, Mayer, and Caruso 2002; Salovey and Sluyter 1997). Differences in musical, athletic, and mechanical abilities can be recognized by even the minimally informed observer. Because these intelligences are not tested or highlighted, they may go unnoticed and possibly wasted.

However, keep in mind Gardner's "reflections" fourteen years after the publication of *Frames of Mind:*

> *MI [multiple intelligences] may be appealing, but it is not for the faint-hearted, nor for those in search of a quick fix. After initial experimentation with the ideas and*

practices of MI, practitioners realize that MI is not an end in itself. To say that one has an MI classroom or an MI school is not meaningful—one has to ask "MI for what?" (1997, 20).

Learning Styles

Students vary greatly in regard to **learning styles,** the approaches to learning that work best for them. These differences have also been called *learning style preferences* or *cognitive styles* (Woolfolk 2001). The National Task Force on

Figure 8.6 The eight intelligences.
Source: Project SUMIT (Schools Using Multiple Intelligence Theory), "Theory of Multiple Intelligences."

The Eight Intelligences

Linguistic intelligence allows individuals to communicate and make sense of the world through language. Poets exemplify this intelligence in its mature form. Students who enjoy playing with rhymes, who pun, who always have a story to tell, who quickly acquire other languages—including sign language— all exhibit linguistic intelligence.

Musical intelligence allows people to create, communicate, and understand meanings made out of sound. While composers and instrumentalists clearly exhibit this intelligence, so do the students who seem particularly attracted by the birds singing outside the classroom window or who constantly tap out intricate rhythms on the desk with their pencils.

Logical-mathematical intelligence enables individuals to use and appreciate abstract relations. Scientists, mathematicians, and philosophers all rely on this intelligence. So do the students who "live" baseball statistics or who carefully analyze the components of problems—either personal or school-related—before systematically testing solutions.

Spatial intelligence makes it possible for people to perceive visual or spatial information, to transform this information, and to recreate visual images from memory. Well-developed spatial capacities are needed for the work of architects, sculptors, and engineers. The students who turn first to the graphs, charts, and pictures in their textbooks, who like to "web" their ideas before writing a paper, and who fill the blank space around their notes with intricate patterns are also using their spatial intelligence.

Bodily-kinesthetic intelligence allows individuals to use all or part of the body to create products or solve problems. Athletes, surgeons, dancers, choreographers, and craftspeople all use bodily-kinesthetic intelligence. The capacity is also evident in students who relish gym class and school dances, who prefer to carry out class projects by making models rather than writing reports, and who toss crumpled paper with frequency and accuracy into wastebaskets across the room.

Interpersonal intelligence enables individuals to recognize and make distinctions about others' feelings and intentions. Teachers, parents, politicians, psychologists, and salespeople rely on interpersonal intelligence. Students exhibit this intelligence when they thrive on small-group work, when they notice and react to the moods of their friends and classmates, and when they tactfully convince the teacher of their need for extra time to complete the homework assignment.

Intrapersonal intelligence helps individuals to distinguish among their own feelings, to build accurate mental models of themselves, and to draw on these models to make decisions about their lives. Although it is difficult to assess who has this capacity and to what degree, evidence can be sought in students' uses of their other intelligences—how well they seem to be capitalizing on their strengths, how cognizant they are of their weaknesses, and how thoughtful they are about the decisions and choices they make.

Naturalist intelligence allows people to distinguish among, classify, and use features of the environment. Farmers, gardeners, botanists, geologists, florists, and archaeologists all exhibit this intelligence, as do students who can name and describe the features of every make of car around them.

Professional Reflection

Identifying Your Learning Style Preferences

Describe your preferred learning environment. Where, when, and how do you learn best? Does certain lighting, food, or music seem to enhance your learning? Think about how you acquire new information–do you prefer being analytical and abstract or commonsensical and concrete? Do you prefer thinking about things or doing things? Do you prefer to learn alone, in a small group, or in a large group? When given an assignment, do you prefer a lot of structure and details, or do you prefer more unstructured or open-ended assignments?

Learning Style and Brain Behavior suggests that there is a "consistent pattern of behavior and performance by which an individual approaches educational experiences. It is the composite of characteristic cognitive, affective, and physiological behaviors that serve as relatively stable indicators of how a learner perceives, interacts with, and responds to the learning environment."

Students' learning styles are determined by a combination of hereditary and environmental influences. Some more quickly learn things they hear; others learn faster when they see material in writing. Some need a lot of structure; others learn best when they can be independent and follow their desires. Some learn best in formal settings; others learn best in informal, relaxed environments. Some need almost total silence to concentrate; others learn well in noisy, active environments. Some are intuitive learners; some prefer to learn by following logical, sequential steps.

There is no one "correct" view of learning styles to guide teachers in their daily decision making. Culture-based differences in learning styles are subtle, variable, and difficult to describe (Zhang and Sternberg 2001); and learning styles change as the individual matures. Moreover, critics maintain that there is little evidence to support the validity of dozens of conceptual models for learning styles and accompanying assessment instruments. Nevertheless, you should be aware of the concept of learning styles and realize that any given classroom activity may be more effective for some students than for others. Knowledge of your own and your students' learning styles will help you to individualize instruction and motivate your students.

How Do Students Vary in Ability and Disability?

Students also differ according to their special needs and talents. Some enter the world with exceptional abilities or disabilities; others encounter life experiences that change their capabilities significantly, and still others struggle with conditions that medical scientists have yet to understand. Where possible, all children and youth with exceptionalities are given a public education in the United States.

Exceptional Learners

Children "who require special education and related services if they are to realize their full human potential" (Hallahan and Kauffman 2003, 7) are referred to as **exceptional learners.** They are taught by special education teachers and by regular teachers into whose classrooms they have been integrated or *included.* Among the many exceptional children that teachers may encounter in the classroom are students who have physical, mental, or emotional disabilities and students who are gifted or talented.

Special-needs students are often referred to synonymously as *handicapped* or *disabled.* However, it is important for teachers to understand the following distinction between a disability and a handicap:

> *A disability . . . results from a loss of physical functioning (e.g., loss of sight, hearing, or mobility) or from difficulty in learning and social adjustment that significantly interferes with normal growth and development. A handicap is a limitation imposed on the individual by environmental demands and is related to the individual's ability to adapt or adjust to those demands (Hardman, Drew, and Egan 2003, 3).*

For example, Stephen W. Hawking, a gifted physicist who has amyotrophic lateral sclerosis (also known as Lou Gehrig's disease), which requires him to use a wheelchair for mobility and a speech synthesizer to communicate. If Hawking had to enter a building accessible only by stairs, or if a computer virus infected his speech synthesizer program, his disability would then become a handicap.

In addition, teachers should know that current language use emphasizes the concept of "people first." In other words, a disabling condition should not be used as an adjective to describe a person. Thus, one should say "a child with a visual impairment," not a "blind child" or even a "visually impaired child."

Teachers should also realize that the definitions for disabilities are generalized, open to change, and significantly influenced by the current cultural perception of normality. For example, the American Association on Mental Retardation (AAMR) has changed its definition of mental retardation seven times since 1950 to reflect shifting views of people with cognitive disabilities.

Cautions about labeling should also apply to gifted and talented students. Unfortunately, people commonly have a negative view of gifted and talented youngsters. Like many ethnic groups, gifted students are "different" and thus have been the target of many myths and stereotypes. However, a landmark study of 1,528 gifted males and females begun by Lewis Terman (Terman, Baldwin, and Bronson 1925; Terman and Oden 1947, 1959) in 1926 and to continue until 2010 has "exploded the myth that high-IQ individuals [are] brainy but physically and socially inept. In fact, Terman found that children with outstanding IQs were larger, stronger, and better coordinated than other children and became better adjusted and more emotionally stable adults" (Slavin 2003, 429).

Students with Disabilities

Table 8.3 shows that the percentage of all students participating in federally supported education programs for **students with disabilities** increased from 8.33 percent in 1976–77 to 13.22 percent in 1999–2000. Nearly 6.2 million students participated in these programs in 2000 (National Center for Education Statistics 2001).

Various tests and other forms of assessment are used to identify persons in various categories of disability. The following brief definitional characteristics are based on the Individuals with Disabilities Education Act (IDEA) and definitions used by professional organizations dedicated to meeting the needs of persons in each category.

1. *Specific learning disabilities (LD)*—Learning is significantly hindered by difficulty in listening, speaking, reading, writing, reasoning, or computing
2. *Speech or language impairments*—Significant difficulty in communicating with others as a result of speech or language disorders
3. *Mental retardation*—Significant limitations in cognitive ability
4. *Serious emotional disturbance (SED)*—Social and/or emotional maladjustment that significantly reduces the ability to learn

5. *Hearing impairments*—Permanent or fluctuating mild to profound hearing loss in one or both ears
6. *Orthopedic impairments*—Physically disabling conditions that affect locomotion or motor functions
7. *Other health impairments*—Limited strength, vitality, or alertness caused by chronic or acute health problems
8. *Visual impairments*—Vision loss that significantly inhibits learning
9. *Multiple disabilities*—Two or more interrelated disabilities
10. *Deaf-blindness*—Vision and hearing disability that severely limits communication
11. *Autism and other*—Significantly impaired communication, learning, and reciprocal social interactions

Table 8.3 Children 0 to 21 years old served in federally supported programs for the disabled, by type of disability: 1976–77 to 1999–2000*

Number served as a percent of total enrollment**

Type of Disability	1976–77	1988–89	1997–98	1998–99	1999–2000
Specific learning disabilities	1.80	4.94	5.91	5.99	6.05
Speech or language impairments	2.94	2.41	2.29	2.29	2.30
Mental retardation	2.16	1.40	1.28	1.28	1.28
Serious emotional disturbance	0.64	0.94	0.98	0.99	1.00
Hearing impairments	0.20	0.14	0.15	0.15	0.15
Orthopedic impairments	0.20	0.14	0.15	0.15	0.15
Other health impairments	0.32	0.11	0.41	0.47	0.54
Visual impairments	0.09	0.06	0.05	0.06	0.06
Multiple disabilities	–	0.21	0.23	0.23	0.24
Deaf-blindness	–	****	****	****	****
Autism and traumatic brain injury	–	–	0.12	0.14	0.17
Developmental delay	–	–	0.01	0.03	0.04
Preschool disabled***	0.44	0.89	1.22	1.22	1.24
Infants and toddlers	–	0.08	–	–	–
All disabilities	8.33	11.26	12.80	13.01	13.22

–Data not available

*Data reported in this table for years prior to 1993–94 include children ages 0–21 served under Chapter 1 of the Elementary and Secondary Education Act. Data reported in this table for years after 1993–94 reflects children ages 3–21 served under IDEA, Part B.

**Based on the enrollment in public schools, K–12, including a relatively small number of PreK students.

***Includes preschool children 3–5 years served under Chapter I and IDEA, Part B.

****Less than .005 percent.

Note: Counts are based on reports from the fifty states and District of Columbia only (i.e., figures from outlying areas are not included). Increases since 1987–88 are due in part to new legislation enacted fall 1986, which mandates public school special education services for all children with disabilities ages 3 through 5. Some data have been revised from previously published figures. Detail may not sum to totals due to rounding.

Source: U.S. Department of Education, Office of Special Education and Rehabilitative Services, *Annual Report to Congress on the Implementation of the Individuals with Disabilities Act*, various years, and unpublished tabulations; and National Center for Education Statistics, Common Core of Data survey. (This table was prepared April 2001.)

Of the six million children in special education, half are identified as having a specific learning disability (President's Commission on Excellence in Special Education 2002). Since the term **learning disability (LD)** was first introduced in the early 1960s, there has been no universally accepted definition. The National Joint Committee on Learning Disabilities states that

> *Learning disabilities is a general term that refers to a heterogeneous group of disorders manifested by significant difficulties in the acquisition and use of listening, speaking, reading, writing, reasoning, or mathematical skills. These disorders are intrinsic to the individual, presumed to be due to central nervous system dysfunction, and may occur across the life span. Problems in self-regulatory behaviors, social perception, and social interaction may exist with learning disabilities but do not, by themselves, constitute a learning disability (National Joint Committee on Learning Disabilities 1997).*

Imagine that you are concerned about two of your new students—Mary and Bill. Mary has an adequate vocabulary and doesn't hesitate to express herself, but her achievement in reading and mathematics doesn't add up to what you believe she can do. Often, when you give the class instructions, Mary seems to get confused about what to do. In working with her one-on-one, you've noticed that she often reverses letters and numbers the way much younger children do—she sees a *b* for a *d* or a *6* for a *9*. Mary may have a learning disability, causing problems in taking in, organizing, remembering, and expressing information. Like Mary, students with learning disabilities often show a significant difference between their estimated intelligence and their actual achievement in the classroom.

Bill presents you with a different set of challenges. He is obviously bright, but he frequently seems to be "out of sync" with classroom activities. He gets frustrated when he has to wait for his turn. He sometimes blurts out answers before you've even asked a question. He can't seem to stop wiggling his toes and tapping his pencil, and he often comes to school without his backpack and homework. Bill may have **attention deficit hyperactivity disorder (ADHD),** one of the most commonly diagnosed disabilities among children. Students with ADHD have difficulty remaining still so they can concentrate. Students with an **attention deficit disorder (ADD)** have difficulty focusing their attention long enough to learn well. Children with ADD/ADHD do not qualify for special education unless they also have another disability in a federally defined category.

Treatment for students with ADD/ADHD includes behavior modification and medication. Since the early 1980s, Ritalin has become the most commonly prescribed drug for ADD/ADHD, and more than one million American children are currently estimated to take Ritalin to increase their impulse control and attention span.

By being alert for students who exhibit several of the following academic and behavioral characteristics, teachers can help in the early identification of students with learning disabilities so they can receive the instructional adaptations or special education services they need.

- Significant discrepancy between potential and achievement
- Inability to solve problems
- Substantial delay in academic achievement
- Lack of involvement in learning tasks
- Poor language and/or cognitive development

- Lack of basic reading and decoding skills
- Lack of attention during lectures or class discussion, distractible
- Excessive movement, hyperactive
- Impulsivity
- Poor motor coordination and spatial relation skills
- Poor motivation
- Overreliance on teacher and peers for class assignments (Smith 2001, 139)

Students Who Are Gifted and Talented

You are concerned about the poor performance of Paul, a student in your eighth-period high school class. Paul is undeniably bright. When he was ten, he had an IQ of 145 on the Stanford-Binet. Last year, when he was sixteen, he scored 142. Paul's father is a physician, and his mother is a professor. Both parents clearly value learning and are willing to give Paul any needed encouragement and help.

Throughout elementary school, Paul had an outstanding record. His teachers reported that he was brilliant and very meticulous in completing his assignments. He entered high school amid expectations by his parents and teachers that he would continue his outstanding performance. Throughout his first two years of high school, Paul never seemed to live up to his promise. Now, halfway through his junior year, Paul is failing English and geometry. Paul seems to be well adjusted to the social side of school. He has a lot of friends and says he likes school. Paul explains his steadily declining grades by saying that he doesn't like to study.

Paul may be gifted. **Gifted and talented** students, those who have demonstrated a high level of attainment in intellectual ability, academic achievement, creativity, or visual and performing arts, are evenly distributed across all ethnic and cultural groups and socioeconomic classes. Although you might think it is easy to meet the needs of gifted and talented students, you will find that this is not always the case. "Students with special gifts or talents often challenge the system of school, and they can be verbally caustic. Their superior abilities and unusual or advanced interests demand teachers who are highly intelligent, creative, and motivated" (Hallahan and Kauffman 2000, 497). The ability of such students to challenge the system is reflected in a recent U.S. Department of Education study that found that gifted and talented elementary schoolchildren have mastered 35 percent to 50 percent of the grade curriculum in five basic subject areas *before* starting the school year.

There are many forms that giftedness may take; Joseph S. Renzulli (1998), Director of the National Research Center on the Gifted and Talented at the University of Connecticut, for example, suggests two kinds of giftedness: "schoolhouse giftedness [which] might also be called test-taking or lesson-learning giftedness" and "creative-productive giftedness." The trend during the last few decades has been to broaden our view of what characterizes giftedness.

Drawing from the work of Renzulli and his colleagues, Woolfolk defines *giftedness* "as a combination of three basic characteristics: above-average general ability, a high level of creativity, and a high level of task commitment or motivation to achieve in certain areas. Truly gifted children are not the students who simply learn quickly with little effort. The work of gifted students is original, extremely advanced for their age, and potentially of lasting importance" (Woolfolk 2001, 123).

Variations in criteria used to identify gifted and talented students are especially evident in the reported incidence of giftedness from state to state; for example, North Dakota identifies only 1.0 percent of its students as gifted and talented, while Wisconsin identifies 15.0 percent (National Center for Education Statistics 1999, 67). Depending on the criteria used, estimates of the number of gifted and talented students range from 3 to 5 percent of the total population.

Strategies for teaching students who are gifted and talented begin with effective teachers. Educational psychologist Anita Woolfolk suggests that "teaching methods for gifted students should encourage abstract thinking (formal-operational thought), creativity, and independence, not just the learning of greater quantities of facts. In working with gifted and talented students, a teacher must be imaginative, flexible, and unthreatened by the capabilities of these students. The teacher must ask, What does this child need most? What is she or he ready to learn? Who can help me to challenge them?" (2001, 126).

Research indicates that effective teachers of the gifted and talented have many of the same characteristics as their students (Davis and Rimm 1998; Piirto 1999). In fact, Feldhusen (1997) suggests that teachers of gifted students should be gifted themselves and should possess the following characteristics:

- Be highly intelligent
- Have cultural and intellectual interests
- Strive for excellence and high achievement
- Be enthusiastic about talent
- Relate well to talented people
- Have broad general knowledge

Several innovative approaches exist for meeting the educational needs of gifted students.

Acceleration—Accelerated programs for intellectually precocious students have proven successful. For example, an analysis of 314 studies of the academic, psychological, and social effects of acceleration practices at the elementary and secondary levels found "generally positive academic effects for most forms of acceleration" and no negative effects on socialization or psychological adjustment

Gifted and talented students benefit from enriched learning experiences and individualized plans that give them the opportunity to grow at an accelerated rate. What are some forms of enrichment you will offer your students?

(Rogers 1991). In addition, the analysis identified the following acceleration options as the most beneficial at different grade levels:

- *Elementary school*—early entrance, grade-skipping, nongraded classes, and curriculum compacting (modifying the curriculum to present it at a faster pace).
- *Junior high school*—grade-skipping, grade telescoping (shortening the amount of time to complete a grade level), concurrent enrollment in a high school or college, subject acceleration, and curriculum compacting.
- *Senior high school*—concurrent enrollment, subject acceleration, advanced placement (AP) classes, mentorships, credit by examination, and early admission to college.

One example of acceleration is a suburban Chicago alternative school where high-potential at-risk students work at their own pace in high-tech classrooms. They engage in "integrative accelerative learning," which offers advanced curricula and encourages individual creativity, positive reinforcement, and relaxation. At the National Research Center on Gifted and Talented Education, teachers in experimental classrooms practice thematic "curriculum compacting," which encourages brighter students to forge ahead in the regular curriculum while all students work to their strengths and less able students still get the time and attention they need. Also, many colleges and universities now participate in accelerated programs whereby gifted youth who have outgrown the high school curriculum may enroll in college courses.

Self-directed or independent study—For some time, self-directed or independent study has been recognized as an appropriate way for teachers to maintain the interest of gifted students in their classes. Gifted students usually have the academic backgrounds and motivation to do well without constant supervision and the threat or reward of grades.

Individual education programs—Since the passage of PL 94-142 and the mandating of Individual Education Programs (IEPs) for special education students, IEPs have been promoted as an appropriate means for educating gifted students. Most IEPs for gifted students involve various enrichment experiences, self-directed study, and special, concentrated instruction given to individuals or small groups in pull-out programs. For example, at Columbia Teachers College in New York, economically disadvantaged students identified as gifted participate in Project Synergy, which pairs students with mentors who nurture their talents and guide them through advanced academic content.

Alternative or magnet schools—Several large-city school systems have developed magnet schools organized around specific disciplines, such as science, mathematics, fine arts, basic skills, and so on. The excellent programs at these schools are designed to attract superior students from all parts of the district. Many of these schools offer outstanding programs for gifted and talented youth. Gary Davis and Sylvia Rimm, experts in education for the gifted and talented, say that such schools "are indeed relevant, and they do meet students' needs" (1998, 137).

What Are Special Education, Mainstreaming, and Inclusion?

Prior to the twentieth century, children with disabilities were usually segregated from regular classrooms and taught by teachers in state-run and private schools. Today, an array of programs and services in general and special education class-

Meeting the Standard

Individualizes Instruction

The teacher understands how children learn and develop, and can provide learning opportunities that support their intellectual, social and personal development. (INTASC Knowledge, Principle #2)

The new professional teachers . . . should be able to apply effective methods of teaching students who are at different developmental stages, have different learning styles, and come from diverse backgrounds (NCATE, Standard 4: Diversity).

Teachers are committed to students and their learning (NBPTS, Proposition 1).

Teacher displays knowledge of typical developmental characteristics of age group, exceptions to the patterns, and the extent to which each student follows patterns (PRAXIS III Framework–"distinguished" level of performance).*

Teachers who meet these standards work from the knowledge that they must address the interdependency associated with a learning community on two fronts by (1) intentionally educating themselves to better understand the learning needs of all members of their learning community, and (2) locating tools and resources that make diversifying the learning environment possible. These teachers have developed a good understanding of their own approach to learning. They also know that what they do and say, or in some cases do not do or say, directly impacts each student in the class.

This chapter and the Companion Website provide a good sampling of the many resources that are available to help teachers develop their knowledge of learning styles and preferences. It is not enough to just complete learning style inventories, however. Action research and teacher reflection on the resulting data informs one's understanding of the dynamics of an entire learning community, and helps to make appropriate differences in the teaching and learning environment.

1. Visit the Performance Learning Systems, Inc., website (http://www.plsweb.com/) and complete the "free learning styles inventory" for educators. When you see the results, spend time looking at the information links connected to the results page. Do you think the results accurately reflect your preferences? Ask two people who know you if they feel the results are accurate. If there is a discrepancy, try to determine why. Think about the impact your strong areas might have in your work with students and how they influence the way you arrange learning environments. Also, try to better understand the areas in which your scores were low. How do you relate with students who have strengths in those areas? What adjustments might be needed based on those observations?
2. Consider having a group of students take the "free inventory for students" on the Performance Learning Systems, Inc., website (http://www.plsweb.com/) and write down the scores for their strong and weak areas. Study that data to determine how these factors might impact the overall learning environment for the class.
3. Visit this website (http://www.learnspanish-online.com/spanish/online_word_challenge.html) and assess what type of learning needs the site is designed to meet. Find other examples of tools and resources that could help you individualize instruction to better meet the learning needs of your students. Consider creating an easy-to-access resource list for future reference. (See Meeting the Standard in Chapter 11 for more information about creating a resource list.)

rooms is aimed at developing the potential of exceptional students. Three critical concepts to promote the growth, talents, and productivity of exceptional students are special education, mainstreaming, and inclusion.

Special education refers to "specially designed instruction that meets the unusual needs of an exceptional student" (Hallahan and Kauffman 2003, 13). Teachers who are trained in special education become familiar with special materials, techniques, and equipment and facilities for students with disabilities. For example, children with visual impairment may require reading materials in large print or Braille; students with hearing impairment may require hearing aids and/or instruction in sign language; those with physical disabilities may need special equipment; those with emotional disturbances may need smaller and more highly structured classes; and children with special gifts or talents may require access to working professionals. "Related services—special transportation, psychological assessment, physical and occupational therapy, medical treatment, and counseling—may be necessary if special education is to be effective" (Hallahan and Kauffman 2003, 13).

Special Education Laws

Until 1975, the needs of students with disabilities were primarily met through self-contained special education classes within regular schools. That year, however, Congress passed the **Education for all Handicapped Children Act (Public Law 94-142).** This act guaranteed to all children with disabilities a free and appropriate public education. The law, which applied to every teacher and every school in the country, outlined extensive procedures to ensure that exceptional students between the ages of three and eighteen were granted due process in regard to identification, placement, and educational services received. As a result of PL 94-142, the participation of students with disabilities in all classrooms and school programs became routine.

In 1990, PL 94-142 was replaced by the **Individuals with Disabilities Education Act (IDEA).** IDEA included the major provisions of PL 94-142 and extended the availability of a free, appropriate education to youth with disabilities between the ages of three and twenty-one years of age. IDEA, which is one of the most important and far-reaching pieces of educational legislation ever passed in this country, has several provisions with which all teachers should be familiar. In 1997, the **Amendments to the Individuals with Disabilities Education Act (IDEA 97)** were passed. IDEA 97, which went beyond IDEA's focus on public school *access* for students with disabilities to emphasize educational *outcomes,* modified eligibility requirements, IEP guidelines, public and private placements, student discipline guidelines, and procedural safeguards.

Least restrictive environment—IDEA requires that all children with disabilities be educated in the **least restrictive environment.** In other words, a student must be mainstreamed into a general education classroom whenever such integration is feasible and appropriate and the child would receive educational benefit from such placement. Figure 8.7 on page 302 shows the educational service options for students with disabilities, from the least restrictive to the most restrictive. Among students with high-incidence disabilities (those with a child count over 100,000), students with speech or language impairments and specific learning disabilities are served in the regular classroom for most of the school day. Students with emotional disturbance, mental retardation, and multiple disabilities typically receive services outside the regular classroom for more than 60 percent of the school day (President's Commission on Excellence in Special Education 2002).

Individualized education plan—Every child with a disability is to have a written **individualized education plan (IEP)** that meets the child's needs and specifies educational goals, methods for achieving those goals, and the number and quality of special educational services to be provided. The IEP must be reviewed annually by five parties: (1) a parent or guardian, (2) the child, (3) a teacher, (4) a professional who has recently evaluated the child, and (5) others, usually the principal or a special-education resource person from the school district.

Related services—IDEA 97 ensures that students with disabilities receive any related services, including "transportation, and such developmental, corrective, and other supportive services as may be required to assist a child with a disability to benefit from special education" (Amendments to IDEA 97).

Confidentiality of records—IDEA also ensures that records on a child are kept confidential. Parental permission is required before any official may look at a child's records. Moreover, parents can amend a child's records if they feel information in it is misleading, inaccurate, or violates the child's rights.

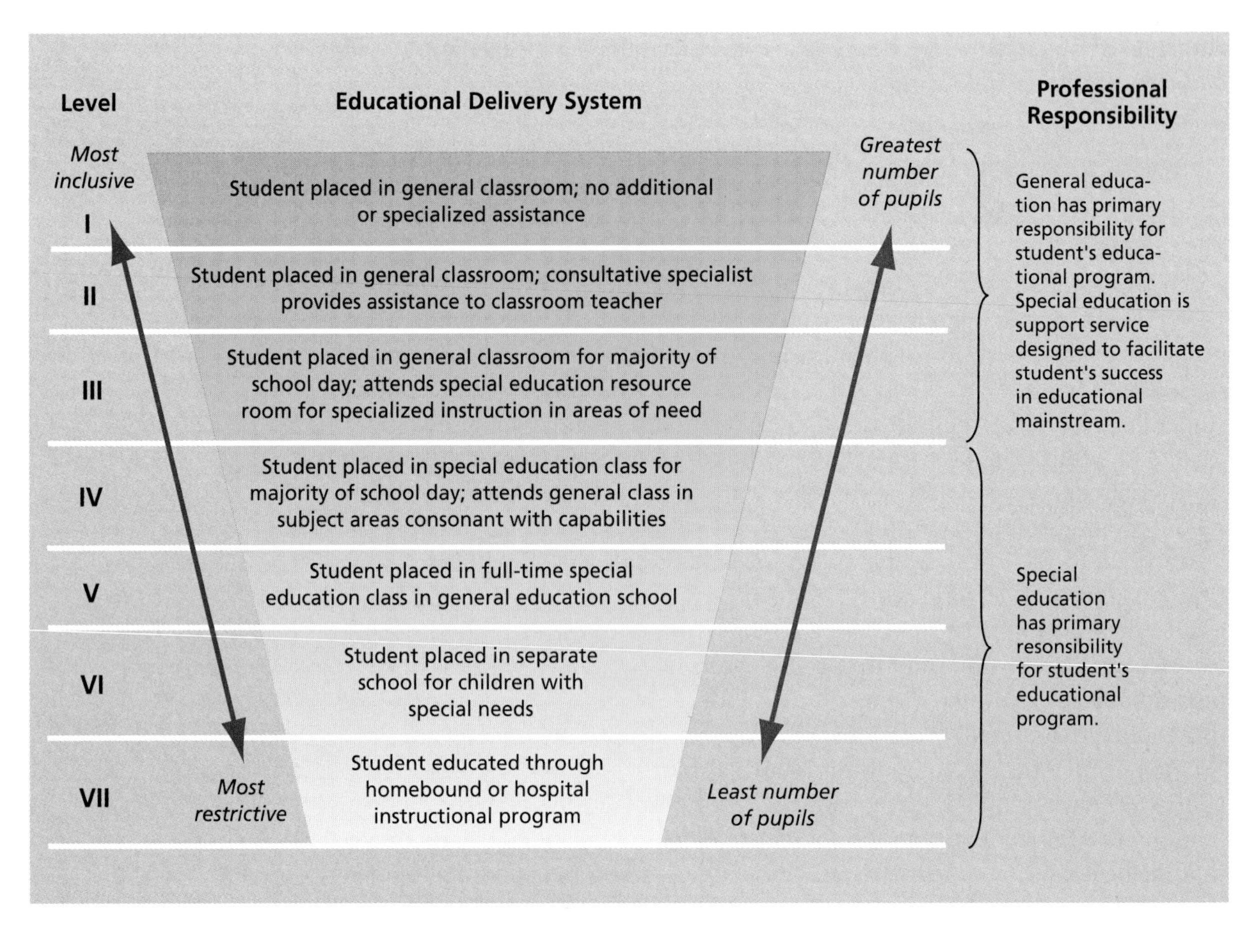

Figure 8.7 Educational service options for students with disabilities.
Source: Michael L. Hardman, Clifford J. Drew, and M. Winston Egan, *Human Exceptionality: Society, School, and Family,* 7th ed., p. 29. Boston: Allyn and Bacon. Copyright © 2002 by Allyn and Bacon. Reprinted by permission.

Due process—IDEA gives parents the right to disagree with an IEP or an evaluation of their child's abilities. If a disagreement arises, it is settled through an impartial due process hearing presided over by an officer appointed by the state. At the hearing, parents may be represented by a lawyer, give evidence, and cross-examine, and are entitled to receive a transcript of the hearing and a written decision on the case. If either the parents or the school district disagree with the outcome, the case may then be taken to the civil courts.

Meeting the Mainstreaming Challenge

To help teachers satisfy the provisions of IDEA, school districts across the nation have developed inservice programs designed to acquaint classroom teachers with the unique needs of students with disabilities. In addition, colleges and universities with preservice programs for educators have added courses on teaching students with special educational needs.

The guidelines for IDEA suggest that schools must make a significant effort to include, or mainstream, *all* children in the classroom. However, it is not clear how far schools must go to meet this **mainstreaming** requirement. For example, should children with severe disabilities be included in general education classrooms if they are unable to do the academic work? Recent court cases have ruled that students with severe disabilities must be included if there is a potential benefit for the child, if the class would stimulate the child's language development, or if other students could act as appropriate role models for the child. In one case, the court ordered a school district to place a child with an IQ of 44 in a regular second-grade classroom and rejected as exaggerated the district's claim that the placement would be prohibitively expensive (*Board of Education, Sacramento City Unified School District v. Holland* 1992). In another case, the court rejected a school district's argument that inclusion of a child with a severe disability would be so disruptive as to significantly impair the learning of the other children (*Oberti v. Board of Education of the Borough of Clementon School District* 1992).

To meet the mainstreaming challenge, teachers must have knowledge of various disabilities and the teaching methods and materials appropriate for each. Since teachers with negative attitudes toward students with special needs can convey these feelings to all students in a class and thereby reduce the effectiveness of mainstreaming (Lewis and Doorlag 1999), general education teachers must have positive attitudes toward students receiving special education. An accepting, supportive climate can significantly enhance the self-confidence of students with disabilities.

In addition, Hallahan and Kauffman suggest that all teachers should be prepared to participate in the education of exceptional learners. Teachers should be willing to do the following:

1. Make maximum effort to accommodate individual students' needs
2. Evaluate academic abilities and disabilities
3. Refer [students] for evaluation [as appropriate]
4. Participate in eligibility conferences [for special education]
5. Participate in writing individualized education programs
6. Communicate with parents or guardians
7. Participate in due process hearings and negotiations
8. Collaborate with other professionals in identifying and making maximum use of exceptional students' abilities (2003, 19–20)

The Debate Over Inclusion

While mainstreaming refers to the application of the least restrictive environment clause of PL 94-142, **inclusion** goes beyond mainstreaming to integrate all students with disabilities into general education classes and school life with the active support of special educators and other specialists and service providers, as well as **assistive technology** and adaptive software. Advocates of inclusion believe that "if students cannot meet traditional academic expectations, then those expectations should be changed. They reject the mainstreaming assumption that settings dictate the type and intensity of services and propose instead the concept of inclusion" (Friend and Bursuck 2002, 4).

Full inclusion goes even further and "represents the belief or philosophy that students with disabilities should be fully integrated into general education classrooms and schools and that their instruction should be based on the abilities, not their disabilities" (Friend and Bursuck 2002, 4). According to the full-inclusion approach, if a child needs support services, these are brought *to the child;* the child does not have to participate in a pull-out program to receive support services. Advocates of full inclusion maintain that pull-out programs stigmatize participating students because they are separated from their general-education classmates, and pull-out programs discourage collaboration between general and special education teachers. Those who oppose full inclusion maintain that classroom teachers, who may be burdened with large class sizes and be assigned to schools with inadequate support services, often lack the training and instructional materials to meet the needs of all exceptional students.

In addition, some parents of children with disabilities believe that full inclusion could mean the elimination of special education as we know it along with the range of services currently guaranteed by federal special education laws. Full inclusion, they reason, would make them depend upon individual states, not the federal government, to meet their children's needs. Moreover, some parents believe that special education classes provide their children with important benefits.

How do classroom teachers feel about inclusion? Lin Chang, an eighth-grade teacher, addresses the concerns general education teachers may have about the availability of resources to help them be successful in inclusive classrooms.

> *At first I was worried that it would all be my responsibility. But after meeting with the special education teacher, I realized that we would work together and I would have additional resources if I needed them (Vaughn, Bos, and Schumm 1997, 18).*

In addition, the following comments by Octavio Gonzalez, a ninth-grade English teacher who has three students with disabilities in two of his five sections of English, express the satisfaction that teachers can experience in inclusive classrooms:

> *At first I was nervous about having students with disabilities in my class. One of the students has a learning disability, one student has serious motor problems and is in a wheelchair, and the third student has vision problems. Now I have to say the adaptations I make to meet their special learning needs actually help all of the students in my class. I think that I am a better teacher because I think about accommodations now (Vaughn, Bos, and Schumm 1997, 18).*

The attitudes of the two teachers quoted above are confirmed in research on teachers' attitudes toward inclusion. Two studies, for example, found that teachers who had experience with inclusion and opportunities for professional development had more positive attitudes toward inclusion and more confidence in their ability to fulfill students' IEPs (Avramidis, Bayliss, and Burden 2000; Van Reusen, Shoho, and Barker 2000).

Equal Opportunity for Exceptional Learners

Like many groups in our society, exceptional learners have often not received the kind of education that most effectively meets their needs. Approximately 10 percent of the population aged three to twenty-one is classified as exceptional; that is, "they require special education because they are markedly different from most children in one or more of the following ways: They may have mental retardation, learning disabilities, emotional or behavioral disorders, physical disabilities, disorders of communication, autism, traumatic brain injury, impaired hearing, impaired sight, or special gifts or talents" (Hallahan and Kauffman 2003, 7).

Just as there are no easy answers for how teachers should meet the needs of students from diverse cultural backgrounds, there is no single strategy for teachers to follow to ensure that all exceptional students receive an appropriate education. The key, however, lies in not losing sight of the fact that "*the most important characteristics of exceptional children are their abilities*" (Hallahan and Kauffman 2003, 6).

To build on students' strengths, classroom teachers must work cooperatively and collaboratively with special education teachers, and students in special education programs must not become isolated from their peers. In addition, teachers must understand how some people can be perceived as "different" and presumed to be "handicapped" because of their appearance or physical condition. Evidence suggests, for example, that people who are short, obese, or unattractive are often victims of discrimination, as are people with conditions such as AIDS, cancer, multiple sclerosis, or epilepsy. Significantly, many individuals with clinically diagnosable and classifiable impairments or disabilities do not perceive themselves as *handicapped.* The term itself means permanently unable to be treated equally.

Officially labeling students has become a necessity with the passage of the laws that provide education and related services for exceptional students. The classification labels help determine which students qualify for the special services, educational programs, and individualized instruction provided by the laws, and they bring to educators' attention many exceptional children and youth whose educational needs could be overlooked, neglected, or inadequately served otherwise. Detrimental aspects include the fact that classification systems are imperfect and have arbitrary cutoff points that sometimes lead to injustices. Also, labels tend to evoke negative expectations, which can cause teachers to avoid and underteach these students, and their peers to isolate or reject them, thereby stigmatizing individuals, sometimes permanently. The most serious detriment, however, is that students so labeled are taught to feel inadequate, inferior, and limited in terms of their options for growth.

How Can You Teach All Learners in Your Inclusive Classroom?

Teachers have a responsibility to address all students' developmental, individual, and exceptional learning needs. Although addressing the range of student differences in the inclusive classroom is challenging, it can also be very rewarding. Consider the comments of three teachers who reflect on their experiences teaching diverse learners:

> *This is a note I wrote on the bottom of her [final] report card: "Sara is a sweet, bright child. As much as she could be a challenge, she made me a better teacher by keeping me on my toes. I will truly, truly miss her!"* (Teacher of a student with Turner syndrome)
>
> *It was a gratifying year. I had no idea at the beginning that we would see the progress that we did. . . . Irina came back for a visit today. She ran right up to me and gave me a hug. A year ago, such an obvious display of emotion would have been unthinkable!* (Teacher of a student with an "attachment disorder" resulting from a lack of human contact during the years she spent in a Romanian orphanage)
>
> *On complex and difficult days, it sometimes feels like it would be a lot easier not to have children with special needs in my classroom. . . . But, you know, I really mourned having to give Daniel up at the end of the schoolyear. There was a special connection I made with that child, and I wanted to be sure that his next teacher felt the same way.* (Teacher of a student with Down syndrome) *(Kostelnik, Onaga, Rohde, Whiren 2002, 55, 92–93, 149)*

Since it is beyond the scope of this book to present in-depth instructional strategies to address students' diverse learning needs you may wish to refer to the Appendix "Selected Resources for Including Exceptional Learners" on this book's website. In addition, attention to three key areas will enable you to create a truly inclusive classroom: collaborative consultation, partnerships with parents, and assistive technology for special learners.

Collaborative Consultation with Other Professionals

One approach to meeting the needs of all students is known as **collaborative consultation,** an approach in which a classroom teacher meets with one or more other professionals (a special educator, school psychologist, or resource teacher, for example) to focus on the learning needs of one or more students. The following first-year teacher describes how collaborative consultation enabled her to meet the needs of a special student.

> *I taught a Down's syndrome child who was very frustrated. I convened a meeting that included district experts, his parent, and a resource teacher, suggesting a change in educational strategy. All agreed to pilot the plan, and things have worked more smoothly ever since. It was a very rewarding experience (Sallie Mae Corporation 1995, 11).*

Collaborative consultation is based on mutuality and reciprocity (Hallahan and Kauffman 2003), and participants assume equal responsibility for meeting students' needs. Friend and Bursuck (2002, 95–96) make the following suggestions for working with a consultant: "prepare for meetings, be open to the consultant's suggestions, use the consultant's strategies systematically, and document the effectiveness of the ideas you try."

To meet the educational goals of a student's IEP, regular education teachers are part of an IEP team that includes special educators, other support personnel, and parents (see Figure 8.8). The following special education professionals are among those who consult with and/or collaborate with regular education teachers:

Consulting teacher—A special educator who provides technical assistance such as arranging the physical setting, helping to plan for instruction, or developing approaches for assessing students' learning

Resource-room teacher—A special educator who provides instruction in a resource room for students with disabilities

School psychologist—Consults with the general education teacher and arranges for the administration of appropriate psychological, educational, and behavioral assessment instruments; may observe a student's behavior in the classroom

Speech and language specialist—Assesses students' communication abilities and works with general education teachers to develop educational programs for students with speech and/or language disorders

Physical therapist—Provides physical therapy for students with physical disabilities

Occupational therapist—Instructs students with disabilities to prepare them for everyday living and work-related activities

Working with Parents

In addition to working with education professionals to meet the learning needs of all students, effective teachers develop good working relationships with parents. Parents of exceptional children can be a source of valuable information about the characteristics, abilities, and needs of their children; they can be helpful in securing necessary services for their children; and they can assist you by reviewing skills at home and praising their children for their learning. The power of partnerships with parents is evident, for instance, in three examples from the U.S. Department of Education's *Schools with IDEAs*

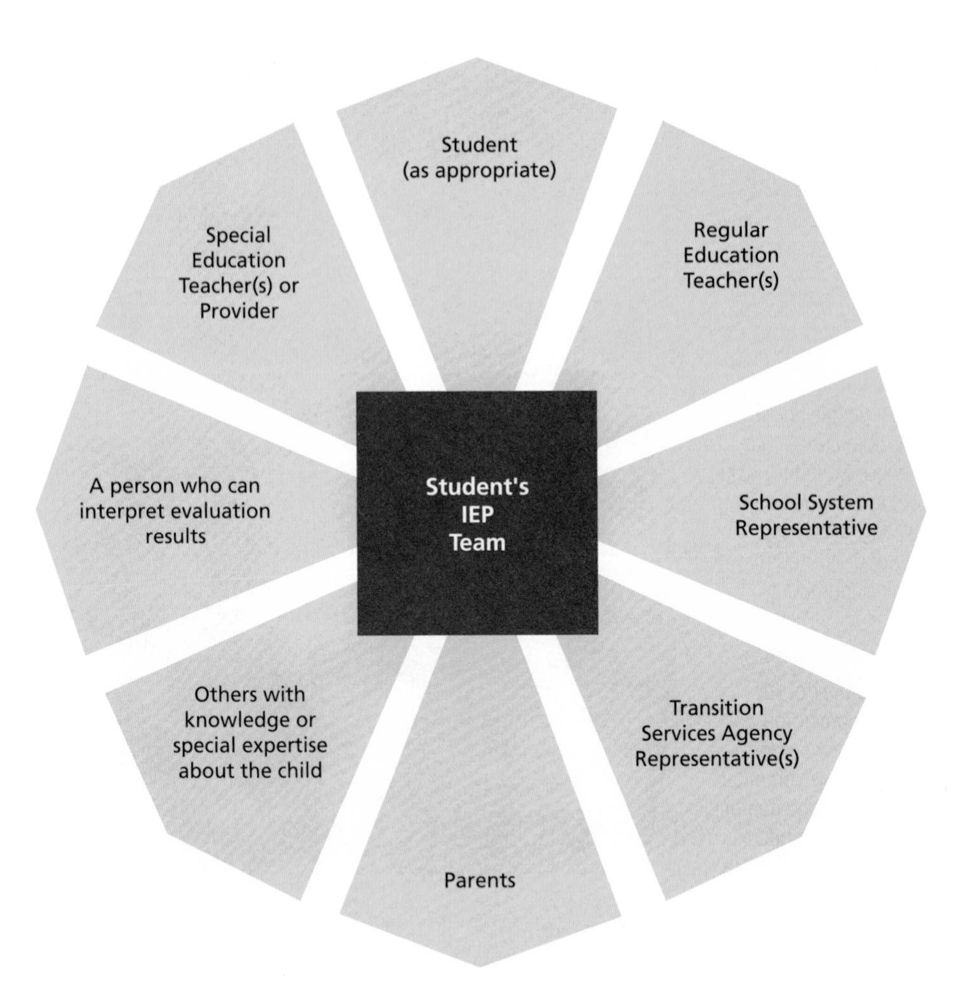

Figure 8.8 **Student's IEP team.**
Source: Office of Special Education Programs and Rehabilitation Services, U.S. Department of Education, *A Guide to the Individualized Education Program,* July 2000, p. 9. Washington, D.C.: U.S. Department of Education.

That Work (1999b), state-by-state descriptions of schools that work closely with parents to implement IDEA.

- *O'Loughlin Elementary School*—At this award-winning school in Hays, Kansas, parents pay for after school programs such as Young Astronauts and O'Loughlin Singers; and students lead the four parent-teacher conferences per year.
- *Sudduth Elementary School*—Since this rural school of approximately 1,000 students in Starkville, Mississippi, has limited fiscal and human resources, parent volunteers come and go throughout the day; during the first eight weeks of school one year, parents had 1,129 contacts with the school.
- *Mirror Lake Middle School*—At this school in Chugiak, Alaska, parents volunteer in the office, classroom, and other areas of the school; and frequently they help teach lessons and serve as guest speakers in classrooms.

Assistive Technology for Special Learners

The ability of teachers to create inclusive classrooms has increased dramatically as a result of many technological advances that now make it easier for exceptional students to learn and communicate. For example, computer-based word

Technology Highlights

How can word prediction software enhance the writing abilities of students with disabilities?

"What should I write?" "What words will best express what I want to say?" Although most people find these questions at least somewhat difficult to answer, students with disabilities may confront unique challenges when they write. Students with learning disabilities may not be able to retain ideas in their memory long enough to express them in writing; others may have difficulty with spelling; and students with motor disabilities may be challenged when forming letters with pen or pencil or making repetitive keystrokes on a word processor.

Students with disabilities that affect their ability to write can be assisted by word prediction software that reduces the number of keystrokes needed to type words. When writing with word prediction software, a student types the first letter of a word, and then a numbered list of words beginning with that letter appears on the computer screen. If the desired word is on the list, the student enters the number and the word is typed automatically. For example, assume a student wants to write the word *tonight* to complete the sentence "I will watch TV tonight." First, she enters a "t" and the list of common "t" words shown in screen #1 appears. Since the word *tonight* is not on this list, she types an "o" and screen #2 appears. Since *tonight* is on this list, she types a number "3" and the word is entered automatically. Thus, the seven keystrokes needed to write *tonight* has been reduced to three.

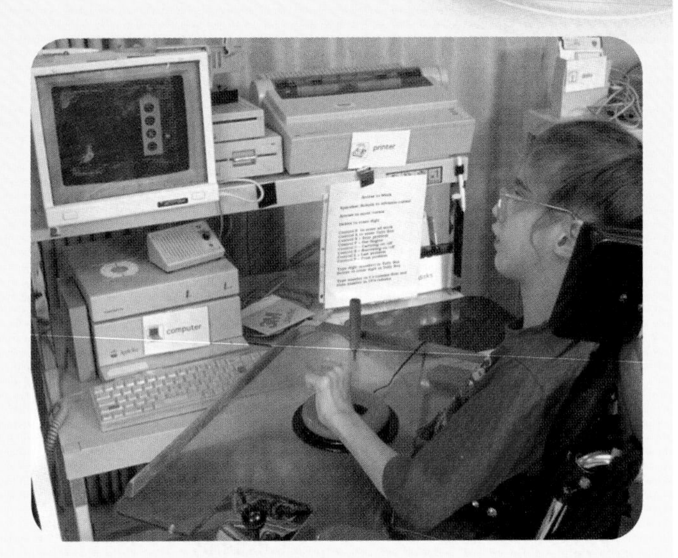

The following list describes additional features of various word prediction software programs.

- *Synthesized speech output*
- *Prediction methods*—Some programs predict on the basis of spelling only, while others consider the words that have come before in the sentence; for example only nouns are listed after the word *a* or *an.*
- *List updating*—After "learning" a student's vocabulary, the word prediction program tailors the word prediction lists to the student's usage. Some programs update automatically, while others allow the user to decide when to update.
- *Prediction window customizing*
- *Keyboard sensitivity adjustment*—Keyboard sensitivity can be adjusted to prevent repetition if keys are not quickly released.

I will watch TV t

Word Prediction Window:

1 talk 2 that 3 the

4 this 5 them 6 they

Screen #1

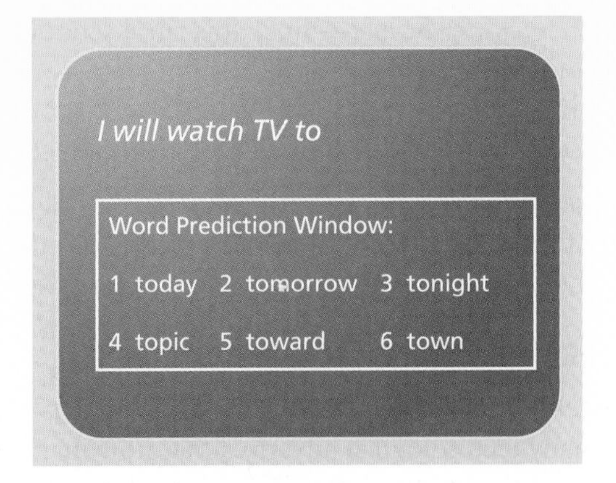

Screen #2

The IEP for this student with multiple disabilities provides for assistive technology, which enables her to create and respond to language.

processing and math tutorials can greatly assist students with learning disabilities in acquiring literacy and computational skills. Students with hearing impairments can communicate with other students by using telecommunications equipment, and students with physical disabilities can operate computers through voice commands or with a single switch or key. Among the recent developments in assistive technology are the following:

1. talking word processor
2. speech synthesizer
3. touch-sensitive computer screens
4. computer screen image enlarger
5. teletypewriter (TTY) (connects to telephone and types a spoken message to another TTY)
6. customized computer keyboards
7. ultrasonic head controls for computers
8. voice-recognition computers
9. television closed captioning
10. Kurzweil reading machine (scans print and reads it aloud)

In addition, assistive technology includes devices to enhance the mobility and everyday activities of people with disabilities (wheelchairs, lifts, adaptive driving controls, scooters, laser canes, feeders).

Many technology-related special education resources and curriculum materials are available on the Internet. One of these sites, The National Center to Improve Practice in Special Education through Technology, Media, and Materials, also maintains discussion forums for teachers of students with disabilities. Clearly, the dazzling revolution in microelectronics will continue to yield new devices to enhance the learning of all students.

Summary

How Do Students' Needs Change as They Develop?

- People move through different stages of cognitive, psychosocial, and moral development throughout their life spans.
- Piaget maintains that children, who reason differently from adults, pass through four stages of cognitive development as they mature. Effective teachers are aware of the characteristics of school-age children's thinking during three of these stages: the preoperational stage, the concrete operations stage, and the formal operations stage.
- According to Erikson's model of psychosocial development, people pass through eight stages of emotional and social development throughout their lives. Each stage is characterized by a "crisis" with a positive and negative pole. Healthy development depends upon a satisfactory, positive resolution of each crisis.
- Kohlberg believes that moral development, the reasoning people use to decide between right and wrong, evolves through three levels. Evidence suggests that males may base their moral reasoning on rights and rules, and females on altruism and self-sacrifice. Many teachers and schools emphasize character education to "teach" moral reasoning and values.
- Maslow suggests that human growth and development depends on how well the individual's biological and psychological needs have been met. According to his hierarchy of needs model, people must satisfy their survival and safety needs before addressing "higher" needs such as self-actualization.
- Teachers must be aware of the developmental stresses and tasks students encounter during childhood and early and late adolescence.

How Do Students Vary in Intelligence?

- There are conflicting definitions of *intelligence;* they range from "what IQ tests measure" to "goal-directed adaptive behavior." Some theorists believe intelligence is a single, basic ability, though recent research suggests that there are many forms of intelligence.
- According to Howard Gardner's theory of multiple intelligences, there are at least eight human intelligences.
- Students differ in their learning styles–the patterns of behavior they prefer to use while learning. Although there is conflict about the concept of learning styles, effective teachers are aware of differences among students regarding their preferences for learning activities.

How Do Students Vary in Ability and Disability?

- Some students are "exceptional" because they have abilities or disabilities that distinguish them from other students. Students with physical, cognitive, or emotional disabilities and students who are gifted and talented have unique learning needs.
- There is a lack of agreement regarding the definition of *learning disability (LD).* Teachers can identify students with learning disabilities by noting difficulties they have acquiring and processing new information. Learning disabilities are the most common disability among students, with attention deficit hyperactivity disorder (ADHD) and attention deficit disorder (ADD) the most common learning disabilities.
- There are many forms of giftedness. Among the approaches used to meet the learning needs of gifted students are acceleration, self-directed or independent study, individual education programs, special or magnet schools, and weekend and summer programs.

What Are Special Education, Mainstreaming, and Inclusion?

- Special education includes a variety of educational services to meet the needs of exceptional students. Key provisions of the Individuals with Disabilities Education Act (IDEA) include least restrictive environment, individualized education program (IEP), confidentiality of records, and due process.
- *Mainstreaming* is the process of integrating students with disabilities into regular classrooms.
- *Inclusion* integrates all students with disabilities into regular classrooms, with the support of special education services as necessary. *Full inclusion* is the integration of students with disabilities in general education classrooms at all times regardless of the severity of the disability.

How Can You Teach All Learners in Your Inclusive Classroom?

- Though challenging, teachers have a responsibility to create inclusive classrooms that address the developmental, individual, and exceptional learning needs of all students.
- Through collaborative consultation, an arrangement whereby the regular classroom teacher collaborates with other education professionals, teachers can meet the needs of exceptional students. Collaborative consultation is based on mutuality and reciprocity, and all participants assume responsibility for meeting students' needs.
- By developing effective relationships with parents of exceptional students, teachers acquire valuable information and support.
- An array of assistive technologies and resources is available to help exceptional students learn and communicate in inclusive classrooms.

Key Terms and Concepts

Amendments to the Individuals with Disabilities Education Act (IDEA 97), **301**
assistive technology, **303**
attention deficit disorder (ADD), **296**
attention deficit hyperactivity disorder (ADHD), **296**
character education, **283**
cognitive development, **278**
collaborative consultation, **306**
concrete operations stage, **279**
Education for all Handicapped Children Act (Public Law 94-142), **301**
exceptional learners, **293**
formal operations stage, **279**
full inclusion, **303**
gifted and talented, **297**
hierarchy of needs, **287**
inclusion, **303**
individualized education plan (IEP), **301**
Individuals with Disabilities Education Act (IDEA), **301**
intelligence, **289**
learning disability (LD), **296**
learning styles, **292**
least restrictive environment, **301**
mainstreaming, **302**
moral reasoning, **278**
multiple intelligences, **291**
preoperational stage, **279**
psychosocial crisis, **280**
psychosocial development, **278**
special education, **300**
stages of development, **278**
students with disabilities, **294**

Applications and Activities

Teacher's Journal

1. Through a series of vignettes, relate Erikson's stages of psychosocial development to your own experiences as a child and as an adolescent. How did sources of stress, psychosocial crises, and your resolutions of them affect your learning in school?
2. Do you know your IQ or recall participating in an IQ test? How do you regard yourself in terms of intelligence and how did you come by your beliefs about your intelligence? Do you think these beliefs influenced your motivation, choices, and achievement as a student? Do you think they influenced your school or class placements? Do you think they influenced the way your teachers and peers responded to you? What criteria would you use now to evaluate the fairness of IQ testing and the appropriateness of use of IQ scores?
3. Recount an experience you had as an exceptional student or one that involved a person with disabilities. What did you learn from this experience or from your reflection on it that could help you as a teacher?

Teacher's Database

1. Investigate sources of information on students with disabilities or exceptional learners in the ERIC Clearinghouse on Disabilities and Gifted Education. The databases in this clearinghouse are maintained by the Council for Exceptional Children (CEC) in Reston, Virginia.

Then visit the National Information Center for Children and Youth with Disabilities (NICHCY) on the SpecialNet. This government clearinghouse answers questions about disability issues, refers you to disability organizations, provides fact sheets, and identifies relevant educational resources in your state.

2. "Observe" children online by locating chat rooms by and for children and youth. As an adult you may not be allowed to participate, but in many cases you will be invited to visit (called "lurking" in Internet jargon). What educational interests, needs, and concerns do students share with one another? How might visiting students' sites online be viewed as an extension of your field experiences as an education major or a student teacher? What teacher observation techniques and protocols could you use in this situation? What are some ethical concerns about this practice? How might any new knowledge of students gained in this way help to make you a more effective teacher?

Observations and Interviews

1. Observe in a classroom that has exceptional students. What steps does the teacher take to meet the needs of these students? Interview the teacher to determine what he or she sees as the challenges and rewards of teaching exceptional students.
2. Observe and interview a student in the age group you wish to teach to conduct a brief case study that focuses on common developmental tasks for that age group and the areas of individual differences highlighted in this chapter. Then

prepare a written portrait of the student. To help you with this activity, ask your instructor for handout masters M8.1, "Who Are the Students in the Classroom?" and M8.2, "Conversations with Students in the School."

3. Visit a school at the level you plan to teach. Interview the counselor, asking questions about the problems that bring students to the counselor most often. If possible, shadow the school counselor for a day.

4. Attend an extracurricular event such as a high school basketball game or Little League soccer game. Observe the students on the field as well as any students watching the players. Notice the differences among the students in terms of their physical appearance, clothing and hairstyles, athletic abilities, social skills, and evidence of personal interests and confidence. Share your observations in class.

Professional Portfolio

For the grade level and content area you are preparing to teach, identify learning activities that address each of the eight multiple intelligences identified by Gardner. For example, you might plan activities such as the following. For one activity in each category, list the preparations you would need to make and/or the materials you would need to gather, and add this information to your portfolio.

Logical-Mathematical

- Design an experiment on . . .
- Describe the rules for a new board game called . . .

Linguistic

- Write a short story about . . .
- Write a biographical sketch of . . .

Musical

- Write song lyrics for . . .
- Locate music that sounds like . . .

Spatial

- Draw, paint, or sculpt a . . .
- Create an advertisement for . . .

Bodily-Kinesthetic

- Role play a person who is . . .
- Do a dance that shows . . .

Intrapersonal

- Assess your ability to . . .
- Describe how you feel about . . .

Interpersonal

- Show one or more of your classmates how to . . .
- In a small group, construct a . . .

Naturalist

- Identify the trees found in . . .
- Classify the rocks found in . . .

Video**Workshop Extra!**

If the VideoWorkshop package was included with your textbook, go to Chapter 8 of the Companion Website (www.ablongman.com/parkay6e) and click on the VideoWorkshop button. Follow the instructions for viewing videoclip 4 and completing this exercise. Consider this information along with what you've read in Chapter 8 while answering the following questions.

1. There are many definitions of intelligence, and theories presenting different aspects of the concept are included in the text. Explain how the practice of peer modeling can boost children's intelligence, and why this practice is a critical feature of inclusion. Videoclip 4 provides additional insight into the concept of inclusion.

2. Compare and define the terms *mainstreaming* and *inclusion* that are presented in your text. Using what you already know about classroom environments and information presented in videoclip 4, which process seems best suited for promoting children's self-esteem?

Appendix 8.1

A SAMPLE INDIVIDUALIZED EDUCATION PLAN (IEP)

Student's Primary Classification: Serious Emotional Disturbance

Secondary Classification: None

Student Name Diane

Date of Birth 5-3-87

Primary Language:

HOME English Student English

Date of IEP Meeting April, 27, 2000

Entry Date to Program April, 27, 2000

Projected Duration of Services One school year

Services Required Specify amount of time in educational and/or related services per day or week

General Education Class 4-5 hours p/day

Resource Room 1-2 hours p/day

Special Ed Consultation in General Ed Classroom

Co-teaching and consultation with general education teacher in the areas of academic and adaptive skills as indicated in annual goals and short-term objectives.

Self-Contained none

Related Services Group counseling sessions twice weekly with guidance counselor. Counseling to focus on adaptive skill development as described in annual goals and short-term objectives

RE. Program 45 min. daily in general ed PE class with support from adapted PE teacher as necessary

Assessment

Intellectual WISC-R

Educational Key Math Woodcock Reading

Behavioral/Adaptive Burks

Speech/Language

Other

Vision Within normal limits

Hearing Within normal limits

Classroom Observation Done

Dates 1/15-2/25/00

Personnel Conducting Observation School Psychologist, Special Education Teacher, General Education Teacher

Present Level of Performance Strengths:

1) Polite to teachers and peers

2) Helpful and cooperative in the classroom

3) Good grooming skills

4) Good in sports activities

Access to General Education Curriculum

Diane will participate in all content areas within the general education curriculum. Special education supports and services will be provided in the areas of math and reading.

Effect of Disability on Access to General Education Curriculum

Emotional disabilities make it difficult for Diane to achieve at expected grade level performance in general education curriculum in the areas of reading and math. It is expected that this will further impact her access to the general education curriculum in other content areas (such as history, biology, English) as she enters junior high school.

Participation in Statewide or District Assessments

Diane will participate in all state and district wide assessments of achievement. No adaptations or modifications required for participation.

Justification for Removal from General Education Classroom:

Diane's objectives require that she be placed in a general education classroom with support from a special education teacher for the majority of the school day. Based on adaptive behavior assessment and observations, Diane will receive instruction in a resource room for approximately one to two hours per day in the areas of social skill development.

Reports to Parents on Progress toward Annual Goals:

Parents will be informed of Diane's progress through weekly reports of progress on short-term goals, monthly phone calls from general ed teachers, special education teachers, and school psychologist, and regularly scheduled report cards at the end of each term.

Appendix 8.1 *(continued)*

Areas Needing Specialized Instruction and Support

1. Adaptive Skills
   - Limited interaction skills with peers and adults
   - Excessive facial tics and grimaces
   - Difficulty staying on task in content subjects, especially reading and math.
   - Difficulty expressing feelings, needs, and interests
2. Academic Skills
   - Significantly below grade level in math—3.9
   - Significantly below grade level in reading—4.3

Annual Review: Date:__________

Comments/Recommendations

____

Team Signatures IEP Review Date__________

LEA Rep. __________

Parent__________

Sp Ed Teacher__________

Gen Ed Teacher__________

School Psych__________

Student (as appropriate) __________

Related Services Personnel (as appropriate) __________

Objective Criteria and Evaluation Procedures__________

IEP—Annual Goals and Short-Term Objectives	Persons Responsible	Objective Criteria and Evaluation Procedures
#1 ANNUAL GOAL: Diane will improve her interaction skills with peers and adults. S.T. OBJ. Diane will initiate conversation with peers during an unstructured setting twice daily. S.T. OBJ. When in need of assistance, Diane will raise her hand and verbalize her needs to teachers or peers without prompting 80% of the time.	General education teacher and special ed teacher (resource room) School psychologist consultation	Classroom observations and documented data on target behavior
#2 ANNUAL GOAL: Diane will increase her ability to control hand and facial movements. S.T. OBJ. During academic work, Diane will keep her hands in an appropriate place and use writing materials correctly 80% of the time. S.T. OBJ. Diane will maintain a relaxed facial expression with teacher prompt 80% of the time. Teacher prompt will be faded over time.	General education teacher and special ed teacher (resource room) School psychologist consultation	Classroom observations and documented data on target behavior
#3 ANNUAL GOAL: Diane will improve her ability to remain on task during academic work. S.T. OBJ. Diane will work independently on an assigned task with teacher prompt 80% of the time. S.T. OBJ. Diane will complete academic work as assigned 90% of the time.	General education teacher and special ed teacher (resource room) School psychologist consultation	Classroom observations and documented data on target behavior

Appendix 8.1 *(continued)*

IEP—Annual Goals and Short-Term Objectives	Persons Responsible	Objective Criteria and Evaluation Procedures
#4 ANNUAL GOAL: Diane will improve her ability to express her feelings. S.T. OBJ. When asked how she feels, Diane will give an adequate verbal description of her feelings or moods with teacher prompting at least 80% of the time. S.T. OBJ. Given a conflict or problem situation, Diane will state her feelings to teachers and peers 80% of the time.	General education teacher and special ed teacher (resource room) School psychologist consultation	Classroom observations and documented data on target behavior
#5 ANNUAL GOAL: Diane will improve math skills one grade level. S.T. OBJ. Diane will improve rate and accuracy in oral 1- and 2-digit division facts to 50 problems per minute without errors. S.T. OBJ. Diane will improve her ability to solve word problems involving t—x—v.	Collaboration of general education teacher and special education teacher through co-teaching and consultation	Precision teaching Addison Wesley Math Program Scope and Sequence Districtwide Assessment of Academic Achievement
#6 ANNUAL GOAL: Diane will improve reading skills one grade level. S.T. OBJ. Diane will answer progressively more difficult comprehension questions in designated reading skills program. S.T. OBJ. Diane will increase her rate and accuracy of vocabulary words to 80 wpm without errors.	Collaboration of general education teacher and special education teacher through co-teaching and consultation	Precision teaching Barnell & Loft Scope and Sequence District wide Assessment of Academic Achievement

Source: Michael L. Hardman, Clifford J. Drew, and M. Winston Egan, *Human Exceptionality: Society, School, and Family,* 7th ed. Boston: Allyn and Bacon, 2002, pp. 123–125.

9 Authentic Instruction and Curricula for Creating a Community of Learners

If I were a teacher, I would want to make my subject exciting and get to know all students well.

—A tenth-grade student quoted in the *MetLife Survey of the American Teacher 2001: Key Elements of Quality Schools*

September 26
I set up a classroom library. We don't use the reading textbook. What for? Grown-ups don't read textbooks unless they're forced. I told them we could read real books so long as they don't steal any. I make a big show of counting the books at the end of the day. The kids sigh audibly when they're all there. They look beautiful, like a bookstore, facing out in a big wooden display my uncle made for me. Plus, it covers the bullet-riddled window that never was repaired.

We don't call the subjects the old-fashioned names in Room 211. Math is "Puzzling," science is "Mad Scientist Time," social studies is "T.T.W.E." which stands for "Time Travel and World Exploring," language arts is "Art of Language," and reading is "Free Reading Time." I did this because I figured kids at this age come to me with preconceived notions of what they are good at. This way, a kid who thinks she's no good in math might turn out to be good at Puzzling, and so on.

In the morning, three things happen religiously. I say good morning, real chipper, to every single child and make sure they say good morning back. Then I collect "troubles" in a "Trouble Basket," a big green basket into which the children pantomime unburdening their home worries so they can concentrate on school. Sometimes a kid has no troubles. Sometimes a kid piles it in, and I in turn pantomime bearing the burden. This way, too, I can see what disposition the child is in when he or she enters. Finally, before they can come in, they must give me a word, which I print on a piece of tagboard and they keep in an envelope. It can be any word, but preferably one that they heard and don't really know or one that is personally meaningful. A lot of times the kids ask for *Mississippi,* just to make me spell it. We go over the words when we do our private reading conferences. I learned this from reading *Teacher* by Sylvia Ashton-Warner, who taught underprivileged Maori children in New Zealand. She says language should be an organic experience. I love her approach.

It takes a long time to get in the door this way, but by the time we are in, I know every kid has had and given a kind greeting, has had an opportunity to learn something, and has tried to leave his or her worries on the doorstep. Some kids from other classrooms sneak into our line to use the Trouble Basket or to get a word card.

Then the national anthem blares over the intercom. The kids sing with more gusto now that we shout "Play ball!" at the end. We do Puzzling until 10:30, then we alternate Mad Sciencing with T.T.W.E., lunch, reading aloud, Free Reading and journaling, and Art of Language.

At the end of the day, as the kids exit, they fill in the blanks as I call out, "See you in the _____ [morning!]." "Watch out for the _____ [cars!]." "Don't say _____ [shut up!]." "I love _____ [you!]." This is a game I played with my father at bedtime growing up. It gives the day a nice closure (Codell 1999, 29–31).

Focus Questions

1. **What determines the culture of the classroom?**
2. **How can you create a positive learning environment?**
3. **What are the keys to successful classroom management?**
4. **What teaching methods do effective teachers use?**
5. **What is taught in schools?**
6. **How is the school curriculum developed?**

Expand your knowledge of the concepts discussed in this chapter by reading current and historical articles from the *New York Times* by visiting the **"Themes of the Times"** section of the Companion Website (**www.ablongman.com/parkay6e**).

The opening scenario for this chapter, taken from *Educating Esmé: Diary of a Teacher's First Year,* by Esmé Raji Codell, a fifth-grade teacher in Chicago, illustrates how one teacher organized her classroom to create a positive learning environment. Sensitivity to the elements that combine to give a day in the classroom a "nice closure" is the hallmark of a professional, reflective teacher. In addition, Codell realized that *what* she taught her students was as important as *how* she taught them. She understood that developing a community of learners requires authentic instruction and curricula. Accordingly, she modified her curricula by relabeling subjects to fit students' "preconceived notions of what they are good at," and she developed vocabulary lessons based on words students found personally meaningful.

For teacher education students such as you, making the transition between the study of teaching and actual teaching can be a challenge. The more you understand how "the classroom learning environment develops gradually, in response to the teacher's communication of expectations, modeling of behavior, and approach to classroom management" (Good and Brophy 2003, 112), the better prepared you will be to make the transition smoothly. The first two-thirds of this chapter, then, focus on creating a community of learners, and the last third on developing the curriculum.

What Determines the Culture of the Classroom?

As you learned in Chapter 7, one definition of *culture* is the way of life common to a group of people. In much the same way, each classroom develops its own culture. The culture of a classroom is determined by the manner in which teachers and students participate in common activities.

The activities that teachers and students engage in are influenced by several factors. As a teacher, you will make countless decisions that will shape the physical and social milieus of your classroom. From seating arrangement, to classroom rules and procedures, to the content and relevance of the curriculum, you will have a strong influence on the culture that emerges in your classroom. You will have many methodological choices to make—when to shift from one activity to another, when to use discussion rather than lecture, or whether to make one requirement rather than another.

Classroom Climate

Part of the environment of the classroom is **classroom climate**—the atmosphere or quality of life in a classroom. The climate of your classroom will be determined by how you interact with your students and "by the manner and degree to which you exercise authority, show warmth and support, encourage competitiveness or cooperation, and allow for independent judgment and choice" (Borich 2000, 346–347).

In addition to promoting learning, the classroom climate should convince students that the teacher cares about them and believes they can learn, is sensitive to their differing needs and abilities, has knowledge of subject matter, and maintains effective classroom discipline. Figure 9.1 shows how important these dimensions of teaching are to a group of roughly two thousand students and the "grades" they would give their teachers for each dimension.

Classroom climates are complex and multidimensional; their character is determined by a wide array of variables, many of which are beyond the teacher's control. Nevertheless, our observations of high-performing teachers have confirmed that they take specific steps to create classroom climates with the following eight characteristics:

- A productive, task-oriented focus
- Group cohesiveness
- Open, warm relationships between teacher and students

Figure 9.1 Most important aspects of teaching and their ratings.
Source: The MetLife Survey of the american Teacher 2001: Key Elements of Quality Schools. New York: Harris Interactive, Inc., 2001.

Question 1: The following is a list of several aspects of teaching, which one do you think is most important?
Question 2: For each item, how would you grade your teacher?
Base: All students (N = 2,049)

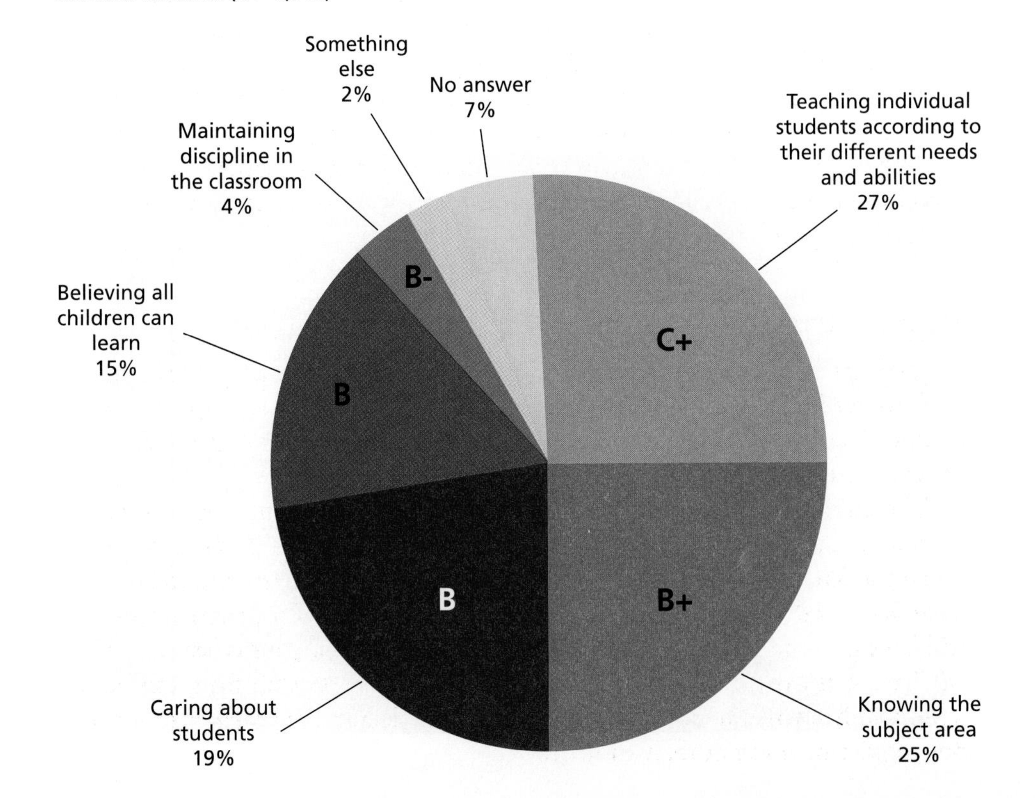

- Cooperative, respectful interactions among students
- Low levels of tension, anxiety, and conflict
- Humor
- High expectations
- Frequent opportunities for student input regarding classroom activities

These dimensions of classroom climates are within teachers' spheres of influence and are promoted, consciously or unconsciously, by their styles of communicating and treating students. As the following reflections by a student teacher indicate, creating a classroom climate characterized by these eight dimensions is not easy; teachers must make moment-to-moment judgments about what actions will enhance students' motivation to learn.

The next day, as I was going over the instructions for a science experiment I noticed Sheila and Devon leaning over and whispering. I immediately stopped my presentation and said, "Sheila and Devon, you need to turn around in your seats and stop whispering while I am talking." Both girls rolled their eyes and slowly turned their bodies around in their seats. Neither of them made eye contact with me as I continued the lesson. Although the class was now quiet, I felt uncomfortable myself. As the students gathered the science materials they needed to carry out the experiment in their cooperative learning groups, I noticed that Theresa was passing a note to Sheila. Trying to hide my anger and frustration, I said, "Theresa, you need to get rid of that note now. You can come up and put it in the wastebasket. It is time to be working on science, not note passing." Although singling out the girls worked in the short term, to tell the truth I did not feel comfortable dealing with the situation as I did.

I didn't want to feel as if I was spending half the time handling misbehavior, but that's just what I was doing. I had learned in school to reach for student strengths, so I am trying to practice the strategy of giving the students a better attitude about themselves through praise. I explained to them that by correcting their behavior I was just trying to create a climate in which they could learn. I am trying to be a supportive teacher who still corrects misbehavior—always with the goal of redirecting students toward meaningful classroom work.

What words would you use to describe the apparent climate of this classroom? In what ways does this classroom appear to be an effective learning environment? What would you look for to determine if this is a caring classroom?

That same afternoon, I began to gather the students together for literature circles. I had four groups reading different novels. Today I was planning to have the students discuss their reactions to the first chapter and make predictions about the rest of the book. For the first five minutes or so, the groups were very productive, and I felt a surge of hope that all would go well. Just then, I noticed Devon lean back in her chair to pass a note to Theresa, who was in a different group. I wanted to shout across the room at them, but I kept my calm and tried to figure out what I should do now (Rand and Shelton-Colangelo 1999, 10–11).

How would you describe this classroom climate using the eight dimensions listed earlier? What changes in the student teacher's behavior could transform the overall climate?

Although teachers influence the classroom climate by the way they regard and treat students, they also shape it by their instructional decisions. David Johnson and Roger Johnson (1999), two researchers in the area of classroom communication and dynamics, delineate three types of interactions promoted by instructional decisions: cooperative or positive interdependence, competitive or negative interdependence, and individualistic or no interdependence. To illustrate the three types, Johnson and Johnson suggest that a group project to measure classroom furniture would promote cooperative interdependence; a race to be the first student to measure the furniture would call for competitive interdependence; and having a student measure the furniture independently would be an example of no interdependence. Johnson and Johnson believe that teachers should use strategies that foster all three forms of interactions, depending on their instructional goals, but that, ideally, the emphasis should be on furthering cooperative interdependence.

Classroom Dynamics

Interactions between teachers and students are the very core of teaching. The quality of these interactions reveals to students how the teacher feels about them. Teachers who empathize with students, genuinely respect them, and expect them to learn are more likely to develop a classroom climate free of management problems. In classrooms with positive group dynamics, teachers and students work toward a common goal—learning. In classrooms with negative interactions, the energy of teachers and students may be channeled into conflict rather than into learning.

There is no precise formula to guarantee success in the classroom; however, educational psychologist Anita Woolfolk (2001, 419–421) suggests four "necessary conditions" to increase student learning through positive interactions:

1. The classroom must be relatively organized and free from constant interruptions and disruptions.
2. The teacher must be a patient, supportive person who never embarrasses students for mistakes.
3. The work must be challenging but reasonable.
4. The learning tasks must be authentic.

Teacher Communication Successful teachers possess effective communication skills. They express themselves verbally and nonverbally (and in writing) in a manner that is clear, concise, and interesting. They "are able to communicate clearly and directly to their students without wandering, speaking above students' levels of comprehension, or using speech patterns that impair the clarity of what is being presented" (Borich 2000, 8). In addition, they are good listeners. Their students feel that not only are they heard, they are understood.

Effective teachers relish the live, thinking-on-your-feet dimensions of classroom communication. Their communication skills enable them to respond appropriately to events that could sabotage the plans of less effective teachers: a student's clowning, announcements on the public address system, interruptions by other teachers or parents, students' private arguments or romances, or simply the mood of the class at that particular time.

Student Interaction In addition to engaging in positive, success-oriented interactions with their students, effective teachers foster positive, cooperative interactions among students. As a result, students feel supported by their peers and free to devote their attention to learning. Richard Schmuck and Patricia Schmuck (2001) describe the climate of such classrooms as "mature" and "self-renewing." Their research on classroom group processes has led them to identify the four sequential stages of group development portrayed in Figure 9.2.

During Stage 1 of a class's group development, students are on their best behavior. Teachers who are aware of this "honeymoon period" use it to their advantage; they discuss and teach classroom rules and procedures, outline their goals, and deliberately set the classroom tone and standards they want. During Stage 2, teachers seeking to promote group development are advised to encourage student participation and communication and to discourage the formation of cliques.

Groups that have met the requirements of the preceding stages move into Stage 3, which lasts for the majority of the expected life of the group (i.e., the semester or the school year). This stage is characterized by the group's willingness to set clear goals, share tasks, and agree on deadlines. At Stage 4, the final stage, group members fully accept responsibility for the group's quality of life, and they continuously strive to improve it.

In addition, teachers who effectively orchestrate group processes in their classrooms recognize that, for good or ill, students as well as teachers exert leadership in classrooms. Wise teachers quickly identify student leaders and develop ways to focus their leadership abilities on the attainment of goals that benefit the entire class. Teachers should also encourage their students to develop leadership skills.

How Can You Create a Positive Learning Environment?

A positive classroom climate and positive classroom dynamics are prerequisites for a good learning environment. Creating and then maintaining a positive

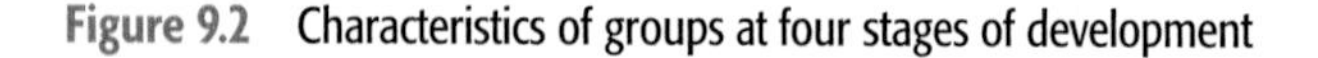
Figure 9.2 Characteristics of groups at four stages of development

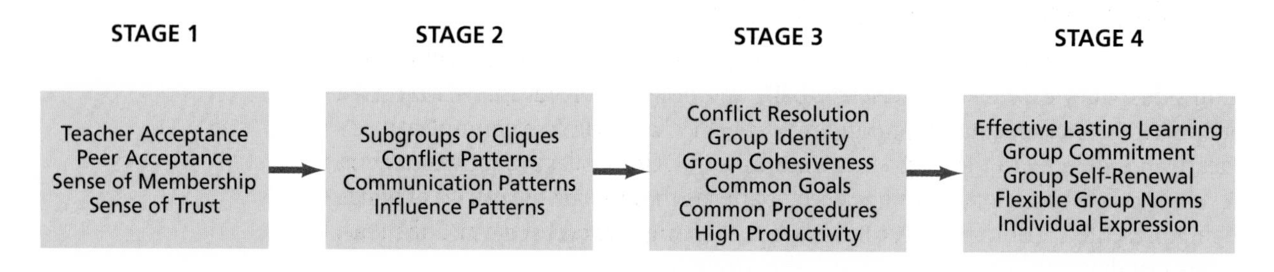

learning environment is a multidimensional challenge. While no single set of strategies will ensure success in all situations, educational researchers have identified teacher behaviors that tend to be associated with high levels of student learning. Effective teachers also know how to use these behaviors and *for what purposes* they are best suited. The following sections address three important dimensions of positive learning environments: the caring classroom, the physical classroom environment, and classroom organization, including procedures for grouping students for instruction and managing time.

The Caring Classroom

At this point in your preparation to become a teacher, you may feel uncertain of your ability to create a positive classroom climate and to orchestrate the complex dynamics of the classroom so that you and your students become a cohesive, productive, and mutually supportive group. In your quest to achieve these aims, it will help to remember that an authentic spirit of caring is at the heart of an effective learning environment. "[C]*aring pedagogy* can . . . create or restore self confidence needed for participating in the positive learning opportunities in the classroom. It can also help form the moral foundation of responsible citizenship, productive community membership and leadership, and lifelong engagement in learning" (italics added) (Paul and Colucci 2000, 45).

How do teachers establish a **caring classroom**? First, teachers demonstrate caring through their efforts to help all students learn to their fullest potential. They learn as much as they can about their students' abilities and what motivates them to do their best. Teachers actually become *students of their students*—as a tenth-grade student states: An effective teacher "[gets] to know all students well" (MetLife Survey 2001). Teachers also support student learning by encouraging and conveying appropriate (neither too high nor too low) expectations.

In addition, teachers realize that how they speak and listen to students determines the extent to which students believe their teachers care about them. In a synthesis of research on classroom environments that enhance students' learning, Herbert Walberg and Rebecca Greenberg (1997, 46) found that "students learn more when their classes are satisfying, challenging, and friendly and they have a voice in decision making. [When] classes are unfriendly, cliquish, and fragmented, they leave students feeling rejected and therefore impede learning." Table 9.1 on p. 325, based on Walberg and Greenberg's work, presents fifteen dimensions of classroom life and how each influences students' learning at the junior and senior high levels.

While students learn best in caring classrooms, Nel Noddings (see Keepers of the Dream feature) has suggested that students also must learn to care for others. Toward this end, she recommends reorganizing the school curriculum around "themes of care" and suggests that "all students should be engaged in a general education that guides them in caring for self, intimate others, global others, plants, animals, the environment, objects and instruments, and ideas" (2002, 99).

The Classroom as a Physical Environment

When you become a teacher, the physical environment you work in will probably be similar to that of schools you attended. However, we encourage you, with the help of your students, to make your surroundings as safe, pleasant, and convenient as possible. Fresh air; plants; clean, painted walls; displays of students' work; a comfortable reading or resource area; and a few prints or posters can enhance the quality of teacher–student relationships. Seating arrangements and the place-

Keepers of *the Dream*

Nel Noddings, Leader in the Challenge to Care

Nel Noddings, author of over one hundred articles and chapters, a philosophy textbook, and a number of books, including the popular and influential works, *Caring* (1984) and *The Challenge to Care in Schools* (1992), is also the mother of ten children, half of whom are adopted. When Noddings suggests that teachers view education as "parents who are engaged in the task of raising a huge heterogeneous family" (1992, 177), she brings her heart and personal experience to the metaphor.

Noddings, a Stanford University professor, leads a movement to emphasize care in schools. She taught mathematics at the secondary level in New Jersey for many years and then earned a doctorate in philosophy at Stanford University. There she remained, teaching courses in philosophy and education, serving as dean, and writing articles on theories of knowledge.

"Keep reflecting on everything you do. . . "

It was through an effort to combine the twin treasures in her life, her family and her superb analytical training, that Noddings developed the concept of caring. When she introduced the idea, the feedback she received was enthusiastic; the timing of her work was well matched with a growing sense of alarm in the United States over the increase of violence and the erosion of character and moral behavior. Schools unwittingly or unwillingly have contributed to the problem. As Noddings observes, "Secondary schools—where violence, apathy, and alienation are most evident—do little to develop the capacity to care. Today, even elementary teachers complain that the pressure to produce high test scores inhibits the work they regard as central to their mission: the development of caring and competent people" (1995, 679).

Noddings contends that educational efforts should promote more than adequate academic achievement. "We will not achieve even that meager success unless our children believe that they themselves are cared for and learn to care for others" (1995, 675–676). Noddings's perception of caring is not that of soft sentimentality, but rather the quality of care that involves deep commitment. "When we care, we want to do our very best for the objects of our care" (1995, 676). She suggests organizing the curriculum around themes of care: caring for self, for intimate others, for strangers and global others, for the natural world and its nonhuman creatures, for the human-made world, and for ideas (1992). She encourages teachers to collaborate in developing curricula according to these broad themes or to emphasize these common themes in their separate curricula. She also recommends that teachers introduce themes of care in response to events that occur in the school or neighborhood. When faced with a tragedy, schools too often rely on outside experts, "when what children really need is the continuing compassion and presence of adults who represent constancy and care in their lives" (1995, 678).

Noddings's advice to teachers is "to keep reflecting on everything you do to see whether, in fact, what you do does promote the growth of loving, lovable, competent, and caring people. When you examine everything you do—how you grade, the rules you make—from this perspective, you will change the way you operate." She agrees with John Dewey's warning: "What the best and wisest parent wants for his own child, that must the community want for all its children. Any other ideal for our schools is narrow and unlovely; acted upon, it destroys our democracy" (Dewey 1902, 3).

Table 9.1 15 Dimensions of classroom environment

		Percent Positive Influence on
Dimension	**Learning**	**Description**
Satisfaction	100% (17)	Students enjoy classroom work and find it satisfying.
Challenge	87 (16)	Students find the work difficult and challenging.
Cohesiveness	86 (17)	Students know one another well and are helpful and friendly toward one another.
Physical Environment	85 (15)	Adequate books, equipment, space, and lighting are available.
Democracy	85 (14)	Students share equally in making decisions that affect the entire class.
Goal Direction	73 (15)	Learning goals are clear.
Competition	67 (9)	Competition among students is minimized.
Formality	65 (17)	Class is informal, with few formal rules to guide behavior.
Speed	54 (14)	Students have sufficient time to finish their work.
Diversity	31 (14)	Students' interests differ and are provided for.
Apathy	14 (15)	Students don't care about what the class does.
Favoritism	10 (13)	All students do not enjoy the same privileges; the teacher has favorites.
Cliquishness	8 (13)	Certain students work only with close friends and refuse to interact with others.
Disorganization	6 (17)	Activities are disorganized and confusing, rather than well organized and efficient.
Friction	0 (17)	Tension and quarreling among students characterize the classroom.

Note: Percent indicates the percentage of research studies that reported a positive influence on learning for that dimension; number in parentheses indicates number of research studies that investigated that dimension.

Source: Adapted from Herbert J. Walberg and Rebecca C. Greenberg, "Using the Learning Environment Inventory," *Educational Leadership*, May 1997, p. 47.

ment of other classroom furniture also do much to shape the classroom environment. Although seating by rows may be very appropriate for whole-group instruction or examinations, other arrangements may be more beneficial for other activities. For example, you can enhance small-group activities by moving desks into small clusters in different parts of the room. Figure 9.3 on page 326 shows the arrangement of a classroom at an exemplary elementary school. The room is designed to encourage students to learn through discovery at learning centers located around the room.

However you design your classroom, take care to ensure that seating arrangements do not reduce the opportunity of some students to learn. For example, students in some classrooms receive more attention if they are seated in the "action zone," the middle front-row seats and seats on the middle aisle. Teachers often stand near this area and unknowingly give students seated there more opportunities to speak.

Classroom Organization

A factor in positive learning environments is **classroom organization**—the way teachers and students are grouped for instruction, the way learning tasks are

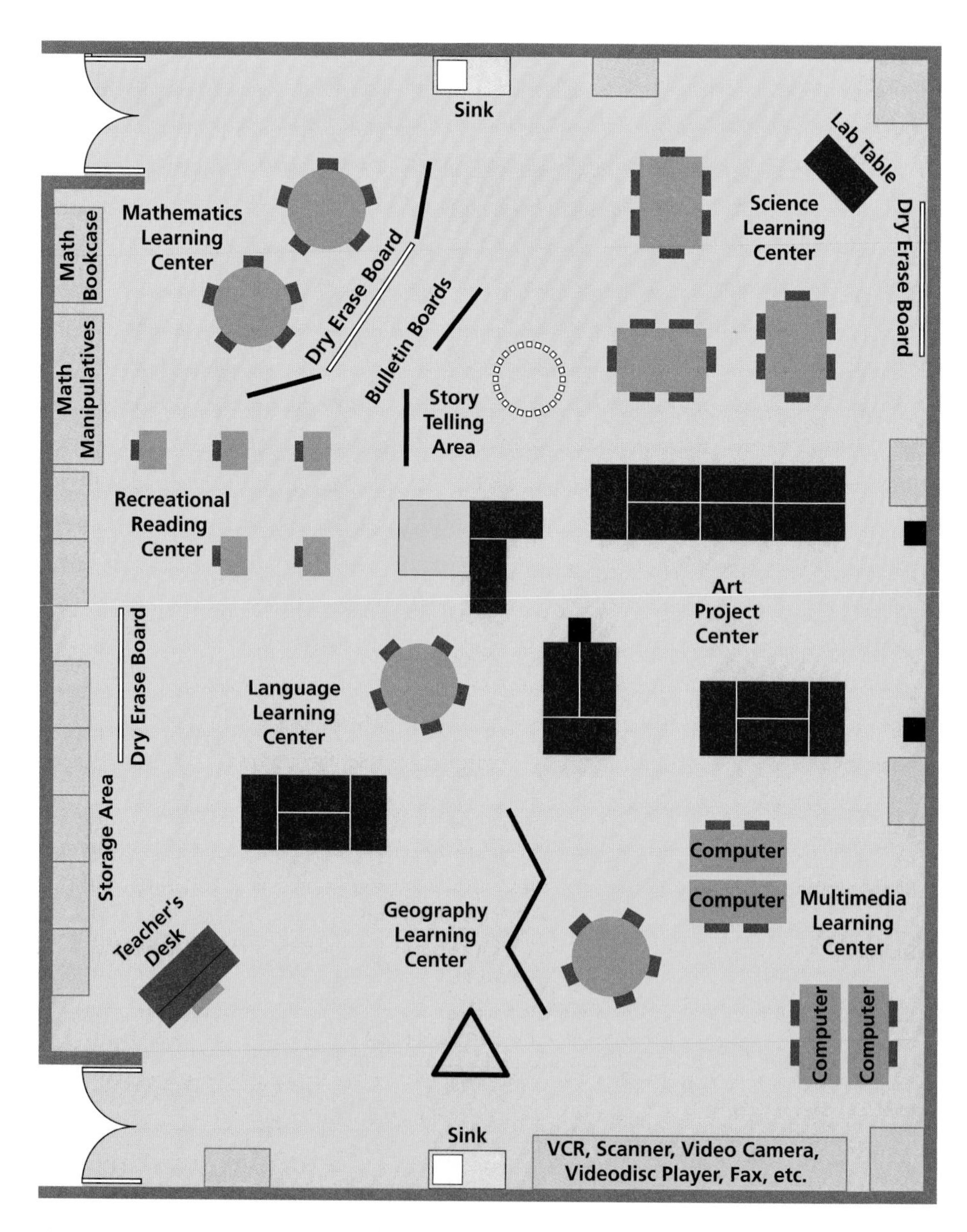

Figure 9.3 Learning centers in an elementary classroom

structured, and other resources used. The following sections focus on these aspects of classroom organization.

Grouping Students by Ability Two common approaches for grouping students on the basis of shared characteristics are between-class ability grouping, often called tracking, and within-class ability grouping. Students who attend schools where **between-class ability grouping** is practiced are assigned to classes on the basis of ability or achievement (usually determined by scores on standardized tests). Another form of between-class ability grouping, especially at the high school level, is based on students' goals after graduation. Many high schools, for example, have a college preparatory track, a vocational track, and a business education track.

Research suggests that, for the most part, between-class ability grouping does not contribute to greater achievement (Good and Brophy 2003). Supporters nevertheless claim that teachers are better able to meet the needs of students in homogeneous groupings. Among the alternatives to between-class ability grouping are heterogeneous (or mixed-ability) grouping, regrouping by subject area, the Joplin Plan (regrouping students for reading instruction by ability across grade levels), and cooperative learning.

Within-class ability grouping often is used for instruction in reading and mathematics within a class, where a teacher instructs students in homogeneous, small groups. Within-class grouping is used widely in elementary classrooms. Perhaps you can recall learning to read in a small group with a name such as the Eagles, the Redbirds, or the Mustangs. Like tracking, within-class ability grouping can heighten preexisting differences in achievement between groups of students, especially if teachers give high-achieving groups more attention. Also, once students are grouped, they tend not to be regrouped, even when differences in achievement are reduced.

At best, evidence to support student groupings is mixed. Whether students are grouped on the basis of ability, curricular interests, or disabling condition, there is a danger that some group labels can evoke negative expectations, causing teachers to "underteach" certain students, and their peers to isolate or reject them. The most serious consequence, of course, is that students so labeled are taught to feel inadequate, inferior, and limited in their options for growth.

Grouping Students for Cooperative Learning **Cooperative learning** is an approach to teaching in which students work in small groups, or teams, sharing the work and helping one another complete assignments. Student-Team-Learning, for example, is a cooperative approach teachers use to increase the basic skills achievement of at-risk students. In cooperative learning arrangements, students are motivated to learn in small groups through rewards that are made available to the group as a whole and to individual members of the group. Cooperative learning includes the following key elements:

- Small groups (four to six students) work together on learning activities.
- Assignments require that students help one another while working on a group project.
- In competitive arrangements, groups may compete against one another.
- Group members contribute to group goals according to their talents, interests, and abilities.

In addition, cooperative learning is an instructional method that can strengthen students' interpersonal skills. When students from different racial, ethnic, and cultural backgrounds and mainstreamed special-needs students all contribute to a common group goal, friendships increase and group members tend to view one another as more equal in status and worth. The contribution that cooperative learning can make to the culture of the classroom is supported by research that indicates that, under cooperative learning arrangements, "African American, Mexican American, and White students develop more positive racial attitudes and choose more friends from outside racial groups" (Banks 2002, 47). In addition, cooperative learning has "a positive effect on the academic achievement of students of color" (Banks 2002, 47).

Cooperative learning also enables students to learn a variety of roles and responsibilities, as the following comments by a fifth-grade science teacher indicate:

I have the class divided into groups of five students and each group works as a team. The job duties are as follows: principal investigator (PI), materials manager (MM), reader, recorder, and reporter. The PI is the leader of the group and helps mediate when problems occur. The PI is the only student who can come to me with questions during the actual procedure. This rule enables me to monitor the groups and also teaches the group to work independently.

Students change job duties within their group [for] each activity and every six weeks students change groups. This plan gives each student the experience of working with different classmates as well as learning the responsibility of group participation through performing the different job duties.

Delivering Instruction The delivery of instruction is a key element in creating positive learning environments. What the teacher does and what students do have powerful influences on learning and on the quality of classroom life. A common activity format in elementary schools consists of students doing seatwork on their own or listening to their teachers and participating in whole-class recitations. In addition, students participate in reading groups, games, and discussions; take tests; check work; view films; give reports; help clean up the classroom; and go on field trips.

A teacher must answer the question "What activity will enable me to accomplish my instructional goals?" Teachers also must realize that learning activities should meet *students'* goals; that is, the activities must be meaningful and authentic for students. **Authentic learning tasks** enable students to see the connections between classroom learning and the world beyond the classroom—both now and in the future. To understand how authentic learning tasks can motivate students to learn, reflect upon your own school experiences. Do you recall memorizing facts only because they would appear on a test? Did you ever wonder why a teacher asked you to complete a learning task? Did you ever feel that a teacher asked you to do "busywork"? What kinds of learning tasks motivated you the most?

A comprehensive nationwide study of successfully restructured schools reported that "authentic pedagogy" helps students to (1) "construct knowledge" through the use of higher-order thinking, (2) acquire "deep knowledge" (relatively complex understandings of subject matter), (3) engage in "substantive conversations" with teachers and peers, and (4) make connections between substantive knowledge and the world beyond the classroom (Newmann and Wehlage 1995; Newmann et al. 1996). In addition, as Figure 9.4 shows, high authentic pedagogy classes boost achievement for students at all grade levels.

Structuring the Use of Time How teachers use time affects student learning. **Allocated time** is the time teachers allocate for instruction in various areas of the curriculum. Teachers vary widely in their instructional use of time. Educational researchers Tom Good and Jere Brophy report, for example, that "some students [may receive] as much as four times more instructional time in a given subject than other students in the same grade" (2003, 29).

Researchers have shown that **time on task**—the amount of time students are actively engaged in learning activities—is directly related to learning. As anyone who has ever daydreamed while appearing to pay attention can confirm, time on task is difficult to measure. In response to this difficulty, researchers have introduced the concept of **academic learning time**—the amount of time a student spends working on academic tasks with a high level of success (80 percent or higher). Not surprisingly, learning time, like allocated time, varies greatly from classroom to classroom. For example, Figure 9.5 shows how the more than one thousand hours most states mandate for instruction at the elementary level actually result in about three hundred hours during which students are truly engaged in meaningful, appropriate tasks.

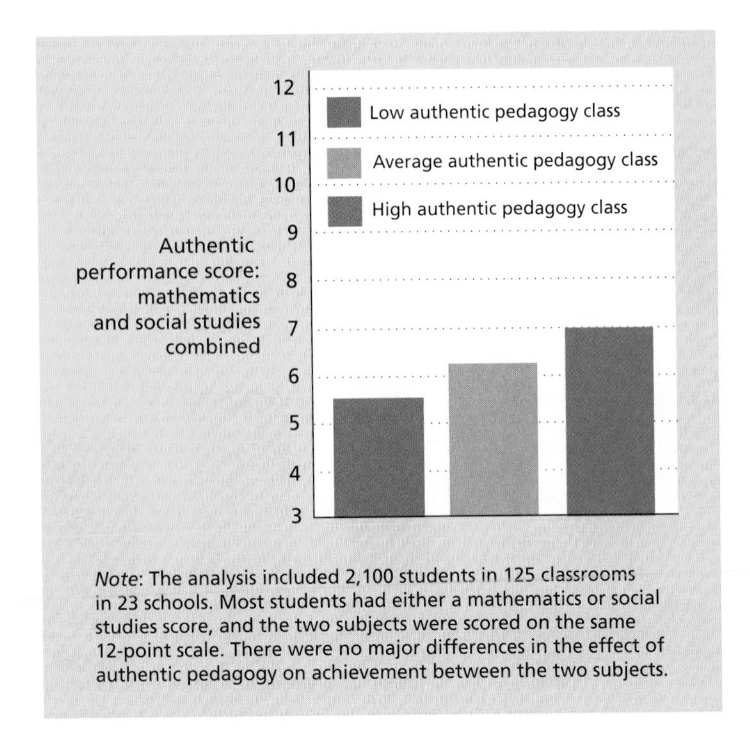

Figure 9.4 Level of authentic student performance for students who experience low, average, and high authentic pedagogy in restructuring elementary, middle, and high schools.
Source: Fred M. Newmann and Gary G. Wehlage, *Successful School Restructuring: A Report to the Public and Educators by the Center on Organization and Restructuring of Schools.* University of Wisconsin-Madison: Center on Organization and Restructuring of Schools, 1995, pp. 21, 55.

An additional concept that is proving useful in understanding teachers' use of time in the classroom is known as **opportunity to learn (OTL).** OTL is based on the premise that teachers should use time to provide all students with challenging content through appropriate instruction. Many states are developing OTL standards for how teachers should use time in the classroom.

To increase the time available for active learning, many high schools have implemented block scheduling arrangements. **Block scheduling** uses longer blocks of time each class period, with fewer periods each day. Longer blocks of time allow more in-depth coverage of subject matter and lead to deeper understanding and higher-level applications. Block scheduling also gives teachers more time to present complex concepts and students more time to practice applying those concepts to authentic problems.

What Are the Keys to Successful Classroom Management?

For most new teachers, classroom management is a primary concern. How can you prevent discipline problems from arising and keep students productively engaged in learning activities? While effective **classroom management** cannot be reduced to a cookbook recipe, there are definite steps you can take to create an effective learning environment in your classroom. First, it is important to understand that classroom management refers to how teachers structure their learning environments to prevent, or minimize, behavior problems; *discipline* refers to the methods teachers use *after* students misbehave. *Classroom management* is prevention-oriented, while *discipline* is control-oriented. Second, it is important to recognize that "the key to good management is use of techniques that elicit student cooperation and involvement in activities and thus *prevent* problems from emerging in the first place" (Good and Brophy 2003, 112). In addition,

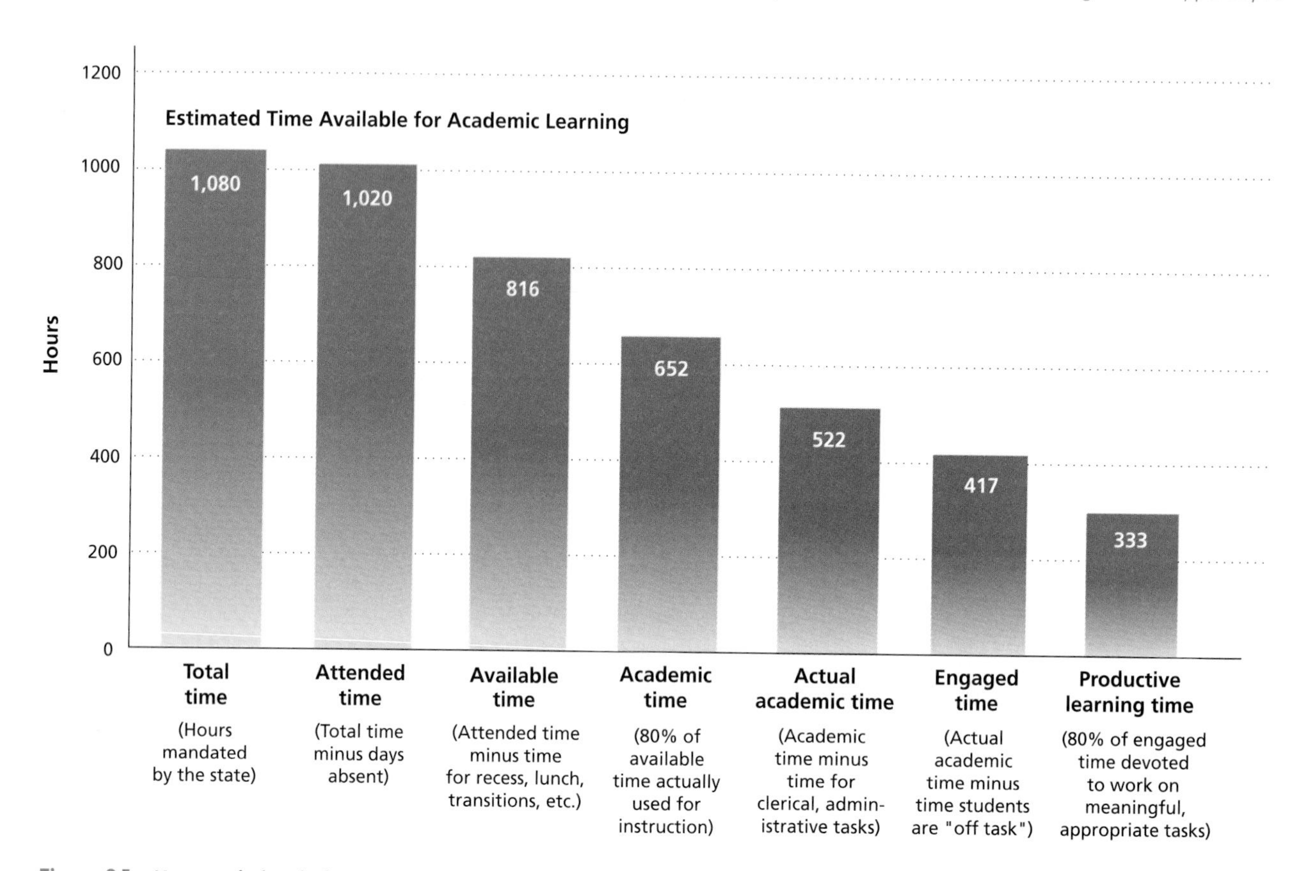

Figure 9.5 How much time is there, anyway? *Source:* From Carol Simon Weinstein and Andrew J. Migano, Jr. *Elementary Classroom Management: Lessons from Research and Practice,* 2nd ed. New York: McGraw-Hill, p. 142. Copyright © 1997 by McGraw-Hill Companies. Adapted with permission of The McGraw-Hill Companies.

sound classroom management techniques are based on the guidelines for creating an effective learning environment presented previously in this chapter—in other words, (1) creating a caring classroom, (2) organizing the physical classroom environment, (3) grouping students for instruction, (4) providing authentic learning tasks, and (5) structuring the use of time to maximize students' learning. Positive leadership and preventive planning thus are central to effective classroom management.

The Democratic Classroom

Research findings suggest that teachers who allow students to participate in making decisions about the physical classroom environment, classroom rules and procedures, modifications to the curriculum, and options for learning activities also have fewer discipline problems. Students in **democratic classrooms** have both more power and more responsibility than students in conventional classrooms. On the premise that if students are to live in a democracy, they must learn to manage freedom responsibly, teachers model democracy by giving their students some choices and some control over classroom activities.

William Glasser, well-known psychiatrist and author of *Quality School* (1998a), *The Quality School Teacher* (1998b), *Choice Theory* (1998c), and (with Karen Dotson) *Choice Theory in the Classroom* (1998), recommends that teachers develop "quality" classrooms based on democratic principles. According to Glasser, many teachers struggle with classroom management because their actions are guided by stimulus-response theory; that is, they try to coerce students through rewards or punishment, or what many teachers term "logical consequences." Instead, Glasser maintains that teachers should establish "quality" environments in the classroom by following *choice theory*—that is, recognizing that human beings make choices that enable them to create "quality worlds" that satisfy four needs: the need to belong, the need for power, the need for freedom, and the need for fun.

From a **choice theory** perspective, misbehavior in the classroom arises when students' learning experiences do not enable them to create quality worlds for themselves. Therefore, teachers "must give up bossing and turn to 'leading' " (Glasser 1997, 600). We follow leaders, Glasser says, because we believe they are concerned about our welfare. To persuade students to do quality schoolwork, teachers must establish warm, noncoercive relationships with students; teach students meaningful skills rather than ask them to memorize information; enable them to experience satisfaction and excitement by working in small teams; and move from teacher evaluation to student self-evaluation.

Preventive Planning

In what other ways can teachers prevent discipline problems from occurring? The key to prevention is excellent planning and an understanding of life in classrooms. In addition, teachers who have mastered the essential teaching skills have fewer discipline problems because students recognize that such teachers are prepared, well organized, and have a sense of purpose. They are confident of their ability to teach all students, and their task-oriented manner tends to discourage misbehavior.

In a seminal study of how teachers prevent discipline problems, Jacob Kounin looked at two sets of teachers: those who managed their classrooms smoothly and productively with few disruptions and those who seemed to be plagued with discipline problems and chaotic working conditions. He found that the teachers who managed their classrooms successfully had certain teaching behaviors in common: (1) they displayed the proverbial eyes-in-the-back-of-the-head, a quality of alertness Kounin referred to as *withitness,* (2) they used individual students and incidences as models to communicate to the rest of the class their expectations for student conduct—Kounin's *ripple effect,* (3) they supervised several situations at once effectively, and (4) they were adept at handling transitions smoothly (Kounin 1970). In addition to the principles of effective classroom management that emerge from Kounin's study, two key elements of preventive planning are establishing rules and procedures and organizing and planning for instruction.

Establishing Rules and Procedures Educational researchers have found that effective classroom managers have carefully planned rules and procedures, which they teach early in the year using clear explanations, examples, and practice (Evertson, Emmer, and Worsham 2003; Good and Brophy 2003). Your classroom rules should be clear, concise, reasonable, and few in number. For example, five general rules for elementary-age students might include: (1) be polite and helpful; (2) respect other people's property; (3) listen quietly while others are speaking; (4) do not hit, shove, or hurt others; and (5) obey all school rules. Rules for the secondary level might stipulate the following: (1) bring all needed materials to class; (2) be in your seat and ready to work when the bell rings; (3) respect and be polite to everyone; (4) respect other people's property; (5) listen and stay seated while someone else is speaking; and (6) obey all school rules (Evertson, Emmer, and Worsham 2003).

It is important to enforce classroom rules consistently and fairly. "Consistency is a key reason why some rules are effective while others are not. Rules that are not enforced or that are not applied evenly and consistently over time result in a loss of prestige and respect for the person who has created the rules and has the responsibility for carrying them out" (Borich 2000, 354).

Procedures—the routines your students will follow as they participate in learning activities—also are essential for smooth classroom functioning and minimizing opportunities for misbehavior. How will homework be collected? How will supplies be distributed? How will housekeeping chores be completed? How will attendance be taken? How do students obtain permission to leave the classroom? Part of developing classroom rules and procedures is to decide what to do when students do not follow them. Students must be made aware of the consequences for failing to follow rules or procedures. For example, consequences for rule infractions can range from an expression of teacher disapproval to penalties such as loss of privileges, detention after school, disciplinary conference with a parent or guardian, or temporary separation from the group.

Organizing and Planning for Instruction The ability to organize instructional time, materials, and activities so that classes run smoothly are skills that will enable you to keep your students engaged in learning, thereby reducing the need for discipline. Time spent planning authentic learning activities that are appropriate to students' needs, interests, and abilities will enable you to enjoy the professional satisfaction that comes from having a well-managed classroom.

In the following, a remedial algebra teacher in an urban school tells how organization and planning helped her effectively teach a class of twenty-seven students, grades 9 through 12, who enrolled in the class "for a myriad of reasons, [including] absenteeism, learning disabilities, failure in college prep classes, unwillingness to do required work in college prep classes, personal problems, nonconformity, and a need for credits":

> *I am consistently rewarded by the creative thinking and quickness of these students when they are asked to do something other than listen to my thinking, take notes, and copy examples from the board. I have learned that planning meaningful activities, choosing engaging tasks, organizing small groups and pair problem-solving experiences, valuing thinking, and carefully assessing understanding promote an improved classroom atmosphere where learning is the objective for everyone (Schifter 1996, 75–76).*

Effective Responses to Student Behavior

When student misbehavior does occur, effective teachers draw from a repertoire of problem-solving strategies. These strategies are based on their experience and common sense, their knowledge of students and the teaching-learning process, and their knowledge of human psychology. There are many structured approaches to classroom management; some are based on psychological theories of human motivation and behavior, while others reflect various philosophical views regarding the purposes of education. None of these approaches, however, is appropriate for all situations or for all teachers or for all students, and the usefulness of a given method depends, in part, on the teacher's individual personality and leadership style and ability to analyze the complex dynamics of classroom life. In addition, what works should not be the only criterion for evaluating structured or "packaged" approaches to discipline; what they teach students about their self-worth, acting responsibly, and solving problems is also important (Curwin and Mendler 1988, 1989).

Severity of Misbehavior Your response to student misbehavior will depend, in part, on whether an infraction is mild, moderate, or severe and whether it is occurring for the first time or is part of a pattern of chronic misbehaviors. For example, a student who throws a wad of paper at another student might receive a warning for the first infraction, while another student who repeatedly throws objects at other students might receive an after-school detention. Definitions of the severity of misbehavior vary from school to school and from state to state. Table 9.2 presents one classification of examples of mild, moderate, and severe misbehaviors and several alternative responses.

Table 9.2 Mild, moderate, and severe misbehaviors and some alternative responses

Misbehaviors	Alternative Responses
Mild misbehaviors	**Mild responses**
Minor defacing of school property or property of others	Warning
Acting out (horseplaying or scuffling)	Feedback to student
Talking back	Time out
Talking without raising hand	Change of seat assignment
Getting out of seat	Withdrawal of privileges
Disrupting others	After-school detention
Sleeping in class	Telephone/note to parents
Tardiness	
Throwing objects	
Exhibiting inappropriate familiarity (kissing, hugging)	
Gambling	
Eating in class	
Moderate misbehaviors	**Moderate responses**
Unauthorized leaving of class	Detention
Abusive conduct toward others	Behavior contract
Noncompliant	Withdrawal of privileges
Smoking or using tobacco in class	Telephone/note to parents
Cutting class	Parent conference
Cheating, plagiarizing, or lying	In-school suspension
Using profanity, vulgar language, or obscene gestures	Restitution of damages
Fighting	Alternative school service (e.g., clean up, tutoring)
Severe misbehaviors	**Severe responses**
Defacing or damaging school property or property of others	Detention
Theft, possession, or sale of another's property	Telephone/note to parents
Truancy	Parent conference
Being under the influence of alcohol or narcotics	In-school suspension
Selling, giving, or delivering to another person alcohol, narcotics, or weapons	Removal from school or alternative school placement
Teacher assault or verbal abuse	
Incorrigible conduct, noncompliance	

Source: Gary Borich, *Effective Teaching Methods,* 4th ed. Upper Saddle River, NJ: Merrill, 2000, p. 386. © 2000. Reprinted by permission of Prentice-Hall, Inc., Upper Saddle River, NJ.

On the Frontlines

Social Cruelty

Once a week you have lunch with the students instead of joining your colleagues in the faculty area. You usually feel a bit awkward in the noisy cafeteria sitting at a long bench table with them, but every time later you are glad you did. You learn things about your students this way that you wouldn't pick up on in the classroom.

Today you overhear a conversation several seats away from you. Maya is talking about something that happened before school. "So Nadia stands there with her hands on her hips and says in a really mean voice, 'I like your sweater; give it to me!' " Maya lowers her voice, "Amy didn't know what to do. She just stood there and looked at Nadia, which made Tiffany mad and she said, 'I mean it. Give it to me! If you don't, I'll make everyone hate you.' "

"Well what did Amy do?" April asks in a loud whisper.

Maya's tone is matter of fact, "She gave Nadia her sweater."

"That's awful," April says. "She's so mean to Amy."

"Oh, Nadia does things like that to Amy all the time. She knows Amy can't stand up to her. I just try stay as far away from Nadia as I can."

You know the girls Maya and April were talking about. Nadia has a history of bullying other students and being disruptive in class. Just her presence creates a different atmosphere in class. As you pick up your tray to go, you wonder, "Is this my business? If I get involved, will it make it worse for Amy? Should I take this seriously?"

Bullying is something to take seriously and something that too many adults overlook or decide to ignore. While the phenomenon of bullying is ages old, a scholarly study of it wasn't conducted until the 1970s, when Norwegian researcher Dan Olweus launched extensive investigations in his country. In 1982, the suicides of three ten- to fourteen-year-old boys in Norway, "in all probability as a consequence of severe bullying by peers," Olweus observes, led to Norway's nationwide campaign against bullying. In his book, *Bullying at School,* Olweus reports that in the 1980s and 1990s a number of countries gave bullying among schoolchildren "some public and research attention."

The post-Columbine investigations of student-instigated school violence in the United States brought the problem of bullying in our schools to the forefront in America. According to the *Safe School Initiative,* the U.S. Department of Education and Secret Service collaborative investigation of thirty-seven incidents of targeted school shootings, "Almost three-quarters of the attackers felt persecuted, bullied, threatened, attacked or injured by others prior to the incident." The report notes that in some cases bullying had been longstanding and extensive: For example, in one incident, most of the attacker's schoolmates described the attacker as "the kid everyone teased." The schoolmates described how at some point virtually every child in the school had thrown the attacker against a locker, tripped him in the hall, held his head under water in the pool, or thrown things at him. Several schoolmates had noted that the attacker acted differently in the days preceding the attack in that he seemed more annoyed by and less tolerant of the teasing than usual.

In early 2000, educators and journalists began writing more about the social dimension of students' worlds in books like *Best Friends, Worst Enemies: Understanding the Social Lives of Children* (2001) and *Odd Girl Out: The Hidden Culture of Aggression in Girls* (2002). In the latter, author Rachel Simmons describes a form of bullying more typical of girls—cruel social ostracism imposed on victims and a hidden physical aggression toward them that adults had difficulty detecting or believing because of the perpetrators' "good girl" images. Noting the power of relationships for girls, Simmons reports that the ostracism had residual impact on the victims she interviewed as adults.

Olweus outlines specific measures to prevent or counter bullying. Among these at the school level are to provide "better supervision during recess and lunch time" hold "a school conference day on bully/victim problems," and pull together "teacher groups for the development of the social milieu of the school." At the class level he proposes creat-

ing "class rules against bullying"; holding regular class meetings to address issues; using literature, role playing, and cooperative learning activities that promote interaction and cooperation among students; and promoting positive class activities, such as service learning projects to develop mutual respect among students. At the individual level he advises teachers to have "serious talks" with bullies and victims and with their parents, to involve "neutral" students, and, when other methods fail, to change the class or school of the bully or victim.

Exploratory Questions

1. Go to http://www.nochildleftbehind.gov and use the search tool to locate "The Final Report of Findings of the Safe School Initiative: Implications for the Prevention of School Attacks in the United States." What are the findings of this report?
2. Why might it be important to address bullying at an early age?
3. What responsibility does the teacher in the vignette have to address this situation? What difficulties does the teacher face?

Your Survival Guide of Helpful Resources

The following resources provide helpful hints for surviving "on the frontlines."

Books and Articles

Beane, A. L. (1999). *The Bully-free Classroom: Over 100 Tips and Strategies for Teachers K-8.* Minneapolis, MN: Free Spirit Publishing, Inc.

Olweus, D. (1993). *Bullying at school: What we know and what we can do.* Cambridge, MA: Blackwell Publishers.

Simmons, R. (2002). *Odd girl out: The hidden culture of aggression in girls.* New York: Harcourt.

Thompson, M., Grace, C. O., and Cohen, L. J. (2001). *Best friends, worst enemies: Understanding the social lives of children.* New York: Ballantine Books.

Websites

Center for the Prevention of School Violence (http://www.ncsu.edu/cpsv)

Colorado Anti-Bullying Project (http://www.no-bully.com/)

Operation Respect: Dont Laugh at Me (http://www.dontlaugh.org)

The Ophelia Project (http://www.opheliaproject.org/)

Companion Website

Constructive Assertiveness The effectiveness of your responses to students' misbehavior will depend, in part, on your ability to use "constructive assertiveness" (Evertson, Emmer, and Worsham 2003). Constructive assertiveness "lies on a continuum of social response between aggressive, overbearing pushiness and timid, ineffectual, or submissive responses that allow some students to trample on the teacher's and other students' rights. Assertiveness skills allow you to communicate to students that you are serious about teaching and about maintaining a classroom in which everyone's rights are respected" (Evertson, Emmer, and Worsham, 2003, 152). Communication based on constructive assertiveness is neither hostile, sarcastic, defensive, nor vindictive; it is clear, firm, and concise.

Evertson and colleagues (2003) suggest that constructive assertiveness has three basic elements:

- A clear statement of the problem or concern
- Body language that is unambiguous (e.g., eye contact with student, erect posture, facial expressions that match the content and tone of corrective statements)
- Firm, unwavering insistence on appropriate behavior

Lee Cantor developed an approach to discipline based on teacher assertiveness. The approach calls on teachers to establish firm, clear guidelines for student behavior and to follow through with consequences for misbehavior. Cantor (1989, 58) comments on how he arrived at the ideas behind assertive discipline: "I found that, above all, the master teachers were assertive; that is, they *taught* students how to behave. They established clear rules for the classroom, they communicated those rules to the students, and they taught students how to follow them." **Assertive discipline** requires teachers to do the following:

1. Make clear that they will not tolerate anyone preventing them from teaching, stopping learning, or doing anything else that is not in the best interest of the class, the individual, or the teacher.
2. Instruct students clearly and in specific terms about what behaviors are desired and what behaviors are not tolerated.
3. Plan positive and negative consequences for predetermined acceptable or unacceptable behaviors.
4. Plan positive reinforcement for compliance. Reinforcement includes verbal acknowledgment, notes, free time for talking, and, of course, tokens that can be exchanged for appropriate rewards.
5. Plan a sequence of steps to punish noncompliance. These range from writing a youngster's name on the board to sending the student to the principal's office (MacNaughton and Johns 1991, 53).

Teacher Problem Solving When a teacher's efforts to get a student to stop misbehaving are unsuccessful, a problem-solving conference with the student is warranted. A problem-solving conference may give the teacher additional understanding of the situation, thus paving the way for a solution. A conference also helps teacher and student understand the other's perceptions better and begin to build a more positive relationship.

The goal of a problem-solving conference is for the student to accept responsibility for his or her behavior and make a commitment to change it. While there is no "right way" to conduct a problem-solving conference, Glasser's choice theory lends itself to a conferencing procedure that is flexible and appropriate for most situations. Students will usually make good choices (i.e., behave in an acceptable manner) if they experience success and know that teachers care about them. The following steps are designed to help misbehaving students see that the choices they make may not lead to the results they want.

1. Have the misbehaving student evaluate and take responsibility for his or her behavior. Often, a good first step is for the teacher to ask "What are you doing?" and then "Is it helping you?"
2. Have the student make a plan for a more acceptable way of behaving. If necessary, the student and the teacher brainstorm solutions. Agreement is reached on how the student will behave in the future and the consequences for failure to follow through.
3. Require the student to make a commitment to follow the plan.
4. Don't accept excuses for failure to follow the plan.
5. Don't use punishment or react to a misbehaving student in a punitive manner. Instead, point out to the student that there are logical consequences for failure to follow the plan.
6. Don't give up on the student. If necessary, remind the student of his or her commitment to desirable behavior. Periodically ask "How are things going?"

Developing Your Own Approach to Classroom Management No approach to classroom management is effective with all students at all times. How you respond to misbehavior in your classroom will depend on your personality, value system, and beliefs about children and will range along a continuum from the "minimum power" of giving students nonverbal cues to the "maximum power" of physical intervention.

Classroom management expert Charles Wolfgang points out that teachers usually present one of three "philosophies" (or attitudes) to students who misbehave:

1. The *relationship-listening* "philosophy" involves the use of minimum power. This reflects a view that the student has the capabilities to change his or her own behavior, and that if the student is misbehaving, it is because of inner emotional turmoil, flooded behavior, or feelings of inner inadequacy.
2. The *confronting-contracting* "philosophy" is one of "I am the adult. I know misbehavior when I see it and will confront the student to stop this behavior. I will grant the student the power to decide how he or she will change, and encourage and contract with the student to live up a mutual agreement for behavioral change."
3. The *rules and consequences* "philosophy" is one that communicates an attitude of "This is the rule and behavior that I want and I will set out assertively to get this action" (Wolfgang 2001, 4–5).

See the Appendix "Beliefs about Discipline Inventory" on this book's website, so you can determine which "philosophy of discipline" best fits your personality.

In your journey toward becoming a professional teacher, you will develop a repertoire of strategies for classroom management; then, when you encounter a discipline problem in the classroom, you can analyze the situation and respond with an effective strategy. The ability to do so will give you confidence, like the following beginning teacher:

I went into the classroom with some confidence and left with lots of confidence. I felt good about what was going on. I established a comfortable rapport with the kids and was more relaxed. Each week I grew more confident. When you first go in you are not sure how you'll do. When you know you are doing OK, your confidence improves.

What Teaching Methods Do Effective Teachers Use?

As we pointed out in our discussion of educational philosophy in Chapter 3, beliefs about teaching and learning, students, knowledge, and what is worth knowing influence the instructional methods a teacher uses. In addition, instruction is influenced by variables such as the teacher's style, learners' characteristics, the culture of the school and surrounding community, and the resources available. All of these components contribute to the "model" of teaching the teacher uses in the classroom. A model of teaching provides the teacher with rules of thumb to follow to create a particular kind of learning environment, or, as Bruce Joyce, Marsha Weil, and Emily Calhoun point out in *Models of Teaching* (2000, 13), a model of teaching is "a description of a learning environment." Table 9.3 presents brief descriptions of four widely used models of teaching.

Effective teachers use a repertoire of teaching models and assessment strategies, depending upon their situations and the goals and objectives they wish to attain. Your teaching strategies in the classroom will most likely be eclectic, that is, a combination of several models and assessment techniques. Also, as you gain classroom experience and acquire new skills and understanding, your personal model of teaching will evolve, enabling you to respond appropriately to a wider range of teaching situations.

Methods Based on Learning New Behaviors

Many teachers use instructional methods that have emerged from our greater understanding of how people acquire or change their behaviors. **Direct instruction,** for example, is a systematic instructional method that focuses on the transmission of knowledge and skills from the teacher (and the curriculum) to the student. Direct instruction is organized on the basis of observable learning behaviors and the actual products of learning. Generally, direct instruction is most appropriate for step-by-step knowledge acquisition and basic skill development but not appropriate for teaching less structured, higher-order skills such as writing, the analysis of social issues, and problem solving.

Extensive research was conducted in the 1970s and 1980s on the effectiveness of direct instruction (Gagné, 1974, 1977; Good and Grouws 1979; Rosenshine 1988; Rosenshine and Stevens 1986). The following eight steps are a synthesis of research on direct instruction and may be used with students ranging in age from elementary to senior high school.

1. Orient students to the lesson by telling them what they will learn.
2. Review previously learned skills and concepts related to the new material.
3. Present new material, using examples and demonstrations.
4. Assess students' understanding by asking questions; correct misunderstandings.
5. Allow students to practice new skills or apply new information.
6. Provide feedback and corrections as students practice.

Table 9.3 Four instructional models

	Goals and Rationale	Methods
Cooperative Learning	Students can be motivated to learn by working cooperatively in small groups if rewards are made available to the group as a whole and to individual members of the group.	• Small groups (four to six students) work together on learning activities. • Assignments require that students help one another while working on a group project. • In competitive arrangements, groups may compete against one another. • Group members contribute to group goals according to their talents, interests, and abilities.
Theory into Practice	Teachers make decisions in three primary areas: content to be taught, how students will learn, and the behaviors the teacher will use in the classroom. The effectiveness of teaching is related to the quality of decisions the teacher makes in these areas.	The teacher follows seven steps in the classroom: 1. Orients students to material to be learned 2. Tells students what they will learn and why it is important 3. Presents new material that consists of knowledge, skills or processes students are to learn 4. Models what students are expected to do 5. Checks for student understanding 6. Gives students opportunity for practice under the teacher's guidance 7. Makes assignments that give students opportunity to practice what they have learned on their own
Behavior Modification	Teachers can shape student learning by using various forms of enforcement. Human behavior is learned, and behaviors that are positively reinforced (rewarded) tend to increase and those that are not reinforced tend to decrease.	• Teacher begins by presenting stimulus in the form of new material. • The behavior of students is observed by the teacher. • Appropriate behaviors are reinforced by the teacher as quickly as possible.
Nondirective Teaching	Learning can be facilitated if teachers focus on personal development of students and create opportunities for students to increase their self-understanding and self-concepts. The key to effective teaching is the teacher's ability to understand students and to involve them in a teaching-learning partnership.	• Teacher acts as a facilitator of learning. • Teacher creates learning environments that support personal growth and development. • Teacher acts in the role of a counselor who helps students to understand themselves, clarify their goals, and accept responsibility for their behavior.

7. Include newly learned material in homework.
8. Review material periodically.

A direct instruction method called **mastery learning** is based on two assumptions about learning: (1) virtually all students can learn material if given enough time and taught appropriately and (2) students learn best when they participate in a structured, systematic program of learning that enables them to progress in small, sequenced steps (Bloom 1981; Carroll 1963):

1. Set objectives and standards for mastery.
2. Teach content directly to students.
3. Provide corrective feedback to students on their learning.

From this photo, what can you tell about this teacher's proficiency in planning and preparation, structuring classroom environment, and instruction?

4. Provide additional time and help in correcting errors.
5. Follow a cycle of teaching, testing, reteaching, and retesting.

In mastery learning, students take diagnostic tests and then are guided to do corrective exercises or activities to improve their learning. These may take the form of programmed instruction, workbooks, computer drill and practice, or educational games. After the corrective lessons, students are given another test and are more likely to achieve mastery.

Methods Based on Child Development

As you learned in Chapter 8, children move through stages of cognitive, psychosocial, and moral development. Effective instruction includes methods that are developmentally appropriate, meet students' diverse learning needs, and recognize the importance of learning that occurs in social contexts. For example, one way that students reach higher levels of development is to observe and then imitate their parents, teachers, and peers, who act as models. As Woolfolk (2001, 327) points out:

> *Modeling has long been used, of course, to teach dance, sports, and crafts, as well as skills in subjects such as home economics, chemistry, and shop. Modeling can also be applied deliberately in the classroom to teach mental skills and to broaden horizons—to teach new ways of thinking. Teachers serve as models for a vast range of behaviors, from pronouncing vocabulary words, to reacting to the seizure of an epileptic student, to being enthusiastic about learning.*

Effective teachers also use **modeling** by "thinking out loud" and following three basic steps of "mental modeling" (Duffy and Roehler 1989):

1. Showing students the reasoning involved
2. Making students conscious of the reasoning involved
3. Focusing students on applying the reasoning

In this way, teachers can help students become aware of their learning processes and enhance their ability to learn.

Since the mid-1980s, several educational researchers have examined how learners *construct* understanding of new material. "Constructivist views of learning, therefore, focus on how learners make sense of new information—how they construct meaning based on what they already know" (Parkay and Hass 2000, 168). Teachers with this constructivist view of learning focus on students' thinking about the material being learned and, through carefully orchestrated cues, prompts, and questions, help students arrive at a deeper understanding of the material. The common elements of **constructivist teaching** include the following:

- The teacher elicits students' prior knowledge of the material and uses this as the starting point for instruction.
- The teacher not only presents material to students, but he or she also responds to students' efforts to learn the material. While teaching, the teacher must *learn about students' learning.*
- Students not only absorb information, but they also actively use that information to construct meaning.
- The teacher creates a social milieu within the classroom, a community of learners, that allows students to reflect and talk with one another as they construct meaning and solve problems.

Constructivist teachers provide students with support, or "scaffolding," as they learn new material. By observing the child and listening carefully to what he or she says, the teacher provides **scaffolding** in the form of clues, encouragement, suggestions, or other assistance to guide students' learning efforts. The teacher varies the amount of support given on the basis of the student's understanding—if the student understands little, the teacher gives more support; conversely, the teacher gives progressively less support as the student's understanding becomes more evident. Overall, the teacher provides just enough scaffolding to enable the student to "discover" the material on his or her own.

The concept of scaffolding is based on the work of L. S. Vygotsky, a well-known Soviet psychologist. Vygotsky (1978, 1986) coined the term *zone of proximal development* to refer to the point at which students need assistance in order to continue learning. The effective teacher is sensitive to the student's zone of development and ensures that instruction neither exceeds the student's current level of understanding nor underestimates the student's ability.

Methods Based on the Thinking Process

Some instructional methods are derived from the mental processes involved in learning, thinking, remembering, problem solving, and creativity. **Information processing,** for example, is a branch of cognitive science concerned with how people use their long- and short-term memory to access information and solve problems. The computer is often used as an analogy for information-processing views of learning:

> *Like the computer, the human mind takes in information, performs operations on it to change its form and content, stores the information, retrieves it when needed, and generates responses to it. Thus, processing involves gathering and representing information, or* encoding; *holding information, or* storage; *and getting at the information when needed, or* retrieval. *The whole system is guided by* control processes *that determine how and when information will flow through the system (Woolfolk 2001, 243).*

Although several systematic approaches to instruction are based on information processing—teaching students how to memorize, think inductively or deductively, acquire concepts, or use the scientific method, for example—they all focus on how people acquire and use information. Table 9.4 presents general teaching guidelines based on ideas from information processing.

Table 9.4 Using information processing ideas in the classroom

- Make sure you have the students' attention. For example, begin a lesson by asking a question that stimulates interest in the topic.
- Help students separate essential from nonessential details and focus on the most important information as it relates to instructional objectives.
- Help students make connections between new information and what they already know.
- Provide for repetition and review of information and the practice of skills.
- Present material in a clear, organized, concrete way. For example, give students a brief outline to follow and summarize lessons.
- Focus on meaning, not memorization.

Source: Adapted from Anita E. Woolfolk, *Educational Psychology*, 7th ed. Boston: Allyn and Bacon, 1998, pp. 265-266.

In **inquiry learning** and **discovery learning** students are given opportunities to inquire into subjects so that they "discover" knowledge for themselves. When teachers ask students to go beyond information in a text to make inferences, draw conclusions, or form generalizations; and when teachers do not answer students' questions, preferring instead to have students develop their own answers, they are using methods based on inquiry and discovery learning. These methods are best suited for teaching concepts, relationships, and theoretical abstractions, and for having students formulate and test hypotheses. The following example shows how inquiry and discovery learning in a first-grade classroom fostered a high level of student involvement and thinking.

> *The children are gathered around a table on which a candle and jar have been placed. The teacher, Jackie Wiseman, lights the candle and, after it has burned brightly for a minute or two, covers it carefully with the jar. The candle grows dim, flickers, and goes out. Then she produces another candle and a larger jar, and the exercise is repeated. The candle goes out, but more slowly. Jackie produces two more candles and jars of different sizes, and the children light the candles, place the jars over them, and the flames slowly go out. "Now we're going to develop some ideas about what has just happened," she says. "I want you to ask me questions about those candles and jars and what you just observed" (Joyce, Weil, and Calhoun 2000, 3).*

Methods Based on Peer-Mediated Instruction

Student peer groups can be a deterrent to academic performance (Steinberg et al. 1996), but they can also motivate students to excel. Because school learning occurs in a social setting, **peer-mediated instruction** provides teachers with options for increasing students' learning. Cooperative learning, described earlier in this chapter, is an example of peer-mediated instruction. Another example is **group investigation,** in which the teacher's role is to create an environment that allows students to determine what they will study and how. Students are presented with a situation to which they "react and discover basic conflicts among their attitudes, ideas, and modes of perception. On the basis of this information, they identify the problem to be investigated, analyze the roles required to solve it, organize themselves to take these roles, act, report, and evaluate these results" (Thelen 1960, 82).

The teacher's role in group investigation is multifaceted; he or she is an organizer, guide, resource person, counselor, and evaluator. The method is very effective in increasing student achievement (Sharan and Sharan 1989/90, 17–21), positive attitudes toward learning, and the cohesiveness of the classroom group. The model also allows students to inquire into problems that interest them and enables each student to make a meaningful, authentic contribution to the group's effort based on his or her experiences, interests, knowledge, and skills.

Other common forms of peer-mediated instruction include peer tutoring and cross-age tutoring. In **peer-tutoring** arrangements, students are tutored by other pupils in the same class or the same grade. **Cross-age tutoring** involves, for example, sixth-grade students tutoring second-grade students in reading. Research clearly shows that with proper orientation and training, cross-age tutoring can greatly benefit both "teacher" and learner (Henriques 1997; Schneider and Barone 1997; Utay and Utay 1997; Zukowski 1997). Pilot programs pairing students at risk of dropping out of school with younger children and with special-needs students have proved especially successful.

What Is Taught in Schools?

Think back to your experiences as a student at the elementary, middle, junior, and secondary schools you attended. What things did you learn? Certainly, the curriculum you experienced included reading, computation, penmanship, spelling, geography, and history. In addition to these topics, though, did you learn something about cooperation, competition, stress, football, video games, computers, popularity, and the opposite sex? Or, perhaps, did you learn to love chemistry and to hate English grammar?

The countless things you learned in school make up the curriculum that you experienced. Curriculum theorists and researchers have suggested several different definitions for ***curriculum,*** with no one definition universally accepted. Here are some definitions in current use.

1. A course of study, derived from the Latin *currere,* meaning "to run a course"
2. Course content, the information or knowledge that students are to learn
3. Planned learning experiences
4. Intended learning outcomes, the *results* of instruction as distinguished from the *means* (activities, materials, etc.) of instruction
5. All the experiences that students have while at school

No one of these five is in any sense the "right" definition. The way we define curriculum depends on our purposes and the situation we find ourselves in. If, for example, we were advising a high school student on the courses he or she needed to take in order to prepare for college, our operational definition of curriculum would most likely be "a course of study." However, if we were interviewing sixth-grade students for their views on the K–6 elementary school they had just graduated from, we would probably want to view curriculum as "all the experiences that students have while at school." Let us posit an additional definition of curriculum: *Curriculum refers to the experiences, both planned and unplanned, that enhance (and sometimes impede) the education and growth of students.*

Kinds of Curriculum

Elliot Eisner, a noted educational researcher, has said that "schools teach much more—and much less—than they intend to teach. Although much of what is taught is explicit and public, a great deal is not" (2002, 87). For this reason, we need to look at the four curricula that all students experience. The more we understand these curricula and how they influence students, the better we will be able to develop educational programs that do, in fact, educate.

Explicit Curriculum The explicit, or overt, curriculum refers to what a school intends to teach students. This curriculum is made up of several components: (1) the goals, aims, and learning objectives the school has for all students, (2) the actual courses that make up each student's course of study, and (3) the specific knowledge, skills, and attitudes that teachers want students to acquire. If we asked a principal to describe the educational program at his or her school, our inquiry would be in reference to the explicit curriculum. Similarly, if we asked a teacher to describe what he or she wished to accomplish with a particular class, we would be given a description of the explicit curriculum.

In short, the **explicit curriculum** represents the publicly announced expectations the school has for its students. These expectations range from learning how to read, write, and compute to learning to appreciate music, art, and cultures other than one's own. In most instances, the explicit curriculum takes the form of written plans or guides for the education of students. Examples of such written documents are course descriptions, curriculum guides that set forth the goals and learning objectives for a school or district, texts and other commercially prepared learning materials, and teachers' lesson plans. Through the instructional program of a school, then, these curricular materials are brought to life.

Hidden Curriculum The hidden, or implicit, curriculum refers to the behaviors, attitudes, and knowledge the culture of the school unintentionally teaches students (Parkay and Hass 2000). What students learn via the **hidden curriculum** can be positive or negative, depending on their day-to-day experiences at school. For example, from teachers who are knowledgeable, well organized, and personable, students are likely to develop positive habits and abilities—cooperating with others, taking responsibility, planning ahead, and forgoing immediate gratification to obtain long-range goals. On the other hand, from teachers who are ill prepared, apathetic, or aloof, students are likely to acquire habits and attitudes that are negative and that discourage personal growth and development—a dislike for learning, the ability to deceive or defy adult authority figures, or a tendency to procrastinate.

Many factors influence the attitudes students display in class. How might a "hidden curriculum" result in negative attitudes among students? How can the concept of a hidden curriculum be used to promote positive behavior?

In the following examples, four students describe the hidden curricula they experienced in school. In examples 1 and 2, excerpts from letters students wrote their teachers, the hidden curricula "taught" students to be more confident in their ability to learn. In examples 3 and 4, the hidden curricula undermined the students' confidence and desire to learn.

Example #1

I was in your grade 10 English class. I sure felt safe to take a risk in your class. I actually tried hard, knowing I might fail, but felt safe enough to do so (Paul, Christensen, and Falk 2000, 23).

Example #2

I was in your grade 9 class and you praised me for my creative writing. Until that time, I had never thought of myself as a very

Meeting the Standard

Creates a Positive Learning Culture

INTASC *The teacher uses an understanding of individual and group motivation and behavior to create a learning environment that encourages positive social interaction, active engagement in learning, and self-motivation (INTASC Knowledge, Principle #5).*

Teachers are responsible for managing and monitoring student learning (NBPTS, Proposition 3).

The new professional teacher should be able to explain instructional choices based on research-derived knowledge and best practice (NCATE, Standard 7: Knowledge, Skills, and Dispositions).

Both students and teacher establish and maintain through planning of learning activities, interactions, and the classroom environment high expectations for the learning of all students (PRAXIS III Framework—"distinguished" level of performance).*

Through the establishment of a safe learning environment and an understanding of learning theory and effective teaching practices, the best teachers strive to do more than teach to the norm. From the first day that students enter a classroom, the decisions that the teacher makes influence the affective, as well as the cognitive aspects of learning, both of which must be present for success to occur.

Tom looked over the sea of heads that belonged to those sitting at newly cleaned desks. This was the moment to enlist his students' imaginations and cooperation in making a "Class Proclamation of Rights and Responsibilities." He had tried this activity during the first week of class last year, and it had been moderately successful in helping his students to focus on the behaviors that led to a classroom in which all students were given equal opportunities to learn. This year, however, he was entering into this activity with a clear list in his own mind of the most important items that he would encourage the students to contribute, along with rewards and consequences. He would need to be a good listener and facilitator to direct the conversation, but he knew that the end result—to be printed on a large piece of bright blue poster paper, signed and dated by all, and displayed on the front wall—would be well worth the effort. He also believed that the students would be more responsive to rules and consequences they had designed than they might be to his—at least at the beginning of a new year!

By enlisting the cooperation of his students in designing a personalized set of rules and consequences for the classroom, Tom modeled leadership skills that encouraged students to take responsibility for their behaviors throughout the upcoming year. With thoughtful anticipation of student responses, Tom would be able to help his students form the basis of a democratic classroom in which their "voices" would lead to a positive learning environment.

1. Write down important guidelines that you think should be present for a class to operate with responsibility and high expectations for learning and behavior. Think of guidelines from both the teacher's and students' points of view. Then, in groups of four or five, pool your guidelines into a "Group Proclamation of Rights and Responsibilities." When you have each agreed that you can abide by the statements written down, sign and date your proclamation. Compare your group proclamation with those of other groups in the class. How are they similar? How do they differ?
2. Why do you think Tom felt he needed to "guide" the list this year?

creative person but your faith in me spurred me on to choose English as my major at the university (Paul, Christensen, and Falk 2000, 23).

Example #3

The teacher just put [material] on the board and if you don't know how, the teacher get angry. I try to get help but when I come after school, they gotta go somewhere and can't help you . . . like when I ask somebody to help me, just because some other kid won't need help, then they think others won't either; some kids are smarter (Wilson and Corbett 2001, 38).

Example #4

I was in your 11th grade biology class. I loved science and biology until I took your class. You gave me a great disdain for the subject. Your teaching methods bored the class to tears. We read each chapter out loud at the beginning of the week and spent the rest of the week working quietly on the questions at the end of the chapter along with the endless dittos you passed out. We never discussed anything and you never taught us anything. We were graded on how well we could come up with the answers you thought were right and heaven forbid if we did not head our paper using the "correct" format. I think the only thing I learned in your class was conformity (Colucci 2000, 38).

As a result of the hidden curriculum of schools, students learn more than their teachers imagine. Although teachers cannot directly control what students learn through the hidden curriculum, they can increase the likelihood that what it teaches will be positive. By allowing students to help determine the content of the explicit curriculum, by inviting them to help establish classroom rules, and by providing them with challenges appropriate for their stage of development, teachers can ensure that the outcomes of the hidden curriculum are more positive than negative.

Null Curriculum Discussing a curriculum that cannot be observed directly is like talking about dark matter or black holes, unseen phenomena in the universe whose existence must be inferred because their incredible denseness and gravitational fields do not allow light to escape. In much the same way, we can consider the curriculum that we *do not* find in the schools; it may be as important as what we *do* find. Elliot Eisner has labeled the intellectual processes and content that schools do not teach "the **null curriculum**—the options students are not afforded, the perspectives they may never know about, much less be able to use, the concepts and skills that are not a part of their intellectual repertoire" (2002, 106–107).

For example, the kind of thinking that schools foster among students is largely based on manipulations of words and numbers. Thinking that is imaginative, subjective, and poetic is stressed only incidentally. Also, students are seldom taught anthropology, sociology, psychology, law, economics, filmmaking, or architecture.

Eisner points out that "certain subject matters have been traditionally taught in schools not because of a careful analysis of the range of other alternatives that could be offered but rather because they have traditionally been taught. We teach

Would this be an extracurricular activity or a cocurricular activity? Explain why. Do you think participation promotes achievement or does achievement promote participation?

Identifying Kinds of Curriculum

Professional Reflection

Reflect on your experiences with the curriculum as an elementary, middle, or high school student. Then, focusing on one part of the explicit curriculum that you experienced–a particular subject or a particular class–identify possible aspects of the hidden curriculum and possible areas of null curriculum. What conclusions might you draw about beliefs and values concerning the curriculum held by educators? local communities? the wider society? How did those beliefs and values affect you and your education?

what we teach largely out of habit, and in the process neglect areas of study that could prove to be exceedingly useful to students" (2002, 103).

Extracurricular/Cocurricular Programs The curriculum includes school-sponsored activities—music, drama, special interest clubs, sports, student government, and honor societies, to name a few—that students may pursue in addition to their studies in academic subject areas. When such activities are perceived as additions to the academic curriculum, they are termed *extracurricular.* When these activities are seen as having important educational goals—and not merely as extras added to the academic curriculum—they are termed *cocurricular.* To reflect the fact that these two labels are commonly used for the same activities, we use the term *extracurricular/cocurricular* activities.

Though **extracurricular/cocurricular programs** are most extensive on the secondary level, many schools at the elementary, middle, and junior high levels also provide their students with a broad assortment of extracurricular/cocurricular activities. For those students who choose to participate, such activities provide an opportunity to use social and academic skills in many different contexts.

Research shows that the larger a school is, the less likely it is that a student will take part in extracurricular/cocurricular activities. At the same time, those who do participate tend to have higher self-concepts than those who do not (Coladarci and Cobb 1996). The actual effects that extracurricular/cocurricular activities have on students' development, however, are not entirely clear. Although it is known that students who participate in extracurricular/cocurricular activities tend to receive higher grades than nonparticipants and are more frequently identified as gifted (Gerber 1996; Jordan and Nettles 1999; Modi, Konstantopoulos, and Hedges 1998), it is not known whether participation influences achievement, or whether achievement influences participation. However, research has shown that participation has a positive influence on the decision to remain in school (Mahoney and Cairns 1997), educational aspirations (Modi, Konstantopoulos, and Hedges 1998), and the occupation one aspires to and eventually attains (Brown, Kohrs, and Lanzarro 1991; Holland and Andre 1987). Furthermore, students themselves tend to identify extracurricular/cocurricular activities as a high point in their school careers.

It is also clear that students who might benefit the most from participating in extracurricular/cocurricular activities—those below the norm in academic achievement and students at risk—tend not to participate. In addition, students from low socioeconomic backgrounds participate less often (National Center for Education Statistics 1995).

Curriculum Content

The nation's schools teach what the larger society believes young people should learn. For example, Table 9.5 on page 348, based on a survey by Public

Table 9.5 What content is essential for the curriculum?

	Absolutely Essential	Important, But Not Essential	Not that Important	Don't Know
Basic reading, writing, and math skills	92%	8%	<0.5%	1%
Good work habits such as being responsible, on time, and disciplined	83%	15%	1%	1%
The value of hard work	78%	20%	1%	1%
Values such as honesty and tolerance of others	74%	23%	2%	1%
Computer skills and media technology	80%	18%	1%	1%

Note: Does not total 100% due to rounding. Methodology: telephone survey of 800 adults.

Source: Adapted from Public Agenda, *Education: A Nation Divided?* New York: Public Agenda, 1999.

Agenda, shows several curriculum content areas that the public believes are "absolutely essential." The public believes that the basics of reading, writing, and mathematics plus the development of good work habits should be the heart of the curriculum. Additional support for these curriculum goals comes from employers and college professors who deal with students after they graduate from high school. For example, when asked whether public school graduates have the skills needed to succeed "in the work world" or "in college," only 32 percent of employers surveyed and 39 percent of professors believe students have the skills (Public Agenda 1999). The following comments by two parents who participated in an earlier Public Agenda survey typify the concern many people have about the position of the basic skills in the school curriculum:

> *Education is becoming more about social issues as opposed to reading, writing, and arithmetic. Some of it's fine, but I think schools need to stay with the basics. . . . You can't get by in the business world on social issues if you can't add and subtract.*
>
> *They all talk all the time about this "whole child educational process." . . . It's not your business to make a "whole child." Your business is to teach these students how to read, how to write, and give them the basic skills to balance their checkbook. It's not to make new Emersons out of them (Johnson and Immerwahr 1994, 13).*

How Is the School Curriculum Developed?

Although there is no easy-to-follow set of procedures for developing curriculum, Ralph Tyler has provided four fundamental questions that must be answered in developing any curriculum or plan of instruction. These four questions, known as the **Tyler rationale,** are as follows (Tyler 1949, 1):

1. What educational purposes should the school seek to attain?
2. What educational experiences can be provided that are likely to attain these purposes?
3. How can these educational experiences be effectively organized?
4. How can we determine whether these purposes are being attained?

Tyler's classic work has been used by a great number of school systems to bring some degree of order and focus to the curriculum development process.

The Focus of Curriculum Planning

In discussing curriculum development, it is helpful to clarify the focus of curriculum planning. Figure 9.6 illustrates two dimensions of this planning process: the target and the time orientation. The target of curriculum planning may be at the macro- or the micro-level. At the macro-level, decisions about the content of the curriculum apply to large groups of students. The national goals for education and state-level curriculum guidelines are examples of macro-level curricular decisions. At the micro-level, curriculum decisions are made that apply to groups of students in a particular school or classroom. To some extent, all teachers are micro-level curriculum developers—that is, they make numerous decisions about the curricular experiences they provide students in their classrooms.

Another dimension of curriculum planning is the time orientation—does the planning focus on the present or the future? In addition to the national goals and state-level curriculum guidelines, the semester-long or monthly plans or unit plans that teachers make are examples of future-oriented curriculum planning. Present-oriented curriculum planning usually occurs at the classroom level and is influenced by the unique needs of specific groups of students. The daily or weekly curriculum decisions and lesson plans that teachers make are examples of present-oriented curriculum planning.

Student-Centered versus Subject-Centered Curricula

A key concern in curriculum development is whether greater emphasis should be given to the requirements of the subject area or to the needs of the students.

Figure 9.6 Two dimensions of curriculum planning

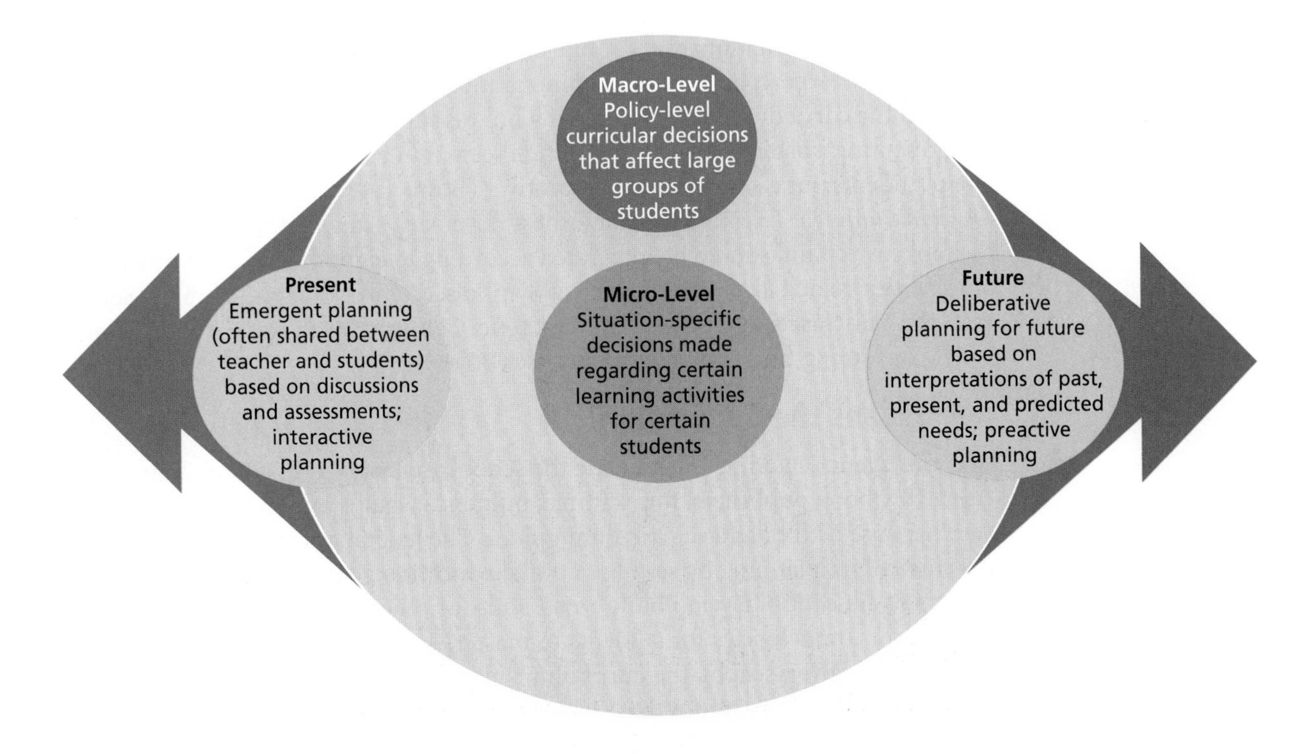

It is helpful to imagine where a school curriculum might be placed on the following continuum.

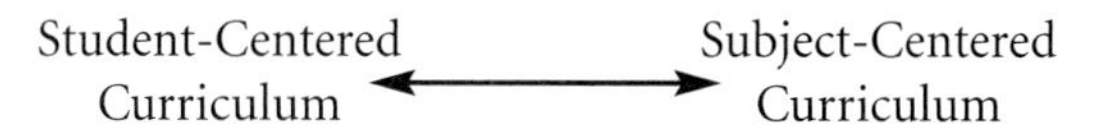

Although no course is entirely subject- or student-centered, curricula vary considerably in the degree to which they emphasize one or the other. The **subject-centered curriculum** places primary emphasis on the logical order of the discipline students are to study. The teacher of such a curriculum is a subject-matter expert and is primarily concerned with helping students understand the facts, laws, and principles of the discipline. Subject-centered curricula are more typical of high school education.

Some teachers develop curricula that reflect greater concern for students and their needs. Though teachers of the **student-centered curriculum** also teach content, they emphasize the growth and development of students. This emphasis is generally more typical of elementary school curricula.

The Integrated Curriculum

To provide students with more meaningful learning experiences, many teachers use an integrated approach to developing the school curriculum. Used most frequently with elementary-age students, the **integrated curriculum** draws from several different subject areas and focuses on a theme or concept rather than on a single subject. Early childhood education expert Suzanne Krogh (2000, 340) suggests that an integrated approach based on thematic "webs" is a more "natural" way for children to learn:

> *[Children] do not naturally learn through isolating specific subjects. These have been determined by adult definition. Children's natural learning is more likely to take place across a theme of interest: building a fort, exploring a sandbox, interacting with the first snow of winter. Teachers can create a good deal of their curriculum by building webs made up of these themes of interest. Done with knowledge and care, a web can be created that incorporates most, or even all, of the required and desired curriculum.*

According to a national survey of elementary teachers' views on the integrated curriculum, 89 percent believed that integration was the "most effective" way to present the curriculum. As one teacher who was surveyed said, "I'm not interested in presenting isolated facts which children seem to memorize and forget. I want to help students put each lesson in perspective" (Boyer 1995, 83). In *The Basic School: A Community for Learning,* the late Ernest Boyer suggested that the elementary school curriculum should be integrated according to eight themes or "core commonalities": The Life Cycle, The Use of Symbols, Membership in Groups, A Sense of Time and Space, Response to the Aesthetic, Connections to Nature, Producing and Consuming, and Living with Purpose (Boyer 1995).

Who Plans the Curriculum?

Where Do You Stand? Visit the Companion Website to Voice Your Opinion.

Various agencies and people outside the school are involved in curriculum planning. Textbook publishers, for example, influence what is taught because many teachers use textbooks as curriculum guides. The federal government contributes to curriculum planning by setting national education goals, and state departments of education develop both broad aims for school curricula and specific minimum competencies for students to master.

Within a given school, the curriculum-planning team and the classroom teacher plan the curriculum that students actually experience. As a teacher you will draw from a reservoir of curriculum plans prepared by others, thus playing a vital role in the curriculum-planning process. Whenever you make decisions about what material to include in your teaching, how to sequence content, and how much time to spend teaching certain material, you are planning the curriculum.

What Influences Curricular Decisions?

From the earliest colonial schools to schools of the twenty-first century, curricula have been broadly influenced by a variety of religious, political, and utilitarian agendas. Figure 9.7 illustrates the influence of community pressures, court decisions, students' life situations, testing results, national reports, teachers' professional organizations, research results, and other factors. The inner circle of the figure represents factors that have a more direct influence on curriculum development (such as students' needs and school district policies). The outer circle represents factors that are more removed from the school setting or have less obvious effects on the curriculum. Individual schools respond to all these influences differently, which further affects their curricula. Let us examine some of these influences in greater detail.

Social Issues and Changing Values Values that affect curriculum planning include prevailing educational theories and teachers' educational philosophies. In addition, curriculum planners respond to social issues and changing values in the wider society. As a result, current social concerns find their way into textbooks, teaching aids, and lesson plans. Often curriculum changes are made in the hope that changing what students learn will help solve social problems or achieve local, statewide, or national goals. Visit this book's Companion Website for bonus information on reform efforts throughout history that have affected curriculum.

Because the United States is so culturally diverse, proposed curriculum changes also reflect divergent interests and values. This divergence then leads to controversies over curriculum content and conflicting calls for reform. Recall, for

Figure 9.7 Influences on the school curriculum

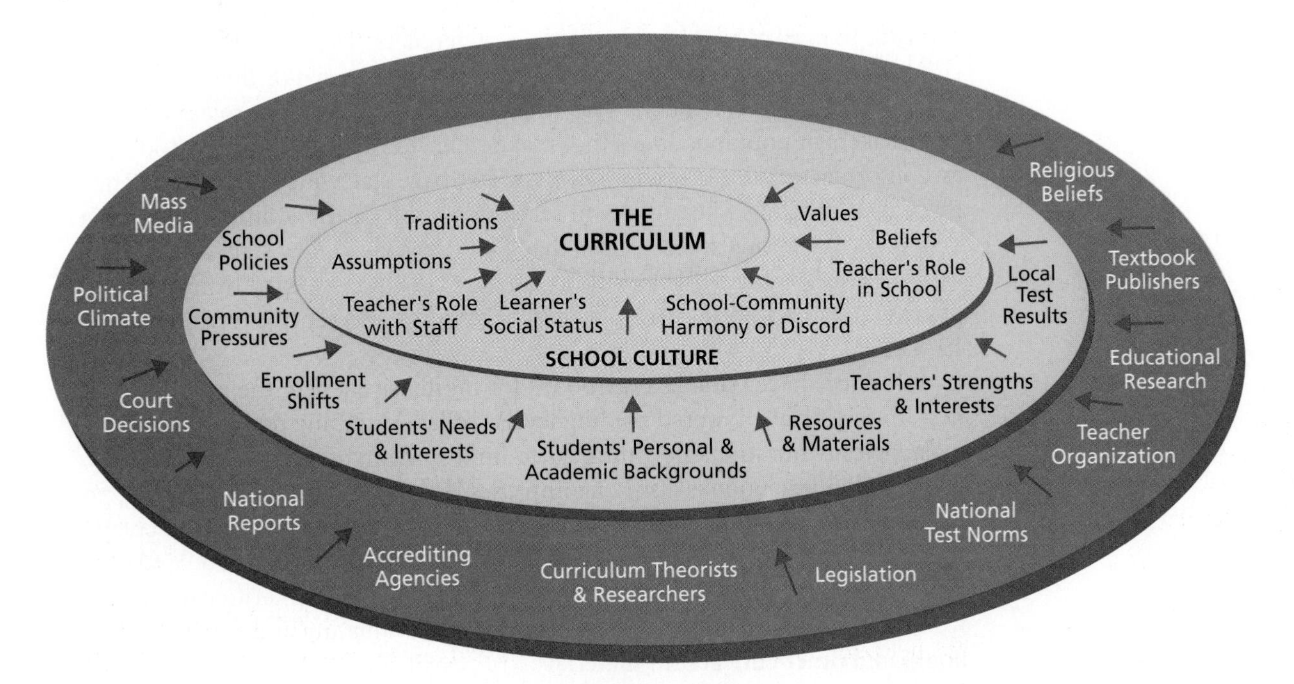

example, the discussion in Chapter 6 of legal issues surrounding the demands of some groups that Christian teachings and observances be included in the public school curricula or that materials regarded as objectionable on religious grounds be censored or banned; or the discussion in Chapter 7 of the trend for states to pass English-only laws and the controversy that erupted in California around the teaching of "ebonics" or "black English." Additional curriculum controversies have arisen over calls for the elimination of all activities or symbols that have their origins in organized religion, including even secularized or commercialized ones such as Halloween and the Easter bunny. Curriculum changes to promote greater social integration or equity among racial or ethnic groups may draw complaints of irrelevancy or reverse discrimination. Traditionalists may object to curriculum changes that reflect feminist views.

As you can imagine, consensus on many curriculum reform issues is never achieved. However, because of their public accountability, schools must consider how to respond to those issues. One survey revealed that during a one-year period, half the school districts in Florida received complaints about curriculum content. Included were complaints claiming that the schools were undermining family values, overemphasizing globalism, underemphasizing patriotism, permitting profanity and obscenity, and teaching taboo subjects such as satanism and sex (Sheuerer and Parkay 1992, 112–118). In the end, the creative and evaluative tasks of choosing and developing curriculum materials are a source of both empowerment and frustration for teachers. Budget constraints, social and legal issues, and state and local curriculum mandates often determine curriculum choices.

Textbook Publishing Textbooks greatly influence the curriculum. Without a doubt, most teachers structure classroom lessons and homework on textbooks. In addition, textbook publishers influence school curricula by providing teaching objectives, learning activities, tests, audiovisual aids, and other supplements to assist their customers.

Like curriculum planners, textbook authors and publishers are influenced by trends in education and by social issues. In response to criticism, for example, publishers now tend to avoid bias in terms of gender, religion, class, race, and culture. However, because the goal of business is profit, publishers are most responsive to market trends and customer preferences. They are often reluctant to risk losing sales by including subjects that are controversial or that may be offensive to their bigger customers. They may also modify textbooks to appeal to decision makers in populous states that make statewide adoptions of textbooks, such as California and Texas. About half the states have statewide adoption policies that school districts must follow in selecting textbooks. In addition, California and Texas are among several states that systematically review state-approved textbooks for accuracy. Texts with too many errors are dropped from state-approved lists, and publishers are levied fines for failing to correct errors (Manzo 1999).

Educators have criticized textbooks for inoffensiveness to the point of blandness, for artificially lowered reading levels (called "dumbing down"), and for pedagogically questionable gimmicks to hold students' attention. "The quality problem [with textbooks also] encompasses [f]actors such as poor writing, poor content 'coverage,' and failure to engage students in the skills needed to create the knowledge contained in a particular area of study" (Sowell 1996, 158). Although the publishing industry continually responds to such criticisms, you would be wise to follow systematic guidelines in evaluating and selecting textbooks and other curriculum materials.

Summary

What Determines the Culture of the Classroom?

- From seating arrangements, to classroom rules and procedures, to the content and relevance of the curriculum, teachers make many decisions that influence the culture of the classroom.
- Classroom climate refers to the atmosphere or quality of life in a classroom. The climates established by high-performing teachers are characterized by a productive, task-oriented focus; group cohesiveness; open, warm relationships between teacher and students; cooperative, respectful interactions among students; low levels of tension, anxiety, and conflict; humor; high expectations; and frequent opportunities for student input regarding classroom activities.

How Can You Create a Positive Learning Environment?

- An important element of a positive learning environment is a caring classroom climate. Teachers show care for students by providing support, structure, and appropriate expectations.
- The physical environment of a classroom–seating arrangements and the placement of other classroom furniture, for example–can make a positive contribution to students' learning.
- Classroom organization, how students are grouped for instruction and how time is used, is an important element of the effective learning environment. Among the patterns for organizing classrooms are grouping students by ability, grouping students for cooperative learning, using activity formats based on authentic learning tasks, and using time to maximize students' learning.

What Are the Keys to Successful Classroom Management?

- The key to successful classroom management is preventing problems before they occur. Teachers who prevent problems foster effective, harmonious interpersonal interactions; understand how their leadership style influences students; and facilitate the development of the classroom group so that it becomes more cohesive and supportive.
- Teachers who establish a democratic classroom climate that allows students to participate in making decisions about the classroom environment, rules and procedures, curriculum materials, and learning activities have fewer discipline problems.
- When management problems occur, effective teachers use a repertoire of problem-solving skills based on experience, common sense, and understanding of the teaching–learning process. Regardless of the management strategy used, effective teachers base their response to problems on three elements of "constructive assertiveness": a clear statement of the problem or concern; unambiguous body language; and a firm, unwavering insistence on appropriate behavior.

What Teaching Methods Do Effective Teachers Use?

- Although it is difficult to identify all the skills teachers need, research indicates that effective teachers use a repertoire of models of teaching based on students' learning behaviors, child development, the thinking process, and peer mediation.
- Direct instruction and mastery learning are based on the view that learning is the acquisition of new behaviors.
- Modeling, constructivism, and scaffolding are based primarily on an understanding of how students construct meaning as they learn new material.
- Information processing, inquiry learning, and discovery learning are based on our understanding of the cognitive processes involved in learning.
- Peer-mediated instruction, which views learning as taking place in social situations, includes cooperative learning, group investigation, and peer- and cross-age tutoring.

What Is Taught in Schools?

- There are many different definitions for the term *curriculum.* A general definition is that *curriculum* refers to the experiences, both planned and unplanned, that either enhance or impede the education and growth of students.
- There are four curricula that all students experience. In addition to learning what teachers intend to teach (the explicit curriculum), students learn from the hidden curriculum, the null curriculum, and extracurricular/cocurricular programs.
- From school policies to national politics, many factors influence what is taught (and not taught) in the schools.

How Is the School Curriculum Developed?

- Curricula are based on the needs and interests of students and also reflect a variety of professional, commercial, local, state, national, and international pressures.
- Teachers must be prepared to assume important roles in the curriculum development process, especially in developing student-centered and integrated curricula.

Key Terms and Concepts

academic learning time, **328**
allocated time, **328**
assertive discipline, **336**
authentic learning tasks, **328**
between-class ability grouping, **326**
block scheduling, **329**
caring classroom, **323**
choice theory, **331**
classroom climate, **319**
classroom management, **329**
classroom organization, **325**
constructivist teaching, **341**
cooperative learning, **327**
cross-age tutoring, **343**
curriculum, **343**
democratic classrooms, **330**
direct instruction, **338**
discovery learning, **342**
explicit curriculum, **344**
extracurricular/cocurricular programs, **347**
group investigation, **342**
hidden curriculum, **344**
information processing, **341**
inquiry learning, **342**
integrated curriculum, **350**
mastery learning, **339**
modeling, **340**
null curriculum, **346**
opportunity to learn (OTL), **329**
peer-mediated instruction, **342**
peer-tutoring, **343**
scaffolding, **341**
student-centered curriculum, **350**
subject-centered curriculum, **350**
time on task, **328**
Tyler rationale, **348**
within-class ability grouping, **327**

Applications and Activities

Teacher's Journal

1. Recall the teachers and classmates you had during your school career. Select one class and analyze its group processes in terms of the stages of group development discussed in this chapter. At what stage of development was the group near the end of the school year? What conditions facilitated or impeded the development of this group?
2. Describe the "ideal" physical classroom environment for you. How would the seating arrangement facilitate the attainment of your instructional goals and objectives? How would you involve students in arranging the classroom?
3. Describe your leadership style as it relates to classroom management. In which aspects of leadership and classroom management do you feel most and least confident? What might you do, or what skills might you acquire, to strengthen your effectiveness in areas you feel you lack confidence? Develop your ideas into a statement of professional goals.
4. List in order of importance the five factors that you believe have the greatest impact on the curriculum. Then list the five factors that you believe ideally should have the greatest influence. What differences do you notice between your actual and ideal lists? What might be done to reduce the differences between the two lists?
5. Reflect on the 12,000 or so hours that you have spent as a student in K–12 classrooms. What did the nonexplicit curricula in the classes teach you about yourself?

Teacher's Database

1. Visit the home pages of three or more of the following research publications on the Web. These journals focus on educational research, learning theories, student and teacher attitudes and behaviors, and the effectiveness of teaching methods. Some journals especially emphasize the implications of educational psychology theory and research for educational policy and applications to teaching practice. Note the kinds of studies and research topics each selected journal reports. How might articles in these journals help you as an education major? As a classroom teacher? As a teaching professional?

   American Educational Research Journal
   Cognition and Instruction
   Contemporary Educational Psychology
   Educational Psychologist
   Educational Psychology Review
   Educational Researcher
   Journal of Educational Psychology
   Journal of Teaching and Teacher Education
   Review of Educational Research
   Review of Research in Education
   Social Psychology of Education

2. What resources are available on the Internet for developments in educational assessment? Begin in the ERIC Clearinghouse on Assessment and Evaluation. This clearinghouse

contains the Test Locator service, searchable testing databases, tips on how to best evaluate a test, and information on fair testing practices.

Then visit CRESST (The National Center for Research on Evaluation, Standards, and Student Testing), which houses a database of alternative approaches to assessment, including portfolio and performance assessments.

3. Visit the online ERIC Clearinghouse for a curricular area you plan to teach and record information for your portfolio on the resources available to you as a teacher in that content area.
4. Survey the Internet to begin locating and creating bookmarks or favorites for websites, schools, networks, and teacher discussion groups that you could use to help develop a subject-area curriculum for your students. To begin, you might wish to visit some of the online resources for developing and implementing the curriculum presented in the Appendix "Online Resources for Developing and Implementing the Curriculum" on this book's website.

Observations and Interviews

1. Observe several teachers at the level for which you are preparing to teach and try to identify the teaching methods they are using as part of their instructional repertoires.
2. Interview a classroom teacher about the assessment of students' learning. How do the assessment methods used by this teacher relate to his or her goals and objectives? To what extent does the teacher use authentic assessments?
3. Spend a half-day at the level you plan to teach and record your impressions regarding the types of curricula. If possible, chat briefly with administrators, teachers, and students about your impressions. Include observations of students outside the classroom during the school day.
4. As a collaborative project, conduct an informal survey on what people think are the four most important subjects to be taught at the elementary, middle, junior, and senior high levels. Compare your data with the information in this chapter.
5. With classmates, as an experiment, practice the process of curriculum development described in this chapter. Assign some members of the group to observe and report on their observations in relation to concepts presented in this chapter.

Professional Portfolio

Prepare a poster depicting a classroom arrangement appropriate for the subject area and grade level for which you are preparing to teach. The poster should indicate the seating arrangement and location of other classroom furniture. In addition, make a list of classroom rules that will be posted in the room. You may wish to organize the rules according to the following categories.

- Rules related to academic work
- Rules related to classroom conduct
- Rules that must be communicated on your first teaching day
- Rules that can be communicated later

Last, prepare a flow chart depicting routine activities for a typical day. This chart could include procedures for the following:

- Handling attendance, tardy slips, and excuses
- Distributing materials
- Turning in homework
- Doing seatwork or various in-class assignments
- Forming small groups for cooperative learning activities
- Returning materials and supplies at the end of class

VideoWorkshop Extra!

If the VideoWorkshop package was included with your textbook, go to Chapter 9 of the Companion Website (www.ablongman.com/parkay6e) and click on the VideoWorkshop button. Follow the instructions for viewing videoclips 2 and 8 and completing this exercise. Consider this information along with what you've read in Chapter 9 while answering the following questions.

1. Videoclip 2 stresses the notion that a stimulating and intriguing environment promotes brain growth in children. A democratic classroom climate, as discussed in the text, may facilitate this brain growth. Discuss how a democratic classroom climate stimulates children, and how children benefit from such a challenge.
2. Thoughtful planning, discussed in videoclip 8, often leads to successful curricula, which are meaningful to children. What predictions can you make about a curriculum for students that emphasizes test scores and performance on exams over individual strengths and alternative assessment? Use information from the text to support your ideas.

10 Curriculum Standards, Assessment, and Student Learning

At the classroom level, assessment can serve two key purposes: (1) it can serve as a powerful teaching tool, particularly when students are involved in the process; and (2) results can inform a variety of instructional decisions.

—Richard J. Stiggins
Student-Involved Classroom Assessment, 2001

During an in-service meeting at your school, a panel of four teachers is discussing the need to develop a schoolwide approach to assessing students' learning. Your state has mandated academic standards and developed the Statewide Assessment of Student Achievement (SASA) test.

A panel member, last year's Teacher of the Year in the district, is explaining how "traditional" norm-referenced tests rely heavily on multiple-choice questions that emphasize basic skills, while the SASA measures the application of those skills to problem-solving tasks and "real world" situations.

"Unlike traditional tests," the teacher says, "the SASA requires students to complete short-answer questions, draw graphs, compare and contrast information from multiple texts, and write short essays. Questions like these require students to do more with their knowledge than they have in the past."

"Also," another panel member adds, "traditional norm-referenced tests evaluate students' performance only with reference to other students. Tests like the SASA, however, evaluate *each* student's performance against a rigorous standard of knowledge and skills."

At this point, Mr. Washington, a well-respected teacher, stands and begins speaking from the back of the cafeteria. "Our emphasis on 'rigorous' standards may be misguided. If we set higher standards, does that result in more learning? I don't think so. Does a coach improve a player's performance merely by saying 'try harder'?"

"But if a coach *believes* a player can improve, that by itself can make a difference," a panel member counters. "Setting high expectations for students is based on a belief that they *can* meet those standards. If we don't believe every child can succeed, failure can become a self-fulfilling prophecy."

"Perhaps," says Mr. Washington, a slight smile suggesting that he is eager to have a substantive conversation on testing and standards. "However, I want to read two comments from recent issues of the *Phi Delta Kappan.*" He holds up two *Kappans,* each folded open to the article.

"The first," he continues, "is by a high school principal in West Chicago. He presents eleven reasons why simply raising standards 'won't work.' Near the end of his article, he says 'We must begin with the experiences children are having in schools. Forget about test scores; forget about the economy; forget about Japan.' What do students think about their experiences? Do they feel safe? Do they like their teachers? Do they talk at the dinner table about the interesting day they had at school?" (Jones 2001, 464).

Mr. Washington places that *Kappan* onto the table in front of him and begins to read from the other. "The next article points out that there is 'little empirical evidence' for a 'causal link between standards and enhanced student learning' " (Nave, Miech, and Mosteller 2000, 128, 132).

"We spend too much time focusing on *what* the standards are," Mr. Washington continues. "We should focus on *how* standards improve students' learning.

Instead, we use standards in a negative, punitive way: Students won't be promoted or graduate unless they master standards; schools and teachers will be 'punished' if their students don't master the standards. If we reflect on how *we* ourselves learn best, most of us would have to admit that the 'big stick' approach doesn't help us learn. If it doesn't work for us, why would it work for the kids?"

Listening to Mr. Washington's comments raises several questions in your mind. Can a standards-based approach help my students learn more? How should I assess my students' learning?

Focus Questions

1. **What role will standards play in your classroom?**
2. **What controversies surround the effort to raise standards?**
3. **What methods can you use to assess student learning?**
4. **How can you develop high-quality classroom assessments?**

Expand your knowledge of the concepts discussed in this chapter by reading current and historical articles from the *New York Times* by visiting the **"Themes of the Times"** section of the Companion Website (**www.ablongman.com/parkay6e**).

As the first *Kappan* article from which Mr. Washington quotes and daily newspaper headlines remind us, the public is concerned about declining test scores, the performance of U.S. students on international comparisons of achievement, and our nation's standing in a competitive global economy. Pressure to get "back to the basics" and drives by parents, citizen groups, and politicians to hold teachers accountable have led to a nationwide push to raise standards and develop more effective ways to assess student learning. As a result, state-level standards and large-scale assessment systems will be "facts of life" during your career as a teacher.

Standards and assessments are key elements in the move to hold educators more accountable for student learning. Parents must know that the schools to which they entrust their children are educating them well, and the community must know that its investment in school buildings, teachers' salaries, and curricular resources is returning educational "dividends."

What Role Will Standards Play in Your Classroom?

Where Do You Stand? **Visit the Companion Website to Voice Your Opinion.**

As adults, we are familiar with standards. To obtain a driver's license, we have to demonstrate the knowledge and skills needed to drive a car. At work, we must meet our employer's standards. In this regard, a *standard* refers to a level of knowledge or skill that is generally acknowledged as necessary to perform a specific task or to occupy a particular role in society. In education, for example, standards represent the criteria students must meet to receive a grade of A, to be promoted to the next grade, or to graduate from elementary or high school.

Educational standards take a variety of different forms. The type of standards most important to the individual often depends on whether one is a school ad-

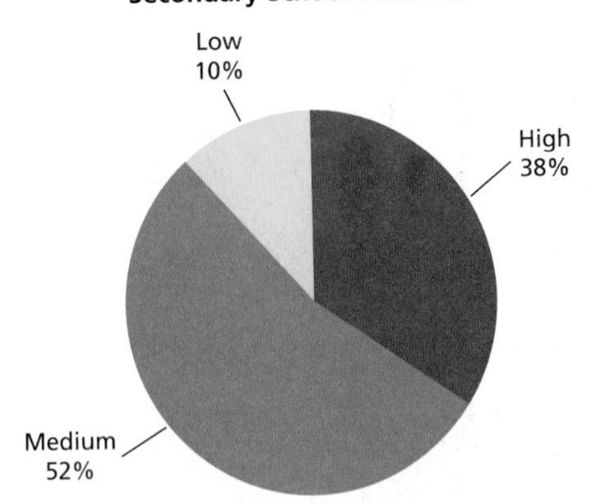

Q240: How would you rate the academic standards at your school?
Base: Secondary school students (N = 2049)

Q305: How would you rate the academic standards at your school?
Base: Secondary school teachers (N = 430)/Secondary school principlas (N = 383)

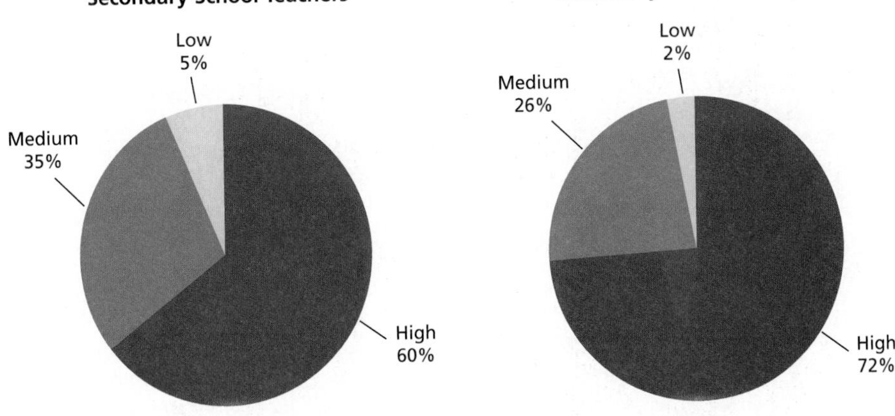

Figure 10.1 Academic standards: students, teachers, and principals
Source: The MetLife Survey of the American Teacher, 2001: Key Elements of Quality Schools. New York: Harris Interactive 2001, p. 46.

ministrator, teacher, or student. Administrators, for example, are very concerned about standards related to *students' performance on standardized tests of achievement.* In such instances, the administrator (and his or her school board) might focus on a standard such as the following: "During the next five years, the percentage of students scoring above the norm will increase by at least 2 percent each year."

Teachers, of course, are also concerned about standards related to students' performance on standardized tests. In addition, teachers understand that another important standard is their *expectations for student performance and behavior at the classroom level.* Teachers demonstrate their commitment to high standards by giving students intellectually demanding reading and writing assignments; providing extensive, thoughtful feedback on students' work; and presenting intellectually stimulating lessons.

Students often have yet another perspective on standards; for them, the school curriculum should meet the *standard of being personally relevant, interesting, and meaningful.* The school curriculum should help them meet the developmental challenges of moving from childhood to adulthood. It should help them realize the goals they have set for themselves.

Most teachers and principals believe their school has high academic standards. Figure 10.1, for example, shows that 72 percent of secondary principals and 60 percent of teachers included in the *MetLife Survey of the American Teacher, 2001: Key Elements of Quality Schools* view their schools as having high standards. However, secondary school students have a different perception of

On the Frontlines

Test-Related Stress

It's 2:00 A.M. and you're still not asleep. You've been churning since this morning's faculty meeting when the principal called everyone together—teachers and aides, even student teachers—to deliver the bad news about the test results. He tried to be encouraging, but his voice cracked mid-sentence as he struggled to maintain his composure. The principal told everyone to be ready for reactions to tomorrow's newspaper that would report that the school's scores were the poorest in the district and poorer than any in the neighboring districts.

The news shocked everyone. Morale has been so high this year. The new math program seems to be going well—students complete homework now and seem eager to do more. The two programs the assistant principal introduced seem to be reducing discipline problems. One orients new students to the school rules and expectations and assigns them a peer trained in being supportive. The other program promotes character development and includes discussions on bullying, peer pressure, and perseverance. Some teachers are convinced the program will help kids stay out of gangs and off drugs. Given the poverty and negative influences in the area and the personal challenges many students face daily, these new programs can make life-changing differences.

This latest news, however, was demoralizing. You fear that you haven't done as good a job as you could have—that you have somehow shortchanged your students.

As the minutes tick away into the night, you wonder what more you could have done; you question whether you're capable of doing more. How will the community react? Worse yet, how will your students take the news? They've worked so hard and this news could be discouraging. Children lean on adults' evaluations of them. The younger they are, the more vulnerable they are to adult judgment. To students, the poor test rankings are the same as adults saying they failed. You fear that some will react by hating school more and rejecting learning. Others might lose confidence in their abilities and will be convinced that they are not good enough, not as smart as others, and never will be. The individual progress made by your students could be undone quickly. You worry about how you should proceed. What can you do to make your students and yourself feel better?

In recent years the introduction of high-stakes testing has brought with it calls for accountability, closer scrutiny of individual practices, and a greater demand for positive results. For many teachers, no feeling is worse than feeling as though they have failed to do everything they could to help their students learn. With job security and student advancement often tied closely to test scores, the resulting environment can be highly pressurized for both students and teachers. As one teacher stated, "There are so many factors [teachers] can't control, and it seems like all they judge teachers on is how their kids did on the tests last year. It affects them, when people are asking why their kids aren't doing [well] on this or that." (*Daytona Beach News Journal* 2002)

Teachers know all too well the various sources of stress in their lives—dealing with disruptive students, angry parents, testy colleagues, unfair directives, excessive paperwork, and schedules filled with unanticipated meetings, to name but a few. The addition of high-stakes testing has simply added a new stressor for many teachers. Dealt with incorrectly, stress can lead to numerous physical ailments, including muscle aches, stomach disorders, and heart disease. Emotionally, stress can result in insomnia, short-temperedness, irritability, difficulty focusing, and an erosion of self-confidence, to name a few.

Historically, however, teachers tend to manage stress well because they have one of the best tools for doing so, a sense of control. In their classrooms, they are "the boss." As noted earlier, high-stakes testing threatens that control. Therefore, experts recommend that, in this era of high stakes testing, teachers need to be prepared psychologically to cope with stress. They need to learn positive coping skills that will help them maintain perspective about testing and, ultimately, provide a positive learning environment for their students.

Teachers can soothe their own stress by analyzing the situation and examining it rationally. New programs take some time before they begin to show results. No single measurement, like an achievement test, is a sound indication of whether or not their students have learned. Although a high value often is placed on those scores these days, individual growth can be measured in other ways and a teacher needs to hang onto these accomplishments.

Teachers also need to remember that learning occurs along a continuum with the student playing a dynamic role in the process. Often what is taught one year doesn't appear until the next. Teachers cannot be certain that the learning their stu-

dents accomplish is due solely to their teaching, and therefore, need to be careful not to connect test results as a sole reflection of his or her own abilities as an educator. Maintaining a positive sense of self is critical in coping with stress.

A bigger challenge is helping students cope with the newfound stress of high-stakes testing. As test results are scrutinized more closely and are used to determine advancement and even graduation, some degree of stress among students is inevitable. By their very nature, standardized tests arouse feelings of anxiety. They are rigidly timed, instructions can be complicated, and the rules often are inflexible. A teacher plays a critical role in helping students maintain a good perspective about test-taking. with test-taking. Perhaps the most important thing teachers can do for their students is to relax! Children will be watching teachers for their reactions to upcoming tests and the resulting news. If teachers are alarmed, children are likely to respond in the same way. Most important in the process will be the teachers' genuine belief in their students' abilities to do well. If they believe their students are capable of doing better, and if they show that in their words and actions, students will respond.

Exploratory Questions

1. What are some ways teachers can help students counter test anxiety?
2. What might be some things parents can do to help ease the pressure over testing?

Your Survival Guide of Helpful Resources

The following resources provide helpful hints for surviving "on the frontlines."

Books and Articles

Clovis, D. L. (2002). Take out your no. 2 pencils: Taking the stress out of standardized tests. New York: Scholastic Online. Retrieved from http://teacher.Scholastic.com/professional/assessment/take_out_pencils.htm

Elkind, D. (2001). *The hurried child: Growing up too fast too soon, 3rd ed.* Cambridge, MA: Perseus.

Mahlios, M. C. (2001). Matching teaching methods to learning styles, in B. H. Stanford & K. Yamamoto (Eds.). *Children and stress: Understanding and helping.* Olney, MD: Association for Childhood Education International.

Teachers, feeling their own standardized test pressure, fall victim to stress. *The Daytona-Beach News-Journal,* April 28, 2002. Retrieved from http://njcnt1.news-jrnl.com/2002/Apr/28/SSTAT1.htm

Companion Website

Websites

The National Center for Fair & Open Testing (http://www.fairtest.org)

National Assessment of Educational Progress (http://nces.ed.gov/nationsreportcard/)

Creative Classroom Online (http://www.creativeclassroom.org)

academic standards at their schools; only 38 percent of students surveyed believe standards are high. Many high school students, it seems, would agree with an eleventh-grade boy quoted in the MetLife Survey: "I can't remember the last time I learned something new. . . . I just get sick of the busy work, and usually just end up throwing it aside and not doing it. I want to be LEARNING things" (Harris Interactive 2001, 44).

While administrators, teachers, students, and parents frequently have different perspectives on standards, during the last decade, **standards** in education (on occasion, called *content standards, goals, expectations, learning results,* or *learning outcomes*) have come to be seen primarily as statements that reflect what students should know and be able to do within a particular discipline or at a particular grade level.

Current efforts at educational reform in the United States emphasize **standards-based education (SBE)**—that is, basing curricula, teaching, and assessment of student learning on rigorous, so-called world-class standards. Roy Romer, former governor of Colorado and a vocal national advocate for higher standards, explains how higher standards can improve education:

> *Setting standards, raising expectations, and assessing student progress in a meaningful way gives students the tools they need to thrive in the 21st century and the tools parents and teachers need to help them. [Content] standards are a compilation of specific statements of what students should know or be able to do. They do not represent the totality of what students should learn at school. They are not curriculum. When standards are well-conceptualized and written, they can focus the education system on common, explicit goals; ensure that rigorous academic content is taught by all teachers in all classrooms and raise expectations for all students (2000, 314–315).*

To meet the demand for higher standards, forty-nine states (Iowa is the exception) have adopted state standards for what students should know and be able to do. For example, here are standards in geometry from three states:

> **Colorado:** Students use geometric concepts, properties, and relationships in problem-solving situations and communicate the reasoning used in solving these problems.

What might be some of the pressures felt by students and teachers as a result of the emphasis on high-stakes testing?

North Dakota: Students understand and apply geometric concepts and spatial relationships to represent and solve problems in mathematical and nonmathematical situations.

Wyoming: Students apply geometric concepts, properties, and relationships in problem-solving situations. Students communicate the reasoning used in solving these problems.

As these examples show, state standards are broad statements of learning outcomes against which student achievement can be measured.

Content and Performance Standards

Standards documents prepared by state education agencies, local school districts, and professional associations typically refer to two types of standards—content standards and performance standards. **Content standards,** as the term implies, refer to the content—or knowledge and skills—students should acquire in various academic disciplines. An oft-repeated phrase in standards documents is that content standards represent "what students should know and be able to do."

Content standards are often subdivided into benchmarks (frequently called indicators). **Benchmarks** are content standards that are presented as specific statements of what students should understand and be able to do *at specific grade levels or developmental stages*—for example, "at the end of the eighth grade, the student understands basic properties of two- and three-dimensional figures."

In addition, many standards documents refer to performance standards. A **performance standard** specifies "how good is good enough." Performance standards are used to assess the *degree to which* students have attained standards in an academic area. Performance standards require teacher judgment about the quality of performance or level of proficiency required. Performance standards differ from content standards because performance standards reflect levels of proficiency—for example: 5 = outstanding, 4 = exemplary, 3 = proficient, 2 = progressing, and 1 = standard not met.

Standards Developed by Professional Associations

In addition to the push for standards at the national, state, and local levels, professional associations are playing a key role in SBE by developing standards that reflect the knowledge, skills, and attitudes students should develop in the subject-matter disciplines. In many cases, professional associations have developed specific, grade-level **performance expectations**—established levels of achievement, quality of performance, or level of proficiency—for recommended standards as well as classroom activities related to standards.

Educators, parents, and community members use standards developed by professional associations in different ways. State departments of education, school districts, and schools can use the standards as a guide for developing curricula and assessments of student learning. At the classroom level, teachers can use standards to develop goals and objectives for units and courses, to evaluate their teaching, and to develop ideas for instructional activities and classroom assessments. And parents and community members can use standards to assess the quality of education in their local schools and to monitor the achievement levels of their children. Figure 10.2 on page 364 presents several professional associations that have recommended curriculum standards in various academic disciplines. You can obtain complete sets of standards from the websites these associations maintain.

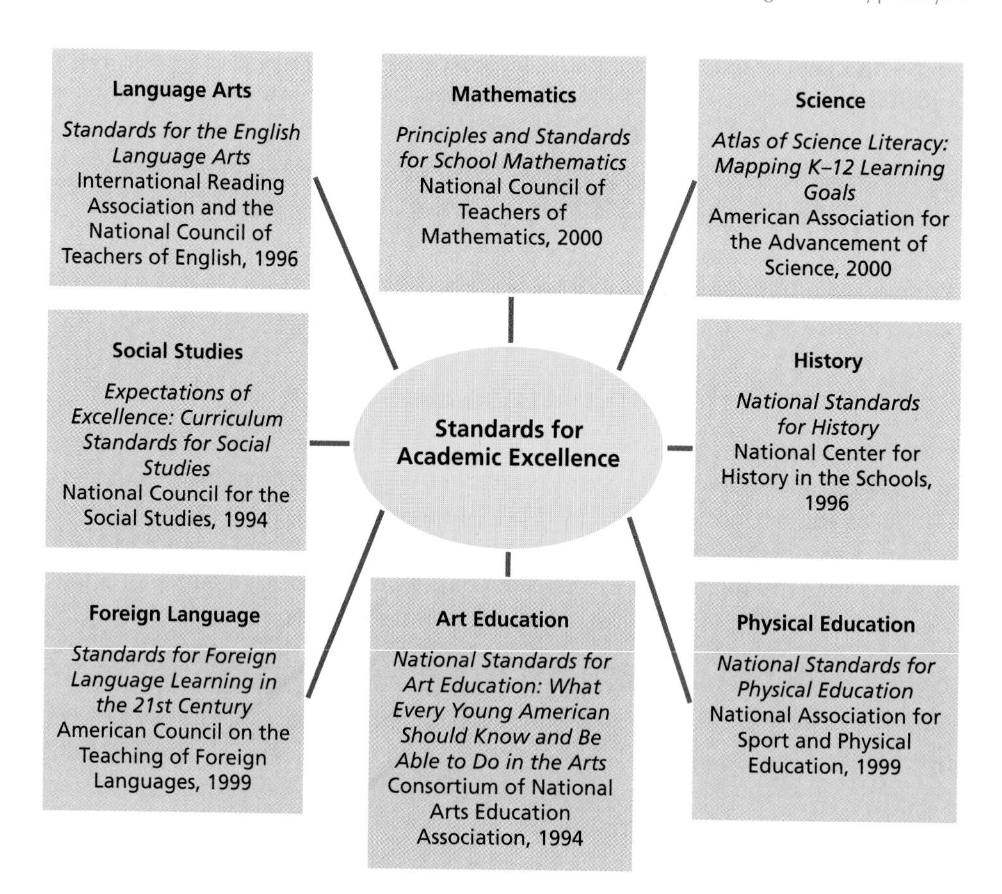

Figure 10.2 Curriculum standards developed by professional associations

Aligning Curricula and Textbooks with Standards and Curriculum Frameworks

An important part of SBE in the United States is aligning curricula and textbooks with national and state standards and "curriculum frameworks." **Curriculum alignment** may take two forms. *Horizontal alignment* occurs when teachers within a specific grade level coordinate instruction across disciplines and examine their school's curriculum to ensure that course content and instruction dovetail across and/or within subject areas. *Vertical alignment* occurs when subjects are connected across grade levels so that students experience increasingly complex instructional programs as they move through the grades.

A **curriculum framework** is a document, usually published by a state education agency, that provides guidelines, recommended instructional and assessment strategies, suggested resources, and models for teachers to use as they develop curricula that are aligned with national and state standards. Curriculum frameworks are usually written by teams of teachers and state agency personnel, and they serve as a bridge between national and state standards and local curriculum and instructional strategies. In Alaska, for example, curriculum frameworks in CD-ROM format and "Frameworks Resource Kits" in specific subjects are given to teachers by the Department of Education & Early Development. The CD-ROM provides state-of-the-art information in different formats, including videoclips of educators explaining standards-based curricula. Figure 10.3, taken from the Alaska frameworks, presents English/language arts process skills for writing.

Like teachers, textbook authors and publishers have been influenced significantly by the development of academic standards throughout the nation. Many publishers are revising their textbooks so they are in alignment with state standards and curriculum frameworks, particularly in populous states that make statewide adoptions of textbooks, such as California and Texas.

Figure 10.3 **English/language arts process skills.**
Source: Used with permission of the Alaska Department of Education & Early Development's Curriculum Frameworks Project. Retrieved from http://www.educ.state.ak.us/tls/frameworks/langarts/30content.htm

The following figure presents graphic explanations of the processes of writing as they have been developed and/or adapted and used by Alaskan educators for the last decade. This figure is meant to be illustrative rather than prescriptive.

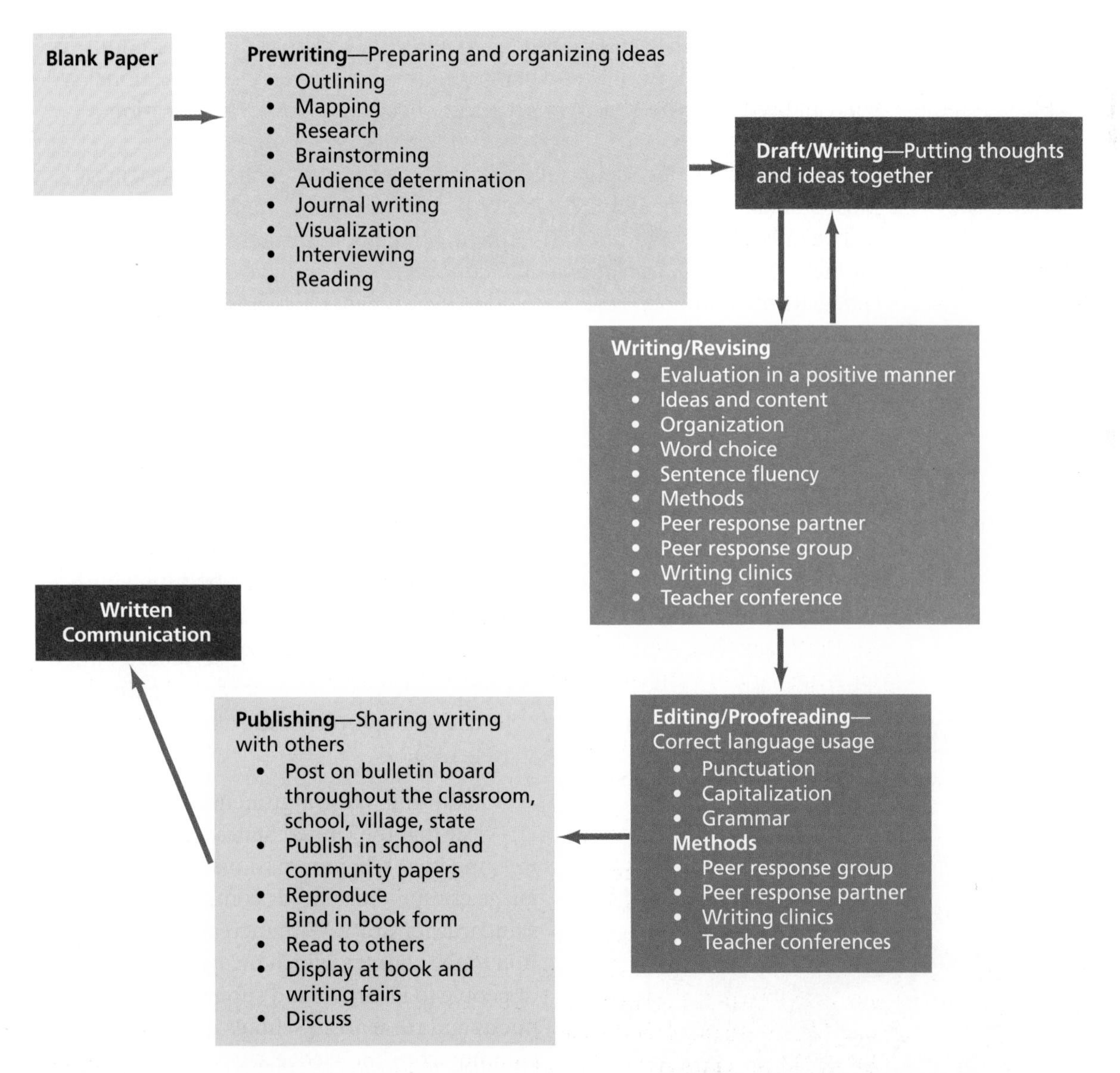

The writing process is recursive thinking leading to writing leading to thinking and writing some more. Not every writer will commit every step in the process to paper. Nor will every idea or piece of writing be carried through the entire process. Only pieces that have completed the process—and not all of those—should be assessed.

What Controversies Surround the Effort to Raise Standards?

Along with the push to raise standards has come an increasingly widespread national dialogue over the role of standards in educational reform. Without a doubt, the response to the effort to raise standards has been mixed.

Arguments in Support of Raising Standards

"We are moving in this country from a local to a national view of education and we need better arrangements to guide the way." So observed the late Ernest Boyer, president of the Carnegie Foundation for the Advancement of Teaching. As Boyer's comment implies, the United States, like other nations of the world, needs national goals and standards to motivate its people to excel. Without them, people may become complacent and satisfied with mediocrity. Also like other countries in our increasingly interdependent world, the United States needs to compare the achievement of its students with those of other countries. Just as a runner will run faster when paced by another, the U.S. educational system can become more effective as a result of comparisons with educational systems in other countries.

As an advocate of raising standards and assessing students' attainment of those standards, Diane Ravitch observed that "[a] failing mark on the state test will be only a temporary embarrassment, but a poor education will stigmatize for life" (1997, 106). In *National Standards in American Education: A Citizen's Guide,* Ravitch outlined several additional arguments in support of the effort to raise standards:

- Standards can improve achievement by clearly defining what is to be taught and what kind of performance is expected.
- Standards (national, state, and local) are necessary for equality of opportunity.
- National standards provide a valuable coordinating function.
- Standards and assessments provide consumer protection by supplying accurate information to students and parents.
- Standards and assessments serve as an important signaling device to students, parents, teachers, employers, and colleges (1996, 134–135).

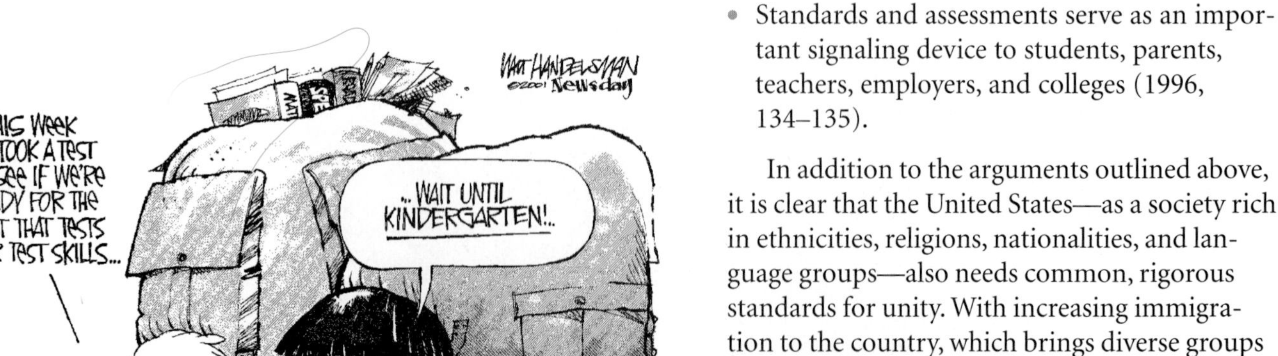

In addition to the arguments outlined above, it is clear that the United States—as a society rich in ethnicities, religions, nationalities, and language groups—also needs common, rigorous standards for unity. With increasing immigration to the country, which brings diverse groups of people to its urban and suburban neighborhoods and rural areas, schools need to provide a common core knowledge about the democratic heritage of our country and a common curriculum based on high academic standards.

As a mobile society, the United States needs common educational standards so that children from one area will not fall behind when they move to another. Children from a farming community in Minnesota should be able to move to the heart of New Orleans without finding themselves behind or ahead of their peers in school. Children from a school in Seattle should be able to transfer to a school in Cincinnati and recognize the curricula studied there.

Concerns about Raising Standards

Opponents of the effort to develop world-class standards that are used as the centerpiece of educational reform point out that our nation's failure to achieve the national standards implicit in the Goals 2000: Educate American Act is evidence that a new approach to educational reform is needed. Instead, they contend, we should become more aware of the lack of uniformity in schools around the country and the needs of the children they serve. As Jonathon Kozol's 1991 book *Savage Inequalities* vividly illustrates, equal education in the United States is an illusion. To compare the performance of a student in a poor Chicago housing project with that of a student in that city's wealthy suburbs is to confront the "savage inequalities" found throughout our educational system.

In addition, test score gains attributed to the standards movement have been shown not to reflect "real" gains in the knowledge and skills the tests were designed to measure. A phenomenon known as "score inflation" results in students' scores on high-stakes tests rising faster than their scores on other standardized tests given at the same time and measuring the same subjects. Students don't actually know as much as we think they do based only on the high-stakes test scores. Actually, the standards movement may result in test scores that are less accurate than they were prior to the addition of high-stakes assessments (Stecher and Hamilton 2002).

Also, sanctions imposed on low-performing schools will not ensure that students in those schools are not left behind. The record of success when sanctions such as staff reassignment and school takeover have been imposed is mixed. Students in low-performing schools may not be helped by sanctions, and there is some risk that they will be harmed (Stecher and Hamilton 2002). Thus, higher standards would further bias educational opportunities in favor of students from advantaged backgrounds, intensify the class-based structure of U.S. society, and increase differences between well-funded and poorly funded schools.

Opponents of efforts to develop world-class standards in U.S. schools have raised numerous additional concerns. The following are among their arguments:

- Raising standards might lead to a national curriculum and an expanded role of federal government in education.
- The push to raise standards is fueled by conservative interest groups that wish to undo educational gains made by traditionally underrepresented groups.
- A focus on higher standards diverts attention from more meaningful educational reform.
- Increased emphasis on tested subjects often results in a decrease in emphasis on subjects not tested.
- World-class standards are often vague and not linked to valid assessments and scoring rubrics.
- Standards frequently describe learning activities, not the knowledge and skills students are expected to learn—for example, "Students will experience various forms of literature."

How might national standards help even the playing field for these students? What are some of the arguments against this belief?

- The scope and sequence of what students should learn with reference to standards and benchmarks has been unclear; in other words, to what degree and in what order should students learn material?
- Grade-level benchmarks have been created that are unrealistic and developmentally inappropriate for some students; often students are hurried through their learning without sufficient time and instruction to acquire underlying concepts and skills.
- SBE and high-stakes tests based on those standards lead to the practice of "teaching-to-the-test," giving priority to academic content covered by the tests and deemphasizing areas of the curriculum not covered. For example, a study of Kentucky's assessment system found that test-related sanctions and rewards influenced teachers to "focus on whatever is thought to raise test scores rather than on instruction aimed at addressing individual student needs" (Jones and Whitford 1997, 277).

As a teacher, you and your colleagues will be responsible for participating in an ongoing dialogue about academic standards at your school. Thus, the role that standards will play in your professional lives will be significant. Accordingly, the following eight questions may help you decide the nature of SBE in your school.

1. Where will we get our standards?
2. Who will set the standards?
3. What types of standards should we include?
4. In what format will the standards be written?
5. At what levels will benchmarks be written?
6. How should benchmarks and standards be assessed?
7. How will student progress be reported?
8. What will we hold students accountable for? (Marzano 1997)

Standards, Testing, and Accountability

Controversy also surrounds widespread efforts to hold schools and teachers accountable for students' attainment of state-mandated educational standards. As part of this push for **accountability,** some states—Florida and South Carolina, for example—rank schools on how well their students learn. In Florida, schools are graded from A through F, and those that receive low grades run the risk of being closed. At the end of the 2001–02 academic year, for example, an elementary school in Pensacola was closed by school officials, though it had managed to move from a grade of F to a D (Sandham, 2002). In South Carolina, schools are graded "good," "average," "below average," or "unsatisfactory." Teachers and principals in high-ranked South Carolina schools receive salary bonuses of up to $1,000 each, while lower-rated schools can face state takeovers or reorganization of their staffs (Richard 2002).

Every state has mandated a standardized test to assess students' mastery of academic standards, and most districts are assisting schools in bringing standards-based reform into classrooms. For example, fourth-, seventh-, and tenth-grade students in Washington State must take the Washington Assessment of Student Learning (WASL) based on the state's Essential Academic Learning Requirements (EALRs) in reading, writing, listening, and mathematics. In Texas, students must take the Texas Assessment of Knowledge and Skills (TAKS) that assesses how well they have mastered the Texas Essential Knowledge and Skills (TEKS) in English language arts, mathematics, science, and social studies. As a result of standards-based reforms at the state level, *how* and *what* teachers teach is changing, and, in many cases, student achievement is increasing.

Similarly, at the national level, efforts are being made to hold schools accountable. Since passage of the Goals 2000: Educate America Act in 1994 (subsequently revised as America's Education Goals in 1999), national policymakers have stressed the role that more rigorous standards can play in educational reform. In 2002, the national push for higher standards became even stronger when President George W. Bush, to fulfill his pledge to "leave no child behind," signed into legislation a $26.5 billion comprehensive educational reform bill mandating statewide testing in reading and mathematics each year in grades 3–8. According to the No Child Left Behind Act of 2001 (NCLBA), schools whose scores fail to improve over a six-year period could lose staff, and low-income students at those schools could receive federal funds for tutoring or transportation to another public school. Also, NCLBA requires that, by the end of the academic year 2013–14, public schools guarantee that all students are prepared to pass state proficiency tests.

High-Stakes Testing

Testing students to assess their learning is not new. However, state-mandated tests often have high-stakes consequences for students, teachers, and administrators. For example, performance on **high-stakes tests** may determine whether a student can participate in extracurricular activities or graduate, or whether teachers and administrators are given merit pay increases. Basing such decisions on a single standardized test is acceptable to the public, as revealed by the 2001 Phi Delta Kappa/Gallup Poll: 53 percent approve linking test scores to grade-to-grade promotion, and 57 percent approve linking test scores to determine eligibility for a high school diploma (Rose and Gallup 2001). Currently, seventeen states require students to pass exit or end-of-course exams to receive a high school diploma, and seven more plan to do so in the future (Olson 2002).

For teachers and administrators, test results are frequently linked to merit rewards, increased funding, or sanctions. Some states and large school districts provide additional funds for high performing schools or bonuses for educators at those schools. For example, California has several merit-based incentive programs for teachers, schools, and administrators, including the "Governor's Performance Awards" that give money to schools based on their "academic per-

Technology Highlights

Will computer-adaptive online testing systems be used to deliver statewide assessment tests?

Some states—Idaho, Oregon, South Dakota, and Virginia, for example—are opting to use online testing systems to deliver their statewide assessments tests. In 2001, South Dakota became the first state to use an online exam linked to state standards of learning.

The online tests used by Idaho and South Dakota differ from pencil-and-paper tests because they are computer-adaptive. The tests "adjust" depending on how well a student is doing. If a student proficient in science keeps getting all the science questions right, the questions become more difficult.

Computer-adaptive testing enables teachers to identify students who are advanced for their grade or below standard grade-level proficiency. Teachers thus get more information about a student's strengths and weaknesses than they receive from paper-and-pencil tests. The South Dakota system uses an artificial intelligence system to determine which grade level a student is testing at in individual units, such as fractions, decimals, and algebraic equations. In one class period, the test can determine exactly where a student is performing at across a twelve-grade range. Test results are then reported, usually within twenty-four hours, with reference to the standards of a specific state or district.

A disadvantage of online testing is that it requires a state-of-the-art technology infrastructure. In South Dakota, for example, every classroom has a T1 line, and the Digital Dakota Network links every school and every K–12 classroom with the state government, technical schools, and higher education institutions. Also, each classroom has broadband access to the Internet, with five or six connection points.

What do you see as some of the advantages and disadvantages of computer-adaptive online testing? Reflect on the standardized tests you have taken. Would you have preferred taking them online?

formance index." Similarly, in New York City, the school system gives bonuses of up to $15,000 to principals and other administrators whose schools show significant gains on test scores. School system administrators group schools into three performance categories—low, middle, and high—taking into account students' economic circumstances. For high schools, factors such as dropout rates are also used.

On the other hand, schools, and even entire districts, that do poorly on tests can be taken over by the state or, in some cases, closed. Currently, more than twenty states give state boards of education the authority to intervene in academically "bankrupt" schools whose students score too low as a group. Of those states, ten allow students to leave low-performing schools, taking their proportional amount of state funding aid with them. Four of these states directly punish low-performing schools by taking aid away from them. While some states use test scores as one of several accountability indicators, many rely solely on scores.

Testing can also have significant consequences when schools are ranked according to how well they attain a state or district's performance goals. Usually, school rankings are reported in relation to schools of similar size and demographics since test results are closely linked to students' economic backgrounds, with the lowest scores often earned by schools that serve the neediest children (Fetler 2001; Lindjord 2000).

High-stakes testing is a hotly debated topic among educators, students, and parents. Many observers worry that "when high-stakes consequences are attached to tests, they hold the potential for great harm" (Falk 2002, 614). Tenth-grade students in Massachusetts expressed their concern by creating SCAM (Student Coalition for Alternatives to the Massachusetts Comprehensive Assessment System [MCAS]). The MCAS stipulates that students must pass the tenth-grade MCAS exams to graduate from high school. Reacting to what she calls "MCAS mania," the headmaster of the Boston Arts Academy worries that high-stakes testing will lead to "[more] money spent on test-prep workbooks and Princeton Review-type courses, but not on lowering class size, providing professional development, or helping students learn the skills necessary to complete complex, long-term goals" (Nathan 2002, 600).

The debate is also heating up at the national level. As part of its effort to educate the public on what it perceives as the abuses, misuses, and flaws of national standardized testing, for example, the National Center for Fair & Open Testing (FairTest) contends that the "leave-no-child-behind" education legislation of 2002 should be called the "Leave No Child Untested Act" because the legislation requires national testing. The Center also maintains that national testing will divert funding from programs not covered on the tests (Toppo 2001).

Clearly, the debate over the effectiveness of testing programs based on state-mandated standards will continue for some time. However, professional teachers understand that participating in these programs is only part of their assessment responsibility—they must develop high-quality classroom assessments *for day-to-day use in the classroom.* The ability to develop and implement high-quality assessments of students' learning is a fundamental part professional accountability for today's teachers. Teachers must know whether their methods of assessing students' learning are, in fact, enhancing students' ability to learn.

What Methods Can You Use to Assess Student Learning?

The assessment of student learning will enable you to make judgments about the performance of students and about your performance as a teacher. Successful teachers use assessment to evaluate their effectiveness because they recognize that how well students learn depends on how well they teach. Furthermore, teachers realize that "assessment is more than a collection of techniques. It is a systematic process that plays a significant role in effective teaching" (Linn and Gronlund 2000, xiii).

Assessment has been defined as "the full range of procedures used to gain information about student learning (observations, ratings of performances or projects, paper-and-pencil tests) and the formation of value judgments concerning learning progress" (Linn and Gronlund 2000, 31). Truly professional teachers work continuously to become aware of the latest approaches to assessing student learning. They understand the critical role that assessment plays in teaching and the importance of "establishing credible performance standards, communicating these standards to students, and providing feedback to students on their progress" (McMillan 2001, xiii). In addition, they follow four "guiding principles" when developing classroom assessments: "(1) Students are the key assessment users, (2) Clear and appropriate targets are essential, (3) Accurate assessment is a must, (4) Sound assessments must be accomplished by effective communication" (Stiggins 2001, 17–23).

To assess student learning, teachers use both quantitative and qualitative approaches. Quantitative approaches make use of measurement and evaluation techniques—such as teacher-made classroom tests comprised of multiple-choice, true-false, matching, or essay items—or performance-based assessments. Qualitative approaches may include formal and informal observations of students' performance on various learning tasks, the manner with which they approach those learning tasks, or students' self-reports of their interests and attitudes. For example, teachers routinely assess students' **work habits.** *Work habits* is a term suggested by the Coalition of Essential Schools (see Chapter 12, pages 458–459) for various dispositions important for effective thinking and learning, including reading with curiosity; reflecting critically on one's own work; developing independence, clarity, and incisiveness of thought; willingness to work hard; an ability to manage time effectively; persistence; accuracy and precision; and working collaboratively.

Teachers also frequently have students conduct a self-assessment by using *rubrics* (guides for evaluating the performance of a learning task) and/or benchmarks to assess their work. When students are involved in **self-assessment,** they are also engaged in self-evaluation—that is, interpreting information from the assessment of their own work.

Purposes of Classroom Assessment

For most people, the term *classroom assessment* brings to mind a four-step process: (1) the teacher prepares a test (or selects a preexisting test) to cover material that has been taught, (2) students take the test, (3) the teacher corrects the test, and (4) the teacher assigns grades based on how well students performed on the test. Classroom assessment, however, involves more—it provides information teachers use (1) to determine how well students are learning the material being taught; (2) to identify the type of feedback that will enhance student learning; (3) to develop strategies for improving their effectiveness as teachers; and (4) to determine if students have reached certain levels of performance.

To assess student learning, teachers use measurement and evaluation techniques. **Measurement** is the gathering of quantitative data related to the knowledge and skills students have acquired. Measurement yields scores, rankings, or ratings that teachers can use to determine the degree to which students have attained specified standards. **Evaluation** involves making judgments about or assigning a value to those measurements. When teachers measure students' attainment of knowledge and skills for the purpose of making decisions about their teaching, they are engaging in **formative evaluation.** When they use those measurements to determine grades at the end of a unit, semester, or year and to decide whether students are ready to proceed to the next phase of their education, they are engaging in **summative evaluation.** Figure 10.4 illustrates the essential elements of effective classroom assessment and the questions that guide teachers' decision making in this important area of teaching.

Emerging Trends in Classroom Assessment

As mentioned at the beginning of this chapter, declining test scores, international comparisons of student achievement, and calls to hold teachers more accountable have fueled a movement to assess student learning with ever-increasing numbers of tests. More recently, however, new forms of assessment are being used. Innovations in assessment are partly in response to criticisms of the fairness and objectivity of standardized tests, such as the Iowa Test of Basic Skills, the Scholastic Assessment Test (SAT), and the American College Test (ACT). Ed-

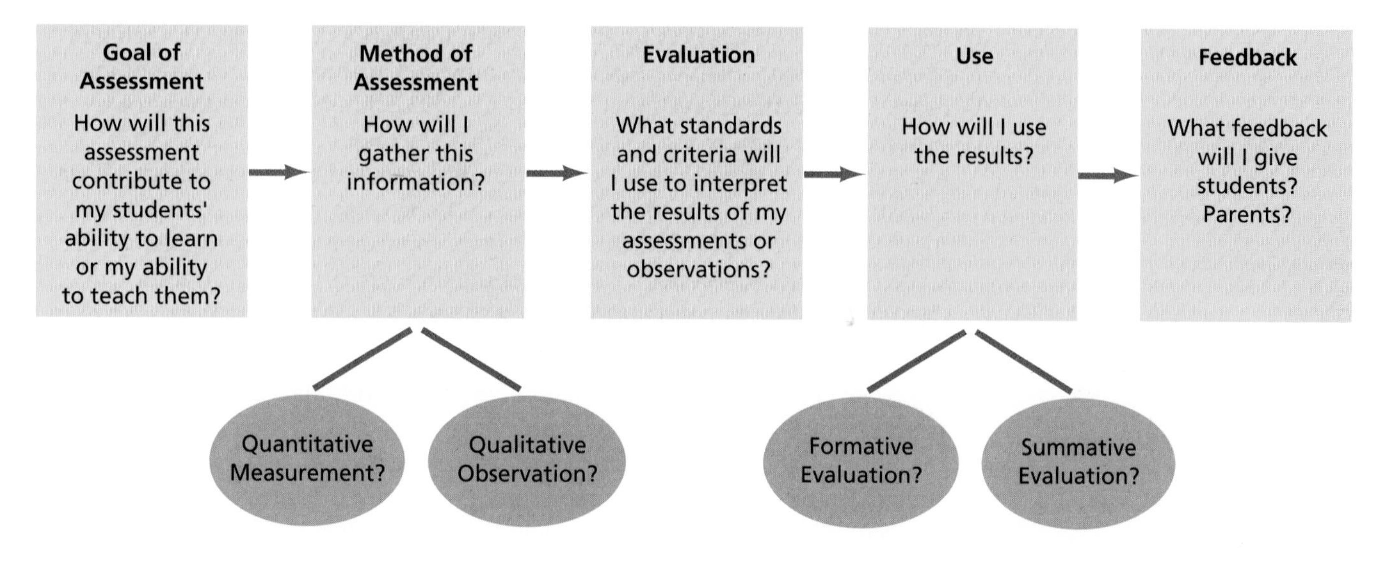

Figure 10.4 Effective classroom assessment

ucators and the public have criticized these tests not only for class and gender bias in their content but also for failing to measure accurately students' true knowledge, skills, and levels of achievement. For all these reasons, educators are increasingly going beyond traditional pencil-and-paper tests, oral questioning, and formal and informal observations. In addition, they are using an array of new assessment tools—individual and small-group projects, portfolios of work, exhibitions, videotaped demonstrations of skills, and community-based activities, to name a few.

Increasingly, teachers are using alternative assessments—that is, "forms of assessment that require the active construction of meaning rather than the passive regurgitation of isolated facts" (McMillan 2001, 14). The following sections examine several forms of **alternative assessments:** authentic assessment, portfolio assessment, performance-based assessment, alternate assessment, and project-based learning.

Authentic Assessment **Authentic assessment** (sometimes called *alternative assessment*) requires students to use higher-level thinking skills to perform, create, or solve a real-life problem, not just choose one of several designated responses as on a multiple-choice test item. A teacher might use authentic assessment to evaluate the quality of individual and small-group projects, videotaped demonstrations of skills, or participation in community-based activities. In science, for example, students might design and conduct an experiment to solve a problem and then explain in writing how they solved the problem.

Authentic assessments require students to solve problems or to work on tasks that approximate as much as possible those they will encounter beyond the classroom. For example, authentic assessment might allow students to select projects on which they will be evaluated, such as writing a brochure, making a map, creating a recipe, writing and directing a play, critiquing a performance, inventing something useful, producing a video, creating a model, writing a children's book, and so on. In addition, authentic assessment encourages students to develop their own responses to problem situations by allowing them to decide what information is relevant and how that information should be organized and used.

When teachers use authentic assessment to determine what students have learned—and the depth to which they have learned—student achievement and attitudes toward learning improve. For example, a study of eleven pairs of K–12 science and math teachers found that when teachers assess student learning in real-life problem-solving situations, learning and attitudes toward school improve (Appalachia Educational Laboratory 1993). Similarly, a synthesis of research on successfully restructured schools (Newmann and Wehlage 1995) revealed that teachers in those schools emphasized authentic assessment. Their assessments focused on students' ability to think, to develop in-depth understanding, and to apply academic learning to important, realistic problems. The Professional Reflection below illustrates the differences between "traditional" classroom assessment and authentic assessment.

Portfolio Assessment **Portfolio assessment** is based on a collection of student work that "tell[s] a story of a learner's growth in proficiency, long-term achievement, and significant accomplishments in a given academic area" (Tombari and Borich 1999, 164). In short, a portfolio provides examples of important work undertaken by a student, and it represents that student's *best* work. For example, a high school physics student might include in a portfolio (1) a written report of a physics lab experiment illustrating how vector principles and Newton's laws explain the motion of objects in two dimensions, (2) photographs of that experiment in progress, (3) a certificate of merit received at a local science fair, and (4) an annotated list of Internet sites related to vector principles and Newton's laws. For students, an important part of portfolio assessment is clarifying the criteria used to select work to be included in the portfolio, and then organizing and presenting that work for the teacher to assess.

Performance-Based Assessment Put simply, **performance-based assessment** is based on observation and judgment (Stiggins 2001). We observe a student perform a task or review a student-produced product, and we judge its quality. We could observe a student's science experiment and judge the quality of the thinking involved, or we could read a student's research report in history and judge the quality of argumentation and writing. Performance assessment is used to deter-

Classroom Assessment

Read the following descriptions of assessment activities in two fifth-grade social studies classrooms. What differences do you notice between the assessment activities in both classes? What do you think Mrs. Allen's students thought about the learning tasks they were asked to complete? Ms. Rodriguez's students? When you were a fifth- or sixth-grade student, which teacher would you have preferred? Why?

Assessment in Mrs. Allen's Classroom

The task for a class of fifth graders required them to copy a set of questions about famous explorers from a work sheet and to add the correct short-answer responses in the appropriate spots. The class spent thirty minutes on this exercise, which was part of a larger unit on exploration and which the teacher, Mrs. Allen, described as very consistent with the typical assessment.

During the four times that [researchers] observed Allen's hour-long classes, students read aloud from the textbook, a routine occasionally punctuated with Allen's asking them factual recall questions. During one class, students copied a chart from the board organizing the facts from the reading into categories. After finding more facts to fill up the chart, the students then completed a work sheet crossword puzzle built from the vocabulary words of the lesson (Marks, Newmann, and Gamoran 1996, 59–60).

Assessment in Ms. Rodriguez's Classroom

As an assessment of their learning, Ms. Rodriguez had her class of fifth and sixth graders research and write a paper on ecology, an assignment that occupied forty hours of class time during the twelve-week grading period. Each student produced several drafts of the paper and met individually with the teacher several times to discuss the drafts. Before they began the project, students received eleven pages of written directions on how to research, organize, and write the paper, including a step-by-step checklist for completing the assignment, a sample outline, and sample bibliography entries. The paper counted for 75 percent of the student's grade for the twelve-week period (Marks, Newmann, and Gamoran 1996, 60).

What type of assessment is taking place in this classroom?

mine what students can *do* as well as what they *know.* In some cases, the teacher observes and then evaluates an actual performance or application of a skill; in others, the teacher evaluates a product created by the student.

Performance-based assessment focuses on students' ability to apply knowledge, skills, and work habits through the performance of tasks they find meaningful and engaging. While traditional testing helps teachers answer the question, "Do students *know* content?," performance-based assessment helps answer the question, "How well can students *use* what they know?"

Students should find that performance tasks are interesting and relevant to the knowledge, skills, and work habits emphasized in the curriculum. If appropriate, students can help teachers construct performance-based assessments. For example, elementary level and high school level students helped their teachers construct the following two performance-based assessments, each of which required students to create graphs.

Example 1—Elementary Level

At various times during the school day, students observe and count, at fifteen-minute intervals, the number of cars and trucks that crossed an unlit intersection near their school. Students also gather the same information for a lit intersection near the school. Using data for both intersections, students construct graphs to illustrate the results. If the data suggest the need for a light at the unlit intersection, the graphs will be sent to the local police department.

As students work on various parts of this performance task, the teacher would observe students and make judgments about the quality of their work. Do the counts of cars and trucks appear to be accurate? Do the graphs illustrate the results clearly? Is the students' decision about the need for a traffic light supported by the data they have gathered?

Example 2—High School Level

Students go online to find data on traffic accidents in their state. Based on the data they locate, students prepare graphs that show, by driver's age, various types of accidents, fatalities, speed at the time of accident, and so on. Exemplary graphs will be displayed in the driver education classroom.

As with the elementary level example, the teacher would make judgments about the quality of the high school students' work. Naturally, these judgments would reflect the teacher's beliefs about the characteristics of exemplary student work at the high school level. Did students visit online sites that have extensive, accurate data on traffic accidents? Were students exhaustive in their online search? Do their graphs show a high degree of technical accuracy? Do the graphs "look professional"?

Alternate Assessments **Alternate assessments** are designed to measure the performance of students who are unable to participate in traditional large-scale assessments used by districts and states. This approach to assessment emerged as a result of the reference to "alternate assessment" in the 1997 reauthorization of the Individuals with Disabilities Education Act (IDEA), which called for states to have alternate assessments in place by the year 2000. An alternate assessment is an alternative way of gathering data about what a student, regardless of the severity of his or her disability, knows and can do. Alternate strategies for collecting data might consist of observing the student during the school day, asking the student to perform a task and noting the level of performance, or interviewing parents or guardians about the student's activities outside of school.

The primary purpose for alternate assessments in state assessment systems is to provide information about how well a school, district, or state is doing in terms of enhancing the performance of *all* students. Gathering data through alternate assessments requires rethinking traditional assessment methods.

An alternate assessment is neither a traditional large-scale assessment nor an individualized diagnostic assessment. For students with disabilities, alternate assessments can be administered to students who have a unique array of educational goals and experiences, and who differ greatly in their ability to respond to stimuli, solve problems, and provide responses.

Most states are in the process of developing alternate assessments for students with severe disabilities. The National Center on Educational Outcomes at the University of Minnesota suggests six principles for developing inclusive assessment and accountability systems:

Principle 1. All students with disabilities are included in the assessment system.

Principle 2. Decisions about how students with disabilities participate in the assessment system are the result of clearly articulated participation, accommodation, and alternate assessment decision-making processes.

Principle 3. All students with disabilities are included when student scores are publicly reported, in the same frequency and format as all other students, whether they participate with or without accommodations, or in an alternate assessment.

Principle 4. The assessment performance of students with disabilities has the same impact on the final accountability index as the performance of other students, regardless of how the students participate in the assessment system (i.e., with or without accommodation, or in an alternate assessment).

Principle 5. There is improvement of both the assessment system and the accountability system over time, through the processes of formal monitoring, ongoing evaluation, and systematic training in the context of emerging research and best practice.

Principle 6. Every policy and practice reflects the belief that *all students* must be included in state and district assessment and accountability systems (Guenemoen, Thompson, Thurlow, and Lehr 2001).

Project-Based Learning (PBL) A growing body of research supports the use of **project-based learning (PBL)** as a way to engage students, cut absenteeism, boost cooperative learning skills, and improve test scores. In project-based learning (PBL), students work in teams to explore real-world problems and create presentations to share what they have learned. Compared with learning solely from textbooks, this approach has many benefits for students, including deeper knowledge of subject matter, increased self-direction and motivation, and improved research and problem-solving skills. Furthermore, as George Lucas, founder of the George Lucas Educational Foundation and Director of *Star Wars,* points out, project-based learning has benefits that go beyond academic learning: "[Project-based learning] promotes emotional intelligence, which is actually much more important in the real world than a high degree of intellectual intelligence, because what you're really doing is working with other people" (George Lucas Educational Foundation 2001).

A three-year 1997 study of two British secondary schools—one that used open-ended projects and one that used more traditional, direct instruction—found striking differences between the two schools in understanding and standardized achievement data in mathematics. Students at the project-based school did better than those at the more traditional school both on math problems requiring analytical or conceptual thought and on those requiring memory of a rule or formula. Three times as many students at the project-based school received the top grade achievable on the national examination in math (George Lucas Educational Foundation 2001).

Project-based learning, which transforms teaching from *teachers telling* to *students doing,* includes five key elements:

1. Engaging learning experiences that involve students in complex, real world projects through which they develop and apply skills and knowledge.
2. Recognizing that significant learning taps students' inherent drive to learn, their capability to do important work, and need to be taken seriously.
3. Learning for which general curricular outcomes can be identified up front, while specific outcomes of the students' learning are neither predetermined nor fully predictable.
4. Learning that requires students to draw from many information sources and disciplines in order to solve problems.
5. Experiences through which students learn to manage and allocate resources such as time and materials (Oaks, Grantman, Pedras 2001, 443).

These five key elements are reflected in the following examples of project-based learning:

- At Mountlake Terrace High School in Mountlake Terrace, Washington, teams of students in a high school geometry class design a state-of-the-art high school for the year 2050. The students create a site plan, make simple architectural drawings of rooms and a physical model, draw up a budget, and write a narrative report. They present their work to real architects, who judge the projects and "award" the contract.

- At Newsome Park Elementary School in Newport News, Virginia, second-graders curious about the number of medicines a classmate takes and her frequent trips to the doctor investigate—with the classmate's permission—the causes of cystic fibrosis. They invite experts to tell them about the disease, write up their research, use graphs and Microsoft PowerPoint to tell the story, sell pledges to a cystic fibrosis walkathon, and participate in the walkathon.
- At the Mott Hall School in New York City's Harlem, a fifth-grade project on kites involves using creative writing skills in poems and stories with kite themes. While designing their own kites on the computer and then making them by hand, students learn about electromagnetism and the principles of ratios and proportions. A casual remark by one student leads to an in-depth study of the role of kites in various cultural celebrations.

How Can You Develop High-Quality Classroom Assessments?

Teachers use various criteria to grade the assignments students complete and the tests they take. Among the criteria teachers may consider are effort, neatness, correctness, how well students did compared with other students or with their own past performance, and how long students had been studying the topic. These criteria, of course, focus on what *students* do to demonstrate their learning. To develop high-quality classroom assessments, however, teachers must focus on what *they* do to ensure that assessments fairly and accurately measure students' knowledge, skills, and levels of achievement. To assess student learning, teachers should be skilled in the following:

- Choosing and/or developing assessment methods appropriate for attaining instructional goals and objectives
- Administering, scoring, and interpreting the results of both externally produced and teacher-produced assessment methods
- Using assessment results when making decisions about individual students, planning teaching, developing curriculum, and school improvement
- Developing valid grading procedures based on high-quality assessment of student learning
- Communicating assessment results to students, parents, other nonteaching audiences, and other educators
- Recognizing unethical, illegal, and otherwise inappropriate assessment methods and uses of assessment information

Validity and Reliability

Two important qualities of classroom assessments—whether teacher-made or commercially prepared—are validity and reliability. Since high-quality assessments are directly related to teaching effectiveness, assessments must be valid and reliable. **Validity** refers to the extent to which assessments measure what they are supposed to measure. If assessments fail to do this, they are useless. Valid assessments, however, ensure that what students are asked to do is a direct reflection of stated standards, goals, expectations, and/or targeted learning

Meeting the Standard

Assesses Student Learning

INTASC

The teacher understands and uses formal and informal assessment strategies to evaluate and ensure the continuous intellectual, social and physical development of the learner (INTASC Knowledge, Principle #8).

Teacher candidates accurately assess and analyze student learning, make appropriate adjustments to instruction, monitor student learning, and have a positive effect on learning for all students (NCATE, Standard 1: Knowledge, Skills, and Dispositions).

Accomplished teachers . . . employ multiple methods for measuring student growth and understanding and can clearly explain student performance to parents (NBPTS, Proposition 3).

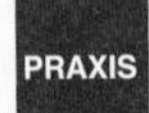

Assessment criteria and standards are clear and have been clearly communicated to students. There is evidence that students contributed to the development of the criteria and standards (PRAXIS III Framework– "distinguished" level of performance).*

Teachers who meet these standards systematically assess student learning because they place a high value on being prepared to adapt learning environments and resources to their students' needs. There are many approaches to assessment, but these teachers are knowledgeable about assessment methods and skilled at selecting the most appropriate ones to use with their students.

The demand for educational accountability has given rise to the standards-based curriculum and to the use of rubrics and the student-learning portfolios. Many useful resources are available on these subjects, including a number of them online. Teachers can access some helpful resources at the following websites:

Companion Website

- *Standards-based curriculum*–A school district in upper New York maintains a comprehensive website that allows educators to link to curriculum standards by subject and by state (http://edstandards.org/standards.html#state)
- *Rubrics*–Kathy Schrock's Guide for Educators provides a comprehensive list of resources for developing rubrics (http://school.discovery.com/schrockguide/assess.html#rubrics).
- *Student learning portfolios*–Useful suggestions and resources for creating and maintaining student learning portfolios have been posted on the Web by David Niguidula, Coalition of Essential Schools, Annenberg Institute for School Reform (http://www.essentialschools.org/pubs/exhib_schdes/dp/getfram.htm), and Dr. Helen Brett, Assistant Professor, Educational Technology, School of Education, University of Alaska Anchorage (http://electronicportfolios.com/portfolios.html).

1. *Curriculum standards*–To develop an appreciation for resources that can help you as a teacher, (a) view an annotated description of assessment methods at the website maintained by the STAR Center (Support Texas for Academic Renewal) (http://www.rmcdenver.com/useguide/assessme/definiti.htm.); (b) scan the list the STAR Center provides that links to some assessment resources (http://www.rmcdenver.com/useguide/assessme/online.htm); (c) find the curriculum standards for your state by using the Wappinger Curriculum Standards search tool (http://edstandards.org/standards.html#state); (d) select a curriculum standard that interests you and then go to the STAR Center (http://www.rmcdenver.com/useguide/assessme/aindex.htm.); or (e) create a plan by following the four-step guide for "Adopting, Adapting, or Developing an Aligned Assessment for Your [Standards-Based] Lesson" (http://www.rmcdenver.com/useguide/assessme/aindex.htm.)
2. *Rubric*–Create a rubric for an assignment you plan to include in an upcoming lesson by using a rubric wizard from the Educator's Network website (http://www.mehs.educ.state.ak.us/portfolios/portfolio.html).
3. *Student learning portfolios*–One retired elementary school teacher offers sound advice about the use of portfolios with young children (http://www.hannahmeans.bizland.com/grading.htm). Another teacher, Todd Bergman, explains how more than eight hundred students (representing various ages, grades, and ability levels) have constructed digital learner portfolios at Mt. Edgecumbe High School (http://www.mehs.educ.state.ak.us/portfolios/portfolio.html). Which approach would you use with your students? What will you need to know or do to begin using the portfolio to assess student learning?

outcomes. If assessments are valid, teachers can use that information to improve their teaching, and students can use that information to improve their learning.

Surprisingly, perhaps, examples of assessments that lack sufficient validity can be found among state-mandated tests of student learning. For example, Beverly Falk observes that

> *Numerous accountability systems use tests that have little relation to the standards they are supposed to evaluate. As recently as 1999, at least 25 states that claimed to be implementing new standards were still using old-style, norm-referenced tests to measure student progress. Although the rhetoric of new and lofty standards is used when discussing what the tests measure, their actual content includes few performance items, and their formats provide scant opportunities for students to demonstrate the higher-order thinking of the new standards (2002, 614).*

Reliability refers to the degree to which an assessment provides results that are consistent over time. In other words, an entire test (or individual test item) is considered to be reliable if it yields similar results at different times and under different conditions. For example, imagine that Mr. Jones wants to assess his students' multiplication and division skills using whole numbers by giving them a forty-point quiz (twenty points for multiplication, twenty points for division). After scoring his students' quizzes, Mr. Jones is uncertain about whether he should begin teaching the more complex skills of multiplying and dividing using fractions. He decides to gather more information by giving another quiz three days later on the same multiplication and division skills. The following table presents the scores several students received on both quizzes.

	Multiplication		Division	
Student	**Quiz #1**	**Quiz #2**	**Quiz #1**	**Quiz #2**
Carlos	20	18	17	9
Kim	14	13	13	17
Shawn	11	11	12	17
Nong	16	17	16	12
Mary	20	19	15	14

The items that assessed students' multiplication skills, Mr. Jones notes, are quite consistent (or reliable). On quiz #1 and #2, all five students received comparable scores, with Carlos and Mary receiving the highest scores on both quizzes, and Shawn and Kim receiving the lowest scores. On the other hand, the items that assessed students' division skills are less consistent (or reliable). On quiz #1, Carlos and Nong received the highest scores on the division items; while Kim and Shawn received the highest scores on the items for quiz #2.

At this point, Mr. Jones must make a judgment about the reliability of the information he has gathered. Since the results for the multiplication items are fairly consistent and those for the division items fairly inconsistent, he decides to spend one more class session instructing students on division using whole numbers before he proceeds to teach multiplication and division using fractions.

Scoring Rubrics

Rubrics are an important element of quality classroom assessments. Sometimes called *scoring guides,* **scoring rubrics** are rating scales that consist of preestablished performance criteria. Teachers use rubrics to differentiate between levels of student performance on a rating scale, and students can even use them to guide their learning. Rubrics can be used to specify performance criteria for a variety of learning activities—writing an essay, conducting a science experiment, or delivering an informative speech.

Since students can benefit from seeing examples of excellent work appropriate to their grade and ability levels, teachers should collect "models" of exemplary performances and products by their students. Besides using a scoring rubric to learn about the specific elements that will be used to assess the quality of their work, students must see what quality looks (sounds, feels, smells, or tastes) like. Over time, teachers collect sets of excellent work such as graphs, nonfiction writing, solutions to open-ended math problems, and designs for science experiments from students. Less than exemplary work may also be used in the process of teaching students how to use the rubrics.

Rubrics are typically used as scoring instruments when teachers evaluate student performances or products resulting from a performance task. There are two types of rubrics: holistic and analytic. A **holistic rubric** requires the teacher to score the overall process or product as a whole, without judging the component parts separately (Nitko 2001). Figure 10.5 presents a "generic" framework for developing a holistic scoring rubric based on a five-point scale.

As an illustration, a high school English teacher might use the framework presented in Figure 10.5 for holistic assessment of students' ability to write a clear, well-organized essay. A score of 5 would mean the essay reflected characteristics such as clear organization, accurate and precise use of words, adequately developed ideas, insightful analysis of the topic, and effective transitions from paragraph to paragraph. An essay with a score of 3 might

Figure 10.5 Generic framework for a holistic scoring rubric

Score	Description
5	Performance or product reflects complete understanding of the assessment task or problem. The performance or product reflects all requirements of the task or problem.
4	Performance or product reflects considerable understanding of the assessment task or problem. The performance or product reflects all requirements of the task or problem.
3	Performance or product reflects partial understanding of the assessment task or problem. The performance or product reflects nearly all requirements of the task or problem.
2	Performance or product reflects little understanding of the assessment task or problem. Many requirement of the task or problem are missing.
1	Performance or product reflects no understanding of the assessment task or problem.
0	Task or problem not undertaken.

	Beginning	Developing	Accomplished	Highly Accomplished	Score
Criteria #1	Performance or product reflects beginning level of performance.	Performance or product reflects emerging performance at the mastery level.	Performance or product reflects performance at the mastery level.	Performance or product reflects performance at the highest level of mastery.	
Criteria #2	Performance or product reflects beginning level of performance.	Performance or product reflects emerging performance at the mastery level.	Performance or product reflects performance at the mastery level.	Performance or product reflects performance at the highest level of mastery.	
Criteria #3	Performance or product reflects beginning level of performance.	Performance or product reflects emerging performance at the mastery level.	Performance or product reflects performance at the mastery level.	Performance or product reflects performance at the highest level of mastery.	
Criteria #4	Performance or product reflects beginning level of performance.	Performance or product reflects emerging performance at the mastery level.	Performance or product reflects performance at the mastery level.	Performance or product reflects performance at the highest level of mastery.	

Figure 10.6 Generic framework for an analytic rubric

have grammatical errors, problems with logic, confusing sentences, and a lack of transitions from paragraph to paragraph. And an essay with a score of 1 might be very confusing and contain only a few sentences that are clear and understandable.

Unlike the holistic scoring rubric, an **analytic rubric** requires that the teacher score separate, individual parts of the product or performance according to prespecified criteria, then add the individual scores to obtain a total score (Moskal 2000; Nitko 2001). Figure 10.6 presents a "generic" framework for developing an analytic scoring rubric based on a five-point scale.

Continuing with the example that focuses on teaching essay writing at the high school level, a teacher might evaluate students' essays with reference to the following four criteria, each of which would be evaluated according to Figure 10.6's description of performances at the "beginning," "developing," "accomplished," and "highly accomplished" levels:

- *Criteria 1:* The essay is organized clearly—the introduction "sets the stage" for what follows and the conclusion summarizes key ideas.
- *Criteria 2:* The essay is free of grammatical errors.
- *Criteria 3:* The essay has a unifying idea that is clear and easy to follow.
- *Criteria 4:* Effective paragraphing and transitions from one paragraph to the next provide an organizing structure and facilitate movement from one idea to the next.

To help you develop scoring rubrics for eventual use in your classroom, Figure 10.7 presents a step-by-step process for designing holistic and analytic scoring rubrics.

Designing Scoring Rubrics: A Step-by-Step Procedure

Step 1: Reexamine the learning objectives to be addressed by the task.

Step 2: Identify specific observable attributes that you want to see (as well as those you don't want to see) your students demonstrate in their product, process, or performance.

Step 3: Brainstorm characteristics that describe each attribute.

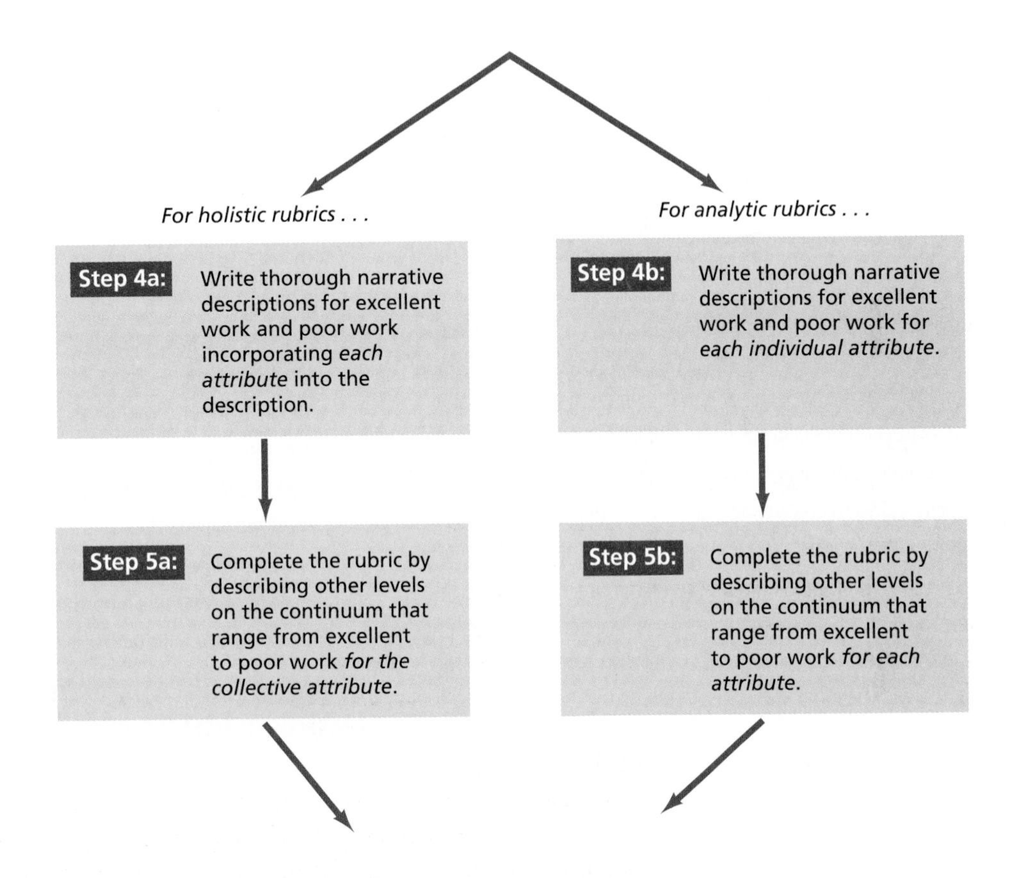

Step 6: Collect samples of student work that exemplify each level.

Step 7: Revise the rubric, as necessary.

Figure 10.7 Designing scoring rubrics: a step-by-step procedure. *Source:* Craig A. Mertler, "Designing Scoring Rubrics for Your Classroom," *Practical Assessment, Research & Evaluation,* 2001, *7*(25). Used with permission.

Summary

What Role Will Standards Play in Your Classroom?

- Standards at the state and national levels are part of the movement to hold educators and schools more accountable for student learning.
- Content standards refer to the content—knowledge and skills—students should acquire in various academic disciplines.
- Performance standards are used to assess how well students have attained standards.
- Benchmarks specify what students should understand and be able to do at specific grade levels or developmental stages.
- Professional associations have developed standards that reflect the knowledge, skills, and attitudes students should develop in the subject-matter disciplines.
- Horizontal curriculum alignment occurs when teachers within a specific grade level coordinate instruction across disciplines and examine their school's curriculum to ensure that course content and instruction dovetail across and/or within subject areas.
- Vertical curriculum alignment occurs when subjects are connected across grade levels so that students experience increasingly complex instructional programs as they move through the grades.
- Curriculum frameworks provide guidelines, recommended instructional and assessment strategies, suggested resources, and models for teachers to use as they develop curricula that are aligned with national and state standards.

What Controversies Surround the Effort to Raise Standards?

- Proponents of higher standards advance several arguments in favor of higher standards, including the role that standards can play in increasing student achievement.
- Opponents of standards-based education advance several arguments against higher standards, including evidence that indicates that higher standards may result in decreased emphasis on subjects not tested.
- To hold educators and schools accountable for student learning, some states rank schools on how well their students learn.
- Some states are using computer-adaptive testing systems to deliver statewide assessment tests.
- State-mandated tests often have high-stakes consequences for students, such as determining eligibility to participate in extracurricular activities or to graduate from elementary or high school.
- For teachers, administrators, and schools, test results can be linked to merit rewards, increased funding, or sanctions.

What Methods Can You Use to Assess Student Learning?

- Classroom assessments of student learning enable teachers to make judgments about the performance of students and about their own performance as teachers.
- To assess student learning, teachers use quantitative and qualitative approaches, measurement and evaluation techniques, and formative and summative evaluation.
- Among the emerging trends in classroom assessment are authentic assessments, portfolio assessments, performance-based assessments, alternate assessments, and project-based learning.

How Can You Develop High-Quality Classroom Assessments?

- Validity and reliability are two qualities of high-quality classroom assessments.
- Scoring rubrics are rating scales that consist of preestablished performance criteria.
- Holistic rubrics are used to evaluate student performances or products related to a performance task.
- Analytic rubrics are used to score separate, individual parts of a performance or product.

Key Terms and Concepts

accountability, **368**
alternate assessment, **376**
alternative assessments, **373**
analytic rubric, **382**
assessment, **371**
authentic assessment, **373**
benchmarks, **363**
content standards, **363**
curriculum alignment, **364**
curriculum framework, **364**
evaluation, **372**
formative evaluation, **372**
high-stakes tests, **369**
holistic rubric, **381**
measurement, **372**
performance-based assessment, **374**
performance expectations, **363**
performance standard, **363**
portfolio assessment, **374**
project-based learning (PBL), **377**
reliability, **380**
scoring rubrics, **380**
self-assessment, **372**
standards, **362**
standards-based education (SBE), **362**
summative evaluation, **372**
validity, **378**
work habits, **372**

Applications and Activities

Teacher's Journal

1. As Figure 10.1 shows, secondary students are less likely than secondary teachers or principals to view their schools as having high academic standards. What might account for this difference in perceptions?
2. Reflect on the 12,000 or so hours that you have spent as a student in K–12 classrooms. How would you characterize the academic standards you were expected to meet? How were these expectations conveyed to you?

Teacher's Database

1. Find the professional curriculum standards for your subject area online and compare them to the curriculum standards for that subject area in a state where you plan to teach; (most state department of education websites include state-mandated standards). For example, you might download the National Council for Teachers of Mathematics (NCTM) standards and then compare them with the mathematics curriculum in the state where you plan to teach.
2. Visit the George Lucas Educational Foundation online (http://www.glef.org/) and, with reference to the subject matter and grade level for which you are preparing to teach, find two examples of project-based learning activities that are featured at the GLEF site. How is student learning assessed in these project-based learning activities? How might you adapt or modify these assessment activities when you become a teacher?

Observations and Interviews

1. Spend a half-day at a school at the level you plan to teach, recording your impressions about the degree to which teachers hold students accountable for meeting high academic standards. If feasible, share your impressions with administrators, teachers, and students.
2. As a collaborative project, conduct an informal survey of what people think about retaining elementary, middle, and secondary students at their current grade level as a solution to the dilemma of what to do with students who do not meet standards for promotion. What differences do you note at the three levels of schooling?

Professional Portfolio

Using Figure 10.4 on page 373 as a guide, prepare an authentic classroom assessment at the grade level and in the subject area for which you are preparing to teach. The following outline may help you organize your portfolio entry:

Subject area: ______________

Activity or learning task: ______________

Materials needed: ______________

Goal of assessment: ______________

Method of assessment: ______________

Standards/criteria for evaluation: ______________

Use of assessment results: ______________

Feedback to students: ______________

VideoWorkshop Extra!

If the VideoWorkshop package was included with your textbook, go to Chapter 10 of the Companion Website (www.ablongman.com/parkay6e) and click on the VideoWorkshop button. Follow the instructions for viewing videoclips 9 and 10 and completing this exercise. Consider this information along with what you've read in Chapter 10 while answering the following questions.

1. Your text discusses the issue of standards, specifically how curriculum can reflect expectations of schools for students' abilities. Performance standards are often visible in the form of standardized tests given throughout a school district or statewide. Videoclip 9 presents the perspective that many high-stakes tests only represent a narrow portion of the curriculum. If a school district decided to take a break from high-stakes testing for five years, what then would parents, teachers, and others use to judge whether a school and its students were "successful"?
2. Use what you know about assessment from your text and videoclip 10 to answer the following question: Does raising standards succeed at holding schools and teachers accountable for students' learning? At what cost?

11 Teaching with Technology

The power of the Internet to transform the educational experience is awe-inspiring.

—The Web-Based Education Commission to the President and the Congress of the United States, 2001

Until Consuelo Molina discovered the San Fernando Education Technology Team (SFETT), she wasn't particularly engaged in school, and her extreme shyness kept her from being anything more than an uncomfortable, silent observer in class. However, through the technology team program and its photography, videotaping, sound recording, editing, and presentation instruction and equipment, Molina's voice is now loud and clear, and her opinions are known around the world.

A Sacrifice for You, Molina's web video on sweatshops, has been praised and used by participants at the Women's Human Rights Conference in Paris, by Apple CEO Steve Jobs, and by a teacher in India, among others.

"Her passion and her interest to talk about something that really bothered her and to have it reach every corner of the world was an experience that she'll never forget," says Marco Torres, the teacher who started the technology team at San Fernando High School, north of Los Angeles. The school has a population of predominantly poor Latino students. Ninety-six percent have no access to computers at home, and 83 percent perform below grade level. So far, about three hundred people have participated in the SFETT program, and all of the eighty SFETT participants who graduated from San Fernando have gone on to college. Torres says the program catches students' interest because it focuses on learning by doing and speaks to their fascination with technology and all things digital.

Torres says, "Media is the language of kids." Students who may not take to learning by reading a textbook or listening to a lecture often jump at the chance to understand complex concepts by presenting finished products in the form of a film, a web documentary, or a Microsoft PowerPoint presentation.

Tools of multimedia are introduced through projects in several different formats: documentaries, music, experimental video, advocacy/selling ideas, and storytelling/feature production. Content of the projects comes from the students and is often based on assignments given in other classes. Molina's sweatshop project fulfilled an assignment in her economics class. Using up-to-date "presentation of learned information makes for realistic, contextual, emotional connections" to what is learned, says Torres (Monsef 2002).

Focus Questions

1. **How are educational technologies influencing schools?**
2. **What technologies are available for teaching?**
3. **How do teachers use computers and the Internet?**
4. **What are the effects of computer technology on learning?**
5. **Should technology be at the forefront of efforts to improve schools in the United States?**
6. **What are the challenges of integrating technology into schools?**

Themes of the Times
The New York Times expect the world
nytimes.com

Expand your knowledge of the concepts discussed in this chapter by reading current and historical articles from the *New York Times* by visiting the **"Themes of the Times"** section of the Companion Website (www.ablongman.com/parkay6e).

Since the early 1980s, teachers have used computers as an *instructional delivery system* to present information to students. Today, teachers use computers not only for highly structured drill-and-practice exercises, but as a *catalyst for group investigation and inquiry.* In the opening scenario, for example, Marco Torres is using up-to-date technology to stimulate his students' higher-order thinking, creativity, and problem solving. For Torres, technology is a tool to achieve his educational goals and to create a rich, stimulating environment that fosters collaboration, inquiry, and decision making.

How Are Educational Technologies Influencing Schools?

Technology has transformed teaching and learning throughout our nation's schools. Each day, students communicate via the Internet with other students around the world. Students use child-oriented search engines such as Yahooligans! and KIDLINK to search the World Wide Web for information about whales, the Brazilian rain forest, or the planet Mars. They go to chat rooms or newsgroups for children, where they can "talk" to other children in other countries or participate in various global networking projects for children.

Torres's classroom at San Fernando High School is representative of how recently developed technologies have transformed the learning environments in thousands of schools around the country. Moreover, the pace of change shows no signs of letting up—as one technology expert said, "We may well assume that we haven't seen anything yet. [If] present trends continue, it seems not unreasonable to expect that digital technologies will have an impact on our classrooms proportionate to that of writing and the printing press" (Withrow 1997, 4). Similarly, one of the nation's foremost futurists, Marvin Cetron, has predicted that "Computers will free educators to adopt much more sophisticated, effective, and rewarding styles of teaching. Future teachers will be facilitators, monitors, and catalysts, rather than lecturers and taskmasters" (1997, 19–20).

Technology and the Challenge to Schools

The Internet, the World Wide Web, and related telecommunications technologies have the potential to transform teaching and learning. However, one of the education issues for the twenty-first century is how committed are teachers, administrators, policymakers, parents, and the general public to enabling students to realize the full impact that technology can have on their learning? As the following statement suggests, the future of schools may depend on educators' response to this challenge:

> *The doubling of technological power through the 1990s morphed us into a high-speed, high-tech society. As a result, we are all experiencing accelerated change at a pace never before experienced in human history. Most of us involved in education are simply unprepared for this, and consequently, we have not been able to respond to it as quickly as the world outside of education has. We must quickly catch up or face the unenviable prospect of becoming irrelevant (McCain and Jukes 2001, 58–59).*

Additionally, educators must develop new assessment techniques to evaluate students' learning that occurs through the use of advanced telecommunications like the Internet and the World Wide Web. The number of correct responses on homework, quizzes, and examinations will no longer suffice to measure students' learning. "If teachers want students to be able to use ditto masters, then they shouldn't spend thousands of dollars on systems that support computer-assisted instruction. If teachers want to reinforce their didactic role and their role as information providers, then they should also leave computers alone" (Morton 1996, 419).

The CEO Forum on Education and Technology (2001) has called on teachers to use technologies to help students develop the following "21st century skills" they will need for life and work in the digital age:

Digital Age Literacy

1. Basic, Scientific, and Technological Literacy
2. Visual and Information Literacy
3. Cultural Literacy and Global Awareness

Inventive Thinking

4. Adaptability/Managing Complexity
5. Curiosity, Creativity, and Risk Taking
6. Higher Order Thinking and Sound Reasoning

Effective Communication

7. Teaming, Collaboration, and Interpersonal Skills
8. Personal and Social Responsibility
9. Interactive Communication

High Productivity

10. Prioritizing, Planning, and Managing for Results
11. Effective Use of Real-World Tools
12. Relevant, High Quality Products

When you think about your future as a teacher who will be expected to help students develop "21st century skills," you may find that future at once exciting and intimidating, enticing and threatening. You may ask, will I be ready to meet the challenge of integrating technologies into my teaching? In a very real sense, it is in the hands of people like you to develop new ways to use new technologies in the classrooms of tomorrow. The Professional Reflection on the following page is designed to help you begin the process of planning for that future.

E-Learning and Virtual Schools

At Hudson High School in Hudson, Massachusetts, ten students are working at computers in a small room marked "VHS Lab." One of the students is working on an assignment for an online media studies course taught by a teacher in Malaysia. Another student is studying technology and multimedia in a course taught by a teacher in Georgia. Their classmates include students from throughout the nation, Asia, Europe, and South America.

Hudson High School is one of a growing number of high schools in the nation that are using **e-learning,** or online education, to supplement the school curriculum. A small school with an enrollment of 880, Hudson has access to 128 courses online, most of which would not be included in the traditional curricu-

Professional Reflection

How Technically Proficient Are You?

Following is a list of educational technologies and instructional strategies that are currently changing teaching and learning. For each, indicate with an X whether you are "proficient," "somewhat proficient," or "not proficient" with that technology or strategy. Then indicate whether you are "highly committed," "somewhat committed," "opposed," or "neutral" toward using that technology or strategy in your teaching.

Space is provided for you to add technologies and strategies not on the list.

After responding to the items, reflect on those to which you are "highly committed" to integrating into your teaching. What steps will you take from this point on to ensure that those technologies and strategies will, in fact, be part of your teaching in the future?

	Proficiency Level			Commitment to Using			
Technology or Instructional Strategy	**Proficient**	**Somewhat proficient**	**Not proficient**	**Highly committed**	**Somewhat committed**	**Opposed**	**Neutral**
1. Student networking via computer	____	____	____	____	____	____	____
2. Video teleconferencing	____	____	____	____	____	____	____
3. Interactive multimedia/hypermedia	____	____	____	____	____	____	____
4. Web page authoring	____	____	____	____	____	____	____
5. CD-ROMs/videodiscs/digital video discs (DVD)	____	____	____	____	____	____	____
6. Computer assisted instruction (CAI)	____	____	____	____	____	____	____
7. Word processing	____	____	____	____	____	____	____
8. Desktop publishing	____	____	____	____	____	____	____
9. Presentation graphics	____	____	____	____	____	____	____
10. Spreadsheets/graphing	____	____	____	____	____	____	____
11. Databases	____	____	____	____	____	____	____
12. e-mail	____	____	____	____	____	____	____
13. Attaching files to e-mail	____	____	____	____	____	____	____
14. Newsgroups	____	____	____	____	____	____	____
15. Electronic gradebook	____	____	____	____	____	____	____
16. Information retrieval on WWW	____	____	____	____	____	____	____
17. Networking with file server	____	____	____	____	____	____	____
18. Scanners	____	____	____	____	____	____	____
19. Faxes	____	____	____	____	____	____	____
20. Digital cameras	____	____	____	____	____	____	____
21. Video cameras	____	____	____	____	____	____	____
22. Other ____	____	____	____	____	____	____	____
23. Other ____	____	____	____	____	____	____	____

lum. E-learning "broadens the curriculum way beyond what we'd normally be able to offer," says the principal (Trotter 2002).

Hudson High receives its online courses through the Virtual High School (VHS), a consortium of high schools run by VHS Inc., a nonprofit foundation. The Hudson School District cofounded the program in 1995, along with the Concord Consortium, a nonprofit research and development organization, under a five-year grant from the federal government. The VHS has two hundred member schools in twenty-eight states and eight countries. Each member school must contribute a teacher to teach at least one online class of twenty students.

The VHS was one of the nation's first two online programs for high schools—the other was the e-school run by the Hawaii Department of Education. Since then, Apex Learning in Bellevue, Washington, the Florida Virtual School, and several colleges and universities offered online courses to high school students. In fact, by the end of the 2001–02 school year, between forty and fifty thousand K–12 students had enrolled in an online course (WestEd 2001). Figure 11.1 shows that twelve states had established **virtual schools** by the end of the 2001–02 school year. Five states—Idaho, Maryland, Mississippi, Oklahoma, and Texas—were developing or piloting virtual schools. Also, twenty-five

Figure 11.1 Virtual schools, 2001–02
Source: Technology Counts 2002: E-Defining Education (2002) *Education Week*. May 2002. Retrieved at http://www.edweek.org/sreports/tc02. Used with permission.

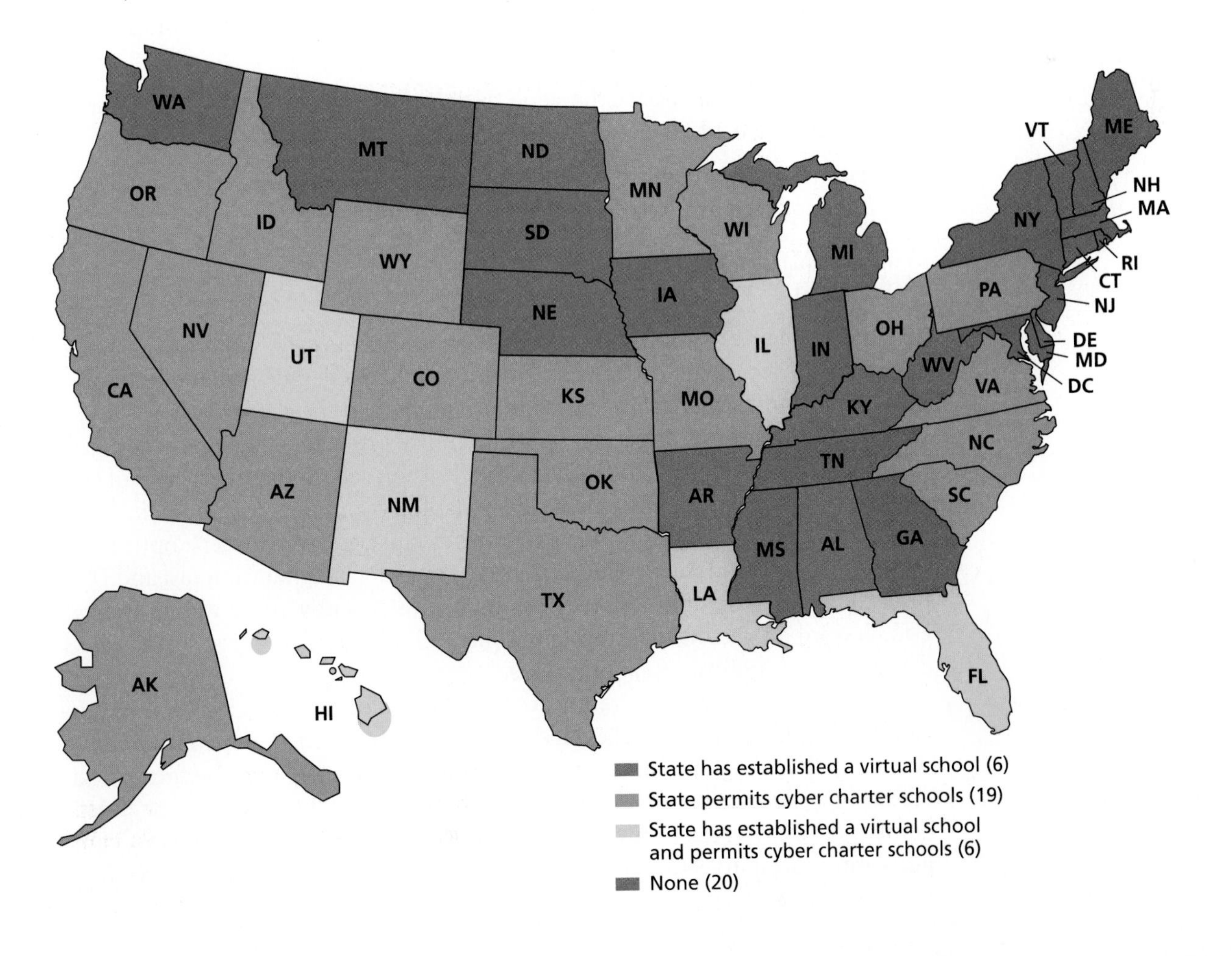

of the thirty-seven states and the District of Columbia that allowed charter schools also permitted cyber charter schools.

With the spread of virtual schools and courses, some educators, policymakers, and researchers have expressed concern about exaggerated claims for online learning. In addition, they are worried about what is lost when students do not meet face-to-face with their classmates and teachers. As Alan Warhaftig, a Los Angeles high school English teacher who earned certification from the National Board for Professional Teaching Standards (NBPTS), said, there is an "overall weakness to that notion that online schools can replace the school environment." He doubts that online classrooms can provide the "looking-in-the-eyes" factor that teachers use to monitor students' understanding of a lesson or how they might be feeling (Trotter 2002).

The trend toward e-learning and virtual schools no doubt will continue. Meanwhile, several questions need to be addressed to ensure that virtual students have quality online learning experiences:

- While online learning may be appropriate for high school students, should online learning be made available to elementary and middle school students?
- Should online courses be aligned with state academic standards?
- Who should provide for students' technological needs while they take an online course?
- Are online teachers trained effectively to teach via the Internet?
- Should parent approval be required before a child enrolls in an online course?
- Should students receive the same credit for an online course as they would for an interactive, face-to-face class?
- How can school officials ensure the quality of online courses, especially those offered by teachers in other states or countries?

What Technologies Are Available for Teaching?

To enhance their classroom instruction, today's teachers can draw from a dazzling array of technological devices. Little more than a decade ago, the technology available to teachers who wished to use more than the chalkboard was limited to an overhead projector, a 16-mm movie projector, a tape recorder, and, in a few forward-looking school districts, television sets. Today, teachers and students use ever-more-powerful desktop and laptop computers with built-in modems, faxes, and CD-ROM players; videodisc players; camcorders; optical scanners; speech and music synthesizers; laser printers; digital cameras; and LCD projection panels. In addition, they use sophisticated software for web browsing, e-mail, word processing, desktop publishing, presentation graphics, spreadsheets, databases, and multimedia applications.

Although the array of currently available technology for the classroom is dazzling, Ted McCain and Ian Jukes, authors of *Windows on the Future: Education in the Age of Technology,* predict even more dazzling technologies in the future: "Electronics have increased in power more than 1,000,000 times since the development of ENIRC [electronic numerical integrator and calculator, an early computer introduced in 1946], but the greatest changes still lie ahead. Fasten your seat belts!" (2001).

While the term *educational technology* is usually taken to mean computers in the classroom, many different forms of technology have influenced education in the United States. If we broadly define **educational technology** as inventions that enable teachers to reach their goals more effectively, it is clear that for some time teachers have been integrating into their classrooms many forms of educational technology, from the humble chalkboard to the overhead projector. One technology that has had a long and perhaps controversial history in education is television.

The Television Revolution

The television revolution in the United States began with great optimism. David Sarnoff, who founded NBC and introduced the first color television at the New York World's Fair in 1939, confidently predicted that television was "destined to provide greater knowledge to larger numbers of people, truer perception of the meaning of current events, more accurate appraisal of men in public life, and a broader understanding of the needs and aspirations of our fellow human beings" (Sarnoff 1940). Since that time, television has become an omnipresent feature of life in the United States, and its effects—both positive and negative—on all facets of American life are still being studied and debated, and for good cause. Children spend an estimated equivalent of two months of the year watching television. The typical child between six and eleven years of age watches about twenty-seven hours a week; and, by the time they graduate from high school, young people have watched an average of 22,000 hours of television (Shenk 1998).

Critics of television point out that it encourages passivity in the young, may be linked to increases in violence and crime, often reinforces sexual and ethnic stereotypes, retards growth and development, and may be linked to learning disorders. Psychologist Jerome Singers contends that "most [heavy-viewing] kids show lower information, lower reading recognition or readiness to reading, [and] lower reading levels; [and they] tend to show lower imaginativeness and less complex language usage" (quoted in Shenk 1998, 61). Some say that television robs children of the time they need to do homework, to read and reflect, and to build bonds with family members and others through interaction.

However, television can enhance students' learning. Excellent educational programs are aired by the Public Broadcasting Service and by some cable and other commercial networks. Television has also had a positive impact on how students are taught in schools. With the increased availability of video equipment, many schools have begun to have students produce their own television documentaries, news programs, oral histories, and dramas. Many schools have closed-circuit television systems that teachers use to prepare instructional materials for students in the district, and many districts have **distance learning networks** that use two-way, interactive telecommunications to provide enrichment instruction to students in remote areas or staff development to teachers.

Channel One One of the most controversial uses of television in the schools is Channel One, started by Christopher Whittle in 1990. Watched daily by about eight million teenagers in more than 12,000 public and private schools in nearly every state, **Channel One** is a twelve-minute news broadcast, with two minutes of commercials for which advertisers pay as much as $200,000 per thirty-second time slot (Walsh 1999a). On agreeing to show Channel One programs to most students on 90 percent of school days (students may opt out of viewing), schools receive the program free, including $25,000 worth of equipment (a satellite dish, two video cassette recorders, nineteen-inch color monitors mounted throughout the school, and internal wiring) that is regularly serviced at no charge. According to the Channel One Network, 99 percent of schools choose to renew their three-year contract to carry Channel One, and the Network has received numerous awards and aired more than $70 million worth of public service announcements. Moreover, the Network points out, schools are encouraged to use the equipment for other educational purposes such as viewing programs on the Learning Channel, CNN, the Discovery Channel, and C-Span; producing student news shows; conducting teacher in-service programs; and making daily announcements.

The Channel One contributions to education notwithstanding, professional associations such as the National Education Association, educational leaders, and politicians have maintained that advertisements have no place in the classroom. At a 1999 Senate committee hearing, consumer advocate Ralph Nader labeled Channel One "the most brazen marketing ploy in the history of the United States" and cited "parental neglect and the delinquency of school boards" as key reasons for the network's popularity (Walsh 1999d). According to William Hoynes (1998), a sociology professor at Vassar College, the primary goal of Channel One is not to inform students but to assemble a vast "teen market" and then sell high-priced advertising slots. His analysis of Channel One programs led him to conclude that they were "fundamentally commercial" and their educational value "highly questionable."

The Computer Revolution

At Consolidated High School District (CHSD) 230 in suburban Chicago, students are using handheld computers—wallet-sized computers many people use to keep track of appointments, e-mail, and the current news on the Internet. The district equipped its three high schools with 2,200 Palm IIIxe's in the form of both classroom sets and individual handhelds that could be bought or rented by students. Students conduct science experiments outdoors with computerized probes and create graphs on the spot as they enter spreadsheet data. Teachers no longer need to write assignments on the blackboard because they can "beam" in-

These students are broadcasting a live program from their school's television studio. How have the television revolution and the computer revolution changed education for the better? For the worse?

Meeting the Standard

Enriches Learning with Teaching Resources

The teacher knows how to enhance learning through the use of a wide variety of materials as well as human and technological resources (e.g., computers, audio-visual technologies, videotapes and discs, local experts, primary documents and artifacts, texts, reference books, literature, and other print resources) (INTASC Knowledge, Principle #4).

PRAXIS

In addition to being aware of school and district resources, teacher actively seeks other materials to enhance instruction. . . . (PRAXIS III Framework–"distinguished" level of performance).*

The new professional teacher . . . should be able to integrate technology into instruction effectively (NCATE, Standard I: Candidate Knowledge, Skills, and Dispositions).

Teachers know about the breadth of options available to them, such as . . . working with computers (NBPTS, Proposition 3).

The teachers meeting these standards are adept at enriching learning with teaching resources, including those that are technology-oriented, and thereby making it meaningful and interesting for their students. Determination to stay knowledgeable about available resources, coupled with an intentional plan to develop the skills needed to enrich student learning, are the key ingredients for their success. Educational resources include such things as guest speakers (local experts, parents, visitors from other parts of the country or other countries), field trips, related pieces of art, related music, drama, computer work, videodiscs, and dances. Incorporating a variety of resources accommodates different learning styles and allows students a variety of opportunities to flourish. For instance, when one class of sixth-graders studied the Middle Ages and Renaissance periods, the teacher had an art professor do a portrait of one of the students, emphasizing that the subjects of art are not only aristocracy and royalty. A local group of entertainers visited the class and demonstrated jousting and medieval dances. The students made stilts, embroidered purses, and other items and sold them at a Renaissance Fair attended by the entire student body. In this case, history was brought to life, and the students were given the opportunity to learn through mediums other than the printed word.

Teachers who meet these standards also seem to find ways to use a variety of resources that increase their professional effectiveness and efficiency, even in today's hectic educational environment. This chapter and its Companion Website provide just a small sample of the countless free or inexpensive online resources available to K–12 teachers and their students.

Easy-to-access resource lists organized around one or several themes can greatly reduce the time it takes teachers to locate ideas and information they can use in their planning. Such lists can be created to include web addresses for web-based resources. They are stored on the computer's desktop or in a familiar document storage area on the teacher's computer. Then the teacher can easily view the web-based resources by simply opening the Word document and clicking on the web addresses. At the following URL you can see how one teacher has created such a list on resources for a one-computer classroom (http://www.kn.pacbell.com/wired/fil/pages/listonecompja.html).

Teacher-created resource lists also can be a potential timesaver for other educators, and the Internet has made it possible for teachers throughout the country or world to share their ideas. Online forms, such as the one at the Filamentality website hosted by SBC Pacific Bell, make posting on the Web simple and encourage teachers to share their findings with other educators. The following websites demonstrate more sophisticated web skills used to post a children's literature resource list (http://www.acs.ucalgary.ca/~dkbrouwn/www.ucalgary.ca/dkbrouwn/index.html) and a list on technology and teaching (http://www.wam.umd.edu/~mlhall/teaching.html#misc).

National or international awards and scholarship programs provide a good starting place to develop a plan for systematic growth in the use of educational resources and technologies. Awards and scholarship program guidelines are often tied to curriculum and technology standards for students, which can be translated into a plan for integration of teaching resources and technology within class activities. The organization's policies and guidelines are generally available at a related website, making it easy to check the compatibility between the program's requirements and the school's policies and expectations. Collaborating with other teachers can make this kind of planning more fun and productive. Many web-based programs now make that kind of sharing among educators easy and interesting.

1. Try creating an easy-to-access list of resources as part of your own technology skills development plan. Begin locating some web-based resources by checking the Companion Website for this and other chapters in this book or by completing your own topical search online. Keep the information you locate in a word processing document on your computer or share it by completing the online form at the Filamentality website (http://www.kn.pacbell.com/wired/fil/).
2. The International Technology Education Association (ITEA) offers educators opportunities to compete for a variety of awards and scholarships built around the implementation of twenty technology standards for students. Study the ITEA website (http://www.iteawww.org) and begin translating the award/scholarship guidelines and technology standards into a skills development plan for yourself.

structions to students' handhelds, often called *personal digital assistants* or PDAs. Students' written reports now include animated pictures, and flash cards to memorize important information have become a fun computer game. According to science teacher Laurie Ritchey, "For once I think education is keeping up with what's going on in the real world and not sitting there chiseling something into a rock" (Curtis 2002).

Although personal computers may not have transformed all schools so that all students have learning experiences like those at CHSD 230, computers have had a significant impact on education. Like the dawn of the television era over sixty years earlier, the widespread availability of personal computers has been heralded as a technological innovation that will change the teaching–learning process. As Bill Gates, founder of Microsoft Corporation, predicted in *The Road Ahead* (Gates, Myhrvold, and Rinearson 1996), "I expect education of all kinds to improve significantly within the next decade . . . information technology will empower people of all ages, both inside and outside the classroom, to learn more easily, enjoyably, and successfully than ever before."

Computers and Instruction Since the early 1980s, the use of computers to enhance instruction has grown steadily. Two of the more common approaches are computer-assisted instruction (CAI) (sometimes called computer-*aided* instruction) and computer-managed instruction (CMI). **Computer-assisted instruction (CAI)** relies on computer programs that provide students with highly structured drill-and-practice exercises or tutorials. Research has shown CAI to be effective with at-risk students and students with disabilities because it accommodates their special needs and instruction is appropriately paced (Bialo 1989; Jones 1994; Kozma et al. 1992; Norris 1994; Signer 1991). Moreover, CAI can provide students with a more positive, supportive environment for learning; students can avoid embarrassment since their inevitable mistakes while learning are not exposed to peers. Figure 11.2 presents several additional student-centered and technology-centered advantages of CAI.

Computer-managed instruction (CMI) relies on programs that evaluate and diagnose students' needs and then, based on that assessment, guide them through the next steps in their learning. CMI also records students' progress for teachers to monitor. CAI and CMI can result in reduced teacher–student interactions, if the teacher interprets his or her role as primarily that of record keeper or manager. On the other hand, CAI and CMI can enhance teacher–student interactions: "Freed from the necessity of conducting routine drills and performing many management duties, the teacher has more time to be the vital human link between student and knowledge. The computer does not supplant teachers; it supports them" (Bitter and Pierson 1999, 249).

An increasingly popular approach to computer-based instruction is computer-enhanced instruction (CEI). Unlike CAI and CMI, **computer-enhanced instruction (CEI)** is less structured and more inquiry-oriented. The following example illustrates how CEI was used at Richmond Academy in New York City to involve students in archeological inquires:

> *Ninth-graders file into their social studies classroom and, before class begins, log on to one of six workstations at tables against the walls. They argue noisily about what they are finding as they unearth an archaeological site in ancient Greece. The students have been working on the computer-based archaeology simulation for about three weeks, and teams of students are each responsible for excavating one of four separate quadrants of the site. It is a welcome break for the ninth-graders, who in their other classes spend much of their time taking lecture notes and learning to parse sophisticated texts as part of their college-prep curriculum. Here they are "dig-*

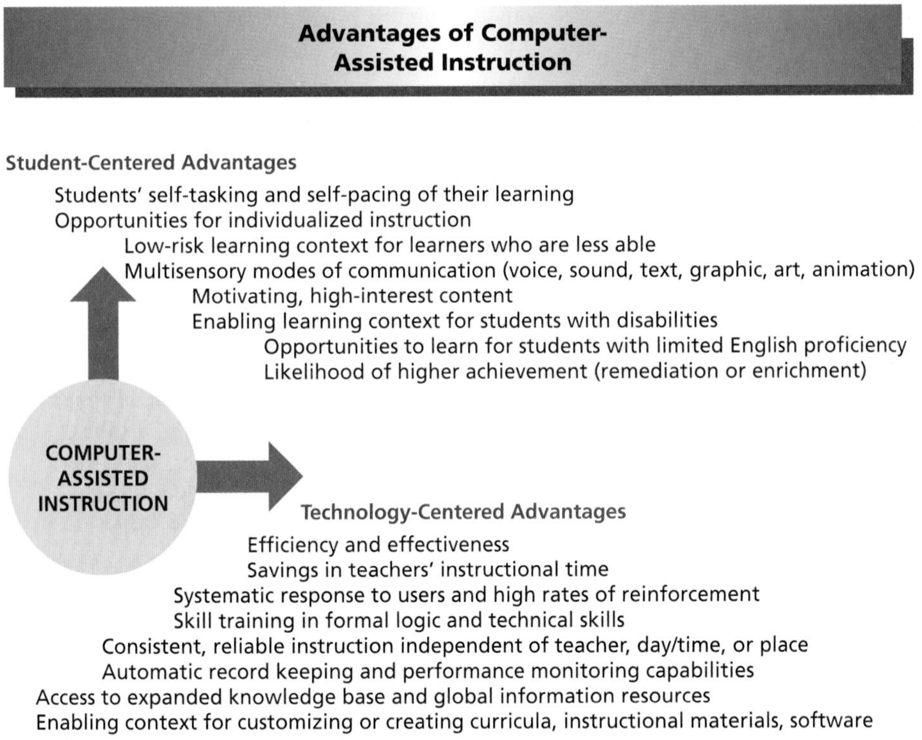

Advantages of Computer-Assisted Instruction

Figure 11.2 Advantages of computer-assisted instruction (CAI)

ging up" pottery shards, fragments of weapons, pieces of masonry, and bits of ancient texts, and trying to identify and interpret each artifact in order to fit it into their emerging picture of the site as a whole. In their research the students visit local museums, consult reference works on Greek history, art, and architecture, and ask other teachers in the school to help translate texts. Cleverly, the students' teachers have filled the site with ambiguous evidence, so that some teams find a preponderance of data suggesting the site was a temple, while others find artifacts mostly suggesting it was a battlefield. In weekly meetings the teams present their latest findings to the rest of the class, and a hot debate ensues as the amateur archaeologists struggle to reconcile the fragmentary and ambiguous data. On this day the classroom is active and noisy, yet controlled, as students take turns at the computer, graph their findings on large wall-charts, call across the room to ask if anyone has a spearhead to compare with one just found, and argue about whose final interpretation of the site will best explain the bulk of the evidence (Brunner and Tally 1999, 24–25).

Unlike CAI or CMI, teachers in CEI play a critical role in facilitating interactions between computer and student—teachers "are [essential] to the learning process, because simply seating students in front of their computers to surf the Net will not result in the same learning curve as when teachers assign well-designed projects in which students use the Net to gather information" (Kirkpatrick and Cuban 1998).

Some schools are using another inquiry-oriented approach to enhancing instruction with computers—the microcomputer-based laboratory (MBL), sometimes called CBL (computer-based laboratory). Through probes and sensors attached to computers, **microcomputer-based laboratories (MBL)** enable students to measure and graph data such as light, sound temperature, voltage, skin resistance, magnetic field, and heat flow. Students can gather data in the school laboratory or use a battery-operated interface to gather data in the field. For example, Concord Consortium, a nonprofit research and development organization dedicated to developing new ways to use technology in teaching, has developed MBL curriculum materials that enable students to learn about rain forests by using a sensor to gather local data for such variables as humidity, light, dissolved oxygen in rivers and streams, and acid rain. Students then compare local data with those obtained in an actual rain forest.

The "Magic" of Media

Personal computers have so revolutionized the instructional media available to teachers that today it is no exaggeration to refer to the "magic" of media. Carol Gilkerson, a Christa McAuliffe Educator, describes how instructional media have transformed her teaching:

> *One of the chief strengths of using technology in the classroom is that it enables me to adapt my instruction to the individual needs and learning styles of the students. As computer activities can be tailored to student needs, the class becomes more student centered. CD-ROM, videodisc, and captioned instructional television present information visually and allow students to learn complex material more easily.*

Some of the most exciting forms of media magic involve CD-ROMs, videodiscs, and interactive multimedia. Recent advances in computer technology have made it possible for students to become much more active in shaping their learning experiences. On a four-inch **CD-ROM,** they can access the equivalent of about 270,000 pages of text, about nine hundred 300-page books; or on a twelve-inch **videodisc** they can access the equivalent of about 54,000 photographic slides. Computer-supported **interactive multimedia** allow students to integrate information from huge text, audio, and video libraries.

Hypermedia Systems consisting of computer, CD-ROM drive, videodisc player, video monitor, and speakers now allow students to control and present sound, video images, text, and graphics with an almost limitless array of possibilities. Students who use such hypermedia systems, the most familiar of which is the World Wide Web, can follow their curiosity, browse through enormous amounts of information, and develop creative solutions for multidimensional, real-life problem situations. On-line databases in many fields are changing the way students conduct library research, as more computerized reference works—such as directories, dictionaries, and encyclopedias—become available.

The term **hypermedia** refers to documents composed of text, audio, and visual information stored in a computer and accessed by the user in a nonlinear fashion. "Rather than reading an information space sequentially in a predetermined order, a user of [hypermedia] explores the information space in his or her own order, usually based on his or her interests" (Schwartz and Beichner 1999, 56), with the computer used to "link" related segments of information into larger "webs" or networks. A hypermedia system is an effective learning tool because it allows students to actively construct their own learning experiences based on their interests, preferences, and learning styles.

Computer Simulations For students, computer simulations can be engaging and very motivational. Simulations model complex, multidimensional events in the real world and can range from the lemonade stand that elementary school students plan and run vicariously, practicing basic arithmetic and problem-solving skills, to a mock trial, which Harvard Law students can participate in via videodisc and computer. As learners work their way through a simulation, they make decisions at critical points, enter their decisions into the computer, and then receive feedback on the consequences of those decisions.

Currently available **computer-based simulations** provide students with contextually rich learning experiences, from visiting the great museums of the world, to exploring the bottom of the Pacific Ocean, to experiencing what it was like to be a pioneer setting out in a wagon train from St. Louis to the coast of Oregon. Figure 11.3, for example, shows a household water use simulator from *Exploring the Nardoo,* a CD-ROM program that focuses on a range of water management investigations related to the Nardoo, an imaginary river in Australia. The Nardoo program, developed by the Interactive Multimedia Learning Laboratory at the University of Wollongong in Australia, requires students to solve problems, measure, synthesize data, and communicate findings as they "conduct" research at the Water Research Centre. After students enter the number of baths, showers, toilet flushes, dish washings, car washes, and so on a hypothetical family uses per day, the simulator calculates the family's water usage and compares it with national averages. Students then implement various water-saving strategies throughout the household and rerun the simulation to determine the amount of water saved.

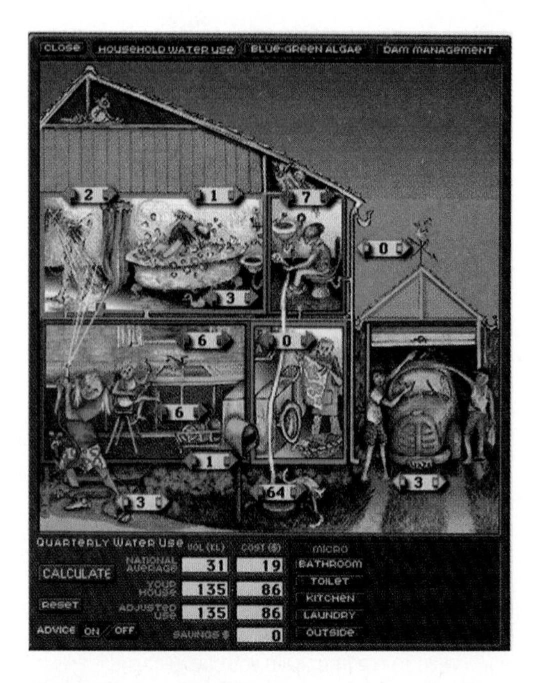

Figure 11.3 Household water use simulator from *Exploring the Nardoo*

Source: Interactive Multimedia Learning Laboratory, Faculty of Education, University of Wollongong, Wollongong, New South Wales, Australia. Used with permission.

Home–School Communication Systems Computer-based home–school communication systems such as the Phone Master Notification System are helping busy teachers and parents exchange information. By interfacing a computer program with its computer-based student records, Georgetown Middle School in Georgetown, Kentucky, enables teachers to use a "Talking Gradebook" to communicate students' progress to parents. Or, by using a touchtone phone and entering a teacher's room number, Georgetown students and parents can access homework assignments, test scores, and current grades. Increasingly, schools are using sophisticated **home–school communication systems** to strengthen their educational programs. Some communication systems even include a "tip line" that uses voice disguising to provide students with an anonymous, safe way to provide tips to help reduce school violence. Schools are also using home–school communication systems to disseminate the following kinds of information:

absence and tardy parent notification

bus schedules

club information

congratulatory calls

invitations to school events

lunch menus

PTA/PTO information

reminders to vote on bond issues

school cancellations, early dismissals

teacher reminders for assignments/activities

The Internet

Observers estimate that the amount of information in the world doubles every nine hundred days (Bitter and Pierson 2002); the Internet, consisting of thousands of interconnected computers around the globe, and the **World Wide Web** (the most popular "entrance" to the Internet) make available to teachers and

Keepers of *the Dream*

Kristi Rennebohm Franz, Technology and Multicultural Educator

First-graders in Kristi Rennebohm Franz's class in Sunnyside Elementary School, Pullman, Washington, think that using the Internet to exchange drawings with children around the world and taking daily Spanish lessons from a teacher in Argentina are just part of going to school. The students also took in stride talking to their teacher while she attended an international conference in Budapest and participating in an hour-long live videoconference with twelve teachers from other countries. "Their communication skills are innate at that young age," Franz explains. "It's so natural for them to want to communicate with people, and technology becomes a natural way to do it."

"... learning with the children."

What moved Franz most, as she watched from Budapest, was seeing her young students in Pullman form a huddle to figure out how to talk with one of the conference teachers who spoke only Spanish. After sharing their bits of knowledge, they said several sentences in Spanish to her. Franz was also pleased to have students discover that people in other countries were interested in learning about them, noting that "multicultural education tends to focus only on learning about *other* people and places."

As an educator and life-long learner, Franz has developed a rich array of skills and talents, which serve her well as she designs motivating future-oriented curricula that tap students' varied learning modalities. In college she studied speech therapy and on graduation became a speech therapist in the public schools in Champaign, Illinois. She later earned a degree in music therapy so she could "use speech and music therapy together to help students with special needs." When she moved to Washington state with her husband, a university professor, she taught cello lessons and chamber music and played in the Washington Symphony. Traveling with her husband for a sabbatical in Nairobi, Kenya, she taught kindergarten at an international school.

Her rich storehouse of experiences contributes to Franz's forward-looking perspective. The title of the project that Franz shared at the 1996 International Education and Resource Network conference in Budapest was "Reweaving the Global Tapestry of Education for Today's Students: Multicultural Education." Franz and her Internet colleague, Jane McLane Kimball, collaborated with teachers in twelve schools around the world, "on every continent except Antarctica," to exchange their young students' drawings of their families along with brief texts written by the children in their native languages explaining what they had drawn. Franz observes that including the brief texts, locally translated, helped the students "comprehend the multilingual aspect of our planet." The children then e-mailed their reactions to each others' drawings and discussed how families are different and alike in different countries. Franz's project was published as an article entitled "Toward a Critical Social Consciousness in Children: Multicultural Peace Education in a First Grade Classroom" in the journal *Theory into Practice* (1996, 264–70).

To teachers who want to begin using educational technology in their classrooms, Franz advises: "Choose what you feel are important curricular concepts and start by looking for ways software and telecommunications can enhance your teaching and learning with the children." She suggests that teachers find two or three recommended websites to explore in depth, well enough to integrate them into their curriculum. "Partnering up with another school to develop a social context for learning" is the next step. Franz's students exchange e-mail daily with another class across their state, sometimes sending a letter with each line contributed by a different child. Her class has also built its own website.

Franz began using computers and telecommunication technology with her students when she realized that it was "a way to enhance their learning about the world." She learned along with the children, discovering a unique form of student–teacher collaborative learning–a process that "is making major changes in how we do our teaching and learning." Franz believes strongly in global awareness, multiculturalism, environmental education, and teaching to all learning modalities, as well as educational technology and telecommunications. As a Visiting Scholar at Harvard University's Graduate School of Education from January through August 1997, Franz assisted in the development of a summer institute on technology for teachers to help prepare students for the global future.

Table 11.1 Growth of the Internet and the World Wide Web (WWW)

	1995	1996	1997	1998	1999	2002
Number of people online (worldwide)*	26,000,000	55,000,000	101,000,000	150,000,000	179,000,000	580,780,000
Number of WWW sites (worldwide)	23,500	299,403	1,681,868	3,689,227	4,389,131	38,000,000
Number of hosts (computers connected to Internet worldwide)	6,642,000	12,881,000	19,540,000	36,739,000	43,230,000	162,128,000

*Figures include both adults and children.
Note: Numbers are estimates.

Source: Data compiled from Nua Ltd., Internet Surveys, 2002; Internet Software Consortium (ISC), 2002; and Robert H. Zakon, Hobbes' Internet Timeline, 2002.

students much of this information. As Table 11.1 shows, the size of the World Wide Web has increased exponentially since 1995. In addition, newsgroups and chat rooms on the Internet enable teachers and students to communicate with people around the world.

Newsgroups Through **newsgroups,** students can create electronic bulletin boards of their own and discuss topics of mutual interest with students at other schools, in the same community, or around the world. Messages are "posted" on the bulletin board for others to read at their convenience. When students "surf" into a newsgroup, they will find messages arranged by subject and author, with responses listed beneath the original message.

Chat Rooms Students can also participate in "live" discussions held in a **chat room.** Chat rooms use Internet Relay Chat (IRC) technology and allow users to participate in live, online, typed discussions. In some chat rooms, students can talk to online experts in a wide array of fields and receive immediate responses to their questions.

KIDLINK, a well-known chat room for children ages ten to fifteen, is carefully monitored and open only to registered users. The goal of KIDLINK is to promote global dialogue among young people, and students must answer four questions when they register: (1) "Who am I?" (2) "What do I want to be when I grow up?" (3) "How do I want the world to be better when I grow up?" and (4) "What can I do now to make this happen?" Teacher-leaders of KIDLINK organize and monitor numerous projects; for example, the "Draw a Story for Me" project for kindergarten and first-grade students around the world has the following objectives.

Students will:

1. Communicate with other kids by means of artwork
2. Learn some easy English words and sentences
3. Learn some computer skills
    - Drawing with a graphic software
    - Using a scanner to import their drawings in the computer
    - Uploading their pictures in KidSpace
    - Sending their pictures as attachments by e-mail to the project moderator

4. Learn some habits and customs of other people
5. Enjoy new friends all over the world (KIDLINK 2002)

Videoconferencing Video conferences can be held over the Internet if users have video cameras connected to their computers and C-U SeeMe, PictureTel, or similar software installed. As with any educational technology, care must be taken that **videoconferencing** is more than a "high tech" way for teachers to lecture to passive students at other locations. "Videoconferencing best supports meaningful learning by helping diverse learners to collaborate and converse with each other in order to solve problems and construct meaning" (Jonassen, Peck, and Wilson 1999, 82).

How Do Teachers Use Computers and the Internet?

As the preceding section illustrates, a dazzling array of technologies is available for teachers to use in the classroom. However, the availability and use of these tools for teaching and learning are two different matters. To what extent and how are teachers actually using new technologies? How useful do they find them? To answer these questions, the U.S. Department of Education sponsored the Teaching, Learning, and Computing (TLC) survey which gathered data from three groups: (1) a nationally representative sample of approximately 2,250 fourth- through twelfth-grade teachers at public and private schools throughout the country, (2) 1,800 teachers at "high-end" technology schools and schools participating in national or regional educational reform programs, and (3) 1,700 principals and school-level technology coordinators (Anderson and Ronnkvist 1999; Becker 1999, 2001; Ravitz, Wong, and Becker 1999).

Preparing Lessons

The Internet has been termed "the world's largest library," and, as such, it can be a remarkable resource for planning lessons. According to the TLC survey, 28 percent of teachers use the Internet weekly or more often to gather information and resources on the Internet for their teaching, and 40 percent do so occasionally. Among teachers who have access to the Internet at school as well as at home, 46 percent report weekly or more frequent use. In Washington state's Kent School District, for instance, teachers learn to use the district's Staff Toolbox website (see Figure 11.4) where they share lesson plans and gather information on students' progress in other classes. Kent teachers also use the Toolbox to complete previously onerous paperwork online and to sign up for in-service training.

Communicating with Other Educators

Compared to their use of the Internet to prepare lessons and gather resources, teachers use the Internet less often to communicate with other educators, according to the TLC survey. Only 16 percent of teachers used e-mail to communicate with teachers in other schools, and 23 percent did so occasionally. However, "by far the most important variable in predicting teachers' Internet use is the teacher's level of classroom connectivity" (Becker 1999, 29). For example, a comparison of e-mail use between teachers who had Internet access at home and at school with teachers who had access only at home revealed that teachers with classroom access were *three times as likely* to e-mail teachers at other schools. Not surprisingly, if teachers don't have ready access to the Internet during their daily professional lives, their use of e-mail is less frequent.

Staff Toolbox

Communication Tools

- Outlook Web Access Check your e-mail and calendar online
  - Outlook Web Access Tutorial
- Groupwise is no longer available

Information Sources

- Staff Directory - phone, building, and e-mail search form
- Calendar - district and school activities
- EduPortal - district policies and procedures plus state and federal resources [password required - call Customer Support Center at x7030]
- Employee Newsletter - staff news and information
- Community Connections - newsletter, events, and cultural information
- Human Resources - applications, benefits, and human resources information
- Risk Management - workers' comp and safety program
- School Web Pages - view school maps, information and Web pages
- Staff Web Pages - directory of staff members' Web sites
- Technology - district technology resources and information
- Athletics and Activities - sports schedules and information
- Kent School District Library - search for school or district materials
- King County Library - catalog and other information online
- News Sources - ProQuest & other magazines, newspapers, radio & television
- Room to Learn - Moving Forward - Follow the progress on KSD's secondary school reconfiguration

Interactive Tools

- Staff Development - sign up online for classes, view transcripts and more
- Student Information - Star Gazer, online IEPs, attendance and grading
- Lunch Menu - order a sub sandwich or view the menu
- Mileage Manager - track your KSD mileage and print out a report
- InformAGENT - sign up for automatic e-mail from KSD sources
- Medicaid Administrative Match - Forms and assistance for Medicaid Match
- Warehouse Support Services Order Form - order tables, chairs, equipment, supplies, basically anything that needs to be moved from one location to another
- Debit Card - Review your Debit Card transactions

Classroom Tools

- Curriculum Resources - lesson plans and resources for teachers

District References

- Kent School District Policies - school board policies
- Kent School District Student Learning Objectives (SLOs)
- Copyright Information - copyright guidelines for educators

State and Community Resources

- Washington State Essential Learnings (EALRs)
- Office of the Superintendent of Public Instruction - OSPI in Olympia
- Emergency Information - school closure information
- Qwest Dex Directory

Site Search: [ ] Go
Advanced Search Search Tips

Figure 11.4 Staff Toolbox, Kent School District

Source: Kent School District, Kent, Washington. Copyright © 1995–2002 by the Kent School District. Used with permission.

Although efforts to integrate technology into schools require information about the extent of teachers' access to and use of the Internet, it is important to ask whether teachers believe the Internet is a valuable tool for teaching. In response to this question, TLC survey data revealed that 49 percent of teachers believe that having a computer with e-mail capabilities on their own desk is "essential," and, similarly, 47 percent believe having web access in the classroom is "essential." In addition, another 38 percent believe e-mail access is "valuable," and 41 percent believe web access is "valuable." These results seem to counter the observation that "a lot of teachers say, '[Technology] is one more thing on my plate and I don't know how it will help me' " (Ortiz 1999).

Posting Information and Student Work on the Web

In addition to using e-mail to communicate with other educators, 18 percent of teachers posted information, professional opinions, or student work at least once on the Web. For instance, as with the use of e-mail, the likelihood of teachers posting information, opinions, or student work was strongly related to connectivity in the classroom. As classroom access to the Internet continues to increase, teachers' use of the Internet to communicate with other educators and to post material will also increase. Many school districts have taken steps to increase teacher professional communications via the Internet. As part of a "Reinventing Education" grant program, teachers in the San Jose Unified School District keep journals of their progress at integrating technology into instruction, and they share these with other teachers online. To ensure that teachers use their training in technology, the principal of Philadelphia's Hill-Freedman Middle School accepts lesson plans only by e-mail and posts daily announcements exclusively on the Internet (CEO Forum on Education and Technology 1999).

Facilitating Students' Learning Via Computers and Cyberspace

In previous sections of this chapter, we have seen several examples of how teachers are using computers and the Internet to enhance students' learning. Figure 11.5, based on TLC survey data, documents the extent of this usage among teachers whose students typically use a computer more than twenty times during a school year. After word processing, the use of CD-ROM references, and games to build skills, using a WWW browser is the most common teacher-directed use of computers by students. As with teachers' use of the Internet, student use is directly related to classroom connectivity; among teachers with modems in the classroom, almost half had students use web search engines on at least three occasions. Moreover, teachers whose classrooms had direct high-speed connections instead of modem connections were 25 percent more likely to have students search the Web ten or more times.

Few teachers have students use the Internet to communicate with others, to collaborate on projects with classes at other schools, and to publish on the Web. The TLC survey revealed that about 5 percent of teachers have students involved

Figure 11.5 Software use by frequent computer-using teachers
Source: Adapted from Henry Jay Becker, *How Are Teachers Using Computers in Education?* Paper presented at the Annual Meeting of the American Educational Research Association, Seattle, April 2001, pp. 4, 12.

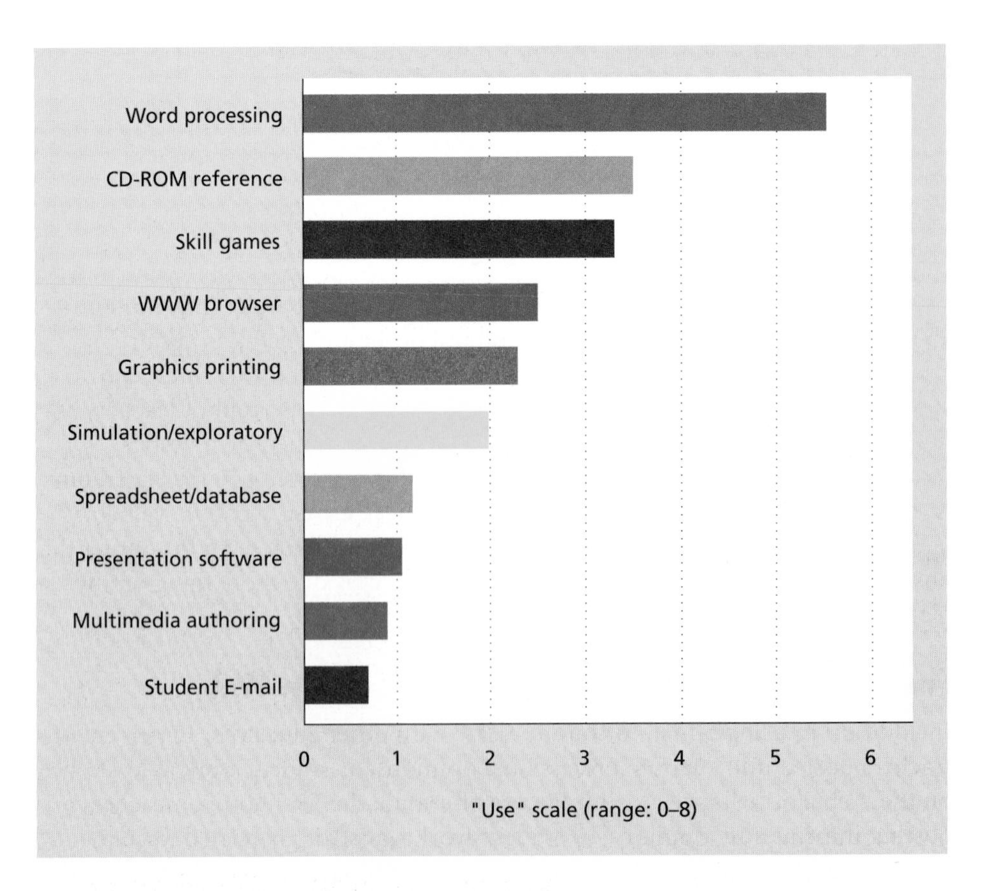

*Use is defined as teachers reporting that a typical student in one of their classes used computers more than 20 times during the school year. Percentage of teachers (by subject taught) who report "frequent computer use": computer, 80%; business, 70%; elementary self-contained, 43%; vocational 42%; English, 24%; science, 17%; social studies, 12%; math, 11%; fine arts, 9%.

in beyond-the-classroom projects and web publishing (Ravitz, Wong, and Becker 1999). One example of a collaborative web-based project is ThinkQuest at Lakeland High School in New York state. As their winning entry for a college scholarship contest, Lakeland students and a faculty sponsor developed a website to help others learn. Though she thought a computer teacher should oversee the project, the music teacher and band director who reluctantly agreed to be faculty sponsor found the project professionally energizing:

> *At first I just wanted to give the team feedback. Then the kids' excitement and motivation got to me—they were doing extraordinary academic work and loving it. I discovered a whole new way to research, learn, and use technology. The kids taught me so much and as they did, they grew intellectually and socially. This has truly been one of the most rewarding and authentic professional development experiences of my career (CEO Forum on Education and Technology 1999).*

What Are the Effects of Computer Technology on Learning?

The use of computers and other technologies in schools has grown enormously since the early 1980s, and, as a director of the North Central Regional Education Laboratory noted, "For policymakers, the honeymoon for technology is over. They are starting to say, 'Show us the results' " (Williams 1999). Regarding the effects of technology on learning, research results are just now beginning to appear.

Apple Classrooms of Tomorrow Project (ACOT)

One of the most informative research studies is based on the Apple Classrooms of Tomorrow (ACOT) project launched in seven K–12 classrooms in 1986. Participating students and teachers each received two computers—one for school and one for home. Eight years later, study results indicated that all ACOT students performed as well as they were expected without computers, and some performed better. More important, perhaps, "the ACOT students routinely and without prompting employed inquiry, collaboration, and technological and problem-solving skills" (Mehlinger 1996, 405). Also, 90 percent of ACOT students went on to college after graduating from high school, while only 15 percent of non-ACOT students did. Furthermore, the behavior of ACOT teachers also changed—they worked "more as mentors and less as presenters of information" (Mehlinger 1996, 404).

An additional positive finding of the ACOT study was how teachers gradually began to use the computers in new ways in the classroom. "When [ACOT] teachers were able to move past that pervasive teacher-centered view of education, students and teachers, as communities of learners, were able to benefit from the range of individual areas of expertise represented by the entire group" (Bitter and Pierson 1999, 43). Teachers rearranged their classrooms to enable students to work collaboratively on projects, and they frequently made arrangements for students who wished to stay after school to work on multimedia projects. Frequently, "students and teachers collaborated together, with the students often in the role of expert or resource person" (Schwartz and Beichner 1999, 33–34).

Integrating Technology Teacher participants in the ACOT study were volunteers, many of whom had little experience with educational technology. As with teachers learning any new instructional strategy, the ACOT teachers frequently struggled to adjust to their new computer-filled rooms. Researchers found that the

On the Frontlines

Motivating Unmotivated Students

Your second year of teaching you're given a sixth-grade class that includes four boys known as troublemakers and poorly motivated students. Poorly motivated academically, that is. You quickly discover they are highly motivated and gifted athletically and that the parents of all four demanded that their sons be held back when they were in fourth grade. "They wanted their boys to be bigger and better-developed when they got to high school and tried out for the football team," a colleague told you. "It's a common practice in this community," he adds.

Recess is the height of their school day. They play kickball with such intensity that their tempers flash. Arguments about the rules and cheating spill over into their afternoon classes. Their math lesson and activities are incidental to their thoughts about the game and ongoing whispered disagreement about the rules, the argument being a new competition for them.

You discover also that they really are behind in their skills, especially in reading and language arts. Their homework and class assignments in all subjects are done in a perfunctory way, as tasks to get behind them or avoid altogether.

You worry about what you can do to motivate the four to improve.

Turning poorly motivated students around in elementary and middle school is easier than in high school and vitally important. For a boat out at sea, the position of the rudder governs the course ahead, and if the direction is a poor one, it will end up far off course. Welcome winds and hampering storms may have their impact, but the course set by the rudder's original angle is likely to prevail. Like the boat, if unmotivated students don't get turned around early and headed in the right direction, the course ahead may be rough. At some point they'll become aware of and embarrassed by their poor academic skills and grades. Even worse, they may begin to expect nothing better from themselves. School will become less and less comfortable for them, and the dreams they have for being on a college football team and having "the good life" are likely to remain just that, dreams. In the worst case, they will seek escape by dropping out of school or getting into trouble. These ideas may seem farfetched for the sixth-grade athletes, but consider a high school dropout and back him or her up in time to see if his or her life direction could have been changed by a teacher. While the effort isn't always successful, no matter how hard a teacher tries, the possibility should encourage teachers to make it a mission to motivate the academically unmotivated.

How can teachers help motivate students? Four helpful suggestions and insights emerge in the current research on motivation and successful students: (1) child-centered teaching and high expectations for all promote learning (Scribner and Scribner 2001); (2) students' perceptions of themselves as learners impact their learning (Bempechat 1999); (3) students working in noncompetitive, cooperative groups worry less about "how smart they are relative to others and focus on learning for its own sake" (Bempechat 1999,); and (4) "service learning is a powerful instructional strategy that can engage students and produce significant academic and social growth" (Carter 2002).

Teachers can also learn how to teach well and develop motivating curriculum from experience-wise colleagues, the teachers who motivated them, and from gifted teachers' accounts written in books—classic and new—such as *Teacher,* by Sylvia Ashton-Warner; *Sometimes a Shining Moment,* by Eliot Wigginton; *The Courage to Teach,* by Parker J. Palmer; and *The Freedom Writers Diary: How a Teacher and 150 Teens Used Writing to Change Themselves and the World Around Them,* by the Freedom Writers and Ziata Filipovic. Most important, the strategies for motivating disengaged students likely lie within novice teachers, themselves, and their beliefs in their students.

Exploratory Questions

1. What are some possible service learning activities for students in the age group you might teach?
2. Bempechat reports that children's self-perceptions as learners impact their success or failure to learn. What do you suppose she means by this? Investigate the concept of "self-fulfilling prophecy" and relate it to Bempechat's thoughts.
3. Go online (e.g., Amazon.com, BarnesandNoble.com) to read a brief description of the books recommended above. Which most reflects a style of motivating students that would suit you?

Your Survival Guide of Helpful Resources

The following resources provide helpful hints for surviving "on the frontlines."

Books and Articles

Ashton-Warner, S. (1986). *Teacher.* New York: Simon & Schuster.

Bempechat, J. (1999, May/June). Learning from poor and minority students who succeed in school. *Harvard Education Letter,* pp. 1–3.

Carter, G. R. (2002). "The power and promise of service learning." Association for Supervision and Curriculum Development Series: Is it good for the kids? Retrieved from http://www.ascd.org/educationnews/kids/kids072002.html

Freedom Writers and Filipovic, Z. (1999). *The freedom writers diary: How a teacher and 150 teens used writing to change themselves and the world around them.* New York: Doubleday.

Palmer, P. J. (1998). *The Courage to teach.* San Francisco: Jossey-Bass.

Scribner, A. P., and Scribner, J. D. (2001). High-performing schools serving Mexican American students: What they can teach us (ERIC Digest: ED459048). Retrieved from http://www.ed.gov/databases/ERIC_Digests/ed459048.html

Wigginton, E. (1986). *Sometimes a shining moment: A foxfire experience.* New York: Doubleday.

Websites

National Service-Learning Partnership (http://www.service-learningpartnership.org)

teachers progressed through five distinct stages as they integrated the technology into their teaching (Sandholtz, Ringstaff, and Dwyer 1997).

1. *Entry stage*—For many teachers, this was a period of painful growth and discomfort; learning to use computers presented challenges similar to those faced by beginning teachers.
2. *Adoption stage*—Becoming more proactive toward the challenge of integrating computers, teachers began to teach students how to use the computers and software.
3. *Adaptation stage*—Teachers turned from teaching the technology to using the technology as a tool to teach content.
4. *Appropriation stage*—Teachers moved from merely accommodating computers in their daily routines to personally exploring new teaching possibilities afforded by the technology.
5. *Invention stage*—Eager to move beyond teacher-centered instruction, teachers began to collaborate with peers in developing authentic, inquiry-oriented learning activities.

As informative as the ACOT study has been, it is important to remember that the project was funded by a computer manufacturer; thus, the outcomes might have been influenced by commercial bias and/or the expectation that computers *could not* have had anything other than a significant positive influence on teaching and learning. In fact, Schwartz and Beichner (1999, 34) suggest that the ACOT project "epitomizes what might be termed the 'Emperor's New Clothes' perspective on technology in education. [To] take the ACOT reports at face value would be to accept the notion that technology is the panacea that education has been searching for for ages."

Findings from Other Research Studies

A powerful way to determine whether certain educational practices actually influence students' learning is to conduct *meta-analyses,* that is, to "take the findings from single studies and calculate a way to compare them with each other. The goal is to synthesize the findings statistically and determine what the studies reveal when examined all together" (Kirkpatrick and Cuban 1998). One such meta-analysis reviewed the results of 133 research studies on educational technology from 1990 through 1994. The results of that study follow:

- Educational technology has a significant positive impact on achievement in all subject areas, across all levels of school, and in regular classrooms as well as those for special-needs students.
- Educational technology has positive effects on student attitudes.
- The degree of effectiveness is influenced by the student population, the instructional design, the teacher's role, how students are grouped, and the levels of student access to technology.
- Technology makes instruction more student-centered, encourages cooperative learning, and stimulates increased teacher–student interaction.
- Positive changes in the learning environment evolve over time and do not occur quickly (Mehlinger 1996, 405).

Another meta-analysis conducted by Heather Kirkpatrick and Larry Cuban (1998) at Stanford University also addressed the complications and difficulties involved in determining the effects of computers on learning, particularly when much of the research in that area is methodologically flawed. Research studies, they pointed out, "are of little use unless they elaborate the children's ages, the subject, the software used, the kinds of outcomes that were sought, and how the study was done." With these limitations in mind, the following is a brief summary of Kirkpatrick and Cuban's findings:

1. Seven of the single studies of elementary and secondary students yielded positive findings related to achievement and attitude change, while seven studies yielded negative or mixed findings.
2. Ten of the single studies on the effectiveness of computers to teach in core areas such as mathematics, reading, science, and social studies yielded results ranging from very positive to "cautiously negative."
3. Ten meta-analyses found higher levels of student achievement in computer-using classrooms.
4. Five meta-analyses found that student attitudes improved and students learned more in less time in computer-using classrooms.

On the basis of their meta-analysis of the research, much of it considered methodologically flawed due to a lack of scientific controls, Kirkpatrick and Cuban conclude that "we are unable to ascertain whether computers in classrooms have in fact been or will be the boon they have promised to be."

The ambiguities of research on computer-based instruction aside, it is clear that educational technology *can* have positive effects on learning and teaching, and indications are that technology will influence all aspects of education even more in the twenty-first century. Thus the question to be asked about the effectiveness of educational technology is not, "Is it effective?" Instead, the question should be, "How and under what circumstances does educational technology enhance students' learning?" As more funds are made available to purchase hardware and software, train teachers, and provide technical support, the benefits of classroom media magic will become even more widespread.

Should Technology Be at the Forefront of Efforts to Improve Schools in the United States?

Where Do You Stand? Visit the Companion Website to Voice Your Opinion.

Daily, the mass media feature stories on schools and classrooms that have been transformed through the use of computer-based modes of teaching and learning. Additional reports appear regularly describing the development of new technologies that hold further promise for the improvement of education in the United States. The advantages outlined in these reports include:

- Systematic, well-structured, and consistent lessons
- The ability of students to pace their learning
- The ability of teachers to accommodate their students' varied learning styles and preferred paces of learning
- Opportunities for students in rural and remote areas to interact with students and teachers in diversely populated urban and suburban areas
- Increased record-keeping efficiency, which allows teachers to spend more time with students
- Immediate feedback and reinforcement for students

- Improved student engagement and motivation that result from learning materials with color, music, video, and animated graphics
- More effective assessment of students' learning
- Cost effectiveness
- The acquisition of computer literacy skills needed for the twenty-first century workplace

For several years, some people have been questioning the role of technology in improving schools in the United States. An *Atlantic Monthly* cover story titled "The Computer Delusion" even suggested that spending money on computers in the classroom was a form of "malpractice" (Oppenheimer 1997). Some critics, like Stanford professor Larry Cuban, believe it is misguided to assume that teaching will benefit from the use of computers, as have other forms of work:

> *The essence of teaching is a knowledgeable, caring adult building a relationship with one or more students to help them learn what the teacher, community, and parents believe to be important. It is an intertwining of emotional and intellectual bonds that gives a tone and texture to teaching and learning unlike what occurs in other work environments. The lure of higher productivity in teaching and learning via computer technologies, however, has seduced reformers to treat teaching like other forms of labor that gained productivity after automation (Cuban 1999a).*

Elsewhere, Cuban (1999b) suggests several seldom-considered factors that might account for why the increase in available educational technologies is not reflected in more effective use of technology in the classroom:

- *Contradictory advice from experts*—During the last two decades, Cuban points out, teachers have been presented with an "ever-shifting menu of ad-

These students receive immediate feedback and reinforcement, are more engaged and motivated, and are acquiring important twenty-first century workplace skills by using computers at school. Should computers and other technology be at the forefront of efforts to improve schools?

vice" about what computer skills to teach students, ranging from how to program computers in the 1980s to how to do hypertext programming or HTML in the 1990s.

- *Intractable working conditions*—While technology has transformed most workplaces, conditions of teaching have changed little. As "people for whom rollerblades would be in order to meet the day's obligations," Cuban says, teachers are hard pressed to find time and energy to integrate new technologies into their teaching.
- *The inherent unreliability of the technology*—Software malfunctions, servers that crash, and the continual need for computers with more memory and speed are among the problems Cuban notes.
- *Policymakers' disrespect for teachers' opinions*—Teachers are seldom consulted about which machines and software are most appropriate and reliable for their teaching.

Other critics, like *Chicago Tribune* columnist Bob Greene, are clear about the place of computers in the classroom: "The key to helping the next generation of American children be bright, literate, intellectually self-sufficient, steeped in the most important areas of knowledge? It all comes down to computers in the classroom. Get rid of them" (Greene 1999). Critics like Greene believe that computers can have a dampening effect on the intellectual development of children, not unlike television, and should not be used extensively in the classroom until the high school level. As Greene puts it: "We are not doing [children] any favors by plopping them in front of yet another set of screens and programming them to tap and stare away."

Lastly, many critics are concerned about what they view as tremendous pressure, much of it coming from technology-oriented corporations, for schools to "go online." As the daily fabric of our lives becomes increasingly shaped by sophisticated technologies and as a disconcerting number of politicians, business leaders, parents, and others continue to proclaim loudly that the United States is falling behind many other countries in educational attainment, technology is mistakenly touted as the "magic bullet," the panacea to turn the schools around.

Are schools falling prey to a tremendous computer-oriented "hype" encouraged by technology corporations, big business, and ambitious superintendents who want their districts to be ahead in the race for the latest technology, and politicians promoting the latest "quick fix" for education? What will be the consequences for the many schools that have cut art, music, and physical education classes to purchase computers? Will computer technology help the United States develop the kind of students and citizens the nation needs? Is there a "fit" between the undeniable power of computers and the educational goals we seek? Are there more cost-effective ways to achieve these educational goals? These are among the difficult questions that are being addressed as the role of technology in educational reform is being debated.

The Opposition: Computers *Will Not* Improve Education

Among the first to question the role of technology in the classroom was Clifford Stoll, one of the pioneers of the Internet. In *Silicon Snake Oil: Second Thoughts on the Information Highway* (1996, 127), Stoll points out that "our schools face serious problems, including overcrowded classrooms, teacher incompetence, and lack of security. Local education budgets hardly cover salaries, books, and paper. Computers address none of these problems. They're expensive, quickly become obsolete, and drain scarce capital budgets. Yet school administrators want them desperately." Similarly, David Shenk concludes his book, *Data Smog: Surviving the Information Glut* (1998, 220), with eight "Principles of Technorealism" endorsed by several of the nation's leading experts on technology; principle No. 5 states:

> **Wiring the schools will not save them.**
>
> The problems with America's public schools—disparate funding, social promotion, bloated class size, crumbling infrastructure, lack of standards—have almost nothing to do with technology. Consequently, no amount of technology will lead to the educational revolution prophesized by President Clinton and others. The art of teaching cannot be replicated by computers, the Net, or by "distance learning." These tools can, of course, augment an already high quality educational experience. But to rely on them as any sort of panacea would be a costly mistake.

Similarly, others critics have cautioned the public against pushing schools into the computer revolution. A sampling of their comments follow:

> Penetration of the education market with computer-based technology has depended more on effective conditioning of the market through a barrage of advertising and ideology than on the effectiveness of the technologies themselves (Noble 1996, 20).

> "Optimistic" is probably the kindest word to describe the current status of educational computing in the United States. The good examples [aren't] always easy to find and [are] far outnumbered by the bad ones (Healy 1998, 78).

> I do not go as far back as the radio and Victrola, but I am old enough to remember when 16-millimeter film was to be the sure-cure. Then closed-circuit television. Then 8-millimeter film. Then teacher-proof textbooks. Now computers. I know a false god when I see one (Postman 1995).

Perhaps the strongest argument that computers will not improve education is the fact that computers can distract educators from what should be their focus—students, their learning, and their lives. Computers can depersonalize education, distancing students from each other and from their teachers. Computers are not sensitive to students' needs, nor do they notice when a student's work habits, communication, demeanor, grooming, or dress change abruptly, signaling trouble. Computers don't know when a student is discouraged, sad, lonely, fearful, or "stuck" in his or her learning. Also, computers are poor substitutes for true companions—they do not laugh, commiserate, or share warmly with their users. Clearly, they cannot provide the human dimension that is needed so greatly in today's schools.

The Advocates: Computers *Will* Improve Education

Despite media stories and articles critical of the call for more computers in schools, enthusiasm for technology in schools remains strong. For example, in an MCI nationwide poll in 1998, almost 60 percent of the public answered "a great amount" when asked, "How much do you think computers have helped improve student learning?" (Trotter 1998, 6). Following are a few representative comments that rebut arguments against computers in the schools.

> *It has become fashionable to say that computers in education are a bust. [However,] the new media can positively change the role of the teacher and student, shifting education from broadcast to interactive learning. When done effectively, [the] results are dramatic (Tapscott 1999).*

> *There are real dangers in looking to technology to be the savior of education. But it won't survive without the technology (Jane David, Apple consultant, quoted in Oppenheimer 1997).*

> *Industrial Age educators will fight Information Age education tooth and nail. [However], in the long run they will probably do no more than slow the implementation of an emerging and vastly improved educational system. Not only is the encroachment of information technology into children's lives inevitable, but it is critical to their future—and ours (Snider 1996).*

As long as educators remember that computers are not an end in themselves but a tool for enhancing the educational experiences of students, computers have great potential to improve education. To avoid using computers, whatever the reason, is to limit learning possibilities. Motion pictures, videos, and television, once viewed as threats to education, have become generally accepted in classrooms. Further development of today's educational technology will do the same.

What Are the Challenges of Integrating Technology into Schools?

Clearly, educational technology *does* have positive effects on learning and teaching, and indications are that technology will influence all aspects of education even more in the future. However, Figure 11.6 illustrates four challenges that must be met so that all students attend "high-end technology schools": (1) providing broadband Internet access for all schools, (2) providing access to technology for all students, (3) obtaining quality educational software, and (4) providing high-quality, continuous training in technology for teachers. To fail to meet these challenges will shortchange students and prevent them from participating fully in the digital age.

Broadband Internet Access for All Schools

Internet access is a vital part of a school's capacity to benefit from the vast resources found in cyberspace. Through the Internet, teachers and students can draw from the world's best libraries, museums, and cultural resources. In

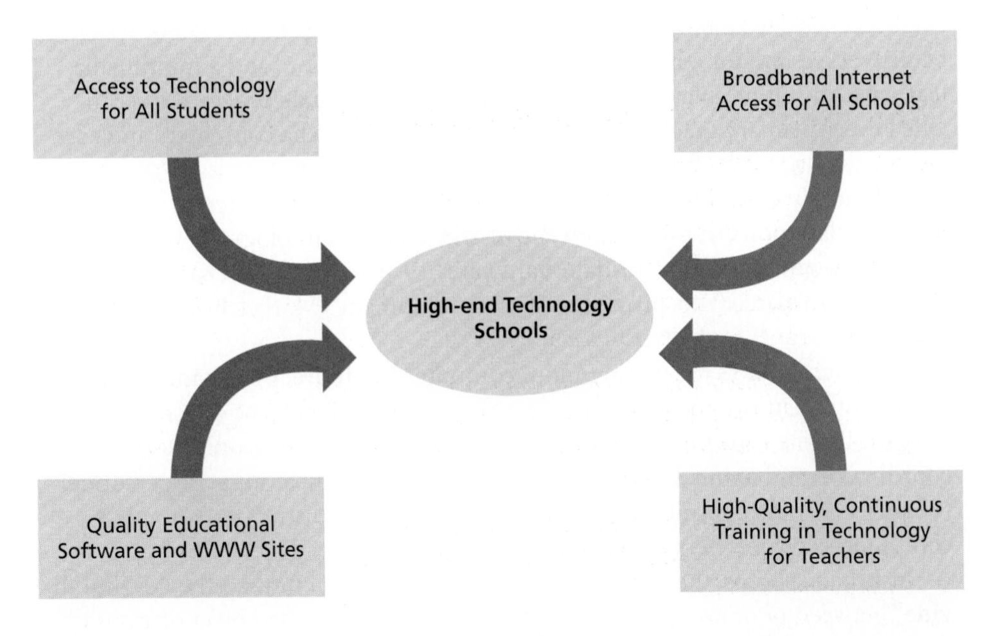

Figure 11.6 Creating "high-end technology schools": four key challenges

1995, President Bill Clinton created the **National Information Infrastructure (NII)** to encourage all schools, libraries, hospitals, and law enforcement agencies to become connected to the "information superhighway." A year later, the Education rate (E-rate) program was established to help schools and libraries connect to the Internet. The **E-rate** program provides schools with Internet access at discounted rates based on the income levels of students' families and whether their location is urban or rural (rural communities receive up to a 10 percent discount). With increased purchasing power from the E-rate program, schools can purchase improved telephone service and greater bandwidth, thus allowing more data to travel across wires for Internet and e-mail use.

The percentage of the nation's public schools with Internet access has risen dramatically since the mid-1990s. Thirty-five percent of public schools had access to the Internet in 1994; by the fall of 2000, 98 percent were connected. In addition, by fall 2000, there were no differences in school access to the Internet by school characteristics such as poverty level or metropolitan status (National Center for Education Statistics 2001).

While schools have made significant progress in their technological capabilities, Table 11.2 shows that about 25 percent of public school classrooms did not have Internet access by 2000. In addition, as the percentage of minority students and/or students eligible for free or reduced-price lunch increases, the percentage of classrooms with Internet access decreases.

The Appendix "The CEO Forum on Education and Technology's STaR Assessment of a School's Effectiveness at Integrating Technology into the Teaching and Learning Process" on this book's website presents an assessment instrument developed by the CEO Forum that yields an approximate measure of a school's access to technology and its effectiveness at integrating technology into the teaching and learning process. The assessment score, ranging from "Low Tech" to "Target Tech," is based on five categories: hardware, connectivity to the Internet, quality of software programs, professional development for teachers, and integration and use of technology.

Funding for Computers and Technical Support To enable schools to participate more fully in the computer revolution, some school districts have passed bond measures to fund educational technology, and a few states have adopted long-term budgets for computers and technical support. In Milwaukee, a comprehensive technology plan called for all 156 buildings in the school system to be networked and for a mini-network, a printer, a television, and a multimedia teacher workstation in every classroom. In Cleveland, a state program has provided every primary grade classroom with three multimedia computers and each teacher with a laptop computer (Harrington-Lueker 1999).

As schools continue to work toward the goal of having Internet access in every classroom, about 66 percent of their total technology spending is devoted to purchasing up-to-date hardware, 19 percent to purchasing software, and 15 percent to providing staff development (Market Data Retrieval 2002).

Although schools are getting more computer hardware, most cannot afford to hire sufficient support staff for technology. About 30 percent of schools employ a full-time coordinator of technology, about 40 percent employ a part-time coordinator, and about 30 percent have no on-site technical support personnel (Furger 1999). As a result, most schools rely on central district personnel or computer-savvy teachers for support.

At urban schools, the ability to narrow what has been termed the **"digital divide"** between poor and more affluent schools is often limited by enormous ob-

Table 11.2 Percent of instructional rooms with Internet access in public schools, by school characteristics: 1994–2000

School Characteristic	Instructional Rooms with Internet Access						
	1994	1995	1996	1997	1998	1999	2000
All public schools	3	8	14	27	51	64	77
Instructional level[1]							
Elementary	3	8	13	24	51	62	76
Secondary	4	8	16	32	52	67	79
School size							
Less than 300	3	9	15	27	54	71	83
300 to 999	3	8	13	28	53	64	78
1,000 or more	3	4	16	25	45	58	70
Metropolitan status							
City	4	6	12	20	47	52	66
Urban fringe	4	8	16	29	50	67	78
Town	3	8	14	34	55	72	87
Rural	3	8	14	30	57	71	85
Percent minority enrollment[2]							
Less than 6 percent	4	9	18	37	57	74	85
6 to 20 percent	4	10	18	35	59	78	83
21 to 49 percent	4	9	12	22	52	64	79
50 percent or more	2	3	5	13	37	43	64
Percent of students eligible for free or reduced-price school lunch[3]							
Less than 35 percent	3	9	17	33	57	73	82
35–49 percent	2	6	12	33	60	69	81
50–74 percent	4	6	11	20	41	61	77
75 percent or more	2	3	5	14	38	38	60

[1]Data for combined schools are included in the totals and in analyses by other school characteristics but are not shown separately.
[2]Percent minority enrollment was not available for some cases. In 1994, this information was missing for 100 schools. In subsequent years, the missing information ranged from 46 schools (1995) to 6 (1997).
[3]The breakouts for the percentage of students eligible for free or reduced-price school lunch have been revised this year and therefore are different from the ones reported in previous Internet access reports.
Note: All of the estimates in this report were recalculated from the raw data files using the same computational algorithms. Consequently, the estimates presented here may differ trivially (i.e., 1 percent) from previously published results.

Source: Taken from National Center for Education Statistics. (May 2001). *Internet Access in U.S. Public Schools and Classrooms: 1994–2000.* Washington, DC: National Center for Education Statistics, p. 4.

stacles, including "limited resources, low expectations, overwhelming poverty, teacher contracts, entrenched bureaucracies, political infighting, and the sheer size of these districts" (Williams 1999). *Barriers and Breakthroughs: Technology in Urban Schools,* a 1999 study by the Education Writers Association, revealed that, while most urban districts have "lighthouse" schools in which sophisticated technologies are fully integrated into the curriculum, they also have schools with woefully limited technologies.

Commercial Computer Labs Confronted with limited budgets to purchase computers, about two thousand public and private schools during the late 1990s accepted "free" computer labs (complete with software, training, and maintenance) from companies such as California-based ZapMe. In exchange, schools agreed that classes would use the labs at least four hours a day and that students would be exposed to onscreen advertisements that ran continuously in a 2″ × 4″ box in a bottom corner of the screen, changing every fifteen seconds. In addition, schools agreed to allow ZapMe and its for-profit partners to use the labs for computer training and related activities.

However, free, commercially oriented computer labs like ZapMe led critics such as Ralph Nader to compare the labs to the controversial Channel One. Eventually, ZapMe bowed to pressure from critics and ceased providing free labs to schools. On the demise of ZapMe, its founder pointed out that school districts and parents were mostly enthusiastic about the labs and stated that "if you're not going to charge more taxes or bond issues, what options do the schools have?" (Tweney 2000).

Access to Technology for All Students

The nation's schools have made significant strides toward reducing the student–computer ratio. In 1999, a survey by Quality Education Data revealed that only 25 percent of K–12 schools could be characterized as "high-end technology schools" with a student–computer ratio of 6:1 or less (Anderson and Ronnkvist 1999). By 2002, however, the average ratio was less than 4:1 per computer used for instruction and less than 6:1 per multimedia computer, according to a survey of 87,100 schools (Market Data Retrieval 2002).

While schools have reduced the number of students per computer, there is evidence of a "digital divide" if computer use at school and at home is compared to family income and minority-group status. In *A Nation Online: How Americans Are Expanding Their Use of the Internet,* the U.S. Department of Commerce (2002) reported that only 33.1 percent of children (ages ten to seventeen) in the lowest income category use computers at home, compared with 91.7 percent of children in the highest income category. However, schools do help equalize the disparity in computer use among children from various income categories; according to *A Nation Online,* 80.7 percent of children in the lowest income category use computers at school, compared with 88.7 percent of children in the highest income category.

What are the potential repercussions for schools that cannot afford to keep investing in technology?

Figure 11.7 shows that Hispanic and African American children—who have lower computer use rates at home—have computer use rates at school that result in their having overall use rates that are comparable to white and Asian American and Pacific Islander children. The overall computer use rate for Hispanic children is 84.4 percent; 88.8 percent for African American children; 94 percent for Asian and Pacific Islander children; and 95.4 percent for white children.

Quality Educational Software and WWW Sites

For students and teachers to benefit from Digital Age technology, high-quality software and WWW sites, not just the latest hardware, must be readily available. Since computers first began to be used extensively in education in the 1980s,

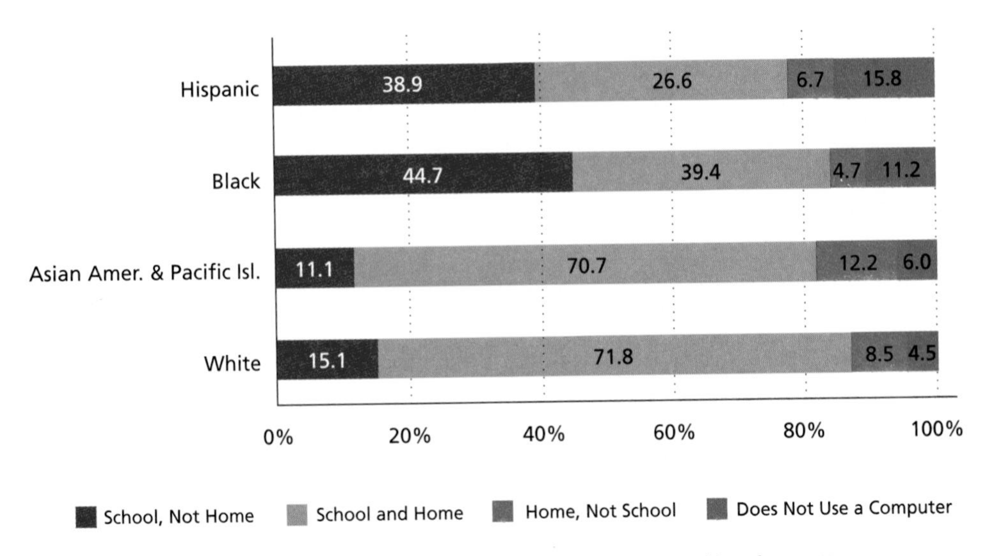

Figure 11.7 Computer use among ten- to seventeen-year-olds by race and location, 2001
Source: NITA and ESA, U.S. Department of Commerce, using U.S. Census Bureau Current Population Survey Supplements. *A Nation Online: How Americans Are Expanding Their Use of the Internet.* February, 2002, p. 48. Washington, D.C.: U.S. Department of Commerce.

inadequacy of software has been a common criticism. By the turn of the century, the situation had not changed much: "Though schools have increased their outlays for software, their choices are few and far between when it comes to superior programs designed specially for classroom use" (Furger 1999). Some programs tend to deemphasize humanistic, holistic, and open-ended fields of knowledge, which are not easily quantified. Others are merely electronic page-turners, known as "drill-and-kill" software, that simply transfer textbooks or workbooks to the computer monitor. As William J. Bennett, the U.S. Secretary of Education who went on to become the chairman of K12, an Internet-based school, and David Gelernter, a Yale professor of computer science and technology advisor for K12, point out:

> *Too often, educational software has promoted glitz, glamour, and graphics instead of serious learning. Too often, the Internet has promoted the "surfing culture" where users click their way across an ocean of information, feeling overwhelmed by the vastness of it all and never dipping below the surface (Bennett and Gelernter 2001).*

These negative appraisals of educational software aside, promising efforts are being made to upgrade the quality of educational software. For example, the International Society for Technology in Education, the largest teacher-based organization devoted to disseminating effective methods for using educational technology and developer of national "Technology Foundation Standards" for preK–12 students, is working with teachers around the country to identify high-quality software to meet their curriculum goals. Steadily, new, more powerful hypermedia learning software programs are appearing that present students with problems to solve that are interesting, multifaceted, and embedded in real-world contexts. For example, the *Astronomy Village: Investigating the Universe,* developed by the National Aeronautics and Space Administration (NASA) and available at a modest cost, promotes ninth and tenth grade students' learning within a virtual observatory community (see Figure 11.8) that includes extensive multimedia resources and sophisticated exploration tools. The *Astronomy Village* requires that teams of three students select one of the following ten investigations, develop a plan, and carry it out.

- *Search for a Supernova*—Uses neutrino data to locate a supernova
- *Looking for a Stellar Nursery*—Views Omega nebula using different wavelengths
- *Variable Stars*—Identifying a Cepheid variable star in another galaxy
- *Search for Nearby Stars*—Movement of stars' positions as Earth circles sun
- *Extragalactic Zoo*—Different galaxies and clusters
- *Wedges of the Universe*—Viewing depths of space in two wedges of sky
- *Search for a "Wobbler"*—Looking for stars that wobble in their motion
- *Search for Planetary Building Blocks*—Examines Orion nebula for proplanetary disks
- *Search for Earth-Crossing Objects*—Looks for asteroids that cross Earth's path
- *Observatory Site Selection*—Selects a site for an observatory (Jonassen, Peck, and Wilson 1999, 94–95)

Included as part of the *Astronomy Village* are a star life-cycle simulator, orbital simulator, and 3D star simulator. In addition, the student teams can use the program's digitized video clips, images from the Hubble space telescope and other instruments, audio clips of astronomers discussing their work, and book chapters, NASA publications, and articles from astronomy journals and magazines. To help you evaluate computer-based instructional materials, Appendix 11.1 presents "Criteria for Evaluating Software Programs," and Appendix 11.2 presents "Criteria for Evaluating World Wide Web Sites."

High Quality, Continuous Training in Technology for Teachers

Using technology to enhance students' learning requires more than investing in the latest hardware, software, and connectivity to the Internet. In the words of *The Technology Literacy Challenge*, "*Upgrading teacher training is key to integrating technology into the classroom and to increasing student learning*" (italics in original). E-mailing students, parents, and peers; conducting classroom demonstrations augmented with multimedia; using presentation graphics to address students' varied learning styles; and designing lessons that require students to use the Internet as a resource for inquiry should be second nature for teachers. Just as new technological skills are needed in the workplace, a high degree of technological literacy is needed in the classroom. Thus acquiring proficiency in the ever-evolving array of technologies should be an important part of professional development for new and veteran teachers. However, teachers frequently complain of a lack of training in how to use technology to reach their curriculum goals. Only 20 percent of teachers believe they are well prepared to integrate educational technology into the curriculum, and among the teachers who seek training in technology, 50 percent pay for their training with their own money (CEO Forum

Figure 11.8 The Astronomy Village: Investigating the Universe
Source: NASA Classroom of the Future, National Aeronautics and Space Administration (NASA) and Wheeling Jesuit University, Wheeling, WV. Copyright 1999 by Wheeling Jesuit University/NASA Classroom of the Future. All Rights Reserved.

on Education and Technology 1999). On average, only 9 percent of a school district's technology budget is spent on teacher training, less than one-third of the U.S. Department of Education's recommendations (Furger 1999).

Although survey data indicate that about half of teachers have participated in technology-related staff development, those training sessions often tend to emphasize the basics of computer use rather than how to integrate technology with instruction in their subject matter (Ravitz, Wong, and Becker 1999). Moreover, 38 percent of teachers reported that at least once a month they needed help integrating computers into their lessons, but only 15 percent reported that they "always" get that help and only 12 percent more say such help is "mostly" available. In the absence of high-quality, continuous training in how to integrate technology into teaching, some students will continue to make observations like the following two high school students quoted in a 2002 report titled *The Digital Disconnect: The Widening Gap Between Internet-Savvy Students and Their Schools:*

> *"Our teachers usually . . . don't really know what to do with [the Internet]." "I never really got an assignment that specifically said you have to use the Internet" (Levin and Arafeh 2002, 16).*

In addition, teachers have similar experiences related to technical support to keep computers working and software programs functioning properly. Forty-six percent of teachers say they need technical help at least once a month, and only 31 percent of these teachers say that such help is "always" or "mostly" available when they need it. After technical help is given, about one-third of teachers say the help was "excellent" or "very good," one-third say it was "good," and the remaining third say it was "fair" or "poor." Not surprisingly, 54 percent of school leaders who responded to a survey by the National School Boards Association (2002) reported that they rely on students to provide assistance with computers and advice about using the Internet.

In response to the uneven quality of professional development and technical support, several state departments of education, school districts, and individual schools are taking steps to ensure that teachers have the help they need to fully integrate technology into their teaching. In North Carolina, for example, all new teachers must take an examination to demonstrate their mastery of basic technology competencies in the following nine areas:

- Computer operation skills
- Setup, maintenance, and troubleshooting
- Word processing/introductory desktop publishing
- Spreadsheet/graphing
- Databases
- Networking
- Telecommunications
- Media communications (including image and audio processing)
- Multimedia integration

In addition, North Carolina is one of two states (along with Vermont) that require new teachers to develop a portfolio demonstrating mastery of "advanced" technology competencies, which is evaluated by public school and university faculty chosen by the new teacher's preservice program. The advanced competencies reflect the ability to use multiple forms of technology as they relate to the following four dimensions of learning:

- Curriculum
- Subject-specific knowledge
- Design and management of learning environments/resources
- Child development, learning, and diversity

In addition, teachers applying for five-year license renewal in North Carolina must have thirty to fifty hours of technology training.

At the school district level, creative approaches are extending teachers' technological literacy. For example, the board of education in Baldwin Park, California, leased nine hundred notebook computers and gave them to teachers and administrators in all of the district's twenty-one schools (Caterinicchia 1999).

Teacher-education programs also will play a key role in preparing technologically competent teachers to fill the roughly two million teaching vacancies the National Center for Education Statistics has projected between 1998 and 2008. However, as the CEO Forum on Education and Technology stated in its *School Technology and Readiness Report* released in 1999: "America's schools of education have only just begun to focus on preparing their students [to] understand, access, and bring technology-based experiences into the learning process." For example, according to the Milken Exchange on Education Technology's report *Will New Teachers Be Prepared to Teach in a Digital Age?,* less than half of student teachers routinely use technology during their field experience, and less than half of field experience supervisors or cooperating teachers can advise them on how to integrate technology into the curriculum (Milken Exchange on Education Technology 1999).

To ensure that preservice teachers possess the ability to integrate technology into the classroom, the National Council for the Accreditation of Teacher Education (NCATE) has developed technology-related guidelines that teacher-education programs must meet as a criterion for accreditation (National Council for the Accreditation of Teacher Education 2002a). Also, many teacher-education programs have taken innovative steps such as the following to ensure that their graduates possess the ability to integrate technology into the classroom.

- At Washington State University, students develop an online portfolio of literacy strategies that are critiqued by teachers around the state.
- At the University of Virginia, students use the Internet to link with students at eleven other universities to analyze case studies based on commonly occurring problems in classrooms; students also write their own cases and post them on the Web.
- At San Diego State University, student teachers, along with classroom teachers and school administrators, participate in a weekly "Multimedia Academy" taught by university staff and former student teachers.
- At the University of Northern Iowa, students learn from television-mediated observations of "live" classrooms at a P–12 laboratory school and conduct question-answer sessions with the laboratory school teachers.
- At Indiana University, students, as well as visitors from around the world, learn about educational technology at the Center for Excellence in Education, a new state-of-the-art facility with seven hundred computers, an "enhanced technology suite," a building-wide video distribution system, and a two-way video distance-learning classroom.
- At Boise State University, students complete a fifteen-hour technology fieldwork internship in a public school classroom with a teacher who effectively integrates technology into the curriculum.

In spite of progress at integrating technology into schools, the following observation by the Web-Based Education Commission accurately sums up the work that remains: "The Internet is perhaps the most transformative technology in history, reshaping business, media, entertainment, and society in astonishing ways. But for all its power, it is just now being tapped to transform education" (Web-Based Education Commission 2001). Schools will need extensive support as they continue striving to meet the four challenges outlined in this section. Teachers, professional associations, the private sector, state and federal governments, and local communities must continue to work together to enable classroom "media magic" to enhance every student's learning. (To assist you in contributing to this effort, see the Appendix "Selected Resources for Integrating Technology into Instruction" on this book's website.)

Fortunately, teachers, along with others who have an interest in education, are becoming more sophisticated in understanding the strengths and limitations of technology as a tool to promote learning. They know full well that like another educational tool—the book—the computer *can* be a powerful, almost unlimited medium for instruction and learning, if they carefully reflect on *how* it will further the attainment of the goals and aspirations they have for their students.

Summary

How Are Educational Technologies Influencing Schools?

- Technology is a tool teachers can use to achieve educational goals and to create particular kinds of learning environments.
- Technology can provide students with a structured, efficient instructional delivery system, or it can spark their interest in open-ended, inquiry-oriented learning.
- In many schools and classrooms, technology has already transformed teaching and learning; however, teachers, administrators, policymakers, and parents must realize that advanced telecommunications will require new approaches to teaching and assessing students' learning.

What Technologies Are Available for Teaching?

- Through technologies such as two-way interactive telecommunications, CD-ROM players, interactive multimedia, handheld computers, computer simulations, and hypermedia, teachers are creating learning environments that allow students to become more active in shaping their learning experiences.
- If *educational technology* is broadly defined as inventions that enable teachers to reach their goals more effectively, then it is clear that for some time all teachers have been using various forms of educational "technology."
- Though considerable evidence suggests that television retards children's growth and development, the medium, if properly used, can enhance students' learning.
- Channel One is a controversial use of commercial-based television in the schools, and many critics question its educational value.
- Three common uses of computers in instruction are computer-assisted instruction (CAI), computer-managed instruction (CMI), and computer-enhanced instruction (CEI).
- Some schools have microcomputer-based laboratories (MBL) that students use to gather and analyze various kinds of data.
- Newsgroups, chat rooms, and videoconferencing on the Internet enable teachers and students to communicate with people around the world.

How Do Teachers Use Computers and the Internet?

- Teachers most frequently use the Internet to gather information and resources for teaching.
- Teachers who have classroom access to the Internet are more likely than those without access to communicate via e-mail and to post information and student work on the World Wide Web.

- After word processing and using CD-ROM references, performing "research" on the Web is the most common teacher-directed use of computers by students.

What Are the Effects of Computer Technology on Learning?

- Although how and to what extent computers and other technologies are being used in schools is not known, research indicates that technology has a positive impact on students' achievement and attitudes.
- The Apple Classrooms of Tomorrow (ACOT) project showed that teachers progress through five stages as they integrate technology into teaching: entry, adoption, adaptation, appropriation, and invention.
- Single research studies and meta-analyses of large numbers of single studies indicate that the effects of computers on students' learning are varied—some report learning gains, some don't, and others report "mixed" outcomes.
- In spite of the ambiguities of research on computer-based instruction, it is clear that technology *can* have positive effects on learning.

Should Technology Be at the Forefront of Efforts to Improve Schools in the United States?

- From the need to acquire computer literacy skills for the twenty-first century to the importance of allowing students to pace their learning, the role that technology should play in improving schools has been widely publicized.
- Some critics believe that schools are under tremendous pressure, much of it coming from technology-oriented corporations, to integrate technology.
- According to some critics, technology has little to add to the art of teaching, and it will not help schools face critical problems such as overcrowding, limited funds, and school violence.
- Despite criticisms of technology in the schools, the public believes that computers have increased students' learning.

What Are the Challenges of Integrating Technology into Schools?

- Four challenges must be met so that all students can attend "high-end technology schools": (1) providing broadband Internet access for all schools, (2) providing access to technology for all students, (3) obtaining quality educational software, and (4) providing high-quality, continuous training in technology for teachers.
- Many schools report inadequate funding for computers and technical support.
- A "digital divide" is evident when access to computers is compared to minority-group status and family income.
- Since the National Information Infrastructure (NII) was developed to encourage all schools to use advanced telecommunications, nearly all schools and 75 percent of classrooms have access to the Internet.
- Though the quality of many software programs is low, new hypermedia programs are being introduced that present students with multifaceted, engaging, and authentic learning experiences.
- Only 20 percent of teachers believe they are well prepared to integrate technology into the curriculum.
- Though school district spending on technology training for teachers is often inadequate and the quality of that training uneven, state departments of education, school districts, and individual schools are developing new approaches to providing teachers with support as they integrate technology.
- Many teacher-education programs have developed innovative approaches to preparing technologically competent teachers.

Key Terms and Concepts

Applications and Activities

Teacher's Journal

1. In your opinion, what are the most important benefits of technology for education, and what are its most important drawbacks?
2. What impact has television had on your life? What steps might teachers take to increase the educational benefits of television in society?
3. A concern voiced by some is that the use of computers in education will lead to a depersonalization of the teacher–learner relationship. How valid is this concern?
4. Write a scenario forecasting how technology will change the teaching profession during the next two decades. During the next four decades.

Teacher's Database

1. With classmates, join or start an online discussion on one or more of the following topics or another topic in Chapter 11.

   computer-assisted instruction (CAI)
   computer-enhanced instruction (CEI)
   computer-managed instruction (CMI)
   computer simulations
   educational software
   educational technology
   hypermedia
   interactive multimedia

2. Find out more about educational newsgroups and distance learning networks. How might you use newsgroups or distance learning networks in your preparation as a teacher? As a teacher, how might you and your students use these two forms of educational technology? What knowledge and skills do you need to start or participate in an educational newsgroup or distance learning network? Using the Internet, develop a list of resources for both.

Observations and Interviews

1. Survey a local school district to determine the educational technologies used by teachers. How and how often are these technologies used for instruction? What is the availability of computers and software for student use?
2. Find an online chat room frequented by teachers and enter (or initiate) a discussion on educational technology. What are the teachers' views of integrating technology into the classroom? What technologies, software, and instructional activities have they found most effective?

Professional Portfolio

Prepare a catalog of interactive multimedia resources and materials that you will use as a teacher. For each entry, include an annotation that briefly describes the resource materials, how you will use them, and where they may be obtained. As with the selection of any curriculum materials, try to find evidence of effectiveness, such as results of field tests, published reviews of educational software, awards, or testimonials from educators. View and report on at least one program you have included in your personal catalog. Explain in your report how you will integrate this multimedia resource into your curriculum. For some ideas to get you started, ask your instructor for handout master M11.6, "Selected Resources for Integrating Technology into the Classroom."

VideoWorkshop Extra!

If the VideoWorkshop package was included with your textbook, go to Chapter 11 of the Companion Website (www.ablongman.com/parkay6e) and click on the VideoWorkshop button. Follow the instructions for viewing videoclip 11 and completing this exercise. Consider this information along with what you've read in Chapter 11 while answering the following questions.

1. Educational technologies are more or less appropriate in a given situation. Using what you know from the text about diverse learners and learning styles, classify the following technologies into a sequence *from least to most helpful* in terms of promoting student comprehension of the events of September 11, 2001: CD-ROMs, television, video, computer programs, library books, guest speakers, the Internet. Explain, using videoclip 11 as support for your ideas.
2. The text and videoclip 11 address the issue about whether technology could ever replace the human student–teacher interaction. Compare the influences of a teacher and a computer on students' learning. What if teachers were replaced with computer software? Discuss.

Appendix 11.1

CRITERIA FOR EVALUATING SOFTWARE PROGRAMS

User friendliness	Poor	Fair	Excellent
How easy is it to start the program?	❑	❑	❑
Is there an overview or site map for the program?	❑	❑	❑
Can students easily control the pace of the program?	❑	❑	❑
Can students exit the program easily?	❑	❑	❑
Can students create their own paths through the program and develop their own links among elements?	❑	❑	❑
After first-time use, can students bypass introductory or orientation material?	❑	❑	❑
Does the program include useful hotlinks to Internet sites?	❑	❑	❑
Inclusiveness			
Can students with hearing or visual impairments make full use of the program?	❑	❑	❑
Can students navigate the program by making simple keystrokes with one hand?	❑	❑	❑
Does the material avoid stereotypes and reflect sensitivity to racial, cultural, and gender differences?	❑	❑	❑
Textual Material			
How accurate and thorough is the content?	❑	❑	❑
Is the content well organized and clearly presented?	❑	❑	❑
Is the textual content searchable?	❑	❑	❑
Can the content be integrated into the curriculum?	❑	❑	❑
Images			
Is the image resolution high quality?	❑	❑	❑
Is the layout attractive, "user friendly," and uncluttered?	❑	❑	❑
Do the graphics and colors enhance instruction?	❑	❑	❑
How true are the colors of the images?	❑	❑	❑
Are the images large enough?	❑	❑	❑
Does the program have a zoom feature that indicates the power of magnification?	❑	❑	❑
Does the program make effective use of video and animation?	❑	❑	❑
Audio			
Are the audio clips high quality?	❑	❑	❑
Does the audio enhance instruction?	❑	❑	❑
Technical			
Is installation of the program easy and trouble-free?	❑	❑	❑
Are instructions clear and easy to follow?	❑	❑	❑
Is user-friendly online help available?	❑	❑	❑
Are technical support people easy to reach, helpful, and courteous?	❑	❑	❑

Appendix 11.1 *(continued)*

Motivational	**Poor**	**Fair**	**Excellent**
Does the program capture and hold students' interest?	❑	❑	❑
Are students eager to use the program again?	❑	❑	❑
Does the program give appropriate, motivational feedback?	❑	❑	❑
Does the program provide prompts or cues to promote students' learning?	❑	❑	❑

Appendix 11.2

CRITERIA FOR EVALUATING WORLD WIDE WEB SITES

Authoritativeness	**Poor**	**Fair**	**Excellent**
The author(s) are respected authorities in the field.	❑	❑	❑
The author(s) are knowledgeable.	❑	❑	❑
The author(s) provide a list of credentials and/or educational background.	❑	❑	❑
The author(s) represent respected, credible institutions or organizations.	❑	❑	❑
Complete information on references (or sources) is provided.	❑	❑	❑
Information for contacting the author(s) and webmaster is provided.	❑	❑	❑
Comprehensiveness			
All facets of the subject are covered.	❑	❑	❑
Sufficient detail is provided at the site.	❑	❑	❑
Information provided is accurate.	❑	❑	❑
Political, ideological, and other biases are not evident.			
Presentation			
Graphics serve an educational, rather than decorative, purpose.	❑	❑	❑
Links are provided to related sites.	❑	❑	❑
What icons stand for is clear and unambiguous.	❑	❑	❑
The website loads quickly.	❑	❑	❑
The website is stable and seldom, if ever, nonfunctional.	❑	❑	❑
Timeliness			
The original website was produced recently.	❑	❑	❑
The website is updated and/or revised regularly.	❑	❑	❑
Links given at the website are up-to-date and reliable.	❑	❑	❑

Reflections on Education

Teaching to Our Changing Demographics

by Paul A. Flores

Educators must be concerned with the education of all children, including minorities, and at no time has this been more evident than now. According to the 2000 Census, of the 281,421,906 people living in the United States, nearly 35 percent are considered part of a minority race, with Hispanics representing the greatest increase (57.9%) in population from 1990 to 2000 (U.S. Census Bureau 2001). Of course any changes to the trends of the general population have an immediate impact on the nation's education system as well. According to the National Center for Education Statistics, minorities represent 40 percent of all students in school districts. In the nation's 500 largest school districts, 58 percent of enrollment were minorities, and in the 100 largest school districts, minority enrollment represented 68 percent of the total student population (NCES 2002). As demographics have indeed changed, so too must education respond in a way that effectively teaches to those changes.

On January 8, 2002, President George W. Bush signed into law the *No Child Left Behind Act of 2001* with a major part of the initiative focused on addressing the achievement gap between minorities and Whites. According to information from the No Child Left Behind website, educating every child is "the greatest moral challenge of our time." Minorities drop out at a higher rate than non-whites and lag behind in reading and math NAEP (National Association of Educational Progress) scores leading to a smaller percentage receiving a college education (No Child Left Behind 2002). The National Center for Education Statistics explains the high dropout rate among some groups as a reflection of a large number of youth with little education who come to the United States to work, not to attend school (NCES 2002). President Bush and Congress have taken this challenge by focusing on results. Public Law 107-110 requires states to create their own standards for what a child should know and learn and then test every student's progress toward those standards. It is expected that each state, school district, and school will make adequate yearly progress with results publicly reported.

There remains concern, however, as to how best to educate all students, including minorities. "No Child Left Behind" refers to proven methods and researched-based pedagogy, but that is a subject of concern as well. What should also be considered is addressing each student from a strength-based perspective or, as some education experts would say, "utilizing cultural capital." Often minority students are addressed from a deficit-based perspective, focusing on what they don't know or don't have and ignoring what they do have. Instead, author Lisa Delpit and others suggest that educators need to change their approach and consider the strengths that each student brings to the educational table. Cultural capital takes into account that students do not enter the classroom as a blank slate, but rather as sources of a variety of experiences and knowledge. Among the strengths of many minority cultures are language, strong sense of family, desire to improve, religious beliefs, and resiliency.

For example, rather than see, in most cases, a first language other than English as a deficit, educators should acknowledge that as a strength, as capital. Researchers have found that primary language can be instrumental in second language and content acquisition. In addition, our global economy encourages bilingual and multilingual skills that minority students often come to school with, yet sometimes leave without. Angela Valenzuela refers to that phenomenon as "Subtractive Schooling." Sometimes Latinos, along with other minorities, leave school with less resources from youth in areas of dismissing their definition of education and through assimilationist policies and practices that minimize their culture and language (Valenzuela 1999). Often minority students come from a strong sense of family, yet that often goes unused in schooling. Educators need to use that as a strength in creating a classroom environment that mirrors family and utilizing "relational teaching," or teaching through relationship. When students feel respected by the teacher and believe the teacher is there for them and is dedicated to improving their academic understanding and inspiring them to greater success, they are more apt to give a maximum effort. Gail Thompson's research with African-American students indicated that they want teachers who exhibit qualities such as explaining things well and making the coursework interesting (Thompson 2002).

Guadalupe Valdez addresses this issue as primary to school success (Valdez 1996). Setting high standards and expectations is part of utilizing the family strength. Most minority or immigrant parents seek a better quality of life for their children, which is often a prime reason for their migration in the first place. Many come to America seeking improvement of their quality of life, taking risks and leaving comforts to pursue the dream of a better life. That strength should be utilized in the classroom when setting goals and inspiring their attainment. In addition, many minorities find affirmation in religious institutions where they experience culturally relevant education and support. These strong religious beliefs often provide and inspire some family members with a sense of hope (DHHS 2001). Teachers can adapt the faith and hope that students bring to the classroom to academics and the pursuit thereof. Finally, many minorities are known for their resiliency; often overcoming the challenges of poverty, lack of education, language, and other hurdles before entering the classroom. Educators can call upon these strengths, or cultural capital, when new standards are addressed, standardized exams given, and additional requirements mandated.

Educators need to assist parents in providing information that will encourage educational success. From resources offered in the school district to courses necessary for college admission, understandable information can fuel academic pursuits. For example, at Azusa Pacific University the C.H.A.M.P. (College Headed And Mighty Proud) project connects university students with mostly Latino fourth-grade students and their parents in an effort to inspire the hope of college attendance. Parents are provided information on higher education, including admission and financial aid. It is the hope of the project that guidance will eliminate fears while encouraging the pursuit of a dream of many minorities, a college degree.

Minorities indeed bring a rich culture to the American classroom. Perhaps what might be missing is the utilization of the strengths of the culture in addressing academic content. Developing strong educational relationships with teachers and college mentors will provide an avenue for acquiring the knowledge and language necessary for academic success. Utilizing cultural strengths in the classroom, maintaining high expectations, along with integrating the possibility of college will help direct minorities and all students down the road of academic success. The big picture not only takes into account demographics, but also the strengths of each student with the belief that all students can learn and thus will not be left behind.

Paul A. Flores is the director of the Liberal Studies Program and an Assistant Professor in the Teacher Education Department at Azusa Pacific University. He is also currently completing his Ph.D. at Claremont University.

References

Delpit, L. (1996). *Other people's children: Cultural conflict in the classroom.* New York: The New Press.

National Center for Education Statistics. (2002). *The Condition of Education: 2000–2002.* Washington, D.C.: U.S. Department of Education. Retrieved at http://www.nces.ed.gov

U.S. Census Bureau. (2002). *United States Census 2000.* Washington, D.C.: U.S. Department of Commerce. Retrieved at http://www.census.gov

U.S. Department of Education. (2002). *No child left behind.* Washington, D.C.: U.S. Department of Education. Retrieved at http://www.nochildleftbehind.gov

U.S. Department of Health and Human Services. (2001). *Mental health: Culture, race, and ethnicity: A Supplement to Mental Health: A Report of the Surgeon General.* Rockville, MD: U.S. Department of Health and Human Services, Substance Abuse and Mental Health Services Administration, Center for Mental Health Services.

Thompson, G. (2002). *African American teens discuss their schooling experience.* Westport, CT: Bergin and Garvey.

Valdez, G. (1996). *Con respeto: Bridging the distances between culturally diverse families and schools: An ethnographic portrait.* Teachers College Press.

Valenzuela, A. (1999). *Subtractive schooling: U.S. Mexican youth and the politics of caring.* Albany: State University of New York Press.

part 4

Your Teaching Future

Dear Mentor

Preparing a Literate Populace

Dear Mentor,

I am a graduate student in a teacher credential program, and in less than a year, I will be seeking a high school English teaching position. As a future English teacher, I have many concerns, but one in particular stands out: illiteracy.

The ability to read is an absolute necessity. However, there are still so many people who are unable to read or who read at a level far below normal. I know that I will have many students who will struggle with reading. Since this skill is such a large part of the English/language arts curriculum, the idea of teaching illiterate students is daunting.

What resources are available to help these students? Also, do you have any tips on how best to communicate with the parents of children who are struggling with reading? I want to know how to convey my concerns and offer suggestions without offending anyone.

Thank you so much for taking the time to read this letter. Any help that you can offer me is greatly appreciated!

Sincerely,
Lyndie J. Okura

Dear Lyndie,

I have been teaching for six years at the elementary level and have taught English as a second language at the college level. To address the illiteracy issue, one needs to begin by filling the reading gaps of the student. Improving students' reading skills may entail revisiting elementary reading concepts and assessments. First, we must examine students' reading strategies and errors. A brilliant book by Marie M. Clay, An Observation Survey of Early Literacy Achievement (1993), provides a tool called the "Running Record." It helps identify students' specific reading strategies as well as makes error analyses. In the area of spelling, Words Their Way (1996) by Donald R. Bear et al. is a great resource to ascertain students' spelling stages and implement activities at their level of development. Mastery of phonemic awareness, in my experience, is one skill that is often deficient when students are illiterate. Jane Greene addresses blending and segmenting concepts in the book Sounds and Letters for Readers and Spellers (1997). For phonics assessment, the "Beginning Phonics Skills Test" by John Shefelbine is also valuable. Combining these assessments will provide a thorough depiction of the student's reading ability. These resources will further assist you by offering specific academic activities to implement.

Education is a shared responsibility, making communication with parents essential. Parents are usually eager to help but are sometimes unsure how. However, parents are able to offer valuable insight regarding their child, and we as teachers need to listen. Then provide parents with specific strategies and activities they can do at home that will help improve their child's reading progress.

Lastly, language arts envelops all subject areas. Therefore, the greatest resource will be your colleagues. At the high school level, when teachers and subjects are departmentalized, collaboration is essential. Coordinating across the curriculum will ensure that students have access to all subject matter and will support their journey in becoming literate.

Sincerely,

Jennifer Hite
Horace Mann Elementary School
Anaheim, CA

12 Teachers as Educational Leaders

Some teachers view their work as taking place solely within their classrooms in what is essentially a private, individual practice. Others view their responsibilities as extending beyond classroom teaching to include participation in the larger community of educators and administrators.

—Henry Jay Becker
"How Are Teachers Using Computers in Instruction?," April 2001

It is November, and you are attending a meeting of the steering committee for a statewide teacher network launched that September. The state department of education divided the state into twelve regions, and you were elected by your peers to be the network leader for your region. The network is based on the premise that teachers should have opportunities to participate in, and to lead, professional development activities of their own choosing, such as curriculum workshops, leadership institutes, internships, and conferences.

The purpose of this two-day meeting at the state capitol is to begin the process of designing a series of two-week summer institutes for teachers. The institutes will be invitational, and institute "fellows" will be selected by the steering committee after an extensive application and interview process. One institute will be held in each region throughout the state, and teachers will receive an $800 stipend plus expenses for attending. To disseminate the knowledge and skills they acquire and to further develop their leadership abilities, the institute fellows will design and deliver staff development programs at their home schools.

The committee chair, a teacher from a school in the state's largest city, has just laid out the group's task for the next two days. "By the end of the day tomorrow, we need to have identified which institutes will be offered in each region. Also, we need to have a 'game plan' for how each of you will facilitate the development of the summer institute in your region."

"Well, the way I see it," says the teacher next to you, "the institutes should accomplish at least two major purposes. First, they should provide teachers with ways to increase their effectiveness in the classroom by acquiring new strategies and materials. Second, and just as important, the institutes should give teachers opportunities to play key leadership roles in school reform efforts around the state."

"That's right," says another teacher. "Teachers should recognize that the institutes give them a voice and meaningful opportunities to function as professionals."

"What I like about the institutes," says the teacher across the table from you, "is that they give teachers a chance to break out of the role of passively *receiving* in-service training. It's no different for teachers than it is for students—we learn best by actively shaping our learning environment and constructing meaning."

As several members of the group, including you, nod in agreement, you reflect on what you've just heard. What does it really mean to be a professional? What are the characteristics of a profession, and to what extent does teaching reflect those characteristics? What new leadership roles for teachers are emerging? What leadership roles will you play in educational reform?

Focus Questions

1. **To what extent is teaching a full profession?**
2. **What is professionalism in teaching?**
3. **To what professional organizations do teachers belong?**
4. **What new leadership roles for teachers are emerging?**
5. **How do teachers contribute to educational research?**
6. **How are teachers providing leadership for school restructuring and curriculum reform?**

Expand your knowledge of the concepts discussed in this chapter by reading current and historical articles from the *New York Times* by visiting the "**Themes of the Times**" section of the Companion Website (www.ablongman.com/parkay6e).

Educational reform, as the preceding scenario illustrates, is continuing to change dramatically what it means to be a teacher. State-sponsored teacher networks, the professionalization of teaching, shared decision making, peer review, and mentor teacher programs are just a few of the changes that are providing unprecedented opportunities for teachers to assume new leadership roles beyond the classroom. In addition, as Joseph Murphy (1999) points out in "Reconnecting Teaching and School Administration: A Call for a Unified Profession," approaches to educational leadership are becoming more collaborative and participatory:

> *The hierarchical, bureaucratic organizational structures that have defined schools over the past 80 years are giving way to more decentralized and more professionally controlled systems that create new designs for school management. In these new postindustrial educational organizations, there are important shifts in roles, relationships, and responsibilities: traditional patterns of relationships are altered, authority flows are less hierarchical, role definitions are both more general and flexible, leadership is connected to competence for needed tasks rather than to formal position, and independence and isolation are replaced by cooperative work.*

We have referred to teaching as a **profession** throughout this book; however, if we compare teaching with other professions—law and medicine, for example—we find some significant differences. As a result of these differences, current opinion is divided as to whether teaching actually is a full profession. Some have labeled teaching a *semi*-profession (Etzioni 1969), a *classless* profession (Mattingly 1975), an *emerging* profession (Howsam et al. 1976), an *uncertain* profession (Powell 1980), an *imperiled* profession (Duke 1984; Sykes 1983; Freedman, Jackson, and Botes 1983; Boyer 1990), an *endangered* profession (Goodlad 1983), and a *not-quite* profession (Goodlad 1990)!

To What Extent Is Teaching a Full Profession?

We use the terms *professional* and *profession* quite frequently, usually without thinking about their meanings. Professionals "possess a high degree of specialized *theoretical knowledge,* along with methods and techniques for applying this knowledge in their day-to-day work. . . . [And they] are united by a high degree of in-group solidarity, stemming from their common training and common adherence to certain doctrines and methods" (Abrahamsson 1971, 11–12).

From several sociologists and educators who have studied teaching come additional characteristics of occupations that are highly professionalized, summarized in Figure 12.1. Before reading further, reflect on each characteristic and decide whether it applies to teaching. Then, continue reading about the extent to which teaching satisfies each of these commonly agreed-upon characteristics of full professions. Do our perceptions agree with yours?

Institutional Monopoly of Services

On one hand, teachers do have a monopoly of services. As a rule, only those who are certified members of the profession may teach in public schools. On the other hand, varied requirements for certification and for teaching in private schools weaken this monopoly. In addition, any claim teachers might have as exclusive providers of a service is further eroded by the practice of many state systems to approve temporary, or emergency, certification measures to deal with teacher shortages or the widespread practice of "out-of-field-teaching." For example, according to an Education Trust (2002) report, about one out of four teachers instructing in grades 7–12 lack even a college minor in the subject being taught. In high-poverty schools, the rate of out-of-field teachers is 34 percent

Figure 12.1 Does teaching meet the criteria for a profession?

Yes	Uncertain	No	
❍	❍	❍	1. Professionals are allowed to institutionalize a monopoly of essential knowledge and services. For example, only lawyers may practice law; only physicians may practice medicine.
❍	❍	❍	2. Professionals are able to practice their occupation with a high degree of autonomy. They are not closely supervised, and they have frequent opportunities to make their own decisions about important aspects of their work. Professional autonomy also implies an obligation to perform responsibly, to self-supervise, and to be dedicated to providing a service rather than meeting minimum requirements of the job.
❍	❍	❍	3. Professionals must typically undergo a lengthy period of education and/or training before they may enter professional practice. Furthermore, professionals usually must undergo a lengthy induction period following their formal education or training.
❍	❍	❍	4. Professionals perform an essential service for their clients and are devoted to continuous development of their ability to deliver this service. This service emphasizes intellectual rather than physical techniques.
❍	❍	❍	5. Professionals have control over their governance, their socialization into the occupation, and research connected with their occupation.
❍	❍	❍	6. Members of a profession form their own vocational associations, which have control over admissions to the profession, educational standards, examinations and licensing, career development, ethical and performance standards, and professional discipline.
❍	❍	❍	7. The knowledge and skills held by professionals are not usually available to nonprofessionals.
❍	❍	❍	8. Professionals enjoy a high level of public trust and are able to deliver services that are clearly superior to those available elsewhere.
❍	❍	❍	9. Professionals are granted a high level of prestige and higher-than-average financial rewards.

compared to about 19 percent in low-poverty schools. Thus, teaching is the only profession that allows noncertified individuals to practice the profession. Furthermore, a decline of inadequately licensed teachers seems unlikely, given the U.S. Department of Education's projection that more than two million teachers would be needed between 1999 and 2009.

Perhaps the most significant argument against teachers claiming to be the exclusive providers of a service, however, is the fact that a great deal of teaching occurs in informal, nonschool settings and is done by people who are not teachers. Every day, thousands of people teach various kinds of how-to-do-it skills: how to water-ski, how to make dogs more obedient, how to make pasta from scratch, how to tune a car's engine, and how to meditate.

Teacher Autonomy

In one sense teachers have considerable autonomy. As Henry Jay Becker suggests in this chapter's epigraph, teaching is, in large measure, "a private, individual practice." Teachers usually work behind a closed classroom door, and only seldom is their work observed by another adult. In fact, one of the norms among teachers is that the classroom is a castle of sorts, and teacher privacy a closely guarded right. Although the performance of new teachers may be observed and evaluated on a regular basis by supervisors, veteran teachers are observed much less frequently, and they usually enjoy a high degree of autonomy.

Teachers also have extensive freedom regarding how they structure the classroom environment. They may emphasize discussions as opposed to lectures. They may set certain requirements for some students and not for others. They may delegate responsibilities to one class and not another. And, within the guidelines set by local and state authorities, teachers may determine much of the content they teach.

There are, however, constraints placed on teachers and their work. Teachers, unlike doctors and lawyers, must accept all the "clients" who are sent to them. Only infrequently does a teacher actually "reject" a student assigned to him or her.

Teachers must also agree to teach what state and local officials say they must. Moreover, the work of teachers is subject to a higher level of public scrutiny than that found in other professions. Because the public provides "clients" (students) and pays for schools, it has a significant say regarding the work of teachers. Nevertheless, it has been suggested that some "leveling" of professions will occur in the United States during the early twenty-first century: "More of the work of the traditional high-status professions, particularly medicine, will occur in bureaucratic or large organizational settings under the watchful eye of managers. [While] doctors are accepting more and more regulation, school teachers . . . will slowly break out of long-established bureaucratic hierarchies and share more of the autonomy previously enjoyed by members of the high-status professions" (Grant and Murray 1999, 231–232).

Years of Education and Training

As sociologist Amitai Etzioni (1969) points out in his classic discussion of the "semi-professions," the training of teachers is less lengthy than that required for other professionals—lawyers and physicians, for example. The professional component of teacher education programs is the shortest of all the professions—only 15 percent of the average bachelor's degree program for a high school teacher is devoted to professional courses. However, as we learned in Chapter 2, several colleges and universities have begun five-year teacher education programs. Similarly, in its comprehensive report, *What Matters Most: Teaching for America's Future,* the National Commission on Teaching and America's Future (1996) recommended that teacher education be moved to the graduate level. If the trend toward five-year and graduate-level teacher education programs continues, the professional status of teaching will definitely be enhanced.

In most professions, new members must undergo a prescribed induction period. Physicians, for example, must serve an internship or residency before beginning practice, and most lawyers begin as clerks in law firms. In contrast, teachers usually do not go through a formal induction period before assuming full responsibility for their work. Practice teaching comes closest to serving as an induction period, but it is often relatively short, informal, and lacking in uniformity. As the National Commission on Teaching and America's Future (1996) noted, "Our society can no longer accept the [s]ink-or-swim induction [of teachers]."

Provision of Essential Service

Although it is generally acknowledged that teachers provide a service that is vital to the well-being of individuals and groups, the public does need to be reminded of this fact from time to time. This importance was driven home on a large scale during the early 1980s when several reports calling for school reform linked the strength of our country to the quality of its schools. In a sense, it is no exaggeration to say that teaching is a matter of life and death:

> *every moment in the lives of teachers and pupils brings critical decisions of motivation, reinforcement, reward, ego enhancement and goal direction. Proper professional decisions enhance learning and life; improper decisions send the learner towards incremental death in openness to experience and in ability to learn and contribute. Doctors and lawyers probably have neither more nor less to do with life, death, and freedom than do teachers (Howsam et al. 1976, 15).*

Degree of Self-Governance

The limited freedom of teachers to govern themselves has detracted from the overall status of the profession. In many states, licensing guidelines are set by government officials who may or may not be educators; and at the local level, decision-making power usually resides with local boards of education, largely made up of people who have never taught. As a result, teachers have had little or no say over what they teach, when they teach, whom they teach, and, in extreme instances, *how* they teach.

However, recent efforts to empower teachers and to professionalize teaching are creating new roles for teachers and expanded opportunities to govern important aspects of their work. At schools throughout the country, teachers are having a greater voice in decisions related to curriculum development, staffing, budget, and the day-to-day operation of schools. Figure 12.2 on page 436, for example, compares public and private school teachers' perceptions of teacher influence or control over curricula, student performance standards, discipline policies, in-service training, teacher evaluation, teacher hiring, and budget. Although public school teachers differ significantly in the amount of influence or control they believe teachers have, public school teachers should experience greater degrees of self-governance as principals respond to increasing pressure to become more effective at facilitating collaborative, emergent approaches to leadership (Parkay, Shindler, and Oaks 1997). As Gerald Grant and Christine Murray

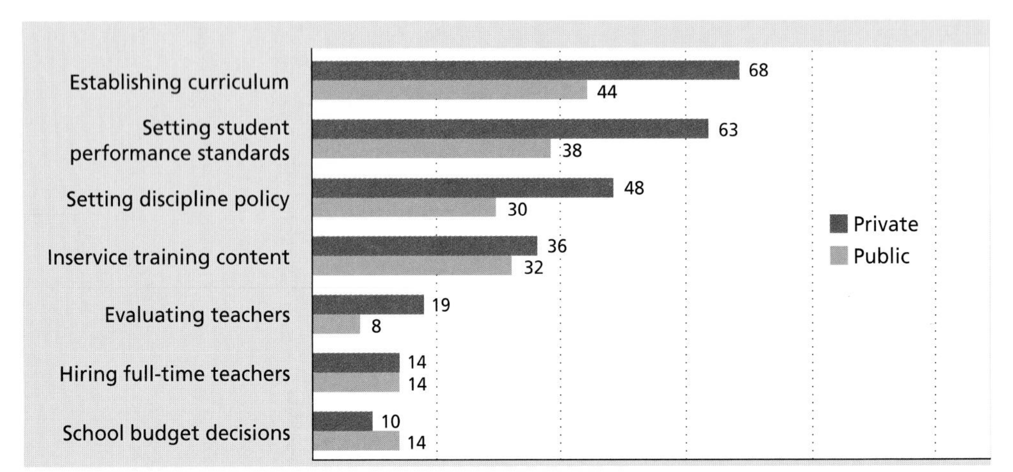

Figure 12.2 Percentage of teachers who thought they had a lot of influence on various school policies, by sector: 1999–2000
Source: U.S. Department of Education, NCES. Schools and Staffing Survey (SASS), Public, Public Charter, and Private School Teacher Surveys, 1999–2000. Taken from National Center for Education Statistics, *Special Analysis 2002–Private Schools: A Brief Portrait,* Figure 5. Washington, D.C.: Author.

point out in *Teaching in America: The Slow Revolution* (1999, 217), "schoolteachers can assert that they have genuine expertise in their subject matter and that there is a body of pedagogical content knowledge that is specific to their work. Most important, they are no longer willing to let the administrators define themselves as the exclusive class of experts controlling either the content of the curriculum or decisions about who is fit to teach it."

Professional Associations

Teachers, like other professionals, have formed a number of vocational associations that are vitally concerned with issues such as admission to the profession, educational standards, examinations and licensing, career development, ethical and performance standards, and professional discipline. It is clear, though, that the more than five hundred national teacher organizations have not progressed as far as other professions have in gaining control of these areas.

Professional Knowledge and Skills

Professionals are granted a certain status because they possess knowledge and skills not normally held by the general public. Within the profession of teaching, however, the requirements for membership are less precise. In spite of the ongoing efforts of educational researchers, there is less than unanimous agreement on the knowledge and skills considered necessary to teach. This lack of agreement is reflected in the varied programs at the 1,300 or so colleges and universities that train teachers.

During the last ten years, the National Board for Professional Teaching Standards (NBPTS) has made significant progress toward clarifying the knowledge base for teaching. As you learned in Chapter 2, the NBPTS (the majority of whose members are teachers) offers board certification to teachers who possess a high level of NBPTS-identified knowledge and skills. Near the end of 2001, the NBPTS had granted national certification to about 6,500 teachers, and the board planned to certify 100,000 teachers by 2006.

Meeting the Standard

Demonstrates Professional Involvement

The teacher recognizes his/her professional responsibility for engaging in and supporting appropriate professional practices for self and colleagues (ITASC Disposition, Principle #9).

Accomplished teachers contribute to the effectiveness of the school by working collaboratively with other professionals on instructional policy, curriculum development and staff development (NBPTS, Proposition 5. Teachers are members of learning communities).

Teacher candidates are able to foster relationships with school colleagues, parents and families, and agencies in the larger community to support students' learning and well being (NCATE, Standard i: Candidate Knowledge, Skills, and Dispositions).

Teacher volunteers to participate in school and district projects, making a substantial contribution, and assumes a leadership role in a major school or district project (PRAXIS III Framework–"distinguished" level of performance).

Professional behavior is more than just a state of mind. Teachers adhere to a high standard of professional practices both inside and outside the classroom. It is an orientation to the teaching profession on the part of the teacher to work collaboratively and ethically with community, school, and educational leadership groups, to continue to expand knowledge about the best ways to reach and teach the "whole child."

Ty had just completed his student teaching, and he had signed a contract for his first teaching job. He was looking forward to entering the teaching profession. Ty thought of Mr. Sendae, his high school algebra teacher, who had such a profound influence on him that he had decided to become a teacher himself. Just last week, he had visited Mr. Sendae, who was still at the same school, to ask him for advice on how to begin to build professionalism into his life. Mr. Sendae advised him to always keep up-to-date with the practices of his discipline by joining and participating in a discipline-based educational organization. He also encouraged Ty to do more than just teach students in class, but to also support them through leadership in extracurricular activities or by attending events in which his students were participating. This, he assured Ty, would keep him connected with the interests and lives of his students, which was what teaching was all about.

By following Mr. Sendae's advice for building professionalism into his new vocation, Ty realizes that there are many ways in which teachers support learners. Seeing the world of teaching as extending beyond classroom walls, Ty is taking his first steps toward supporting his students through the educational network that surrounds the teaching profession.

1. Investigate appropriate professional educational organizations within your content area or desired school teaching level. What are the requirements for joining? Does the organization offer student memberships? What types of benefits does it offer? Does this organization feature conferences, workshops, or special-interest groups in which you might participate? How might participation in this organization benefit you as a future professional in education?
2. Attend an event at either a local school or in your hometown (e.g., a musical performance, sporting event, Open House, Science Fair, authors' day) and report back on the goal for this event, as well as faculty, staff, and student participation. How do you believe the event was planned–for example, was an individual or a team approach taken? What type of pre-event preparation needed to be in place before the event? Participation during the event? Clean-up or follow-up for the event? Was the goal successfully met? If you were in charge of the event next year, which successful strategies would you implement again? What new recommendations would you make?

Level of Public Trust

The level of trust the public extends to teachers as professionals varies greatly. On the one hand, the public appears to have great confidence in the work that teachers do. Because of its faith in the teaching profession, the public invests teachers with considerable power over its children. For the most part, parents willingly allow their children to be molded and influenced by teachers, and this willingness must be based on a high degree of trust. In addition, most parents expect their children to obey and respect teachers.

Though all professions have some members who might be described as unprofessional, teaching is especially vulnerable to such charges. The sheer size of the teaching force makes it difficult to maintain consistently high professional standards. Moreover, teaching is subject to a level of public scrutiny and control that other, more established, professions traditionally have not tolerated. However, the era of widespread public trust may be running out for these other professions as well. Mushrooming malpractice suits against doctors, for example, may be a sign that here, too, public confidence has significantly eroded.

Prestige, Benefits, and Pay

While "many teachers and school administrators . . . are thought to be of a more elite social class than the majority of the population in the United States" (Parker and Shapiro 1993, 42) this higher status is based on level of education attained rather than wealth. Thus teachers have not received salaries in keeping with other professions requiring approximately the same amount of schooling. Nevertheless, there is significant support for reducing the salary gap—as mentioned in Chapter 1, 83 percent of the public surveyed for the 2002 poll, *A National Priority: Americans Speak on Teacher Quality,* favor increased salaries for teachers even if it means paying higher taxes (Hart and Teeter 2002).

What Is Professionalism in Teaching?

The current goal among teachers, teacher educators, policymakers, and the general public is to make teaching a full profession. Toward this end, teachers are willing to take risks and learn new roles as they press for greater self-governance, better working conditions, and increased financial rewards. In addition, teachers are acquiring the analytical skills needed to understand and provide leadership for the complex processes of educational reform. The following sections look at the three key dimensions of professionalism in teaching presented in Figure 12.3: professional behavior, life-long learning, and involvement in the profession.

Figure 12.3 Professionalism in teaching

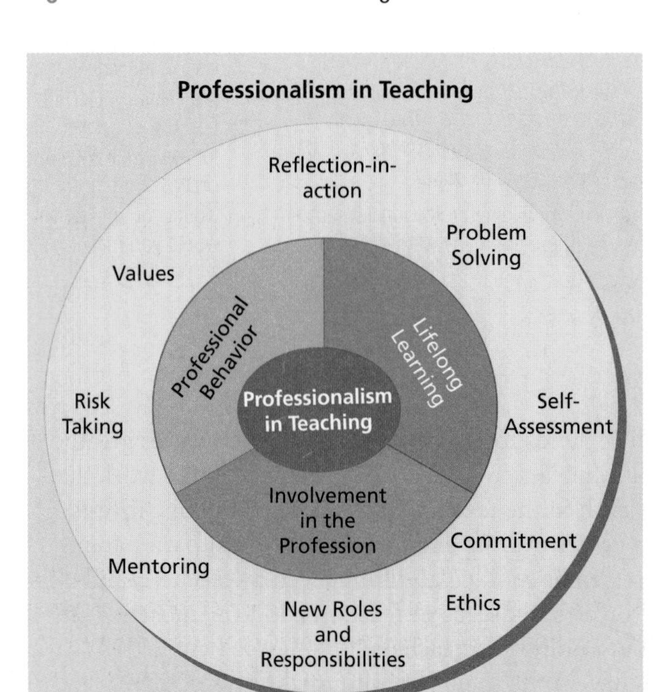

Professional Behavior

The professional teacher is guided by a specific set of values. He or she has made a deep and lasting commitment to professional practice. He or she has adopted a high standard of professional ethics and models behaviors that are in accord with that code of ethics. The professional teacher also engages in serious, reflective thought about how to teach more effectively. Moreover, he or she does this while teaching, continually examining experiences to improve practice.

Reflection-in-Action Donald Schön (1987, 1991, and 2000) has described this professional behavior as **reflection-in-action,** and he describes how a teacher might use it to solve a problem in the classroom:

> *An artful teacher sees a child's difficulty in learning to read not as a defect in the child but as a defect "of his own instruction." And because the child's difficulties may be unique, the teacher cannot assume that his repertoire of explanations will suffice, even though they are "at the tongue's end." He must be ready to invent new methods and must "endeavor to develop in himself the ability of discovering them" (2000, 66).*

The professional teacher Schön describes makes careful, sensitive observations of classroom events, reflects on the meaning of those observations, and then decides to act in a certain way. A former public school teacher in low-income urban neighborhoods explains professional reflection further: "Reflection is not (educational) reflection unless it is linked to teaching action. Reflection involves conflicting thoughts and questions. It is hard work and it can be painful. . . . Acting professionally on reflection requires true grit" (Freppon 2001, 2).

Becoming a Mentor Because of their positions and their encounters with young people, teachers may find opportunities to become mentors to some of their students. Accepting this responsibility is another example of professional behavior. The role of **mentor** is unique in several ways. First, mentorship develops naturally and is not an automatic part of teaching, nor can it be assigned to anyone. True mentorships grow from teaching relationships and cannot be artificially promoted. Second, the role of mentor is a *comprehensive* one: Mentors express broad interest in those whom they mentor. Third, the role of mentor is *mutually* recognized by student and teacher; both realize that their relationship has a special "depth." Fourth, the role of mentor is significant and has the potential to change the quality and direction of students' lives. And fifth, the opportunity to work with a mentor is free, what Gehrke (1988) terms the mentor's "gift of care."

The longer you teach, the more you will encounter opportunities for mentorships to develop, discovering that you can mentor less experienced teachers and student teachers as well as students. The rewards that come from the unique role of mentor are among the most satisfying.

Lifelong Learning

The professional teacher is dedicated to continuous learning—both about the teaching-learning process and about the subject taught. No longer is it sufficient for career teachers to obtain only a bachelor's degree and a teaching certificate. Rather, teachers are life-long members of learning communities.

Several states have mandated continuing education for teachers. The content of the curriculum as well as methods and materials for teaching that content are changing so rapidly that teachers must be involved in continuous learning to maintain their professional effectiveness. In addition, we feel that teachers must practice what they preach. A teacher who is not continuously learning raises

A good mentor can make an incredible difference in the professional life of a new teacher. What qualities might make someone a good mentor?

serious questions for students: If it's not important for our teachers to learn, why should we? The attitude toward learning that teachers model for students may be as important as the content they teach.

Many opportunities are available for teachers to learn new knowledge and skills. Nearly every school district makes provisions for in-service training or staff development. Topics can range from classroom-focused issues such as authentic assessment, using the Internet, classroom management, integrated curricula, or learning styles to schoolwide management issues such as restructuring, shared governance, or school–community partnerships. Beyond these in-service opportunities, professional teachers actively seek additional avenues for growth, as a teacher of children from low-income homes in Appalachia observes:

> *My journey toward becoming an effective teacher and a person who is proud of his work has not been easy. However, it has been necessary—I don't think one can be an effective teacher without being proud of one's teaching. For me professional development (being in a constant learning state and networking with other teachers) is the key in maintaining my commitment and building my expertise (Freppon 2001, 50).*

Many teachers have attained National Board Certification, a professional growth experience several board-certified teachers describe this way:

- "One of the best professional development experiences—it gave me lots of self-confidence."
- "The certification process was a real eye-opener. I realized I've done an awful lot—the process helps document your accomplishments."
- "It was like the final stages of a major graduate course or a cumulative comprehensive exam or thesis."
- "The certification process far exceeds everything I've ever done, including my M.A."
- "The certification process was more focused than a master's program and more valuable because it was what I was really doing in the classroom" (Rotberg, Futrell, and Lieberman 1998, 463).

Learning to Become a Leader For professional teachers, an important goal of life-long learning is to acquire leadership skills. Successful educational reform in the twenty-first century will require teacher participation in leadership, as data presented in Table 12.1 imply. The data suggest that public school teachers believe principals do not provide sufficient leadership in many areas of instruction and school management. Only 11 percent of teachers report that the "principal often discusses instructional practices," and less than half believe "school goals are communicated clearly" by their principals. Teachers who have a leadership orientation, however, understand that *they,* as well as the principal, have an obligation to initiate schoolwide discussions of instructional practices or school goals. They also understand, as John Gardner (1990) pointed out in his best-selling book *On Leadership,* that "no individual has all the skills—and certainly not the time—to carry out all the complex tasks of contemporary leadership."

As teachers assume broader leadership roles, collaborative decision making will become more common in schools (Parkay, Shindler, and Oaks 1997). One such school is Anzar High School in San Juan Bautista, California whose teachers are "committed to collaborative decision-making regarding teaching and learning, devoting faculty meetings and professional development time to discussing student progress, curriculum, and assessment" (Davidson 2002). The success of the collaborative leadership model is the result of teachers' commitment to the "Anzar Communication Guidelines" comprised of ten "individual guidelines" and twelve "group guidelines." The following are included among the guidelines:

- I commit to practice these guidelines.
- I listen to the message and not the messenger.
- We are all part of the same team; we collectively own problems, and we collectively solve them.
- We help and support others.
- We allow conflict and differing ideas to exist, and we recognize that tension may be normal (*Horace* 2002).

Table 12.1 Percentage of teachers who strongly agreed with various statements about the school's principal and management, by sector and private school type: 1999–2000

Sector and type	Principal enforces school rules	School goals are communicated clearly	Administration is supportive and encouraging	Necessary materials are available	Principal expresses expectations for staff	Staff are recognized for good work	Principal often discusses instructional practice
Public	47.4	48.1	41.8	37.2	49.7	25.7	11.0
Private	62.7	61.3	59.9	60.2	56.5	39.8	15.4
Private school type							
Catholic	59.2	59.1	56.1	53.2	55.9	36.5	14.1
Other religious	68.3	66.4	67.3	64.0	60.5	45.7	18.1
Nonsectarian	59.4	56.5	53.6	64.5	51.1	35.7	12.9

Source: U.S. Department of Education, National Center for Education Statistics. Schools and Staffing Survey (SASS), "Public, Public Charter, and Private School Teacher Survey," 1999–2000. Taken from National Center for Education Statistics, *Special Analysis 2002–Private Schools: A Brief Portrait,* Table 10. Washington, D.C.: Author.

Professional Reflection

Group Collaboration

Reflect on your experiences working in two groups—one group whose members collaborated successfully, the other whose members did not. In retrospect, what might have accounted for the ability of one group to collaborate and the inability of the other group? Review the "individual" and "group" communication guidelines developed by the Anzar High School teachers. What additional "individual" and "group" guidelines are necessary if members of a group are to collaborate effectively?

Involvement in the Profession

Today's teachers realize that they have the most important role in the educational enterprise and that, previously, they have not had the power they needed to improve the profession. Therefore, they are taking an increasingly broader view of the decisions that, as professionals, they have the right to make.

Across the country, professional teachers are deeply involved with their colleagues, professional organizations, teacher educators, legislators, policymakers, and others in a push to make teaching more fully a profession. Through their behaviors and accomplishments, they are demonstrating that they are professionals, that the professional identity of teachers is becoming stronger. During the last decade, for example, teachers have become more involved in teacher education reform, teacher certification, and professional governance. And, through the efforts of scores of teacher organizations, teachers have also made gains in working conditions, salaries, and benefits.

To What Professional Organizations Do Teachers Belong?

The expanding leadership role of teachers has been supported through the activities of more than five hundred national teacher organizations (*Directory of National Trade and Professional Associations of the United States* 2002). These organizations and the scores of hardworking teachers who run them support a variety of activities to improve teaching and schools. Through lobbying in Washington and at state capitols, for example, teacher associations acquaint legislators, policymakers, and politicians with critical issues and problems in the teaching profession. Many associations have staffs of teachers, researchers, and consultants who produce professional publications, hold conferences, prepare grant proposals, engage in school improvement activities, and promote a positive image of teaching to the public. In the quest to improve the professional lives of all teachers, two national organizations have led the way: the National Education Association (NEA) and the American Federation of Teachers (AFT). These two groups have had a long history of competition for the allegiance of teachers.

The National Education Association

Membership in the **National Education Association (NEA),** the oldest and largest of the two organizations, includes both teachers and administrators. Originally called the National Teachers Association when it was founded in 1857, the group was started by forty-three educators from a dozen states and the District of Columbia (West 1980, 1).

The NEA has affiliates in every state plus Puerto Rico and the District of Columbia, and its local affiliates number more than 15,000. About two-thirds of the teachers in this country belong to the NEA. More than 78 percent of NEA's 2.7 million members are teachers; about 12 percent are guidance counselors, librarians, and administrators; almost 3 percent are university professors; about 2 percent are college and university students; about 3 percent are support staff (teacher aides, secretaries, cafeteria workers, bus drivers, and custodians); and about 2 percent are retired members.

Where Do You Stand? Visit the Companion Website to Voice Your Opinion.

To improve education in this country, the NEA has standing committees in the following areas: affiliate relationships, higher education, human relations, political action, teacher benefits, and teacher rights. These committees engage in a wide range of activities, among them preparing reports on important educational issues, disseminating the results of educational research, conducting conferences, working with federal agencies on behalf of children, pressing for more rigorous standards for the teaching profession, helping school districts resolve salary disputes, developing ways to improve personnel practices, and enhancing the relationship between the profession and the public.

Currently, more than two-thirds of states have passed some type of collective bargaining laws that apply to teachers. There is little uniformity among these laws, with most of the thirty-one states permitting strikes only if certain conditions have been met. The NEA has gone on record as supporting a federal statute that would set up uniform procedures for teachers to bargain with their employers.

The NEA continues today to focus on issues of concern to teachers, primarily in the area of professional governance. Efforts are being made to broaden teachers' decision-making powers related to curriculum, extracurricular responsibilities, staff development, and supervision. To promote the status of the profession, the NEA conducts annual research studies and opinion surveys in various areas and publishes *NEA Today* and *Tomorrow's Teachers* for NEA student members.

The American Federation of Teachers

The **American Federation of Teachers (AFT)** was founded in 1916. Three teachers' unions in Chicago issued a call for teachers to form a national organization affiliated with organized labor. Teacher unions in Gary, Indiana; New York City; Oklahoma; Scranton, Pennsylvania; and Washington, D.C., joined the three Chicago unions to form the AFT.

The AFT differs from the NEA in that it is open only to teachers and nonsupervisory school personnel. The AFT is active today in organizing teachers, collective bargaining, public relations, and developing policies related to various educational issues. In addition, the organization conducts research in areas such as educational reform, bilingual education, teacher certification, and evaluation, and also represents members' concerns through legislative action and technical assistance.

The AFT has more than 1.2 million members who are organized through 2,265 local affiliates. The AFT is affiliated with the American Federation of Labor–Congress of Industrial Organizations (AFL-CIO), which has over thirteen million members. To promote the idea that teachers should have the right to speak for themselves on important issues, the AFT does not allow superintendents, principals, and other administrators to join. As an informational brochure on the AFT states, "Because the AFT believes in action—in 'getting things done' rather than issuing reports, letting someone else do the 'doing'—a powerful, cohesive structure is necessary."

Unlike the NEA, the AFT has been steadfastly involved throughout its history in securing economic gains and improving working conditions for teachers. Though the AFT has been criticized for being unprofessional and too concerned with bread-and-butter issues, none other than the great educator and philosopher John Dewey took out the first AFT membership card in 1916. After twelve years as a union member, Dewey made his stance on economic issues clear:

> *It is said that the Teachers Union, as distinct from the more academic organizations, overemphasizes the economic aspect of teaching. Well, I never had that contempt for the economic aspect of teaching, especially not on the first of the month when I get my salary check. I find that teachers have to pay their grocery and meat bills and house rent just the same as everybody else (1955, 60–61).*

Traditionally, the AFT has been strongest in urban areas. Today, the AFT represents teachers not only in Chicago and New York but in Philadelphia, Washington, D.C., Kansas City, Detroit, Boston, Cleveland, and Pittsburgh. NEA membership has tended to be suburban and rural. The NEA has always been the larger of the two organizations, and it is presently more than twice the size of its rival.

The NEAFT Partnership

For decades, many people within both the NEA and the AFT believed that the interests of teachers and students could best be served through a merger of the two organizations. One national teachers' union with enormous political strength, they believed, could do more to advance the teaching profession than two independent, often competing, organizations. However, until the turn of the century, differences between the two organizations thwarted periodic efforts to merge.

By the end of the 1990s, differences between the NEA and the AFT had become less apparent. Collective bargaining and the use of strikes, long opposed by the NEA, were now used by both organizations. Eventually, a "conceptual agreement" to merge the organizations was announced in 1998 by the presidents of the NEA and the AFT. The presidents cited an "assault" on public education in the form of voucher plans, charter schools, and other approaches to school privatization as a primary reason to merge (Bradley 1998). In 2001, NEA and AFT Unity Discussion Teams and Advisory Committees forged the **NEAFT Partnership** and endorsed the following goals:

- **Building Relationships** to increase knowledge, promote trust and collaboration and involve leaders and affiliates in both our unions at the national, state and local levels.
- **Making Collaboration Work** to more effectively use our combined resources to focus on promoting the welfare of children, public education and our members.
- **Creating Value** from the power of our collaboration to strengthen our ability to resist the challenges by the enemies of public education and collective bargaining.
- **Demonstrating Visibly** our united strength and ability to improve the institutions in which our members work and further signal our commitment to public education and unionism (NEAFT Partnership 2002).

Other Professional Organizations

In addition to the NEA and AFT, teachers' professional interests are represented by more than 500 other national organizations. Several of these are concerned with improving the quality of education at all levels and in all subject areas. **Phi Delta Kappa (PDK),** for example, is an international professional and honorary fraternity of educators concerned with enhancing quality education through research and leadership activities. Founded in 1906, Phi Delta Kappa has a membership of more than 90,000. Members, who are graduate students, teachers, and administrators, belong to one of more than 666 chapters. To be initiated into Phi Delta Kappa, one must have demonstrated high academic achievement, have completed at least fifteen semester hours of graduate work in education, and have made a commitment to a career of educational service. Phi Delta Kappa members receive *Phi Delta Kappan,* a journal of education published ten times a year.

Another example is the **Association for Supervision and Curriculum Development (ASCD),** a professional organization of teachers, supervisors, curriculum coordinators, education professors, administrators, and others. The ASCD is interested in school improvement at all levels of education. Founded in 1943, the association has a membership of 160,000. ASCD provides professional development experiences in curriculum and supervision, disseminates information on educational issues, and encourages research, evaluation, and theory development. ASCD also conducts several National Curriculum Study Institutes around the country each year and provides a free research information service to members. Members receive *Educational Leadership,* a well-respected journal printed eight times a year. ASCD also publishes a yearbook, each one devoted to a particular educational issue, and occasional books in the area of curriculum and supervision.

In addition, as you will see in Appendix 12.1 many professional associations exist for teachers of specific subject-areas, such as mathematics, English, social studies, music, physical education, and so on, as well as for teachers of specific student populations, such as exceptional learners, young children, and students with limited English proficiency.

What New Leadership Roles for Teachers Are Emerging?

Teachers' roles are changing in fundamental and positive ways at the beginning of the twenty-first century. Greater autonomy and an expanded role in educational policymaking has led to unprecedented opportunities for today's teachers to extend their leadership roles beyond the classroom. To prepare for this future, today's teachers will need to develop leadership skills to a degree not needed in the past.

Teacher Involvement in Teacher Education, Certification, and Staff Development

Teacher input into key decisions about teacher preparation, certification, and staff development is on the rise. Through their involvement with professional development schools and the National Board for Professional Teaching Standards (see Chapter 2), state professional standards boards (see Chapter 2), and scores of local, state, and national education committees, teachers are changing the character of pre- and in-service education. For example, the National Board for Professional Teaching Standards (NBPTS) established a network designed to allow nearly 7 percent of the nation's 2.5 million teachers to participate in field-testing various components of the NBPTS certification system. The NBPTS allocated $1 million to teachers, in the form of honoraria, for helping to field-test

What characteristics distinguish teaching as a profession? What are some new leadership roles teachers are taking on these days?

the NBPTS assessment materials. One participant in the field test reflects on how teacher participation in the NBPTS can positively influence the profession of teaching:

> *I am proud to say I was one of the first teachers in the country to participate in NBPTS. At its best, NBPTS can help us validate our skills as teachers; it can help us focus on areas of needed improvement; it can encourage a core of committed teacher-thinkers. . . . As more and more teachers participate and are certified, we will find our voices. We will be able to speak in an articulate fashion about what is important for us and our students. We will be heard (Hletko 1995, 36).*

Teachers who have received National Board Certification are recognized as professionals not only in their schools, but also in their districts and beyond. For example, after receiving Board Certification, these teachers had the following professional opportunities:

- Helene Alolouf (Early Adolescence/English Language Arts certificate) of Yonkers, New York, was invited to teach at the Manhattanville Graduate School of Education as an adjunct professor.
- Sandra Blackman (Early Adolescence/English Language Arts certificate) of San Diego, California, was promoted to resource teacher for the Humanities Departments for fifty-five schools, where she provides staff development for a standards-based system.
- Edward William Clark Jr. (Early Childhood/Generalist certificate) of Valley, Alabama, helped the State Department of Education and the Alabama Education Association develop National Board Certification training modules to assist Alabama teachers with National Board Certification.
- Linda Lilja (Middle Childhood/Generalist certificate) of Scranton, Kansas, was invited to serve as a member of the task force for the National Teachers Hall of Fame.
- Donna W. Parrish (Early Adolescence/Generalist certificate) of Shelby, North Carolina, was appointed curriculum specialist at a middle school.

Teacher-Leaders

As the titles of the following books suggest, the term ***teacher-leader*** has become part of the vocabulary of educational reform:

- *Reframing the Path to School Leadership: A Guide for Teachers and Principals* (Bolman and Deal 2002).
- *Leadership Strategies for Teachers* (Merideth 2000).
- *Reflective Action Planning for Teachers: A Guide to Teacher-Led School and Professional Development* (Frost 1997).
- *Teacher Leaders: Making a Difference in Schools* (Gehrke and Romerdahl 1997).
- *Who Will Save Our Schools? Teachers as Constructivist Leaders* (Lambert et al. 1997).

- *Deciding to Lead: The English Teacher as Reformer* (Wolfe and Antinarella 1997).
- *Every Teacher as a Leader: Realizing the Potential of Teacher Leadership* (Ackerman, Moller, and Katzenmeyer 1996).
- *Awakening the Sleeping Giant: Leadership Development for Teachers* (Katzenmeyer and Moller 1996).
- *Collaborative Leadership and Shared Decision Making: Teachers, Principals, and University Professors* (Clift et al. 1995).
- *Educating Teachers for Leadership and Change: Teacher Education Yearbook III* (O'Hair and Odell 1995).
- *A Handbook for Teacher Leaders* (Pellicer and Anderson 1995).
- *Becoming a Teacher Leader: From Isolation to Collaboration* (Boleman and Deal 1994).
- *Classroom Crusaders: Eleven Teachers Who Are Trying to Change the System* (Wolk and Rodman 1994).
- *Teachers as Leaders: Perspectives on the Professional Development of Teachers* (Walling 1994).
- *When Teachers Lead* (Astuto 1993).
- *Teachers as Leaders: Evolving Roles* (Livingston 1992).

"In their new leadership roles, teachers are being called upon to form new partnerships with business and industry; institutions of higher education; social service agencies; professional associations; and local, state, and federal governmental agencies. In this new role, teachers will be the key to promoting widespread improvement of our educational system" (Gmelch and Parkay 1995, 50–51). A brief look at the professional activities of Sandra MacQuinn, a teacher-leader who worked with the first author and a colleague on a major restructuring effort at Rogers High School in Spokane, Washington, illustrates the wide-ranging roles of a teacher-leader. In addition to teaching, here are just a few of MacQuinn's leadership activities while serving as liaison and onsite coordinator of a school-university partnership between Rogers High School and Washington State University's College of Education:

- Writing grant proposals for teacher-developed projects
- Helping other teachers write grant proposals
- Facilitating the development of an integrated school-to-work curriculum
- Preparing newsletters to keep faculty up-to-date on restructuring
- Organizing and facilitating staff development training
- Developing connections with area businesses and arranging "job shadowing" sites for students
- Working with a community college to create an alternative school for Rogers High students at the college
- Scheduling substitute teachers to provide Rogers teachers with release-time to work on restructuring
- Making presentations on the Rogers High restructuring at state and regional conferences

On the Frontlines

Schools with Relational Trust

While home for spring break, you return to your high school to meet with Ms. Ondula, the teacher who inspired you to become a teacher and who has been your mentor. You want her advice on what to look for when interviewing for a job and how to decide which school is right for you. As you walk down the hall, you realize that something has changed. It's 4:30, school let out at 3:15, and a lot of people are still here. Clusters of students and parents talk with teachers, animated and laughing. It wasn't like this when you attended. Teachers used to stay only up to the time required in their contracts. When you sit down with Ms. Ondula, you ask her what caused the change.

> *It's Mr. Thomas, the new principal. He started last year and things have been different ever since! He's clearly here for us—and he has great ideas! With his help we launched a formal new-teacher induction program and developed plans for monthly professional development meetings to help the new teachers. Actually, though, we're all benefiting from them. We share our strategies and brainstorm for better ways to deal with class troublemakers, bullying, parent conflicts, time management, student test anxiety and our own stress. All of the new teachers partner and regularly meet with one or two of us veterans. They helped us create the in-service topics.*
>
> *Mr. Thomas is open to our ideas, too. Like the Friday Clubs Program for the fourth through sixth grades. We presented the idea and he was all for it; he felt it was worth a try. Friday afternoons are no longer a wasteland. Students love Fridays, and the club courses are fascinating. Each teacher offered several they wanted to teach, and the students chose the ones they wanted. This session they're taking film animation, medieval games, Monet, local architecture, city government, Spanish, investing in the stock market, and film critiquing. Mr. Thomas suggested that we see if parents wanted to participate, and they did. They're great additions.*
>
> *We feel like a community now. It has been especially good for the new teachers. But enough of that. Let's talk about what you came here for. What should you look for in the schools that offer you a position?*

New teachers need to choose the schools where they'll teach, as well as be chosen by them. They can tell a lot about a school by simply walking through the hallways and observing how teachers talk to their students and each other. They can pick up on or seek out principals' attitudes toward students, teachers, and parents in their interviews with them. Attention to the emotional dimensions of the school culture they might enter can serve them well.

While we instinctively know that people do better in positive environments, it was not until a recent study that empirical evidence was found to support the concept and to connect trusting environments with academic achievement. Anthony S. Bryk and Barbara Schneider (2002) based these findings on their tenth-year, mixed-method, longitudinal study of schools in Chicago during a period of educational reform. Through observations, interviews, and case studies, they were able to describe "four vital signs for identifying and assessing trust in schools." These factors can be used in assessing a school environment.

The first vital sign of trust in a school is *Respect:* "Do we acknowledge one another's dignity and ideas? Do we interact in a courteous way?" The second is *Competence:* "Do we believe in each other's ability and willingness to fulfill our responsibilities effectively?" Trust is hard to maintain when a perception of incompetence exists. The third is *Personal Regard:* "Do we care about each other both professionally and personally?" Birthday celebrations, department picnics, and social gatherings with parents may seem like distractions to busy task-oriented teachers, but their benefits are great in terms of strengthening trust.

The fourth vital sign for trust in a school is *Integrity*. "Can we trust each other to put the interests of children first, especially when tough decisions have to be made? Do we keep our word?"

Because of new teacher retention problems, attention is being given to finding ways to smooth the transition into teaching. A research study to follow is the Project on the Next Generation being conducted by the Harvard Graduate School of Education. These are promising times of change for new teachers.

Exploratory Questions

1. By examining trust in relationships between principals and teachers, teachers and teachers, and school professionals and parents, Bryk and Schneider also examined how the quality of these relationships affect reform efforts and academic achievement. What do you suppose they found?
2. What kind of affect might the relationships and culture of a school have on determining a new teacher's commitment to the profession?

Your Survival Guide of Helpful Resources

The following resources provide helpful hints for surviving "on the frontlines."

Books and Articles

Bryck, A., and Schneider, B. L. (2002). *Trust in schools: A core resource for improvement.* New York: Russell Sage Foundation.

Gordon, D. T. (2002, July/August). Fuel for reform: The importance of trust in changing school. *Harvard Education Letter,* pp. 1–4.

Gordon, D. T. (2002, July/August). Wide open and welcoming: How trust helped transform a small Chicago school. *Harvard Education Letter,* pp. 4–6.

Johnson, S. M., and Kardos, S. M. (2002/March). Redesigning professional development: Keeping new teachers in mind. *Educational Leadership,* pp. 12–16. Retrieved from http://www.ascd.org/readingroom/edlead/0203/johnson.html

Websites

Project on the Next Generation of Teachers New York:
(http://www.gse.harvard.edu/~ngt)

Tips and Strategies from First-Year Teachers
(http://www.ed.gov/pubs/FirstYear/ch3.html)

- Arranging for Rogers students to visit Washington State University (WSU)
- Meeting with the principal, assistant principals, WSU professors, and others to develop short- and long-range plans for implementing site-based management; chairing meetings of the site-based council, the restructuring steering committee, and other restructuring-related committees

Three hundred sixty teachers will participate in the Teacher Leaders in Research-Based Science Education (TLRBSE) between 2002 and 2007. Funded by the National Science Foundation, TLRBSE enables experienced teacher-leaders to mentor teachers new to the profession, participate in a year-round online course, and implement research-based science education in the classroom. The teacher-leaders also participate in a combination of in-residence workshops at Kitt Peak National Observatory and the National Solar Observatory. Participants also receive a stipend, airfare, room and board, and support to attend a meeting of the National Science Teachers Association (Rector, Jacoby, Lockwood, and McCarthy 2002).

Dimensions of Teacher Leadership Beyond the Classroom

Figure 12.4 illustrates eleven dimensions of teacher leadership beyond the classroom. The many teachers whom we have assisted on school restructuring projects during the last few years have used these skills to reach an array of educational goals. These teachers are similar to those described by Henry Jay Becker in this chapter's epigraph—they "view their responsibilities as extending beyond classroom teaching to include participation in the larger community of educators and administrators."

At schools around the country, teachers and principals are using a "collaborative, emergent" approach to leadership; that is, the person who provides leadership for a particular schoolwide project or activity may or may not be the principal or a member of the administrative team (Parkay, Schindler, and Oaks

Figure 12.4 Eleven dimensions of teacher leadership beyond the classroom

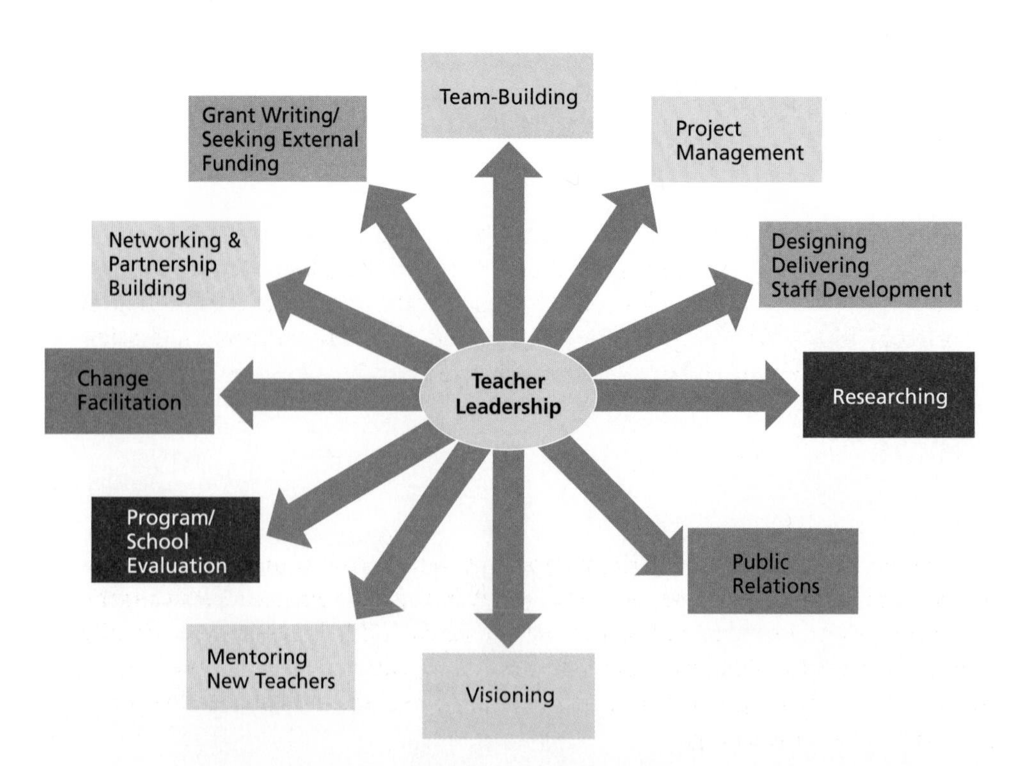

Five Principles That Guide the Actions of Teacher-Leaders

PRINCIPLE 1

Teacher-leaders accept their responsibility to increase the degree and quality of daily interactions with other teachers, administrators, and staff members. They know that "even if done on a small scale regularly, this can make a very significant difference for other individual teachers and for oneself."

PRINCIPLE 2

Teacher-leaders recognize that they have a responsibility to understand and to improve the culture of the school. "Every teacher must be concerned about the health of the school as an organization. This does not mean getting obsessively involved in every aspect of school life, but it does mean taking some responsibility for the welfare of one's colleagues and the wider life of the school."

PRINCIPLE 3

Teacher-leaders recognize that every teacher is a leader, and that a teacher's leadership role will vary according to the stage of the teacher's life and career. However, "all teachers have a leadership contribution to make beyond their own classrooms and should take action accordingly."

PRINCIPLE 4

Teacher-leaders recognize that they have a responsibility to become informed about the development of educational policies as well as professional and research issues. "This does not mean having a second career as an academic. But it does mean connecting with the knowlege base for improving teaching and schools. The more knowledgeable a teacher is about global educational and professional issues, the more resourceful he or she will be for students as well as for other teachers."

PRINCIPLE 5

Teacher-leaders recognize that all teachers have a responsibility for helping to shape the quality of the next generation of teachers. Teachers can make a contribution by working with student teachers, mentoring new teachers, and supporting and praising other teachers who assume those roles.

Figure 12.5 Five principles that guide the actions of teacher-leaders
Source: Adapted from Michael Fullan and Andy Hargreaves, *What's Worth Fighting for in Your School?* New York: Teachers College Press, 1996.

1997). Teachers who accept the challenge of becoming teacher-leaders and redefining their roles to include responsibilities beyond the classroom recognize the importance of five principles Michael Fullan and Andy Hargreaves present in their book, *What's Worth Fighting for in Your School?* (1996); they use these principles to guide their professional actions (see Figure 12.5).

How Do Teachers Contribute to Educational Research?

Today's teachers play an increasingly important role in educational research. By applying research to solve practical, classroom-based problems, teachers validate the accuracy and usefulness of educational research and help researchers identify additional areas to investigate. As consumers of educational research, teachers improve their teaching, contribute to educational reform, and enhance the professional status of teaching.

In addition, increasing numbers of teachers are becoming competent researchers in their own right and making important contributions to our understanding of teaching and learning. Prior to the mid 1980s, teachers were the missing "voice" in educational research. However, as teachers and staff developers Holly and McLoughlin (1989, 309) noted more than a decade ago, "We've moved from research on teachers to research with teachers and lately to research by teachers." Since their observation, we have seen the emergence of the **teacher-researcher,** the professional teacher who conducts classroom research to improve his or her teaching.

Part of being a professional is the ability to decide *how* and *when* to use research to guide one's actions. For example, Emmerich Koller, a teacher of German at a suburban high school, describes in an article he wrote for the book *Teachers Doing Research: Practical Possibilities* (Burnaford, Fischer, and Hobson 2001) how he experimented with new teaching methods based on the latest findings from brain research and "accelerated learning," a strategy for optimizing learning by integrating conscious and unconscious mental processes. After determining how and when to put that research into practice, he commented, "At age 50, after 27 years of teaching, I have found something that has made teaching very exciting again" (Koller 1996, 180).

Sources of Educational Research

Research findings are reported in scores of educational research journals. In addition, there are several excellent reviews of research with which you should become familiar during your professional preparation, such as the fourth edition of the *Handbook of Research on Teaching* (published by the American Educational Research Association, 2001). Its more than 1,200 pages synthesize research in several areas, including research on teaching at various grade levels and in various subject areas. Other comprehensive, authoritative reviews of research you might wish to consult include the following:

- *Encyclopedia of Educational Research,* 6th ed., four volumes (Macmillan, 1992)
- *Handbook of Research in Middle Level Education* (Information Age Publishing, 2001)
- *Handbook of Research on the Education of Young Children* (Macmillan, 1993)
- *Handbook of Research on Improving Student Achievement* (Educational Research Service, 1999)
- *Handbook of Research on Mathematics Teaching and Learning* (Macmillan, 1992), sponsored by the National Council of Teachers of Mathematics
- *Handbook of Research on Multicultural Education* (Macmillan, 1995)
- *Handbook of Research on Music Teaching and Learning* (Macmillan, 1992), sponsored by the Music Educators National Conference
- *Handbook of Research on Science Teaching and Learning* (Macmillan, 1994), sponsored by the National Science Teachers Association
- *Handbook of Research on Social Studies Teaching and Learning* (Macmillan, 1991), sponsored by the National Council for the Social Studies

Technology Highlights

How are teachers playing a leadership role in the development and dissemination of multimedia software?

As pointed out in Chapter 11, a key to the effective use of technology to enhance students' learning is the availability of high-quality educational software. Since computer-enhanced instruction (CEI) first began to be used widely in the schools during the early 1990s, there has been a consistent call for higher-quality educational software and a realization that teachers, with their deep understanding of students' learning needs, would need to play a central role in the development of that software. As a software publisher stated in the U.S. Department of Education's publication *Getting America's Students Ready for the 21st Century: Meeting the Technology Literacy Challenge* (1996a): "We definitely need teachers to help identify good software–to put some models out there that producers can emulate. Teachers need to be involved in separating the wheat from the chaff."

In response to that call, scores of teachers have become directly involved in developing and disseminating innovative, cutting-edge educational software. Perhaps the best known teacher-developed software is Roger Wagner's HyperStudio®, with more than two million users in the United States alone. As a science and mathematics teacher in California, Wagner launched HyperStudio® in 1978. According to Wagner, "We wanted to make multimedia authoring a reality for students on the humble Apple IIGS. [The] world at large sets the stage for what is happening in classrooms now. As students increasingly use electronic sources of information for their research, and see the pervasion of multimedia around them, they expect to create their own projects in the same manner" (Davitt, 1997). Currently, dozens of teachers provide Wagner with input as he continues to develop newer versions of HyperStudio®.

Many other teachers around the country are working with instructional technology laboratories to develop and field-test multimedia software. For example, scores of teachers have collaborated with researchers at Wheeling Jesuit University's Center for Educational Technologies (CET), also home of NASA's Classroom of the Future program, to develop Astronomy Village and Investigating the Solar System, two of the most innovative computer simulations currently available.

Still other teachers are providing leadership for the integration of technology into teaching and learning environments. For example, dozens of teachers have attended the CET's Teacher-Leader Institutes, where they acquire strategies for integrating technology into education. Similarly, other teachers have completed the Teacher2Teacher Technology Leadership programs in San Jose, California, where they can earn Teacher Technology Integration Certification (TTIC), Train the Trainer Certification (TTC), or Technology Leadership (TL) Certification.

Clearly, teachers will play three vital leadership roles in the development of multimedia software for classrooms of the twenty-first century:

1. Developing and disseminating increasingly powerful versions of multimedia software
2. Developing strategies for the most effective ways to use that software in the classroom
3. Training other teachers to use that software

- *Handbook of Research on Teaching the English Language Arts* (Macmillan, 1991), sponsored by the International Reading Association and the National Council of Teachers of English
- *Handbook of Research on Teaching Literacy through the Communicative and Visual Arts* (Macmillan, 1997)
- *Research Ideas for the Classroom: Early Childhood Mathematics, Middle School Mathematics, and High School Mathematics* (Macmillan, 1993), three volumes sponsored by the National Council of Teachers of Mathematics

This teacher is conducting classroom research on the ways students come to understand a problem and to apply appropriate problem-solving skills. What are several ways the teacher might use this research as a professional?

Government Resources for Research Application

The federal government supports several efforts designed to help teachers improve their practice through the application of research findings. In 1966, three agencies were created to support and disseminate research: **Educational Resources Information Center (ERIC), Research and Development Centers,** and **Regional Educational Laboratories.** ERIC is a national information system made up of sixteen **ERIC Clearinghouses** and several adjunct clearinghouses—all coordinated by the central ERIC agency in Washington, D.C. (see the Appendix "Educational Resources Information Center (ERIC) Clearinghouses" on this book's website). The ERIC system, available in most college and university libraries, contains descriptions of exemplary programs, the results of research and development efforts, and related information that can be used by teachers, administrators, and the public to improve education. Each clearinghouse specializes in one area of education and searches out relevant documents or journal articles that are screened according to ERIC selection criteria, abstracted, and indexed.

Within the **Office of Educational Research and Improvement (OERI)** in Washington, D.C., the Office of Research (formerly the National Institute of Education) maintains twelve research centers at universities around the country (see the Appendix "Selected National Educational Research and Improvement [OERI] Centers" on this book's website). The centers are devoted to high-quality, fundamental research at every level of education, with most of the research done by scholars at the host university. Among the areas these centers focus on are the processes of teaching and learning, school organization and improvement, the content of education, and factors that contribute to (or detract from) excellence in education.

OERI also maintains ten regional educational laboratories and sponsors a number of Assistance Centers (see the Appendix "Department of Education Regional Assistance Centers" on this book's website). Each laboratory serves a geographic region and is a nonprofit corporation not affiliated with a university. Laboratory staff work directly with school systems, state educational agencies, and other organizations to improve education through the application of research findings.

Conducting Classroom Action Research

Almost four decades ago, Robert Schaefer (1967, 5) posed the following questions in *The School as the Center of Inquiry:*

> *Why should our schools not be staffed, gradually if you will, by scholar-teachers in command of the conceptual tools and methods of inquiry requisite to investigating the learning process as it operates in their own classroom? Why should our schools not nurture the continuing wisdom and power of such scholar-teachers?*

Schaefer's vision for teaching has become a reality. Today, thousands of teachers are involved in action research to improve their teaching. Using their classrooms as "laboratories," these teacher-researchers are systematically studying the outcomes of their teaching through the application of various research methods. In addition, they are disseminating the results of their research at professional conferences and through publications, including *Networks: An On-line Journal for Teacher Research.*

Simply put, **action research** is the classroom-based study by teachers, individually or collaboratively, of how to improve instruction. As in the *reflection-in-action* approach described earlier in this chapter, action research begins with a teacher-identified question, issue, or problem. For example, Laura Jordan, a middle school teacher, explains how she designed an action research study (published in *Networks*) in response to her students' lack of involvement in class activities:

> *The students enrolled in my sixth grade advanced language arts class are particularly difficult to engage in discussions and frequently do not put forth their best efforts in completing assignments. [As] a result of my reflections, I discovered that I spend the majority of instructional time lecturing and directing students, as well as giving too few assignments that allow students to express their creativity and individual learning styles.*
>
> *In light of this realization, I came to the conclusion that I needed to seek a way to engage my students, making learning experiences meaningful and creating in students a spark of excitement for learning. [As] I began this project my goal was to determine whether students would take more ownership of their learning and produce higher quality work if they were allowed to choose responsive activities that reflected their individual learning styles (Jordan and Hendricks 2002).*

Action research is also "a natural part of teaching. [T]o be a teacher means to observe students and study classroom interactions, to explore a variety of effective ways of teaching and learning, and to build conceptual frameworks that can guide one's work. This is a personal as well as a professional quest, a journey toward making sense out of and finding satisfaction in one's teaching. It is the work of teacher-researchers" (Fischer 1996, 33). Figure 12.6 presents five steps in the classroom-focused action research cycle.

Not surprisingly, becoming a teacher-researcher is hard work, given the daily demands of teaching itself. However, more schools are redefining the teacher's role to include doing action research. These schools realize that action research can provide data on the effectiveness of educational programs, enhance student learning, and energize teachers for professional growth. Four teachers who are

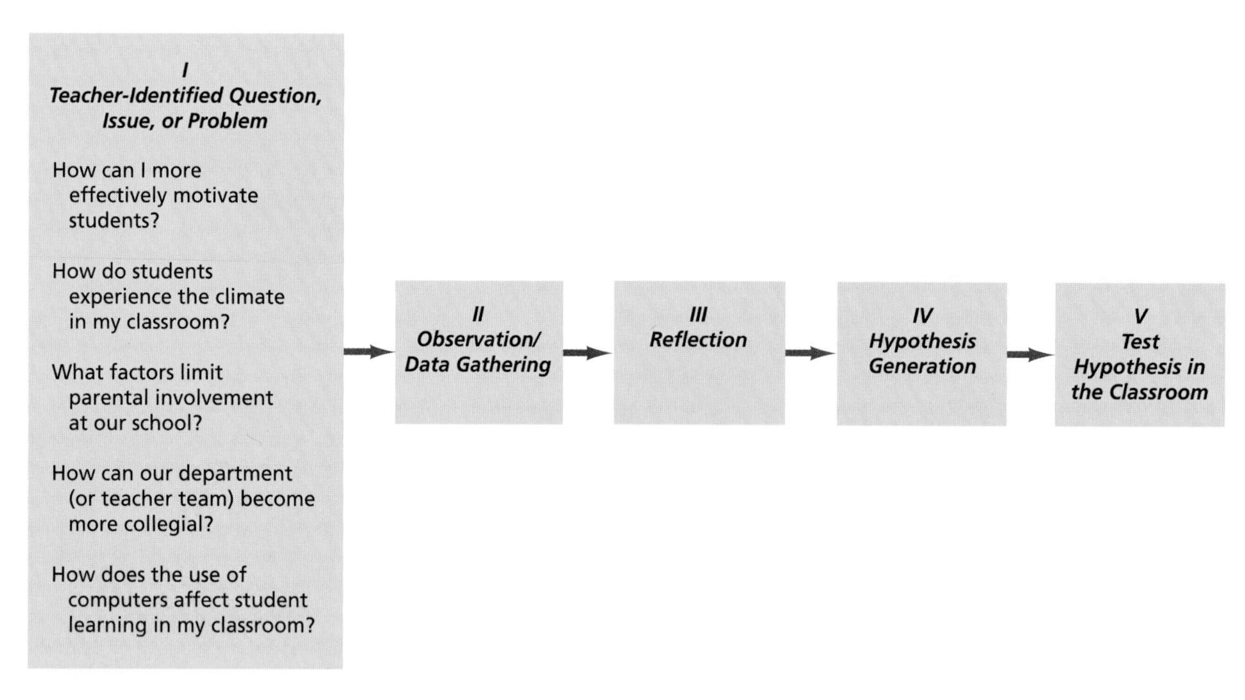

Figure 12.6 A classroom-focused action research cycle

members of the Action Research Laboratory at Highland Park High School near Chicago comment on the benefits of action research:

> *By far the most rewarding part of working on an action research team was the opportunity to learn and grow with a small group of teacher colleagues. This experience of mutual commitment provided a wonderful staff development experience; by working with these colleagues consistently throughout the year, we were able to explore new ideas and take risks in the classroom with a type of "safety net" in place. For that reason alone, as well as our desire to explore the new questions and challenges raised by our research, we will continue to conduct action research into the effectiveness of our teaching and grading practices (Mills 2000, 97).*

How Are Teachers Providing Leadership for School Restructuring and Curriculum Reform?

Today's teachers welcome opportunities to provide leadership for school restructuring and curriculum reform. Although teachers may have played a limited role in school governance in the past, there are currently many opportunities for teachers to become educational leaders beyond the classroom. Figure 12.7 presents five clusters of educational reform, each of which will offer teachers opportunities to shape policies during the twenty-first century.

Leadership and Collaboration for School Reform

The key to successful school restructuring and curriculum reform is teacher leadership and collaboration. At the National Teacher Forum on Leadership, sponsored by the U.S. Department of Education, participating teachers identified the following ways in which teachers can lead and collaborate for school reform. To illustrate each form of leadership, we provide one example from among the thousands of teachers exercising similar leadership.

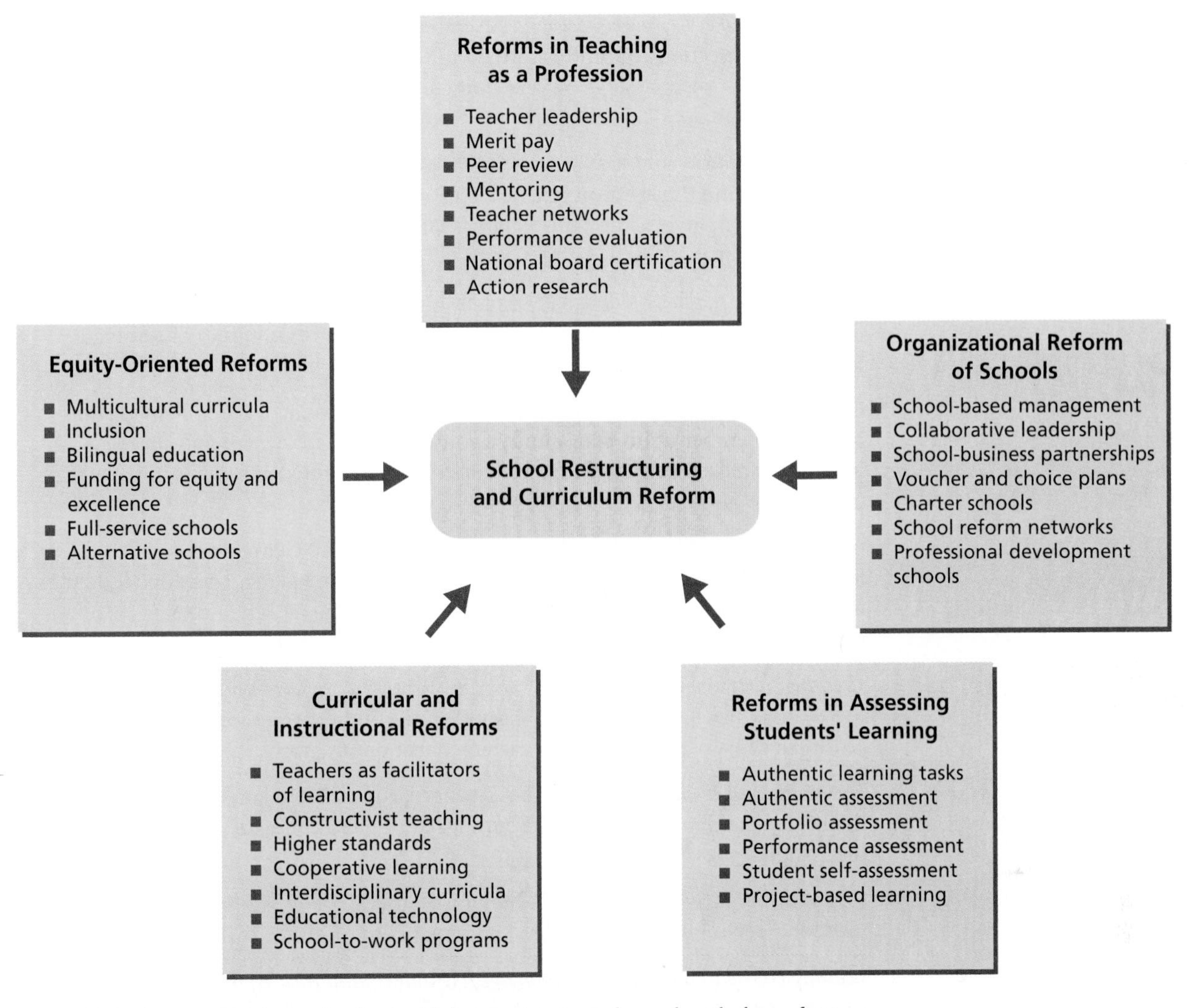

Figure 12.7 Opportunities for teacher leadership in school restructuring and curriculum reform

Participating in professional teacher organizations—As President of the Wisconsin Science Teachers' Association, Sharon Nelson worked with the National Science Teachers Association, Goals 2000, to disseminate national science education standards in her state.

Taking part in school decisions—Melisa Hancock, an elementary school teacher in Kansas, became a clinical instructor at Kansas State University and played a key role in engineering a partnership with the university that led to her school becoming a professional development school.

Defining what students need to know and be able to do—Delaware teacher Jan Parsons was one of several teachers who took leadership roles on Delaware commissions that wrote standards for mathematics, science, social studies, and language arts; teachers also wrote and piloted new statewide assessments in line with the new standards.

Sharing ideas with colleagues—Tom Howe and other Wisconsin teachers developed a "Share Net Program" that allows teachers to make formal presentations to their peers on effective instructional practices.

Being a mentor to new teachers—Science teacher Fie Budzinsky serves as a Teacher Mentor for the State of Connecticut; Budzinsky had, in turn, been mentored earlier in her career by Dick Reagan, another science teacher.

Helping to make personnel decisions—North Carolina teacher Mary Ostwalt served on a selection committee formed to replace a teacher who resigned; other teachers in her district serve on selection committees for the hiring of new principals.

Improving facilities and technology—Ray Hasart and other teachers were the driving force behind the creation of a new $3.5 million technology facility at a Redmond, Oregon, high school; the facility is visited regularly by people throughout the West Coast.

Working with parents—Martina Marquez and a team of colleagues in New Mexico visit Native American villages and surrounding communities to disseminate math and reading activities parents can do with their children.

Creating partnerships with the community—North Carolina teacher Scott Griffin became a member of his community's volunteer fire department and spearheaded the redesign of the fire safety curriculum presented at schools in the community.

Creating partnerships with businesses and organizations—Georgia teacher Stephanie Blakney took the lead in developing a systemwide Partnership with Education program that led to the creation of a food bank and the Atlanta Coca-Cola Bottling Company "adopting" her school.

Creating partnerships with colleges and universities to prepare future teachers—Former Kansas Teacher of the Year Christy McNally and other award-winning teachers organized a partnership with teacher education programs throughout Kansas.

Becoming leaders in the community—Teacher Jacqueline Omland is President of the Legion auxiliary in Aberdeen, South Dakota, and a colleague is Chairman of the Legion.

Becoming politically involved—Washington State teacher Ivy Chan served as treasurer for a person who ran for State Superintendent of Public Instruction.

Leading efforts to make teachers more visible and communicate positive information—High school teacher Larry Torres started a weekly news column in his New Mexico community paper that focuses on positive articles about education; the column has now expanded to a full page.

Collaborative School Reform Networks

Many teachers are involved in restructuring and curriculum change through their schools' participation in collaborative networks for reform. Networks provide teachers with training and resources for restructuring, and they create opportunities for teachers at network schools to help teachers at nonnetwork schools with their restructuring efforts. Among the many collaborative reform networks are the Coalition of Essential Schools, the National Network for Educational Renewal, Accelerated Schools, and state-based networks, such as the League of Professional Schools.

Coalition of Essential Schools The **Coalition of Essential Schools (CES),** started in 1984 by Theodore R. Sizer at Brown University, consists of nineteen regional centers that offer direct support to hundreds of schools in the areas of school organization, classroom practice, leadership, and community connections. The regional centers, with the support of CES National, coach schools through a systematic process of change at the school site. No two Coalition schools are alike; each develops an approach to restructuring suited to its students, faculty, and community. However, the efforts of Coalition schools to restructure are guided by ten Common Principles extrapolated from Sizer's (1997a, 1997b, 1997c; Sizer and Sizer 1999) books on redesigning U.S. schools and the beliefs that top-down, standardized solutions to school problems don't work and that teachers must play a key role in the operation of their schools. Recently, the Coalition organized resource centers so teachers at Coalition schools can provide non-Coalition schools with restructuring assistance.

National Network for Educational Renewal The Center for Educational Renewal at the University of Washington created the **National Network for Educational Renewal (NNER)** to encourage new opportunities for teachers to become involved in school restructuring, curriculum reform, and the preparation of teachers. The NNER consists of nineteen settings in eighteen states, and its members include forty-one colleges and universities, more than one hundred school districts, and over 750 "partner" schools. The NNER is based on nineteen postulates for reforming teacher education that John Goodlad presented in *Educational Renewal: Better Teachers, Better Schools* (1994). For a school to become a member of the NNER, its teachers must demonstrate that they "understand their appropriate role in site-based management and school renewal" (89).

Accelerated Schools Stanford economist Henry M. Levin has developed a nationwide network of **accelerated schools** that provide enriched, rigorous curricula to "speed up" the learning of students at risk. Instead of placing at-risk students into remedial classes, accelerated schools provide students with challenging learning activities traditionally reserved for gifted and talented students. Accelerated schools are based on the belief that teachers—in collaboration with administrators, parents, and community members—must be able to make important educational decisions, take responsibility for implementing those decisions, and take responsibility for the outcomes of those decisions. The National Center for the Accelerated Schools Project at Stanford operates eleven regional Accelerated Schools Satellite Centers across the country. The satellite centers provide assistance to teachers and administrators who wish to restructure their schools according to the accelerated schools model.

State-Based Educational Partnerships Many states have established state-based partnerships between a state university or college and a coalition of public schools. Several of these partnerships are patterned after the League of Professional Schools started by Carl Glickman at the University of Georgia. The overall goal of the League is to improve student learning by using shared governance and action research to focus on instructional and curricular issues. Following guidelines Glickman has outlined in *Renewing America's Schools: A Guide for School-Based Action* (1993) and *Revolutionizing America's Schools* (1998), League schools usually begin the restructuring process by developing a *covenant,* a set of mutually agreed on beliefs about how students learn best, and a *charter,* a set of democratically developed guidelines for how shared governance will operate at the school. Presently, nearly one hundred League schools exchange resources and ideas and support one another in their restructuring efforts.

Summary

To What Extent Is Teaching a Full Profession?

- Teachers are assuming new leadership roles beyond the classroom as educational systems become more decentralized and approaches to school leadership become more collaborative and participatory.
- For an occupation to be considered a profession, it must satisfy several criteria. Of the following nine criteria for a profession, teaching meets some more fully than others: (1) institutional monopoly of services, (2) teacher autonomy, (3) years of education and training, (4) provision of essential service, (5) degree of self-governance, (6) professional associations, (7) professional knowledge and skills, (8) level of public trust, and (9) prestige, benefits, and pay.
- Although teaching does not currently satisfy all criteria for a profession, the collaborative efforts of individuals and groups such as the National Commission on Teaching and America's Future and the National Board for Professional Teaching Standards are rapidly professionalizing teaching.

What Is Professionalism in Teaching?

- The most potent force for enhancing the professional status of teaching is for teachers to see that their actions are professional and to commit themselves to lifelong learning and active involvement in the profession.
- Professional behavior as a teacher is characterized by reflection-in-action (the ability to observe sensitively in classrooms, reflect on those observations, and then act accordingly) and a willingness to serve as a mentor to those entering the profession.
- As lifelong learners, professional teachers actively seek opportunities for growth—from participating in training provided by a school district to arranging one's own "in-service" activities, to acquiring new leadership skills.

To What Professional Organizations Do Teachers Belong?

- Teachers help shape education as a profession through their leadership roles in more than five hundred national teacher organizations.
- As the oldest and largest professional organization for educators, the National Education Association has played a key role in addressing issues of concern to the 78 percent of its members who are teachers.
- Affiliated with organized labor and open only to teachers and nonsupervisory personnel, the American Federation of Teachers has done much to secure greater financial rewards and improved working conditions for teachers.
- After years of competition and conflicting views about collective bargaining, teacher strikes, and affiliation with organized labor, the NEA and AFT formed the NEAFT Partnership to work toward shared goals for improving the profession of teaching.
- Teachers are members of professional associations for specific subject areas and student populations.

What New Leadership Roles for Teachers Are Emerging?

- Through their involvement with professional development schools, the National Board for Professional Teaching Standards, and local, state, and national education committees, teachers participate in making key decisions about teacher preparation, certification, and staff development.
- In their new role as teacher-leaders, many teachers are playing a key role beyond the classroom as they form partnerships that focus on the transformation of schools in the United States.
- Teachers who work collaboratively with principals on school improvement are involved in eleven dimensions of teacher leadership beyond the classroom: team-building, project management, designing and delivering staff development, researching, public relations, visioning, program/school evaluation, change facilitation, networking and partnership building, grant writing/seeking external funding, and mentoring new teachers.

How Do Teachers Contribute to Educational Research?

- Teachers validate the accuracy and usefulness of educational research and identify additional areas to research when they put "research into practice."
- When conducting action research, teachers follow a five-step classroom-focused action research cycle to understand the dynamics of their classrooms and to improve their teaching: identify a question, issue, or problem; observe/gather data; reflect; generate a hypothesis; and test hypothesis.

How Are Teachers Providing Leadership for School Restructuring and Curriculum Reform?

- Five "clusters" of educational reform provide teachers with many opportunities to provide leadership for school restructuring and curriculum reform: reforms in teaching as a profession, equity-oriented reforms, organizational reform of schools, reforms in assessing students' learning, and curricular and instructional reforms.

- Through collaborative school reform networks such as the Coalition of Essential Schools, the National Network for Educational Renewal, Accelerated Schools, and the League of Professional Schools, teachers provide leadership for restructuring their schools and help other teachers promote school reform at nonnetwork schools.

Key Terms and Concepts

accelerated schools, **459**
action research, **455**
American Federation of Teachers (AFT), **443**
Association for Supervision and Curriculum Development (ASCD), **445**
Coalition of Essential Schools (CES), **458**
Educational Resources Information Center (ERIC), **454**
ERIC Clearinghouses, **454**
mentor, **439**
National Education Association (NEA), **442**
National Network for Educational Renewal (NNER), **459**
NEAFT Partnership, **444**
Office of Educational Research and Improvement (OERI), **454**
Phi Delta Kappa (PDK), **445**
profession, **432**
reflection-in-action, **439**
Regional Educational Laboratories, **454**
Research and Development Centers, **454**
teacher-leader, **446**
teacher-researcher, **452**

Applications and Activities

Teacher's Journal

1. In your opinion, what accounts for public trust and lack of trust in the teaching profession? What might be the best way to increase that trust?
2. Review several recent issues of the NEA publication, *NEA Today,* and the AFT publication, *American Teacher.* Compare and contrast concerns or issues that each publication addresses. What overall differences do you find between the NEA and AFT publications?
3. Do you plan to join a teacher's association such as the NEA or AFT? What are your reasons? What advantages and disadvantages are most important to you?

Teacher's Database

1. With classmates, join an online discussion on one or more of the following topics or another topic in Chapter 12 of this text.

   action research
   educational reform
   grant writing
   mentoring
   National Board for Professional Teaching Standards (NBPTS)
   school restructuring
   teacher leadership
   teacher–principal collaboration
   teacher strikes
   teacher unions

2. Using your favorite search engine, gather online information and resources about school networking and teacher networking. How might online networking contribute to your preparation as a teacher? As a teacher, how might you and your students use networking in connection with your curriculum? What knowledge and skills do you need to start to participate in a school-based networking project?

Observations and Interviews

1. Survey adults who are not involved in education to get their views on teaching as a profession. What images of teachers and teaching emerge? How do you account for these views?
2. Interview teachers about their involvement in professional associations and the teachers' union. What benefits do teachers obtain from their professional involvement?

3. Find out if teacher strikes are legal in your state. What risks do striking teachers face? How are disputes between teachers and school districts settled?

4. Collaborate with classmates to study a school that is involved in restructuring and participants' roles in the change process. Compare teachers' activities with the new leadership roles for teachers discussed in this chapter. Are any of the teachers involved in action research in the classroom? How does teacher research contribute to restructuring efforts?

5. Visit a school that has developed a partnership with one or more community agencies, schools of higher education, businesses, parent groups, or neighborhood associations. Arrange to observe a planning meeting between the school and the community representatives. Write a narrative account of the meeting followed by an evaluation of the effectiveness of this partnership. To help you with this activity, ask your instructor for handout masters M12.1, "Observing a School-Community Partnership," and M12.2, "Evaluating the Effectiveness of a School-University Partnership."

Professional Portfolio

Focusing on the grade level and subject area for which you are preparing to teach, consult several of the sources of educational research listed in this chapter and prepare a set of research findings to guide your teaching. For each entry, include a bibliographic citation and an annotation that briefly describes the research and the results of that research.

Video**Workshop Extra!**

If the VideoWorkshop package was included with your textbook, go to Chapter 12 of the Companion Website (www.ablongman.com/parkay6e) and click on the VideoWorkshop button. Follow the instructions for viewing videoclip 10 and completing this exercise. Consider this information along with what you've read in Chapter 12 while answering the following questions.

1. Teachers contribute to educational research by practicing daily what theories present, thereby refuting or validating findings. What is the role of authentic assessment, as discussed in the text and videoclip 10, in educational research, and who gains most from such practice—students or teachers?

2. Do you believe that teaching is a full profession? The criteria presented in the text emphasize different aspects of a profession. Where would you place the practice of assessment in the list of criteria, bearing in mind that assessment incorporates self-assessment, instructional assessment, alternative assessment, and performance assessment. Discuss your opinions.

Appendix 12.1

SAMPLER OF PROFESSIONAL ORGANIZATIONS FOR TEACHERS

American Alliance for Health, Physical Education, Recreation and Dance (AAHPERD)

1900 Association Drive
Reston, VA 20191
(703) 476-3400
Fax (703) 476-9527
info@aahperd.org

Students and educators in physical education, dance, health, athletics, safety education, recreation, and outdoor education. Purpose is to improve its fields of education at all levels through such services as consultation, periodicals and special publications, leadership development, determination of standards, and research. Publications: *AAHPERD Update; Health Education; American Journal of Physical Education, Recreation and Dance; Leisure Today; News Kit on Programs for the Aging; Research Quarterly.*

American Alliance of Teachers of French (AATF)

57 E. Armory Avenue
Champaign, IL 61820
(217) 333-2842
Fax (217) 333-2842

Teachers of French in public and private elementary and secondary schools, colleges, and universities. Maintains Pedagogical Aids Bureau, conducts annual French contest in elementary and secondary schools, awards scholarships to teachers for study in France, maintains placement bureau and a pen pal agency. Publications: *AATF National Bulletin, French Review.*

American Association of Teachers of German (AATG)

112 Haddontowne Court, No. 104
Cherry Hill, NJ 08034
(609) 795-5553
Fax (609) 795-9398
73740.3231@compuserve.com

Teachers of German at all levels. Offers in-service teacher-training workshops and awards and scholarships to outstanding high school students and teachers of German. Publications: *American Association of Teachers of German—Newsletter, Die Unterrichtspraxis: For the Teaching of German, German Quarterly.*

American Association of Teachers of Spanish and Portuguese (Hispanic) (AATSP)

University of Northern Colorado
Gunter Hall
Greeley, CO 80636
(970) 351-1090
lsandste@bentley.univnorthco.edu

Teachers of Spanish and Portuguese languages and literatures and others interested in Hispanic culture. Operates placement bureau and maintains pen pal registry. Sponsors honor society, Sociedad Honoraria Hispanica, and National Spanish Examinations for secondary school students. Publication: *Hispania.*

American Classical League (Language) (ACL)

Miami University
Oxford, OH 45056
(513) 529-7741
Fax (513) 529-7742
americanclassicalleague@muohio.edu

Teachers of classical languages in high schools and colleges. To promote the teaching of Latin and other classical languages. Maintains placement service, teaching materials, and resource center. Publications: *Classical Outlook, Prima* (handbook for elementary school teachers).

American Council on the Teaching of Foreign Languages (ACTEL)

6 Executive Plaza
Yonkers, NY 10701-6801
(914) 963-8830
Fax (914) 963-1275

Individuals interested in the teaching of classical and modern foreign languages in schools and colleges. Operates materials center, conducts seminars and workshops, and presents awards. Publications: *ACTFL Newsletter, Foreign Language Annals* (professional journal covering teaching methods and educational research).

American Federation of Teachers (Education) (AFT)

555 New Jersey Avenue NW
Washington, DC 20001

(202) 879-4400
(800) 242-5465

Works with teachers and other educational employees at the state and local level in organizing, collective bargaining, research, educational issues, and public relations. Conducts research in areas such as educational reform, bilingual education, teacher certification, and evaluation. Represents members' concerns through legislative action; offers technical assistance. Operates Education for Democracy Project. Publications: *American Educator, American Teacher, On Campus, Public Service Reporter,* and others.

Association of American Educators (AAE)

26012 Marguerite Parkway #333
Mission Viejo, CA 92692
(800) 704-7799
(949) 595-7979

A nonpartisan, nonprofit professional association designed to provide an "alternative to the partisan politics and social agendas of the national teacher unions." Membership open to any employee of an educational entity. According to the AAE, "the 'values-neutral' teaching experiment has been a monumental failure and has led to much of the public's negative opinion of our profession. We believe our schools must once again integrate academics, character, and citizenship."

Association for Childhood Education International (ACEI)

11501 Georgia Avenue, Suite 315
Wheaton, MD 20902
(301) 942-2443
(800) 423-3563
aceihq@aol.com

Teachers, parents, and other caregivers in thirty-one countries interested in promoting good educational practices for children from infancy through early adolescence. Conducts workshops and travel/study tours abroad, bestows awards, conducts research and educational programs, maintains speakers bureau. Publications: *ACEI Exchange, Childhood Education, Journal of Research in Childhood Education.*

Association for Supervision and Curriculum Development (ASCD)

1250 N. Pitt Street
Alexandria, VA 22314-1403
(703) 549-9110
Fax (703) 549-3891
member@ascd.org

Professional organization of supervisors, curriculum coordinators and directors, consultants, professors of education, classroom teachers, principals, superintendents, parents, and others interested in school improvement at all levels of education. Provides professional development experiences and training in curriculum and supervision; provides Research Information Service. Publications: *ASCD Update, Curriculum and Supervision.*

Council for Exceptional Children (Special Education) (CEC)

1920 Association Drive
Reston, VA 22091-1589
(703) 620-3660
cec@sped.org
http://www.cec.sped.org

Teachers, school administrators, teacher educators, and others with a direct or indirect concern for the education of the disabled and gifted. Provides information to teachers, parents, and others concerning the education of exceptional children. Maintains 63,000 volume library. Operates the ERIC Clearinghouse on Handicapped and Gifted Children. Publications: *Exceptional Child Education Resources, Exceptional Children, Teaching Exceptional Children.*

Education International (EI)

Boulevard Emile Jacqmain 155 (8th floor)
1210 Brussels, Belgium
32-2-224-06-80
Fax 32-2-224-06-06

World's largest educators' federation, representing 23 million members in more than 150 countries. EI's 294 member organizations include the NEA.

Foundation for Exceptional Children (Special Education) (FEC)

1920 Association Drive
Reston, VA 22091
(703) 620-1054

Institutions, agencies, educators, parents, and persons concerned with the education and personal welfare of gifted or disabled children. Established to further the educational, vocational, social, and personal needs of the disabled child or youth and the neglected educational needs of the gifted. Publication: *Foundation for Exceptional Children—Focus.*

International Reading Association (IRA)

800 Barksdale Road
P.O. Box 8139
Newark, DE 19714-8139
(302) 731-1600
Fax (302) 731-1057
73314.1411@compuserve.com

Teachers, reading specialists, consultants, administrators, supervisors, researchers, psychologists, librarians, and parents interested in promoting literacy. Seeks to improve the quality of reading instruction at all educational levels; stimulate and promote the lifetime reading habit and an awareness of the impact of reading; encourage the development of every reader's proficiency to the highest possible level. Disseminates information pertaining to research on reading. Publications: *Desktop Reference to the International Reading Association, Journal of Reading Reading Teacher, Reading Today.*

Music Teachers National Association (MTNA)

617 Vine Street, Suite 1432
Cincinnati, OH 45202
(513) 421-1420
Fax (513) 421-2503
mtnaadmin@aol.com

Professional society of music teachers in studios conservatories, music schools, and public and private schools, colleges, and universities; undergraduate and graduate music students. Seeks to raise the level of musical performance, understanding, and instruction. Publications: *American Music Teacher Magazine, Music Teachers National Association—Directory of Nationally Certified Teachers.*

National Art Education Association (Arts) (NAEA)

1916 Association Drive
Reston, VA 22091-1590
(703) 860-8000
Fax (703) 860-2960
naea@dgs.dgsys.com

Teachers of art at elementary, secondary, and college levels; colleges, libraries, museums, and other educational institutions. Studies problems of teaching art; encourages research and experimentation. Serves as clearinghouse for information on art education programs, materials, and methods of instruction. Maintains placement services and library on art education. Publications: *Art Education, Studies in Art Education.*

National Association for Bilingual Education (Bilingualism) (NABE)

1220 L Street NW
Suite 605
Washington, DC 20005-4018
(202) 898-1829
Fax (202) 789-2866

Educators, administrators, paraprofessionals, community and laypeople, and students. Purposes are to recognize, promote, publicize bilingual education. Seeks to increase public understanding of the importance of language and culture. Utilizes and develops student proficiency and ensures equal opportunities in bilingual education for language-minority students. Works to preserve and expand the nation's linguistic resources. Educates language-minority parents in public policy decisions. Promotes research in language education, linguistics, and multicultural education. Coordinates development of professional standards. Publications: *Annual Conference Journal, Journal, Newsletter.*

National Association of Biology Teachers (NABT)

11250 Roger Bacon Drive, No. 19
Reston, VA 22090
(703) 471-1134
nabter@aol.com

Professional society of biology and life science teachers and teacher educators at all educational levels. Works to achieve scientific literacy among citizens. Promotes professional growth and development; fosters regional activities for biology teachers; confronts issues involving biology, society, and the future; provides a national voice for the profession. Publications: *American Biology Teacher, National Association of Biology Teachers—News and Views,* and others.

National Association for the Education of Young Children (Childhood Education) (NAEYC)

1509 16th Street NW
Washington, DC 20036
(202) 232-8777
(800) 424-2460
Fax (202) 328-1846
naeyc@org/naeyc

Teachers and directors of preschool and primary schools, kindergartens, child care centers, cooperatives, church schools, and groups having similar programs for young children. Open to all individuals interested in serving and acting on behalf of the needs and rights of young children, with primary focus on the provision of educational services and resources. Offers voluntary accreditation for early childhood schools and centers through the National Academy of Early Childhood Programs. Publications: *Early Childhood Research Quarterly, Young Children.*

National Association for Gifted Children (NAGC)

1707 L Street NW
Suite 550
Washington, DC 20036
(202) 785-4268

Teachers, university personnel, administrators, and parents. To advance interest in programs for the gifted. Seeks to further education of the gifted and to enhance their potential creativity. Distributes information to teachers and parents on the development of the gifted child; sponsors annual convention to provide training in curriculum planning, program evaluation, and parenting and guidance relevant to gifted children. Maintains speakers' bureau. Publication: *Gifted Child Quarterly.*

National Association for Trade and Industrial Education (NATIE)

P.O. Box 1665
Leesburg, VA 22075
(703) 777-1740

Educators in trade and industrial education. Works for the promotion, development, and improvement of trade and industrial education. Supports instructional programs for members to prepare for job instruction, apprentice training, adult retraining, and special training for industry. Publications: *NATIE News Notes, State Supervisors/Consultants of Trade and Industrial Education,* and others.

National Business Education Association (NBEA)

1914 Association Drive
Reston, VA 22091
(703) 860-8300

Teachers of business subjects in secondary and postsecondary schools and colleges; administrators and research workers in business education; businesspeople interested in business education; teachers in educational institutions training business teachers. Publication: *Business Education Forum.*

National Council for the Social Studies (NCSS)

3501 Newark Street, NW
Washington, DC 20016
(202) 966-7840
Fax (202) 966-2061
ncss@ncss.org

Teachers of elementary and secondary social studies, including instructors of civics, geography, history, economics, political science, psychology, sociology, and anthropology. Publications: *Social Education, The Social Studies Professional, Social Studies and the Young Learner, Theory and Research in Social Education.*

National Council of Teachers of English (NCTE)

1111 West Kenyon Road
Urbana, IL 61801
(217) 328-3870
Fax (217) 328-9645

Teachers of English at all school levels. Works to increase the effectiveness of instruction in English language and literature. Presents achievement awards for writing to high school juniors and students in the eighth grade, and awards for high school literary magazines. Provides information and aids for teachers involved in formulating objectives, writing and evaluating curriculum guides, and planning in-service programs for teacher education. Publications: *English Education, English Journal, Language Arts, Research in the Teaching of English,* and others.

National Council of Teachers of Mathematics (NCTM)

1906 Association Drive
Reston, VA 22091-1593
(703) 620-9840
Fax (703) 476-2970
infocentra@nctm.org

Teachers of mathematics in grades K–12, two-year colleges, and teacher educators. Publications: *Arithmetic Teacher, Journal for Research in Mathematics Education, Mathematics Teacher, National Council of Teachers of Mathematics—Yearbook,* and others.

National Education Association (NEA)

1201 16th Street, NW
Washington, DC 20036
(202) 833-4000

Professional organization and union of elementary and secondary school teachers, college and university professors, administrators, principals, counselors and others concerned with education. Publications: *NEA Today, Thought and Action,* and others.

National Middle School Association (NMSA)

4151 Executive Parkway, Suite 300
Westerville, OH 43081
(800) 528-NMSA (6672)
info@NMSA.org

Professional organization for teachers, administrators, parents, and others interested in the education of young adolescents (ten to fifteen years of age). The only national organization devoted to improving the education of young adolescents, NMSA has more than 20,000 members worldwide. State, provincial, and international affiliates work to provide support for middle-level education at the local level. Publications: *Middle School Journal, Middle Ground,* and others.

National Science Teachers Association (NSTA)

1840 Wilson Blvd.
Arlington, VA 22201-3000
(703) 243-7100
Fax (703) 243-7177

Teachers seeking to foster excellence in science teaching. Studies students and how they learn, the curriculum of science, the teacher and his or her preparation, the procedures used in classroom and laboratory, the facilities for teaching science, and the evaluation procedures used. Affiliated with American Association for the Advancement of Science. Publications: *Journal of College Science Teaching, Quantum, Science and Children, Science Scope, The Science Teacher.*

Phi Delta Kappa (Education)

8th and Union
P.O. Box 789
Bloomington, IN 47402-0789
(812) 339-1156
(800) 766-1156
Fax (812) 339-0018
headquarters@pdkintl.org

Professional, honorary, and recognition fraternity—education. To enhance quality education through research and leadership activities. Conducts seminars and workshops. Publications: *Phi Delta Kappan,* and others.

Pi Lambda Theta (Education)

4101 E. 3rd Street
P.O. Box 6626
Bloomington, IN 47407-6626
(812) 339-3411
members@pilambda.org

Honor and professional association—education. Presents biennial awards. Sponsors comparative education tours and educational conferences. Publication: *Educational Horizons.*

Reading Is Fundamental (RIF)

600 Maryland Avenue, SW, Suite 800
Washington, DC 20024
(202) 287-3220
Fax (202) 287-3196

Volunteer groups composed of community leaders, educators, librarians, parents, and service club members who sponsor local grassroots reading motivation programs serving three million children nationwide. Purpose is to involve youngsters, preschool to high school age, in reading activities aimed at showing that reading is fun. Provides services to parents to help them encourage reading in the home. Publication: *RIF Newsletter.*

Speech Communication Association (SCA)

5105 Backlick Road, Bldg. E
Annandale, VA 22003
(703) 750-0533
Fax (703) 914-9471

Elementary, secondary, college, and university teachers, speech clinicians, media specialists, communication consultants, students, theater directors, and others. To promote study, criticism, research, teaching, and application of the artistic, humanistic, and scientific prin-ciples of communication, particularly speech com-munication. Sponsors the publication of scholarly volumes in speech. Conducts international debate tours in the United States and abroad. Maintains placement service. Publications: *Communication Education, Speech Communication Teacher, Text and Performance Quarterly,* and others.

Teachers of English to Speakers of Other Languages (TESOL)

1600 Cameron Street, Suite 300
Alexandria, VA 22314-2751
(703) 836-0774
Fax (703) 836-7864
tesol@tesol.edu

School, college, and adult education teachers who teach English as a second or foreign language. Aims to improve the teaching of English as a second or foreign language by promoting research, disseminating information, developing guidelines and promoting certification, and serving as a clearinghouse for the field. Offers placement service. Publications: *Directory of Professional Preparation, TESOL Journal, TESOL Quarterly,* and others.

For complete information on professional organizations, see *Encyclopedia of Associations* (2000), Gale Research, Inc.

13 Your First Teaching Position

I slept about two hours last night. I was finally a teacher, the experience I had talked about for the past two years.

I walked in, introduced myself, pushed the nervousness aside, and got right to it. The butterflies went away and excitement reigned!

A veteran teacher was sent in to help me during homeroom, but after five minutes, she said, "You obviously don't need my help," and left. My ego soared!

—Melissa Balog, first-year middle school teacher
quoted in *NEA Today,* September 2002

"Hey . . . , you gonna teach here?"

I looked up from my desk that Monday morning and saw three boys crowded into the open doorway of room 207, my new classroom for the year.

"Yeah, I be talkin' to you, man! Is you a teacher or something?"

"Yes, I'm a new English teacher here," I said, getting up from my desk and my preparations for my new students who were to arrive in 30 minutes. The three tall, slender youths eyed me with bemusement as though I not only was of a different skin color but wore antlers as well.

The boy [who] spoke to me began to laugh and the others quickly joined in.

"What you teach? Sewing?"

They laughed again and then turned to leave.

"You'll be sorry you came here . . . ," one of them called out just before he slammed the door.

That was my formal introduction to [my new high school's] student body—an introduction that made me feel that my students might be more prepared for me than I was for them.

I was, on that first day [of my teaching career], frightened. If I had been told that I would spend the next eight years of my life at [the school], I would have quit—right then. As it was, though, I had no crystal ball with which to foretell my future—and so I began my slow, often painful, professional growth as [a] teacher at a school most Chicagoans knew as a "dumping ground" for underachievers and delinquents.

[*Reflections after teaching at _____ High School for eight years*]

I realize just how much those eight years at _____ have influenced me as a teacher and as a person. I recognize, too, how much I owe the hundreds of students with whom I shared so much time. Their names have faded, but their faces and voices are as clear as ever. They opened my eyes and forced me to recognize the importance of being able to understand the richness and complexity inherent in any classroom.

They also made me see that being a "good" teacher involves much more than subject matter competence or being able to show kids "who's boss." What I needed, as all teachers anywhere need, was to grow in the skills of observing and interpreting the dynamics of interaction in the classroom.

Finally, they helped me to see that building relationships—caring, loving, educative relationships—with kids is what teaching has always been about. For their authenticity, for their energy, and for their courage, I respect—and, yes, love—my former [high school] students. In a very real sense, they held me accountable. And they did it in a way that seemed logical to them and, I must confess, to me as well. When I bored them, they told me. When I made them angry, they told me. And when I taught them something important, and taught it well, they told me that, too (Parkay 1983, 211–212).

Focus Questions

1. **How will you become certified or licensed to teach?**
2. **Will you have difficulty finding a teaching job?**
3. **How will you find your first teaching job?**
4. **What can you expect as a beginning teacher?**
5. **How can you become a part of your learning community?**
6. **How can you participate in teacher collaboration?**
7. **How will your performance as a teacher be evaluated?**

Expand your knowledge of the concepts discussed in this chapter by reading current and historical articles from the *New York Times* by visiting the "**Themes of the Times**" section of the Companion Website (**www.ablongman.com/parkay6e**).

The first half of the preceding scenario is based on the first author's experiences at the start of his teaching career; in the second half, he reflects on his first eight years of teaching. The scenario illustrates in highly compressed form how he came to view teaching at his school as professionally rewarding and personally satisfying. Your experiences as a beginning teacher will be different, of course, but you, too, will undergo a transformation and come to see that teaching is tremendously rewarding and satisfying.

It is natural that you feel both excited and a bit fearful when thinking about your first job. While taking the courses required in your teacher education program, you probably feel secure in your role as a student; you know what is expected of you. As a teacher, however, you will assume an entirely new role—a role that requires some time before it becomes comfortable. The aim of this chapter, then, is to help make the transition from student to professional teacher a positive, pleasant one. Preparing well for this transition will go a long way toward helping you begin teaching with confidence. We first look at the steps you can take to become certified or licensed to teach and to identify current trends related to teacher supply and demand.

How Will You Become Certified or Licensed to Teach?

State certification is required for teaching in the public schools, and in many private schools as well. In some cases, large cities (e.g., Chicago, New York, Buffalo) have their own certification requirements that must be met. And certain local school districts have additional requirements, such as a written examination, before one can teach in those districts.

A **teaching certificate** is actually a license to teach. The department of education for each of the fifty states and the District of Columbia sets the requirements for certification. A certificate usually indicates at what level and in what content areas one may teach. One might, for example, be certified for all-level (K–12) physical education or art, secondary English, elementary education, or middle-level education. Currently, about two-thirds of the states offer certification for teaching at the middle school or junior high level—an increase from 1987 when about half of the states offered such certification. In addition, a certificate may list other areas of specialization, such as driver's training, coaching, or journalism. If you plan to go into nonteaching areas such as counseling, librarianship, or administration, special certificates are usually required.

State Certification Requirements

For a person to receive a teaching certificate, all states require successful completion of an approved teacher education program that culminates with at least a bachelor's degree. To be approved, programs must pass a review by the state department of education approximately every five years. In addition to approval at the state level, most of the nearly 1,300 programs in the nation have regional accreditation, and more than 525 voluntarily seek accreditation by the **National Council for Accreditation of Teacher Education (NCATE)** (2002b). Currently, all states require an average of six to eight semester credits of supervised student teaching. Alabama, Colorado, Idaho, Indiana, Nevada, New York, and Virginia require a master's degree for advanced certification; and Arizona, Maryland, Montana, Oregon, and Washington require either a master's degree or a specified number of semester credits after certification (Kaye 2001). Additional requirements may also include U.S. citizenship, an oath of loyalty, fingerprinting, or a health examination.

A few states, including Iowa, New Mexico, North Carolina, and Oklahoma, waive state licensing requirements for teachers certified by the National Board for Professional Teaching Standards (NBPTS). About half of the states will issue a license to a person from another state who holds a valid NBPTS certificate. For a current listing of state and local action supporting NBPTS certification, call the NBPTS at (800)-22TEACH.

Nearly all states now require testing of teachers for initial certification. States use either a standardized test (usually the National Teacher Examination [NTE] or Praxis) or a test developed by outside consultants. Areas covered by the states' tests usually include basic skills, professional knowledge, and general knowledge. Many states also require an on-the-job performance evaluation for certification (see Table 13.1 on pages 472–473).

There is a trend away from granting teaching certificates for life. Some states, for example, issue three- to five-year certificates, which may be renewed only with proof of coursework completed beyond the bachelor's degree. And, amid considerable controversy, several states, including Connecticut, Maryland, Massachusetts, New Hampshire, Rhode Island, South Carolina, and Wisconsin have enacted testing for **recertification** of experienced teachers. Though each state's policy differs, all have moved away from allowing teachers to take any education-related classes to renew their certification. New Hampshire and South Carolina, for instance, require that teachers pursue professional development in their subject areas, as well as in technology, to become recertified (Boser 2000).

Certification requirements differ from state to state, and they are frequently modified. To remain up-to-date on the requirements for the state in which you plan to teach, it is important that you keep in touch with your teacher placement office or certification officer at your college or university. You may also wish to refer to *Requirements for Certification for Elementary and Secondary Schools* (The University of Chicago Press), an annual publication that lists state-by-state certification requirements for teachers, counselors, librarians, and administrators. Or, you may contact the teacher certification office in the state where you plan to

Table 13.1 Assessment requirements for the initial teaching certificate

	Basic Skills Exam					Subject Matter Exam	General Knowledge Exam	Knowledge of Teaching Exam	Assessment of Teaching Performance	
State	Reading 1	Math 2	Writing 3	Spelling 4	Other 5	6	7	8	9	Footnotes
Alabama	(1)	(1)	(1)	(1)		(2)		(2)	X	(1) For admission to program (2) Institution's exit exam
Alaska	X	X	X							
Arizona						X		X	X	
Arkansas	X	X	X			X		X		
California	X	X	X			(1)				(1) Or completion of an approved subject matter program
Colorado						X				
Connecticut	X	X	X			X				Praxis I–CBT and Praxis II
Delaware	X	X	X							Praxis I Pre-Professional Skills Test
District of Columbia	X	X	X			X			X	Praxis I Pre-Professional Skills Test
Florida	X	X	X			X	X	X	X	
Georgia	(1)	(1)	(1)			X				(1) Praxis I required in Georgia approved programs, eff. 3/1/99
Hawaii	X	X	X			X		X		
Idaho										
Illinois	X	X	X		(1)	X				(1) Grammar
Indiana	X		X		(1)	X	X	X		(1) Listening
Iowa										
Kansas	X	X	X					X		
Kentucky	(1)	(1)	(1)	X		(2)		(2)	X	(1) Required for admission to teacher education (2) Fingerprint check is required for employment
Louisiana	X	X	X		(1)	X	X	X	X	(1) Communication skills
Maine					(1)		X	X		(1) Communication skills
Maryland	X	X	X			X		X	X	
Massachusetts (1)										(1) Two-part exam covering communication and literacy skills and the subject matter knoweldge for the certificate
Michigan	X	X	X			X	(1)			(1) Elementary Certificate exam (subject-area exam)
Minnesota	X	X	X		(1)					(1) PPST required
Mississippi						X		X		
Missouri	(1)	(1)	(1)	(1)		X		(2)		(1) For entry into teacher education (2) If no subject knowledge test is designated
Montana	X	X	X							
Nebraska	X	X	X							
Nevada	X	X	X			X		X		
New Hampshire	(1)	(1)	(1)			X				Praxis I and Praxis II
New Jersey						X	(1)		X	(1) For elementary education
New Mexico	X	X	X				X	X		

Table 13.1 (Continued)

State	Basic Skills Exam: Reading 1	Basic Skills Exam: Math 2	Basic Skills Exam: Writing 3	Basic Skills Exam: Spelling 4	Basic Skills Exam: Other 5	Subject Matter Exam 6	General Knowledge Exam 7	Knowledge of Teaching Exam 8	Assessment of Teaching Performance 9	Footnotes
New York							X	X		
North Carolina	(1)	(1)	(1)			X				(1) Prior to entry into teacher education
North Dakota	(1)	(1)	(1)	(1)			X	X		(1) Prior to entry into teacher education
Ohio	X	X	X			X		X	(1)	(1) Entry year Perf. Assess-2002
Oklahoma	X	X	X			X	X	X	X	
Oregon	X	X	X			X			(1)	(1) For Oregon graduates
Pennsylvania	X	X	X		(1)	X	(2)	X		(1) Listening (2) Includes Math
Rhode Island (1)							X			(1) Principles of Learning Teaching Test
South Carolina	X	X	X			X		X	X	
South Dakota (1)	X	X	X			X			X	(1) Required within the institutional program requirements
Tennessee (1)						X		X		(1) Basic skills exams in reading, math, and writing are covered in PPST.
Texas (1)						X		X		(1) Screening for admission to a teacher preparation progam includes college level skills in reading, oral and written communication, critical thinking, and mathematics
Utah								(1)		(1) Entry year requirement
Vermont	X	X	X			(1)				(1) See Emerging Trends
Virginia	X	X	X			X				
Washington	(1)	(1)	(1)							(1) Required prior to entering teacher education
West Virginia	X	X	X			X		X	X	
Wisconsin	X	X	X							
Wyoming										

Source: The NASDTEC Manual 2001: Manual on the Preparation and Certificate of Educational Personnel. Mashpee, MA: National Association of State Directors of Teacher Education & Certification, pp. B-6–B-7. Used with permission.

teach (see the Appendix "Directory of State Teacher Certification Offices in the United States" on this book's website).

Currently, forty-seven states and the District of Columbia are members of the **Interstate Certification Agreement Contract,** a reciprocity agreement whereby a certificate obtained in one state will be honored in another. If you plan to teach in a state other than the one in which you are currently studying, you should find out whether both states share a reciprocity agreement.

About 404,000 teachers, many of whom are noncertified, teach in the United States' growing system of private, parochial, for-profit, and charter schools (National Center for Education Statistics 2002e). Private and parochial schools supported largely by tuition and gifts, and for-profit schools operated by private educational corporations, usually have no certification requirements for teachers. Also, teacher-created and teacher-operated charter schools, though they are public, are often free of state certification requirements. A school's **charter** (an agreement between the school's founders and its sponsor—usually a local school board) may waive certification requirements if the school guarantees that students will attain a specified level of achievement.

Alternative Certification

Despite the national movement to make certification requirements more stringent, concern about meeting the demand for two million new public school teachers by the year 2008–09 (American Federation of Teachers 2001) and attracting minority-group members into the teaching profession has resulted in increasing use of alternative teacher certification programs. In 1983, only eight states offered alternatives; by 2002, forty-five states had alternative routes to certification (Feistritzer 2002; Roach and Cohen 2002).

Alternative certification programs are designed for people who already have at least a bachelor's degree in a field other than education and want to become licensed to teach. It is estimated that about 175,000 people have been licensed through alternative certification programs since 1983 (Feistritzer 2002). Most alternative certification programs are collaborative efforts among state departments of education, teacher education programs in colleges and universities, and school districts. For example, Washington State University, in collaboration with area school districts, has a federally funded program to prepare paraprofessional educators (teachers' aides, for example) in southwest Washington to become bilingual/ESL teachers. Compared with recent college graduates who enter teaching directly from a traditional college-based teacher preparation program, those who enter teaching through alternate routes tend to

- Have degrees with majors in subjects other than education
- Be more likely to have work experience in occupations other than education

What are some alternatives for becoming certified or licensed to teach? What are some current trends in certification and what conditions might account for those trends?

- Be older
- More likely be people of color
- More likely be men (Feistritzer 2002)

All but two states may grant certification to those who do not meet current requirements. About half of the states may even give a substandard credential to those who hold less than a bachelor's degree. In response to occasional shortages of teachers in particular subject and grade-level areas, many state systems approve temporary measures such as **emergency certification.** Nationwide, more than 12 percent of newly hired teachers enter the profession without any training at all, and another 15 percent enter without having fully met state standards, according to the National Commission on Teaching and America's Future.

Emergency certification is strongly resisted by professional teacher organizations and several state departments of education. Though strongly resisted by professional teacher organizations, alternative certification is likely to become even more widespread in the event of a teacher shortage.

The Praxis Series

Thirty-five of the forty-three states that include tests as part of their certification process require completion of the **Praxis Series: Professional Assessments for Beginning Teachers** developed by Educational Testing Service (ETS) in consultation with teachers, educational researchers, the National Education Association, and the American Federation of Teachers. The Praxis Series (*praxis* means putting theory into practice) enables states to create a system of tests that meet their specific licensing requirements.

The Praxis Series, which replaced the National Teacher Examination in the mid-1990s, consists of three components:

> *Praxis I: Academic skills assessments*—Praxis I covers the "enabling skills" in reading, writing, and mathematics that all teachers need, regardless of grade or subject taught. Two formats, computer-based and pencil-and-paper, are available for the Praxis I assessment, which is given early in a student's teacher education program. To help students pass Praxis I, ETS offers online practice test items and, for students who need help in improving basic academic skills, LearningPlus, an interactive computer software program that provides instruction and diagnostic placement tests in reading, writing, and mathematics.

> *Praxis II: Subject assessments*—Praxis II measures teacher education students' knowledge of the subjects they will teach. In most cases, Praxis II tests are taken on completion of an undergraduate program. The tests, available in more than seventy subject areas, have a core content module required by every state, with the remaining modules selected on an individual basis by the states. Each state can base its assessment on multiple-choice items or on candidate-constructed-response modules. In addition, Praxis II includes the Principles of Learning and Teaching (PLT) test and the Professional Knowledge test; each is a two-hour test to assess teachers' professional knowledge. The PLT is available in three versions: K–6, 5–9, and 7–12.

> *Praxis III: Classroom performance assessments*—Praxis III is a performance-based assessment system, not a test. Developed after extensive job analyses, reviews of research, and input from educators, Praxis III involves the assessment of actual teaching skills of the beginning teacher. The assessments focus on the four domains of the Praxis Framework for Teaching as presented in Chapter 1's Meeting the Standard feature (see pages 28–29): planning and preparation, the classroom environment, instruction, and professional responsibilities. In addition, Praxis III

assesses the teacher's sensitivity to developmental levels and cultural differences among students. In-class assessments and pre- and post-observation interviews conducted by trained state and local personnel are the main components of Praxis III. The observations are supplemented by work samples—for example, lesson plans. Following Praxis III assessments, which normally are completed by the end of the first year of teaching, the state makes a decision about whether to grant a license to teach.

Will You Have Difficulty Finding a Teaching Job?

When you think ahead to a career in teaching, a question you are likely to ask yourself is, How hard will it be to find a job? From time to time, **teacher supply and demand** figures have painted a rather bleak picture for those entering the teaching profession. At other times, such as now, finding a position has not been difficult.

In 2002, the U.S. Department of Education announced that approximately 2.4 million teachers would be needed during the next eleven years because of teacher attrition and retirement and increased student enrollment (National Center for Education Statistics 2002c). This projection jumped as high as 2.7 million if declining student–teacher ratios based on nationwide class size reduction efforts were considered (National Center for Education Statistics 2002d).

Even during times of teacher surplus, talented, qualified teachers are able to find jobs. Teaching is one of the largest professions in the United States; out of a national population of about 288 million, about 47.4 million attended public elementary and secondary schools in fall 2002, where they were taught by approximately 3.2 million teachers (National Center for Education Statistics 2002b). Within such a large profession, annual openings resulting from retirements and career changes alone are sizable.

Demand by Geographic Region and Specialty Area

Although public elementary and secondary school enrollments are projected to rise less than 1 percent between 1999 and 2011, growth will vary widely across the nation. Enrollment will increase in the western and southern regions by 8 percent and 1 percent, respectively. On the other hand, a decrease of 4 percent is projected for the northeastern region, while a decrease of 3 percent is expected in the midwestern region. Figure 13.1 shows the percent of change in public K–8 and 9–12 enrollment by region.

The ease with which you will find your first teaching position is also related to your area of specialization. In 2002, for example, job seekers able to teach bilingual education, special education, English as a second language (ESL), mathematics, chemistry, or physics were in an especially favorable position. For current employment opportunities according to specialty area and geographic region and for other job-search resources, check the following publications by the American Association for Employment in Education, Inc. (AAEE) (3040 Riverside Drive, Suite 125, Columbus, OH 43221-2550, (614) 485-1111, fax (614) 485-9609, http://www.aaee.org, aaee@osu.edu). Be aware, however, that the AAEE does not provide placement services or maintain lists of vacancies.

- *The Job Search Handbook for Educators*—Supply-demand data, interview techniques, résumé advice, and other job-search suggestions, $8
- *The Job Hunter's Guide: Services and Career Fairs for Educators*—Includes job fairs across the nation (dates, times, locations, contact information),

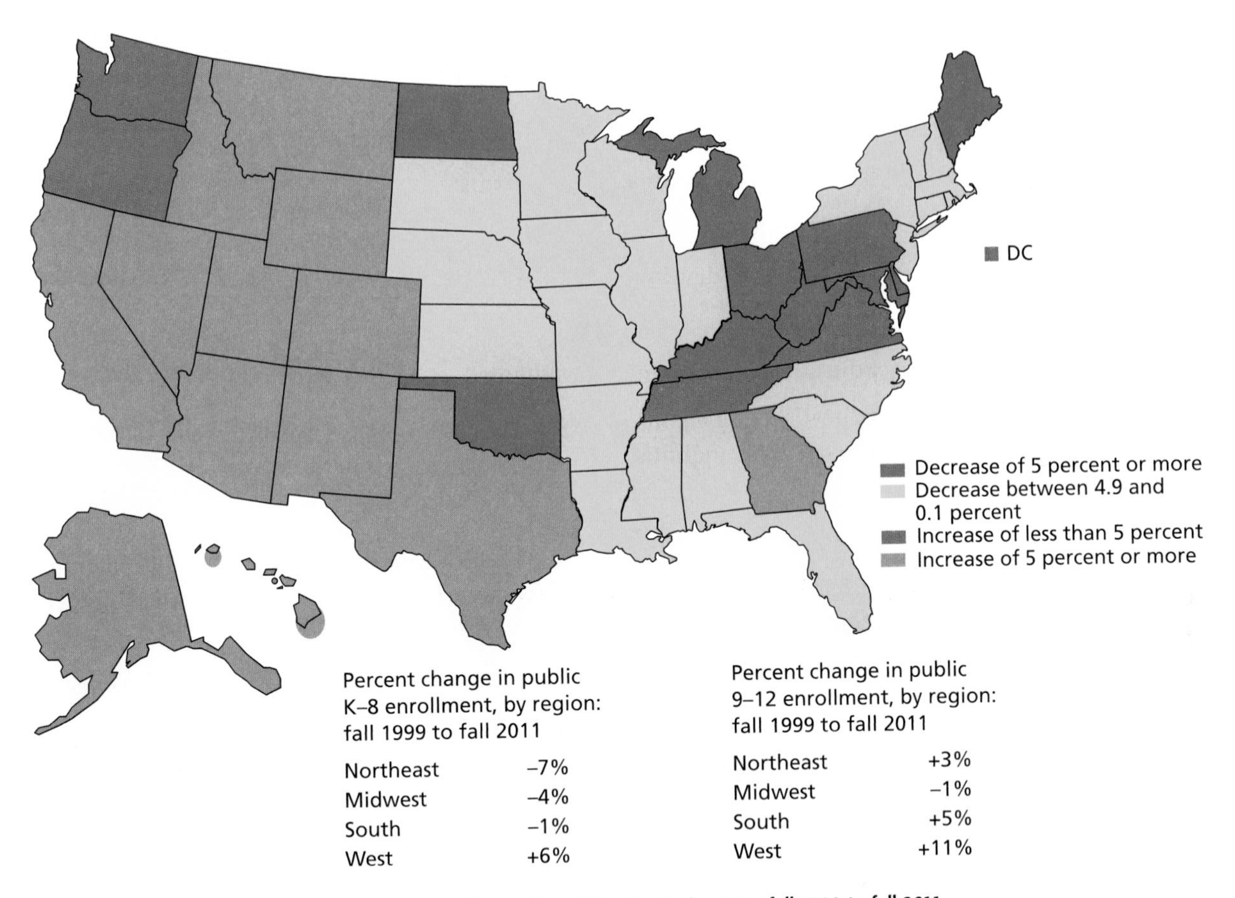

Figure 13.1 Percent change in grades K–12 enrollment in public schools, by state: fall 1999 to fall 2011
Source: U.S. Department of Education, National Center for Education Statistics, Common Core of Data surveys, and State Public Elementary and Secondary Enrollment model. Adapted from *Projections of Education Statistics to 2011.* Washington, DC: National Center for Education Statistics, 2001.

listing of colleges and universities that offer services to students who are not their own graduates, teacher certification reciprocity among states, subscriptions to vacancy listings or websites, computer referral systems, and other resources, $15

- *Directory of Public School Systems in the U.S.*—Names, addresses, and phone numbers of contact persons, district size, school grade levels, and other information, $80 for complete directory; from no charge to $12 for individual state directories

When considering supply and demand estimates, remember that jobs are to be had in oversupplied areas. Job hunting will be more competitive, though, and you may have to relocate to another region of the country.

Other Career Opportunities for Teachers

There are also a great many nonteaching jobs in education and education-related fields, such as principal, assistant principal, librarian, and counselor. In addition, there are many jobs that, although removed from the world of the classroom, would nevertheless enable you to use your teaching skills.

The following outline lists several places other than schools where individuals with teaching backgrounds are often employed. The number of education-related careers is likely to increase in the coming decades.

Industry

- Publishers
- Educational materials and equipment suppliers
- Specialized educational service firms
- Communications industries
- Research and development firms
- Management consulting firms
- Education and training consultants
- Educational divisions of large corporations—Xerox, IBM, CBS, General Electric, Westinghouse, etc.

Government

- Federal agencies—U.S. Office of Education, Bureau of Prisons, Department of Labor, Office of Economic Opportunity, Department of Justice, Department of Health, Education and Welfare, etc.
- Federal programs—Bureau of Indian Affairs Schools, Bureau of Prisons Schools, Job Corps, Overseas Dependent Schools, Peace Corps, Teacher Corps, Upward Bound, VISTA, etc.
- Regional educational networks—Research and development centers, regional educational laboratories, sixteen clearinghouses of the Educational Resources Information Center (ERIC), etc.
- Jobs in state departments of education

Education-Related Associations

- Research centers and foundations
- Professional associations—National Council of Teachers of English, National Association of Mathematics Teachers, National Education Association, American Federation of Teachers, Phi Delta Kappa, Kappa Delta Pi, Educational Testing Service, etc.

Community Organizations

- Community action programs—Upward Bound, neighborhood health centers, legal services, aid to migrant workers, etc.
- Social service agencies—United Fund agencies, Boy Scouts, Girl Scouts, YMCAs and YWCAs, settlement houses, boys' and girls' clubs, etc.
- Adult education centers
- Museums
- Hospitals

How Will You Find Your First Teaching Job?

During the last year of your teacher education program, you will probably become increasingly concerned about finding a teaching position. The "Job Search Timetable Checklist" presented in Appendix 13.1 may help you plan your job search. Also, Figure 13.2 presents an overview of the data and impressions that more than two hundred school hiring officials consider most important when they are considering first-time teachers for employment. In the remainder of this

CANDIDATE

Employers evaluate first-time teachers' job applications for:

(a) Letters of recommendation from public school personnel
(b) A mentoring teacher's evaluation
(c) Examples of teaching skills and classroom management skill
(d) Experience with specific programs used in the school district
(e) Number of certifications which the candidate holds (e.g. elementary *and* special education).

Employers evaluate first-time teachers' academic preparation for:

(a) Knowledge of subject matter
(b) Success in student teaching
(c) Computer knowledge and skill

Important factors about candidates' work experience in paid employment not related to teaching include:

(a) A positive work ethic
(b) Punctuality
(c) Good quality work
(d) Low absenteeism

The following factors influence the decision to invite an applicant for an interview:

(a) Correct spelling, punctuation, and English usage of the candidate's application
(b) Letters of recommendation from those who have seen the candidate work with students
(c) Neatness of the applicant's materials
(d) Evaluation from the mentoring teacher

Employers use interview questions to assess the ways in which first-time teachers respond to:

(a) "Real life" and "what if" situations
(b) Classroom management issues
(c) Enthusiasm about teaching
(d) Demonstrating their knowledge of subject matter
(e) Describing and evaluating their own strengths
(f) Structured questions that range from impersonal to personal

In evaluating interviews, employers look for the following:

(a) The candidate's commitment to teaching
(b) Knowledge of the teaching field
(c) Interpersonal skills
(d) The candidate's understanding of the role of a teacher
(e) Professional judgment

Figure 13.2 Moving from "candidate" to "teacher"

Note: Items arranged in order of importance.
Source: Adapted from Judy McEnany and Patricia Reuss, "Fascinating Facts for First-Time Teachers," *2001 Job Search Handbook for Educators,* American Association for Employment in Education, p. 30. Used with permission.

section we discuss five critical steps in that sequence: finding out about teaching vacancies, preparing a résumé, writing letters of inquiry and letters of application, being interviewed, and selecting a position.

Finding Out About Teaching Vacancies

Your college or university probably has a **placement service** designed to help graduates find jobs. On a regular basis, placement offices usually publish lists of vacancies, which are posted and, in many cases, mailed to students who have registered with the office and set up a credentials file. In addition, you can use the Internet to connect with other universities that have accessible online placement services.

A **credentials file** (known as placement papers at some institutions) usually includes the following: background information on the applicant, the type of position sought, a list of courses taken, performance evaluations by the applicant's cooperative teacher, and three or more letters of recommendation. With each job application, the candidate requests that his or her credentials be sent to the appropriate person at the school district, or the school district itself may request the applicant's papers. Placement offices usually charge a small fee for each time a candidate's papers are sent out.

A job announcement describes the position and its requirements and provides the name and address of the individual to contact at the school district. For each position you are interested in, send a letter of application to the appropriate person along with your résumé. In addition, you may have your placement office send your credentials file. Placement offices also frequently set up on-campus interviews between candidates and representatives of school district personnel departments.

State department of education employment offices help teachers locate positions. Like college and university placement offices, states publish lists of job openings, which are then distributed to registered candidates. Because most of these states will assist out-of-state candidates, you can register in more than one state.

Personal networking will play an important role in landing the right job. Let people know you are looking for a job—friends, teachers at schools you've attended, faculty at the school where you student teach, and people you meet at workshops and conferences. Also, with access to the Internet, you can conduct a global job search and even make your résumé available to millions of people. The following noncommercial Internet sites can be helpful in your job search efforts:

- School district websites
- State departments of education websites
- *Project Connect*—After obtaining a free user name and password, you can search teaching vacancies on the Web and post information about yourself, sponsored in part by the AAEE
- *America's Job Bank*—A comprehensive, free job-search service linked to two thousand state employment offices

Preparing Your Résumé

A **résumé** presents a concise summary of an individual's professional experiences, education, and skills. Résumés must be typed and preferably no longer than one page, two pages at most. Though there is no right way to prepare a résumé, it should present—in a neat, systematic way—key information that will help an employer determine your suitability for a particular position. Because your résumé will most likely be your first contact with an employer, it must make a good impression.

Ordinarily, a résumé contains the following information:

- Personal data
- Education
- Certificates held
- Experience
- Activities and interests
- Honors and offices held
- Professional memberships
- References

Figure 13.3 on page 482 is a résumé prepared by Linda M. Rodriguez that you can use as a model. To prepare an effective résumé, read "Résumé Advice for Educators" in Appendix 13.2.

Writing Letters of Inquiry and Applications

As a job seeker, you will most likely have occasion to write two kinds of letters: letters of inquiry and letters of application. A **letter of inquiry** is used to determine if a school district has, or anticipates, any teaching vacancies. This type of letter states your general qualifications and requests procedures to be followed in making a formal application (see Figure 13.4 on page 483). A letter of inquiry should also include your résumé as well as a self-addressed, stamped envelope for the school district's convenience. Be prepared not to receive a reply for each letter of inquiry you send out. Many school districts are unable to respond to all inquiries.

A **letter of application** (often called a cover letter) indicates your interest in a particular position and outlines your qualifications for that job. As most districts have several vacancies at any given time, it is important that the first sentence of your letter refer to the specific position for which you are applying. The body of the letter should then highlight why you would be an excellent choice to fill that position. Also, inform the reader that your credentials file will be sent on request or is being sent by your placement office. Close the letter by expressing your availability for an interview (see Figure 13.5 on page 484).

Participating in a Job Interview

The interview is one of the most important steps in your search for an appropriate position. As job applicants realize after they have participated in a few interviews, school district representatives may ask a wide range of questions, both structured and open-ended.

In some districts, you might be interviewed by the principal only; in others, the superintendent, the principal, and the department chairperson might interview you; and in still others, classroom teachers might interview you. Regardless of format, the interview enables the district to obtain more specific information regarding your probable success as an employee, and it gives you an opportunity to ask questions about what it is like to teach in the district. By asking questions yourself, you demonstrate your interest in working in the district. The Appendix

Linda M. Rodriguez

Personal Data

Born: October 16, 1983

Address and Phone: 948 W. Third
Spokane, WA 99206
(509) 924-1234
lmrodrig@abc.com

Education

B.A., Elementary Education, Washington State University, June 2004.

Certificates Held

Major Area: Elementary Education, K–8

Minor Area: Bilingual Education

Experience

Student Teaching, Garden Springs Elementary, W. 5116 Garden Springs Road, Spokane, WA 99204, Spring 2004. Cooperating teacher: Mrs. Becky Jones. Observed, assisted, and taught regular and accelerated 3rd grade classes in a multilingual setting. Organized after-school tutoring program and developed a unit on using the World Wide Web in the classroom. Attended site-based council meetings with Mrs. Jones and assisted in the development of community-based partnerships.

Camp Counselor and Recreation Director, YWCA Summer Camp, Spokane, WA.
Directed summer recreation program comprised of 10 counselors and 140 elementary aged girls.

Volunteer Telephone Counselor, Spokane County Crisis Hotline, June 2002–June 2004.

Activities and Interests

Spokane County Historical Society, Secretary, 2004.

Member, Washington State University Community Service Learning Center.

Hobbies: Jogging, Aerobics, Piano, Water Skiing.

Honors

B.A. with Honors, Washington State University, June 2004.

Washington State Scholarship, 2002–2004.

Professional Memberships

Washington Association for Supervision and Curriculum Development.

Kappa Delta Pi.

Instructional Technology Skills

Word processing, Internet and World Wide Web, optical scanner, interactive electronic whiteboard,

LCD computer projection panel, NovaNET (computer-based learning system).

Career Objective

Seeking K–8 position in multicultural/multilingual setting.

References

References and credentials file available upon request.

Figure 13.3 Résumé

Linda M. Rodriguez
948 W. Third
Spokane, Washington 99206

April 5, 2004

Dr. Lawrence Walker
Office of Personnel Services
City School District
100 Post Oak Boulevard
Houston, Texas 77056

Dear Dr. Walker:

This letter is to express my interest in a teaching position in the Houston City School District. Specifically, I would like to know if you anticipate any vacancies at the elementary level for fall of 2004. This June I will receive my B.A. (with honors) in elementary education from Washington State University. My supporting endorsement will be in bilingual education.

As a student teacher this spring semester, I taught regular and accelerated 3rd grade classes at Garden Springs Elementary School in Spokane, Washington. One class had 25 students, 3 of whom were diagnosed as having learning disabilities. At Garden Springs, I introduced students to science resources on the World Wide Web, and each student learned how to send e-mail messages to students in other countries.

My education at Washington State University, I believe, has prepared me well to teach in today's classrooms. I have had a course that focuses on meeting the needs of at-risk learners, and my supporting endorsement in bilingual education has prepared me to meet the challenges of working with students from diverse linguistic backgrounds. If possible, I would like a position that would allow me to develop programs for students with non–English backgrounds.

Enclosed you will find my résumé, which provides additional information about my experiences and activities. If there are any positions for which you think I might be suited, please send application materials in the enclosed stamped, self-addressed envelope. I appreciate your consideration, and I look forward to hearing from you.

Sincerely,
Linda M. Rodriguez
Linda M. Rodriguez

Figure 13.4 Letter of inquiry

"Sample Interview Questions for Candidates to Ask" on this book's website presents seventeen questions you can ask. In addition, at some point in the interview process you may wish to present brief highlights from your professional portfolio. Or, if you have created Internet and/or CD-ROM versions of your portfolio, you could give the hiring official(s) the URL for the portfolio or a copy of the CD-ROM itself.

Accepting an Offer

One day you are notified that a school district would like to hire you. Your job search efforts have paid off! In the competition for positions, you have been

Linda M. Rodriguez
948 W. Third
Spokane, Washington 99206

May 5, 2004

Dr. Mary Lamb
Associate Superintendent for Personnel
Metropolitan School District
Wacker Office Building
773 Ranier Avenue
Seattle, Washington 98504

Dear Dr. Lamb:

This letter is in support of my application for the position of 4th grade teacher at City Elementary School. This June I will receive my B.A. (with honors) in elementary education from Washington State University. My supporting endorsement will be in bilingual education.

As my enclosed résumé indicates, I just completed my student teaching at Garden Springs Elementary School in Spokane. During that 16-week period, I taught regular and accelerated 3rd grade classes. One class had 25 students, 3 of whom were diagnosed as having learning disabilities. I also organized an after-school tutoring program and assisted my cooperating teacher in developing community-based partnerships.

A major interest of mine is using technology in the classroom. I am familiar with various hypermedia programs and NovaNET, a computer-based learning system. At Garden Springs, I introduced students to science resources on the World Wide Web, and each student learned how to send e-mail messages to students in other countries.

As a result of my rewarding experiences at Garden Springs Elementary and in light of my preparation in bilingual education, I believe I could make a significant contribution to the educational program at City Elementary.

I have arranged for my credentials to be forwarded from Washington State University's placement office. If you require additional information of any sort, please feel free to contact me. At your convenience, I am available for an interview in Seattle. I thank you in advance for your consideration.

Sincerely,
Linda M. Rodriguez
Linda M. Rodriguez

Figure 13.5 Letter of application

successful. However, accepting your first teaching position is a major personal and professional step. Before signing a contract with a district, you should carefully consider job-related questions such as the following:

- In regard to my abilities and education, am I suited to this position?
- Would I like to work with this school's students, administrative staff, and teachers?

- Is the salary I am being offered sufficient?
- Will this position likely be permanent?
- Would I like to live in or near this community?
- Would the cost of living in this community enable me to live comfortably?
- Are opportunities for continuing education readily available?

What questions might you be asked in an interview for a teaching position? What questions should you have about the teaching position? about the school?

If you accept the offer, you will need to return a signed contract to the district along with a short letter confirming your acceptance. As a professional courtesy, you should notify other districts to which you have applied that you have accepted a position elsewhere. The Professional Reflection can help you identify the type of school that would be most satisfying for your first teaching position.

What Can You Expect as a Beginning Teacher?

Once you accept the professional challenge of teaching, it is important to prepare well in advance of the first day of school. In addition to reviewing the material you will teach, you should use this time to find out all you can about the school's students, the surrounding community, and the way the school operates. Also reflect on your expectations.

Professional Reflection

What Elements Are Essential for Your Job Satisfaction?

Job satisfaction as a teacher depends on many factors: the size and location of a school; the backgrounds of students; the surrounding community; and the climate, or culture, of the school itself, to name a few. The following sentence completion items can help you determine what conditions are essential for your job satisfaction. Write your responses on a separate sheet or in your teacher's journal. For each item, write at least a few additional sentences to elaborate on how you completed the sentence.

1. Ideally, my first position would be teaching students who had the following backgrounds and characteristics
2. For me, an ideal work setting would be a school that
3. My fellow teachers would help me during my first year of teaching by
4. When not in school, my colleagues and I would enjoy
5. My principal and/or supervisor would appreciate the way I
6. In his or her feedback on my teaching, my principal and/or supervisor would be most impressed with
7. During my first year at the school I would volunteer to
8. Five years after I began teaching at this school, I would like to be

The First Day

The first day of school can be frightening, as the following beginning teacher admits:

> *My first day of teaching in the classroom—alone! All of the other teachers look calm and are even smiling. I'm so nervous about fitting in at this school, making friends with my colleagues, and being respected by my students. What if the students misbehave and I don't handle it properly? Or what if the principal walks in unannounced? (Hauser and Rauch 2002, 35)*

Veteran teachers can also feel anxious on the first day of school; however, anxiety can be used to set a positive tone for the rest of the school year, as the following experienced teacher points out:

> *The anxiety level for both teachers and students about [the] first day is high. Taking advantage of these feelings can make for a good beginning.*
>
> *Students like to have guidelines on how the class will be run as well as what is expected of them academically. I always begin by welcoming the students into my class and immediately giving them something to do. I hand them their textbook and an index card. On the card, they write their name, address, telephone number, and book number.*
>
> *While the students are filling out their cards and looking at the textbook, I set up my seating chart and verify attendance. Within ten minutes of meeting the students, I begin my first lesson. By keeping clerical chores to a minimum, I try to have more time on task. After a closure activity, somewhere in the middle of the class period I take a few minutes to explain how their grade will be determined, the rules of the class, and when extra help sessions are available.*
>
> *Next, we deal with some curriculum content, and then I make a homework assignment. I tell the students that any homework assignment will be written on the chalkboard every day in the same location.*
>
> *Setting high standards on the first day makes the following days easier. We will always need to monitor and adjust, but this will be within the framework set on the first day (Burden and Byrd 1999, 177).*

Creating a pleasant, learning-oriented climate on the first day, as this teacher has done, will contribute greatly to your success during the first year. On the first day, students are eager to learn and are hopeful that the year will be a productive one. In addition, nearly all students will be naturally receptive to what you have to say. To them, you are a new, unknown quantity, and one of their initial concerns is to find out what kind of a teacher you will be. It is therefore critical that you be well organized and ready to take charge.

Advice from Experienced Teachers

In our work with schools and teachers, we have gathered recommendations on preparing for the first day from experienced K–12 teachers in urban, suburban, and rural schools. Teachers' recommendations focus on planning, establishing effective management practices, and following through on decisions.

> *There are little things you can do, such as having a personal note attached to a pencil welcoming each child. You may want to do a few little tricks in science class or read them your favorite children's story. But, don't put all your energy into the first day and have that day be the highlight of the year. Be well prepared and have plenty of things to do. Don't worry if you don't get everything done. Remember, you have all year.*
>
> —*Middle school science teacher*

Keepers of *the Dream*

Advice from "Sophomores"

Throughout this book, words of advice from and stories of achievement of veteran educators have provided guidance in your career choice as a future teacher. This guidance has been practical as well as inspiring. However, anyone who has ever taught knows that *everyone* who stands before a roomful of children–whether eight years old or eighteen years old–is a "keeper" of the dream. Stepping in front of a class for the first time can be scary; surviving that first year represents a major achievement, the first of many. So it is time to hear from the "sophomores"–teachers who went through that first year–and survived! In a survey of second-year teachers from across the country, *Education World* found the teachers agreed upon several key points when asked to reflect on their successes and failures and offer their best advice to the next year's *Dreamkeepers*.

"Have a blast!"

- **Take charge.** Wisconsin teacher Dawn Schurman recommended "having a clear discipline plan set up, with both rewards and consequences. Explain it to the kids on day 1 and review throughout the first week. In addition, I'm very glad that I sent home a copy of the discipline plan. I asked parents to read it with their child and for parents and children to sign and return a contract stating that they agreed to the rules. This has come in handy a few times."
- **Keep students busy and engaged.** First-year teacher Jean Federico said "I have one big piece of advice for first-year teachers: Before the first day of school, have plenty of activities prepared for emergency use. I learned the hard way that kids *will* misbehave if they have nothing to do. A class full of bored kids won't all sit quietly for ten minutes waiting for you to figure out what is next."
- **Get peer support.** Retta Threet, a teacher in Sumter, South Carolina, admitted "My biggest mistake was not insisting on a mentor, or at least a peer teacher. If I had it to do again, I would make a good friend whom I could go to for advice."
- **Get parental support.** North Carolina teacher Jana Lippe suggested: "Use your parents as much as you can. Every time I needed supplies for a celebration, I just sent a note home asking for donations. Every time, the parents came through."
- **Organize yourself.** Arizona English teacher Alana Morales advised: "Find an organization system that you can live and work with and stick with it. With 120-plus students, it's crucial that you stay organized!"
- **Organize your students.** Said Mississippi teacher Lisa Packard: "Don't assume they know how to organize themselves, because they don't. Show them how to organize their notebooks and folders. Show them exactly what you want on their papers and homework."
- **Write and reflect.** Teacher Mike Powell advised: "Start keeping a professional journal. After the course of the year, this journal will allow you to reflect on your professional practices and to witness what is probably going to be enormous personal growth."
- **Have fun.** "Do your best and have fun doing it. Once I finally relaxed, I had a great time," said teacher Tracy Keirns.

Finally, keep in mind the words of Philadelphia teacher Lew Clark: "Have a blast! You are about to begin a remarkable adventure."

For further tips and resources for first-year teachers, including The ABCs for First Year Teachers and connections to helpful websites for beginning teachers, visit Education World online at the website listed below.

Source: Adapted from L. Starr (2002). Advice for first-year teachers–from the "sophomores" who survived last year! *Education World.* Wallingford, CT. Retrieved from http://www.educationworld.com/a_curr/curr152.shtml.

> *It really helps on the first day to have plenty of material to cover and things to do. I'd recommend taking the material you plan to cover that day and doubling it. It's better to have too much than to run out. What you don't use the first day, you use the next. It takes awhile to get a feeling for how fast the kids are going to go.*
>
> —*Third-grade teacher*

> *The first day is a good time to go over rules and procedures for the year. But don't overdo it. Be very clear and specific about your expectations for classroom behavior.*
>
> —*Sixth-grade teacher*

> *From the beginning, it's important to do what you're there to do—that's teach. Teach the class something, maybe review material they learned last year. That lets them know that you're in charge, you expect them to learn. They'll look to you for direction—as long as you give it to them, you're fine.*
>
> —*Junior high language arts teacher*

How Can You Become a Part of Your Learning Community?

Your success in your first year of teaching will be determined by the relationships you develop with the pupils, their families, your colleagues, school administrators, and other members of the school community. All of these groups contribute to your effectiveness as a teacher, but the relationships you establish with students will be the most important (and complex) you will have as a teacher.

Relationships with Students

The quality of your relationships with students will depend in large measure on your knowledge of students and commitment to improving your interactions with them. As a first-year teacher put it:

> *It is amazing when every student is involved and enjoying the lesson. At moments like these, I realize that I'm educating real people and making a difference in their futures.*
>
> *I really connected with my students because they saw that learning can be fun. They realized that I, too, am a person who cares about them and wants them to succeed. It makes my job feel complete and I know I'm in the right profession (Hauser and Rauch 2002, 36).*

Your relationships with students will have many dimensions. Principally, you must see that each student learns as much as possible; this is your primary responsibility as a professional teacher. You will need to establish relationships with a great diversity of students based on mutual respect, caring, and concern. Without attention to this personal realm, your effectiveness as a teacher will be limited. In addition, teachers are significant models for students' attitudes and behaviors.

Relationships with Colleagues and Staff

Each working day, you will be in close contact with other teachers and staff members. As the experience of the following teacher suggests, it will definitely be to your advantage to establish friendly, professional relationships with them:

I was on a staff with a group of teachers who really supported me. They made it a part of their day to come into my room and see how I was doing and to share things. They made it easy to ask questions and work with them. They started me on the track of cooperating with other teachers and sharing my successes and failures with them.

They did such a good job of taking care of each other that my needs were always met. I had plenty of supplies, counseling help, administrative help. The school was a community. Anything I needed to be successful was provided.

During your first few months at the school, it would be wise to communicate to colleagues that you are willing to learn all you can about your new job and to be a team player. In most schools it is common practice to give junior faculty members less desirable assignments, reserving the more desirable ones for senior faculty. By demonstrating your willingness to take on these responsibilities with good humor and to give them your best effort, you will do much to establish yourself as a valuable faculty member.

Your colleagues may also appreciate learning from you about new approaches and materials—if you share in a manner that doesn't make others feel inferior. The following comments by a high school department chair, for example, illustrate a first-year Spanish teacher's positive influence on others:

She won the respect of all her colleagues in the school who have dealt with her almost immediately, not because she's so competent in Spanish and not because she's so competent as a teacher, but because she handles everything with such sensitivity and sensibleness.

Because of the way she operates—which is quietly but effectively—she has raised the whole tenor of expectations in the department. We have some very fine faculty in Spanish, but I would speculate they don't see their group self-image as intellectuals but rather as "people people." Because of what Elizabeth has brought to the school: the knowledge about how to use computers, her knowledge of foreign language oral proficiency, her knowledge of Spanish film and Spanish authors, she has kind of lifted everybody up and helped her colleagues see themselves in a little bit different light and to improve professionally (Dollase 1992, 49).

It is important that you get along with your colleagues and contribute to a spirit of professional cooperation or **collegiality** in the school. Some you will enjoy being around; others you may wish to avoid. Some will express obvious enthusiasm for teaching; others may be bitter and pessimistic about their work. Be pleasant and friendly with both types. Accept their advice with a smile, and then act on what you believe is worthwhile.

Relationships with Administrators

Pay particular attention to the relationships you develop with administrators, department heads, and supervisors. Though your contacts with them will not be as frequent as with other teachers, they can do much to ensure your initial success. The following comments illustrate the information new teachers often desire from their school principals:

- *"I would like affirmation from my principal that I am doing things OK. If not, I would like to know about it so I can address and correct the situation."*
- *"I would like to meet monthly with my principal to discuss things like 'hidden agendas,' culture and traditions of the school, expectations, regular events, and what to expect, as well as an opportunity to bitch and gripe a bit."*

- *"The principal should express the expectations that he has for students in the school. I needed to know about the parameters of the grading system. I needed to know expectations for lesson plans"* (Brock and Grady 2001, 18–19).

Principals are well aware of the difficulties you might encounter as a first-year teacher, and they are there to help you succeed. However, since the demands on their time are intense, you should not hesitate to be proactive about meeting with them to discuss issues of concern.

The principal of your new school will, most likely, be the one to introduce you to other teachers, members of the administrative team, and staff. He or she should inform you if there are assistant principals or department heads who can help you enforce school rules, keep accurate records, and obtain supplies, for example. The principal may also assign an experienced teacher to serve as a mentor during your first year.

Relationships with Parents

Developing positive connections with your students' parents can contribute significantly to students' success and to your success as a teacher. In reality, teachers and parents are partners—both concerned with the learning and growth of the children in their care. As U.S. Secretary of Education Rod Paige pointed out, "We need to build a bridge between powerful scientific research, homes, and preschools and make sure that adults know how vital it is that children have strong cognitive development, even before they enter school. Teachers and parents around the country [must work together] to ensure that no child is left behind" (U.S. Department of Education 2001). Figure 13.6 shows the percentage of stu-

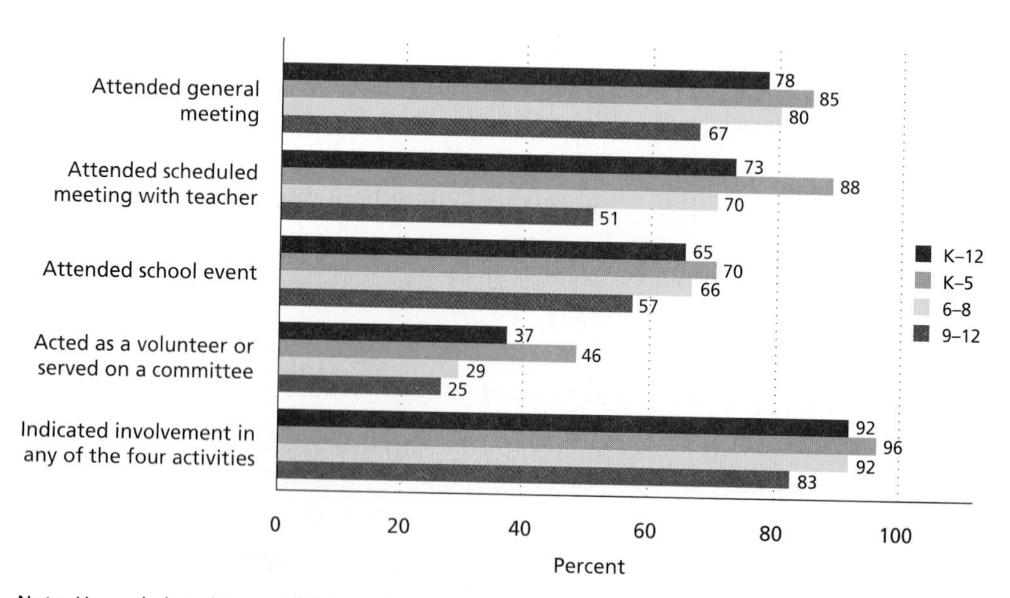

Note: Ungraded students or children who were home schooled were not included in this analysis; these students accounted for 1.6 percent of students in grades K–12. Data have been revised from previously published figures.

Figure 13.6 Parental involvement: percentage of students in grades K–12 whose parents reported involvement in specific activities in their child's school, 1999
Source: U.S. Department of Education, NCES. National Household Education Surveys Program (NHES), 1999 (Parent Interview Survey). Taken from *The Condition of Education 2001–Societal Support for Learning: Family Support.* Washington, D.C.: Department of Education.

Parents can be a teacher's greatest partners in determining the success of his or her students. What are some ways you can reach out to know your students' parents and gain their support?

dents in grades K–12 whose parents reported involvement in activities at their child's school.

It is important that you become acquainted with parents at school functions, at meetings of the Parent Teacher Association or Organization (PTA or PTO), at various community events, and in other social situations. To develop good communication with parents, you will need to be sensitive to their needs, such as their work schedules and the language spoken at home.

Where Do You Stand? Visit the Companion Website to Voice Your Opinion.

By maintaining contact with parents and encouraging them to become involved in their children's education, you can significantly enhance the achievement of your students. One research study, based on interviews with the parents and guardians of almost 17,000 K–12 students, showed that parental involvement is associated with higher levels of student achievement, more positive attitudes toward school, greater participation in extracurricular activities, fewer suspensions and expulsions, and fewer grade repetitions (Nord and West 2001). In light of such significant findings, it is important that you be willing to take the extra time and energy to pursue strategies such as the following for involving parents:

- Ask parents to read aloud to the child, to listen to the child read, and to sign homework papers.
- Encourage parents to drill students on math and spelling and to help with homework lessons.
- Encourage parents to discuss school activities with their children and suggest ways parents can help teach their children at home. For example, a simple home activity might be alphabetizing books; a more complex one would be using kitchen supplies in an elementary science experiment.
- Send home suggestions for games or group activities related to the child's schoolwork that parent and child can play together.
- Encourage parents to participate in school activities such as a sports booster club, career day, and music and drama events.

- Involve parents in their children's learning by having them co-sign learning contracts and serve as guest speakers.

The Goals 2000: Educate America Act funded parent resource centers in each state plus the District of Columbia (see the Appendix "Parent Information and Resource Centers" on this book's website). To help families get involved in their children's learning, these centers offer training for parents, hotlines, mobile training teams, resource and lending libraries, support groups, and referral networks. The U.S. Department of Education also sponsors the Partnership for Family Involvement in Education, designed to help students act as a link between their teachers and schools and their families and communities. (For information, call 1-800-USA-LEARN.)

Family involvement resources are also available on the Internet through the National Parent Information Network (NPIN), a project sponsored by the ERIC system. (For information, call (800) 583-4135.) NPIN resources include information for parents on child development, testing, working with teachers, and home learning activities. AskERIC Question & Answer Service provides forums for parents and teachers to address mutual concerns, listings of useful and inexpensive learning materials, and descriptions of model parent involvement programs. Other online resources for parental involvement in schools can be obtained from the Consortium for School Networking.

Community Relations

Communities provide significant support for the education of their young people and determine the character of their schools. In addition, communities often help their schools by recruiting volunteers, providing financial support for special projects, and operating homework hotline programs. For example, school–community partnerships have been formed through "The Employer's Promise," a national effort to involve communities in supporting the family's central role in children's learning:

- John Hancock Financial Services sponsors "Kids-to-Go," a program of daylong supervised activities for employees' school-age children during school holidays in Boston.
- Southern California Edison supports the Parent Institute for Quality Education, which has trained 7,500 parents from East Los Angeles to participate actively in their children's education.
- Hewlett-Packard staggers start times for employees who volunteer at the corporation's on-site elementary school and accommodates the schedules of employees with school-age children.
- American College Testing's "Realize the Dream" program provides workshops and resources to involve parents in their children's education.

How Can You Participate in Teacher Collaboration?

The relationships that build a learning community involve **collaboration**—working together, sharing decision making, and solving problems. As a member of a dynamic, changing profession, your efforts to collaborate will result in an increased understanding of the teaching–learning process and improved learning for all students. By working with others on school governance, curriculum development, school–community partnerships, and educational reform, you will play an important role in enhancing the professional status of teachers.

Meeting the Standard

Collaborates with Colleagues

INTASC

The teacher draws upon professional colleagues within the school and other professional arenas as supports for reflection, problem-solving and new ideas, actively sharing experiences and seeking and giving feedback (INTASC Performance, Principle #10).

Teacher candidates reflect on their practice and make necessary adjustments to enhance student learning (NCATE, Standard 1: Candidate Knowledge, Skills, and Dispositions).

Support and cooperation characterize relationships with colleagues. Teacher takes initiative in assuming leadership among the faculty (PRAXIS III Framework–"distinguished" level of performance).

Teachers are members of learning communities (NBPTS, Proposition 5).

Teachers meeting these standards value lifelong learning so it is no surprise that they are skilled in their abilities to collaborate with colleagues. They continually seek opportunities to spend time with experienced teachers, who are often more than happy to share their wealth of knowledge and experience. They also demonstrate the willingness to collaborate with colleagues in problem-solving and team-teaching opportunities and to serve as mentors and confidantes to less experienced teachers. Collaborative teachers recognize that colleagues also exist outside the geographic confines of their own school and use the Internet to share ideas and pick up helpful practical teaching tips, lesson plans, and even ready-to-use activities like Webquests. To expand their minds and professional knowledge, they routinely read professional journals, attend workshops or seminars, and scan web-based briefs like the ones sent to subscribers via e-mail from the Association for Supervision and Curriculum Development (ASCD) (described at http://www.smartbrief.com/ascd/).

The ability to productively collaborate with professional colleagues begins with an understanding of oneself as a professional educator. One way of developing a deeper self-understanding is to maintain a professional teaching portfolio. Web-based systems, such as the ones available from commercial companies such as LiveText.com or TaskStream.com, make that process more doable and useful than the paper portfolio systems. These companies promote colleague collaboration, provide the tools needed to create and maintain electronic teaching portfolios, and, at the same time, allow the teacher to control the level of security the portfolio documents and artifacts should have. Even teachers without sophisticated web development skills can collect, store, and post their teaching artifacts to the Web with either of these systems.

Commercial systems also often offer helpful tools such as the curriculum standards and rubric wizards that ease the work related to standards alignment and rubric development. The system provides electronic libraries that can store the artifacts to document a teacher's use of curriculum standards and rubrics. System users can collect their entire curriculum as well as annotated links to resources on the Internet in the system and then share the germane portions of their work with other people, who can also be linked to the portfolio through the system. That feature makes it possible to demonstrate curricular activities, including the district-required elements to a supervisor, parents, or other colleagues. Such a system can also be set to notify others each time a new learning activity is added.

Companion Website

1. At the following websites, you can see how two teachers share some of their knowledge with other teachers. The first is a veteran elementary school teacher with a wealth of knowledge and experiences (http://www.hannahmeans.bizland.com/). The other educator received the 2002 Global School Network Award (GSN) in recognition of collaboration with others (http://www.globalschoolnet.org/GSNawards/index.html). Check out the "Awards Info" section of the site to identify the qualifications for the award. Do you know a teacher who qualifies for the GSN Award? Write a brief letter of nomination for this person and then watch the GSN website for the chance to submit your nomination.
2. One seventh-grade teacher uses her website to document that she is "a highly motivated and organized instructor" with "the highest academic standards" who is able to get her "students [to] enjoy their classes and [to] perform with excellence." Take a few minutes and view this portfolio (http://www.mandia.com/kelly/portfolio.htm). Do you think the teacher has succeeded in documenting these skills? Why or why not? What skills do you think she needed to create this electronic portfolio?
3. Visit the LiveText.com (http://www.livetext.com) to see an example of a standards-based electronic portfolio. Enter "Haymond" in the search box or enter this address in your web browser: http://www.livetext.com/doc/4170. To view additional electronic portfolios at this website, return to the "LiveText" home page and enter the word "portfolio" in the search box. Write down some of the ideas you like or bookmark them in your web browser. To learn more about what you need to know and do to create your own electronic portfolio, "Take a Tour" at the LiveText website.

The heart of collaboration is meaningful, authentic relationships among professionals. Such relationships, of course, do not occur naturally; they require commitment and hard work. Friend and Bursuck (2002, 76–77) have identified seven characteristics of collaboration which are summarized in the following:

- Collaboration is voluntary; teachers make a personal choice to collaborate.
- Collaboration is based on parity; all individuals' contributions are valued equally.
- Collaboration requires a shared goal.
- Collaboration includes shared responsibility for key decisions.
- Collaboration includes shared accountability for outcomes.
- Collaboration is based on shared resources; each teacher contributes something—time, expertise, space, equipment, or other resource.
- Collaboration is emergent; as teachers work together, the degree of shared decision making, trust, and respect increases.

Schools that support the essential elements of collaboration are collegial schools "characterized by purposeful adult interactions about improving schoolwide teaching and learning" (Glickman, Gordon, and Ross-Gordon 2001, 5). In the following, we examine four expressions of teacher collaboration: peer coaching, staff development, team teaching, and co-teaching.

Peer Coaching

Experienced teachers traditionally help novice teachers, but more formal peer coaching programs extend the benefits of collaboration to more teachers. **Peer coaching** is an arrangement whereby teachers grow professionally by observing one another's teaching and providing constructive feedback. The practice encourages teachers to learn together in an emotionally safe environment. According to Bruce Joyce and Marsha Weil, peer coaching is an effective way to create communities of professional educators, and all teachers should be members of coaching teams:

> *If we had our way,* all *school faculties would be divided into coaching teams—that is, teams who regularly observe one another's teaching and learn from watching one another and the students. In short, we recommend the development of a "coaching environment" in which all personnel see themselves as coaches (Joyce, Weil, and Calhoun 2000, 440).*

Through teacher-to-teacher support and collaboration, peer coaching programs improve teacher morale and teaching effectiveness.

Staff Development

Increasingly, teachers are contributing to the design of staff development programs that encourage collaboration, risk-taking, and experimentation. Some programs, for example, give teachers the opportunity to meet with other teachers at similar grade levels or in similar content areas for the purpose of sharing ideas, strategies, and solutions to problems. A day or part of a day may be devoted to this kind of workshop or idea exchange. Teachers are frequently given released time from regular duties to visit other schools and observe exemplary programs in action.

One example of a collaborative staff development program is at Sherman Oaks Community Charter School in San Jose, California. Every school day between 11:30 A.M. and 1 P.M., Sherman Oaks teachers meet for ninety minutes of professional development. The teachers discuss and debate instructional theory and practice, try to solve problems that have come up or are likely to come up in their classrooms, discuss curriculum, seek advice, offer encouragement, or quietly reflect. As one teacher put it, "It's always wonderful stuff—things that get your brain stretched. I feel like a professional" (Curtis 2000).

Another collaborative program is the Maryland Electronic Learning Community (MELC), a teacher development and support group that provides formal training in technology integration followed by ongoing collaboration and support. Funded in part by the U.S. Department of Education, the MELC project is a coalition of partners who form an electronic learning community using technologies such as digitized video, Internet resources, two-way video and audio for distance learning, and e-mail to support and enhance middle school curriculum and professional development (Fulton and Riel 1999).

Team Teaching

In **team teaching** arrangements, teachers share the responsibility for two or more classes, dividing up the subject areas between them, with one preparing lessons in mathematics, science, and health, for instance, while the other plans instruction in reading and language arts. The division of responsibility may also be made in terms of the performance levels of the children, so that, for example, one teacher may teach the lowest- and highest-ability reading groups and the middle math group, while the other teaches the middle-ability reading groups and the lowest and highest mathematics group. In many schools, team teaching arrangements are so extensive that children move from classroom to classroom for 40- to 50-minute periods just as students do at the high school level.

The practice of team teaching is often limited by student enrollments and budget constraints. As integrated curricula and the need for special knowledge and skills increase, however, the use of collegial support teams (CSTs) will

What are some forms of professional collaboration in which you will participate as a teacher? In what types of co-teaching arrangements might these teachers cooperate?

On the Frontlines

Advice for the First Year

Seven women sit in student chairs around a low table in the science room in an elementary school in South Central Los Angeles. Outside, the playground is empty and silent, the other classrooms dark, and the winter sun is ready to drop and end another day. But the energy in the science room is newborn, alive with earnest talk, laughter, and excitement. The university researcher sits at one end, launching each discussion with a question. The six others begin to soar from there, taking turns at first, then layering their answers on top of another's. The researcher catches their attention then, pulls them back, and asks the next question. The soaring begins again.

Her goal is to gather the advice the six veteran teachers have for students and new teachers planning to teach in urban schools. The three African American and three Euro-American women, in their mid-thirties to late fifties, teach in different elementary schools in the area. Their principals selected them, along with ten others who were also interviewed, because they matched the researcher's profile of "teachers with high morale and career perseverance."

"What advice would you give to someone taking classes to be a teacher?" the researcher asks.

"Not to take yourself too seriously—the children won't, be persistent. [Know that] there's a light at the end of the tunnel, growth is a process—[it becomes like an] old shoe that starts to fit," Margaret replies.

Janet jumps in next, "Make sure this is the professional area they're supposed to be [in]. If they're not dedicated to children, it's a losing battle. Teaching is a calling."

"Zero in on filling the needs of children," says Beatrice. "When parents come in, deal with them on the level they are. Know their children's environment, parents, the type of kids, homes."

"Be prepared—in the sense of an open mind. Keep it open. College bookwork doesn't teach you per se—how to be a successful teacher. You have to experience quite a bit with different children. Student teaching is not enough," Lesley adds.

And the group starts to soar again.

The teachers in the study above counseled novices to have realistic expectations for themselves and of their schools. Teaching well takes time and experience, and it isn't mastered in the first year. Schools are not always equipped with the equipment, books, and supplies that teachers might expect, especially in poor school districts. They advised novice teachers who want to teach in urban schools to do so for the right reasons—because they cared deeply about the children and their community. They recommended that those getting ready to teach prepare well and to even "over prepare." And they stressed the importance of having a "child-focus."

The success and enjoyment of teachers' first-year experiences will depend in good measure on the schools they select to work at and the quality of their cultures, regardless of their locations. Schools that make new teachers feel welcome have "integrated professional cultures" according to Susan Moore Johnson, Director of The Project on the Next Generation of Teachers at the Harvard Graduate School of Education. She and her research team (2001) also note that in such schools "all colleagues within the school" shared responsibility for the school and its students. The team found that good teacher induction programs incorporated key factors: "Well-matched mentors, curriculum guidance, collaborative lesson planning, peer observation, and inspired leadership all support new teachers in ways that recruitment incentives never can."

New teachers can also find advice and resources on the Internet. Years ago, such ready access to tips and ideas didn't exist. Today, technology has opened up the possibilities. The Internet, other novice teachers, experienced teachers, university faculty, and former classmates in other school districts can all be sources of help to smooth that first-year experience.

Exploratory Questions

1. Visit the website for the Survival Guide for New Teachers. (See address below.) What does it say are the benefits and negative aspects of seeking advice from experienced teachers?
2. Visit the website for Harvard's The Project on the Next Generation of Teachers. (See address below.) What are the latest findings?

Your Survival Guide of Helpful Resources

The following resources provide helpful hints for surviving "on the frontlines."

Books and Articles

Johnson, S. M., Birkeland, S., Kardos, S. M., Kauffman, D., Liu, E., and Peske, H. G. (2001/July/August). Retaining the next generation of teachers: The importance of school-based support. *Harvard Education Newsletter,* pp. 6, 8.

Ladson-Billings, G. (1994). *The dreamkeepers: Successful teachers of African American children.* San Francisco, CA: Jossey Bass.

Websites

The Project on the Next Generation of Teachers (http://www.gse.harvard.edu/~ngt/)

Survival Guide for New Teachers (http://www.ed.gov/pubs/survivalguide/)

Teachers.net Lesson Plan Bank (http://teachers.net/lessons/)

become more common. A **collegial support team** (**CST**) provides teachers with a "safe zone" for professional growth, as one teacher commented:

> *[The CST] allows me much discretion as to the areas I'd like to strengthen. Therefore, I am truly growing with no fear of being labeled or singled out as the "teacher who is having problems." I am aware of problem spheres and I work to correct these with the aid of my colleagues (Johnson and Brown 1998, 89).*

The members of a team make wide-ranging decisions about the instruction of students assigned to the team, such as when to use large-group instruction or small-group instruction, how teaching tasks will be divided, and how time, materials, and other resources will be allocated.

Co-Teaching

In **co-teaching** arrangements, two or more teachers, such as a classroom teacher and a special education teacher or other specialist, teach together in the same classroom. Co-teaching builds on the strengths of two teachers and provides increased learning opportunities for all students (Friend and Bursuck 2002). Typically, co-teaching arrangements occur during a set period of time each day or on certain days of the week. Among the several possible co-teaching variations, Friend and Bursuck (2002) have identified the following:

- *One teach, one support*—one teacher leads the lesson; the other assists.
- *Station teaching*—the lesson is divided into two parts; one teacher teaches one part to half of the students while the other teaches the other part to the rest. The groups then switch and the teachers repeat their part of the lesson. If students can work independently, a third group may be formed, or a volunteer may teach at a third station.
- *Parallel teaching*—a class is divided in half, and each teacher instructs half the class individually.
- *Alternative teaching*—a class is divided into one large group and one small group. For example, one teacher may provide remediation or enrichment to the small group, while the other teacher instructs the large group.

How Will Your Performance as a Teacher Be Evaluated?

Most teachers are evaluated on a regular basis to determine whether their performance measures up to acceptable standards, if they are able to create and sustain effective learning environments for students. Performance criteria used to evaluate teachers vary and are usually determined by the school principal, district office, the school board, or a state education agency. In most schools, the principal or a member of the leadership team evaluates teachers.

Teacher evaluations serve many purposes: to determine whether teachers should be retained, receive tenure, or be given merit pay. Evaluations also help teachers assess their effectiveness and develop strategies for self-improvement. In fact, "teachers who receive the most classroom feedback are also most satisfied with teaching" (Glickman, Gordon, and Ross-Gordon 2001, 315).

Quantitative and Qualitative Evaluation

Typically, supervisors use quantitative or qualitative approaches (or a combination) to evaluate teachers' classroom performance. **Quantitative evaluation** includes pencil-and-paper rating forms the supervisor uses to record classroom events and behaviors objectively in terms of their number or frequency. For example, a supervisor might focus on the teacher's verbal behaviors—questioning, answering, praising, giving directions, and critiquing. The Florida Performance Measurement System (FPMS), discussed in Chapter 2, is an example of a quantitative approach to teacher evaluation (see Appendix 2.1 for the "Screening/ Summative Observation Instrument" used by the FPMS).

Qualitative evaluation, in contrast, includes written, open-ended narrative descriptions of classroom events in terms of their qualities. These more subjective measures are equally valuable in identifying teachers' weaknesses and strengths. In addition, qualitative evaluation can capture the complexities and subtleties of classroom life that might not be reflected in a quantitative approach to evaluation.

Clinical Supervision

Many supervisors follow the four-step **clinical supervision** model in which the supervisor first holds a preconference with the teacher, then observes in the classroom, analyzes and interprets observation data, and finally holds a postconference with the teacher (Acheson and Gall 1997; Goldhammer, Anderson, and Krajewski 1993; Pajak 1999; Smyth 1995; Snyder and Anderson 1996). During the preconference, the teacher and supervisor schedule a classroom observation and determine its purpose and focus and the method of observation to be used. At the postconference, the teacher and supervisor discuss the analysis of observation data and jointly develop a plan for instructional improvement.

Fulfilling the clinical supervision model is difficult and time-consuming, and time-pressed administrators must often modify the approach. For example, Kim Marshall, principal at a Boston elementary school with thirty-nine teachers, makes four random, unannounced five-minute visits to classrooms each day. This schedule allows him to observe every teacher during a two-week period, and each teacher about nineteen times during a year. To make the most of his five-minute classroom visits, he follows these guidelines:

- Be a perceptive observer in order to capture something interesting and helpful to say during the feedback session.
- Give teachers a mixture of praise, affirmation, suggestions, and criticism.
- When sharing critical observations with teachers, be tactful and nonthreatening but totally honest.
- Use good judgment about when to deliver criticism and when to hold off (Marshall 1996, 344).

Regardless of the approach a school district will use to evaluate your performance as a beginning teacher, remember that evaluation will assist your professional growth and development. Experienced teachers report that periodic feedback and assistance from knowledgeable, sensitive supervisors is very beneficial; such evaluation results in "improved teacher reflection and higher-order thought, more collegiality, openness, and communication, greater teacher retention, less anxiety and burnout, greater teacher autonomy and efficacy, improved attitudes, improved teaching behaviors, and better student achievement and attitudes" (Glickman, Gordon, and Ross-Gordon, 2001, 329).

Summary

How Will You Become Certified or Licensed to Teach?

- State certification is required for teaching in public schools and in many private schools. Some large cities and local school districts have additional criteria for certification. Certification requirements for teachers vary from state to state and are frequently modified. Some states waive licensing requirements for teachers certified by the National Board for Professional Teaching Standards (NBPTS).
- Most states require testing of teachers for initial certification, and some require recertification after a three- to five-year period.
- States that are members of the Interstate Certification Agreement Contract honor teaching certificates granted by certain other states.
- Private, parochial, for-profit, and charter schools employ about 404,000 noncertified teachers. Many states offer alternative and emergency certification programs.
- The Praxis Series: Professional Assessments for Beginning Teachers is required in most states for initial certification. The Praxis Series includes assessments of academic (basic) skills, subject matter knowledge, and classroom performance.

Will You Have Difficulty Finding a Teaching Job?

- Teacher supply and demand in content areas and geographic regions influences finding a teaching position.
- Teaching is a large profession, involving more than 47 million students in public K–12 schools and more than 3 million teachers.
- Job vacancies result from retirements, relocation, and career changes. Elementary and secondary enrollments and the demand for new teachers will increase through 2011.
- Education-related career opportunities for teachers include principal, assistant principal, librarian, counselor, and teaching roles in government and the private sector.

How Will You Find Your First Teaching Job?

- Information about teaching vacancies may be obtained through placement services, state departments of education, and personal networking on the Internet.
- A résumé is a concise summary of an individual's experiences, education, and skills. A letter of inquiry is used to find out if a school district has any teaching vacancies, and a letter of application (or cover letter) indicates an individual's interest in and qualifications for a teaching position.

What Can You Expect as a Beginning Teacher?

- Beginning teachers should prepare instructional strategies and materials and learn about their students and the community well in advance of the first day of school.
- Experienced teachers' recommendations for beginning teachers focus on planning, organizing, and following through.

How Can You Become a Part of Your Learning Community?

- The learning community includes students, their families, colleagues, and members of the community.
- Research indicates that parental involvement is a key factor in children's academic achievement.
- Training programs, hotlines, referral networks, and partnership programs are among the resources teachers can use to involve parents and members of the community.

How Can You Participate in Teacher Collaboration?

- Teachers collaborate through participation in school governance, curriculum development, school-community partnerships, and educational reform.
- Four approaches to teacher collaboration are peer coaching, staff development, team teaching, and co-teaching.

How Will Your Performance as a Teacher Be Evaluated?

- Performance criteria for evaluating teachers are developed by school principals, districts, school boards, or states.
- Quantitative approaches to teacher evaluation focus on the incidence, frequency, or amount of teacher or student behavior in various categories.
- Qualitative approaches to teacher evaluation are usually written narratives focusing on the qualities of classrooms and events, such as classroom climate and teaching style.

Key Terms and Concepts

alternative certification, **474**
charter, **474**
clinical supervision, **499**
collaboration, **492**
collegiality, **489**
collegial support team (CST), **498**
co-teaching, **498**
credentials file, **480**
emergency certification, **475**
Interstate Certification Agreement Contract, **473**
letter of application, **481**
letter of inquiry, **481**
National Council for Accreditation of Teacher Education (NCATE), **471**
peer coaching, **494**
placement service, **480**
Praxis Series: Professional Assessments for Beginning Teachers, **475**
qualitative evaluation, **499**
quantitative evaluation, **498**
recertification, **471**
résumé, **480**
teacher supply and demand, **476**
teaching certificate, **470**
team teaching, **495**

Applications and Activities

Teacher's Journal

1. Record in your journal your plan for becoming certified or licensed to teach.
2. Develop answers to possible interview questions and brainstorm questions to ask.
3. Envision your first day as a teacher and describe what you see.
4. When you become a teacher, in what collaborations and partnerships will you participate? How might these activities contribute to your effectiveness as a teacher? How might your involvement enhance students' learning and your relationships with them?

Teacher's Database

1. Explore and compare teacher proficiencies and teaching standards according to state boards of education, national standards organizations, and teacher and subject area organizations. Begin by locating the following organizations online and information about your school's education program in relation to state and national standards.

   National Association for State Boards of Education (NASBE)

   National Association of State Directors for Teacher Education and Certification (NASDTEC)

   National Board for Professional Teaching Standards (NBPTS)

   National Council for Accreditation of Teacher Education (NCATE)

   Continue your search by accessing the government or education department of a locality, region, or state where you plan to teach and gathering information about becoming a teacher there.

2. Formulate a research question concerning demographic aspects of teachers and schools in the United States. Then go online to gather current national and state statistics on your question. For example, your question might relate to one or more of the following topics.

   attitudes of teachers

   characteristics of parochial schools

   characteristics of the teaching force

   independent and private schools

   information about school districts

   public schools compared to private schools

   teacher recruitment

   teacher shortages

   teaching salaries and benefits

   Begin your data search in the U.S. Department of Education's National Center for Education Statistics (NCES).

Observations and Interviews

1. If you can arrange it, observe the first day of classes at a local school. What strategies did the teachers use to begin the year on a positive, task-oriented note? What evidence did you see that the teachers followed the advice given by the experienced teachers in this chapter? Record your qualitative observations on handout master M13.3 "Qualitative

Observation Log," and share them with your classmates. What common themes do you detect in the data?

2. Survey teachers at a local school to get information about how they prepare for the first day of school. To help you develop questions for your survey, ask your instructor for handout master M13.1, "Developing and Conducting a Survey 1."

3. Prepare a questionnaire and then survey a group of experienced teachers for their recollections about the triumphs and defeats they experienced as beginning teachers. What lessons are evident in their responses to your questionnaire? Are there common themes that characterize the triumphs they recall? The defeats? For help in developing the items for your questionnaire, ask your instructor for handout master M13.2, "Developing and Conducting a Survey 2."

4. Interview teachers and administrators about their experiences with professional collaboration and parental involvement. What examples do they provide, and how do these reflect the seven characteristics of collaboration presented in this chapter? How do students benefit from collaboration and parental involvement? What suggestions do the teachers and administrators have for improving collaboration and parental involvement?

Professional Portfolio

1. Draft a preliminary professional résumé. Review the section in this chapter titled "Preparing Your Résumé" and Appendix 13.2 "Résumé Advice for Educators." In addition, examine the résumé prepared by Linda M. Rodriguez (see Figure 13.3).

   In your résumé, under "Personal Data," provide a current address and a permanent address. Also, under "Education," specify an anticipated graduation date. Under "Experience," include work experience that indicates your ability to work with people. Begin with your most recent experiences and present information in reverse chronological order.

   When you have finished your preliminary résumé, critique it against "Résumé Advice for Educators."

2. Draft an essay describing what you will bring to your first year of teaching. It may help to review the essay you wrote for the Chapter 1 portfolio entry on what has drawn you to teaching.

VideoWorkshop Extra!

If the VideoWorkshop package was included with your textbook, go to Chapter 13 of the Companion Website (www.ablongman.com/parkay6e) and click on the VideoWorkshop button. Follow the instructions for viewing videoclip 8 and completing this exercise. Consider this information along with what you've read in Chapter 13 while answering the following questions.

1. It is common knowledge that beginning teachers should prepare instructional strategies and materials prior to the first day of instruction. The text and videoclip 8 reinforce this idea. Explain how such preparation can help teachers with both classroom management and classroom discipline.

2. After you have watched videoclip 8, compare team teaching and co-teaching methods discussed in the text. How do these approaches influence the curricula teachers prepare?

Appendix 13.1

JOB SEARCH TIMETABLE CHECKLIST

This checklist is designed to help you make good use of your time as you conduct your job search. We encourage you to use this checklist in conjunction with the services and resources available from your college or university career services office.

August/September *(12 months prior to employment)*	______ Review your career services' Web site for information relating to your field. ______ Register with your career services office and become oriented to their programs. ______ Begin to define the type and size of school systems in which you have an interest.
October *(11 months prior to employment)*	______ Begin to identify references and consider where you want to deposit letters of recommendation, résumés, etc. (e.g., your career services office, a commercial service). ______ Meet with a counselor in your career services office to discuss your job-search plan.
November/December *(8–10 months prior to employment)*	______ Begin developing résumés which can be scanned, used for online applications, e-mailed, and mailed. You will need cover letters for résumés which you mail. ______ Begin networking by contacting friends, faculty members, past teachers, etc., to inform them of your career plans. ______ Finalize your résumé(s) and have them critiqued in your career services office. For those to be mailed, check out reproduction processes. ______ Attend appropriate career planning workshops. ______ Begin developing a list of school systems in which you are interested. ______ Check out school system Web sites and contact to obtain necessary application materials. ______ If relocating away from your geographic area, contact a career services office in the area to which you are moving and request reciprocity of services. ______ Determine certification requirements. Make sure you have completed testing requirements for your field(s). If you are applying to out-of-state school systems, contact the appropriate State Department of Education or Professional Standards to determine requirements.
January *(8 months prior to employment)*	______ Complete online or paper applications for school systems and send with appropriate résumés and cover letters. ______ Inquire about school systems that will be recruiting at your institution, or at regional job fairs, or virtual career fairs. Inquire about the processes for interviewing with these systems. ______ Research school systems with which you will be applying and interviewing.
February/March/April *(5–7 months prior to employment)*	______ Participate in on-campus interviews and career fairs (virtual or otherwise) related to education. Send thank you letters as appropriate. ______ Register with online job search systems. ______ Monitor the job vacancy listings available on the Internet in your state, in your career services office, etc.
April–August *(1–5 months prior to employment)*	______ Stay up-to-date with job openings through online systems and your career services office. ______ Maintain communication with your network of contacts. ______ Contact school systems by phone or e-mail to stay in touch with potential job openings. ______ Aggressively network with educational contacts. Keep them up to date on your progress. ______ Accept an offer that is appropriate to your particular situation. ______ Inform those associated with your search once you have accepted a position. This includes those systems in which your application is still active. Then celebrate!

Source: Checklist prepared by Bruce Brewer, State University of West Georgia, for American Association for Employment in Education (AAEE), *2002 Job Search Handbook for Educators.* Columbus, OH: American Association for Employment in Education, p. 6. The *Handbook* is available for $8.00 from AAEE.

Appendix 13.2

RÉSUMÉ ADVICE FOR EDUCATORS

A modern-day résumé is a written advertisement focused toward a prospective employer. In a résumé, however, the "product" being advertised is you, the candidate.

Many job applicants become confused about what to include on a résumé. This article covers the most common informational categories, but you should strive to include any information that you feel will enhance your chances of being selected for an interview.

Seeking the "Perfect" Résumé

Just as every individual is different, each résumé presents a distinct combination of skills, abilities, and qualifications about its author. This is why it is impossible to find a perfect sample résumé and simply copy it. Your background is unique, and cannot be found in a book. However, reviewing other résumés will certainly be helpful because they will provide a rich supply of ideas and perspectives for your document.

While the perfect résumé may be an elusive concept, excellent résumés have many characteristics in common. An excellent résumé is one to two pages in length. It is free of typographical errors, produced on high-quality bond paper, accentuates your most salient qualities and qualifications, is organized and easy to read, and conveys a sense of who you are to the reader. This is easier said than done!

You need to remember that in today's job market, school principals are inundated with résumés. One or two pages is about the maximum they are willing to read about each candidate. As a prospective teacher, a résumé with any typographical error is a signal that you are poorly prepared to instruct others, so be sure to have your final document read by others, until all errors are eliminated.

Résumés for teaching and résumés for business have both similarities and differences. Organization, style, appearance, neatness, and punctuation issues apply to both. (If you need help with these issues, you will find useful books on the topic in your institution's career planning and placement office or at local bookstores.) However, educators' résumés typically include additional categories: student teaching, clinical experience, and certification information.

As you work to write the "perfect" résumé you will undoubtedly receive a variety of well-intentioned advice, and some of it will be conflicting. Everyone will have an opinion to offer. One of your most difficult tasks will be to evaluate what you hear. Pursue different opinions, and then decide what makes sense for you.

Statement of Teaching Objective

It is appropriate to include a "Career Objective" or "Teaching Objective" statement on your résumé. While optional, this statement is highly recommended because it helps identify the specific areas in which you wish to teach. Consider the advantages and disadvantages of the following three sample objectives, then develop your own to fit your requirements.

1. Elementary Teaching Position, K–6.
2. Seeking a classroom position in the upper elementary grades that provides an opportunity to facilitate academic, social, and personal growth of students.
3. Secondary or middle school position in science/math, in a suburban location. Qualified and interested in coaching track, volleyball, or swimming.

Objective 1 is descriptive and to the point. However, additional elements are incorporated into examples 2 and 3. Objective 3 is well thought out and developed, although unless you intend to decline all offers other than those in suburban locations, you should avoid using a phrase which defines location too tightly. The reader will assume that you mean what you say.

Student Teaching Information

It is important that beginning teachers provide information about their student teaching experiences. Do not assume that all student teaching experiences are alike, and therefore need not be described. Some principals remain interested in your student teaching experience even after you have several years of professional experience.

Review the following two examples, and then develop a section that accurately portrays your own experience.

1. Northwestern High School
   Rolling Hills, Illinois
   Student Teacher
   Taught 11th grade chemistry and math courses in an open classroom format. Coordinated field study trips, and a "Careers in Science" day.
2. MacKenzie Elementary School
   Chicago, Illinois
   Student Teacher
   September–December, 1995
   Observed, assisted, and taught regular and accelerated classes. Developed daily lesson and unit plans. Assisted in after-school tutoring program. Coordinated a revised parent conference format that increased teacher–parent interaction. Refined an existing computer database for classroom record keeping.

Note how the examples include pertinent details of student teaching experiences beyond the routine aspects, it is this information that demonstrates ways in which you made yourself valuable. In your narrative, try to focus on how your presence made something better to make your experience stand out from those who merely developed lesson plans and assisted teachers.

Past Employment Information

Normally, an employer wants to know about your last ten years of professional experience. As a prospective teacher, you should include any experiences in which you worked with K–12-age individuals. Examples of pertinent positions would include camp counselor, teacher's aide, tutor, Scout troop leader, and so forth.

Many candidates dismiss nonteaching experiences as unrelated, and fail to include them on their résumés. However, principals and school administrators can draw valuable inferences regarding your work habits from this information. Dependability, responsibility, and leadership potential are just a few of the desirable traits you can document with information about jobs you have held.

Related Activities and Interests

Information about activities and interests helps you present the image of a well-rounded and versatile teacher. The following categories represent just a few of the areas you may want to include.

- Volunteer activities
- Professional memberships
- Special interests
- Honors and awards
- Committee work
- Training
- Study abroad
- Community involvement
- Fluency in languages other than English
- Computer skills
- Leadership activities
- Professional development activities
- Class projects
- Scholarships

Remember, the more areas of knowledge and expertise that you demonstrate, the more likely you are to become a desirable candidate in the eyes of school administrators. School districts actively seek candidates who are flexible and willing to take on a variety of tasks in the school.

A Few Final Do's and Don't's

Make sure that your résumé is not a jigsaw puzzle of unrelated odds and ends, expecting that the principal will be able to piece them together. If those who receive your résumé have to work hard to figure it out, it is likely that they will just move on to the next résumé!

When your résumé is complete, print your final copy on a laser-jet printer, and have copies made at a printing service on high-quality, bond paper. Conservative paper—white, off-white, or ivory—is always suitable. Your printing service can help you select a paper which has matching envelopes to enhance you presentation. Be sure to purchase blank paper that matches your résumé so your cover letters will also match your presentation package.

Writing your résumé should be an introspective, exhilarating, positive, pat-yourself-on-the-back experience. If you approach it with this spirit, your résumé will be one of which you are justifiably proud.

Source: Lorn B. Coleman, *2001 Job Search Handbook for Educators.* Columbus, OH: American Association for Employment Education, pp. 15–16. Used with permission.

Reflections on Education

Preparing a Literate Populace

by Maria Pacino

"Why Johnny can't read and Maria can't write" seem to be popular themes in print and nonprint media in the United States and other countries. This literacy crisis is apparent in academic work from kindergarten through higher education and adulthood. Although statistics indicate that modern democratic countries have eliminated illiteracy, many citizens seem unprepared for the demands of technology-oriented, morally challenged, global democracies.

According to a 2002 Carnegie report, "The Urban High School's Challenge: Ensuring Literacy for Every Child," literacy in the United States has given an advantage to the upper middle class, leaving women and minorities on unequal footing in terms of educational access and resources; such a disadvantage has resulted in high dropout rates, high school students reading at a sixth-grade level, and a significant number of college freshmen needing remedial courses in English and math. Challenges arise as more and more immigrants from varied cultural backgrounds attempt to navigate and negotiate an educational system often at odds with democratic schooling. U.S. students are often seen as less literate than peers in other nations. Yet the struggles and challenges of literate citizenship is a global concern. With the federal government pushing for an increase in standardized reading scores as a measure of accountability, teachers often feel the need to teach for the test, rather than to nurture a child-centered curriculum and pedagogy. Little time is left to link literacy to life experiences.

Although reading and writing are at the core of literacy skills, literacy allows individuals to define themselves and to bring their voices and experiences into shaping their view of the world and their relationship with others. Paulo Freire, the late Brazilian educator, maintained that before children are introduced to reading and writing, they need to read "the world," or to be given opportunities to understand the global and cultural influences that help define their world and their place as citizens in a pluralistic democracy. U.S. schools struggle with the challenges of defining literacy and identifying effective strategies for teaching reading and writing, including bilingual education.

The definition of literacy goes beyond the ability to read and write; it is the ability to think critically, to be self-reflective, and to make informed, ethical decisions in a democratic society. Traditional notions of literacy in Western democracies tend to exclude and devalue cultures that emphasize oral tradition, observational skills, and non-Western modes of discourse, which are often characteristic of immigrant populations in the United States. Literacy develops in cultural context. It is dangerous to assume that there is only one sure way, "a quick fix," to increase literacy skills because the very notion of literacy is complex and involves a variety of skills: verbal, critical inquiry-based, quantitative, technological, cross-cultural, information processing and management, ethical decision making and problem solving.

Schools and libraries play a very important role in the literacy development of individuals in a free society. Consequently, the American Library Association has established standards of information literacy in terms of the following five abilities:

1. To access and process information efficiently and effectively and to evaluate it critically in terms of authenticity, validity, and reliability
2. To use information in a discerning way, while relating it to personal interests, as well as for generating knowledge
3. To appreciate literature and other creative expressions of information
4. To contribute to the learning community and understand the importance of information in a democratic society
5. To make ethical decisions regarding information and technology.

Literate citizens must be able to filter and evaluate critically large amounts of information available through multiple media sources and understand the sociocultural, economic, and legal ramifications of ethical media access, use, and dissemination. Information literacy should be the foundation for lifelong learning.

What is the role and responsibility of teachers and schooling in the literacy development of culturally diverse democratic societies? How do teachers collaborate with parents and other societal institutions to provide holistic literacy development in a pluralistic democracy? In what ways can we promote self-directed learning and a lifelong love for literacy development? As educators, we need to encourage other representational forms of literacy as complementary to text-based literacy. Teachers must provide safe classroom environments in which students feel that their voices are heard and praised. Democratic classrooms are communities of learners who engage in intellectual inquiry and participatory decision making.

As educators face the challenges of teaching literacy skills, they need to understand how language develops, the sociocultural context of language, and the influence of books and technology as a foundation for acquiring literacy. Educators need to rediscover their own literacy experiences to facilitate the literacy experiences of their students. My experience as a tutor in a public library adult literacy program helped me gain a more in-depth understanding of the relationship between reading and writing, the cultural context of language, and the role of libraries in the literacy development of democratic societies. When the workshop leader held up cards written in Arabic language and asked us to read the cards, I and others who neither read nor speak Arabic felt lost. The words and symbols and the reading format were totally different from our Western literacy experiences. My own Portuguese immigrant experience was reawakened, and I remembered taking a community college math course in which I had to show the long division process. I was shocked to find out that the way I learned long division was different from my instructor, yet we achieved the same correct response. So I learned from him, but he also learned from me. Language, reading, writing, and other literacy expressions are developed in cultural context. Our students' cultural backgrounds and experiences influence their literacy development.

As we attempt to redefine literacy for the twenty-first century, schools, teachers, and parents need to develop partnerships in assisting students to become lifelong learners—learners who engage in critical inquiry as consumers of information and knowledge delivered through many print and nonprint formats and learners who use this information and knowledge to make ethical decisions in a global democracy. Educators, parents, and schools need to view the role of libraries as essential in literacy development. In teaching reading and writing, we must view these processes as intricately woven—writers read! Reading other people's work informs our own writing process. A balanced approach to teaching reading and writing (whole language and phonics), along with bilingual education, are effective in acquiring literacy skills. Interdisciplinary and cooperative teaching and learning strategies enable learners to see the relationships between the arts and the sciences, including technology, and to understand their application in the real world. Character development, conflict resolution, and cross-cultural awareness are also essential literacy skills in a global democracy.

The theme issue of the October 1999 *Educational Leadership* was entitled "Redefining Literacy." One of the articles included a list of representative types of literacy from *The Literacy Dictionary: The Vocabulary of Reading and Writing:* academic, adult, basic, community, computer, critical, cultural, family, media, multilingual, quantitative, workplace, among many others. There are models of successful holistic literacy programs for elementary and secondary school settings. One example is Van Ness Elementary School in Washington, D.C., where K–3 students develop literacy skills in a working community with a store, a newspaper, a post office, a museum, and a banking system. A middle school teacher's use of books by Latino authors in his classroom has been a success with Latino students and parents. One of my students, who teaches at a continuation high school, has encouraged her students to write essays and poems about their life experiences; these troubled students look forward to reading and writing.

There are many examples of successful literacy experiences. For example, multicultural materials (authentic cultural portrayals of universal problems and conflicts), skits, simulations, role playing, community involvement, and service learning show connections between reading and writing. Literature circles and discussions, writers' workshops, and dramatizations are effective in K–12 and adult literacy development. Other useful strategies include literature-based reading, strategic reading, storytelling, scaffolded writing, interactive journaling, and peer editing. Literacy education is a developmental, holistic, lifelong commitment in a free society. Schools and educators need to provide meaningful literacy experiences connecting schools with families and communities.

Maria Pacino, Ed.D. is the Chair of the Department of Advanced Studies in Education at Azusa Pacific University. Much of her work focuses on diversity, social justice, children's literature, educational technology, and character education.

References

*References marked with an asterisk are new to this edition.

Abrahamsson, B. (1971). *Military professionalization and political power.* Stockholm: Allmanna Forlagret.

Acheson, A. A., and Gall, M. D. (1997). *Techniques in the clinical supervision of teachers: Preservice and inservice applications,* 4th ed. New York: Longman.

Ackerman, R. H., Moller, G., and Katzenmeyer, M. (Eds.). (1996). *Every teacher as a leader: Realizing the potential of teacher leadership.* San Francisco: Jossey-Bass.

Acton v. Vernonia School District, 66 F.3d 217 (9th Cir. 1995), 115 S. Ct. 2386 (1995).

Adler, M. (1982). *The paideia proposal: An educational manifesto.* New York: Macmillan.

Alan Guttmacher Institute. (1999). *Teenage pregnancy: Overall trends and state-by-state information.* New York: Author.

Alexander, C. J. (1998). Studying the experiences of gay and lesbian youth. *Journal of Gay and Lesbian Social Services, 8.*

Alfonso v. Fernandez, 606 N.Y.S.2d 259 (N.Y. App. Div. 1993).

Alvin Independent School District v. Cooper, 404 S.W.2d 76 (Tex. Civ. App. 1966).

American Association for the Advancement of Science. (2000). *Atlas of science literacy goals: Mapping K–12 learning goals.* New York: Oxford University Press.

American Association of University Women (AAUW). (1991). *Shortchanging girls, shortchanging America.* Washington, DC: Author.

American Association of University Women (AAUW). (1992). *How schools shortchange girls: The AAUW report.* (Researched by The Wellesley College Center for Research on Women). Washington, DC: The AAUW Educational Foundation.

American Association of University Women (AAUW). (1993). *Hostile hallways: The AAUW survey on sexual harassment in America's schools.* New York: Louis Harris and Associates.

American Association of University Women Educational Foundation. *Hostile Hallways: Bullying, Teasing, and Sexual Harassment in School.* New York: Harris Interactive 2001.

*American Council on the Teaching of Foreign Languages. (1999). *Standards for foreign language learning in the 21st century.* Lawrence, KS: American Council on the Teaching of Foreign Languages.

*American Federation of Teachers. (2001, September). *Educational issues policy brief,* No. 13. Washington, DC: Author.

*American Federation of Teachers. (July, 2002). *Do charter schools measure up? The charter school experiment after 10 years.* Washington, DC: Author.

American Federation of Teachers. (1998). *Student achievement in Edison schools: Mixed results in an ongoing experiment.* Washington, DC: Author.

**American School Board Journal.* (2001, December). Education vital signs.

Anderson, J. D. (1997). Supporting the invisible minority. *Educational Leadership, 54,* 65–68.

Anderson, R. E., and Ronnkvist, A. (1999). The presence of computers in American schools. The University of California, Irvine, and the University of Minnesota: Center for Research on Information Technology and Organizations.

Anderson, R. J., Keller, C. E., and Karp, J. M. (Eds.). (1998). *Enhancing diversity: Educators with disabilities.* Washington, DC: Gallaudet University Press.

Annie E. Casey Foundation. (1999). *Kids count data book, 1999.* Baltimore: Author.

*Annie E. Casey Foundation. (2002). *Kids count data book, 2002.* Baltimore: Author.

Anyon, J. (1996). Social class and the hidden curriculum of work. In E. Hollins (Ed.), *Transforming curriculum for a culturally diverse society* (pp. 179–203). Mahwah, NJ: Lawrence Erlbaum.

*Appalachia Educational Laboratory. (1993). *Alternative assessment in math and science: Moving toward school a moving target.* Charleston, WV: Author.

Aronson, E., and Gonzalez, A. (1988). Desegregation, jigsaw, and the Mexican-American experience. In

P. A. Katz, and D. A. Taylor (Eds.), *Eliminating racism: Profiles in controversy.* New York: Plenum Press.

Artz, S. (1999). *Sex, power, and the violent school girl.* New York: Teachers College Press.

Ashton-Warner, S. (1963). *Teacher.* New York: Simon and Schuster.

Asian Americans/Pacific Islanders in Philanthropy. (1997). *An invisible crisis: The educational needs of Asian Pacific American youth.* New York: Author.

Astuto, T. (Ed.). (1993). *When teachers lead.* University Park, PA: University Council for Educational Administration.

*Avramidis, E., Bayliss, P., and Burden, R. (2000). A survey into mainstream teachers' attitudes towards the inclusion of children with special educational needs in the ordinary school in one local education authority. *Educational Psychology, 20*(2), 191–211.

*Ayers, W. C., and Miller, J. L. (Eds.). (1998). *A light in dark times: Maxine Greene and the unfinished conversation.* New York: Teachers College Press.

Baker, K. A. (1991). *Bilingual Education.* Bloomington, IN: Phi Delta Kappa.

Ballantine, J. H. (1997). *The sociology of education: A systematic analysis,* 4th ed. Upper Saddle River, NJ: Prentice Hall.

Banks, J. A. (1997). *Teaching strategies for ethnic studies,* 6th ed. Boston: Allyn and Bacon.

Banks, J. A. (1999). *An introduction to multicultural education,* 2nd ed. Boston: Allyn and Bacon.

*Banks, J. A. (2001). *Cultural diversity and education: Foundations, curriculum, and teaching,* 4th ed. Boston: Allyn and Bacon.

*Banks, J. A. (2002). *An introduction to multicultural education,* 3rd ed. Boston: Allyn and Bacon.

*Banks, J. A. (2003). *Teaching strategies for ethnic studies,* 7th ed. Boston: Allyn and Bacon.

Banks, J. A., and Banks, C. A. (Eds.). (2002). *Multicultural education: Issues and perspectives,* 4th ed. New York: John Wiley & Sons.

Battles v. Anne Arundel County Board of Education, 904 F. Supp. 471 (D. Md. 1995), *aff'd,* 95 F.3d 41 (4th Cir. 1996).

Becker, H. J. (1999). *Internet use by teachers: Conditions of professional use and teacher-directed student use.* The University of California, Irvine, and The University of Minnesota: Center for Research on Information Technology and Organizations.

*Becker, H. J. (2001, April). *How are teachers using computers in instruction?* Paper presented at the annual meeting of the American Educational Research Association, Seattle, WA.

Bennett, C. I. (1999). *Comprehensive multicultural education: Theory and practice,* 4th ed. Boston: Allyn and Bacon.

*Bennett, C. I. (2003). *Comprehensive multicultural education: Theory and practice,* 5th ed. Boston: Allyn and Bacon.

Bennett, L. (1997). Break the silence: Gay and straight students in Massachusetts team up to make a difference. *Teaching Tolerance, 6,* 24–31.

Bennett, W. (1987). *James Madison High School: A curriculum for American students.* Washington, DC: U.S. Department of Education.

Bennett, W. J., and Gelernter, D. (2001, March 14). Improving education with technology. *Education Week on the Web.*

Berliner, D. C., and Biddle, B. J. (1995). *The manufactured crisis: Myths, fraud, and the attack on America's public schools.* Reading, MA: Addison Wesley.

Bernstein, B. B. (1996). *Pedagogy, symbolic control and identity: Theory, research, critique (critical perspectives on literacy and education).* New York: Taylor and Francis.

Besner, H. F., and Spungin, C. I. (1995). *Gay and lesbian students: Understanding their needs.* Washington, DC: Taylor and Francis.

Bialo, E. (1989). Computers and at-risk youth: A partial solution to a complex problem. *Classroom Computer Learning, 9*(4), 48–55.

Bitter, G. G., and Pierson, M. E. (1999). *Using technology in the classroom,* 4th ed. Boston: Allyn and Bacon.

*Bitter, G. G., and Pierson, M. E. (2002). *Using technology in the classroom,* 5th ed. Boston: Allyn and Bacon.

Bloom, B. S. (1981). *All our children learning: A primer for parents, teachers, and other educators.* New York: McGraw-Hill.

Board of Education of Oklahoma City Public Schools v. Dowell, 498 U.S. 237, 249–250 (1991).

Board of Education, Sacramento City Unified School District v. Holland, 786 F. Supp. 874 (E.D. Cal. 1992).

Boleman, L. G., and Deal, T. E. (1994). *Becoming a teacher leader: From isolation to collaboration.* Thousand Oaks, CA: Corwin Press.

*Boleman, L. G., and Deal, T. E. (2002). *Reframing the path to school leadership: A guide for teachers and principals.* Thousand Oaks, CA: Corwin Press.

*Borich, G. D. (2000). *Effective teaching methods,* 4th ed. Upper Saddle River, NJ: Merrill.

*Boser, U. (2000, May 3). States stiffening recertification for teachers. *Education Week on the Web.*

Boyer, E. (1983). *High school: A report on secondary education in America.* New York: Harper and Row.

Boyer, E. (1990). Teaching in America. In M. Kysilka (Ed.), *Honor in Teaching: Reflections.* West Lafayette, IN: Kappa Delta Pi.

Boyer, E. (1995). *The basic school: A community for learning.* Princeton, NJ: The Carnegie Foundation for the Advancement of Teaching.

Bracy, G. W. (1993). "Now then, Mr. Kohlberg, about moral development in women . . ." In G. Hass and F. W. Parkay (Eds.), *Curriculum planning: A new approach,* 6th ed. Boston: Allyn and Bacon.

Bradley, A. (1998, February 4). Unions agree on blueprint for merging. *Education Week on the Web.*

Brameld, T. (1956). *Toward a reconstructed philosophy of education.* New York: Holt, Rinehart and Winston.

Brameld, T. (1959). Imperatives for a reconstructed philosophy of education. *School and Society, 87.*

*Brock, B. L., and Grady, M. L. (2001). *From first-year to first-rate: Principals guiding beginning teachers.* Thousand Oaks, CA: Corwin Press.

*Brown, A. H. (1999). Simulated classrooms and artificial students: The potential effects of new technologies on teacher education. *Journal of Research on Computing in Education, 32*(2), 307–318.

Brown, F. B., Kohrs, D., and Lanzarro, C. (1991). The academic costs and consequences of extracurricular participation in high school. Paper presented at the Annual Meeting of Educational Research Association.

Brown, M. E. (1994). *Computer simulation: Improving case study methods for preservice and inservice teacher education.* ERIC Document Reproduction Services No. ED371 730.

Brown v. Board of Education of Topeka, Kansas, 347 U.S. 483, 74 S. Ct. 686 (1954).

Brown v. Hot, Sexy and Safer Productions, Inc., 68 F.3d 525 (1st Cir. 1995), *cert. denied,* 116 S. Ct. 1044 (1996).

**Brown v. Unified School District No. 501,* 56 F. Supp. 2d 1212 (D. Kan. 1999).

**Brunelle v. Lynn Public Schools,* 702 N.E.2d 1182 (Mass. 1998).

Brunner, C., and Tally, W. (1999). *The new media literacy handbook: An educator's guide to bringing new media into the classroom.* New York: Anchor Books.

Bryk, A. S., Sebring, P. B., Kerbow, D., Rollow, S., and Easton, J. Q. (1998). *Charting Chicago school reform: Democratic localism as a lever for change.* Boulder, CO: Westview Press.

Bucky, P. A. (1992). *The private Albert Einstein.* Kansas City: Andrews and McMeel.

Burch v. Barker, 651 F. Supp. 1149 (W.D. Wash. 1987).

Burch v. Barker, 861 F.2d 1149 (9th Cir. 1988).

Burden, P. R., and Byrd, D. M. (1999). *Methods for effective teaching,* 2nd ed. Boston: Allyn and Bacon.

Burnaford, G., Fischer, J., and Hobson, D. (2001). *Teachers doing research: The power of action through inquiry.* Mahwah, NJ: Lawrence Erlbaum.

Burton v. Cascade School District Union High School No. 5, 512 F.2d 850 (9th Cir. 1975).

Button, H. W., and Provenzo, E. G. (1989). *History of education and culture in America, 2nd ed.* Englewood Cliffs, NJ: Prentice Hall.

*Campbell, D. M., Cignetti, P. B., Melenyzer, B. J., Nettles, D. H., and Wyman, R. M. (2001). *How to develop a professional portfolio: A manual for teachers,* 2nd ed. Boston: Allyn and Bacon.

Cantor, L. (1989). Assertive discipline—more than names on the board and marbles in a jar. *Phi Delta Kappan, 71*(1), 57–61.

Carnegie Council on Adolescent Development. (1989). *Turning points: Preparing American youth for the 21st century.* New York: Author.

Carroll, J. (1963). A model of school learning. *Teachers College Record, 64.*

Caterinicchia, D. (1999, June 18). Teachers' limited tech know-how prompts laptop lease. *CNN Interactive.*

Centers for Disease Control and Prevention. (1998). *Youth risk behavior surveillance—United States, 1997.* Atlanta: Author.

Center for Research on Effective Schooling for Disadvantaged Students. (1992). Helping students who fall behind, Report no. 22. Baltimore: Johns Hopkins University.

CEO Forum on Education and Technology. (1999). *School Technology and Readiness Report.* Washington, DC: Author.

*CEO Forum on Education and Technology. (2001). *The CEO forum school technology and readiness report: Key building blocks for student achievement in the 21st century.* Washington, DC: Author.

Cetron, M. (1997). Reform and tomorrow's schools. *TECHNOS Quarterly, 61,* 19–22.

Clift, R. T., et al. (1995). *Collaborative leadership and shared decision making: Teachers, principals, and university professors.* New York: Teachers College Press.

Codell, E. R. (1999). *Educating Esmé: Diary of a teacher's first year.* Chapel Hill, NC: Algonquin Books.

Cohen, S. (Ed.). (1974). *Massachusetts school law of 1648. Education in the United States.* New York: Random House.

Coladarci, T., and Cobb, C. D. (1996). Extracurricular participation, school size, and achievement and self-esteem among high school students: A national look. *Journal of Research in Rural Education, 12*(2), 92–103.

Coleman, J. S., Campbell, E. Q., Hobson, C. J., McPartland, J., Mood, A. L., Weinfeld, F. D., and York, R. L. (1966). *Equality of educational opportunity.* Washington, DC: U.S. Government Printing Office.

*Colucci, K. (2000). Negative pedagogy. In J. L. Paul and K. Colucci (Eds.), *Stories out of school: Memories and reflections on care and cruelty in the classroom.* Stamford, CT: Ablex, pp. 27–44.

Combs, A. (1979). *Myths in education: Beliefs that hinder progress and their alternatives.* Boston: Allyn and Bacon.

Comer, J. P. (1997). *Waiting for a miracle: Why schools can't solve our problems—and how we can.* New York: Dutton.

Committee for Economic Development. (1994). *Putting learning first: Governing and managing schools for high achievement.* New York: Research and Policy Committee, Committee for Economic Development.

Cornfield v. Consolidated High School District No. 230, F.2d 1316 (7th Cir. 1993).

Costa, A. L. (1984). A reaction to Hunter's knowing, teaching, and supervising. In P. L. Hosford (Ed.), *Using what we know about teaching.* Alexandria, VA: Association for Supervision and Curriculum Development.

Coughlin, E. K. (1993, March 24). Sociologists examine the complexities of racial and ethnic identity in America. *Chronicle of Higher Education.*

Counts, G. (1932). *Dare the school build a new social order?* New York: John Day.

Cuban, L. (1999a, January). High-tech schools, low-teach teaching. *The Education Digest.*

Cuban, L. (1999b, August 4). The technology puzzle: Why is greater access not translating into better classroom use? *Education Week,* pp. 47, 68.

*Curtis, D. (2000, October 1). Treating teachers as professionals. *Edutopia.* San Rafael, CA: The George Lucas Educational Foundation. (Retrieved from http://glef.org/orlandpk.html)

*Curtis, D. (2002, March 12). Handhelds go to class. *Edutopia.* The George Lucas Educational Foundation.

Curtis v. School Committee of Falmouth, 652 N.E.2d 580 (Mass. 1995), *cert. denied,* 116 S. Ct. 753 (1996). (Retrieved from http://www.glef.org/principals.htm)

Curwin, R., and Mendler, A. (1988). Packaged discipline programs: Let the buyer beware. *Educational Leadership, 46*(2), 68–71.

Curwin, R., and Mendler, A. (1989, March). We repeat, let the buyer beware: A response to Canter. *Educational Leadership, 46*(6), 83.

Cziko, G. A. (1992, March). The evaluation of bilingual education: From necessity and probability to possibility. *Educational Researcher,* pp. 10–15.

Danielson, C. (1996). *Enhancing professional practice: A framework for teaching.* Alexandria, VA: Association for Supervision and Curriculum Development.

*Danielewicz, J. (2001). *Teaching selves: Identity, pedagogy, and teacher education.* Albany, NY: State University of New York Press.

Danzberger, J. P. (1994, January). School board reform in West Virginia. *Phi Delta Kappan.*

*Davidson, J. (2002). Democratic leadership in coalition schools: Why it's necessary, how it works. *Horace, 18*(3).

Davis, G. A., and Rimm, S. B. (1998). *Education of the gifted and talented,* 4th ed. Boston: Allyn and Bacon.

Davis v. Meek, 344 F. Supp. 298 (N.D. Ohio 1972).

Davis v. Monroe County Board of Education, Supp. 97-843 (Georgia 1999).

Davitt, J. (1997, January 3). The ultimate good shepherd. *Times Educational Supplement.*

Deal, T. E., and Peterson, K. D. (1999). *Shaping school culture: The heart of leadership.* San Francisco: Jossey-Bass.

*Degnan, E., and Bozeman, W. (2001). An investigation of computer-based simulations for school crisis management. *Journal of School Leadership, 11*(4), 296–312.

*DeRoche, E. F., and Williams, M. M. (2001). *Character education: A guide for school administrators.* Lanham, MD: Scarecrow Press.

Dewey, J. (1902). *The child and the curriculum.* Chicago: University of Chicago Press.

Dewey, J. (1955). Quoted in *Organizing the teaching profession: The story of the American Federation of Teachers.* Glencoe, IL: The Commission on Educational Reconstruction.

**Directory of national trade and professional associations of the United States 2002.* (2002). B. Downs (Ed.). New York: Columbia Books.

Doe v. Renfrow, 635 F.2d 582 (7th Cir. 1980), *cert. denied,* 451 U.S. 1022, *reh'g denied,* 101 S. Ct. 3015 (1981).

Dollase, R. H. (1992). *Voices of beginning teachers: Visions and realities.* New York: Teachers College Press.

Doyle, W. (1986). Classroom organization and management. In M. Wittrock (Ed.), *Handbook of research on teaching,* 3rd ed. New York: Macmillan.

Dryfoos, J. G. (1994). *Full-service schools: A revolution in health and social services for children, youth, and families.* San Francisco: Jossey-Bass.

Dryfoos, J. G. (1998). *Safe passage: Making it through adolescence in a risky society.* New York: Oxford University Press.

**Dubuclet v. Home Insurance Co.,* 660 So. 2d 67 (La. Ct. App. 1995).

Duffy, G., and Roehler, L. (1989). The tension between information-giving and mediation: Perspectives on instructional explanation and teacher change. In J. Brophy (Ed.), *Advances in research on teaching,* vol. 1. Greenwich, CT: JAI Press.

Duke, D. L. (1984). *Teaching—the imperiled profession.* Albany, NY: State University of New York Press.

*Dunklee, D. R., and Shoop, R. J. (2002). *The principal's quick-reference guide to school law: Reducing liability, litigation, and other potential legal tangles.* Thousand Oaks, CA: Corwin Press.

Durlak, J. A. (1995). *School-based prevention programs for children and adolescents.* Thousand Oaks, CA: Sage Publications.

Edelman, M. W. (1997, November 9). Young families shut out of the American dream. *Seattle Times,* p. B5.

*Edison Schools, Inc. (2002, September 30). *Annual report.* New York: Author.

*The Education Trust. (2002). *All talk, putting an end to out-of-field teaching.* Washington, DC: Author.

Education Week. (1999a, March 31). N.M. governor digs in his heels on vouchers.

Education Week. (1999b, June 2). Substituting the privilege of choice for the right to equality.

Education Week. (2000). Quality counts 2000: Who should teach? Retrieved from www.edweek.org/sreports/qc00

Educational Testing Service. (1995, Spring). Bringing volunteers into teacher education programs. *ETS Policy Notes,* pp. 8–9.

*Eduventures. (2002, August). *School reform news.*

Edwards, A. T. (1997). Let's stop ignoring our gay and lesbian youth. *Educational Leadership, 54.*

Edwards, P., and Young, L. (1992). Beyond parents: family, community, and school involvement. *Phi Delta Kappan, 74*(1), pp. 72, 74, 76, 78, 80.

Edwards v. Aguillard, 482 U.S. 578 (1987).

Eisner, E. W. (1998). *The kind of schools we need: Personal essays.* Ports-mouth, NH: Heinemann.

*Eisner, E. (2002). *The educational imagination: On the design and evaluation of school programs,* 3rd ed. New York: Macmillan College.

Elam, S. M., Rose, L. C., and Gallup, A. (1994, September). The 26th annual Phi Delta Kappan/Gallup Poll of the public's attitudes toward the public schools. *Phi Delta Kappan,* pp. 41–56.

Emmer, E. T., Evertson, C. M., and Worsham, M. E. (2002). *Classroom management for secondary teachers,* 6th ed. Boston: Allyn and Bacon.

Engel v. Vitale, 370 U.S. 421 (1962).

Erikson, E. H. (1963). *Childhood and society.* New York: W. W. Norton.

Erikson, E. H. (1997). *The life cycle completed: Extended version with new chapters on the ninth stage of development by Joan M. Erikson.* New York: W. W. Norton.

Essex, N. L. (1999). *School law and the public schools: A practical guide for educational leaders.* Boston: Allyn and Bacon.

Etzioni, A. (1969). *The semi-professions and their organization: Teachers, nurses, social workers.* New York: The Free Press.

Etzioni, A. (1999, June 9). The truths we must face to curb youth violence. *Education Week on the Web.*

*Evertson, C. M., Emmer, E. T., and Worsham, M. E. (2003). *Classroom management for elementary teachers,* 6th ed. Boston: Allyn and Bacon.

Fagen v. Summers, 498 P.2d 1227 (Wyo. 1972).

*Falk, B. (2002, April). Standards-based reforms: Problems and possibilities. *Phi Delta Kappan,* pp. 612–620.

**Falvo v. Owasso Independent School District*, 233 F.3d 1203 (10th Cir. 2000).

Fashola, O. (1999). Review of extended-day and after-school programs and their effectiveness. Baltimore: Johns Hopkins University, Center for Research on the Education of Students Placed at Risk.

*Feistritzer, C. E. (1999). *A report on teacher preparation in the U.S.* Washington, DC: National Center for Education Information.

Feistritzer, E. (2002). *Alternative teacher certification: A state-by-state analysis.* Washington, DC: National Center for Education Information.

Feldhusen, J. F. (1997). Educating teachers for work with talented youth. In N. Colangelo and G. A. Davis (Eds.), *Handbook of gifted education.* Boston: Allyn and Bacon.

*Fetler, M. (2001). Student mathematics achievement test scores, dropout rates, and teacher characteristics. *Teacher Education Quarterly, 28*(1), 151–168.

Fischer, J. C. (1996). Open to ideas: Developing a framework for your research. In G. Burnaford, J. Fischer, and D. Hobson, *Teachers doing research: Practical possibilities.* Mahwah, NJ: Lawrence Erlbaum.

Franklin, B. (1931). Proposals relating to the education of youth in Pennsylvania, in T. Woody (Ed.), *Educational views of Benjamin Franklin.* New York: McGraw-Hill.

Franklin v. Gwinnett County Public Schools, 112 S. Ct. 1028 (1992).

Franz, K. R. (1996, Autumn). Toward a critical social consciousness in children: multicultural peace education in a first grade classroom. *Theory into Practice, 35*(4), 264–270.

Freedman, S., Jackson, J., and Botes, K. (1983). Teaching: An imperiled profession. In L. Shulman and G. Sykes (Eds.), *Handbook of teaching and policy.* New York: Longman.

Freeman v. Pitts, 503 U.S. 467 (1992).

*Freppon, P. A. (2001). *What it takes to be a teacher: The role of personal and professional development.* Portsmouth, NH: Heinemann.

*Friend, M., and Bursuck, W. D. (2002). *Including students with special needs: A practical guide for classroom teachers.* Boston: Allyn and Bacon.

Frost, D. (1997). *Reflective action planning for teachers: A guide to teacher-led school and professional development.* London: D. Fulton.

Fuligni, A. J., and Stevenson, H. W. (1995). Home environment and school learning. In L. W. Anderson (Ed.), *International encyclopedia of teaching and teacher education,* 2nd ed. (pp. 378–382). Oxford: Pergamon.

Fullan, M., and Hargreaves, A. (1996). *What's worth fighting for in your school?* New York: Teachers College Press.

*Fulton, K. P., and Riel, M. (1999, May 1). Professional development through learning communities. *Edutopia, 6*(2), 8–9. San Rafael, CA: The George Lucas Educational Foundation.

Furger, R. (1998). *Does Jane compute? Preserving our daughters' place in the cyber revolution.* New York: Warner Books.

Furger, R. (1999, September). Are wired schools failing our kids? *PC World.*

Gaddy, B. B., Hall, W. W., and Marzano, R. J. (1996). *School wars: Resolving our conflicts over religion and values.* San Francisco: Jossey-Bass.

Gagné, R. M. (1974). *Essentials of learning for instruction.* Hinsdale, IL: Dryden.

Gagné, R. M. (1977). *The conditions of learning,* 3rd ed. New York: Holt, Rinehart and Winston.

Gallup, G. H. (1975, September). The 11th annual Gallup poll of the public's attitudes toward the public schools. *Phi Delta Kappan,* pp. 227–241.

Gandara, P., and Fish, J. (1994, Spring). Year-round schooling as an avenue to major structural reform. *Educational Evaluation and Policy Analysis,* p. 16.

Garbarino, J. (1999). *Lost boys: Why our sons turn violent and how we can save them.* New York: The Free Press.

Gardner, H. (1983). *Frames of mind.* New York: Basic Books.

*Gardner, H. (September, 1997). Multiple intelligences as a partner in school improvement. *Educational Leadership,* pp. 20–21.

Gardner, H. (1999). *The disciplined mind: What all students should understand.* New York: Simon and Schuster.

*Gardner, J. W. (1990). *On leadership.* New York: The Free Press.

*Garet, M. S., Porter, A. C., Desimone, L., Birman, B. F., and Yoon, K. S. (2001). What makes professional development effective? Results from a national sample of teachers. *American Educational Research Journal, 38*(4), 915–945.

Gates, B., Myhrvold, N., and Rinearson, P. M. (1996). *The road ahead.* New York: Penguin.

*Gauld, L., and Gauld, M. (2002). *The biggest job we'll ever have: The Hyde School program for character-based education and parenting.* New York: Scribner.

Gaylord v. Tacoma School District No. 10, 88 Wash. 2d 286, 599 P.2d 1340 (1977).

Gehrke, N. (1988, Summer). Toward a definition of mentoring. *Theory into Practice,* pp. 190–194.

Gehrke, N. J., and Romerdahl, N. S. (1997). *Teacher leaders: Making a difference in schools.* West Lafayette, IN: Kappa Delta Pi.

*George Lucas Educational Foundation. (2001, November). *Project-based learning research.* Retrieved from http://www.glef.org./index.html

Gerber, S. B. (1996). Extracurricular activities and academic achievement. *Journal of Research and Development in Education, 30*(1), 42–50.

Gilligan, C. (1993). *In a different voice: Psychological theory and women's development.* Cambridge, MA: Harvard University Press.

Gipp, G. (1979, August–September). Help for Dana Fast Horse and friends. *American Education,* p. 15.

Glasser, W. R. (1997, April). A new look at school failure and school success. *Phi Delta Kappan,* pp. 596–602.

Glasser, W. R. (1998a). *Quality school,* 3rd ed. New York: Harper Perennial.

Glasser, W. R. (1998b). *The quality school teacher: Specific suggestions for teachers who are trying to implement the lead-management ideas of the quality school.* New York: Harper Perennial.

Glasser, W. R. (1998c). *Choice theory: A new psychology of personal freedom.* New York: HarperCollins.

Glasser, W. R., and Dotson, K. L. (1998). *Choice theory in the classroom.* New York: Harper Perennial.

Glickman, C. D. (1993). *Renewing America's schools: A guide for school-based action.* San Francisco: Jossey-Bass.

Glickman, C. D. (1998). *Revolutionizing America's schools.* San Francisco: Jossey-Bass.

*Glickman, C., Gordon, S. P., and Ross-Gordon, J. M. (2001). *SuperVision and instructional leadership,* 5th ed. Boston: Allyn and Bacon.

Gmelch, W. H., and Parkay, F. W. (1995). Changing roles and occupational stress in the teaching profession. In M. J. O'Hair and S. J. Odell, *Educating teachers for leadership and change: Teacher education yearbook III.* Thousand Oaks, CA: Corwin Press.

Goldhammer, R., Anderson, R. H., and Krajewski, R. J. (1993). *Clinical supervision: Special methods for the supervision of teachers,* 3rd ed. Fort Worth: Harcourt Brace Jovanovich.

*Good, T. E., and Brophy, J. E. (2003). *Looking in classrooms,* 9th ed. Boston: Allyn and Bacon.

Good, T. E., and Grouws, D. (1979). The Missouri mathematics effectiveness project: An experimental study in fourth-grade classrooms. *Journal of Educational Psychology, 71,* 355–362.

Goodlad, J. (1983, Spring). *Teaching: An endangered profession. Teachers College Record,* pp. 575–578.

Goodlad, J. (1990). *Teachers for our nation's schools.* San Francisco: Jossey-Bass.

Goodlad, J. (1994). *Educational renewal: Better teachers, better schools.* San Francisco: Jossey-Bass.

*Goodlad, J. (1998). *Educational renewal: Better teachers, better schools.* New York: John Wiley and Sons.

Gordon, D. T. (1999, September/October). Rising to the discipline challenges. *Harvard Education Letter, 15*(5), 1–4.

Goss v. Lopez, 419 U.S. 565 (1975).

Grant, C. A. (1994, Winter). Challenging the myths about multicultural education. *Multicultural Education,* pp. 4–9.

Grant, G., and Murray, C. E. (1999). *Teaching in America: The slow revolution.* Cambridge, MA: Harvard University Press.

Grant, P. G., Richard, K. J., and Parkay, F. W. (1996, April). *Using video cases to promote reflection among preservice teachers: A qualitative inquiry.* Paper presented at the annual meeting of the American Educational Research Association, New York.

Greene, B. (1999, July 7). A 21st century idea for schools: Log off and learn. *Chicago Tribune,* sect. 2, p. 1.

*Greene, M. (1995a). *Releasing the imagination.* San Francisco: Jossey-Bass.

Greene, M. (1995b). What counts as philosophy of education? In W. Kohli (Ed.), *Critical conversations in philosophy of education.* New York: Routledge.

Griego-Jones, T. (1996). Reconstructing bilingual education from a multicultural perspective. In C. A. Grant and M. L. Gomez, *Making schooling multicultural: Campus and classroom.* Englewood Cliffs, NJ: Merrill.

*Grimes, G. F. (2000). What teacher salary averages don't show. Atlanta: Southern Regional Education Board.

Grossman, D., and Siddle, P. (1999). Combat. In L. Kurtz (Ed.), *The encyclopedia of violence, peace, and conflict.* San Diego: Academic Press.

*Guenemoen, R. F., Thompson, S. J., Thurlow, M. L., and Lehr, C. A. (2001). *A self-study guide to implementation of inclusive assessment and accountability systems: A best practice approach.* Minneapolis, MN: University of Minnesota, National Center on Educational Outcomes.

Haberman, M. (1995, June). Selecting "star" teachers for children and youth in urban poverty. *Phi Delta Kappan,* pp. 777–781.

Hale-Benson, J. E. (1986). *Black children: their roots, culture, and learning styles.* Baltimore: Johns Hopkins University Press.

Hallahan, D. P., and Kauffman, J. M. (2000). *Exceptional children: Introduction to special education,* 8th ed. Boston: Allyn and Bacon.

*Hallahan, D. P., and Kauffman, J. M. (2003). *Exceptional children: Introduction to special education,* 9th ed. Boston: Allyn and Bacon.

Hansen, D. T. (1995). *The call to teach.* New York: Teachers College Press.

*Hardman, M. L., Drew, C. J., and Egan, M. W. (2002). *Human exceptionality: Society, school, and family,* 7th ed. Boston: Allyn and Bacon.

Harrington-Lueker, D. (Ed.). (1999). *Barriers and breakthroughs: Technology in urban schools.* Washington, DC: Education Writers Association.

*Harris Interactive, Inc. (2001). *The MetLife Survey of the American Teacher: Key Elements of Quality Schools.* New York: Author.

*Hart, P., and Teeter, R. (2002). *A national priority: Americans speak on teacher quality.* Princeton, NJ: Educational Testing Service.

*Hauser, M., and Rauch, S. (2002). New teacher! An exciting and scary time. *2002 Job search handbook for educators.* Columbus, OH: American Association for Employment in Education.

Hazelwood School District v. Kuhlmeier, 56 U.S.L.W. 4079, 4082, 484 U.S. 260, 108 S. Ct. 562 (1988).

Healy, J. M. (1998). *Failure to connect: How computers affect our children's minds—for better and worse.* New York: Simon and Schuster.

Heath, S. B. (1983). *Ways with words.* Cambridge: Cambridge University Press.

Hedges, L. V. (1996). Quoted in Hedges finds boys and girls both disadvantaged in school. *Education News.* The Department of Education, The University of Chicago.

Hendrie, C. (1999, May 5). Battle over principals in Chicago: Administration vs. local councils. *Education Week on the Web.*

Henriques, M. E. (1997, May). Increasing literacy among kindergartners through cross-age training. *Young Children,* pp. 42–47.

Henry, E., Huntley, J., McKamey, C., and Harper, L. (1995). *To be a teacher: Voices from the classroom.* Thousand Oaks, CA: Corwin Press.

Henry, M. (1993). *School cultures: Universes of meaning in private schools.* Norwood, NJ: Ablex.

Henry, M. E. (1996). *Parent-school collaboration: Feminist organizational structures and school leadership.* Albany, NY: State University of New York Press.

*Hess, F. M. (2002). *Revolution at the margins: The impact of competition on urban school systems.* Washington, DC: Brookings Institution Press.

Hess, G. A., Jr. (2000). *Changes in student achievement in Illinois and Chicago, 1990–2000.* Chicago: Northwestern University, Center for Urban School Policy.

*Hiebert, J., Gallimore, R., and Stigler, J. W. (2002). A knowledge base for the teaching profession: What would it look like and how can we get one? *Educational Researcher, 31*(5), 3–15.

Hirshfelder, A. B. (1986). *Happily may I walk: American Indians and Alaska Natives today.* New York: Scribner.

*Hletko, J. D. (1995). Reflections on NBPTS. *Voices from the middle, 2*(4), 33–36.

Hole, S. (1998). Teacher as rain dancer. *Harvard Educational Review, 68*(3), 413–421.

Holland, A., and Andre, T. (1987, Winter). Participation in extracurricular activities in secondary schools. *Review of Educational Research,* pp. 437–466.

Holly, M. L., and McLoughlin, C. (Eds.). (1989). *Perspectives on teacher professional development.* New York: Falmer Press.

Holmes, M., and Weiss, B. J. (1995). *Lives of women public schoolteachers: Scenes from American educational history.* New York: Garland.

The Holmes Group. (n.d.). *Tomorrow's schools: Principles for the design of professional development schools.* East Lansing, MI: Author.

*Holmes Partnership. (2001). *Origins of the Holmes Partnership (1987–1997).* Auburn, AL: Author.

Holt, J. (1964). *How children fail.* New York: Delta.

Holt v. Shelton, 341 F. Supp. 821 (M.D. Tenn. 1972).

Holt-Reynolds, D. (1999). Good readers, good teachers? Subject matter expertise as a challenge in learning to teach. *Harvard Educational Review, 69*(1), 29–50.

Hopkins, B. J., and Wendel, F. C. (1997). *Creating school-community-business partnerships.* Bloomington, IN: Phi Delta Kappa Educational Foundation.

*Hopson, J. L., Hopson, E., and Hagen, T. (2002, May 8). Take steps to protect latchkey children. Knight Ridder/Tribune News Service.

**Horace.* (2002, Spring). Anzar High School communication guidelines. *Horace, 18*(3).

Hortonville Joint School District No. 1 v. Hortonville Education Association, 426 U.S. 482, 96 S. Ct. 2308 (1976).

*Howard, V. F., Williams, B. F., Port, P. D., and Lepper, C. (2001). *Very young children with special needs.* Upper Saddle River, NJ: Merrill Prentice Hall.

Howsam, R. B., Corrigan, D. C., Denemark, G. W., and Nash, R. J. (1976). *Educating a profession.* Washington, DC: American Association of Colleges for Teacher Education.

Hoynes, W. (1998, Summer). News for a teen market: The lessons of Channel One. *Journal of Curriculum and Supervision,* pp. 339–356.

Hoyt, W. H. (1999). An evaluation of the Kentucky Education Reform Act. In *Kentucky Annual Economic Report 1999* (pp. 21–36). Lexington, KY: University of Kentucky, Center for Business and Economic Research.

Huling-Austin, L. (1990). Teacher induction programs and internships. In W. R. Houston (Ed.), *Handbook of research on teaching.* New York: Macmillan.

Hurwitz, S. (1999, April). New York, New York: Can Rudy Crew hang tough on vouchers and pull off a turnaround in the nation's biggest school system? *The American School Board Journal,* pp. 36–40.

Hutchins, R. M. (1963). *A conversation on education.* Santa Barbara, CA: Fund for the Republic.

Idol, L. (1998). Optional extended year program, Feedback, Publication No. 97.20. Austin Independent School District, TX, Office of Program Evaluation.

Igoa, C. (1995). *The inner world of the immigrant child.* New York: Lawrence Erlbaum.

Imber, M., and van Geel, T. (1993). *Education law.* New York: McGraw-Hill.

*Imber, M., and van Geel, T. (2001). *A teacher's guide to education law,* 2nd ed. Mahwah, NJ: Lawrence Erlbaum.

Indiana University. (February 1999). IU school of education programs offer life-changing experiences. Bloomington, IN: Indiana University, Office of Communication and Marketing.

Ingraham v. Wright, 430 U.S. 651 (1977).

*Institute for Social Research. (2002). *Monitoring the future: National results on adolescent drug use, Overview of key findings, 2001.* Ann Arbor, MI: The University of Michigan, Institute for Social Research.

*International Reading Association, National Council of Teachers of English. (1996). *Standards for the English language arts.* Newark, DE: International Reading Association; Urbana, IL: National Council of Teachers of English.

Interstate New Teacher Assessment and Support Consortium. (1993). *A model standards for beginning teacher licensing and development: A Resource for state dialogue.* Washington, DC: Council of Chief State School Officers.

Jackson, P. (1990). *Life in classrooms.* New York: Teachers College Press.

Jacobson, L. (1996, November 22). Gay student to get nearly $1 million in settlement. *Education Week on the Web.*

Jeqlin v. San Jacinto Unified School District, 827 F. Supp. 1459 (Cal. 1993).

Jencks, C., et al. (1972). *Inequality: A reassessment of the effect of family and schooling in America.* New York: Basic Books.

Jencks, C., and Phillips, M. (Eds.). (1998). *The black-white test score gap.* Washington, DC: Brookings Institution Press.

Jersild, A. (1955). *When teachers face themselves.* New York: Teachers College Press.

Johnson, D. W., and Johnson, R. T. (1999). *Learning together and alone: Cooperative, competitive, and individualistic learning,* 5th ed. Boston: Allyn and Bacon.

Johnson, J., and Immerwahr, J. (1994). *First things first: What Americans expect from the public schools, a report from Public Agenda.* New York: Public Agenda.

Johnson, M. J., and Brown, L. (1998). Collegial support teams. In D. J. McIntyre and D. M. Byrd (Eds.), *Strategies for career-long teacher education: Teacher education yearbook VI.* Thousand Oaks, CA: Corwin Press.

Jonassen, D. H., Peck, K. L., and Wilson, B. G. (1999). *Learning with technology: A constructivist perspective.* Upper Saddle River, NJ: Merrill.

*Jones, A. A. (2001, February). Welcome to standardsville. *Phi Delta Kappan,* pp. 462–464.

Jones, J. (1994). Integrated learning systems for diverse learners. *Media and Methods, 31*(3).

*Jones, K., and Whitford, K. (1997, December). Kentucky's conflicting reform principles: High-stakes accountability and student performance assessment. *Phi Delta Kappan,* pp. 276–281.

*Jones, R. (1999). "I don't feel safe here anymore": Your legal duty to protect gay kids from harassment. *American School Board Journal, 186*(11), 26–31.

Jordan, K. M., Vaughan, J. S., and Woodworth, K. J. (1997). I will survive: Lesbian, gay, and bisexual youths' experience of high school. *Journal of Gay and Lesbian Social Services, 7,* 17–33.

*Jordan, L., and Hendricks, C. (2002, March). Increasing sixth grade students' engagement in literacy learning. *Networks: An on-line journal for teacher research.*

Jordan, W. J., and Nettles, S. M. (1999). *How students invest their time out of school: Effects on school engagement, perceptions of life chances, and achievement.* Baltimore: Center for Research on the Education of Students Placed at Risk.

Joyce, B., Weil, M., and Calhoun, E. (2000). *Models of teaching,* 6th ed. Boston: Allyn and Bacon.

Karp, J. M., and Keller, C. E. (1998). Preparation and employment experiences of educators with disabilities. In R. J. Anderson, C. E. Keller, and J. M. Karp (Eds.), *Enhancing diversity: Educators with disabilities.* Washington, DC: Gallaudet University Press.

Karr v. Schmidt, 401 U.S. 1201, 91 S. Ct. 592, 27 L. Ed. 2d 797 (1972).

*Katz, Y. J. (1999). Kindergarten teacher training through virtual reality: Three-dimensional simulation methodology. *Educational Media International, 36*(2), 151–156.

Katzenmeyer, G. M., and Moller, G. (1996). *Awakening the sleeping giant: Leadership development for teachers.* Thousand Oaks, CA: Corwin Press.

Kavarsky, M. (1994). Salome Urena Middle Academies. *Journal of Emotional and Behavioral Problems,* 3(3), 37–40.

*Kaye, E. A. (Ed.). (2001). *Requirements for certification of teachers, counselors, librarians, administrators for elementary and secondary schools—sixty-sixth edition, 2001–2002.* Chicago: The University of Chicago Press.

*Keller, B. (2002, March 27). Unions turn cold shoulder on charters. *Education Week on the Web.*

Keller, C. E., Anderson, R. J., and Karp, J. M. (1998). Introduction. In

R. J. Anderson, C. E. Keller, and J. M. Karp (Eds.), *Enhancing diversity: Educators with disabilities.* Washington, DC: Gallaudet University Press.

*Kennedy, M. (1999). Ed schools and the problem of knowledge. In J. D. Raths and A. C. McAninch (Eds.), *Advances in teacher education,* vol. 5. *What counts as knowledge in teacher education?* (pp. 29–45). Stamford, CT: Ablex.

*The Kentucky Institute for Education Research. (2001). *KIER 2000 Review of Research.* Georgetown, KY: Georgetown College Conference and Training Center.

Keresty, B., O'Leary, S., and Wortley, D. (1998). *You can make a difference: A teacher's guide to political action.* Portsmouth, NH: Heinemann.

*KIDLINK. (2002). Kidproj in KidSpace. KIDLINK Society. Retrieved from http://www.kidlink.org/KIDPROJ/projects.html

Kirkpatrick, H., and Cuban, L. (1998). Computers make kids smarter—right? *TECHNOS Quarterly, 7*(2), 26–31.

Kleinfeld, J. (1998). *The myth that schools shortchange girls: Social science in the service of deception.* Washington, DC: The Women's Freedom Network.

Kohl, H. R. (1968). *36 children.* New York: Signet.

Kohlberg, L. (2000). The cognitive-developmental approach to moral education. In F. W. Parkay and G. Hass (Eds.), *Curriculum planning: A contemporary approach,* 7th ed. (pp. 136–148). Boston: Allyn and Bacon.

Koller, E. (1996). Overcoming paradigm paralysis: A high school teacher revisits foreign language education. In G. Burnaford, J. Fischer, and D. Hobson (Eds.), *Teachers doing research: Practical possibilities.* Mahwah, NJ: Lawrence Erlbaum.

*Kostelnik, M. J., Onaga, E., Rohde, B., and Whiren, A. (2002). *Children with special needs: Lessons for early childhood professionals.* New York: Teachers College Press.

Kounin, J. (1970). *Discipline and group management in classrooms.* New York: Holt, Rinehart and Winston.

Kozma, R., et al. (1992). Technology and the fate of at-risk students. *Education and Urban Society, 24*(4), 440–453.

Kozol, J. (1967). *Death at an early age.* Boston: Houghton Mifflin.

Kozol, J. (1991). *Savage inequalities: Children in America's schools.* New York: Crown.

Krizek v. Cicero-Stickney Township High School District No. 201, 713 F. Supp. 1131 (1989).

Krogh, S. L. (2000). Weaving the web. In F. W. Parkay and G. Hass (Eds.), *Curriculum planning: A contemporary approach,* 7th ed. (pp. 338–341). Boston: Allyn and Bacon.

Lambert, L., et al. (1997). *Who will save our schools? Teachers as constructivist leaders.* Thousand Oaks, CA: Corwin Press.

*LaMorte, M. W. (2002). *School law: Cases and concepts,* 7th ed. Boston: Allyn and Bacon.

Larry P. v. Riles, 793 F.2d 969 (9th Cir. 1984).

Lau v. Nichols, 414 U.S. 563 (1974).

Lee, V. E., Chen, X., and Smerdon, B. A. (1996). *The influence of school climate on gender differences in the achievement and engagement of young adolescents.* Washington, DC: American Association of University Women.

*Lefton, L. A., and Brannon, L. (2003). *Psychology,* 8th ed. Boston: Allyn and Bacon.

*Leinhardt, G. (1990). Capturing craft knowledge in teaching. *Educational Researcher, 19*(2), 18–25.

Lemon v. Kurtzman, 403 U.S. 602, 91 S. Ct. 2105, 291 L. Ed. 2d 745 (1971).

*Levin, D., and Arafeh, S. (2002). *The digital disconnect: The widening gap between Internet-savvy students and their schools.* Washington, DC: The Pew Internet and American Life Project.

Levine, D. U., and Levine, R. F. (1996). *Society and education,* 9th ed. Boston: Allyn and Bacon.

Levy, F. (1996, October). What General Motors can teach U.S. schools about the proper role of markets in education reform. *Phi Delta Kappan,* pp. 108–114.

Lewis, R. B., and Doorlag, D. H. (1999). *Teaching special students in general education classrooms,* 5th ed. Upper Saddle River, NJ: Merrill.

*Lindjord, D. (2000). Families at the century's turn: The troubling economic trends. *Family Review, 7*(3), 5–6.

Lindsay, D. (1996, March 13). N.Y. bills give teachers power to oust pupils. *Education Week.*

*Linn, R. L., and Gronlund, N. E. (2000). *Measurement and assessment in teaching,* 8th ed. Upper Saddle River, NJ: Merrill.

**Lipsman v. New York City Board of Education,* No. 98 Civ. 2008 (SHS), 1999 WL 498230 (N.Y.).

Livingston, C. (Ed.). (1992). *Teachers as leaders: Evolving roles.* Washington, DC: National Education Association.

**Los Angeles Times.* (2002, August 6). Florida judge overturns state's school voucher program.

Louis Harris and Associates, Inc. (1995). *The Metropolitan Life survey of the American teacher, 1984–1995: Old problems, new challenges.* New York: Author.

Louis Harris and Associates, Inc. (1997). *The Metropolitan Life survey of the American teacher, 1997: Examining gender issues in public schools.* New York: Author.

MacLeod, J. (1995). *Ain't no makin' it: Aspirations & attainment in a low-income neighborhood.* Boulder, CO: Westview Press.

MacNaughton, R. H., and Johns, F. A. (1991, September). Developing a successful schoolwide discipline program. *NASSP Bulletin,* pp. 47–57.

Mahoney, J., and Cairns, R. B. (1997). Do extracurricular activities protect against early school dropout? *Developmental Psychology, 33*(2), 241–253.

Mailloux v. Kiley, 448 F.2d 1242, 323 F. Supp. 1387, 1393 (1st Cir. 1971).

Mann, H. (1868). Annual reports on education. In Mary Mann (Ed.), *The life and works of Horace Mann,* vol. 3. Boston: Horace B. Fuller.

Mann, H. (1957). Twelfth annual report. In Lawrence A. Cremin (Ed.), *The republic and the school: Horace Mann on the education of free men.* New York: Teachers College Press.

Manning, M. L., and Baruth, L. G. (1996). *Multicultural education of children and adolescents.* Boston: Allyn and Bacon.

Manzo, K. K. (1999, June 2). States setting strategies to reduce mistakes in textbooks. *Education Week on the Web.*

Marcus v. Rowley, 695 F.2d 1171 (9th Cir. 1983).

*Market Data Retrieval. (2002). *Technology in education 2002.* Shelton, CT: Author.

Marks, H. M., Newmann, F. M., and Gamoran, A. (1996). Does authentic pedagogy increase student achievement? In F. M. Newmann, et al. (Eds.), *Authentic achievement: Restructuring schools for intellectual quality* (pp. 49–76). San Francisco: Jossey-Bass.

Marshall, K. (1996, January). How I confronted HSPS (hyperactive superficial principal syndrome) and began to deal with the heart of the matter. *Phi Delta Kappan,* pp. 336–345.

*Marzano, R. J. (1997). *Eight questions you should ask before implementing standards-based education at the local level.* Aurora, CO: Mid-Continent Research for Education and Learning.

Maslow, A. (1954). *Motivation and personality.* New York: Basic Books.

Maslow, A. (1962). *Toward a psychology of being.* New York: Basic Books.

*Mattingly, P. H. (1975). *The classless profession.* New York: New York University Press.

*McCain, T., and Jukes, I. (2001). *Windows on the future: Education in the age of technology.* Thousand Oaks, CA: Corwin Press.

McCarthy, M. M., Cambron-McCabe, N. H., and Thomas, S. B. (1998). *Public school law: Teachers' and students' rights,* 4th ed. Boston: Allyn and Bacon.

*McMillan, J. H. (2001). *Classroom assessment: Principles and practice for effective instruction,* 2nd ed. Boston: Allyn and Bacon.

Mehlinger, H. D. (1996, February). School reform in the Information Age. *Phi Delta Kappan,* pp. 400–407.

*Merideth, E. M. (2000). *Leadership strategies for teachers.* Arlington Heights, IL: SkyLight Professional Development.

*Miller, S. R., Allensworth, E. M., and Kochanek, J. R. (2002). *Student performance: Course taking, test scores, and outcomes.* Chicago: Consortium on Chicago School Research.

Milken Exchange on Education Technology. (1999). *Will new teachers be prepared to teach in a digital age? A national survey on information technology in teacher education.* Santa Monica, CA: Author.

Mills, G. E. (2000). *Action research: A guide for the teacher researcher.* Upper Saddle River, NJ: Merrill.

Missouri v. Jenkins, 515 U.S. 70 (1995).

Modi, M., Konstantopoulos, S., and Hedges, L. V. (1998). *Predictors of academic giftedness among U.S. high school students: Evidence from a nationally representative multivariate analysis.* Paper presented at the annual meeting of the American Educational Research Association, San Diego. Eric Document Number ED422 356.

Molino, F. (1999). My students, my children. In M. K. Rand and S. Shelton-Colangelo, *Voices of student teachers: Cases from the field* (pp. 55–56). Upper Saddle River: Merrill.

*Monsef, P. (2002, July 1). Students find their voices through multimedia. *Edutopia.* San Rafael, CA: The George Lucas Educational Foundation.

Montagu, A. (1974). *Man's most dangerous myth: The fallacy of race,* 5th ed. New York: Oxford University Press.

Moore, D. R. (1992). Voice and choice in Chicago. In W. H. Clune and J. F. Witte (Eds.), *Choice and control in American education: Volume II. The practice of choice, decentralization and school restructuring.* Philadelphia: The Falmer Press.

Moore, J. P., and Terrett, C. P. (1999). *Highlights of the 1997 national youth gang survey. Fact sheet.* Washington, DC: U.S. Department of Justice, Office of Justice Programs, Office of Juvenile Justice and Delinquency Prevention.

Moran v. School District No. 7, 350 F. Supp. 1180 (D. Mont. 1972).

Morris, J. E., and Curtis, K. E. (1983, March/April). Legal issues relating to field-based experiences in teacher education. *Journal of Teacher Education,* pp. 2–6.

Morris, V. C., and Pai, Y. (1994). *Philosophy and the American school: An introduction to the philosophy of education.* Lanham, MD: University Press of America.

Morrison v. State Board of Education, 82 Cal. Rptr. 175, 461 P.2d 375 (Cal. 1969).

Morton, C. (1996, February). The modern land of Laputa: Where computers are used in education. *Phi Delta Kappan,* pp. 416–419.

*Moskal, B. M. (2000). Scoring rubrics: what, when, and how? *Practical Assessment, Research, & Evaluation, 7*(3).

Moyers, B. D. (1989). *A world of ideas: Conversations with thoughtful men and women.* New York: Doubleday.

Mozert v. Hawkins County Board of Education, 827 F.2d 1058 (6th Cir. 1987), *cert. denied,* 484 U.S. 1066 (1988).

Murphy, J. (1999, April). *Reconnecting teaching and school administration: A call for a unified profession.* Paper presented at the annual meeting of the American Educational Research Association, Montreal.

Murray v. Pittsburgh Board of Public Education, 919 F. Supp. 838 (Pa. 1996).

*Nathan, L. (2002, April). The human face of the high-stakes testing story. *Phi Delta Kappan,* pp. 595–600.

National Association for Sport and Physical Education. (1999). National standards for physical education. Reston, VA: Author.

*National Association for Year-Round Education. (2002). History of year-round education. San Diego: Author. Retrieved from http://www.nayre.org

National Board for Professional Teaching Standards. (1994). *Toward high and rigorous standards for the teaching profession.* Arlington, VA: Author.

National Board for Professional Teaching Standards. (1995). *An invitation to national board certification.* Arlington, VA: Author.

*National Board for Professional Teaching Standards. (2002). *Quick facts.* Arlington, VA: Author.

National Center for Education Statistics. (1980). *High school and beyond study.* Washington, DC: U.S. Department of Education: Author.

*National Center for Education Statistics. (1995). *Educational policy issues: Statistical perspectives: Extracurricular participation and student involvement.* Washington, DC: U.S. Department of Education: Author.

National Center for Education Statistics. (1999). *Digest of education statistics 1998.* Washington, DC: U.S. Department of Education, Office of Educational Research and Improvement.

*National Center for Education Statistics. (2001). *Projections of education statistics to 2011.* Washington, DC: U.S. Department of Education: Author.

*National Center for Education Statistics. (2002a). *The condition of education 2002.* Washington, DC: U.S. Department of Education: Author.

*National Center for Education Statistics. (2002b). *The digest of education statistics 2001.* Washington, DC: U.S. Department of Education: Author.

*National Center for Education Statistics. (2002c). *Predicting the need for newly hired teachers in the U.S. to 2008–09.* Washington, DC: U.S. Department of Education: Author.

*National Center for Education Statistics. (2002d). *Projections of education statistics to 2008.* Washington, DC: U.S. Department of Education: Author.

*National Center for Education Statistics. (2002e). *Special analysis—private schools: A brief portrait.* Washington, DC: U.S. Department of Education: Author.

*National Center for History in the Schools. (1996). *National standards for history.* National Center for History in the Schools: University of California-Los Angeles, Dept. of History.

*National Clearinghouse for English Language Acquisition. (2002). *Survey of the states' limited English proficient students and available educational programs and services.* Washington, DC: George Washington University, National Clearinghouse for English Language Acquisition.

*National Clearinghouse on Child Abuse and Neglect. (2002). *National child abuse and neglect data system (NCANDS): Summary of key findings from calendar year 2000.* Washington, DC: Author.

National Commission on Excellence and Education. (1983). *A nation at risk: The imperative for educational reform.* Washington, DC: U.S. Government Printing Office.

National Commission on Teaching and America's Future. (1996). *What matters most: Teaching for America's future.* New York: Author.

*National Council for Accreditation of Teacher Education. (2002a). *Professional standards for the accreditation of schools, colleges, and departments of education—2002 edition.* Washington, DC: Author.

*National Council for Accreditation of Teacher Education. (2002b). *NCATE: Quick facts.* Washington, DC: Author.

National Council for the Social Studies. (1994). *Expectations of excellence: Curriculum standards for social studies.* Washington, DC: Author.

*National Council of Teachers of Mathematics. (2000). *Principles and standards for school mathematics.* Reston, VA: Author.

*National Education Association. (2002a). *Status of the American public school teacher.* Washington, DC: Author.

*National Education Association. (2002b). *Results of poll on potential teachers: Answering the call . . . for all the right reasons.* Washington, DC: Author.

*National Governors' Association and NGA Center for Best Practices. (2002). *After-school plus (+) program: Hawaii.* Washington, DC: Author.

National Institute for Mental Health. (1999). *Suicide fact sheet.* Washington, DC: Author.

National Joint Committee on Learning Disabilities. (1997). *Operationalizing the NJCLD definition of learning disabilities for ongoing assessment in schools.* Rockville, MD: Author.

*National School Boards Association. (2002). *Are we there yet? Research and guidelines on school's use of the Internet.* Alexandria, VA: Author.

*Nave, B., Miech, E., Mosteller, F. (2000, October). A lapse in standards: Linking standards-based reform with student achievement. *Phi Delta Kappan,* pp. 128–132.

*NEAFT Partnership. (2002, April 23–24). NEAFT Partnership Joint Council Communique. Washington, DC: Author.

Neill, A. S. (1960). *Summerhill: A radical approach to child rearing.* New York: Hart.

Nelson, J. L., Carlson, K., and Palonsky, S. B. (2000). *Critical issues in education: A dialectic approach,* 4th ed. New York: McGraw-Hill.

New Jersey v. Massa, 231 A.2d 252 (N.J. Sup. Ct. 1967).

New Jersey v. T.L.O., 221 Cal. Rptr. 118, 105 S. Ct. 733 (1985).

Newmann, F. M., et al. (Eds). (1996). *Authentic achievement: Restructuring schools for intellectual quality.* San Francisco: Jossey-Bass.

Newmann, F. M., and Wehlage, G. G. (1995). *Successful school restructuring: A report to the public and educators by the Center on Organization and Restructuring of Schools.* Madison, WI: University of Wisconsin, Center on Organization and Restructuring of Schools.

Nieto, S. (1992). *Affirming diversity: The sociopolitical context of multicultural education.* White Plains, NY: Longman.

*Nitko, A. J. (2001). *Educational assessment of students,* 3rd ed. Upper Saddle River, NJ: Merrill.

Noble, D. (1996, November). The overselling of educational technology. *Educational Leadership,* pp. 18–23.

Noddings, N. (1992). *The challenge to care in schools: An alternative approach to education.* New York: Teacher's College Press.

Noddings, N. (1995, May). Teaching themes of care. *Phi Delta Kappan, 76*(9), 675–679.

*Noddings, N. (2002). *Educating moral people: A caring alternative to character education.* New York: Teachers College Press.

*Nord, C. W., and West, J. (2001). *National household education survey: Fathers' and mothers' involvement in their children's schools by family type and resident status.* Washington, DC: U.S. Department of Education, National Center for Education Statistics.

Norris, C. (1994). Computing in the classroom: Teaching the at-risk student. *Computing Teacher, 21*(5), 12, 14.

Null v. Board of Education, 815 F. Supp. 937 (D.W. Va. 1993).

*Oaks, M. M., Grantman, R., and Pedras, M. (2001). Technological literacy: A twenty-first century imperative. In F. W. Parkay and G. Hass (Eds.), *Curriculum planning: A contemporary approach,* 7th ed. (pp. 439–445). Boston: Allyn and Bacon.

Oberti v. Board of Education of the Borough of Clementon School District, 789 F. Supp. 1322 (D.N.J. 1992).

Odden, A., and Busch, C. (1998). *Financing schools for high performance: Strategies for improving the use of educational resources.* San Francisco: Jossey-Bass.

O'Hair, M. J., and Odell, S. J. (Eds.). (1995). *Educating teachers for leadership and change: Teacher education yearbook III.* Thousand Oaks, CA: Corwin Press.

Ohman v. Board of Education, 301 N.Y. 662, 93 N.E.2d 927 (1950).

Olson, L. (January 9, 2002). Two new projects to examine quality, impact of exit exams. *Education Week on the Web.*

Oppenheimer, T. (1997, July). The computer delusion. *The Atlantic Monthly,* pp. 45–62.

Orfield, G., and Yun, J. T. (1999). *Resegregation in American schools.* Cambridge, MA: Harvard University, The Civil Rights Project.

*Ormrod, J. E. (2003). *Educational psychology: Developing learners,* 4th ed. Upper Saddle River, NJ: Merrill Prentice Hall.

Ortiz, M. G. (1999, April 19). Urban schools lag in technology. *Detroit Free Press.*

**Owasso Independent School District No. 1 v. Falvo,* 233 F.3d 1203 (10th Cir. Ct. 2002).

Ozmon, H. W., and Craver, S. M. (1999). *Philosophical foundations of education,* 6th ed. Upper Saddle River, NJ: Merrill.

*Pajak, E. (1999). *Approaches to clinical supervision: Alternatives for improving instruction.* Norwood, MA: Christopher-Gordon.

Pang, V. O. (1994, December). Why do we need this class: Multicultural education for teachers. *Phi Delta Kappan.*

*Parkay, F. W. (1983). *White teacher, black school: The professional growth of a ghetto teacher.* New York: Praeger.

Parkay, F. W. (1988, Summer). Reflections of a protégé. *Theory into practice,* pp. 195–200.

Parkay, F. W., and Hass, G. (2000). *Curriculum planning: A contemporary approach,* 7th ed. Boston: Allyn and Bacon.

Parkay, F. W., Potisook, P., Chantharasakul, A., and Chunsakorn, P. (1999). *New roles and responsibilities in educational reform: A study of Thai and U.S. principals' attitudes toward teacher leadership.* Bangkok: Kasetsart University, Center for Research on Teaching and Teacher Education.

Parkay, F. W., Shindler, J., and Oaks, M. M. (1997, January). Creating a climate for collaborative, emergent leadership at an urban high school: Exploring the stressors, role changes, and paradoxes of restructuring. *International Journal of Educational Reform,* pp. 64–74.

Parker, L., and Shapiro, J. P. (1993). The context of educational administration and social class. In C. A. Capper (Ed.), *Educational administration in a pluralistic society* (pp. 36–65). Albany, NY: State University of New York Press.

PASE (Parents in Action on Special Education) v. Hannon, 506 F. Supp. 831 (E.D. Ill. 1980).

Patchogue-Medford Congress of Teachers v. Board of Education of Patchogue-Medford Union Free School District, 70 N.Y.2d 57, 510 N.E.2d 325 (1987).

*Paul, J. L., Christensen, L., and Falk, G. (2000). Accessing the intimate spaces of life in the classroom through letters to former teachers: A protocol for uncovering hidden stories. In J. L. Paul and T. J. Smith (Eds.), *Stories out of school: Memories and reflections on care and cruelty in the classroom* (pp. 15–26). Stamford, CT: Ablex.

*Paul, J. L., and Colucci, K. (2000). Caring pedagogy. In J. L. Paul and T. J. Smith (Eds.), *Stories out of school: Memories and reflections on care and cruelty in the classroom* (pp. 45–63). Stamford, CT: Ablex.

*Paul, J. L., and Smith, T. J. (Eds.). (2000). *Stories out of school: Memories and reflections on care and cruelty in the classroom.* Stamford, CT: Ablex.

Pellicer, L. O., and Anderson, L. W. (1995). *A handbook for teacher lead-*

ers. Thousand Oaks, CA: Corwin Press.

Peter Doe v. San Francisco Unified School District, 131 Cal. Rptr. 854 (1976).

**Picarella v. Terrizzi,* 893 F. Supp. 1292 (Pa. 1995).

Piirto, J. (1999). *Talented children and adults: Their development and education.* Upper Saddle River, NJ: Merrill.

Pitton, D. E. (1998). *Stories of student teaching: A case approach to the student teaching experience.* Upper Saddle River, NJ: Merrill.

Portner, J. (1999, May 12). Schools ratchet up the rules on student clothing, threats. *Education Week on the Web.*

*Posner, G. J. (2000). *Field experience: A guide to reflective teaching,* 5th ed. New York: Longman.

Postman, N. (1995, October 9). Virtual students, digital classroom. *The Nation.*

Powell, A. G. (1980). *The uncertain profession: Harvard and the search for educational authority.* Cambridge, MA: Harvard University Press.

Power, E. J. (1982). *Philosophy of education: Studies in philosophies, schooling, and educational policies.* Englewood Cliffs, NJ: Prentice Hall.

*President's Commission on Excellence in Special Education. (2002). *A new era: Revitalizing special education for children and their families.* Washington, DC: Author.

Public Agenda. (1999). *Reality check: The status of standards reform.* New York: Author.

Rand, M. K., and Shelton-Colangelo, S. (1999). *Voices of student teachers: Cases from the field.* Upper Saddle River, NJ: Merrill.

*Randall, V. R. (2001). *Institutional racism.* Dayton, OH: The University of Dayton School of Law.

Ravitch, D. (1983). *The troubled crusade: American education, 1945–1980.* New York: Basic Books.

Ravitch, D. (1996). *National standards in American education: A citizen's guide.* Washington, DC: Brookings Institute.

Ravitch, D. (1997, December 15). The fight for standards. *Forbes, 160*(13), 106.

Ravitz, J. L., Wong, Y. T., and Becker, H. J. (1999). Report to participants. The University of California, Irvine, and The University of Minnesota: Center for Research on Information Technology and Organizations.

Ray v. School District of DeSoto County, 666 F. Supp. 1524 (M.D. Fla. 1987).

RCM Research Corporation. (1998). *Time: Critical issues in educational change.* Portsmouth, NH: Author.

*Rector, T. A., Jacoby, S. H., Lockwood, J. F., and McCarthy, D. W. (2002, January 7). *Teacher leaders in research based science education.* Paper presented at the 199th meeting of the American Astronomical Society, Washington, DC.

Renzulli, J. S. (1998). The three-ring conception of giftedness. In S. M. Baum, S. M. Reis, and L. R. Maxfield. (Eds.), *Nurturing the gifts and talents of primary grade students.* Mansfield Center, CT: Creative Learning Press.

Rice, R., and Walsh, C. E. (1996). Equity at risk: The problem with state and federal education reform efforts. In C. Walsh (Ed.), *Education reform and social change: Multicultural voices, struggles, and visions.* Mahwah, NJ: Lawrence Erlbaum.

*Richard, A. (2002a, January 9). Report card days. *Education Week on the Web.*

*Richard, A. (2002b, May 15). Memphis school board wants uniforms for all. *Education Week on the Web.*

Rippa, S. A. (1997). *Education in a free society: An American history,* 8th ed. New York: Longman.

Ripple, R. E., and Rockcastle, V. E. (Eds.). (1964). *Piaget rediscovered: A report of the conference on cognitive studies and curriculum development.* Ithaca, NY: School of Education, Cornell University.

*Roach, V., and Cohen, B. A. (2002). *Moving past the politics: How alternative certification can promote comprehensive teacher development reforms.* Alexandria, VA: National Association of State Boards of Education.

Roberts v. City of Boston, 59 Mass. (5 Cush.) 198 (1850).

Rogers, C. (1961). *On becoming a person.* Boston: Houghton Mifflin.

Rogers, C. (1982). *Freedom to learn in the eighties.* Columbus, OH: Merrill.

Rogers, K. (1991). *The relationship of grouping practices to the education of the gifted and talented learner.* Storrs, CT: National Research Center on the Gifted and Talented, University of Connecticut.

Romans v. Crenshaw, 354 F. Supp. 868 (S.D. Tex. 1972).

*Romer, R. (2000). Today standards—tomorrow success. In F. W. Parkay and G. Hass (Eds.), *Curriculum planning: A contemporary approach* (pp. 314–317). Boston: Allyn and Bacon.

Rose, L. C., and Gallup, A. M. (1998, September). The 30th annual Phi Delta Kappa/Gallup poll of the public's attitudes toward the public schools. *Phi Delta Kappan,* pp. 41–56.

*Rose, L. C., and Gallup, A. M. (2001, September). The 33rd annual Phi Delta Kappa/Gallup poll of the public's attitudes toward the public schools. *Phi Delta Kappan,* pp. 41–58.

*Rosenkranz, T. (2002). *2001 CPS test trend review: Iowa Tests of Basic Skills.* Chicago: Consortium on Chicago School Research.

Rosenshine, B. (1988). Explicit teaching. In D. Berliner and B. Rosenshine (Eds.), *Talks to teachers.* New York: Random House.

Rosenshine, B. (1995). Advances in research on instruction. *The Journal of Educational Research, 88*(5), 262–268.

Rosenshine, B., Meister, C., and Chapman, S. (1996). Teaching students to generate questions: A review of the intervention studies. *Review of Educational Research, 66*(2), 181–221.

Rosenshine, B., and Stevens, R. (1986). Teaching functions. In M. C. Wittrock (Ed.), *Handbook of research on teaching,* 3rd ed. New York: Macmillan.

Rossell, C. H. (1990, Winter). The research on bilingual education. *Equity and Choice,* pp. 29–36.

*Rossell, C., and Baker, K. (1996). The educational effectiveness of bilingual education. *Research in the Teaching of English, 30*(1), 7–74.

Rotberg, I. C., Futrell, M. H., and Lieberman, J. M. (1998). National board certification: Increasing participation and assessing impacts. *Phi Delta Kappan, 79*(6), 462–466.

Rothstein, R. (1998, May). Bilingual education: The controversy. *Phi Delta Kappan,* pp. 672, 674–678.

Ruenzel, D. (1999, April). Pride and prejudice. *Teacher Magazine on the Web.*

Sallie Mae Corporation. (1995). *A report from the 1994 Sallie Mae symposium on quality education.* Washington, DC: Author.

*Salovey, P., and Feldman-Barrett, L. (Eds.). (2002). *The wisdom of feelings: Psychological processes in emotional intelligence.* New York: Guilford Press.

*Salovey, P., Mayer, J. D., and Caruso, D. (2002). The positive psychology of emotional intelligence. In C. R. Snyder & S. J. Lopez (Eds.), *The handbook of positive psychology* (pp. 159–171). New York: Oxford University Press.

Salovey, P., and Sluyter, D. J. (Eds.). (1997). *Emotional development and emotional intelligence: Educational implications.* New York: Basic Books.

*Sandham, J. L. (2002, February 6). Board to close Fla. "voucher" school. *Education Week on the Web.*

Sandholtz, J. J., Ringstaff, C., and Dwyer, D. C. (1997). *Teaching with technology: Creating student-centered classrooms.* New York: Teachers College Press.

Sarason, S. B. (1997). *How schools might be governed and why.* New York: Teachers College Press.

Sarnoff, D. (1940). Foreword. In L. R. Lohr, *Television broadcasting.* New York: McGraw-Hill.

Sartre, J.-P. (1972). Existentialism. In John Martin Rich (Ed.), *Readings in the philosophy of education.* Belmont, CA: Wadsworth.

*Scales, P. C. (2001). The public image of adolescents. *Society 38*(4), 64–70.

Schaefer, R. (1967). *The school as the center of inquiry.* New York: Harper and Row.

Schaill v. Tippecanoe School Corp., 864 F.2d 1309 (7th Cir. 1988).

Schifter, D. (Ed.). (1996). *What's happening in math class? Envisioning new practices through teacher narratives,* vol. 1. New York: Teachers College Press.

Schmidt, P. (1991, February 20). Three types of bilingual education effective, E. D. study concludes. *Education Week on the Web.*

*Schmuck, R. A., and Schmuck, P. A. (2001). *Group processes in the classroom,* 8th ed. Boston: McGraw-Hill.

Schneider, R. B., and Barone, D. (1997, Spring). Cross-age tutoring. *Childhood Education,* pp. 136–143.

Schön, D. (1983). *The reflective practitioner: How professionals think in action.* New York: Basic Books.

Schön, D. (1987). *Educating the reflective practitioner: Toward a new design for teaching and learning in the professions.* San Francisco: Jossey-Bass.

Schön, D. (1991). *The reflective turn: Case studies in an educational practice.* New York: Teachers College Press.

Schön, D. (2000). *The reflective practitioner: How professionals think in action.* New York: Basic Books.

**School Board News: Conference Daily.* (2002, April 8). Paige urges school boards to play large roles in implementing new education law.

School District of Abington Township v. Schempp, 374 U.S. 203, 83 S. Ct. 1560, 10 L. Ed. 2d 844 (1963).

Schwartz, J. E., and Beichner, R. J. (1999). *Essentials of educational technology.* Boston: Allyn and Bacon.

Scopes, J. (1966). *Center of the storm.* New York: Holt, Rinehart and Winston.

Scoville v. Board of Education of Joliet Township High School District 204, cert. denied, 400 U.S. 826, 91 S. Ct. 51 (1970); 425 F.2d 10 (7th Cir. 1971).

*Search Institute. (2002). *Help your youth grow up healthy.* Minneapolis, MN: Author.

Sears, J. T. (1991). Educators, homosexuality and homosexual students: Are personal feelings related to professional beliefs? *Journal of Homosexuality, 22.*

Shade, B. J. (1982). Afro-American cognitive style: A variable in school success? *Review of Educational Research 52*(2), 219–238.

Shanley v. Northeast Independent School District, 462 F.2d 960 (5th Cir. 1972).

Sharan, Y., and Sharan, S. (1989/90, December/January). Group investigation expands cooperative learning. *Educational Leadership,* pp. 17–21.

Shenk, D. (1998). *Data smog: Surviving the information glut.* New York: HarperEdge.

Sheuerer, D., and Parkay, F. W. (1992). The new Christian right and the public school curriculum: A Florida report. In J. B. Smith and J. G. Coleman, Jr. (Eds.), *School library media annual: 1992,* vol. 10. Englewood, CO: Libraries Unlimited.

*Shulman, L. (1987, August). *Teaching alone, learning together: Needed agendas for the new reform.* Paper presented at the Conference on Restructuring Schooling for Quality Education, San Antonio.

Signer, B. (1991). CAI and at-risk minority urban high school students. *Journal of Research on Computing in Education, 24*(2).

Simonetti v. School District of Philadelphia, 308 Pa. Super. 555, 454 A.2d 1038 (Pa. Super. 1982).

Singer, A. (1994, December). Reflections on multiculturalism. *Phi Delta Kappan,* pp. 284–288.

Sizer, T. (1997a). *Horace's compromise: The dilemma of the American high school,* 3rd ed. Boston: Houghton Mifflin.

Sizer, T. (1997b). *Horace's school: Redesigning the American high school.* Boston: Houghton Mifflin.

Sizer, T. (1997c). *Horaces hope: What works for the American high school.* Boston: Houghton Mifflin.

Sizer, T., and Sizer, N. F. (1999). *The students are watching: Schools and the moral contract.* Boston: Beacon Press.

Skinner, B. F. (1972). Utopia through the control of human behavior. In J. M. Rich (Ed.), *Readings in the philosophy of education.* Belmont, CA: Wadsworth.

*Slavin, R. E. (2000). *Educational Psychology: Theory and Practice,* 6th ed. Boston: Allyn and Bacon.

*Smith, D. D. (2001). *Introduction to special education: Teaching in an age of opportunity.* Boston: Allyn and Bacon.

Smith v. Board of School Commissioners of Mobile County, 655 F. Supp. 939 (S.D. Ala.), *rev'd,* 827 F.2d 684 (11th Cir. 1987).

Smyth, J. W. (1995). *Clinical supervision: Collaborative learning about teaching.* New York: State Mutual Book and Periodical Service.

Snider, J. H. (1996, May–June). Education wars: The battle over information-age technology. *The Futurist,* pp. 24–29.

*Snyder, K. J., and Anderson, R. H. (Eds.). (1996). *Clinical supervision: Coaching for higher performance.* Lanham, MD: Scarecrow Press.

Sommers, C. H. (1994). *Who stole feminism? How women have betrayed women.* New York: Simon and Schuster.

Sommers, C. H. (1996, June 12). Where the boys are. *Education Week on the Web.*

Sowell, E. J. (1996). *Curriculum: An integrative introduction.* Boston: Allyn and Bacon.

Spokesman Review. (1993, June 4). Harassment claims vex teachers.

Spring, J. (1997). *The American school 1642–1996,* 4th ed. New York: McGraw-Hill.

Spring, J. (1998). *Conflict of interests: The politics of American education,* 3rd ed. Boston: McGraw-Hill.

Spring, J. (1999). *American education,* 8th ed. New York: McGraw-Hill.

St. Michel, T. (1995). *Effective substitute teachers: Myth, mayhem, or magic?* Thousand Oaks, CA: Corwin Press.

Stanford, B. H. (1992). Gender equity in the classroom. In D. A. Byrnes and G. Kiger (Eds.), *Common bonds: Anti-bias teaching in a diverse society.* Wheaton, MD: Association for Childhood Education International.

State v. Rivera, 497 N.W.2d 878 (Iowa 1993).

Station v. Travelers Insurance Co., 292 So. 2d 289 (La. Ct. App. 1974).

Stecher, B., and Hamilton, L. (2002, February 20). Test-based accountability: Making it work better. *Education Week on the Web.* (Retrieved from http://www.edweek.org/ew/newstory.cfm?slug=23Stecher.h21)

*Sternberg, R. J. (2002). Beyond g: The theory of successful intelligence. In R. J. Sternberg and E. L. Grigorenko (Eds.), *The general factor of intelligence: How general is it?* (pp. 447–479). Mahwah, NJ: Lawrence Erlbaum.

*Stiggins, R. J. (2001). *Student-involved classroom assessment,* 3rd ed. Upper Saddle River, NJ: Merrill Prentice Hall.

Stoll, C. (1996). *Silicon snake oil: Second thoughts on the information highway.* New York: Anchor.

Stover, D. (1992, March). The at-risk kids schools ignore. *The Executive Educator,* pp. 28–31.

*Strang, H. R. (1997). The use of Curry Teaching Simulations in professional training. *Computers in the Schools, 13*(3–4), 135–145.

*Substitute Teaching Institute. (2002). *Fact sheet.* Logan, UT: Utah State University, Substitute Teaching Institute.

Sue, D. W., and Sue, D. (1999). *Counseling the culturally different: Theory and practice,* 3rd ed. New York: John Wiley and Sons.

Sullivan v. Houston Independent School District, 475 F.2d 1071 (5th Cir.), *cert. denied,* 414 U.S. 1032 (1969).

**Swanson v. Guthrie Independent School District No. 1-1,* 135 F.3d 694 (10th Cir. 1998).

Swisher, K., and Deyhle, D. (1987). Styles of learning and learning styles: Educational conflicts for American Indian/Alaskan Native youth. *Journal of Multilingual and Multicultural Development, 8,* no. 4.

Sykes, G. (1983, October). Contradictions, ironies, and promises unfulfilled: A contemporary account of the status of teaching. *Phi Delta Kappan,* pp. 87–93.

Tapscott, D. (1999, July 6). Kids, technology and the schools. *Computerworld.*

Teacher Centers of New York State. (1999). What is a teacher center? (Retrieved from http://www.tier.net/tcenters/class.htm)

Teach for America. (1999). About us. New York: Author. (Retrieved from http://www.teachforamerica.org)

Tellijohann, S. K., and Price, J. H. (1993). A qualitative examination of adolescent homosexuals' life experiences: Ramifications for secondary school personnel. *Journal of Homosexuality, 26.*

Terman, L. M., Baldwin, B. T., and Bronson, E. (1925). Mental and physical traits of a thousand gifted children. In L. M. Terman (Ed.), *Genetic studies of genius,* vol. 1. Stanford, CA: Stanford University Press.

Terman, L. M., and Oden, M. H. (1947). The gifted child grows up. In L. M. Terman (Ed.), *Genetic studies of genius,* vol. 4. Stanford, CA: Stanford University Press.

Terry, W. (1993, February). Make things better for somebody. *Parade Magazine.*

Thelen, H. A. (1960). *Education and the human quest.* New York: Harper and Row.

Tinker v. Des Moines Independent Community School District, 393 U.S. 503 (1969).

Tombari, M. L., and Borich, G. D. (1999). *Authentic assessment in the classroom: Applications and practice.* Upper Saddle River, NJ: Merrill.

*Toppo (2001, December 19). New law requires standardized school tests. *Spokesman Review,* p. A10.

Tozer, S. E., Violas, P. C., and Senese, G. (1993). *School and society: Educational practice as social expression.* New York: McGraw-Hill.

Trotter, A. (1998, October 1). A question of effectiveness. *Education Week on the Web.*

*Trotter, A. (2002, May 9). E-learning goes to school. *Education Week on the Web.*

Trueba, H. T., Cheng, L. R. L., and Kenji, I. (1993). *Myth or reality: Adaptive strategies of Asian Americans in California.* Washington, DC: Falmer Press.

*Tweney, D. (2000, December 7). No more free ride. Tampa, FL: Business 2.0 Media, Inc.

Tyler, R. (1949). *Basic principles of curriculum and instruction.* Chicago: University of Chicago.

Unified School District No. 241 v. Swanson, 717 P.2d 526 (Kan. App. 1986).

United Press International. (1998, November 15). Teachers may soon make $100,000.

The University of Memphis. (Winter 1994/95). Technology provides field experiences. *Perspectives.* Memphis: The University of Memphis, College of Education.

Uribe, V., and Harbeck, K. M. (1991). Addressing the needs of lesbian, gay and bisexual youth. *Journal of Homosexuality, 22.*

U.S. Census Bureau. (September 1993). *We the . . . first Americans.* Washington, DC: Author.

U.S. Census Bureau. (1998). *Statistical abstract of the United States 1998.* Washington, DC: Author.

U.S. Census Bureau. (1999). *The Asian and Pacific Islander population in the United States: March 1997.* Washington, DC: Author.

*U.S. Census Bureau. (2002). *Statistical abstract of the United States 2002.* Washington, DC: Author.

*U.S. Department of Commerce, U.S. Census Bureau. (2000). *Current population survey* (CPS). Washington, DC: Author.

*U.S. Department of Commerce. (2002). *A nation online: How Americans are expanding their use of the Internet.* Washington, DC: Author.

U.S. Department of Education. (1996). *Getting America's students ready for the 21st century: Meeting the technology literacy challenge.* Washington, DC: Author.

U.S. Department of Education. (1999). *Schools with IDEAs that work.* Washington, DC: Author.

*U.S. Department of Education. (2001, July 27). *Ready to read, ready to learn* [news release]. Washington, DC: Author.

*U.S. Department of Education. (2002, July 28). Paige announces new "No Child Left Behind-Blue Ribbon Schools" program [new release]. Washington, DC: Author.

*U.S. Department of Health and Human Services. (2002). *HHS Fact Sheet, February 26, 2002.* Washington, DC: Author.

*U.S. Department of Justice. (2001). *Indicators of school crime and safety: 2001.* Washington, DC: Author.

Utay, C., and Utay, J. (1997). Peer-assisted learning: The effects of cooperative learning and cross-age peer tutoring with word processing on writing skills of students with learning disabilities. *Journal of Computing in Childhood Education, 8.*

*Van Reusen, A. K., Shoho, A. R., and Barker, K. S. (2000). High school teacher attitudes toward inclusion. *High School Journal, 84*(2), 7–20.

Vaughn, S., Bos, C. S., and Schumm, J. S. (1997). *Teaching mainstreamed, diverse, and at-risk students in the general education classroom.* Boston: Allyn and Bacon.

*Ver Velde, P., Ver Velde, R., Prater, G., and Minner, S. (1999). School-based teacher education "en la Frontera": Preparing special education teachers on the Arizona-Mexico border. ERIC Document No. ED429-775.

Vygotsky, L. S. (1978). *Mind in society: The development of higher mental process.* Cambridge, MA: Harvard University Press.

Vygotsky, L. S. (1986). *Thought and language.* Cambridge, MA: MIT Press.

Walberg, H. J., and Greenberg, R. C. (1997, May). Using the learning environment inventory. *Educational Leadership,* pp. 45–47.

Waller, W. (1932). *The sociology of teaching.* New York: John Wiley.

Walling, D. R. (Ed.). (1994). *Teachers as leaders: Perspectives on the professional development of teachers.* Bloomington, IN: Phi Delta Kappa Educational Foundation.

Walsh, M. (1999a, April 2). Conservatives join effort to pull the plug on Channel One. *Education Week on the Web.*

Walsh, M. (1999b, April 14). Most Edison schools report rise in test scores. *Education Week on the Web.*

Walsh, M. (1999c, May 5). Shootings raise host of legal questions. *Education Week on the Web.*

Walsh, M. (1999d, May 26). Nader, Schlafly lambaste Channel One at Senate hearing. *Education Week on the Web.*

*Walsh, M. (2002, June 5). Home school enrollment surge fuels "cottage" industry. *Education Week on the Web.*

Warger, C. (1999, September). Positive behavior support and functional assessment. (Retrieved from http://www.ed.gov/databases/ERIC_Digests/ed434437.html)

Washington, W. (1998). Optional extended year program feedback. Austin Independent School District, TX, Department of Accountability, Student Services, and Research.

Wasserman, S. (1994, April). Using cases to study teaching. *Phi Delta Kappan,* pp. 602–611.

Webb, L. D., Metha, A., and Jordan, K. F. (1999). *Foundations of American education,* 3rd ed. Englewood Cliffs, NJ: Prentice Hall.

*Web-Based Education Commission. (2001). *The power of the Internet for learning: Moving from promise to practice.* Washington, DC: Author.

Wechsler, D. (1958). *The measurement and appraisal of adult intelligence,* 4th ed. Baltimore: Williams and Wilkins.

*Wentz, P. J. (2001). *The student teaching experience: Cases from the class-*

room. Upper Saddle River, NJ: Merrill Prentice Hall.

West, A. M. (1980). *The National Education Association: The power base for education.* New York: The Free Press.

West v. Board of Education of City of New York, 187 N.Y.S.2d 88, 8 A.D.2d 291 (N.Y. App. 1959).

*WestEd. (2001). *Virtual schools: Trends and issues, a study of virtual schools in the United States.* San Francisco: WestEd.

William Randolph Hearst Foundation. (1999). *United States Senate youth program survey.* San Francisco: Author.

Williams, J. (1999, April 18). Urban schools' obstacles hindering technology. *Milwaukee Journal Sentinal.*

Willig, A. C. (1987, Fall). Examining bilingual education research. *Review of Educational Research,* pp. 363–376.

Willingham, W. W., and Cole, N. S. (1997). *Gender and fair assessment.* Mahwah, NJ: Lawrence Erlbaum.

*Wilson, B. L., and Corbett, H. D. (2001). *Listening to urban kids: School reform and the teachers they want.* Albany, NY: State University of New York Press.

Wirt, F. M., and Kirst, M. W. (1997). *The political dynamics of American education.* Berkeley: McCutchan.

Withrow, F. B. (1997). Technology in education and the next twenty-five years. *T.H.E. Journal, 24*(11), 59–61.

Wohlstetter, P., and Anderson, L. (1994, February). What can U.S. charter schools learn from England's grant-maintained schools? *Phi Delta Kappan,* pp. 486–491.

Wolfe, D. T., and Antinarella, J. (1997). *Deciding to lead: The English teacher as reformer.* Portsmouth, NH: Boynton Cook.

*Wolfgang, C. H. (2001). *Solving discipline problems: Methods and models for today's teachers,* 5th ed. Boston: Allyn and Bacon.

*Wolk, R. A., and Rodman, B. H. (1994). *Classroom crusaders: Eleven teachers who are trying to change the system.* San Francisco: Jossey-Bass.

Woolfolk, A. E. (1998). *Educational psychology,* 7th ed. Boston: Allyn and Bacon.

*Woolfolk, A. E. (2001). *Educational psychology,* 8th ed. Boston: Allyn and Bacon.

Yamamoto, K., Davis, O. L., Jr., Dylak, S., Whittaker, J., Marsh, C., and van der Westhuizen, P. C. (1996, Spring). Across six nations: Stressful events in the lives of children. *Child Psychiatry and Human Development,* pp. 139–150.

Young, C. (1999). *Ceasefire! Why women and men must join forces to achieve true equality.* New York: The Free Press.

Zehm, S. J., and Kottler, J. A. (1993). *On being a teacher: The human dimension.* Newbury Park, CA: Corwin Press.

*Zhang, L., and Sternberg, R. J. (2001). Thinking styles across cultures: Their relationships with student learning. In R. J. Sternberg and L. Zhang (Eds.), *Perspectives on thinking, learning, and cognitive styles.* Mahwah, NJ: Lawrence Erlbaum, pp. 197–226.

Zucker v. Panitz, 299 F. Supp. 102 (S.D.N.Y. 1969).

Zukowski, V. (1997, Fall). Teeter-totters and tandem bikes: A glimpse into the world of cross-age tutors. *Teaching and Change,* pp. 71–91.

Glossary

A

Academic freedom (p. 201): the right of teachers to teach, free from external constraint, censorship, or interference.

Academic learning time (p. 328): the amount of time students spend working on academic tasks with a high level of success (80 percent or higher).

Academies (p. 95): early secondary schools with broader and more practical curricula than those found in grammar schools of the previous era.

Accelerated schools (p. 459): a national network of schools that provide enriched, rigorous curricula to "speed up" the learning of students at risk.

Accountability (p. 107, 368): the practice of holding teachers responsible for adhering to high professional and moral standards and creating effective learning environments for all students.

Action research (p. 455): classroom-based study, by teachers, of how to improve their instruction.

Aesthetics (p. 84): the branch of axiology concerned with values related to beauty and art.

Afrocentric schools (p. 253): schools that focus on African American history and cultures for African American pupils.

Allocated time (p. 328): the amount of time teachers allocate for instruction in various areas of the curriculum.

Alternate assessment (p. 376): an alternative way of measuring the performance of students who are unable to participate in "traditional" approaches to assessment.

Alternative assessments (p. 373): approaches that assess students' ability to complete "real-life" tasks rather than merely regurgitate facts.

Alternative certification (p. 474): a provision allowing people who have completed college but not a teacher education program to become certified teachers.

Alternative school (p. 145): a small, highly individualized school separate from a regular school; designed to meet the needs of students at risk.

Amendments to the Individuals with Disabilities Education Act (IDEA 97) (p. 301): amendments to IDEA that emphasize educational outcomes for students with disabilities and provide greater access through changes in eligibility requirements, IEP guidelines, public and private placements, student discipline guidelines, and procedural safeguards.

American Federation of Teachers (AFT) (p. 443): a national professional association for teachers, affiliated with the AFL-CIO.

Analytic rubric (p. 382): a rating scale, or scoring guide, for evaluating part of a student's product or performance.

Assertive discipline (p. 336): an approach to classroom discipline requiring that teachers establish firm, clear guidelines for student behavior and follow through with consequences for misbehavior.

Assessment (p. 371): the process of gathering information related to how much students have learned.

Assistive technology (p. 303): technological advances (usually computer-based) that help exceptional students learn and communicate.

Association for Supervision and Curriculum Development (ASCD) (p. 445): a professional organization for educators interested in school improvement at all levels.

Attention deficit disorder (ADD) (p. 296): a learning disability characterized by difficulty in concentrating on learning.

Attention deficit hyperactivity disorder (ADHD) (p. 296): a learning disability characterized by difficulty in remaining still so that one can concentrate on learning.

Authentic assessment (p. 373): an approach to assessing students' learning that requires them to solve problems or work on tasks that approximate as much as possible those they will encounter beyond the classroom.

Authentic learning tasks (p. 328): learning activities that enable students to see the connections between classroom learning and the world beyond the classroom.

Axiology (p. 83): the study of values, including the identification of criteria for determining what is valuable.

B

Back-to-basics movement (p. 107): a movement begun in the mid-1970s to establish the "basic skills" of reading, writing, speaking, and computation as the core of the school curriculum.

Behaviorism (p. 89): based on behavioristic psychology, this philosophical orientation maintains that environmental factors shape people's behavior.

Benchmarks (p. 363): statements of what students should understand and be able to do at specific grade levels or developmental stages.

Between-class ability grouping (p. 326): the practice of grouping students at the middle and high school levels for instruction on the basis of ability or achievement, often called *tracking*.

Bicultural (p. 260): the ability to function effectively in two or more linguistic and cultural groups.

Bilingual education (pp. 243): a curriculum for non-English-speaking and English-speaking students in which two languages are used for instruction and biculturalism is emphasized.

Block grants (p. 181): a form of federal aid given directly to the states, which a state or local education agency may spend as it wishes with few limitations.

Block scheduling (p. 329): a high school scheduling arrangement that provides longer blocks of time each class period, with fewer periods each day.

Brown v. Board of Education of Topeka (p. 104): a 1954 landmark U.S. Supreme Court case rejecting the "separate but equal" doctrine used to prevent African Americans from attending schools with whites.

Buckley Amendment (p. 221): a 1974 law, the Family Educational Rights and Privacy Act, granting parents of students under eighteen and students over eighteen the right to examine their school records.

Burnout (p. 19): an acute level of stress resulting in job dissatisfaction, emotional and physical exhaustion, and an inability to cope effectively.

C

Caring classroom (p. 323): a classroom in which the teacher communicates clearly an attitude of caring about students' learning and their overall well-being.

Categorical aid (p. 182): state-appropriated funds to cover the costs of educating students with special needs.

CD-ROM (p. 398): a small plastic disk (usually 4.72 or 5.25 inches in diameter) that holds 600 or more megabytes of information that can be read by a computer.

Censorship (p. 213): the act of removing from circulation printed material judged to be libelous, vulgar, or obscene.

Channel One (p. 393): a controversial twelve-minute news broadcast, including two minutes of commercials, aired daily in more than 12,000 public and private schools; schools receive Channel One programs, equipment, and service free of charge on agreeing to show the programs to students.

Character education (p. 283): an approach to education that emphasizes the teaching of values, moral reasoning, and the development of "good" character.

Charter (p. 474): an agreement between a charter school's founders and its sponsors specifying how the school will operate and what learning outcomes students will master.

Charter schools (p. 186): independent schools, often founded by teachers, that are given a charter to operate by a school district, state, or national government, with the provision that students must demonstrate mastery of predetermined outcomes.

Chat rooms (p. 401): Internet sites where students can participate in online discussions by typing in their comments and questions.

Chief state school officer (p. 174): the chief administrator of a state department of education and head of the state board of education, often called the *commissioner of education* or *superintendent of public instruction.*

Choice theory (p. 331): an approach to classroom management, developed by psychiatrist William Glasser, based on a belief that students will usually make good choices (i.e., behave in an acceptable manner) if they experience success in the classroom and know that teachers care about them.

Classroom climate (p. 319): the atmosphere or quality of life in a classroom, determined by how individuals interact with one another.

Classroom culture (p. 128): the "way of life" characteristic of a classroom group; determined by the social dimensions of the group and the physical characteristics of the setting.

Classroom management (p. 329): day-to-day teacher control of student behavior and learning, including discipline.

Classroom organization (p. 325): how teachers and students in a school are grouped for instruction and how time is allocated in classrooms.

Clinical supervision (p. 499): a four-step model supervisors follow in making teacher performance evaluations.

Coalition of Essential Schools (p. 458): a national network of public and private high schools that have restructured according to nine Common Principles.

Code of ethics (p. 195): a set of guidelines that defines appropriate behavior for professionals.

Cognitive development (p. 278): the process of acquiring the intellectual ability to learn from interaction with one's environment.

Cognitive science (p. 90): the study of the learning process that focuses on how individuals manipulate symbols and process information.

Collaboration (p. 492): the practice of working together, sharing decision making, and solving problems among professionals.

Collaborative consultation (p. 306): an approach in which a classroom teacher meets with one or more other professionals (such as a special educator, school psychologist, or resource teacher) to focus on the learning needs of one or more students.

Collective bargaining (p. 200): a process followed by employers and employees in negotiating salaries, hours, and working conditions; in most states, school boards must negotiate contracts with teacher organizations.

Collegiality (p. 489): a spirit of cooperation and mutual helpfulness among professionals.

Collegial support team (CST) (p. 498): a team of teachers—created according to subject area, grade level, or teacher interests and expertise—who support one another's professional growth.

Common schools (p. 97): free state-supported schools that provide education for all students.

Compensatory education programs (p. 144): federally funded educational programs designed to meet the needs of low-ability students from low-income families.

Computer-assisted instruction (CAI) (p. 396): the use of computers to provide individualized drill-and-practice exercises or tutorials to students.

Computer-based simulations (p. 399): computer programs that present the user with multifaceted problem situations similar to those they will encounter in real life.

Computer-enhanced instruction (CEI) (p. 396): the use of computers to provide students with inquiry-oriented learning experiences such as simulations and problem-solving activities.

Computer-managed instruction (CMI) (p. 396): the use of computers to evaluate and diagnose students' learning needs and record students' progress for teachers to monitor.

Concrete operations stage (p. 279): the stage of cognitive development (seven to eleven years of age) proposed by Jean Piaget in which the individual develops the ability to use logical thought to solve concrete problems.

Constructivism (p. 90): a psychological orientation that views learning as an active process in which learners construct understanding of the material they learn—in contrast to the view that teachers transmit academic content to students in small segments.

Constructivist teaching (p. 341): a method of teaching based on students' prior knowledge of the topic and the processes they use to construct meaning.

Content standards (p. 363): the content—or knowledge and skills—students should acquire in various academic disciplines.

Cooperative learning (p. 327): an approach to education in which students work in small groups, or teams, sharing the work and helping one another complete assignments.

Copyright laws (p. 210): laws limiting the use of photocopies, videotapes, and computer software programs.

Corporal punishment (p. 224): physical punishment applied to a student by a school employee as a disciplinary measure.

Cost of living (p. 12): the amount of money needed, on average, for housing, food, transportation, utilities, and other living expenses in a given locale.

Co-teaching (p. 498): an arrangement whereby two or more teachers teach together in the same classroom.

Credentials file (p. 480): a file set up for students registered in a teacher placement office at a college or university, which includes background information on the applicant, the type of position desired, transcripts, performance evaluations, and letters of recommendation.

Cross-age tutoring (p. 343): a tutoring arrangement in which older students tutor younger students; evidence indicates that cross-age tutoring has positive effects on the attitudes and achievement of tutee and tutor.

Cultural identity (p. 242): an overall sense of oneself, derived from the extent of one's participation in various subcultures within the national macroculture.

Cultural pluralism (p. 242): the preservation of cultural differences among groups of people within one society. This view is in contrast to the melting-pot theory that says that ethnic cultures should melt into one.

Culture (p. 242): the way of life common to a group of people; includes knowledge deemed important, shared meanings, norms, values, attitudes, ideals, and view of the world.

Curriculum (p. 343): the school experiences, both planned and unplanned, that enhance (and sometimes impede) the education and growth of students.

Curriculum alignment (p. 364): the process of ensuring that the content of curricula and textbooks reflects desired learning outcomes, or academic standards, for students.

Curriculum framework (p. 364): a document that provides guidelines, instructional and assessment strategies, resources, and models for teachers to use as they develop curricula aligned with academic standards.

D

Dame schools (p. 92): colonial schools, usually held in the homes of widows or housewives, for teaching children basic reading, writing, and mathematical skills.

Democratic classroom (p. 330): a classroom in which the teacher's leadership style encourages students to take more power and responsibility for their learning.

Departmentalization (p. 127): an organizational arrangement for schools in which students move from classroom to classroom for instruction in different subject areas.

Desegregation (p. 104): the process of eliminating schooling practices based on the separation of racial groups.

"Digital divide" (p. 414): inequities in access to computer technology that are related to minority-group status, family income, and gender.

Direct instruction (p. 338): a systematic instructional method focusing on the transmission of knowledge and skills from the teacher to the students.

Discovery learning (p. 342): an approach to teaching that gives students opportunities to inquire into subjects so that they "discover" knowledge for themselves.

Dismissal (p. 199): the involuntary termination of a teacher's employment; termination must be made for a legally defensible reason with the protection of due process.

Distance learning (p. 49): the use of technology such as video transmissions that enables students to receive instruction at multiple, often remote, sites.

Distance learning networks (p. 393): two-way, interactive telecommunications systems used to deliver instruction to students at various locations.

Diversity (p. 241): differences among people in regard to gender, race, ethnicity, culture, and socioeconomic status.

Due process (p. 196): a set of specific guidelines that must be followed to protect individuals from arbitrary, capricious treatment by those in authority.

E

Education Consolidation and Improvement Act (ECIA) (p. 181): a 1981 federal law giving the states a broad range of choices for spending federal aid to education.

Education for All Handicapped Children Act (Public Law 94-142) (p. 110, 301): a 1975 federal act that guarantees a free and appropriate education to all handicapped children (often referred to as the *mainstreaming law* or *Public Law 94-142*).

Educational malpractice (p. 207): liability for injury that results from the failure of a teacher, school, or school district to provide a student with adequate instruction, guidance, counseling, and/or supervision.

Educational philosophy (p. 79): a set of ideas and beliefs about education that guide the professional behavior of educators.

Educational reform movement (p. 47): a comprehensive effort made during the 1980s and into the 1990s to improve schools and the preparation of teachers.

Educational Resources Information Center (ERIC) (p. 454): a national information system made up of sixteen clearinghouses that disseminate descriptions of exemplary programs, results of research and development efforts, and related information.

Educational technology (p. 393): computers, software, multimedia systems, and advanced telecommunications systems used to enhance the teaching-learning process.

E-learning (p. 389): education that is delivered via the Internet, satellite broadcast, interactive TV, or CD-ROM.

Elementary and Secondary Education Act (p. 105): part of President Lyndon B. Johnson's Great Society Program, this act allocated federal funds on the basis of the number of poor children in school districts.

Emergency certification (p. 475): temporary, substandard certification requirements set by a state in response to a shortage of teachers.

Entitlements (p. 181): federal programs to meet the educational needs of special populations.

Epistemology (p. 82): a branch of philosophy concerned with the nature of knowledge and what it means to know something.

E-rate (p. 414): a controversial program that uses fees from telecommunications companies to provide discounts on telecommunications services and wiring to schools and libraries.

ERIC Clearinghouses (p. 454): sixteen Educational Resources Information Center Clearinghouses that disseminate descriptions of exemplary educational programs, the results of research and development efforts, and related information.

Essentialism (p. 85): formulated in part as a response to progressivism, this philosophical orientation holds that a core of common knowledge about the real world should be transmitted to students in a systematic, disciplined way.

Ethical dilemmas (p. 195): problem situations in which an ethical response is difficult to determine; that is, no single response can be called "right" or "wrong."

Ethics (p. 83): a branch of philosophy concerned with principles of conduct and determining what is good and evil, right and wrong, in human behavior.

Ethnic group (p. 242): individuals within a larger culture who share a racial or cultural identity and a set of beliefs, values, and attitudes and who consider themselves members of a distinct group or subculture.

Ethnicity (p. 246): a shared feeling of common identity that derives, in part, from a common ancestry, common values, and common experiences.

Evaluation (p. 372): making judgments about, or assigning a value to, measurements of students' learning.

Exceptional learners (p. 293): students whose growth and development deviate from the norm to the extent that their educational needs can be met more effectively through a modification of regular school programs.

Existentialism (p. 87): a philosophical orientation that emphasizes the individual's experiences and maintains that each individual must determine his or her own meaning of existence.

Expenditure per pupil (p. 177): the amount of money spent on each pupil in a school, school district, state, or nation; usually computed according to average daily attendance.

Explicit curriculum (p. 344): the behavior, attitudes, and knowledge that a school intends to teach students.

Extracurricular/cocurricular programs (p. 347): Activities perceived as additions to the academic curriculum.

F

Fair use (p. 210): the right of an individual to use copyrighted material in a reasonable manner without the copyright holder's consent, provided that use meets certain criteria.

Female seminaries (p. 96): schools established in the early nineteenth century to train women for higher education and public service outside the home.

Field experiences (p. 49): opportunities for teachers-in-training to experience firsthand the world of the teacher, by observing, tutoring, and instructing small groups.

Formal operations stage (p. 279): the stage of cognitive development (eleven to fifteen years of age) proposed by Jean Piaget in which cognitive abilities reach their highest level of development.

Formative evaluation (p. 372): an assessment, or diagnosis, of students' learning for the purpose of planning instruction.

For-profit schools (p. 187): schools that are operated, for profit, by private educational corporations.

Freedom of expression (p. 213): freedom, granted by the First Amendment to the Constitution, to express one's beliefs.

Fringe benefits (p. 12): benefits (i.e., medical insurance, retirement, and tax-deferred investment opportunities) that are given to teachers in addition to base salary.

Full-funding programs (p. 182): state programs to ensure statewide financial equity by setting the same per-pupil expenditure level for all schools and districts.

Full inclusion (p. 303): the policy and process of including exceptional learners in general education classrooms.

Full-service schools (p. 141): schools that provide students and their families with medical, social, and human services, in addition to their regular educational programs.

G

Gender bias (p. 271): subtle bias or discrimination on the basis of gender; reduces the likelihood that the target of the bias will develop to the full extent of his or her capabilities.

Gender-fair classroom (p. 271): education that is free of bias or discrimination on the basis of gender.

G.I. Bill of Rights (p. 175): a 1944 federal law that provides veterans with payments for tuition and room and board at colleges and universities and special schools, formally known as the Servicemen's Readjustment Act.

Gifted and talented (p. 297): exceptional learners who demonstrate high intelligence, high creativity, high achievement, or special talents.

Grievance (p. 200): a formal complaint filed by an employee against his or her employer or supervisor.

Group investigation (p. 342): an approach to teaching in which the teacher facilitates learning by creating an environment that allows students to determine what they will study and how.

H

Hidden curriculum (p. 344): the behaviors, attitudes, and knowledge the school culture unintentionally teaches students.

Hierarchy of needs (p. 287): a set of seven needs, from the basic needs for survival and safety to the need for self-actualization, that motivate human behavior as identified by Abraham Maslow.

High-stakes tests (p. 369): achievement tests that have "high-stakes" consequences for students, teachers, and administrators—for example, a test that determines if a student is eligible to graduate or whether educators receive merit pay increases.

Holistic rubric (p. 381): a rating scale, or scoring guide, for evaluating a student's overall product or performance.

Holmes Group (p. 48): a group of ninety-six colleges of education that prepared *Tomorrow's Teachers,* a 1986 report calling for all teachers to have a bachelor's degree in an academic field and a master's degree in education.

Holmes Partnership (p. 48): a consortium of professional organizations—including the Holmes Group, the National Board for Professional Teaching Standards, the National Education Association, and the American Federation of Teachers—committed to the reform of teacher education.

Home-school communication systems (p. 399): computer-based systems that allow schools to disseminate information to parents and, in turn, enable parents to communicate directly with school personnel.

Horn book (p. 93): a copy of the alphabet covered by a thin transparent sheet made from a cow's horn.

Humanism (p. 89): a philosophy based on the belief that individuals control their own destinies through the application of their intelligence and learning.

Humanistic psychology (p. 89): an orientation to human behavior that emphasizes personal freedom, choice, awareness, and personal responsibility.

Hypermedia (p. 398): an interactive instructional system consisting of a computer, CD-ROM drive, videodisc player, video monitor, and speakers. Hypermedia systems allow students to control and present sound, video images, text, and graphics in an almost limitless array of possibilities.

I

Inclusion (p. 303): the practice of integrating all students with disabilities into general education classes.

Indian Education Act of 1972 and 1974 Amendments (p. 259): a federal law and subsequent amendment designed to provide direct educational assistance to Native American tribes and nations.

Individualized education plan (IEP) (p. 301): a plan for meeting an exceptional learner's educational needs, specifying goals, objectives, services, and procedures for evaluating progress.

Individual racism (p. 248): the prejudicial belief that one's ethnic or racial group is superior to others.

Individuals with Disabilities Education Act (IDEA) (p. 301): a 1990 federal act providing a free, appropriate education to disabled youth between three and twenty-one years of age. IDEA superseded the earlier Education for all Handicapped Children Act (Public Law 94-142).

Induction programs (p. 57): programs of support for beginning teachers, usually during their first year of teaching.

Information processing (p. 341): a branch of cognitive science concerned with how individuals use long- and short-term memory to acquire information and solve problems.

Inquiry learning (p. 342): an approach to teaching that gives students opportunities to explore, or inquire into, subjects so that they develop their own answers to problem situations.

In-service workshops (p. 62): onsite professional development programs in which teachers meet to learn new techniques, develop curricular materials, share ideas, or solve problems.

Institution (p. 125): any organization a society establishes to maintain, and improve, its way of life.

Institutional racism (p. 248): institutional policies and practices, intentional or not, that result in racial inequities.

Integrated curriculum (p. 350): a school curriculum that draws from two or more subject areas and focuses on a theme or concept rather than on a single subject.

Intelligence (p. 289): the ability to learn; the cognitive capacity for thinking.

Interactive multimedia (p. 398): computer-supported media that allow the user to interact with a vast, nonlinear, multimedia database to combine textual, audio, and video information.

Interactive teaching (p. 24): teaching characterized by face-to-face interactions between teachers and students in contrast to preactive teaching.

Internship programs (p. 57): programs of assistance and training for beginning teachers, usually for those who have not gone through a teacher education program.

Interstate Certification Agreement Contract (p. 473): a reciprocity agreement among approximately thirty states whereby a teaching certificate obtained in one state will be honored in another.

Interstate New Teacher Assessment and Support Consortium (INTASC) (p. 46): an organization of states established in 1987 to develop performance-based standards for what beginning teachers should know and be able to do.

J

Job analysis (p. 44): a procedure for determining the knowledge and skills needed for a job.

K

Kentucky Education Reform Act (KERA) (p. 171): comprehensive school-reform legislation requiring all Kentucky schools to form school-based management councils with authority to set policies in eight areas.

Kindergarten (p. 100): a school for children before they begin formal schooling at the elementary level; based on the ideas of German educator Friedrick Fröebel, *kindergarten* means "garden where children grow."

Knowledge base (p. 42): the body of knowledge that represents what teachers need to know and be able to do.

L

Latchkey children (p. 135): children who, because of family circumstances, must spend part of each day unsupervised by a parent or guardian.

Latin grammar school (p. 93): colonial schools established to provide male students a precollege education; comparable to today's high schools.

Learning disability (LD) (p. 296): a limitation in one's ability to take in, organize, remember, and express information.

Learning styles (p. 292): cognitive, affective, and physiological behaviors through which an individual learns most effectively; determined by a combination of hereditary and environmental influences.

Least restrictive environment (p. 301): an educational program that meets a disabled student's special needs in a manner that is identical, insofar as possible, to that provided to students in general education classrooms.

Lemon test (p. 228): a three-part test, based on *Lemon v. Kurtzman,* to determine whether a state has violated the separation of church and state principle.

Letter of application (p. 481): a letter written in application for a specific teaching vacancy in a school district.

Letter of inquiry (p. 481): a letter written to a school district inquiring about teaching vacancies.

Limited English proficiency (LEP) (p. 244): a designation for students with limited ability to understand, read, or speak English and who have a first language other than English.

Local school council (p. 168): a group of community members that is empowered to develop policies for the operation of local schools.

Local school district (p. 161): an agency at the local level that has the authority to operate schools in the district.

Logic (p. 84): a branch of philosophy concerned with the processes of reasoning and the identification of rules that will enable thinkers to reach valid conclusions.

M

Magnet school (p. 123): a school offering a curriculum that focuses on a specific area such as the performing arts, mathematics, science, international studies, or technology. Magnet schools, which often draw students from a larger attendance area than regular schools, are frequently developed to promote voluntary desegregation.

Mainstreaming (p. 110, 302): the policy and process of integrating disabled or otherwise exceptional learners into regular classrooms with nonexceptional students.

Massachusetts Act of 1642 (p. 93): a law requiring each town to determine whether its young people could read and write.

Massachusetts Act of 1647 (p. 94): a law mandating the establishment and support of schools; often referred to as the Old Deluder Satan Act because education was seen as the best protection against the wiles of the devil.

Mastery learning (p. 339): an approach to instruction based on the assumptions that (1) virtually all students can learn material if given enough time and taught appropriately and (2) learning is enhanced if students can progress in small, sequenced steps.

McGuffey readers (p. 98): an immensely popular series of reading books for students in grades 1 through 6, written in the 1830s by Reverend William Holmes McGuffey.

Measurement (p. 372): the gathering of data that indicate how much students have learned.

Mentor (p. 61, 439): a wise, knowledgeable individual who provides guidance and encouragement to someone.

Mentoring (p. 61): an intensive form of teaching in which a wise and experienced teacher (the mentor) inducts a student (the protégé) into a professional way of life.

Metaphysics (p. 82): a branch of philosophy concerned with the nature of reality.

Microcomputer-based laboratories (MBL) (p. 397): the use of computers to gather and then analyze data that students have collected in a school laboratory or in the field.

Microteaching (p. 51): a brief, single-concept lesson taught by a teacher education student to a small group of students; usually designed to give the education student an opportunity to practice a specific teaching skill.

Minorities (p. 247): groups of people who share certain characteristics and are smaller in number than the majority of a population.

Modeling (p. 340): the process of "thinking out loud" that teachers use to make students aware of the reasoning involved in learning new material.

Modes of teaching (p. 28): different aspects of the teaching function—for example, teaching as a way of being, as a creative endeavor, as a live performance, and so on.

Montesorri method (p. 102): a method of teaching, developed by Maria Montessori, based on a prescribed set of materials and physical exercises to develop children's knowledge and skills.

Moonlight (p. 12): the practice of holding a second job to increase one's income.

Moral reasoning (p. 278): the reasoning process people follow to decide what is right or wrong.

Morrill Land-Grant Act (p. 99): an 1862 act that provided federal land that states could sell or rent to raise funds to establish colleges of agriculture and mechanical arts.

Multicultural curriculum (p. 264): a school curriculum that addresses the needs and backgrounds of all students regardless of their cultural identity and includes the cultural perspectives, or "voices," of people who have previously been silent or marginalized.

Multicultural education (p. 262): education that provides equal educational opportunities to all students—regardless of socioeconomic status; gender; or ethnic, racial, or cultural backgrounds—and is dedicated to reducing prejudice and celebrating the rich diversity of U.S. life.

Multiculturalism (p. 244): a set of beliefs based on the importance of seeing the world from different cultural frames of reference and valuing the diversity of cultures in the global community.

Multiple intelligences (p. 291): a perspective on intellectual ability, proposed by Howard Gardner, suggesting that there are at least seven types of human intelligence.

N

National Board for Professional Teaching Standards (NBPTS) (p. 44): a board established in 1987 that began issuing professional certificates in 1994–95 to teachers who possess extensive professional knowledge and the ability to perform at a high level.

National Council for Accreditation of Teacher Education (NCATE) (p. 471): an agency that accredits, on a voluntary basis, almost half of the nation's teacher education programs.

National Defense Education Act (p. 104): a 1958 federally sponsored program to promote research and innovation in science, mathematics, modern foreign languages, and guidance.

National Education Association (NEA) (p. 442): the oldest and largest professional association for teachers and administrators.

National Governor's Association (NGA) (p. 172): an association of state governors that influences policies in several areas, including teacher education and school reform.

National Information Infrastructure (NII) (p. 414): a federal plan to create a telecommunications infrastructure linking all schools, libraries, hospitals, and law enforcement agencies to the Internet and the World Wide Web.

National Network for Educational Renewal (NNER) (p. 459): a national network of colleges and universities that collaborate with school districts and partner schools to reform education according to nineteen postulates in John Goodlad's *Teachers for Our Nation's Schools* (1990).

A Nation at Risk (p. 26): a 1983 national report critical of U.S. education.

NEAFT Partnership (p. 444): an agreement between the National Education Association and the American Federation of Teachers to work collaboratively to attain mutually desired goals for the teaching profession.

Negligence (p. 207): failure to exercise reasonable, prudent care in providing for the safety of others.

Newsgroups (p. 401): Internet sites where students can post and exchange information on electronic "bulletin boards."

Nondiscrimination (p. 197): conditions characterized by the absence of discrimination; for example, employees receive compensation, privileges, and opportunities for advancement without regard for race, color, religion, sex, or national origin.

Normal schools (p. 98): schools that focus on the preparation of teachers.

Null curriculum (p. 346): the intellectual processes and subject content that schools do not teach.

O

Observations (p. 50): field experiences wherein a teacher education student observes a specific aspect of classroom life such as the students, the teacher, the interactions between the two, the structure of the lesson, or the setting.

Office of Educational Research and Improvement (OERI) (p. 454): a federal agency that promotes educational research and improving schools through the application of research results.

Open-space schools (p. 127): schools that have large instructional areas with movable walls and furniture that can be rearranged easily.

Opportunity to learn (OTL) (p. 329): the time during which a teacher provides students with challenging content and appropriate instructional strategies to learn that content.

Outcome-based teacher education (p. 43): an approach to teacher education emphasizing outcomes (what teachers should be able to do, think, and feel) rather than the courses they should take.

P

Parochial schools (p. 92): schools founded on religious beliefs.

Pedagogical content knowledge (p. 41): the knowledge accomplished teachers possess regarding how to present subject matter to students through the use of analogies, metaphors, experiments, demonstrations, illustrations, and other instructional strategies.

Peer coaching (p. 494): an arrangement whereby teachers grow professionally by observing one another's teaching and providing constructive feedback.

Peer counseling (p. 141): an arrangement whereby students, monitored by a school counselor or teacher, counsel one another in such areas as low achievement, interpersonal problems, substance abuse, and career planning.

Peer-mediated instruction (p. 342): approaches to teaching, such as cooperative learning and group investigation, that utilize the social relationships among students to promote their learning.

Peer-tutoring (p. 343): an arrangement whereby students tutor other students in the same classroom or at the same grade level.

Perennialism (p. 85): a philosophical orientation that emphasizes the ideas contained in the Great Books and maintains that the true purpose of education is the discovery of the universal, or perennial, truths of life.

Performance-based assessment (p. 374): the process of determining students' ability to apply knowledge, skills, and work habits to the performance of specific learning tasks; determining what students can do as well as what they know.

Performance-based teacher education (p. 43): an approach to teacher education emphasizing performances (what teachers should be able to do, think, and feel) rather than the courses they should take.

Performance expectations (p. 363): established levels of achievement, quality of performance, or level of proficiency.

Performance standard (p. 363): academic standards that reflect levels of proficiency—for example, "1 = outstanding," "2 = exemplary," "3 = proficient," "4 = progressing," and "5 = standard not met."

Personal-development view (p. 43): the belief that teachers become more effective by increasing their self-knowledge and developing themselves as persons.

Phi Delta Kappa (PDK) (p. 445): a professional and honorary fraternity of educators with 650 chapters and 130,000 members.

Placement service (p. 480): a school, government, or commercial service that matches job applicants with job openings and arranges contacts between employers and prospective employees.

Portfolio assessment (p. 374): the process of determining how much students have learned by examining collections of work that document their learning over time.

Practicum (p. 54): a short field-based experience during which teacher education students spend time observing and assisting in classrooms.

Praxis Series: Professional Assessments for Beginning Teachers (p. 475): a battery of tests available to states for the initial certification of teachers. Consists of assessments in three areas: academic skills, knowledge of subject, and classroom performance.

Preactive teaching (p. 24): the stage of teaching when a teacher prepares to teach or reflects on previous teaching experiences in contrast with interactive teaching.

Preoperational stage (p. 279): the stage of cognitive development (two to seven years of age) proposed by Jean Piaget in which the individual begins to use language and symbols to think of objects and people outside of the immediate environment.

Privatization movement (p. 185): Umbrella term for reform initiatives that seek to run public schools as private enterprises.

Problem-solving orientation (p. 47): an approach to teaching that places primary emphasis on the teacher's role as a decision maker and problem solver.

Profession (p. 432): an occupation that requires a high level of expertise, including advanced study in a specialized field, adherence to a code of ethics, and the ability to work without close supervision.

Professional development schools (PDS) (p. 48): schools that have formed partnerships with a college or university for the purpose of improving the schools and contributing to the improvement of teacher preparation programs. Activities at a PDS may include collaborative research, team teaching, demonstration lessons by teacher education faculty, and various professional growth opportunities for teachers and teacher educators.

Professional empowerment (p. 19): a trend for teachers to have expanded opportunities to make decisions that affect their professional lives.

Professional portfolio (p. 59): a collection of various kinds of evidence (e.g., projects, written work, and video demonstrations of skills) documenting the achievement and performance of individuals in an area of professional practice.

Professional standards boards (p. 49): state agencies to regulate and improve the professional practice of teachers, administrators, and other education personnel.

Progressive movement (p. 101): a movement during the 1920s and 1930s to create schools that emphasized democracy, children's interests and needs, and closer connections between school and community.

Progressivism (p. 86): a philosophical orientation based on the belief that life is evolving in a positive direction, that people may be trusted to act in their own best interests, and that education should focus on the needs and interests of students.

Project-based learning (PBL) (p. 377): an approach to learning in which students work in teams on complex, "real-world" projects that allow them to develop and apply skills and knowledge.

Property taxes (p. 179): local taxes assessed against real estate and, in some areas, against personal property in the form of cars, household furniture and appliances, and stocks and bonds.

Prosocial values (p. 120): values such as honesty, patriotism, fairness, and civility that promote the well-being of a society.

Psychosocial crisis (p. 280): a life crisis at one of eight different stages of growth and development. According to psychologist Erik Erikson, individuals must resolve each crisis to reach the next stage.

Psychosocial development (p. 278): the progression of an individual through various stages of psychological and social development.

Q

Qualitative evaluation (p. 499): the appraisal of teacher performance through the use of written, open-ended descriptions of classroom events in terms of their qualities.

Quantitative evaluation (p. 498): the appraisal of teacher performance by recording classroom events in terms of their number or frequency—for example, teacher verbal behaviors such as questioning, praising, or critiquing.

R

Race (p. 246): a concept of human variation used to distinguish people on the basis of biological traits and characteristics.

Reading and writing schools (p. 93): colonial schools, supported by public funds and fees paid by parents, that used a religiously oriented curriculum to teach boys reading and writing skills and, to a lesser degree, mathematics.

Realities of teaching (p. 19): actual conditions teachers face in the classroom; the demands as well as the rewards.

Recertification (p. 471): the practice in some states of requiring experienced teachers to undergo periodic testing to maintain their teaching certificates.

Redistricting (p. 182): the practice of redrawing district boundaries to equalize educational funding by reducing the range of variation in the ability of school districts to finance education.

Reflection (p. 47): the process of thinking carefully and deliberately about the outcomes of one's teaching.

Reflection-in-action (p. 439): the process of engaging in serious, reflective thought about improving one's professional practice while one is engaged in that practice.

Reflective teaching log (p. 56): a journal of classroom observations in which the teacher education student systematically analyzes specific episodes of teaching.

Regional Educational Laboratories (p. 454): nine federally supported, nonprofit agencies that serve a region of the country and work directly with educators to improve schools.

Regional Educational Service Agency (RESA) (p. 174): a state educational agency that provides supportive services to two or more school districts; known in some states as education service centers, intermediate school districts, multicounty education service units, board of cooperative educational services, or educational service regions.

Reliability (p. 380): the degree to which an assessment provides results that are consistent over time.

Research and Development Centers (p. 454): fourteen federally supported, university-based centers, each conducting research and development activities in a different area of education.

Research-based competencies (p. 43): specific behaviors that educational research has identified as characteristic of effective teachers.

Restructuring (p. 167): reorganizing how schools are controlled at the local level so that teachers, principals, parents, and community members have greater authority.

Résumé (p. 480): a concise summary of an individual's professional experiences and education.

S

Scaffolding (p. 341): an approach to teaching based on the student's current level of understanding and ability; the teacher varies the amount of help given (e.g., clues, encouragement, or suggestions) to students based on their moment-to-moment understanding of the material being learned.

School-based interprofessional case management (p. 144): an approach to education in which professionally trained case managers work directly with teachers, the community, and families to coordinate and deliver appropriate services to at-risk students and their families.

School-based management (p. 167): various approaches to school improvement in which teachers, principals, students, parents, and community members manage individual schools and share in the decision-making processes.

School-based teacher education (p. 58): a model of teacher preparation through which professional coursework is presented onsite at a school, usually to students who have a bachelor's degree.

School board (p. 164): the primary governing body of a local school district.

School choice (p. 183): various proposals that would allow parents to choose the schools their children attend.

School culture (p. 126): the collective "way of life" characteristic of a school; a set of beliefs, values, traditions, and ways of thinking and behaving that distinguish it from other schools.

School traditions (p. 127): those elements of a school's culture that are handed down from year to year.

School-within-a-school (p. 145): an alternative school (within a regular school) designed to meet the needs of students at risk.

Scientific management (p. 99): the application of management principles and techniques to the operation of big business and large school districts.

Scoring rubrics (p. 380): rating scales that consist of preestablished criteria for evaluating student performance on learning tasks.

Search and seizure (p. 217): the process of searching an individual and/or his or her property if that person is suspected of an illegal act; reasonable or probable cause to suspect the individual must be present.

Self-assessment (p. 62, 372): the process of measuring one's growth in regard to the knowledge, skills, and attitudes possessed by professional teachers.

Self-contained classroom (p. 127): an organizational structure for schools in which one teacher instructs a group of students (typically, twenty to thirty) in a single classroom.

Service learning (p. 122): an approach to teaching in which students participate in community-based service activities and then reflect on the meaning of those experiences.

Sex-role socialization (p. 268): socially expected behavior patterns conveyed to individuals on the basis of gender.

Sex-role stereotyping (p. 268): beliefs that subtly encourage males and females to conform to certain behavioral norms regardless of abilities and interests.

Sexual harassment (p. 225): unwanted and unwelcome sexual behavior directed toward another person, whether of the same or opposite sex.

Social reconstructionism (p. 88): a philosophical orientation based on the belief that social problems can be solved by changing, or reconstructing, society.

Socratic questioning (p. 84): a method of questioning designed to lead students to see errors and inconsistencies in their thinking, based on questioning strategies used by Socrates.

Special education (p. 300): a teaching specialty for meeting the special educational needs of exceptional learners.

Stages of development (p. 278): predictable stages through which individuals pass as they progress through life.

Standards (p. 362): statements that reflect what students should know and be able to do within a particular discipline or at a particular grade level.

Standards-based education (SBE) (p. 362): basing curricula, teaching, and assessment of student learning on rigorous academic standards.

State aid (p. 180): money given by a state to its cities and towns to provide essential services, including the operation of public schools.

State board of education (p. 172): the highest educational agency in a state, charged with regulating the state's system of education.

State department of education (p. 173): the branch of state government, headed by the chief state school officer, charged with implementing the state's educational policies.

Stereotyping (p. 248): the process of attributing behavioral characteristics to all members of a group; formulated on the basis of limited experiences with and information about the group, coupled with an unwillingness to examine prejudices.

Student-centered curriculum (p. 350): curricula that are organized around students' needs and interests.

Student diversity (p. 8): differences among students in regard to gender, race, ethnicity, culture, and socioeconomic status.

Student-mobility rates (p. 15): the proportion of students within a school or district who move during an academic year.

Students at risk (p. 132): students whose living conditions and backgrounds place them at risk for dropping out of school.

Students with disabilities (p. 294): students who need special education services because they possess one or more of the following disabilities: learning disabilities, speech or language impairments, mental retardation, serious emotional disturbance, hearing impairments, orthopedic impairments, visual impairments, or other health impairments.

Student variability (p. 8): differences among students in regard to their developmental needs, interests, abilities, and disabilities.

Subject-centered curriculum (p. 350): a curriculum that emphasizes learning an academic discipline.

Substitute teaching (p. 58): Temporary teachers who replace regular teachers absent due to illness, family responsibilities, personal reasons, or professional workshops and conferences.

Summative evaluation (p. 372): an assessment of student learning made for the purpose of assigning grades at the end of a unit, semester, or year and deciding whether students are ready to proceed to the next phase of their education.

Superintendent (p. 165): the chief administrator of a school district.

T

Teach for America (p. 9): a program that enables recent college graduates without a teaching certificate to teach in districts with critical shortages of teachers and, after taking professional development courses and supervision by state and school authorities, earn a teaching certificate.

Teacher accountability (p. 28): society's expectations that teachers will adhere to high professional and moral standards and create effective learning environments for all students.

Teacher centers (p. 63): centers where teachers provide other teachers with instructional materials and new methods and where teachers can exchange ideas.

Teacher-leader (p. 446): a teacher who assumes a key leadership role in the improvement and/or day-to-day operation of a school.

Teacher-researcher (p. 452): a teacher who regularly conducts classroom research to improve his or her teaching.

Teacher–student ratios (p. 14): a ratio that expresses the number of students taught by a teacher.

Teachers' craft knowledge (p. 42): the knowledge teachers develop about teaching that derives from their experiences in the classroom, particularly the actions they have taken to solve specific problems of practice.

Teachers' thought processes (p. 25): the thoughts that guide teachers' actions in classrooms. These thoughts typically consist of thoughts related to planning, theories and beliefs, and interactive thoughts and decisions.

Teacher supply and demand (p. 476): the number of school-age students compared to the number of available teachers; may also be projected based on estimated numbers of students and teachers.

Teaching certificate (p. 470): a license to teach issued by a state or, in a few cases, a large city.

Teaching contract (p. 198): an agreement between a teacher and a board of education that the teacher will provide specific services in return for a certain salary, benefits, and privileges.

Teaching simulations (p. 54): an activity in which teacher education students participate in role-plays designed to create situations comparable to those actually encountered by teachers.

Team teaching (p. 495): an arrangement whereby a team of teachers teaches a group of students equal in number to what the teachers would have in their self-contained classrooms.

Tenure (p. 12, 198): an employment policy in which teachers, after serving a probationary period, retain their positions indefinitely and can be dismissed only on legally defensible grounds.

Time on task (p. 328): the amount of time students are actively and directly engaged in learning tasks.

Title IX (p. 110): a provision of the 1972 Education Amendments Act prohibiting sex discrimination in educational programs.

Tort liability (p. 205): conditions that would permit the filing of legal charges against a professional for breach of duty and/or behaving in a negligent manner.

Tyler rationale (p. 348): a four-step model for curriculum development in which teachers identify purposes, select learning experiences, organize experiences, and evaluate.

V

Validity (p. 378): the degree to which assessments measure what they are supposed to measure.

Vertical equity (p. 182): an effort to provide equal educational opportunity within a state by providing different levels of funding based on economic needs within school districts.

Videoconferencing (p. 402): the use of computer-mounted video cameras to conduct two-way interactive conferences over the Internet.

Videodisc (p. 398): a twelve-inch plastic disc, each side of which holds about thirty minutes of motion video, or 54,000 frames of video; each frame can be frozen with a high degree of clarity.

Virtual schools (p. 391): educational institutions that offer K–12 courses through the Internet or by means of web-based methods; an online learning space where teachers and students interact.

Voucher system (p. 183): funds allocated to parents that they may use to purchase education for their children from public or private schools in the area.

W

Within-class ability grouping (p. 327): the practice of creating small, homogeneous groups of students within a single classroom for the purpose of instruction, usually in reading or mathematics, at the elementary level.

Women's Educational Equity Act (WEEA) (p. 269): a 1974 federal law that guarantees equal educational opportunity for females.

Work habits (p. 372): dispositions important for effective thinking and learning—for example, reading with curiosity and willingness to work hard.

World Wide Web (WWW) (p. 399): the most popular connection to the Internet; composed of home pages that users access through browser programs such as Netscape Communicator, Microsoft Explorer, or America Online.

Name Index

G

H

Subject Index

B

C

E

F

M

N

O

P

S

T

U

V